The Child

The Child

Infants, Children, and Adolescents

Nancy J. Cobb
California State University, Los Angeles

Mayfield Publishing Company
Mountain View, California
London • Toronto

Library of Congress Cataloging-in-Publication Data

Cobb, Nancy J.
    The Child: infants, children, and adolescents / Nancy J. Cobb.
       p.   cm.
    Includes bibliographical references and indexes.
    ISBN 1-55934-633-7
    1. Child psychology 2. Child development. I. Title.
  BF721.C5622000
  305.231—dc21   00-053291

Manufactured in the United States of America
10   9   8   7   6   5   4   3   2   1

Sponsoring editor, Franklin C. Graham; developmental editor, Barbara Armentrout; production editor, Melissa Williams Kreischer; manuscript editor, Margaret Moore; design manager and cover designer, Susan Breitbard; text designer, Ellen Pettengell; art editor, Robin Mouat; illustrators, Lineworks and John and Judy Waller; manufacturing manager, Randy Hurst; permissions editor, Marty Granahan. Cover photo © Martin Klimek/Jeroboam, Inc. The text was set in 10.5/12 Legacy Serif Book by GTS Graphics, Inc., and printed on acid-free 45# Somerset Matte by R. R. Donnelley and Sons Company.

Brief Contents

Contents

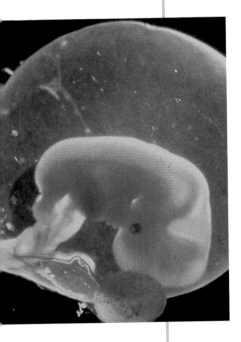

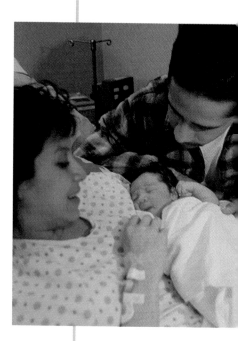

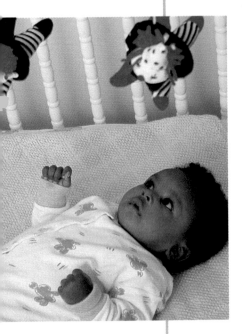

chapterfourteen Adolescence
Cognitive Development   531

Research Focus Boxes

Social Policy Focus Boxes

Narratives

Preface

What do you remember of your own childhood or the games you played? Imagine yourself sitting on a park bench watching children at play. Over next to the trees, you notice a few school-age children taking turns on the swings. Close by, you can make out four young children playing contentedly by themselves in a sandpit, one with a shovel and the others with various toys. In the distance is a skateboard park seemingly used only by boys, each doing their own thing on the ramps or clustered in small knots around the perimeter. A number of girls their age are walking through the park by two's and three's, involved intensely in conversation. You continue watching. Have you ever really looked at children playing before? Is there more than meets the eye in the way children of different ages play?

What is play, you wonder? Do toddlers usually play alone, even if they are right next to each other? When do children learn to take turns? Why were only boys at the skateboard park? Is the scene at this park typical for children of these ages? You were a child once, presumably much like these children. But, you're surprised to find you don't have answers to these questions. And then you wonder what makes some children aggressive and others shy? What brought aggression to mind? You remember seeing a news story on TV only this morning about a school shooting. Several experts in child development talked about possible signs of disturbance that could have told the parents or teachers that something was going wrong, or already had gone wrong, in the lives of those children. Others commented that many times there are no reliable signs to distinguish children who are truly troubled from those who are not. They also said that troubled children can come from homes that are just as loving and supportive as those of other children.

Last Sunday's newspaper profiled a very different child. The Teen Life section described the day-to-day life of a teenage boy—active in 4-H, a merit scholar bound for the university next fall—whose favorite activity is serving as a volunteer at an after-school day care center near his home. Three days a week, for 3 years now, he has helped children with their homework, played games with them, and just kept them company. What makes children so different? How much of a difference is there to begin with from one child to the next? How do circumstances change life outcomes, you wonder? As a casual observer you may never discover the answers to these questions. But, as a student of child development, some questions may be answered and others that you never imagined may come to mind.

This book introduces you to ordinary children, such as those in the park, with the hope that you will see things about them that you previously never noticed or thought about. Instead of simply talking about children, as many textbooks do, this book will let children talk to you as well. This textbook relies on the use of narrative, using children's own words as well as stories about children and their families, to help you understand developmental concepts. In addition, three features distinguish this textbook's approach: This book will emphasize a constructive perspective to development, it will highlight ethnic and gender diversity, and it will stress continuity of development.

A Narrative Approach

As you read this text, you will be invited to see things from the perspective of the children as well as from that of the researchers who study them. The things children say and do, as well as narrative accounts of their experiences by others, provide a rich database from which to study development. You will be encouraged to analyze and make sense of children, as developmentalists do, by observing them and their families firsthand through these narrative accounts. Instead of simply presenting you with various theories or research findings, you will be included in the process of discovery itself by being introduced to the developmental issues, in the form of narrative accounts, that research and theory were designed to address.

A Constructive Perspective

As you begin to look at things from the vantage point of children, you will see that they frequently see things differently than do adults. The constructive perspective assumes that individuals actively "construct" reality rather than passively react to events. In doing so, they organize experience in meaningful ways that change predictably with age. Individuals continually interpret the events they experience. As a consequence, a single event can mean different things to different people. Perceiving the world, whether listening to someone talk or making sense of what we are seeing, is an active process. Reality does not come at us packaged for passive absorption. In order to experience a coherent, meaningful world, a person must construct or assemble it from the moment, from less coherent raw material. This view of perception as an active, constructive process is termed the constructive perspective and will inform the pages of this text.

Gender and Ethnic Diversity

In reading this book, you will discover how differences of gender and ethnicity contribute to the way children construct their reality. Few differences are as important to children, or to individuals of any age, for that matter, as those associated with their gender. Some differences are biologically based, whereas others are socially determined and reflect what a particular culture expects of children depending on gender. Culture contributes to development in even more general ways, affecting everything from which foods children like (preferences that may be established even before birth) to which language they use when talking to a grandparent. The very rituals, beliefs, and rhythms to life that a culture provides furnish the perspective from which children learn to view the world. Culture, whether this is provided by children's sex or their ethnicity, provides the interpretive lens through which they look when constructing the events they experience.

Continuity of Development

You may be surprised to discover yourself in the experiences of the children you are reading about. Development brings many changes—in size, skills, maturity and understanding—but each of us still carries within us the self we were at different points in our lives. Continuity of development assumes that within every adult there lurks an adolescent and an even younger child. Issues of intimacy, for instance, are salient not only in early adulthood but also in infancy. A concern with autonomy is central not only to adolescence, but also to toddlerhood, and emerges again as an issue in later adulthood. As you discover how children at different ages deal with various issues, you may discover new things about yourself as well.

Continuity exists in yet another way. Despite obvious differences between groups of children defined by factors such as ethnicity or gender, the differences *among* children within any group are greater than the differences *between* those groups. Underlying commonalities may suggest ways of conceptualizing solutions to some of the social ills that affect children's lives. With respect to this point, each chapter contains a social policy box that highlights a policy related to some aspect of children's well-being. Issues covered in these policy boxes include substance abuse in pregnancy and how to balance the rights and responsibilities of the individual with those of the community, genetic testing and the human genome project, and how best to teach schoolchildren who are not proficient in English.

Additional Features

What else distinguishes this book? One of the most important features of this text is one that you may *not* notice at first. The writing style of this book is designed to be "reader friendly" and conversational. The text is intended to read much the way someone would sound when speaking to you—informal and personal. When this approach is successful, you, the reader, become aware only of the concepts you are asked to think about and not the process of reading about them. Don't be misled by the informal tone to the text; you will be getting a sophisticated analysis of developmental concepts, research, and theory.

In addition to boxes highlighting social policy, this book contains boxes highlighting research. The study of child development involves two quite different types of knowledge. One of these describes *what* we know about children's development, the ways they change with age and the factors that are responsible for those changes. The other describes *how* we know what we know, the research methods that generate the findings you'll be reading about. The Research Focus boxes introduce you to this second type of knowledge: the basic methods of developmental research. These boxes are important because they provide you with the tools you will need to actively analyze what you're reading rather than simply taking in the facts. Each box begins with a practical problem and then illustrates how researchers used a particular approach to solve it. Some examples are "Descriptive Statistics: How harmful *Is* Secondhand Smoke?" "Ethics: Kangaroo Care for Low-Birthweight Infants," and "Internal and External Validity: 'Tuning Out' Powerless Adults." All together, the boxes cover all of the basic topics important for understanding the methodologies used by developmental researchers.

Organization of This Text

The book is divided into five parts: Foundations, Infancy and Toddlerhood, Early Childhood, Middle Childhood, and Adolescence. Each part contains three chapters: physical development, cognitive development, and psychosocial development. All chapters begin with an outline of the material that is to be covered. Each chapter begins with a brief vignette or opening section designed to draw you into the chapter, and ends with a summary that describes the major points of the chapter. Key terms appear in a running glossary in the margins of the text, to highlight developmental concepts as you read. Also, each chapter contains Stop-and-Think questions that are designed to engage you with the material as you read.

Teaching and Learning Tools

- *Instructor's Manual and Test Bank.* This is a comprehensive resource for instructors. Part One of the manual includes, for each chapter: chapter outlines, summaries, and learning objectives; lecture organizers (the text of the PowerPoint slides available on the Instructor's CD and *The Child* Web site); lecture suggestions; discussion and critical thinking questions; suggested answers to the text's Stop-and-Think questions; activities; and student worksheets. Part Two offers Internet Resources, with suggested Web sites and worksheets to guide students through Internet-related assignments. Part Three, Video Resources, gives detailed descriptions and reviews of suggested videos for each chapter. The Test Bank contains over 1,500 questions in multiple choice, true-false, short answer, and essay formats. Answers with page references and topic identification are provided.

- *Computerized Test Bank.* MicroTest III, developed by Chariot Software Group, contains the complete test bank, including answers, topic identification and page references. MicroTest allows you to design tests using the questions included with *The Child* and/or to incorporate your own questions. The testing program is available in both Windows and Macintosh formats.

- *Transparency Acetates.* Provided to enhance lectures, the 50 acetates, many in full-color, include selected art and other images from the text. They are also available on the Instructor's CD and the Web site.

- The Child *Web Site (http://www.mayfieldpub.com/cobb).* Instructor's resources on the site include a syllabus builder (which allows instructors to customize a syllabus and post it at a unique Web address), the Instructor's Resource Guide, PowerPoint slides, an image bank, electronic transparencies, and Internet links. The entire instructor's section is password-protected. Student's resources on the site include an interactive study guide, Internet activities, and a Web tutorial.

- *The Mayfield Child and Adolescent Development Custom Video.* This video, developed to accompany *The Child*, contains more than 15 video clips ranging from 5 to 10 minutes in length. With at least one clip per chapter, the video is a valuable resource for encouraging class discussion. Topics include classical and operant conditioning, pediatric brain development, the diagnosis and treatment of Attention Deficit Disorder, differences between the sexes, memory, and depression in children and adolescents.

- *Instructor's CD-ROM.* This CD contains PowerPoint slides, electronic transparencies, an image bank of images from the text, and the Instructor's Resource Guide. The PowerPoint slides, as shown in the lecture organizers section of the Instructor's Manual, provide a lecture outline for each chapter and can be combined with the electronic transparencies for an integrated classroom presentation. The Instructor's Manual can be downloaded from the CD and materials customized to fit any course organization. This complete package of presentation resources can be used with both IBM-compatible and Macintosh computers.

- *Study Guide.* Written to coordinate with the materials found in the Instructor's Manual and Test Bank, this guide uses the SQ4R method and offers for each chapter: chapter outline, summary, and learning objectives; flash cards; questions for reflection and application; activities and observations; worksheets; and practice quizzes.

Acknowledgments

I would like to thank all of those who have helped with the writing of this book. To all of you at Mayfield who have been involved in this project, my sincerest thanks. This book would not have come into being without the work that you have contributed to it. I am deeply thankful for this, as I am for the opportunity to have worked with you. My sincere thanks go to Barbara Armentrout, the developmental editor for this project, who helped to flesh out and develop the manuscript at every stage of the writing. Your contributions have enriched this text in ways that are too numerous to mention. To Melissa Williams, the production editor, many thanks for your creative touch and your attentiveness to detail as you shepherded this project through to completion. Your efforts in its production have resulted in a beautiful book. Thanks also go to Joan Pendleton for your expert and careful reading and copyediting of the manuscript. Finally, I am especially thankful for the opportunity of working once again with Frank Graham, the sponsoring editor for this project. For your vision for this project, your integrity as an editor and a person, for your good spirits, and for being a friend, Frank, I thank you.

Thanks also to talented and creative students past and present, and to their supportive spouses, to Jennie Euler, who found references when I could not, and to Larry Albinski, who dropped these off at all hours of the day and night. Thank you, thank you! To Anita Rosenfield and Andrea Weyermann, for doing an outstanding job on the ancillaries, my sincere thanks for making this book a more meaningful experience for those who will use it.

To my prayer partners, Roberta Veit, Monteene Ivey, and Holly Tone, my deepest thanks for your friendship, prayers, and encouragement. To Bill Cobb, for your humor, CDs, and nostalgia, thank you; these made writing, not to mention my life, so much easier. To Joshua and Jenny, I thank you for the brave way you live your lives; you have been my tie to what is real as a parent and as a person. To Michael, if one can thank another for wisdom and love, I thank you for these, and for your courageous honesty and generosity of spirit, for always taking the time to listen to ideas and read pages of manuscript, even when this was time that you took from your writing. I could not have written this, nor done much else, without you—nor would I want to.

My thanks also go to those colleagues who have reviewed the manuscript and offered both helpful suggestions and informed criticism: Nancy Ahlander, Ricks College; Eric Ansel, Weber State University; Daniel R. Bellack, Trident Technical College; Kenneth S. Bordens, Indiana University, Purdue University at Fort Wayne; Kathleen W. Brown, California State University, Fullerton; Joan B. Cannon, University of Massachusetts–Lowell; Elaine Cassel, Marymount University; Melonye

Curtis, Amarillo College; Denise Davidson, Loyola University of Chicago; Deborah Davis, Chaffey College; Nancy E. Dye, Humboldt State University; Diane Widmeyer Eyer, Cañada College; William J. Gnagey, Illinois State University; Dale Goldhaber, University of Vermont; Janet Gonzalez-Mena, Napa Valley College; Mary Jo Graham, Marshall University; Allen Keniston, University of Wisconsin–Eau Claire; Kina Leitner, New York University; Terry F. McNabb, Coe College; Philip J. Mohan, University of Idaho; Linda C. Monahon, Simmons College; Marilyn Moore, Illinois State University; David L. Morgan, Spalding University; Peggy Perkins, University of Nevada, Las Vegas; Jay B. Pozner, Jackson Community College; Joe Price, San Diego State University; Wanda L. Ruffin, Hood College; Jane A. Rysberg, California State University, Chico; Marie Saracino, Stephen F. Austin State University; Rochelle Robinson Warm, Palm Beach Community College; and Valjean Whitlow, Belmont University.

For I know the thoughts I think concerning you,
says the Lord, thoughts of peace and not of hurt,
to give you a future and a hope.

Jeremiah 29:11

Introduction and Theories of Development

The French call memories *souvenirs*—a part of the past we take with us. Impossible? Time, after all, can't be put in a pocket, to be carried off for another day. Just as with sand, by which it's been measured, time slips through fingers like water and light. "Souvenirs" exist nonetheless. But how? How does one hold on to a moment? Remember a childhood? The answer, I believe, is that *we* become the souvenirs. The souvenirs we carry are *ourselves,* changed by the act of collecting them.

In *Salt Dancers,* Ursula Hegi describes a scene from childhood:

> When I turned four, my father taught me the salt dance: he sprinkled a line of salt on the living room floor, positioned my bare feet on top of his shoes, and told me to leave everything I feared or no longer wanted behind that line. His gold-flecked eyes high above me, he walked me across that salt border into my brand-new year—he backward, I forward—my chin tilted against the buttons of his silk vest. . . . Though I no longer recall what I left behind the salt line that day or chose to take with me, I can still evoke the tingling in my arms as they encircled my father's lanky waist. Below his right eyebrow curved the moon-sliver scar where a dog had bitten him when he was a boy. Rooted to his feet, I didn't slip off as we danced, careful at first—"Two steps to the right, Julia, one to the left"—then spinning through the rooms, past the radiant faces of my mother and brother. (p. 11) ◄

In a sense, all children dance into the future on the feet of their parents. We carry the past within us, measuring our steps to its rhythms. The cadence of the

familiar provides us with footholds to the present—the past and the present meeting in the assembling of the moment. Listen for such a "meeting" in this young boy's account of his first day at school, as he makes sense of his experiences in the only way he can, in terms of what he brings with him, the "souvenirs" of experience:

> I spent that first day picking holes in paper, then went home in a smoldering temper.
>   "What's the matter, Love? Didn't he like it at school then?"
>   "They never gave me the present."
>   "Present? What present?"
>   "They said they'd give me a present."
>   "Well, now, I'm sure they didn't."
>   "They did! They said: 'You're Laurie Lee, aren't you? Well just you sit there for the present.' I sat there all day but I never got it. I ain't going back there again." (Donaldson, 1978, p. 9) ◄

Laurie Lee's misunderstanding of what the teacher said illustrates the way his expectations colored his experiences (in Scotland, Laurie Lee is a common name for boys). But the "present" is not a simple reality. Events are not necessarily perceived in the same way by each of the persons experiencing them. There are, in fact, as many realities—presents—as there are people to experience them. In order for any one of these realities to emerge for a person, the person must construct, or "assemble," that particular reality and not any of the others. This understanding of human activity, referred to as a **constructive approach,** will inform the pages of this text.

Children and adults alike continually put together the events to which they respond, doing so effortlessly, imbuing these with meaning. This activity is so centrally human that Robert Kegan (1982), a psychologist at Harvard, calls us "meaning makers."

In *Sula*, Toni Morrison (1973) describes the reactions of two girls, Sula and Nell, who are responsible for the accidental drowning of a young boy. Each has constructed the event in a different way. Sula is from "a household of throbbing disorder constantly awry with things, people, voices and the slamming of doors," whereas Nell is daily "surrounded by the high silence of her mother's incredibly orderly house, feeling the neatness pointing at her back." The two friends have spent the hot afternoon by the bank of a river, lying in the grass, wordlessly sharing the day. Chicken, a small boy whom they know, appears and Sula invites him over to play. Nell is put off by the child, who is dressed in clothes too large and is digging his finger in his nose, but Sula playfully grasps the boy's hands and, to his terror and delight, swings him in circles by the river's edge. Sula's grasp slips and Chicken sails out over the river, disappears beneath the water, and drowns. Nell calms the distraught Sula and makes sure they leave no trace of their presence by the river's bank. The girls are silent about their part in the death; and, as Sula cries at the boy's funeral, Nell assures herself she has done nothing wrong. Years later, Nell is stunned when Sula's grandmother interrupts the polite chatter of Nell's social call by asking her how she had killed that little boy. Nell assures the grandmother that it had been Sula, not she. But the grandmother responds, "You. Sula. What's the difference? You was there. You watched, didn't you?" (p. 168). ◄

Despite its terrible finality, the child's death is no more a simple reality than was Laurie Lee's misunderstanding of the teacher's remark. Chicken's death meant different things to those involved—sorrow to one girl, self-protective concern to the other, and grief to still others. The "real" meaning of the story is made

constructive approach The theoretical perspective that individuals' expectations color their experiences of the world; that each individual constructs a particular reality from experience.

**FIGURE 1.1 The Process of
Constructing Meaning**

no clearer by examining the objective event—the drowning—to which each character responds. Instead, it is the grandmother's remark that focuses our attention on what Kegan (1982) calls "that most human of 'regions' *between* an event and a reaction to it . . . the place where the event is privately composed, made sense of, the place where it actually *becomes* an event for that person . . . this zone of mediation where meaning is made" (p. 2). This process is schematically represented in Figure 1.1.

In this zone, Nell had composed a reality in which she had no responsibility for the drowning. Chicken's death carried no meaning of loss or guilt for her as it did for Sula. However, in making sense of the grandmother's question, she is surprised by another reality—that she shares responsibility for the drowning with Sula, that the "neatness pointing at her back" is not a salt line behind which she can leave what she has feared all her life—death and loss, and the impotence of an orderly life to change either.

You will meet many children in the pages of this text, children like Laurie Lee, Sula, and Nell. Each has a story to tell, and each will bring to life the developmental themes and concepts of the book. The book itself has three organizing themes: it adopts a constructive perspective on development, it focuses on issues of diversity, and it stresses the continuity of development.

The Constructive Perspective on Development

Children do not necessarily see things the way adults see them, nor even the way children a bit older or younger do. The Swiss developmentalist, Jean Piaget, has given us a powerful way of understanding these differences; his approach illustrates the constructive developmental perspective. Piaget was fascinated by differences in the way children and adults understood their world. By simply talking with children, he discovered, for instance, that they believed that dreams came

Differences in cognitive development at different ages affect how children make sense of the world. This small child doesn't understand why he can't always have the ball whenever he wants it.

in through the window at night, that taller people had to be older than shorter ones, or that how much there was to something had more to do with how many pieces there were than with the size of the pieces. Observations such as these convinced Piaget that what we call knowledge is more than a simple copy of reality. Piaget assumed, instead, that we actively construct what we know of the world and that we organize this understanding in qualitatively different ways with age, each new organization resulting in a distinctly different stage of thought.

Robert Kegan (1982) illustrates one such stage difference humorously with the following story in which a mother of two young sons had just about "had it" with their continual squabbling. They had bickered their way through the day, and her patience was nearing its end as she watched them quarrel over the dessert she had just given them—little pastries of different sizes filled with assorted jams. She had given her 4-year-old the biggest of three pastries and her 10-year-old the two smaller ones. The 4-year-old was tearfully complaining that his brother had "more," and that he wanted two pieces as well. His mother and his brother assured him that his one piece was just as big as the two smaller ones put together, but he was unmoved by the logic of their argument. Kegan describes the situation as the mother, now well beyond the limits of her patience:

> "in a fit of sarcasm . . . swept down on his plate with a knife, saying, 'You want two pieces? Okay, I'll give you two pieces. Here!'—whereupon she neatly cut the younger boy's pastry in half. Immediately, all the tension

What might Piaget suggest as a way to help children sleep through the night when they are scared of bad dreams?

FIGURE 1.2 Letter Recognition

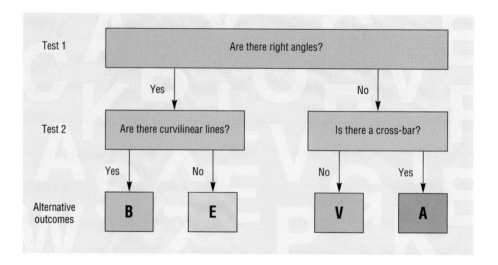

went out of him; he thanked his mother sincerely, and contentedly set upon his dessert. The mother and the older son were both astonished. They looked at the boy the way you would look at something stirring in a waste-basket. Then they looked at each other; and in that moment they shared a mutually discovered insight into the reality of their son and brother, a reality quite different from their own" (pp. 27–28). ◄

The constructive perspective maintains that a child's reality is not *of necessity* one that is shared by others, as this mother and older brother discovered. However, instead of then dismissing children's reality as bizarre or simply "mistaken," the constructive perspective assumes that their reality reflects a logic of its own, one that is internally consistent and through which they make sense of their world.

Assuming that individuals *do* continually interpret their experience, composing or making sense of the events to which they react, how, you might ask, do they do this? How, in other words, are we to understand such a constructive process?

We can begin an explanation by examining the activity you are engaging in at this very moment—reading. The constructive approach assumes that perception is an active process. To perceive the letters that make up a sentence, in other words, one must do something other than simply keep one's eyes open and on the page. The nature of this perceptual activity takes the form of scanning the lines that form the letters to determine which features are present. Features are the characteristics of letters that enable us to distinguish one letter from another, such as whether the lines are straight or curved, open or closed, form angles, and so on. Perceptual scanning is directed by expectations of what a letter *might* be, based on what has preceded it. Given the number of letters that are possible, each of which is distinguished by multiple features, such expectations play a major role in perception.

Look at Figure 1.2. Are there right angles? Could that letter be a B? An E? An E has the same number of right angles as a B, but lacks curvilinear lines. Are there curvilinear lines? Research on letter recognition lends substantial support to this type of analysis. Confusion errors in tasks calling for individuals to quickly identify letters flashed on a screen confirm that the more features two letters have in common, the more likely they are to be confused with each other (Neisser, 1967).

Given the explanation of the constructivist theory of reading, why is it so difficult to proof your own written work?

If you are still not convinced that we actively "construct" the events to which we respond, take a moment to look at Figure 1.3. Notice that the very same lines that form the letter B in the top row also form the number 13 in the bottom row. What determines whether you will see these lines as a letter or as a number? The answer, obviously, is not in the physical arrangement of the lines themselves, since this arrangement is the same in either case. Rather, it is your, the reader's, expectation of seeing one or the other figure that determines how the arrangement of lines will be read. This expectation, in turn, is derived from the context in which the lines appear—that context being either a row of letters or a row of numbers. Whether you eventually perceive a letter or a number, the event itself will be assembled in Kegan's "zone of mediation where meaning is made," constructed in the process of perceiving it.

This same active, constructive process occurs at each of many levels of human functioning, from the relatively molecular level of perceptual processing that we have just examined to the molar level of social interactions. An experiment by Condry and Ross (1985) illustrates how the same constructive process occurs in the perception of social behavior. The investigators showed college students a videotape of two children rough-and-tumbling in the snow. The actual sex of the children couldn't be determined because of their bulky snowsuits; some viewers were told the children were boys and others that they were girls. Viewers who believed the children to be boys perceived the children's behavior as playful. However, those who thought they were looking at girls perceived the identical behavior (remember, they all viewed the same videotape) as aggressive. Boys' play, you see, is expected to be rough; and actions such as wrestling or pummeling someone with snowballs fit the viewers' expectations of how boys play. In other words, it was easy for them to "read" such actions as playful. Conversely, girls' play is expected to be quiet. Given that expectation, wrestling and pummeling could only be perceived as aggressive.

What determined what each viewer saw? Just as in the previous example, the answer is not to be found in the videotape of the two children. The same videotape was seen by all subjects. Rather, it is to be found in the expectations of the viewers. What they saw is what they constructed, guided by their expectations, as these gave meaning to the activity they were viewing. See the Research

An Experiment: "Who You Pushin', Buddy!"— Perceptions of Aggressiveness BY MICHAEL WAPNER

People interpret experience by literally constructing or piecing together the events to which they respond. One of the most important manifestations of this interpretive construction occurs in determining the intentions of others. Even when an action is so obvious that it leaves little to interpretation, the motives behind the action still need to be understood, and this usually requires a good deal of cognitive construction. Observers may all agree that George bumped into Ira. But what the observers feel and do about it depends more on why they think George did it than the mere fact that he did. If George stumbled and could not keep from bumping Ira, that's one thing. But if George bumped Ira to get ahead of him in line, that's entirely different.

What determines how observers interpret the intentions behind an act? Mary Lynne Courtney and Robert Cohen (1996) designed an experiment to investigate this question. In particular, they looked at the contribution of two variables to the interpretation of intention: (1) prior information and (2) the personality of the observer. These two variables, in addition to influencing an observer's interpretation of the intentions behind an action, illustrate, by their difference, something fundamental about the design of experiments in general.

Briefly, boys between 8 and 12 were shown a videotape of two boys playing tag on a playground. At a critical point in the middle of the tape, the boy being chased falls down after being tagged by the other boy. The fallen boy slowly gets up and resumes the game. The variables were introduced as follows:

1. Prior Information: An Independent Variable Previous research, and common sense, would suggest that observers' interpretation of the intention behind an act should depend on what else they know about the actors. Thus, one would guess that the subjects would more likely attribute hostile intent to the tag that caused the fall if they were told beforehand that the two boys were enemies and had just recently been fighting. Conversely, the likelihood of seeing the tag as accidental should increase if the observers believed the boys to be good friends. But what if the observers knew nothing about the boys? These three conditions— let us call them hostile, benign, and ambiguous—constitute the independent variable in the experiment.

In an *experiment*, each group of subjects is treated differently than the others. In all other respects the groups are equivalent. If the groups differ afterward, we can assume the difference is due to the way they were treated. In order to be confident about this assumption, however, we must be sure that the groups are the same at the outset. The simplest way to ensure this would be to start with identical groups. But because no two individuals are ever the same in all respects, such a tactic is impossible. An equally good approach is to make sure the groups don't differ in any *systematic* way. We can accomplish this by assigning individuals at random to each condition. If each person has the same chance of being assigned to each group, and if we assign enough people to each, the differences among the people would balance out among the groups. *Random assignment* will distrib-

Focus, "An Experiment: 'Who You Pushin,' Buddy!—Perceptions of Aggressiveness," for more information on how individuals might construct the meaning of aggressiveness.

Diversity

A second theme to the book is its emphasis on diversity. The proportion of children born to cultural and ethnic minorities has increased steadily in the United States over the past 50 years. Estimates based on the latest U.S. Census data project that by 2050, one out of four individuals in our society will belong to an ethnic minority (Day, 1996). There is a pressing need to understand the effects of such diversity on the lives of children and on the society in which they live.

Individuals reflect their cultural heritages, and the meaning that events have for them—that is, the sense they make of their experiences—will vary with differences in their cultural backgrounds. Meaning, in other words, is relative. This text will highlight the cultural diversity that increasingly distinguishes our society. Laurie Lee's frustration with school arose because, in an important sense, he and the teacher did not speak the same language. Yet his difficulties are magnified tenfold in the hundreds of thousands of children for whom not only their language but also their customs differ from the ones they encounter at school. In this

ute any initial differences more or less evenly among the groups. Contrast this type of independent variable with a second variable these investigators studied.

2. Aggressiveness of the Observer: A Classification Variable

Aggressive boys have been found to attribute hostile intentions to the actions of others more frequently than less aggressive boys. Courtney and Cohen incorporated the variable of aggressiveness by having classmates rate each boy for aggressiveness. Notice that, unlike assignment to the prior knowledge variable, aggressiveness scores could not be assigned randomly. Rather, subjects were *classified* based on judgments of a preexisting characteristic—that is, aggressiveness. Thus, if we find a difference between aggressive and unaggressive boys, we cannot be sure that the difference is not due to something else that might be correlated with aggressiveness.

Now let's look at the results of the study. The subjects (randomly assigned and classified as described above) were shown the videotape and asked to "segment" the action by pressing a button whenever one action stopped and another began. These points of segmentation are labeled "breakpoints." Of course, most natural behavior does not have discrete breakpoints. Rather, one activity flows into another. Thus, segmenting the flow of action is not simply marking what already objectively exists; rather, it is an act of cognitive construction and will vary from observer to observer.

A dramatic example of segmentation as a cognitive construction lies in the fact that we hear our native language spoken in discrete word segments although the sound issuing from the speaker's mouth is continuous, as can be demonstrated by visualizing normal speech on the screen of an oscilloscope. It is our knowledge of the rhythms and sounds of our native language, as well as familiarity with the vocabulary and current context, that allows us to segment accurately. You can test this proposition. Rent a film in an unfamiliar foreign language. Then gather a few friends who are equally ignorant of the language and all try to count the number of words spoken in two minutes of dialogue. You will be surprised at the wildly different counts.

Segmenting the action in Courtney and Cohen's videotape is roughly the same kind of cognitive task. But unlike speech, there is no cultural consensus as to where the breakpoints belong. Because the number of breakpoints should increase when an individual is seeking more information, it was expected that identifying breakpoints would be a function of how much information the boys had about the action. Recall, each boy got information from two sources: (1) from what he was told about the boys' friendship (the condition of prior information to which he had been assigned) and (2) from what he assumed (based on his level of aggressiveness). When subjects were given information that the boys were enemies, aggressiveness did not predict the amount of segmentation. Everyone "knew," in other words, what was going on and didn't have to look for it. When subjects were told the boys were friends, or were told nothing at all, subjects who were more aggressive identified more breakpoints than less aggressive ones, suggesting that their perception of ongoing behavior differed from that of less aggressive boys. Aggressiveness relates not only to the motives one attributes to others, but also to the ways in which one organizes one's perception of ongoing events.

text, we will frequently look at the families of children and often at their cultural and ethnic backgrounds as well. Each of these affects the lives of children in intimate and pervasive ways.

Sex, as well as culture, contributes to diversity. Another important theme of this text is the impact of differences related to sex on children's development. All cultures hold up one set of expectations for females and a different set for males. These expectations powerfully influence our perceptions of children even when we are not aware of their doing so. At no age are children immune from such expectations. For instance, when first-time parents were interviewed about their infants, who were by this time only hours old, the parents had already started to perceive their infants in terms of existing stereotypes for children of either sex. Thus, parents of females saw their infants as softer and having finer, more delicate features than did parents of males. In contrast, the latter saw their infants as hardier, stronger, and more coordinated than did parents of females. It should be pointed out that measures of such characteristics as alertness, coordination, or physical appearance revealed no differences between infants of either sex (Rubin, Provenzano, & Luria, 1974).

Because of expectations based on sex, females and males are likely to follow different developmental paths. These paths give rise to important differences in personality development, as well as different definitions of maturity. As we trace

Can parents' expectations of their children influence development of preference, such as favorite color or most-played-with toy? Why or why not?

*Cultural background and gender affect
how we make sense of our experiences.*

these differences through the chapters of this text, we will question prevailing definitions of maturity. It is important to keep in mind, however, that differences
within groups defined by culture and gender are larger than the differences that
exist *between* these groups.

Continuity

As a final theme, this text will emphasize the continuities that are present in development as well as the more obvious changes that occur with age. A day in the life
of a toddler, a teenager, and a grandparent are very different. And yet each may
be coping with many of the same issues: closeness and separation, competence
and autonomy, dependence and independence. The toddler and grandparent, for
example, may face problems in dressing themselves—the one due to fingers not
yet under fine motor control and the other to fingers immobilized by arthritis. The
teenager's problem, on the other hand, may arise from restrictions on what clothes
she can get away with wearing. Yet each is struggling with an issue of independence versus dependence.

Not only do individuals face many of the same issues at different points in
their lives, but, in addition, the way they cope with these bears the particular

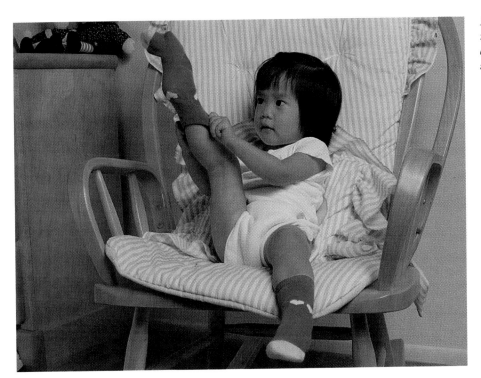

How we resolve issues such as independence/dependence may be determined by our personality and shows some continuity over time.

stamp of their personalities. How people resolve issues such as these affects their sense of self and gives their behavior over time a certain continuity.

Defining Development

How are we to define *development*? Briefly, we can say that **development** is the orderly set of changes that occur over time as individuals move from conception to death. Three features characterize these changes: growth, differentiation, and complexity. Although each of these aspects of development is most apparent in the very young, development itself is a lifelong process.

Growth is the result of metabolic processes in which proteins are broken down and used to make new cells. In a process called *mitosis,* cells divide to produce new cells, eventually producing the trillions of cells that form the adult body. Although growth at certain points in development can be very rapid, it is always an orderly process.

Growth progresses from the general to the specific. This aspect of development is known as **differentiation.** During prenatal development, for example, a single cell, the zygote, develops into the many different types of cells that will form the liver, the eyes, the fingernails, and the eyelashes of the fetus. Differentiation characterizes behavioral as well as physical development. Toddlers, for example, catch a ball with their whole bodies, clasping it to themselves; preschoolers can catch it with two hands; and, somewhere in middle childhood, children learn to catch with a single hand.

Differentiation brings new *complexity,* and with it comes a need to organize cells into a functioning whole. The nervous system and endocrine system accomplish this integration. As the central nervous system assumes control over activity, for example, the jerky reflexes of the fetus give way to fluid movements.

development The orderly set of changes that occur over the life span.

growth The result of metabolic processes in which proteins are broken down and used to make new cells.

differentiation A developmental trend characterized by a progression from the general to the specific.

Development is the result of growth,
differentiation, and complexity.

Similarly, in adolescence, the endocrine system integrates much of the body's functioning through the action of hormones, although adolescents will attest that the integration achieved is less than perfect. A girl can have the figure of a woman before she ever begins to menstruate, and a boy can be inches taller than his father and have not a wisp of hair on his chin.

Describing Development

Do you remember as a child riding a merry-go-round and trying to grab the brass ring as you passed by? Remember having to lean out over the horse, straining to reach the ring, balancing all the while as your horse moved up and down? It wasn't easy. That was probably what made it so much fun. Studying human development is a bit like riding a carousel—reaching for the brass ring on a moving horse. So much is changing in children at any given moment that it is hard to get a fix on any one thing. Just as they begin to walk, they are also speaking their first words and charming those around them with new social skills. All this in one who has tripled in size from birth! In order to simplify our study of development, we will consider separately three aspects that make up the whole of development (Figure 1.4). *Physical development* covers such things as growth of the brain and body and can be seen in such "simple" activities as being able to pick up a crayon, use scissors, or kick a ball. *Intellectual development* covers perceiving, remembering, thinking, and language and includes developments such as, in the example of the two brothers, the understanding that two pastries are not necessarily more than one if they also differ in size. Finally, *psychosocial development* covers the development of emotions, personality, and relationships with others.

These three aspects of development will be covered in separate chapters at each of the four ages covered in this text: infancy and toddlerhood, early child-

FIGURE 1.4 The Three Domains of Development

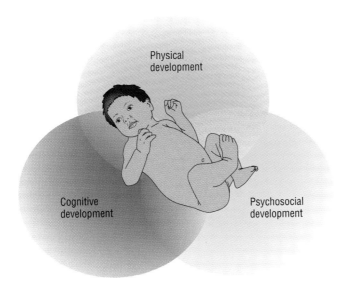

Physical development

Cognitive development

Psychosocial development

hood, middle childhood, and adolescence. As you read these chapters, however, keep in mind that this division is simply heuristic; it works because it simplifies our view of development, reducing it to manageable proportions. In actuality, changes in any of these areas of development affect each of the others.

The constructive perspective adopted in this text is not new. It derives from a set of assumptions, known as the organismic model, that have appeared in one form or another in the writings of many developmentalists. An alternative set of assumptions influencing developmental thought, known as the environmental model, can be seen in the work of early and contemporary behaviorists. We turn now to an examination of these models, or ways of looking at development, and to some of the theories they have spawned.

Models and Theories

Beneath the surface of every scientific theory are the beliefs we hold about the world we live in. We believe, for instance, that boys and girls *are* different. Many of us believe that there *has to be* a difference. Many of us believe that without differences the human species would be less viable than it is. These assumptions can be so fundamental that they go unnoticed, yet they exert powerful influences on the theories they generate.

A Model Defined

The assumptions we make about the world determine which questions appear reasonable and which seem foolish. If a developmentalist assumes that children's behaviors are primarily reactions to events in the environment, then it makes sense to inquire what is different about the events that precede their different behaviors. If another developmentalist assumes that behavior reflects goal-directed decisions, then it is reasonable to ask children about their goals and how they make their decisions. Notice that the first developmentalist is likely to observe what children do and what's going on around them when they do it. The second is likely to ask children *why* they do what they do. In each case, the beliefs that direct

Is nature or nurture most responsible for how similar or different twins turn out to be?

scientific investigation are collectively called a **model.** It is important to know just what a model is and how it serves our understanding of development.

You might think that only scientists have models of human behavior. Actually, we all do. Do you think behavior is intentional and goal-directed, or does it simply reflect past reinforcements? What motivates us? A succession of rewards and punishments? Inner goals? How much are we influenced by our biology? Does our genetic inheritance shape our interests and drives? Or do our interests and drives reflect acquired tastes and passions?

Not all of us share the same model. Models are easiest to see when the differences between them are extreme. Consider a teenage baby-sitter putting a young child to bed. The child lost a tooth that day and insists on placing it under his pillow. The child's belief system (model) includes tooth fairies. The baby-sitter's does not. What would the baby-sitter think if the child were to run up to her later with money in his hand and explain that he found it under the pillow? The teenager would question her sanity before admitting to anything like the tooth fairy—and with good reason. Scientists and teenagers alike base their theories on assumptions about what is real and what is not, and most adolescents assume that fairies are not real (Kuhn, 1962; Reese & Overton, 1970).

Models are useful because they generate theories. But models themselves are too general and often too vague to test. Theories, on the other hand, are specific explanations of particular phenomena that can be confirmed or disconfirmed. The baby-sitter dismisses the child's explanation because she assumes that a person, not a fairy, must have put the money under the pillow. We can even imagine her reviewing each alternative: "The money was there all along . . . I put it there and forgot . . . His mom or dad put it under the pillow before leaving . . . He took the money from his piggy bank just to put one over on me?" Each possibility reflects

model A set of assumptions about reality and human nature from which theories proceed.

a model in which *people* put money under pillows, a model that bestows reality on some events—whether they be people, quarks, or electromagnetic fields—and nonreality on others.

A Theory Defined

Theories reflect the models from which they derive. A look at our example shows us why. A **theory** consists of statements arranged from the very general to the very specific. The most general statements derive directly from the model and are called **axioms;** they are the assumptions one never thinks to question. An axiom that might be derived from the teenager's belief system would be that only things occupying space and existing in time are real. This axiom would exclude all but the most substantial of fairies. A **law** is at the next level. Derived from axioms, laws state relationships that are either true or false. Careful observations inform us of the validity of laws. A law from the preceding example might be that inanimate objects (such as teeth) remain stationary unless moved by some external force. Laws make it possible to predict specific events. We might predict that a tooth placed under a pillow would be there the next morning unless someone moved it.

All developmental theories have one thing in common: Each is an attempt to explain the constancies and changes in functioning that occur throughout the life course. Rather than embrace all aspects of functioning, developmental theories have limited themselves to particular aspects. Some, for instance, are concerned with personality development, others with social or intellectual development, still others with moral and ethical development. Whatever their focus, each theory looks at the similarities and differences that occur with age and attempts to explain them in terms of their sources or causes (Lerner, 1986).

Developmental Questions

Questions concerning the source of development have traditionally divided theorists into two camps. The division reflects their position on the **nature-nurture controversy:** Is nature—that is, heredity—primarily responsible for development, or is nurture—that is, the environment—responsible? Those who view nature as organizing developmental variables emphasize the importance of factors such as genetic inheritance and maturation. Developmentalists who look to nurture for explanations emphasize conditions such as the home environment and learning.

A second question, following from the first, also distinguishes developmental theories. This question concerns the form of the developmental laws that relate behavior to either source: the **continuity-discontinuity issue.** Can one explain behavior at any, and every, point in the life cycle without formulating new sets of laws? Do the same laws apply to other species as well (continuity)? Or do lawful relationships change with age and across species (discontinuity)? Figure 1.5 illustrates the contrasting concepts. Developmentalists who stress the importance of genetic inheritance and maturation typically assume that different sets of laws are needed for species with different genetic endowments and, within a species, at different points in development due to maturation. These theorists see development as occurring in discrete stages. Conversely, those who trace development to environmental sources are more likely to see these forces as exerting the same influence independent of age or species (Lerner, 1986).

Finally, developmentalists differ in the assumptions they make when explaining the occurrence of new behavior. Those who assume that the same set of laws

theory A set of testable statements derived from the axioms of a model.

axioms The unquestioned assumptions that form the basis of a theory.

laws Relationships that are derived from axioms and that can be proven to be true or false.

nature-nurture controversy The controversy concerning whether heredity (nature) or the environment (nurture) is primarily responsible for development.

continuity-discontinuity issue The question of whether the same set of developmental laws applies to all stages of the life cycle and to all species (continuity assumption) or whether different laws apply to different stages and different species (discontinuity assumption).

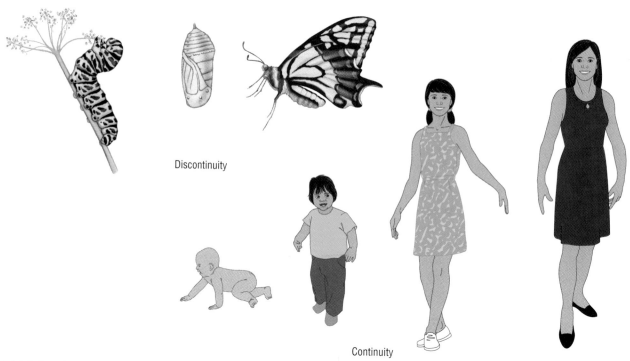

Discontinuity

Continuity

FIGURE 1.5 Continuity Versus Discontinuity of Development

Would a researcher who assumes that toddlers and middle adults experience disappointment for the same reasons be a reductionist or an epigenesist?

reductionism The explanation of complex behaviors by reducing them to their simpler components.

epigenesis At each stage of development, the emergence of new complexities that cannot be predicted from, or reduced to, earlier forms.

is sufficient to describe behavior at all points in the life cycle believe in **reductionism,** which is an attempt to explain complex behavior by reducing it to its simpler components. Developmentalists who assume that new laws are needed at different ages argue from the standpoint of **epigenesis,** holding that new complexities in development emerge that cannot be predicted from earlier forms (Lerner, 1986).

Differences in these sets of assumptions characterize different models of behavior: the environmental and the organismic. The first considers the environment to be the primary source of behavior, assumes continuity in developmental laws, and is reductionist in nature. The second looks to genetic or maturational forces—that is, nature—to explain development, assumes a noncontinuity position, and views development as epigenetic. All the theories deriving from a model bear a strong "family resemblance." Even so, you will find that the degree to which they reflect the assumptions characterizing the model will vary. Some theories reflect each of the model's assumptions perfectly; others are only a good approximation.

One organismic theory, the psychodynamic theory of Freud, is sufficiently broad in scope and has spawned enough offshoots that it is given separate treatment as a model. The psychodynamic approach gives importance to environmental as well as biological forces. This model adopts a compromise position with respect to continuity of developmental laws and assumes certain relationships to hold at all developmental periods and others to be specific to each particular period (Lerner, 1976).

Of the three models we will consider, the organismic model most directly represents the constructive approach adopted in this text, catching the dynamic interplay between the child's expectations and its experiences. Since the environmental model puts least emphasis on this active, constructive process, I have chosen to begin with that model and move to the one that best captures this dynamic developmental process.

The Environmental Model

The environmental model traces development to environmental forces. These forces affect behavior in lawful ways; the laws are assumed to apply at all levels of development. The assumption of continuity to behavioral laws underlies a strong reductionist approach in environmental theories. Since everything from silicon chips to bones and brain tissue is made of atoms and molecules, the laws that describe their actions should describe the functioning of humans as well as the workings of a computer. To explain vision, an environmentalist would speak of the amount of light necessary to stimulate receptors in the retina or of the exchange of sodium and potassium ions across the membrane of a neuron as the impulse is propagated along the neural fiber. Everything from a toddler taking first steps to the virtuosity of a concert cellist playing a Bach fugue is understood as a sequence of simple reactions, each prompted by the completion of the last and all traceable to an external force. In other words, "there is nothing special about the complex pattern of events we call psychological function. In the final analysis these events involve the functioning of the very same atoms and molecules that are involved in the workings of a liver, a kidney, or a shooting star" (Lerner, 1986, p. 45).

Reductionism reduces psychological phenomena to simple components that operate, in principle, no differently than do those in a machine. The metaphor of a machine is helpful in understanding the environmental model, because it translates otherwise abstract assumptions into an everyday example. Based on what we know about the example, we can predict certain outcomes and events that otherwise might remain unclear.

In order to get a machine to work, you have to start it; a machine does not start on its own. You have to plug it in, push a button, or whatever. This sets off a chained sequence of events that takes the same form each time it unfolds. As long as the parts bear the same relationship to each other, tripping one will set the next in motion. Machines do only what they are constructed to do. Vacuum cleaners do not give off light, and refrigerators don't suck up dirt. But, if you know what kind of machine you have and just what point in the sequence is unfolding, you should be able to predict what it will do next.

Is human behavior this predictable? The environmental model assumes it is—ideally. In actuality, it is difficult, if not impossible, to specify the myriad parts that make up the human machine. Even if one could, must our actions be started by something external to ourselves, or are we capable of self-initiated behavior? The environmental and organismic models give us different answers (Reese & Overton, 1970).

If the model of the machine is correct, behavior is always a response to an external event. Actions are *re*actions to forces external to us. The environment becomes the source of our behavior. We, like machines, remain quiescent until something stimulates us to act. Does an engine fail to start because it doesn't "want" to? Intention and desire are reduced by the environmentalist to links in the chain of human behavior. The burden for explaining and changing behavior remains with the environment. Is a first-grader disruptive in school? Look for the events in the classroom that cause this behavior. Is a child anxious in new situations? Have that child list situations from the most to the least anxiety-producing, and then tackle the easiest. Success will make the next situation more

Is it events (environmental) that explain this child's precocity, or is it how the child made sense of and reacted to those events?

approachable. While it is often difficult to trace behaviors to the events that occasion them, it is infinitely easier than it would be if organisms could, at any moment, choose to alter what they were doing just because they felt like it. Human behavior is, at least in the abstract, predictable for those who hold to this model.

Notice that, in this model, there is no reference to what takes place "*between* an event and a reaction to it . . . the place where the event is privately composed, made sense of . . . where it actually *becomes* an event for that person," as Kegan (1982) would say. Such a constructive process is not thought to be a necessary precursor to one's response to events. However, just such a process does characterize the organismic model.

The Organismic Model

The organismic model, from which the constructive perspective derives, takes the living, biological system as its metaphor for human behavior. This model explains human development in terms of variables closely tied to the nature of the organism and governing its growth. Organismic theorists differ sharply from environmentalists, practically point by point, in their views of human nature (Table 1.1).

One method used to train pre-school children to stop wetting the bed is an alarm installed under the sheets that sounds when the child has wet the bed. What would organismic theorists probably think about this technique?

Three points summarize these differences. Organismic theorists view the human organism as active rather than passive. They believe this activity to be internally organized, and not just a reaction to external events. Finally, they understand behavior as the unfolding of genetically programmed processes, which produce discontinuous development, marked by qualitatively different stages. Environmentalists, on the other hand, view developmental change as continuous, with ever-more-complex behaviors being formed from the same simple building blocks (Lerner, 1986; Reese & Overton, 1970).

TABLE 1.1 Comparison of Developmental Models

	Environmental Model	Organismic Model
Organism Is	Reactive	Active
Behavior Is	Structured by environment	Internally organized
Development Is Due to	Behavioral conditioning	Environmental-genetic interactions
Focus Is on	Behavior	Cognition, perception, motivation
Developmental Stages?	No	Yes

The Active Organism   Organismic theorists point out that environmental events become clear only when we respond to them. It takes an action from us to define the conditions that will then be perceived as events. Noam Chomsky (1957), a psycholinguist at MIT, has pressed this argument effectively (John Dewey made the same argument in 1896). Chomsky argues that many sentences appearing to have a single meaning actually have many. They appear clear because we have *already* assumed a context in which they are unambiguous. Consider the sentence, "They are eating apples." Seems clear enough. What are they doing? They are eating apples. Yet if the sentence is a response to the question "What kind of apples are those?" its meaning changes. There are different kinds of apples. Some are for cooking and others for eating. And what are those? They are eating apples.

Organized Activity   Let's look at a simple experiment to illustrate the point: Individuals heard a click every 20 seconds for several minutes. With the first click, heart rate, brain-wave activity, sensory receptivity, and electrical conductance of the skin changed. These changes make up the *orienting response,* a general reaction to novel events. With each recurrence of the click, the orienting response decreased until it barely occurred at all (Sokolov, 1963). When **habituation,** or decreased response, had been pretty well established, the click was stopped, and everyone reacted with a full-scale orienting response. What was the stimulus for their reaction? Could it have been the *absence* of sound? The same silence, however, did not produce a reaction before the procedure began.

The phenomenon of habituation tells us that organisms detect regularities in their surroundings and anticipate them. Events that match, or confirm, their anticipations provoke no further reaction. Those that do not conform prompt a reaction. Notice that our definition of a stimulus has changed. The stimulus is no longer an external event. Nor is it simply an internal event. It is a product of both. The stimulus is the match, or mismatch, of input with what is anticipated. As such, the original meaning of stimulus, as a goad or prod to action, is lost (Miller, Galanter, & Pribram, 1960).

Developmental Stages   Organismic theorists argue that as children age, they organize experience in different ways than they did during the preceding period of development. Each period is a separate **stage** with its own characteristics. For example, Jean Piaget, a Swiss developmentalist, described several stages in the development of thought, the last of which begins in adolescence. In the first stage, infants do not have symbols through which they can represent their experiences, and thought in the absence of symbols is very different from the symbolic thought of adults, or even of slightly older children. When language first develops, young children organize their experience in personal ways, not according to the linguistic categories used by older children or adults (Piaget, 1952, 1954).

habituation Decreased responsiveness to a stimulus with repeated exposure to it.

stage A level of development that is assumed to be qualitatively different from the earlier level from which it evolves. Stages are assumed to occur in a fixed sequence and to occur universally within a species.

You can see this difference for yourself with a simple procedure. Just ask a preschooler and an adolescent to say the first word that comes to mind after you say each of two words. To "fork" the preschooler is likely to say "eat"; the adolescent will most likely say "spoon." To "chair" the preschooler will likely respond "sit"; the adolescent, "table." Preschoolers organize experience in terms of what they do with things. They answer with functional categories: One eats with a fork and sits on a chair. Adolescents organize experience in terms of linguistic categories: "Fork" and "spoon" are both utensils, and "chair" and "table" are furniture.

A final point before leaving our discussion of this model concerns the way we know our world. Recall that the environmental model views perception as a passive copy of reality. The organismic model maintains, predictably enough, just the opposite—that perception is an active, constructive process. The example given earlier in the chapter, of the way we recognize words by actively scanning the features of letters when we read, illustrates this position.

These two models have generated a lively debate in the scientific community. The third model offers yet another perspective and, along with it, fuel for more debate.

The Psychodynamic Model

Psychodynamic theories, like many other organismic theories and some environmental ones such as social-cognitive theory, combine elements of both approaches. They hold that development is organized around stages that take form as maturation enables the organism to interact with its surroundings in new ways. Like environmentalists, they emphasize the way the environment contributes to the personal experiences that focus inner organization. Freud, for example, assumed that young boys experience horror when they first see a little girl naked, believing that she has been castrated. Their reaction to this experience both reflects and redirects inner psychic forces. Freud (1925b/1961) would argue that maturation has brought them to a stage in which sexual tensions receive genital focus and also involve them in a dangerous rivalry with their fathers. To protect themselves from a fate similar to the girls', boys must repress their sexual fantasies, thus resolving the Oedipal complex and moving them into the next stage of development.

For psychodynamic theorists, life is a battle, and we are all on the front lines. Two opposing forces, one within us and the other outside, fight for control. Since each is an integral aspect of our personalities, the victory of either one means a sure defeat to the individual. This model emphasizes both inner processes and external events.

The psychodynamic model stresses a balance between strong biological instincts and social constraints. We achieve this balance only with time and at some personal cost. As in any war, there are casualties. True spontaneity may be the first to go. The second takes the form of compromise: We learn to make do with lesser delights to avoid the anxiety provoked by indulging our first instincts. There are victories as well. We gain control over instinctual urges that otherwise, these theorists say, could destroy us and our civilization (Hall, 1954).

Like organismic theorists, psychodynamic theorists believe that development occurs over distinct stages that unfold in different zones of the body, focusing the expression of psychic energy. This energy, which Freud termed **libido,** takes different forms depending on the body zone through which it is channeled. Expression of the libido moves from the region of the mouth in infancy (*oral stage*), to

libido In psychoanalytic theory, the psychic energy that is expressed through different zones of the body and motivates much of behavior.

the sphincters in toddlerhood (*anal stage*), to the genital region in early childhood (*phallic stage*). Because genital expression of the libido in early childhood is associated with tremendous anxiety, it goes underground (*latency stage*), so to speak, and does not arise again until it emerges full-force with puberty (*genital stage*), once again pressing for genital expression (Freud, 1961).

Different aspects of the personality express or inhibit these instincts. The **id** demands immediate gratification of the biological impulses which it houses. It operates according to the pleasure principle. The **ego** attempts to satisfy impulses in the most diplomatic way without getting the organism into really deep trouble. It operates according to the reality principle. Even so, Freud assumed that reality for most of early childhood does not include issues of right and wrong, only what one can get away with without getting punished. Moral concerns arise when the **superego** emerges, and with it the conscience. This part of the personality internalizes social standards and comes about when the child identifies with the parent of its own sex. (The emergence of the superego is discussed later in this chapter.)

Although Freud included both biological and environmental forces in his theory, he embodied each in a separate aspect of the personality: biological forces in the id and social standards in the superego. The ego, like a clever general, is given the job of leading the weary troops between these warring factions. The functions of the ego—such as planning, comparing, and evaluating—emphasize the active role we take in structuring our experiences, an assumption shared with organismic theorists. Perhaps because the psychodynamic model does not require us to choose between environmental and biological influences, by relegating each to different aspects of personality functioning, it has remained immensely popular. And, since it is willing to address unconscious motives and thoughts, it permits us to explain much of human behavior that otherwise would remain obscure (Hall, 1954).

Is the psychodynamic model better than the others for these reasons? Or perhaps the environmental model is more "scientific," because it focuses on behaviors that can be observed and precisely measured? Comparisons all too frequently lead to evaluations, and someone ends up holding the short end of the theoretical stick. Comparisons can also be misleading. Each model addresses different aspects of human function. We need all three to begin unraveling the knotty problems of development. The psychodynamic model helps us understand motives and feelings that otherwise would never see the light of day. The environmental model gives us objective and easily testable theories of behavior. The organismic model offers sophisticated approaches to cognition and perception. Unless we are willing to settle for theories about children who act but don't think and feel, or children who think and feel but can't act, we need the insights each model offers.

But what about the developmental theories spawned by these models? Remember, a single model can parent many theories. We will look at several theories for each. Examining more than one theory should help distinguish the assumptions of the model from the particular form they take in a theory.

Environmental Theories

Environmental theories, recall, look to forces outside the individual to explain development. These theories assume that behavior is essentially a reaction to surrounding events. As a consequence, these theories attempt to describe development in terms of lawful changes that relate behavior to external events.

id In psychoanalytic theory, the aspect of the personality that demands immediate gratification of biological impulses; operates according to the pleasure principle.

ego In psychoanalytic theory, the executive aspect of the personality that attempts to satisfy impulses in socially acceptable ways.

superego In psychoanalytic theory, the aspect of the personality that represents the internalized standards and values of society and emerges when the child identifies with the parent of its own sex.

FIGURE 1.6 Pavlov's Conditioning Apparatus

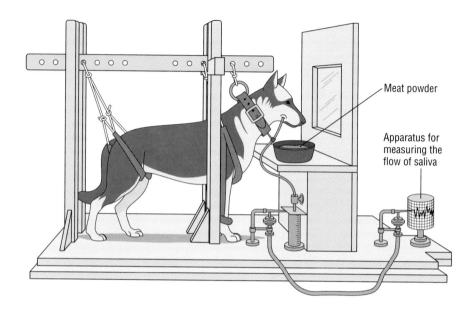

Meat powder

Apparatus for measuring the flow of saliva

Ivan Pavlov

How might Pavlov explain the response we have to familiar smells like Mom's pancakes or the smell of a family barbeque?

Ivan Pavlov, a Russian physiologist, noticed that his laboratory animals began salivating at the sounds of their evening meal being prepared. Many of us have probably noticed the same thing when feeding a pet. To a physiologist, salivation in response to a *sound* is highly unusual—and requires explaining. Salivation, you see, is a reflex that should occur only when triggered by its own stimulus. The trigger is a chemical reaction caused by food touching the membranes lining the mouth. Pavlov's dogs were salivating *before* food ever reached their mouths (Pavlov, 1927). His conditioning apparatus is shown in Figure 1.6.

Pavlov had identified a simple form of learning, which he termed **respondent conditioning.** Respondents are reflexes that occur involuntarily, in response to particular stimuli, such as salivation in response to food in one's mouth or the knee jerk in response to a sharp tap beneath the knee. Respondents can be brought under the control of other environmental stimuli through respondent conditioning, also known as classical conditioning.

Pavlov identified four elements in respondent conditioning. The food that triggers the salivation is the **unconditional stimulus (UCS),** and reflexive salivation to the food is the **unconditional response (UCR).** The food-preparation sounds are the **conditional stimulus (CS),** and salivation in response to the sounds is the **conditional response (CR).** To make sure you have the components of respondent conditioning down pat, try analyzing the following example for the UCS, UCR, CS, and CR.

A 10-year-old who had difficulty waking for school in the morning solved his problem by placing an alarm clock inches away from his pillow. Each morning, as the first rays of light appeared through the blinds, the alarm went off and he was startled awake. He was especially annoyed during spring vacation to find that he continued to awaken at the first rays of light, even though he had not set the alarm. What are the UCS and the UCR in this example? Can you identify the CS? The CR? (The answers appear at the end of the chapter.)

respondent conditioning A simple form of learning in which an involuntary reflex is brought under the control of another environmental stimulus.

unconditional stimulus (UCS) In respondent conditioning, the stimulus that triggers a reflexive, or unconditional, response.

unconditional response (UCR) In respondent conditioning, the reflexive response to a particular stimulus.

conditional stimulus (CS) In respondent conditioning, the new environmental stimulus used to elicit a reflexive, or conditional, response.

conditional response (CR) In respondent conditioning, the reflex learned in response to a new stimulus.

B. F. Skinner

Most human behavior is not reflexive. B. F. Skinner, an American psychologist, referred to voluntary, or nonreflexive, actions as *operants,* to distinguish them from respondents. He pointed out that operants frequently do not have identifiable stimuli to elicit them. Instead, Skinner reduced the nuances and complexities of human behavior to the events that follow it rather than to what might have preceded it. His approach is a radical departure from the way most people understand their behavior. Most of us think that what we do is a response to inner states, to our feelings and thoughts. Skinner told us our behavior is under the control of external events. He called his approach radical behaviorism.

Skinner said it is senseless to talk about inner states such as motives and intentions. We can't measure or observe them. He believed we can only understand behavior by describing the conditions under which it occurs. When antecedent conditions cannot be identified, he suggested looking at what follows the behavior. When we do, lawful relationships emerge. Operants, just like respondents, can be brought under the control of environmental events. Skinner studied this simple form of learning—operant conditioning—extensively (Skinner, 1938, 1953, 1961).

Skinner successfully used operant conditioning in laboratories, classrooms, and mental hospitals. The breadth of his successes supports his conviction that the environment exerts a pervasive influence on human behavior. Together, these two forms of learning, respondent and operant, tie many aspects of behavior to environmental sources. Reflexive responses ranging from behavioral reflexes to emotional responses (the involuntary nervous system is involved in emotional expression) can be respondently conditioned, and nonreflexive actions, whether a simple tap of a toe or the double axel of an Olympic skating champion like Kristi Yamaguchi, can be explained in terms of operant conditioning (Skinner, 1953).

Skinner's (1938) first subjects were rats. He constructed a small box with a metal lever protruding from one wall and selected a simple behavior—pressing the lever—for study. Since there was little for an animal to do in such a small space, its explorations soon brought it near the lever. Skinner waited until the animal touched the lever and then dropped a food pellet into a chute that ended in a dish beneath the lever. Each time the rat pressed the lever, a pellet of food dropped into the dish. In no time the rat began to steadily press the lever. Skinner had brought a voluntary behavior—putting a paw on a metal lever and depressing it—under the control of its consequences. By making food contingent on lever pressing, he controlled the frequency with which the rat pressed the lever.

Critics reacted by saying that humans are different from animals or, at the very least, different from rats. Our behavior reflects motives and intentions, not contingencies. Skinner's reply to these objections was that our intentions reflect our reinforcement histories. Consider a teenager who has a favorite color—purple, for instance—and buys many of her clothes in that color. Skinner would explain this preference for purple in terms of past reinforcements when wearing purple. She may have worn a purple skirt one day and received several compliments. When next shopping for clothes, she tried on several items that were purple, finally buying one. She spent a few extra minutes with her appearance the day she wore her new clothes and once again received several compliments. Skinner would suggest that this history of reinforcements shaped her preference for purple.

Some reinforcements are pleasant. When they follow a behavior, the behavior becomes more frequent; this procedure is called **positive reinforcement.** Other reinforcements can be unpleasant, and behavior that *removes* them becomes more frequent; this procedure is called **negative reinforcement.** Positive and negative reinforcement have powerful and pervasive effects on behavior.

We can analyze many social interactions in terms of positive and negative reinforcement. Sometimes such an analysis seems especially appropriate with children and their parents. Let's look at an exchange between a 5-year-old and

How might Skinner describe a room full of people gambling on slot machines?

positive reinforcement An event that increases the frequency of the behavior on which its occurrence is made contingent.

negative reinforcement An event that increases the frequency of the behavior on which its removal is made contingent.

his mother. The mother has just told him to pick his clothes up from the living room floor. "Awhh," he whines. She reacts quickly and sharply, with more animation than he has seen all morning. He picks up his clothes and carries them off to his room.

Now take a closer look at what has just taken place. The mother reinforced her son when she allowed herself to become "engaged" by his whining. She paid more attention to him than she had all morning. Attention is a powerful reinforcer. Even though this may not be the kind of attention the child, or anyone, seeks, if it is more than he usually gets and if he frequently whines when his mother scolds, she is very likely reinforcing a behavior that in fact annoys her.

Also notice that *he* reinforced *her* scolding. By picking his clothes up when she scolded (removing something that displeased her), he negatively reinforced her scolding—the very behavior that maintains his whining. We can analyze many parent-child interactions in terms of the reciprocal effects of positive and negative reinforcement. Children frequently develop the very behaviors their parents find most objectionable. According to behaviorists such as Skinner, this is no accident. Those are the very behaviors parents are most likely to notice.

Reinforcement is a powerful force in shaping and maintaining behavior. But must we actually do something or receive reinforcement in order to learn? Critics of radical behaviorism point out that we can know *what* to do before we ever do it. Many actions are novel, yet they unfold in smooth, successful sequences, not in the on-again, off-again manner one would expect if trial and error governed their performance. Language itself is perhaps the most intricate of all human activities and the most difficult for Skinner to explain. We produce endless numbers of novel sentences each day. Has each been shaped through reinforcement? How is radical behaviorism to account for each of these?

Albert Bandura

Albert Bandura, a psychologist at Stanford University, stresses the social nature of learning; his approach is called social-cognitive theory. Bandura believes that most human learning is **observational learning,** not conditioning, and occurs by *observing* what others do and *imitating* what one sees. One need not actually perform the behavior oneself. Inner processes such as attention and memory focus behavior. This theory departs from strict environmentalist assumptions by emphasizing inner, cognitive processes by which individuals interpret their experiences. Bandura supported his position in a dramatic study of aggression in children.

Children at play watched a model punch and kick a large inflated doll in unusual ways (Bandura, Ross, & Ross, 1963). The model sat on it, shouted "Sock him in the nose," punched the doll, and then hit it with a hammer and yelled "Pow!" Later, when the children were left alone with the doll and other toys, they imitated the same unusual sequences, often copying exactly what they had seen. Other children who had watched a model play with Tinkertoys showed none of the same aggressive behaviors. Numerous studies support the importance of observation and imitation in human learning (Bandura, 1977, 1980).

Social-cognitive theorists are willing to talk about many of the same processes as organismic theorists, such as thoughts and motives. Many of these processes suggest that the learner actively use information instead of being a passive receiver of input. Yet social-cognitive theorists, just like other environmentalists, assume that developmental changes are continuous. Unlike organismic theorists, they do not explain change as a succession of stages distinguished by qualitatively different features. Psychodynamic theorists give us a very different view of things.

observational learning In social-cognitive theory, learning by observing what others do and imitating what one sees.

How important are observation and information in human learning? Bandura's bobo doll experiment supports the idea that aggression is learned through imitation.

Psychodynamic Theories

Psychodynamic theories, like environmental ones, assume that environmental forces significantly contribute to development. However, these theories also assume there are powerful forces within each of us that interact with environmental ones in giving shape to development.

Sigmund Freud

As a young physician with a private practice in neurology, Sigmund Freud might have been more surprised than anyone else at the direction his career would take. Were it not for some of his patients who complained of mysterious ailments, he might have remained an obscure but successful Viennese doctor.

The mysterious symptoms were no different from those he saw daily, such as numbness and paralysis from damaged nerves. But the nerves in these patients were unaffected; he found only healthy neural tissue when he examined them. How could patients suffer neurological symptoms with no physical damage? Fortunately, a Frenchman named Jean Charcot had just concluded a series of studies in which healthy people were told under hypnosis that they would awake with physical symptoms (among those suggested were numbness and paralysis). When they awoke, they had no memory of the suggestion, yet they exhibited the symptoms, just as Freud's patients did (Thomas, 1979).

The Unconscious Freud (1961) eventually solved the mystery, but only by tossing aside current notions about the mind. He asserted that we have an active mental life of which we remain completely unaware, an unconscious that affects our actions in direct ways. Thoughts, feelings, or problems that are too disturbing to face or that cannot be solved immediately are pushed out of the conscious mind, repressed to the unconscious realm of thought. Although **repression**

repression A defense mechanism that operates by relegating distressful thoughts and feelings to the unconscious.

Sigmund Freud

momentarily reduces the distress, it does not get rid of the problem. The thoughts and feelings continue to exist and continue to push for expression, like a teapot that has been brought to a boil: If you cover the spout, the pressure within continues to build until the steam is released through some other opening, perhaps by blowing off the lid. The repressed ideas and feelings escape in many ways—in dreams, actions, or even physical symptoms, as with Freud's patients. The only requirement limiting their expression is that the person remain unaware of their true meaning, thereby protected from the distress they occasion. The treatment that Freud eventually devised involved discovering the unconscious source of the patient's distress and bringing it to light in the safe atmosphere of therapy.

Freud formulated his theory of personality development while treating these unusual symptoms. He believed that they resulted from an inner war between conflicting aspects of the personality. Although Freud first noticed these aspects of personality in his patients, he believed them to be present in all of us.

Three Facets of the Personality   For Freud, all thought and action are motivated. He termed the life force that motivates these the *libido* (see "The Psychodynamic Model," earlier in the chapter). Different aspects of the personality control the expression or inhibition of libido. Its expression is highly pleasurable (assuming a sexual nature even in infancy), and the pressure resulting from its blockage is painful. The facet of the personality that seeks immediately to satisfy the libido's expression is the *id*. Present from birth, the id has limited means for gratifying libidinal impulses. The infant can only cry its displeasure or fantasize about the food and comfort it desires.

The *ego* soon emerges as a means of realistically satisfying these instinctual impulses. The ego can distinguish the id's fantasies from actual goals and can negotiate the realities of the environment. It also realizes that while some forms of expression will be tolerated, others will bring more pain than they're worth. The ego seeks to gratify as many of the id's demands as possible without bringing on the wrath of parents, peers, and society. It operates according to the reality principle, both facilitating and blocking the expression of the libido.

A final aspect of the personality, emerging from the ego when the child is about 4 or 5, contains the moral values acquired from our culture and dictates what we should and should not do. Freud called this the *superego*. It has two aspects, the conscience and the ego-ideal. The conscience embodies the "should-nots," those thoughts and actions for which we have been punished in the past; the ego-ideal represents the "shoulds," the positive values we have learned as children. These two aspects of the superego gradually assume the controls that once had to be exercised by parents and others, so that, with the ego and superego working in concert, behavior becomes self-regulated (Hall, 1954).

The baton Freud carried was passed to a successor who also viewed development as unfolding in a single, universal sequence for females and males alike—a sequence that again takes a male perspective.

According to Freud, is it reasonable to expect a 3-year-old to know the difference between "good" and "bad" behavior?

Erik Erikson

As a restless young man, Erik Erikson traveled about Europe, earning a living as an artist and eventually teaching art in a school for young children. The position at the school proved to be a turning point in his life, for the school had been founded by Freud's daughter Anna, who herself was an analyst and involved in establishing the new discipline of child analysis. Erikson became part of the intimate circle of associates and friends of the Freuds, eventually entering into analysis with Anna Freud and completing his training as a psychoanalyst (Coles, 1970).

Erikson built on Freud's analysis of the personality as id, ego, and superego and on his stages of psychosexual development. Yet he differed from Freud in several important respects. Perhaps the most significant is Erikson's emphasis on the healthy personality. Freud regarded health as the *absence* of something—neurosis. Erikson regarded it as the *presence* of something—vitality. Erikson (1968) cites Marie Jahoda's definition of a healthy personality in enumerating three things essential to vitality: *mastery* of one's surroundings, *unity* of the personality, and *accuracy* in perceiving one's world and oneself. See the Research Focus, "Erikson's Psychohistorical Approach: A Clinician's Notebook from the Dakota Prairies," for a discussion of Erikson's view of development within a social community.

Erik Erikson

Psychosocial Stages of Development   Erikson (1963) believed that new aspects of the person emerge through inner growth, making new types of social encounters possible. As with other stage theorists, he assumed that development occurs in the same set sequence for all, reflecting an internal ground plan in which each stage has its own period of ascendance, a time in which the individual is especially vulnerable to certain influences and insensitive to others. (This assumption is known as Erikson's **epigenetic principle**.) Society challenges us with new demands as we age. We experience these as crises. Each takes a slightly different form and gives each age its unique characteristics. Table 1.2 describes each of Erikson's life stages.

Each of the first four crises equips individuals to meet the central challenge of achieving an ego identity. Trust establishes the confidence in themselves and in

TABLE 1.2 Erikson's Developmental Stages	
Stage	**Psychosocial Crisis**
Birth to Adolescence	
Infancy	Trust versus mistrust. Realization that needs will be met leads to trust in others and self.
Toddlerhood	Autonomy versus shame and doubt. Physical maturation gives sense of being able to do things for self.
Early childhood	Initiative versus guilt. Increasing abilities promote exploration and expand experience.
Middle childhood	Industry versus inferiority. Accomplishments and skills provide basis for self-esteem.
Adolescence to Old Age	
Adolescence	Identity versus identity diffusion. Biological and social changes of adolescence occasion a search for continuity of self.
Early adulthood	Intimacy versus isolation. Sense of self provides the basis for sexual and emotional intimacy with another adult.
Middle adulthood	Generativity versus stagnation. Concern for children and future generations reflects need to leave something of oneself.
Late adulthood	Integrity versus despair. Acceptance of one's life as having meaning gives one a sense of dignity.

Source: E. Erikson. (1963). *Childhood and society.* New York: Norton.

epigenetic principle Erikson's assumption that an internal plan governs the timing or period of ascendance for each new development.

Erikson's Psychohistorical Approach: A Clinician's Notebook from the Dakota Prairies WITH MICHAEL WAPNER

When we neared the simple, clean homestead, the little sons were playing the small Indian boy's favorite game, roping a tree stump, while a little girl was lazily sitting on her father's knees, playing with his patient hands. Jim's wife was working in the house. We had brought some additional supplies, knowing that with Indians nothing can be settled in a few hours; our conversation would have to proceed in the slow, thoughtful, shy manner of the hosts. Jim's wife had asked some women relatives to attend our session. From time to time she went to the door to look out over the prairie which rolled away on every side, merging in the distance with the white processions of slow-moving clouds. As we sat and said little, I had time to consider what Jim's place among the living generations of his people might be. (Erikson, 1963, pp. 120–121)

So begins Erikson's description of the conversations that contributed to his understanding of the Sioux's early childhood experiences and their difficulty as adults in finding meaning to life. More generally, these observations led to his understanding of the ways in which one's society influences the course of each person's development.

Erik Erikson developed a unique style of research that combined the tools of clinical analysis with those of fieldwork. His insights into human development reflected the same psychoanalytic training that Freud and others practiced in urban European offices. Erikson took these skills to the rolling plains of the Dakotas, and later to the forested dwellings of the Yurok in the Northwest, and, in doing so, opened new vistas in our understanding of human development.

His observations made him keenly aware that human development takes place within a social community. Each community raises its children to participate in the world as adults—but there are as many worlds as there are communities. Children are indulged or controlled, taught to give away or to hoard, and so on, depending on the wisdom of their group—a wisdom that reflects the peace their group has made with the realities of geography and the historical moment. The area in which one lives determines the form life takes, whether in the specifics of what one eats or wears or in abstractions such as notions of goodness and propriety (Coles, 1970).

The Sioux, for instance, value generosity and regard the accumulation of wealth as tantamount to evil. Erikson traces these attitudes to a nomadic life in which they followed the buffalo across the plains. The buffalo existed in great numbers and the Sioux rarely experienced need. As nomads, the Sioux learned to live lightly, without the encumbrances of possessions. Generosity, because it reflected a more basic harmony with their surroundings, was a virtue. Conversely, the Yurok value thrift and a meticulous management of resources. They live in settlements along the Klamath River. Once a year, when the salmon return to breed, they experience the abundance that the Sioux lived with in every season. For the rest of the year, they must cautiously manage that brief harvest to avoid hunger and need.

These particular differences are less important than the common function served by the communal practices of either group. Ritual ways of living provided each with a group identity. It is from this group identity that members of the community derived a sense of their own identity. Erikson arrived at this observation after noting what he referred to as a "cultural pathology" among the present-day Sioux. He traced this problem to their inability to find "fitting images to connect the past with the future" (Erikson, 1963, p. 117). The Sioux's lifestyle had been tied to the buffalo, the provider of meat for food; pelts for clothing and shelter; bones for needles, ornaments, and toys; and even dried droppings for fuel. The destruction of the buffalo herds by White settlers resulted in the destruction of the Sioux's way of life—and the group identity from which new generations could derive a sense of themselves. Speaking of the present generation of Sioux, Erikson (1963) noted that

the majority of them have as little concept of the future as they are beginning to have of the past. This youngest generation, then, finds itself between the impressive dignity of its grandparents, who honestly refuse to believe that the white man is here to stay, and the white man himself, who feels that the Indian persists in being a rather impractical relic of a dead past. (p. 121)

If Erikson's theory is correct, that without "fitting images to connect the past with the future" young people are lost, what are the images that performed this function for you? Is there any single or even small set of recurrent experiences that anchor you in your community and physical environment the way the buffalo anchored the Sioux? Is it possible that our present society in the United States has no such single image? Perhaps these images belong to subgroups rather than the culture as a whole. For instance, is the gang for the East Los Angeles gang member in any way analogous to the buffalo for the Sioux? What functions would the gang have to fulfill for its members to qualify as an image? If it is an image in the Eriksonian sense, then what will it take to discourage gang membership in East Los Angeles and similar urban communities?

others that is needed to begin the task. Autonomy gives self-direction and purpose, the ability to follow goals that one sets for oneself rather than those set by others. Initiative allows individuals to explore options as these open up, and industry allows them to realistically evaluate these options and select the ones they will commit themselves to (Erikson, 1963, 1968).

The establishment of identity involves the individual in a succession of commitments to life goals that serve to define the self. The young adult faces the crisis of sharing that self with another—of intimacy, first with a mate and then, for most, with children. Middle adulthood extends the adult's concerns beyond this intimate group to others in the community. Older adults face a final crisis of reviewing their lives and accepting the decisions they have made. Erikson calls this last crisis one of personal integrity.

Like Freud's, Erikson's theory reflects a male bias. Erikson considers the achievement of identity to be the central crisis of adolescence, even though he asserts that a different sequence exists for females. Most females resolve the crisis of intimacy, which Erikson places in early adulthood, *before* they complete identity issues. Their sense of themselves derives more from their relationships than from commitments to work and ideology. Although Erikson notes these differences, he does not change his sequence of life stages; that is, he equates the male experience with development in general (Bardwick & Douvan, 1971; Josselson, 1988).

Nancy Chodorow

Nancy Chodorow

Another theorist, also influenced by Freud, gives us a different view of development. Nancy Chodorow offers an alternative to the universal developmental sequence charted by Freud and Erikson. Chodorow (1978) attributes psychological differences in the makeup of females and males to the social fact that for most children the first intimate relationship is with a woman—their mother. This initial relationship has different consequences for girls than it does for boys.

Chodorow (1978) asserts that infants experience themselves as continuous with the mother. They live within the boundless security of her presence, little caring which smile is theirs or whose hand reaches out to the other, all of it part of the same encircling awareness. Mothers, too, empathically relate to their infants and experience a continuity with them:

> In a society where mothers provide nearly exclusive care and certainly the most meaningful relationship to the infant, the infant develops its sense of self mainly in relation to her. Insofar as the relationship with its mother has continuity, the infant comes to define aspects of its self . . . in relation to internalized representations of aspects of its mother. (p. 78)

Important to Chodorow are the necessary differences in the way children of either sex develop beyond this point. Girls can continue to define themselves within the context of this first relationship. Mothers, as well, can see their daughters as extensions of themselves. Girls can experience a continuing attachment to the mother while still defining themselves as females. None of this is possible for boys. They must separate themselves from the mother much earlier than girls do in order to develop as males. Mothers, too, experience their sons as separate and different from themselves, unlike their daughters. Thus, boys embark on a developmental path marked not by attachment but by separation and increasing individuation.

Chodorow argues that since the primary caregiver is the same sex for girls, there is less need for the girl to differentiate herself in terms of ego boundaries.

The Declining Fortunes of Children: How Best to Help? BY ANDREA HAYES

Historically, attitudes toward the poor in this nation have vacillated between believing that their poverty was due to undisciplined behavior and believing them to be truly disadvantaged through no fault of their own. Consequently, assistance has been divided into "workfare" and "welfare" approaches. August 1996 brought one of the most radical pieces of legislation regarding public assistance since the 1930s, shifting the swing of the legislative pendulum in the direction of "workfare" rather than "welfare." The Personal Responsibility Work Opportunity and Reconciliation Act (PRWORA), or welfare reform law of 1996, indicated that legislators no longer saw welfare as helpful assistance to the disadvantaged, but rather as a handout that fostered continued dependence.

The 1996 welfare reform law replaces the former Aid to Families with Dependent Children (AFDC), a program that offered guaranteed federal income support to economically disadvantaged families, with a new program, Temporary Assistance to Needy Families (TANF), in which individual states determine assistance eligibility. TANF represents a significant departure from AFDC in several important respects. The new bill imposes a lifetime limit on public assistance of no more than 5 years, introduces work requirements, and ties support to limitations on the size of families.

Will requirements and limitations such as these prompt the parents of children living in poverty to find jobs and limit the size of their families? Or do they impose additional hardships on children by failing to take child welfare issues into consideration (Wise, Chavkin, & Romero, 1999)?

Mothers complying with the "workfare" requirements of TANF are most likely to find work in physically demanding, entry-level jobs that allow little flexibility for attending to family responsibilities. Typically, employment does not include leave time to attend to children's health care, nor is it likely to include paid vacation leave. Factors such as these can significantly affect children's welfare in that mothers previously on AFDC are significantly more likely than those never receiving welfare to have a child with some type of chronic health condition. They are also more likely to be single parents, with all the additional demands on their time that single parenthood places (Heymann & Earle, 1999).

PRWORA addresses some of these potential hardships by adding certain provisions to the bill. The State Child Health Insurance Plan of 1997, for instance, ensures that children can have health coverage even if their parents do not. Additionally, certain states have passed legislation exempting women who are victims of domestic violence from TANF's time limit requirements through the Family Violence Option. In this way victims of violence can receive support while both learning new job skills and ensuring their child's safety (Wise et al., 1999). Communities have also stepped in, developing special programs to foster the health and cognitive development of children living in poverty (see Chapter 5, the Social Policy Focus on early intervention programs).

Social problems are multifaceted and complex. As a consequence, social policy introduces a host of questions, all addressing the issue of "how best to help."

Chodorow brings us to a point made earlier by Freud: The personalities of women are frequently less differentiated than those of men and are more closely tied to their relationships. But she sees this difference as an asset, as a strength rather than a weakness. Girls can experience continuity with others and relate to their feelings. Chodorow points to the heavy costs males pay for their greater individuation. In curtailing their emotional attachment to the mother, they also limit their ability in general to relate empathically to others. Thus, differences in ego boundaries lay the foundation for a greater capacity for empathy in females. In fact, Chodorow sees the capacity for empathy to be a core part of the feminine personality, giving women a sense of connectedness with others (Chodorow, 1978; Gilligan, 1982). See the Social Policy Focus, "The Declining Fortunes of Children: How Best to Help?"

Organismic Theories

Organismic theories share with psychodynamic ones the assumptions that forces within the organism give shape to development and that development progresses through a succession of qualitatively different stages. Individuals are seen as actively interpreting the events to which they respond, imbuing these with meaning in the process of doing so.

Jean Piaget

By training, Jean Piaget was a biologist. However, his first job, after getting his degree in biology, was in the new field of intelligence testing. Piaget left his native Switzerland and went to Paris to work with Alfred Binet, standardizing questions for Binet's scales of intelligence. Perhaps because Piaget was first interested in biology, he approached human intelligence with questions a biologist might ask if discovering a new organism. How does a creature adapt to its surroundings? What does it do that allows it to survive? How is it changed by the processes that maintain it? For Piaget, intelligence was a means of adapting to one's environment, and only those forms of thought that promoted adaptation survived with increasing age.

Jean Piaget

Piaget regarded intelligence as an adaptive process through which we maintain an equilibrium with our environment. Adaptation takes place through two related processes, assimilation and accommodation. **Assimilation** is the process by which individuals fit new information into their present ways of understanding, as when they act on a new object in a way that is similar to previous actions on other objects. Quite often—but not always—we can understand new experiences in terms of what we already know. And sometimes the actions by which we attempt to gain understanding are modified by the process of gaining it. **Accommodation** is the process by which cognitive structures are altered to fit new experiences.

A closer look at children's behavior reveals these two processes frequently to be at work. For instance, consider a young child who has spent the day at the beach, learning to build sand castles by first shoveling wet sand into a bucket, inverting the bucket, and then pulling it off to make a castle. Several days later at the park, the child may spot a play area filled with sand and attempt to make more castles. This sand, however, is dry; and when the child inverts the bucket, it all runs out. The child has attempted to assimilate this new situation into her understanding of sand castles. That is, she has acted here just as she did with the sand at the beach. In order to be successful, she would need to revise this understanding to include an awareness that the sand must be wet. Such a revision illustrates accommodation.

The processes of assimilation and accommodation must be complementary for us to remain in equilibrium with the environment. If assimilation predominates, the organism imposes its own order on the environment; and, if accommodation predominates, the converse occurs. Neither one by itself represents the homeostatic state of balance between organism and environment that characterizes adaptation. Thus with each assimilation, accommodation must occur. Piaget referred to the balance thus achieved as **equilibration:** the process responsible for the growth of thought.

Not surprisingly, given his background, Piaget (1971) viewed intellectual development as biologically based: He assumed that differences in intellectual functioning with age reflected an underlying maturation of the nervous system. This emphasis did not prevent him from giving equal importance to environmental contributions. In fact, a singularly distinctive feature of his theory is the manner in which it accounts for intellectual development through the interaction of environmental and biological forces. Rather than viewing maturation as providing "ready-made knowledge" or "pre-formed structures," Piaget viewed it as

assimilation Piaget's term for the process by which individuals fit new information into their present ways of understanding.

accommodation Piaget's term for the process by which individuals alter cognitive structures to fit new experiences or events.

equilibration Piaget's term for the balance between assimilation and accommodation that is responsible for the growth of thought.

TABLE 1.3 Piaget's Four Stages of Cognitive Development	
Stage	**Description**
Sensorimotor (birth–2 years)	Infants' awareness of their world is limited to their senses and their reactions to general action patterns (such as sucking, grasping) through which they incorporate their experiences.
Preoperational (2–7 years)	Children can use symbols such as words and images to think about things, but confuse the way things appear with the way they must be.
Concrete operational (7–11 years)	Thinking becomes more flexible, allowing children to consider several dimensions to things simultaneously, to realize that though an object may look different, it has not necessarily changed.
Formal operational (11 years–adulthood)	Thinking becomes abstract, embracing thought itself; adolescents can consider things that are only possible, as well as those that are real.

"open[ing] up new possibilities . . . which still have to be actualized by collaboration with the environment" (p. 21).

Piaget's theory of intelligence illustrates the central assumptions of the organismic model, and of the constructivist approach taken in this text, perhaps better than any other. Piaget believed knowledge to be more than a copy of reality, as it might be if all it reflected were a faithful detecting and recording by an ever-more-mature nervous system. On the contrary, Piaget assumed that we actively construct what we know of the world—that we are active, not passive, organisms. He also assumed that we organize our experiences in qualitatively different ways with age, leading to distinctly different apprehensions of reality or stages of intellectual development.

Piaget (1954) assumed that all knowledge is based initially on actions. Actions are transformed into thought through a process of **reflective abstraction,** in which features of the actions become abstracted so that they can be applied in other contexts. The way we interact with our environment changes with age; and, as a result, our experience also changes. Initially, infants have no way of holding experience in mind, and their awareness is limited to immediate sensations. Through repeatedly interacting with things around them, infants develop ways of representing these experiences, though at first the objects they recall are not distinguished from the activities leading to their discovery. For example, an infant who delights in a game of finding a toy hidden under a pillow may again look under the pillow even thought she has just watched her parent hide the toy in a new place. Why? Because seeing the toy is part of the same experience as pulling away the pillow. With time, children separate the way they have come to represent their world from the way they act on it. As adolescents, once they can free their ideas from objects, they can relate these ideas to other ideas, and thought becomes abstract. Each form of knowledge evolves from the preceding one. In all, Piaget argued that we progress through four stages. Table 1.3 presents the major characteristics of each of Piaget's four stages.

Piaget studied many aspects of cognitive development, from understanding time and space to the use of rules in children's games. He regarded the latter as important because he believed they provided the foundation for later social and moral development. His approach was always the same, whether studying children's concept of number or of social justice: He watched children and asked them questions about what they were doing. In the matter of moral development, Piaget

reflective abstraction Piaget's term for the process in which features of actions become abstracted, turning the actions into thought.

watched children play marbles, a game common at the time. When he questioned them about the rules of the game, he began to construct a view of the stages of cognitive and moral thinking.

Younger and older children answered his questions in different ways. The youngest boys (the players were rarely girls) regarded the rules as absolute and didn't think they could be changed. When asked where the rules came from, they assumed they had always existed in their present form. They didn't realize that rules are important only for the purpose they serve, making it possible to continue with the game when disagreements arise. Older boys knew that rules are a matter of convenience and are worked out by the players. They also knew rules can be changed if all agree (Piaget, 1965).

Piaget (1965) found that girls and boys approached rules differently. Girls were more lax, more pragmatic, and willing to break the rules as the need arose. Piaget believed the girls' approach was not as well developed as that of boys, who had a better sense of the legal function of rules. Since Piaget is one of the most influential theorists in child development, his belief that this sense of rules is critical for moral development has important implications for our view of the sexes.

Piaget is not the only theorist to measure females against a yardstick developed with males (marbles is a boys' game) and find them lacking. Freud and Erikson did the same. Harvard psychologist Carol Gilligan (1982), commenting on psychological theorists in general, writes

> Implicitly adopting the male life as the norm, they have tried to fashion women out of a masculine cloth. It all goes back, of course, to Adam and Eve—a story which shows, among other things, that if you make a woman out of a man, you are bound to get into trouble. In the life cycle, as in the Garden of Eden, the woman has been the deviant. (p. 6)

Lev Vygotsky

Just like Piaget, Lev Vygotsky believed that individuals acquire knowledge of their world simply in the course of doing whatever they happen to be doing, without having to be formally instructed. But Vygotsky differed from Piaget in an important respect. For Vygotsky (1978), acquisition of this knowledge is fundamentally a social process, taking place under the tutelage of another simply as a natural consequence of working alongside someone who has already discovered a better way of doing things. Vygotsky pointed out that for much of the time children and adolescents play or engage in the tasks they must do in the presence of someone who is older—and more skilled at the very activity in which they are engaged. The discoveries of others, what Vygotsky refers to as cultural tools, get passed on to children in this social context, without ever breaking the flow of the activity itself or being labeled "learning" as such.

Take, as an example, a weekend project—painting a room. Everyone pitches in, the room gets painted, and the furniture is moved back into place. Mom, a veteran of many painted rooms, heads over to the window with a razor blade, handing another to her son on the way. He watches her slide the blade under the dried paint on the pane and does the same until they have cleaned paint off all the panes. The use of a tool—not the razor blade, but the wisdom that it is easier to scrape paint *off* than to put masking tape *on*—has been acquired in a social context, without the need for direct instruction.

Both Piaget and Vygotsky analyze, or view, the course of cognitive development in terms of progressive adaptations to one's environment. But they differ in what they take as the proper unit of analysis (Rogoff, 1990). Piaget takes as this

This girl is able to benefit from her older sister's help using the computer because she has reached a zone of proximal development where she is close to being able to grasp the skills needed.

How might Vygotsky have regarded questions on intelligence tests about the best or right way to complete tasks or think through problems?

zone of proximal development
Vygotsky's term for the closeness between a person's current performance and what it might optimally be; readiness to learn something new.

unit the solitary individual, gaining a sense of his or her world through inspecting the objects that make it up. By observing what a person does and says, Piaget "enters" the mind of the individual and examines the processes by which that person grasps hold of his or her reality. Thinking, for Piaget, is a mental activity taking place *in the mind* of a person as that person adapts to his or her environment. As such, thinking is a *property* of the individual (Rogoff, 1990).

Vygotsky takes as his unit of analysis not the solitary individual, but a social person playing or working alongside others, engaging in activities that are characteristic of the group, whether these be learning the best way to remove paint from window panes or to program the VCR. By observing people as they acquire the skills of those they live with—that is, of their culture—Vygotsky identifies thought in terms of the "tools" that have enabled the members of the culture to "grasp" things more easily than they might otherwise have done. Thinking, for Vygotsky, develops as a person internalizes these tools through interacting with those who already use them. As such, thinking is a *process*, one that is fundamentally social in nature, that occurs as a result of living within a social group. The "mind" that Piaget observed within the individual (that is, the individual's grasp on reality) exists, for Vygotsky, in the society in which that person lives, in the form of the cultural wisdoms which the child internalizes through its interactions with those who are already skilled in their use. Thinking takes the form of the person's internalization of these cultural "tools." It is no accident that Vygotsky (1978) titled the book in which he set forth this theory *Mind in Society* (emphasis added).

Vygotsky believed that, just as with tools, the mind of the apprentice learner "grasps" these cultural wisdoms. He believed, as did Piaget, that their acquisition changes the way the mind apprehends reality; but, unlike Piaget, he did not regard them as being forged anew by the individual, through her or his own interaction with the physical world. Instead, he saw them as handed down from those who are more skilled to those who are less skilled in their use.

For something to be passed on in this manner, the learner must be close enough to reach out for it. Vygotsky termed this closeness the **zone of proximal development.** This zone is the distance separating a person's current performance from what it optimally might be. *Proximal* means "near" or "close to." Thus, in order for people to profit from working alongside those who are more skilled, their own performance must come close to, or approximate, the behavior of the other person. The zone represents the range of skills that individuals must possess in order to profit from exposure to those who are more skilled. We see this zone illustrated in the example of removing paint from the windows. This boy was able to internalize the cultural wisdom that it's easier to scrape the paint off than to put something else on only because his own behavior was sufficiently close to the behavior he eventually acquired; in other words, he was already skilled in using tools such as the one his mother handed him.

Barbara Rogoff

Regarding the expertise of a culture as tools to be used by its members has implications for the way one thinks of intellectual development. Barbara Rogoff, a psychologist at Stanford, speaks of this development as an "apprenticeship" in thinking.

The term *apprenticeship* suggests that development is fundamentally a social process and that thinking, rather than a private event occurring within a person's head, is an activity that is shared with others. Thinking, in other words, is not so much a process by which we "produce thoughts" as one that guides "practical action" (Rogoff, 1990). This action can be as playful as it is practical when it involves children and caregivers. Rogoff describes a scene in which 9-month-old twins, who were eating dry Cheerios in their high chairs, were surprised when their mother walked by and popped some of their cereal in her mouth. How silly for Mom to be eating their food! Each time the mother snatched some cereal, the twins would laugh. The mother then put a Cheerio in one twin's fingers and, opening her mouth, bent down close to her: "Valerie began putting the Cheerio in her own mouth reflexively but stopped abruptly when her mother opened her mouth. Valerie looked at her mother's open mouth and began laughing hilariously with her hand poised in midair" (p. 17). This child's thought (I could pop this in *Mom's* mouth!) arises out of the shared activity of their game.

For Rogoff, as for Vygotsky, the unit of analysis is the activity in which the child is engaged. For Vygotsky, however, this activity is initially only a social activity, taking part "outside" the child, and must be internalized in order to regulate behavior as thought. Rogoff does not make such a distinction. Rogoff's focus on the *shared* activity as the crucible of development avoids the age-old developmental question of what is on the "outside" and what on the "inside" of the child. Rogoff does not regard the child, the mother, or the social context (the game) as separable elements, but sees each as a part of the other. Instead of thinking of context as an influence *on* behavior, Rogoff sees behavior as embedded *in* context, taking its particular shape and direction from context. The activity (popping Cheerios into mouths) is the unit of analysis—not the child, not the Cheerio, and not the child *and* the Cheerio. By focusing on the activity and not the Cheerio (or Mom's mouth) for instance, we can predict that once the child knows that the Cheerio can be popped into Mom's mouth, the child also knows that she can pop it into her brother's mouth—and she knows that other digestibles (and indigestibles) can be similarly "popped."

Rogoff does not need to explain how this knowledge is internalized—that is, to explain how it moves from a social realm that is "outside" the child to a realm of thought that is "inside." Such a distinction would suggest a barrier of some kind across which the activity must pass, changing form in the process. Instead, Rogoff sees children as appropriating features of an activity in which they are already engaged with another. What they have practiced with the other is not on the "outside," nor does it need to be brought "inside," or internalized. "The

Carol Gilligan

'boundaries' between people who are in communication are already permeated; it is impossible to say . . . 'whose' a collaborative idea is" (Rogoff, 1990, p. 195). Valerie was already putting *her* Cheerios into her own mouth—as was her mother. Popping a Cheerio into her mother's mouth was "appropriated from," or fit into, this activity. Both activities, in other words, were on the same side of the "barrier."

Valerie's discovery illustrates Rogoff's concept of **guided participation.** This concept extends Vygotsky's concept of the zone of proximal development. Guided participation captures the notion that the child shares with an adult an activity in which both participate to decrease the distance between their respective contributions to the activity in which they are engaged. Rogoff (1990) focuses more than Vygotsky on the ways in which children actively participate in their development: "Children see, structure, and even demand the assistance of those around them in learning how to solve problems of all kinds" (p. 16). She also places greater emphasis than Vygotsky on the importance of tacit, or unspoken, forms of communication, as in the example of Valerie and the Cheerio.

Rogoff points out that the child's strategies for learning its culture are the same one would recommend to any visitor to a foreign culture: Stay close to your guide, watch what the guide does, get involved whenever you can, and pay attention to what the guide may tell or show you. The "guide" complements the child's activity by adjusting the difficulty of the activity to match the child's abilities, modeling the behavior that is sought while the child is watching, and accommodating his or her own behavior to what the child can grasp.

Rogoff views development as multidirectional. Unlike Piaget, for instance, she does not see development as moving toward a single "end point," toward a universal set of achievements, such as Piaget's formal thought. Instead, the course of development can take any of a number of forms, depending on the types of skills that are valued in the child's culture. These skills, whether they be literacy or goat herding, establish the developmental goals that are local to each culture. Thus, Piaget's developmental end point of logical, abstract thought reflects the value placed in our society on scientific reasoning. Formal thought, in other words, represents the "local" goals of Western societies.

Another theorist also views development as progressing toward more than a single end point. Carol Gilligan argues that children of either sex are likely to follow quite different developmental paths.

Carol Gilligan

Carol Gilligan notes striking differences in the ways males and females think of themselves. These differences extend to the ways they resolve issues involving others. Gilligan (1982) finds that males tend to see themselves as separate from others; females describe themselves in terms of their relationships with others. These themes of separation and connectedness appear over and over again in her research, whether she is studying morality and choice, descriptions of the self, or interpersonal dynamics.

Notice the way two children interviewed by Gilligan, an 11-year-old boy and an 11-year-old girl, describe themselves (their descriptions are in Box 1.1).

Jake describes himself at length. He first identifies himself by his age and name and then his status within his community. We never know what his mother does, but we know that her job doesn't contribute to his sense of position the way his father's occupation does. He then identifies his abilities and interests. He ends with a description of an important physical characteristic. We get the impression of a distinct personality from this description. Gilligan agrees. Jake has described himself in terms of the things that distinguish him from others. His self-description emphasizes his uniqueness and separateness.

guided participation Rogoff's term for the shared activity of a novice and one who is more skilled, in which both participate to decrease the distance between their respective contributions to the activity; an extension of Vygotsky's zone of proximal development that assumes a more active role for the learner.

Box 1.1 *Self-Descriptions of Two Adolescents*

How would you describe yourself to yourself?

JAKE: Perfect. That's my conceited side. What do you want—any way that I choose to describe myself?

AMY: You mean my character?

What do you think?

Well, I don't know. I'd describe myself as, well, what do you mean?

If you had to describe the person you are in a way that you yourself would know it was you, what would you say?

JAKE: I'd start off with 11 years old. Jake [last name]. I'd have to add that I live in [town], because that is a big part of me, and also that my father is a doctor, because I think that does change me a little bit, and that I don't believe in crime, except for when your name is Heinz; that I think school is boring, because I think that kind of changes your character a little bit. I don't sort of know how to describe myself, because I don't know how to read my personality.

If you had to describe the way you actually would describe yourself, what would you say?

I like corny jokes. I don't really like to get down to work, but I can do all the stuff in school. Every single problem that I have seen in school I have been able to do, except for ones that take knowledge, and after I do the reading, I have been able to do them, but sometimes I don't want to waste my time on easy homework. And also I'm crazy about sports. I think, unlike a lot of people, that the world still has hope. . . . Most people that I know I like, and I have the good life, pretty much as good as any I have seen, and I am tall for my age.

AMY: Well, I'd say that I was someone who likes school and studying, and that's what I want to do with my life. I want to be some kind of a scientist or something, and I want to do things, and I want to help people. And I think that's what kind of person I am, or what kind of person I try to be. And that's probably how I'd describe myself. And I want to do something to help other people.

Why is that?

Well, because I think that this world has a lot of problems, and I think that everybody should try to help somebody else in some way, and the way I'm choosing is through science.

Source: C. Gilligan. (1982). *In a different voice* (pp. 35–37). Cambridge, MA: Harvard University Press.

Amy's description of herself is brief. We know only that she enjoys school and wants to be a scientist. Otherwise she describes herself in terms of her relationship with others. We know nothing about Amy apart from the qualities she believes will allow her to help others. Being short, tall, freckled, funny, well-off, or disadvantaged—things that set her apart from others—receives little attention. Gilligan stresses that this sense of responsibility for and connectedness to others frequently appears in girls' and women's descriptions of themselves. It is, she notes, a real difference between most females and males.

We see this difference clearly when Jake and Amy are asked how one should choose when responsibility to oneself and responsibility to others conflict (Box 1.2). Jake believes we are mostly responsible to ourselves. Being independent means taking care of ourselves and making sure that our actions don't hurt others. (If you want to kill yourself, use a hand grenade instead of an atom bomb so you don't take your neighbors with you!) Jake starts with the assumption that individuals are separate and proceeds with the need for rules to protect each person's autonomy. Thus, for Jake, responsibility is *not* doing certain things.

Box 1.2 *Choosing Between Responsibility to Self and Responsibility to Others*

When responsibility to oneself and responsibility to others conflict, how should one chose?

JAKE: You go about one-fourth to the others and three fourths to yourself.

AMY: Well, it really depends on the situation. If you have a responsibility with somebody else, then you should keep it to a certain extent, but to the extent that it is really going to hurt you or stop you from doing something that you really, really want, then I think maybe you should put yourself first. But if it is your responsibility to somebody really close to you, you've just got to decide in that situation which is more important, yourself or that person, and like I said, it really depends on what kind of person you are and how you feel about the other person or persons involved.

Why?

JAKE: Because the most important thing in your decision should be yourself, don't let yourself be guided totally by other people, but you have to take them into consideration. So, if what you want to do is blow yourself up with an atom bomb, you should maybe blow yourself up with a hand grenade because you are thinking about your neighbors who would die also.

AMY: Well, like some people put themselves and things for themselves before they put other people, and some people really care about other people. Like, I don't think your job is as important as somebody that you really love, like your husband or your parents or a very close friend. Somebody that you really care for—or if it's just your responsibility to your job or somebody that you barely know, then maybe you go first—but if it's somebody that you really love and love as much or even more than you love yourself, you've got to decide what you really love more, that person, or that thing, or yourself.

And how do you do that?

Well, you've got to think about it, and you've got to think about both sides, and you've got to think which would be better for everybody or better for yourself, which is more important, and which will make everybody happier. Like if the other people can get somebody else to do it, whatever it is, or don't really need you specifically, maybe it's better to do what you want, because the other people will be just fine with somebody else so they'll still be happy, and then you'll be happy too because you'll do what you want.

What does responsibility mean?

JAKE: It means pretty much thinking of others when I do something, and like if I want to throw a rock, not throwing it at a window, because I thought of the people who would have to pay for that window, not doing it just for yourself, because you have to live with other people and live with your community, and if you do something that hurts them all, a lot of people will end up suffering, and that is sort of the wrong thing to do.

AMY: That other people are counting on you to do something, and you can't just decide, "Well, I'd rather do this or that."

Are there other kinds of responsibility?

Well, to yourself. If something looks really fun but you might hurt yourself doing it because you don't really know how to do it and your friends say, "Well come on, you can do it, don't worry," if you're really scared to do it, it's your responsibility to yourself that if you think you might hurt yourself, you shouldn't do it, because you have to take care of yourself.

Source: C. Gilligan. (1982). *In a different voice* (pp. 35–37). Cambridge, MA: Harvard University Press.

Amy's answer is much longer than the one she gave in describing herself. She puts her responsibility to others first—not always, of course, but she differs in an important way from Jake in her view of responsibility. Amy sees responsibility as an action, as a positive response. She assumes a connectedness with others. She talks about people and caring, all on a personal level, whereas Jake mentions the community and seems to imply a need for rules to regulate the actions of its members.

Amy and Jake have taken different paths through childhood. They are likely to follow different paths into adulthood. Amy experiences herself in terms of her connection with others, Jake through his separateness. Each is also developing different strengths: Amy in interpersonal relations, Jake in functioning autonomously. At this point, the strengths of one are the weaknesses of the other.

Susan Pollak and Gilligan (1982) noticed unusual violence in men's fantasies about seemingly peaceful, intimate scenes. When asked to tell a story about a couple seated on a bench, more than one fifth of the men described some act of violence—murder, rape, kidnapping, or suicide. None of the women did. Gilligan reminds us that males, from an early age, define themselves through their separateness and uniqueness. Intimacy and closeness with others pose threats to their sense of themselves, and they react to this danger with themes of violence.

Pollak and Gilligan reasoned that because relationships contribute substantially to females' experience of themselves, females would be more likely to experience danger in impersonal settings. As expected, they found that females wrote 3 times as many violent stories about scenes that depicted situations of isolation, such as those involving competitive achievement, as they did about scenes depicting closeness with others.

Gilligan brings a new awareness to the study of personality. She identifies two distinct perspectives on human experience, each more dominant in one sex than in the other. The first is individualistic, defining the self in terms of its uniqueness and separateness. Relationships with others are governed by a consideration of individual rights, rules, and the application of an impartial justice. Gilligan finds this approach more characteristic of males. The second perspective reflects a sensitivity to and connectedness with others. The self is defined through interpersonal relationships. Rather than rights and rules governing relationships, a sense of responsibility toward others arising out of one's connectedness with them shapes relationships. An ethic of care—rather than abstract justice—dictates personal responsibility in dealings with others. This second approach is more characteristic of females.

Before leaving Gilligan's approach, let's go back to a point raised earlier when discussing Paiget: the differences he observed between girls' and boys' use of rules. Gilligan cites research by Janet Lever (1976, 1978) in which it was noted that boys' games occur in larger groups, are more competitive, and last considerably longer than girls' games. Of special interest is the fact that although boys quarreled throughout the games, they never let the quarreling disrupt their play. They were always able to settle their disputes through the rules of the game. Girls play in smaller, more intimate groups, usually with a best friend. When disagreements occur among girls, they tend to stop the play.

On the face it it, these findings seem to support Piaget's contention that boys' moral (and social) development outpaces girls'. Gilligan interprets the data differently. She points to different priorities in the play of either sex. The game has first priority for boys, and rules enable them to continue it. With girls, the relationship comes first, and the need for rules to negotiate play signals danger. Girls will end the game in order to preserve the relationship. Is this a less-developed sense of morality? Surely not. But it *is* a very different dynamic, one that has been addressed by only a handful of developmental theorists to date.

In a collectivist society, the most advanced stage of moral development is one that sacrifices rules and individual competition for the good of the group. In such a society, is it likely that boys' moral development will fit Piaget's model?

Older and younger children viewing this scene from an observation tower would have different perceptions of the people below.

Robert Kegan

Among the various theories we have reviewed, those of Freud and Piaget have dominated the developmental field, the one emphasizing motives and feelings and the other perception and thought—the heart and mind of the child. Of these, Piaget's will be of greater importance in this text. Its importance, however, reaches beyond the developmental *domain* of perception and thought that it embraces and stems, rather, from the developmental *process* that Piaget has elaborated.

Building on the constructive process elaborated by Piaget, Robert Kegan (1982, 1994) has developed a theoretical approach that encompasses both domains. Kegan elaborates a way of understanding, in other words, that integrates heart and mind. Kegan believes that the most central human activity is that of "meaning making," of constructing from the moment a reality that makes sense, given the balance one has already struck with the world. Such balances are represented in Piaget's stages, which Kegan refers to as "evolutionary truces."

Kegan argues that, at every age, individuals partition experience into two "rough cuts" of reality—that which is "me" and that which is "not-me." Development occurs when aspects of the "me" become differentiated from that which one has regarded as "not-me." This differentiation has the effect of simultaneously defining new aspects of one's surroundings and of the self. In a manner similar to Newton's second law of motion, in which every action has an opposite and equal reaction, when one gives meaning to events "out there," one's sense of self in relation to these events also changes.

Kegan gives the example of two young boys surveying a street scene from the observation deck of a skyscraper. They exclaim their wonderment in different ways. The younger one says, "Look at the people. They're tiny ants." The older one says, "Look at the people. They look like tiny ants." There is a complexity to the older boy's remark that is lacking in the younger boy's. We hear in his remark a comment that has to do as much with *how* he is perceiving as with *what* he has perceived. His awareness of people looking *like* ants, rather than simply being the size of ants, adds a reflective quality in which the percept is evaluated, giving him an awareness both of the percept and of the evaluating self—both of what he is seeing and of himself seeing it.

Kegan speaks of differentiation as involving a "moving-over" in the subject-object balance that the child has struck with the world, a balance that represents the child's current grasp on reality. In order to envision this process, it might help to think of an actual balance, the old-fashioned kind with two pans positioned on either side of a fulcrum, or balance point. For the scale to balance, whatever is placed in one pan must be countered by an equivalent weight in the other pan.

Differentiation, just like weights in a scale, adds something to each "pan" of the subject-object balance. Consider again the example of the two boys looking down at people on the street below. Differentiation has enabled the older boy to see as an object what previously had been embedded on the subject side of the balance; that is, something has moved over from the "me" to the "not-me" pan. He can distinguish the people from his own viewing perspective (they only *look* as small as ants). This moving-over is balanced by a comparable "weight" that is added to the subject side of the scale. He is aware not only of what he is looking at, the size of the people below, but also of the way he perceives them. This second awareness, of his own perceptual activity—distinct from the people he is perceiving—is the "weight" that is added to the subject side of the balance.

Kegan extends this developmental analysis to impulses and feelings as well as perception and thought. Thus, he explains the protests of an 8-month-old when its mother leaves as being due to the same process of differentiation. Kegan (1982) assumes, along with many other personality theorists, that infants at first do not have a sense of themselves that is distinct from the mother. Infants' experiences of themselves are embedded in the way they experience themselves with the mother. In other words, both the infant and the mother are on the *subject* side of the balance. As infants emerge from this embeddedness, they stand to lose not so much the mother as their own sense of themselves. The distress "seems to be not so much a matter of separation from the object as separation from myself, from what is gradually becoming the old me, from which I am not yet sufficiently differentiated to integrate as other" (p. 82).

A Concluding Note

Each of these theorists has seen fit to question and challenge what others have accepted. I encourage you to do the same. Rogoff, for instance, has pointed to a bias in most theorists' adoption of a single cultural perspective. She warns that a failure to acknowledge differences among cultures, and even between subcultures within a society, can lead to a trivialization of developmental theory and findings.

Gilligan points out that science has not been neutral. Our theories reflect "a consistent observational and evaluative bias." We tend to interpret "different" as either better or worse, since we have a tendency to work with a single scale. Since most scales are also standardized in terms of male development, male behavior is taken as the norm and female behavior as a departure from the norm. This approach is perpetuated by the fact that most research is done by males, with many important studies using only males as subjects (Gilligan, 1982; Yoder & Kahn, 1993).

Gilligan remarks that since human development has been charted, to date, in male terms—that is, in terms of increasing separation and individuation—when females have problems with individuation, these are seen as a developmental immaturity. Males' problems with relationships, however, do not evoke a parallel interpretation. Gilligan (1982) pointedly notes that "women's failure to separate then becomes by definition a failure to develop."

Theorists such as Rogoff and Gilligan offer us a challenge. Can we see human behavior from other than a single perspective? Gilligan, for instance, dares us to ask not only why females' feelings "get in the way" of their reasoning when thinking about others (a quality she does not regard as a weakness), but also why males' feelings do not. Instead of just asking why more females than males have problems with individuation, we need also to ask why more males have problems with intimacy and relationships. Until we begin to ask and find answers to all of these questions, our psychology of human development will remain incomplete.

Answers for page 22
UCS: alarm going off
UCR: waking to the alarm
CS: light appearing through the blinds
CR: waking to the light

Summary

The Constructive Perspective

The constructive approach to development assumes that children and adults actively construct the events to which they respond, imbuing these with meaning. This constructive process occurs at each of the many levels of human functioning, from the molecular level of perceptual processing to the molar level of social interactions, and contributes to the diversity with which individuals make sense of and respond to their experiences.

Two major sources of diversity in children's experiences are ethnicity and gender. Children reflect their cultural heritages; the sense they make of their experiences will vary with differences in their cultural background. Gender also contributes to diversity, both through physiological differences associated with being female or male and through gender stereotypes that reflect shared beliefs that some qualities characterize one sex and others characterize the other sex.

In addition to diversity, continuity also characterizes development. Not only do children face many of the same issues at different points in their lives, but the way they cope with these as they age can be similar as well.

Models and Theories

Models are sets of assumptions about the nature of reality. These assumptions are too general to be tested; however, theories, which derive from models, are more specific explanations of phenomena and can be confirmed or disconfirmed.

The assumptions that make up a model can frequently be expressed as a metaphor. The machine is a popular metaphor for human behavior, and models based on this metaphor assume that behavior is as predictable as that of a machine. Such models, however, allow no room for self-initiated action. Three models of human behavior are the environmental, organismic, and psychodynamic.

The environmental model views humans as passive and sees their actions as *re*actions to environmental events. People are assumed to remain quiescent until something stimulates them to act. Behavior is linked to external events through simple associations; these are formed through respondent and operant conditioning.

The organismic model takes the living, biological system as its metaphor for human behavior. Theories derived from this model assume that variables tied to the nature of the organism structure development. These theorists assume that the human organism is active and does not passively await stimulation and that activity is internally organized instead of structured by environmental events. Behavior is seen as an unfolding of developmental stages, each of which is qualitatively different from the last.

The psychodynamic model emphasizes both inner processes and external events in explaining behavior. Freud, the major theorist for this model, assumed that biological impulses are housed in the id and social standards in the superego; the ego balances the demand for expression of the id against the realities of social constraints.

Environmental Theories

Ivan Pavlov identified a simple form of learning in which reflexive behavior can be brought under the control of environmental events that predictably precede the behavior.

The theory of B. F. Skinner is a radical departure from the way most people understand their behavior. Skinner assumes that behavior is under the control of the events that follow it instead of reflecting preceding motives or intentions. Skinner refers to these subsequent events as reinforcers.

Albert Bandura also emphasizes the importance of learning in development, but believes that most human learning occurs through observing others rather than through direct conditioning. Inner processes such as attention and memory are important in Bandura's social-cognitive theory.

Psychodynamic Theories

Freud assumed that all thoughts and actions are motivated; he termed the life force motivating these the libido. Different aspects of the personality control the expression of the libido. The id, present from birth, has limited means for gratifying libidinal impulses. The ego, next to develop, seeks to gratify as many libidinal impulses as possible within social constraints. The last aspect of the personality to develop, the superego, contains the moral values of one's culture and dictates what one should and should not do.

Erik Erikson assumed, as did Freud, that personality develops through a sequence of stages, but he carried these through the life span. He assumed that society challenges us with new demands as we age and that we experience these as crises. Each crisis takes a slightly different form and gives each stage its unique characteristics. Achievement of a personal identity is the central crisis of adolescence; this involves adolescents in a set of commitments to life goals that give definition to the self.

Nancy Chodorow builds on a foundation provided by Freud but attributes gender differences to the social fact that for almost all children the first intimate relationship is with a female—the mother. Girls can continue to define themselves within the context of this first relationship, but boys must separate themselves in order to develop as males. As a consequence, girls' development is characterized by attachment, and boys' by separation and individuation.

Organismic Theories

Jean Piaget viewed intelligence as a means of adapting to one's environment, with only those forms of thought that promote adaptation surviving over the years. Piaget viewed intelligence as biologically based. He assumed that knowledge, rather than being a simple copy of reality, is an active construction of what we know of the world. He also assumed that our experiences are organized in qualitatively different stages with age.

Like Piaget, Lev Vygotsky believed that events do not have meaning until people actively interpret and internalize them. He differs from Piaget, however, in his notion that thinking and learning are fundamentally social in nature, rather than the result of individual experience. For Vygotsky, cognitive development is the internalization of the tools of cultural wisdom.

Barbara Rogoff extends Vygotsky's concept of the zone of proximal development with her concept of guided participation; the child doesn't simply copy the adult's behavior but actively participates in the activity. Rogoff, unlike Piaget, sees development as multidirectional, depending on the goals and values of the particular culture.

Carol Gilligan focuses on the interpersonal aspects of development. She notes striking gender differences in the ways individuals of either sex define themselves. Males tend to view themselves as separate from others; females typically describe themselves in terms of their relationships with others.

Robert Kegan has built on the constructive process described by Piaget. Kegan argues that the most central human activity is meaning making, or constructing a reality that corresponds to our sense of self in relation to events and other people. Development, for Kegan, is a cumulative process of differentiating the "me" from the "not-me." As our sense of "me" changes, so do our ways of relating to others and responding to events—and those changes lead to further changes in our sense of self.

Key Terms

accommodation (p. 31)
assimilation (p. 31)
axioms (p. 15)
conditional response (CR) (p. 22)
conditional stimulus (CS) (p. 22)
constructive approach (p. 3)
continuity-discontinuity issue (p. 15)
development (p. 11)
differentiation (p. 11)
ego (p. 21)
epigenesis (p. 16)
epigenetic principle (p. 22)

equilibration (p. 31)
growth (p. 11)
guided participation (p. 36)
habituation (p. 19)
id (p. 21)
laws (p. 15)
libido (p. 20)
model (p. 14)
nature-nurture controversy (p. 15)
negative reinforcement (p. 23)
observational learning (p. 24)
positive reinforcement (p. 23)

reductionism (p. 16)
reflective abstraction (p. 32)
repression (p. 25)
respondent conditioning (p. 22)
stage (p. 19)
superego (p. 21)
theory (p. 15)
unconditional response (UCR) (p. 22)
unconditional stimulus (UCS) (p. 22)
zone of proximal development (p. 34)

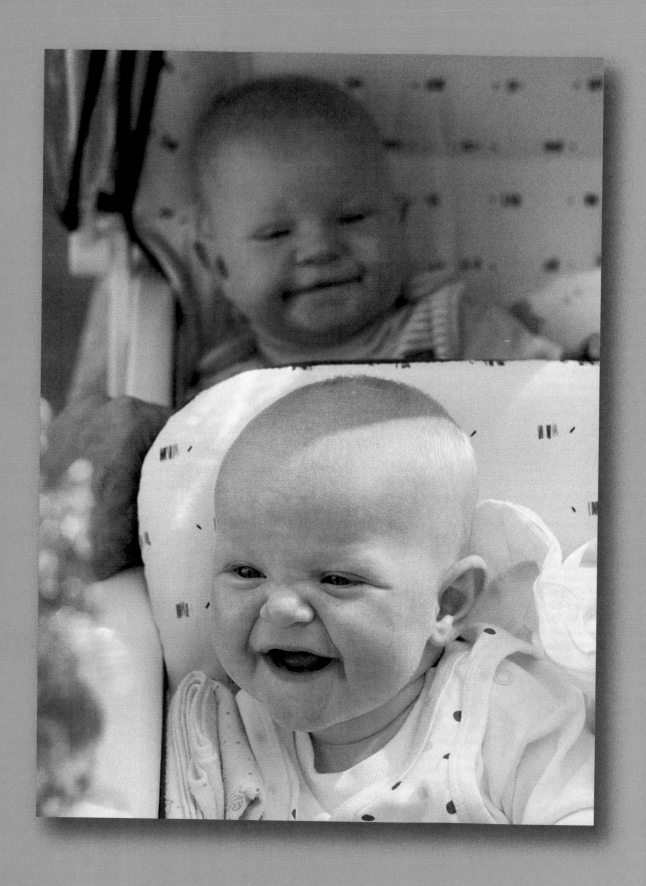

chapter two

The Context of Development
Genetic Action and Environmental Influences

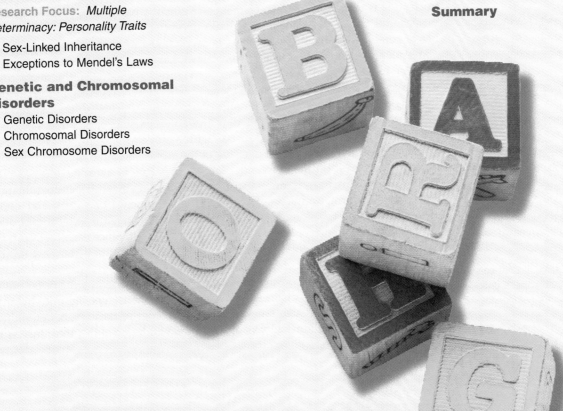

This time the sea of waters pressed too forcefully against the straining membrane. It burst and the massive body within rode the exploding corona of fluids toward freedom and the beginnings of life. This drama repeats itself monthly within the body of every sexually mature female as an egg ripens and breaks its protective covering within one of the ovaries. It is the first leg of the long journey into life. This chapter charts the beginnings of this journey, examining genetic and environmental influences on the developing organism.

The Beginnings: DNA and Life

They worked quickly. Pacing, talking, they went over it once again. The solution was so close, and yet it eluded them. They knew that any moment another team might break the code. Like many codes, it was simple. Just a handful of elements made up the ancient alphabet. Millions of years old, the alphabet disclosed how life reproduced itself.

James Watson, an American geneticist, and Francis Crick, an English biologist, broke the code when they arrived at the structure of deoxyribonucleic acid (DNA). **DNA** is the tightly coiled molecule of which chromosomes are formed (represented schematically in Figure 2.1). Not until 1944 was it known that DNA was the material in chromosomes responsible for genetic transmission. Nine years later Crick and Watson, working with Rosalind Franklin, whose crystallography data confirmed their model, discovered how it provided the genetic blueprint for all living things (Watson, 1968).

Traits are passed on from one generation to the next through **genes,** short segments of the DNA strand. Thousands of genes are carried within each of the chromosomes making up the 23 pairs found in every cell in the body. In a remarkable excess of nature, each cell, with the exception of mature sex cells, contains all the genetic information needed to replicate the entire organism, some 150,000 genes in all (Tjian, 1995).

DNA is composed of units called **nucleotides,** which, in different combinations, spell out the plans for everything from eyelashes to elbows. Since each nucleotide is made of just three elements—a sugar, a phosphate, and one of four nitrogenous bases—the genetic code looks deceptively simple. And yet, the number of combinations of these elements is myriad, just as is the number of words and sentences that can be formed from our alphabet of 26 letters.

One can think of DNA as a zipper. As Figure 2.1 illustrates, the nucleotides form two twisted strands of genetic material held loosely together in the middle. The edges of the zipper are sugars and phosphates. Attached to each sugar and phosphate is a nitrogenous base: adenine, thymine, cytosine, or guanine. The bases form the teeth of the zipper. And just as with a zipper, the teeth "fit" each other. Whenever adenine is a tooth on one side of the zipper, thymine must be the tooth corresponding to it on the other side. The same is true of cytosine and guanine. When DNA unzips, as it does in cell division, enzymes attract free-floating nucleotides to form complementary halves. The sequence of sugars and phosphates making up the side of the zipper remains unchanged by division as does the ascending sequence of "teeth" attached to either half. Since each tooth can fit, or bond with, only one of the three remaining possible types, the new strand becomes a mirror likeness of the old, reproducing itself.

The blueprint for the construction of new cells is provided by the order of the bases, or the teeth, in the chain. On average, each gene is "spelled out" by anywhere from 900 to 1,500 such pairs of bases. The order of these pairs determines which proteins, the building blocks of the body, will be manufactured. Just as in

Q Does a strand of DNA duplicate through growth or by each enzyme finding a perfect match?

DNA Deoxyribonucleic acid, the double-stranded molecule in chromosomes that encodes genetic information.

genes Short segments of the DNA strand, responsible for transmission of particular traits; thousands of genes are carried within each chromosome.

nucleotides Subunits of DNA consisting of a sugar molecule, a phosphate molecule, and a nitrogenous base.

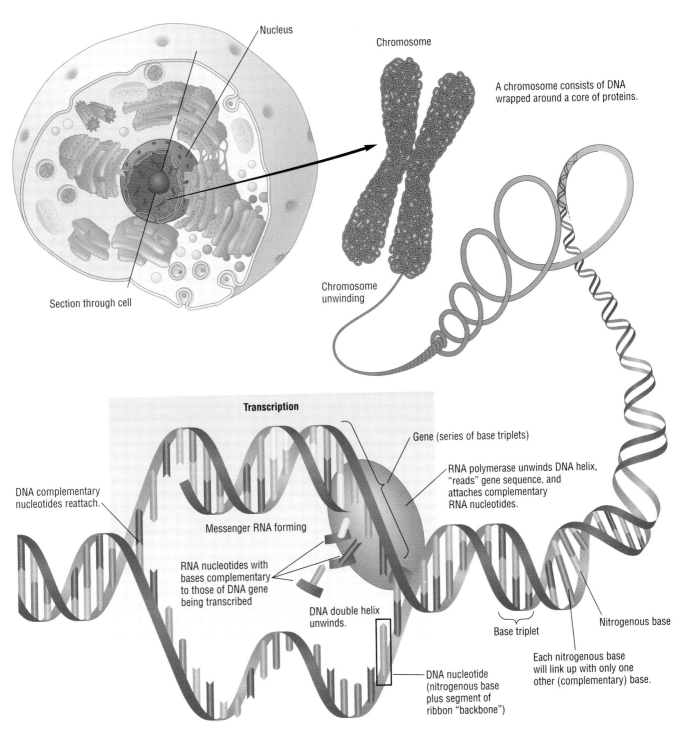

Nucleus

Chromosome

A chromosome consists of DNA wrapped around a core of proteins.

Section through cell

Chromosome unwinding

Transcription

Gene (series of base triplets)

RNA polymerase unwinds DNA helix, "reads" gene sequence, and attaches complementary RNA nucleotides.

DNA complementary nucleotides reattach.

Messenger RNA forming

RNA nucleotides with bases complementary to those of DNA gene being transcribed

DNA double helix unwinds.

Base triplet

Nitrogenous base

Each nitrogenous base will link up with only one other (complementary) base.

DNA nucleotide (nitrogenous base plus segment of ribbon "backbone")

FIGURE 2.1 Cell Structure and the Transcription Process

the spelling of a word, changing a single letter can change the entire meaning, as in "si*t*" versus "si*p*". So, too, changing a single base pair in the hundreds of bases spelling out a trait can change the "meaning" of that trait. Of the more than 400 base pairs that form the gene related to red blood cells, for instance, a single base pair makes the difference between the production of normal blood and blood with the distorted cells known as sickle-cell anemia (Meryash, 1995).

Genes

DNA directs the manufacture of proteins with the aid of two related substances, messenger RNA (m-RNA) and transfer RNA (t-RNA). **Messenger RNA** is a copy of DNA, in much the same way a photograph is of a negative; m-RNA serves as the model for the new construction (see Figure 2.1). **Transfer RNA,** a smaller copy which matches only short segments of the model, picks up molecules from the surrounding cytoplasm and carries these "piggyback" to the chain under construction.

Two functionally distinct types of genes make up the DNA strand. **Structural genes** provide the actual codes for the construction of new proteins, the biological building blocks that make up the various cells of the body. **Regulatory genes** control which genes are copied. The transcription, or copying, process involves a number of steps. Initially, many different proteins converge on the DNA molecule, forming what Robert Tjian (1995), a biochemist and molecular biologist at Berkeley, calls a "transcription engine." Tjian likens the DNA molecule itself to a track. Certain stretches of the track provide the code for the construction of new proteins; these stretches are made up of the structural genes. Other stretches of the track contain the regulatory genes that control the coding process.

The transcription engine enters the DNA track on a stretch of the molecule containing the regulatory genes, usually just preceding the stretch to be copied. The engine rides along the DNA, sliding over the coding region containing the structural genes. The actual work of copying is done by an enzyme, **RNA polymerase,** which copies the DNA into messenger RNA as it rolls along the track. Since RNA polymerase will copy anything it rolls over, additional regulatory elements are involved that program it to copy only certain segments of the DNA. These regulatory genes are often located some distance either up or down the track from the segment that is being copied. Certain regulatory genes facilitate the copying and are known as *enhancers.* Others, called *silencers,* work to inhibit copying (Tjian, 1995).

How do regulatory genes influence an activity taking place sometimes at a great distance from them? Tjian and his co-workers found the existence of other proteins, **activators** and **repressors,** that "dock" at these regulatory sites along the DNA track, picking up their messages to copy or to inhibit copying, and relaying them on to other molecules, **coactivators,** which integrate signals from many such proteins before sending the product on to **basal factors,** which communicate directly with RNA polymerase. These different regulatory elements work together to influence the rate at which genes are copied (Tjian, 1995).

Although identical enhancers and silencers can be shared by several genes, no two genes have exactly the same combination of these, thus making it possible for each cell to control the transcription of genes individually. Because each cell in the body contains all the genetic information needed to replicate the entire organism, regulatory genes serve an important function by suppressing genes that are unrelated to the replication of a particular cell, thereby enabling that cell to replicate only itself. Thus, liver cells, for instance, are able to produce additional

messenger RNA (mRNA) The form of ribonucleic acid (RNA) that carries genetic codes from the DNA in the cell nucleus to the sites of protein synthesis in the cytoplasm.

transfer RNA (tRNA) The form of ribonucleic acid (RNA) that carries amino acids to the cytoplasm, where proteins are assembled according to the genetic code carried by the messenger RNA.

structural genes Genes in the DNA strand that provide the codes for the construction of new proteins.

regulatory genes Genes in the DNA strand that regulate which genes are copied.

RNA polymerase An enzyme that copies DNA into messenger RNA during the transcription process.

activators Proteins that facilitate the copying of DNA segments by picking up messages at regulatory sites along the DNA track and relaying them to coactivators.

repressors Proteins that inhibit the copying of DNA segments by picking up messages at regulatory sites along the DNA track and relaying them to coactivators.

coactivators Molecules that integrate signals from activators and repressors and send them on to basal factors.

basal factors Factors that communicate directly with RNA polymerase.

Nettie Stevens discovered XX and XY chromosomes when she was a postdoctoral student with Theodor Boveri.

liver cells, and not bone or kidney cells, because the genes for the latter, also contained within the cell nucleus, are suppressed.

How do the regulatory genes distinguish which genes in the cell nucleus to turn off and which to turn on? Definitive answers await further research. However, we do know that cells are sensitive to their environments, just as individuals are. For instance, up to a certain point in development, if cells from the brain region of a developing newt, or salamander, are transplanted to another part of the body, such as its back, they develop into skin cells and not brain cells. Depending on where a cell is and what is taking place around it, the cell will behave in quite different ways (Gilbert, 1994).

Chromosomes

Thousands of genes, segments of coiled DNA, make up a single chromosome. **Chromosomes** are microscopic filaments within the nucleus of a cell. Each cell contains 23 pairs of chromosomes, one member of the pair coming from the mother and the other from the father. Twenty-two of these are matching pairs, called **autosomes**. Research at the turn of the century by Nettie Stevens (as cited in Gilbert, 1994), however, revealed that the 23rd pair, which determines the sex of the child, matches for females but not for males. As Figure 2.2 shows, in females, both **sex chromosomes** are relatively long and X-shaped (XX), whereas in males one is considerably shorter and Y-shaped (XY). The sex chromosome received from the mother is always an X (females do not have a Y chromosome

Why can't cells from different parts of the body, such as neurons, bone cells, and heart cells, replicate into other kinds of cells?

chromosomes Microscopic filaments within a cell nucleus carrying genetic information and composed of DNA and protein.

autosomes The 22 matching pairs of chromosomes that, together with the sex chromosomes of the 23rd pair, are found in the cell nucleus.

sex chromosomes The 23rd pair of chromosomes that determine the sex of the child; females have two X chromosomes, and males have one X and one Y chromosome.

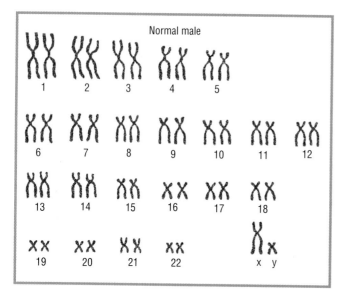

FIGURE 2.2 *The 23 pairs of chromosomes in the normal male and normal female human being. The sex chromosomes are the 23rd pair.*

to pass on); that from the father can be either an X or a Y. The sex of a child is determined by one or more genes located along the Y chromosome, which trigger the production of androgens, male sex hormones that masculinize the developing organism. Without the presence of these hormones, the organism would develop as a female (Page, Fisher, McGillivray, & Brown, 1990; Sinclair et al., 1990).

Gametes: The Ovum and Sperm

The sex cells that unite at conception are known as **gametes.** Within the nucleus of each gamete are the chromosomes containing the genetic material that will direct the formation of the developing organism. However, before the gametes can ever serve their reproductive function, they themselves must develop. Immature sex cells, just like all other cells within the body, contain 23 pairs of chromosomes. Sex cells mature through a series of cell divisions, termed **meiosis,** which leaves them with half the number of chromosomes. Like strangers bearing an important message, each gamete carries half a torn ticket to identify itself.

Were it not for meiosis, the union of ovum and sperm would result in a cell containing twice the normal number of chromosomes, instead of the 46 per cell that characterize humans—and the number would double with each generation. All other body cells divide through a process of **mitosis,** in which the resulting cells each end up with 23 pairs of chromosomes. Meiosis progresses in similar ways in ova and sperm, but with important differences (Figure 2.3). We will consider this process first in ova.

Each infant girl is born with several million ova, contained within the ovaries that flank the uterus. Only about 400 of these will mature in her lifetime (Gilbert, 1994). At puberty, increases in follicle stimulating hormone (FSH) and luteinizing hormone (LH) stimulate the ovaries to begin producing **estrogens,** female sex hormones. Each month an ovum in one of the ovaries matures through two cell divisions. The first division results in two "daughter" cells, each still with 23 pairs of chromosomes. With the second cell division, the chromosomes forming each pair separate, migrating to opposite sides of the nucleus as it pulls apart, resulting in cells that contain only half of each pair, or 23 *single* chromosomes. Meiosis produces only a single mature ovum, instead of the four that one might expect from

gametes Sperm and ova, which, when mature, have 23 individual instead of 23 pairs of chromosomes.

meiosis The process of cell division in which sex cells mature, reducing the number of chromosomes from 23 pairs to 23 individual chromosomes.

mitosis The process of cell division in which body cells replicate; the chromosomes of each new cell are identical to those of the parent cell.

estrogens Sex hormones produced primarily by the ovaries.

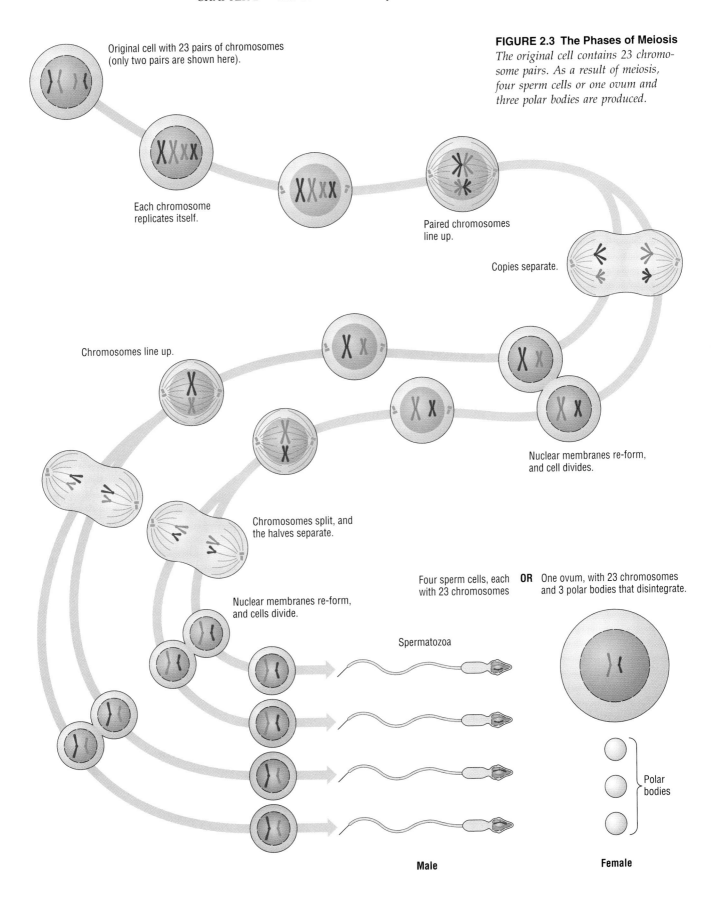

FIGURE 2.3 The Phases of Meiosis
The original cell contains 23 chromosome pairs. As a result of meiosis, four sperm cells or one ovum and three polar bodies are produced.

Original cell with 23 pairs of chromosomes (only two pairs are shown here).

Each chromosome replicates itself.

Paired chromosomes line up.

Copies separate.

Chromosomes line up.

Nuclear membranes re-form, and cell divides.

Chromosomes split, and the halves separate.

Nuclear membranes re-form, and cells divide.

Four sperm cells, each with 23 chromosomes

OR One ovum, with 23 chromosomes and 3 polar bodies that disintegrate.

Spermatozoa

Polar bodies

Male

Female

There are approximately 200 million sperm produced in a single ejaculation. Typically, following ejaculation during intercourse, fewer than 100 will reach a fallopian tube where an ovulated oocyte may be present.

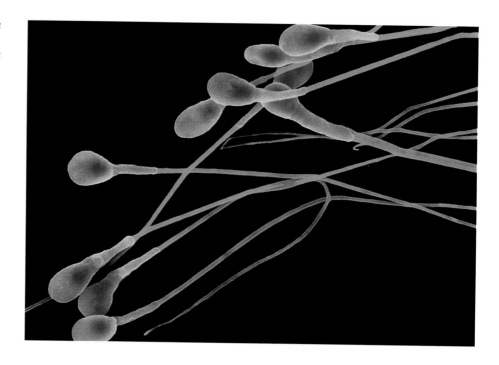

What would be the possible consequence for a man who does not have the ability to produce Sertoli cells?

Which parent is responsible for the sex of a child?

two cell divisions, since three of the cells receive very little cytoplasm and eventually disintegrate (Gilbert, 1994).

In contrast to the single ovum that matures in the female each month, a mature male produces several hundred million sperm each hour, and in any ejaculate there are approximately 200 million mature sperm (Harper 1988). Sperm develop in tubules in the testes, which are contained within the scrotal sac hanging beneath the penis. Here they are maintained at a temperature ideal for their breeding, several degrees less than that found inside the body. At puberty, increases in FSH and LH, the same hormones that stimulate the ovaries, stimulate the testes to secrete **testosterone,** a male sex hormone, which is involved in the production of sperm.

Two types of cells line the tubes in which sperm develop: sperm-producing cells (germinal epithelial cells) and nurse cells (Sertoli cells). Division of the germinal cells produces sperm. One part remains for later cell divisions (unlike the female, the male will continue to produce sex cells throughout his life); the other will mature as sperm. Sertoli cells function as "nurses" for the immature sperm, which nestle among them to receive nourishment while they develop. As with the ovum, the first cell division produces two cells, each still with 23 pairs of chromosomes. The members of all 23 pairs are similar, with the exception of the two chromosomes making up the 23rd pair. A close inspection shows that one of these is X-shaped and the other is shaped like a Y. With the last cell division, one sperm receives the X chromosome and the other the Y. These chromosomes determine the sex of the child. If an X-bearing sperm fertilizes the ovum, the child will be a female; a Y-bearing sperm produces a male. Thus, which type of sperm fertilizes the ovum will determine the sex of the child.

One might almost say that "sex differences" are apparent right from the start. Y-bearing sperm, called androsperm, have sleeker, narrower bodies and swim faster than the more rounded and heavier X-bearing spermatids, or gynosperm. The X chromosome carried by the latter is 5 times the size of the Y carried by the androsperm, and differences in the size and weight of their genetic cargo slow the

testosterone A sex hormone produced by the testes.

X-bearing sperm. As a consequence of the greater speed of the androsperm, it is estimated that 400 to 500 males are conceived for every 100 females. Were it not for the fact that androsperm are also more vulnerable to "environmental" stresses once within the vagina and uterus, there would be a very real imbalance in the sexes. As it is, for every 100 females born, there are 105 males (Lips, 1997).

Increasingly, parents are turning to technology to select the sex of their child, some because they carry genes for disorders affecting one sex but not the other and others to add a child of one sex to a household where children are exclusively of the other sex. In interviews with women considering such procedures, Lisa Belkin (1999), a contributing writer for the *New York Times Magazine*, writes, "We care about the sex of our children. Some of us care more than others, but we all care. It is the first question asked about a baby, almost from conception, certainly at the moment of birth" (p. 27).

Genetic Diversity

Recall that in the fertilized ovum, or **zygote,** one chromosome in each pair comes from the mother and the other from the father. The combination of these chromosomes results in an individual who is distinct from either parent. The process of meiosis itself, by which these two sex cells have matured, has further contributed to diversity. Meiosis reduces the number of chromosomes in the mature sex cell by half, shuffling the members of each pair into either one gamete or the other as the cell divides. The number of possible different combinations of chromosomes making up the two mature gametes that result from the shuffling of 23 pairs is 2 to the 23rd power, or about 8 million different possible gametes from the maturation of a single sex cell. A similar number of gametes results from cell division in the other parent. Since any one of these gametes can fertilize, or be fertilized by, any of the others, the number of chromosomally different zygotes that could result is very large—64 trillion (Plomin, DeFries, & McClearn, 1990).

Geneticists note that this figure is only the beginning of diversity. Additional genetic diversity occurs through a process of **crossing over,** which takes place during cell division. During meiosis, the members of each pair line up, and segments of the chromosomes making up each pair break off and cross over to corresponding positions along the other chromosome, resulting in two different chromosomes, neither of which resembles the ones that were inherited from either parent.

Twins

Some of you at this point might be thinking of individuals you know who have a twin sibling. Wouldn't such twin pairs prove the exception to nature's rule of diversity? Although at first glance the answer might appear to be yes, such is not always the case. Identical twins are individuals who share identical genetic makeups. The technical term for identical twins is **monozygotic,** referring to the fact that each twin originates from the same fertilized ovum, or zygote (Figure 2.4). The diversity resulting from the combination of each parent's chromosomes, as well as from meiosis and crossing over, virtually guarantees that each and every *zygote* will be different from the next. However, since identical twins originate from the same zygote, they will have identical genes (100% genetic relatedness). Identical twins are formed when a single zygote separates into two clusters of cells, instead of continuing as a single cluster, during initial cell division. The frequency of monozygotic twins is approximately 4 of every 1,000 births and is unrelated to any known factors.

zygote A single cell resulting from the union of the ovum and sperm at conception.

crossing over During meiosis, the exchange of corresponding genes in homologous chromosomes; one of the sources of genetic diversity.

monozygotic twins Twins who develop from the same fertilized ovum, or zygote.

Identical (Monozygotic) Twins

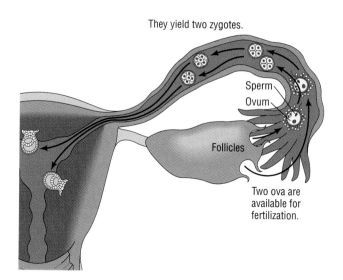

It yields one zygote.

The zygote divides, and the two new zygotes separate.

Sperm
Ovum

Follicle

One ovum is available for fertilization.

Fraternal (Dizygotic) Twins

They yield two zygotes.

Sperm
Ovum

Follicles

Two ova are available for fertilization.

Two genetically identical embryos develop.

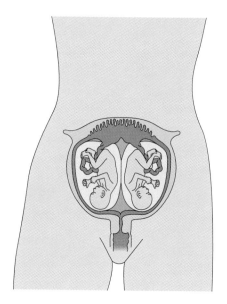

Two genetically different embryos develop.

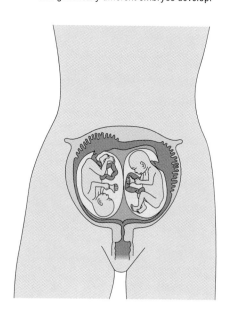

FIGURE 2.4 The Genetics of Identical and Fraternal Twins

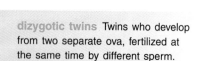

Can a boy and a girl be monozygotic twins?

dizygotic twins Twins who develop from two separate ova, fertilized at the same time by different sperm.

Twins can also be fraternal, or **dizygotic.** Fraternal twins originate when two ova are released during ovulation, and each is fertilized (see Figure 2.4). Dizygotic twins, although born at the same time, are no more alike genetically than any other two siblings with the same parents (50% genetic relatedness). The frequency of dizygotic twins has been found to vary with a number of factors, such as ethnicity, the mother's age, and the use of fertility drugs. Fraternal twins occur twice as frequently among Whites (8 per 1,000 births) as among Asians (4 per 1,000). Among African Americans, fraternal twins are even more frequent, 12 to 16 for every 1,000 births. The incidence of fraternal twins increases with the mother's

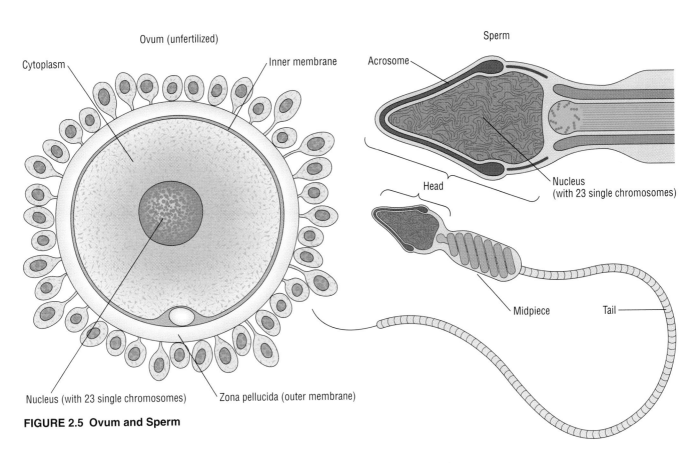

FIGURE 2.5 Ovum and Sperm

age and with the number of children she has already had. The use of fertility drugs also increases the likelihood of multiple births (Keith & Luke, 1993).

Fertilization

The ovum is one of the largest cells in the body, just large enough to be seen without magnification. Its size reflects the nutrients it stores, not the size of the organism it will produce. Human ova are about the same size as those of mice—and whales (Phillips & Dryden, 1991). When fertilized, elements in the cytoplasm will provide a biochemical support system to the developing organism (Wasserman, 1988). The ovum is covered with a tough outer membrane, the zona pellucida (Figure 2.5). Under this thick outer coat, a second membrane encases the cell nucleus and the surrounding cytoplasm, the rich storehouse of nutrients on which the dividing cells, should fertilization occur, must rely before they receive nourishment from the mother's body. The latter is possible only when implantation occurs, nearly a week away. Until then, the long journey down the Fallopian tubes is, at the cellular level at least, the equivalent of "backpacking."

It has been estimated that all of the eggs necessary to reproduce the population of North America could be placed in a 3-inch cube. All the sperm needed for this could be put on the head of a pin (Arey, 1954). These cells are quite obviously different, each uniquely specialized for the function it will serve—ova for providing life-sustaining nourishment and sperm for delivering a genetic cargo. Sperm are composed of a compact head carrying the nucleus with its genetic message; a short neck, or midpiece; and a long lashing tail that propels it forcefully in a swimming motion (see Figure 2.5). The head of the sperm is covered with a

Only a single sperm completely fuses with the membrane of the ovum to achieve fertilization. All other sperm trying to fuse are shed from the surface of the ovum.

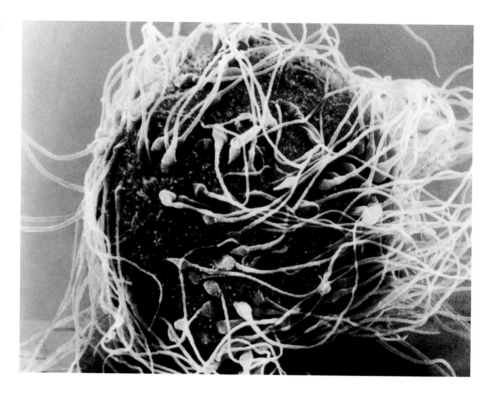

cap, termed the **acrosome,** that is filled with enzymes. In contrast to ova, which contain much cytoplasm, the sperm has almost none. Its structure reflects its function: Everything has been given over to motility.

Fertilization occurs near the top of the Fallopian tube. Unlike sperm, the ovum has no movement of its own. Instead, it must depend on muscular contractions of the Fallopian tube and on tiny hairlike cilia that line the walls of the tube to sweep it along its course. The Fallopian tube, or oviduct, is a tight fit for the ovum. Cilial action forceful enough to move the inert ovum would be too great a force for sperm to swim against. Secretory cells lining the oviduct may play a part in sperm transport. During ovulation, a tide of mucus rises from the cells lining the Fallopian tubes, impeding the action of the cilia; this subsides only after ovulation. These secretory tides, controlled by hormones, may help the microscopic sperm to reach the ovum lodged at the top of the Fallopian tube. At present, however, there is no conclusive evidence implicating one mechanism as more important than any other (Harper, 1988; Jansen, 1984).

Of the millions of sperm present in an ejaculate, only several hundred reach the ovum; and, of these, only a single sperm will get through the protective layers of the ovum to have its nucleus unite with that of the ovum. Because sperm are highly motile, there is a tendency to think of them as playing a more active rule than the ovum in the fertilization process. Such is not the case. Some evidence suggests that the ovum may actually signal the sperm by secreting a chemical signal and, when the sperm get within reach, anchoring them to its surface with tiny hairlike filaments (Roberts, 1991). Even before this, however, chemicals in the female reproductive tract trigger a process known as **capacitation** in sperm. In capacitation, the outer membrane of the sperm fuses with the membrane of the acrosome. This fusion allows the enzymes contained within the acrosome to be released, a process known as the **acrosomal reaction.**

A complex molecular mechanism allows the sperm and the ovum to recognize each other. On the membrane of the ovum are "docking sites" to which the

acrosome The cap on the head of the sperm containing enzymes that digest the outer surface of the ovum.

capacitation A change in the outer membrane of the sperm, triggered by chemicals in the female reproductive tract, that allows the acrosome's enzymes to be released.

acrosomal reaction The release of the enzymes by the acrosome as a result of capacitation.

Ernest Just was the first to identify membrane depolarization and zona reaction.

sperm binds. Once the sperm reaches a docking site, microvilli on the ovum's surface tether the sperm in place; at this time the enzymes covering the surface of the sperm soften the tough outer membrane of the ovum. Only a single sperm fuses with the membrane of the ovum (Gilbert, 1994). What prevents more than one sperm from doing so?

Ernest Just (1919) identified two distinct gating mechanisms that are precipitated by this fusion. Fusion with the ovum's membrane triggers an action potential, a change in the surface polarization that radiates across the membrane. Much like an electric gate that swings shut, this **membrane depolarization** bars entrance by other sperm. Like a toppled row of dominoes collapsing the spaces between, a change in voltage makes substances within the ovum's membrane unavailable for further fusion with other sperm. The sperm's fusion with the ovum's membrane triggers a second, slower reaction known as the **zona reaction.** Sacs that lie just below the membrane release granular particles and enzymes that affect the membrane's ability to bind with sperm. Thus sperm that may have begun this process at other binding sites can no longer maintain it and are shed from the ovum's surface (Gilbert, 1994).

The nuclei of the sperm and ovum have yet to exchange their genetic contents, however. The sperm's nucleus is still near the outer perimeter of the egg, which in volume is 85,000 times that of the sperm. Further, only wreckage remains of the capsule that crashed against the egg's surface before depositing its cargo safely inside. Now, it is the nucleus of the ovum that migrates toward that of the sperm. The two nuclei meet and, migrating to the center of the zygote, combine genetic materials, forming a single cell with 23 pairs of chromosomes. One member of each pair has been contributed by the mother and the other by the father (Longo, 1987).

A woman is fertile for approximately 6 days each month, for approximately 5 days preceding ovulation and on the day of ovulation itself. The sooner intercourse occurs before ovulation, the greater the chance of conceiving. Investigators using daily urine samples to estimate time of ovulation, have found the likelihood of conception to increase from 8% on the 5th day preceding ovulation to 36% on

membrane depolarization The neutralization of the surface polarity of the ovum after a sperm succeeds in fusing with the ovum's membrane; this change bars entrance by other sperm.

zona reaction A release of granular particles and enzymes beneath the ovum's outer membrane, triggered by the sperm's fusion with the ovum's membrane, that affects the membrane's ability to bind with sperm.

When during her menstrual cycle is a woman most likely to become pregnant if she has intercourse?

the day of ovulation. No conceptions occurred for intercourse on days following ovulation or when intercourse preceded ovulation by more than 6 days (Wilcox, Weinberg, & Baird, 1995).

How long the ovum remains viable and capable of fertilization cannot be said with certainty. It is not known, for instance, whether the sudden drop in the probability of conceiving immediately following ovulation reflects the viability of the ovum itself or the inability of any additional sperm to reach the ovum due to cervical mucus. The fact that intercourse 5 days prior to ovulation can result in conception indicates that sperm are viable for at least that long. Some research has found live sperm even after 7 days (Glezerman, 1993). How old the sperm is does not appear to be related to the viability of the embryo, given conception, since differences in live births were not found for infants conceived at different days within the 6-day interval. However, relatively few (6%) infants were conceived with sperm 3 or more days old. Given conception, the same has been found for ova. Simpson (1995) reports no difference in live births for the few conceptions he observed to occur following ovulation than for those preceding it. Additionally, no relationship was observed between the timing of intercourse and the sex of the infant (Wilcox, Weinberg, & Baird, 1995).

Most women are unaware of the time at which they ovulate. Few symptoms accompany its occurrence, and it rarely occurs at exactly the same time in the cycle from month to month. On the average, ovulation occurs about 10 days prior to the start of the next period.

Patterns of Genetic Action

Genes at corresponding positions along the lengths of a pair carry related information. We know much of the functioning of these gene pairs, or **alleles,** from the work of an obscure 19th-century Augustinian monk, Gregor Mendel, whose study of the ordinary garden pea become the basis for the science of genetics.

Mendel noticed that many characteristics of the pea appeared in either of two forms. Their flowers, for example, were either white or red, their pods yellow or green, and the seeds within either wrinkled or smooth. He thought that each characteristic must be controlled by a pair of factors. Exactly how these factors passed their characteristics from one generation to the next was not so obvious, however. For one thing, plants of the next generation did not always show the same characteristics as the parent generation. Were the factors controlling those characteristics lost? Did they merge with other, more dominant, factors, or did they pass hidden but unchanged to the next generation?

What would happen, Mendel asked, if the pollen from white flowering plants were used to fertilize red flowering plants? Would some of the seedlings mature into white flowering plants and others into red flowering plants? Would they all be red? Or all be white? With hoe in hand, Mendel set about to get an answer and, in spring, neat rows of plants all blossomed in red. Since all the plants had red flowers, Mendel reasoned that the factor controlling this characteristic must be **dominant.** Whenever it is present, the trait it carries will occur.

But what of the other factor, that for white flowers? Was it lost? Mendel bred the second generation of red flowering plants with each other and found that, though most of the following generation had red flowers, some bloomed in white. The other factor, which he called **recessive,** had been masked by the first but was passed to the next generation. In order for the trait carried by the recessive gene to occur, *both* members of the allele pair had to be recessive.

alleles The complementary forms of a gene located at the same site on the autosomes that determine the expression of a particular trait.

dominant allele The gene of an allele pair that produces a particular trait.

recessive allele The gene of an allele pair that governs the expression of a trait only in the presence of another recessive allele.

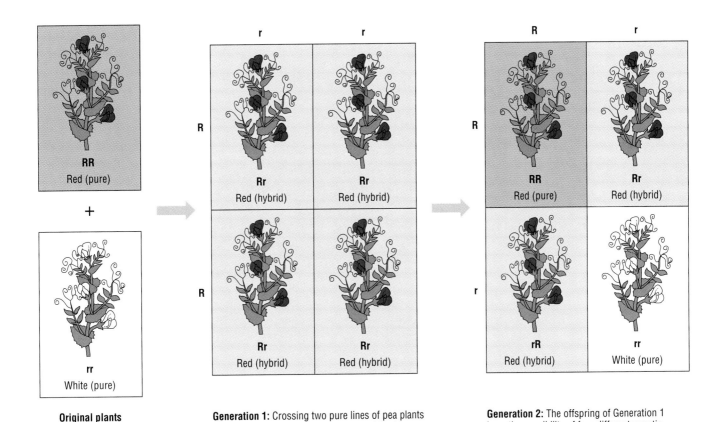

Original plants

Generation 1: Crossing two pure lines of pea plants —one with red flowers (RR) and one with white flowers (rr)—creates hybrid offspring (Rr), each with one red gene and one white gene. Because red is dominant, all the flowers appear red.

Generation 2: The offspring of Generation 1 have the possibility of four different genetic combinations: RR (pure red), rr (pure white), Rr (hybrid red), and rR (hybrid red).

FIGURE 2.6 Mendel's Pea Plants

If there were an equal likelihood of receiving either a dominant or a recessive gene from either parent, there should be approximately equal numbers of plants in which both genes are dominant (AA), one gene is dominant and one is recessive (Aa and aA), and both genes are recessive (aa). Only in the last group of plants will the recessive trait appear. A count of the blossoms in Mendel's garden showed that just one fourth of the plants flowered in white—as one would expect. Figure 2.6 diagrams this process.

What holds for peas holds for people—in many respects. As with peas, human genes function in pairs and the members of a pair can be dominant or recessive. Because some genes are recessive, it is not always possible to know whether a person carries the genes for certain traits. The observable or measurable characteristics displayed by a person make up that person's **phenotype.** These traits reflect the action of dominant genes, either paired or singly, or of pairs of recessive genes. However, many hidden recessive genes are carried in the **genotype,** the set of genes acquired at conception that constitutes each person's genetic makeup. Box 2.1 lists some traits inherited by humans.

Most traits result from the combination of many gene pairs working together in complex ways to produce the trait. In some cases, the action of one pair adds to that of other pairs, each contributing something to the final result. In others, genes may contribute only a "go ahead" for the action of other pairs or, conversely,

phenotype The observable or measurable characteristics of an organism, resulting from the interaction between the genotype and the environment.

genotype The total set of genes inherited at conception.

Box 2.1 *Some Inherited Traits*

Allergic reactions

- Asthma—recessive trait
- Allergic sensitivity to ragweed pollen—dominant trait
- Hypersensitivity to insect stings—may be dominant trait

Ears

- Earlobes may be present or absent, free or attached—probably dominant trait
- Ability to wiggle ears without touching them—probably dominant trait
- Earwax may be dry (as in about 85% of Japanese) or wet (as in most Caucasians and Blacks)—dominant traits

Eyes

- Earlier idea that blue eye color is a simple autosomal recessive trait is no longer accepted
- Unusually long eyelashes—probably dominantly inherited

Facial features

- Cheek dimples—dominant trait
- Chin dimple (cleft chin)—dominant trait

Gastrointestinal tract

- Celiac disease (a failure to absorb foods normally, especially fats)—polygenic; risk to child of affected person is about 3%
- Crohn disease (an autoimmune inflammation of the bowel)—polygenic; risk to child of affected person is probably 0.4%–1%
- Peptic ulcer—may be polygenic or autosomal dominant; risk to child of affected person is probably 5–10%

Hair

- Male-pattern baldness—recessive trait
- Curly hair—probably dominant trait
- Hair on middle segments of fingers—dominant trait
- Very blond hair—may be recessive trait
- Very red hair—may be recessive trait (however, red pigment in hair is dominantly inherited)

Joints

- Dislocation of hips—polygenic, but dominant inheritance may also be responsible
- Rheumatoid arthritis—polygenic, more frequent in females than in males; risk to child of affected person is 3–5%

Skin

- Painful calluses over pressure points in hands and feet—dominant trait
- Susceptibility to chilblain—dominant trait that especially affects young women
- Pigmented moles—probably dominant trait
- Psoriasis—polygenic; risk to child of affected person is about 1%

Smell

- Absent or deficient sense of smell—usually dominant trait, but sex-linked forms also occur
- Inability to smell cyanide—may be sex-linked
- Inability to smell musk—recessive trait affecting about 7% of Caucasians but no Blacks
- Inability to smell skunk—probably recessive trait

Speech

- Stammering (stuttering)—dominant trait that is unusually frequent in Japanese, very infrequent in Polynesians, and almost completely absent in American Indians

Teeth

- Peg-shaped, conical, variably sized, or pitted teeth—dominant trait
- Overbite due to upper front teeth that jut out too far—dominant trait
- Impacted teeth—may be sex-linked trait

Toes

- First toe (big toe) longer than the second—probably recessive trait
- Second toe longer than the first—probably dominant trait

Tongue

- Ability to roll or curl sides of tongue and form trough down center—probably dominant trait
- Ability to fold up tip of tongue—probably recessive trait

Vision

- Difficulty seeing blue and yellow but not red and green—may be dominant or sex-linked trait
- Severe myopia—can be dominant, recessive, or sex-linked trait

Other traits

- Achoo syndrome (sneezing stimulated by sudden exposure to sunlight or other intense light)—dominant trait
- Aspirin intolerance—recessive trait
- Hypersensitivity to cold (resulting in skin wheals and possibly pain, swelling of joints, chills, fever)—dominant trait
- Double groin hernia—probably dominant trait
- Apnea (periods of not breathing during sleep)—dominant trait
- Abundant sweating, especially on forehead, tip of the nose, and upper lip, while eating spicy or sour foods—dominant trait
- Tone deafness—probably dominant trait
- Varicose veins—may be due to both autosomal and sex-linked inheritance

Source: From Aubrey Milunsky; *Choices, Not Chances.* Copyright © 1977, 1989 by Aubrey Milunsky, MD.

Multiple Determinancy: Personality Traits

BY MICHAEL WAPNER

Yes or no, is intelligence inherited? Yes or no, does being raised in a poor neighborhood lead to delinquency? Yes or no, does watching violence on TV lead to aggressive behavior? How often have we all heard these kinds of questions? How often have we witnessed arguments about whether some such life circumstance does or does not lead to a particular consequence? Life certainly would be simpler, although probably not as interesting, if things like emotional adjustment, delinquency, intelligence, and aggression each were determined by a single variable. Certainly it would make it easier to predict later behavior from childhood experience. Did you watch violent programs on TV when you were a kid? Then you will be violent. Were you raised in poverty? Then you will be delinquent. Did your parents score low on intelligence tests? Then you will score low also.

While each of these statements is false as presented, each may contain a grain of truth. There *is* a relationship between the intelligence of parents and their children, between socioeconomic status and delinquency, between exposure to TV violence and aggressive behavior. So what's wrong with these statements?

What is wrong is that characteristics such as violence, intelligence, and delinquency are **multiply determined.** Each is the result of *many contributing factors* that combine in complex ways to produce the final behavior, and it is grossly misleading to single out only one factor as the "cause." When the behavior or condition under consideration is undesirable, these contributing

factors are termed **risk factors.** As the number of risk factors that are present increases, the likelihood of the behavior occurring also increases. Thus, for instance, while poverty is not "the cause" of delinquency in boys, it is a risk factor. So is growing up in a single-parent family. And when both are present, the probability of a boy becoming a delinquent is greater than when only one is present. However, there are generally also factors that oppose risk factors and reduce the probability of the undesirable result. These are termed **protective factors.** The presence of involved men in the community is a protective factor. Thus, a behavior as complex as delinquency is the net result of both risk and protective factors. You can see how ignoring all but one of them can lead to misunderstanding.

Of course, multiple determinacy also presents problems for research. How do we investigate the way many risk and protective factors combine? Happily, a number of research techniques have been developed for this purpose. One of them is a statistical technique called **multiple regression.** While the details are more technical than we need go into here, we can illustrate its use. Greenberg, Coie, Lengua, and Pinderhughes (1999) were interested in the relationship between a number of risk factors in the preschool years and social competence, as evaluated by the teacher, in first-grade children. (Actually, the study by Greenberg et al. was extensive, investigating the relationship between the listed risk factors and a number of different

multiply determined Of characteristics that are the result of many contributing factors.

risk factors Factors associated with an increased rate of undesirable behavior or disease.

protective factors Factors that counter risk factors and reduce the probability of undesirable developmental results.

multiple regression A statistical technique designed to investigate the relationship between a set of predictor variables and an outcome variable.

may inhibit their action. In other cases, single genes result in the expression of different traits depending on the presence or absence of other genes. And in yet other cases, genes require certain environmental conditions to be present for their expression. The fur of the Himalayan rabbit, for instance, is white, although its ears, feet, and tail are black. The genes governing the expression of fur color are sensitive to temperature, "turning on" only when the body temperature is low, as it is in the extremities. The action of this gene only in low temperatures becomes apparent if one shaves a patch of fur off the rabbit's back and straps on a cold pack, making that part of the back as cold as the animal's ears, feet, or tail: The fur that previously had grown in white will grow in black. The complexity of attributing cause to either genetic or environmental factors is discussed in the Research Focus, "Multiple Determinacy: Personality Traits."

Sex-Linked Inheritance

In some cases, genes are not paired. When this occurs, even recessive genes will determine the presence of a trait. Sex-linked traits, such as color blindness, illustrate the operation of unpaired recessive genes. Males are more likely to be affected by these genes than are females. Recall that in males, the Y chromosome of the 23rd pair is substantially shorter than the X chromosome, leaving many of the genes along the X chromosome with no matching allele. All of the traits influ-

outcome variables. We have chosen to look at only one.) The risk factors they investigated are listed below, organized in categories.

1. Specific demographics	2. SES–Race	3. Family risk
No. of siblings	Education	Life stress
Mother's age	Occupation	Family expressiveness
Single parenthood	Race	Social support
Marital stress		
Home environment		

4. Mother's depression

5. Neighborhood risk

Each of these factors has been shown, in one context or another, to be associated with emotional and/or academic problems in school. Each risk factor was assigned a value, with the higher scores reflecting greater risk. Thus, for instance, a child who lived with both parents might be given a 0, while a child living with only its mother would be given a 1 on the *single parenthood* risk factor. Similarly, on the *neighborhood* risk factor, a child living in a high-crime neighborhood might be given a 3, while a child living in a more law-abiding community might be given a 1. Thus, each child was assigned a score on each risk factor— the higher the score, the greater the risk. Similarly, each child was rated on social competence by the first-grade teacher and given an *outcome* score.

Basically, multiple correlation allows us to determine what proportion of the differences among the outcome scores (referred to as outcome variance) can be attributed to each risk factor. In the study by Greenberg et al., all of the risk factors taken together accounted for 24% of the outcome variance. That means that 24% of the differences among all the children with respect to social competence could be related to the 13 risk factors selected. Seventy-six percent of the differences in social competence must have been due to something else or, more likely, *a number of other things*. Of the 24% of the outcome variance accounted for, *demographic factors* (number of siblings, mother's age at time of child's birth, one- or two-parent household) accounted for 7%. *Socioeconomic status and race* (parents' occupation, level of education, and race) accounted for another 7%, and *family risk* (levels of stress and support within the family) accounted for 6%. All the remaining factors together accounted for only 4% of the outcome variance.

With these results in mind, consider how complex is the mix of factors underlying the social competence of first-graders. Consider what a small part of the differences among children can be attributed to any single variable (risk or protective factor) and how an accurate picture begins to emerge only when we recognize the *multiplicity of contributing factors*.

So, yes or no, does being raised by a single parent make a child less socially competent? If you are less comfortable now than you would have been a little while ago with that question, phrased exactly that way, then you have grasped the point of this box.

enced by these unpaired genes will be expressed in males, even when these genes are recessive. Females, who have two chromosomes of equal length, are less likely to be affected by a recessive gene, since all alleles are paired, and the other member of any pair may be dominant. Since these females still carry the recessive gene, however, they can pass it on to their children.

Exceptions to Mendel's Laws

Mendel's laws specified patterns of genetic action solely in terms of dominant and recessive genes. As long as a pair contained a dominant gene, the trait would be expressed. It was not supposed to matter *which* parent contributed that gene; alleles of either the form Aa or aA should be functionally equivalent. Recent gene research shows that this assumption doesn't always hold. It appears that some genes, at least, are marked for parentage, for whether they are received from the mother or from the father. When such a gene is inherited from one parent, it will have one effect; and it will have a different effect when inherited from the other parent. For instance, if a particular segment of genetic material along the 15th chromosome is missing, it will result in a form of mental retardation. The particular type of retardation, however, will depend on whether the child receives that chromosome from the father or from the mother (Nicholls, 1993). In other cases, inheriting a gene from the father can result in a genetic disorder that will *not*

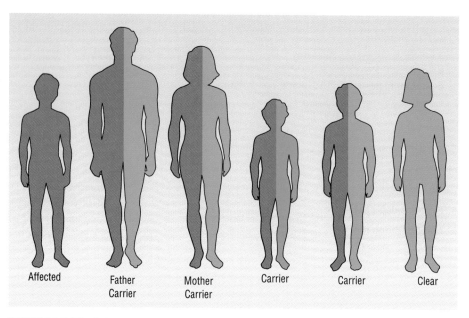

Affected   Father   Mother   Carrier   Carrier   Clear
              Carrier   Carrier

FIGURE 2.7 The Inheritance of Cystic Fibrosis *The gene for the disease is carried by symptomless individuals. A child will be affected only if he or she inherits a copy of the cystic fibrosis gene from both parents. On average, one child in every four born in such a family will be affected by the disease; two out of four will be symptomless carriers; and one will be entirely free of the gene. This pattern follows the rules laid down by Gregor Mendel.*

appear if that same gene is inherited from the mother. Thus a father can pass the gene in question on to both a son and a daughter, both of whom will develop the disorder. The son and daughter, in turn, can pass the gene on to their children. The son's children, because they receive the gene from their father, will develop the disorder. Their cousins, who receive the same gene, but from their mother, will not (Hoffman, 1991).

Other exceptions to Mendel's laws exist. Among each pair of alleles, one member of the pair was always thought to be inherited from the mother and the other from the father. However, recent research shows that, on occasion, both members of a pair can come from the same parent. This exception to the rules happens when the nucleus of a gamete contains more than its share of genetic material. When this nucleus unites with the other, any excess DNA is "shed." If the DNA that is shed is from the nucleus of the *other* gamete, the one parent will have supplied all, as opposed to half, the DNA along those segments of that chromosome.

In the case of certain recessive disorders, the consequences for parents and child can be disastrous. Cystic fibrosis, for instance, is a genetic disease characterized by the accumulation of excessive mucus in the lungs. Because this is a recessive disorder, it occurs only when both parents carry the recessive gene and pass it on to the child (Figure 2.7). When one parent has two dominant normal genes, the child will not inherit the disorder. If tested for cystic fibrosis, a couple like this would be told that none of their children could inherit the disorder even though one parent carried the recessive gene. However, if excess genetic material from the carrier parent were to cause "shedding" of the dominant genes from the other parent, and if the excess material consisted of copies of the recessive gene, a child could be born with cystic fibrosis. As more and more parents go for genetic

TABLE 2.1 Frequency of Selected Genetic Disorders

Disease	Description	Genetic Transmission	Incidence
(Cooley's anemia (thalassemia)	Abnormal blood cells, resulting in lethargy and listlessness, reduced populations resistance to infection, and retarded growth	Recessive	1 in 100 (can be higher) among Mediterranean, some Asian, and African
Cystic fibrosis	Secretion of excessive mucus, resulting in breathing and digestive problems	Recessive	Most common among Caucasians, affecting 1 in 2,000
Hemophilia	Failure of blood to clot, resulting in excessive bleeding	Recessive, sex-linked	Occurs in males, affecting 1 in 10,000
Huntington's disease	Progressive degeneration of central in nervous system, resulting in difficulties movement and breathing; symptoms appear in mid-30s	Dominant	1 in 20,000
Muscular dystrophy	Wasting of muscles, resulting in difficulties in motor coordination, inability to walk	Recessive; some forms are sex-linked	Incidence varies widely with type of disorder
Phenylketonuria (PKU)	Inability to metabolize certain proteins, resulting in severe mental retardation, but treatable with special diet	Recessive	1 in 15,000
Sickle-cell anemia	Abnormal red blood cells, resulting in swelling and pain, reduced resistance to infection, and retarded growth	Recessive	Among African Americans, 1 in 500
Tay-Sachs disease	Inability to metabolize fatty substances, resulting in neurological degeneration, blindness, deafness, and death before the age of 5	Recessive	1 in 3,500 Eastern European Jews

screening, geneticists are discovering that such exceptions to Mendel's laws, though rare, can occur. A small number of children, for instance, whose parents were told they could not *possibly* inherit cystic fibrosis have been identified (Dahl, Tybjaerg-Hansen, Wittrup, Lange, & Nordestgaard, 1998).

Genetic and Chromosomal Disorders

Genetic Disorders

As noted, Mendel's work has special significance for humans in cases of genetic disorders, many of which are carried by a single pair of genes. In all but the most unusual of cases, in recessive single-gene disorders, both parents must be carriers of the disorder for any of their children to be affected. The chances that a child will receive the recessive gene from each parent and inherit the disorder are one in four. There is a 50% chance, though, of receiving the gene from only one parent and being a carrier of the disorder, even though not actually affected by it. Cystic fibrosis, Cooley's anemia, Tay-Sachs disease, and sickle-cell anemia are all carried by a single pair of recessive genes (Table 2.1).

Some genetic disorders are carried by a single dominant gene. In these, a gene from just one parent can result in the disorder. Each conception carries with it a 50% risk if only one parent carries the gene. Huntington's disease, a neurological disorder, is carried by a single dominant gene. This disease, like so many others, would have remained obscure were it not for the personal bravery of individuals whose lives have been affected. In the case of Huntington's disease, Marjorie Guthrie, the wife of the folk singer Woody Guthrie, who succumbed to the disease, was largely responsible for establishing a committee to support research and to help affected families.

Chromosomal Disorders

Some developmental disorders can be traced to irregularities affecting the chromosomes during meiosis. During cell division, chromosomes can fail to separate, or part of a chromosome can break off, leaving either too much or too little genetic material. Since these irregularities involve stretches of DNA and not single genes, they frequently affect a broader range of behaviors than do genetic disorders.

Down syndrome is one of the more common chromosomal disorders, increasing in frequency with the mother's age. For women under 30, the risk of giving birth to a child with Down syndrome is 1 in 1,000 births, but increases to 1 in 20 for women over 45. Down syndrome results when the 21st pair of chromosomes fails to separate during meiosis, resulting in 47 rather than the normal 46 chromosomes. Children with Down syndrome share a number of physical and psychological characteristics. They tend to be shorter than average, with a stocky build. Certain facial features are present, such as almond-shaped eyes resulting from a fold along the eyelid, a slightly pug nose and flattened face, and a thick tongue. Motor development tends to be slower in these children, and mental retardation is present in almost all cases, but varies in severity, differing with the particular nature of the disorder and with the amount of stimulation and support in the child's environment. In some, retardation is severe; others learn to read and write and live semi-independent lives. Down syndrome children characteristically have a sweet disposition and a mischievous humor. These children are more likely to experience a number of physical problems, such as congenital heart defects and certain visual and hearing problems; are more subject to certain types of cancer; and have a reduced life expectancy.

Sex Chromosome Disorders

Instead of inheriting the normal pair of sex chromosomes, either two X chromosomes or an X and a Y for females and males, respectively, children with sex chromosome disorders have either a single X chromosome or an additional X or Y chromosome.

Approximately 1 in 2,000 females have a single X chromosome, or **Turner's syndrome.** A number of irregularities characterize their development. In terms of their physical appearance, these females tend to be short, have a broad chest, and a characteristic webbing on the neck. The ovaries fail to develop, resulting in infertility. Secondary sex characteristics fail to develop at puberty unless estrogen replacement therapy is given. Even though intelligence is normal, deficiencies in spatial perception are characteristic.

Approximately 1 in 1,000 males have an extra Y chromosome, or **XYY syndrome.** These males tend to be somewhat taller than average, with large body builds, and they may have severe acne. They are of normal intelligence, develop normal secondary sex characteristics, and are fertile. With respect to personality characteristics, their parents report somewhat higher activity levels and more impulsiveness than for XY males (Thompson & Thompson, 1986).

Anywhere from 1 in 400 to 1 in 1,000 males have an extra X chromosome, or **Klinefelter's syndrome.** These males, though taller than normal, may have a somewhat feminized body build and incomplete development of secondary sex

---

Q Why is Down syndrome a chromosomal, rather than a genetic, disorder?

Down syndrome A chromosomal disorder caused by an extra 21st chromosome (trisomy 21); characterized by distinctive facial features, slow motor development, and some degree of mental retardation.

Turner's syndrome A rare genetic disorder in females caused by the absence of one X chromosome; characterized by a distinctive physical appearance (such as webbing of the neck and drooping eyelids) and failure of the ovaries to develop.

XYY syndrome A genetic disorder in males caused by an extra Y chromosome; symptoms may include above-average stature, speech delays, learning disabilities, some degree of mental retardation, and behavior disturbance. Also known as polysome Y syndrome.

Klinefelter's syndrome A genetic disorder in males caused by an extra X chromosome; symptoms include small testes, insufficient production of testosterone, and infertility.

Down syndrome is a common chromosomal disorder with characteristic features.

characteristics at puberty. Most report problems of sterility in adulthood. Intelligence is normal, although verbal skills are frequently affected.

Detecting Birth Defects

Most conceptions in which the fetus is severely compromised spontaneously abort early in pregnancy, usually before the mother even realizes she has been pregnant. Genetic and chromosomal disorders vary widely in the extent to which they can compromise the quality of a child's life. Some disorders, such as Down syndrome, even though affecting both mental and physical functioning, do not always prevent children from living meaningful lives, with supportive family environments. Other diseases do; for example, Tay-Sachs disease, which results in a progressive deterioration of the nervous system, causes profound mental retardation and leads to a painful early death, usually by the age of 2.

Prospective parents can receive genetic counseling, in which they go over their family histories with someone who can help them interpret patterns in family illnesses that suggest an inherited disease. Even though most prospective parents do not receive such counseling, it is especially recommended for couples who have a family member with a genetic disease, either a child who has already been born or a relative in one or the other's family. Also, those who have had difficulty conceiving or carrying a pregnancy to term should receive such counseling, since many such difficulties actually represent spontaneous abortions of compromised conceptions. Genetic counseling is usually offered to prospective parents who are older, since a number of chromosomal abnormalities are associated with parental age, especially that of the mother. Couples who receive genetic counseling are in a better position to weigh the risks of having a child with a birth defect and to consider the alternatives. The Social Policy Focus, "Genetic Testing and the Human Genome Project," explores some of the complications of deciding to get genetic testing.

A number of tests enable prospective parents to determine whether they might pass a disorder on to their children. A simple blood test can be used to detect whether the genes for a number of the more common genetic disorders are carried by one or both prospective parents, who can then make informed decisions about parenting, knowing the potential risks of giving birth to a child with a disorder. Other tests can reveal, once pregnancy has occurred, whether a fetus

Genetic Testing and the Human Genome Project

BY MICHAEL WAPNER

More information is not always better, especially when it's about things over which we have no control. Until fairly recently, screening for health problems has been accompanied by available treatments should the tests bring bad news. For instance, early detection of cancer (mammograms, pap smears, and the like) allowed earlier treatment and a better prognosis. However, the incredible advances in medical technology triggered by the Human Genome Project are increasingly making possible prediction of health threats for which no treatment yet exists. For some people with a family history of hereditary disease, genetic testing may bring reassurance that they have been spared. But for others the results of testing will be ominous. What do you do with the news that you, your child, the fetus that you are carrying, or your yet-to-be-conceived offspring do, or will likely, carry the genes for eventual schizophrenia, Alzheimer's disease, some form of cancer, or depression?

A number of questions regarding the psychological problems produced by genetic testing need to be answered, but health professionals have just recently begun to investigate them:

1. What determines the decision to seek genetic testing? Early results already suggest that fewer people than expected take advantage of the opportunity when it is available (Codori, Hanson, & Brandt, 1994; Lannfelt, Axelman, Lilius, & Basun, 1995).

2. What sorts of response can we expect from those for whom screening brings bad news? Will shock and worry outweigh the benefits of early knowledge? A few studies have already been published—with inconsistent results. Some studies report few or no negative reactions. Other studies report stronger emotional responses. However, these studies did not use the same methods to assess emotional reactions. Some only asked the patient general questions and did not follow up after the initial meeting. Other studies used more probing assessments, followed the patient for a longer period of time, or did both. Some published accounts of individual cases report quite serious reactions. In one case, an individual who was told that he carried the gene for Alzheimer's disease reacted with "anxiety, sorrow, . . . depression, and . . . suicidal thoughts" lasting 6 months. In another case, being told that she carried the genes for Huntington's disease brought a woman to the brink of suicide (Salkovskis & Rimes, 1997). Are these last examples extreme cases? Or, with deeper assessment and longer follow-ups, will they turn out to be fairly typical?

3. Given the likelihood of strong emotional reactions in some cases of genetic screening, can mental health professionals provide counseling and other psychological support to mitigate this distress? And if so, what kind? Should it be provided before the patient takes the test? Or should it be on receiving the results? Or both? Should everyone receive counseling, or only those with obvious negative reactions?

An article prepared for the World Health Organization (Wertz, Fletcher, & Borg, 1995) focuses on pretest genetic counseling and warns that the supportive aspects are at least as important as the informational aspects. The article goes on to suggest nondirective counseling except where there is "high risk of serious harm." (Nondirective counseling emphasizes active listening, empathy, and reflecting back to the patient what seem to the counselor to be the patient's own feelings. There is an avoidance of behavioral or medicinal prescriptions, interpretations, or advice.) However, a review article by Salkovskis and Rimes (1997) is critical of the use of nondirective counseling. These authors, along with calling for much more research, suggest the use of a cognitive-behavioral approach both to assessing the individuals' reaction to screening and to treatment should the reaction be problematic. The cognitive-behavioral approach emphasizes the importance of the way people think about the information they receive. Individuals who habitually interpret ambiguous information in a pessimistic way, who quickly feel hopeless and helpless in the face of threats, are more likely to have serious negative reactions to the results of genetic screening. Thus, by evaluating an individual's beliefs and attitudes toward health and illness, predictions might be made about that person's reaction to the results of genetic tests. The cognitive-behavioral approach also has developed various techniques and exercises for changing beliefs and attitudes and hence one's emotional reactions. Thus, this model provides an approach for both assessment and treatment. Whether it is as good or better than a nondirective approach remains to be seen.

As you can see, there is still a lot to be learned about the emotional impact of genetic screening and how to deal with it. But there is something we can say about this problem now. History tells us that whatever we can do, we do. There is no undoing of our knowledge about the human genome. It will be used to predict our future, whether those predictions are happy or frightening. Thus, the only intelligent response to the negative effects of this new knowledge is still more knowledge. It is important, therefore, that along with support for the Genome Project itself, there be adequate financing for research into coping with the emotional consequences.

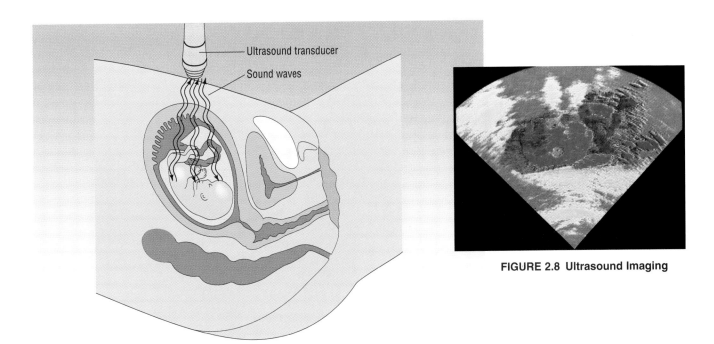

FIGURE 2.8 Ultrasound Imaging

is affected by a particular disorder. Sometimes the damage to the fetus is so extensive that it cannot develop normally. Many times these fetuses spontaneously abort. Other times chromosomal damage is so slight as to be negligible. And at still other times, the problem lies somewhere in between.

Ultrasound Imaging

This procedure uses ultra-high-frequency sound waves that bounce off the fetus, creating an image that is useful in detecting abnormalities in head growth and organ or limb development (Figure 2.8). This procedure is totally noninvasive, as there is no need to sample fetal or placental cells or even maternal blood, and carries no risk of infection or danger to the fetus or the mother. It does not reveal, however, some of the genetic and chromosomal disorders that can be detected through the use of amniocentesis, alpha-fetoprotein screening, and chorionic villus sampling.

Amniocentesis

The most common procedure for genetic screening samples fluid from the amniotic sac that surrounds the fetus. After the position of the fetus and the placenta is determined through the use of ultrasound, a needle is inserted through the mother's abdomen, and amniotic fluid is drawn out (Figure 2.9). The amniotic fluid contains skin cells sloughed off by the fetus, each of which contains a full set of chromosomes. These are analyzed to determine the presence of chromosomal damage. The sex of the fetus can also be determined at this time. When is amniocentesis called for? When specific genetic or chromosomal diseases are suspected. It is not practical, however, to use amniocentesis to screen for multiple genetic disorders, since each test would necessitate examining individual genes, an extremely time-intensive and expensive procedure.

Amniocentesis is usually done between 16 and 17 weeks following the last menstrual period. The results may not be available for up to 2 more weeks. The

FIGURE 2.9 Amniocentesis

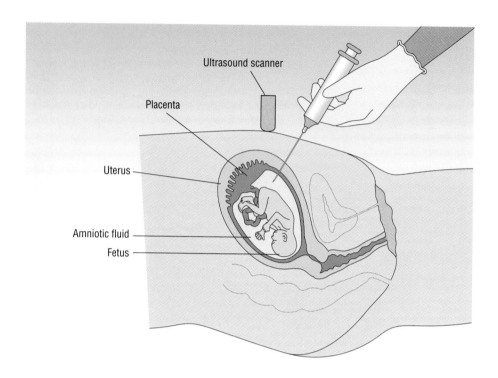

most important drawback to the use of this particular test is the fact that it cannot be done before mid-pregnancy.

Alpha-Fetoprotein Screening

Unlike amniocentesis, which—because of its invasiveness and the late stage of the pregnancy at which it is done—is recommended only for pregnancies where specific genetic questions arise, alpha-fetoprotein screening (AFP) is a reasonable screening procedure in all pregnancies, as it involves a simple blood test. A sample of the mother's blood is analyzed for elevated levels of alpha fetoprotein, which may indicate neural tube defects. Since there is a high rate of false positives with this test, additional screening measures are necessary to evaluate the condition of the fetus (O'Shea, 1995).

Chorionic Villus Sampling

Like amniocentesis, chorionic villus sampling (CVS) obtains cells not from the mother, but from those surrounding the fetus. Under the guidance of ultrasound, a sample of the placenta is biopsied (Figure 2.10). The advantage of CVS over amniocentesis is that it can be done as early as the 2nd month of pregnancy. However, it is not quite as accurate, and positive results need to be confirmed by amniocentesis (O'Shea, 1995).

Which type of prenatal test is most accurate in detecting genetic and chromosomal disorders, and why?

Huntington's disease highlights some of the special problems that surround issues of genetic counseling. People with Huntington's live normal lives, unaffected by the disease, until their late 30s. Then there is a progressive impairment of speech and movement and frequently of mental functioning. The disease is fatal, but only after years of illness. Many people who are likely to be affected by the disease may not want to know whether they actually have it. However, since it appears late in their childbearing years, there is a 50% chance they will unknow-

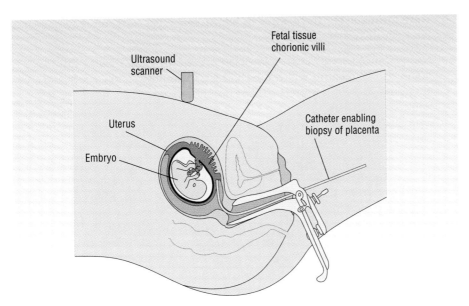

FIGURE 2.10 Chorionic Villus Sampling

ingly pass it on to their children. What are the emotional costs to all concerned? If such individuals are diagnosed before the symptoms emerge, they can choose to avoid passing the disorder on, yet they would then live with the knowledge that they have an incurable disease.

The Contexts of Genetic Action

The exceptions to Mendel's laws discussed earlier indicate that the way genes direct the expression of various characteristics is not simple, nor is it always direct. The presence of various other factors can determine which effects genes have; their final expression will depend on the environment in which they are present. The environment can be intracellular, involving the presence of other genes that inhibit or facilitate genetic expression, or it can be the environmental surround provided by a family. In the latter case, environments assume various forms through interactions with family members and aspects of the home itself.

Genetic and Environmental Contributions

Sandra Scarr (1992, 1993), at the University of Virginia, takes a constructivist approach in explaining the interplay of genetic and environmental factors, arguing that children construct their "realities" from many possible realities that are latent in their environments. The events that make up their daily lives, for instance, can be perceived in quite different ways by different children; and, because of this, these events will not have the same impact from one child to the next.

Scarr adds that not only do environments not exist for children apart from being constructed by them, but also the processes that children bring to bear in constructing reality are themselves influenced by genetic factors, making it impossible to separate "environmental" and "genetic" contributions to development. A child's genotype, in other words, will predispose that child to take in certain environmental experiences and not others, even though the latter may be present to the same degree. Such experiences simply will not be as salient for a child with that genotype.

Scarr distinguishes three ways in which genotypes structure environments: passive, evocative, and active.

- *Passive:* Since parents are responsible for both the child's genes and the home environment in which the child grows up, the child's genes and environment will be correlated. For instance, parents who enjoy reading will read to their children and talk about books. In this way the parent's own enjoyment of reading, which is genetically influenced, in turn influences both the child's environment and the child's genotype.

- *Evocative:* In this pattern of influence, genetically influenced behaviors, such as sociability, mood, or intelligence, evoke responses in others that contribute to the child's interpersonal environment and to the child's self-image. It is possible, for instance, that parents' behavior is more similar with siblings who are themselves more similar, as is the case with identical twins. Genetically influenced traits serve as self-fulfilling prophecies. Infants, for instance, with sunny personalities elicit positive responses in others, which in turn occasion positive moods in the infants. Fussy infants, in comparison, are more likely to experience negative reactions in others, which contribute to their negative moods.

- *Active:* Children select environments that fit their genetically influenced personalities. Thus, the way that children spend their time, either with others or alone, and what they do will reflect their personalities and talents. Children will sort themselves into different types of environments based on the interests and abilities resulting from different genotypes. This third way in which genetic predispositions structure children's experiences, sometimes called "niche picking," is increasingly likely to occur with age, as children have more opportunities to choose their own activities.

One Particular Environment: The Family

The notion that children create their own environments runs counter to many parents' beliefs concerning the importance of their influence. Yet research examining similarities among siblings differing in degrees of relatedness supports substantial genetic contributions (Plomin & Daniels, 1987). Scarr (1992) points out that the variability that exists among children from the same family is as great as that among children from different families. This observation suggests that family environments have fewer important effects on children than has been supposed, providing, of course, that the environment furnished by the family is sufficient to support the development of genetically influenced individual differences. In other words, Scarr believes that differences in environments, given that these are adequate, are not important determinants of differences among children. Some parents, at least, may find comfort in Scarr's words, namely that "children's outcomes do not depend on whether parents take children to the ball game or to a museum so much as they depend on genetic transmission, on plentiful opportunities, and on having a good enough environment that supports children's development to become themselves" (p. 15).

Support for Scarr's position comes from research examining similarities in the way children perceive their family environments as a function of the degree to which the children are genetically related to each other. When identical twins (100% genetic relatedness), fraternal twins (50% relatedness), full siblings (50% relatedness), half siblings (25% relatedness), and genetically unrelated children (0% relatedness) were asked to evaluate their family environments along a number of dimensions, such as parental warmth and the way parents monitor their

Identical twins are likely to perceive their environments quite similarly whether they grow up in the same or different homes.

children's behavior and deal with conflict, investigators found significant genetic effects for most of their measures. That is, the closer the genetic relatedness among the siblings, the more similar the siblings' perceptions of their environments. In general, over 25% of the variance of environmental measures was attributable to genetic similarities among children (Plomin, Reiss, Hetherington, & Howe, 1994).

Yoon-Mi Hur and Thomas Bourchard (1995) also examined identical and fraternal twins' perceptions of their childhood family environments. However, their twins had been separated early in childhood (mean age at separation was 1 year) and grew up in different homes. Even so, these investigators found that identical twins were much more likely than were fraternal twins to share similar perceptions of parental support. With respect to issues of parental control, however, genetic contributions were minimal. Since the twins grew up with different sets of parents and in different homes, these findings suggest a very real biological basis to differences among individuals in the ways in which they perceive, or construct, their surroundings. They suggest, in other words, that children help to create the environments which they experience.

A number of scholars have criticized Scarr's position (Baumrind, 1993; Jackson, 1993). Diana Baumrind (1993) has argued that Scarr has not made clear what makes a family environment "good enough." In the absence of specifying what contributes to a family's environment, Scarr's argument that factors such as

Factor Analysis: Fertility Procedures

"What a darling baby!" exclaimed the woman in line next to Molly. "She looks just like you."

She certainly does, Molly smiled to herself with pleasure; she looks just as happy and just as pleased with life as I feel whenever I look at her.

Molly had felt that same pleasure ever since she first set eyes on her daughter in the delivery room, still joined to her by a freshly clamped umbilical cord, with her husband Jake beaming down at the two of them.

Despite some similarities in their appearance, such as the wreath of curls surrounding each of their faces and eyes that turn up slightly at the corners, and despite the fact that Molly had given birth to her daughter, mother and daughter were genetically unrelated to each other.

Like 15% of married couples, Molly and Jake had tried for over a year to have children with no success. The birth of their daughter was possible only as a result of recent reproductive technologies. Because of difficulties with ovulation, which made it impossible for Molly's ova to be used, Molly and Jake had used a procedure known as **egg donation,** in which an ovum that had been removed from another woman was fertilized in the laboratory using Jake's sperm. Once cell division had begun, the resulting embryo was inserted into Molly's uterus where it developed as an otherwise normal pregnancy. In a procedure such as this, the child is genetically related to the father, but not to the mother. In a similar procedure, known as **in vitro fertilization,** the mother's own ova are removed and fertilized in the laboratory with sperm from the father, making the child genetically related to both the mother and the father (see figure). In cases where the father's sperm cannot be used, sperm obtained from a donor are injected through the cervix at the time of ovulation. In this procedure, known as **donor insemination,** the child is genetically related to the mother but not the father.

It is also possible, of course, to use donor sperm to fertilize ova obtained from another woman and then insert the resulting embryo into the uterus of the mother. In this procedure, known as **egg and sperm donation,** the child is genetically related neither to the mother or the father. Finally, an embryo resulting from any of these techniques can be inserted into the uterus of another woman, in a procedure involving a **surrogate birth mother.** Thus, it is possible for a child to have anywhere from two to five parents. We're all familiar with the case of two parents. What about five? The parents in such a case would be an egg donor, a sperm donor, a surrogate birth mother, and the two people the child would eventually call "Mom" and "Dad."

What are the psychological consequences, if any, of reproductive technologies such as these? Are relationships within the family affected, for instance, by whether one parent but not the other is genetically related to the child? Will children be confused as to their identity when they have been conceived through the use of donor sperm or donor ova? Might parents have unresolved issues about infertility that could affect their relationship with each other or their children?

Susan Golombok, Rachel Cook, Alison Bish, and Clare Murray (1995) looked for answers to questions such as these by comparing families in which children were conceived through in vitro fertilization (41 families) and donor insemination (45 families) with those in which children were born to two biological parents (43 families) or were adopted at birth (55 families).

In each type of family, parents responded to a number of questionnaires designed to measure the quality of the marital relationship, aspects of their mental health, their attitudes about parenting, and the stress they experienced as parents. Additionally, mothers supplied information through extensive interviews about qualities of parenting such as warmth and emotional involvement. Information was obtained from the children as well, concerning such things as their emotional attachment to their parents and their perceptions of relationships within the family.

For each family, then, hundreds of answers to literally

egg donation A fertility procedure in which an ovum removed from a donor woman is fertilized with the father's sperm, and the resulting embryo is inserted into the birth mother's uterus.

in vitro fertilization A fertility procedure in which ova are taken from the birth mother and fertilized in a laboratory with sperm from the father.

parental disciplinary patterns or family income are not important loses its force. In fact, Hur and Bourchard's finding that children's perceptions of certain dimensions of the family environment (such as parental support) reflect a biological component, whereas other dimensions (such as parental control) do not, underscore Baumrind's point. Baumrind also argues that research into genetic and environmental contributions to development is limited by the inadequacies of the instruments currently available for measuring family environment. Research by Baumrind and others clearly underscores the contribution of parenting styles to developmental outcomes such as social competence and independence (Baumrind, 1991; Smetana & Berent, 1993).

In *The Blue Jay's Dance,* Louise Erdrich (1996) writes of the everyday mysteries of parenting children, of bathing babies, waking in the night with them, feed-

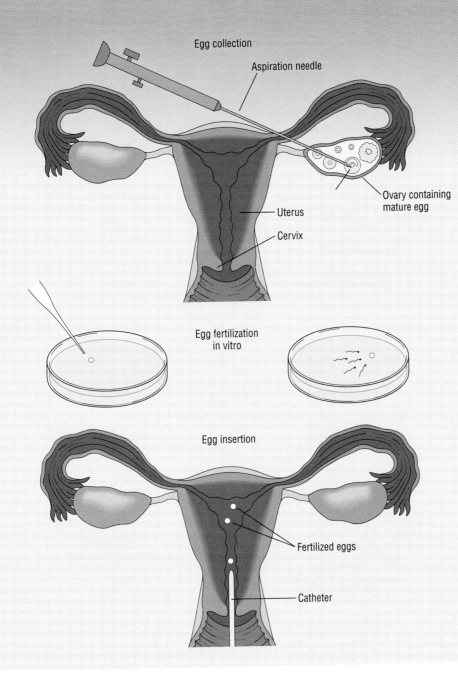

Egg collection

Aspiration needle

Ovary containing
mature egg

Uterus

Cervix

Egg fertilization
in vitro

Egg insertion

Fertilized eggs

Catheter

In Vitro Fertilization

The woman receives hormone injections to stimulate production of ova. Additional hormones are given to stimulate ovulation and to prepare the uterus to receive the fertilized ovum. The follicles are viewed through a laparoscope inserted through an incision at the navel. The ova are retrieved by being drawn into a long, hollow needle. (The ovary may also be viewed and the ova extracted through the vagina.) Each ovum, or egg cell, is placed in a laboratory dish containing a culture that is chemically similar to the uterine environment. Sperm are added. Two days later, the fertilized ova (usually no more than three) are injected into the uterus.

ing and soothing them. One of the greatest mysteries, though, is that of conceiving them. Of this she writes, "We conceive our children in deepest night, in blazing sun, outdoors, in barns and alleys and minivans. We have no rules, no ceremonies, we don't even need a driver's license. Conception is often something of a by-product of sex, a candle in a one-room studio, pure brute chance, a wonder. To make love with the desire for a child is to move the act out of its singularity, to make the need of the moment an eternal wish. But of all passing notions, that of a human being for a child is perhaps the purest in the abstract, and the most complicated in reality" (p. 3). ◀

For some couples, that reality is complicated from the very beginning. The Research Focus, "Factor Analysis: Fertility Procedures," discusses the psychological consequences of reproductive technologies.

donor insemination A fertility procedure in which sperm from a donor are injected into the birth mother's uterus at the time of ovulation.

egg and sperm donation A fertility procedure in which donor sperm are used to fertilize donor ova, and the resulting embryo is inserted into the birth mother's uterus.

Factor Analysis: Fertility Procedures *(continued)*

hundreds of questions were obtained. How, you might wonder, could these researchers make sense of all that data? How, in other words, does one go about looking for, and finding, meaningful patterns?

Factor analysis is a statistical procedure designed to do just that. Using this procedure, researchers can identify underlying dimensions or *factors* that account for the ways in which individuals respond to different measures such as the ones mentioned above. Several steps are involved in factor analysis. The first step, already described, consists in choosing a set of measures that are conceptually related to each other. For instance, Golombok and her associates used a number of questionnaires as well as data gathered from interviews to assess parental attitudes and practices. In the second step, each measure is correlated with each of the other measures to yield a matrix of correlation coefficients (see the table). Correlation coefficients indicate the degree to which two variables are related (see the Research Focus, "Bias and Blind Controls" in Chapter 13) or both measure the same thing. An index of the proportion of variance that is shared by each of these measures can be obtained by squaring this correlation coefficient. Thus, a corre-

lation of .70 between a questionnaire measuring the quality of the marital relationship and one measuring mental health would indicate that 49% of what was being measured by the marital relationship questionnaire was also being measured by the questionnaire on mental health.

Let's take a look at a matrix of correlations to see what it is that factor analysis needs to accomplish (keep in mind that the data are fictitious). Looking at these correlations, we can see that parental warmth is highly correlated with emotional involvement, but not with parental stress. Looking over the rest of the table, can you see a pattern to any of the other correlations?

One of the first things you might notice is that warmth and emotional involvement are highly correlated with each other, and the correlation for each with parental stress and parent-child dysfunction is low. Similarly, the latter two measures are themselves highly correlated. Mental health appears to be only moderately correlated with any of the other items. Judging from this matrix, then, we might say that there are two factors accounting for the relationships among these five measures. Warmth and emotional involvement are associated with one of these factors, and parental stress and parent-child dysfunction

Infertility

Just as with high-performance cars and toys on Christmas morning, reproductive systems do not always function according to the manual. Approximately 15% of couples in the United States are infertile, incapable of becoming pregnant within a year of trying. Infertility has risen over the decades. We live with increasing numbers of environmental toxins and occupational hazards that can affect the production of gametes. A rise in sexually transmitted diseases is also implicated. These are infections of the reproductive tract that, when healed, leave scar tissue that can block the passage of gametes. Also, a trend toward postponing childbearing contributes to increased infertility rates. For instance, infertility affects approximately 5% of women in their early 20s, but nearly 3 times that number of women in their early 30s (Menken, Trussell, & Larsen, 1986).

It comes as a surprise to most individuals that, when contraceptives are finally put aside, conception does not occur. They have been worrying about finding a convenient and safe way to prevent pregnancy, having assumed that unless precautions were taken, pregnancy would ensue. This assumption underlies basic attitudes most adults hold about themselves. Fertility and potency are central to what it means to be female and male. Infertility challenges these assumptions and, with these, one's sense of self.

Infertility also transforms the sexual encounter. For infertile couples sex is easily stripped of romance and passion and becomes scheduled by the calendar, visits to the doctor, and morning basal temperature charts (indicating time of ovulation) rather than by desire. The American Fertility Society estimates that 70% of infertile couples can be helped. However, treatment is costly, frequently lengthy, sometimes painful, and always emotionally intrusive.

surrogate birth mother A woman who becomes pregnant usually by artificial insemination or surgical implantation of a fertilized egg for the purpose of carrying the fetus for another woman.

factor analysis A statistical procedure designed to identify underlying dimensions, or factors, that account for the relationship among several variables.

Table of Matrix of Correlations

	1	2	3	4	5
1. Parental warmth	1.00	.25	.75	.22	.55
2. Parental stress	.25	1.00	.19	.70	.51
3. Emotional involvement	.75	.19	1.00	.26	.49
4. Parent-child dysfunction	.22	.70	.26	1.00	.50
5. Mental health	.55	.51	.49	.50	1.00

with the other factor. Mental health appears to be associated to some degree with both of these factors.

With only a few measures, such as in the example here, it is not that difficult to see patterns as they arise. However, when many measures are involved, a statistical procedure must be used to identify the underlying factors. These procedures enable researchers not only to identify factors, but also to estimate the importance of each in accounting for the overall variability of scores.

And what did Golombok and her associates discover about parent-child relationships in families created by new reproductive technologies?

The quality of parenting was actually superior in assisted reproduction families, irrespective of whether the children were genetically related to one or both of the parents. Assisted reproduction mothers showed more warmth and more emotional involvement (the latter was also true for adoptive mothers) toward their children than did those who naturally conceived their children. Additionally, mothers and fathers of assisted reproduction children, as well as adoptive parents, interacted more with their children than did parents who naturally conceived their children. Factor analysis of the parenting variables identified from the interview data (warmth, emotional involvement, mother-child interaction, and father-child interaction) and of the parental stress index yielded a single factor that accounted for 43% of the variance. Overall, these findings suggest that how well a family functions is affected less by the genetic similarity among family members than by the parents' desire to have a child. Furthermore, fathers who were genetically unrelated to their children, as in the case of donor insemination and adoption, did not have difficulty relating to their children.

In about 40% of the cases, infertility can be traced to the woman. Another 40% can be traced to the man, and in many couples the problem lies with both partners. Dramatic advances in science and medicine now make it possible to treat many causes of infertility. Synthetic hormones, microsurgery, in vitro fertilization, and donor procedures offer new hope to childless couples.

Among women, failure to ovulate is a frequent cause of infertility. Synthetic hormones can stimulate the hypothalamus, a brain center that regulates bodily functions, to release hormones that in turn stimulate the pituitary to release FSH and LH, thus starting the ovulatory cycle. These hormones, however, lack the delicate touch of nature and may cause several follicles to ripen at the same time, thus increasing the chance of multiple births.

Another common cause of infertility among women is endometriosis, a disorder in which the tissues lining the uterus grow within the abdominal cavity, enveloping the ovaries and Fallopian tubes and blocking the passage of gametes. This condition can be treated with drugs that shrink the abnormal tissue or by surgical removal of the tissue. Blocked Fallopian tubes resulting from adhesions and scar tissue are another common cause of infertility in women. Microsurgery can often be used to open the blocked tubes.

In men, an inadequate sperm count is a frequent cause of infertility. Sperm are either too few, not sufficiently motile, or insufficiently developed. Many factors can be responsible. Childhood diseases such as mumps can damage the cells that produce sperm; infections can leave scar tissue blocking the passageways the sperm must travel; and occupational hazards such as chemicals, radiation, or excessive heat can permanently or temporarily alter sperm production (see Chapter 3).

78 PART 1 • Foundations

Summary

Genes and Chromosomes

Traits are passed from one generation to the next through genes, segments of the DNA strand making up a chromosome. DNA provides the blueprint for the construction of new cells by directing the manufacture of proteins with the aid of messenger RNA and transfer RNA. Two distinct types of genes are involved. Structural genes provide the actual codes for the construction of new proteins, whereas regulatory genes determine which genes are copied.

Twenty-three pairs of chromosomes are contained within the nucleus of each body cell; one member of each pair comes from the mother and the other from the father. Twenty-two of these are matching pairs called autosomes. The 23rd pair, which determines the sex of the child, contains two matching X chromosomes in females and an X and a Y chromosome in males. Since a Y chromosome can be received only from the father, it is the father that determines the sex of the child.

Gametes: Ovum and Sperm

The chromosomes making up the 23rd pair are known as gametes. Gametes mature through a process of cell division termed meiosis, in which the number of chromosomes is reduced to 23 single chromosomes. In comparison, cell division in body cells, termed mitosis, maintains 23 pairs of chromosomes in each of the resulting cells. Females are born with all of the ova they will ever produce, with generally only one of these maturing each month. Males continue to produce sperm throughout their lives, and as many as 200 million may be contained in a single ejaculate.

Genetic Diversity

With the exception of identical twins, each individual is genetically distinct from every other individual. Genetic diversity is achieved in a number of ways. Individuals are distinct from either of their parents since one chromosome of each pair is from one parent and the second from the other. Meiosis further contributes to diversity by shuffling the members of each pair into either one gamete or the other as cell division occurs. Additional diversity occurs through crossing over, a process occurring during cell division in which segments of the chromosomes making up each pair break off and cross over to corresponding positions along the other chromosome.

Twins

Identical, or monozygotic, twins share identical genetic makeups since they result from the same fertilized ovum, or zygote, which then separates into two clusters of cells during initial cell division. Fraternal, or dizygotic, twins originate when two ova are released during ovulation and each is fertilized by a separate sperm.

Fertilization

Fertilization occurs near the top of the Fallopian tube. Once inside the female reproductive tract, sperm undergo a process known as capacitation, which allows the release of enzymes that enable the sperm to fuse with the membrane of the ovum. Only a single sperm can fertilize an ovum due to a dual-action gating mechanism triggered by this fusion. A woman is fertile for approximately 6 days each month, approximately 5 days preceding ovulation and on the day of ovulation itself.

Patterns of Genetic Action

Genes at corresponding positions along the lengths of paired chromosomes carry related information. These gene pairs, or alleles, can contain two types of genes: Members of a pair can be dominant or recessive. When a dominant gene is present, the trait that it determines will be expressed. In order for a trait carried by a recessive gene to occur, both members of the allele pair must be recessive. The observable or measurable characteristics displayed by a person make up that person's phenotype. These traits reflect the action of dominant genes, either paired or singly, or of pairs of recessive genes. Additionally, many recessive genes are carried in a person's genotype, or the set of genes acquired at conception that constitutes each person's genetic makeup.

Genetic and Chromosomal Disorders

Most genetic disorders are caused by a single recessive gene; children must receive the recessive gene from each parent to be affected. Chromosomal disorders can be traced to irregularities affecting the chromosomes during meiosis that result in either extra or insufficient genetic material. Down syndrome is one of the more common chromosomal disorders and results from the 21st pair of chromosomes failing to separate during meiosis. Sex chromosome disorders result from inheriting either a single X chromosome or an additional X or Y chromosome rather than two X chromosomes or an X and a Y for females and males, respectively.

Detecting Birth Defects

A number of tests enable prospective parents to determine whether they might pass a disorder on to their children. Ultrasound imaging is useful in detecting abnormalities in head growth and organ or limb development, but does not reveal some of the genetic and chromosomal disorders that can be detected through other procedures. Both amniocentesis and chorionic villus sampling obtain cells, either from the amniotic fluid or from the placenta, which can be tested to detect genetic and chromosomal disorders, whereas alpha-fetoprotein screening utilizes a blood test to screen for certain specific disorders.

The Contexts of Genetic Action

Depending on the presence of other factors, genes can have different effects; their final expression will depend on the environment in which the genes are present. This environment can be intracellular, involving the presence of other genes, or it can be the surroundings provided by a family or community.

Infertility

Infertility affects approximately 15% of couples within the United States. In 40% of these the problem can be traced to the woman, and in another 40% the problem lies with the man. New techniques such as microsurgery, the use of synthetic hormones, and donor gametes allow the successful treatment of infertility in approximately 70% of affected couples.

Key Terms

acrosomal reaction (p. 56)
acrosome (p. 56)
activators (p. 48)
alleles (p. 58)
autosomes (p. 49)
basal factors (p. 48)
capacitation (p. 56)
chromosomes (p. 49)
coactivators (p. 48)
crossing over (p. 53)
dizygotic twins (p. 54)
DNA (p. 46)
dominant allele (p. 58)
donor insemination (p. 75)
Down syndrome (p. 66)
egg and sperm donation (p. 75)

egg donation (p. 74)
estrogens (p. 50)
factor analysis (p. 76)
gametes (p. 50)
genes (p. 46)
genotype (p. 59)
in vitro fertilization (p. 74)
Klinefelter's syndrome (p. 66)
meiosis (p. 50)
membrane depolarization (57)
messenger RNA (mRNA) (p. 48)
mitosis (p. 50)
monozygotic twins (p. 53)
multiple regression (p. 62)
multiply determined (p. 62)
nucleotides (p. 46)

phenotype (p. 59)
protective factors (p. 62)
recessive allele (p. 58)
regulatory genes (p. 48)
repressors (p. 48)
risk factors (p. 62)
RNA polymerase (p. 48)
sex chromosomes (p. 48)
structural genes (p. 48)
surrogate birth mother (p. 76)
testosterone (p. 52)
transfer RNA (tRNA) (p. 48)
Turner's syndrome (p. 66)
XYY syndrome (p. 66)
zona reaction (p. 57)
zygotes (p. 53)

chapterthree

Prenatal Development

T ime plays on itself fast or slow, depending on the measure of change. Suspended between worlds the fertilized ovum marks the passage of time to its own rhythms. Within its gated perimeter, the two nuclei combine their genetic contents while on its surface the beating tails of remaining sperm cause the giant body beneath to rotate with their movement. Like an expanding universe, the timeless capsule divides, first once, then twice, increasing exponentially in number with each division, drawing the spinning sphere into the pull of time.

Stages of Prenatal Development

The course of development can be charted according to the inner world of the developing organism or the calendar months of the world it has yet to enter. The first alternative chronicles development in terms of gestational age, measured from conception, and divides prenatal development into three stages: the germinal stage, the embryonic stage, and the fetal stage. The second alternative, that of the calendar, divides pregnancy into three trimesters, each approximately 13 weeks long. The germinal and embryonic stages together correspond roughly to the first trimester. The fetal stage, lasting from the 9th week to birth, encompasses the second and third trimesters. Since most women are unaware of the time of conception, the first trimester is measured from the beginning of the last monthly period, adding 2 weeks for a 38-week gestation period (Singer, 1995).

Development in the Germinal Stage (Conception Through the 2nd Week)

The germinal stage begins with fertilization and ends when the organism becomes attached to the uterine wall. Fertilization, you may recall, is the process by which the nuclei of the two gametes fuse, combining their genetic contents as the chromosomes within each of the two nuclei arrange themselves into corresponding pairs. Fertilization initiates a number of processes, not only restoring the number of chromosomes to 23 pairs, but also determining the sex of the child and initiating **cleavage,** or cell division (Sadler, 1990) (Figure 3.1).

Cleavage is a unique form of cell division that differs from mitosis in an important respect. In mitosis, each cell division is preceded by a period of growth in which the cell doubles in size before dividing. Such growth does not precede cleavage. As a consequence, each new generation of cells is smaller than the last. Since only the nuclear contents are replicated, whereas the cytoplasm is not, the size of the cell nucleus changes in respect to that of the rest of the cell, which must do with an ever-diminishing amount of cytoplasm. A change in this ratio, in fact, may trigger the activation of genes that begin the transcription process in which cell differentiation begins to take place (Gilbert, 1994).

The first cell division occurs approximately 24 hours after the two nuclei merge. In this division, as in all later ones, each pair of chromosomes replicates before the cell pulls apart. Each new cell again divides, with subsequent divisions occurring at about 12-hour intervals. The resulting cluster of cells is termed a **morula,** deriving its name from the Latin word for a mulberry, which it resembles slightly in appearance (Singer, 1995). As the morula divides, it moves down the Fallopian tube, propelled by repeated contractions of the tube and by the beating fingers of millions of cilia, tiny hairlike filaments lining the tube, which set up powerful currents within the fluid interior of the oviduct. Approximately a week

cleavage The form of cell division initiated by fertilization; unlike ordinary mitosis, the cells do not double in size before dividing.

morula A solid cluster of cells resulting from the cleavage of a fertilized ovum.

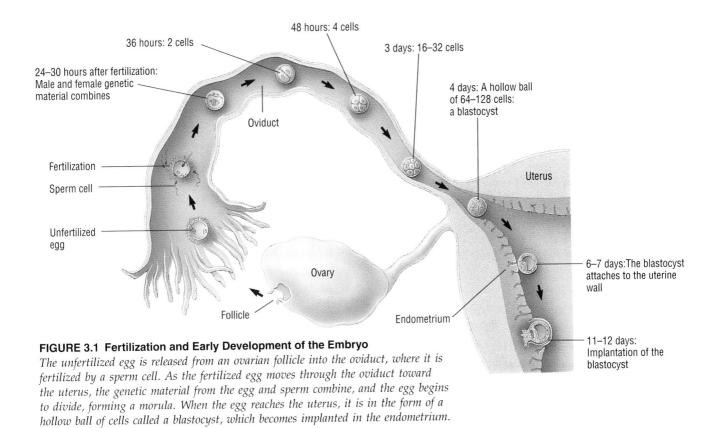

FIGURE 3.1 Fertilization and Early Development of the Embryo
The unfertilized egg is released from an ovarian follicle into the oviduct, where it is fertilized by a sperm cell. As the fertilized egg moves through the oviduct toward the uterus, the genetic material from the egg and sperm combine, and the egg begins to divide, forming a morula. When the egg reaches the uterus, it is in the form of a hollow ball of cells called a blastocyst, which becomes implanted in the endometrium.

after conception, the tiny cluster of cells, now termed a **blastocyst,** reaches the entrance to the uterus.

Just as news of a distant event often spreads by word of mouth before any of the characters themselves arrive, news of fertilization reaches the uterine environment before the tiny organism does. Hormones, the body's chemical messengers, have signaled its imminent arrival. Immediately following ovulation, cells lining the ruptured follicle from which the ovum was released begin secreting *progesterone,* which, in combination with several other hormones, causes the lining of the uterus to become thick and spongy and rich with blood vessels. The journey down the Fallopian tube provides just enough time for the lining of the uterus, the **endometrium,** to become sufficiently thick to be hospitable to the tiny organism. Were it to arrive any sooner, or much later, the organism could not embed itself within the endometrium.

The ruptured follicle, now known as the **corpus luteum,** plays a critical role in the pregnancy for the next several months. The follicle increases in size until it becomes nearly half as large as the ovary itself. Its secretion of progesterone prevents the uterus from shedding the lining in which the organism is embedded. Not until the end of the 4th month does the placenta become capable of producing enough progesterone to maintain the pregnancy (Sadler, 1990).

At first only individual cells are recognizable as the zygote, encased within its transparent membrane, moves down the Fallopian tube to the uterus. Once the zygote sheds its protective covering within the uterine cavity, however, one can discern the emergence of *structure* in the arrangement of its cells: An outer layer

blastocyst A thin-walled hollow sphere resulting from the differentiation of morula cells into the trophoblast and the inner cell mass.

endometrium The inner lining of the uterus.

corpus luteum The ruptured ovarian follicle formed by the release of an ovum; important source of progesterone early in pregnancy.

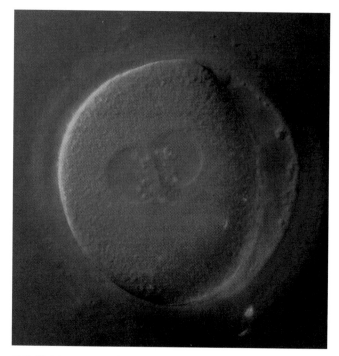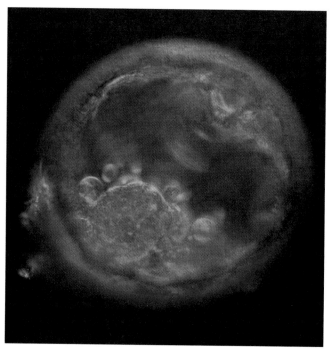

Cell division creates changes in a cell's environment as dramatic as those within the cell itself. Shown are the first cell division at about 24 hours—the morula (left) and a cluster of cells at about 4 days—the blastocyst (right).

surrounds an inner mass. On the one hand, the emergence of distinct structures is what development is all about. On the other hand, this poses an interesting question. Each cell, you may recall, contains all of the genetic instructions necessary to reproduce the entire organism, yet only certain of these instructions will be used as the cell divides; the remaining instructions will not be, resulting in the many different types of cells that eventually make up the human body. Cell differentiation remains one of the most intriguing aspects of development. How do different types of cells emerge if each cell contains the same genetic information as all other cells? How does a cell "know," in other words, whether it is to be a bone cell, a blood cell, or a heart cell?

Cell Differentiation   Very early in development, specialized regions in the embryo organize the way cells will develop. These regions are set up, much like coordinating "headquarters," to direct the differentiation of cells under their command. As different parts of the body develop, activity in these regions switches on or off. For instance, research with chicks has identified a region located in the posterior limb bud, called the zone of polarizing activity, which organizes the development of the limb bud into a jointed leg and foot. This region switches on when the limb is developing and turns off once development of the limb is completed (Tickle, Summerbell, & Wolpert, 1975).

These organizer regions contain something akin to "genetic generals," genes that operate by sending out signals to cells, telling them which part of the body they will become (Johnson, Laufer, Riddle, & Tabin, 1994). These genes, referred to as **hedgehog genes,** operate by directing the manufacture of molecules called **morphogens,** literally "form-givers." Morphogens are proteins that diffuse across the cells, tagging different cells for the functions they will assume, telling them where to go and what they are to become (Smith, 1994).

You might be saying at this point, "Wait a minute, how does the *hedgehog gene* know whether a cell is to be a bone cell, a blood cell, or a heart cell?" Luckily, it

hedgehog genes Genes that direct the manufacture of morphogens.

morphogens Proteins that tag different embryonic cells for different functions.

doesn't have to. Jill Heemskerk and Stephen DiNardo (1994), at Columbia University, found that the particular message that a cell receives is determined by a gradient of dispersion. The signal is encoded, in other words, by the concentration of the protein reaching it. Cells that are closest to the hedgehog gene get more of the protein and so receive one message, whereas those that are further away get less of the protein and receive a different message. As a limb bud develops into a leg and foot, for instance, those cells that receive the heaviest concentration of the morphogen develop as the big toe and those receiving the lightest develop as the little toe (Smith, 1994).

Precisely how the proteins communicate their instructions to the genes within a cell remains unclear. We do know that the cells they reach contain two types of genes: regulatory genes and structural genes (see Chapter 2). The regulatory genes, called "smart genes" by Eric Davidson (1990), an embryologist at California Institute of Technology, control the transcription of DNA, selecting which structural genes are to be copied. Only those structural genes that are copied will direct protein growth in the new cell (see Chapter 2). These smart genes function like computers, arriving at decisions based on information as to what is taking place in other parts of the cell, as well as acting on information from outside the cell (Beardsley, 1991). Not only the genes themselves, but also the larger cellular environment in which they operate, then, determine the unfolding developmental process. The same cell, in other words, would develop in different ways if placed in a different environment.

The environment of the cell, as well as the cell itself, changes with cell division. With the first division, for instance, each new cell becomes part of the other's chemical and structural surround. The metabolism of one cell creates by-products that, passing through its membrane, affect the neighboring cell. Similarly, each cell is bounded on one side by a second cell instead of the medium in which it previously existed. Cell division, in other words, creates changes in a cell's environment as dramatic as those within the cell itself, changes that in turn affect subsequent developments within the cell, supporting the copying of only those genetic instructions that are appropriate to that environment. An infant need not yet be born, in other words, for environmental influences to be present. Environments exist at all levels, whether in the form of neighboring cells or the welcoming arms of a parent. An environment is simply whatever surrounds something else, the medium in which the other exists.

As cells multiply, they surround other cells, forming a cellular environment. Cells in the center of the developing mass of cells encounter a different environment that do those on the perimeter; the former are bounded by other cells within the mass, while the latter come into contact with the cells of the outer membrane.

Implantation As the blastocyst divides and cells differentiate, two distinct groups of cells appear. One group of cells, bunched up together at one end of the sphere (the **inner cell mass**), will develop into the embryo. A second group of cells (the **outer cell mass**) forms a surrounding layer, the **trophoblast,** from which the placenta will develop. The blastocyst has remained encased within the outer shell of the zona pellucida during its journey to the uterus. However, it must shed this shell before implantation can occur within the uterine wall. As the blastocyst enters the uterus, the zona pellucida begins to disintegrate, allowing fluids to seep in and fill the space within, forming an inner cavity. The outer cell mass flattens out, forming an outer wall. Together, the cluster of cells now numbers more than 100.

The blastocyst is now ready for the final, and somewhat perilous, leg of its journey—implantation in the lining of the uterus. The trophoblast sends out tiny

inner cell mass The group of cells in the blastocyst from which the embryo is formed.

outer cell mass The outer layer of cells (the trophoblast) of the blastocyst that will develop into tissues supporting the developing organism.

trophoblast The outer layer of blastocyst cells from which develop the tissues that support the developing organism.

A fertilized ovum at about 11 days burrows completely beneath the surface of the endometrium, thus becoming the blastocyst. Secreting a hormone, the new blastocyst helps to keep the uterine lining "friendly" to the organism.

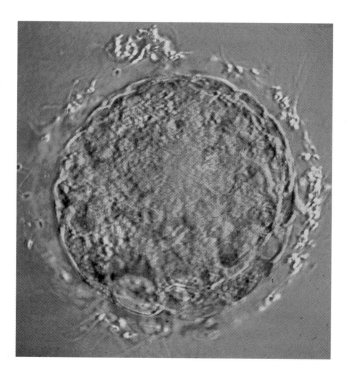

fingerlike filaments that reach within the cells making up the endometrium, breaking a few blood vessels as they do. These villi anchor the blastocyst and supply nutrients for its growth. Viewed under magnification, it looks like a tiny blister with a crimson halo (the broken vessels) on the pale lavender lining of the uterus. Implantation begins by the end of the 1st week. It will take another week for the process to be completed, during which time the blastocyst burrows completely beneath the surface of the endometrium (Sadler, 1990).

Implantation is not without its risks. It is estimated that more than 50% of conceptions spontaneously abort without the mother ever realizing that she has been pregnant (Sadler, 1990). A number of hazards attend the process. One is the possibility that the blastocyst will be rejected by the mother's immune system. Because the blastocyst is genetically distinct from other tissues within the mother's body, it could be treated as a foreign body. A hormone secreted by the blastocyst, human chorionic gonadotrophin (HCG), helps to keep the uterine lining "friendly" to the tiny organism. The uterine lining, in turn, produces substances that promote the activity of the blastocyst. Implantation is thus mutually regulated by an exchange of hormones between the tiny organism and the mother's body (Sadler, 1990; Strong & DeVault, 1999).

The flurry of hormonal messages and directions by which the organism and its host interact prompts changes not only within the uterus, but also throughout the woman's body. These produce, in many women, the first signs of pregnancy: tiredness, tender breasts, a slight queasiness, and sometimes a change in the way things taste and smell. Some of these changes offer important protections for the developing organism. For instance, a glass of wine or a cigarette—for some women a means of relaxing—may occasion feelings of nausea early in pregnancy. Thus, even before they know they should be avoiding substances like alcohol or cigarettes, many women are prompted to change habits that could otherwise endanger the new organism.

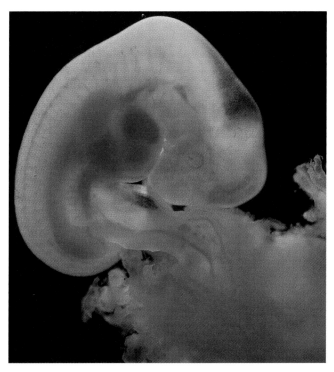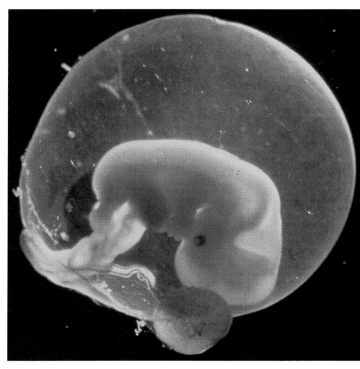

By the 5th week, the embryo has developed a rudimentary brain, spinal cord, and heart (left). At 6 weeks (right), you can also see the development of fingers and eyes.

Development in the Embryonic Stage (3rd Through the 8th Week)

The embryonic stage begins with implantation and ends with the appearance of true bone cells by the end of the 7th week. These signal the end of this stage and the beginning of the fetal stage since they also coincide with the completion of all the body parts. Prior to the appearance of bone cells, the embryo develops a complete skeleton of cartilage, as in the tip of one's nose, rather than of bone.

One of the first events in the embryonic stage is **gastrulation,** the formation of three distinct layers of cells from the inner cell mass; all parts of the body will be formed from these layers. The outer layer **(ectoderm)** will develop into those parts that bring the organism into contact with its environment: the outer layer of skin, the nervous system, and sensory organs. The middle layer **(mesoderm)** gives rise to the muscles and bones forming the skeletal structure, the inner layers of skin, and the circulatory, excretory, and reproductive systems. The innermost layer **(endoderm)** gives rise to the digestive and respiratory tracts and to internal glands and organs.

The outer cell mass, the trophoblast, develops into structures that will nourish and support the growth of the embryo: the amniotic sac, the placenta, the umbilical cord, and the yolk sac. The **amniotic sac** is a transparent, watertight membrane that develops around the embryo. Filled with amniotic fluid, it provides support for the developing organism by permitting the movement of limbs that otherwise would be too heavy to lift and offering protection from sharp edges and jarring.

The **placenta** is a spongy mass of tissue attached to the uterine lining and connected to the embryo by the umbilical cord. It is the embryo's life-support

gastrulation The formation of three layers of embryonic cells: the ectoderm, the mesoderm, and the endoderm.

ectoderm The outer layer of the inner cell mass, which will develop into the outer layer of skin, the nervous system, and the sensory organs.

mesoderm The middle layer of the inner cell mass; it will develop into the muscles, bones, and circulatory, excretory, and reproductive systems.

endoderm The inner layer of the inner cell mass, which will develop into the digestive and respiratory tracts and internal glands and organs.

amniotic sac A transparent, watertight membrane that develops around the embryo and is filled with amniotic fluid.

placenta A spongy mass of tissue attached to the uterine lining and connected to the embryo by the umbilical cord from which the fetus receives oxygen and nutrients and through which waste products are excreted.

system, supplying oxygen-rich blood and nutrients to the embryo and removing waste products from the embryo's blood. The exchange of these materials takes place in tiny villi that reach, like the roots of a tree, deep within the uterine lining where they come into contact with the mother's blood supply. The walls of the villi are semipermeable, allowing some molecules to pass through but not others. Smaller molecules carried in the blood, such as oxygen, carbon dioxide, some proteins and sugars, can pass through the membranes; but larger molecules, such as the blood cells themselves, cannot. The placenta thus keeps the two blood systems separate.

The placenta serves other functions as well. It produces hormones that initiate and orchestrate the transactions taking place between the developing organism and the mother's body. For instance, just prior to birth, the placenta, together with the fetus, produces enormous amounts of estrogens each day, generating as much as normally would be produced by the woman's ovaries over a 3-year period. These hormones prepare the mother's body for birth, causing the cervix to soften prior to labor and readying the breasts for lactation. The placenta will also supply maternal antibodies, which provide immunity against a number of infectious diseases (Coustan, 1995a).

The **umbilical cord,** through which oxygenated blood is carried to the fetus and waste products are removed, is about 2 feet long and carries 300 quarts of liquid a day. Blood travels at 4 miles an hour through the cord. This force gives the cord the properties of a garden hose filled with water, making it rigid and resistant to knotting that might otherwise cut off vital supplies of oxygen and nutrients (Coustan, 1995a).

A **yolk sac,** external to the body, produces blood cells until the organism's liver, spleen, and bone marrow are sufficiently developed to take over this function.

The embryo changes dramatically from day to day. By the end of the 1st month, the embryo is only ½-inch long. Yet a rudimentary brain and spinal cord are visible, and the heart, which is disproportionately large in comparison to the rest of the body, has begun to beat and pump blood. On closer inspection, the embryo also has what looks like a tail as well as ridges on either side of the head that resemble gill slits. The "tail" is actually the end of the spine. It covers the spinal cord, which is oversized at first, anticipating the complex nervous system that will develop, and is temporarily longer than the body. The "gills" are folds of tissue for the chin, cheeks, jaw, and ears.

By the end of the 2nd month, the embryo has more than doubled in size, measuring over an inch in length. Limb buds, which were just visible at the end of the 5th week, have developed into long, thin arms and legs, and movements appear from 7 weeks on (Nijhuis, 1995). Delicate fingers and toes have formed on the tiny hands and feet, and the rims of ears appear on either side of the oversized head. The face is distinctly human, with eyes, ears, nose, lips, and tongue. There are even milk teeth buds within the gums.

Brain growth has progressed at a phenomenal pace, with 100,000 neurons, or brain cells, appearing every minute. Subdivisions of the central nervous system are apparent by the 2nd month, in the form of two zones from which new neurons are created. One zone is associated with the part of the brain that regulates basic bodily functioning and the other with the cortex, which is responsible for intentional, conscious action (Nowakowski, 1987). The cortex itself is divided, left to right, into two cerebral hemispheres, which begin to emerge as early as the 5th week (Sadler, 1990).

The brain sends out signals to the functioning organs, the heart beats, the stomach secretes digestive fluids, the liver produces blood cells, and the kidneys take uric acid from the blood. Sensitivity to touch begins to develop, first in the region of the head, and then, over the next few weeks, over the rest of the body.

umbilical cord The cord connecting the embryo to the placenta through which oxygenated blood and nutrients are carried to the organism, and waste products are removed.

yolk sac A sac outside the body of the embryo that produces blood cells until the embryo's liver, spleen, and bone marrow are sufficiently developed to take over this function.

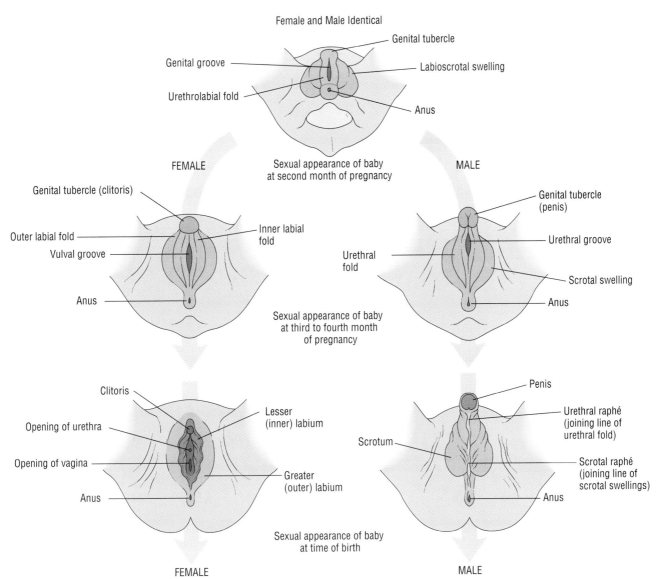

Female and Male Identical

Genital groove — — Genital tubercle
Urethrolabial fold — — Labioscrotal swelling
— Anus

FEMALE — Sexual appearance of baby at second month of pregnancy — MALE

Genital tubercle (clitoris) — Inner labial fold
Outer labial fold —
Vulval groove —
Anus —

Urethral fold —
Genital tubercle (penis)
— Urethral groove
— Scrotal swelling
— Anus

Sexual appearance of baby at third to fourth month of pregnancy

Clitoris —
Opening of urethra —
Opening of vagina —
Anus —
— Lesser (inner) labium
— Greater (outer) labium

Penis —
Scrotum —
— Urethral raphé (joining line of urethral fold)
— Scrotal raphé (joining line of scrotal swellings)
— Anus

Sexual appearance of baby at time of birth

FEMALE — MALE

FIGURE 3.2 Three Stages of External Genital Differentiation in the Human Fetus *Source:* J. Money & A. A. Ehrhardt. (1972). *Man and woman, boy and girl* (p. 44). Baltimore: Johns Hopkins University Press.

Perhaps most surprising of all, the tiny organism can react to things. If the lip is brushed with a hair, a global, reflexive reaction occurs, the head pulling back and turning to the side and arms and legs moving in synchrony (Hooker, 1952; Nilsson & Hamberger, 1990).

Development follows two predictable patterns. The first of these is the **cephalocaudal trend,** growth proceeding from the region of the head downward. This pattern is illustrated in the growth of the arms and legs, in which the arms form several days before the legs, just as do the fingers before the toes. It is the size of the head in relation to the rest of the body, however, that best illustrates this trend. The head makes up nearly half of the entire body length at the end of the embryonic period (at birth, it is one fourth the body's length and, in adults, about one eighth). The second pattern to growth is the **proximodistal trend,** development proceeding from the center of the body outward to the extremities. Illustrating this trend, first the shoulder, then the arm, and last the hand develops. Only then do fingers begin to form. A similar progression occurs with the legs, feet, and toes.

In the 8th week the external genitals begin to differentiate into those of a male or a female. The genitals of either sex develop from the same structures (Figure 3.2), the genital tubercle becoming either a penis or a clitoris, and the labioscrotal swelling

What will develop first, the shoulders or the hands and fingers?

cephalocaudal trend The tendency of physical development to proceed from the region of the head downward.

proximodistal trend The tendency of physical development to proceed from the center of the body outward to the extremities.

By the 15th week, the face of the fetus looks like that of a baby. The whole body is sensitive to touch and most of the movements that can be seen in the third trimester and even after birth, have already emerged.

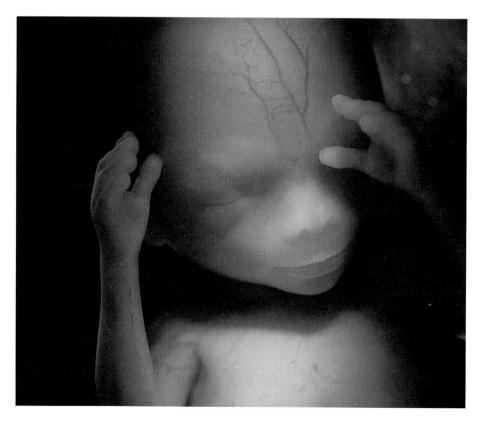

At what point in development might the sex of the baby be detected by ultrasound picture?

either closing to form the scrotal sac in males or remaining open to form the labia in females. By the 12th week, these developments are clearly visible (Lips, 1997).

At the end of the embryonic period, all of the body parts have been formed and are in place. The tiny organism has a complete skeleton, the organs have begun to function, and the embryo can react reflexively to events in its surround if stimulated.

Development in the Fetal Stage (9th Week to Birth)

The fetal stage includes the second and third trimesters and ends with the birth of the baby.

Second Trimester   The physical structures that were largely complete by the end of the embryonic period are refined in the fetal period. The bone cells that appeared by the end of the 7th to the 8th week have begun to replace the carti-lage cells forming the skeleton. In the 3rd month, the eyes move from the sides of the face closer to the nose, eyelids form and close over the eyes, and ears that were low on the sides of the head move up to the level of the eyes. The result is a face that is more distinctly that of a baby. By the end of the 2nd month, the fetus has begun to move on its own, moving its arms and legs, stretching, kicking, suck-ing, and swallowing (Table 3.1). By the middle of the 3rd month (14 weeks), the whole body is sensitive to touch (Hepper, 1992), and most of the movements that can be seen in the third trimester, and even after birth, have already emerged (de Vries, 1992).

Even though all of the body parts were formed in the embryonic stage, fin-ishing touches have yet to be added. The fetus develops eyelashes, eyebrows, baby

TABLE 3.1 First Appearance of Movement Patterns During the First Trimester in 12 Fetuses

Movement Patterns	First Appearance: Range in Weeks Postmenstrual Age
Startle	8.0–9.5
General body movements	8.5–9.5
Stretch	10.0–15.5
Turning of the body	10.0
Hiccups	8.5–10.5
Breathing movements	10.0–11.5
Arm and leg movements	9.0–10.5
Finger movements	12.0
Head movements	
backward	9.5–12.5
turning	9.5–12.5
forward	10.5–14.5
Mouth opens	10.5–12.5
Sucking and swallowing	12.5–14.5
Tongue movements	11.0
Hand-face contact	10.0–12.5
Yawn	11.5–15.5
Eye movements	
slow	16.0
rapid	23.0

Source: Adapted from J. I. P. de Vries. (1992). The first trimester. In J. I. P. de Vries (Ed.), *Fetal behavior: Developmental and perinatal aspects* (pp. 3–16). New York: Oxford University Press.

hair, fingernails, and toenails. The familiar lines forming handprints and footprints appear, forever sealing its individuality. Bodily organs grow in size and begin to function more efficiently. The fetus adds inches and ounces, growing to half its birth size in the 4th month (Figure 3.3).

The brain continues to develop at a rapid pace. By the end of the second trimester, all of the neurons—some 100 billion—have formed. Glial cells, which surround and nourish the neurons, continue to develop throughout pregnancy. Once formed, neurons must migrate to their final destinations, following paths laid down by the glial cells, before undergoing the special developments that make it possible for them to communicate with other nerve cells. The neuron develops an **axon,** a long filament extending out from the cell body, enabling one neuron to reach another, even across great distances (Figure 3.4). **Dendrites,** looking like the branches of a tree, extend from the other end of the cell, making connections with many different neurons possible. Neurons also develop **neurotransmitters,** chemicals by which they communicate with neighboring neurons. Connections between neurons begin to be established as soon as the cells migrate to their proper locations. Bundles of fibers connecting the two hemispheres begin to form in the 10th week (Sadler, 1990). Electrical impulses, which signal the activity of the brain, take the characteristic form of brain-wave patterns by the end of the second trimester (Goldman-Rakic, 1987; Nowakowski, 1987).

With the development of the brain, the activity of the fetus changes and behaviors emerge. By the 7th month, characteristic cycles of sleeping and waking and even positions for sleeping appear. For instance, the fetus typically assumes the same position each time it sleeps. Many fetuses even suck their thumbs

axon A long filament extending from the cell body of a neuron along which neural impulses are conducted, enabling it to communicate with other nerve cells.

dendrites Fibers extending from a neuron that receive input from neighboring neurons.

neurotransmitters Chemicals released into the synapse that mediate the transmission of impulses.

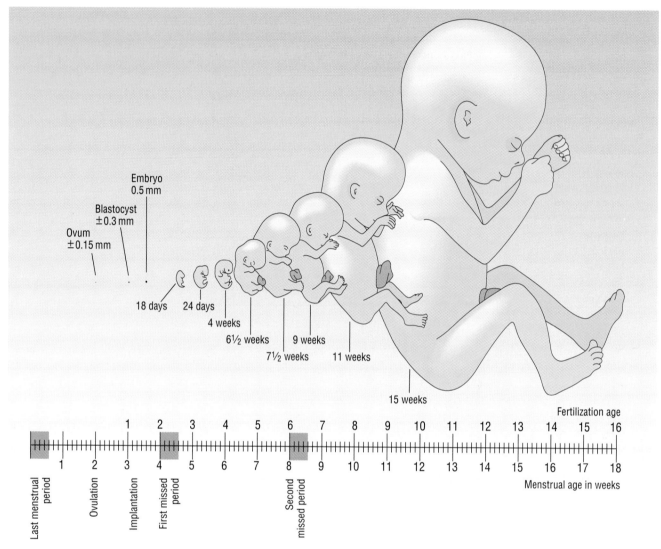

FIGURE 3.3 Growth of the Embryo and Fetus *The actual sizes of the developing embryo and fetus are shown here, from conception through the first 15 weeks.*

quiet sleep A sleep state characterized by relative inactivity except for brief startles; rapid eye movements (REM) are absent in quiet sleep.

active sleep A sleep state characterized by frequent body movement; also known as REM sleep because of the presence of rapid eye movements.

(Hepper, 1992). Patterns of sleeping and waking become more regular with passing weeks, until behavioral states indistinguishable from those of the newborn can be detected just prior to birth. Two of these states describe types of sleep, and two describe waking states.

The fetus spends most of its time, by far, asleep. About 30% of the time it is asleep, it is in a state of **quiet sleep,** not moving its body except for brief startles. Rapid eye movements (REM) also are absent in quiet sleep. The remaining time the fetus is sleeping, nearly 60%, it is in a state of **active sleep,** in which it frequently stretches its body and moves its arms and legs (Groome, Bentz, & Singh, 1995). This state is also known as REM sleep because of the presence of rapid eye movements. REM sleep is intriguing since, metabolically, it is an expensive state to maintain, using much more oxygen and glucose (about 30% more) than quiet sleep, suggesting that it benefits the organism in some way. One possible way would be in cortical development. We know, for instance, that the proportion of time spent in REM sleep declines rapidly with age, dropping from 60%, or approximately 14 hours a day, in the newborn, to 10% in late adulthood, and that sup-

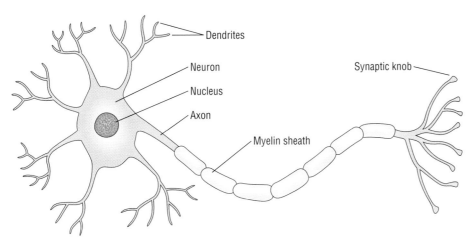

Dendrites

Neuron

Nucleus

Axon

Myelin sheath

Synaptic knob

FIGURE 3.4 Neuron

pression of REM sleep in fetal rats reduces the size of their cortex, as well as affecting their behavior (Mirmiran, 1995).

In the remaining two states, the fetus is awake. When the fetus is **quietly awake,** it moves its eyes about, but is otherwise still, not moving its body as much as in active sleep. When **actively awake,** the fetus frequently and vigorously moves its body, as well as moving its eyes. Characteristic changes in heart rate also accompany changes in each of these states (Nijhuis, 1995). Just how active or quiet a particular fetus is varies considerably (Nijhuis, 1995).

The fetus also develops a biological clock that regulates periods of activity and inactivity. This diurnal, or daily, 24-hour cycle develops several months earlier (at 20 weeks) than the cycle of sleeping and waking, and is independent of the latter. The cycle is interesting in that it is a reversal of the adult's daily cycle, the fetus being most active in the evening and least active in the morning. Unlike the sleep-wake cycles that are regulated by cortical development, the diurnal cycle appears to be regulated by maternal hormones (Arduini, Rizzo, & Romanini, 1995).

The senses have also begun to develop, enabling the fetus to react to its surroundings. The fetus, in fact, is surrounded by a kaleidoscopically changing world of sense impressions. It experiences the gentle jostlings of its mother's movements as well as the ripple of its own, hears the sounds unique to its uterine life and those reaching it from the outside world. Sensitivity to touch, first seen as early as 7 weeks, develops over the entire body by the 14th week. The fetus experiences a variety of tastes, since the sense of taste is well developed before birth. Taste buds appear by the 4th month and the fetus has been shown to have taste "preferences." When the amniotic fluid is sweetened, for instance, through injections of a saccharin solution, the fetus swallows more. Similarly, when an unpleasant-tasting substance is injected, sucking movements decrease (Hepper, 1992).

The sense of smell is also well developed before birth. Although odors can be sensed better when carried in the air, they are nonetheless discernible when dissolved in a liquid such as the liquid environment of the fetus. The amniotic fluid takes on various odors, reflecting the maternal diet. Obstetricians, for instance, have reported being able to smell spices such as curry and cumin in the amniotic fluid when assisting at the birth of infants delivered shortly after their mothers had eaten food strongly flavored with these spices (Schaal, Orgeur, & Rognon, 1995). We know, in addition, that preterm infants as young as 28 weeks react to strong smells, just as do full-term infants 3 months later.

Why do mothers in the second half of pregnancy often report that their baby won't "let" them get any sleep?

quietly awake A waking state characterized by quiet wakefulness.

actively awake A waking state characterized by frequent and vigorous movements.

Vision and hearing also develop relatively early. The fetus reacts to external sounds by 4 months, blinking, moving, and showing changes in its heart rate (Hepper, 1992). In addition, the fetus is surrounded by the sounds and movements of its internal world: the rhythmic beating of the mother's heart, the pulsing of her blood, even the sounds of her voice as she talks. The latter reaches its watery world as a muffled, but nevertheless distinctive, voice (Hepper, 1992). One team of investigators asked prospective mothers to read *The Cat in the Hat* out loud each day during the last 6 weeks of pregnancy. Following the birth, their infants were given an electronic nipple to suck that "switched on" either *The Cat in the Hat* or another, unfamiliar story, depending on the frequency with which they sucked. Infants changed their sucking to hear the story they had heard in the womb (DeCasper & Spence, 1986). Of course, other sounds reach the fetus from the outside world as well, and most prospective mothers will tell you that, just like a newborn, the fetus can be wakened by loud sounds. Also, by about 6½ months, the fetus can respond to light. However, little patterned stimulation is available in the dark uterine interior.

By the 6th month the fetus can open and close its eyes, and buds for the permanent teeth have appeared in the gums above the milk teeth. The amniotic fluid that cushions and protects the fetus maintains it at a constant temperature; this feature of the amniotic environment is important since the fetus has yet to develop the layer of subcutaneous fat that insulates the newborn from temperature changes. The fluid surroundings of the fetus also free it from the force of gravity. Like an astronaut, the fetus floats weightlessly, moving arms and legs and a head that will be too heavy to lift for months after birth. Its skin is covered with a greaselike coating, called **vernix,** and a fine downy hair, **lanugo.** The fetus could not survive on its own if born now, since its lungs, digestive system, and the neural centers regulating its breathing are still immature.

Third Trimester   In the 7th month, the fetus sheds its covering of lanugo and gains weight, 1 pound in the 7th month and another 4 pounds in the next 6 weeks. The once-roomy uterus starts to become a tight fit by the 8th month, and activity is restricted by the cramped quarters. The fetus usually settles into a head-down position by the 9th month. Its quarters are so close that its movements can be seen as ripples on the mother's swollen abdomen, and a good kick can upset something in her lap.

The fetus becomes viable by the 7th month, although it weighs a mere 2–2½ pounds and lacks the layer of fat that holds in heat in full-term infants. Infants born at this age require special postnatal care, needing to be maintained on a respirator while their lungs develop. Before 6½ months, the tiny air pockets in the lungs have not developed sufficiently to permit the absorption of adequate amounts of oxygen or to get rid of carbon monoxide. In adults and children, a layer of fat containing the protein **surfactant** lines these air pockets and keeps them from collapsing when air is breathed out. Surfactant is absent before 6½ months and does not begin to be produced in any quantity until 7½ or 8 months. In addition to respiratory problems, preterm infants also experience digestive problems. Their digestive systems are not sufficiently developed to permit an adequate absorption of nutrients. Also, sucking and swallowing are not coordinated prior to about 34 weeks (Ensher & Clark, 1994). Most premature infants lose weight initially as a result. They are also more susceptible than full-term infants to infection since they have not received the immunities to many diseases that are transmitted as antibodies in the mother's blood during these last important months (Ensher & Clark, 1994).

If a father wants to increase his ability to soothe his newborn and foster a stronger connection to him or her before birth, what might he do?

vernix A protective white, greasy coating that covers the skin of the fetus.

lanugo Fine, downy hair that covers the skin of the fetus.

surfactant A substance that lines the air pockets in the lungs.

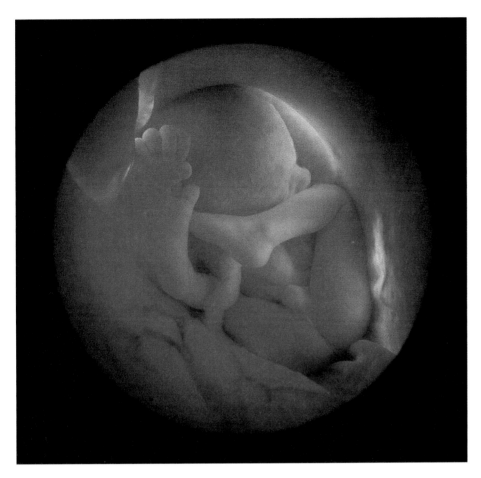

By the 8th month, the uterus starts to become a tight fit for the fetus.

By the end of the 9th month, the fetus has been readied for life outside the uterus as much as possible. The first preparation for birth is the "lightening"; the uterus drops slightly, and the fetus's head (or buttocks if a breech birth) fits snugly into the pelvic area, wedged in place. The fetus stops growing about a week before birth. The placenta is now aging and less able to supply nutrients and manage the by-products of metabolism. The fetus participates actively in the changes in the mother's body that trigger labor, communicating with the maternal system through chemical messages that modify the tone of the uterus and the activities of the placenta (Menticoglou, Manning, Harmon, & Morrison, 1995). A final change in hormone levels will trigger the birth process, ending one of the most intimate of human relationships—and beginning another.

Maternal Changes

One of the most common first signs of pregnancy is missing a monthly period, since the uterine lining is not sloughed off in the form of a menstrual flow if conception has occurred. However, monthly cycles are not a reliable index. Many women have highly variable cycles. Stress, tension, diet, activity, and body weight can all affect the menstrual cycle. Many women experience some nausea, frequently referred to as morning sickness, early in pregnancy. Despite its name, "morning sickness" is no more likely to occur in the morning than at any other time throughout the day. The hormonal changes contributing to nausea can also cause sleepiness and emotional ups and downs. These mood changes can be heightened by how a woman feels toward the pregnancy. Even pregnancies that are planned can be greeted with some ambivalence (Coustan, 1995b).

Numerous physical changes occur throughout the mother's body during pregnancy. One of the most noticeable of these is weight gain, anywhere from 20 to 30 pounds being typical. Most women gain from 2 to 6 pounds during the first trimester, adding another 10 to 12 pounds in each of the remaining trimesters (Coustan, 1995b). Only about 11 pounds is contributed by the infant (7.5 pounds) and its support system, the placenta, the amniotic sac and its fluid (3.5 pounds). The remaining weight is gained by the mother. Increases in fluids and fat are responsible for about 10 pounds of this gain. The remainder is due to the increased weight of the uterus (about 2.5 lbs), the breasts (1 lb), and the increased volume of circulating blood (3.5 lbs) (Coustan, 1995b). Of course, gaining more than 20–30 pounds is not unusual either. Apart from changes due to the pregnancy itself, simply gaining weight can cause women to feel uncomfortable, lethargic, or otherwise different from usual.

What are some of the earliest signs of pregnancy, and how early in pregnancy are they experienced?

Thyroid activity increases after the first 8 weeks of pregnancy, sometimes causing more than the usual amount of sweating. Even though the uterus is still quite small, it presses against the bladder, and so women often need to urinate frequently during the first trimester. The uterus rises in the second trimester, relieving the pressure. The rapidly growing fetus again crowds the bladder in the third trimester.

Other changes are less noticeable to the mother. Her rib cage expands, and muscles and ligaments soften and stretch throughout the body, including the joints between the pelvic bones, making the birth of the baby easier. Metabolism becomes more efficient; blood volume increases, lungs take in more air, and kidneys function more efficiently.

Many women report feeling in peak condition during the second trimester. Their bodies have adjusted to the additional demands made by pregnancy, and the fetus has not yet grown to a size where it is a source of discomfort. By the third trimester, with a larger and more active fetus, the prospective mother may have difficulty sleeping and may also experience backaches and some swelling of hands and ankles. Swelling sometimes signals a condition called toxemia and should always be reported immediately to one's doctor.

In the 9th month, just when it seems that pregnancy has become a permanent condition, the "lightening" occurs. The uterus drops about 2 inches, relieving pressure on the rib cage and making it possible to breathe more comfortably, and the fetus's head slips into the pelvic region. With the fetus again pressing against the bladder, there is a need to urinate more frequently. Toward the end of pregnancy, the prospective mother will experience some contractions. These are short and irregular. Unlike labor, they do not increase in intensity; and after an hour or so they stop.

The Prenatal Environment

The fetus becomes a part of the family long before it is born, contributing to the plans of the parents and sharing in their pastimes. "Having a baby" frequently means changes in work schedules and living arrangements for parents. Also, parents' routines and habits can affect the fetus just as they affect other siblings in the family. Eating habits, such as the mother's diet, are obviously important. So, too, are other habits that may introduce substances into the maternal bloodstream. It was once thought that the placenta acted as a barrier protecting the fetus against harmful substances; however, any substance that can enter the mother's bloodstream, whether vitamins and minerals or nicotine and other drugs, can affect the fetus. Infectious diseases are no exception. Surprisingly, even the *father's* health habits and type of work can affect the health of the fetus.

Health Factors and Health Hazards

Factors that interfere with normal development are called **teratogens.** Teratogens can interfere with development at any point in pregnancy. They can prevent ovulation, damage sperm, diminish chances of fertilization, interfere with implantation, or do direct or indirect damage to the embryo or fetus. Not all of their effects may be apparent at birth as, for instance, those affecting neural development. Some teratogens have sweeping effects, and others produce very specific effects. The effect of a teratogen will vary with its timing, the amount of exposure, and individual differences in susceptibility to it.

The average infant will be exposed to approximately 20 drugs from the moment of conception through the first several days of life. Most pregnant women know better than to take pills indiscriminately, but most women do not know initially when they are pregnant. Furthermore, medicine cabinets are chock-full of things that many Americans fail to think of as drugs—aspirin, laxatives, cold pills, antihistamines, cough medicines, and tablets for upset stomachs, to mention just a few; and many of these can affect the fetus. More potential teratogens can usually be found in the kitchen in the form of megavitamins and alcoholic beverages.

Research on teratogens reveals that their effects are rarely simple. Whether a substance will harm the fetus or leave it unaffected, in other words, depends on more than whether the fetus has been exposed to the teratogen. One of the most important factors contributing to a substance's effect is *when* the fetus is exposed—its timing, in other words. Not all parts of the body are vulnerable at the same time. An organ is most vulnerable during the time of its most rapid growth, when it is being formed (Figure 3.5). Since different parts of the body develop at different times, a substance can affect one organ or body part and leave others unaffected. Also, some teratogens affect specific parts of the body, leaving others untouched. The antibiotic tetracycline, for instance, can create staining in the teeth and affect bone growth, but does not affect other parts of the body, such as the central nervous system or organ development.

The *amount* of a teratogen the fetus is exposed to also determines its effect. Some teratogens have simple cumulative effects: The more the fetus is exposed to the substance, the greater the effect. With cigarettes, for instance, each one that is smoked is associated statistically with a reduction in the birthweight of the fetus by a certain average amount. Other teratogens must reach a critical level before they have an effect, affecting the fetus only once a threshold has been passed. The danger with any potential teratogen, however, is that its effect frequently depends on what other substances are present. Alcohol taken in combination with a barbiturate, for instance, can affect the fetus in ways that cannot be predicted by knowing the effect of either the alcohol or the barbiturate alone.

The manner in which any of the potential disabilities resulting from a teratogen will affect an infant depends to a great extent on the larger developmental context for that infant. An infant born with a disability, for instance, with parents who provide a warm, loving, and stimulating environment, who encourage independence, and who can afford corrective medical intervention will develop in

teratogens Agents that interfere with normal prenatal development.

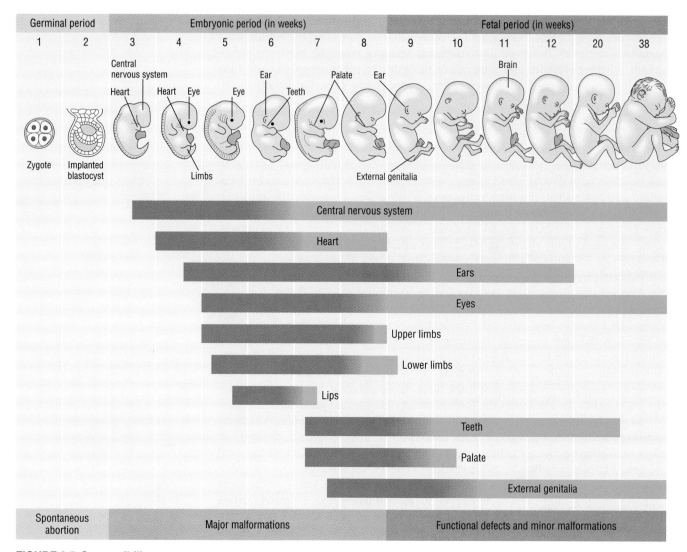

FIGURE 3.5 Susceptibility to Teratogenesis for Organ Systems

Solid bar denotes highly sensitive periods. Source: T. W. Sadler. (1990). *Langman's medical embryo* (6th ed.). Baltimore: Williams & Wilkins.

different ways than will an infant with the same impairments and equally loving parents, but ones who may be fearfully overprotective, limit the child's independence, and fail to take advantage of available interventions.

Maternal Nutrition

Maternal nutrition is one of the most important factors affecting prenatal development. The mother's diet supplies not only the nutrients she needs but all of those needed by the fetus as well. In addition to meeting the specific nutritional needs of the fetus, an adequate diet protects against low birthweight, a general index associated with health complications. Eating a variety of foods, including fresh vegetables and fruits, will supply most of the minerals and vitamins needed. There are, of course, some exceptions. One is the need for iron, which is typically not met by diet alone. Daily supplements of iron, especially for the last two trimesters, are recommended (Lynch, 2000). Calcium, another important mineral, may also need to be supplemented, especially in younger women (under 25). The best sources of calcium, however, remain the dairy products consumed in one's

Why are women encouraged to have regular prenatal visits during their entire pregnancy, even if they "feel" healthy and the pregnancy appears to be going well?

Adequate maternal nutrition protects against low birthweight, a general index associated with health complications.

diet, such as milk, cottage cheese, yogurt, eggs, and cheese. Pregnant women also need somewhat greater amounts of protein.

Additionally, if women of childbearing age—whether they knew themselves to be pregnant or not—simply took a multivitamin containing folic acid each day, the number of children born with a variety of birth defects could be significantly reduced (Shaw, O'Malley, Wasserman, Tolarova, & Lammer, 1995). Additional vitamin and mineral supplements need to be taken with caution. Too much can cause harm as well as too little. For instance, excessive amounts of iron can result in a zinc deficiency, which can cause birth complications. Similarly, megadoses of vitamin A, which are involved in some treatments of severe acne, can produce a variety of birth defects, ranging from cleft lip to heart problems, when such use occurs early in pregnancy (Rosa, Wilk, & Kelsey, 1986).

It is also important to eat enough of the right things. And this, of course, means that the woman is going to gain weight. How much is enough? The weight a woman needs to gain during pregnancy will depend, for the most part, on how much she weighed prior to getting pregnant. A woman who is of normal weight for her height should expect to gain from 25 to 34 pounds, gaining about 1 pound a week in the last two trimesters. Women who were underweight may need to gain as much as 40 pounds, depending on their initial weight and height. Overweight women, conversely, need to gain considerably less, from 15 to 24 pounds (Cogswell, Scanlon, Fein, & Schieve, 1999).

Much of what we know concerning the importance of nutrition comes from the experiences of pregnant women who have been malnourished. One of the most severe "natural experiments" on the effects of malnutrition comes from a famine imposed on certain parts of the Netherlands during the last 7 months of World War II, in which many pregnant women lived on a diet of 400 calories a day (Stein, Susser, Saenger, & Marolla, 1975).

As might be expected, the famine affected not only birthweight, but also infant survival. Infants who experienced the famine during the last trimester, the time of most rapid weight gain, weighed almost a pound less and were more likely to die in the first several months following birth than were those born to well-nourished mothers. However, even infants who were well nourished for the last two trimesters and experienced malnutrition only during the first trimester were less likely to survive infancy. These infants were also more likely to have birth defects affecting the central nervous system, which undergoes rapid development in the first trimester.

Malnutrition need not be this severe to affect the developing fetus. Similar defects, including spina bifida and anencephaly, have been found to occur in infants born in the United States to women with inadequate amounts of folic acid in their diets. Folic acid is a vitamin B compound found in green leafy vegetables and some fruits, such as bananas. Dietary supplements of folic acid taken during pregnancy dramatically reduce the number of infants with birth defects involving the central nervous system (T. K. Estes, 1998; Oakley, 1997; Shaw, O'Malley, Wasserman, Tolarova, & Lammer, 1995). Since most pregnancies are not planned and many women are not aware initially that they are pregnant, daily use of a multivitamin that contains folic acid is important for all women of child-bearing age.

One of the most surprising findings to emerge from the study of the Dutch victims of famine concerns not the children, or even their mothers, but the grandchildren of the mothers who experienced famine during pregnancy. Adult daughters who were malnourished as fetuses in the first or second trimester were more likely to give birth to low-birthweight babies themselves than were their well-nourished counterparts, even though these infants received adequate nutrition throughout their prenatal development. The severe malnourishment of their mothers, when they themselves were fetuses, is likely to have affected the course of oogenesis, or the formation of ova in these females. Immature ova begin to form as early as the 3rd week, migrating to the ovaries by the 5th week, where they begin cell division, replicating their DNA. The maximum number of ova is not reached until the 5th month, in the second trimester (Sadler, 1990). Findings such as these demonstrate the far-ranging effects of developmental experiences and the difficulties, as a result, in anticipating their consequences. They also underscore the importance of social programs, such as supplemental food programs for pregnant women and infants, and free prenatal care, including advice on nutrition.

Such programs can benefit a society for generations to come. Nutrition, like most factors that either safeguard the health or present hazards to the developing fetus, does not work in isolation. The ameliorating effects of supportive programs are evidence of this.

Maternal Stress

It has long been suspected that a mother's emotional state can affect fetal development. A recent study of pregnant women, comparing those who were severely stressed with those who were not, provides support for the adverse effects of maternal stress on fetal development. Women who were severely stressed during pregnancy, because of divorce, a death in the family, or a physical attack, for instance, gave birth to infants with lower birthweights. The infants also had smaller head circumferences, even when corrected for their smaller size, suggesting that severe stress may affect brain growth. Responses to a neurological inventory, given several days after birth, supported the notion that, at least initially, cognitive functioning as well as head size was affected (Lou et al., 1994).

It is always difficult for research such as this to rule out alternative explanations. For instance, women who were stressed drank and smoked more, as might be expected, than did those who were not stressed. However, when these differences were corrected for statistically, the results remained unchanged (Lou et al., 1994). Of course, other differences might still exist. Women under stress might fail to eat and sleep as regularly, or otherwise not take as good care of their health, as do women whose pregnancies were free of stress.

Clearly, though, physical mechanisms exist by which stress can affect the developing fetus. When stressed, the body releases corticoids that stimulate the cardiovascular system and increase available sources of energy, enabling the body to cope better with the stressor. However, by redirecting the body's available resources, these hormones also inhibit cell division. If chronically present, they could well affect fetal growth. Typically, the placenta secretes an enzyme that protects the fetus from excessive levels of such hormones; however, inordinate amounts of these hormones will inhibit the enzyme.

A certain amount of stress is to be expected. After all, pregnancy itself is a major life transition, and transitions bring their own stresses, even when they are positive. Is divorce stressful? Yes; however, so is marriage. Similarly, a promotion is stressful, just as is losing a job, and birth as well as death is stressful. In addition to bringing physical and psychosocial changes, pregnancy involves a number of life adjustments. Work and living arrangements may change. Some women may decide to cut back on their work schedules while others may increase their work hours to pay for the additional expenses of a baby. An apartment that was just the right size for two might soon become too small. Relationships, also, can change in subtle or not-so-subtle ways.

The effects that these or other stresses will have depend on the larger context of the pregnancy. Women who can count on the supporting presence of others find stress more manageable. What constitutes support? Support can be simply having someone to talk to or just relaxing with friends. At other times, it may take the form of someone else's taking over household responsibilities, such as grocery shopping or child care.

Not only pregnancy, but also the anticipation of labor can be a source of stress for some women. In *The Blue Jay's Dance,* Louise Erdrich (1996) writes, "I look down into my smooth, huge lap, feel my baby twist, and I can't figure out how I'll ever stretch wide enough. I fear I've made a ship inside a bottle. I'll have to break. I'm not me. I feel myself becoming less a person than a place, inhabited, a foreign land"(p. 9). ◄

TABLE 3.2 Some Maternal Conditions Associated with Problems in a Fetus or Infant

Condition	Potential Effects
Chlamydia	Eye infections, pneumonia
Cytomegalovirus (CMV)	Small head, mental retardation, blindness
Diabetes (insulin-dependent)	Malformations of the brain, spine, and heart
Gonorrhea	Eye infection leading to blindness if untreated
Hepatitis B	Liver failure, hepatitis infection, jaundice, fever
Herpes	Brain damage, death
HIV infection	Impaired immunity, death
Rubella (German measles)	Malformation of eyes or ears causing deafness or blindness; small head; mental retardation
Syphilis	Fetal death and miscarriage, prematurity, physical deformities
Toxoplasmosis	Small head, mental retardation, blindness, hearing impairments, seizures, learning disorders

Source: P. M. Insel & W. T. Roth. (2000). *Core concepts in health* (8th ed.). Mountain View, CA: Mayfield.

Infections

Infections that initially affect the mother can cross the placenta to infect the fetus which can also be infected during birth itself by coming into contact with organisms in the birth canal. The first type of infection, known as **transplacental infections,** most commonly includes a number of viruses—rubella, cytomegalovirus, HIV, and hepatitis B, as well as syphilis, a bacterial infection, and toxoplasmosis, a parasitic infection. The most common infections transmitted during birth, known as **ascending infections,** are the herpesvirus and gonorrhea, a bacterial infection. Infants can be infected with HIV during delivery as well as during the pregnancy. Breast-feeding can also lead to infection with HIV. Table 3.2 compares these infections and their potential effects.

Rubella (German measles) was once a common cause of birth defects in the United States. Currently, an aggressive national immunization program targeting children under the age of 3 has resulted in over 90% of young children being immunized for measles; this program has virtually eliminated congenital rubella in the United States, with only five cases reported in 1997 (National Center for Health Statistics, 1999).

The importance of immunization programs such as this cannot be overemphasized. Rubella can severely affect the fetus, causing partial deafness (about 87% of infected infants), blindness (about 34%), heart disease (about 46%), and mental retardation (about 40%). The likelihood and severity of damage depend on when the mother contracts the disease and are greatest if she is infected in the first trimester. Women who are not sure whether they possess immunity to rubella can get a blood test and, if they are not already immune, can be immunized before getting pregnant (Ensher & Clark, 1994).

Cytomegalovirus, a member of the herpes family, has become the most common form of fetal viral infection now that rubella has been controlled through immunization. This virus has effects similar to those of rubella and, just as with rubella, the timing of the infection determines the way in which the fetus is likely to be affected, with infections occurring in the first trimester having more serious consequences than those occurring later. At present, no immunization against this virus exists; and, once acquired, the infection remains throughout life (Ensher & Clark, 1994).

transplacental infections Infections of the fetus due to organisms that initially infect the mother and then cross the placenta.

ascending infections Infections transmitted during birth; the most common are the herpesvirus and gonorrhea.

rubella German measles; once a common cause of birth defects in the United States.

cytomegalovirus A member of the herpes family that has become the most common form of fetal viral infection.

The **human immunodeficiency virus (HIV),** attacks the immune system, making the infant vulnerable to infections and eventually leading to death. Approximately 2% of women of childbearing age in the United States are HIV-positive; and, of these, anywhere from 15 to 30% will transmit the virus to the fetus. Translated into numbers, these percentages mean that about 7,000 infants are born each year to HIV-positive women; and, of these, 1,000 to 2,000 are infected with the virus (CDC, 1995c). The incubation period for the disease is shorter in infants than in adults, perhaps because their immune systems are less well developed. Most infected infants are healthy at birth, but show symptoms of severe immunodeficiency by 5 to 10 months. Seventy-five percent die within the first year after AIDS symptoms appear. Since recent advances in drug therapy have made it possible to reduce the risk of transmitting HIV to the infant, pregnant women who are at risk for infection should know their HIV status (CDC, 1995c; Ensher & Clark, 1994).

Hepatitis B is a virus that can cause liver failure and less-severe symptoms of jaundice and fever in infants infected with it, even though it is symptomless in 40% of adult carriers. This virus poses an increasing risk to infants born in the United States due to large numbers of immigrants from countries in which it is prevalent. An infant born to an infected mother has a 50% risk of being infected. Since the incubation period is from 1½ to 6 months, infants born to infected mothers need to be followed closely and treated with protective immunoglobulins (Ensher & Clark, 1994). A vaccine is available, and the percentage of preschool children vaccinated against hepatitis B has increased significantly in recent years (National Center for Health Statistics, 1999).

Toxoplasmosis results from a parasite transmitted by the mother, who usually has no symptoms. The parasite can be acquired by eating undercooked meat or contaminated foods or by inhaling the eggs when emptying out cat litter. The parasite develops in the intestinal tract and is carried in the blood to organs in the body, where it forms cysts. Infection in the first trimester can produce a range of birth defects, from auditory and visual problems to impairments in brain growth and the development of body organs.

Syphilis and **gonorrhea** are sexually transmitted bacterial infections. Syphilis can cause damage to the central nervous system as well as to developing organs and bones. It may go unnoticed at birth, however, if the mother's symptoms are subtle; and infants may receive medical attention for it only when they develop swelling in the joints or difficulty moving their limbs. Syphilis is easily treated with antibiotics. Gonorrhea is more frequently transmitted to the infant during birth. If not treated with antibiotics, the infection can lead to blindness. Almost all newborns are given antibiotic ointment or drops of silver nitrate in the eyes at birth to prevent damage to the eyes.

Herpes is a viral infection that is most frequently transmitted during birth. The most common symptom is lethargy. Many infants also experience respiratory problems. The virus targets the central nervous system and can cause blindness, seizures, and mental retardation. Even mothers who have no symptoms at the time of birth can transmit the disease to the fetus; cesarean delivery reduces the infant's risk of infection. Once acquired, the infection remains throughout life and can be reactivated when resistance is low (Ensher & Clark, 1994).

Legal Drugs

The most commonly used drugs with the potential to harm the fetus are not "street drugs," such as cocaine, heroin, or marijuana, but legal ones—cigarettes and alcohol. The risks to the fetus from smoking and drinking during pregnancy have been

human immunodeficiency virus (HIV) Can be transmitted by an infected mother to her fetus; the risk of transmission can be reduced with drug therapy.

hepatitis B A virus that can cause liver failure, jaundice, and fever in infected infants.

toxoplasmosis A parasitic disease, often transmitted in cat feces, that can cause birth defects if the mother is infected during the first trimester.

syphilis A sexually transmitted bacterial infection that can cause damage to the central nervous system and to developing organs and bones; easily treated with antibiotics.

gonorrhea A sexually transmitted bacterial infection that can be transmitted to an infant during birth and can lead to blindness; damage can be averted with preventive measures at birth.

herpes A viral infection that can be transmitted during birth; can damage the central nervous system.

FIGURE 3.6 Percentage of Low-Birthweight Infants Born to Women As a Function of Number of Cigarettes Smoked *Source:* B. Zuckerman. (1988). Marijuana and cigarette smoking during pregnancy. In I. J. Chasnoff (Ed.), *Drugs, alcohol, pregnancy, and parenting* (pp. 73–89). Hingham, MA: Kluwer Academic.

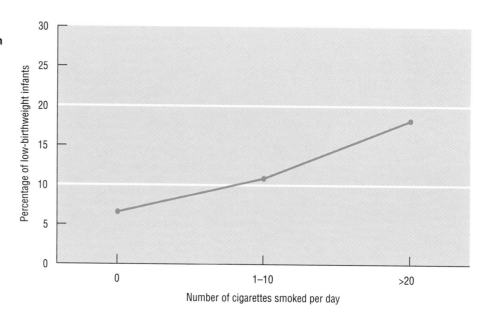

extensively studied. This body of research unequivocally documents the risks to the fetus that attend the use of cigarettes and alcohol during pregnancy and, with cigarettes, the risks associated with their use subsequent to birth (Ensher & Clark, 1994; Klonoff-Cohen et al., 1995; Zhang, Savitz, Schwingl, & Cai, 1992).

Cigarettes Smoking when pregnant poses a significant and serious risk to the fetus. Women who smoke have smaller babies (Dejin-Karlsson, Hanson, Oestergren, Sjoberg, & Marsal, 1998; Horta, Victora, Menezes, Halpern, & Barros, 1997), have more miscarriages and stillbirths (Ness et al., 1999), and give birth to infants with more health complications (Hanna, Faden, & Dufour, 1997). They are also more likely to have an infant die of sudden infant death syndrome during the 1st year of life (Guntheroth, 1995; Mitchell et al., 1997).

The association between smoking and low birthweight is well established (Muscati, Koski, & Gray-Donald, 1996; Nieto, Matorras, Serra, Valenzuela, & Molero, 1994; Olsen, 1992). As can be seen in Figure 3.6, the likelihood of giving birth to a low-birthweight infant increases with the number of cigarettes a woman smokes (Horta et al., 1997; Roquer, Figueras, Botet, & Jimenez, 1995; Zuckerman, 1988). Additionally, the nicotine content of the cigarettes a woman smokes has been found to be related to retarded fetal growth (Olsen, 1992). Not only is maternal smoking associated with reduced birthweight, but so is passive exposure from partners who smoke (Dejin-Karlsson et al., 1998; Horta et al., 1997; Roquer, Figueras, Botet, & Jimenez, 1995). Birthweight can be reduced by approximately 4 ounces for each pack of cigarettes smoked a day by a partner (Rubin, Krasnilikkoff, Leventhal, Weile, & Berget, 1986). Finally, infants born to mothers who smoke may also be somewhat shorter as toddlers (Eskenazi & Bergmann, 1995; Fried & Watkinson, 1990; Leger, Limoni, & Czernichow, 1997).

Several nutrients important to fetal development have been found to differ in smoking and nonsmoking women. Levels of vitamins A, B$_{12}$, and C as well as of zinc and folate and of several amino acids are lower in those who smoke. These nutritional differences are likely to play a role in the greater number of premature births to women who smoke during pregnancy, as well as in fetal growth retardation (Witter & Keith, 1993). Smoking can also affect the ratio of blood gases reaching the fetus, reducing oxygenation by affecting the efficiency of the placenta

Why is it important that a woman stop smoking during pregnancy as well as stay away from secondhand smoke from her mate and others?

in exchanging blood gases. In addition, blood levels of hemoglobin and hematocrit differ between women who do and do not smoke during pregnancy (Witter & Keith, 1993).

Maternal smoking is implicated in a host of health complications in infancy—from lower Apgar scores to congenital heart problems (Malloy, Kleinman, Land, & Schramm, 1988). Some of the most serious findings implicate cigarette smoking in **sudden infant death syndrome (SIDS).** SIDS, commonly known as crib death, is the principal cause of death in infants from the 1st month to the 1st year of life. These deaths are sudden and unexpected, striking infants with no discernible health problems. Smoking during pregnancy increases the risk of SIDS. The increase is dose-dependent, with even half a pack of cigarettes a day significantly affecting the risk (Mitchell et al., 1991). Smoking habits of the fathers, as well as those of the mothers, were associated with greater risk of infant death. Infants whose fathers smoked throughout the pregnancy, even when the mother did not smoke, were 3 times more likely to die from SIDS than were those whose fathers did not smoke.

Paternal smoking has also been found to be associated with slight increases in the risk of birth defects, such as anencephaly, cleft palate, and peculiarities in skin pigmentation. These risks increase with the number of cigarettes smoked by fathers. It cannot be said with any certainty at this point whether smoking has an effect on sperm or whether it exerts its effect in other ways, such as by changing the uterine environment through passive maternal smoking (Zhang et al., 1992).

According to the National Center for Health Statistics (1999), one quarter of women who are of childbearing age smoke. Although many women attempt to quit during pregnancy, doing so is difficult, since cigarette smoking is highly addictive (CDC, 1995b). A national household survey on drug use, for instance, found that cigarette smokers were more likely than those using alcohol, marijuana, or cocaine to say they had tried to cut back, but were twice as likely to have failed. In fact, only 2.5% of cigarette smokers each year are successful in kicking the habit, even though most smokers say they want to quit (CDC, 1995b). Cigarette smokers who decide to quit during pregnancy, even if they have smoked for part of the pregnancy, immediately reduce the risk of health complications to their infants (Ahlsten, Cnattinguis, & Lindmark, 1993).

Alcohol Alcohol is a powerful teratogen that can affect many aspects of fetal development. The particular damage that is done will depend on when the fetus is exposed to alcohol and how much it is exposed to. Women who are heavy drinkers during pregnancy are more likely to give birth to infants with a pattern of deficits that include mental retardation, low birthweight, heart defects, and atypical facial features. However, even women who do not consider themselves to be drinkers, but who may have a number of drinks over a short period of time expose the fetus to increased risk because of the threshold-dependent effects of alcohol (Rosenthal, 1990).

It is difficult to predict how much alcohol is dangerous since the level of alcohol in the blood must reach a certain level, or threshold, before it becomes dangerous to the fetus. This threshold varies from individual to individual and differs as well for different organs within the body. The use of alcohol carries a special risk for brain development, since the brain develops throughout pregnancy and since the threshold for damage to the brain may be lower than that for other organs. Because of the difficulty in predicting when this threshold is reached for any individual, the safest course to follow during pregnancy is abstinence.

Secondhand smoke from fathers has been associated with birth defects.

sudden infant death syndrome (SIDS) Also called crib death, the principal cause of death in infants from the 1st month to the 1st year of life; smoking during pregnancy increases the risk.

Fetal alcohol syndrome is a pattern of disabilities affecting children whose mothers drank during pregnancy.

The risk to the fetus is significantly increased among women who drink heavily. The pattern of deficits mentioned earlier, known as **fetal alcohol syndrome (FAS),** affects all aspects of development. FAS children have smaller heads, retarded physical growth, and characteristic facial features, such as flat, upturned noses and widely spaced eyes with droopy lids. In addition, mental retardation is typical, as are problems with attention and judgment. FAS children also are likely to have poor social skills and behavior problems (Miller et al., 1995).

In *The Broken Cord* (1989), Michael Dorris describes the moment he realized his teenage son Adam, adopted as a toddler, suffered from this syndrome. Until this moment, he had assumed that his son's problems reflected the quirks of his own personality rather than a profile of damage wrought by alcohol. As he stands talking to the director of Project Phoenix, a Native American treatment center for teenagers, several boys suffering from FAS enter the room:

> There was a noise behind us, and I moved to make room for three young boys, "clients" the director called them, to enter. Ignoring our presence, they turned on the TV, dropped onto chairs and couches, and stared straight ahead.
>
> I stared too. They could have been Adam's twin brothers. They resembled him in every facial feature, in every gesture, in body type. They came from a living situation as different as possible from an eighteenth-century farmhouse in rural New Hampshire; they were bare survivors of family cri-

fetal alcohol syndrome (FAS) A pattern of disabilities, including mental retardation, low birthweight, heart defects, and atypical facial features, resulting from consumption of alcohol during pregnancy.

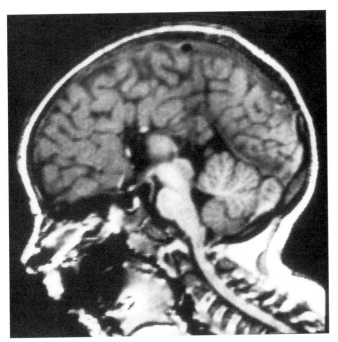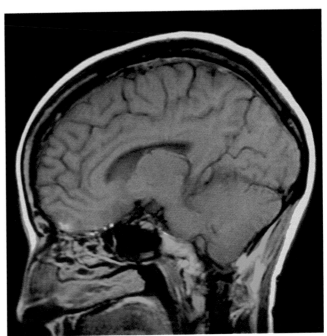

Brain of child with FAS (left) compared with the brain of a normal child (right).

sis, of violence, of abuse—otherwise they wouldn't be at Project Phoenix—and Adam, after the dislocations of his first three years, had been protected, defined as "special," monitored in his every phase of development. Yet there was something so uncannily familiar to me about these boys, about their facial expressions and posture, their choice of television program, their screening out of all but a few elements in the environment that surrounded them. The correspondences seemed too great for mere coinci-dence; they were not superficial either. The fact that these boys and Adam shared the same ethnic group was far less central to their similarities than was the unmistakable set of fine tunings that transformed disparate individuals into the same general category. Some common denominator was obvious—clear as it would have been if in a gathering of people only a few had blue skin, were seven feet tall, spoke a language no one else understood. (p. 137) ◄

A related pattern, which is less severe than FAS, is that of **fetal alcohol effects (FAE).** These infants are not retarded and do not have the distinguishing facial features characteristic of FAS. However, they share a pattern of disabilities that implicate involvement of the central nervous system, including impulsivity, difficulty in initiating and carrying through with actions, problems with attention and memory, and hyperactivity. Many of these children also experience problems in their relationships with others and have difficulty maintaining friendships. Because of the absence of distinguishing features at birth, most are not diagnosed until childhood (Streissguth, 1994).

Approximately 20% of women drink during pregnancy. Most of these women have at most three, or fewer, drinks a month (National Center for Health Statistics, 1999). Is this a "safe" amount, or is it harmful? How much alcohol is dangerous to the developing infant? What effect will a glass of wine or a toast to one's health have on the developing fetus? As with other teratogens, the effect that

fetal alcohol effects (FAE) A pattern of disabilities related to, but less severe than, fetal alcohol syndrome.

drinking will have on any particular pregnancy cannot be predicted. Even among heavy drinkers, not every fetus chronically exposed to alcohol develops fetal alcohol syndrome (Fried, O'Connell, & Watkinson, 1992). On the other hand, a woman who drinks infrequently but has more than a few drinks at any one time can risk harming the fetus because the threshold for toxicity is more easily reached with "binge" drinking. Something to keep in mind while awaiting a definitive answer is that alcohol distributes evenly throughout all the tissues of the body—which means that the blood level of the mother and the fetus will be the same after a drink. Until data indicate just how much is too much, or whether any amount at all is safe, the most prudent course of action is to refrain from having *any* alcohol during pregnancy. Just as with cigarettes, the use of alcohol carries risks to the infant that can last a lifetime. The Social Policy Focus, "Drinking While Pregnant: Who Should Protect the Unborn?," looks at the question of whether society has a role in protecting embryos and fetuses from the mother's use of alcohol.

Illegal Drugs

Estimates of cocaine use vary widely with age and geographic area, ranging from 3% to nearly 50% of women of childbearing age. Over 15% of women receiving routine prenatal care, in one study, admitted to having used cocaine at least once while pregnant. Across all socioeconomic groups, it is estimated that from 10% to 20% of infants are exposed to cocaine during pregnancy. However, this figure can approach 50% for inner-city populations (Lester, Freier, & LaGasse, 1995, Mayes & Bornstein, 1995).

Cocaine is a central nervous system stimulant that inhibits the uptake of certain neurotransmitters, chemicals that facilitate the passage of impulses from one neuron to that next, thereby producing a state of arousal. It can have both direct and indirect effects on the fetus. Cocaine freely crosses the placenta and can directly affect brain development. It is also a vasoconstrictor, indirectly affecting the fetus by restricting the supply of maternal blood to the fetus. Even more indirectly, frequent cocaine use is associated with a host of health hazards, such as poor nutrition, environmental stress, lack of social supports, and multidrug abuse.

Infants born to mothers who have a history of cocaine use during pregnancy have a greater risk of weighing less at birth and having smaller head sizes. Behaviorally, these infants can be more excitable and irritable or, paradoxically, more lethargic, more difficult to wake or to keep alert (Lester, Freier, & LaGasse, 1995). It is important to note that these infants are not a homogeneous group, and not all infants born to women who have used cocaine during pregnancy have symptoms. At present we know little about the long-term effects of cocaine use, in part because longitudinal studies have only recently begun to follow infants exposed prenatally to cocaine into childhood (Olson, Grant, Martin, & Streissguth, 1995) and in part because of the welter of methodological complexities involved in separating out the effects of cocaine from the host of other risk factors that are frequently present. For instance, not only is exposure to cocaine frequently confounded with the use of other drugs, but also what we know is based on the study of low-income children, where the effects of cocaine are inextricably mixed with those of poverty. (Table 3.3 summarizes the effects of various drugs and environmental contaminants on fetuses and infants.) Comparable studies of middle- and upper-income children do not exist. Finally, most research has focused on potential cognitive and intellectual effects, with the result that we know little about other areas of functioning, such as its social-emotional consequences (Lester, Freier, & LaGasse, 1995).

Drinking While Pregnant: Who Should Protect the Unborn? WITH MICHAEL WAPNER

Michael Dorris (1989), whose oldest adopted son was identified as having fetal alcohol syndrome (FAS), writes of his reaction one day at overhearing a pregnant woman at a nearby table in a restaurant order a martini:

> "Excuse me," I said. "But it's really not safe to drink when you're pregnant. I'm working on a book, and . . . "
>
> "Mind your own business," she snapped back, then turned to her friend and loudly complained about how typical it was for a man to think he knew more than she about her own body. When her drink arrived, she caught my eye and held up the glass in my direction. "Cheers," she said, and took her first sip.

Dorris recounts his feelings at this point:

> There was a part of me that wanted to whip out my wallet, show her Adam's picture, tell her his story. There was a part of me that wanted to make a citizen's arrest or to plead for her baby's brain cells. There was a part of me that wanted to ask her if she intended to fill a formula bottle with gin and vermouth, to feed that to her child when it was born—since there would probably be less harm done at that stage than what she was doing today. But I kept silent, turned away in embarrassment. (p. 199)

No one knew better than this father the developmental implications of consuming alcohol during pregnancy. At the age of 5, his son Adam suffered from seizures, was still not toilet-trained, and hadn't yet learned to count to 5 or name the basic colors. Nor did he seem to connect to his world in the way most children do, imaginatively and inquisitively. Dorris recalls one of the many small behaviors that bespoke the enormity of his son's problems:

> Every morning and late afternoon, as I drove him to and from his school, I talked a steady stream, pointing out interesting sights, asking about his activities, recounting tales of my adventures at work. At its midpoint our route traversed a railroad track. . . .
>
> "Choo choo train!" he sang the first time.
>
> . . . He did the same the next morning and the next evening, and the next and the next. For the two years he attended his day care, he never once failed to chime in, but he rarely said anything else. . . .
>
> It was a small thing, a silly thing to have been upset about. Now that I don't drive that way anymore and that Adam thinks about some other things, those trips can even be fashioned into a funny story of parental overreaction. But at the time, after the first month, there was nothing

humorous about it to me. Adam always crossed those tracks in the same way, as if he had never done so before. . . . He had grasped a single connection in the universe that resonated to him, and it was enough, it was sufficient, it obscured from his view everything behind it. He lacked the quality so celebrated in our species: the desire to see over the top of the next hill. (pp. 43–44)

Adam's mother had been an alcoholic, who drank heavily throughout her pregnancy and who died several years after Adam's birth from acute alcohol poisoning. For many of us, it is all too easy to think of the potential abuse of substances as limited to chemically dependent women living in desperate circumstances. But in an upscale restaurant? With crisp white tablecloths and the sounds of conversation mingled with those of ice clinking softly in water goblets? How many women continue to drink, smoke, or use other dangerous substances during pregnancy? And how many of them are aware of the potential consequences to the fetus of the substances they are using?

Was Michael Dorris's response to this woman out of line? Was her reaction irresponsible and uncaring? More generally, what is the role of society, if any, in protecting the fetus from potential harm? And, conversely, what is the point beyond which society's interest would constitute an intolerable encroachment on personal privacy? *Roe v. Wade* (1973), by legalizing abortion up to a certain point in pregnancy, established that up to that point the embryo or fetus is a part of the mother's body and hence its welfare is the mother's, and not society's, concern. On the other hand, that same Supreme Court decision, by fixing a point beyond which a pregnancy cannot be terminated, also implicated society in protecting the fetus (Cohen, 1995). Does that protection include monitoring the mother's intake of alcohol? If it does, then is the point of transition from personal privacy to public concern the same as for abortion— even though the vulnerability of the unborn begins much earlier? And if the public is given the right to involve itself in a pregnant woman's alcohol intake, what about smoking? What about diet? What about vitamins or regular visits to the doctor? On the other hand, if the conduct of pregnancy is totally the mother's business, then do we imply that society has nothing to say about the willful or ignorant behavior that results in tragedies such as those recounted by Michael Dorris?

Simple answers are not forthcoming. However, a combination of education, social policy, and the funding of supportive structured environments for pregnant women with substance abuse problems is urgently needed.

TABLE 3.3 Some Drugs and Other Substances Associated with Problems in a Fetus or Infant

Drug or Substance	Potential Effects
Accutane (acne medication)	Small head, mental retardation, deformed or absent ears, heart defects, cleft lip and palate
Alcohol	Fetal alcohol syndrome (FAS) or fetal alcohol effect (FAE): unusual facial characteristics, small head, heart defects, mental impairment, defective joints
Antiseizure medications	Small head and possible mental retardation, cleft lip and palate, genital and kidney abnormalities, spina bifida
Cigarette smoking	Miscarriage, stillbirth, low birthweight, increased risk of respiratory problems and sudden infant death (SIDS)
Cocaine	Miscarriage, stillbirth, low birthweight, small head, defects of genital and urinary tract
Lead	Reduced IQ, learning disorder
Lithium	Heart defects
Marijuana	Impaired fetal growth; increase in alcohol-related fetal damage
Mercury	Brain damage
Radiation (high dose)	Small head, growth and mental retardation, multiple birth defects
Streptomycin	Deafness
Tetracycline	Pigmentation of teeth, underdevelopment of enamel
Vitamin A (excess)	Miscarriage; defects of the head, brain, spine, and urinary tract

Source: P. M. Insel & W. T. Roth. (2000). *Core concepts in health* (8th ed.). Mountain View, CA: Mayfield.

Paternal Factors

The father's occupation and lifestyle have come under increasing scrutiny as potential sources of toxicity that might affect fetal development. It can't be said with any certainty whether such exposure brings about genetic changes in the sperm or affects other factors such as the seminal fluid—or whether potentially harmful substances contaminate the home, thereby entering the maternal system and crossing the placenta (Friedler, 1996). Research on the effects of any particular toxin is complicated by numerous difficulties. Even ascertaining exposure is problematic. Some toxins, for instance, can accumulate in parental tissues and not be released until pregnancy, years after the initial exposure occurred (Marcus, Silbergeld, Mattison, & the Research Needs Working Group, 1993). In any case, certain occupations are associated with increased risks to the fetus.

Women whose husbands are agricultural workers or who work in petroleum refineries, rubber manufacturing plants, and operating rooms, for instance, are more likely to spontaneously abort (Olshan & Faustman, 1993). Fathers who are exposed to X-rays and certain chemicals, such as benzene, run a greater risk of having their wives deliver preterm (Savitz, Whelan, & Kleckner, 1989). Also, fathers who work in petroleum and chemical industries and those exposed to paint have a somewhat greater risk of their children having certain types of cancer (Savitz & Chen, 1990; Savitz, Whelan, & Kleckner, 1989). Similarly, male firefighters, who risk exposure to toxic elements in smoke, have a greater risk of birth defects in their children (Olshan, Teschke, & Baird, 1990). Even excessive heat may pose a problem, such as with factory workers who must work close to furnaces. Since researchers have just begun to investigate the potential ways in which men's reproductive capacities can be affected by workplace hazards, we know relatively little about the dangers of different substances. In the absence of clear research findings and because clear guidelines do not exist, industries usually do not alert their male workers to the danger of potential reproductive hazards (Kenen, 1993).

The father's lifestyle can also affect the fetus. There is a modest association, for instance, between paternal smoking and increased risk of stillbirth, preterm deliveries, birth defects, and childhood cancers (as there is for maternal smoking). For instance, Esther John, David Savitz, and Dale Sandler (1991) found that males who were smokers when their infants were conceived had a somewhat greater chance of having their child develop certain childhood cancers than did those who did not smoke, even when the mother was not a smoker. The Research Focus, "Descriptive Statistics: How Harmful *Is* Secondhand Smoke?" considers the effects of passive smoking on birthweight.

The father's use of alcohol prior to conception has also been implicated in fetal development, although not consistently. One study of over 350 fathers found that men who were regular drinkers—that is, who had 1 or more ounces of alcohol a day or one binge (five or more drinks at a time) during the month prior to conception—had infants who weighed 137 g (nearly 5 ounces) less at birth, even when corrections were made for differences in other factors such as paternal smoking and drug use and maternal drinking (Little & Sing, 1987). A larger epidemiological study of over 10,000 births, however, found no relationship between paternal use of alcohol and birthweight (Savitz, Zhang, Schwingl, & John, 1992). These latter researchers point out, however, that most of the fathers in their study drank considerably less than those in the study reporting an effect for alcohol. In other respects, the samples were similar, both being primarily middle-class and healthy. It appears that modest use of alcohol by fathers carries little or no risk to the fetus; however, heavier use may pose a risk. Further research is needed before we can say whether there actually is a risk or just how great that might be.

Older fathers (over 35) are somewhat more likely to have children born with certain types of birth defects, such as cleft palate, heart defects, and hydrocephalus than are younger fathers (Savitz, Schwingl, & Keels, 1991). Most of the previous research has looked only at the effects of the mother's age on birth defects, such as the increase in the frequency of Down syndrome with advanced maternal age (see Chapter 2).

Are there any negative effects to the baby from prenatal paternal behaviors? If so, what are they?

How might factors such as the father's use of alcohol prior to conception or exposure to chemicals on the job affect an infant that has not as yet even been conceived? Gladys Friedler (1988, 1996), a researcher at Boston University School of Medicine who has investigated male-mediated effects of toxicity, suggests that more than one mechanism is likely, given the diverse effects that have been observed and the variety of toxins that are involved. It is possible, for instance, for toxins to directly affect sperm, altering the genetic code. Toxins need not cause genetic mutations to be damaging, however, and can affect other factors, such as the motility of sperm or even the rate at which they mature. Conversely, toxins might leave sperm unaffected, but change the composition of the semen in which they are carried, introducing elements that could then be absorbed into the maternal system and affect the developing organism once conception has occurred.

Just how much risk any particular teratogen poses to the fetus or the infant cannot be said in any absolute sense. The risk varies with the presence of other factors. Infants born to very young and older mothers, for instance, are more vulnerable, as are those whose mothers' health and diet are poor. Potential teratogens such as cigarettes, alcohol, or other drugs are capable of exerting both direct and indirect effects. For each of these substances, clearly established physical pathways exist through which development can be affected. For instance, smoking can

Descriptive Statistics: How Harmful *Is* Secondhand Smoke?

Wally left the others in the living room and stepped out onto the front porch, reaching in his shirt pocket and drawing out a cigarette as he did so. Shivering a bit in the crisp night air, he stared off at the surrounding mountains, listening to the coyotes in the distance. When had it become customary, he wondered, for members of his family to not smoke in the house? Thinking back, he couldn't really remember. At this point, he and all the others automatically headed for the door whenever they wanted a cigarette. At times he felt resentful. After all, just how bad could it be for someone to breathe in a little cigarette smoke? It wasn't like actually smoking a cigarette, was it? What was all the fuss about?

Wally, like so many smokers, didn't know just how much of a problem his cigarette smoke could pose for others. He also didn't realize that for infants problems could start well before birth. But how can one link such problems to secondhand cigarette smoke?

Elizabeth Dejin-Karlsson and her associates (1998) in the Department of Community Medicine at Malmoe University Hospital in Sweden asked the same question. They wanted to know whether women who were exposed to the cigarette smoke of others, sometimes referred to as passive smoking, were more likely to give birth to infants who suffered problems as a result of this exposure. They used birthweight as their measure of well-being, with low birthweight signaling problems.

It turns out that one of the best predictors of well-being in infants is how much they weigh at birth, with infants whose weight is below the range of what is considered to be normal being more likely to experience problems. Infants can be low birthweight for a number of reasons. One group of low-birthweight infants that experiences more than its share of problems consists of those who are small for gestational age, weighing less than would be expected for their gestational age even when born full-term.

Dejin-Karlsson and her associates obtained information from nearly 900 women early in their pregnancies concerning a number of lifestyle variables, including the presence of passive smoking ("Do other people smoke near you at home or at work?"). They also obtained information concerning the weight of their infants at birth. They defined low-birthweight infants as those whose weight fell below the range of what is considered to be normal. But how, precisely, is one to say what constitutes a normal range? Weight in newborns, after all, can differ widely and still be considered normal, ranging anywhere from 5½ pounds to 9½ pounds. Who is to say what is "normal" and what is not?

These investigators used a statistical approach in defining a normal range for birthweight. They knew that weight, just like height or intelligence, is **normally distributed.** That is, given a relatively large sample, such as the one they were studying, if one were to plot the frequency with which each possible birthweight occurred, the resulting distribution would be shaped like a bell (see figure). In addition to their shape, normal distributions are defined by the percentages of cases that fall different distances from the mean. These distances are measured in standardized units that express the average variability among the scores. Just as one can compute the average score for a set of scores, one can also compute the average variability among that set of scores. One such measure of variability is termed the **standard deviation.** In a normal distribution, 66.7% of the cases fall within +1 and −1 standard deviations on either side of the mean, 95% of all the cases fall within +2 and −2 standard deviations, and 99% fall within +3 and −3 standard deviations.

These investigators defined normal birthweight as anything falling within two standard deviations from the mean in either direction. Thus, infants who were small for gestational age were defined as those whose weight was *more* than two standard deviations below the mean. Using this criterion, 6.7% of the infants born to women in this sample were identified as small for gestational age. Of greater importance, however, Dejin-Karlsson and her associates found that passive smoking during early pregnancy was significantly linked to an infant being small for gestational age. In fact, exposure to the cigarette smoke of others *doubled* the chances that a woman would give birth to a small-for-gestational-age infant.

These investigators concluded that the prevalence of small-for-gestational-age infants could be substantially reduced if women were not exposed to others' smoke during pregnancy. This fact, together with the fact that maternal smoking has been identified as a major risk factor for sudden infant death syndrome (Mitchell et al., 1997), should be enough to keep pregnant women a healthy distance from shivering souls such as Wally, as well as to alert them to the very real dangers of smoking cigarettes themselves.

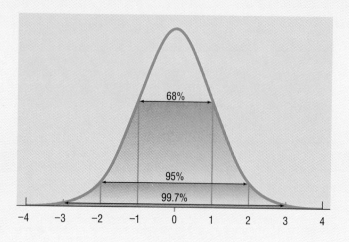

directly affect fetal growth and development by reducing oxygenation in the maternal blood supply. Cigarettes also can indirectly affect development to the extent that smoking affects eating habits; a woman might choose to have a cigarette, for example, instead of a snack, reducing her intake of essential nutrients. Similar examples exist for alcohol and other drugs.

In addition to either the direct or indirect effects of a substance are the broader effects of the physical and social environment into which the child is born. The use of substances such as cigarettes, alcohol, marijuana, and cocaine cuts across all socioeconomic levels. One study found that approximately 15% of pregnant women use alcohol or one or more illegal drugs during pregnancy. The incidence of use differs little between women who go to public clinics (16.3%) or to private physicians (13.1%) or between White women (15.4%) and Black women (14.1%). Despite these similarities in use across socioeconomic and racial lines, however, low-income women are more likely to be studied than middle- or upper-income women, and Black women are 10 times more likely to be studied than are White women (Chasnoff, Landress, & Barrett, 1990). Most of our information about the effects of various substances, in other words, comes from studying children in low-income homes. We do not know whether the same findings would be seen in children raised in middle- or upper-income families. Does this larger developmental context mediate the effects of drug exposure? Factors such as the quality of prenatal care, the number of books in the home, and the caliber of schooling, to mention just a few, have been found to have a developmental impact; and each of these also vary with income level (Ensher & Clark, 1994).

Our understanding of the effects of most teratogens has been guided by an "insult" model. Such models outline the ways in which a substance can alter normal development. However, little is known of how the body or brain compensates for exposure to a substance. Such "recovery" models incorporate protective as well as risk factors in predicting outcomes of exposure, such as differences in the supportiveness of the environment into which exposed infants are born (Lester, Freier, & LaGasse, 1995). In fact, research on newborns with medical complications has found that the quality of the home into which infants are born, rather than their initial condition at birth, is the best predictor of their eventual outcome (Werner, 1994). Margaret Bendersky and her colleagues (1995), examining a variety of predictors of eventual outcome, similarly find that, even with brain insults such as those arising from intraventricular hemorrhage (IVH), environmental factors account for significantly more of the outcome. Both children's language development and their understanding of number, although not their motor development, were affected more by environmental conditions than medical ones (Figure 3.7).

Birth

In the weeks preceding labor, the cervix, the muscular opening to the uterus, begins to soften and dilate, so that with the first gentle contractions, the mucous plug that has sealed off the entrance to the uterus, protecting the fetus from infection, becomes dislodged and is expelled (called the "showing"). Labor involves the work of the uterus, which must accomplish two things. The contractions of the uterus cause the cervix to dilate, or open, enough for the infant to pass through, and they expel the infant. By far the longest part of labor is taken up with dilation of the cervix, in the first stage of labor. The second stage, expulsion of the infant, moves the infant through the birth canal and is much shorter, usually lasting under an hour. In the third stage, the placenta is expelled, taking only a matter of minutes (Figure 3.8).

normally distributed Frequency distributions in which most scores cluster around the middle, or the mean, in the shape of a bell curve.

standard deviation A standardized unit that expresses the average variability among scores.

FIGURE 3.7 Three-Year Outcome Measures *Environmental factors account for more of the outcome in language development and understanding of number than do intraventricular hemorrhage or medical condition at birth. Source: Adapted from M. Bendersky, S. M. Alessandri, M. W. Sullivan, & M. Lewis (1995). Measuring the effects of prenatal cocaine exposure. In M. Lewis & M. Bendersky (Eds.), Mothers, babies, and cocaine: The role of toxins in development (pp. 163–178). Hillsdale, NJ: Erlbaum.*

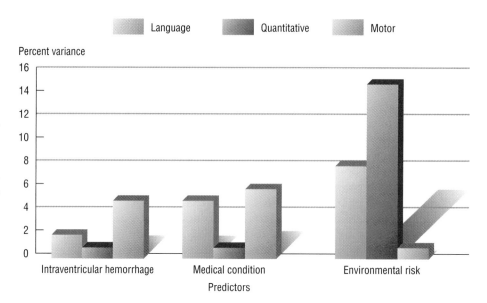

The uterus contracts at the top, where it bunches up and thickens, pulling itself thin at the bottom. With each contraction, the muscle shortens ever so slightly, gradually pulling the cervix open. Contractions are mild at first, increasing in intensity only as labor progresses. The pain of labor comes when the infant's head is forced against the cervix and pelvis. Tightening and tensing the muscles, an involuntary response to pain, works against the uterus. Courses in prepared childbirth teach ways of relaxing during contractions to minimize the pain and speed the course of labor.

The first stage begins with the onset of regular contractions and ends when the cervix has dilated enough to allow passage of the infant's head, approximately 4 inches (10 cm). Contractions initially are brief and spaced far apart, occurring every 15 to 20 minutes. This stage of labor usually takes from 8 to 12 hours for first births and from 6 to 8 hours for subsequent births, although the duration of labor varies considerably. Some of this time will be spent at home. Depending on the hours of the day or night, it is possible to catnap, talk with friends, sit in the sun, count the stars, watch the snow fall, practice one's breathing, repack the bag for the hospital, or wonder about the infant soon to arrive.

The course of labor, once the mother arrives at the hospital, is carefully monitored. Monitoring can be done at regular intervals by a nurse or physician who checks the fetal heartbeat and the dilation of the cervix, or an instrument can be used to continuously monitor the fetus's heart rate and the frequency of contractions. Ultrasound can also be used to determine the position of the infant, so that decisions can be made as to whether to intervene when the infant is in a breech, or feet first, position. For high-risk mothers, the availability of technological support, such as monitoring and surgical intervention, saves lives. However, the use of sensitive monitors may cause physicians to intervene too quickly, interrupting a labor that would otherwise progress safely. For instance, roughly 21% of all births in the United States are by cesarean (National Center for Health Statistics, 1999).

Uterine contractions increase in frequency and intensity with time. When the cervix is nearly completely dilated, contractions reach a peak, coming every 2 to 3 minutes and lasting for as long as a minute apiece. This phase of labor, known as **transition,** is the most difficult for the mother. It is also the shortest part of the first stage and usually lasts under an hour. The presence of a "labor coach," such as the father or a close friend, can help the mother to relax and shortens the actual duration of labor.

transition The phase of labor when uterine contractions reach a peak and the cervix is nearly completely dilated.

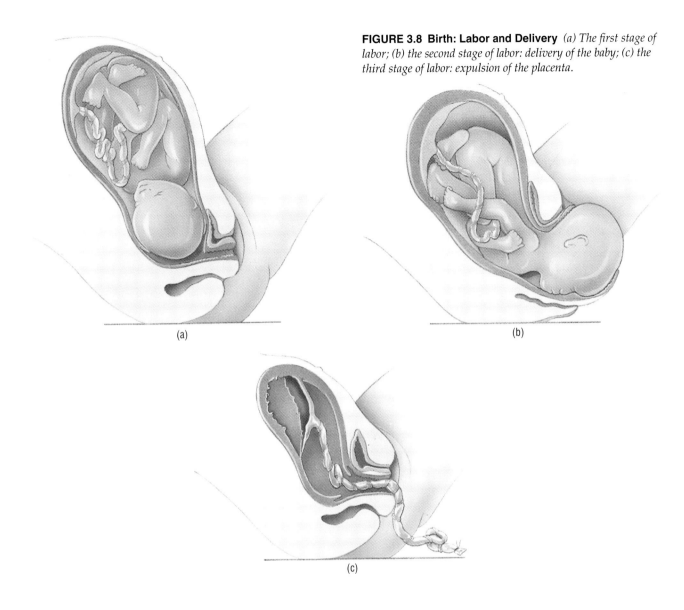

FIGURE 3.8 Birth: Labor and Delivery *(a) The first stage of labor; (b) the second stage of labor: delivery of the baby; (c) the third stage of labor: expulsion of the placenta.*

(a)

(b)

(c)

Louise Erdrich (1996) in *The Blue Jay's Dance*, describes her experience of labor. Though each birth is uniquely personal, her description has a universal quality to it:

> The first part of labor feels, to me anyway, like dance exercises—slow stretches that become only slightly painful as a muscle is pulled to its limit. After each contraction, the feeling subsides. The contractions move in longer waves, one after another, closer and closer together until a sea of physical sensation washes and then crashes over. In the beginning I breathe in concentration, watching Michael's eyes. I feel myself slip beneath the waves as they roar over, cresting just above my head. I duck every time the contraction peaks. As the hours pass and one wave builds on another there are times the undertow grabs me. I struggle, slammed to the bottom, unable to gather the force of nerve for the next. Thrown down, I rely on animal fierceness, swim back, surface, breathe, and try to stay open, willing. Staying *open and willing* is difficult. Very often in labor one must fight the instinct to resist pain and instead embrace it, move toward it, work with what hurts the most.

Lamaze classes teach the mother breathing and relaxation techniques and the father how to be supportive and help her use them.

> The waves come faster. Charlotte asks me to keep breathing *yes, yes.* To say yes instead of shuddering in refusal. Whether I am standing on the earth or not, whether I am moored to the dock, whether I remember who I am, whether I am mentally prepared, whether I am going to float beneath or ride above, the waves pound in. At shorter intervals, crazy now, electric, in storms, they wash. Sometimes I'm gone. I've poured myself into some deeper fissure below the sea only to be dragged forth, hair streaming. (pp. 45–46)◄

Labor is difficult for the infant as well. Contractions reduce the amount of oxygen reaching the infant, by constricting the placenta and the umbilical cord. In response, the infant's adrenal glands secrete stress hormones, adrenaline and noradrenaline, which increase its heart rate and redirect more blood to the brain, the part of the body that is most sensitive to a reduction in oxygen. These same hormones also ready the respiratory system for breathing.

Grantly Dick-Read, an English physician, argued that the pain of labor could be greatly minimized by reducing the mother's fear, which causes her to tense her muscles, making the work of the uterus more difficult and even prolonging labor. Elizabeth Bing and Rosemary Carmel promoted a similar approach, known as the Lamaze method, in the United States. Each of these approaches encourages an attitude of active work, rather than an attitude in which suffering is anticipated. Couples attend classes where they learn about childbirth. The father is encouraged to take an active, supportive role in the birth process, serving as the mother's labor "coach," assisting her throughout labor and delivery.

In childbirth classes, couples learn breathing techniques that help the woman relax during contractions, thereby lessening pain. Even without these techniques, simply having a supportive companion present can cut the number of hours of labor significantly (Kennell, Klaus, McGrath, Robertson, & Hinkley, 1991). The presence of a labor companion also leads to fewer birth complications for mother

TABLE 3.4 APGAR SCORES

Sign	Score		
	0	1	2
Appearance (color)	Blue or pale	Pink body with blue extremities	Completely pink
Pulse (heart rate)	Absent	Slow (<100/min)	>100/min
Reflex irritability	No response	Grimace	Coughing, sneezing, or crying
Muscle tone	Limp	Some flexion	Active movement
Respiration	Absent	Slow, irregular	Good, crying

and infant and less fetal distress. Prepared childbirth makes labor manageable without heavy medication, and parents have an exhilarating sense of participating in one of the most important dramas of their lives.

The second stage of labor begins unmistakably with the urge to push with each contraction. This stage is reached when the cervix has dilated sufficiently for the infant's head to pass through. When the head shows at the vaginal opening, known as "crowning," the surrounding tissue is stretched to its limits, and the obstetrician may make an incision, called an **episiotomy,** which prevents tearing. Frequently a local anesthetic is given for this, although the pressure of the infant's head against the nerve endings provides a natural analgesic to pain. Once the head emerges, birth is completed in a matter of minutes. The umbilical cord is "stripped" of blood toward the infant, giving the baby another 2½ ounces of blood, before it is cut and tied. A jellylike substance inside the cord swells when it meets the air, sealing the cord off naturally.

The third stage of labor is the briefest of all, lasting only a few minutes. In this stage, the placenta separates from the uterine wall and is expelled.

A decrease in the level of oxygen and an increase in carbon dioxide in the infant's blood help to trigger the first breath. The dramatic changes attending birth probably also play a role. The infant is naked, wet, and colder by 20 degrees and, for the first time, experiences the pull of gravity. Sharp noises, loud voices, bright lights, and prodding fingers replace the softly muffled sounds of its velvety dark surround. One or two gasps are usually sufficient to initiate breathing.

Assessing the Newborn

Moments after birth, the physical condition of the infant is checked using the **Apgar scale.** Virginia Apgar, an anesthesiologist who had assisted in countless births, noticed that just a handful of signs were key in predicting the physical condition of newborns. Using these, she devised a simple scale to assess the overall state of the newborn, enabling medical staff to quickly determine whether an infant needed immediate medical care (Table 3.4). The Apgar scale assigns a score from 0 to 2 on each of five measures: (1) appearance, or color, (2) heart rate, (3) reflex irritability, ranging from no response to coughing, sneezing, or crying, (4) muscle tone, and (5) respiration, or effort required in breathing. The Apgar is given twice, once immediately after birth and again 5 minutes later to distinguish infants who may have only momentary trouble adjusting to life outside the uterus from those with more serious problems. Infants with an Apgar of 7 or higher are considered to be in good condition. Those with a score of 4 to 6 will need help in regulating one or more aspects of functioning. Infants with an Apgar of 3 or less receive immediate medical attention.

If a newborn is given an Apgar score of 3, what does that mean?

episiotomy An incision made in the mother's vaginal opening to prevent tearing of the tissue during delivery.

Apgar scale A method of rating the physical state of a newborn in terms of appearance or color, heart rate, reflex irritability, muscle tone, and respiration.

Many new parents are surprised how small their newborn seems.

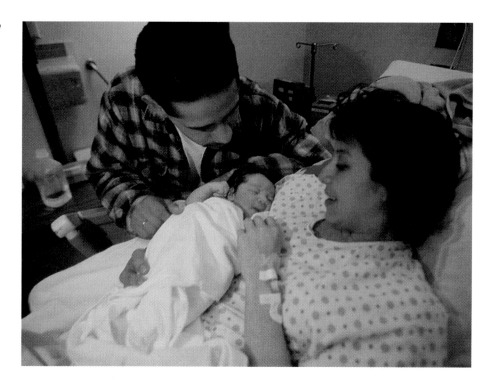

Meeting the Newborn

The newborn's appearance is likely to be a surprise to most first-time parents. Most parents aren't prepared for just how small a newborn is—weighing a little over 7 pounds and measuring 20 inches in length. The infant's bodily proportions are surprising as well. The head is nearly one fourth of the body's length (in adults, it is only one eighth) and may be slightly elongated, molded by its passage through the birth canal. And, as if dressed in clothes a size too large, the skin is too loose for the tiny body, awaiting the layer of fat that will soon fill it out to size.

But most startling are the eyes, eyes that stare at one, taking in a face in one long look. When protected from the bright lights of the delivery room and if not heavily medicated from the birth, the newborn will stare at a face, alert and sensitive to the movements and voices of others. This immediate responsiveness to the presence of others is perhaps the most striking aspect of all.

Low-Birthweight and Preterm Infants

Most newborns weigh a little over 7 pounds (about 3,000 g), and are born after 38 weeks of gestation. Newborns, just like their parents, vary considerably in weight, and differences of over 3 pounds are still within the normal range (Table 3.5). Infants who weigh in under 5½ pounds (2,500 g), however, are considered **low birthweight.** Birthweight is one of the best indices of overall health, and these infants are at greater risk for complications surrounding birth and during infancy. Approximately 6% of infants born in the United States are low birthweight. The incidence of low birthweight is significantly affected by whether the mother seeks prenatal care: The risk is more than 3 times higher for infants who do not receive prenatal care than for those who do. The likelihood that an infant will receive prenatal care, however, depends on the resources available to the family, and infants born into low-income families are significantly more likely to be low birthweight.

low birthweight Newborns who weigh less than 5½ pounds, or 2,500 g.

TABLE 3.5 Approximate Birth Weights at Different Gestational Ages	
Gestational Age (in weeks from date of conception)	Birthweight (average)
20	7 oz
23	1 lb, 2 oz
28	2 lb, 5 oz
32	3 lb, 5 oz
36	5 lb, 8 oz
40	7 lb, 8 oz
42	7 lb, 15 oz

Source: D. B. Singer & P. A. O'Shea. (1995). Fetal and neonatal pathology. In D. R. Coustan, R. V. Haning, Jr., & D. B. Singer (Eds.). *Human reproduction: Growth and development.* New York: Little, Brown.

Low birthweight results from two quite different causes: intrauterine growth retardation and preterm birth. The first type of low-birthweight infant is considered to be **small for gestational age (SGA).** These infants weigh less than do 90% of the infants at the same gestational age. These infants may be either full-term or preterm, but, in either case, they are smaller than other infants their gestational age. Although the causes of SGA are not always known, it frequently is associated with poor maternal nutrition or maternal use of substances such as cigarettes, alcohol, or street drugs. These infants not only weigh less at birth, but also have lower Apgar scores, indicating poor muscle tone, unresponsiveness to events around them, and respiratory problems. Differences frequently persist into infancy; however, the quality of the care and rearing they experience following birth can substantially affect subsequent development (Gorman & Pollitt, 1992).

Just as considerable variability exists in newborns' weights, so too is there considerable variability in the timing of their arrival. Infants who are born within several weeks, in either direction, of the due date are considered full-term. When birth precedes the due date by more than 3 weeks, however, the infant is considered **preterm.** Figure 3.9 shows survival rates at various gestational ages. Just under 10% of all live births in the United States are preterm (Witter & Keith, 1993).

Some premature births can be forestalled. The chances of doing so increase with regular prenatal care. One woman, an investment banker and the mother of a school-age son, recalls the day she discovered that her routine pregnancy, following an earlier miscarriage, had become problematic:

I really took care of myself during the first three months, because from everything I'd read, I figured if you get past that point, you're home free. So I got past the first three months, and then the next three months, and then suddenly I was faced with a new problem.

Again, I had no idea that I had a problem. I was leaving on another business trip, and I figured I could fly now. I went to the obstetrician and asked him to check me out thoroughly before I got on the plane. I just wanted to know everything was O.K. So he examined me, and—I think he was as shocked as I was—all he said was, "Look, you've got to go to the hospital. I'm going to send my nurse with you. . . . You need to have a stitch put in, because you're already starting to dilate. Otherwise, you'll lose the baby."

. . . I just followed the nurse into the cab; I didn't even call my husband. I just went. I ended up on the labor floor at Mt. Sinai. The doctor

small for gestational age (SGA) Low-birthweight infants who weigh less than 90% of the infants of the same gestational age.

preterm Infants born more than 3 weeks before the due date.

FIGURE 3.9 Survival Rates at Various Weeks of Gestational Age *Source:* D. R. Coustan. (1995). Obstetric complications. In D. R. Coustan, R. B. Haning, Jr., & D. B. Singer (Eds.), *Human reproduction: Growth and development.* New York: Little, Brown.

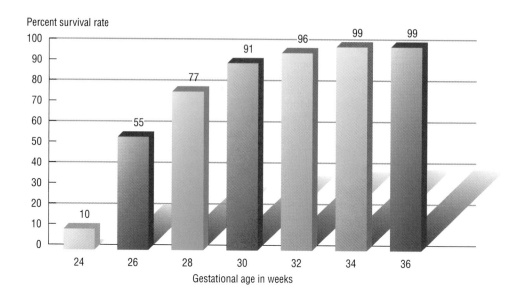

Percent survival rate

came in and explained that he was going to put this stitch in and give me a drug that would stop any contractions, although I didn't feel any. He said I had a condition called "incompetent os"—a weakening of the cervix area—but that if I stayed off my feet and followed all their instructions, they would try to hold everything together for as long as they possibly could. That was the end of the business trip—the end of everything for a while.

It was the twenty-sixth week when this happened. (Sorel, 1984, pp. 61–62)◄

With bed rest and medication, many women are able to maintain their pregnancies long enough to significantly decrease the risks of an early premature birth. This woman, for example, was able to maintain her pregnancy for another 10 weeks. Even with this additional time and despite weighing 6 pounds at birth, her son had difficulty breathing and spent 10 days in a neonatal nursery before being able to go home. The hospital stay for this infant, however, was much briefer than that for very early preterms.

Preterm infants face a number of challenges. Some of the most basic of these involve what others simply take for granted: breathing, eating, digesting our food, and falling into a restful sleep. The newborn intensive care units in which preterm infants are placed following birth are designed to meet their physical and medical needs. Incubators provide oxygen-enriched air and constant temperatures, and tube feeding supplies nourishment—completing a job begun, but not finished, by nature. Even so, many preterm infants must struggle to survive. T. Berry Brazelton, both a developmentalist and a physician, writes of one such infant:

What are some of the challenges faced by preterm infants?

Clarissa D. was born prematurely to a thirty-one-year-old mother who had had several miscarriages. . . . When she went into labor at twenty-seven weeks . . . the two-pound baby was delivered. The infant survived despite many complications. She was in severe distress with Apgar scores of 5 at one minute, 7 at five minutes, requiring oxygen for resuscitation. Respiratory distress ensued and, for seven weeks, Clarissa was given constant artificial respiratory support with a tube in her throat and numerous medications. Jaundice appeared and, on the second day, an exchange transfusion was necessary. . . . She required pulmonary surgery and developed an infection and pneumonia, for which she received antibiotics for fourteen days.

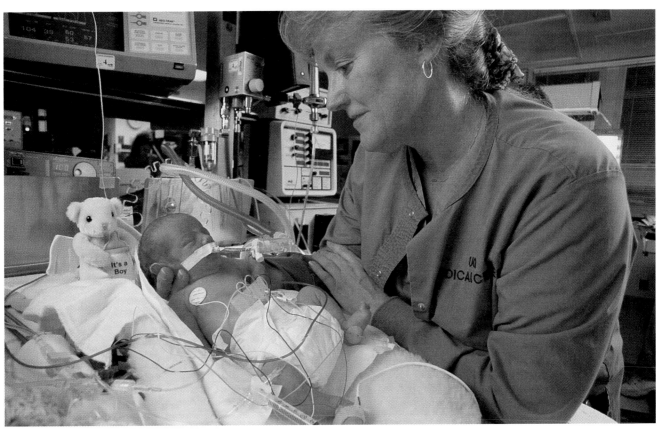

Preterm infants may require intensive care, including oxygen-enriched air and constant temperatures, and tube feeding to provide nourishment.

Despite all of these complications, Clarissa survived and was placed in room air at the age of thirty-five weeks, eight weeks after her birth. . . . She still had respiratory problems and evidence of cerebral hemorrhage, which we suspected might have left her with mild neurological damage.

When the baby was examined at eighteen months, Brazelton reports that

She was still potentially disorganized, but she appeared to know her own capabilities and could defend herself from "falling apart." . . . She played by herself creatively. Her mother talked about how difficult it had been to let Clarissa learn to play alone and to ignore her constant demands. . . . she had found that Clarissa could be independent and resourceful, if her initial whines were ignored. This was hard for Mrs. D., but she had been shown by the physiotherapist that Clarissa could be more outgoing and independent than she had realized. The child's vision had improved markedly with the aid of glasses. She spoke now in three- and four-word phrases, and her receptive language was entirely adequate.

. . . On the Bayley exam, she now performed somewhat above her age, with above-average scores on energy level and coordination of fine and gross motor skills.

Her parents described her as "fun, talking all the time, and rewarding." Indeed, she was delightful, determinedly stubborn, and charming in a social situation. (Brazelton & Cramer, 2000, pp. 16–19) ◄

A preterm birth is never simply a medical problem, however. Because preterm infants are born before critical aspects of brain development are completed, their

FIGURE 3.10 Prenatal Development of Human Brain *Source: Scientific American*, September 1979, p. 116. Illustration by Tom Prentiss. Reprinted with permission from Nelson H. Prentiss.

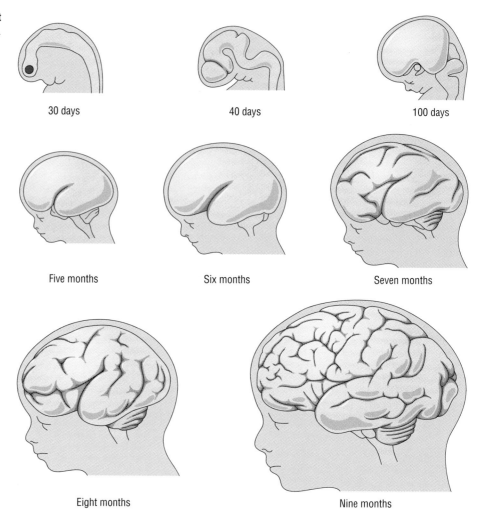

30 days   40 days   100 days

Five months   Six months   Seven months

Eight months   Nine months

experiences outside the womb have the potential for influencing the very course of brain development. Brain growth and development involve a number of inter-related processes (Figure 3.10). Two of these, the production of brain cells and the migration of those cells to the areas in which they will function, are completed by the end of the second trimester. A third aspect of brain development, however, the organization of cortical areas and the growth of neural connections, occurs largely in the third trimester, a time when most preterm infants are born and the period of most rapid brain growth. A fourth aspect, myelinization of neural fibers, also continues through the third trimester until well past birth (Dawson & Fischer, 1994).

Even though the general structure of the cortex has been genetically pro-grammed, the particular configurations it eventually assumes are influenced by experience. Experience, in other words, is not only *picked up* by the nervous sys-tem but also, in the process, *programs* cortical development. The most basic argu-ment for the transactional nature of experience, perhaps, is that there simply are not enough genes in the genotype to program the complexities that characterize the nervous system. The more than 150,000 genes constituting each individual's genotype do not in themselves contain sufficient information to fully determine the complex neural connections that make up even one of the sensory systems. In the visual system alone, there are millions of connections between neurons, making it unlikely that these are established through the matching of proteins under the direction of particular genes (Bower, 1982; Lund & Chang, 1986). Instead, it is more likely that genetic instructions program interactions between categories of neurons (Changeux & Danchin, 1976). Research with organisms that share identical genotypes, the one being cloned from the other, reveals that, despite the same overall structure to their sensory systems, there were substantial differences in the patterns of neural organization (specifically, in the branching of dendrites and their synapses), differences that can be accounted for only by differences in their experiences, since they shared identical genetic makeup. Such research strongly supports the notion that experience contributes to the "hardwiring" of neural circuitry (Changeux & Danchin, 1976).

The brain responds to stimulation in two quite distinct but related ways: The presence of stimulation facilitates the formation of connections between neurons, and the *absence* of stimulation results in selective cell death. William Greenough, James Black, and Christopher Wallace (1987), at the University of Illinois, suggest that ultimately the way the brain responds to external stimulation depends on the patterning of these two quite different mechanisms, each designed to deal with a different type of experience.

Some experiences are idiosyncratic and unique, differing from child to child, such as the sound of a mother's voice or the pattern of a mobile over the crib. The brain responds to these experiences with **experience-dependent mechanisms,** which come into play when the child is exposed to unique experiences. Characteristic of this first type of responsiveness is the ability to establish *new* connections between neurons, thus enabling the child to hold on to the new information (Greenough, Black, & Wallace, 1987).

Other experiences are common to virtually all children. Examples of these would be hearing the sounds of language or being exposed to patterned light. The environment, in other words, will reliably expose all children to these types of stimulation. Greenough, Black, and Wallace argue that the brain responds to this type of stimulation with **experience-expectant mechanisms,** such as those specialized for language use or for pattern detection. Characteristic of such experience-expectant mechanisms is that more connections exist initially between neurons than are required for adequate functioning in any specific environment. An important aspect of this second type of mechanism is the elimination of excess connections based on the child's actual experiences. For instance, there are far more neurons at birth than there are several months later. Only those that are stimulated will form connections with other neurons; those that are not will die out.

The type of stimulation afforded by the intrauterine environment differs from that of the extrauterine environment both in the absence of certain types of stimulation and the presence of others. The most dominant sounds for the fetus are those of the mother's heartbeat and the pulse of her bodily functions. These have a familiarity that divests them of stimulatory properties, such that only when they are absent will they be noticed or "heard." The same is true for cutaneous and visual experiences. The fetus is surrounded by a bath of fluid the same temperature as its body, vastly reducing cutaneous stimulation. Additionally, patterned visual stimulation is absent. The uniformity of these experiences presumably contributes to the development of numerous experience-expectant mechanisms. Exposure to vastly different types of stimulation, such as occurs with life outside the womb for preterm infants, may prematurely activate certain pathways, interfering with the course of cortical organization as this normally would occur (Als, 1995).

experience-dependent mechanisms Neural processes that enable the organism to establish new connections between neurons when exposed to unique experiences.

experience-expectant mechanisms Neural processes, such as those specialized for language use or for pattern detection, that enable the organism to respond to common environmental stimuli.

Ethics: Kangaroo Care for Low-Birthweight Infants

BY MICHAEL WAPNER

At no other time and in no other relationship will the attachment be as intimate as the perinatal bond between mother and child. In the period just before and just after birth the most powerful influences of both biology and culture converge. Mother and child need and are ready for each other. It is against this symbiotic connection that we must understand the wrenching separation necessitated by premature, low-birthweight infants. Intrauterine development is cut short by too-early birth. And then the underdeveloped, vulnerable infants must be further distanced from their mothers by the glass walls of an incubator—sometimes for weeks, sometimes for months—until they are able to regulate their own temperature, show an adequate daily weight gain, reach an acceptable body weight, and be expected to thrive on their own. Touching, nursing, mirroring, bonding—all the normal nurturing communications between mother and child are, for the duration, at best interrupted, at worst lost.

Unless, that is, some safe, effective alternative to the incubator were to be found.

Such an alternative may exist in the form of KMC—"kangaroo mother care." KMC was proposed and has been investigated in one of the largest obstetric facilities in Colombia. In this procedure, the mother is used as the "incubator" and as the main source of food and stimulation. The infant remains bound to its mother's chest around the clock in an upright position. The constant contact with the mother's skin maintains the baby's body temperature; and breast feeding, which can be supplemented with formula if required, is constantly available. This intense closeness is continued as long as required or until the baby's behavior indicates it is no longer comfortable. KMC, if shown to be safe and effective, is obviously a wonderful alternative to incubation—the closeness between mother and infant is preserved (indeed, intensified), and (no trivial consideration) the immense financial cost of special hospital care is avoided.

The crucial question, of course, is whether KMC is as safe and effective as the incubator. A team of Colombian physicians, headed by Dr. Nathalie Charpak, set out to answer just this question. The study they designed compared low-birthweight infants treated traditionally in incubators with comparable infants given KMC. To make the research as experimentally sound as possible, it was desirable to *randomly* assign infants to experimental (KMC) or control (traditional incubator) conditions. (See the Research Focus in Chapter 12, "Coding.") It is at this point that the research encountered *ethical* questions, as almost all research does at one point or another. Ethical considerations demand that participants in research first be informed of the nature of the treatment to which they will be subjected and then given the opportunity to agree or refuse to participate.

Heidelise Als (1995), at Harvard Medical School, argues that the preterm infant experiences sensory overload. The infant is thrown into a world of harsh sounds, bright lights, physical discomfort, and occasional pain. Sounds, once muffled and familiar, clamor intrusively for attention. The liquid darkness explodes into brilliant color, and the warm, muscular cradle of the uterus is replaced by hands attaching electrodes, changing diapers, and pricking feet for blood samples. For the preterm infant, these events can be more than disruptive. They can be lifeshaping, since they occur when the growth of neural connections and the organization of cortical areas is most rapid. The extrauterine environment of the preterm infant represents a poor match for the expected input provided by the intrauterine experiences of the fetus, those that ordinarily shape brain growth and cortical development in the last trimester.

Als compared healthy infants born 26 to 32 weeks (very early preterms), those born 33 to 37 weeks (middle preterms), and those born between 38 and 41 weeks (full-terms) on a measure assessing their ability to modulate their response to stimulation. How much energy, as measured by changes in heart rate and breathing, for example, must infants expend in order to attend to an event? Perhaps not surprisingly, the full-term infants could more easily respond to events with less disruption to their overall functioning. In general, preterm infants had greater difficulty moving from one state to another—for instance, from sleep to alert atten-

This is termed *informed consent*. In this study, informed consent was requested only after patients were randomly assigned to one group or the other, and then it was requested only of parents assigned to the experimental (KMC) condition. The investigators explain this unusual procedure in the following way. Because mothers in the KMC group are able to leave the hospital with the infants much earlier than mothers in the control group, the KMC group is much more appealing. It was very likely that a majority of the parents would have asked to be in the KMC group. (Indeed, the researchers report a situation in Guatemala where research on KMC had to be terminated because overwhelming parental desire to be in the KMC group disrupted the study.) Consultation with the Ethics Committee of the University to which the hospital belonged led the researchers to conclude that since the control group was receiving the usual care provided in these cases there was no ethical problem in not informing them. In support of this conclusion, it should be noted that this study is different from medical studies in which the experimental group is selected for possibly effective treatment from among sufferers of a condition for which no other adequate treatment is available. In such cases, *untreated controls* are without benefit of any treatment except possible *placebo effects*.

In general, the overriding principle governing any research with humans is to protect the *dignity and welfare* of the subjects who participate in the research. Investigators must inform *all* prospective subjects that their participation is *voluntary* and can be discontinued at any point—assuming that the nature of the research is such that sudden or unscheduled withdrawal is not itself harmful, as might be the case in certain drug studies, a situation of which the subjects must, of course, also be informed. Once individuals agree to serve as subjects, investigators assume responsibility for protecting them from *physical or psychological distress*. Avoidance of "psychological distress" to the subjects is particularly important in psychological or behavioral research where physical dangers are fewer than in medical research, but the possibility of emotional discomfort is still present.

After the data have been collected, it is important for the investigator to *debrief* the subjects, informing them about the nature of the study and removing any misconceptions that may have arisen. If the investigators suspect any undesirable consequences, they have the responsibility to correct them. Any information gained about the participants is, of course, confidential. And should the results of the research be made public, then the *anonymity* of the participants must be maintained.

As it turned out, kangaroo mothering care does seem promising. Growth and body weight were essentially the same among both groups of infants. The number and proportion of deaths were lower among the KMC infants, although not significantly so. The occurrence of serious infections was the same in both groups. But while the frequency of mild-to-moderate infections was higher among KMC infants, the total number of infectious episodes was lower among KMC babies. However, the data gathered do not mention what must have been the enormous psychological and emotional benefits which accrued to both mothers and children in the kangaroo care group.

tion—a frequent predictor of distractibility and attentional problems later in infancy.

Findings such as these perhaps are not that surprising. Most parents of a preterm infant have been warned that their infant will experience somewhat more difficulty falling asleep, waking up, or attending to what is going on. Parents are also told that their child will catch up. And these children do. But not in any simple fashion. Als and her co-workers followed the preterm infants and tested them for various aspects of cognitive functioning 8 years later. These children displayed tremendous variability in their performance on the various measures of intellectual functioning, a child placing as high as three standard deviations above the mean on some subtests (in the very superior range of intellectual functioning) and falling more than a standard deviation below the mean on other measures (in the dull normal to borderline range) (see the Research Focus, "Descriptive Statistics" for an explanation of standard deviation). Figure 3.11 illustrates such variability for one child across the various subscales of the Wechsler Intelligence Scale for Children. Thus, these children will have trouble with some things and be very good at others. Als speculates that the sensory experiences of these children, occurring as they did at a time when their brains were still developing, may have reorganized the normal course of cortical development, accounting for "peaks of excellence" alongside "valleys of disability."

FIGURE 3.11 Test Profile of Early-Born, Medically Healthy Preterm Child *Source:* H. Als. (1995). The preterm infant: A model for the study of fetal brain expectation. In J. P. Lecanuet, W. P. Fifer, N. A. Krasnegor, & W. P. Smotherman (Eds.), *Fetal development: A psychobiological per-spective* (pp. 439–471). Hillsdale, NJ: Erlbaum.

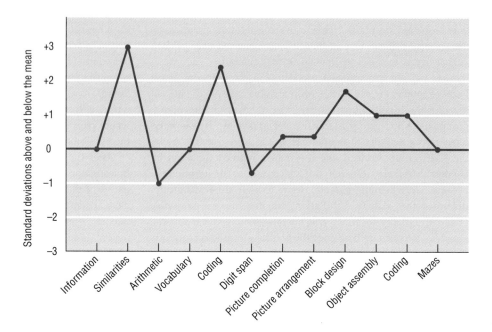

Als (1995) recommends that the experiences of the intensive-care nursery be brought more closely in line with the expected intrauterine experiences for sensory input, with the best index of what is expected being the infant's own behavior. Excessive stimulation, such as loud noises and bright fluorescent lighting is reduced, and nurses are trained to give individualized care, being sensitive to the infant's reactions and guided by the way the infant contributes to its care. Infants assigned at random to individualized care do significantly better than those randomly assigned to traditional care, spending less time on the ventilator, gaining more weight, and leaving the hospital earlier.

Infants also benefit from gentle touch. Tiffany Field and her colleagues investigated the effects of touch by stroking and moving the limbs of preterm infants for 15 minutes, 3 times a day. These investigators have found that infants who are touched gain weight faster than those who are maintained solely in incubators. They also have shorter stays in the hospital before going home (Field et al., 1986; Dawson & Fischer, 1994). A number of studies also have examined the effects of placing preterm infants on waterbeds, since these more closely approximate intrauterine life by moving with the infant's own movements. These infants have been found to have fewer breathing problems than do those on regular mattresses (Dawson & Fischer, 1994).

In many neonatal intensive-care units, preterm infants are benefiting from KMC, "kangaroo mother care," an approach in which the infant is removed from its incubator for several hours each day and placed directly on the mother's or father's chest, skin-to-skin, where it is warmed by the parent's body and soothed by the familiar sounds of a heartbeat. Parents also have a chance to gently touch and stroke the infant. The contact helps regulate the infant's body temperature and breathing. These infants also put on weight faster and show more organized body states, falling asleep better and being more attentive when awake (Dawson & Fischer, 1994). The Research Focus, "Ethics: Kangaroo Mother Care for Low-Birthweight Infants," discusses a study that compared KMC to traditional neonatal intensive care.

What are some of the ways parents and nursing staff can improve the health of and decrease hospital stay time for preterm infants?

Summary

Stages of Prenatal Development

The three stages of prenatal development can be measured from conception, termed gestational age, or from the beginning of the last monthly period. This chapter charts development according to gestational age.

Germinal Stage

The germinal stage begins with fertilization and ends with implantation, approximately 1 week later. Fertilization accomplishes three things: it restores the number of chromosomes to 23 pairs, determines the sex of the child, and initiates cleavage.

Cell Differentiation

Specialized regions in the embryo organize the way cells will develop when they divide. These regions contain hedgehog genes that operate by directing the manufacture of proteins known as morphogens, which tag different cells for the functions they will assume. The tag, or message, is communicated to cells by a gradient of dispersion. Within each cell, regulatory genes control the transcription of DNA, selecting which structural genes will be copied.

Implantation

The cluster of cells, termed a blastocyst, that implants within the lining of the uterus contains two distinct groups of cells, an inner cell mass that will develop into the embryo and an outer cell mass that will develop into the placenta.

Embryonic Stage

The embryonic stage begins with implantation and ends with the appearance of true bone cells, by the 7th or 8th weeks. One of the first events in this stage is gastrulation, in which three distinct layers of cells form from the inner cell mass. Structures that will nourish and support the growth of the embryo—the amniotic sac, the placenta, the umbilical cord, and the yolk sac—develop from the outer cell mass. Two trends characterize development during this and all subsequent stages of development. Development proceeds according to cephalocaudal trend in which growth proceeds from the region of the head downward. A second pattern of growth is the proximodistal trend in which development proceeds from the center of the body outward to the extremities. At the end of the embryonic period, all of the body parts have been formed. The tiny organism has a complete skeleton, the organs have begun to function, and the embryo can react reflexively to events in its surround if stimulated.

Fetal Stage

The physical structures that were largely complete by the end of the embryonic period are refined in the fetal period. By the end of the 2nd month, the fetus has begun to move on its own and by the middle of the 3rd month the whole body is sensitive to touch. Brain growth continues at a rapid pace throughout this stage. With the development of the brain, the activity of the fetus changes and behaviors emerge, such as characteristic cycles of sleeping and waking. The senses have also begun to develop, enabling the fetus to react to its surroundings. The fetus becomes viable by the 7th month, although infants born at this age require special postnatal care.

Maternal Changes

Many women experience some nausea early in pregnancy. The hormonal changes contributing to nausea can also cause sleepiness and emotional lability. Many women report feeling in peak condition during the second trimester. Their bodies have adjusted to the additional demands made by pregnancy, and the fetus has not yet grown to a size where it is a source of discomfort. By the third trimester, because of the increasing size of the fetus, women may again experience some discomfort and have difficulty sleeping.

Health Factors and Health Hazards

Substances that interfere with normal development are called teratogens. The extent to which any particular teratogen will affect a fetus depends on the timing and the amount of exposure. An organ is most vulnerable during the time of its most rapid growth. Since different parts of the body develop at different times, a substance can affect one organ and leave others unaffected. The amount of a teratogen the fetus is exposed to also determines its effect. Some teratogens have cumulative effects; the more the fetus is exposed to the substance, the greater the effect. Other teratogens must reach a critical level before they have an effect.

Maternal Nutrition and Stress

Maternal nutrition is an important factor affecting prenatal development. Eating a variety of foods supplies most of the minerals and vitamins needed; however, some supplements, such as of iron, calcium, and folic acid, are recommended. Supplements need to be taken with caution, as too much can cause as much harm as too little. There is also some evidence that maternal stress can adversely affect fetal development.

Infections

The fetus can be infected by exposure to organisms that initially infect the mother and then cross the placenta to infect the fetus, or it can be infected during birth by coming into contact with organisms in the birth canal.

Cigarettes

Smoking during pregnancy poses a significant and serious risk to the fetus. Women who smoke have smaller babies, more miscarriages and stillbirths; give birth to infants with more health complications; and are more likely to have an infant die of sudden infant death syndrome during the 1st year of life. Secondhand smoke has also been associated with increased risks to the fetus.

Alcohol

Alcohol is a powerful teratogen that can affect many aspects of fetal development. Women who are heavy drinkers during pregnancy are more likely to give birth to infants with a pattern of deficits that includes mental retardation, low birthweight, heart defects, and atypical facial features. However, because alcohol's effects are threshold-dependent, even women who do not consider themselves to be drinkers, but who may have a number of drinks over a short period of time, expose the fetus to increased risk.

Paternal Factors

Occupations in which men are exposed to certain chemicals, X-rays, or excessive heat have been found to affect men's reproductive capacities, and fetal development. Leisure activities, such as smoking and use of alcohol, have also been associated with effects on fetal development.

Birth

The first stage of labor takes from 8 to 12 hours for first births and begins with the onset of regular contractions. The second stage of labor begins when the cervix has dilated sufficiently for the infant's head to pass through; once the head is in the birth canal, the actual birth is completed in a matter of minutes. In the third stage of labor, the placenta separates from the uterine wall and is expelled; this stage is the briefest of all.

Assessing the Newborn

The physical condition of the infant is checked using the Apgar scale, which assesses heart rate, breathing, reflexes, muscle tone, and color.

Low-Birthweight and Preterm Infants

Infants who weight less than 5½ pounds (2,500 g) are considered low birthweight. Low birthweight results from two distinct causes: intrauterine growth retardation and preterm birth. The first type of infant is considered to be small for gestational age. Infants whose birth precedes the due date by more than 3 weeks are considered preterm. Because preterm infants are born before critical aspects of brain development are completed, their experiences following birth have the potential for influencing the course of subsequent brain development. The brain responds to stimulation in two related ways: the presence of stimulation facilitates the formation of connections between neurons, and the absence of stimulation results in selective cell death. The stimulation experienced by preterm infants may contribute to both types of responsiveness in ways that differ from those of full-term infants.

Key Terms

active sleep (p. 92)

actively awake (p. 93)

amniotic sac (p. 87)

Apgar scale (p. 117)

ascending infections (p. 102)

axon (p. 91)

blastocyst (p. 83)

cephalocaudal trend (p. 89)

cleavage (p. 82)

corpus luteum (p. 83)

cytomegalovirus (p. 102)

dendrites (p. 91)

ectoderm (p. 87)

endoderm (p. 87)

endometrium (p. 83)

episiotomy (p. 117)

experience-dependent mechanisms
    (p. 123)

experience-expectant mechanisms
    (p. 123)

fetal alcohol effects (FAE) (p. 107)

fetal alcohol syndrome (FAS) (p. 106)

gastrulation (p. 87)

gonorrhea (p. 103)

hedgehog genes (p. 84)

hepatitis B (p. 103)

herpes (p. 103)

human immunodeficiency syndrome
    (HIV) (p. 103)

inner cell mass (p. 86)

lanugo (p. 94)

low birthweight (p. 118)

mesoderm (p. 87)

morphogens (p. 84)

morula (p. 82)

neurotransmitters (p. 91)

normally distributed (p. 113)

outer cell mass (p. 86)

placenta (p. 88)

preterm (p. 119)

proximodistal trend (p. 89)

quiet sleep (p. 92)

quietly awake (p. 93)

rubella (p. 102)

sudden infant death syndrome
    (SIDS) (p. 105)

small for gestational age (SGA)
    (p. 119)

standard deviation (p. 113)

surfactant (p. 94)

syphilis (p. 103)

teratogens (p. 97)

toxoplasmosis (p. 103)

transition (p. 114)

transplacental infections (p. 102)

trophoblast (p. 86)

umbilical cord (p. 88)

vernix (p. 94)

yolk sac (p. 89)

chapterfour

Infancy and Toddlerhood
Physical Development

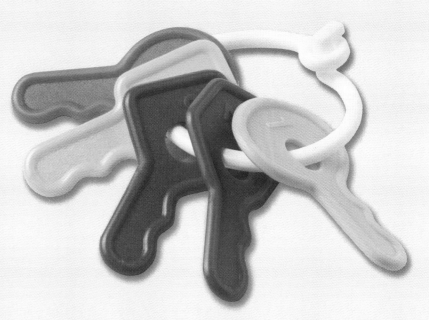

S oon smiles dapple the sunlight, and gurgles soften the edges of silence. The newborn emerges from its warm cocoon and balances on each new moment, unfolding a pattern of expressions and moods to the delight of all. Routines of feeding and sleeping shape the hours of parents and infant alike. Parents report that their infant's personality becomes more recognizable with each new day, few realizing the ways in which theirs are changing as well. Like partners in a dance, the steps taken by one determine the other's next movements. This chapter looks at the rhythms of growth within the first 2 years of life and at the steps, first tentative and then flowing, of the social dance.

The Newborn: The Biological Beat to Life

Birth involves neonates in the basics—breathing, keeping warm, eating, and sleeping. All of these require adjustment to life outside the uterus. Breathing is irregular, control of body temperature uneven, and swallowing unsteady. Infants startle easily and cry and sneeze at the drop of a feather. Instead of sustained behavior, they show fitful activity. Neither sleeping nor waking are well defined (Sahni, Schulze, Stefanski, Myers, & Fifer, 1995). Almost everything requires more effort than it did before or will later. As a result, neonates tire quickly.

Breathing

With the first breath, a valve inside the heart closes. The flow of blood shifts from the umbilical arteries that took it to the placenta for oxidation to the lungs. Breathing is usually irregular for the first 2 or 3 days. It is also noisy. Most neonates cough, sneeze, and wheeze, all of which helps to clear passages of mucus and fluids. Initially, infants are "belly breathers," relying on the muscles of the diaphragm to breath. When they begin to sit upright, however, additional muscles come into play, the rib cage expands, and breathing becomes more efficient (Cech & Martin, 1995).

Body Temperature

Keeping warm is another problem the newborn faces. In the uterus, regulation of body temperature, like everything else, was taken care of by the mother's body. With birth, this changes. The delivery room is 20 degrees colder than the uterine world—an especially noticeable change for the infant, who arrives naked and wet. Even when diapered and dry, neonates lack the protective layer of fat that insulates older infants from rapid changes in temperature. A light covering, even in rooms comfortable to adults, may be necessary until body temperature stabilizes.

Eating

Nourishment is no longer automatically supplied as it was prior to birth, and hunger, as such, is a new experience. Most infants lose approximately 6 to 10 ounces immediately following birth. Fluids previously supplied by the maternal system are no longer taken in, and more are lost through elimination. Once infants start to nurse or take in formula, they begin to put on weight.

States of Arousal

Patterns of sleeping and waking change dramatically in the 1st year of life. In adults, the sleep-wake cycle consists of a period of sleep lasting anywhere from 6

Active sleep accounts for about 50% of a newborn's sleep time.

to 10 hours and a longer period of wakefulness lasting from 14 to 18 hours. This cycle is sometimes referred to as a circadian cycle (from the Latin words *circa*, which means "about," and *dies*, which means "day"). Most infants will establish a stable circadian rhythm between 2 and 4 months of age. Prior to this time, they are on a 4-hour sleep-wake cycle, in which they alternate among a number of states of arousal, ranging from quiet sleep to active wakefulness (see Chapter 3). In **quiet sleep,** the body is relaxed, heart rate and breathing are slow, and brain wave activity is regular; eyelids are closed and the eyes are motionless. In **active sleep,** the infant's arms and legs occasionally twitch, facial expressions appear, and the eyes dart back and forth beneath closed eyelids. This sleep state is often referred to as REM sleep, referring to the **rapid eye movements (REM)** that characterize it. Even though the infant is clearly asleep, heart rate and breathing are irregular and the brain wave activity is similar to that of a waking state (Blumberg & Lucas, 1996). In **drowsiness,** a state in which infants are either waking up or falling asleep, the body is almost as relaxed as in quiet sleep; breathing is regular; and the eyes, though frequently open, have a glassy look to them. **Quiet wakefulness** is one of two waking states, in which the infant is relaxed, moving its body little, but keeping its eyes open and attentive. **Active wakefulness** is punctuated with brief bodily activity; breathing becomes irregular, and facial expressions appear. Crying also occurs in this state (Nijhuis, 1995).

When they are asleep, infants, just like adults, can be seen to move in and out of active, or REM, sleep. In fact, newborns spend about 50% of the time they are asleep in active sleep, in contrast to 20% for adults. This percentage steadily declines until, somewhere between the ages of 3 and 5 years, the adult level is reached. Developmental trends such as this one are intriguing and prompt developmentalists to ask why very young infants spend as much time as they do in REM sleep. In adults, dreaming most frequently occurs in REM sleep; however, it is doubtful that rapid eye movements are a sign of dreaming in very young infants. Instead, active sleep appears to plays a role in the development of the central nervous system. The spontaneous neural activity that occurs in this state may be critical in establishing neural pathways, as well as in determining which

quiet sleep A sleep state characterized by relative inactivity except for brief startles; there are no rapid eye movements (REM); also known as NREM (non-REM) sleep.

active sleep A sleep state characterized by frequent body movements; also known as REM sleep because of the presence of rapid eye movements.

rapid eye movements (REM) Rapid movements of the eyes beneath closed lids during certain sleep stages.

drowsiness A state of either falling asleep or waking up when the body is relaxed, breathing is regular, and the eyes have a dreamy stare.

quiet wakefulness A waking state in which an infant is relaxed and attentive and moves its body little.

active wakefulness A waking state characterized by frequent and vigorous movement.

Box 4.1 *Sudden Infant Death Syndrome (SIDS)*

Every year thousands of infants in the United States with no obvious health problems die in their sleep. Typically, these infants are several months old, have begun to put on weight, are happy, sociable, and well cared for. They die from sudden infant death syndrome (SIDS), the second leading cause of death among infants in the United States. They die because they simply stop breathing during the night.

Despite extensive research, the cause or, more likely, causes of SIDS remain unknown. However, a number of risk factors have been identified. One of the most important of these is the position in which an infant sleeps. A 3-year nationwide study in New Zealand identified the prone sleeping position as the leading risk factor associated with SIDS. Infants who are placed prone—that is, on their stomachs or abdomens—were more than twice as likely to die of SIDS than were infants placed on their backs (Mitchell et al., 1997). A review of other studies reports even higher odds in many of these (Henderson-Smart, Ponsonby, & Murphy, 1998; Oyen et al., 1997). Although not as dangerous as the prone position, the side sleeping position is also associated with a greater risk of SIDS (Fleming et al., 1996; Mitchell et al., 1997). Before research investigating the effects of sleeping position was done, pediatricians had actually recommended the prone and side positions over the supine position (sleeping on one's back), assuming that infants would be less likely to choke if they spit up during the night. This concern, however, has turned out to be unfounded. A large-scale study of over 8,000 infants in Britain found that infants in the supine position were not more likely to regurgitate milk or choke. In fact, sleeping in the prone position was somewhat more likely to lead to choking if infants vomited during sleep (Hunt, Fleming, & Golding, in press).

A second factor that significantly increases the risk of SIDS is parental smoking. Maternal smoking alone contributes substantially to the risk that infants will die while sleeping; and when both parents smoke, this risk is increased even further (Mitchell et al., 1997). Hillary Konoff-Cohen, an epidemiologist at the University of San Diego, found that infants exposed to cigarette smoke, either from mothers who continue to smoke during the months of breast-feeding, from caretakers, or fathers, are from 2 to 3 times more likely to die of SIDS than are those not passively exposed to cigarette smoke. In this research, a group of 200 infants who had died of SIDS was compared with a similar group of healthy infants. Care had been taken to equate the two groups for other factors associated with SIDS, such as sleeping position and whether the baby had been breast-fed

Why might very young infants need to spend so much time in REM sleep?

neurons will continue to exist (many more are initially produced than are needed), eliminating excessive interconnections among neurons and their targets, and in promoting the organization of neural centers (Blumberg & Lucas, 1996).

The most significant change in patterns of sleeping and waking is not so much the *amount* of time infants spend asleep or awake, but *how long* they stay in either state. Year-old infants sleep almost as much as newborns, about 13 hours in comparison to the newborn's 16 hours. However, they sleep longer when they nap, and they can stay awake for longer periods of time in between. For the 1st month, infants are awake for only short periods of time, taking as many as six or seven naps a day. By 2 months, the number of naps decreases to three or four longer ones, and by 7 months to one or two a day. Also, by this time, most infants sleep through the night. Of course, there are wide individual differences in the amount of sleep infants need and in how active they are when awake. Although parents

(Klonoff-Cohen et al., 1995). Infants with the highest risk were those who were routinely in the same room as someone who smoked, the risk of death being as much as 8 times higher than that of infants not passively exposed to cigarette smoke. As in previous research, the risk to the infant was "dose-dependent," increasing with the amount of smoke the infants were exposed to (Klonoff-Cohen et al., 1995).

Based on data collected in a Nordic epidemiological SIDS study, it is estimated that the number of SIDS deaths could have been reduced by nearly half (46.7%) had mothers not smoked during pregnancy (Oyen et al., 1997). The increased risk to the infant from smoking is dose-dependent, increasing with the number of cigarettes that the mother smokes (Henderson-Smart, Ponsonby, & Murphy, 1998). Since it is difficult to stop smoking, prospective parents should ask for help from their doctor or seek out other professional help. Smoking increases the risk not only of SIDS but also of a multitude of medical and health problems in infants.

Another condition that has been found to place infants at risk for SIDS is being too warm or, less frequently, too cold. Infants who are dressed too warmly when put to bed, who are covered with too many blankets, or who sleep in an excessively warm room are at a greater risk of SIDS. This risk is further increased if they are placed in the prone position, since the face is the primary region for heat loss when infants are covered in thick clothing or bedding. Becoming too cold is also a problem. A general rule is to clothe infants as one would dress oneself in order to be comfortable. However, if the infant has a fever, one should use fewer coverings than otherwise (Henderson-Smart, Ponsonby, & Murphy, 1998).

Finally, bed sharing is also associated with an increased risk of SIDS if either parent smokes. There does not appear to be a risk of SIDS from sleeping in the same bed with parents who do not smoke, although parents should take care that the infant does not slip beneath the covers or have its breathing blocked by pillows. In summary, parents can significantly reduce the risk of sudden infant death syndrome by

- Laying the infant on its back
- Keeping the infant in a smoke-free environment
- Preventing the infant from getting too hot while sleeping
- Not sharing a bed with the infant if the parents smoke

are always relieved to have their children sleep through the night, they also worry about SIDS; Box 4.1 discusses risk factors.

One of the landmark events, for most American parents, occurs when their infant sleeps through the night. Prior to this, new parents stumble awake several times each night to feed a hungry infant. Many attempt to forestall the inevitable by getting in one last feeding before putting the infant down for the night, hoping for an uninterrupted night's sleep. These challenges are not universally experienced in other cultures; they have more to do with the sleeping arrangements of most North American families than with the sleeping patterns of individual infants. In our culture, many infants are put to bed in a room separate from that of their parents. When infants wake in the night, parents must get out of bed and go into the other room for a feeding. By that time, everyone is completely awake. In many cultures, including industrialized ones such as Japan, infants sleep in the

Weight in pounds

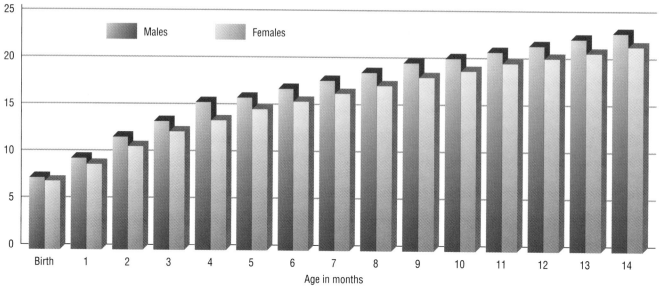

FIGURE 4.1 Mean Weight of Infants from Birth to 14 Months *Source:* S. J. Foman & S. E. Nelson. (1993). Size and growth. In S. J. Foman (Ed.), *Nutrition of normal infants*. St. Louis: Mosby.

same room as their parents, often in the same bed or in a cradle beside the bed. When the infant wakes, it is a simple matter to reach over and tend to its needs.

As basic rhythms of sleeping and waking stabilize, larger rhythms develop that include other members of the family. These rhythms are achieved largely through trial and error, learning when, for instance, to expect smiles and rapt glances with a feeding and when milk will be a sleepy punctuation to the night. Before such rhythms become established, life with a new baby has a jet set quality to it—late hours, an unfamiliar partner, and the feeling of always being on the move.

Many new parents simply have no idea of what it will be like having a new baby or of what parenting an infant will require of them. An infant's cries are particularly demanding. As Anne Lamott wrote of her infant son, "Between the tears and the cooing and his crazy drunken-old-man smiles, it's almost unbearable. There's so much joy and pain and love." Despite the complexity and maturity of her response, this mother was still not prepared for all that was involved in being a parent, at one point writing in the journal she was keeping, "I just can't get over how much babies cry. I really had no idea what I was getting into. To tell you the truth, I thought it would be more like getting a cat" (Lamott, 1993, p. 66). ◄

Physical Growth

At birth, infants weigh about 7 pounds and are about 20 inches long. Growth in the first year is rapid. Weight triples and body length increases by half again. When their first birthday comes around, most infants weigh just over 20 pounds and measure approximately 30 inches. Growth is less rapid in the 2nd year, infants adding another 5 pounds and growing 5 inches. Most children continue to add 4 to 5 pounds a year, and another 2 to 3 inches, for the next 3 years (Figures 4.1 and 4.2).

As infants grow, the proportions of their bodies also change. At birth the head accounts for one quarter of the infant's entire body, the legs contributing only one third of its length. By 2 years of age, the lower half of the body begins to catch up, and the legs account for almost half the body's length. Not all parts of the body, in other words, grow at the same rate. Growth during infancy, as well as prior to birth, reflects two growth trends, the **cephalocaudal growth trend**, in

cephalocaudal growth trend The developmental pattern in which growth begins in the regions of the head and proceeds downward.

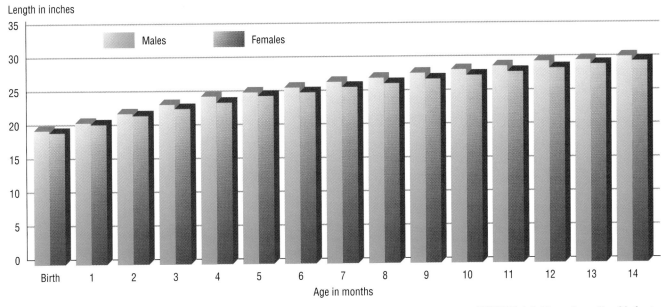

FIGURE 4.2 Mean Length of Infants from Birth to 14 Months *Source:* S. J. Foman & S. E. Nelson. (1993). Size and growth. In S. J. Foman (Ed.), *Nutrition of normal infants.* St. Louis: Mosby.

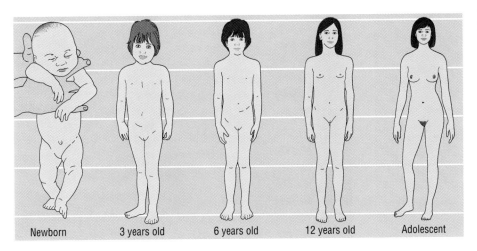

FIGURE 4.3 Changes in Body Proportions with Age *Source:* V. G. Payne & L. D. Isaacs. (1995). *Human motor development: A lifespan approach.* Mountain View, CA: Mayfield.

which growth begins in the region of the head and proceeds downward, and the **proximodistal growth trend,** in which growth progresses outward from the center of the body to the extremities (see Chapter 3). This latter growth trend can be seen in the early growth of the chest and trunk, then of the arms and legs, and finally the hands and feet (Figure 4.3).

Growth of Body Fat and Muscle

The ounces and pounds that infants add in the first weeks and months of life are due primarily to increases in body fat. Infants begin to add a layer of fat directly beneath the skin in the weeks just preceding birth and continue to do so after birth, with increases in body fat peaking by about 9 months. Body fat serves a number of useful functions, providing a protective layer of insulation that helps infants regulate their body temperature and also serving as an emergency reserve of nutrients.

Increases in muscle tissue develop more slowly. In the 2nd year, infants begin to add muscle, slimming out as they do. A spurt in the development of muscle occurs at about 2 years, followed by a relatively steady increase in muscle throughout childhood. As muscle tissue develops, the type of muscle tissue also

Why is it healthy for infants to have a layer of body fat directly beneath the skin?

proximodistal growth trend The developmental pattern in which growth progresses outward from the center of the body to the extremities.

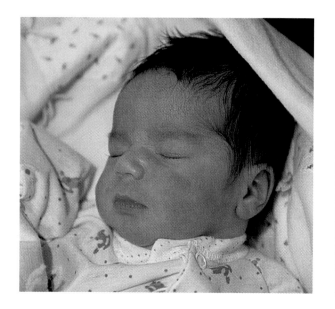

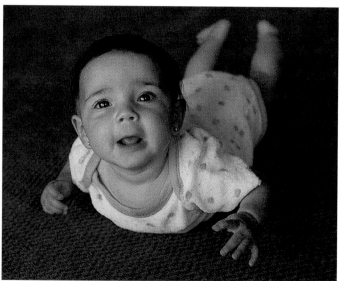

Not all parts of the body grow at the same rate, as illustrated by this girl shown at birth, six months, age 1, and age 3. At birth the head is 1/4 of the infant's entire body. By age 3, growth of the chest, trunk, arms, legs, hands, and feet increasingly define a child's overall shape and proportions.

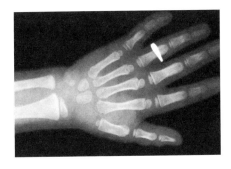 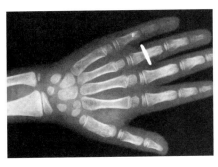 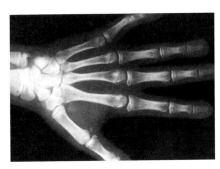

FIGURE 4.4 The Growth of Small Bones in the Wrists—at 3, 5, and 14 Years *Source:* V. G. Payne & L. D. Isaacs. (1995). *Human motor development: A lifespan approach.* Mountain View, CA: Mayfield.

changes. For the 1st year of life, muscles are predominantly fast-contracting ones. At about 1 year, slow-contracting muscles begin to develop, allowing infants greater control over their movements (Wilder, 1995).

Skeletal Growth

Bone growth occurs rapidly during both infancy and early childhood, with existing bones increasing in size and density, new bones emerging, and the overall alignment of bones changing.

The Growth of Existing Bones Prior to birth, a complete skeleton develops out of a supple substance known as cartilage, which calcifies and becomes bone. During infancy and childhood, existing bones grow both in length and in thickness. Bone growth takes place in each of two growth centers, or **epiphyseal growth plates,** near either end of the bone. These growth centers produce new cells that eventually harden into bone. As the bone reaches its adult length, the growth plates narrow and finally fuse with the ends of the bone, preventing any further bone growth (Cech & Martin, 1995).

The Emergence of New Bone Skeletal growth also occurs through the emergence of new bones. The small bones forming the wrists and ankles, for instance, develop from ossification centers, which turn into spongy bone tissue that, over time, hardens into bone (Cech & Martin, 1995). Figure 4.4 shows how new bones form in a child's wrist with age.

The bony plates forming the skull also grow in this way. At birth, the skull bones are separated by gaps, or **fontanels.** These allow the bones of the skull to overlap each other as the head squeezes through the birth canal. Following birth, in fact, an infant's head may be somewhat pointed, molded by the narrow birth canal. The fontanels also allow the skull to grow to accommodate increases in brain size. The fontanels gradually close after the 1st year (Figure 4.5).

Skeletal Alignment

As infants begin to move about, putting stresses on the skeletal system, various bones realign themselves to accommodate the forces of movement. The spine in infants, for instance, is initially much straighter than it is in adults, with the curvature in the upper region occurring as infants begin to sit upright and that in the lower region occurring as they begin to walk. Similarly, the alignment of the leg bones changes, as does that of the pelvis, once the infant begins to move about. For instance, in comparison to infants, who are bow-legged, the knees of 3-year-olds turn in, giving them a knock-kneed gait. Surprisingly, sitting upright and walking also have implications for breathing. In infants, the ribs extend out

epiphyseal growth plates In a child, areas near the ends of a bone that produce new cells.

fontanels In an infant, gaps between the bony plates of the skull.

FIGURE 4.5 The Bony Plates, or Fontanels, Forming the Skull in the Newborn *Source:* T. W. Sadler. (1990). *Langman's medical embryology* (6th ed.). Baltimore: Williams and Wilkins.

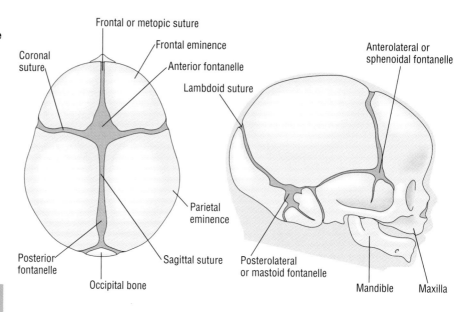

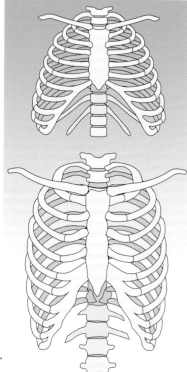

FIGURE 4.6 Changes in Skeletal Alignment with Age *The rib cage of an infant (top) and of an adult (bottom).* Source: D. Cech & S. Martin. (1995). *Functional movement development across the life span.* Philadelphia: W. B. Saunders.

neurons Brain cells responsible for the conduction of nerve impulses.

glial cells Cells that support and nourish neurons and produce myelin.

horizontally, rather than sloping downward as they do in adults. Gravity and the use of abdominal muscles, both involved in maintaining an upright position, pull the ribs down, increasing the space between them and, as a result, making breathing all that much easier. Figure 4.6 shows these changes (Cech & Martin, 1995).

Nutrition plays an important role in skeletal growth. Adequate amounts of protein, calcium, and vitamins C and D are essential for bone growth. Also, because bone growth is so rapid in the early years, children's bodies are especially responsive to corrective therapies of disorders such as club foot or hip dislocation.

Brain Development

The brain continues to develop following birth, doubling in weight by 6 months, at which point it weighs about half that of the adult brain. Development of the brain proceeds unevenly, with spurts of brain growth occurring between 3 and 10 months and again between 15 and 24 months. Most of the 100 billion **neurons,** or brain cells responsible for the conduction of nerve impulses, are present at birth. The increase in the size of the brain is due to the proliferation of **glial cells,** which support and nourish the neurons. Glial cells outnumber neurons 10 to 1, but since they are much smaller than neurons, they make up only about half of the brain tissue (Cech & Martin, 1995).

In addition to nourishing the neurons, the rapidly spreading glial cells serve another important function. They produce **myelin,** a fatty substance that coats the **axon** of the neuron, the long filament extending out from the cell body, by which the neuron makes contact with other nerve cells, thereby transmitting neural messages (Figure 4.7). Fibers coated with a myelin sheath conduct impulses at higher speeds than do those without a myelin covering.

Myelination of nerve fibers progresses at different rates for different parts of the brain. The **peripheral nervous system,** which connects the sensory receptors and muscles to the brain and spinal cord, as well as connecting the internal organs and glands to the brain, is first to be myelinated. These fibers are largely myelinated at birth, thus ensuring that the newborn is able to receive and act on information from the various sensory systems. The one exception are the fibers in the optic tract, those responsible for vision, which is the least mature of the senses at birth (Cech & Martin, 1995).

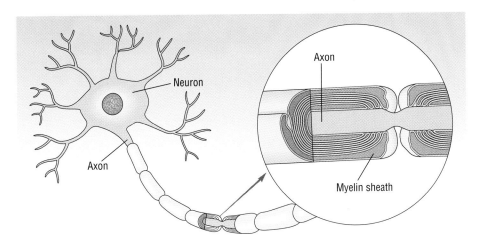

FIGURE 4.7 Myelin Sheath Coating Axon

Myelination of neurons within the **central nervous system,** the spinal cord and the brain itself, is completed later. Here, too, the order of myelination mirrors the order in which various areas of the brain begin to function at more mature levels. For instance, fibers in the spinal cord and the part of the brain controlling vital functions such as breathing, regulating temperature, eating, and sleeping are first to be myelinated. Myelination underlies other developments as well, which are reflected in the infant's behavior. For instance, the 24-hour cycle of sleeping and waking that develops between 2 and 4 months of age can be seen to correspond to new patterns of electrical activity in the brain. With increasing periods of alertness, there is greater opportunity for social interaction, and most parents see social smiles starting at about 2 months of age. Some of the last fibers to myelinate are those in the frontal cortex, the area most responsible for thought, conscious experience, and intentional behavior (Cech & Martin, 1995).

Even though the number of neurons does not increase following birth, the neurons themselves continue to develop with age. The length of axons increases, and tiny branchlike fibers, or dendrites, at the end of the axon increase in density over the first 2 years of life (Figure 4.8). These increases make possible many more interconnections between neurons than previously were possible.

Recall from Chapter 3 that the infant's experiences are thought to contribute in different ways to the brain's development, some types of stimulation being necessary for the *establishment* of neural connections, thereby enabling the infant to hold on to new experiences, and other types of stimulation being necessary for the *maintenance* of connections laid down by the nervous system in anticipation of usage, connections that would be lost in the absence of experience (Greenough, Black, & Wallace, 1987). The importance of early experiences is supported by research with laboratory animals which finds, for instance, that rats reared from infancy in living conditions that have been enriched with interesting things to do, such as mazes, activity wheels, and the presence of other animals, have more synaptic connections than do those reared alone in empty cages. Their brains also weigh more and produce more of an enzyme that is important in learning (Globus, Rosenzweig, Bennett, & Diamond, 1973; Rosenzweig, 1984).

The specialization of function that occurs with different types of experiences begins from birth on. With age, different areas within the cortex become specialized in their control over different types of functions. As a consequence, injuries to the brain that occur early in infancy typically have less damaging effects than do those occurring later.

How does an infant benefit from having toys, such as rattles and over-the-crib mobiles?

Why do injuries to the brain in early infancy frequently have less serious consequences than those occurring later?

myelin A fatty substance that coats axons and increases the speed of conduction of nerve impulses.

axon A long filament extending from a nerve cell, through which neural impulses are transmitted.

peripheral nervous system That part of the nervous system that connects the sensory receptors and muscles and glands and internal organs to the central nervous system.

central nervous system The brain and the spinal cord.

FIGURE 4.8 The Growth of Dendrites in the First 2 Years Following Birth *Source:* J. L. Conel. (1975). *The postnatal development of the human cerebral cortex.* Cambridge, MA: Harvard University Press.

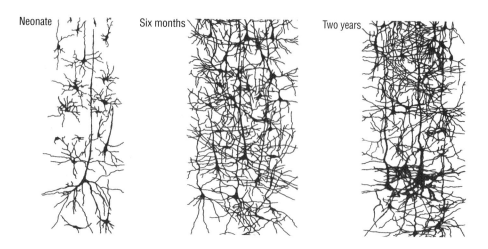

Neonate   Six months   Two years

Development of the Senses

Once thought to be passive, socially unresponsive, and possessed of senses dimmer than those of an octogenarian, our view of the newborn has changed dramatically. Only moments old, the newborn will turn toward the sound of a voice, searching for its source, or will follow a face, turning head and eyes to keep it in view. The newborn can distinguish speech from nonspeech sounds and moves in synchrony to the sounds of human voices. Newborns, in fact, appear to obtain many of the same pleasures from their senses as do individuals at any age, distinguishing not only sounds and sights, but tastes and smells as well.

Taste and Smell

Taste may provide one of the infant's first pleasures. Infants can distinguish sweet, salty, sour, and bitter tastes. They also have taste preferences right from the start, being born with a "sweet tooth," it seems, and showing an aversion to substances that taste bitter or sour.

In addition to allowing infants to savor their food, taste receptors may serve a more practical function. Research with newborn animals finds that when drops of plain water, sweetened water, or milk reach the larynx, the animals momentarily stop breathing, which prevents them from inhaling the liquid. When the water is salty, however, this protective mechanism is not triggered. A similar mechanism in neonates coordinates breathing and swallowing, taste receptors on the epiglottis triggering a reflex that stops breathing. Just like the experimental animals, neonates are less likely to inhale milk or water, both low in natural salts, than a salty solution. On a practical note, breast milk has less salt than commercial formulas (Lawrence, 1994). This is not to suggest that infants will experience difficulties when bottle-fed with a commercially prepared formula, but if an infant is choking while feeding, it might pay to check the salt content of the formula or to switch brands (Acredolo & Hake, 1982).

Much of one's sense of taste is actually provided by smell. The sense of smell, or olfaction, is triggered by molecules in the air that reach receptors inside the nose. Preterm infants as young as 28 weeks (38 weeks is full term) react to strong smells, just as do full-term infants months later (Acredolo & Hake, 1982). The sense of smell is highly developed. In fact, infants who are breast-fed can even discriminate the smell of their mother's milk from that of other nursing women, turning their head in the direction of a breast pad soaked with their mother's milk

The sense of smell in newborns is so acute that infants who are breast-fed can recognize the smell of their mother's milk.

in preference to one soaked with the milk of another mother (MacFarlane, 1975). Even infants who are not breast-fed appear to prefer the smell of breast milk to that of their formula, turning more to the breast milk when given a choice (Porter, Makin, Davis, & Christensen, 1992).

Vision

Of all the senses on which we humans rely, vision is the most important. It is also the least mature at birth. Dramatic changes occur within the 1st year in infants' ability to follow moving objects with their eyes, in visual acuity, and even in perceiving the very unity of objects at first (Johnson & Aslin, 1995).

In previous chapters, we have spoken of children as "meaning makers," continually engaged in a process of putting together, or constructing, the events to which they respond. But at what age do such constructive activities begin? Do *infants* assemble reality from the perceptual scraps offered up by their senses? And if they do, what patterns do they bring with them by which to fashion a larger whole?

Marshall Haith (1980, 1993), a psychologist at the University of Denver, has studied the way infants obtain information about their visual world. Haith recorded the eye movements of newborns, 24 to 96 hours old, as they scanned their environment. Haith discovered that, rather than passively waiting for objects to come into view, newborns actively search for things in the visual field. Comparisons of eye movements from one infant to the next revealed that all infants

Vision is the least mature of the senses at birth. As dramatic changes occur within the first year, what some research suggests are "rules for scanning" as inborn capacities emerge by which the infant actively engages the world.

engage in the same types of searches, using what Haith refers to as **"rules" for scanning.** Since these rules are present shortly after birth, Haith assumes infants are "wired at birth" for them.

What rules do infants use? Haith (using an infrared TV camera) found that in a dark room infants open their eyes very wide and intensely scan the darkness with very small eye movements. Should even the faintest image of anything be there, such activity will improve their chances of discovering it. In contrast to the way they scan in the dark, infants scan a light-filled room with large, sweeping movements. Such scans increase the likelihood of "bumping" into an edge or a contour. When they detect a contour, infants stop scanning the field and focus on the edges of the object (Haith, 1980).

The scanning rules that infants use, whether in a darkened room or in the light, optimize their chances of discovering something if anything is there. These particular rules, however, also make it likely that infants will miss other types of information. Specifically, by focusing on the edges of objects, very young infants miss what is inside the perimeters. When shown a picture of a face, for instance, a 1-month-old will concentrate on the outer contour of the face. Not until 2 months of age will the infant scan the actual features of the face. You can see these differences in Figure 4.9. The 1-month-old, whose scanning pattern is shown on the left, seems to concentrate on the perimeter of the face, the chin and the hairline, while the 2-month-old, whose scanning pattern is on the right, spends the most time scanning the face's features, the eyes and mouth (Haith, Bergman, & Moore, 1977).

By 4 months, most infants scan objects in their visual world the way adults do, by quickly processing the global configuration, or shape, of an object and then analyzing its internal features. Janet Frick and John Columbo (1996), at the Uni-

"rules" for scanning Patterns of scanning used by infants to actively search for things in their visual field.

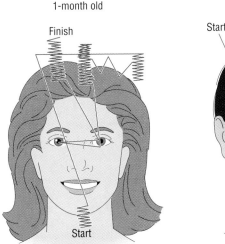
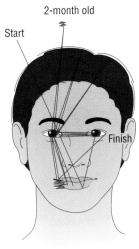

1-month old

Finish

Start

2-month old

Start

Finish

FIGURE 4.9 **Differences in the Visual Scanning of a Face by 1- and 2-Month-Old Infants** *Source:* P. Salapatek. (1975). Pattern perception in early infancy. In L. B. Cohen & P. Salapatec (Eds.), *Infant perception: From sensation to cognition.* New York: Academic Press.

versity of Kansas, found that by 4 months, differences among infants can be striking, with infants differing both in their speed of processing and in the strategies they use. Infants who take longer to process information also appear to use less mature strategies, being more likely to scan only the perimeter of objects as do younger infants.

Gordon Bronson (1994), at Mills College, points out that the infant's visual system undergoes rapid changes within the 2nd and 3rd months. Changes in scanning patterns parallel these developments. By 3 months, for instance, infants are able to scan a much larger visual field and do so more systematically, focusing on all of the figures that are present and comparing them by looking at first one and then the other.

Being able *not* to look at things also develops with age. The ability to inhibit automatic sweeps of the eye, or saccades, which are triggered by peripheral movement, allows infants to more systematically inspect the objects they *are* looking at (Johnson, 1995). This type of control becomes increasingly important as infants are better able to anticipate where interesting things will appear and to look in their direction. By 3 months, for instance, infants who are shown a picture first to the left of them and then to the right can detect the alternating pattern to the picture's location and will look in the expected direction. In contrast, infants younger than 3 months are unable to anticipate where an object will next appear (Haith, Hazen, & Goodman, 1988; Haith, Wentworth, & Canfield, 1993). This inability, combined with their, as yet, relatively poor motor coordination, can lead to interesting encounters with their own bodies. Anne Lamott (1993) writes of her infant son, "His arms and hands still have wills of their own. They float erratically above him, suddenly darting into his field of vision like snakes, causing him to do funny little Jack Benny double takes" (p. 101). ◄

By 6 months of age, infants not only look at the objects that interest them in more adult ways, but they also process peripheral, or contextual, visual information the way adults do, swiftly and automatically detecting features of the background without attending to it (Early, Bhatt, & Rovee-Collier, 1995).

Just as infants' ability to visually explore their world changes significantly within the first 6 months, so, too, does their **visual acuity,** or their ability to see fine detail. At birth, acuity is actually quite poor, being only one twentieth that of an adult. Acuity improves dramatically month by month until, by the end of the 1st year, it reaches that of an adult (Courage & Adams, 1990). Improvements in acuity can be traced to a number of factors, such as neurological maturation,

What information are young infants most likely to pick up when scanning a person's face, and what are they most likely to miss?

visual acuity Ability to see fine detail.

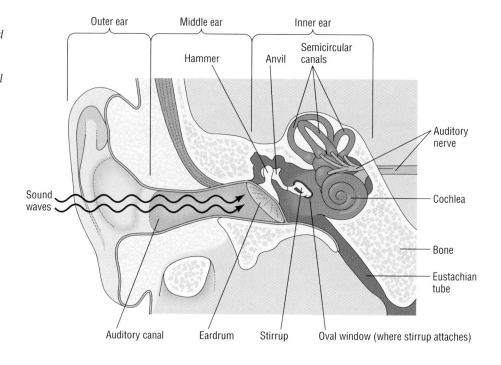

FIGURE 4.10 The Mechanism of Hearing *The outer ear funnels sound waves to the eardrum. The bones of the middle ear amplify and relay the eardrum's vibrations through the oval window into the fluid-filled cochlea.*

myelination of neural fibers, and changes in the eye itself. With respect to the latter, the fovea, a receptor-rich area of the retina on which images are focused, continues to develop until the 4th month. The most mature part of the visual system at birth is the "secondary visual system," cells distributed throughout the retina that are responsive to movement and gross characteristics of objects, such as changes in brightness and size (Bronson, 1982). Perhaps not surprisingly, given their relatively poor acuity, infants initially prefer to look at things that move, as well as at large patterns and bright objects, simply because it is easier for them to see these.

An object's distance from the infant is also important in determining how well it can be seen. Objects that are 8 to 12 inches away are seen most clearly. Vision blurs when the retinal image of an object does not maintain the same size, relative to the object, at all distances. In adults, the lens of the eye thickens as we focus on objects close at hand and thins out as they move further away, changing the angle at which light is refracted through the lens (and hence where the image will fall), thus accommodating for distance. Accommodation fails to occur in young infants, in part because objects are not seen well enough to prompt an attempt to bring them into focus. With foveal development, the ability to see objects either at a distance or close at hand improves to that of an adult (Maurer & Maurer, 1988).

Why might infants find it difficult to bring objects into focus as they look at them?

Audition

In comparison to vision, hearing is relatively well developed at birth. Sounds, whether the clatter of dishes or the rise and fall of a human voice, are transmitted as waves of pressure changes that differ in frequency (in how quickly the pattern of change repeats itself). These waves are picked up by the eardrum, which is set in motion, in turn transmitting the patterns to the cochlea of the inner ear (Figure 4.10). The cochlea contains hair cells that translate the waves to neural

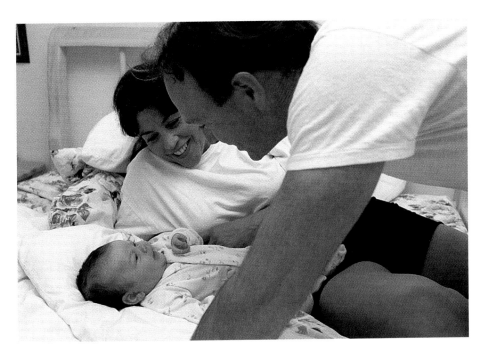

Very young infants can hear sounds that older infants and adults cannot, which suggests that they lose the ability to hear some sounds depending on their language community.

impulses. Newborns have the same number of hair cells as adults, though not all are mature at birth (Acredola & Hake, 1982).

Newborns can be seen to startle to loud sounds or to sudden changes in sound. Although their threshold for detecting sounds is not as low as that of most adults, neither are differences between them and adults that great. Electrophysiological measures, which record impulses along the auditory pathway, show that for most newborns sounds need be only twice as loud to be heard as they need to be for an adult to hear them (in comparison to vision, where objects need to be 20 times as close for a newborn to see them as well as an adult would). Considerable variation exists from one infant to the next, and some infants hear nearly as well as adults. Infants hear high-frequency sounds most easily, and, by 6 months of age, can hear these as well as adults. Their ability to hear low-frequency sounds, however, continues to improve throughout the first 18 months (Siegler, 1998).

Infants also get better with age at localizing where sounds are coming from. This improvement takes a surprising turn, in that newborns are actually better at localizing sounds than are infants several months older. Only by the age of 4 months do infants surpass the ability of newborns. This U-shaped curve reflects the operation of two separate mechanisms. Initially, in the 1st month, spatial localization is thought to be under the control of subcortical centers within the brain. As cortical activity increases in the succeeding months, subcortical centers are replaced. Even so, cortical activity is initially not fully developed, and spatial localization is not as accurate as it eventually becomes at 4 months (Siegler, 1998).

Not only can infants localize sounds, but they can also distinguish among them and show preferences right from the start. Infants only 3 days old can identify their mother's voice from those of other speakers and appear to prefer to listen to the voice of their mother. Researchers have to be ingenious when working with infants, since babies can neither answer nor understand the questions one might want to ask. To determine listening preferences, these investigators gave infants a nipple to suck. When the infants sucked, they heard either their mother's voice or that of another woman. Infants sucked more to hear their mother's voice (DeCasper & Fifer, 1980).

How do researchers use the principle of habituation to determine whether one sound can be discriminated from another?

Although infants can distinguish many types of sounds, not all are equally interesting to them. Those that are most interesting are the sounds of the human voice (Ecklund-Flores & Turkewitz, 1996). From the first days on, infants react differently to speech and nonspeech sounds, moving their faces and fingers rhythmically to the patterns of speech and turning their heads in its direction. These movements are "paced" by the rhythmic features of speech, occurring in synchrony to the rise and fall of the speaker's voice (Condon & Sander, 1974).

Speech sounds appear to be processed in a way that is qualitatively different from the way nonspeech sounds are processed. Infants, for example, are able to distinguish highly similar sounds, such as "pa" and "ba" or "s" and "z," when these are heard in the context of speech more easily than when they are not. The two hemispheres, or sides, of the brain show specialization in their processing of speech from early infancy on (Best, 1988). Sounds entering the two ears travel to the different hemispheres of the brain; but, in an interesting twist of nature, those picked up by the left ear go to the right side of the brain and those entering the right ear go to the left. Language is processed in the left hemisphere. Specialization of the hemispheres is apparent even in early infancy, in that speech sounds presented to the left ear, and processed by the right hemisphere, are not as easily distinguished as those presented to the right ear (Best, 1988).

With respect to hearing the sounds of speech, infants less than a month old can hear sounds that older infants and adults cannot, which suggests that the experience of living within a language community contributes to the development of language as much by *decreasing* the likelihood of hearing differences among sounds (those that are not meaningful in that language) as by enhancing distinctions among others. Speech sounds, you see, are actually composed of continuous signals differing along many dimensions, yet the speakers of a language hear these signals categorically—that is, as either one type of sound or another. One such dimension is voice onset time (VOT), when the vocal cords begin to vibrate in making a sound. The VOT for "ba," for instance, is short (the cords vibrate at the very beginning of the sound), whereas the VOT for "pa" is quite long. Despite very real differences along this dimension, all sounds with VOTs that are shorter than a certain value are heard as "ba" and all sounds that are longer than this VOT as "pa." As Robert Siegler (1991), a psychologist at Carnegie-Mellon University, says, "A sound is either a *ba* or a *pa,* never something in between." Except, that is, for infants less than a month old.

Perceptual Exploration

Claus von Hofsten (1982), at the University of Uppsala in Sweden, photographed arm movements from two different camera angles, giving three-dimensional information regarding the infant's actions. Von Hofsten found that although neonates were no more likely to touch an object when they were looking at it (we look at the things we reach for) than when they were not, their arm movements could be seen to come closer to the object, and the hand slowed down as it neared the object. One should not overinterpret these early reaches. Even though reaching is more likely to occur when an object is present than in the absence of an object, reaching does not necessarily mean that the infant "intends" to grab something. This type of means-end understanding develops over the course of the 1st year.

Von Hofsten suggests that the eye-hand coordination evident in neonates' reaches constitutes an "information gathering system." He views reaching as an attentional act rather than a manipulative one. According to von Hofsten (1982), looking at and reaching toward something are merely different, related ways of gaining information. From this perspective, vision becomes a way of exploring and making sense of one's surroundings. Perception, rather than a passive process triggered by external events, becomes an active process and one that is internally guided.

Ulric Neisser (1967, 1976), at Cornell, suggests that anticipatory schemata direct the pickup of information and are, themselves, refined and altered in the process. Picking up certain information creates a "readiness" for related information, preparing us to see or hear certain things and not others. The information that is received modifies the schema. The modified schema, in turn, directs the next exploration. Perception, for Neisser, is an active, constructive process. Figure 4.11 illustrates the dynamic nature of this process.

To illustrate how such schemata could account for the selective nature of perception—that is, seeing one thing and not another—Neisser devised a simple experiment in which adults watched a videotaped basketball game. Neisser assumed that the movements of the players and the ball would create anticipatory schemata based on the trajectories of each. Vision guided by these schemata should fail to pick up other, unrelated movements with different trajectories. At one point, a second videotape of a woman with an umbrella walking across the court, was superimposed over the game. People monitoring the fast action of the game failed to notice the woman. What we fail to notice, the woman with the umbrella in this case, simply is not picked up with anticipatory schemata. In a similar type of task, 4-month-old infants also failed to notice an irrelevant stimulus while attending to another (Bahrick, Walker, & Neisser, 1981). Neisser argues that, through the action of such schemata, we put together, or construct, the events to which we respond and that these constructions are fundamental to perception. Anticipatory schemata bridge perception and memory. Because the schemata are anticipations, they are the medium by which the past effects the future, information already acquired determining that which will next be experienced.

Perceptual Integration

Thus far, we have considered the senses separately. But does the activity of one sensory system ever contribute to the ability to sense something in a different modality? You have probably experienced how tasteless food becomes when your nose is stopped up with a cold or how much easier it is to hear a sound when you look in the direction of its source, even when the source is not visible. Do we taste with our noses, or hear with our eyes? Bats and dolphins can make their way unerringly in darkness, guided by echoes—forms shaped in patterns of sounds. Can we, too, use the structure of sound to see? For most of us, the answer is obscured by the very ease with which we see and hear. A look at some work with handicapped infants offers the intriguing possibility that the senses may overlap, the same information being picked up by more than one sense.

In a remarkable demonstration, a sonic guide was strapped to the forehead of a blind infant. An echoing signal indicated the presence of objects. The echo increased in pitch and loudness with size and nearness to an object. Surface texture was broadcast through the clarity of the echo, a pure tone indicating smooth surfaces and a gravelly tone rough ones. Within minutes, the infant was able to use the spatial information given by the sonic guide. At one point, as she moved her hand in front of her face, her expression changed; and, then, probing the textured darkness, she moved her hand again, this time following the movement with her head, her face sparkling in smiles (Bower, 1982). Since this initial demonstration, sonic guides have been used experimentally in programs for the blind (Humphrey & Humphrey, 1985).

The ability of infants to make almost immediate use of a sonic guide offers the promise of new aids for the visually handicapped. But how are we to understand their ability to use this information? If sensory experience is specific to each

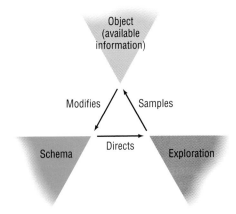

FIGURE 4.11 Neisser's Perceptual Cycle *Anticipatory schemata both direct and are modified by the pickup of information.* Source: U. Neisser. (1976). *Cognition and reality.* San Francisco: Freeman.

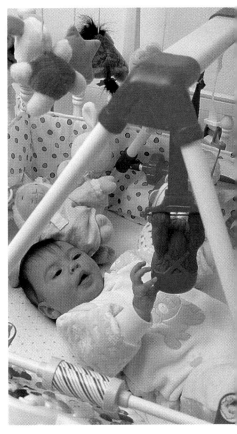

Eye-hand coordination is a way for infants to make sense of their surroundings.

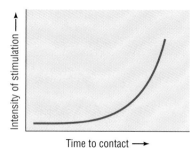

FIGURE 4.12 Changes in the Intensity of Stimulation with the Nearness of an Approaching Object *Source:* T. G. R. Bower. (1982). *Development in infancy* (2nd ed.). San Francisco: W. H. Freeman.

modality, how does the infant translate an auditory signal into a structured space that corresponds in important ways to what is seen?

T. G. R. Bower (1982), a developmentalist at Edinburgh University, explains what happens visually when an object approaches. As the object moves closer, there is a change in the pattern of retinal stimulation, the image that it projects on the retina expanding. The optical expansion that occurs with increasing proximity follows a time course. With increasing nearness, or *decreasing* time to "contact," the amount of stimulation increases (Figure 4.12). The relationship between distance and amount of stimulation is not, however, specific to vision. It can, in fact, be communicated through several senses (Bower, 1982).

To a similar approaching object, the sonic guide echoes back a change in pitch and loudness, the tone becoming both higher and louder with increasing nearness of the object. Both of these changes have the same time course—a time course that is identical to the one for optical expansion. The *information* is the same, in other words, irrespective of the sensory modality (Bower, 1982; Gibson, 1966).

Bower suggests that there may be other "amodal" variables to which infants are responsive. Consider the ability to detect radial direction. The amodal variable for straight ahead is symmetrical stimulation of both receptors, whether these be nostrils, ears, or eyes. Asymmetrical stimulation, arriving at one side before the other, signals a source that is off from the center. The order of stimulation cues direction, and the amount of difference in the time it takes the source to reach the left versus right receptors informs us as to the degree to which the object is to the side (Bower, 1982). Infants' perception of their own leg movements, also, appears to be determined, at least in part, by their detection of intermodal invariants that indicate the position of the body in its spatial surround (Rochat & Morgan, 1995). Similarly, infants respond to amodal cues, as well as specific visual and auditory ones, in listening to speech (Lewkowicz, 1996).

As already suggested, one advantage to intersensory coordination is practical; it offers therapeutic uses with handicapped infants. Bower notes a theoretical advantage, as well—that of parsimony. As pointed out in Chapter 3, the genotype does not carry sufficient information to fully specify the functioning of the nervous system. Even though the genotype can code several million proteins, this figure is still short of that necessary to explain the operation of all the senses, and the environment is believed to play an important part in modulating the process of genetic expression (see Chapter 3).

There is little doubt, however, that the genotype carries sufficient information to program amodal structures in the nervous system. For radial direction, for instance, one would only need a symmetry-asymmetry detector that would receive input from all senses. Thus one could expect a neonate to be perceptually competent despite the dramatic neural development that occurs after birth. This latter growth could be seen as fleshing out the skeletal worldview given by amodal variables (Bower, 1982). In fact, the transfer of control from subcortical to cortical centers for activities such as localizing sounds or scanning visual patterns suggests just such a development (Bronson, 1974).

Some of the simplest questions concerning perception can set the occasion for complicated answers indeed. How, for example, does an infant distinguish the sights and sounds that emanate from a single source, such as a person talking, for example, from those that merely occur together by chance? Must sensory impressions be "fused" together through the repeated association of images with sounds, smells, textures, and tastes? If the senses functioned independently of each other, as separate channels for sensory experiences, such might be necessary. If, however, perception is viewed as an *activity*, involving one or more sensory systems, by which one explores one's surroundings, what is picked up is information, and much of this can be amodal (Lewkowicz, 1996). Sensory receptors still respond to changes in stimulation, of course. However, only those changes that reflect invariant features of stimulation, those that maintain similar relationships despite differences in pitch, loudness, or size, for instance, carry the information that results in perception (Gibson, 1966).

Infants are remarkably competent at birth, having been readied for life outside the uterus in a multitude of ways. Yet there is a paradox to the richly equipped "utility kit" of biological rhythms and sensory capacities with which infants are supplied; their innate abilities place infants in a better position to explore and learn—and be influenced all the more by their experiences. This brings us to the topic of motor development and the infant's increased ability to grasp, move about, and discover more about its world and itself.

Motor Development

Perhaps nothing excites parents more than the "firsts" of motor development, seeing the first time their infant reaches out for an interesting object, for instance, or takes a first step. Physical growth and the maturation of the brain enable infants to develop new control over their bodies. Changing body proportions also contribute to increased control of movement. Were the head to remain proportionally as large, for instance, as it is in the newborn, walking would be as difficult as balancing a pumpkin on popsicle sticks. As it is, changes in body proportions, growth, and neuromuscular maturation contribute to some of the most noticeable developments of infancy—the kind that find their way into baby books—as voluntary actions begin to supplant the newborn's repertoire of involuntary reflexes.

Reflexes

Reflexes are specific responses that occur automatically to particular types of stimuli, our bodies being "prewired" to respond in distinct ways. A light tap just beneath the knee, for instance, will cause the leg to swing up in the familiar knee-jerk reflex. Tapping the tendon causes the muscle to which it is attached to stretch. Information about the muscle's movement is carried to the spinal cord along an **afferent, or sensory, pathway,** where it connects with an **efferent, or motor, pathway** leading out to the same muscle, causing it to contract, correcting for the initial movement. Simple reflexes such as this are relayed at the level of the spinal cord (Figure 4.13). More complex reflexes, such as sucking, which require the coordination of a number of related movements, involve relays within the **brain stem,** an area beneath the cortex that controls basic body functions such as breathing, eating, heart rate, body temperature, and emotional arousal.

Reflexes abound in individuals of all ages, not just newborns. Salivating to the taste of a lemon, blinking at a fast-approaching object, and swinging one's leg to a tap beneath the knee are all reflexes. Reflexes in the newborn serve highly adaptive functions, such as obtaining food, maintaining an unobstructed flow of air, and holding on to the caretaker.

Sucking and rooting are both reflexes by which the infant initially receives nourishment. The **sucking reflex** can be triggered by anything that touches the infant's mouth, whether this be a nipple, a finger, or a shirtsleeve. Simply brushing the infant's lips is sufficient to cause the lips to purse and sucking to begin. A related reflex, the **rooting reflex,** helps the infant locate the source of nourishment. Brushing the infant's cheek will prompt the infant to turn its head in that direction and to start sucking.

afferent, or sensory, pathway A series of neurons carrying impulses from the periphery (skin, muscles, joints, and internal organs) to the central nervous system.

efferent, or motor, pathway A series of neurons carrying impulses from the central nervous system to the periphery (skin, muscles, joints, and internal organs).

brain stem The area at the base of the brain that contains the midbrain, the pons, and the medulla oblongata and controls basic functions such as breathing and heart rate.

sucking reflex Sucking in response to a touch on the mouth; an adaptive reflex in infants.

rooting reflex Turning the head and starting to suck in response to a brush on the cheek; an adaptive reflex in infants.

FIGURE 4.13 A Simple Spinal Reflex

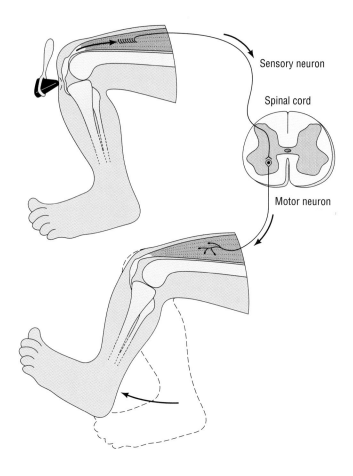

In another adaptive reflex, head turning, infants will turn their heads away from something covering their nose, thereby maintaining an adequate supply of air. As with other reflexes, this is nature's *first* defense and is not necessarily adequate in all situations. Parents need to be sure that the crib is free of objects such as pillows and soft toys that, though inviting to an adult, can be dangerous to a newborn. Breathing itself is a reflexive activity that does not require conscious monitoring. In another reflex, the swimming reflex, infants will momentarily hold their breath and kick with a swimming motion if placed face down in water. It cannot be emphasized too much that this reflex will not keep an infant from drowning if left unattended in a bath, *even if only for a moment.* An infant can drown in mere inches of water simply because it is "top heavy," and if it falls face down, its muscles are not yet sufficiently developed for it to lift its face out of the water.

A sudden loss of support or a loud noise will prompt the **Moro reflex,** in which the infant arches its back, throws its arms out, and then quickly brings them in again toward the body. The adaptive significance of this reflex is disputed. It may, in times past, have helped our ancestors cling to their caretakers, or it may have more current adaptive value in enhancing mother-infant bonding. In perhaps a related reflex, the **grasp reflex,** the infant spontaneously grasps an object that is pressed against the palms of the hands. A newborn can actually be lifted into the air as it grasps a forefinger in either hand. The Research Focus, "Science as Self-Correcting: 'The Case of The Disappearing Reflex,'" discusses the stepping reflex.

In addition to their adaptive value, reflexes are useful diagnostically, since reflexive behavior changes with age, many reflexes dropping out as the central nervous system matures. Checking an infant's reflexes is one way of assessing whether such maturation is progressing normally.

Moro reflex A reflex in infants in response to a sudden loss of support or loud noise, in which they arch their back, throw their arms out, and quickly bring them in.

grasp reflex Spontaneously grasping an object pressed against the palm of the hand.

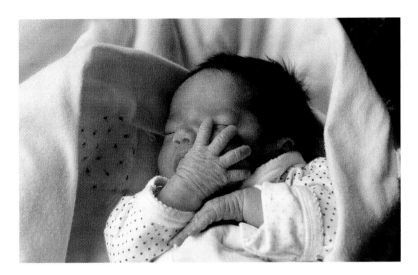

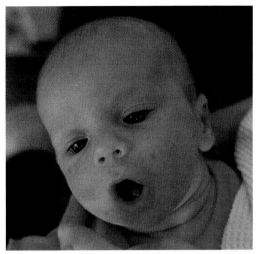

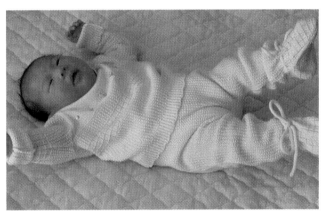

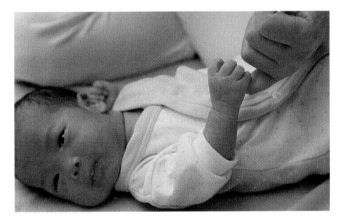

Sucking reflex (top left), rooting reflex (top right), swimming reflex (middle left), moro reflex (middle right), grasp reflex (bottom left).

Voluntary Actions

As neurons within the cerebral cortex increase in size and complexity, and as they become myelinated, new behaviors emerge. One of the first areas to be myelinated is the **primary motor cortex,** one of two cortical areas that are important in controlling voluntary actions. This area is responsible for governing the activity of discrete muscles within the body. Figure 4.14 illustrates the way in which muscles in different parts of the body are "mapped" onto the motor cortex. As you can see, some parts of the body, such as the hands and face, are allotted more space than others. Another area that is important in the control of voluntary movement

primary motor cortex The area of the cortex responsible for governing the voluntary movement of discrete muscles.

Science as Self-Correcting: "The Case of the Disappearing Reflex"

Theoretical assumptions serve as lenses through which we view behavior. Frequently they lead us to look for, and enable us to see, things we otherwise would not have been able to detect. At times, however, they can blur our vision, preventing us from seeing things that are actually there. A case in point is that of the "disappearing" reflex (Thelen, 1995).

Newborn infants can be seen to make stepping movements when they are held upright with their feet touching a surface. This stepping reflex disappears after a few months, and coordinated stepping does not occur again until infants, many months later, take their first steps as they begin to walk. Presumably, the early reflexive stepping has been inhibited due to the maturation of the higher cortical centers that will eventually control the later voluntary stepping.

Esther Thelen and Donna Fisher (1982) began to question this assumption when they noticed that the movements involved in kicking, when infants are lying on their backs or stomachs, are highly similar to those of stepping. In fact, subsequent comparisons of the movement patterns involved in kicking and stepping revealed *no difference* either in the muscles that were activated or in the pattern of the movements themselves. Kicking, in other words, was essentially the same as stepping except that it involved horizontal leg movements rather than vertical ones. Yet kicking continues to occur throughout infancy and does not drop out, whereas stepping does. Surely, they reasoned, one could not expect the cortex to inhibit movements that occurred in one position and yet leave intact the very same movements when they occurred in another.

Thelen and Fisher entertained a theoretical heresy. What if movement is not simply governed by neural impulses? Isn't it just as reasonable to assume that our movements are also governed by bodily and environmental constraints, as well as by neural programming? How might these considerations explain the disappearance of stepping but not of kicking?

Thelen and Fisher noted that when posture changes from being held upright to lying down, one also has a change in the relationship between body mass and gravity. Because of this change, infants require more strength to flex their legs when in an upright position than when lying down. Also, infants are gaining weight in the months prior to the disappearance of stepping. Since most of this weight is fat and not muscle, their legs have become heavier but not correspondingly stronger. These investigators reasoned that the stepping reflex disappears not because of cortical inhibition, but because of environmental and physical constraints such as these.

When viewed from this perspective, one might expect to see the reappearance of the stepping reflex if one could counter the effects of such mechanical and environmental factors. Thelen and Fisher arranged such a test: Infants in whom the stepping reflex had dropped out were held upright in chest-high water. They found, as they had expected, that stepping once again occurred. Conversely, when weights were added to these infants' legs, they failed to kick when placed on their backs. So much for "disappearing" reflexes!

What is it about the scientific method as it was pursued by these and previous investigators that enables science to be self-correcting? First, science is *empirical;* scientists gather observations about behavior rather than basing their statements on assumptions as to what might be taking place. Second, scientists are *self-critical,* not only examining their own work for possible faults, but also publishing their work so that it can be examined by others. Third, theories, even when well established, are never considered to be proven, but instead to be *supported* or *refuted* by empirical findings.

Why do muscles of the hands and face correspond to larger areas of the motor cortex than other parts of the body do?

secondary motor cortex The area of the cortex responsible for voluntary patterned movements of groups of muscles.

cerebellum A large structure located behind the cerebral cortex that coordinates sensory input and muscle responses.

is the **secondary motor cortex.** This area, in contrast to the first, is responsible for patterned movements, in which the activity of discrete muscles is coordinated into a single action. In addition to these two regions of the cortex, the **cerebellum** also plays a critical role in movement. The cerebellum, lying beneath the cortex in the brain stem, acts as a clearing center for all of the many ingoing and outgoing signals that collectively communicate the infant's current body position. The cerebellum undergoes rapid development early in infancy, at a time when the infant is making rapid gains in the postural control and balance that are needed for walking (Malina & Bouchard, 1991).

Control over muscles in different parts of the body progresses unevenly, illustrating the cephalocaudal growth trend. Thus infants are first able to move their heads, 90% being able to lift their heads by 2 months of age. They next gain control over their shoulders, by about 3 months, raising themselves up to look around when placed on their stomachs; and, at 4 months, they can use their arms to support their weight when they do so. Similarly, the proximodistal trend is also apparent. Infants gain control over their shoulders before being able to move their

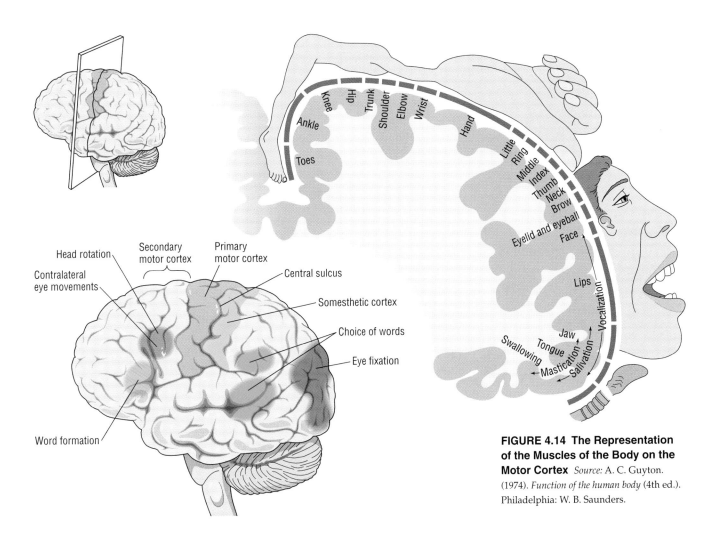

FIGURE 4.14 The Representation of the Muscles of the Body on the Motor Cortex *Source:* A. C. Guyton. (1974). *Function of the human body* (4th ed.). Philadelphia: W. B. Saunders.

arms with accuracy (their first reaches are more like swipes), only much later developing the control over their fingers that allows them, by opposing thumb and index finger, to pick up even the smallest of objects, by about 1 year of age. Box 4.2 and Figure 4.15 present the different ages at which infants accomplish the major milestones of motor development. Keep in mind, when looking at these ages, that considerable variability exists in the timing of accomplishments from one infant to the next.

Flow

Not only are parents delighted by these accomplishments, but infants appear to be as well. Anyone who has watched an infant successfully roll over after a number of abortive attempts or pick something up that has been difficult to grasp will recognize the unmistakable signs of pleasure that attend such successes. Actions that have become second nature to adults carry the heady excitement of victory for the infant.

Mihaly Csikszentmihalyi (1990), a psychologist at the University of Chicago, has analyzed what makes activities enjoyable, whether these involve perfecting one's backhand or navigating the kitchen floor in a crablike crawl. He began his study of enjoyment serendipitously, initially being interested in creativity. He noticed as he studied artists engaged in their work how absorbed they became in

What emotions are infants likely to experience as they master new motor skills?

Box 4.2 *Major Milestones in Motor Development*

1 Month

Lifts Head When Held at Shoulder
Holds Head Erect for 3 Seconds (Vertical)
Adjusts Posture When Held at Shoulder
Holds Head Erect and Steady for 15 Seconds
Holds Head Steady While Being Moved
Lifts Head (Dorsal Suspension)
Adjusts Head to Ventral Suspension
Turns from Side to Back

2 Months

Holds Head Erect and Steady for 15 Seconds
Holds Head Steady While Being Moved
Balances Head
Lifts Head (Dorsal Suspension)
Adjusts Head to Ventral Suspension
Turns from Side to Back
Maintains Head at 45° and Lowers with Control
Sits with Support

3 Months

Holds Head Steady While Being Moved
Balances Head
Adjusts Head to Ventral Suspension
Turns from Side to Back
Turns from Back to Side
Maintains Head at 45° and Lowers with Control
Maintains Head at 90° and Lowers with Control
Shifts Weight on Arms
Sits with Support
Sits with Slight Support for 10 Seconds
Sits Alone Momentarily
Uses Whole Hand to Grasp Rod

4 Months

Balances Head
Turns from Back to Side
Pulls to Sitting Position
Maintains Head at 45° and Lowers with Control
Maintains Head at 90° and Lowers with Control
Shifts Weight on Arms
Sits with Support
Sits with Slight Support for 10 Seconds
Sits Alone Momentarily
Sits Alone for 30 Seconds
Sits Alone While Playing with Toy
Uses Whole Hand to Grasp Rod
Uses Partial Thumb Opposition to Grasp Cube

5 Months

Turns from Back to Side
Turns from Back to Stomach
Shifts Weight on Arms
Grasps Foot with Hands
Pulls to Sitting Position
Sits Alone Momentarily
Sits Alone for 30 Seconds
Sits Alone Steadily
Sits Alone While Playing with Toy
Uses Whole Hand to Grasp Rod
Uses Partial Thumb Opposition to Grasp Cube
Uses Pads of Fingertips to Grasp Cube
Makes Early Stepping Movements

6 Months

Turns from Back to Stomach
Grasps Foot with Hands
Attempts to Raise Self to Sit
Pulls to Sitting Position
Pulls to Standing Position
Sits Alone Momentarily
Sits Alone for 30 Seconds
Sits Alone Steadily
Sits Alone While Playing with Toy
Uses Whole Hand to Grasp Rod
Uses Partial Thumb Opposition to Grasp Cube
Uses Pads of Fingertips to Grasp Cube
Raises Self to Sitting Position
Moves Forward, Using Prewalking Methods
Makes Early Stepping Movements
Supports Weight Momentarily
Shifts Weight While Standing

7 Months

Turns from Back to Stomach
Grasps Foot with Hands
Attempts to Raise Self to Sit
Pulls to Standing Position
Sits Alone While Playing with Toy
Sits Alone Steadily
Rotates Trunk While Sitting Alone
Uses Pads of Fingertips to Grasp Cube
Raises Self to Sitting Position
Moves Forward, Using Prewalking Methods
Moves from Sitting to Creeping Position
Makes Early Stepping Movements
Supports Weight Momentarily
Shifts Weight While Standing

8 Months

Attempts to Raise Self to Sit
Pulls to Standing Position
Rotates Trunk While Sitting Alone
Uses Partial Thumb Opposition to Grasp Rod
Grasps Pencil at Farthest End
Moves Forward, Using Prewalking Methods
Moves from Sitting to Creeping Position
Raises Self to Sitting Position
Raises Self to Standing Position
Supports Weight Momentarily
Shifts Weight While Standing
Attempts to Walk
Walks Sideways While Holding on to Furniture
Walks with Help

9 Months

Rotates Trunk While Sitting Alone
Uses Partial Thumb Opposition to Grasp Rod
Grasps Pencil at Farthest End
Moves from Sitting to Creeping Position
Raises Self to Standing Position
Attempts to Walk
Walks Sideways While Holding on to Furniture
Walks with Help
Stands Alone
Walks Alone

10 Months

Uses Partial Thumb Opposition to Grasp Rod
Grasps Pencil at Farthest End
Moves from Sitting to Creeping Position
Raises Self to Standing Position
Attempts to Walk
Walks Sideways While Holding on to Furniture
Walks with Help
Stands Alone
Walks Alone
Walks Alone with Good Coordination
Throws Ball

11 Months

Uses Partial Thumb Opposition to Grasp Rod
Grasps Pencil at Farthest End
Walks Sideways While Holding on to Furniture
Walks with Help
Stands Alone

Walks Alone
Walks Alone with Good Coordination
Throws Ball
Walks Backward
Walks Up Stairs with Help
Walks Down Stairs with Help

12 Months

Grasps Pencil at Farthest End
Grasps Pencil at Middle
Walks with Help
Stands Alone
Walks Alone
Walks Alone with Good Coordination
Throws Ball
Walks Backward
Walks Sideways
Stands on Right Foot with Help
Walks Up Stairs with Help
Walks Down Stairs with Help

13 Months

Grasps Pencil at Middle
Uses Pads of Fingertips to Grasp Pencil
Uses Hand to Hold Paper in Place
Stands Alone
Walks Alone
Walks Alone with Good Coordination
Throws Ball
Walks Backward
Walks Sideways
Stands on Right Foot with Help
Stands on Left Foot with Help
Walks Up Stairs with Help
Walks Down Stairs with Help

14–16 Months

Grasps Pencil at Middle
Uses Pads of Fingertips to Grasp Pencil
Uses Hand to Hold Paper in Place
Walks Alone with Good Coordination
Throws Ball
Walks Backward
Walks Sideways
Stands on Right Foot with Help
Stands on Left Foot with Help
Runs with Coordination
Jumps off Floor (Both Feet)
Walks Up Stairs with Help
Walks Up Stairs Alone, Placing Both
    Feet on Each Step
Walks Down Stairs with Help

17–19 Months

Grasps Pencil at Middle
Uses Pads of Fingertips to Grasp Pencil
Uses Hand to Hold Paper in Place
Walks Backward
Walks Sideways
Stands on Right Foot with Help
Stands Alone on Right Foot
Stands on Left Foot with Help
Runs with Coordination
Jumps off Floor (Both Feet)
Walks Up Stairs with Help
Walks Up Stairs Alone, Placing Both
    Feet on Each Step
Walks Down Stairs with Help
Walks Down Stairs Alone, Placing Both
    Feet on Each Step
Jumps from Bottom Step

20–22 Months

Grasps Pencil at Middle
Uses Pads of Fingertips to Grasp Pencil
Uses Hand to Hold Paper in Place
Walks Sideways
Stands on Right Foot with Help
Stands Alone on Right Foot
Stands on Left Foot with Help
Stands Alone on Left Foot
Runs with Coordination
Walks Forward on Line
Walks Backward Close to Line
Swings Leg to Kick Ball
Jumps off Floor (Both Feet)
Walks Up Stairs Alone, Placing Both
    Feet on Each Step
Walks Down Stairs Alone, Placing Both
    Feet on Each Step
Jumps from Bottom Step

23–25 Months

Uses Hand to Hold Paper in Place
Grasps Pencil at Nearest End
Manipulates Pencil in Hand
Laces Three Beads
Imitates Hand Movements
Tactilely Discriminates Shapes
Stands Alone on Right Foot
Stands Alone on Left Foot
Jumps off Floor (Both Feet)
Jumps Distance of 4 Inches
Runs with Coordination

Walks Forward on Line
Walks Backward Close to Line
Swings Leg to Kick Ball
Walks on Tiptoe for Four Steps
Walks Up Stairs Alone, Placing Both
    Feet on Each Step
Walks Down Stairs Alone, Placing Both
    Feet on Each Step
Jumps from Bottom Step

26–28 Months

Grasps Pencil at Nearest End
Manipulates Pencil in Hand
Copies Circle
Laces Three Beads
Imitates Hand Movements
Tactilely Discriminates Shapes
Stands Alone on Right Foot
Stands Alone on Left Foot
Jumps off Floor (Both Feet)
Jumps Distance of 4 Inches
Walks Forward on Line
Walks Backward Close to Line
Swings Leg to Kick Ball
Walks on Tiptoe for Four Steps
Walks Up Stairs Alone, Placing Both
    Feet on Each Step
Walks Up Stairs, Alternating Feet
Walks Down Stairs Alone, Placing Both
    Feet on Each Step
Jumps from Bottom Step

29–31 Months

Grasps Pencil at Nearest End
Manipulates Pencil in Hand
Copies Circle
Laces Three Beads
Imitates Hand Movements
Imitates Postures
Tactilely Discriminates Shapes
Buttons One Button
Walks Forward on Line
Walks Backward Close to Line
Swings Leg to Kick Ball
Walks on Tiptoe for Four Steps
Walks on Tiptoe for 9 Feet
Jumps Distance of 4 Inches
Walks Up Stairs, Alternating Feet
Uses Eye-Hand Coordination in Tossing
    Ring
Stops from Full Run

Source: N. Bayley, (1993). *Manual for the Bayley Scales of Infant Development*, 2nd Edition. San Antonio: The Psychological Corporation.

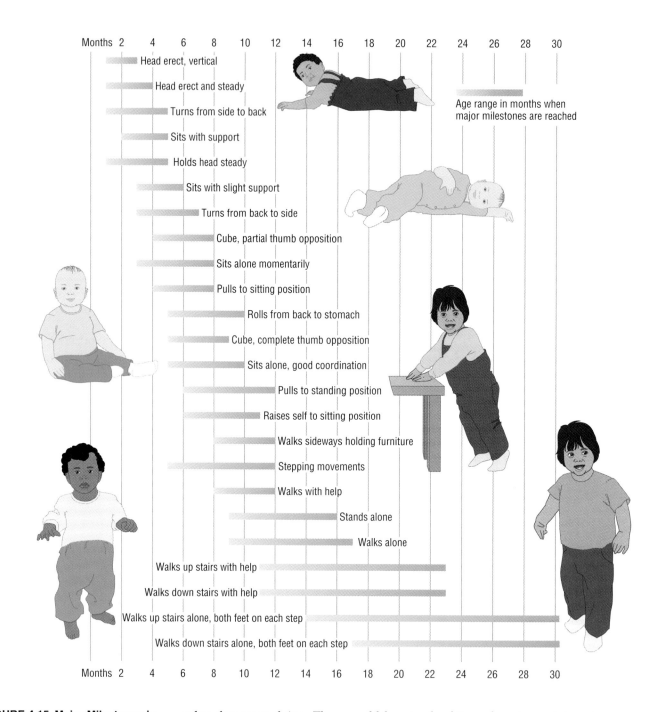

Months 2 4 6 8 10 12 14 16 18 20 22 24 26 28 30

Head erect, vertical
Head erect and steady
Turns from side to back
Sits with support
Holds head steady
Sits with slight support
Turns from back to side
Cube, partial thumb opposition
Sits alone momentarily
Pulls to sitting position
Rolls from back to stomach
Cube, complete thumb opposition
Sits alone, good coordination
Pulls to standing position
Raises self to sitting position
Walks sideways holding furniture
Stepping movements
Walks with help
Stands alone
Walks alone
Walks up stairs with help
Walks down stairs with help
Walks up stairs alone, both feet on each step
Walks down stairs alone, both feet on each step

Months 2 4 6 8 10 12 14 16 18 20 22 24 26 28 30

Age range in months when major milestones are reached

FIGURE 4.15 Major Milestones in Motor Development

flow The experience of becoming totally absorbed in a challenging activity.

what they were doing. They would lose track of time, forget appointments, even forget to eat as their work began to take shape. Once the work was finished, however, their intense interest in it was gone. Their enjoyment came not so much from having a finished product as from the process by which it was created. As Csikszentmihalyi studied others who were good at what they did, he noticed that they described their experiences in much the same way, whether the activity was acting, tennis, or chess—they described the feeling of being carried away by something that took place so smoothly it occurred effortlessly. He called this experience **flow.**

T. G. R. Bower made an interesting observation of something similar in infants, one resembling Csikszentmihalyi's observation concerning *what* it is that makes something enjoyable for adults. Bower (1982) noted that early attempts to demonstrate simple forms of learning in infants frequently ran into difficulty

Infants can experience "flow" when learning to master a difficult task, such as standing up.

because the events used to reinforce the learning soon failed to hold the infants' attention. Paradoxically, the infants often learned difficult tasks, with reinforcement presented according to a complex schedule, better than simple tasks, with reinforcement presented every time the infant responded. He noticed, too, that it mattered little *what* the reinforcement was. A simple flashing light worked just as well as much more elaborate events, such as a jack-in-the-box. What appeared to be most important in holding the infants' attention was not the reinforcement at all, but the schedule by which it occurred.

"What is it about a schedule of reinforcement," Bower asked, "that can be more motivating than a reinforcement itself?" Bower's answer was that the schedule poses a problem, much like a puzzle, and *solving* the problem becomes motivating. In other words, what is enjoyable, to use Csikszentmihalyi's term, is the process of mastery. In this case, mastery involves discovering the pattern to the reinforcement. Once infants master that, they, just like Csikszentmihalyi's artists, lose interest in the task.

Under what conditions, then, might an infant, or an adult, experience flow? Paradoxically, it is not when we are relaxing, but when we are engaged in activities that are difficult enough to stretch our current level of ability—in other words, when we are involved in mastering something new. It makes sense, in that case, to expect to see evidence of flow in infants as they master the challenges of new activities, whether in discovering the pattern to a reinforcement schedule or in mastering the movements involved in crawling.

Louise Erdrich (1996) describes her infant daughter's initial attempts to move about on her own, attempts that, though not actually crawling, would lead to her discovery of this. Erdrich had bought herself time for writing by scattering toys about on the floor, knowing that she would have time to write only until her daughter reached the toy that was furthermost from her, a musical bird:

> This will last fifteen minutes, until she explores the last toy, a musical blue-bird with an orange beak and great black cartoon eyes. She has learned how to prop herself, how to swivel on her stomach, but she can't crawl, not yet. Instead, she lunges. She props herself on her arms and pushes with her knees, lands with a solid thump, pushes up, and throws herself again and again toward the toy. It is a paradigm of something, I think, idly, pausing to study her absolute striving concentration, but what? Turning back to this page, I know. It is what I am doing now. My face is hers. Unyielding eagerness. That is her work, just as this page is my play, just as all this is our life. It is what we do, afraid and avid, full of desire, hurling ourselves again and again toward the musical object. (p. 133) ◄

The intense concentration that Erdrich observed both in her daughter and in herself is characteristic of flow. Csikszentmihalyi refers to this aspect of flow as a *focusing of attention.* Infants, for instance, will simply become oblivious to what is going on around them as they concentrate all their efforts on what they are doing. The match between the skills the infant brings to the task and those that are required for its mastery is also critical for the experience of flow. The disparity must be just great enough to require the infant to "stretch," but not so great as to place mastery beyond the infant's reach. Finally, the nature of the activity itself is also important in determining whether flow will be experienced. Activities that provide continuous *feedback,* so that one can monitor one's performance relative to reaching a goal, are those in which one is most likely to experience flow, activities such as tennis or chess—or crawling, if one is very young (Csikszentmihalyi, 1990).

Csikszentmihalyi points out that as we focus attention on the activity, we lose awareness of ourselves, "becoming" what we are doing, losing ourselves in time. Paradoxically, the mastery that is involved in experiences in which one loses the boundaries of the self also contributes to self-definition.

Mastery and the Self

To experience the self, one must also be aware of that which is *not* part of the self. Robert Kegan (1982) speaks of the way individuals of all ages partition their experience into *subject* and *object,* into that which is "me" and that which is "not-me." I am not suggesting, by this, that young infants have a sense of self. That does not develop until about 1½ years of age. However, I am suggesting that infants begin this elemental partitioning of experience in the very first months of life and that this partitioning enables them to distinguish which of their experiences come from within and which are external to themselves. The alternative, as Kegan puts it, is to be embedded in one's senses, taking these to be what one *is* rather than what one *does,* confusing one's sensory impressions, in other words, with the self that senses.

Differentiating oneself from one's world takes a quantum leap when infants become able to coordinate their movements with the sights and sounds around them, when they can reach out to grasp an interesting toy or creep across a room

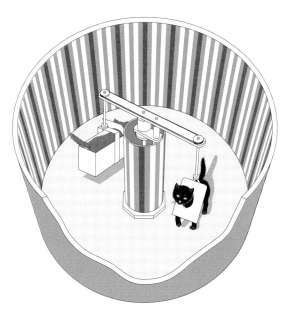

FIGURE 4.16 The Kitten Carousel Used in Held and Hein's Classic Experiment *A demonstration of the importance of active experience to development.*

they could previously only explore with their gaze. Research with laboratory animals points to the importance for understanding one's world of being able to move about in it. In a now-classic study, Richard Held and Alan Hein (1963) raised kittens in total darkness; the kittens' only chance to see anything came when they were placed, two by two, in a "kitten carousel" (Figure 4.16). One kitten was strapped into a harness attached to the end of an elevated arm that swept a circular space. The second kitten was placed in a basket hanging from the other end of the arm. As the first kitten walked, it pulled the other kitten along. Both of the kittens saw exactly the same thing, but only the first was able to coordinate what it was seeing with what it was doing. When placed in a new situation, the kitten that had been able to move about on its own was able to use visual information to position its body with respect to the things it saw. To turn an old phrase, seeing may be believing, but moving makes it real.

The development of voluntary movements, by which infants grasp, manipulate, and explore the objects around them, enables infants to discover not only the objects they are holding in their hands, but things about themselves as well. In making sense of objects "out there," in other words, the infant's sense of self in relation to these objects also changes. Infants' intense focusing on activities at this stage and their obvious enjoyment in exploring the things about them may have as much to do with the pleasures of self-discovery as with mastering the individual movements by which they explore their world. The Research Focus, "Operational Definitions: Anything You Can Do, I Can Do Too," discusses mastery motivation for those with developmental disabilities.

Nutrition and Health

It is said that an army moves on its stomach. The same can be said of development in infancy. Given that infants triple their birthweight within the 1st year and increase in length by half again, the nutritional demands of the 1st year are enormous. Because of the rate at which they grow, infants are almost always hungry, or so it seems to parents, waking every 2 to 4 hours for a feeding.

The best food for meeting infants' needs is breast milk (Hervada & Hervada-Page, 1995; Lawrence, 1994). In fact, breast milk is such a perfect food that infants

Although breast milk is the ideal food for infants, by about 6 months, additional foods can be added to the infant's diet in strained forms.

Operational Definitions: Anything You Can Do, I Can Do Too

Carl stood quietly in the middle of the kitchen floor, looking down at his 2-year-old son, Gil, who was deliberately, and with considerable effort, putting one object after another into a large kitchen drawer that had been cleared for him to use. The 2-year-old surveyed the scattered objects on the floor about him and selected a large wooden spoon from among them. Securing his balance by gripping the drawer handle, the child painstakingly lifted the spoon over the lip of the open drawer and then, with a smile, released his grip, letting the spoon fall with a satisfying clatter to the bottom of the drawer.

The sound brought a smile to Carl's face as well. After experiencing the emotional devastation that followed Gil's diagnosis, he had thought his face might break if he ever smiled again. He had been told that Gil would never be like other kids, that he had a "developmental disability" that would prevent him from developing normally. Well, Carl thought, he might not be able to get around as well as other toddlers or hold on to things as easily, but that didn't stop him from trying just as hard. Once he set his mind to something, that little kid wouldn't give up until he'd mastered it. One thing seemed sure: Gil wasn't a quitter. Carl was proud of his son.

Was Gil unusual in this respect? Did he experience the same motive for mastery as other children his age? Mastery motivation has been assumed to serve as the basis for much of development, stimulating children to explore and rise to challenging situations. But are children with developmental disabilities as motivated to explore and master their environments as children without such disabilities?

Before one can begin to gather answers to questions such as these, an essential step has to be taken. The concepts under consideration (developmental disabilities and mastery motivation) have to be *operationally defined*. Because concepts are, by definition, abstract, there are usually a number of different ways of interpreting them. Operationally defining a concept pins it down by expressing it in terms of the methods used to measure it. Operationalizing is a fundamental process employed in all empirical science. Even a seemingly simple concept like "friendliness," in order to be studied, might be operationally defined in terms of the number of times a child smiles at others or through a questionnaire filled out by a parent. By operationalizing a concept, investigators define it in a way that others can use and follow in order to be sure they are studying the same concept.

But not all operational definitions are equally adequate. Suppose, in studying friendliness, we operationally define a "friendly" child as "any child who is smiling the first time that child is observed." Although that phase does fulfill the minimum requirement for an operational definition—that is, it specifies what operation to perform to determine if a child is friendly (observe the child and see if that child is smiling)—it is not likely to be a satisfactory definition. It is likely to be deficient with respect to the two most important criteria for any measure—*reliability* and *validity*—that is, its consistency and the degree to which it measures what we assume it is measuring.

Penny Hauser-Cram (1996) notes that previous research with children who are *developmentally delayed*, or suffer a mental disability, has found them to have lower levels of mastery motiva-

who are breast-fed need nothing else for the first 6 months, though there is debate as to whether this includes the need for some supplements, such as iron. Even though there is less iron in breast milk than in iron-fortified formulas, nearly 50% of the iron in breast milk is absorbed, compared to only 4% of the iron in fortified formulas (Lawrence, 1994). Since the composition of commercial formulas is closely patterned after that of breast milk, mothers who cannot, or simply choose not to, breast-feed need not be concerned that their infants will not be properly nourished. Infants fed with breast milk or a commercially prepared formula will receive all the nutrients they need. Parents should not feed their infant the milk they drink, however, since it contains little usable iron and almost no vitamins, has too much sodium, and can cause rectal bleeding if consumed as a steady diet (Hervada & Hervada-Page, 1995).

One of the many advantages of breast milk is that it is more easily digested than commercial formulas. As a consequence, breast-fed infants are less likely to suffer gastric discomforts; problems such as diarrhea or constipation are less likely to occur. However, they also get hungry about every 2 hours, in comparison to every 3 to 4 hours for infants who are bottle-fed.

Another advantage to breast milk is the protection that it offers infants against disease. Breast milk contains antibodies that are transferred from mother to infant,

tion. Such research, however, has examined only school-age children, leaving open the question of whether differences in mastery motivation are inherent to this type of disability or develop only with time. Furthermore, previous research has looked exclusively at children who are developmentally delayed, leaving unanswered whether the findings extend to physically disabled children. To examine the first issue, Hauser-Cram examined nondisabled infants and toddlers, comparing them to developmentally disabled children of a comparable mental age. To address the second issue, she included children who were motor-impaired (physical disability) as well as developmentally delayed.

To assess, or operationally define, children who were developmentally delayed, Hauser-Cram administered the Bayley Scales (1969) Mental Development Index (MDI). The MDI contains questions designed to distinguish children in terms of mental development. Children were considered to be developmentally delayed if they were at least one standard deviation below the mean in at least two subtests (see the Research Focus, "Descriptive Statistics," in Chapter 3). Hauser-Cram relied on determinations made by caseworkers to assess motor impairment. To assess mastery motivation, children were given problem-posing toys, such as puzzles, and were scored for such things as their persistence and focus on the task.

Were these measures reliable? One way of determining reliability is to give the measure to the same individuals on two separate occasions, assessing consistency in responding to questions from one time to the next. This method is termed *test-retest reliability*. One of the strengths of the MDI is its reliability, with children obtaining close to the same score when tested at different times. Similarly, reliability for assessments of mastery motivation was determined by having two independent ob-servers score each child's performance. Each observer's scores were compared

to yield a measure of *interobserver reliability*. Thus, rather than comparing a child's performance on two different occasions, the same performance is assessed by two different observers. Using this approach, interobserver reliability for assessments of mastery motivation was found to be high.

Of equal, if not greater, interest is whether a measure is a valid one. One way to determine a measure's validity is to see how well the measure relates to other measures of the construct. This measure of validity is known as *construct validity*. The Bayley Scales have been found to predict mental functioning in other settings, such as classrooms. Since classroom learning is assumed to reflect mental ability, this has been taken as a mea-sure of the construct validity of this test. Similarly, the assessments of motor impairment made by caseworkers were confirmed by compar-isons with children's medical records. One might question whether the measure of mastery motivation that was chosen was as valid as it was reliable. Will children focus on a task as much when being tested by an unfamiliar person with another observer present, and possibly at a time of day when they would rather be doing something else, as when they choose to sit down with a toy and play with it by themselves? Or is involvement with toys even the best measure of such a broad concept? Such questions point to the inherent difficulty in operationally defining concepts. Operational definitions, because they define concepts in terms of a set of specific procedures, are at least in principle reliable. But how well these procedures capture the underlying concept is a more difficult matter.

But back to Gil. Just how representative was this toddler of other developmentally disabled children? Hauser-Cram found that children like Gil, whether motor-impaired or developmentally delayed, did not differ from nondisabled children in measures of mastery motivation when working at tasks of comparable levels of difficulty.

protecting the infant from a number of illnesses and allergies. This advantage is particularly important in nonindustrialized nations in which death rates among infants who are not breast-fed can be up to 5 times higher than those who are (Lawrence, 1994). Even when the mothers themselves are malnourished, the nutri-ents contained in their breast milk do not differ significantly from those in the milk of mothers with an adequate diet. They simply produce less milk (Lawrence, 1994).

Not all mothers choose to breast-feed. For some, it is a matter of preference. Others may experience embarrassment at nursing an infant outside the home or inconvenience at having to pump their own milk into bottles for feedings when they cannot be there, such as during work hours if they are employed outside the home. For mothers who want to breast-feed but experience difficulty doing so, the La Leche League, a national organization devoted to promoting breast-feeding, pro-vides information concerning problems such as these. Other mothers may be unable to breast-feed for medical reasons, such as a disease that could be trans-mitted to the infant through the milk or medication they may be taking that also would reach the infant through their milk. Although breast milk is unquestionably the best food source available to infants, the mother's comfort is also an important consideration. And mothers who choose to bottle-feed can stare with rapt delight into their infant's eyes just as well as do those who choose to breast-feed.

Supplemental Food Programs

Worldwide, approximately 190 million children below the age of 5 suffer from malnutrition (Pollitt et al., 1996). Malnutrition occurs when diets are deficient in protein, calories, or micronutrients. The first of these components, protein, provides amino acids, the body's building blocks, and is essential for growth. Calories provide energy. When diet affords too few calories, the body breaks down amino acids for energy instead of using them to build new cells. Micronutrients include essential vitamins and minerals, such as vitamin A, iodine, iron, and zinc. Deficiencies in these can result in lowered resistance to infection, goiter, anemia, and retarded growth, respectively (Brown & Pollitt, 1996). Since children who are deficient in one of these dietary components are usually deficient in others, the effects of malnutrition can be myriad. Malnourished children not only experience hunger, weight loss, and even stunted growth, but they also feel listless, are less curious, have difficulty paying attention, and get sick more often. Additionally, severe malnutrition in early childhood can impair cognitive functioning and affect later intellectual development, as well as interfere with children's emotional development and the very quality of their most intimate relationships, those they have with their parents (Brown & Pollitt, 1996; Meeks Gardner, Grantham-McGregor, Chang, Himes, & Powell, 1995; Pollitt et al., 1996).

How effective are existing intervention programs at reducing the effects of malnutrition? That depends on the degree of malnutrition, the timing of the intervention, and the presence of other conditions that frequently accompany malnutrition, such as poverty, neglect, poor medical care, and poor schools. The bottom line, however, is that when malnourished children are given supplemental food, the benefits are profound. In one such supplemental feeding program, over 2,000 pregnant women and young children living in each of several villages in Guatemala were given either of two simple nutritional supplements for a period of 8 years. One of the supplements ("atole") was a cereal that is rich in protein, an ingredient believed to be deficient in the diet of many of these children. The other supplement ("fresco") was a fruit drink containing no protein, but an equivalent supply of vita-

mins and minerals. Both supplements also supplied calories, though only a third as many were in the fruit drink as in the cereal.

The protein-rich cereal reduced infant mortality by 69%, and the vitamin supplement by 24%. But beyond saving lives, the supplements had long-term impact on the quality of those lives as well. Ten years later, the effects of the supplemental protein on intellectual ability were still evident, effectively counteracting differences due to income level (see left side of the figure). Dietary supplements also enabled the children to benefit from schooling in a way not possible had they remained malnourished (see right side of the figure).

These effects are not only striking in themselves but also offer the means to counter some of the most crippling effects of poverty in children's lives, even when other conditions remain unchanged. Supplemental food programs, in other words, can mitigate against the cognitive deficits that otherwise go hand in hand with poverty (Brown & Pollitt, 1996; Meeks Gardner et al., 1995; Pollitt, 1994; Pollitt et al., 1996). The importance in terms of social policy of findings such as these cannot be overstated.

In the United States some 12 million children have diets that are significantly deficient in one or more important nutrients. For instance, iron-deficiency anemia, which affects children's psychomotor development and intellectual performance, is one of the most serious of the nutritional deficiencies, affecting approximately 20% of children under 2 years of age (Yip et al., 1992). The United States currently has a number of food assistance programs, authorized under the National School Lunch and Child Nutrition Act Amendments of 1975 (Public Law 94-105). These programs provide food rich in protein, iron, calcium, and vitamins A and C to pregnant women, new mothers, infants, and children; and they provide nutritious snacks and lunches to low-income schoolchildren. Given that one in four infants and toddlers in this nation lives in poverty, such programs remain vitally important (Children's Defense Fund, 1994). Food assistance programs not only provide a better return for each tax dollar spent on education, but they also help to improve the quality of life for millions of children.

By about 6 months, additional foods can be added to the infant's diet in the form of strained cereals, fruits and vegetables, and meats; and by about 1 year of age, most infants have enough teeth to tackle whatever is served to the rest of the family, if it is cut into tiny pieces.

 When speaking of feeding infants, developmentalists talk for the most part about which foods best meet the nutritional needs of infants. And rightly so. However, getting the nutritionally right foods *into* the infant, as opposed to on the walls or in your shoes is quite another thing. As Anne Lamott (1993) writes after feeding her son his newest strained vegetable, "Sam had strained carrots again tonight. Big huge mess, carrots everywhere, all over the kitty who passed by at a bad time,

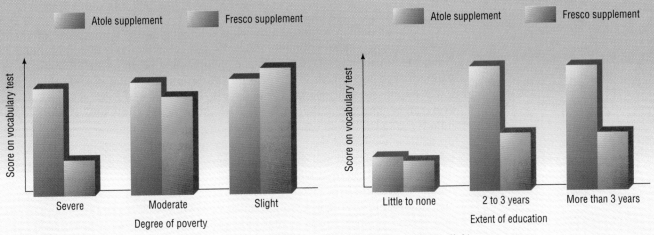

The effects of a supplemental food program on intellectual performance as a function of poverty (left). The effects of education as a function of supplemental food (right). Source: Brown & Pollitt (1996).

Guidelines for Good Nutrition

Food Category	Servings per Day	Serving Size*		
		Age 1 to 3 Years	4 to 6 Years	7 to 10 Years
Whole-grain or enriched breads, cereals, rice, pasta	6 or more	1/2 slice bread or 1/4 cup rice or noodles	1 slice bread or 1/2 cup rice or noodles	1 to 2 slices bread or 1/2 to 1 cup rice or noodles
Vegetables	3 or more	2 to 4 tbsp or 1/2 cup juice	1/4 to 1/2 cup or 1/2 cup juice	1/2 to 3/4 cup or 1/2 cup juice
Fruits	2 or more	2 to 4 tbsp or 1/2 cup juice	1/4 to 1/2 cup or 1/2 cup juice	1/2 to 3/4 cup or 1/2 cup juice
Lean meats, fish, poultry, eggs, nuts, beans	2 or more	1 to 2 oz	1 to 2 oz	2 to 3 oz
Milk and cheese	3 to 4	1/2 to 3/4 cup milk or 1/2 to 3/4 oz cheese	3/4 cup milk or 3/4 oz cheese	3/4 to 1 cup milk or 1/2 to 3/4 oz cheese

*Data from Growth and nutrient requirements of children, by P. M. Queen and R. R. Henry. In *Pediatric Nutrition*, edited by R. J. Grand et al. Butterworth, 1987. *Source:* Brown & Pollitt (1996).

on Sam's socks, in his hair, in my hair. I can see that things are going to begin deteriorating around here rather rapidly" (p. 150). ◄

Malnutrition

Maintaining adequate nutrition during infancy is vitally important, not only for physical growth, but also for intellectual development. Children who do not receive an adequate diet during infancy can suffer a number of consequences, from lethargy and loss of curiosity to physical stunting to impaired cognitive functioning. Recall that not only does the infant add inches and pounds at a rapid rate, but the brain also continues to develop following birth, with spurts of brain growth occurring between 3 and 10 months and again between 15 and 24 months. Adequate nutrition is vital for optimal development. Children who are sufficiently malnourished to have their physical growth stunted usually perform somewhat lower on measures of mental ability as well. Supplemental food programs, however, can be effective in reversing these trends. A recent study of undernourished infants found that those who were placed on a supplemental food program caught up to their well-nourished age-mates after being on the program for a year, at which point they did not differ in measures of mental ability. Another group of undernourished children who had not received supplemental food, however, continued to perform at a lower level than those receiving an adequate diet (Gardner, Grantham-McGregor, Chang, Himes, & Powell, 1995). The potential benefits to a society of such supplemental food programs cannot be overestimated. The cost of providing nutritional supplements is relatively low, certainly when compared to the misery and loss of human potential resulting from malnourishment or the costly corrective measures, such as special education classes, that may be required further down the road. See the Social Policy Focus, "Supplemental Food Programs," for a discussion of the effectiveness of these programs.

 Summary

The Newborn

Birth requires adjustments in breathing, regulating temperature, eating, and sleeping. Breathing is usually irregular for the first 2 or 3 days. Most neonates cough and sneeze frequently, which helps to clear passages of mucus and fluids. Keeping warm can also be problematic in that newborns lack the protective layer of fat that insulates older infants from rapid changes in temperature. Since several days lapse before infants begin to take nourishment in the form of breast milk or formula, most also lose several ounces immediately following birth.

States of Arousal

Most infants establish a stable circadian rhythm between 2 and 4 months of age, in which they sleep for longer periods of time than they did initially. Prior to this time, they are on a 4-hour sleep-wake cycle. Both sleeping and waking are characterized by quiet and active states. In quiet sleep the body is relaxed, eyelids are closed, and the eyes are motionless. In active sleep, body movements, facial expressions, and rapid eye movements occur. Similar distinctions between states of wakefulness can be made. In drowsiness, the body is relaxed, but the eyes are open. In quiet wakefulness, the infant is relaxed and attentive, and in active wakefulness, the infant is physically and mentally active.

Physical Growth

Growth in the 1st year is rapid; weight triples and body length increases by half again. Growth is less rapid in the 2nd year, with infants adding another 5 pounds and growing 5 inches. Growth reflects two trends: the cephalocaudal trend in which growth begins in the region of the head and proceeds downward, and the proximodistal trend in which growth progresses outward from the center of the body to the extremities. Physical growth includes increases in body fat and muscle tissue as well as bone growth. The latter involves both the growth of existing bones and the emergence of new bones.

As infants move about, they put stress on the skeletal system, which causes the bones to realign. This realignment results in the familiar curvatures in the upper and lower regions of the spine and realignment of the leg bones and the pelvis as well as of the bones forming the rib cage. Nutrition plays an important role in all aspects of skeletal growth.

Brain Development

The brain continues to develop following birth. Development proceeds unevenly, with spurts of brain growth occurring between 3 and 10 months and 15 and 24 months. This growth is due largely to the proliferation of glial cells, which both nourish the neurons and produce myelin, the substance that coats the axons of neurons, thereby facilitating the conduction of neural impulses. Myelination progresses at different rates for different parts of the brain. The peripheral nervous system is first to be myelinated; among the last is the frontal cortex. Early experience also contributes to brain development, being necessary for the establishment of neural connections and for the maintenance of already-established ones.

Development of the Senses

Newborns have a well-developed sense of taste; they are able to distinguish sweet, salty, sour, and bitter substances. Their sense of smell is also highly developed. Vision, however, is the least developed of the senses at birth, maturing within the 1st year. Newborns actively scan a visual surround. These scanning patterns change markedly with age, paralleling development of the visual system. Visual acuity and distance perception also develop significantly within the first 6 months.

In comparison to vision, hearing is relatively well developed at birth. For most newborns, sounds need only be twice as loud to be heard as they need to be for an adult, whereas objects need to be 20 times as close to be seen. Infants also get better with age at localizing where sounds are coming from. Even newborns react differently to speech sounds than to nonspeech sounds, the former being processed in a qualitatively different way than the latter.

The senses can be thought of as ways of exploring and making sense of one's surround. It is suggested that anticipatory schemata guide this process, directing the pickup of information and in turn being modified by what is perceived. This information need not be tied to a particular sensory modality. Rather than functioning as separate and isolated systems, the activity of one sensory system has been shown to contribute to the ability to sense things in a different modality.

Motor Development

Both physical growth and brain development enable infants to develop new control over their bodies. Prior to the development of this control, much of their behavior is reflexive. These reflexes are highly adaptive, such as the sucking, rooting, head turning, and grasp reflexes. In addition to their adaptive value, reflexes are useful diagnostically, since reflexive behavior changes with age, and many reflexes drop out as the central nervous system matures.

Myelination of fibers within the motor cortex makes possible the emergence of new, voluntary behaviors. The primary motor cortex is responsible for governing the activity of discrete muscles within the body; the secondary motor cortex is responsible for patterned movements, in which the activity of discrete muscles is coordinated. Control over muscles in different parts of the body progresses unevenly, illustrating the cephalocaudal trend. Considerable variability also exists from one infant to the next. All infants, however, appear to experience pleasure at the mastery of new skills. The process of mastering motor skills embodies many of the same characteristics as do the activities that produce the experience of flow in adults.

The development of voluntary movements, by which infants grasp, manipulate, and explore the objects around them, enables infants to discover not only the objects they are manipulating, but things about themselves as well.

Nutrition and Health

The best food for meeting the nutritional needs of infants is breast milk. Infants who are breast-fed need nothing else for the first 6 months, with the possible exception of some supplements, such as iron. Since the composition of commercial formulas is closely patterned after that of breast milk, infants who are bottle-fed will similarly receive all the nutrients they need from the formula; however, they will not receive the antibodies contained in breast milk that protect infants from many illnesses and allergies. By about 6 months, additional foods can be added to the infant's diet in the form of strained cereals, fruits and vegetables, and meats.

Maintaining adequate nutrition during infancy is important not only for physical growth but also for intellectual development. Malnutrition can result in physical stunting and impaired cognitive functioning. Supplemental food programs, however, have been found effective in reversing both of these trends.

 Key Terms

active sleep (p. 133)
active wakefulness (p. 133)
afferent, or sensory, pathway (p. 151)
axon (p. 141)
brain stem (p. 151)
central nervous system (p. 141)
cephalocaudal growth trend (p. 136)
cerebellum (p. 154)
drowsiness (p. 133)
efferent, or motor, pathway (p. 151)

epiphyseal growth plates (p. 139)
flow (p. 158)
fontanels (p. 139)
glial cells (p. 140)
grasp reflex (p. 152)
Moro reflex (p. 152)
myelin (p. 141)
neurons (p. 140)
peripheral nervous system (p. 141)
primary motor cortex (p. 153)

proximodistal growth trend (p. 137)
quiet sleep (p. 133)
quiet wakefulness (p. 133)
rapid eye movements (REM) (p. 133)
rooting reflex (p. 151)
"rules" for scanning (p. 144)
secondary motor cortex (p. 154)
sucking reflex (p. 151)
visual acuity (p. 145)

chapter**five**

Infancy and Toddlerhood
Cognitive Development

L isten, Paula. I am going to tell you a story, so that when you wake up you will not feel so lost." Thus, Isabel Allende, a master at storytelling, begins a narrative for her seriously ill daughter, one intended to anchor her firmly in this world. Infants, too, are told stories, by all of us. And with each story, they are tied ever more securely to their surroundings. However, these stories are rarely in words. Instead, they take other forms—of faces moving to the rhythm of language, or mobiles spinning when touched, of shadows and light, and footsteps and fingers, and the dazzling complexity of the ordinary. For infants, you see, discover through the narrative of experience what we, as adults, no longer notice. They discover the way a door appears to change as it opens, morphing from rectangle to trapezoid, yet all the while remaining a door. Or the sameness of color as light and shadow move across surfaces. They discover the way things reappear, momentarily obscured from view, such as a hand at the end of a sleeve or a toy beneath a blanket. These daily narratives fix infants in a stable world of increasing predictability, one that invites, and yields to, their exploration.

Perceiving and Making Sense of the World

Infants are curious about their surroundings and begin to explore them from their first moments on. While still in the delivery room, infants will turn their heads in the direction of a sound, look intently at a face, and attend to the sounds of the human voice. With age, infants get increasingly better at perceiving the things around them, becoming more efficient at locating objects, following things that move with their eyes, and grasping onto what they reach for.

Getting better at the things we do is something many of us take for granted. But how is this accomplished? As you might expect, numerous explanations have been offered. Just as we saw in Chapter 1, these can be grouped as to whether they emphasize conditions that are external to the individual as primarily responsible for the changes (an environmental perspective) or whether they stress inborn processes through which individuals organize experience (an organismic or constructive perspective). Each perspective acknowledges the importance of both environmental and inner processes, but they differ in the emphasis they give to either of these in explaining developmental change.

Consider the seemingly simple activity of locating where an interesting event is likely to appear next. Marshall Haith and his associates (1993) showed 3-month-old infants pictures that sometimes appeared to the left of them and sometimes to the right. For some of the infants, the location of the pictures alternated in a predictable sequence (left, right, left, etc.), whereas for others, the sequence was unpredictable. Unlike infants for whom the pictures appeared randomly, those shown the alternating sequence quickly learned where to look for the next picture. Clearly, infants who were given a predictable sequence had gotten better at knowing where to look. But what precisely accounted for their improvement?

With age, infants get better at locating and looking at things around them.

operant conditioning A simple form of learning in which the probability of a behavior is affected by its consequences.

The Environmental Perspective: Looking Outside the Organism

Those adopting an environmental perspective would argue that the infants had learned to turn left, then right, and so on; and in each case their looking had been rewarded by actually seeing the picture when they turned their head in that direction. This type of learning, known as **operant conditioning,** accounts for changes in behavior as a result of the events that follow a behavior (see Chapter 1). An event that, when it is made contingent on behavior, increases the frequency of that behavior, is termed **reinforcement.** The behavior which is reinforced is known as an *operant*. Thus the operant in this instance would be turning to the left or right, and the reinforcement would be seeing the picture.

The Constructive Perspective: Looking Within the Organism

Ulric Neisser (1976), a psychologist at Cornell University, suggests that what is changed is not so much the behavior of looking to the left or the right as what guides the behavior. Neisser traces the infants' improvement to the development of anticipatory schemata (see Chapter 4). These are cognitive structures that prepare us to take in certain types of information and not others. Anticipatory schemata direct the way we explore things, determining the features that are sampled and guiding the pickup of information. The schemata are in turn modified and refined by the information that is picked up. This perceptual process takes the form of an ongoing activity in which what is anticipated directs the way new objects and events will be explored, with the outcome modifying and refining one's initial expectations. These tie one ever more closely to the events one is monitoring.

Neisser points out that infants come into the world with considerable "perceptual equipment." We have seen evidence of such equipment, in the last chapter, such as infants' rules for scanning in dark versus well-lit rooms. Other equipment exists in the form of their ability to visually track moving objects, reflexively reach out toward things they see, or grasp those that are placed in their hands. Even though this basic perceptual equipment does not provide infants with all they will need to know about their surroundings, it is enough to show them how to find what they need to know (Neisser, 1976). Anticipatory schemata can be thought of as plans for perceptual activity, plans that guide the constructive process by which we make sense of experience. As Haith (1993) has commented, infants don't just look at things. Instead they are analyzing what they see and creating little hypotheses as they do. But where might these hypotheses, or plans, come from?

Piaget's Developmental Constructivism

A central issue for Jean Piaget, one that gave shape to his theory of intellectual development, concerned this very question, "How do we come to know what we know?" Paiget believed that our understanding of the world begins with the development of sensorimotor schemas that are rooted in, and evolve out of, the basic reflexes that are present at birth. Piaget traced intellectual development over four stages. The first, the **sensorimotor stage,** lasts from birth to the age of 2, and is the stage that concerns us in this chapter. Like the reflexes from which they evolve, sensorimotor schemas are assumed initially to be activated only when something is actually present. With age, these become modified, spanning time to "hold" a thing in mind, whether it is there or not. For Piaget, this ability represents one of the most important cognitive achievements of infancy, the capacity to represent experience in one's mind. Before this, the infants' world is one of the here and now, a world that coincides with what they can see, hear, or touch. Only with age will they reach for things hidden from sight or be stilled by the sound of familiar footsteps. With age, also, they begin to relate to things in new and more intentional ways, at first doing so only with their hands, but eventually mentally

reinforcement An event that, when it is made contingent on behavior, increases the frequency of that behavior.

sensorimotor stage Piaget's first stage of intellectual development, during which sensory experiences are coordinated with motor behaviors.

TABLE 5.1 Stages of Sensorimotor Development in Infants and Toddlers

Stage	Approximate Age	Characteristic Behaviors
Substage 1: Reflex modification	Birth to 1 month	Repeats reflexive behaviors, such as sucking, and becomes able to perform them efficiently
Substage 2: Primary circular reactions	1 to 4 months	Intentionally repeats actions for their own sake, such as opening and closing hands, touching them together, or making bubbles
Substage 3: Secondary circular reactions	4 to 8 months	Repeats actions directed at objects in the environment, such as kicking a crib mobile or shaking a rattle, and observes what happens
Substage 4: Coordination of secondary circular reactions	8 to 12 months	Acts for a purpose, such as crawling across room to get a desired toy, or pushing aside an obstacle, such as an adult's hand, to reach a toy
Substage 5: Tertiary circular reactions	12 to 18 months	Experiments with objects, feeling their texture, watching what happens when they are dropped or pushed; begins to use trial and error to solve problems; begins mimicking adult behaviors
Substage 6: Mental representation	18 to 24 months	Engages in make-believe play; looks at pictures in books; can point to named body part

as well, manipulating images of things that previously yielded only to their touch. Piaget distinguished six substages to this development; these are described below and summarized in Table 5.1.

Substage 1: Modification of Basic Reflexes (Birth to 1 Month)

The reflexes that infants are born with, such as rooting, sucking, and grasping, initially occur only when triggered by specific stimuli. Thus, touching the infant's cheek will trigger the rooting reflex, causing the infant to turn its head. Similarly, brushing the infant's lips will cause the infant to suck, and stroking the palm of its hand will cause it to reflexively close its fingers in a tight grasp. These reflexes soon become modified in two ways. First, they become altered, in seemingly small but nonetheless important ways, such that they provide a better fit with the conditions imposed by the immediate situation. Second, they begin to occur in the absence of the stimuli that initially had triggered them.

Consider the reflex of sucking. In the first few days of life, the infant will purse its lips and position its tongue in much the same way when it nurses, irrespective of how its head is positioned with respect to the nipple or even to differences in the shape of the nipple itself. As you might expect, the same way of sucking will not work equally well under different circumstances, and only those modifications of the reflex that produce enough suction will result in an even flow of milk. Infants soon adjust, or *accommodate,* their sucking in order to adapt to the conditions of the situations in which it is evoked.

These basic reflexes function in ways similar to Neisser's anticipatory schemata. Thus, sucking can be thought of as a biological blueprint, or plan, for drawing fluid into one's mouth. These plans are modified on an ongoing basis, involving the organism in a dynamic interaction with the environment. Thus, the infant's experience of the activity that is being guided by the schema provides information that in turn serves to modify the original schema, bringing it more closely into alignment with the requirements of the immediate situation. The way the infant initially positions its lips and places its tongue to create the pressure necessary to draw in milk is adjusted as it experiences that more or less pressure (and more or less milk) results from positioning its tongue one way or another relative to the nipple.

One soon notices a second modification. The infant can be seen to suck to the *sight* of the nipple as well as to the touch of the nipple on its lips. Similarly, other events that regularly accompany nursing, such as being held in a certain position or the sound of a bottle being prepared, will occasion sucking before the nipple touches its lips. We saw this type of modification in the discussion of classical conditioning (Chapter 1), in which reflexes were seen to occur in response to an event that predicts the arrival of the triggering stimulus. In the earlier example, dogs salivated to the sounds (CS) that preceded the arrival of food (UCS). Here, we see the infant sucking to cues, whether these are the sight of the nipple or being held in a certain position, that precede nursing. This second modification illustrates the process of *assimilation,* in which the infant incorporates new elements, such as the sight of the nipple, into an existing schema, a reflex that was originally triggered only by the touch of the nipple.

Substage 2: Primary Circular Reactions (1 to 4 Months)

In the second substage, basic reflexes are further modified, evolving into **schemas,** or action patterns, that become divorced from the stimuli that initially triggered them. This development enables the behavior to occur in new situations and to be repeated without subsequent stimulation. Infants, in other words, become able to prolong an interesting event by repeating the behavior that brought it about. The activity by which they do this takes a cyclic form, in that the completion of the behavior serves to trigger its repetition. Note, it is now the behavior itself, rather than the onset of a stimulus, that governs its occurrence. Piaget referred to these behaviors as **primary circular reactions,** primary in that they are limited to actions that involve the infant's own body and circular in that the behavior is prompted by its own completion. Thus, an infant can be seen to purse its lips as it does when sucking, but without a nipple in its mouth. When bubbles form, as they do, the infant will blow new ones as the first ones pop. Similarly, an infant may kick, enjoying the way this causes its body to wiggle, and then, once the movement stops, kick again.

Substage 3: Secondary Circular Reactions (4 to 8 Months)

In the third substage, circular reactions are extended to include objects outside the infant's body and are termed **secondary circular reactions.** Thus, an infant lying on its back with a mobile overhead might kick, and then notice the mobile moving, and kick again. Or an infant given a rattle might wave its arms, hear the sound, and then delightedly wave them again, producing the sound again. Recall that infants at this age can sit up with support and look around and are much

schemas Piaget's term for the mental structures through which the child represents experience through actions.

primary circular reactions Substage 2 of Piaget's sensorimotor stage in which infants (1–4 months) repeat a physical behavior involving their own body.

secondary circular reactions Substage 3 of Piaget's sensorimotor stage in which infants (4–8 months) repeat behaviors affecting objects outside their body.

This child is showing purposeful exploration, an indication that he has reached Piaget's fourth substage.

During which substage of the sensorimoter period outlined by Piaget might an infant begin to delight in bathtime activities?

better at focusing on things that interest them. Their interest in the sights and sounds around them increases dramatically, and they incorporate these into their action schemas. In doing so, they become better at differentiating themselves from the things about them. For example, moving one's arms without the rattle in one's hand does not produce any interesting sounds. Piaget also believed infants first become able to imitate the actions of others at this stage, although only if this involves actions they are already capable of performing.

Substage 4: Coordination of Secondary Circular Reactions (8 to 12 Months)

Actions can be seen to become more coordinated and complex and also to reveal an intentional, goal-directed quality in the fourth substage. Piaget assumed that infants are first able to coordinate previously isolated actions into a single purposeful activity in this substage. Infants are interested in discovering all they can about the objects around them. Unlike the earlier circular reactions of the second and third substages, both of which were prompted by the accidental occurrence of an interesting event, behavior at this stage shows purposeful exploration. No longer content simply to look at something, infants pick things up, drop them, grasp them again and squeeze them, before putting them into their mouths for a final inspection. Through actions such as these, infants learn which things break, which bounce, and which quietly spill out their contents. They pursue these investigations with the determination of little scientists. As Anne Lamott (1993) writes of her son,

> He's heavily into flinging things. He dismantles everything he can get his hands on. . . . It's gratuitous looting. He almost never actually takes anything and crawls away with it, but he'll get to the coffee table and system-

atically, often without any expression, lift and then drop or fling every single magazine, book, cup, or whatever to the ground. His grim expression suggests he's got a lot to do and just really doesn't want to be bothered until he's done. (p. 219) ◄

By such activity, Piaget would observe, infants are learning what they need to know about the world they live in.

How would Piaget explain why infants repeatedly drop things from their high chair?

Substage 5: Tertiary Circular Reactions (12 to 18 Months)

Whereas infants in the fourth substage directed their attention to the objects around them, in the fifth substage they become fascinated with the effects of their own actions. Piaget places the beginnings of problem solving at this substage. Infants are no longer content simply to repeat a behavior that produces some interesting event; they now vary this, experimenting with all the different ways they can accomplish something. **Tertiary circular reactions** are the action schemas by which they explore new ways of acting on things. Unlike primary circular reactions in which the focus of interest is simply the activity, or secondary reactions in which focus shifts to the object, in tertiary reactions, infants focus on the relationship between their actions and the objects they are exploring, between what they are doing and the effects this has on things. The child who has noticed that a pea will bounce over the edge if she hits her high-chair tray with her hand may try to do the same by banging her cup against the tray, or her plate, looking to see with each attempt if something pops over the edge.

Substage 6: Mental Representation (18 to 24 months)

The sensorimotor period ends with the sixth substage, since Piaget believed the emerging ability to represent experiences mentally moves the child into the preoperational stage, the second of his four stages of development. Up to this point, the child's interactions with the world have been prompted by what it can see or touch, by what is actually present. But with the ability to mentally represent objects, children can think of things that are not present, thus opening up a world of imagination and fantasy. This ability is made possible by the development of *symbols*, internalized images of objects. With the ability to imagine, or anticipate, some outcome of an action, exploration is no longer a matter of trial and error, of "let's see what will happen next," but can be guided by the expected outcomes of different actions, and thought becomes symbolic and conceptual.

Object Permanence

Piaget assumed that infants only gradually become able to hold things in mind when these are not present and that it takes them 2 years to develop a full understanding of the nature of objects. Boldly put, he assumed that, initially, objects simply cease to exist for infants when they are out of sight. Piaget traced infants' understanding of objects over a series of six stages that correspond roughly to the substages of sensorimotor thought, with the last being reached only as infancy ends. Piaget developed his assumptions about infants' understanding of their world by noting their reactions to the disappearance of their toys. Many a parent has similarly observed changes in the way infants react to objects disappearing from view. For instance, Anne Lamott (1993) writes of her infant son's reactions to dropping a toy:

tertiary circular reactions
Substage 5 of Piaget's sensorimotor stage in which infants (12–18 months) begin to experiment with different ways of accomplishing something; the beginning of problem solving.

During the first 2 years, children gradually acquire an understanding of object permanence (which is why peekaboo is fun for them).

Enjoying a game of peek-a-boo is a sign of what kind of development in young infants?

He's figuring out little concepts all the time these days, like that if something falls out of his hands, it is not instantly vaporized but just might be found somewhere on the floor. Even a week ago Sam was like some rich guy who drops some change and doesn't even give it a second glance, but now when he drops something, he slowly cranes his neck and peers downward, as if the thing fell to the floor of a canyon. (p. 187) ◄

Piaget observed that in the first stage of the development of object permanence (birth to 2 months), infants show no reaction when something they have been following with their eyes disappears from view. They neither look for it nor reach after it. In the second stage (2 to 4 months), infants will follow something with their eyes as it moves out of sight, but do so in peculiar ways. For instance, they will continue to track an object even after it has stopped moving. By the third stage (4 to 6 months), these tracking errors disappear. Infants also begin to reach for things, such as toys, that are only partially visible. However, they will stop in midreach if a toy is completely covered from view before they contact it. Even after grasping hold of the toy, if their hand is covered before they pull the toy out, they can be seen to look idly about, eventually pulling back an empty hand. Nor do they appear to be surprised if the hidden object is spirited away, revealing nothing there when the cover is removed. All of these reactions suggested to Piaget that objects cease to exist for infants when perceptual contact with them is lost.

In the fourth stage (6 to 12 months), infants will retrieve objects that are completely hidden from view. However, they make "place errors," looking for things where they have been found previously even when they have just seen them moved somewhere else. Unlike infants a few months younger, they show surprise when an object hidden under a cover is not there when the cover is removed, and another object has taken its place. However, they will still play with the new toy rather than looking for the first. In the fifth stage (12 to 18 months), they continue to look for the first object. They also no longer make place errors, looking for things where they last saw them. However, one last confusion remains. They have difficulty understanding that something can be moved while out of sight. If, for example, you were to show them a ball in your hand, then hide it with a fist, place your fist behind your back and transfer the ball to the other hand, and show them your empty hand, they would not think to look in the other hand. This inability to imagine movements that cannot be seen, what Piaget referred to as errors of "invisible displacement," is overcome in the sixth stage of object permanence (Piaget, 1954).

Critique of Piaget's Theory

Piaget has given us a remarkably detailed record of infants' developing abilities over the first 2 years of life, one that rings true to those familiar with infants. As a consequence, critics of his theory are less likely to take issue with the behaviors that he documented than they are to quarrel with the assumptions he based these on. For Piaget assumed, despite the significant changes that he chronicled over these years, that infants were not capable of thinking until they were approximately 2 years old. He believed not only that they lacked concepts for things, but also that, for the first half of the sensorimotor period, they did not even perceive their world as made up of three-dimensional objects. Piaget also assumed that infants had no way of bringing previously experienced events to mind or of imagining future ones. In fact, until the achievements of the sensorimotor period were completed, he believed that infants had no way of symbolically representing their world, or even had a world to represent. Why would Piaget think this?

Piaget assumed that our experience of the world is filtered through our actions on and reactions to the things around us. For the infant, these first actions take the form of reflexes, each triggered by a particular stimulus, the way a touch to the lips triggers sucking or movement in the visual field triggers tracking. Furthermore, like most of his contemporaries, Piaget believed that stimulation was specific to each sensory modality and that, as a consequence, the actions prompted by different stimuli provided information about only that one modality. Thus, one of the first things an infant had to accomplish was to integrate the different components of sensory information into a unitary percept. Only then could the infant experience a world of objects that moved and made sounds and were solid to the touch. Much of the first half of the sensorimotor period was assumed to be devoted to the construction of schemas that integrated information from the separate senses. Until this perceptual integration was achieved, objects as such could not exist for the infant nor, of course, could they be conceptualized (Piaget, 1952, 1954).

Thus, according to Piaget, an infant looking at a toy bear beating a drum would not connect the *movements* of the bear with the *sounds* of the drum. Before that connection could be made, the infant had to coordinate the various sensations arriving at the eyes, ears, and fingertips. Until then, the world was experienced as fleeting images and disconnected sounds. Piaget believed infants accomplished this integration through the development of schemas, action patterns that had become freed from the modality-specific stimuli that triggered reflexes, thus becoming available to coordinate information received from several or more senses. This integration of sensory input became one of the major accomplishments of the first year (Mandler, 1990, 1992). (The Research Focus: "Cross-Sectional Design—Slices Through Time: Visual Scanning," describes how scanning works and the way it changes from ages 6 to 13 weeks.)

Are the senses initially unconnected, and do they need to be integrated through the types of experiences Piaget has documented in the six substages of sensorimotor thought? Or do infants recognize much earlier than this that the various sights and sounds and feel of things are aspects of a single object? Can infants recognize something by sight, for instance, that they have only had a chance to feel, using information provided by one modality to recognize something they have experienced only in another? There is considerable evidence, in fact, that they

Cross-Sectional and Sequential Designs— Slices Through Time: Visual Scanning BY MICHAEL WAPNER

Look around—at your hand, at a chair, at someone near you. As you fix your gaze on that object, you see it totally and immediately. In other words, the object does not "resolve" into view like those scenes in movies that begin out of focus and gradually become clear. Nor do you experience a bunch of isolated features assembling themselves into an object—first a patch of color, then a corner, and then an edge. Whatever object you see, you see "all at once." And yet, although you are not conscious of it, seeing an object does take time.

To be seen in its detailed entirety, an object must be *scanned.* Scanning involves movement of the eyes back and forth across the relevant portion of the visual field. The scanning movement consists of two parts—(1) brief fixations where the eye rests on some portion of the visual field and (2) intervening movements, or *saccades,* which carry the eye from one fixation point to another. Information collected by scanning must be integrated. What is seen at any given moment does not come from any single fixation, but from the integration of successive fixations— just as what is seen at any given moment on a movie screen does not correspond to any single film frame, but results from the integration of successive frames. To accomplish this integration, visual information must be circulated through various brain structures where it is collected and organized. Information from other sensory modalities (hearing, smell, touch, and the rest) and from past experience also aid in this process. What you finally see is the product of these scanning and integrative *processes.* This is what it means to say that visual perception is *constructed.*

The way we scan is not random. We do not move our eyes here and there unsystematically. Fixations must take in relevant parts of the visual field. And, especially where the environment is changing, fixations must occur in appropriate order. Depending on how well the eye is guided in its pattern of fixations and movements, it will gather more or less relevant information more or less rapidly. Because visual scanning can be more or less accurate, more or less efficient, it is a skill. And, as you might expect, this skill improves over time, with practice and maturation.

Gordon Bronson, of Mills College, undertook to assess the improvement in visual scanning by infants over different stages of development. As infants of different ages scanned simple geometric figures, their eye movements were monitored by a video camera. A computer, connected to the camera, matched location

on the figure with eye position and recorded the location, duration, and pattern of fixations. The procedure was quite complex, both because of its advanced technology and because 6- to 13-week-old infants are not much impressed with the requirements of scientific research.

Bronson chose three different age groups of infants to study—6 weeks old, 10 weeks old, and 13 weeks old. Although the 7-week age difference between the youngest and oldest groups is short, it is a time of rapid change within an infant's visual system (Bronson, 1994).

Subjects who are of the same chronological age are said to belong to the same *cohort.* Thus, in Bronson's study, 6-week-old infants constituted one cohort, 10-week-old infants another cohort, and so on. His decision to compare different cohorts made Bronson's research design *cross-sectional.* Cross-sectional research seeks to determine how a phenomenon changes over time by comparing different cohorts at a single point in time. An advantage that cross-sectional research has over longitudinal methods (see the Research Focus, "Longitudinal Designs," in Chapter 13) is that because it can be done at one time, one need not wait around while individuals grow older. However, there may also be drawbacks.

In Bronson's study, cohorts differed only by weeks, but in many studies cohorts differ by several or more years. The greater the time separating cohorts, the more likely it is that a cross-sectional approach will confront a particular difficulty. Not all differences between cohorts are attributable to age. Subjects who differ in age may also differ in other ways. Suppose, for instance, that a study is interested in whether political attitudes change with age. Suppose further that the attitudes of an adolescent cohort are compared with those of an adult cohort, a frequently used cross-sectional research strategy. We may well find that political attitudes differ between these cohorts. But we might be seriously mistaken in attributing these differences to age. They may have more to do with the social-historical context in which the members of a cohort reached a certain age than with age itself. For instance, adolescents today live in relatively plentiful times, and most grow up in urban or suburban settings. Adolescents born in 1930 grew up in the shadow of the Depression and were more likely to live in rural areas. Such *cohort differences* would likely be reflected in measures of political attitude and mistakenly attributed to age. Thus, in contrast to *longitudinal research,* which risks confounding age with times of measurement, cross-sectional research risks confusing age with cohort differences.

Is there a way around this difficulty in cross-sectional designs that also avoids the problems of longitudinal designs? A research technique called *sequential design,* which combines cross-sectional and longitudinal approaches, provides one solution. This technique tests several different cohort groups at several different times. In a way, the sequential design is a number of longitudinal studies, each starting with a different age group, as shown in the figure. By looking at the blocks that form the diagonals in the figure, we can compare 5-year-olds with 10-year-olds and 15-year-olds. The means for each of those diagonals will reflect age differences as well as cohort differences and time of measurement differences.

By taking an average of the scores for the blocks in the top row, we get a mean for the 1980 cohort. By averaging the scores for the blocks in the middle row, we get a mean for the 1985 cohort. And by averaging the scores for the blocks in the bottom row, we get a mean for the 1990 cohort. Differences among these three means provide an estimate of the amount of variability that is contributed by cohorts.

We can also estimate the effect of time of measurement. We can compare performance measured in 1990 (the blocks in the second column), for example, with performance measured in 2000 (the blocks in the fourth column). Thus, by using appro-priate statistical techniques, we can isolate cohort and time of measurement effects and subtract these out; differences that remain reflect age changes.

To return to Bronson, when adults view figures similar to those presented to the infants, they show a characteristic pattern of scanning—long strings of brief fixations (0.3 to 0.6 seconds). On the other hand, the scanning patterns of 6-week-old infants consist of much longer fixations—some well over a second. Bronson found that the older the cohort, the greater the percentage of brief, adult-like fixations. Thus at 6 weeks the infants averaged only 27% brief fixations; at 10 weeks the average was 41%, and at 13 weeks the average was 87%. Further, even when brief fixations did occur in the younger cohorts, they tended to occur singly, between the longer, infantile fixations. The older the cohort, the more prevalent were long sequences of brief fixations. Thus, for the 6-week group only 6% of the brief fixations occurred in long strings, while by 13 weeks almost all did. Clearly then, visual scanning does change with age. And it would seem that given the small age differences between cohorts in the Bronson study and the nature of the phenomenon studied, there was little danger of cohort effects. But exercise your imagination anyway. Can you suggest some possible cohort effects that might have influenced Bronson's results? Think mobiles. Think wallpaper. Think siblings. Think HMOs.

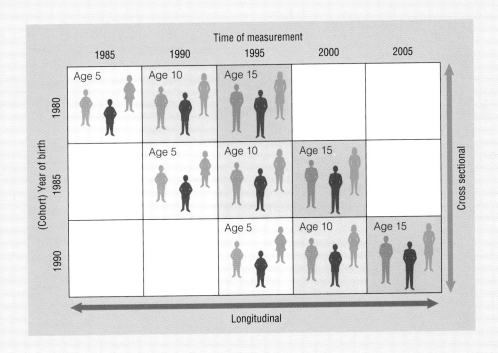

FIGURE 5.1 Pacifiers Used in Melt-zoff and Borton's Study *Infants who had been given the bumpy pacifier (on the left) spent more time looking at it than at the smooth pacifier (on the right) when both pacifiers were presented for visual inspection. The reverse was true for infants who had been given the smooth pacifier. Looking longer at the pacifier they had explored in their mouth than at the one they had not tactually explored demonstrates that infants can recognize something by sight that they have previously experienced only by touch.* Source: A. N. Meltzoff and R. W. Borton, (1979, November). Intermodel matching by human neonates. *Nature,* Vol. 282, p. 403.

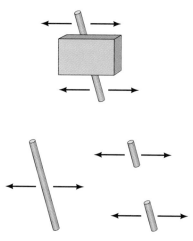

FIGURE 5.2 *Habituation display (top) and test displays from an experiment on perception of partly hidden objects.* Source: From Elizabeth S. Spelke, Perceptual development in infancy: the Minnesota symposium on child psychology, Vol. 20, p. 200.

habituation Decreased responsiveness to a stimulus with repeated exposure to it.

can. In one early demonstration of this, Andrew Meltzoff and Richard Borton (1979) gave 1-month-old infants one of two kinds of pacifiers to suck on, either a smooth one or a bumpy one. When the pacifier they had been sucking on was removed from the infants' mouths and shown to them along with the other one, infants were able to visually identify the pacifier they had only felt in their mouths but never seen (Figure 5.1).

How, you might ask, could these investigators be sure that the infants had indeed recognized the pacifier that had been in their mouths? Infants, you may recall, are curious and will spend more time looking at something that is novel, or unexpected, than at something that is familiar. Meltzoff and Borton's infants stared longer at the pacifier that had *not* been in their mouths, the one with which they were not familiar. In a comparable study, 4- and 5-month-old infants were allowed to play with two rings, one in each hand, that were connected either by a rigid bar or an elastic band. The infants' hands, as well as the rings, were hidden from their view by a cloth. Nonetheless, when the infants were presented with both pairs of rings under conditions in which they could visually, but not manually, inspect them, they recognized the ones they had explored only through touch (Streri & Spelke, 1988).

Similarly, there is large body of research indicating that infants perceive their world as made up of solid, three-dimensional objects, and that they do so well before they have mastered the action schemas Piaget believed responsible for this. Elizabeth Spelke (1988), at Cornell University, showed 3- and 5-month-old infants a moving object that was partially hidden behind another (Figure 5.2). Adults who are shown this display describe it as a stick partially blocked from view by a cube. The question is, what would infants see this as? Would they also see the two ends as belonging to a single object? Or would they see only what was visibly present, two short pieces extending from the top and bottom of a cube, without inferring the existence of a stick behind the cube?

Spelke used a **habituation** procedure to determine what the infants had perceived. In this procedure, infants were shown the figure until they lost interest and looked away. Then they were shown, on alternating trials, either a full-length stick or two short sticks as far apart as they would be if actually separated by the object that had appeared in front of them. Knowing that infants would spend more time looking at something that was unexpected, Spelke compared the time they looked at each alternative as a measure of what they expected to see when the cube was no longer there. By 4 months, infants look longer at the two separate pieces than at the single stick, indicating that they expected to see a whole stick,

Principle of Cohesion: A moving object, such as a ball, follows a single path and does not divide or move along two paths.

Illustrates cohesion

Violates cohesion

FIGURE 5.3 Three Types of Information Carried by a Moving Object *The arrows show the direction of movement.*

Principle of Continuity: There can be no breaks in the path followed by a moving object.

Illustrates continuity

Violates continuity

Principle of Contact: A moving object can affect the movement of another object only by coming into contact with it.

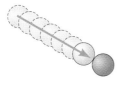

Illustrates contact

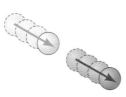

Violates contact

even though they could only have inferred the existence of such an object, since they had never seen it. It might be argued that two things are more interesting to look at than one, thus accounting for the longer looking time. However, Spelke controlled for this possibility by pretesting infants with each of the test displays and found no difference initially in the time they spent looking at either of these.

Important differences remain, however, in what infants and adults appear to infer about partially hidden objects. When infants are shown the same arrangement of stick and cube, but without the stick's moving, they do not, as do adults, perceive an object behind the cube (Spelke, 1988). Only when there is common motion between the several parts do they see these as belonging to a single whole (Johnson & Aslin, 1995; Johnson & Nanez, 1995).

Gretchen Van de Walle and Elizabeth Spelke (1996) suggest that infants rely on three types of information carried by movement: cohesion, continuity, and contact. *Cohesion* refers to the knowledge that a moving object follows a single path and does not divide or move along two paths. *Continuity* is the knowledge that there can be no breaks in the path followed by a moving object; that is, objects do not disappear and reappear somewhere else. *Contact* refers to the understanding that an object can have no effect at a distance, but can affect the movements of another object only if it comes into contact with the other (Figure 5.3). They found that whereas 5-month-old infants effectively use motion cues such as these to infer the existence of an object from the parts of it they can see, they are not as successful in using these cues to infer the shape of the object. In fact, cues such as shape and color, commonly relied on by adults in recognizing objects, appear not to become salient for infants until 6 to 12 months (Craton, cited in Van de Walle & Spelke, 1996).

How can we know when infants are paying attention to the sights and sounds around them, such as special toys and nursery rhymes?

FIGURE 5.4 *Schematic representation of the habituation and test events shown to the infants in the experimental and control conditions.* Source: L. Baillargeon, (1987), Object-permanence in 3½ and 4½-month-old infants. *Developmental Psychology,* 23, 655–664.

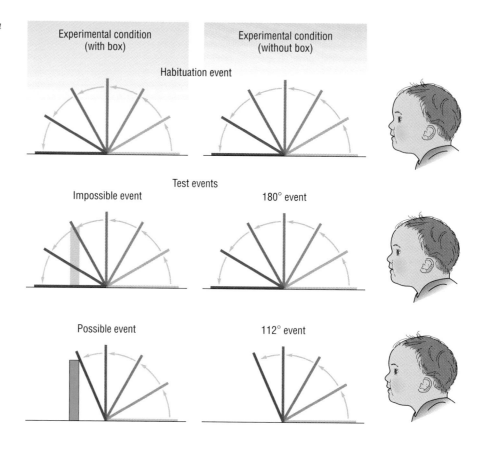

Nonetheless, a world of very real objects clearly exists for infants at an early age. By 3 months, they can determine the boundaries of objects and by 4 months they expect these objects to occupy a space of their own, to be solid and substantial, and to remain where they last saw them (Baillargeon, 1995; Spelke, 1988). Renee Baillargeon (1987) showed infants a screen, initially lying face down on a table in front of them, which swung backward through a 180 degree arc, becoming vertical at 90 degrees and proceeding back until, at 180 degrees, it again lay flat on the table. Infants watched the screen moving in this manner until they habituated, or lost interest in it. Then, with the screen again lying face down on the table, she placed an object on the table in the path of the screen's movement. The screen, as it rotated backward, soon hid the object from view. Would infants still expect the object to remain where it had been placed, even though they could no longer see it? Had they developed, in other words, a concept of object permanence?

To answer this, Baillargeon compared infants' reactions to two test conditions. In one condition, the screen stopped moving when it reached the point at which the object, now hidden by the raised screen, had been placed. In a second condition, the screen continued to rotate backward, moving through the point at which the object had been placed, until it lay flat on the table (Figure 5.4). In each case, once the screen had stopped moving, it reversed direction and rotated back until it lay on the table in front of the infant, again revealing the object behind it. Baillargeon found that infants showed surprise at the second of these tests, but not at the first, indicating that they believed the object was still behind the screen even though they could no longer see it.

How are we to reconcile findings such as these with Piaget's observations concerning object permanence? For T. G. R. Bower, the issue is not one of object per-

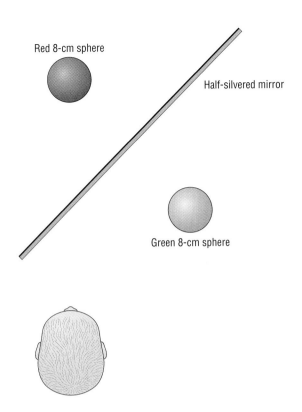

Red 8-cm sphere

Half-silvered mirror

Green 8-cm sphere

FIGURE 5.5 Object Identity Experiment *Depending on which side of the mirror is illuminated, the infant will see either the red or the green ball. By turning on the light in the side containing the green ball while turning off the light in the other side, the red ball appears to have turned into a green ball.* Source: T. G. R. Bower, (1982). Development in infancy.

manence, but one of object identity. An object's size, shape, and color, which are salient aspects of its identity for adults, appear not to be as important to young infants as other features, such as movement. Consider a 3-month-old watching a colorful toy train. The train moves down a short track, first to the right, then to the left, back and forth in front of the infant, stopping for 10 seconds each time it reaches either end. Then, instead of moving off in the other direction, the train remains in place. The infant, on schedule, removes its gaze from the motionless train and looks down the track, registering surprise when it fails to see the moving train. Surely it didn't expect to see the train after just having looked away from it? But this and other demonstrations lead one inevitably to this conclusion (Bower, 1982; Jusczyk, Johnson, Spelke, & Kennedy, 1999).

Bower (1982) suggests that the stationary train is not the same object to the infant as the train that moves. Up to 5 months of age, infants appear to rely almost exclusively on movement to determine the identity of objects. Prior to this age, a moving object that they are visually tracking can change in size, shape, and color, yet, if it reappears on the same course from behind a screen, infants will continue to follow it with their eyes, never looking back for the original object (Bower, Broughton, & Moore, 1971).

For stationary objects, place appears to enjoy a similar, privileged role in determining identity. If one object is substituted for another in the same place, by changing the illumination of different sides of a mirrored glass, thus making one or the other object disappear, the infant will continue to stare at the new object without looking around for the old one (Bower, 1982). Figure 5.5 illustrates such a procedure. Until infants reach the age of 5 months, they continue to look at the substitute object, showing no disruption in their gaze and no searching for the first object. After 5 months, movement and place lose their unique status. Infants appear to relate movement to place, realizing that movement is responsible for an object being in different places. With this, movement and place are less a part of an object's identity than of its activity or nonactivity (Bower, 1982).

How are an adult and a very young infant likely to differ in their recognition of objects?

The work of Baillargeon, in which infants as young as 3 months show evidence of object permanence, suggests that we have misinterpreted motor difficulties as conceptual difficulties. Infants who are too young to reach out and pull away a cover to expose an object hidden underneath nonetheless express surprise at events which suggest that an object hidden from view is no longer where they last saw it, such as when a screen rotates through the location in which they have seen an object placed.

Categorizing Experience

Given that infants share our understanding, more or less, of the things around them, in what other ways might their understanding of the world be similar to ours? What, for instance, do they understand about such basic dimensions as time and space? Or number? Or of ways of categorizing the things with which they come into contact, even those they cannot see or touch, such as the feelings and thoughts of others?

The Timing of Things

We take time as a given, yet it cannot be seen, heard, touched, or smelled. One might argue that time exists only as a mental construction, that we impose a grid of minutes and hours on an otherwise seamless flow of experience. If so, how is time to be experienced by infants and toddlers before they, too, weave the net of seconds, minutes, and hours through which we capture time?

Implicit in the notion of time is the experience of the succession or simultaneity of events. With respect to the first of these, infants can be shown to readily detect regularities to sequences, anticipating when as well as where something will next occur. Recall that infants who are shown photos that appear to the left or right of them in a predictable pattern anticipate when the next event will occur, turning their head in that direction before the photo appears (Haith, Wentworth, & Canfield, 1993). These investigators found that even infants as young as 3½ months can form expectations based on temporal regularities.

Many of the temporal sequences to which infants are exposed are unidirectional in nature, representing processes that naturally occur in one direction but not in another as, for example, the sequence observed when something falls or when an object breaks into pieces. William Friedman (1997, 1999), at Oberlin College, looked at infants' awareness of several temporally unfolding processes, such as liquid being poured from one container to another, blocks falling out of a hand, or a cookie being broken into pieces. Events such as these occur over an extended period of time and unfold only in a given sequence or order. At what age are infants sensitive to the temporal sequence of these events?

Friedman showed 4- to 17-month-old infants videotapes, played forward or backward, of these unidirectional events and measured how long they looked at either type of sequence. If infants can be expected to show greater attention to sequences that are discrepant with what they expect to see, they should stare longer at the backward sequences. Friedman's findings suggest that infants are aware of temporal sequence and that this awareness is related to what they have been exposed to. Thus, sequences that are readily interpretable as violating a natural direction, such as a liquid being unpoured or something falling up, show preferential staring earlier than those that are less clear violations, such as a broken cookie being reassembled. The experience of things falling down, as opposed to up, is universal; however, interpreting a unidirectional temporal sequence to

As infants' and toddlers' ability to move increases, so does their perception of things in space around them.

viewing a cookie broken into pieces is less clear, given infants' experience with blocks and puzzle pieces that can be assembled into a whole, or soft foods or clay that fuse neatly into a mass.

Space

As infants' and toddlers' activities expand, so does their perception of the space around them. At first limited to what they can follow with their eyes and then to what they can grasp within their reach, their awareness of the arrangement of things in space takes a quantum leap when they become able to crawl about. Through crawling and then walking, infants and toddlers become better able to judge distance, detour around objects in their way, and stop in time to avoid tumbling down stairs. Infants who can move about in space, either by creeping or crawling or by using a walker, are much better able to locate where things are than are infants of the same age who have not yet begun to crawl or otherwise had experience in getting about on their own (Bertenthal, Campos, & Kermoian, 1994).

How does infants' ability to get about on their own affect the way they perceive their environment?

Infants' and toddlers' perception of the form of things develops with their ability to grasp things and move them about.

Movement, either of other objects or of ourselves, informs us of space. For instance, some early work with inverted lenses by Ivo Kohler (1962), a German psychologist, suggests that our own activity is highly important in defining space. Kohler constructed a pair of glasses with lenses that inverted the images projected on the retina. When he first put these lenses on, the world flipped upside down, requiring him to cautiously feel his way about rather than rely on visual cues. With time, a most interesting thing happened. The particular things he was handling appeared right-side up, even though everything else remained upside down. However, as soon as he stopped working with these things, they too flipped upside down. Later still, the space around him appeared right-side up as long as he was moving about in it, but when he stopped moving, it turned upside down again. Only eventually did everything appear right-side up, despite the fact that the retinal images were still inverted. The research of Kohler, and of others, indicates that our perception of things, as well as of the space they occupy, is intimately related to our actions (Church, 1961; Held & Hein, 1963).

What does this research suggest about infants' experience of space? Infants' and toddlers' perception of the form of things, just like their perception of space, develops with their ability to take hold of things, to grasp them and move them about. Thus infants who can be seen to judge the size of something, by the way they adjust their grasp as they reach out to grab hold of it, can make surprising errors of judgment when simply looking at an object (Robinson, McKenzie, & Day,

1996; Sitskoorn & Smitsman, 1995). Infants will position their hands around an object similarly to the way adults do but, unlike adults, fail to anticipate the way they will have to grasp it prior to making contact with it. When a screen is placed between them and the object, with an opening through which the object can be seen, they have even more difficulty, frequently even failing to adjust the position of their hands to squeeze through the screen. Interestingly, they are better at getting their hand through when the object behind the screen is too large to pull through and can only be "petted" or touched. They appear to be better at assessing the spatial relations between themselves and an object than between one object and another (Robinson, McKenzie, & Day, 1996).

These spatial relations are important in another respect as well; they serve initially as a way of representing, or remembering, where things are located. Children's increasing ability to get about on their own and, once they get where they are going, to pick things up and move them about, contributes immensely to their understanding and memory for their surroundings. Anne Lamott (1993) captures this aspect of development as she describes her son's ability to remember the places where he previously did things that had fascinated him:

> This memory thing is really interesting. Before, every time Sam went into a room—the bathroom, for instance—he would be almost beside himself with wonder and amazement, like it was his first trip to FAO Schwartz. Now he recognizes it. It's not quite old-hat yet, but he sees the bathtub and he remembers that he loves it and he tries to thrust and squirm his way over to it. It's funny that he loves the bathtub so much. He didn't always. But mostly he loves to toss stuff into the tub when it's empty, and then he loves to gaze endlessly down into it, with wonder, like it's a garden in full bloom. (p. 218) ◄

Initially, children's understanding of space is subjective, or experienced in relation to themselves. With age, their understanding becomes more objective, and their knowledge of where things are is less dependent on their own position with respect to these. One of the earliest ways in which children represent the location of objects in space is by encoding or representing the position of the object relative to themselves. This is termed **egocentric representation.** Linda Acredola (1978), at the University of California at Davis, taught infants to crawl down a pathway and turn left to find a toy. Once they had learned this, she reversed the position from which they approached the path to the toy, such that they had to turn right, and not left. Infants continued to turn left, finding it difficult to compensate for the different location of the toy relative to their own bodies. Only by the age of 16 months were infants able to successfully turn toward the toy.

A second way of representing spatial relations, or **landmark representation,** locates objects in relation to something else in the environment. Infants can be seen to use landmarks as soon as they begin to move about on their own, by about the age of 6 months, and can even use them successfully in locating objects whose position has changed relative to their own—as in Acredola's experiment, in which they had to approach a toy from a direction opposite to the one they had previously followed. If a sufficiently distinctive landmark is available, such as Mom standing on the side nearest the toy, they are more likely to turn in the right direction (Rieser, 1979).

A third way of representing spatial relations, **allocentric representation,** does so in relation to some abstract frame of reference, such as use of a map. This form of representation comes into play when one cannot see the target destination either because it is too far away or because there is something in the way. In order to reach the target, one must envision it relative to its surround and envision these

egocentric representation Representing the location of objects in relation to oneself; typical of young children's subjective understanding of space.

landmark representation Representing the location of objects in relation to environmental landmarks.

allocentric representation Representing the location of objects in relation to an abstract frame of reference, such as a map.

Sequence of events 1+1=1 or 2

1. Object placed in case

2. Screen comes up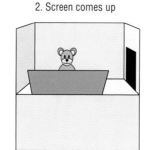

3. Second object added

4. Hand leaves empty

Then either: possible outcome   **or: impossible outcome**

5. Screen drops . . .   revealing 2 objects

5. Screen drops . . .   revealing 1 object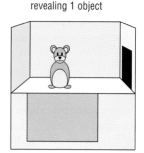

FIGURE 5.6 Sequence of Events Illustrating Infants' Understanding of Amount

If an infant uses an allocentric method of finding a toy, what might be the most important cue?

in relation to oneself. Doing so requires one to organize multiple sources of information into a single system. Not only must one determine the spatial relationship between one position and another on the map, but one must also determine how that relationship corresponds to one's own position relative to where one wants to go and to the map. Despite the abstract nature of such representation, even 1-year-olds have been found to represent spatial relationships in this way (Siegler, 1998). Infants shown a toy hidden in a corner of a room have been found to use an allocentric representation of spatial relationships to locate the toy. The room in which the toy was hidden was rectangular, with identically painted white walls on all sides. It thus afforded no landmarks, but did provide allocentric information in the form of the relative lengths of the two walls forming the corner. To ensure that the infants could not use egocentric cues, they were blindfolded and then turned in a circle before being allowed to search for the toy. Only by representing the location of the toy in terms of the layout of the room—for example, the corner with the long wall on the left—could they find the toy. Since there were two corners that fit that description (remember, they had been turned in a circle), they should go to either of these corners with equal frequencies if they were relying on allocentric cues, and this is precisely what they did (Hermer & Spelke, 1994).

The Number of Things

Karen Wynn (1992, 1995), at the University of Arizona, has studied infants' understanding of arithmetic operations, such as addition and subtraction. To determine their understanding of addition, for instance, she showed 5-month-old infants a hand placing a doll on a stage and then, after a screen came up hiding the stage, the hand adding a second doll to the first behind the screen (Figure 5.6). Would infants add the second doll to the first that was already behind the screen and expect to see two dolls? Since infants will look longer at things that are unexpected, Wynn measured the time they looked when the screen dropped to reveal either two dolls (possible outcome) or a single doll (impossible outcome). Infants spent more time looking at the single doll, suggesting they knew that $1 + 1 = 2$. Similarly, to access their understanding of subtraction, she placed two dolls on the stage and then, once the screen came up, removed one of these. Again, infants were tested with either one doll (possible outcome) or two (impossible outcome) and were found to look longer at the latter outcome.

These findings show that infants know that adding or subtracting a doll results in a different number of dolls. It could be argued, however, that they could do this without being able to compute the actual number of dolls that should appear. Thus, in testing for addition, a test containing three dolls might evoke as much interest as a test with two dolls, since both represent a change from what the infant has seen. Wynn tested for this possibility with 4½-month-old infants by again showing the $1 + 1$ addition procedure, and this time testing with either two or three dolls. Infants stared longer at the three dolls, indicating they were actually performing arithmetic calculations and not responding simply to a change. By the age of 5 months, infants are also able to enumerate repetitive actions, such as those of a puppet jumping up and down, distinguishing among sequences differing in the number of repetitions (Wynn, 1996).

There is, nonetheless, disagreement as to just how competent infants actually are numerically. For instance, infants who were shown displays of objects side by side, one display consisting of two objects and the other consisting of three, and who heard a drum beating out either two or three beats, looked longer at the display that matched the number of sounds they heard (Starkey, Spelke, & Gelman, 1990), prompting these investigators to assume that infants are not only capable of enumerating something that occurs in separable elements, but that they are also able to represent numerosity in different modalities in a way that allows them to relate these in a one-to-one fashion. Not all investigators, however, have been able to replicate such findings (Mix, Levine, & Huttenlocher, 1997).

From a very early age, infants seem to be able to categorize things and distinguish between same and different. This child is well aware that he's in an environment he's not used to.

Types of Things

At what age do infants begin to classify their experiences into different types of things, such as distinguishing cats from dogs or birds from bees? Research addressing this question suggests that infants begin at a very early age indeed. Once again, since young infants are limited in the ways in which they can communicate their knowledge of the world, researchers have had to be ingenious. A procedure that has been commonly used in this type of research shows infants various members of a category and then tests them with a pair of novel items, one of which is a member of the same category and the other of a different one. Knowing that infants look longer at things that are novel, and given that each of the test items is new to them, looking longer at the item from a different group would indicate they have formed some basis for categorizing, or seeing as similar, the ones they had previously seen.

"Well and good," you might say, "but *how* do they do that?" What does one do when one categorizes? There are several ways in which we might form categories. We will consider three of these: using defining features, using a probabilistic approach, and forming a theory of why things go together (Siegler, 1998).

The first of these explanations for forming categories, representing categories in terms of defining features, assumes that all instances of a category possess certain characteristics, or **defining features,** in common that identify them as a

defining features Characteristics that identify items as members of a category.

member of that category. An example of such a feature might be "wings" for the category of birds or "gills" for the category of fish. This approach assumes that when we categorize on this basis, we represent the category in terms of these defining features. Other items that possess the same defining features are also considered to be members of that category. Of course, many things with wings are not birds. Insects and airplanes come to mind. And most categories are defined by more than one feature. Birds, for instance, have feathers, lay eggs, and sing, as well as have wings and fly.

At this point, someone may say, "Wait, don't lizards and snakes lay eggs too? And ostriches have wings, but they can't fly or sing like other birds." Due to difficulties such as these in identifying which features are necessary and sufficient for category membership, Eleanor Rosch and Carolyn Mervis (1975), at Stanford University, proposed a *probabilistic* approach to defining membership in categories. Rosch and Mervis argued that we distinguish items as belonging to a category on the basis of family resemblances rather than an invariant set of features possessed by all members of a category. That is, all members of a category need not have the same set of features in common as long as they have enough in common to resemble other instances of the category.

Rosch and Mervis proposed that four factors are important in assigning items to a category: cue validity, basic-level categories, correlated features, and prototypes. *Cue validity* is the likelihood that an item is a member of a category given that a particular feature, or cue, is present. The validity of a cue refers to the extent to which a particular feature is present in members of the category and absent among members of other categories. Thus, the cue validity of wings is high for the category of birds since the likelihood of birds having wings is high relative to that of other things. Cue validity also explains how some items can be better instances of a category than others. Why are canaries better examples of birds than ostriches are? Because, even though both have wings, other cues found in canaries, such as their size, body proportions, and whether they sing and can fly, are more valid cues for birds than are those of ostriches.

Rosch and her associates note that categories are naturally arranged in a nested fashion, such that being a member of one category means that one necessarily belongs to another, more general, category as well. Thus all canaries are also birds, and all birds are animals. Most categories are arranged in such three-tiered hierarchies, with the *subordinate* level being most specific (canaries), the *superordinate* level the most general (animals), and the middle, or *basic level,* intermediate in generality (birds) and possessing the highest cue validities (Figure 5.7). Thus, "bird" is a basic-level category because the features describing birds, such as having wings, feathers, and beaks, and being able to fly and sing, have high cue validities. That is, most birds have these in common, whereas few other things do. In contrast, cue validities for "animals" are not as high as those for birds; some animals have wings, others have fins, and still others have neither. Similarly, members of subordinate categories, such as canaries, possess all the features found in basic-level categories, but are not as reliably distinguished among each other as is one basic-level category from another.

Rosch and her associates point out that the features that distinguish a category tend to be grouped, or correlated, such that the presence of one feature is highly predictive of another. Thus, things that have gills also tend to have fins and scales, whereas those with wings are likely to have feathers and beaks. This clustering of *correlated features* is characteristic of most categories. Some instances of a category are simply better examples of that category than are others. These are the ones that are the most representative, or have the highest cue validities. Such instances are termed *prototypes* in that they represent the category better than

How do infants use cue validity in order to classify objects?

Superordinate level: Animals

Basic level: Birds

Subordinate level: Canaries

FIGURE 5.7 Levels of Categories

any of its other instances. Canaries, for example, are prototypical birds not only because they have wings, feathers, and beaks, but also because they sing, fly, and are the right size.

Finally, we often categorize objects because of the relationships that exist among them, even when they bear little physical resemblance to each other. Robert Siegler (1998) cites the example of a category that includes children, antiques, jewelry, and family photos, an unlikely assortment unless one is asked to think of what one would remove first from a house that is on fire. Because items such as these derive their similarity from what we know about them, rather than from any physical features they might have in common, the grouping reflects a theory of why these things go together. For adults, at least, an important element in judging which things go together is the issue of whether they are the same *kind* of thing—that is, whether they are similar in nature (Mandler, Bauer, & McDonough, 1991). This basis for categorizing experience represents a theory-based approach. What makes something an animal? Is it simply that animals have legs or eyes and ears? Or is it the notion that animals are capable of self-initiated movement and this, despite large differences in how they look or in the ways they move, is what makes them animals?

By age 2½, children can distinguish basic-level categories and tell a dog from a goat, for example.

Do infants and children use any or all of these ways to categorize experience? If so, what are they most likely to base their categories on? A common assumption is that initially categories are based on perceptual similarity, and only with time do they evolve into conceptually based categories (Eimas & Quinn, 1994; Mervis, 1987). If infants and children at first categorize things based on the way they look, then basic-level categories should be the first ones that they form, since these are made up of items that are most similar in appearance to each other. Presumably when basic-level categories have been formed, children begin to group these into more inclusive, or superordinate, categories, arriving at the conceptually based hierarchical system of classifying things used by adults.

Paul Quinn and Peter Eimas (1996) found that even infants as young as 3 to 4 months of age could distinguish basic-level categories from each other. They showed infants a series of photographs of either cats or dogs and then tested them with a pair of photographs, neither of which had been seen before, one of which was a cat and the other a dog, to see which they would look at longer. Since infants look longer at things that are unexpected, their looking time was taken as a measure of whether they had formed a category based on the series they had seen. They looked longer at the photograph of the animal that differed from the series they had seen. Furthermore, when Quinn and Eimas subsequently presented only the heads or the bodies of these animals, they were able to show that infants distinguished the categories on the basis of distinctive facial features and head contours.

Jean Mandler, Patricia Bauer, and Laraine McDonough (1991) question whether basic-level categories are always the first to be formed. They suggest that children initially form rather broad categories, which they refer to as *domains* to distinguish them from superordinate categories, pointing out that the latter assume a hierarchical organization that is not necessarily present at first. They found that 18-month-olds could distinguish animals from vehicles, for instance, while still not being able to differentiate the basic-level categories, such as dogs from horses, or cars from trucks, that made these up. Only when children reached the age of 2½ did they consistently distinguish the component basic-level categories. These data suggest that, in some domains, children form broad, conceptual categories before making basic-level distinctions among the items within these.

Beliefs About Things

Given that infants and toddlers form categories for things in the world around them, what might they understand about the inner world of their own, or others', minds? Do they have a theory, that is, of the mind? Considerable data suggest that an understanding of mental states in others begins to develop relatively early. Toddlers, for instance, can be seen to establish joint attention with their mothers while engaged in an activity (Goldsmith & Rogoff, 1997), and infants can be seen to scrutinize their mother's face when in an ambiguous situation for cues as to whether the situation is threatening or safe (Hornik, Risenhoover, & Gunnar, 1987). Behaviors such as these suggest that even relatively young infants attribute inner states to others.

One of these inner states is that of desire. Betty Repacholi and Alison Gopnik (1997), at the University of California, Berkeley, explored the age at which young children, 14- and 18-month-olds, begin to understand the desires of others. These investigators used a situation that is familiar to children of any age, asking for something that tastes good. Two types of foods were used, one known to be desirable to children (goldfish crackers) and the other to be undesirable (broccoli flowerets). Children observed the experimenter take a taste of each, reacting positively to one and negatively to the other. For half of the children the experimenter expressed pleasure with the food they themselves liked (cracker) and for the other half this was reversed. What would children give the experimenter when she asked for more? The food she appeared to enjoy? Or the food they preferred? Infants who were 14 months old offered the food they preferred. However, by 18 months, infants could infer what the experimenter wanted and offered her the food she expressed delight in even when it was personally distasteful to them.

Why may showing a toddler how much we love vegetables perhaps not be helpful in getting her to learn to enjoy them herself?

The Meaning of Things

What do infants understand of the categorical distinctions they make? Are these first categories conceptual in nature, or are they only perceptual? Asked another way, do the categorical representations infants make consist only of perceptual cues that have been abstracted from instances of the category, such as features distinguishing the faces of cats from dogs (Quinn & Eimas, 1996)? Or do they include what we would call meaningful distinctions as well? Jean Mandler (1990, 1992), at the University of California at San Diego, argues for the latter, pointing out that if language acquisition is dependent on the existence of preverbal concepts, and if infants' first words occur at about 10 months, or even earlier if they are signing (Padden & Humphries, 1989), these concepts must already be in place.

Mandler suggests that perceptual analysis results in *image-schemas* which map, or redescribe, spatial structure into conceptual structure. Such schemas represent basic forms of understanding, such as the notion of up versus down, or what it means to be supported or contained, or to follow a path. Image-schemas are thought to be based on innate perceptual processes that analyze perceptual features such as movement, border and edge, and the like. The image-schema of "path," for instance, might refer simply to an object moving along a trajectory, without necessarily identifying the object as such. Recall that infants reflexively follow a moving object with their eyes. Recall, too, that the object can appear to change in color, size, and shape, but as long as it continues along the same path, infants will not attend to differences in these dimensions. The notion of "path," Mandler argues, is a perceptual primitive, communicating information to which we are innately attentive. She suggests that image-schemas such as this make up the most fundamental level of the infant's understanding of the world.

Infants use motion cues to judge animacy.

Mandler warns that image-schemas, rather than being thought of as similar to innate concepts, should be regarded as the means by which infants derive their most basic concepts, that which equips or enables infants to conceptually order experience. Recall that Neisser (1976), too, pointed out that infants come into the world fully loaded with all the perceptual equipment they will need in order to discover *what* they will need to know.

Image-schemas, as stripped down abstractions of perceptual processes, would be capable of capturing the active interrelationships among parts. Because of their ability to capture these relational components, image-schemas could yield a syntax of sorts, one capable of specifying "truth conditions," of representing the "what's so" of experience, such as "A hits B, B moves." Possessing such a syntax would make it possible for infants to think about experience in the absence of logical, propositionally based thought, such as awaits the development of language. Mandler cautions that she is not suggesting that infants are conscious of these image-schemas. One would need at least another level of analysis in order to be aware of such processes, since consciousness, by definition, is reflective, requiring a second level from which to view the first. These image-schemas would simply provide the meaning on which concepts that are accessible to consciousness are based.

As an example of such an early image-schema, consider what it means to know that something is animate, or alive. Mandler proposes that judgments of animacy are based on three things. The first of these is *self-motion*, something that moves by itself without having to be started. *Animate motion*, or moving in a rhythmic, up-and-down fashion as we do when pushing off from a surface with every step, is thought to be a second component. In contrast to this type of motion, inanimate objects are more likely to move in a smooth trajectory, as does a missile or a ball. A third component, *contingency motion*, refers to actions that are contingent on the behavior of another, yet are prompted from a distance. We needn't be "bumped" into action, in other words; instead, we respond to the requests and behaviors of others, such as when a parent reacts to an infant's vocalizations. Infants are sensitive to such information. By 4 months, for instance, they notice the difference between an object being set in motion when another bumps into it and an object that starts to move when the first object stops just a fraction short of touching it (Leslie, 1982, 1988).

Do infants use cues such as these to form a notion of animacy? If so, things that move contingently, whether puppies, puppets, or mobiles, should initially be confused with humans. Frye, Rawling, Moore, and Myers (1983) observed 3- and 10-month-old infants' reactions to either their mothers or to toys, each of which either acted contingently or noncontingently to the infants' behavior. They found that 3-month-old infants reacted in a similar way to both their mothers and to toys when the behavior of each was contingent on their own behavior, and that in each case the infants' reactions were different than for noncontingent interactions. By 10 months, however, infants reacted differently to contingent-mothers than to contingent-toys.

Another important image-schema which Mandler discusses is that of containment. This notion, too, develops relatively early. By 5½ months, infants show surprise when containers without bottoms look like they are holding something (Kolstad, as cited in Mandler, 1992), a finding which also suggests that the notions of containment and support are closely related. George Lakoff (1987), a cognitive linguist, notes that containment connotes not only "in," but notions of "out" and "boundary" as well. He argues that containment is basic to understanding logical relations such as "A versus not-A" (that is, *in* versus *not-in*), that when we understand a set, we do so through our knowledge of containment. This notion of containment may also contribute to the meaning of the word "or," in that an object can be in *or* out, but not both. Likewise, just as containment contributes to an understanding of "in," the notion of support provides a basis for understanding the meaning of "on." Mandler points out that these two terms for indicating where something is located, "in" and "on," are among the first locative terms to develop, irrespective of the language studied and that even when children are first learning these words, they make almost no errors.

Mandler (1992) suggests that image-schemas such as these, because they represent meaningful, and not just perceptual, distinctions, can form the basis for the conceptual categories that young children will soon put into words. We turn to this achievement next.

The Development of Language

The very young think with their bodies, their intentions etched in movement. Soon thoughts slip free, loosed by words, and language branches into phrases that span place and time. Observing children as they begin to talk, however, can leave one with more questions than answers as to how they master language. How do they learn so quickly? Must they be taught? Or do they acquire language simply by listening to others? For that matter, need the voices they hear be those of people who are actually present, or could they learn just as easily by listening to a television or the radio?

It is difficult to know for certain when children actually start to acquire a language. We can note when they say their first words, but an infant's first word is only a milestone marking a journey begun much earlier. From birth on, infants are attentive to the sounds of speech, making relatively fine distinctions among these. Even newborns are able to discriminate different stress patterns in otherwise similar words (Sansavini, Bertoncini, & Giovanelli, 1997). Infants also show preferences for certain types of speech over others. They are highly attuned, for instance, to the prosodic features of speech—that is, to the rise and fall of the voice and to the rhythmic stressing of words. In fact, they prefer, when given the alternative, to listen to speech that is directed at them, in which adults characteristically exaggerate these prosodic features, than to speech directed at adults (Fernald, 1985). This is true for newborns as well as for older infants (Cooper & Aslin, 1990; Pegg, Werker, & McLeod, 1992). Infants also prefer to listen to the prosody of their own language than to that of another (Moon, Cooper, & Fifer, 1993).

First Sounds

Infants begin **babbling,** producing vowel and consonant sounds, in the 2nd to 3rd month (Menn & Stoel-Gammon, 1995). Babbling initially follows a common pattern irrespective of the language spoken at home. For the first 6 months or so all infants sound alike, from Brooklyn to Bangkok. Infants first make guttural sounds such as \g\ and \k\ combined with vowels produced mid-mouth (such as \a\). Sounds are added as other consonants (such as \b\, \p\) replace the early guttural ones. This sequence occurs in all infants, even those whose native language has many of the early guttural sounds. It thus appears that an important determinant of babbling is the child's own developing articulatory control. This control, rather than the speech sounds infants hear spoken around them, appears to determine when babbling begins and which sounds will be the first to occur. Deaf infants, for instance, begin to babble at the same age as hearing infants. The persistence of babbling, however, seems to be dependent on the ability of infants to

babbling The production of vowel and consonant sounds by infants in the 2nd to 3rd month.

Infants are highly attuned to prosodic features of speech and prefer to listen to speech directed to them.

How does babbling relate to learning more than one language?

practice and hear the different sounds they make, as well as hear the speech of others (Menn & Stoel-Gammon, 1995). Deaf children stop babbling at about the age that babbling peaks in hearing infants, at about 9 to 12 months. Also in this later stage, differences in babbling emerge that reflect the sounds infants hear in their native language. Infants begin to reproduce the intonation, rhythmic structure, and pitch of speech. This form of babbling is sometimes called **jargon babbling** for, if one is not listening closely, it sounds very much like speech (Kent & Miolo, 1995).

Just as words themselves communicate meaning, so, too, do the prosodic features of speech. Anne Fernald (1993), at Stanford University, notes that the rise and fall of the voice, what might be thought of as the musical contours of speech, as well as the pattern of stresses, or rhythm, given to words, differ with different types of messages. Expressions of approval, such as "Good girl!" are typically drawn out, with the voice dipping and rising, whereas warnings, such as "No!" are short and staccato. Infants have been found to use cues such as these in determining how to respond in ambiguous situations. Donna Mumme, Anne Fernald, and Carla Herrera (1996) tested 12-month-old infants in a social-referencing situation in which infants, confronted with an ambiguous situation, typically look to their caregiver for cues concerning its nature. Mothers were instructed to communicate either through their voices alone, by turning their backs to the child and using words the child could not understand, or through facial expressions alone. The investigators found that infants responded more to the prosodic features of the mother's speech when communicating fear than to fearful expressions on the mother's face.

jargon babbling Babbling that reproduces the intonation, rhythmic structure, and pitch of speech.

One wonders whether infants might use prosody in other ways as well. Cynthia Fisher and Hisayo Tokura (1996), at the University of Illinois, suggest that the rhythms of speech may provide cues about grammatical structure, helping children identify phrases and grammatical units. How well can one hear prosodic cues in speech directed at children? These investigators recorded mothers as they talked to their young children (13 to 14 months old) and found that these cues were easily detectable in the mothers' speech. For the most part, their sentences or phrases were separated by long pauses, with the pauses being preceded by very long vowels and an exaggerated rise and fall to the voice. Because infant-directed speech uses short, simple sentences in which there are relatively few long pauses within a sentence, the relationship between phonologically marked units and grammatical ones is high. Fisher and Tokura carried out the same procedure with native Japanese-speaking mothers and again found that the last syllable in a phrase was consistently different from preceding ones. Thus, whether in Japanese or English, the characteristic melodies of the languages were clearly present in child-directed speech. Since pauses are a reliable cue to the end of one grammatical unit and the beginning of another, they may help infants isolate, or bracket, utterances for linguistic analysis. The Research Focus, "Sampling: Baby Talk in Three Languages" describes a study that examined the way parents speak to babies in three different languages.

Infants' sensitivity to cues such as these changes with their age. Infants 7 months of age or younger, for instance, prefer to listen to speech with pauses between, rather than within, sentences. Not until they reach 9 months of age is there a similar preference at the phrase level, with infants preferring to listen to sentences in which pauses between phrases are greater than those within the phrases. These differences suggest that, with age, a more finely grained analysis of speech becomes possible (Jusczyk et al., 1992).

Infants are learning more than the sounds of words when listening to others speak. They are learning about language itself, that language is part of the way people interact with each other, a way of communicating. John Holt (1969) describes this process:

> A year or more ago, some friends and I dropped in on some people who had a six-month-old baby. She was well-rested and happy, so they brought her in to see the visitors. We all admired her before going on with our talk. She was fascinated by this talk. As each person spoke, she would turn and look intently at him. From time to time she would busy herself with a toy in her lap; then after a few minutes she would begin watching and listening again. She seemed to be learning, not just that people talk, but that they talk to each other, and respond to each other's talk with smiles, and laughter, and more talk; in short, that talk is not just a kind of noise, but messages, communication. (pp. 57–58) ◄

 Why is it good for infants and toddlers to hear adults conversing?

First Words

Usually, somewhere around the first birthday infants say their first word. Considerable variability exists from one infant to the next in the timing of this event, with some doing so as early as 9 months of age and others as late as 15 months (Kent & Miolo, 1995). Also, some infants stop babbling when they start to speak, while others continue to babble as they add words to their vocabulary. On average, infants can be expected to use about 10 words by the time they reach 13 months and 45 words by 16 months. However, they understand many more words than this, comprehending over 100 words at 13 months and more than 180 at 16 months (Fenson et al., 1993).

Sampling: Baby Talk in Three Languages

After once more listening to the tape and reviewing again the last set of words, Carla hit the off button. "Enough for today," she thought. Her difficulty with this last tape had made her realize again that learning a second language wasn't that easy, and she wondered how well she'd be doing by the time she met her host family. It was exciting to think of spending a year on an exchange program, especially after hearing that her host mother had just given birth to a little boy. "Wonder how well that little guy is learning the language," she muttered to herself. "Hope he's doing better than I am." She'd never even *heard* half the sounds she was supposed to be making. "How do infants do it?" she wondered. "One thing's for sure, they don't do it by practicing with language tapes."

They definitely don't. But they appear to do something better. By simply listening to the language being spoken around them, infants' very perception of speech is modified, increasing their sensitivity to the rhythm and sounds of their native language, the sounds Carla found so difficult to hear and reproduce in a language other than her own. In other words, infants' ability to hear the sounds that distinguish their language from others is fine-tuned by the very act of listening to speech itself.

Infants are helped enormously in this task by the way people talk when they are around them. Irrespective of the particular language being spoken, speech that is addressed to infants exhibits certain characteristics. Not only do we speak in shorter and simpler sentences when talking to an infant, we also speak in a higher voice, talk more slowly, and exaggerate the cadence, or the rhythm, to our speech. Language addressed to infants has been found to exhibit these properties around the world, despite differences in the actual words that make it up. This manner of speaking is called "parentese," and, as a form of speech, it is ideal for learning one's mother tongue.

But are the individual sounds making up the words pronounced differently as well? In adult-directed speech, vowels and consonants are frequently slurred, providing a poor model of the sounds an infant needs to learn. Is this a natural handicap infants must overcome in learning their language? Or do we also articulate more distinctly the individual sounds, or phonemes, making up each word when speaking to infants? In order to answer this question, Patricia Kuhl and her associates (1997) compared the phonetic units in infant-directed and adult-directed speech by tape-recording women as they spoke either to infants or adults. Specifically, they examined the way vowels were pronounced in either form of speech. Would these be spoken more clearly in speech directed to infants?

The speech of 10 women was recorded in each of three languages—English, Russian, and Swedish—resulting in thousands of tape-recorded words. From these tapes, individual words were selected for further analysis. But how can we be sure, you might wonder, that the acoustic properties of the words that were selected are representative of all the others? Mustn't one analyze every word in order to know with certainty whether the acoustic properties of vowels differ when speech is directed to infants?

The words that were analyzed were sampled from the larger population of all tape-recorded words. The population represents the entire set of events, or, in this case, of vowels, in which one is interested. The *sample* is a subgroup drawn from this population. If the sample is drawn at random from the population, we can be reasonably certain that it will be *representative* of that population. This is because in random sampling, each person or event has an equal chance of being chosen. How might this procedure apply to vowel sounds?

One might organize the recorded conversations into segments of a specified duration, each, for instance, lasting for 10 seconds (conversations generally lasted for 20 minutes). Such an organization would yield 6 segments per minute, or 120 segments, on average, per conversation. One could then randomly select one target word for phonetic analysis within each segment. To see how this might work, let's assume that 12 words are spoken in a given speech segment. To imagine how any given word might be sampled, think of a hat containing 12 slips of paper, one for each of the recorded words. The number written on the slip you pull would be the word that is sampled for analysis.

What did the samples of vowel sounds show? For all three languages, phonemes are spoken differently in speech addressed to infants. Specifically, vowels are stretched when speaking to infants, making them acoustically more distinct than when speaking to adults. Differences in the way in which phonemes, the building blocks of words, are articulated indicate yet one more way in which the speech to which infants are exposed provides a clear model of the language they are to acquire. This model, in turn, is thought to initiate a process by which infants' perception of speech sounds is modified, altering their ability to detect the sounds peculiar to a particular language.

Infants acquire words slowly at first, usually adding one to three new words a week. However, once their vocabulary reaches anywhere from 20 to 40 words, many infants experience a **vocabulary explosion** in which they add up to eight or more words per week, with the number of words they understand increasing even faster. Considerable variability exists from one child to the next in the timing of this event. The vocabulary explosion typically occurs late in the 2nd year, at around 19 months, but, as with other aspects of language, can vary by as much as 6 months; and in some infants it may not occur at all (Gershkoff-Stowe, Thal, Smith, & Namy, 1997). There is also a slight gender difference in how quickly children learn words, with girls doing so slightly faster than boys, although this difference is small relative to overall differences among children (Barrett, 1995).

Children's first words, just like the sounds they babble, appear to be determined as much by their ability to articulate as by their understanding of the relationship between words and what they name (Gershkoff-Stowe et al., 1997). As we have seen, children understand the meaning of many words before they can speak them. Also, research with deaf children shows that they sign their first words earlier than hearing infants speak theirs, at about 8 months rather than at 10 to 15 months. The greater ease of signing with fingers than of controlling articulatory muscles is most likely responsible for this difference.

Certainly, the regularities of articulation errors in children's first words suggest that it is quite literally a "mouthful" for them to speak. Their errors simplify pronunciation. A common error, for instance, is to reduce multisyllabic words to repetitions of the first syllable. Baby becomes "baba" or mommy is "mama." Children also simplify pronunciation by reducing words of one syllable to a single consonant and vowel. "Ba" serves for *ball* or "tu" for *shoe*. Similarly, children may delete syllables from multisyllabic words, "banana," for example, becoming "nana." Or they may reduce an initial consonant cluster to a single consonant; "stop" becomes "top" or "spoon" is pronounced as "poon." Mastery of consonant clusters continues to develop over the next several years. Some children may have difficulty with these until 4 or 5.

Children also simplify pronunciation by using the same place of articulation for all consonants in a word. "Kitty" becomes "titty" or "doggy," "doddy." Another common form of pronunciation is to replace unvoiced initial consonants, such as \t\, \p\, or \k\, with voiced ones, such as\d\, \b\, or \g\, at the beginning of words. Words such as "toe" and "pie" become "doe" and "bie" (Menn & Stoel-Gammon, 1995). Some errors arise as well from hearing adult speech incorrectly. Perception of speech sounds continues to improve through the 2nd and 3rd years. Even so, children initially are better at perceiving words than at producing them.

Children's use of single words has intrigued parents and psycholinguists alike. How much do they intend to communicate with that one word? Do children use single words to function as phrases or even whole sentences, commenting on their experiences in addition to simply labeling them? Some have suggested they do (McNeill, 1970). Used in this way, single words are termed **holophrases.** "Milk," for instance, might be an observation that the milk is all gone, a request for more milk, or a comment that the cup has milk in it and not juice. While such interpretations of early words are intriguing, they are challenged by others who caution that interpreting single words as holophrastic speech is not warranted by the data. The evidence from single words is simply not sufficient to convict an infant of having a sentence in mind.

Patricia Greenfield and Joshua Smith (1976) suggest, instead, that single words are one component of a communicative expression that, along with gesture, expresses a thought. Thus, "up," combined with raising both arms over the head,

Which do you think comes first, the ability to understand language or the ability to use speech to express language?

vocabulary explosion The rapid addition of new words to a toddler's vocabulary; usually occurs late in the 2nd year.

holophrase A single word used to represent a phrase or sentence; typical of the first stage of language acquisition.

In the early stages of speaking, single words are often combined with gestures to communicate a thought.

communicates one thought ("Pick me up"), whereas the same word combined with pointing to a balloon that has floated free communicates a different thought ("The balloon is going up"). Thus, although the word itself is not the equivalent of a sentence, the combination of word with gesture functions as one.

Whether used as holophrases or simply to name, many of the child's first words may refer only to some, but not all, of the instances for which they are used by adults. Examples of such **underextensions** would be using "bottle" to refer only to plastic nursing bottles or "cut" only to cutting with a knife (Barrett, 1995). Conversely, in **overextensions,** children use a word to refer not only to all members of the group that it labels for adults, but to other referents as well. Thus, "doggie" might be used for all dogs, but also for cats and lambs, or "bath" might be used for the tub, water, or the toys that float in the bath. Some of these overextensions last for months; others will be used only briefly until the correct name for another object is learned. Children typically have no trouble distinguishing the objects they group this way. When asked to bring the rubber ducky, for instance, a child will correctly bring that and not another toy, even though both may be called "bath." Recall, children's comprehension of words far exceeds their ability to spontaneously produce them at first (just as does ours when learning a second language). In a pinch, they will use whatever word comes closest to what they have in mind. They may even deliberately overextend a word as a way of finding an object's name, knowing that parents will supply the right word when correcting them (Barrett, 1995). All children display these regularities of speech, irrespective of their gender, ethnicity, or social class. Despite such regularities, tremendous differences can exist in richness of the experience their environments provide. The Social Policy Focus, "Early-Intervention Programs: Money Well Spent?" describes the success of early intervention programs in countering the effects of impoverished environments.

Naming Things

What is the "right" word to use when naming things for children? One could supply any of several possible names, from the specific to the general. One could refer to the family car, for instance, as a Mustang, a Ford, or simply a car. Similarly, one could refer to a banana or an apple by name or as a piece of fruit. Naming things is something that most of us do without thinking. Yet, despite the many ways we might refer to things, we are amazingly consistent in the way we name things for children. Roger Brown (1958, 1965), at Harvard University, has noted that the names we supply correspond to the distinctions we anticipate children will need to make in using what we are naming. Thus, children are told to get into the "car" and not the "Mustang" unless, of course, there happens to be more than one car in the family. Similarly, cats remain undistinguished as to ancestry or Persian pedigree—all are "kitty." It is enough for toddlers to distinguish a car from a truck, or a cat from a cow, without knowing which type of car or cat it is. Which type of fruit they want for breakfast, however, is a meaningful distinction. As a consequence, most fruits are identified specifically by name. With a few exceptions, we tend to call things by base-level names—children live in a world of cars and cats, not Mustangs and Persians and not vehicles and animals (Lakoff, 1987).

These names, furthermore, tend to be associated with distinctive actions. We name things in meaningful contexts, as part of an ongoing and natural dialogue, in which we might bounce a ball that rolls underfoot, calling it "ball" in the process; peel a piece of banana, offering some "banana" to a child; or smell a

underextension A child's use of a word to refer to only some but not all of the instances for which it is used by adults.

overextension A child's use of a word to refer not only to all members of the group that the word labels for adults but also to other referents.

Early-Intervention Programs: Money Well Spent?

BY ANDREA HAYES

How important are the years from birth to age 3? Do infants' and toddlers' earliest experiences affect their ability to profit from later ones, contributing to their cognitive and social skills in middle childhood and adolescence? Conversely, do impoverished environments contribute to later problems, such as academic failure or youth violence? What might a toddler's environment, for instance, have to do with social problems such as school dropout rate, teen pregnancy, or joblessness? Given the possibility of such influences, might intervention programs that provide rich, stimulating environments for at-risk infants affect the general well-being of all, disadvantaged and advantaged alike?

For the past 25 years, a program at the University of North Carolina has been laying the groundwork for answers to questions such as these. The program is known as the Abecedarian Project, named for the first four letters of the alphabet (Campbell, Helms, Sparling, & Ramey, 1998). Starting at the age of 6 months, 111 at-risk infants from low-income families were placed in an intensive child care program with one supervisory adult for every three infants and were given year-round child care 8 hours a day until they were ready to enter school. Once they reached school age, children received additional intervention until they entered the 2nd grade. The program also offered assistance to their families, providing such things as training in parenting and encouraging parents to become involved in their children's schooling (Burchinal, Campbell, Bryant, Wasik, & Ramey, 1997).

Children who were enrolled as infants in the Abecedarian Project were followed until they reached the age of 21. A comparison of the Abecedarian children with a comparable group of children not enrolled in the program shows that intensive early intervention can significantly improve the odds for at-risk children. Specifically, children who had been enrolled in the project had higher reading and math scores when they reached school age, lower school dropout rates and delayed pregnancy as adolescents, and higher rates of college attendance and higher rates of employment as young adults.

In contrast to the success of the extended intervention provided by the Abecedarian Project, research has repeatedly discovered that 1- or 2-year early-intervention programs fail to protect children against poor academic outcomes (Reynolds & Temple, 1998). Similar research finds that children enrolled in intervention programs that do not cover the transition period from preschool to 2nd grade are less likely to maintain the gains they initially make in reading, math, and grade progression (Reynolds & Temple, 1998). Such findings, together with those demonstrating the effectiveness of intensive long-term intervention that covers the transitional period, call for a renewed examination of existing social policy with respect to early intervention programs. Although the funding of intensive programs such as the Abecedarian Project may seem expensive when compared to conventional preschool programs (roughly $10,000 covers one child for 1 year), such programs are likely to offer society a savings in the long run. It has been estimated that for every $1.00 spent on such programs, society saves $7.00 in reduced costs for crime, premature births, and increased unemployment (Maugh, 1999). In addition to more effectively utilizing public and private funds on social programs, the savings in human potential are incalculable, in the form of reclaiming purposeful and productive lives for at-risk youth. Results from the Abecedarian Project, and others similar to it, focus our attention on *what works*, not what *might* work.

flower we have just named (Brown, 1965; Iverson & Goldin-Meadow, 1997). Most verbs in child-directed speech, for instance, name actions that the child or others are currently engaging in. Such actions distinguish these objects as neatly as do their names, the proof of which is seen in games such as charades. Thus our first names for things are names that correspond to distinctive ways of interacting with, or acting on, those things (Brown, 1965). However, the very actions so helpful in distinguishing flowers from, say, bananas or balls are of no help in distinguishing one type of flower from another. Brown (1965) notes that categorizing experience "begins at the level of distinctive action" and only proceeds upward to superordinate categories by "achievements of the imagination" (as quoted in Lakoff, 1987).

Even when illuminated by gesture, when spoken by others, a new word can refer to any of a myriad of different things that may be present. Which of these does it name? Despite the daunting demands that naming places on young children, children are often able to learn the meaning of new words after hearing

If this girl is like most children her age, many of the names she learns for things will be associated with distinctive actions.

them used a single time. **Fast mapping** refers to children's ability to map the meaning of a new word onto a referent after hearing the word used in context just once. This first mapping does not capture all of the word's meaning. The full meaning of a word can develop over years, but fast mapping enables children to establish a lexicon with many entries, which in itself contributes to language development by making it easier for children to talk to others, putting them in a position to learn even more (Clark, 1995). In one study, children were asked by an adult to bring "the chromium tray, not the blue one, the chromium one." Even though they had never heard the word "chromium" before, they brought the right tray and a week later remembered that the new word referred to a color (Carey, 1978).

Children apparently assume that a new word refers to something for which they presently have no name. Names, in other words, are assumed to be *mutually exclusive*; if a thing has one name, it is not likely to be called by another. Hence children look for unnamed, or novel, items or actions on hearing a new word (Merriam, Evey-Burkey, Marazita, & Jarvis, 1996; Merriam & Stevenson, 1997). Children, for instance, who were shown *Sesame Street* characters performing familiar or unfamiliar actions and were asked "Which one is glorping?" picked the unfamiliar action as a referent for the novel verb. They also extended the meaning of this novel verb to a later picture of another character performing the same action (Golinkoff, Jacquet, Hirsh-Pasek, & Nandakumar, 1996).

fast mapping Children's ability to map the meaning of a new word onto a referent after hearing the word used in context just once.

More than assumptions of mutual exclusivity are important in learning names for things. Young children also appear to rely on social criteria in establishing whether unfamiliar words are actually being used as names for things. One of the most powerful social cues is that of joint attention with another person to something that is present or going on. In one study, 18- to 20-month-olds heard a new word ("peri") spoken by someone while they were looking at a new toy. In one case, the new word was spoken by someone who was also looking at the new toy. In the other case, it was spoken by someone out of view of the infant and the toy. When infants were shown the new toy, together with another one, and asked "Where is the peri?" they correctly identified the new toy only when they had heard it named by someone who was also looking at the toy, even though in both instances, the toy was the only new object around to be named. In order for a new word to be taken as a name for something, then, it cannot simply be uttered in the presence of the object. It must be clear that the speaker is referring to that object—that is, naming it (Baldwin et al., 1996).

Children use other strategies, as well, in learning names for things. In **bootstrapping,** children appear to use their knowledge of word class, of whether a word is a verb or a noun, for instance, to learn the meaning of new words (Clark, 1995). To those of us who didn't get the parts of speech right until we reached the 7th grade, this may sound implausible. Yet Roger Brown offers convincing support for this idea. Brown (1957) showed children a picture of hands working on a spaghetti-like substance in a bowl. To some he said the picture showed "how *to sib*"; to others he said it showed "*a sib*"; and to some others he referred to it as "*some sib*." Different aspects of the picture, in other words, were isolated by the syntactic cues of "to (+ verb)," "a," and "some." The verb "to sib" cues children to look for movement. Similarly, the cue "a" denotes a noun whose referent should have a well-defined shape. In contrast, "some" is used to refer to something with ill-defined borders, such as milk, sand, or spaghetti.

After describing the picture in one of these three ways, Brown showed separate pictures of the hands, the bowl, and the spaghetti, and asked which one "sib" referred to. Those who had been told that the picture showed "how to sib" picked the hands, those who had heard "a sib" picked the bowl, and those who had heard "some sib" picked the spaghetti. Each had learned the meaning of a strange word by relying on syntactic cues, cues that told them to look for movement, something with a well-defined shape, or an amorphous substance. By assuming that a word is one type or another, children know what to look for when hearing a new word.

How can parents help their child to learn words more quickly?

First Sentences

At about 18 months to 2 years, children begin putting words together. Their sentences are simple at first, never more than two words. The number of these two-word combinations initially develops slowly, and then takes off, increasing rapidly. Over a period of 7 months, for example, one child put together 14, 24, 54, 89, 350, 1,400, and then over 2,500 different combinations (Braine, 1963). Children can express most of the same relationships expressed in adult speech in these early constructions. They can identify agents and objects of actions, who did what (Doggie run) and what happened to whom (Bump head), as well as indicate possession (Jenny shoe), location (Kitty chair), recurrence (More cookie), and disappearance (Allgone milk). Word order, important in communicating meaning in adult speech, is similarly important in children's first sentences; the meaning of sentences such as "Davey hit" (Davey hit me) is clearly different from that of "Hit Davey" (I hit Davey).

bootstrapping A strategy children use to learn names for things through their knowledge of word classes and syntactic cues.

What children talk about reflects their understanding of their world. Children are beginning to understand what causes things to happen, and distinctions between agent and object sprinkle their observations of events. Similarly, frequent mention of possession, as in "Mommy cup" or "Billy sock," reflects their awareness of which things they are allowed to touch or play with and which are forbidden. And always, as they explore, they are ever mindful of where others are in relation to them.

Another milestone in language development is reached when children begin putting three or more words together. The age at which this occurs varies considerably, from 2 years in one child to 3 years in the next. These sentences, just like earlier ones, have their own organization. Children frequently begin with a short, two-word sentence and expand it, inserting another phrase similar to the first, "Fix it . . . Joshua fix it." The presence of units in these sentences is revealed by the child's intonation, by hesitations in the pattern of speaking, as well as by the choice of words. Pauses occur at the borders of a unit, as in "Put . . . big boots . . . on." The length of these utterances increases with their developing language skills. In fact, the **mean length of utterance,** determined by counting the number of different units, or **morphemes,** that communicate meaning, is a more reliable measure of language development than is age. Using this measure, "Kick boots" would have a MLU of 3, since it contains three morphemes ("kick," "boot," "s"), even though the sentence contains only two words.

The length of children's utterances has been found to correspond to their use of ever-more-complex rules for communicating meaning (Brown, 1973). Brown has identified five such stages of language development. In the first stage, corresponding to an MLU of 1.0 to 2.0, children speak in two-word sentences, adopting the rule of word order in communicating meaning. Examples would be "Davey hit" or "Billy sock," the order of the words in each communicating agency or possession, respectively. In the second stage, with an MLU of 2.0 to 2.5, children can use rules to inflect words, adding "s" to form plurals and "ed" to indicate past tense, as in "Two kitties" or "Ellie jumped." In the third stage, with an MLU of 2.5 to 3.0, children use rules to get from one form of a sentence to another, known as transformation rules ("Kristina hugged Ginger" or "Ginger was hugged by Kristina"). Some of the first transition rules children use are for questions— the who, what, where, and why ones. Children follow an interesting progression in their mastery of these.

One of the first rules children use in this third stage is the rule of preposing, or putting first, the "wh-" word (*What* does she want? Or *Where* does he sit?). Unlike adults, however, children do not invert the subject and auxiliary verb, as in "What *does she* want?" or "Where *does he* sit?" Instead, they say "What she want?" or "Where he sit?" At about the same time that they ask questions using the preposing rule, they also begin to use another rule, the rule of inverting, or transposing, the subject and predicate—"*Can I* go out?" as opposed to "I can go out." Though both preposing and inverting rules are available to them in this stage, children do not use both in the same question. It seems that early sentences are limited by performance factors such as memory span or just how much can be programmed and thought out at once.

Children appear to be able to employ only a limited number of rules in producing a sentence. Initially, they are limited to one rule ("What she can ride?" or "Can she ride?"). Then they can use two rules within a single sentence, preposing and transposing ("What can she ride?"). But at this point, they cannot produce sentences requiring the use of three rules: preposing, negating, and inverting, as in "Why can't she ride?" Instead, they ask "Why she can't ride?"

In the fourth and fifth stages, with MLUs of 3.0 to 3.75 and 3.75 to 4.5, respec-

mean length of utterance (MLU) The average number of morphemes in a child's sentences.

morphemes Units of language that communicate meaning.

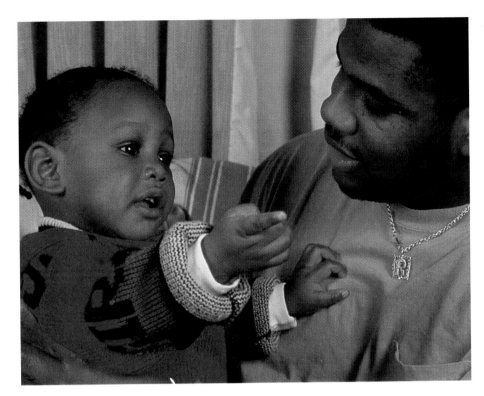

In the third stage of language development, children learn to ask questions using who, what, where, why.

tively, children's sentences become increasingly complex. They begin to use clauses and compound and complex sentences. Language continues to develop through early childhood, and continues to develop even through the school years. Table 5.2 charts milestones in language development.

Theories of Language Development

How are we to explain the development of language? What role, for instance, does the language that children hear spoken around them play in language learning? Or are environmental influences, such as spoken language, relatively unimportant? Noam Chomsky (1965), at MIT, devalued the importance of the speech children hear, assuming it was not an adequate model of grammatical speech. Chomsky assumed instead that children are born with a language-acquisition device, neural centers that are prewired for detecting the phonological, semantic, and syntactic categories that constitute a spoken language. The evidence that language is indeed biologically based is abundant and convincing. Such evidence in itself, however, does not rule out the importance of other factors.

Research examining the way individuals speak to young children reveals important differences between that and speech directed toward adults, differences that make child-directed speech ideal for someone new to a language. Sentences are short, simple, and grammatical. Speakers use familiar words, refer to things in the here-and-now, and talk about whatever the child is paying attention to. All of these aspects of child-directed speech make it an excellent model of language. Thus, it seems that adults *fine-tune* the way they speak to infants and young children, adjusting their speech to correspond to what the child can understand and to capture the child's attention (Snow, 1995).

Why is reading to a child so important to language development?

TABLE 5.2 Milestones in Language Acquisition

By Age 1

Milestones	Activities to Encourage a Child's Language
• Recognizes names • Says 2 to 3 words besides "mama" and "dada" • Imitates familiar words • Understands simple instructions • Recognizes words as symbols for objects	• Responding to coos, gurgles, and babbling • Talking to the child throughout the day • Reading colorful books to the child every day • Telling nursery rhymes and singing songs • Teaching the child the names of everyday items and familiar people • Taking the child to new places and situations • Playing simple games, such as peek-a-boo and pat-a-cake

Between Ages 1 and 2

Milestones	Activities to Encourage a Child's Language
• Understands "no" • Uses 10 to 20 words, including names • Combines two words, such as "daddy bye-bye" • Waves good-bye and plays pat-a-cake • Makes the "sounds" of familiar animals • Gives a toy when asked • Uses words such as "more" to make wants known • Points to his or her toes, eyes, and nose • Brings object from another room when asked	• Reading children's stories to the child • Talking to the child about what you're doing as you do it • Talking simply and clearly • Talking about new situations before you go, while you're there, and after you return • Looking at the child when he or she talks to you • Describing what the child is doing, feeling, hearing • Playing children's records and tapes • Praising the child's efforts to communicate

Fine-tuning takes its cues from the child. This sensitive interplay between speaker and child can first be seen in the way we talk to infants. "Baby talk" is characterized by a high-pitched voice and exaggerated prosodic features, or the rise and fall of the voice and the stress given to words (Garnica, 1977). These same characteristics are true of speech to infants in languages other than English as well. It is noteworthy that these speech characteristics are precisely the ones that are most likely to capture an infant's attention (see Chapter 4).

When young children begin to say their first words, we again fine-tune our speech, but this time by enunciating our words more clearly. Sounds, such as final consonants, that would ordinarily be "swallowed" in speech that is directed toward another adult are now carefully articulated. We usually stop doing this by the time children reach the age of the vocabulary spurt. Even in terms of syntax, there is evidence of fine-tuning. Thus, we see a close correspondence between the degree to which parents will add words, elaborating on the speech of the child, and the degree to which children drop them. That is, the more telegraphic the child's speech, the more likely the parent will elaborate. Elaboration decreases as children spontaneously add the parts of speech they originally had omitted in telegraphic speech. Fine-tuning is most evident in the speech of mothers, and less so in that of fathers and siblings (Snow, 1995).

So far, our discussion of the factors that contribute to language development has stressed input from adults. How active a role do children assume in these dialogues? Lois Bloom and colleagues (1996) propose that children, and not adults,

TABLE 5.2 Milestones in Language Acquisition

Between Ages 2 and 3

Milestones	Activities to Encourage a Child's Language
• Identifies body parts	• Repeating new words
• Carries on "conversation" with self and dolls	• Helping the child listen and follow instructions by playing games: "pick up the ball," "touch my nose"
• Asks "What's that?" and "Where's my . . . ?"	
• Uses two-word negative phrases, such as "no want"	• Taking the child on trips and talking about what you see before, during, and after the trip
• Forms some plurals by adding *s*	• Letting the child tell you answers to simple questions
• Has a 450-word vocabulary	
• Gives first name; holds up fingers to tell age	• Reading books every day, perhaps as part of the bedtime routine
• Combines nouns and verbs, such as "mommy go"	• Listening attentively as the child talks to you
• Understands simple time concepts, such as "last night" and "tomorrow"	• Describing what you are doing, planning, thinking
• Refers to self as "me" rather than by name	• Having the child deliver simple messages for you
• Tries to get adult attention: "Watch me"	• Carrying on conversations with the child
• Likes to hear same story repeated	• Asking questions to get the child to think and talk
• May say "no" when meaning "yes"	• Showing that you understand what the child is saying by answering, smiling, and nodding your head
• Talks to other children as well as adults	
• Solves problems by talking instead of hitting or crying	• Expanding what the child says. If the child says, "more juice," you say, "You want more juice?"
• Answers "where" questions	
• Names common pictures and things	
• Uses short sentences like "me want more" or "me want cookie"	
• Matches 3 to 4 colors, knows big and little	

Source: Adapted from Learning Disabilities Association of America. (1997, July 9). *Speech & language milestone chart.* KidSource OnLine. Retrieved from the World Wide Web: http://www.kidsource.com/LDA/speech_language.html.

take the lead in these early conversations. In her **intentionality model** of language development, Bloom assumes that the impetus for language development comes from the child, fueled by the growth of the child's mind rather than by the conversational skills of the adult. Consequently, the rate at which language is acquired reflects children's growing understanding of their world and their desire to communicate this. It is primarily the abilities of the child, rather than structure provided by the adult, that determine the course of language learning in general and the nature of conversational discourse in particular.

In contrast to Bloom's intentionality model is the **scaffolding model** (Bruner, 1983). This model assumes that adults are the ones to take charge of these early conversations, both by initiating them and by providing a structure, or scaffold, which supports the emergence of new language forms. The concept of a scaffold is similar to Vygotsky's zone of proximal development, in which the adult models forms of speech that are just beyond the capacity of the child to perform independently, yet still within the child's reach when assisted. Different predictions follow from the two models about the form that early conversations between children and their caregivers will take. The intentionality model assumes that

intentionality model Lois Bloom's model of language development, which assumes that the impetus for language development is the growth of the child's mind rather than the conversational skills of the adult.

scaffolding model A model of language development that assumes that the impetus for language development is adults' initiation of conversation and providing of a scaffold, or structure, to support the emergence of new language forms.

children will be the ones to initiate a conversation and that when mothers do initiate a conversation, they will be more likely to state what is on their mind than ask questions to foster speech in the child. Conversely, the scaffolding model predicts that mothers will initiate most conversations and that they will use questions rather than statements in order to prompt turn-taking and help the child build on what they have just said.

At least some evidence seems to favor the intentionality model. Bloom, Margulis, Tinker, and Fujita (1996) followed children from the ages of 9 months to 2 years, recording their conversations with their mothers. They found that most conversations were initiated by children and that when mothers responded, they were more likely to do so with a statement than a question. Thus these early conversations appear to reflect children's desire to communicate and do not appear to require elaborate scaffolding from their conversational partners.

What might children want to talk about? Children talk about what they see ("Ball go"), what they are doing ("Shoe on"), and what they are feeling ("Billy sleepy"). Jean Mandler (1992), recall, has suggested that children's ongoing analysis of activities such as looking at moving objects, understanding agency, and animacy results in image-schemas which represent basic forms of understanding. She further suggests that such image-schemas provide the foundation for the conceptual vocabulary that children later put into words.

What forms of understanding would such a vocabulary include? The narrative of experience suggests some answers. Consider an event such as a cat tapping a ball with its paw. As we have seen earlier in the chapter, even very young infants can abstract information about agency (the cat), action (tapping), object (the ball), location (a room in the house), and path (of the ball). Such preverbal conceptualizations translate into the more familiar questions of what happened, who did it, to what or to whom, and where it took place.

Mandler suggests that these image-schemas function at an intermediate level between perception and language, with preverbal concepts being based on a perceptual analysis of actual ongoing events taking place in space and time. This earliest of grammars, rather than being an abstract formal system, becomes spatial in nature and thus continuous with the way we process other information about our physical world (Armstrong, Stokoe, & Wilcox, 1995; Lakoff, 1987).

How might image-schemas serve as a primitive grammar? These schemas, recall, are assumed to have an internal structure, to consist, in other words, of parts. For instance, the image-schema for "path," as in the path a moving ball follows, would join the beginning, the trajectory, and the destination of the ball. This structure, then, would allow the child's gaze to anticipate and more easily follow points along the path and be surprised should the ball deviate. The analogue nature of such schemas makes it possible for them to embed information about regularities of relationships among the parts. A child following the path of the ball, for instance, can shift her attention from where it starts to where it will be the next moment. The relationship among these elements is rule-governed, just as it is among the words of a spoken language. We know that infants are aware of these rules from the work of investigators such as Van de Walle and Spelke, Baillargeon, and others. Infants are aware, for instance, that objects do not simply disappear and then reappear as they move along a path (principle of continuity) and that for something to start to move, it must be set in motion by something else or itself be animate.

In attending first to one element and then to another within such schemas, children are guided by their knowledge of such rules. In this grammar of experience, they can distinguish such things as agent (the animate cat) from action (the tap which sets the ball in motion) or object (that which moves when it is hit) or

What is this toddler likely to notice? In addition to sharp teeth or furry ears, children can distinguish agent from action, object, or location, and this "grammar of experience" is reflected in the grammar of their speech.

location (the path followed by the moving ball) (Fillmore, 1982). This grammar, since it is based on the same analysis of experience as other perceptual and cognitive processes, provides a foundation for talking about what infants are experiencing.

A perceptually based approach to language such as the one proposed by Mandler assumes that language is processed the way we process other information about our physical world, in terms of basic schemas that capture fundamental distinctions such as part-whole, agent-object, container, support, and the like. Approached this way, grammar, just like other forms of thought, can be traced to the way we perceive and interact with our physical world. Language, rather than beginning as an abstract, formal system that must later be connected to other aspects of experience, becomes continuous with such basic cognitive processes as object recognition or perceptually guided movements such as walking or reaching (Armstrong, Stokoe, & Wilcox, 1995).

 ## Summary

Making Sense of the World

Infants begin to explore their surroundings from the moment of birth. With age, they become increasingly better at perceiving the things around them. These improvements can be interpreted as reflecting the operation of both reinforcing contingencies present in infants' surroundings and internal anticipatory schemata. Reinforcers are events that increase the frequency of the behaviors on which they are contingent. Anticipatory schemata are cognitive structures that direct perceptual exploration, preparing individuals to take in certain types of information and not others. The schemata are in turn modified by the information that is sampled.

Piaget's Developmental Constructivism

Piaget believed that infants' understanding of the world begins with the development of sensorimotor schemas that evolve out of reflexes present at birth. Piaget believed that sensorimotor thought, characteristic of infancy, develops over six substages. In the first substage (modification of basic reflexes) inborn reflexes become modified, providing a better fit with the conditions under which they have occurred and occurring in the absence of the stimuli that initially triggered them. In the second substage (primary circular reactions) infants develop circular reactions in which they are able to repeat behaviors that lead to interesting outcomes. In a third substage (secondary circular reactions) circular actions are extended to include objects outside infants' own bodies. In a fourth substage (coordination of secondary circular reactions) intentional, goal-directed behavior can be seen; and in a fifth stage (tertiary circular reactions) the use of trial and error in problem solving is believed to first occur. In a final substage (mental representation) Piaget believed infants become able to represent their experiences mentally with the emergence of symbolic thought.

A central concept in Piaget's theory of infant intelligence is that of object permanence. Piaget assumed that it takes infants several years to develop a full understanding of the nature of objects; and in the first substages of this development, objects cease to exist for infants when they are out of sight.

Critique of Piaget's Theory

Piaget assumed that each of the sense modalities functioned independently of the other and that only through experience did infants come to integrate these. More recent evidence shows that infants can use information provided by one modality to recognize something they have experienced in another modality. Similarly, research strongly suggests that infants are aware of objects' existence, even when these can't be seen, well before Piaget believed they are able to do so.

Categorizing Experience

Infants' awareness of time, like that of adults, appears to be based on their sensitivity to the temporal sequencing of events. Infants' perception of space and of the form of things develops with their ability to move about and with their ability to take hold of things and grasp them. Initially, infants represent the location of objects in relation to themselves (egocentric representation). Infants come to locate objects in relation to other things in their environments (landmark representation) when they begin to move about on their own. Finally, infants become able to represent spatial relations according to some abstract frame of reference (allocentric representation). Infants also show a rudimentary understanding of simple arithmetic operations that result in an object being added to or taken away from a set.

Even young infants have been shown to be able to classify objects into different categories. Three explanations for forming categories were considered: using defining features, using a probabilistic approach, and forming a theory of why things go together. Categories could be represented in terms of defining features, or features that all members of a category possess in common. A probabilistic approach assumes that we distinguish items as belonging to a category on the basis of family resemblance rather than an invariant set of features. This approach assumes that four factors are important in assigning items to a category: cue validity, basic-level categories, correlated features, and prototypes. Finally, objects can be categorized on the basis of the relationships that exist among them, reflecting a theory of why things go together. The first categories are most likely conceptual in nature, reflecting image-schemas, which map spatial structure into conceptual structure.

The Development of Language

From birth on, infants are attentive to the sounds of speech and prefer to listen to the sounds of their native language. Infants begin to babble in the 2nd to 3rd month. Later, their babbling reflects the sounds they hear in their native language. Infants also attend to the prosodic features of speech, using these as cues in ambiguous situations. Infants typically utter their first word at about the age of 12 months. Word acquisition occurs slowly at first, but late in the 2nd year a vocabulary explosion often occurs. Difficulties in articulation underlie regularities in children's pronunciation errors.

Children may use single words not only to name things but also, in combination with gestures, to communicate more complex thoughts; this usage is referred to as a *holophrase.* When naming things for children, adults use names that correspond to the distinctions they anticipate children will need to make in using the objects named. Children are often able to learn the meaning of new words after hearing them used a single time. *Fast mapping* refers to their ability to map the meaning of a new word onto a referent on hearing the word used in context just once. In learning the names for things, names are assumed to be mutually exclusive: If a thing has one name, it is not likely to be called by another. Children also use a bootstrapping strategy in learning names for things, in which they use their knowledge of word class to learn the meaning of new words.

Children begin putting two words together at about 18 months, and three or more words together anywhere from 2 to 3 years of age. The length of children's utterances (mean length of utterance) has been found to correspond to their use of ever-more-complex rules for communicating. Using this index, five stages of language development have been identified. In the first, children speak in two-word sentences. In the second, children use rules to inflect words, indicating plurality and tense. In the third, children can use rules to transpose meaning from one form of a sentence to another. In the fourth and fifth stages, their sentences become increasingly complex.

Theories of Language Development

There is abundant evidence indicating that language is biologically based; this does not, however, rule out the importance of other factors. Child-directed speech, using sentences that are short, simple, and grammatical, provides an excellent medium through which children can learn aspects of language. Adults fine-tune the way they speak to children, adjusting their speech to correspond to what the child can understand. Children also play an active role in these dialogues, often taking the lead in directing early conversations. In contrast, the scaffolding model of language acquisition assumes that adults are the ones to take charge of conversations, providing a scaffold that supports the emergence of new language forms.

 ## Key Terms

allocentric representation (p. 187)
babbling (p. 195)
bootstrapping (p. 203)
defining features (p. 189)
egocentric representation (p. 187)
fast mapping (p. 201)
habituation (p. 180)
holophrase (p. 199)
intentionality model (p. 206)

jargon babbling (p. 196)
landmark representation (p. 187)
mean length of utterance (MLU) (p. 204)
morphemes (p. 204)
operant conditioning (p. 170)
overextension (p. 200)
primary circular reactions (p. 173)
reinforcement (p. 171)

scaffolding model (p. 207)
schemas (p. 173)
secondary circular reactions (p. 173)
sensorimotor stage (p. 171)
tertiary circular reactions (p. 175)
underextensions (p. 200)
vocabulary explosion (p. 199)

chaptersix

Infancy and Toddlerhood
Psychosocial Development

A toddler stands, legs planted in the doorway, casting a brief shadow, and then with a squeal steps into the outside. Horizons widen in infancy, and beginning steps quicken to a run as mastery brings surer footing and a firmer sense of self. Parents who kept pace initially may find it hard to keep up, as the emotional security of deepening relationships enables infants and then toddlers to move beyond the familiar. The infant's exploration of the world without enables the toddler to discover a world within, one which reveals a realm of emotions and the startling discovery of the self. Households and schedules are rearranged to avoid the wreckage that comes with life in the fast lane, as first the infant and then the toddler fine-tunes shifting emotions and masters corners on the run. It is a fast, wild, joyous, and tumultous ride into childhood.

This chapter marks the developmental route taken. We will stop first to look at the bonds of attachment that form between infants and their caregivers. Much of the exuberance of these first years can be traced to the emotional foundation provided by secure and trusting relationships in infancy. Infants contribute to the building of this foundation just as do their caregivers. In a second stop, we will look at differences in temperament among infants that are apparent even at birth and that give shape to these first relationships. In a final stop along the route into childhood, we will look at the emotional developments that accompany an emerging sense of self. Emotions such as guilt and shame emerge as infants move from reactivity to self-regulation and as toddlers move from stormy demands for autonomy to a more relaxed exploration of their limits. Not all of the moves are smooth, however. There's many a "glitch" as those youngest on the road of life shift gears, find their own pace, and learn to coordinate their needs with those who care for them.

Infants are biologically prepared to become attached to those who care for them.

Attachment: The Bonds of Love

In the first days and weeks of life, infants react in the same way to everyone, showing little preference for one person over another. In a sense, any shoulder or lap will do. This sweet indiscretion becomes less true with time, until by the end of the first 6 months, infants clearly prefer those closest to them, such as parents or siblings, to others. **Attachment** refers to the affectional bonds that infants form with those who care for them and to the ways in which infants organize their behavior around these people, using them as a base from which to explore and to which to return for safety when stressed (Seifer & Schiller, 1995; Waters, Vaughn, Posada, & Kondo-Ikemura, 1995).

Are infants biologically prepared to become attached to those who care for them? It would appear that they are. Not only are they equipped perceptually to discover what they will need to know about their world, as we noted in the last chapter, but they are also equipped socially in much the same manner. This is not to say that infants have social skills, but simply that their initial behaviors are sufficient to ensure that, under most circumstances, their needs will be met. Among the most important behaviors equipping infants for social encounters are their reflexive cries to changes in their body states. Infants need not wait for others to wonder whether they might be hungry or cold. Their cries clearly signal their needs (Seifer & Schiller, 1995). Similarly, a second factor equipping them socially is their soothability. They *stop* crying when fed, are soothed when picked up, grasp fingers that are offered, stare quietly at faces, and still to voices. Each of these responses to those who care for them knits infants and their caregivers ever more closely into a social unit.

Why do infants become attached to their caregivers? Is it because these are the ones who feed them when they are hungry, keep them warm when cold, and amuse them with whispers and kisses? Is love won by sweet talk and warm milk? Initial assumptions about the basis for affectional bonds in infants focused on the satisfaction of physical needs, such as the reduction of hunger, cold, or discomfort.

How does attachment differ form affection?

attachment The affectional bonds that infants form with those who care for them; the ways in which infants organize their behavior around these caregivers, using them as a base from which to explore and to which to return for safety when stressed.

In Harlow's experiments with attachment in monkeys, infants preferred the cloth surrogate mother to the one that gave milk.

Sigmund Freud (1933/1961) assumed that the behavior of humans as well as of other organisms is motivated by biological drives. These drives are experienced as states of arousal, such as hunger and thirst, which individuals seek to reduce. Satisfying biological drives such as these is not only necessary for our survival, but is also pleasurable. The reduction of drives is so pleasurable, in fact, that Freud believed it to serve as one of the basic motivating principles throughout life. Freud assumed that infants associate the pleasure derived from reducing the drive of hunger with the very person who is most closely associated with this activity, the mother. Thus, for Freud, drive reduction became the basis for attachment.

Harry Harlow, a psychologist at the University of Wisconsin, was one of the first to actually put these assumptions to the test. Harlow raised rhesus monkeys with inanimate surrogate mothers, wire forms with plastic faces. These surrogates provided either milk, in the form of a bottle that protruded below the neck, or contact comfort, a soft terry cloth covering the wire form. When allowed to spend time with these surrogates, infants would bound over to the surrogate with the milk. But after satisfying their hunger, they left her for the terry-cloth surrogate. In an even more dramatic test of surrogate preferences, the infants were scared with a raucous toy to see which surrogate they would seek for comfort. Once again, the infants preferred the surrogate they could cling to and cuddle against over the one that gave milk (Harlow & Zimmerman, 1959). This research argues strongly against any simple explanation of attachment in terms of hunger reduction.

The Development of Attachment

John Bowlby, a British psychiatrist, approached attachment in terms of its adaptiveness. Infants are completely helpless at first and must rely on others to meet all of their needs. Survival depends on staying close to those who will care for them. However, infants also experience a growing curiosity about their world, one which increases with age and which can lure them from the safety of their mother's side. The attachment bond balances these competing needs, the need for

Infants will venture off on their own, but they make sure of their parent's whereabouts as they do so.

safety and the need to explore and experience new things. Functioning much like an invisible elastic band, infants stretch the attachment bond as they venture out to explore things around them, until the tension this produces pulls them back within safe limits (Bowlby, 1969). One can actually see this tension in infants' behavior as they scramble away, only to check over their shoulders to make sure Mom is still there. Bowlby would argue that it is no coincidence that attachment can be seen to intensify when the infant becomes mobile at about 6 or 7 months.

Bowlby outlined four phases in the development of attachment. In the *preattachment phase* (birth to 6 weeks), even though infants may be cared for exclusively by a single person, they experience no distress if they happen to be left in the care of someone else.

At about a month and a half, however, infants begin to notice, and care about, whom they are with. When an unfamiliar person approaches or makes overtures, they are likely to become quiet and wary. One can see them look to their mother and then to the stranger, and then back again to the mother. Bowlby referred to this phase as *attachment in the making* and believed it to last until infants are about 6 months old.

At about the time infants begin to crawl around on their own, they enter the third of Bowlby's phases, that of *clear-cut attachment*. This phase is marked by the presence of several distinctive types of behavior: proximity seeking, separation anxiety, and secure-base behavior. **Proximity seeking** can be seen in the infant's attempts to stay close to the mother and follow after her, asking to be picked up or attempting to crawl into a lap. **Separation anxiety** is the evident distress infants experience when the mother or other caregiver is out of sight. Infants have come to feel secure in the mother's presence and become anxious when she leaves. The mother functions as a **secure base** from which they venture forth to explore and to which they periodically return to get recharged. The third phase lasts until the age of 18 to 24 months.

In the fourth and final phase of attachment, that of *reciprocal relationships*, the toddler is able to comfortably spend longer periods of time away from the mother, a development coinciding with increased reliance on representational thought.

proximity seeking An infant's attempts to stay close to the mother and follow after her, asking to be picked up or attempting to crawl into her lap; a behavior seen during the clear-cut attachment phase.

separation anxiety The evident distress infants experience when the mother or other caregiver is out of sight; a behavior seen during the clear-cut attachment phase.

secure base The use of the caregiver by infants as a base from which to venture forth to explore and to periodically return for comfort and reassurance.

This ability to hold things in mind, or mentally represent their experiences, presumably enables toddlers to be by themselves for longer periods of time. Toddlers can be away from the mother, in other words, because they can mentally carry her with them. In a similar way, infants' increased mobility was presumed to solidify the development of a clear-cut attachment bond. Thus, the better infants are able to get away from the mother, the more they need to know she is near, whereas the better toddlers are able to keep her near, the more they can stay away. Each of these developments reflects the adaptability and the elasticity of the attachment bond. Finally, Bowlby believed the child could also represent aspects of the attachment relationship itself and that these served as an internal *working model* for subsequent relationships. This final phase in the development of attachment is assumed to become the foundation on which later relationships are built and lasts for several years.

Types of Attachment Relationships

Mary Ainsworth, a Canadian psychologist who worked with Bowlby, has conducted extensive research on the affectional ties that develop between infants and their parents. Central to Ainsworth's (1973, 1993) understanding of attachment is the concept of security. Infants who experience the warmth and comfort of having their basic needs met feel secure. This sense of security, in turn, frees them to venture out and explore things around them. It also affords a safe haven to which they can return when they feel threatened. This "back-and-forthing" to their secure base, as Ainsworth puts it, enables them to get "recharged" before going out again to explore. The paradox to attachment is that, rather than taking the form of a clinging dependency, it leads to a healthy and inquisitive independence. Thus, the behavior of infants who are securely attached is characterized by a balance between proximity seeking on the one hand and exploring on the other.

Ainsworth believes attachment is biologically based and, as a consequence, should develop in all children, with the exception, perhaps, of those who have been reared under conditions of extreme neglect or isolation. The fact that secure-base behaviors are evident in children from diverse cultures, as well as in other primates, such as Harlow's monkeys, supports this assumption. Cross-cultural comparisons of children in China, Colombia, Germany, Israel, Japan, Norway, and the United States have found that children organize their behavior with respect to using the mother as a secure base in similar ways, being as alike across cultures as they are within their own culture. Secure-base behavior, in other words, is not something unique to middle-class children in the United States (Posada et al., 1995).

Ainsworth assessed differences in attachment security through the use of a procedure that she called the **strange situation.** In this procedure, mothers sit with their infants in a comfortable room, toys scattered about on the floor. After some time, a stranger enters, sits down, and talks with the mother. Then, when the infant is not noticing, the mother leaves; and the infant is alone with the stranger until the mother returns. Differences in the ways infants reacted to each aspect of this procedure, particularly in their reactions to the mother's return, allowed Ainsworth to classify them into one of several types of attachment relationships. Attachment security when initially measured this way was highly stable (Waters, 1978). More recent assessments of attachment have been lower, possibly due to greater flux in contextual variables affecting parenting (Belsky, Campbell, Cohn, & Moore, 1996; Mangelsdorf, Shapiro, & Marzolf, 1995). The three types of attachment relationships Ainsworth identified are securely attached infants, anxious-avoidant infants, and anxious-resistant infants.

strange situation A procedure used by Mary Ainsworth to assess differences in attachment security: The mother sits with the infant in a comfortable room until a stranger enters; she and the stranger talk a while and she leaves when the infant is not looking, leaving the infant alone with the stranger.

Securely Attached Infants   Children who are securely attached derive a sense of security from the presence of the mother, playing contentedly on the floor with only an occasional glance to assure that she is nearby. When the stranger enters, they typically look to the mother, may vocalize or hold out a toy to the stranger, and then return to their play. These infants react with visible distress when they discover the mother is no longer present. Although they may allow the stranger to pick them up and may quiet their crying, they are not completely consoled by her attempts to comfort them. When the mother returns, they immediately reach out or run over to her, snuggle into her arms, become calm, and return again to their play. Most infants (65%) are securely attached.

Anxious-Avoidant Infants   Infants who are anxious-avoidant also play happily when their mother is present, but engage in fewer behaviors designed to assure themselves of her presence. They show little distress when the stranger enters and may also show little distress when the mother leaves. If they do begin to cry, they are as easily consoled by the stranger as they are by their mother's return. Unlike the securely attached infants who run to their mother when she returns, these infants are just as likely to turn away. Nearly 25% of infants show this pattern of attachment.

Anxious-Resistant Infants   Infants who are anxious-resistant are wary and stay close to their mothers in the new situation, yet appear to derive little security from her presence. Although they are the most distressed of all the infants by their mother's leaving, they show the least comfort on her return. They may cry to be picked up, but unlike the securely attached infants who snuggle into their mother's arms, may immediately struggle to be put down. They continue to fuss after her return and have difficulty returning to their play. Slightly over 10% of infants fall into this attachment category.

What factors might be responsible for differences such as these in attachment relationships? Both infants and parents contribute to the quality of the relationship. Ainsworth and Marvin (1995) note, however, that it is the infants who make things happen, "it is *they* who take the initiative. They are not passive little things to whom you do things" (p. 5). Although infants play an active role in the developmenting attachment relationship, the way parents respond to the infant is critically important in determining the type of relationship that eventually develops.

Early research by Mary Ainsworth and Sylvia Bell (1969) revealed two important maternal behaviors related to the attachment relationship: sensitivity and responsiveness. These investigators observed mothers interacting with their infants when they were 3 months old and again when they were 1 year old. One-year-olds whose mothers had sensitively responded to their needs as young infants cried less and were more secure in their relationships with them. Ainsworth defined **sensitivity** in terms of accurately "reading" the infant's signals and **responsiveness** in terms of how promptly she responds to these. Many parents voice concerns that they will spoil their children by picking them up when they cry, fearing that they will reinforce crying by responding to it with their attention (see Chapter 1). However, Ainsworth and Bell's research indicates that with young infants there is little to fear in this respect and that prompt attention to an infant's crying results in children who cry less, and not more.

Mothers of securely attached infants are also more flexible when they interact with their infants, supporting rather than interfering with the infant's behavior. This doesn't put a 3-month-old in the driver's seat of the relationship, but it

What behaviors would you look for to distinguish an infant who is securely attached from one who is not?

sensitivity The ability to accurately "read" an infant's signals; a behavior related to the attachment relationship.

responsiveness Promptness in responding to an infant's signals; a behavior related to the attachment relationship.

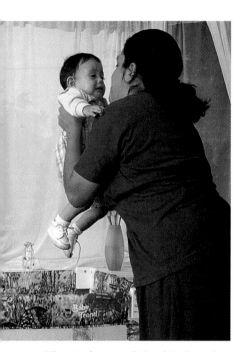

The attachment relationship depends on both the infant's crying and the parent's response; prompt attention to a crying infant results in an infant who cries less, according to Ainsworth & Bell's research.

What are some maternal behaviors that illustrate sensitivity?

does establish the type of cooperative atmosphere that characterizes good relationships at any age, one in which the intentions of the other are taken into consideration. Sometimes small details offer the most telling examples. Ainsworth and Bell conducted some of their observations when mothers were feeding their infants and noted differences in such things as whether mothers watched for when their infants were ready for the next spoonful or how they dealt with infants who were easily distracted while eating. Less-sensitive mothers would attempt to force the procedure, whereas sensitive mothers might deal with distractibility by taking the child to another room with fewer distractions where the child would happily attend to lunch.

In contrast to the sensitivity and responsiveness of mothers of securely attached infants, mothers of anxious-avoidant infants were relatively insensitive to their infants' distress. Furthermore, when these mothers did respond, they were less likely to tend to the infant's emotional needs than they were to try to distract the infant. These mothers typically were not comfortable with physical expressions of emotion, being more likely to give a "peck" on the top of the head, for instance, than a "smooch" on the face, thus maintaining an emotional distance. Infants raised by such mothers were more likely to try to comfort themselves than try to get comfort from the mother (Pederson & Moran, 1995).

The characteristics of anxious-resistant relationships are not as well understood as those of the other attachment relationships, in part because of their infrequency. In general, these mothers were found to be relatively unresponsive and inconsistent. The infants, for their part, were demanding and fussy. Both partners in the relationship tended to be emotionally volatile, "blowing up" at each other in unpredictable ways. The infants' negativity may have been an expression of frustration in response to the mothers' unpredictable behavior. However, it is also possible that the mother's negativity may have been, at least in part, a response to fussiness in the infant (Pederson & Moran, 1995).

How reasonable is it to expect that patterns of attachment will be passed down, like emotional heirlooms, from one generation to the next? Are mothers who were themselves securely attached as children more likely to respond to their own children in ways that foster secure attachment? Conversely, are those who were avoidantly or resistantly attached as children likely to parent as they were parented, resulting in similar patterns of attachment among their infants? In a longitudinal study, Diane Benoit and Kevin Parker (1994) interviewed expectant mothers in order to determine their attachment type and then, a year later, used the strange situation to assess attachment in their infants. Taking things one step further, these investigators also assessed attachment in the maternal grandmothers of the infants. As they had expected, the mother's attachment pattern predicted the pattern of attachment seen in their infants in over 80% of the cases. Also, knowing the mother's attachment pattern predicted the attachment pattern in *their* mothers in 75% of the cases. Thus, the early attachment relationships that children form with their parents appear to provide working models for future relationships, much as Bowlby had suggested.

Jay Belsky (1984, 1990), at the University of Pennsylvania, argues that we need to look beyond the immediate interactions between infants and their parents to the larger context in which these occur. Belsky maintains that no one factor, such as a parent's personality, is likely to determine the security of attachment. Rather, the attachment bond develops within a "well-buffered system" in which stressors are balanced by supports. In other words, there are multiple paths leading to secure attachment. It is the cumulative effect of maternal characteristics with those of the father and the child, along with contextual factors such as the quality of the

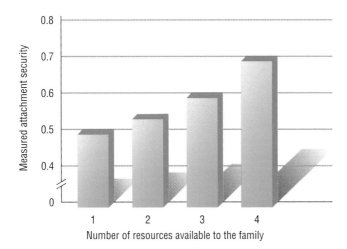

FIGURE 6.1 Security of Attachment Between Fathers and Their Sons As a Function of the Personal and Collective Assets Within the Family *Source:* J. Belsky, (1996). Parent, infant, and social-contextual antecedents of the father-son attachment security. *Developmental Psychology*, 32, 905–913.

marriage, job satisfaction, the family's financial situation, and the presence of social supports that together predict attachment security. For instance, it has been found that mothers who experience satisfaction with their maternal role are more likely to have securely attached infants. The degree to which mothers experience role satisfaction, however, is affected by the amount of social support they receive (Isabella, 1994). The Social Policy Focus, "The Importance of Fathers: Child Support Versus Emotional Support" examines two contextual factors: the absence of the father and the absence of financial support from the father.

Most of the research on attachment has focused on infants' relationships with their mothers. Still, we know that by the end of the 1st year, the affectional bonds infants establish with their fathers are very similar to those with their mothers (Lamb, 1977, 1981). But are similar processes at work in each case? That is, are contextual factors similarly important in determining the quality of infants' attachment to their fathers? Belsky (1996) examined father-son attachment at 1 year of age using the strange-situation procedure. He also assessed the presence of factors that could serve as stressors or supports, such as personality types, quality of the marriage, and work-family relations. He found, just as with mothers, that as the number of resources available to the family increased, so did the security of attachment between fathers and their sons. We can see this relationship in Figure 6.1, in which attachment security is shown to increase with the number of resources that fall above the median.

One of the most obvious factors contributing to the quality of the relationship that develops between parents and their children is the sheer amount of time they have to spend together. For a majority of mothers, this translates into the length of their maternity leave. By the late 1990s, 60% of women with children under the age of 6 were employed, and a majority of mothers returned to work within the 1st year of their child's life (U.S. Bureau of Labor Statistics, 1999).

Is length of the maternity leave related to the quality of mother-child interactions? Roseanne Clark, Janet Shibley Hyde, Marilyn Essex, and Marjorie Klein (1997), at the University of Wisconsin, examined this relationship in the context of what the infant and the mother each bring to it. These investigators were not as interested in determining whether employment in itself affected the relationship as in determining the conditions under which it might and the processes responsible for this.

The Importance of Fathers: Child Support Versus Emotional Support BY ANDREA HAYES

An American father recently spent 11 years searching for his two children, who had been abducted by their mother. The mother had a severe drug addiction and yet effectively kept their whereabouts unknown. This father repeatedly attempted to gain some sort of support or assistance from police and other agencies to help find his children, but to no avail. Predictably, the children ended up in foster care. At the time, the foster care agency claimed the father could not be located for dependency proceedings. Interestingly, this same public entity eventually tracked him down as a "deadbeat dad" in order to garnish his wages to pay for the benefits his children received while they were on welfare. Is it fair to say that this agency was more interested in tracking down a "deadbeat dad" than in helping him to function as a real one?

As a result of welfare reform, Congress has addressed the growing concern for children's health and welfare by passing legislation that strengthens child-support enforcement. Child support is defined as "payments to children from nonresident parents." One third of American families were headed by a single parent in 1996 (Rockefeller, 1998), yet only 60% of this nation's eligible children have a legal agreement for child support. Of those, 25% receive no payment at all. When we consider that the number of eligible children grew from 10% in 1960 to 33% in 1990, it leaves many children at risk for poverty-related problems such as poor nutrition, inadequate health care, and unsafe housing (Garfinkel, Miller, McLanahan, & Hanson, 1998).

Through the 1998 Child Support Performance and Incentive Act, the federal government rewards individual states for better performance and enforcement of child-support laws. The actual implementation of this policy began in the year 2000. While the development of this policy seems logical and necessary, is it an example of the tail wagging the dog?

Some researchers believe that the money spent on incentives for states that enforce child support could be better spent on intervention programs. Certain studies seem to point to fathers' involvement being interdependent on their developmental life stage, economic situation, ability to pay, and relations with other family members. Without attending to these underlying issues, forced payment may actually cause further estrangement (Coley & Chase-Lansdale, 1999). One intervention program called the Parent's Fair Share Demonstration seeks to increase child-support payments and paternal involvement through education, job training, social support groups, and mediation services. Time and further research will tell which approach is most effective: broad legislation or community intervention.

The development and implementation of social policy always has pros and cons. Due to the tax burden on most working Americans, the drain of welfare made reform imperative, and part of this reform requires fathers to take personal responsibility for their children. However, one can't help but wonder if future research will find more children *monetarily* cared for, but *emotionally* bereft due to the absence of their father.

When mothers were depressed or when they perceived their infants as difficult, shorter leaves of absence (6 weeks) were associated with less sensitivity and responsiveness and less pleasure in being with their infants. However, these effects disappeared with longer leaves of absence (12 weeks). It may be that longer maternity leaves provide the opportunity for working mothers to resolve the competing demands of family roles and work. Longer leaves may be especially helpful with difficult infants, by increasing the mother's sense of effectiveness and competence. By 3 months, infants are more responsive and their habits are more regular. Each of these can increase a mother's feelings of competence, which in turn can affect the way she interacts with her infant, enabling her to be more sensitive and simply to enjoy her infant more.

These findings have implications for public policy. The Federal Family and Medical Leave legislation of 1993 guarantees the mother's job and her benefits for a minimum of 12 weeks' leave; but the leave is unpaid, and many working mothers cannot afford to take this length of leave without pay. A shorter 6-week disability leave is currently mandated and often includes pay. While this may be adequate for many mothers, these findings indicate that individual differences in mothers and infants make a longer leave desirable for some. Following the birth of an infant, parents need time not only to care for the infant, but also to develop relationships with the infant and to adjust to new roles within the family.

High-quality day care has no negative developmental effects and may benefit children's social and intellectual development.

Day Care

The number of mothers with young children who work outside the home has increased substantially over the past three decades, with just over 60% of mothers whose children are 6 years of age or less being employed outside the home (U.S. Bureau of Labor Statistics, 1995). As a result, many more young children today experience day care for some number of hours each week than did so in the past.

What effect does early day care have on children's development? Is attachment security likely to be affected? Are other aspects of development, such as intelligence and social behavior, affected? And will the family still continue to exert as strong an influence on a child's development as it might were the child not being cared for by others? Questions such as these have arisen for parents who face the need to find alternate sources of care when they return to work.

Initial research on the effects of day care did not offer comfortable assurances to concerned parents. In fact, based on a review of the existing research to that point, Jay Belsky (1986) suggested that placing infants in day care for 20 hours or more a week during the 1st year of life could pose a risk to the development of secure attachment. Additionally, the effects of extended early day care were thought to carry over into childhood, resulting in poorer social adjustment once children reached school age. Subsequent research has not supported these early generalizations. Research focusing only on the number of hours a child is in day care each week, without considering the many contextual conditions that are present, can lead to more confusion than clarity. See the Research Focus, "The 'File Drawer Problem': Day Care and Attachment."

What contextual conditions need to be considered? The two contexts that are most important, as one might expect, are the day care facility itself and the context of the family. We will consider each of these in turn.

With respect to the day care facility, research has found that when the quality of child care is high, day care has no negative developmental effects and may even beneficially affect aspects of social and intellectual development (Burchinal,

The "File Drawer Problem": Day Care and Attachment BY MICHAEL WAPNER

1. Every year over a thousand tickets pay off more than $500 in the lottery.
2. At least 500 cases of cancer have improved after treatment with medicines made of apricot pits.
3. I personally know of four people who have had bad luck after breaking a chain letter.

What's wrong with these claims as guides to behavior? What's wrong is that they don't tell the whole story. They trumpet the number of *positive outcomes*—that is, the number of times some event or behavior was followed by a particular effect. But they omit the *negative results*—the number of times that the particular effect did not follow. Consequently the claims are misleading. Consider:

1. It may be true that every year more than 1,000 lottery tickets pay over $500. Does that make it a good idea to buy lottery tickets? What if you knew that every year over 10 billion lottery tickets pay nothing? That would make the probability of getting a winning lottery ticket 1 in 10 million.
2. Perhaps 500 cases of cancer did improve after being treated with medicines made of apricot pits. But in how many cases did no change or even deterioration follow the same treatment? Maybe the improvement had nothing to do with apricots.
3. Perhaps I do know four people to whom bad things happened after they failed to respond to a chain letter. But how many people experienced nothing unusual after doing the same thing? (Not to mention the number of people to whom bad things occurred even though they did respond or never received a chain letter.)

We have come to expect that people who are trying to sell something may "forget" to report the negative cases. But that the same problem may occur in science is a bit more surprising. And yet it may occur, not out of an intentional desire to mislead, but as the unintended consequence of the way the results of research are disseminated.

The failure to report negative outcomes in science is called the "File Drawer Problem." The phrase refers to the effect of two related tendencies: First, scientists tend not to submit negative results to journals (but to "file" them); and, second, journals tend not to publish research with negative results. In the extreme, the consequence of the file drawer problem would be that in some cases only the handful of positive results that occur by chance would be published, while the much larger proportion of negative results would remain unknown.

One antidote for the file drawer problem is for researchers to replicate studies that had positive outcomes and to publish the results even (or particularly) if they are negative. Lori Roggman and her colleagues did precisely that in an area of particular social and psychological importance—the relationship between infant day care and mother-infant attachment. The authors chose for replication four published studies which had found that infant day care was significantly related to insecure attachment to the mother. Appropriate to the point in question, the replication (Roggman, Langlois, Hubbs-Tait, and Reiser-Danner, 1994) used data from research which had not been published because it had produced no significant results. However, because the procedures and the subjects in the research by Roggman and her associates were comparable to the studies being replicated, it made sense to reanalyze the unpublished data. In contrast to the earlier published studies, Roggman and her associates did not find a consistent relation between day care and attachment. This is not to say that no significant effects were found. It did appear that anxiety in the mother-infant relationship was greater for infants in part-time day care than for infants in no day care or full-time day care. However, part-time day care also tended to be more irregularly scheduled, with a greater variety of caregivers, reflecting the parents' partial and irregular employment. Thus, the greater insecurity in mother-infant attachment might well have come from factors more complex than day care itself. But in any case, no simple statement about the relation between day care and attachment could be made.

The authors discuss a number of factors which might account for the conflicting results between these studies, including different ways of selecting subjects and different definitions of day care. And certainly there must be reasons for the differences. But the bottom line is that unless negative results, when they occur, are published, there will be no differences to explain.

Ramey, Reid, & Jaccard, 1995; Pungello & Kurtz-Costes, 1999). Determining what constitutes high-quality care, however, is not always that easy for parents.

What does one look for in determining whether a facility offers high-quality care? To get answers, parents need to be able to walk into a facility and look for various conditions. The first thing to notice is the number of children in the facility and the ratio of children to caregivers. For infants and toddlers especially, these ratios should be low. A ratio of one caregiver for every three infants or every six toddlers is desirable, whereas a higher ratio of one to eight is possible with preschoolers (Berezin, 1990; McCartney, Scarr, Phillips, & Grajek, 1985). Another thing to look for is whether children have ample opportunity to interact with the adults who are caring for them. Are they able, that is, to be held, to climb into a lap, or to be listened to or read to? Keep in mind that day care centers with larger numbers of children are likely to have more rules in place and be less flexible in accommodating the interests and needs of individual children than are smaller facilities. Irrespective of the size of the facility, parents should be able to stop by at any time, unannounced and with no appointment necessary.

In addition to the number of staff, both their training and their commitment to caregiving are also important. Day care facilities have been found to differ widely in these respects. For instance, sensitivity and responsiveness, the two dimensions of interaction that Ainsworth found to be important in the formation of attachment, have been found to differ markedly among caregivers. In this respect, parents could follow Ainsworth's lead and notice how responsive adult caregivers are to children's overtures as they show them through the facility, just as Ainsworth noticed how responsive mothers were to their infants while being interviewed. Do caregivers respond promptly? Are they attentive to expressions of delight and pleasure as well as those of distress (Pungello & Kurtz-Costes, 1999)? Additionally, the consistency of staff over time is important for children's emotional comfort. A high turnover of staff can be problematic not only with respect to children's comfort in relating to their caregivers, but also in terms of signifying underlying administrative problems.

Day care facilities also need ample space, both inside and out, for a variety of activities to be going on at any one time. Finally, it is important to be sure that health and safety standards are met. A personal tour of a facility can reveal some things, such as whether dirty diapers are disposed of in a sanitary way or adequate protections exist around stairs and the sharp edges of furniture. It is also important to make sure that the facility has met state licensing requirements.

Even so, parents may not always be able to see what they need to see in order to judge the quality of a facility. They simply can't be there throughout the day to observe, and often find it difficult to interpret the meaning of the things they do see. For instance, how is one to interpret signs of distress in a child? Does a child's tearful clinging simply indicate separation anxiety or a real problem in the type of care the child is experiencing? Perhaps the best measure of a facility's quality is the overall attitude and behavior of the children themselves. Is their behavior spontaneous? Are they busily engaged in play with each other? Do they appear to be happy?

A disturbing finding to emerge from studies assessing the quality of child care is that most facilities, whether child care centers or family day care homes, do not offer high-quality care. Among child care centers offering care for infants and toddlers, only 8% were found to provide good care and as many as 40% were found to have health or safety problems (Helburn et al., 1995). Similarly, irrespective of age, for children cared for in homes, either by relatives or in family day care homes, just under 10% were found to receive good-quality care whereas 35% received care that was potentially harmful to development (Kontos, Howes, Shinn, & Galinsky, 1995). Box 6.1 is a checklist for day care quality.

The quality of care has been found to vary with the income level of the children attending the facility. Children from upper-income homes generally receive the highest quality of care. Interestingly, children from low-income homes receive higher quality care than do those from middle-income homes, with the exception that care providers in these centers have been found to be less sensitive and more emotionally detached than are those in centers attended by children from middle- or high-income homes (Pungello & Kurtz-Costes, 1999).

What should parents look for in a day care center to determine whether it offers high-quality care?

Box 6.1 *Checklist for Day Care Quality*

How can parents determine the quality of care provided by a facility? Child Care Aware, a joint venture of the National Association of Child Care Resource & Referral Agencies (NACCRRA), suggests asking the following questions.

Caregivers/Teachers

- Do the caregivers/teachers seem to really like children?
- Do the caregivers/teachers get down on each child's level to speak to the child?
- Are children greeted when they arrive?
- Are children's needs quickly met even when things get busy?
- Are the caregivers/teachers trained in CPR, first aid, and early childhood education?
- Are the caregivers/teachers involved in continuing education programs?
- Does the program keep up with children's changing interests?
- Will the caregivers/teachers always be ready to answer your questions?
- Will the caregivers/teachers tell you what your child is doing every day? Are parents' ideas welcomed? Are there ways for you to get involved?
- Do the caregivers/teachers and children enjoy being together?
- Is there enough staff to serve the children? (Ask local experts about the best staff/child ratio for different age groups.)
- Are caregivers/teachers trained and experienced?
- Have they participated in early childhood development classes?

Setting

- Is the atmosphere bright and pleasant?
- Is there a fenced-in outdoor play area with a variety of safe equipment? Can the caregivers/teachers see the entire playground at all times?
- Are there different areas for resting, quiet play, and active play? Is there enough space for the children in all of these areas?

Activities

- Is there a daily balance of play time, story time, activity time, and nap time?
- Are the activities right for each age group?
- Are there enough toys and learning materials for the number of children?
- Are toys clean, safe, and within reach of the children?

In General

- Do you agree with the discipline practices?
- Do you hear the sounds of happy children?
- Are children comforted when needed?
- Is the program licensed or regulated?
- Are surprise visits by parents encouraged?
- Will your child be happy there?

Source: Child Care Aware. (1999). A project of the National Association of Child Care Resource and Referral Agencies (NACCRRA), Washington, D. C.

How can we promote the selection of high-quality care facilities by parents? Educating parents is a first step. Providing information about the potential impact of low-quality care as well as guidelines on what to look for in high-quality care is important. Also important are public policy changes that would institute better regulation of such facilities as well as the training of increased numbers of qualified providers. Training, however, will accomplish little unless there are sufficient incentives for individuals to pursue this line of work. Thus, the suggestions just made need to go hand in hand with legislation guaranteeing adequate compensation for child care providers. Finally, we need public policies aimed at helping parents pay for high-quality care, making such care accessible, in other words, to all income groups.

What can we say with respect to the second context, that of the family? Will parents continue to exert as strong an influence on their children's development as they might were their children not being cared for by others? Comparisons of children in day care with those cared for at home by their mothers have found that dimensions of family life are no less closely related to children's development when they attend day care than when they are cared for at home. Rather, exposure to developmentally sound experiences, such as less authoritarian attitudes toward child rearing and more sensitive mothering, is related to more positive development in children whether they are cared for at home or in day care (NICHD, 1998).

Finally, how might the effect of day care vary as a function of differences in family contexts? Although research has found that high-quality day care can have beneficial effects, it is nonetheless true that not all children are equally likely to benefit by such care. Rather, day care appears to have a buffering effect with respect to family variables. In other words, day care appears to serve as a protective factor, mitigating the negative effects of family variables that have been found to be associated with poorer cognitive, social, or emotional functioning. Conversely, however, the very same buffering effects may work in the opposite direction as well, in that beneficial family variables may also have less impact on children's development (Burchinal et al., 1995; NICHD, 1998).

Temperament

Perhaps because infants are small enough to fit in the crook of an arm and are dependent on others for their every need, it is all too easy to think that they would be "putty" in the hands of adults. But are infants so many lumps of biological clay, to be shaped by their caretakers? Observations of a single infant, no matter how carefully they are conducted, would do little to resolve this question. However, even a casual comparison of two newborns reveals noticeable differences between them, and a glance at a roomful of babies, such as in a hospital nursery, would leave no doubt as to the individual nature of each. Infants differ from one another from the moment of birth. They differ not only in their weight, the length of their fingers, and the shape of their ears, but also in what one might refer to more generally as their disposition, or their characteristic mode of responding. Infants begin life very much as individuals.

Differences in infants' characteristic ways of responding are referred to as temperament. More specifically, **temperament** consists of the underlying predispositions contributing to infants' activity level, emotionality, and sociability (Goldsmith et al., 1987). Since differences in temperament are evident even in very young infants, they are assumed to be biologically based, genetically predisposing an infant to

temperament Underlying predispositions contributing to an infant's activity level, emotionality, and sociability.

From birth, infants differ from one another in their temperament.

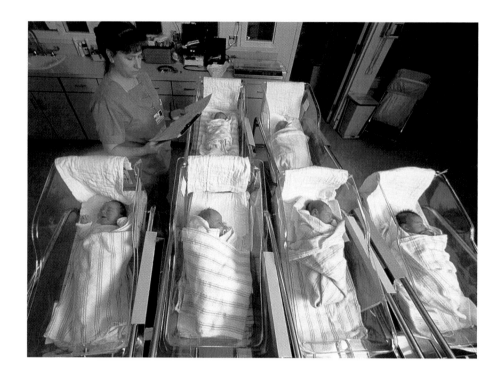

react in certain ways rather than in others (Emde et al., 1992; Kagan, 1997). This is not to say that the resulting behaviors are fixed at birth, but simply that, for any infant, certain ways of behaving are more likely than are others. In the final analysis, the characteristics that infants eventually develop are as much a function of the ways in which their caretakers *respond* to what infants initially do as they are to any behavioral predispositions themselves. Thus, not only would an infant who shies away from new situations be likely to develop in different ways from one who excitedly approaches them, but the first infant would also be likely to develop in different ways from one who, though initially just as shy, is gently encouraged to explore new things (Kagan & Snidman, 1991).

Genetic and Cultural Contributions to Temperament

The influence of heredity on temperament has been studied in a number of ways. One approach is to compare the correspondence in traits among individuals with different degrees of genetic similarity to each other, such as is done in twin and adoptive studies. A second approach is to identify certain index behaviors that, because they are presumably related to temperament types through underlying processes that are partially inherited, predict later differences in temperament among children.

Comparisons of identical (monozygotic) with fraternal (dizygotic) twins illustrate the first of these approaches. Because monozygotic twins (see Chapter 2) develop from the same fertilized ovum, they are genetically identical. Dizygotic twins, on the other hand, develop from two separate fertilized ova and are no more similar genetically than any other two siblings with the same set of parents, sharing 50% genetic relatedness. Greater similarity in a given trait among monozygotic twins than dizygotic twins can be taken as an index of the contribution of heredity to that trait.

Shyness and emotionality appear to be genetically influenced.

There are presently several large-scale longitudinal studies examining genetic contributions to temperament, one comparing identical with fraternal twins and another comparing adopted and matched nonadopted children with their biological and adoptive parents. These are the Louisville Twin Study (Wilson & Matheny, 1986) and the Colorado Adoption Project (Plomin, DeFries, & Fulker, 1988), respectively. Although it is somewhat difficult to generalize across the various situations and measures used in various studies, two temperament traits emerge as showing some genetic influence. These are emotionality and shyness (Goldsmith, Buss, & Lemery, 1997; Plomin et al., 1988; Wilson & Matheny, 1986). Together, these traits describe a more general characteristic that might be described as behavioral inhibition, which other research has also identified as having an hereditary component (Kagan, 1997). Of equal interest, however, is the broad range of genetic influence for different aspects of temperament, ranging from virtually no influence for some traits to moderate levels of influence for others (Emde et al., 1992).

Jerome Kagan and his associates (1981, 1997), at Harvard University, have explored the contributions of heredity to temperament through the second of these two approaches. These investigators assumed that the biological processes that predispose a child to some, although not necessarily all, temperament traits are genetically influenced and that these processes are indexed by the presence of certain behaviors. These investigators found, for instance, that infants who become agitated when exposed to unfamiliar events, reacting by arching their backs and sticking out their tongues, are likely to later be shy as children, whereas those who do not exhibit these behaviors are more likely to be sociable. Thus, the behaviors of arching the back and sticking out the tongue can be used as *index behaviors* for later shyness.

Kagan (1997) began by classifying 4-month-olds according to behavioral differences in the way they reacted to unfamiliar events. Differences were assumed to be indicative of different thresholds of excitability in neural centers that are involved in organizing responses to novelty. Would these differences predict later temperament differences? Specifically, would they predict which infants would be inhibited and which would be uninhibited as toddlers?

Using crying and physical agitation as index behaviors, they identified 4-month-old infants as either *high reactive* or *low reactive.* Approximately 20% and 40% of the 462 infants they studied fell into these two categories, respectively. The index behaviors for these categories were assumed to reflect genetically influenced differences in the processing of information. When these infants were tested with unfamiliar situations at 14 and 21 months of age, a third of the high-reactive infants proved to be extremely fearful, with very few (3%) showing little fear. Just the opposite pattern of responding was observed in the other group. A third of these infants showed very little fear, with very few (4%) being highly fearful.

Thus, the constellation of behavioral reactions that were associated with a lower threshold of excitability was in fact predictive of which infants would become most fearful as toddlers in new situations. These findings strongly suggest that these traits, those of being either inhibited or uninhibited, are influenced by heredity. Furthermore, differences between these groups persisted into childhood. When these two groups of children were tested again when they were 4–5 years old, those who had originally been identified as inhibited smiled less and talked less than did those who had been identified as uninhibited.

To what extent are differences in temperament apparent across cultures? A number of studies have found reliable differences. A comparison of Japanese and Caucasian infants found the former to be less likely to show distress during well-baby examinations (Lewis, Ramsay, & Kawakami, 1993). Comparisons of Chinese and Caucasian infants have found the former to be calmer and more easily soothed when distressed. They were less likely, for instance, to pull off a cloth that had been placed over their face and, when placed in a crib, tended to stay in that position, whereas Caucasian infants were more likely to reposition themselves, lifting their heads or turning them to one side (Freedman & Freedman, 1969). A more recent comparison of 4-month-old Chinese and Caucasian infants found Caucasian infants to have higher levels of arousal and to differ more among themselves than did Chinese infants. They moved more, fretted more, vocalized more, and cried more (Kagan et al., 1994).

Temperament Types

Some differences can clearly be seen to persist into childhood, such as differences in fearfulness or reactions to the unfamiliar (Kagan & Snidman, 1991). And some have been found to persist into early adulthood (Newman, Caspi, Miffitt, & Silva, 1997). However, for most differences in temperament, the link with behavior becomes increasingly complex with age (Goldsmith et al., 1987). How well one can predict temperament qualities in children from assessments made in infancy depends in part on the age of the infant when temperament is first assessed (Rothbart, 1986). By 4 months of age, individual differences in infants' temperament clearly exist, although multiple observations over several sessions may be necessary for these to be reliably assessed (Seifer, Sameroff, Barrett, & Krafchuk, 1994).

Using procedures involving such multiple measurements, Alexander Thomas, Stella Chess, and Herbert Birch (1963) conducted the New York Longitudinal Study, a pioneering study of newborns in which they interviewed parents over several years. These investigators identified nine aspects to temperament.

1. *Activity.* Some infants are more active than others. They move more when held or even when simply lying awake in their cribs. They also move about more in their sleep. Differences in activity are also apparent before birth, in

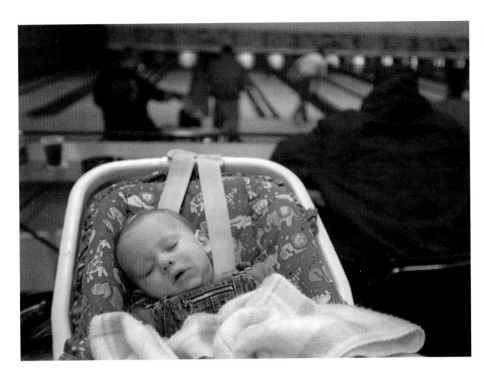

Infants differ in the intensity of stimulation required to elicit a reaction.

movements of the fetus. Parents of these children seem always to be chasing after them. In contrast, less active children can sit quietly in one spot, amusing themselves for long times at a stretch.

2. *Regularity.* Infants and toddlers differ in the regularity of their biological functioning. Some children become hungry at the same time each day and have predictable nap and bed times, enabling parents to plan day and evening activities around them. Other children never seem to be hungry at the same time, are wide awake at nap time, and wired by bedtime.

3. *Approach versus withdrawal to new situations.* Infants and toddlers also differ in the way in which they respond to new situations. Some welcome new experiences and change, whether these involve people, foods, toys, or routines, whereas others are cautious and uncomfortable.

4. *Adaptability.* Infants differ in how quickly they modify their responses to new situations, irrespective of whether they tend to welcome change or withdraw from anything new.

5. *Sensory responsiveness.* There are differences as well in the intensity of stimulation that is required to bring about a reaction. Some infants and toddlers can sleep through a loud party, while others startle awake when the lights to their room softly click on.

6. *Quality of mood.* One can characterize children in terms of their overall mood, by whether they are predominantly happy or unhappy. Some children fuss when they wake up, cry when they go to bed, and mumble over their food and toys in between. Others smile or hum to themselves.

7. *Intensity of response.* Infants and toddlers differ in the energy with which they react to things, irrespective of whether their reactions are positive or negative. Whereas some will smile or whine, others will laugh out loud and howl.

8. *Distractibility.* Infants differ in their ability to concentrate, some, for example, taking a bottle no matter what is happening around them and others being distracted at the slightest sound or movement. Distractibility, however, is not always a disadvantage; distractible children can also be diverted when crying or hurt.

9. *Attention span and persistence.* Infants as well as older children and adults differ in their persistence. For instance, one infant can be seen to persevere in trying to reach something just beyond its fingertips while another will give it only a passing swipe. Children also differ in the length of time they can focus on a task, some jumping from one toy to the next and others playing for a long time at a single activity.

Thomas and Chess (1977) distinguished three temperament types based on clusters of the characteristics listed above. These types identified some infants as easy, others as difficult, and still others as slow-to-warm. These researchers caution that temperament types simply reflect *how* children do what they do and not *why* they do these things. Temperament, in other words, describes the style that characterizes a child's behavior and does not explain the motives that may underlie this.

Easy infants tend to be cheerful and playful, regular in their biological functioning, such as in patterns of sleeping and waking and becoming hungry, and easily adaptable to changes. Approximately 40% of the infants originally studied by Thomas and Chess fell into this category. **Difficult infants** tend to be negative in mood, have irregular body functions, and be slow to adapt to changes. They cry a lot as infants, have irregular sleep patterns, do not take new foods well, and react intensely when frustrated. About 10% of the original sample could be classified as belonging to this temperament type. **Slow-to-warm infants** have low activity levels, give mild reactions, are slow to adapt to changes, tend to withdraw from new situations, are slightly negative in mood, and react to situations in a mild way. Fifteen percent of infants studied could be placed in this category.

Not all infants "fit" into one of these categories, of course. Thirty-five percent of the original sample studied by Thomas and his co-workers could not be categorized according to any of these temperament types. In fact, some researchers, such as Mary Rothbart, at the University of Oregon, prefer not to include a "difficult" category, pointing out that behavior that might be considered difficult in one situation is not necessarily difficult in another. For example, persistence in play, such as when a child is called away by a parent or teacher to do something else, might be labeled as "difficult," yet the same persistence when fitting pieces of a puzzle together would be seen as laudatory. Similarly, what might be perceived as problematic at one age can be an advantage at another. A preschooler who is easily distracted may have trouble getting dressed in time in the morning, but a similar distractibility becomes an advantage for an infant who, by being distracted from sources of discomfort, can be more easily soothed. Instead of labeling a particular constellation of traits as being of one type or another, Rothbart reminds us that each trait has its "social costs" as well as its benefits.

An alternative to classifying infants into temperament types is to identify higher-order factors, or more general temperamental differences, that can be derived from the nine or so traits originally identified. When this is done, five factors emerge (Rothbart & Ahadi, 1994). Two factors, fearfulness and irritability, describe a general negativity, and a third describes a positive mood, as seen in a general tendency to approach things. A fourth factor is related to activity level and the fifth to persistence. These factors roughly correspond to similar dimensions of the adult personality (Eysenck & Eysenck, 1985; Rothbart & Ahadi, 1994; Watson,

easy infants Infants who tend to be cheerful and playful, regular in their biological functioning (such as in patterns of sleeping and waking and becoming hungry), and able to adapt easily to changes; a temperament type identified by Thomas and Chess.

difficult infants Infants who tend to be negative in mood, irregular in their biological functioning (such as in patterns of sleeping and waking and becoming hungry), and slow to adapt to changes; a temperament type identified by Thomas and Chess.

slow-to-warm infants Infants who have low activity levels, give mild reactions, are slow to adapt to changes, tend to withdraw from new situations, and react to situations in a mild way; a temperament type identified by Thomas and Chess.

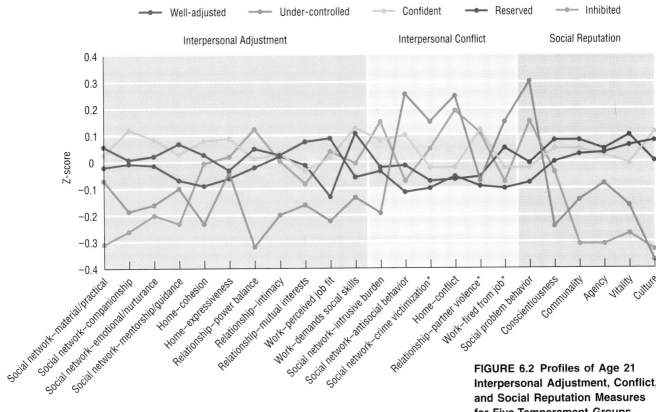

FIGURE 6.2 Profiles of Age 21 Interpersonal Adjustment, Conflict, and Social Reputation Measures for Five Temperament Groups
Measures with asterisks are interpolated z-scaled percentages of cases in groups. Source: D. L. Newman, A. Caspi, T. E. Moffitt, and P. A. Silva (1997). Antecedents of adult-interpersonal functioning: Effects of individual differences in age 3 temperament. *Developmental Psychology*, 33, p. 213.

Clark, & Harkness, 1994). Thus, fearfulness and irritability correspond to a tendency in some adults toward negative affect or mood. Similarly, the factor of positive mood, as well as that of activity, corresponds to differences in adults in positive emotion or extroversion, in which individuals seek out and approach situations. Finally, the factor of persistence corresponds to differences among adults in control or constraint, presumably resulting from attentional factors involved in regulating behavior.

But do differences in temperament in childhood predict different styles of behavior in adulthood? A longitudinal study that followed 3-year-olds into adulthood suggests that they do (Newman et al., 1997). Over 900 3-year-olds were classified into one of five behavioral styles on the basis of three temperament differences: sociability, activity level, and behavioral control. Eighteen years later, when these children reached adulthood, they were again assessed for the way they functioned in a variety of settings, such as at home, at work, and in romantic and social relationships. Young adults who as children were classified as either well-adjusted, reserved, or confident differed little among themselves. However, those who had been inhibited or undercontrolled differed as adults from the others in ways that could be anticipated based on their temperament. For instance, young adults who had been undercontrolled as children reported more conflictual relationships, more difficulty at work, and scored higher on measures of antisocial behavior. Conversely, young adults who had been inhibited as children were described as less outgoing, confident, and popular. These trends can be seen in Figure 6.2: Both undercontrolled and inhibited 3-year-olds scored lower as adults on measures of interpersonal adjustment and social reputation. With respect to measures of interpersonal conflict, only the former were higher (Newman et al., 1997).

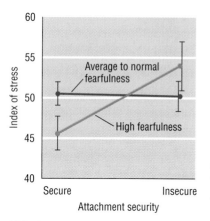

FIGURE 6.3 Attachment Security Moderates the Relationship Between Temperament and Stress
The number of infants in each condition were: secure, high fearful = 9; insecure, high fearful = 8; secure, average-to-low fearful = 32; insecure, average-to-low fearful = 14.

How might parents help a fearful child cope with new situations?

How might temperament affect attachment?

Temperament and Attachment

Differences in temperament not only thread their way into adult personalities but can also affect the ways in which parents interact with their infants. Researchers are still untangling the complex ways in which children and parents influence each other and how this relationship affects the child's development. Does temperament, for instance, affect the quality of attachment? Or does attachment affect the manner in which temperamental traits are expressed? For instance, might children who are predisposed to fearfulness evidence this trait only when they do not have a secure attachment relationship or when their caregiver is not present? Megan Gunnar, at the University of Minnesota, has explored the intricate relationships between temperament and attachment within the context of children's reactions to stressful situations.

Gunnar and her associates (1996) assumed that patterns of attachment actually moderate the way children of different temperaments would cope with stress. Thus, the attachment relationship should serve to buffer or protect children when stressed, and this buffering should be particularly evident in those who are temperamentally most in need of it. Put another way, one should not be able to predict how successful children are at coping simply by observing differences in their temperament. One would also need to know something about their attachment relationships. Gunnar and her associates observed toddlers who were either high or average in fearfulness in a mildly stressful situation. Would children who were temperamentally fearful, or inhibited, but securely attached cope better than those who were equally fearful yet insecurely attached? As expected, fearful toddlers showed greater evidence of stress than those who were less fearful. However, this was true only for those who were insecurely attached. Among toddlers who were securely attached, those who were high in fearfulness actually coped better than the less fearful (Figure 6.3).

Can temperament similarly be shown to affect attachment? For instance, might infants who are temperamentally irritable be more at risk for developing insecure attachment relationships, perhaps because of the difficulty mothers may have in sensitively responding to their demands?

Dymphna van den Boom (1989), at the University of Leiden, wondered whether one could predict the quality of attachment in older infants from assessments of their irritability, or proneness to distress, shortly after birth. Following the same group of infants and their mothers over a year's time, she found that irritability was a better predictor of attachment than the mother's sensitivity and responsiveness. Intrigued by this, van den Boom looked more closely at the way these infants and their mothers interacted. She found that irritable infants were not only more easily distressed, but also less fun in general to be with. They cooed and smiled less and fussed and cried more than other infants, with the result that mothers devoted a disproportionate amount of time to "fixing" things rather than to having fun and playing with their infants. Also, when the infants stopped fussing, their mothers appeared loath to initiate any new activities for fear they might provide more fussing. Thus, an unhealthy pattern of interaction had become established.

In a follow-up study, van den Boom (1994) was interested in whether mothers of irritable infants such as these could be taught to interact in more positive ways with their babies. As before, all of the infants were assessed for irritability shortly after birth; however, only those who were prone to distress were selected this time. When the infants were 6 months old, they and their mothers were randomly assigned to either an intervention or a control condition lasting for several months. Mothers who were given the intervention training were shown how to be more attentive to their infant's signals and how to respond more appropriately.

They were also instructed to play more with their infants. At 1 year of age, 78% of the infants in the intervention condition were securely attached, whereas only 26% of those in the control condition were. Infants in the intervention condition also were more sociable, better able to soothe themselves, cried less, and explored their surroundings more. In subsequent research, van den Boom (1995) found the effects of the intervention to persist into early childhood. Furthermore, there was a spillover from the mothers who participated in the intervention group to their husbands, with the latter also becoming more responsive with their children.

Temperament Types and Parenting

Most parents are unsure of themselves at first, and infants can do much to either make them feel competent or reinforce their initial fears. Parent-child relationships, in other words, show *bidirectional effects* in which infants influence their parents as well as being influenced by them. Easy infants, for instance, more often than not make parents feel effective. They stop crying when they are picked up, relish a bottle when it is offered, and snuggle into the fold of one's arms. These simple reactions of being soothed, comforted, and quieted allow parents to feel competent. They also make it likely that parents will respond to their infants' needs in similar ways in the future. By way of contrast, few experiences are more frustrating to a parent than not being able to soothe a crying infant. Parents of irritable or difficult infants face such frustrations on a daily basis. When infants cannot be soothed, refuse a bottle, or stiffen when held, parents feel helpless, and can even feel resentful or hurt. They are also likely to become inconsistent in the approaches they adopt when such infants fuss, since what they have done in the past has only occasionally been successful. The way infants respond to their parents, in other words, can influence the consistency of the care that they receive.

Children, as well as parents, try to maintain the other's behavior within a range acceptable to them.

Until relatively recently, attempts to understand the course of development have focused on factors outside the child, such as the home environment or parenting practices. Only occasionally have trained eyes been turned toward children themselves to see what they contribute to their own development (Bell, 1968; Scarr, 1993). When one does look at development from this perspective, one sees that children, as well as parents, exert an influence. This influence frequently takes the form of *upper and lower limits* for the other's behavior. These limits reflect how much or how little activity each one expects, or can tolerate, from the other, such as how intense a reaction can be or the extent of physical contact needed by one or the other. Both parents and children will try to maintain the other's behavior within a range that is acceptable to them. When an upper limit to a behavior has been exceeded, the other will act to reduce the behavior in some way. This reaction is termed an *upper-limit control.* Similarly, when a lower limit has been surpassed, attempts will be made to increase the behavior, by exercising a *lower-limit control.*

We should expect the control behaviors that parents use to be stepped, with each successive action depending on what has been tried before. Thus, with toddlers, first an explanation may be offered in a soft voice, then a request for a change, then crisp demands, and finally physical restraints. We might also expect to see more upper-limit controls with difficult children or with those who are extremely active or impulsive. These parents have a long history in which they have learned that other approaches, such as verbal reasoning or subtle changes in their emotional expression, frequently have little or no effect.

The behaviors of children will also be stepped, as they attempt to maintain their interaction with parents within limits that are most comfortable to them.

Consider a toddler who attempts to engage her busy mother's attention with a soft "Mommy." If the mother fails to respond, the toddler is likely to raise her voice a bit the next time, calling out more loudly until, if the mother is still unresponsive, her initial verbal request may become physical, as she tugs at the mother while loudly demanding her attention. It is all too easy for parents to respond only when children's stepped requests reach an upper limit such as this.

The way children cope, their eventual feelings of self-esteem and their willingness to step out on their own, evolve out of their early relationships with parents. Children, as well as parents, give shape to the form these relationships take. Whether children are easy, slow-to-warm, or difficult will influence the ways their parents approach them. Each of these temperament types can bring about, and react differently to, differences in the approaches parents bring to the situation. These early relationships shape the course of future development for parents and children alike.

Emotional Development

Many a new mother or father has watched smiles play across a sleeping infant's face. But do the smiles of newborns signal pleasure? Do infants' cries mean they are unhappy? When do babies first laugh? And when are they first angry? For that matter, what does it *mean* to experience emotions such as pleasure, happiness, anger, or joy? Can emotional states such as these be reduced simply to feelings, or do they play some larger role in our lives? And what do we know of the emotional life of infants and toddlers?

The feelings that emotions occasion in us are certainly one of their most immediate aspects. However, emotions are also highly adaptive behavioral states, organizing the way we react to events. A large, noisy dog occasions not only the experience of fear in a toddler, for instance, but also prompts a characteristic pattern of behavior that includes a physical drawing back or turning away and a general mobilization of the body. Thus, emotions have not only a felt, or experiential, component but also a behavioral component, so that they play a role in motivating behavior (Barrett, 1995; Mascolo & Fisher, 1995). Most emotions also have a cognitive component as well. Whether a child experiences one emotion or another results from that child's evaluation, or appreciation, of the particular significance of a situation. Thus, children may experience anger or amusement at such actions as having ice dropped down their shirts or a hand thrown over their eyes, depending on whether they interpret these actions to be hostile or friendly.

Not all emotions depend on such an appraisal for their instigation, leading some researchers to classify emotions as either basic or complex (Lewis, 1995; Lewis & Michaelson, 1983). According to this distinction, basic emotions are present from early infancy and, since they are not assumed to involve an appraisal of the event occasioning the emotional reaction, their expression is thought to be universal, occurring in all members of the species and taking much the same form from one culture to the next (Ekman, 1984, 1994; Izard & Maletesta, 1987). Complex emotions are assumed to be derived from, or differentiate out of, these more fundamental emotions and to reflect a cognitive appraisal of events.

By what age do infants express emotions such as happiness, surprise, and sadness?

The Growth of Emotions in Infancy

There is less than perfect agreement on which emotions are present in very young infants. Carroll Izard (1983, 1994), who developed a system for reliably coding infants' facial expressions, believes that newborns are likely to experience only

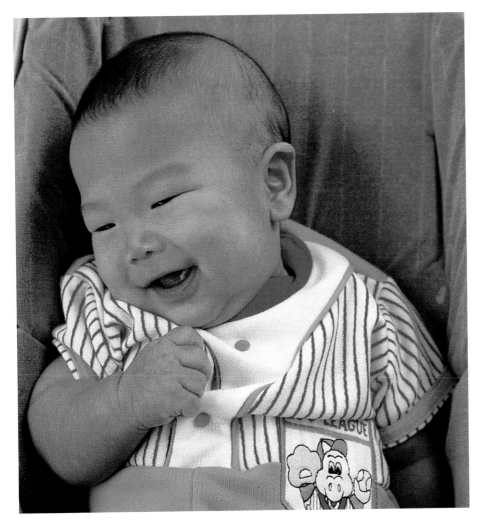

By 3 to 4 months, infants begin to laugh at things that tickle their fancy.

interest, distress, and disgust. Other investigators distinguish only calm or distress in the newborn (Rothbart & Ahadi, 1994). By the age of 1 month, however, mothers report they can detect a number of distinct emotions, such as interest, happiness, fear, anger, surprise, and sadness, based on their infants' facial expressions and their vocalizations (Johnson, Emde, Pannebecker, Stenberg, & Davis, 1982).

Also at about this age, between 4 and 6 weeks, infants begin to smile in response to what is taking place around them, or to engage in **social smiling** (Emde & Harmon, 1972; Izard, 1983). Infants smile much earlier than this, even when they are only days old, but they do so at first only when they are sleeping. Robert Emde and Jean Robinson (1979) traced the development of smiling in infants over the first several months of life. They noted that these earliest smiles appear to be prompted by changes in brain-wave activity in the brain stem, rather than to reflect emotions such as pleasure or happiness, and referred to them as **REM smiles.** By the 2nd week, infants begin to smile when they are awake. These smiles, however, are accompanied by the same brain-wave pattern as those that occurred in their sleep and are unrelated to what is taking place around them. REM smiles decrease in frequency over the next several weeks and are gradually replaced by smiles that occur in response to events that are taking place around the infant. Not until the age of 2 to 3 months, however, do infants appear to

social smiling Smiling in response to what is taking place around one; expression of emotion that begins between 4 and 6 weeks.

REM smiles Early smiles in infants prompted by changes in brain-wave activity in the brain stem.

discriminate between people and other interesting things, smiling back at others who are smiling at them. And by 3 to 4 months, infants begin to laugh at things that tickle their fancy (Maletesta, Culver, Tesman, & Shepard, 1989). Many of the things infants find fanciful are the commonplace events that we take for granted. Anne Lamott (1993) describes her 6-month-old son's reactions to the family cat:

> We were in the kitchen and Sam was lying on his back on a blanket on the floor, and suddenly the cat came in and started rolling around on the floor near him. . . . Sam laughed for ten straight minutes. He wounded like a brook. The kitty would stop rolling for a moment, and Sam would kind of get a grip, catch his breath, and all but wipe his eyes like an old man, and then the kitty would fling herself into the rolling motion again and Sam would just go nuts. (p. 156) ◄

At the opposite end of the emotional spectrum is another behavior familiar to parents—that of crying. This, too, shows a developmental progression. At birth, infants have two distinct types of cries: cries of pain and cries of hunger. Just as with infants' first smiles, these initial cries are involuntary, or reflexive, being coordinated at the level of the brain stem, rather than involving the cerebral cortex. The pattern of sound for each type of cry differs. Pain cries are loud and have a sudden onset, without any preliminary fussing, whereas hunger cries are more likely to build in intensity over a period of time. Most adults, even those who are not parents, can distinguish between these two cries (Gustafson & Harris, 1990; Zeskind, Klein, & Marshall, 1992).

Just as with smiling, after several months, crying comes under voluntary control as centers within the cortex become involved in its coordination. Not only does the crying of an older infant sound different, becoming somewhat lower in pitch, but it can now also be prompted by different circumstances. Voluntary, or *instrumental crying,* can be in response to things such as boredom as well as to hunger or pain (Lester, Boukydis, & Zachariah, 1992). This change introduces a new problem for parents. In addition to wondering whether their infant is hungry or in pain, now they may also wonder whether they will make crying more likely in the future by picking their infant up if the occasion for crying is simply restlessness or boredom.

Q Do parents need to worry they will spoil their infant by picking it up when it cries?

With respect to such fears, parents can feel reassured that picking up a crying infant will not "spoil" their child. Instead, doing so has just the opposite effect. Despite one or two discrepant findings (Gewirtz, 1976), research in this area strongly supports the notion that being responsive to an infant's cries—that is, picking the infant up and soothing it—promotes the development of trust and security in the infant. These emotions translate into a healthy independence, just the opposite of the excessive crying seen in insecure or emotionally dependent children. Recall, Ainsworth and Bell (1969) found that mothers who were responsive to their infants' cries when they were 3 months old, had infants who cried less at the age of 12 months than did less responsive mothers who were less likely to comfort their infants when they cried.

At about 6 months, infants develop a wariness of unfamiliar people and new situations, pulling back or looking away when someone unknown to them tries to talk to them or pick them up, even though a familiar caregiver such as the mother may be present. Shortly afterward, at about 8 months, they can also be seen to look to the mother or caregiver for cues as to how to respond when confronted with someone new. "Is this person okay?" they seem to ask both with their eyes and with their general body language, "or is this someone to be afraid of?" This behavior, known as **social referencing,** signals a significant conceptual development as well as an emotional one, because it suggests that infants at this age

social referencing Checking with a caregiver or other familiar figure for cues about how to respond to a new or ambiguous event.

become aware of mental states in others. For instance, they will look at what is being pointed at rather than at the hand that is pointing, or they will follow another's gaze, establishing joint attention with respect to some object or event, suggesting that they understand that the emotion or interest of the other is in response to the object or event. This referencing is an attempt to "read" others, either through their facial expressions or the intonation of their voices, for emotional messages concerning their world.

By 6 to 8 months, then, infants are capable of expressing a range of emotions, such as interest, disgust, joy, fear, anger, sadness, surprise, and wariness (Lewis, 1993, 1995). These emotions continue to develop throughout infancy and toddlerhood, both in the ways in which they are expressed and in the situations that occasion them.

Emotional Development in Toddlerhood

As infants enter the 2nd year of life, new emotions appear. Toddlers are capable of feeling pride, guilt, shame, and jealousy in addition to basic emotions such as happiness, anger, and fear. These new emotions differ from earlier ones in having an evaluative and self-conscious quality to them. They reflect toddlers' increasing concerns with "measuring up." The yardstick toddlers hold up to themselves reflects their emerging sense of standards and an increasing self-awareness. Because of the self-reflective component to these new emotions, we might expect them to follow a developmental course, one that mirrors toddlers' developing capacity to evaluate their own actions and also their growing awareness of the self (Lewis, 1995).

A Sense of Standards   Jerome Kagan (1996) argues that a singularly human characteristic is our tendency to symbolically evaluate things. Whether these are our own actions, those of others, or naturally occurring events such as rainstorms and traffic jams, we habitually appraise things along a dimension of "good versus bad." He further argues that this evaluative aspect of our nature emerges early in life, at about the age of a year and a half. Thus, 14-month-olds who are given toys to play with that are dented or marred in some way will happily play with them. But by the age of 19 months, toddlers notice and even comment on these imperfections, telling the experimenter the toys need to be "fixed" and preferring to play instead with toys that are not marred (Kagan, 1981). Similarly, Grazyna Kochanska, Rita Casey, and Atsuko Fukomoto (1995), at the University of Iowa, found that toddlers preferred to play with whole, and not flawed, toys even though they expressed more interest in the flawed toys. This interest underscores their developing sensitivity to violations of standards concerning the "way things should be."

Furthermore, toddlers' tendency to evaluate the things around them extends to themselves. Deborah Stipek and her associates (1992, 1995), at the University of California at Los Angeles, looked for toddlers' first signs of pride in accomplishing something. One of the difficulties in determining when self-conscious emotions such as pride are first experienced is in knowing what toddlers are actually feeling from simply observing their behavior. Can a smile after accomplishing something be taken as a sign of pride? Or is it simply an indication of pleasure?

Stipek observed the way 13- to 39-month-old children reacted when a pin was knocked down by a ball, either by themselves or an adult. When the pin fell, they noticed that the children frequently smiled or looked up at the adult. They found, however, that children were no more likely to smile when they themselves had

Why do emotions such as pride, guilt, and shame not appear until children become toddlers?

TABLE 6.1 Percentage of Children Engaging in Social Referencing (Looking at the Experimenter) Following Another's or Their Own Success

Age (in months)	Other	Self
13–21	22	30
22–29	15	45*
30–39	10	65*

*statistically significant

Source: D. Stipek, S. Recchia, & S. McClintic. (1992). Self-evaluation in young children. *Monographs of the Society for Research in Child Development, 57* (1, Serial No. 226).

knocked the pin over than when the adult had. Smiles, apparently, are as much a reflection of simple pleasure as they are of pride. Looking up at the adult, however, was a different matter. Starting at about the age of 22 months, toddlers looked up at the adult more frequently when they had been the ones to successfully knock the pin over than when the adult had (Table 6.1). This behavior suggests that as children near the age of 2, they develop an interest in others' reactions to what they do—in social recognition for their accomplishments. For children 2½–3½ years old, this difference was even more pronounced, with only 10% looking over at an adult who had knocked the pin down, but 65% doing so when they had accomplished the same thing.

We've seen that even very young children react to success with pride. Do their reactions change as they get older? And are there similar self-conscious reactions to failure? These same investigators compared reactions to success and failure in 2- to 5-year-olds by giving them tasks that were possible to complete in a matter of minutes, such as fitting pieces of a puzzle together or arranging a set of nested cups, or that were impossible to complete because of missing or wrong pieces. Irrespective of age, when children were successful, they acted the same way—smiling, saying things like "I did it," looking at what they had done or calling attention to it, and looking up at the experimenter. Even their posture communicated pride, with head up, shoulders back, and arms wide. Thus, despite the large difference in their ages, toddlers and kindergartners alike reacted to success in highly similar ways.

Similarly, their reactions to failure did not noticeably differ with age. Even 2-year-olds would sigh, attempt to divert the adult's attention from their efforts, avoid eye contact, and sit with hunched shoulders and their arms crossed over their bodies. However, with children younger than 2, these investigators found it impossible to create a situation that they would experience as failure. When 18-month-olds, for instance, couldn't do something the experimenter had shown them how to do, they just changed the task, happily playing with the pieces according to their own whims. Thus, below the age of 2, children appear not to take an adult's behavior as a standard for their own or to feel self-conscious for not matching it.

Standards can be defined in a number of ways. They can be set by the requirements of the task itself or established by the accomplishments of others. Completing a puzzle in which the pieces obviously fit together is an example of the first, whereas racing to see who is the fastest is an example of the second. When standards are defined competitively, as in the second example, failure is then experienced as losing and success as winning. At what age, wondered Stipek and her associates, would young children begin to judge their accomplishments in terms of competitive standards such as this? These investigators found that 2-year-olds were oblivious to the competitive standards set by having another child work

Between 2 and 3 years of age, children start to show pride in their accomplishments.

alongside them at the same task, expressing just as much pleasure when they finished after the other had as when they finished first. But by 33 months of age, things changed. Those who finished first were obviously more pleased with themselves than were those finishing second. Furthermore, although the youngest children continued to work at their task even after the other child had "won," by the age of 3½, a fourth of those who did not finish first stopped working when the other child "won"; and by the age of 4 to 5, approximately half stopped working. What makes for success? For the very young, it is the sheer pleasure of completing what they have set out to do. Only with age is one's success at something also measured against the accomplishments of others.

A Sense of Self   Emotions such as pride, guilt, or shame have a self-conscious quality to them as well as an evaluative component. Toddlers are aware of themselves in a way that infants are not. One might think that something as abstract as self-consciousness would be hard to observe and measure. Yet, an ingenious procedure has made this development relatively easy to study. A spot of rouge is surreptitiously dabbed on the child's nose, and the child is then placed in front of a mirror. Before the age of 15 months, infants do not touch their noses when they see the reflection in the mirror. They act instead as if they were seeing another

Toddlers begin to have a consciousness of self, as can be seen by their delight in finding themselves in a mirror.

child in the mirror and attempt to look behind the mirror, or they reach out to touch the image. Starting at about 18 months, however, one can see them reach up and touch their own noses when they see the rouge on their nose in the reflection. Three quarters of the 18-month-olds who were tested in this way and all of the 24-month-olds touched their noses, indicating that they recognized the image in the mirror as themselves (Lewis & Brooks-Gunn, 1979).

There is more than one way in which we are aware of ourselves, however. Over a hundred years ago, William James (1890) distinguished between the "I" and the "Me." The I is that part of the self that is the agent; it is the "do-er" and "knower." The Me is the part of the self that is known; it is what we know *about* ourselves. Sandra Pipp-Siegel and Carol Foltz (1997), at the University of Colorado, studied the development of these aspects of self-knowledge in 12-, 18-, and 24-month-olds, along with their growing ability to distinguish themselves from others. They found that the sense of self as an agent, or the I, increased as one would expect with age. Two-year-olds, although not those who were younger, clearly distinguished themselves from others. Furthermore, as expected, there was a corresponding increase with age in toddlers' knowledge about the self, although even 12-month-olds had more knowledge about themselves than about others.

Perhaps it should not be surprising that toddlers readily distinguish themselves from others, since one of the issues they face at this age is that of autonomy, of separating self from other. Toddlers, in short, are full of themselves. They are, in fact, one of their biggest discoveries. New bodily control informs them that they can do things or not do things. Physical maturation makes many new skills

A toddler's claiming something as "mine" may be an expression of a developing sense of self rather than selfishness.

and types of control possible. They can pick up, hold on to, or throw away, and in doing so they experience themselves as separate from the things around them. However, even while their maturing bodies place new skills within their reach, they also inform them of their limited grasp on what they hold.

Although toddlers are quick to master activities such as running, grabbing hold, and throwing, inner restraints are slower to develop. Parents often find themselves several steps behind, cautioning *not* to run, touch, drop, or throw. With the development of control over events outside themselves, toddlers learn to control their inner worlds as well. Toddlers almost burst with an awareness of themselves as they claim new territories with flags of "me" and "mine." They prize having things their way. Yet they are dependent on others too. It is a time of contradictions. At one moment, a toddler will snuggle into a parent's lap, only in the next to squirm free.

The toddler's developing sense of self divides the world into two opposing encampments—mine and yours. The presence of others may only increase toddlers' need to define their boundaries by claiming things. For instance, toddlers high in self-definition were found to claim toys more and comment on a peer more than those low in self-definition. The latter were more likely to hold toys up and show them or exchange them, but were not as likely to claim them. Once the issues of "me" versus "you" and "mine" versus "yours" were settled, however, toddlers high in self-definition showed an interest in the other child (Levine, 1983). Claiming toys, in other words, is not always simply selfish. Toddlers do this even when there are plenty of toys to play with. Parents who expect their toddlers to share before boundaries have been established may be expecting too much.

By being allowed to do some things on their own, toddlers develop feelings of accomplishment and self-worth. Children's emotional needs are similar to their parents' in this respect. They value their independence, which, because it is newly won, is all the more precious, and they want the respect of others. Their desire to do things themselves can take the form of being demanding and stubborn, however; and Erikson (1963) suggests that parents be firm, so that toddlers' desires to do things on their own do not lead to premature efforts and a sense of failure and shame.

Ethnographic Field Research: Who's Telling This Story, Anyway? BY MICHAEL WAPNER

Life is continuous from fertilization to death. But the self is defined by episodes—salient events in which we participate as the star or victim or hero or supporting player or simply as onlooker. Whatever role we play in the episode itself, its self-defining significance is not fully realized there. What the episode means to and about us is more deeply defined, is reinforced or modified, in its subsequent telling and retelling. It is in these narrative acts that we present ourselves and our experiences to our group—family, friends, colleagues, tribe. For one's stories to be listened to is itself to be affirmed as a participant in the life of the group and thus to have one's selfhood acknowledged. Wiley, Rose, Burger, and Miller (1998) observe that

> selves are constructed in interaction with others, . . . they develop through participation in sociocultural practices. . . . children come to enact certain kinds of selves by virtue of their everyday participation with other people in characteristic self-relevant practices—what Markus, Mullally, and Kitayama (1997) called "selfways."

The way our narratives are listened to communicates how autonomous a participant we are considered. May we initiate a story or must we wait to be asked? Is there silence once we begin to speak or do others continue to talk? Are we interrupted? And most important, are we truly the authors of our own stories (with *narrative autonomy*) and hence of our own experience, or does our narrative become a *co-narrative* in which our story is "corrected" and modified by the perspective of oth-

ers? (When two or more people participate in the telling of a story it is termed a co-narrative.)

The way a group structures storytelling is termed its *narrative practice*. And at no other time in life does narrative practice have more importance for the development of an individual's social self than in his or her third year, for it is then that issues of personal autonomy are likely to appear. Not every culture grants such young children "speakers' rights," for all cultures do not value individual autonomy equally. In Western Samoa, "young children are not considered appropriate conversational partners for parents" (Ochs, 1988, cited in Wiley et al., 1998), and when the children are allowed to speak, "their speech is directed by a higher status person . . . and therefore not 'authored' by the child." In Taiwanese families, parents frequently co-narrate stories with their young children and insist that the child accept their version of the story. Thus, children are granted the right to speak but are denied authorship of the story. These observations suggest that these cultures value deference to authority over individual autonomy. European American families, on the other hand, do place a high value on individual autonomy, and their narrative practices reflect this. However, even within this group there may be differences.

Hypothesizing that family narrative practices will differ across socioeconomic levels, Wiley and associates (1998) compared middle-class with working-class families in the way they allowed their 2-year-old children to tell their stories. The methodology the researchers employed was an **ethnographic**

Shame is the feeling of being exposed, of being visible before being ready to be seen. Feelings of shame increase a child's sense of smallness. Rather than causing toddlers to try harder, shame prompts them to try to get way with things, to not be caught or seen. *Guilt*, on the other hand, is the result of some wrongdoing that one has committed and involves a sense of responsibility for it. Karen Barrett, Carolyn Zahn-Waxler, and Pamela Cole (1993) reasoned that children who experience shame should try to hide, whereas those who experience guilt should try to repair what they have done. These investigators gave toddlers a toy clown to play with, one which they identified as a "favorite doll," and then left the child alone in a room with the mother, who was busily filling out forms. The doll was constructed so that when the toddler picked it up, its leg fell off. Children could be expected to experience either shame or guilt at this occurrence, shame at having violated some standard of care for someone's favorite doll or guilt at having broken something.

They found that some toddlers were prone to shame ("avoiders"), whereas others were prone to guilt ("amenders"). Those who experienced shame averted their eyes when the experimenter returned, were more likely to hide what had happened (only one of them "confessed" about the doll), and were less likely to try to remedy the situation, with less than half trying to fix the doll before the experimenter mentioned the leg. Of those who reacted with guilt, all tried to fix the doll, and three quarters of them promptly told the experimenter what had happened as soon as she came into the room.

field study. That is, the investigators went into the homes of their subjects and observed the interactions of interest as they occurred in their natural settings. The investigators did not establish the conditions under which the behavior would take place and did not control it as it occurred. The authors describe their presence in the following way:

> During the taping sessions the researchers tried to behave in a way that was least disruptive to the communicative norms of the family. . . . They aimed not to be invisible or silent nor to "lead" the conversation but to observe and participate in a relaxed, low-key way, joining in the conversation when appropriate, following up on narrative topics when appropriate. This stance on the part of the observer was intended to maximize the ecological and cultural validity of the samples of narrative talk.

The researchers selected 12 children (half male, half female) and their families, six from each socioeconomic level. The neighborhoods from which the families were selected were heavily Catholic, and so were all of the families selected. All 12 were two-parent families, and in all families the mothers were not currently employed outside the home. In the working-class families, the parents were high-school graduates; the fathers were employed in blue-collar jobs such as truck driver, grave digger, and construction worker. The parents in the middle-class families were college educated, and the fathers held white-collar jobs such as businessman, lawyer, salesman.

Data were collected on two occasions, when the child was 2 years, 6 months and when the child was 3 years old. But because no age differences were found, the data form the two occasions were combined. On each occasion the researchers videotaped the family for 2 hours on each of 2 successive days. In almost all cases the father had already left for work and thus interactions were between the child and her or his mother.

The researchers found patterns of both similarities and differences in the narrative practices of the two groups. In both groups, it was common for children at 2½ and 3 years of age to participate as speakers. There were no differences in the extent to which children began the narratives—in both groups children initiated stories as frequently as half of the time. In both groups the mothers participated in the telling of almost all stories, either by asking questions, coaching, or correcting. Thus at this age, children's narratives are really co-narratives.

The differences between the two groups were primarily in the frequency of occurrence of co-narratives and the way disagreement was handled. Both the frequency and duration of co-narratives was far greater in working-class than in middle-class homes. In both groups, when conflict occurred as to the details of the child's story, it was usually the mother who initiated the conflict by disagreeing or correcting. However, the way disagreements were handled differed significantly between the two communities. Children were allowed more latitude to express their stories in the middle-class homes. When a conflict arose, middle-class mothers were more willing to allow an obviously incorrect telling rather than infringe on the child's authorship. In contrast, working-class mothers were more likely to insist on a correct rendition, and thus their children were forced to defend their version of the story if they wished to retain authorship. Apparently, narrative practice in working-class homes is also a lesson in standing up for one's views.

Guilt and shame are social emotions. They derive their significance, in other words, from involvement with other people. As a result, we would expect socialization to play an important role in the development of these emotions. Socialization not only provides information about the standards that toddlers are increasingly expected to live up to, but it also imbues these standards with significance because they are valued by people whom toddlers look up to. As a consequence, we might expect that parenting practices, because they communicate social values, would be related to the development of these emotions. And they are. Toddlers are most likely to attempt to remedy a wrongdoing, for instance, when parents give explanations as to why it is important. These explanations are most effective when they are accompanied by appropriate feelings. Recall that, by late infancy, children engage in social referencing, reading the emotions of others from their facial expressions and tones of voice. The emotional overtones of parents' explanations most likely help children understand the personal relevance of what parents are saying (Barrett, 1995). See the Research Focus, "Ethnographic Field Research: Who's Telling This Story Anyway?" for a discussion of one form of parent-child communication about events.

Toddlers' emerging ability to regulate their behavior coincides with the onset of parental demands that they control their behavior. In fact, a high proportion of the expectations for toddlers relates to the development of inhibitory control. Grazyna Kochanska, Kathleen Murray, and Katherine Coy (1997) suggest that aspects of temperament that are related to inhibitory control in toddlers have

ethnographic field study Observational research conducted in natural settings that facilitates the study of the unique contributions of the social groups to which individuals belong.

conscience That part of the personality that is concerned with issues of right and wrong.

implications for the later development of **conscience.** These investigators followed toddlers into the early school years in a longitudinal study. Measures of inhibitory control included such things as the ability to slow down an ongoing activity, such as walking a line on the floor or drawing a circle, or suppressing or initiating a behavior when instructed, such as in the game of "Simon says." Conscience was assessed by such things as compliance with mothers' requests, even when the mother was not present, resistance to temptation to violate a rule, or internalizing another person's rules concerning the way to play a game.

These investigators found inhibitory control to increase with age and to be a remarkably stable characteristic of children; that is, a child's position relative to others in the group changed little from toddlerhood to early school age. Such stability is what one would expect in a traitlike characteristic and suggests this to be a genuine individual difference.

Summary

Attachment: The Bonds of Love

Attachment refers to the affectional bonds that infants form with those who care for them and to the ways in which infants use caregivers as a secure base from which to explore and to which to return for safety when stressed. Freud assumed that drive reduction was the basis for attachment, due to infants' association of the mother with hunger reduction. However, research with infant monkeys reared with cloth or wire surrogate mothers showed that infants preferred the cloth surrogate they could cling to over the wire one that gave milk.

Bowlby distinguished four phases in the establishment of attachment. In the preattachment phase, infants experience no distress when cared for by someone other than their primary caregiver. In the attachment-in-the-making phase, infants become wary in the presence of unfamiliar persons. In the phase of clear-cut attachment, infants attempt to stay close to the mother (proximity seeking), show distress when they cannot (separation anxiety), and use the mother as a secure base from which to explore their surroundings (secure base). In the phase of reciprocal relationships, the toddler is able to comfortably spend longer periods of time away from the mother. Bowlby assumed that children develop an internal working model for subsequent relationships based on their initial attachment to the mother.

Types of Attachment Relationships

Ainsworth's research on attachment focused on the security infants derive from their relationship with the mother. Three types of attachment relationships were identified:

infants who are securely attached, anxious-avoidant infants, and anxious-resistant infants. Ainsworth attributed differences in attachment security to the accuracy with which the mother interpreted the infant's signals (sensitivity) and the promptness with which she responded (responsiveness), with both sensitivity and responsiveness being positively related to security of attachment and to less frequent crying in infants. Similar processes contribute to attachment with fathers. The quality of attachment of the infant with either parent is affected as well by contextual factors that can both support and strengthen the relational bond between infant and parent and create stress in the relationship. Attachment security increases with the number of supportive factors present in a family.

Day Care

An increase in the number of mothers with young children who work outside the home has resulted in many more young children experiencing day care today than in the past. When the quality of child care is high, day care has no negative developmental effects and may even beneficially affect aspects of social and intellectual development. Furthermore, comparisons of children in day care with those cared for at home by their mothers have found that dimensions of family life are no less closely related to children's development when they attend day care than when they are cared for at home. Rather, exposure to developmentally sound experiences, such as less authoritarian attitudes toward child rearing and more sensitive mothering, is related to more positive development in children whether they are cared for at home or in day care.

Temperament

Temperament consists of underlying predispositions contributing to infants' activity level, emotionality, and sociability. Nine aspects of temperament have been identified: activity, regularity, approach versus withdrawal to new situations, adaptability, sensory responsiveness, quality of mood, intensity of response, distractibility, and attention span and persistence. Based on clusters of these characteristics, three temperament types have been distinguished: infants who are easy, difficult, and slow to warm. An alternative to classifying infants into temperament types is to identify higher-order factors that can be derived from these traits. The nature of infants' attachment relationship has been found to moderate the way children of different temperaments react. Similarly, temperament has been found to affect attachment.

Temperament Types and Parenting

Parent-child relationships show bidirectional effects in which infants influence their parents and are, in turn, influenced by them. This influence often takes the form of upper and lower limits for the other's behavior, with both parents and children attempting to maintain the other's behavior within a range that is acceptable to them.

Emotional Development

Basic emotions, which are not assumed to involve an appraisal of the event occasioning the emotional reaction, take the same form from one culture to the next. Complex emotions are assumed to reflect a cognitive appraisal of events and occur later in development. By 1 month, distinct emotions such as interest, happiness, fear, anger, surprise, and sadness can be detected. Both smiling and crying initially occur involuntarily but come under voluntary control by 6 to 8 weeks following birth. By 6 months, infants develop a wariness of unfamiliar people and situations and by 8 months engage in social referencing as a means of appraising unfamiliar situations. By this age as well, infants are capable of expressing a range of emotions, which continue to develop throughout infancy and toddlerhood, both in the ways they are expressed and in the situations occasioning them. New emotions of pride, guilt, shame, and jealousy appear in toddlerhood. These emotions differ from earlier ones in that they reflect toddlers' increasing self-awareness.

Key Terms

attachment (p. 215)
conscience (p. 244)
difficult infants (p. 232)
easy infants (p. 232)
ethnographic field study (p. 245)
proximity seeking (p. 217)

REM smiles (p. 237)
responsiveness (p. 219)
secure base (p. 217)
sensitivity (p. 219)
separation anxiety (p. 217)
slow-to-warm infants (p. 232)

social referencing (p. 238)
social smiling (p. 237)
strange situation (p. 218)
temperament (p. 227)

chapterseven

Early Childhood
Physical Development

Young children know what we have forgotten. They know the pure joy of simple actions, of running wild into the wind, or splashing light in puddles like sparks, and spinning under the moon to the heaving breath of the night. They know these things as they know the taste of sweat and dew in their mouths. They have no need to be told. Other things, those we would try to tell them, await their understanding. They know just as surely, despite our protests, that dolls and stuffed animals have feelings too and that, though they themselves sort their world into "big" and "small," they will never be big like us.

Ursula Hegi (1995) captures this perception in describing a young child and her mother in *Salt Dancers:*

> My mother woke me up, whispered for me to get dressed, and brought me along on her moon-walk which she usually took alone when the moon was at its brightest . . . and when my legs grew tired, my mother swirled me into the air and propped me on her shoulders in one fluid motion; her hands spanned my ankles—light, yet secure—and as she took steps longer than any I could have managed, I was rocked by the motion of her body.
>
> "Someday," she said, "you'll be tall too."
>
> My hands in her hair, I smiled to myself, knowing better than to believe that old story which most adults seemed compelled to tell children. I'd figured out a long time ago that children didn't grow up—they stayed children, just as adults stayed adults. (pp. 17–18) ◄

Children make their own sense of the stories we tell them, just as they figure out so many other things, by understanding these in terms of what they already know. And they know that at times they still need to be carried, just as they know

Walking with a grandparent can make a child feel big and small all at once.

that their steps are not as sure as ours. Their experiences of what they can do, or not do, influence their perceptions of themselves and others—of the reality they take as a given.

This take on reality illustrates the constructive approach adopted in this text. Events are rarely perceived in the same way by those who experience them. The reality to which each person responds will differ depending on that person's experiences, for reality is constructed, or assembled, from what we bring with us to each moment. The reality of children's knowledge, such as the idea that they will never be big, comes from the immediacy of their experiences—of having to take two steps to every one of ours or looking down from the dizzying heights of our shoulders. Our reality comes from the same experiences, seen from the other side.

Children not only grow in size during these years, but they also become increasingly adept at the things they do, whether simply running without falling or managing the complexities of silverware or dressing themselves. These developments, in turn, change their relationship to their world. Growth is never simply a matter of inches and pounds. Instead, each new skill necessitates in some way a readjustment on the part of the child to the world as it has been known. The environment that the child experiences is not arbitrarily given by circumstances but, as Erikson (1968) puts it, is an "expectable environment" that itself is differentiated out of many potential ones by the child's own maturation, which makes possible new ways of reacting and, as a consequence, the possibility of new experiences. Thus, a child who can walk enters an environment where interesting things can be approached or where one can get lost. Similarly, a preschooler who is toilet-trained becomes part of an environment where she can be a "big girl" by not soiling her pants versus one where, as a baby, she needed "changing."

This chapter examines the physical growth that takes place during the preschool years and the implications this growth holds for broader aspects of development. Before considering growth itself, we will look at three developmental snapshots to give us an overview of the preschool years. Physical development has both behavioral and psychological consequences for young children, making possible not only a host of new skills but also a new sense of self. These receive attention in separate sections of the chapter. Concluding sections of the chapter examine issues of health and well-being: children's nutritional needs, injuries resulting either from accidents or maltreatment, and the reserves of social capital on which children and their families can rely.

Developmental Profiles

Three-year-olds can be just as animated as toddlers, but can also sit quietly and play, inhibiting movements that a year ago were a nervous jitter throughout the house. Crayons and puzzles suit their improved motor coordination. They have better control of larger movements as well. They can stop and turn when running and take corners in stride. Perhaps because of their improved coordination, they are tidier. There is a "sense of order" in the 3-year-old (Gesell et al., 1940). Despite their new control, modulating behavior can still be a challenge, whether it involves lowering their voices or slowing down at the curb. It will be another year before they develop this flexibility. By that time they will be more responsive to instructions as well, waiting their turn or putting down a noisy toy when asked.

Four-year-olds enjoy showing off, even practicing in order to accomplish something new. Increased skills reflect individuation, a developmental process in which structures and functions become increasingly separate with growth. For

New skills make four-year-olds more self-reliant and independent.

Why do preschoolers lose the "potbellied" look of toddlers?

example, by 4, children begin to throw a ball with their arms instead of their whole bodies. Children now dress themselves easily, buttons and zippers yielding to their fingers. New skills, whether buttoning a shirt or wielding scissors, make 4-year-olds more self-reliant and independent. Yet a 4-year-old who has just told you "I can do it myself" may be afraid to hang a jacket in the closet, for fear there could be something lurking in one of its corners.

By 5, children have good balance and are more agile than before. Increased control can be seen in fine motor movements as well, which are more precise than they were a year earlier, enabling children to pick up small things quickly and easily. In mental games as well, they are nimbler than 4-year-olds, adopting a more flexible approach when they encounter problems. Independent, self-sufficient, assured, and confident, they can dress themselves, go off to kindergarten, make their own friends, and help out around the house. Despite their maturity, they are still very much children. Fantasy and fact are easily confused (perhaps explaining a deadpan response to an adult's humor). Emotionally, too, they are just gaining the controls that will allow them to be less impulsive and more in control of themselves. They may be entering a new world, but fairies and giants can still be found there. For 5-year-olds, the tooth fairy is as real as their kindergarten teacher.

Physical Growth

Three-year-olds stand just over 3 feet tall and weigh a little over 30 pounds. Growth in early childhood occurs at a more even pace than during infancy and toddlerhood, and preschoolers gain 2 to 3 inches in height and add 3 to 5 pounds a year (Figure 7.1). By the time they are ready to go to school, most will weigh 38 to 45 pounds and be 42 to 46 inches tall (Allen & Marotz, 1989).

One can still clearly see evidence of the cephalocaudal trend in patterns of growth. Some of the first visible changes, in 3-year-olds, involve a lengthening of the neck and torso. Recall that in infants and toddlers, the head is much larger in proportion to the rest of the body than it is in adults. With the lengthening of the torso and then the legs, body proportions come closer to those of older children and adults. Also, the longer torso means that internal organs fit more easily within the body cavity, eliminating the "potbellied" look of the toddler.

Bone growth occurs rapidly in early childhood. The long bones of the arms and legs grow noticeably, giving the 3-year-old a more lithe and streamlined appearance than the toddler has. The normal pressures of movement placed on the skeleton through activities such as walking and running contribute to a realigning of the bones in early childhood, causing the legs to rotate from the bow-legged gait of the toddler to the knock-kneed gait of the 3-year-old. In infancy, recall, we saw a similar effect on the curvature of the spine from the pressures of sitting upright and then walking. By 4, most children walk with a mature gait, swinging their arms in synchrony with their legs; and by the age of 5, body proportions have become adultlike.

Bodily strength also increases throughout the preschool years. The muscles develop more rapidly in early childhood than do other aspects of the body. This is especially true for muscles in the legs, since children are continually using them. In fact, approximately 75% of the increase in body mass during the 5th year can be attributed to the development of muscles throughout the body. Along with increases in strength, there are also increases in stamina, or endurance, due to changes in the respiratory and cardiovascular systems. Breathing becomes deeper and slower as lung volume increases and as the chest muscles, as well as the diaphragm, contribute to breathing. With respect to the cardiovascular system, the

Weight-for-age percentiles (girls)

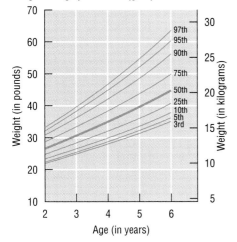

Weight-for-age percentiles (boys)

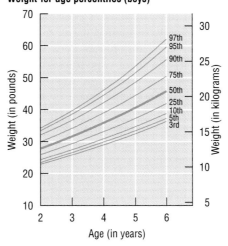

FIGURE 7.1 Growth Charts for Ages 2–6 *Source:* Centers for Disease Control (CDC) (2000), Washington, D. C.

Body mass index-for-age percentiles (girls)

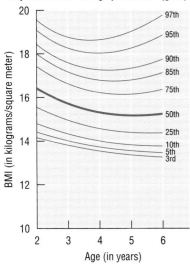

Body mass index-for-age percentiles (boys)

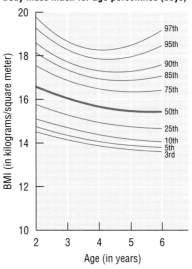

Stature-for-age percentiles (girls)

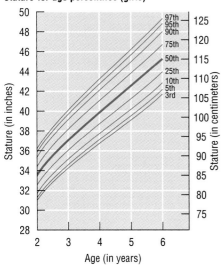

Stature-for-age percentiles (boys)

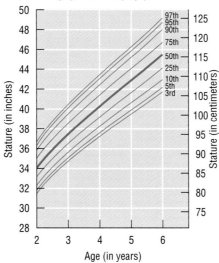

By preschool age, most children lose the toddler's potbelly and their arms and legs are more elongated. This girl is more streamlined than her little sister.

heart beats more slowly and steadily, and blood pressure gradually increases. These changes make it possible for children to be more active, as well as faster and more coordinated (Cech & Martin, 1995; Mitchell, 1990; Wilder, 1995).

Physical differences between boys and girls remain insignificant. Although boys have a slight edge in height and weight, children of both sexes are about the same in muscle strength. Also, there are few differences in physical skills, such as speed, balance, endurance, or agility. Differences in their behavior, however, are apparent. Boys are more active and "rowdy" in their play; and, when disagreements arise, they are more likely to resolve these physically. Chances are, the bully on the playground is a boy, even though a girl is physically just as able to push someone else around. This is not to say that girls don't do their share of pushing. But, as Charlie Brown would tell you, they are more likely to do so, as Lucy does, with words.

Differences in height and, to a lesser degree, weight tend to remain fairly stable from early childhood on. Three-year-olds who are tall for their age, for instance, are likely to be tall at 5 as well, and one can even predict adult height with some accuracy from about the age of 3 (Tanner, 1978). This stability does not mean, of course, that factors such as diet, exercise, or neglect cannot affect a child's weight and even a child's height. However, height and weight are more highly correlated among monozygotic, or identical, twins who share the same genotype than among dizygotic, or fraternal, ones, whose genotypes are no more similar than those of ordinary siblings, suggesting that heredity contributes substantially to stature, or body build (Bouchard, Malina, & Perusse, 1997; Cratty, 1986).

Behavioral Consequences of Physical Development

Preschoolers, especially the youngest among them, have an abundance of energy, coupled with less-than-perfect control over their motor activities. As a consequence, one of the tasks they face is developing self-restraint, learning, for instance, that they cannot simply reach over to grab hold of something that looks interesting or run through a crowded room. They are learning to regulate their movements, to sit still and not fidget, and to put things down or stop when asked. "Simon says" is fun for preschoolers precisely because it's a challenge for them: It is hard for them to restrain actions that have been mentioned without first asking "May I?"

The implications of this challenge became all too clear to me, many years ago now, when I took our 3-year-old son, Joshua, shopping with me at the local mall. We had been to a number of stores, looking at such things as bed linens, mice, and shoes and had accumulated a number of packages. Standing by the escalator to the second level, I released his hand briefly to get a better grip on the packages, only to discover, when I reached for his hand again, that he was no longer by my side. I frantically scanned the area, knee-high to the floor, where we had been standing, but he was nowhere to be seen. As moments passed, anxiety turned to panic. Then, my eyes were caught by a man coming *down* the escalator, holding Joshua in his arms. He explained that Joshua had placed his hands on the outer handrail of the escalator and, as the railing moved up with the rising steps, had been lifted off the ground, hanging outside the escalator as it climbed to the second floor. Only because this stranger had dashed up the steps and grabbed hold of my son was Joshua saved from a terrible fall. One of the developmental challenges facing young families is that parents and children often learn from many of the same experiences, especially with their oldest child.

Compounding problems of restraint is the fact that preschoolers have more aerodynamic bodies than toddlers, making them faster and more agile, a surprise to parents who still expect a trail of carnage as their children move through a

By age 5, children have mastered the use of utensils.

room. Because stopping and turning corners is difficult for toddlers, 2-year-olds frequently find themselves in unexpected situations—two steps from the stairs and at a full run or riding the tray of the highchair on its way to the floor. Three-year-olds, however, can turn corners while running and stop at will. Their agility, however, does not extend to such things as balancing or moving backwards. And, because they run with their heads tilted back for better balance, they often trip and bump into things. Only by about the age of 5 can preschoolers routinely navigate obstacles at a full run.

Especially during the early years, most preschoolers are still mastering the basic routines of daily life, such as dressing, eating, making it to the bathroom in time, falling asleep at night, and navigating a body that is changing almost weekly. At meals, for instance, 3-year-olds can observe such niceties as chewing with their mouths closed and using utensils, feeding themselves with a spoon, or spearing their food with a fork. Knives, however, have yet to be mastered and remain of interest primarily for entertainment purposes, serving as catapults or seesaws, rather than implements for cutting. Five-year-olds, by contrast, can not only manage tableware but can also fix themselves simple meals, such as a bowl of cereal for breakfast or a peanut-butter-and-jelly sandwich for lunch.

By 3, most preschoolers can stay dry through the day, with periodic reminders to use the bathroom. However, even 5-year-olds can have occasional accidents, for the most part due to poor timing. Most 3-year-olds also begin to sleep dry through the night, though this is a transitional time and children who have been successful for nights or even weeks in a row can then wet the bed again for a while. Bladder control continues to develop over the next year and a half. Mature bladder control becomes possible when the bladder can hold nearly double the amount of urine that has been voided during the day, usually before the age of 4½ (Cech & Martin, 1995).

Even the nature of sleep changes in early childhood. Normally, individuals move into and out of two types of sleep states throughout the night: NREM sleep and REM sleep. NREM sleep is associated with a slowing down of bodily functions such as blood pressure, rate of breathing, and basal metabolic rate, as well as the development of characteristic slow-wave brain activity, with decreases in

Children's fears of monsters are the downside of the same active imagination evident in their fantasy play.

How might improved coordination and new skills contribute to tension and outbursts in preschoolers?

brain-stem activity. In REM sleep, the state in which dreaming occurs, brain-wave activity does not become slower, the heartbeat becomes irregular, and rate of breathing actually increases. REM sleep in adults lasts anywhere from 5 to 40 minutes, punctuating NREM sleep every hour and a half or so (Cech & Martin, 1995).

The development of mature sleep patterns involves a fundamental change in the alternation of these two states. In infancy, sleep begins with REM sleep and moves to NREM sleep, whereas in adulthood, sleep begins in the NREM state and is punctuated with episodes of REM sleep. After about the age of 5, children experience the same amount of REM sleep as do adults (Short-DeGraff, 1988), perhaps reflecting the ability of an increasingly mature central nervous system to inhibit REM sleep. The increase in NREM sleep during early childhood is important because it is associated with the release of growth hormone and increased protein synthesis (Cech & Martin, 1995).

More obvious differences to many parents are the fears that children can develop in early childhood that affect both how well they sleep and how easily they fall asleep. Some children wake with nightmares; others have difficulty falling asleep in the first place, imagining monsters in the closet or under the bed or simply being afraid of the surrounding darkness. Each of these fears is the downside of the same active imagination evident in their fantasy play during the day, either alone or with others, talking to themselves, to others, or their toys.

Throughout the preschool years, children continue to become more coordinated and skillful in what they do, whether their activities are as simple as carrying things without dropping them or more complex, such as getting themselves dressed or using a knife to cut their food. Continuing improvements in ordinary activities such as these lead to increased self-confidence and independence. The somewhat uneven progress that young children experience, however, often results in frustration. Perhaps as a result, they still find it easiest to do things when adults are around, a condition that can lead to a test of wills. Having once done something on their own, even young children are not as compliant or cooperative when help is offered as they had been earlier. On the positive side, their testiness over seeming challenges to their independence is offset by their genuine desire to help.

As preschoolers increase in size and become better coordinated, more is also expected of them in both physical coordination and impulse control. Physical development, in other words, has its psychological costs. Parents who might still see the toddler in a 3-year-old and overlook accidents or errors in judgment, for instance, are willing to hold 4-year-olds accountable for their actions in ways they would not have earlier. Perhaps as a result, 4-year-olds live with more tensions and are more likely to have emotional outbursts and tantrums or engage in other nervous outlets, such as biting nails, than are 3-year-olds. They also tire easily. Muscles are not yet attached firmly to the skeleton, with the result that children at this age experience muscle fatigue and need opportunities to rest during the day (Mitchell, 1990). By 5, preschoolers are calmer, have more emotional control, and are more self-confident. Box 7.1 summarizes the self-care and daily routines that 3-, 4-, and 5-year-olds are usually able to manage.

With respect to the routines of daily life, preschoolers have well-formed daily schemas, ordering their day in terms of predictable sequences of activities. They know, for instance, to dress before coming to breakfast or that it is time to get up when they hear a parent switch on the morning news or that bedtime comes after a bath and a story or favorite TV show. Changing the order of activities as familiar as these can be as disorienting as entering a different time zone, or jet lag, is to adults. I recall one futile attempt to rush our two young children as they dawdled through a late dinner one night after arriving home from visiting relatives. I flew around the kitchen throwing together something for us all to eat. We were

Box 7.1 *What Preschoolers Can Do: Self-Care and Daily Routines*

A 3-Year-Old

Dressing and Caring for Self

- Can dress and undress self, with help.
- Has very few toilet accidents, but needs to be reminded to go to the bathroom (boys may still have occasional bladder accidents).
- Can wash and dry face and hands, take a bath, and brush teeth with help.

Eating

- Can feed self at table without help.
- Can use spoon, but spears food with fork.
- Pretty good appetite, but "dawdles" when not hungry.

Sleeping

- Can get ready for bed with some help, likes stories.
- Needs 10–12 hours of sleep a night and a nap or quiet time in afternoon.
- Beginning to sleep dry through the night, with periods of success followed by short periods of bed-wetting.
- Begins to have nightmares.

A 4-Year Old

Dressing and Caring for Self

- Can dress self, managing buttons as well as zippers, but may need to pass "inspection" to make sure shirts and blouses are on right-side out. Tying shoes remains problematic, but can fasten buckles on sandals.
- Can manage most toileting needs, such as brushing teeth, washing faces and hands, and bathing self, but needs help shampooing hair (to keep shampoo out of eyes).
- Can go to the bathroom without help, but may need to be reminded to flush.
- Frequently expect privacy when in bathroom.

Eating

- Can eat with fork and spoon; can spread jelly on bread, cut soft things with knife.
- Develops food dislikes.
- Frequently prefers talking to eating when at the table.
- Enjoys helping out, setting the table, putting things on plates.

Sleeping

- Goes off to bed without much trouble, especially if bedtime is part of a regular routine.
- May be afraid of the dark; a small light helps.
- Needs 10–12 hours of sleep each night; may need a nap in the afternoon or a quiet time.
- Can wake during the night to go to the bathroom, but may need help getting settled down again.

A 5-year Old

Dressing and Caring for Self

- Can dress self, notices if clothes are inside-out.
- Learning to tie shoes.
- Has full bladder and bowel control, but occasional accidents due to putting things off.

Eating

- Can make self breakfast (cereal) or lunch (sandwich).

Sleeping

- Can get ready for bed by self, even helping a younger sibling.
- Sleeps 10–12 hours a night; few need an afternoon nap.
- May have difficulty falling asleep if excited about the next day.
- Dreams and nightmares are common.

Source: Allen & Marotz (1989).

hungry, and it was well past their bedtime. Tomorrow would be another full day, and we still had the evening ritual of a bath, pajamas, and a story ahead of us before the lights went out. My comments about how late it was, pointing out that it was already past their bedtime, went unnoticed as they walked peas, stuck to the tines of their forks, across their plates and made snowbanks with the mashed potatoes. Only much later, after the shouting was over, did I realize why they hadn't paid any attention to me. It simply wasn't bedtime to them. It was dinner time. Why? Because bedtime comes after a bath, when they are in their pajamas, and have been read a story. When one is fully dressed and sitting at the table, it's obviously dinner time. Had I wanted them to hurry, I should have gotten them into their pajamas before sitting down to eat. Then they would have realized that it was time for bed.

Brain Maturation

The brain develops faster during early childhood than does any other part of the body, reaching 90% of its adult size before the age of 6 (Lecours, 1982; Reiss, Abrams, Singer, Ross, & Denckla, 1996). This development makes possible the many motor skills that emerge in early childhood. The maturation of different regions of the brain parallels their anticipated functions. For instance, one of the earliest regions to develop is the cerebellum, a region involved in coordinating movement and maintaining balance; it matures in time for the postural control that is necessary as infants begin to walk. In general, during early childhood all brain regions undergo rapid maturation (Hudspeth & Pribram, 1992).

Brain maturation takes a number of forms. In addition to significant growth in volume, there is the progressive myelination of neural fibers, or the formation of an insulating sheath of myelin around the axons of neurons. This sheath facilitates the conduction of neural impulses, enabling neurons to communicate more effectively with neighboring ones (see Chapter 4). Neural communication, in turn, contributes to what Reiss and his associates (1996) refer to as a remodeling of the brain through the selective elimination of neuronal connections that are not frequently stimulated (Thatcher, 1997). The Research Focus, "Inferential Statistics: Children as Witnesses," on pages 260–261 examines issues related to children's memory.

Robert Thatcher (1997) has found two nearly identical cycles of change in cortical activity with age, the first occurring in early childhood and the second in middle childhood. These cycles involve the establishment of neural interconnections between the frontal lobes and other cortical areas, making possible the creation of new psychological units or ways of functioning. Robbie Case (1992) has suggested that these units underlie not only the motor developments that are so evident in early childhood but also developmental changes in self-awareness. The frontal lobes are involved in monitoring cognitive activity and, as a consequence, in the awareness of oneself engaged in various activities. Interconnections involving the frontal lobes also contribute to children's developing ability to restrain, or inhibit, responses, as is involved in the regulation of activity.

How does brain maturation affect preschoolers' behavior?

Motor Development

Gross motor skills involve large-muscle movements, such as those used in activities that require moving the whole body—running, skipping, or riding a bike, for example. In contrast, fine motor skills involve precise movements controlled by small muscles and usually entail the hands and fingers; examples are the skills involved in using crayons and scissors or fastening buttons. Of course, many activities, such as throwing a ball, require both types of motor skills. Although most basic motor skills develop by the end of the preschool years, there is considerable variability in motor coordination from one child to the next, and significant percentages of even 6- and 7-year-olds are not adept at all basic skills. There is considerable variability even from one day to the next in early childhood. Thus a child who can repeatedly catch a ball on one day may just as consistently fail to do so on the next (Malina & Bouchard, 1991). Box 7.2 summarizes typical skill development in preschoolers.

Gross Motor Skills

One can predict with fair accuracy what a preschooler can do by knowing the child's age. Individual differences, even when extreme, are unlikely to place a child in the next age or skill category. Thus, even well-coordinated 3-year-olds are

Box 7.2 *Skill Development in Preschoolers*

A 3-Year-Old

- Can go up stairs alternating feet, but not down
- Can jump and hop on one foot
- Can kick a ball, if it's a large one
- Can throw a ball overhand
- Can pedal a tricycle or "big wheeler"
- Can draw a circle or a square, and make some letters

A 4-Year-Old

- Better control in drawing, can copy shapes of letters
- Is able to cut with scissors
- Can go up and down stairs alternating feet
- Can pedal a tricycle, turn and stop and not bump into things
- Can skip and stop and turn corners when running
- Good at climbing, whether jungle gyms, stairs, or trees

A 5-Year-Old

- Has good control using pencils and crayons; can color within the lines
- Can cut following a line with scissors
- Walks down stairs as easily as up
- Can walk backwards
- Has good balance; can stand on one foot or walk a balance beam
- Can catch a ball that is thrown a short distance

Source: Allen & Marotz (1989).

unlikely to run as well as an average 4-year-old (Mitchell, 1990). Most 3-year-olds, for instance, run with a flat-footed gait, never completely leaving the ground when they run, and have difficulty with sudden turns. However, by 4, children have a longer stride, actually getting airborne at one point, with both feet off the ground. They are also better at stopping and starting. By 5, coordination has improved even more, enabling them to maneuver sharp turns without falling.

One sees a similar progression with respect to hopping. Three-year-olds can hop with both feet, but have difficulty doing so on one, moving their arms a lot as if they were flying. Even 4-year-olds still hop stiffly, but by 5 most hop by springing from their ankles, knees, and hips. One sees similar progressions with skipping, jumping, and climbing. There are few sex differences in motor skills in the preschool years. One exception is in throwing; boys can throw farther and faster than girls. Since this difference is not reduced when girls later join athletic teams, it may be biologically based (Mitchell, 1990; Thomas & French, 1985).

Fine Motor Skills

Fine motor skills also improve rapidly. Children get better not only in picking things up, but also in manipulating what is already in their hands; this is referred to as **in-hand manipulation.** Thus, they become more adroit at moving an object around in one hand without the help of the other hand—in getting a crayon from the palm of their hand to their fingertips, for example. Three-year-olds can hold

in-hand manipulation The ability to move an object around in one hand without the help of the other hand, such as moving a crayon from the palm of the hand to the fingertips.

Inferential Statistics: Children as Witnesses

BY MICHAEL WAPNER

Imagine you have been falsely accused of a crime. Imagine also that the main witness against you is a 4-year-old child who says she recognizes you as the one in the store who took the watch from the counter and put it in your pocket. True, you were in the store. And when you passed the child, your eyes met, you smiled, and she smiled back, so you know she saw you. But you are innocent of shoplifting. However, unless the child remembers that it was not you she saw at the counter or unless the child's testimony changes or is not believed, you are in danger of being convicted anyway. To add to your danger your lawyer tells you that children of that age are very suggestible and the more you are mentioned to the child in relation to the crime, the more likely the child will "remember" that you committed it.

Of course, this scenario is fictitious. But the problem that it depicts is real. Unfortunately, it is not unheard of for preschool children to be called to give testimony as a witness to a crime. And when they are, it is natural for there to be concern. "Can children adequately process, retain, recall, and report events?" ask James Lampinen and Vicki Smith, of Northwestern University. These authors point to two competing views of children as witnesses. "On the one hand, children are perceived as innocent and truthful; on the other hand, they are viewed as suggestible and prone to fantasy." Actually, both views are correct. When simply asked to tell what they witnessed (called "free recall"), young children are quite accurate (Cole and Loftus, 1987; Marin, Holmes, Guth, & Kovac, 1979, both cited in Lampinen and Smith, 1995). But their accounts tend not to include much detail. If, to fill in the details, they are asked suggestive and misleading questions, their memory may well be distorted.

The reason that such questioning may distort memory is that while a question is presumably a way of *eliciting* information, it is really, to one degree or another, also a way of transmitting information. Of course, how much information is transmitted by the question depends on how the question is phrased. Sometimes the question establishes a context or has an embedded assumption, restricting the range of appropriate answers. "Did you see this defendant put the object in his pocket?" is such a question, since it assumes the defendant put something in his pocket and asks only whether the witness saw it. Other times the questioner may simply add or change details of the event and ask the witness to affirm or deny that it happened that way. However the questioning takes place, the interrogated witness receives information about the event from two sources—the event itself and the questioner. Moreover, misleading interrogation is only one of several possible ways that misinformation can influence what people recall of an earlier event. Another way is simply for the witness to hear a different, false version of the event told by another (alleged) witness.

Lampinen and Smith (1995) raise an interesting question about the suggestibility of children. Does the effect of misinformation on children's memory depend on the credibility of the source of that misinformation? Earlier research had shown that adults' memory is more influenced by misleading suggestions from people with acknowledged authority than from people with less or no authority. The effect on children, however, was not as clear. Lampinen and Smith designed research to clarify this issue.

The experimental design was fairly simple. There were three stages. First, children were given information to be remembered. Second, some of them were exposed to misleading information (while the rest received correct information) about what they had just heard and seen. The (mis)information in this second stage came from sources of varying degrees of credibility. Finally, the children were tested to see whether their memory for the original information had been influenced by the misinformation and whether the credibility of the source made a difference.

One hundred and twenty preschool children from 3 to 5 years old participated in the study. Each child was read a story, which he or she would later be asked to recall, about a girl named Lauren. The story was accompanied by illustrations, including two drawings, one of Lauren eating eggs, the other of Lauren with a stomachache. The information about the eggs and the stomachache was available only in these two drawings and not in the spoken narrative. Ten minutes later the child viewed a videotape of another person, "Anthony," who had also heard the story of Lauren and was now being questioned about it. Depending on the condition, Anthony was either an adult or a child of the same age as the subject. For some subjects the adult was simply introduced as a 24-year-old who had heard the story. For others the adult was introduced as a *silly* 24-year-old who had heard the story. Thus, for each subject, Anthony in the videotape was one of the following: a child, an adult, or a "silly" adult. Thus, the researchers established three levels of credibility. For the 3- to 5-year-old subjects a 24-year-old adult is presumably a credible authority. However, when he is described as "silly," we would expect this credibility to be undermined. And finally, a child who is the same age as the subject would be expected to have less credibility than an adult, although where he would stand with respect to a "silly adult" remained to be seen.

All the videotapes showed Anthony being questioned about what Lauren had for breakfast and in what way she got sick. In half of the videos Anthony answered correctly. In the other half he answered incorrectly, saying Lauren had cereal for breakfast and got a headache. This latter condition, of course, constituted the misleading suggestive information.

Ten minutes later all children were shown two pairs of pictures. One of each pair illustrated the actual event in the story (the ones they had originally seen of Lauren eating eggs and Lauren with a stomachache). The other picture in each pair, which they had never previously seen, illustrated the misleading information of Lauren eating cereal and Lauren with a

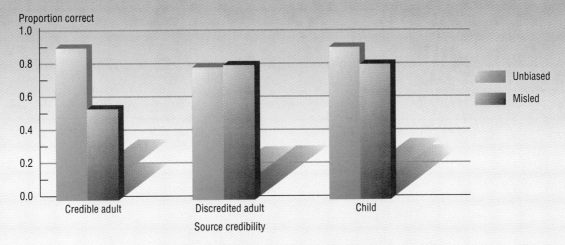

Proportion correct

Source credibility

headache. Each child was asked to choose the picture that had been in the original story.

The figure shows the results. The red bars show the number of questions answered correctly by the children who had seen the misleading videotape. Children who were misled by the credible adult made more errors (got fewer correct) than those who were misled by the discredited (silly) adult or the child. So it does seem, as Laminen and Smith supposed, that children's memory is more vulnerable to misinformation from credible sources than from sources that are discredited or nonauthoritative.

One general but very basic question remains to be asked. To what extent can we rely on these results? To answer this question we must turn to *statistical inference,* a method that allows one to generalize from a sample to the larger population from which that sample was drawn. After all, we are interested not just in the subjects of this study but in children in general. But how can we conclude anything about children in general without having tested all children? It is because, although we actually compare only a *sample* of children, we *infer* that whatever differences we find hold for more than our sample. For such an inference to be justified a number of requirements must be satisfied. First, we must assume that the members of our sample are not systematically different from the members of the population to which we wish to generalize. (See the Research Focus, "Sampling," in Chapter 5.) Second, we must assume that our findings were not the result of chance differences. You will notice from the figure that although *on the average* the children were more misled by the credible adult, not all were misled. (Over 50% answered correctly despite hearing wrong answers from the credible adult.) And although fewer children were misled by incorrect information from the silly adult or the child, about 20% were misled. Finally, even some of the children hearing the correct information answered incorrectly. What these results indicate is that whether a child remembered the actual details or got them wrong did not totally depend on the variables of the study. Each group had variability, and its sources aren't clear. Unexplained variability not due to the variables being studied is termed *random error.* Maybe *all* the differences observed in this study (or any study), including the ones attrib-

uted to the different treatments, were due to random error. It is the probability of differences occurring due to different treatments versus random error that *inferential statistics* is designed to estimate. Given the existence of random error, what is the probability that the differences found in a given study occurred just by chance?

The basic concept of inferential statistics is the *sampling distribution.* The sampling distribution is derived in the following way: First, assume that there is no difference between the populations being compared (in our case between the effects of credible and discredited sources on children's memory). This is called the *null hypothesis.* Second, assume that we repeat our experiment an indefinitely large number of times using the same size sample every time. Because of random error (that is, simply by chance) the difference between the groups will not be the same each time. If the variables that we are studying really make no difference (by the null hypothesis), then most of the chance differences between our groups will be very small and in no particular direction. But if we do the experiment over and over enough times, sometimes large differences will occur just by chance. The sampling distribution tells us the probability of differences of various sizes occurring by chance. Thus, if we compare the results of the current study with the sampling distribution, we can determine the probability of getting a difference this size just by chance. This comparison is called a *test of significance* (which is really not a very good name for it since it does not indicate the "significance" or importance of the result, but only how likely we would be to get one this large simply by chance).

Frequently used inferential statistics (that is, tests of significance) are chi-square, t-tests, and F-tests (or analysis of variance). Limpinen and Smith used an F-test to assess the significance of the differences due to the source of misinformation. Their results were significant at the .01 level. This means that a difference between groups as large as the one they found could be expected to occur by chance about one time in a hundred. Whether this is enough security depends on how important the results are and how the conclusions will be used. For instance, if the results of an experiment could send someone to prison, we might demand that the test of significance be set at one in a thousand.

Fine motor skills improve with age and by age 5, most children can cut with scissors.

bimanual coordination The ability to use both hands simultaneously but to do different things, such as holding a paper with one hand and cutting with scissors with the other.

hand preference The tendency to use one hand instead of the other to do such things as throw a ball, write, or use a fork, even when marked superiority is not apparent with the preferred hand.

hand dominance The superiority of one hand to the other for doing such things as throwing a ball, writing, or using a fork; occurs at the time of brain lateralization.

a crayon between the first two fingers and their thumb, rather than encircling it in their fist as they did earlier (see Figure 10.5). Four-year-olds have even better control in using crayons and pencils and can begin to copy the shapes of letters; some can print their names. Five-year-olds have good control when using pencils and crayons and can cut along a line with scissors (Allen & Marotz, 1989).

Children also improve in **bimanual coordination,** or using both hands simultaneously, one for doing one thing and the other for doing another, as in holding a paper with one hand while using the other hand to cut with scissors or in opening a jar by turning the top in one direction and the jar in the other. As a result, activities such as grasping hold of and using things of different shapes and sizes, such as buttoning a shirt while dressing oneself or holding a doll to brush her hair, improve greatly. Children who may have difficulty with these when attempting them alone are frequently successful when they can watch someone else. Thus a 4-year-old attempting to use scissors is often able to do so better when an older, already-adept child is present (see Chapter 1 for a discussion of Vygotsky's zone of proximal development).

Hand preference also develops during the preschool years, becoming well established by 4 to 6 years. Hand preference refers to the tendency to use one hand over the other for such things as throwing a ball, writing, or using a fork, even when marked superiority is not apparent with the preferred hand. When brain lateralization occurs, however, by the age of 6 or 7, **hand dominance** occurs; and with this, the use of one hand becomes superior to that of the other (Vansant, 1995).

Being allowed to do some things on their own contributes to children's feelings of accomplishment and self-worth.

Psychological Implications of Physical Development

Children develop a sense of themselves in early childhood. The issue for them is no longer *whether* they are autonomous and separate beings, as it was in toddlerhood, but rather of discovering what *kind* of person they are, a task characterized by Erikson as involving **initiative.** Physical development plays an important role in this discovery. New skills, whether simply walking without bumping into things, climbing a jungle gym, or sitting quietly with crayons and scissors or a picture book, make it possible for them to attempt new things, gaining a sense of mastery and success.

New skills also equip preschoolers to play a more active role in the daily routines of their lives. Young children are ready to have a say in things and can profit from being given choices. Being allowed to do some things on their own contributes to their feelings of accomplishment and self-worth. In this sense, their emotional needs are similar to those of their parents. They value their independence, which, newly won, is all the more precious. Although their need to do things for themselves can at times lead to stubborn demands, discernment on the part of parents as to what they can reasonably attempt is usually sufficient to protect them from failure (Erikson, 1959).

In what ways might physical development contribute to a child's sense of self?

initiative The term used by Erik Erikson for a child's sense of purposefulness and effectiveness.

Physical development, by its very nature, seems to prompt comparisons with others. Such comparisons fuel preschoolers' seemingly endless curiosity about who is biggest, strongest, and so on. Their new skills also prompt them to imagine themselves in the roles of others, envisioning possibilities that only the future holds. The most significant comparisons they make, of course, are with those who are closest to them, the very people whom they most want to be like—their parents. Erikson suggests that children's perceptions of their parents are not as simple as we might imagine, that though they see them as "powerful and beautiful," they also perceive them as "often quite unreasonable, disagreeable, and even dangerous" (Erikson, 1968, p. 115).

Why do giants and monsters seem so real to young children?

Children can also regard their own thoughts and feelings as dangerous, confusing these, as they do at times, with real events. With age, they come to separate feelings from actions, knowing that they cannot kill with a wish or a word. Until this time, fantasy and feeling receive little balance from reality testing (Elkind, 1978a). Just as new freedom of movement expands children's outer world, imagination expands their inner one. This, together with increasingly sophisticated language skills, allows children to conjure up the unknown and to question everything. The giants and monsters that rule the dark places in children's minds are a reminder of how small they still feel in comparison to their rapidly expanding world. Rational explanations by parents that monsters don't exist have little impact on this netherworld.

When are children ready to abandon one explanation for their feelings and experiences and accept another? An explanation, at 5 or 50, is a way of relating something new to what we already know. Children have to be ready for a new idea for it to make sense. Piaget, for instance, described children's reactions to his explanation for the origin of Lake Geneva. He had first asked them to explain how the lake had come into being. One of the common explanations they gave was that a giant threw a rock and rain had filled in the hole that it made. Piaget listened and then offered an alternative, scientific explanation, talking about the movement of glaciers that carved out the basin of the lake and then melted, filling it with water. Although the children could accurately repeat what Piaget had told them, when later asked how the lake had been formed, they earnestly explained that a giant had done it. There is a time for giants and myths and another for science. For something to be an explanation, it must fit what one knows; and at 5, one knows there are giants.

Impulse Control

It is not at all simple for young children to stop doing something when they have been told to or to wait to do something until told it is okay.

Inhibition and Verbal Control   Toddlers can do something that is asked of them, but they cannot as easily stop what they are doing when they are asked. By 3, children can inhibit an activity when asked but they have difficulty not acting if they see someone else doing what they want to do—a difficulty shared by 4-year-olds as well. When verbal instructions are inconsistent with visual cues, in other words, the latter are likely to win out (Saltz, Campbell, & Skotko, 1983).

The difficulty young children have in inhibiting an ongoing activity can create problems with parents who may interpret noncompliance with their requests as a power struggle. Toddlers and young children cannot easily bring their behavior under verbal control, either theirs or anyone else's, including an angry parent's. If another toy or activity is substituted for the prohibited one, however, compliance is easier. A harried mother, tired from a day at work and driving home

Scenes like these become less frequent with age as children develop better control over their behavior.

from day care, may find herself dangerously close to the edge after repeatedly telling her 3-year-old *not* to blow the whistle on her spare set of keys. However, if she offers her sunglasses or the photo foldout in her wallet as a substitute, the child is likely to accept the trade happily.

Verbal control over behavior develops gradually. The process is usually not complete until about age 5. Certainly before this age, children have difficulty inhibiting a behavior, especially if tempers flare and parents shout. We know this from research in which children were given a game to play requiring that they follow instructions either to do, or not do, simple things. The instructions were given in a loud, medium, or soft voice. Younger children found it more difficult to inhibit an action when instructions were shouted. However, children older than 5 were more likely to comply under these conditions. Just a note of warning, however. Children who are shouted at will learn to shout like their parents (Saltz et al., 1983).

Children develop better control over their behavior with age. Not only can they stop what they are doing when asked, but they are also better at modulating the pace of their activities. However, even this is difficult for young children. For a preschooler, it is easier to run than walk, to shout instead of talk, to throw rather than hand something, or do anything fast instead of slow. Cautions to slow down, stop running, or wait at the curb go unheard. In addition to this high activity level, preschoolers may be easily distracted from the task at hand. When these behaviors continue into childhood, they may be a sign of attention-deficit disorder, the topic of the Research Focus, "Within-Subjects Designs: Attention-Deficit Hyperactivity Disorder."

Parents can help by anticipating the difficulty young children have in bringing their behavior under control. Instead of telling children what to do, or not do, it is more effective to build habits through consistent routines and consequences for behavior that children can anticipate. David Elkind (1978b) reminds us that young children do not learn through rules. Admonitions such as "Don't hit," "Say please," or "It's not nice to hurt someone" go in one ear and out the other.

Young children learn best by experiencing the consequences of their actions. The liberal and consistent use of positive consequences, such as praise and hugs, and the consistent use of negative ones, such as time out or benching, is effective with young children. Even young children can anticipate the consequences of their

Why do young children not always stop an activity when they are told to stop?

Within-Subjects Designs:
Attention-Deficit Hyperactivity Disorder

Although most preschoolers are not likely to be characterized in terms of their capacity for self-restraint or sustained attention, these qualities are considerably less evident in some than in others. For a small percentage of children, the inability to sit still and pay attention to anything for very long reaches clinical proportions. Attention-deficit hyperactivity disorder (ADHD) is thought to affect upwards of 5% of children (American Psychiatric Association, 1994). Children with this disorder are distractible and impulsive; most are also in seemingly constant motion (those who are not hyperactive are said to have attention-deficit disorder, or ADD).

Paradoxically, despite the difficulty these children have in attending to things, they appear to have no trouble watching television. In this, they are like most children their age. Even so, one might wonder whether they are as likely to remember what they have watched as are other children. Most children, in fact, have no difficulty remembering a program they have watched even though playing with toys while doing so. Presumably they are able to successfully divide their attention by monitoring auditory cues accompanying the program; these cues direct their attention back when something is about to happen.

Steven Landau, Elizabeth Lorch, and Richard Milich (1992) wondered whether ADHD children would be able to control their attention in similar ways. They videotaped both ADHD boys and control boys as they watched a television program, either with appealing toys present or without toys in the room, and, once the program was over, asked both groups of boys what they recalled of the program they had seen.

These investigators used a *within-subjects design.* In this type of design, each boy experienced both of the experimental conditions; that is, each boy watched television once with appealing toys present and once with no toys present. This design can be compared with a between-subjects design in which each subject experiences only one condition (see the Research Focus, "Between-Subjects Design," in Chapter 11). Within-subjects designs are *economical,* requiring fewer subjects because the same subjects react to all conditions. They are also *sensitive.* A design is sensitive to the extent that it can pick up, or detect,

differences resulting from the experimental treatment. Within-subjects designs are sensitive because they use the same subjects in all conditions, thus reducing variability due to individual differences.

Despite these important advantages, this type of design has several serious disadvantages. One runs the risk of *carryover effects,* in which the effect of one treatment is still present when the next is given. In this example, boys might confuse the contents of the first program with that of the second, resulting in poorer memory for the second program. Carryover effects are not necessarily symmetrical for each of the orders in which different subjects watch programs. Watching the first program with distracting toys present may result in less carryover, if the toys actually do distract subjects from the program, than watching without toys present. In addition to carryover effects, there can be *order effects* with this design. These reflect systematic changes in performance over time due to factors such as practice, fatigue, boredom, and so on.

Both carryover and order effects introduce the potential for *confounding.* Confounding exists when the difference between treatments can be explained in more than one way—that is, when an experiment lacks internal validity (see the Research Focus, "Internal and External Validity," in Chapter 14). Landau, Lorch, and Milich *counterbalanced* the order in which boys watched programs under the two toy conditions. Counterbalancing presents each condition an equal number of times in each order, thus balancing any effects due to order equally across conditions.

What did these researchers find? When no toys were present, ADHD boys spent as much time watching television as did the control boys. When toys were present, however, they spent only half the time watching that the control boys spent. Nonetheless, ADHD boys recalled just as much of the program's content as did control boys. These findings suggest that although ADHD children are more distractible, under some circumstances, at least, they can utilize the same cues to guide their attention as used by other children.

actions when these are consistent and predictable. Soon, even the thought of a misdeed is enough to cause anxiety—and restraint. This is not to say that parents should not accompany a hug with a remark such as "That was so kind," or to comment, as a child is benched, that one can play with others when one does not hurt them. But words alone are not sufficient for the very young.

Finally, parents should know when to use external restraints. Childproof doors handles, locked cabinets, a gate to the yard, hand-holding when crossing the street, and seat-belt use are all simple precautions that help children who are at an age when external constraints are more reliable than internal ones.

Waiting: Delay of Gratification   Perhaps even harder for young children than total restraint is waiting for something they have been told they can have. Children's ability to delay gratification has been studied using a number of procedures. In one of these, they are shown two snacks, one more desirable than the other, and told they must wait in order to get the more desirable one, but can have the less desirable whenever they want—but taking the less desirable snack means forfeiting their chances of ever getting the better one. Thus, they might be shown a marshmallow and a pretzel; the adult leaves, taking both, explaining that they can have the marshmallow if they are willing to wait but if they call the adult back beforehand, they get the pretzel. The first thing social scientists found, something any parent could have told them, is that ability to delay gratification, to wait for the better reward, increases with age (Mischel & Rodriguez, 1993).

Even 3-year-olds will consider how long they must wait if they are told in familiar terms how long it will be, such as "until bedtime" or "when Sesame Street ends." However, it seems that while younger children can make choices that are just as adaptive as those of older children, they cannot carry them out as well. That is, they may choose to wait for something better, but they do not have the strategies that help them wait for what they have chosen (Schwartz, Schrager, & Lyons, 1983).

Older children have learned that it is easier to wait if they do not look at what they want. It is also easier to wait if they do not think about what they are waiting for, if they distract themselves with other thoughts or with other things to do. They have learned that "hot thoughts," about how sweet, chewy, or yummy a promised treat will be, make it harder to wait. "Cool thoughts" that focus on abstract qualities of the goal, such as its shape or color, make it easier. Also, when children focus on what they are doing, such as "I am waiting for _____," they can wait longer than when they focus on the reward itself, as in "The _____ is yummy" (Cole & Newcombe, 1983, Miller, Weinstein, & Karniol, 1978).

But how much do young children know about these strategies? Mischel and Mischel (1983) asked preschoolers and third- and sixth-graders what makes it easier to wait. Preschoolers did not seem to know any of the strategies for waiting. Third-graders, however, were more knowledgeable, and sixth-graders were downright sophisticated. Preschoolers, for example, could not spontaneously think of any delay strategies when asked. Third-graders knew that it helped to think about the relationship between waiting and the reward, as in "If I wait, I will get more." Sixth-graders used sophisticated techniques to reduce the temptation to opt for a smaller or less desirable reward that could be had right away. For example, one child repeated over and over, "It would taste soapy." Another said, "I don't want this now, but I will when the experimenter comes back."

These investigators found an interesting trend among the preschoolers. The youngest children, those under 4, showed no preference either for covering up or looking at what they were waiting for, but 4-year-olds thought it would actually help them wait if they could look at what they were waiting for. This seems to be a genuine strategy rather than simple wish fulfillment, since they also suggested it for others (Mischel & Mischel, 1983; Mischel, Shoda, & Rodriguez, 1992).

These same 4-year-olds also knew they would have to distract themselves while waiting, but they did not realize the difficulty they would have in doing so. Thus, they set up self-defeating situations by putting the tempting object in full view, not realizing how difficult it would be to overcome temptation. By 4½, children realize it will not help to look at what they are waiting for, but they also do not think to cover the source of temptation from view. Only by the end of the 5th year do they think to remove the tempting object from view (Mischel & Mischel, 1983; Mischel et al., 1992).

Finally, children find it easier to wait for things when they trust adults to keep promises. Parents who want their children to be able to wait must be prepared to follow through with what they have said. In this case, it is better to promise something that is within one's reach, even if it is small, than something bigger that may not be. Children can wait more easily when they experience a sense of control over the situation and over themselves, when they can trust themselves as well as others to "deliver the goods" (Maccoby, 1984).

Erikson believed children's experience of their parents' trustworthiness to be the foundation on which all later development builds. Keeping promises to children, both the spoken ones and the unspoken ones implicit in the orderly nurturing care they give, is central to this trust. Sam Keen (1970) describes the power of promises kept in an essay about his relationship with his father. He begins

> Once upon a time when there were still Indians, Gypsies, bears, and bad men in the woods of Tennessee where I played and, more important still, there was no death, a promise was made to me. One endless summer afternoon my father sat in the eternal shade of a peach tree, carving on a seed he had picked up. With increasing excitement and covetousness I watched while, using a skill common to all omnipotent creators, he fashioned a small monkey out of the seed. All of my vagrant wishes and desires disciplined themselves and came to focus on that peach-seed monkey. Finally, I marshaled my nerve and asked if I might have the monkey when it was finished (on the sixth day of creation). My father replied, "This one is for your mother, but I will carve you one someday." ◄

His father didn't carve that peach-seed monkey for him that summer, and Keen soon forgot his fascination with it. Years later, as an adult listening to his father taking stock of his life just before dying, Keen told his father how trustworthy he had always been with him, "In all that is important you have never failed me. With one exception, you kept the promises you made to me—you never carved me that peach-seed monkey."

Shortly after this conversation—two weeks before he died—his father gave him a peach-seed monkey that he had carved. For Keen, that carving became a symbol of "all the promises which were made to me and the energy and care which nourished and created me as a human being."

Developing Restraints: How Parents Can Help

Children differ in the amount of control they have over their activity, as well as in their ability to wait for what they want. But initially, all are impulsive compared to later, and parents need to provide many of the controls children need until they develop their own. Parents can help in a number of ways. Especially important for developing restraints as structuring situations, regulating the child's activities, and being controlled themselves (Maccoby, 1984).

How can parents help children develop necessary restraints in their behavior?

Structuring Situations   Regular predictable routines and settings help children to cope with new experiences. It is not by chance that preschoolers are likely to be at their crankiest when Grandma and Grandpa come to visit. Schedules are disrupted; naps are missed; meals, baths, play time, and quiet time are all likely to differ. Young children have difficulty integrating their activities into those of others. It is even difficult for them to integrate one activity of their own with another. Their actions are prompted more by immediate, external conditions than by a planned ordering of events. A predictable schedule, familiar routines of eating, sleeping, and such, give a structure to their experience that is not easily provided from within.

Because preschoolers have trouble anticipating future needs, parents need to plan for them by bringing things for them to do.

Parents frequently need to structure play activities. Young children find it difficult to sustain play over any amount of time. It is not unusual for a parent to hear "I have nothing to do" from a child standing in the middle of a room filled with toys. Children may have the toys to play with, but they lack the plans that will transform them into play. Parents can help by supplying plans. Although one might think first to shoot back a testy remark, it is just as easy to suggest a way to play. "Why don't you build a house with those, make a bridge, give your dolly a meal?" Each of these suggestions is a blueprint for play (Maccoby, 1984).

Parents can help young children manage their impulses by not making them wait. Children lack strategies for filling time and can get out of control when asked to wait. Running, squirming, teasing, fighting, and shouting soon follow.

Regulating Children's Activities   Young children have difficulty anticipating future needs. Five minutes out the door they can announce, "I have to go potty." "Why didn't you think of this before?" an exasperated parent retorts. "I didn't have to go then," is the answer. Children who are told to bring along crayons, skates, paper dolls, or airplanes are likely to answer that they won't be bored, and then drive an adult crazy every 10 minutes with "I'm bored," "Can't we go yet?" and "I want to go home NOW." They weren't bored when told to bring something along and couldn't imagine feeling any way other than how they felt then. Some of these problems can be avoided by building in routines. Trips in the car, whether to the market or the next state, mean going to the bathroom first and bringing along something to do—books, puzzles, crayons, dolls, or action figures.

Because young children find it difficult to anticipate the consequences of their decisions, parents need to make some decisions for them. "Can I have a pet mouse, bird, puppy, kitten, water buffalo? Please, Mom, please? I'll take care of it. Please, pretty please, P-L-E-A-S-E?" Many a tender-hearted parent has fallen prey to such pleadings only to regret it while cleaning out the mouse cage, chasing the bird, or picking up buffalo chips. Preschoolers fail to anticipate that a pet must be fed, bathed, and cared for. Parents who are unwilling to share the burden of these consequences by building in new routines of pet care may find it easier to make their children wait until they are ready to assume the responsibilities themselves. One may feel like a heel when denying a small child, yet the alternative of giving in may be setting the child up for failure ("You promised you would feed it, walk it...") and feelings of guilt or inadequacy (Maccoby, 1984).

Many decisions can be shared by parent and child. Parents can simplify choices to several alternatives, any of which would be manageable and acceptable for the child. The child decides between these. When the number of alternatives is small, children can consider each and reach a decision that they and their parents can live with.

Parental Self-Control   Parents can also help their children develop control through their own self-control. Children can manage their emotional outbursts more easily when parents control their tempers. A child's angry outbursts can lead to anger in the parent, making it all too easy to shout back or spank, leading to more tears and precluding further communication. But when parents are calm and firm, children can take in information even while being disciplined.

Parents can help children develop habits that provide structure when they themselves are predictable and regular. Even though a parent may be dying to skip the nightly routine of chores, homework, bath, and bedtime stories, routines that are set aside too frequently fail to be routine and do not provide structure to the child's daily experiences.

Similarly, children will think of strategies to help them wait or to remember things if parents teach such strategies through example. If children see parents bringing something along to occupy themselves while they wait at the car wash or the dentist's office, it becomes natural for them to do the same. Similarly, strategies for remembering can be built in by teaching children to routinely put the item to be remembered where it will be seen, such as homework by the front door or milk money on the kitchen counter (Maccoby, 1984).

Helping children develop controls requires an investment of time. It takes time, in other words, to teach the skills children need to do things on their own, and it takes time to follow through to see that they carry out what they have been given to do in a responsible way. When children have skills, they have options. Teaching children how to do things on their own, gradually introducing them to difficult tasks and letting them experience success with each new level of difficulty, builds tolerance for frustration and fosters the development of inner controls (Maccoby, 1984).

Health and Well-Being

The dramatic changes in height and weight that take place during the preschool years depend on adequate nutrition. These very same changes also make it possible for preschoolers to increasingly get about on their own, getting into just about anything, and increasing their risk of accidental injuries as a consequence. We will look at the dietary needs of preschoolers and the risk of injury in the following sections.

Nutrition

Rapid skeletal and muscular development, as well as continuing brain growth, all require adequate nutrition. As a consequence, preschoolers need more energy per ounce than do adults. However, because the rate of growth slows in early child-

hood, they need less than they did as toddlers. As a result, their appetites are likely to decrease, often causing some alarm in parents. Preschoolers can even become "finicky," picking through their plates for just the right things to eat. Food not only has to taste good, it also has to look "right," and so foods that are the wrong color or texture are frequently rejected, with little consistency from one day to the next. However, unless parents notice a marked change in weight or persistent fatigue, a diminished appetite is not a problem (Mitchell, 1990).

It is not how much children eat but what they eat that contributes to their health during these years. A healthy diet should include an adequate supply of fruits and vegetables, whole grains, and foods rich in calcium and protein, such as dairy products and meats. Colorful foods, such as oranges, apples, tomatoes, and green vegetables are not only appealing to preschoolers, but also highly nutritious.

Why do preschoolers have less of an appetite than they did as toddlers?

TABLE 7.1 Sources of Essential Vitamins and Minerals

Young children are most likely to be deficient in vitamins A, C, and B$_6$, folic acid, calcium, iron, and zinc. The following foods adequately supply these nutrients.

Whole grains, fortified cereals, and breads	6 servings	Iron, zinc, vitamin B$_6$, folic acid
Fruits	2 servings	Vitamins A, B$_6$, C, folic acid
Milk, cheese, yogurt group	3 servings	Calcium, zinc, vitamins A, B$_6$
Meat, fish, poultry group	2 servings	Iron, zinc, vitamin B$_6$
Vegetables (dark yellow; leafy greens; potatoes)	2 servings	Vitamins A, B$_6$, C, folic acid

Source: W. H. Dietz and L. Stern (eds.). (1999). *American Academy of Pediatrics: Guide to your child's nutrition.* New York: Villard.

TABLE 7.2 Substituting Foods for a Balanced Diet

Vitamins

For children who don't like vegetables	Vitamin A: apricots, cantaloupe, mango, peaches, plums, prunes; milk; eggs Vitamin C: grapefruit, oranges, cantaloupe and other melons, strawberries

Calcium

For children who don't drink milk	Part-skim and low-fat cheeses, yogurt; broccoli, dark-green leafy vegetables; chickpeas, lentils; canned sardines, salmon, and other fish with bones; calcium-fortified orange juice. Some pediatricians recommend an over-the-counter antacid containing calcium carbonate

Protein

For children who don't eat meat	Lentils, tofu; beans, and other legumes in combination with grains; peanut butter; eggs; fish; nuts; dairy foods

Source: W. H. Dietz and L. Stern (eds.). (1999). *American Academy of Pediatrics: Guide to your child's nutrition.* New York: Villard.

A number of deficiencies, however, are sufficiently common to bear mention. One common form of malnutrition during these years, and one not limited to poor or developing countries, is protein deficiency. Adequate supplies of protein are necessary to support rapidly developing muscles and body tissues. Malnutrition, when chronic, can stunt physical growth and affect brain development. Even mild forms of malnutrition, however, can result in fatigue, poor concentration, apathy, and a generally decreased ability to cope with the demands of one's environment (Pollitt et al., 1996).

Most children's eating habits in the United States fail to meet established nutritional guidelines. Only about a third of children in a recent national survey met the daily recommendations for the five food groups of fruits, vegetables, grains, meat, and dairy products. In general, fats and sugars were found to provide about 35% to 40% of the energy children consumed daily from food, much more than is considered healthy. Objectives for healthier eating include eating more complex carbohydrates and high-fiber foods by having at least five servings a day of fruits and vegetables and at least six of grains (that is, breads and cereals), increasing daily calcium intake, and reducing the intake of fat to about 30% of the caloric intake (Munoz, Drebs-Smith, Ballard-Barbach, & Cleveland, 1997). Table 7.1 summarizes a healthy daily diet for young children, and Table 7.2 suggests alternatives for finicky eaters.

Public school lunch programs help to combat inadequate nutrition among children from low-income families.

The total energy consumed daily by children is related to their income level (Munoz et al., 1997). Not surprisingly, children who live in poverty are not as well nourished as those who do not. What may be surprising, however, is that inadequate nutrition poses a serious health problem not only to children living in poor countries, but to significant numbers of low-income children in the United States as well. Paradoxically, we have come to downplay the importance of biological risk factors such as poor nutrition for development because of the very success of our nation's public health system during the first part of this century, which improved children's nutritional status and dramatically reduced communicable childhood diseases (Pollitt, 1994).

What are the nutritional consequences of poverty, and how can these be corrected? The most serious nutritional deficiency among low-income children in the United States is iron-deficiency anemia (Pollitt, 1994). Overall, about 17% of children from low-income families are estimated to have iron-deficiency anemia, whereas only 3% to 5% of middle-income children are estimated to suffer this nutritional deficiency. Iron deficiency can result in retarded growth, greater susceptibility to infectious diseases, and diminished physical and cognitive functioning (Filer, 1995).

Many of these effects are reversible with daily supplements of iron. Research in which iron-deficient infants and toddlers were randomly assigned to either a supplemental iron or a placebo condition found a reversal of such developmental delays in the children treated with iron but not in those given the placebo. Since these studies included double-blind controls, in which neither those receiving the supplements nor those evaluating their effects knew which of these conditions the children were in, the initial symptoms as well as their reversal could clearly be attributed to the deficiency itself and not to social or environmental conditions typically associated with poor nutrition (Idjradinata & Pollitt, 1993).

Just as programs giving supplemental iron have been found to be effective in combating iron deficiency, those giving supplemental food to low-income children have been found effective in combating malnutrition. Support for the effectiveness of supplemental food programs comes primarily from research conducted in other countries (Engle, Gorman, Martorell, & Pollitt, 1992; Joos, Pollitt, & Mueller, 1982; Super, Herrera, & Mora, 1990). In this research, children have been assigned at random either to control conditions in which they did not receive nutritional supplements or to those in which they received supplemental food. Research of this nature has found that supplemental feeding results in improved motor and mental development in children. Furthermore, this improvement carries over into the preschool years, even after the supplemental program has terminated. In one long-term follow-up, in which children were again tested 11 years later, benefits of such programs extended even into adolescence (Engle et al., 1992). In this study, nutritional supplementation was so effective that differences in performance ordinarily associated with socioeconomic status disappeared for the low-income adolescents who had received supplemental food as young children (Engle et al., 1992; Joos et al., 1982; Super et al., 1990).

Overweight

Quite a different problem is faced by other children. The percentage of children in the United States who are overweight has increased substantially in recent years, paralleling a similar trend among adults (Troiano & Flegal, 1998). Given that wide differences in weight are common among children at any age, how is one to determine what constitutes overweight? Body mass index, or BMI, offers a convenient formula for calculating both overweight and underweight. BMI expresses one's weight relative to one's height, by dividing one's weight by the square of one's height (see Table 7.3 for the formula). Is a 3-year-old who weighs 33 pounds overweight? It depends. For a boy who is 37 inches tall, this weight yields a BMI of 16.9, which places him at the 50th percentile. However, a boy weighing 33 pounds who is only 35 inches tall has a BMI of 18.9, placing him at the 95th percentile in weight for that age. Children who are **overweight** are at or above the 85th percentile of weight for their height. Since body fat varies not only with age but also with sex, separate growth charts are necessary for girls and for boys.

Children slim down in the preschool years due both to rapid bone growth, which adds inches to their height, and to muscle development. These developmental changes are reflected in growth charts that use BMI as an index-for-age (see Figure 7.1). One can see a decline in BMI from the age of 2 to approximately 6. After age 6, BMI increases, and approximately 10% to 15% of 6- to 17-year-olds are overweight, which is twice the number who were overweight 30 years ago (CDC, 2000). A number of factors are most likely responsible for this trend in weight gain among children, some of the more important being changes in patterns of physical activity and in eating habits (CDC, 2000; Hill & Trowbridge, 1998).

Both children and adults are less physically active today than in the past. This change is important since being overweight is negatively correlated with physical activity. That is, the *less* active one is, the *more* likely one is to be overweight (Harsha, 1995). What might account for today's more sedentary lifestyle? Both work and leisure pursuits are likely culprits. The work habits of parents, for instance, can affect the entire family's activities. Working parents do not always have time to spend tying on roller skates, balancing a child on a bicycle, or playing catch. And more children today are being raised in families where both parents work or in families with a single working mother. Many days of the week parents may arrive home from work at the same time as their children, having picked them up from day care on the way, only to face the need to fix dinner before beginning the evening's activities. Depending on the quality of the day care, children may or may not have had ample opportunity to run and play outside.

With respect to leisure activities, children today spend more time in sedentary recreational activities than in the past. For some children this decision is

overweight A condition in which children are at or above the 85th percentile of weight for their height.

TABLE 7.3 Body Mass Index Formula

English Formula

BMI = (Weight in pounds ÷ Height in inches ÷ Height in inches) × 703

Fractions and ounces must be entered as decimal values.

Fraction	Ounces	Decimal
1/8	2	.125
1/4	4	.25
3/8	6	.375
1/2	8	.5
5/8	10	.625
3/4	12	.75
7/8	14	.875

Example: A 33 pound 4 ounce child is 37⅝ inches tall.

(33.25 pounds divided by 37.625 inches, divided by 37.625 inches) × 703 = 16.5.

Metric Formula

BMI = Weight in kilograms ÷ (Height in meters)^2

or

BMI = (Weight in kilograms ÷ Height in cm ÷ Height in cm) × 10,000

Example: A 16.9 kg child is 105.2 cm tall.

(16.9 divided by 105.2 cm, divided by 105.2 cm) × 10,000 = 15.3 BMI

For a BMI calculator from the Centers for Disease Control and Prevention, see http://www.cdc.gov/nccdphp/dnpa/bmi/calc-bmi.htm.

Source: Centers for Disease Control and Prevention. (2000, May 30). *What is BMI?* Retrieved June 30, 2000 from the World Wide Web: http://www.cdc.gov/nccdphp/dnpa/bmi/bmi-definition.htm.

The number of hours children spend watching television is related to being overweight.

imposed on them, whereas for others, it is voluntary. In general, children are more active when they are out of doors, yet some children cannot go outside to play as frequently as they might want because their neighborhoods are not safe. Other children prefer spending time inside, engaging in more sedentary activities such as watching television. The number of hours children spend watching television is related to being overweight, with each additional hour spent in front of the television associated with a 2% increase in the likelihood of obesity (Dietz & Gortmaker, 1985). What might account for this association? It might simply be that watching television affords more opportunity for snacking than do more physical activities, such as riding a bike or playing on a swing. Television also provides messages about food and models for eating, influencing preferences for certain foods over others. Most commercials during children's programming, for instance, are for food; and most of these foods—such as cereals high in simple carbohydrates or snacks high in sugar, salt, and fat—have low nutritional value. Children are more likely to request the foods they see on television than other foods.

There may also be a metabolic base to the association between weight gain and television viewing. Resting energy expenditures, for instance, have been

How might watching television contribute to overweight?

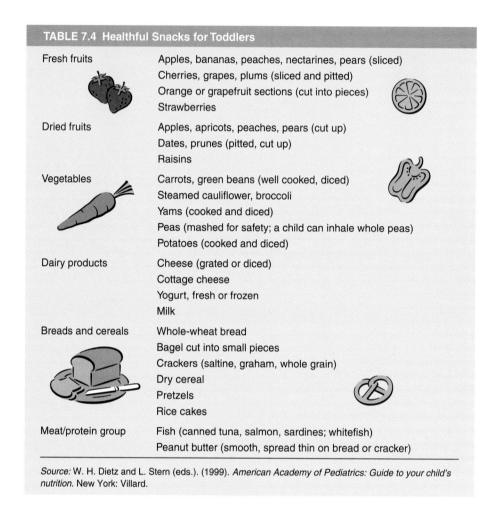

TABLE 7.4 Healthful Snacks for Toddlers

Fresh fruits	Apples, bananas, peaches, nectarines, pears (sliced)
	Cherries, grapes, plums (sliced and pitted)
	Orange or grapefruit sections (cut into pieces)
	Strawberries
Dried fruits	Apples, apricots, peaches, pears (cut up)
	Dates, prunes (pitted, cut up)
	Raisins
Vegetables	Carrots, green beans (well cooked, diced)
	Steamed cauliflower, broccoli
	Yams (cooked and diced)
	Peas (mashed for safety; a child can inhale whole peas)
	Potatoes (cooked and diced)
Dairy products	Cheese (grated or diced)
	Cottage cheese
	Yogurt, fresh or frozen
	Milk
Breads and cereals	Whole-wheat bread
	Bagel cut into small pieces
	Crackers (saltine, graham, whole grain)
	Dry cereal
	Pretzels
	Rice cakes
Meat/protein group	Fish (canned tuna, salmon, sardines; whitefish)
	Peanut butter (smooth, spread thin on bread or cracker)

Source: W. H. Dietz and L. Stern (eds.). (1999). *American Academy of Pediatrics: Guide to your child's nutrition.* New York: Villard.

found to decrease with television viewing, both in obese children and in children of normal weight (Klesges, Shelton, & Klesges, 1993). Also, the sheer amount of energy expended in watching television is less than that for many other activities. We know that children are more active out of doors than inside, and television viewing is an indoors activity. Most likely a combination of these factors is at work (Kohl & Hobbs, 1998).

Not only their physical activity, but also what children eat affects their weight. For both adults and children, being overweight is associated with diets that are high in fat and low in complex carbohydrates. Control of fat intake appears to be critical in controlling body weight for a number of reasons. For one thing, fat is calorie-dense. That is, it has more calories per volume than other substances, and volume is an important contributor to how full one feels. Also, foods high in fat simply taste good, and we tend to eat more of them. Fat is also stored more efficiently than other nutrients, such as protein or carbohydrate, meaning that more of what you eat stays with you. And because foods with fat taste so good, they are likely to supplant other foods that are better for you (Birch & Fisher, 1998).

Even dietary habits that are effective in reducing fat intake do not necessarily increase children's consumption of complex carbohydrates, such as are found in fruits and vegetables. When schoolchildren were asked, in one study, what they had eaten that day, 40% indicated they had eaten no vegetables. In contrast, 35% said they had eaten at least four different types of snack foods (Wolf & Campbell,

TABLE 7.5 Foods That Are Unsafe for Toddlers
Because children don't begin to chew with a grinding motion until approximately 4 years of age, toddlers can easily choke on the following foods. 　Hot dogs (unless cut in quarters lengthwise before being sliced) 　Hard candies, including jelly beans 　Nuts 　Chunks of peanut butter—spread peanut butter thinly on bread or cracker—never give 　　chunks of peanut butter to a toddler 　Popcorn 　Raw carrots, celery, green beans 　Seeds (such as processed pumpkin or sunflower seeds) 　Whole grapes, cherry tomatoes (cut them in quarters) 　Large chunks of any food such as meat, potatoes, or raw vegetables and fruits
Source: Adapted from W. H. Dietz and L. Stern (eds.). (1999). *American Academy of Pediatrics: Guide to your child's nutrition.* New York: Villard.

1993). Even when children eat vegetables, these are not always the ones a dietitian would choose. Among children who said they ate five or more servings of fruits and vegetables a day, 25% of the vegetables they listed were french fries (Krebs-Smith et al., 1996).

Establishing Healthy Patterns

A number of factors affect children's food choices and eating patterns. Perhaps the most obvious of these is the accessibility of various foods. Children eat what is available. Those who attend day care centers and schools, for instance, where more fruits and vegetables are served, eat more fruits and vegetables (Birch & Fisher, 1998). The same holds for preschoolers at home. Parents can establish healthy eating patterns by offering cut-up vegetables or fruits as snacks instead of sweets or crackers; by replacing fast-food meals with microwavable meals that contain less fat; by using low-fat milk instead of whole milk; and by limiting high-calorie drinks, including juices, offering fruit or water to drink instead (Christoffel & Ariza, 1998). Table 7.4 lists some other healthful snacks and Table 7.5 lists foods that are unsafe for children under 4.

Children do what they see others doing. Preschoolers who see other children eating vegetables, even those that they do not especially like, will nonetheless increase the frequency with which they select and eat those vegetables (Birch, 1980). Modeling is a pervasive and powerful influence, even when it comes to establishing food preferences. Very young children are more likely to put different foods in their mouths, for instance, when they see these being eaten by their mother than by a stranger (Harper & Sanders, 1975). Similarly, when weight is a salient issue in families, due to obesity or dieting, children's eating patterns are likely to be influenced by those of their parents (Fisher & Birch, 1996).

Controlling the availability of different foods can sometimes backfire. Parents run the risk of inadvertently increasing children's preferences for certain foods by making them forbidden. The old adage, "Forbidden fruit tastes sweeter," holds true at all ages. Restricting children's access to certain types of foods can increase their value to children (Birch & Fisher, 1998; Smith & Epstein, 1991). We frequently send mixed messages to children about such foods, saying they are bad for them on the one hand, but on the other hand offering them as the food to be eaten on festive occasions, such as birthday parties and other celebrations. It might be better to include these foods in children's daily fare, teaching them to enjoy them in moderation.

How sensitive are children to their energy needs, such that they could be expected to regulate what and when they eat? Research in which children are given food over a series of two courses suggests that they are sensitive. Two groups of children were given the same amount to eat in the first course, but the energy content of the food differed for the two groups, by varying the amount of carbohydrates and fat. After the first course, all were given a second course in which they were allowed to self-select their food. Those who ate the energy-dense food in the first course ate less in the second course (Birch & Deysher, 1986; Birch, McPhee, Shoba, Steinberg, & Krehbiel, 1987). Children's responsiveness to the energy content of food, furthermore, is evident in the foods they select over an extended period of time. Thus, if more energy-dense foods are consumed in one meal, fewer will be consumed even in a much later meal (Birch, Johnson, Andersen, Peters, & Schulte, 1991).

Children's responsiveness to internal cues such as these is reduced when they are encouraged to rely on external cues, such as how much is left on their plate. There appears to be a natural tension between parental attempts to regulate what children eat, which must for the most part rely on external cues, and children's own self-regulatory patterns, which are based primarily on internal cues. Thus, research in which children are fed over two courses has found that children whose parents exercise a high degree of control over what they eat do not adjust their food selections in the second course to compensate for the energy they have taken in as much as do children whose parents exercise less control (Johnson & Birch, 1994). For most children, the tension between parental control and self-regulation introduces few problems. But for those where there are issues related to eating within the family, this tension may be problematic. Parents are more likely to attempt to regulate what their children eat when they have problems themselves in terms of eating, the very conditions under which external cues are likely to be least reliable.

Illnesses, Injuries, and Accidents

The health status of children differs significantly with ethnicity, presumably due to associated differences in socioeconomic status. Thus, African American children are nearly twice as likely to be in fair or poor health as White children, and children from low-income families 3 times more likely to be in poor health than those from middle-income families. Statistics such as these strongly suggest that low-income minority children are more likely to be affected by common illnesses and less likely to receive the medical care they need (Pollitt, 1994).

Comparisons of children from a nationally representative sample give support to this concern. When children at risk due to low income, minority status, or lack of health insurance were compared with a control group of middle-income, White children who were covered by insurance, substantial differences were found in the availability and type of care they received. In addition to being less likely to be cared for by a particular doctor familiar with their health history, at-risk children also had to spend more time traveling to the doctor and more time waiting once they got there. They were also less likely to have access to after-hours medical care in case of emergencies. Perhaps as a result of their difficulty in seeing a doctor, children in the at-risk groups were less likely to be taken for treatment when they were ill than were control children and were less likely to have received all their vaccinations (Newacheck, Hughes, & Stoddard, 1996).

Immunization Programs

Due to widescale immunization programs in developed nations, many infectious diseases that were once life-threatening to children, such as smallpox, diphtheria, polio, and measles have been effectively controlled. In the United States, for instance, rubella (German measles) was a common childhood disease and a common cause of birth defects. Due to a national immunization program, the Centers for Disease Control (1995d) reported only five cases of congenital rubella in 1994. In underdeveloped nations, measles continues to be a common childhood disease and kills upwards of a million children a year (CDC, 1993). Given the success of immunization programs and the potential dangers to children in their absence, one might expect parents, to the extent they are able, to make sure their children are current in all their vaccinations. Such is not the case for many children, however. Paradoxically, the very achievements of these programs threaten to undermine their continued success, as parents and the public in general have become less aware of the potential danger of the diseases that immunization programs control.

Although 90% of children in the United States are immunized by the time they enter elementary school, immunization rates for 2-year-olds frequently fall well below this figure. This discrepancy is especially true for children living in major urban areas. For example, a 1993 survey of families in the Houston area revealed that only 36% of 2-year-olds had received all their immunizations by their 2nd birthday. This figure, though alarmingly low, is not unrepresentative for children living in major U.S. cities. The percentage of 2-year-olds living in Los Angeles and Dallas who were fully immunized, for instance, was 27%; the percentage was 48% for those living in San Diego (Hanson et al., 1996, as reported in McCormick et al., 1997).

Given the low rate of immunizations of young children, it is important to understand why parents are not keeping their children's immunization status up-to-date. It is one thing to be able to say that parents of children living in major urban areas are less likely to have their children immunized. But it is another thing to be able to say *why* they are less likely to do so. Some of the research aimed at understanding the causes behind parents' behavior has started with the assumption that to have their children immunized, parents must *plan* for it and that their plans are affected by their beliefs (Prislin, Dyer, Blakely, & Johnson, 1998). When parents of young children were interviewed, a clear link emerged between parents' beliefs and their likelihood of maintaining up-to-date immunizations.

Such links can improve educational programs aimed at increasing immunization. Well-educated parents, for instance, were somewhat more likely than parents with less education to incorrectly believe that a child with a cold should not get immunized. *All* parents, not only less-educated ones, need accurate information concerning contraindications for immunization.

Other beliefs, however, were found to differ as a function of sociodemographic groups. For instance, low immunization rates among African Americans were related to beliefs in natural immunity. Thus, educational programs targeting this particular group, to be effective, should emphasize the effectiveness of vaccines over natural immunity. Similarly, parents with little formal education were found to be concerned about the safety of vaccines, an issue needing to be addressed in educational programs directed to this segment of the population. An encouraging finding to emerge from this research was the effectiveness of the WIC program (see Chapter 4) in promoting immunization. Those participating in this program were more likely to believe that immunizations protected their children from disease and to perceive fewer barriers to immunization.

Thus, there are nonfinancial as well as financial barriers to health care for many children. Some of these are being addressed through increased federal funding for community health centers and training for health care providers who are willing to practice in low-income neighborhoods. Additional steps will need to focus on improving the availability of transportation and child care, arranging office hours that meet the needs of working single parents, reducing waiting times, and providing more trained providers who are "culturally competent" with respect to those for whom they are caring (Newacheck, Hughes, & Stoddard, 1996). The Social Policy Focus, "Immunization Programs," looks at the effectiveness of parent education programs in improving the immunization rate.

Because they are so active, running across yards or playgrounds at full tilt, climbing anything that's higher than they are, and exploring whatever presents itself as new, preschoolers experience their share of accidental injuries. Most of these do not require medical attention. However, girls have a 25% chance of sustaining an injury that does; and for boys, this figure rises to 33% (Fried, Makuc, & Rooks, 1998).

The increased use of child-restraint devices is primarily responsible for the prevention of automobile fatalities among preschoolers.

Injuries are, in fact, the leading cause of death for children between the ages of 1 and 4. Death from an accidental injury is 4 times more common than the next most common cause (Scholer, Mitchel, & Ray, 1997). The percentage of injury-related deaths among children, however, has decreased substantially. Over a 14-year period from 1978 to 1991, the death rate due to unintentional injuries decreased by 39%. The largest decreases involved motor vehicle deaths and deaths due to drowning (Rivara & Grossman, 1996).

The increased use of child-restraint devices, such as seat belts, is primarily responsible for the prevention of automobile fatalities among children under the age of 5. In 1991, for instance, 63% of the children who died in automobile accidents were not using seat belts or, if younger, were not belted into infant car seats. Belts securing a child across the lap alone are not as effective as lap-shoulder restraints and, though they decrease the risk of fatal injuries, may be a source of serious nonfatal injuries in themselves (Viano, 1995).

Drowning is the second most frequent cause of accidental fatalities among children and adolescents, most of which involve preschoolers. Drowning in swimming pools is largely preventable by making sure that these are fenced in on all sides and secured with a self-latching gate and by having an adult present at all times whenever children are in the pool. Drowning in bathtubs, accounting for approximately 10% of all drownings, is similarly preventable (Rivara & Grossman, 1996). Most of these deaths involve toddlers or children who suffer seizures, such as those with epilepsy. Toddlers should never be left in a bath by themselves, and it is best for children who suffer seizure disorders to take showers rather than baths, even beyond the preschool years.

The risk to a child of dying from an accidental injury increases under certain conditions. Seth Scholer, Edward Mitchel, and Wayne Ray (1997), who studied the population of children born in Tennessee between 1985 and 1994, found a substantial association between injury death rates and certain maternal and child characteristics. Injuries were more than 50% more likely when the mother had less than 12 years of education, had more than two other children in the family, and was less than 20 years old. Race and income level were not related to injury mor-

Box 7.3 *Types of Maltreatment*

Abuse

- *Physical abuse:* Involves substantial injuries that last for at least 48 hours and often, as in the case of burns, broken bones, or internal injuries, longer. Examples might include bruises or fractures from being hit or punched, burns from cigarettes, or cerebral hemorrhages from being shaken. Fifty-one percent of children who are abused are physically abused.
- *Sexual abuse:* Involves exposure, molesting or fondling, or actual penetration. Examples might include a father fondling his 4-year-old son during visitations, or a daughter being molested by her mother's live-in boyfriend. Twenty-nine percent of children who are abused are sexually abused.
- *Emotional abuse:* Involves behavior that undermines a child's sense of well-being and self-esteem. Examples could include denigrating or derisive remarks ("You stupid little brat!"), locking a child in a closet as a form of punishment, or threatening physical or sexual abuse, such as a father taking his children to a gun store to buy a gun which he said he would use to kill their mother. Twenty-eight percent of children who are abused are emotionally abused.

Neglect

- *Physical neglect:* Involves a failure to provide for a child's physical or medical needs or to provide adequate supervision. Examples might include failure to provide treatment for a medical condition, driving while intoxicated, leaving a child unattended in a car, or not attending to obvious hazards around the home. This type of neglect has more than tripled over the past two decades.
- *Educational neglect:* Involves permitting truancy (approximately 5 days/month), not enrolling a child in school, or keeping a child home to care for other siblings. This is the most common form of neglect.
- *Emotional neglect:* This differs from emotional abuse in that this is a passive emotional rejection of the child, taking the form of giving little or no emotional support, attention, or affection. Although the least common form of neglect, it has also risen substantially in the past two decades.

Source: Sedlak & Broadhurst (1996).

tality when other variables were controlled for. When children were classified according to these three variables, those identified as high-risk had an injury mortality rate more than 15 times greater than that of low-risk children. If all children had the same risk of injury as the low-risk children, more than 75% of deaths from injury would not have occurred (Scholer, Mitchel, & Ray, 1997).

Most serious accidents are preventable. Thus, using smoke detectors and child car seats, lowering the thermostat on the water heater, not putting infants in walkers, and instituting home visitation programs for young or poorly educated mothers can all substantially reduce injuries to young children.

Maltreatment

Not all injuries to children are accidental. **Maltreatment** refers to instances of harm to children that are nonaccidental and avoidable, whether from abuse or neglect. Abuse can be physical, sexual, or emotional in nature and often involves some combination of these. Similarly, neglect is categorized as a failure to provide for

maltreatment Nonaccidental and avoidable harm done to children, whether from abuse or neglect.

the child's physical, educational, or emotional needs. Box 7.3 distinguishes among these types of maltreatment.

Well over a million children are maltreated in the United States each year, somewhat over half of these through neglect and just under half through abuse. When one also includes children who are *endangered*, for whom there is no proof of harm but reason to believe they are in danger, the number of children affected by maltreatment is closer to 3 million (Sedlak & Broadhurst, 1996; U.S. Dept. of Health and Human Services, 1998). How do we turn statistics such as these into meaningful figures? An estimate of approximately 3 million children translates, when counting by hundreds, into 4 children out of every 100, or 1 child in 25, an easier figure to put a face to and a figure where 1 becomes a very large number indeed.

How believable are figures such as these? Is maltreatment this common a problem? A national sample of over 3,000 families surveyed by phone suggests that it is. Parents were asked how they resolved family conflicts when these arose and were asked specifically whether acts such as hitting a child with an object, kicking, biting, burning, or using a gun or a knife had occurred during the course of the conflict. By parents' own reports, 110 children per 1,000 had experienced one or more of these forms of violence (Straus & Gelles, 1986). Given that this survey was conducted over a decade ago and that the frequency of maltreatment has increased over the past two decades (U.S. Dept. of Health and Human Services, 1998), these figures are not likely to overestimate the problem.

The toll of abuse extends beyond the immediate effects of the violence, permeating children's lives with a quiet dread. Scott Peck (1995) describes this dread, as a young boy, living with an abusive stepfather in *All American Boy:*

> Somewhere in this night, it is all still happening.
>
> We sit together on the grass, we three. My mother, her dancer's legs drawn up tightly against her chest, her face looking old in the glow of our block's lonely street lamp.
>
> Quiet. She is quietly afraid, quietly listening for sounds from the porch where he sits—her husband, my stepfather. I can see the red tip of his cigarette, flaring on cue every two minutes as he inhales, flaring and sending illuminated little butterflies twitching to the floor. He sits in darkness, still and silent in his rocking chair, like some Mayan king, while his wife and children huddle closely together on the grass of the front lawn. Floridian night breezes, soaked in the smell of gardenias, lap around our heads and necks, chilling.
>
> He will dictate this night to us; we wait for his decree.
>
> When he stands, we scatter like frightened sparrows, Mother grabbing each of us by a wrist and moving out toward the sidewalk.
>
> "Get ready," she hisses. (p. 9) ◄

Most children who experience maltreatment (74%) are maltreated by their parents. Another 13.6% are maltreated by another adult in the home, such as a stepparent or a foster parent. The type of maltreatment children are likely to experience differs as a function of the perpetrator. Mothers, or some other female caretaker, are responsible for 87% of neglect. In contrast, all forms of abuse are more likely to be committed by a male: 89% for sexual abuse, 63% for emotional abuse, and 58% for physical abuse (Sedlak & Broadhurst, 1996).

Rather than assuming that a single factor, such as family income level or characteristics of the child or the parent, is responsible for maltreatment, taking an approach that views contributing factors at many levels is more reasonable (Bronfenbrenner, 1979). These factors could either predispose toward or protect a child from maltreatment. Predisposing factors at the level of the microsystem might take the form of a parent's loss of a job, whereas at the level of the macrosystem, predisposing factors may be the acceptance of violence in society or media portrayal of conflict resolution. Conversely, protective factors at the level of the microsystem might consist of a family income sufficient to buffer stresses, and at the level of the macrosystem they might take the form of cultural beliefs about the innocence of children and legal protections against abuse.

Both risk and protective factors can be either enduring or transient. *Enduring risk factors* represent relatively permanent conditions, such as a parent's inability to tolerate stress. In contrast, *transient risk factors* are short-term challenges, such as the loss of a job, an illness, or a child's entering a difficult developmental period. Similarly, *enduring protective factors* might be the parent's own history of good parenting as a child or the existence of other supportive relationships within the family. *Transient protective factors* buffering a child from maltreatment might be improvement in conditions at work or a new neighbor with a child the same age to play with (Cicchetti & Lynch, 1995).

What can lead parents to maltreat their children? Is it lack of love? Can one look to mental illness as an explanation? Or to catastrophic life circumstance? No simple answers are to be found. Most of these parents love their children and experience genuine remorse for what they do. Similarly, relatively few would be diagnosed as suffering from a mental illness. Nor could one predict maltreatment simply by knowing their life circumstances. In fact, research on maltreatment has failed to identify any single factor that necessarily leads to maltreatment (Cicchetti & Lynch, 1995). Most maltreating parents in many ways are not that different from average parents.

Even so, some differences have been found. One important difference concerns the way they respond under stress. Parents who maltreat their children appear to experience more difficulty coping with stress than do other parents. Not only are they likely to find the normal stresses of life more aversive than are other individuals, but they also tend to overreact when they are stressed, experiencing more difficulty controlling their impulses. In addition, parents who maltreat their children are more likely to interpret events as being outside their control and to react angrily and defensively than are other parents (Brunquell, Crichton, & Egeland, 1981). Thus, although parents who maltreat their children may behave in ways that are similar to the ways other parents behave under most circumstances, they are likely to respond differently when stressed.

Maltreating parents also appear to differ in what might be termed their worldview. They are less likely to have a positive outlook on life, seeing the world instead as a hostile place and life as a struggle, with them on the defensive. This defensive attitude can extend to their interactions with their children, in which they are more likely than are other parents to interpret their children's behavior as intentionally disobedient or otherwise "aimed" at them. A tired toddler's tearful outburst, for instance, is apt to be seen as an expression of anger directed at them rather than as distress experienced by the child. With their own feelings so much in the foreground, it also becomes easy for parent-child relationships to undergo a reversal in which the child is expected to be responsive to their feelings and meet their needs. This reversal, in which the child is *parentified*, places the burden for caring for the parents' needs on the children. In fact, maltreated children frequently are more nurturing than are their parents (Cicchetti & Lynch, 1995; Macfie et al., 1999).

Maltreating parents also tend to hold inappropriate expectations concerning what children of different ages are capable of. These unrealistic expectations can fuel their tendency to perceive their children's behavior as willfully disobedient rather than as normal behaviors for children of that age. Thus, a preschooler who continues to toot on a toy horn after being told to be quiet is likely to be seen as defiant rather than as having difficulty inhibiting an ongoing behavior to a verbal command. Similarly, unrealistic expectations that very young children be able to stay dry through the night, avoid accidents during the day, understand complicated instructions, or keep even younger siblings out of trouble can lead to children being seen as irresponsible or careless and deserving of punishment.

Maltreating parents differ as well from average parents in the types of discipline they are likely to use, being less likely to use effective parenting styles. They are more likely instead to punish, threaten, and otherwise use coercive measures with their children, and they are less likely to use reasoning. They are also less consistent in their discipline and less warm and affectionate in general in their relationships (Cicchetti & Lynch, 1995).

Maltreating parents are not only able to bring fewer personal resources to bear when facing stressful life events, but they also have fewer interpersonal resources on which they can rely. Perhaps the most important of these for most parents is their relationship with their spouse. These relationships are less satisfying for maltreating parents. Partners of maltreating parents have been found to be less supportive and warm than those of comparison parents, as well as more aggressive (Cicchetti & Lynch, 1995; Howes & Cicchetti, 1993). In general, relationships within the home, whether these be with spouse or children, are less positive and warm than in other homes.

None of these characteristics, in themselves, can be regarded as responsible for maltreatment. Maltreatment typically results from a combination of conditions rather than a single factor. Thus, a parent who has difficulty coping with stress may still be able to function adequately unless something untoward happens. The loss of a job, however, or a child entering a "difficult" developmental stage may be enough to precipitate maltreatment. One such condition that places families under significant stress is poverty. Although maltreatment is by no means limited to low-income families, it is unusually high among such families. Life below the poverty line can involve cascading stress on an almost daily basis. A case in point might involve something as simple as an appliance, such as a refrigerator, breaking down and needing repair. But when money is short, food that has spoiled may be difficult to replace. To repair the appliance would leave nothing for groceries; however, without a refrigerator, frequent trips to the market become necessary, taxing the reserves of an already overtaxed parent. Coupled with inadequate transportation and perhaps the need to take along cranky, hungry children, an event that might have been an ordinary stressor in another family can precipitate maltreatment in an impoverished one.

How might poverty increase the likelihood of a child being maltreated?

We have talked so far about characteristics of parents that are associated with maltreatment, but are there characteristics of children as well that affect the likelihood of maltreatment? That is, are some children more likely to be maltreated than others? We need to be very clear that in asking such a question we are not suggesting that children who are maltreated are in any way responsible for the treatment they receive. Rather, to ask about characteristics of children who are maltreated is to look for factors that are associated with an increased risk of abuse when coupled with other risk factors. When we do so, we find a number of such characteristics. Plainly put, children who present special difficulties to parents are more likely to be maltreated than are those who do not. These difficulties can take a number of forms.

Children who are in poor health are more likely to be maltreated. Thus children who because of discomfort or developmental lags are fussy, cry a lot, are difficult to soothe, or require special attention are more likely to be maltreated. Not only are maltreating parents more easily stressed under such conditions, but these parents are also more attuned to their own needs than they are to those of their children, and they expect their children as well to be responsive to these parental needs. When children continue to fuss, maltreating parents can react angrily and defensively. Consider, as an example, a mother who attempts to soothe her crying infant, first by offering a bottle that is spurned with a wail and then by placing the infant on her shoulder, only to have the baby stiffen and cry even harder. Even though very little is expected of infants by way of "appropriate" behavior, most parents expect their infants to be soothed when they are held, their bodies relaxing as they tuck their heads into the crook of one's shoulder. Infants who continue to cry can be perceived as rejecting by maltreating parents. It is all too easy for such parents to lash out in anger. But a parental education program might give this mother permission to let her child cry after she has checked on its well-being and attempted to soothe the infant, enabling her to close the door on a potentially abusive situation and have a much needed cup of tea or a supportive chat with a neighbor.

Children are also at greater risk for abuse when their temperaments or personalities are a poor match with those of their parents. That is, it's not so much the energy level of the child per se that can become problematic, but the degree to which this complements the needs and expectations of the parent (see Chapter 6 for a discussion of upper-limit and lower-limit controls). An active child might ideally match the temperament of one parent but be perceived as unduly demanding by another. Additionally, children whose temperaments fall outside the range of most children, being either hyperactive or, at the other extreme, lethargic, are also at greater risk for some forms of maltreatment.

All forms of maltreatment are more likely among children from lower-income families. Comparing just two income levels, families earning $30,000 or more a year and those earning less than $15,000, children from the latter are more than 22 times as likely to be maltreated. They are also nearly 14 times as likely to be harmed by some form of abuse and more than 44 times as likely to be neglected (Sedlak & Broadhurst, 1996).

One might ask whether these differences in maltreatment are actual or are merely due to differences in reporting. It could be argued, for instance, that maltreatment is simply more visible when families must interface with social workers and public health agencies. This argument is unlikely, however, since agencies such as these are responsible for relatively few (12%) of the reported cases of maltreatment, whereas schools are responsible for most instances of detection (59%), with the consequence that most maltreated children are identified by persons who come into contact with children from all income levels. Furthermore, to assume that differences are due to a failure to report maltreatment among families with incomes of greater than $15,000 a year is to assume that there are vast numbers of children as yet unidentified who are being maltreated (Sedlak & Broadhurst, 1996). Rather, the myriad factors that are associated with poverty, such as fewer social support systems, poorer neighborhoods, fewer educational and occupational opportunities, higher incidence of crime and of substance abuse, are likely contributors to maltreatment (Sedlak & Broadhurst, 1996).

Each of the factors listed can pose either an enduring or a transient risk, raising the level of stress within a family or in other ways reducing the ability to cope. We see, for instance, that maltreatment is also more likely in single-parent households. This is not to say that the custodial parent is necessarily the abusive one, but it does suggest there are additional responsibilities and stresses in single-parent families and a greater likelihood that these will tax or exceed the personal resources of the parent. Similarly, maltreatment is also more likely in larger families, with four or more children, than in those with two to three children or with a single child, again suggesting the importance of stress and reduced family resources in contributing to maltreatment (Sedlak & Broadhurst, 1996).

The overall incidence of maltreatment has risen steadily over the last two decades. The risk of a child suffering some form of maltreatment was more than 2⅓ times greater in 1993 than it was in 1980, and it continues to increase (U.S. Dept. of Health and Human Services, 1998). Furthermore, the increase is greatest for those seriously injured and those suffering emotional abuse (Sedlak & Broadhurst, 1996).

How are we to interpret this increase? Does it reflect an increase in the actual numbers of children who are maltreated or, once again, does it simply mean that professionals in the community are better able to recognize maltreatment when they see it? The answer this time is, most likely, both. The very fact that there has been an increase in the number of children seriously injured argues strongly for the former. Injuries such as these would be difficult *not* to notice. These cases do not, in other words, require a heightened awareness of maltreatment in order to receive attention, and the number of them has quadrupled since 1986 (Sedlak & Broadhurst, 1996). It also seems likely that professionals are better able to recognize abuse than previously. Support for this can be found in the increase in the number of children perceived as endangered—that is, children *without* any visible signs of maltreatment but recognized as potential victims nonetheless. Box 7.4 describes cues to possible abuse.

Just as no single factor can predict the occurrence of maltreatment, no single factor can predict its effects on a child. In attempting to assess these effects, one must consider not only the type of maltreatment but also its severity and how frequently it occurred, as well as the relationship of the perpetrator to the child and the point in development at which the maltreatment occurred (Cicchetti & Lynch, 1995). Protective factors, such as the personal strengths and coping strategies of the child or the general healthiness of relationships within the family must also be entered into the equation (Finkelhor, 1990).

What are the effects of maltreatment on children? Its effects are more far-reaching than any visible injuries a child may have suffered, serious as these frequently are. Physically, these effects can take the form of specific injuries or a general failure to thrive. Behaviorally, maltreatment can result in fearfulness, nightmares, poor peer relations, and aggressive play with other children. Most children, however, do not become delinquent as youths or violent as adults. Similarly, with respect specifically to children who have been physically abused, most do not perpetuate the cycle of abuse when they become parents themselves, although figures are somewhat higher than for those who have not been abused (Cicchetti & Lynch, 1995).

Children who are maltreated also often have difficulty in school, with problems paying attention and concentrating. However, perhaps no single effect of maltreatment is more significant than its potential for affecting a child's trust. Erikson (1968) believed trust to include not only the child's awareness of living in a stable world in which one's needs will be met, but also the awareness that one is worthy of having one's needs met. The myriad effects of maltreatment, influencing as it does everything from the way children play with their peers and their performance in school to the development of language, suggest that maltreatment touches the very core of a child's sense of self (Cicchetti & Lynch, 1995).

The effects of sexual abuse, both the immediate and long-term, are especially marked. Among the more common immediate effects are fearfulness, problems in sleeping, distractedness, depression, anger, and sexually inappropriate behavior.

Box 7.4 *Cues to Possible Abuse*

When is an injury likely to have resulted from abuse, rather than accidental causes? Angelo Giardino, Cindy Christian, and Eileen Giardino offer the following as cues:

- *Nonplausible injuries:* These are injuries that are not likely given the events that are mentioned as happening. Examples might be "minor" accidents that result in extensive injuries, such as internal injuries from falling off a bike. Conversely, other types of accidents, such as falling down stairs or out of bed, do not typically result in extensive harm even though they appear to be major. For instance, one study of 363 children treated in a pediatric emergency department after falling down a stairway found that most needed to be treated only for scrapes and bruises and that none required extensive treatment. Such falls are unlikely to result in fractured bones or abdominal injuries (Joffe & Ludwig, 1988).
- *Peculiar injuries:* This class of injuries includes such things as pattern burns, as would come from a cigarette lighter, "stocking" burns resulting from holding a child's feet in hot water, or patterned welts suggesting the use of a stick or switch for beating.
- *"Magical" injuries:* These are injuries for which the parent has no knowledge of cause; that is, the parent was not present, did not see/hear anything, etc. Of course, many times children do hurt themselves when a caregiver is not present as a witness. However, abuse becomes increasingly suspect as the age of the child decreases. For the first 6 months, infants simply are not capable of inflicting serious injury on themselves. With toddlers and preschoolers, who can run into another room or outside by themselves, this is more likely.
- *Self-inflicted injuries:* The child is reported to have been responsible for its own injuries, but because of the nature of the injuries, this explanation doesn't make sense given the developmental level of the child. Most injuries that children bring about by themselves are minor, although serious ones are certainly possible, such as a toddler pulling a pot from the stove over on itself. Similarly, although fights between siblings and peers are common, few result in serious or multiple injuries.
- *Delay in getting treatment:* Abuse is more likely when caregivers do not immediately bring the child in for treatment. Frequently, following abuse, they will wait until the injuries are partially healed or will try to treat these themselves; for example, treatment may be sought only when burns that have failed to heal have become infected. Other reasons for delay can reflect real obstacles in the parent's life, such as low income, lack of transportation, no one to care for other siblings, or an inability to get off work.

Source: Giardino, Christian, & Giardino (1997).

Long-term effects frequently persist into adulthood and include anxiety, anger, depression, lowered self-esteem, self-destructive behaviors, substance abuse, and sexual problems (Finkelhor, 1990). Children of either sex respond to sexual abuse in similar ways, with the exception that girls are somewhat more likely to be depressed and boys to be more aggressive (Finkelhor, 1990; Swanston, Tebbutt, O'Toole, & Oates, 1997).

Children draw strength from their communities, such as these children attending church.

Once the sexual abuse terminates, children typically begin a process of recovery in which symptoms can be seen to lessen. The most obvious improvements, usually occurring within the first year to a year and a half, involve a lessening of fearfulness and fewer sleeping problems, although a sizable number of children show a worsening of symptoms (Gomes-Schwartz, Horowitz, & Cardarelli, 1990). A recent follow-up of sexually abused children found the effects of abuse to be strikingly present 5 years later. Children who had been sexually abused showed more disturbed behavior, had lower self-esteem, and were more depressed and anxious than were a nonabused comparison group of children (Swanston et al., 1997). Findings such as these underscore the importance of state and federal commitments to the prevention of abuse and care of children who have been abused.

Wellness and Resiliency: With a Little Help from Their Friends

Children do not grow up by themselves. Development unfolds in the multiple contexts of their lives, in families and neighborhoods, day care settings and schools, and churches and synagogues. Children draw their strength from these surroundings, just as they do from the food they eat and the medical attention they receive. **Social capital** refers to the personal relationships that contribute to resiliency in children, both within the family and in the community. These relationships promote children's development not only through the love they provide them but also through the expectations and obligations to which others hold them (Coleman, 1988).

How effective are these reserves of strength in the face of various risk factors? Desmond Runyon and his associates (1998) followed a large group of preschoolers over time, all of them sharing certain factors that placed them at risk for abuse or neglect. Some of these children were eventually reported for maltreatment; however, others were not. These investigators compared the two groups of children, those who fared well with those who did not, first matching them in terms of their sex, socioeconomic status, and ethnicity, so that they differed simply in terms of their social capital. The measures of social capital used were (1) two parents, or parent figures, in the home, (2) the mother's sense of personal support, such as having someone to talk with, (3) no more than two children in the home, (4) a supportive neighborhood, such as neighbors who could be counted on to look out for each other, and (5) a mother who attended church at least several times a month.

Children who fared well were found to have greater reserves of social capital on which they could rely. "Doing well," in other words, was not a function of demographic variables such as ethnicity, gender, or maternal education. Instead, variables indicative of social capital, or relationship variables, predicted how well children were likely to fare. In fact, the greater the number of social capital indicators that were present in a child's life, the greater the odds of that child doing well. The three indicators that were found to be of greatest importance were church affiliation, mothers' perceptions of personal support, and support from the neighborhood. Thus, just as the accumulation of risk factors increases the likelihood of developmental problems, so does the accumulation of social capital indicators increase the likelihood of doing well (Runyon et al., 1998).

Do some children have personal attributes that enable them to "bankroll" more social capital than others, establishing the relationships and receiving the affirmation from others that contribute to their personal reserves of strength? Children who fare well, even in the face of adversity, have been found to have a number of characteristics in common (Cohler, Stott, & Musick, 1995). These children

social capital The relationships, both within the family and the community, that contribute to resiliency in children.

One of the most important things contributing to a child's resiliency is the presence of an adult who cares about that child.

tend, as a group, to be good with people. As a consequence, people enjoy being around them. These children tend to be intelligent, personable, and positive in their approach to life, an attitude that includes both good self-esteem and a sense of humor. They also tend to be self-reliant. Rather than sitting around feeling blue, for instance, they will find something to do. Other people usually feel good about themselves just by being around these children. Perhaps this is because these children are sensitive to those they are with and responsive to them, listening to what they say, being attentive to their feelings, and caring for them. These dimensions of personal interaction are the very same ones that have been found to be important in parents as well (Ainsworth & Bell, 1969).

What personal attributes of children are likely to affect how well they fare when risk factors are present in their lives?

Attributes of children's families also contribute to resiliency and faring well in the face of adversity. Perhaps the most important of these is the presence of a single adult who cares about that child and, in Bronfenbrenner's (1990) words, finds the child "somehow special, especially wonderful, and especially precious" (p. 31). This adult need not be the child's parent. A grandparent, aunt or uncle, or sibling can also provide this caring presence in a child's life. What *is* important is the continuity of the child's relationship with this person (Cohler, Stott, & Musick, 1995; Kaufman, Grunebaum, Cohler, & Gamer, 1979; Musick, Stott, Spencer, Goldman, & Cohler, 1987).

Characteristics of children's neighborhoods also contribute to their reserves of personal strength. Attending schools with supportive classroom environments and, once again, the concern of even just one teacher for the child's welfare; living in a neighborhood where the streets are safe; and the absence (or minimal presence) of conditions related to poverty, such as gangs and substance abuse, are all important (Cohler et al., 1995).

These findings are consistent with those of other research that finds that the type of neighborhood children live in can exert a strong influence, especially on children from high-risk families (Garbarino & Sherman, 1980). What distinguishes one type of neighborhood from another? The most important differences do not necessarily go hand in hand with income level. For instance, neighborhoods that might otherwise be classified as "poor" nonetheless differ among themselves in important ways. Perhaps the most important of these differences is in terms of the network of supporting relationships which they provide to those who make them up. Neighborhoods with a higher percentage of families that could be said to be functioning well are characterized by what one might call "a sense of community." Individuals living in these neighborhoods have an investment in where they live and who they live with. They keep up their property, talk to their neighbors, watch out for each other, and belong to various community groups and organizations. This investment is only loosely tied to income level (Coulton, Korbin & Su, 1999; Korbin & Coulton, 1995).

Income becomes increasingly important, however, as families function closer to the poverty level. And roughly 20% of children in the United States live in poverty, a figure that is twice as high as that for most other industrialized nations. Additionally, the percentage of children living in poverty is disproportionately high for African American and Hispanic children. The experience of poverty itself is also likely to differ for White than for many ethnic minority children, for whom it is more likely to be chronically present and who are more likely to live in neighborhoods with fewer supports and greater risks (Huston, McLoyd, & Coll, 1994).

Although official definitions of poverty are based on income, poverty should not be confused with low income or low socioeconomic status. Poverty, in fact, does not result from a single condition, such as how much money a parent makes, but varies along a number of dimensions (Huston, McLoyd, & Coll, 1994). Thus, a mother and child could live for several years on a poverty-level income in a low-income neighborhood while the mother finishes her education, making ends meet by buying clothes, furniture, and toys at thrift stores, yet not be considered poor by other socioeconomic status indicators, such as the parent's educational level or occupational objective. Furthermore, such a child may even experience an enriched environment, in terms of indices such as the number of books in the home, conversational patterns, exposure to various cultural events (music, museums), and attendance at a university-sponsored day care. Home environments that are supportive and stable, irrespective of income level, contribute to healthy development (Bradley et al., 1994).

Two important dimensions defining the experience of poverty are the duration of the poverty and the surrounding context (Huston, McLoyd, & Coll, 1994). The longer children live below the poverty level, for instance, the more the quality of their home life decreases (Garrett, Ng'andu, & Ferron, 1994). The neighborhoods in which children live also contribute significantly to their experience of poverty or well-being. Neighborhoods differ not only in immediately obvious ways, such as the exteriors of their homes or buildings, but also in the quality and safety of recreational areas, access to and quality of health care facilities, the availability of libraries, the safety of being on the street, and the sense of order to life given by living in a neighborhood that is well tended and cared for, irrespective of the size of the homes, versus one that is not. These are not simply physical properties of neighborhoods, but affect the ways in which people interact with each other. Thus, having a safe and inviting park near one's home means that neighbors are likely to use it and, in the process, get to know each other, establish friendships, perhaps work out cooperative day care arrangements, arrange to shop for each other, organize a car pool, and so on.

Even when one is looking for differences in neighborhoods, they are not always obvious. Thus, day care facilities attended by high-income children have been found to provide better quality care than those attended by low-income children. The difference, however, is subtle, and not likely to be caught by a simple count of the better known indices of quality, such as the ratio of caregivers to children. Comparisons of day care centers have found this ratio to be similar across income levels. Only when the interactions between the caregivers and the children were observed did differences emerge, showing that caregivers in low-income neighborhoods were less sensitive and harsher with the children (Phillips, Voran, Kisker, Howes, & Whitebook, 1994).

Further, children's sense of well-being depends on how parents communicate their own concerns about the family's welfare. Edgar Bledsoe (1996) writes of his experiences as a youth when his family was going through hard times. After he was laid off from his job, his mother, the only other person bringing in any money, became ill and could not work. When bills could not be paid, first one utility and then the next was cut off until finally the family was reduced to eating vegetables from their garden cooked over a fire in the backyard. Then, as he describes it,

> One day my younger sister came skipping home from school saying, "We're supposed to bring something to school tomorrow to give to the poor."
>
> Mother started to blurt out, "I don't know of anyone who is any poorer than we are," when her mother, who was living with us at the time, shushed her with a hand on her arm and a frown.
>
> "Eva," she said, "if you give that child the idea that she is 'poor folks' at her age, she will be 'poor folks' for the rest of her life. There is one jar of that home-made jelly left. She can take that."
>
> Grandmother found some tissue paper and a little bit of pink ribbon with which she wrapped our last jar of jelly, and Sis tripped off to school the next day proudly carrying her "gift to the poor." After that, if there ever was a problem in the community, she just naturally assumed that she was supposed to be part of the solution. ◄

Summary

Developmental Profiles

Control over both small- and large-muscle movements continues to develop through the preschool years, enabling children to work at tasks requiring fine motor coordination, such as puzzles and coloring, and those involving larger movements, such as running, skipping, or riding a bike. However, preschoolers continue to be impulsive and to have difficulty inhibiting their behavior in response to instructions.

Physical Growth

Preschoolers gain 2 to 3 inches in height a year and add 3 to 5 pounds. Growth reflects the cephalocaudal trend, with the neck and torso first lengthening, followed by the legs. Bone growth is rapid in early childhood, as is muscular development, contributing to increases in body size and strength. Physical differences between boys and girls remain insignificant.

Behavioral Consequences of Physical Development

Preschoolers are learning to regulate their movements, in terms of both physical coordination and impulse control. They also become increasingly better with age at self-help routines such as dressing and feeding themselves. By 3, most can stay dry through the day and are beginning to sleep dry through the night. Mature bladder control becomes possible at about 4½, though many children have occasional accidents for the next several years. Sleep patterns also change during the preschool years, from a pattern that starts with REM sleep and moves to NREM sleep to sleep beginning in the NREM state and being punctuated with episodes of REM sleep. As preschoolers increase in size and become better coordinated, more is expected of them, both in terms of physical coordination and impulse control.

Brain Maturation

The brain develops faster during early childhood than does any other part of the body, reaching 90% of its adult size before the age of 6. The brain increases both in volume and in the progressive myelination of neural fibers. Resulting increases in interneural communication contribute to a remodeling of the brain through the selective elimination of neuronal connections that are not frequently stimulated. Cortical activity undergoes cycles of change, involving the establishment of connections between the frontal lobes and other cortical areas, contributing to a greater ability to monitor and regulate activity.

Motor Development

Both gross motor skills, which involve large-muscle movements, and fine motor skills, which involve precise movements controlled by small muscles, improve with age. With respect to fine motor skills, improvements can be seen in in-hand manipulation and bimanual coordination. Few sex differences in motor skills are evident during the preschool years.

Psychological Implications of Physical Development

Children develop a sense of themselves in the preschool years. New skills contribute to a sense of mastery and equip them to assume a more active role in the daily routines of their lives. Being allowed to do some things on their own contributes to feelings of accomplishment and self-worth. Just as new physical skills expand children's outer world, imagination expands their inner one, often leading them to confuse feelings with fantasy.

Impulse Control

Verbal control over behavior develops gradually. Before the age of 5, children have difficulty inhibiting an ongoing behavior when instructed to. Parents can help children through the use of consistent routines, providing consequences for behavior, in addition to stating rules, and using external restraints. The ability to delay gratification increases with age, facilitated by the development of strategies.

Developing Restraints: How Parents Can Help

Parents can help children develop restraint by structuring situations, regulating children's activities and by being controlled themselves. Structuring situations means using predictable routines to provide a structure to children's experience that is not provided from within. Regulating activities means limiting alternatives to manageable choices and then letting children decide among these. Being controlled means being calm, firm, and self-controlled.

Health and Well-Being

Rapid skeletal and muscular development and continuing brain maturation all require adequate nutrition. However, because rate of growth slows in early childhood, preschoolers need to eat proportionately less and may have a diminished appetite. Both protein deficiency and iron-deficiency anemia are relatively common. Supplemental food programs have been found to be effective in counteracting the effects of specific deficiencies as well as of malnutrition more generally. In the United States, most children's diets fail to meet established national guidelines. Recommended dietary objectives include eating more complex carbohydrates, foods high in fiber, and fruits and vegetables, as well as increasing intake of calcium and reducing intake of fat.

Overweight

The percentage of children in the United States who are overweight has substantially increased. Children are less active physically, spending more time in sedentary recreational activities than in the past. Overweight children also are more likely to have diets that are high in fat and low in complex carbohydrates.

Establishing Healthy Patterns

One of the most important factors affecting children's food choices is the accessibility of various foods. Healthier eating patterns can be established by offering vegetables and fruits as snacks instead of sweets or crackers, replacing fast-food meals with those containing less fat, using low-fat milk instead of whole milk, and limiting high-calorie drinks. Modeling is also an important influence in determining food preferences, and children's eating patterns are likely to be influenced by those of their parents. Children are also responsive to internal cues such as the energy content of foods.

Illnesses, Injuries, and Accidents

Low-income and minority children are more likely to be affected by common illnesses and less likely to receive the medical care they need than are middle-income children. Recommended steps for reducing barriers to health care among these children include increasing the number of community health centers, training health care providers willing to practice in low-income neighborhoods, improving the availability of transportation, and extending office hours to meet the needs of working single parents.

Death due to accidental injury is 4 times more common than the next most common cause among preschoolers. The use of child-restraint devices such as seat belts and car seats has significantly reduced fatal injuries. Accidental injuries could be further reduced by instituting home visitation programs for young or poorly educated mothers.

Maltreatment

Maltreatment refers to instances of harm to children that are nonaccidental and avoidable; it includes both abuse and neglect. Abuse can be physical, sexual, or emotional and often involves some combination of these. Neglect refers to a failure to provide for a child's physical, educational, or emotional needs. Over a million children in the United States are maltreated each year, most of these by their parents. Maltreating parents are more likely than other parents to experience difficulty coping with stress, to have difficulty controlling their impulses, to interpret their

children's behavior as intentionally disobedient, to hold inappropriate expectations for their children's behavior, to use less effective modes of discipline, and to have fewer personal resources. The likelihood of maltreatment increases with children who require special attention or are exceedingly active or lethargic. Maltreatment has cognitive and emotional effects as well as physical ones, leading to difficulties in school and in relationships with peers.

Wellness and Resiliency

A number of factors contribute to resiliency in children. The presence of stable, caring relationships within the family and in the community are important. Characteristics of the children themselves, such as good social skills, intelligence, self-reliance, and having a positive outlook on life, also contribute. Attributes of the community, such as supportive classroom environments, safe streets, and the minimal presence of conditions related to poverty, are also important. Two important dimensions defining the experience of poverty are the length of time a child's family income is below the poverty level and the stability and orderliness of the neighborhood in which the child lives.

Key Terms

bimanual coordination (p. 262)
hand dominance (p. 262)
hand preference (p. 262)

in-hand manipulation (p. 259)
initiative (p. 263)
maltreatment (p. 281)

overweight (p. 274)
social capital (p. 288)

chaptereight

Early Childhood
Cognitive Development

Margery, age 3, dimpled and adorable, carefully poured tea into a cup, giving a satisfied sigh after doing so, for she had spilled not a drop, and handed it to the bear on her right. Less successful with the second cup, she murmured a soft "Ohhh," as she had so often heard her mother do, and wiped the imaginary spill with her fingers—for there was no tea in the pot—before handing the cup to the one-eyed doll on her left. Passing the cookies, she opened the conversation by remarking that Grandma was coming to visit today.

A voice from the other room, that of her mother, called out that it was time for a bath. Margery protested that her favorite television show hadn't come on yet, so it couldn't be time for a bath. Appearing at the door with a towel and clean clothes, her mother said they had to hurry in order to meet Grandma at the train station. Margery, still busy with tea, replied that it would be dark by then—and Grandma wouldn't see if she were dirty or not.

Frequently, we are so caught by the imaginary creatures that populate the world of preschoolers that we fail to notice the neatness of their logic. Margery's logic is impeccable. She reasons that it can't be time for a bath since she has not yet seen her favorite show, the one that always precedes taking a bath. Or, in the words of a logician, "If A, then B; and if not A, then not B." Since she has not seen her show, in other words, it can't be time for her bath. Further, she notes that by the time she has taken a bath and they have driven to the station, it will be too dark for her grandmother to see anything clearly.

This mix of fantasy and logic is one of the most striking characteristics of preschoolers' thought, an aspect of their development that we will explore more closely in this chapter. We will look at what young children understand, as well as what they don't, and at how this understanding develops. Along the way, we will consider some of the practical implications of cognitive development, such as how to answer their questions, how much they can be expected to remember, and just what they will understand.

Piaget's Stage of Preoperational Thought

Cognitive development, for Piaget, is a gradual freeing of thought from experience, enabling children to imagine the fanciful as well as consider the actual. Preschoolers' thought illustrates this new freedom. Their understanding of their world is imaginative and playful, as well as serious and sensible, a construction of fantasy and fact pieced together from everyday experiences. Like artisans who have been given a mix of traditional and unusual materials to work with, the resulting product at times gives a curious twist to an otherwise familiar model of the world we live in.

Piaget believed these characteristics to result from the emergence of **preoperational** thought, a way of thinking that is qualitatively different from the sensorimotor thought of infancy. The underlying competence that develops and is presumed responsible for the emergence of preoperational thought is the ability to use symbols to represent experience. As infants become able to hold objects in mind, representing them symbolically, they can differentiate the "existence" of the object from their "experience" of it. With symbolic representation, the external world of objects emerges from the inner world of experience, and the sensorimotor stage of infancy comes to an end (Piaget, 1952).

Thus, the most significant aspect of preschoolers' thought for Piaget was their use of symbols, something that is evident both in their play and in their approach

preoperational thought Piaget's second stage of intellectual development, thought to characterize toddlerhood and early childhood, during which experience is represented symbolically.

to everyday problems. Piaget believed their use of symbols, however, not only freed but also constrained their vision of the world. At this point, we will look more closely at this aspect of preschoolers' thought.

Symbolic and Imaginative Play

Preschoolers chatter to themselves when alone, talk to their stuffed animals, tell their troubles to their pets, assume the identities of their action figures, and spend hours in make-believe play, enacting fantastic adventures as well as the more familiar routines of their lives. In all of this, they are representing their world symbolically, through language, imagination, fantasy, and playful pretense.

Vivian Paley (1997), a teacher at a nursery school maintained by the University of Chicago, tape-recorded children's conversations for a year, enabling her to capture their dialogue as they engaged in imaginative play. Typical of these conversations is that of Mollie, a 3-year-old. Paley describes Mollie's conversation as follows:

> Today, for example, she puts "Mushroom in the Rain," "The Three Pigs," and "Hansel and Gretel" into a Wonderwoman story. In the original "Mushroom in the Rain," a butterfly, a mouse, and a sparrow are drenched in a heavy downpour, then sheltered under a mushroom by a kindly ant. A frightened rabbit and a hungry fox also enter the story, but Mollie gives star billing to the wet butterfly.
>
> "I want to be the wet butterfly and Wonderwoman. First he goes under the mushroom. Now we got to do the big, bad wolf and the three pigs and the fox is going to catch the butterfly and put it in the cage, that one from Hansel. Then Wonderwoman comes. Then I open the cage and the wet butterfly goes under the mushroom because the ant says to come in."
>
> How has Mollie learned to integrate these bits and pieces into a sensible whole? No one else offers Christopher [another child at the nursery school] blackberries and milk if he is good or unites the big, bad wolf with a fox to make trouble for a butterfly. However, it is the sort of storytelling that is heard every day during play: Cinderella and Darth Vader put the baby to bed while Superman serves tea and saves the baby from the witch just as Daddy comes home from work and sits down to eat a birthday cake. (pp. 139–140) ◄

Children, of course, engage in symbolic play well before they reach the preschool years (Bornstein, Haynes, O'Reilly, & Painter, 1996). But their earlier play differs in at least three important respects from the symbolic play of preschoolers. It involves simpler sequences of activities, is dependent more on the characteristics of the objects with which they are playing, and is not well coordinated with the play of other children (Singer & Singer, 1990).

With respect to the first of these differences, for instance, toddlers may "quack" as they push a floating duck around the bath, pretending that the toy is alive or that they themselves are a duck. In contrast, bath time for preschoolers can involve extended battles with bobbing toys, with armaments lined up along the rim of the tub for future battles, or elaborate psychodramas enacting the roles of various family members in familiar daily routines. Second, the objects preschoolers incorporate into their play need not bear as close a resemblance to what they are imagining as these must for toddlers. Thus, a stone can serve as a turtle, a mountain, or a rocket ship for a preschooler, depending on the imaginative script being enacted. In contrast, for a 2-year-old to call a stone a turtle, the

These 4-year-olds aren't bothered by their messy playroom as they enact a script for familiar daily routines—one of the advantages to fantasy play.

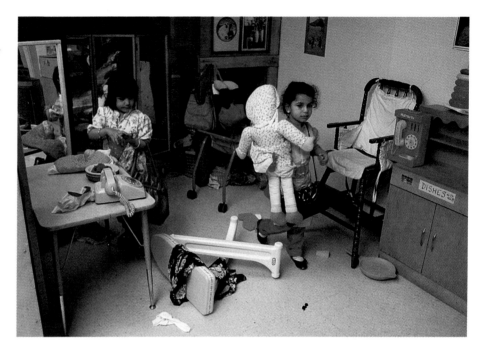

scripts Schematic representations of familiar routines used by young children to organize and recall everyday events.

stone must bear some resemblance to a turtle; and, once seen that way, it cannot easily be transformed into a rocket ship. Finally, preschoolers are able to coordinate their fantasy play with that of other children, all sharing in the same imaginary world. Toddlers, however, even when playing near another child their age, do not share in one another's fantasy worlds and simply play alongside one another.

By the age of 4, children engage in pretend play both by themselves and with others for extended periods of time, assuming different roles as they act out various **scripts,** or schematic representations of familiar routines. Examples of scripts familiar to preschoolers might be going to the market, eating in a restaurant, or visiting the doctor. Of course, there are wide individual differences among children in the extent to which they engage in fantasy play, just as there are among adults in so many aspects of their behavior (Taylor & Carlson, 1997).

Fantasy play with others involves considerable social skill as well as imagination, in that children must first enlist the interest of another child, assign each other various roles, and develop a shared reality. How do they go about accomplishing all of this? Children in our culture do this primarily by explaining what they are doing and negotiating with their play partner—for example, "I'll be the teacher this time and you can be teacher next time." But do children from other cultural backgrounds establish a shared reality in this way as well?

Jo Ann Farver and Yoolim Shin (1997) reasoned that the strategies children use to communicate with each other when playing should reflect the broader social conventions of their culture. North Americans, for instance, value individualism and "saying what you think." In contrast, Asian cultures value group harmony and sensitivity to the needs of others, such that the others need not even voice them. Would these differences be reflected in the strategies preschoolers use to organize and maintain their play with each other?

The investigators compared the social pretend play of children in a predominantly Anglo-American preschool with that of children in two all-Korean preschools. As expected, communication strategies were found to differ as a function of the children's cultural backgrounds. The Anglo-American children's strategies reflected both individualism and self-expression, these preschoolers being more likely to describe their own actions (*"I'm* going into the forest"), use directives when speaking to the other (*"Put the king over there"*), and reject suggestions made by their partner (A: "You can be the princess. B: *"No, I'm the queen!"*). Similarly, Korean American children communicated in ways that both minimized conflict and promoted harmony and also reflected their sensitivity to their partner's intentions. Thus, they were more likely to agree with suggestions made by their partner (A: "Let's put these bad guys in the dungeon." B: *"Yes, let's lock them up"*), make polite requests (*"Could I be the . . . ?"*), use tag questions as a way of eliciting agreement ("We're playing prince and princess, *right?"*), and describe what their partner was doing (*"You're* going into the forest").

Pretend play also involved different themes for children from the two cultures. Korean American children were more likely to act out everyday activities, such as putting a child to bed, and to portray family roles. The pretend play of Anglo-American children, on the other hand, was more likely to be about fantastic or dangerous situations. These differences held for girls and boys alike. In fact, the pretend play of children of either sex differed little in the strategies they used to communicate their fantasies or the themes they played out together.

Knowing What Is "Real"

How real *is* pretend play for preschoolers? Adults, at least, have little difficulty distinguishing reality from fantasy. We know better than to squeeze life into a teddy bear or offer seconds to a doll. Clear lines have been drawn. For children, sorting fantasy from reality is an ongoing task. So too is discovering who shares their inner world—who knows what they know, which of their experiences are held in common with others, and which are private and known only to them. When one is 3 or 4, fairies and giants are no more fantastic than ballerinas and firefighters and more may be fuzzy than the stuffed bear in one's arms.

In a classic children's story, *The Velveteen Rabbit,* Margery Williams (1983) gives voice to this earliest of realities for children, an inner world where desires can take precedence over beliefs. In this story, a toy horse, much loved by the little boy who plays with him, explains to a recent arrival to the toy closet what it means to be real:

Like most preschoolers, this young boy most likely believes he's really talking to Mickey, even though his brother may have told him it's just a person wearing a costume.

> "What is REAL?" asked the Rabbit one day. . . .
>
>   "Real isn't how you are made," said the Skin Horse. "It's a thing that happens to you. When a child loves you for a long, long time, not just to play with, but REALLY loves you, then you become Real." ◄

Children understand the Skin Horse's description of what makes things real. It is an explanation that makes sense to them, given their own need to be loved and the way they feel toward their favorite toys. But does this understanding mean that they *actually* think toys talk and have feelings? Would they unblinkingly accept it if one of their stuffed animals audibly answered them back? Or would they run out of the room in wide-eyed amazement to tell anyone within earshot what had just happened? How firmly are their feet planted in the same sod as ours?

Piaget, for one, believed their tread to be considerably lighter than ours. Despite their capacity to symbolically represent their experiences, his observations of young children suggested that they often accepted as fact what others easily recognized as fiction. He attributed this confusion to the absence of **mental operations,** a concept that is reflected in his use of the term *pre*operational thought to refer to this stage. Piaget defined a mental operation as any action that could be

Do we as adults ever think in ways that are characteristic of preoperational thought?

mental operations Piaget's term for actions that can be carried out in one's head and then reversed or undone.

carried out in one's head and then reversed, the mental equivalent of taking a step forward and then back. What possible advantage could come from taking a step such as this, considering that one ends up in the same spot as before? The advantage, argues Piaget, is one of perspective. Being able to envision an action that one can undo gives individuals two perspectives from which to view a situation, rather than a single one. Piaget believed that—in the absence of mental operations—preschoolers' thought suffered from a number of characteristic limitations.

Piaget noticed that when thinking through a problem, preschoolers tended to focus on one aspect of, or approach to, the problem to the exclusion of others. Piaget referred to this characteristic of thought as **centration.** Typically, when a second approach was pointed out, they lost sight of the first, illustrating their difficulty in considering several aspects of a situation at once. Piaget's measures of **conservation** illustrate this quality of thought. Tests of conservation assess a child's ability to see that something actually remains the same despite changes in its appearance. Since many of these tests are quite simple to do, you may want to carry out one or two, with a child, for yourself.

In one of these, Piaget showed children two identical balls of clay and asked if there were the same amount of clay in each. When they agreed that there was, Piaget rolled one of the balls into a sausage shape and again asked if there were still the same amount of clay in each. Preschoolers frequently said "no," usually indicating that the sausage now had more because it was longer. However, when Piaget pointed out that the sausage was also thinner, they would agree that the ball had more, since it was fatter. Thus, they either focused on the sausage's length, in which case it was judged as having more, or on its thickness, and believed it to have less. Piaget believed centration to result from preschoolers' inability to undo, or reverse, the action he had performed by mentally rolling the sausage into a ball again and thereby see that the two were still equivalent.

This inability to move something around in one's mind and catch it from another angle gives thought a static, or "stuck," quality. How something looks to the preschooler is how it is, and there is no moving beyond this by inference to how it must be. Piaget identified this second limitation by referring to preschooler's thought as *intuitive,* noting that their thought was dominated by the appearance of things. In one of his measures of this, Piaget showed a child two sheets of green cardboard, each the same size, and placed a plastic cow on each "field," asking, "Do the two cows have the same amount to eat?" The child assures him that they do. Piaget then places a block on one of the fields, calling it a barn, and again asks if each cow has the same amount of grass. The child answers "no" this time, indicating that some of the grass is covered by the barn. However, when Piaget adds a barn to the second field, the child again agrees that the two cows have the same amount of grass to eat.

Barns are added, one field at a time. With each addition, the child points out that the amount of grass is unequal, until a barn is added to the other field. In adding barns, Piaget was careful to arrange them neatly along the edge of one field while scattering them randomly across the other. At some point in the process of adding barns, a critical mass of "barn-ness" is reached, and the child's reasoning that the amount of grass must remain the same breaks down in the face of the overwhelming perceptual evidence to the contrary. Simply put, anything that looks that different can't be the same.

Piaget believed that preschoolers' thought was characterized by yet another limitation, which he referred to as **egocentrism,** also reflecting a failure in perspective. Piaget did not mean by this term that children are selfish, but rather that they are self-centered, simply failing to realize that the way they see something is not the way it may look to others. Because young children are unaware of their

Will preschoolers agree that glasses of different shapes filled from identical cans of soda will contain the same amount of soda?

Why might a preschooler be distressed if her mother dyes her hair a different color?

centration Piaget's term for the tendency to focus on one aspect of an object to the exclusion of others; characterizes preoperational thinking.

conservation The realization that something remains the same despite changes in its appearance.

egocentrism The failure to realize that one's perspective is not shared by others.

When asked to describe what the train engineer sees, preschoolers will describe what they see from their own vantage point, an example of Piaget's concept of egocentrism.

view as a perspective, they assume that others see things the same way. Piaget used a model of three mountains, one covered with snow, one with a house at the top, and one with a red cross at the peak, to demonstrate egocentrism. Children were first asked what they saw and then what a doll saw as it was placed at different positions around the mountains. Each time the doll was moved to a new position, children were asked what the doll saw. Could children literally take another's point of view and recognize that the same set of mountains seen from a different position would not look the same? Children younger than 6 or 7 typically described how the mountains appeared from where they were sitting rather than from where the doll was positioned, demonstrating egocentrism.

Piaget noted that preschoolers have difficulty distinguishing other aspects of their own and others' knowledge as well. In particular, they are unsure which aspects of what they know are private, and known only to them, and which are public, and hence knowable by others too. Thus, preschoolers fail to realize that what they know is not automatically known by others. As a consequence, they frequently give themselves away by denying something for which they otherwise would not be caught. A preschooler who tips over an ink bottle might never be picked out of a "line-up" of siblings and household pets were it not for crying out in alarm, "I didn't spill the ink!" Such denials are only necessary if you assume that others know what you know.

Margaret Donaldson (1978) has questioned whether tasks such as those used by Piaget to identify egocentrism actually make sense to young children. She points out that when children are tested with tasks that do make sense, they can be shown to adopt the other person's perspective. Martin Hughes (as cited in Donaldson, 1978) presented children with two dolls, one a policeman and the other a little boy. These were separated from each other by two walls that intersected in a cross, forming four open areas, each hidden from the others (Figure 8.1). When the policeman stood at the end of one wall, he could see into only the two sectors

FIGURE 8.1 A Measure of Perspective-Taking in Preschoolers

on either side of the wall he faced; the remaining two were hidden from him. The little boy was placed in each of the four sectors and children were asked each time if the policeman could see him. Preschoolers made virtually no mistakes on this task.

Even when a second policeman was added and they were told to hide the boy so that he could not be seen by either of them, they still performed well, even though doing so required them to coordinate two separate perspectives. When children 3½ to 5 years old were given this task, 90% of their answers were correct. Donaldson points out that hiding makes sense to young children. They can understand the motives of the little boy, who does not want to be seen by the policemen. Piaget's task, on the other hand, had no interpersonal motives to give it intelligibility. As Donaldson (1978) remarks, "It is totally cold-blooded. In the veins of three-year-olds, the blood still runs warm" (p. 17).

Donaldson also suggests that preschoolers' failure to do well on other of Piaget's measures reflects the way his questions were worded. Based on their answers to his questions about classification, for instance, Piaget assumed that preschoolers could not classify a group of related objects into subclasses while still realizing they retained their membership in the larger class. Piaget believed that in order to group objects into subclasses, children had to be able to view the objects from several perspectives. Thus, the class of animals can be divided into cats and all other animals. One knows that all cats are animals, that some animals are not cats, and so on. A central inference is that the number of items in the class (animals) is greater than the items in any of the subclasses (such as cats).

When Piaget gave tasks such as this to young children, they consistently made mistakes. In one of these tasks, Piaget showed children ten flowers, seven of them red and the remaining three white, and asked, "Are there more red flowers or more flowers?" Most preschoolers answer that there are more red flowers. Piaget assumed from their answer that they are not able to think of the class (flowers) at the same time as the parts (red or white ones) and so cannot compare the parts with the class. In other words, centration limits their performance here as it did with the sausages. Donaldson suggests, instead, that they misunderstand Piaget's question. She points out that there are natural and unnatural, or strange, ways of saying things. For instance, it is natural to say that the flowers are on the television. It is strange, however, to say that the television is under the flowers. It is also strange to ask, "Are there more red flowers or more flowers?" She argues that children do their best to make sense of questions such as this. Surely, this person must mean something by asking that, they think, and so they give a "reasonable" answer. Donaldson calls it "acquiescing in the bizarre." When children were asked, for instance, "Is milk bigger than water?" they all tried to give serious answers. "Yes," said one, "cuz it's got color." Only a 4-year-old didn't try to answer the question. According to Donaldson (1978), he just "grinned his head off."

Despite these criticisms, Piaget has contributed more to our understanding of children's thinking than perhaps any other single person. For some he has helped by providing a theoretical framework for explaining the course of development. For others, he has helped primarily by stimulating research aimed at disproving his theory. In either case, we know considerably more about the course of intellectual development because of Piaget than we would otherwise have known.

Making Wishes and Living with Superheroes

Preschoolers live in a world in which magic, making wishes, and superheroes are served up to them with their morning cereal, yet they show considerable skill in distinguishing fantasy from reality. Jacqueline Woolley (1997), at the University of Texas at Austin, argues that even 3-year-olds can distinguish their thoughts from those of others and know the difference between "pretend" and what is really so. Nonetheless, fantasy and reality still mix somewhat more freely in the world of young children than of adults.

Perhaps one of the most common areas in which fantasy and reality mix in children's minds concerns what it means to make a wish and what to expect after one does. Most preschoolers, when asked, believe that wishing is more than simply thinking about something and probably involves some magic. They also believe that some people are better at making wishes than others. For wishing to be effective, one must know how to do it. As we might expect, children's beliefs in the effectiveness of wishing decrease with age and vary, as well, from one child to the next, with some children being much more credulous than others (Vikan & Clausen, 1993; Woolley, 1997).

Even young children know the difference between events that are possible and those that are not, but when faced with explaining occurrences of the latter, most preschoolers are open to the possibility that magic may be involved (Phelps & Woolley, 1994). The youngest among them believe magic to entail the exercise of special powers. By 5, however, preschoolers are more likely to believe magic to be a trick that anyone can learn to do (Woolley, 1997). Whether children offer magical explanations appears to be more a function of their knowledge about the physical causes of the event they are trying to explain than of their age (Taylor & Carlson, 1997). When children are aware of more naturalistic explanations, even young preschoolers prefer these. Nonetheless, when something happens for which they have no explanation, especially when this runs counter to everything they would normally expect to see, preschoolers resort to magic as an explanation. These conditions, by the way, are pretty much the same as those in which adults become superstitious.

Children also know that fantasy figures, such as Batman, Barney, and Cookie Monster, are not real in the way that other rarely encountered things, such as parrots, bullfrogs, and porpoises are, but the distinctions they make are not as clear as they will later become (Woolley, 1997). In part, these distinctions may blur because children are continually invited by adults to believe in such fantasy figures. Books, movies, logos on T-shirts, and references in everyday speech underscore their existence. With some fantasy figures, such as Santa Claus, there is even what one might call a cultural conspiracy to promote their acceptance. Children are taken to shopping malls to sit on his lap, are encouraged to write him letters, and wake on Christmas morning to find that their stockings have been filled, as

Most preschoolers believe that wishing probably involves some kind of magic.

Q Under what circumstances are preschoolers most likely to rely on magic to explain things?

promised, and that the cookies they left the night before have been eaten, all of this orchestrated by conspiring adults (Taylor & Carlson, 1997). In the absence of information to the contrary, there are many situations in which children do not know what is most reasonable to believe. As one young child explained to a researcher, "I didn't know; I'm still little" (Subbotsky, 1993, as quoted in Taylor & Carlson, 1997).

Consider a 3-year-old, standing at the top of a short flight of stairs in his Superman shirt and a pillowcase cape. The child raises his hands over his head and utters what he believes to be the "important words." "Up, up to the way [sic]," he says. After waiting several moments, poised for flight, he walks down to level ground, muttering to himself, "I guess I wasn't going fast enough," and gathering himself in his cape, prepares to try again with a running start. What part of this sequence represents fantastical thought and what part the use of an adultlike logic? Only by experimenting with such things as capes and "important words" do preschoolers discover what is likely to happen and what is not.

Similarly, I remember mailing out bills, many years ago, licking stamps and pressing them on each envelope in turn as our daughter Jenny, then 3, looked on. When I next looked up, I saw her pull off a stamp, turn to the wall next to her, and press the stamp onto the wall. Since she had missed the part about licking the stamp first, it slid to the floor. Perplexed, she took another stamp and tried again, pressing even harder. No cape and incantation were involved here, but getting a stamp to stick to the wall must have seemed to involve as much magic as flying.

Woolley (1997) points out that the fantasy figures associated with holidays and actual events, such as Santa is with Christmas or the tooth fairy is with losing a tooth, are more likely to be taken as real than those, such as monsters and dragons, that are not. Perhaps this difference reflects the very real evidences of their appearances that are left behind, such as toys, colored eggs, and money under one's pillow, as well as the degree of cultural endorsement they receive. With respect to the latter, it is important to keep in mind the cultural context for children's beliefs. Our culture, like so many others, invites children to believe in the fantastical. As a consequence, figures such as Santa Claus and Cookie Monster, not to mention Disney creations such as Pluto and Mickey, can have more recognizable personalities than the neighbor next door (Woolley, 1997).

Not all developmentalists accept Woolley's arguments. Michael Chandler (1997), at the University of British Columbia, takes issue with her suggestion that differences between children's and adults' willingness to accept the fantastic are due primarily to children lacking the knowledge by which they could realize the fantastical nature of their beliefs or to their living in a subculture in which they are both invited by others to participate in fantastical beliefs and less likely to have their view of the world challenged. Chandler retorts that children, unlike isolated primitive peoples who are rarely exposed to alternative perspectives, are continually exposed to other perspectives. Their failure to attempt to reconcile these perspectives with their own assumptions he takes as evidence, in fact, of a very different way of approaching discrepant beliefs than one finds in adults.

Given that children can distinguish fantasy from reality as well as they so often do, why, then, do they become afraid of things that are obviously fantastic, such as monsters under their beds at night? Woolley suggests that in considering the possibility of such things, negative emotions such as fear are aroused and that these emotions *are* very real. Children, also, may not be as good as adults at dismissing their thoughts by saying such things as "monsters aren't real" and deriving comfort from such assurances. One of the cognitive abilities that appears to develop with age is the ability to recruit related information to either confirm or

Some beliefs are harder to give up than others. Preschoolers like this girl may wonder who brings the presents each year if there isn't a Santa—and what will become of what she has just whispered in this Santa's ear.

disconfirm ideas and events. This ability is probably related to increases in domain-specific knowledge with age, and to information-processing capabilities, which we will consider later in the chapter (Woolley, 1997).

Paul Harris (1997), at Oxford University, argues that it is incorrect to think of logical thought as necessarily displacing magical thinking, pointing out that magical and scientific thinking cannot always be separated as neatly as we might believe, even among scientists. Harris notes, for instance, that Newton developed his theory of gravity, which has become a fundamental scientific law, from his belief in alchemy, which was regarded as magical. The alchemists believed in hidden forces of attraction and repulsion. And gravity is, after all, an "invisible pull." At the time, many considered direct impact (one object hitting another) as the only "scientifically valid" cause of movement. Some even criticized Newton for "magical thinking." We see a similar blending of different forms of thought when anyone looks beneath the surface to explain some action. Thus, we don't mechanistically talk only about bodies in motion when explaining goal-directed behavior, but infer beliefs and desires which, like gravity, exist as unseen forces. The fact that preschoolers sometimes attribute motives to inanimate things, such as trees or clouds, does not mean they have abandoned reason for magic.

Distinguishing Appearances from Reality

Even though preschoolers are relatively successful in distinguishing fantasy from reality, they nonetheless improve with age. John Flavell, Eleanor Flavell, and Frances Green (1983) showed 3-, 4-, and 5-year-olds objects that looked like one thing but were actually another, such as a sponge that had been painted to look like a rock and a stone that had the same shape and color as an egg. After letting the children touch and play with these, so that they could discover the objects' true properties, they asked them what the objects looked like and what they "really, really" were. Five-year-olds nearly always answered each of these questions correctly, easily distinguishing what things looked like from what they actually were. Four-year-olds also answered correctly most of the time, demonstrating that they, too, knew that things are not always as they appear to be. Three-year-olds, however, had difficulty distinguishing appearances from reality, saying, for instance, that the sponge not only looked like a rock but actually was a rock.

Most 3-year-olds encounter few sponges painted to look like rocks or rocks that look like eggs. However, other equally deceptive experiences are a common part of their everyday world. Among these are the images they see on their television screens. Do young children understand that these are in fact images, or do they believe them to be real objects inside the television? Flavell and his associates first showed 3- and 4-year-olds a real bowl of popcorn, tipping it over to show that the popcorn spilled out, and then a photograph of a bowl of popcorn, showing that the popcorn did not spill when the photo was turned upside down. Following this, they played a videotape showing popcorn in a bowl and asked whether the popcorn would spill if the television were turned upside down. Once again, 4-year-olds are relatively good at distinguishing what they see on television from real objects. Nearly 90% of the 4-year-olds in this study answered the question correctly, indicating, when asked what they were really seeing, that they were looking at pictures and not real objects ("No, the popcorn wouldn't spill"). Three-year-olds, predictably, were more likely to interpret the television images as real objects, agreeing that the popcorn could spill if the television were tipped (Flavell, Flavell, Green, & Korfmacher, 1990).

Are there conditions under which 3-year-olds understand that things actually can be different from the way they appear? Catherine Rice and her associates (1997) suggested that children "fail" tests such as the above because of the way they are presented. If the questions are embedded within a meaningful, real-life type of experience with which children are familiar, even 3-year-olds should be able to make the appropriate distinctions. For instance, 3-year-olds are familiar with the experience of playing tricks on people. These investigators first showed children the rock-sponge and asked them what it looked like. When children responded that it looked like a rock, they answered, "That's right, it looks like a rock." Then they allowed the children to touch it and asked them what it felt like, indicating, "That's right, it's really and truly a sponge." At this point, they said, "I played a trick on you with this tricky sponge. Let's play a trick on someone else who's never seen this before and hasn't touched it." When asked under these conditions what the object really was, and whether the other person would think it looked like a rock or a sponge, nearly 80% of 3-year-olds answered correctly, saying that it was really a sponge but that the other would think it a rock.

Children who are given training in understanding the beliefs of others also do better on standard tasks measuring their understanding of the mental states of others (Slaughter & Gopnik, 1996). However, when the tasks themselves are made intuitively understandable, such as when they are related to children's own experiences of tricking others, even 3-year-olds need no training to do well. Thus, providing children with a familiar context, such as tricking someone, in which questions such as these become meaningful makes the task intelligible to them.

A corollary to this observation is that preschoolers will function in a more adultlike manner in their everyday world than they do in a social scientist's laboratory. In the former, they are the ones to set goals, plan, and make decisions, all of which imbue the activities they are engaged in with intrinsic meaning. In the latter situation, they can only guess as to the exotic interests of the adults who have invited them to play, making the best sense they can of the strange situa-

Why might preschoolers be better at understanding another person's false belief when they have intentionally tried to deceive that person?

tions to which they are introduced, before returning to their own world of purposeful action. This is not to say that there are not important differences in the ways in which preschoolers and older children think. There are. But the differences are not as consistently evident as preschoolers' lapses in the labs of social scientists might lead one to expect.

In general, preschoolers, just like adults, think best when the situations they are asked to think about are familiar to them. When they are asked to think through problems that can be related to immediate, real-life situations, where goals and intentions are evident, they perform well. Reason breaks down, however, when they are asked to think about problems that are removed from daily experience. Thus, one of the things that appears to develop with age is the ability to think about things that are increasingly abstract. Perhaps one of the most important differences between the thought of younger and older children is not so much the particular form it takes, but whether it can move beyond familiar experience. The Research Focus, "Formulating Hypotheses: What Does It Mean to Be Rich?" examines the ways children's surroundings can affect their development, including their intelligence.

What Children Know About the Mind

"Come on, Jenny, move over. I can't see," says Joshua with a tug, peering over the pages of the book his mother is holding.

"Here, you hold one page of the book, Joshua, and you hold the other, Jenny. Now, let's see what happens next," says Mom, continuing with the story.

> "Who is it?" called the grandmother in a weak voice.
>
> "It's Red Riding Hood, Grannie, bringing you fresh bread and cakes," answered the wolf, making his voice small.
>
> "Just press the latch, child," the grandmother cried.
>
> The wolf pressed the latch and pushed open the door. He walked in and before the poor grandmother knew what was happening he opened his mouth and with one gulp swallowed her up. Then he put on a nightgown and cap and got into bed and drew the curtains. . . ." (Tudor, 1980)

"See, the wolf is pretending to be Grannie," says the mother, pointing at a picture of the wolf in Grannie's clothes. "Will the wolf try to trick Red Riding Hood and eat her too?"

Jenny, age 3, staring at a picture of the wolf innocently dressed as a grandmother, answers that the wolf will be nice to Red Riding Hood. But Joshua, age 5, knows better and says that the wolf is only pretending to be innocent so that he can eat her as well.

How much do preschoolers actually understand of the stories we read them? The wolf in this story is pretending to be other than he is in order to deceive someone. Are young children able to distinguish the intentions of the characters from the way the characters present themselves to others? Children's everyday activities suggest that they should be able to, since these activities so frequently involve a world of make-believe. Preschoolers spend endless hours in pretend play, and even the very youngest can understand deception when it is they who are planning to play a trick on others. Since both pretense and deceit involve a form of make-believe, in that each involves making up a separate version of reality, one would expect children to be able to follow bedtime stories such as this with ease, participating as well in the fabricated reality.

Formulating Hypotheses: What Does It Mean to Be Rich?

Dorrie's family was poor, but her life was rich. Although she was only 3, she knew everyone who lived on her floor of the building. Two doors down there was old Miss Casterline. Dorrie and her Mom would pick things up for her at the market. And next to her were the Garcias. Sometimes Dorrie had supper at their house when her mother went to night school. Across the hall from Miss Casterline were the Ramsey twins; they went to Head Start every day with Dorrie. Yes, Dorrie knew everyone, and they all knew her.

How much do Miss Casterline, the Garcias, and the Ramseys contribute to the quality of Dorrie's development? And how can their contributions be distinguished from those of Dorrie's home life? One might expect that how well children fare in life will reflect the quality of the environments to which they are exposed, but it is another matter to disentangle the effects of the many environments that are present in any child's life. Such environments surround children at a number of levels, like the concentric layers of an onion, and include, as in Dorrie's case, not only their families but also their neighbors and their neighborhoods. Do each of these environments exert the same effect on a child's development irrespective of the child's age, or does the impact of a particular environment, such as the family or the neighborhood, change with the child's age? And how does one go about separating the immediate effects of children's families from those of the neighborhoods in which they and their families live? Questions such as these are interesting, but difficult to answer. What does one look for first?

What one looks for, or expects to see, takes the form of a research hypothesis. Hypotheses are guesses as to why something might happen. When these guesses are formulated concretely enough to be empirically tested, they take the form of research hypotheses. A *research hypothesis* is a statement specifying the particular conditions under which one expects to observe certain events (Ray & Ravizza, 1985). Hypotheses are based on prior research findings either alone or in conjunction with existing theory (see the Research Focus, "The Role of Theory in Research," later in this chapter). Research by Pamela Kle-

banov, Jeanne Brooks-Gunn, Cecelia McCarton, and Marie McCormick (1998) illustrates how, building on the findings of other investigators, these researchers were able to arrive at a conceptual framework for characterizing the quality of both neighborhoods and families and for separately examining the influence of each on development.

Much research on neighborhood effects has categorized neighborhoods simply in terms of their economic level. But how do neighborhoods affect the families living within them? Is it through the positive effects of having affluent neighbors or the negative effects of living among those who are poor? With respect to problem behavior in adolescents, for instance, research has found the presence of affluent neighbors, not poverty per se, to be more important (Crane, 1991). Similarly, among school-age children, having affluent neighbors has been found to be associated with verbal ability (Chase-Lansdale, Gordon, Brooks-Gunn, & Klebanov, 1997). Klebanov and her associates suspected that for preschoolers, as well, the most important determinant of a neighborhood's quality would be the presence of affluent neighbors, not simply the presence of poverty. In order to translate this expectation into a testable research hypothesis, they had to specify what they meant by affluence versus poverty as well as specify the particular way in which preschoolers' development would be affected.

With respect to the first of these tasks, they defined neighborhood affluence and poverty in terms of the percentage of neighbors who earned over $30,000 a year. Affluent neighborhoods were thus defined as those in which 30% or more of the neighbors earned over $30,000 a year. Conversely, poor neighborhoods were defined as those in which fewer than 10% of neighbors earned over $30,000. To determine whether it was affluence or poverty that affected development, children from each of these types of neighborhoods were compared with those living in middle-income neighborhoods, defined as those in which 10%–29% of neighbors earned over $30,000.

With respect to the second task, these investigators chose to look at the way intelligence in preschoolers might be affected,

Understanding Pretense and Deception

Joan Peskin (1996), at the University of Toronto, read illustrated stories to 3-, 4-, and 5-year-olds about a villain who disguises himself in order to deceive the main character, Susan, in a fashion directly analogous to what the wolf does in Red Riding Hood. After listening to the story, children are asked who the villain really is, who he is pretending to be, who Susan thinks he is, and whether he will still be mean even though he is disguised to look nice. Almost all of the children, irrespective of their age, understood that the villain was pretending and had not actu-

again concretely defining this in terms of scores on standard scales of intelligence. Thus, their research hypothesis was that intelligence scores in preschoolers would be higher for children living among affluent neighbors than for those living among poor neighbors. To test this hypothesis, they compared the intelligence of preschoolers from families *of the same income level* who lived either in affluent neighborhoods or poor neighborhoods, in each case making their comparisons with those living in middle-income neighborhoods.

To assess the quality of the home environment, they used the Home Observation and Measurement of the Environment (HOME), a scale that evaluates such things as parental warmth, types of discipline, and the availability of stimulating experiences. Based on previous research findings, these investigators hypothesized that the effects of neighborhood and family poverty on children, specifically on measures of their intelligence, are likely to be mediated by the quality of children's home environment. For home environment to act as a mediator, however, three conditions must be present: (1) both neighborhood and family poverty should be correlated with the home environment, (2) the home environment should be correlated with measures of intelligence, and (3) the relationships between neighborhood poverty and intelligence, and between family poverty and intelligence, should be significantly reduced when the influence of the child's home environment is removed (see figure).

Because these investigators had defined the quality of children's neighborhoods and of their home environments in the precise way that they did, they were able to determine whether the data they collected supported their research hypotheses. As they had expected, these investigators found that by the time children reached the age of 3, it was the proportion of neighbors who were relatively affluent, such as the Garcias, rather than the proportion of those who were poor, that was associated with higher intelligence in children. They also found, as they had hypothesized, that the relationship between neighborhood affluence and children's intelligence was mediated by the quality of home environment. Finally, these investigators found that environmental effects are ordered in terms of their proximity to children's lives. At 1 year of age, lower intelligence scores reflect only conditions present in a child's immediate environment, such as having a mother who is very young, has little education, or is depressed. By the age of 2, more general family variables, such as family income, can be seen to be related to children's intelligence, perhaps through such things as the ability to buy interesting toys or books or go on family outings. And by the age of 3, when children such as Dorrie begin stepping out into their neighborhoods, we see the effects of even larger, and more distal, surrounds.

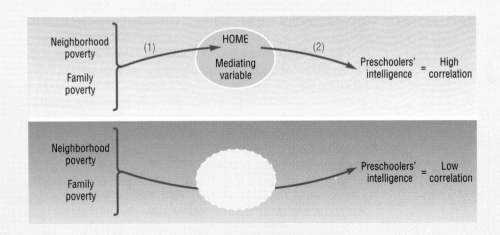

ally changed character, confirming that children as young as 3 actually do understand the difference between make-believe and real. The 4- and 5-year-olds also understood that the villain was attempting to deceive Susan by changing his appearance and knew as well that since Susan had agreed to play with the villain, she must have been deceived, falsely believing the villain to be other than he was. Three-year-olds, however, failed to understand the implications of the deception, fully half of them believing that the villain would act in a way consistent with his new appearance and not try to trick Susan. Nor did they understand that Susan must have been deceived.

Does all of this mean that we should pick simpler stories, ones that do not involve deception, or even forget about stories altogether until we are sure children can understand what the story is about? Not in the least! Stories can be appreciated at many levels. The sense of excitement, danger, and adventure are certainly there for even the youngest children, even if they miss the intrigue of deception. Mention of hungry wolves, dangerous forests, or houses made of candy guarantees their interest. Moreover, of far greater importance than understanding the story is the time children spend together with parents and those who love them.

In fact, most classic children's stories involve an element of deception, whether this is the wolf in Red Riding Hood, the witch in Hansel and Gretel, or the queen in Snow White dressed as a kindly old lady with an apple. How is it that young children fail to understand deception in stories such as these when we know from other research (Rice, Koinis, Sullivan, & Tager-Flusbergf, 1997) that 3-year-olds understand very well what it means to play tricks on others? One possibility is that in order for children to understand the deception, they must be the ones trying to deceive the other and that simply hearing about the actions of someone else may not be enough. Recall that Rice had to involve children in the actual trick for them to understand that someone would be deceived.

Most measures of children's understanding of deception involve creating false beliefs in others, typically by telling the children a story. In a typical task, children are told about a boy who puts candy in a box for safekeeping, only to have it removed to another box by some other child. Children are then asked which box the boy will look in to find his candy when he returns. The box he initially put it in (false belief)? Or the box which they themselves know it to be in (correct belief)? Only answers that the boy will look where he falsely believes the candy to be indicate that children understand that the other has been deceived.

Suzanne Hala and Michael Chandler (1996) argue that because 3-year-olds have no personal stake in understanding what another person might believe in such tasks, they do not perform well on them. When the tasks are structured such that they can participate in the deception, their answers should demonstrate a better understanding of the other's perspective. Thus, when children are allowed to move the candy themselves, they should correctly predict that the person whom they are tricking will believe the candy to be where it had been left and not where they themselves know it to be.

But what, precisely, is responsible for children's improved performance? Is it involving them in the procedure, by having them choose a place to move the candy, or is it making the procedure itself meaningful, by involving them in the goal of deception? Hala and Chandler (1996) argue that it is the latter. They compared two conditions for establishing false belief, each of which required 3-year-olds to remove cookies placed in a container by someone else and put them in a second container without that person's knowledge. In one condition, the cookies were removed because the first container was found to be wet. However, in the second condition the cookies were removed specifically to deceive the person. When asked where the person would look for the cookies, only children who had attempted to deceive the other were more likely to answer that the person would look for the cookies in the first container.

These findings suggest that it is the planning to deceive that is important, by making salient what others know and think. In order for children to plan how they will deceive someone, in other words, they must take into consideration what that person is thinking, or knows to be true, as well as their own goal, which is to make that belief false and so "trick" the other. Older preschoolers, on the other hand, have already developed an appreciation for this on their own.

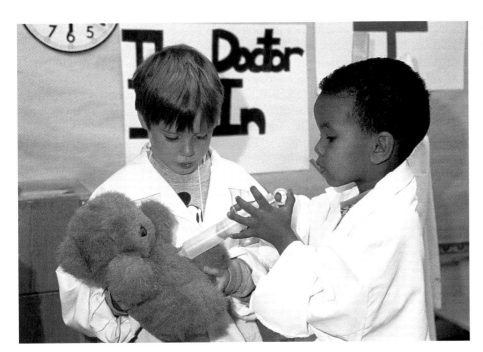

One of the ways in which children develop an appreciation of what others know and think is by constructing a shared reality in pretend play.

Awareness of Mental States

One of the ways in which children develop such an appreciation is by talking about their own and others' mental states in their play together. Jane Brown, Nancy Donelan-McCall, and Judy Dunn (1996) analyzed 4-year-olds' conversations with each other for their references to mental states. They reasoned that children should refer to mental states frequently when playing together, since much of their play involves pretense and, with this, the need to construct a shared reality. As anticipated, children made frequent reference to mental states when playing, clearly revealing their awareness of such states in others as well as themselves. In this respect, the conversations of these 4-year-olds differed little from those of younger children. However, it was also evident from what they said that, unlike younger children, 4-year-olds were aware that they could mentally construct one reality or another in any given play situation and hence needed to communicate which direction they wanted their play to take. Thus, their view of mental states reflected a more active, "agentic" role to the mind. One 4-year-old, for instance, was heard to direct a friend as to how they would find a pile of gold when pretending to be pirates:

CHILD: All the silver things hafta go in here, and then you can use the swords when they find the gold.

FRIEND: You mean it's gonna be under the bed like that?

CHILD: No, it's gonna be on top of the bed so that we can find it.

FRIEND: But we'll still know where it is.

CHILD: I know, that's okay. That's okay, cause we're gonna walk from that way.
    (Brown et al., 1996, p. 847)

As Brown and her associates remark, "the activity of creating fantasy worlds and sustaining interactive games with other children must surely provide multiple opportunities for the fledgling theorists to appreciate the workings of the mind" (p. 847).

Not only play, of course, but also other types of interactions, such as garden-variety household routines, contribute to preschoolers' understanding of the mind. These interactions can be especially helpful if they involve children with those who are older than they are. In a sense, children become social apprentices, being tutored by those who are older in reading the mental states of others. Support for the importance of children's social environments in contributing to this understanding comes from research showing that preschoolers who have older siblings or friends to play with, and who interact more with adults, have a better understanding of mental states in others (Lewis, Freeman, Kyriakidou, Maridaki-Kassotaki, & Berridge, 1996).

Mental Representation

Research investigating children's understanding of pretense and deception is interesting in its own right. However, it is also interesting for the insights it provides into the ways children understand what the mind does. Consider, for a moment, what it means to pretend. Typically, when one pretends, one *does* something, as when a child pretends to be a kangaroo and hops. What distinguishes something as pretense, however, is not the way one acts but the way one represents oneself mentally, which may or may not be evident in one's behavior. No matter how well one hops, in other words, if one does not see oneself as a kangaroo, one is not pretending to be a kangaroo (Lillard, 1996).

Do preschoolers understand this distinction? The research of Angeline Lillard (1993), at Stanford University, suggests they do not. Lillard found that even 4- and 5-year-olds, when told of a troll who had never heard of kangaroos and didn't know they could hop, still believed the troll was pretending to be a kangaroo when it hopped like a kangaroo, thus judging pretense on the basis of action rather than mental representation. Similarly, when preschoolers were shown pictures of children either pretending to be something, thinking about something, or performing some action and were asked whether each of these was something one could do "just inside your head," without using your body, or using only your body and not your mind, she found that fewer than half of the 3-, 4-, and 5-year-olds believed that pretending involved the mind. Thus, only 42% thought you needed your mind to pretend to be a kangaroo, but 96% thought that you needed your mind to think about things, in contrast to only 5% who thought you needed your mind to perform an action such as falling over if pushed (Lillard, 1996).

Similarly, Craig Rosen, David Schwebel, and Jerome Singer (1997) found that preschoolers who were shown episodes from a children's television show could distinguish those that involved pretense from those portraying realistic activities well before they could infer what the characters were thinking about when they were pretending. Thus, after viewing an episode in which characters were pretending to be in an airplane while sitting on a bench, children were asked, "Are they really in an airplane or just pretending to be in an airplane?" and then "Are they thinking about being on an airplane or sitting on a bench?" As can be seen in Figure 8.2, close to half of all 3-, 4-, and 5-year-olds could identify pretense but not infer the pretenders' thoughts. One can also see from this figure that the ability to do the latter systematically increases with age, with 9% of 3-year-olds, 24% of 4-year-olds, and 56% of 5-year-olds being successful in this.

Understanding the Actions of Others

Findings like those illustrated in Figure 8.2 should not be taken to mean that preschoolers cannot understand why people do what they do. Beginning with the preschool years, children's language reveals that they are aware of mental states,

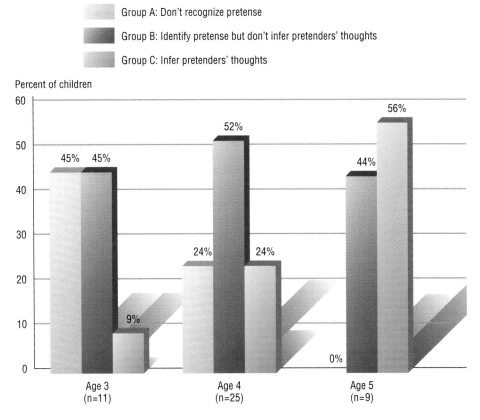

Percent of children

Group A: Don't recognize pretense
Group B: Identify pretense but don't infer pretenders' thoughts
Group C: Infer pretenders' thoughts

FIGURE 8.2 Age Differences in Children's Ability to Identify Pretense and Infer the Pretender's Thoughts *Source*: C. S. Rosen, D. C. Schwebel and J. L. Singer (1997). Preschoolers' attributions of mental states in pretense. *Child Development*, 68, 1133–1142.

both in themselves and others. How does their understanding compare with that of adults? Adults know, for instance, that others' actions are motivated by thoughts and feelings. But do children also attempt to understand the actions of others in terms of underlying beliefs and desires? In order for children to understand behavior as adults do, they must be able to understand that individuals' actions are prompted by what they believe to be so, rather than by what may actually be, by their beliefs *about* reality versus reality itself. They must be able to think of the mind, in other words, as *representing* reality. Do they do this?

Karen Bartsch, at the University of Wyoming, and Henry Wellman (1995), at the University of Michigan, studied children's everyday language as a way of discovering how they conceive of the mind. These investigators found that preschoolers routinely refer to both their own and others' thoughts and feelings in their conversations. Looking for evidence, first, of children's awareness of thinking, they found that children start to use words such as *thinking* and *knowing* in their everyday speech just before they turn 3. Furthermore, it was clear from the way children were using these terms that they were doing so to refer to mental states. Listen to one 3-year-old as he explains a remark he has just made in terms of what he had been thinking:

ABE (3 years, 4 months): Hey, don't eat it.

ADULT: I'm not.

ABE: I thought you were. (Bartsch & Wellman, 1995)

Or consider the exasperated remark of one 4-year-old, "He (Mark) thinks finished is not finished. Marky, not finished is not finished." This child is clearly making reference to what Mark is thinking and distinguishing that from what he knows to be so. Similarly, another 3-year-old explains an adult's behavior in terms of what he knows the adult must have been thinking:

ADAM (3 years, 11 months): No, dat not de right wheels.

ADULT: Oh, why isn't that the right one?

ADAM: Dis de right wheel to de bus.

ADULT: Oh.

ADAM: You thought that was the wheel to that. (Bartsch & Wellman, 1995, p. 45)

How can we know that pre-schoolers are aware of mental states in others?

What can be seen in each of these examples is that even very young children are aware of thinking and that they distinguish their own thoughts from those of others.

Children refer to feelings even earlier than they do to thoughts, starting anywhere from 1½ to 2 years of age. Again, the way they do so clearly indicates they are referring to a psychological state and are not simply using these words as a way of asking for something, such as saying "I want the ball" for "Hand me the ball." Thus, Ross (2 years, 6 months) says to his father

ROSS: You want it (a button) off?

FATHER: No, thank you.

ROSS: You want it on? (Bartsch & Wellman, 1995)

If all Ross asked were the first question, he could be understood as saying "Can I take it off?" But Ross does not try to do anything with the button. Instead he tries to find out what his father wants, as we see in the second question. He is clearly trying to figure out what his father's goal is, not expressing his own. Even at an early age, then, children's use of desire terms indicates that they understand that desires are feelings within a person that motivate a person's behavior, yet are themselves different from the actual behavior.

Thus, very young children appear to share many similarities with adults in the way they understand the actions of others. There are, however, important differences. Children, as you may recall, talk about desires before they begin to talk about beliefs, suggesting the possibility that, at least initially, they may not take people's beliefs into consideration as a way of understanding their behavior. Bartsch and Wellman suggest, in fact, that children progress through several phases in understanding why people do and say what they do. In the first of these, the *desire phase,* children are not yet aware of their own or others' thoughts and understand people's behavior only in terms of their feelings. At about the age of 3, children enter a second phase, the *desire-belief phase.* At this point, they are aware of others' thoughts and beliefs, but fail to realize that these are important in explaining what people do. Thus, children still explain behavior the way they did earlier, by referring only to people's desires.

How reasonable is it to assume that children, even though they recognize beliefs in themselves and others, still do not take these into account in explaining their behavior? Bartsch and Wellman draw an analogy to adults' understanding of imagination. Adults know that people imagine things—that is, that they frequently think about things that do no exist. Yet we rarely take what they imagine into consideration when explaining their behavior. We simply know that people do not act on the basis of the fictional accounts they make up, real as these may be. Similarly, children in this transitional phase may recognize the existence of beliefs but do not have to regard them as important in explaining what people do. Three-year-olds' predictions of where a story character would look for a desired object in a false-belief task were found to support such a transitional phase (Bartsch, 1996).

At about the age of 4, children enter the third and final phase, the *belief-desire phase*. At this point, they realize not only that people have beliefs and thoughts but also that these are central to explaining their actions. They understand, in other words, that what people do is largely determined by their beliefs—specifically, that what they do is what they *believe* will be effective in getting what they want.

Part of the problem may be that preschoolers fail to realize at first that their thoughts can affect their feelings. When asked, for instance, what strategies they might use to regulate their emotional states, preschoolers do not usually suggest mental strategies, such as changing their thoughts. Instead, they suggest changing the situation, which suggests they believe that feelings follow directly from events.

At what age do children understand the relationship between thinking and feeling? Kristin Lagattuta, Henry Wellman, and John Flavell (1997) asked specifically whether children understood that remembering something that had happened to them could cause them to feel happy or sad. Children were read a story in which the character, Mary, felt sad because of some event, such as a dog chasing her pet rabbit away. Later in the story, the character was said to feel sad when a friend asked her to play with a puppy that looked similar to the one that chased her rabbit. The children were then asked why the character felt sad.

Although preschoolers were aware that the character's thoughts could affect her feelings, their knowledge of the relationship between thought and emotions clearly develops in these years. Thus, although a majority of 4-year-olds and even some 3-year-olds understood why the character felt sad, only the older children could put this into words, explaining that Mary felt sad because she was reminded of a sad event. Once again, it's important to emphasize that children's ability to articulate their understanding of a situation will vary from child to child and from one situation to the next, depending on how closely it relates to their own experiences.

All in all, preschoolers understand quite a bit about thinking. They know that thinking is something people do. More generally, they know that something must be alive to think. They also know that thinking is a mental event, as opposed to a physical event, and that thinking is something you do in your head. That is, they know that one thinks with one's brain and that the brain is in one's head. They are also beginning to realize that thoughts are internal, not external—that is, public or tangible—and that a person who is not seen to be doing anything could still be thinking (Flavell, Green, & Flavell, 1995).

Preschoolers gradually realize that thoughts are internal mental events and not necessarily reflected by physical action.

Where Understanding Breaks Down

From here on, however, things start to get murky. One of the big differences between preschoolers and older children is the former's failure to realize how *much* people think. They, unlike older children, do not appear to understand that people are constantly experiencing one mental state or another, whether thinking, noticing something, or simply being aware of feelings; that is, they don't understand that there is a continuous stream of consciousness. Older children, for instance, will attribute consistent mental activity to a person who outwardly appears to be doing nothing, whereas preschoolers do not. Thus, when shown a picture of a person sitting quietly on a bench, fewer than 40% of 4-year-olds agreed with the statement "something is always going on in people's minds, so there *must* be something going on" in this person's mind (Flavell, Green, & Flavell, 1993). Because preschoolers lack this awareness, they are more likely to rely on observable cues, such as a person's actions or aspects of the situation that would prompt

Why might a preschooler interrupt his father when he is reading, even though his father has already told him that he is busy?

thought. However, even when they see people engaged in activities that are known to require thought, such as seeing someone reading a book, listening to or looking at something, or even talking to someone, preschoolers do not necessarily assume that the other is thinking.

Even when preschoolers do recognize that a person is thinking, they still have difficulty guessing what that person is thinking about. Flavell, Green, and Flavell (1995) describe a procedure used to study preschoolers' awareness of thinking in which one person asks another a question about one of two objects. The second person responds, "That's a hard question. Give me a minute. Hmmm," and turns to look at the object. When preschoolers are asked which of the two objects the person is thinking about, they do not, as one might expect, automatically choose the correct object. Even with additional cues, such as the person actually touching the object while looking at it, some of the youngest preschoolers fail to guess correctly.

Part of the problem may be that preschoolers do not understand that attention is focused—that is, that when one is thinking about one thing, one is not simultaneously thinking about something else. Flavell likens focused attention to a flashlight, something one can point in one direction or another, but not in several directions at the same time. Preschoolers appear to think of attention, or focused thinking, more like turning on a light in a room, allowing one to simultaneously take in any number of things. Given this understanding, it makes sense that they would not necessarily know which of two objects a person is attending to even though that person has every appearance of being deep in thought.

We can see similar limitations to preschoolers' understanding when they talk about their own thoughts. One of their more noticeable difficulties is in recalling the content of their thoughts. Thus, when 5-year-olds are given questions to answer—such as "What room do you keep your toothbrush in?"—many fail to recognize that they had been thinking when coming up with an answer. Even when they do realize this and are asked what they had been thinking about, they do not necessarily mention either their toothbrush or the bathroom (Flavell, Green, & Flavell, 1995).

Adults, on the other hand, understand that individuals are continually involved in some mental activity and that this activity can be prompted either internally, such as by another thought, or externally, by events outside ourselves, but that in either case, what is set in motion is a train of related thoughts. This understanding illustrates a central assumption we make about thoughts—namely, that they are part of a causal network of mental events.

Young children are not as aware of their thoughts as are adults and are not likely to spontaneously think about them. As a consequence, when they are asked to do so, they tend to regard their thoughts as isolated mental events, rather than as a chain of interrelated events that can arise as a result of either some other thought or something that has happened. Thus, preschoolers have no explanation for what causes their thoughts, nor do they see thoughts as causes of anything else. As a consequence, thoughts remain outside the flow of explainable behavior. For this reason, preschoolers underestimate the extent to which others engage in mental activity in going about their ordinary activities. And because they conceive of thoughts as isolated events, rather than as part of a stream of consciousness, they find it difficult to understand how one might go beyond the information immediately given to arrive at an interpretation of an event that might differ from that given by another person. Simply put, preschoolers are literalists (Flavell, Green, & Flavell, 1995).

If preschoolers are in fact not aware of the pervasiveness of thought in themselves or in others, we should expect to see evidence of this in their behavior. They should, for instance, have more difficulty than older children in saying how they arrived at an answer or a decision, since they would not be as aware of the mental steps leading up to it. And because they are less aware of the process of attending to something, they should be less aware of having their attention or thoughts distracted from what they were doing. By the same token, they should have difficulty realizing when they are distracting others, not being likely to assume that others are engaged in any mental process from which they could be distracted. They should also be less likely to know when something is beyond their understanding, since they are less aware of the processes contributing to various aspects of problem solving (Flavell, Green, & Flavell, 1995).

Thus a 4-year-old, enthusiastically driving his "big wheels" through the house, would be surprised to hear his father, who is sitting nearby quietly thinking about a problem, tell him that the noise he is making is distracting his thoughts. Similarly, a preschooler would be amazed that his mother could know he was the one who had stained the carpet when he unwittingly answers "grape juice" when she muses as to what might have been spilled. So, too, preschoolers fail to realize that they will not necessarily be able to later remember a list of things simply because they can readily identify them all at the moment.

What Children Know About the Body

"Why aren't there any more dinosaurs?" "Is it the same time of day all around the world?" "What's a nymphomaniac?" Only the last of these is likely to cause a parent to blush, stammer out an answer, or develop sweaty palms. Very few parents think their children will become paleontologists when answering questions about dinosaurs, yet many harbor fears that questions about sex reveal childhood obsessions.

Preschoolers have questions about nearly everything, including questions about their bodies and sex. They want to know how mosquitoes find you in the dark, why ice is cold, how come animals don't talk, and, yes, where babies come from. When questions are answered in ways they can understand, their curiosity is satisfied and they move on to something else.

Birth

Children typically ask questions about their bodies by the age of 3 or 4. These first questions are usually about such things as the function of different parts of their bodies or pregnancy and birth. Many of the questions that preschoolers have are prompted by the birth of a younger sibling. Most parents who are expecting another child have carefully prepared answers to questions about how people get babies. However, most are not prepared for the way their children will interpret their answers. Hours spent thinking of ways to translate the action of ova and sperm into familiar examples involving birds and bees can be reduced in a micromoment to misunderstandings of gigantic proportions. "It's where? . . . You swallowed a baby?"

Children understand the answers we give them in terms of what they already know. A child who has been told, for instance, that babies grow within the mother's womb, may nonetheless confide to a friend that babies come from the mommy's tummy. What most children know about how things get inside you is that you swallow them; this knowledge is garnered from the alarmed reactions of their parents to things the children have put in their mouths. It sometimes helps

The first questions a 3 or 4-year-old asks are typically about the function of different body parts and about pregnancy and birth.

to ask children what they think the answer to a question might be before giving them one of your own. At least this way you can know what you are dealing with.

Many parents, and educators as well, assume that if they can translate the facts into terms that are simple enough, children will automatically understand. The weight of the evidence is against this. Children translate the facts, whether simple or not, into their own way of understanding. And initially they do not understand that things must come into being, rather than having always existed. Anne Bernstein and Philip Cowan (1975), at the University of California, Berkeley, found that part of preschoolers' difficulty in understanding birth is their limited grasp of biological causation, of understanding that a baby is *created* rather than having arrived from some other place. The question of how people get babies is understood, instead, in terms of knowing where to look. The 3- and 4-year-olds they interviewed assumed that the newest addition to a family had always existed. They simply didn't know where the child had been before. Questions about the origin of babies were interpreted spatially, in other words, and not in terms of causation. As one child responded when asked about a younger sibling prior to the child's own birth:

ADULT: You said the baby wasn't in there when you were there.

CHILD: Yeah, then he was in the other place. In . . . in America.

ADULT: In America?

CHILD: Yeah, in somebody else's tummy. (Bernstein & Cowan, 1975, p. 86)

Adoption

Similar misunderstandings can exist concerning what it means to be adopted, specifically as this concerns preschoolers' understanding of the ways in which children can be expected to resemble their birth parents or their adoptive parents. Gregg Solomon, Susan Johnson, Deborah Zaitchik, and Susan Carey (1996) read 4-year-olds an illustrated story in which a woman who gives birth to a daughter dies without ever seeing the baby, and the infant is adopted by a second woman who "brought her home to live with her." Children were then asked which woman the girl would resemble in terms of both physical and nonphysical traits when she was older. Children had difficulty understanding that the child would be likely to resemble the birth parent in terms of her appearance, but would resemble the adoptive parent in her beliefs. Instead, young preschoolers appear to expect that members of a family will simply resemble each other, and that's that. The mechanisms that might underlie biological inheritance await their understanding (Johnson & Solomon, 1997). By the age of 5, they are better at differentiating which traits are inheritable when judging family resemblances, but continue to improve with age (Springer, 1996).

Preschoolers may have difficulty understanding the concept of adoption and distinguishing adoptive parents from birth parents.

Many adoptive parents want to know the best time to tell their children they are adopted. Most agencies tell parents to begin early and to add more facts as the child gets older. However, there are few guidelines on what to say and when. The guidelines that exist mostly concern how to tell the child initially and not how to handle later questions. As a result, many parents remain unsure about how to answer their children's questions. This issue has become increasingly salient as adoption policies have changed from requiring that the identities of each set of parents be withheld from the other to allowing varying degrees of contact between them. The issue is no longer simply whether to inform children of their adoption but how much information about, and contact with, their birth parents is best.

Gretchen Wrobel, Susan Ayers-Lopez, Harold Grotevant, Ruth McRoy, and Meredith Friedrick (1996) interviewed adopted children to determine whether the amount of information they had been given was related to various outcome variables. Measures of self-esteem were high for all adopted children, as were measures of global self-worth, irrespective of how much they had been told. These investigators also found that children's satisfaction with how much they knew was unrelated to how much their parents had told them. However, they caution that one cannot conclude from this that children would remain that satisfied if they understood all that they might know. Most children, irrespective of how much they had been told, indicated being curious about their birth parents. In general, these findings suggest that giving adopted children information about their birth parents has little affect on their feelings about themselves or their satisfaction with their present state.

Perhaps a more fundamental problem than one of giving children information is the issue of how children will understand the information they are given. David Brodinsky, Leslie Singer, and Anne Braff (1984) interviewed several hundred adopted and nonadopted children ranging in age from 4 to 13 to determine their knowledge of adoption. They found that most preschoolers are not likely to understand adoption even though they may have discussed it with parents. Even children who spontaneously refer to themselves as adopted may fail to distinguish adoption from birth, assuming the same biological process explains both. The fact that adopted children overall knew no more about adoption than nonadopted children suggests that what children know is not just what they have been told, since adopted children are much more likely to have been told about adoption, but what they are able to understand.

By 6, most children distinguish adoption from birth as different ways of becoming a parent. They also know that adoption is a permanent relationship, but not necessarily how it takes place or why. They simply know that children cannot be taken away from their adoptive parents. Most likely, they have been told this by parents and have accepted the information on faith. By middle childhood, uncertainties about the permanence of adoption can arise. Fears that the biological parents can reclaim an adopted child may bother some children. Others may see the relationship with the adopted parents as less secure than before. Not until adolescence are children likely to understand that adoption is a legal procedure that transfers rights and responsibilities from biological to adoptive parents and, because of this, is permanent (Brodinsky, Singer, & Braff, 1984).

Most adoptive parents are encouraged to tell their children early of their adoptive status. One advantage to doing so is that children learn they can trust their parents to tell them about important issues. Early telling is also recommended so children are first likely to hear of their adoption at home in a loving context rather than as a taunt or a casual remark disclosed unintentionally by someone else. The findings from Brodinsky and his associates suggest, however, that children may not understand the meaning of adoption, just as they don't understand birth, even when they are told. This can come as a surprise to parents who may think their children know more than they do. After having told them of their adoptive status and hearing their children spontaneously refer to themselves as adopted, parents may not be prepared for children's concerns later on, when they do distinguish adoption from birth. Being told that one is adopted can have the same impact on young children as being told that one has brown hair or red hair—perhaps less, since they cannot see differences between adopted children and those living with their biological parents the way they can see differences in hair color. And what small child can imagine having any parents other than Mom and Dad?

Perhaps the best course is to tell children early, so that the term is familiar and not threatening. Parents should anticipate, however, that very young children will not fully understand what adoption means. By telling their children, they have merely neutralized a word that could hurt if used thoughtlessly by others. Parents and concerned adults need to know that children's ability to understand concepts such as adoption and birth develops with age and that children who comfortably refer to themselves as adopted may nonetheless at some later point experience fears about their adoptive status that need to be discussed.

Information Processing: Acquiring Basic Skills

Some things are so second nature to us that we hardly pay them any mind, such as making inferences from our experiences, knowing that "three" is more than "two," or that we are likely to forget unless we do something to remember. What do preschoolers grasp of the knowledge we have come to take for granted? And how does this develop? Those who adopt an information-processing approach to cognition focus on the specific processes involved in developmental change, rather than on the characteristics of any stage of thought. Such processes include the way information is coded, the ways in which it is stored, and how it is retrieved from memory. A central assumption of this approach is that individuals face real constraints on their ability to process information at any age. In studying the ways individuals approach different types of problems, the strategies they use to overcome these constraints, and the particular demands of the tasks, investigators guided by this approach attempt to explain the mechanisms underlying developmental change.

Reasoning

Reasoning allows one to know something without checking it out. It is a way of extending one's knowledge, in other words, without having to experience things directly. How easily do preschoolers discover new things in this way? In deduction, for instance, one reasons from a premise, concluding that if one thing is true, something else must be. If Princess is a dog, for example, one knows she cannot also be a cat, or if Alisa is older than Anthony, and Anthony is older than Eddie, then one knows that Alisa must also be older than Eddie.

Laboratory tests of preschoolers' ability to reason through simple problems such as these often find they have difficulty doing so. Margaret Donaldson (1978) argues that their failure is due more to the nature of the tasks preschoolers are given than to their ability to reason. Simply put, some laboratory tasks are sufficiently removed from the routines of daily life that preschoolers are not sure what is being asked of them. However, in observing preschoolers as they go about their normal activities, one finds that examples of spontaneous reasoning are common. For instance, Donaldson tells of one 4-year-old's confusion when shown a picture of a wedding in which the groom had shoulder-length hair, giving him the appearance of a woman. When told this was a wedding picture, the child retorted, "But how can it be? . . . You have to have a man too" (p. 52). Rephrasing what the child said in a way that shows reasoning from premises to conclusions, the remark takes the form

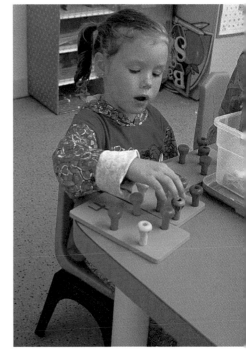

Premise: If there is a wedding, there is a man in it (If P, then Q).

Premise: There is no man (Not P).

Conclusion: Therefore, this is not a wedding (∴ Not Q).

When children's reasoning falters, it is usually because they do not argue from the premises, either bringing in their own instead or ignoring the given ones. A young mother, for instance, who wistfully says, "If this were Saturday, we could go to the beach," is likely to be corrected by her preschooler that this is a weekday. Young children, more so than older ones, have difficulty isolating a problem from the rest of experience, from what they know to be true. However, even adults can find this difficult at times, especially when the premises are at all controversial or touch them personally. The Social Policy Focus, "Schooling Children Not Proficient in English" looks at issues of bilingualism and cognitive abilities.

Counting and Numbers

Preschoolers are also developing an understanding of numbers and what it means to count. By age 3 most preschoolers are beginning to count, know more from less, and can add and "take away." For instance, one 3-year-old, on being passed a plate of cookies a second time around, was heard to mutter, "Someone musta' took one cuz there's only two now. There were three."

Touching each object as it is counted helps the preschooler count each one only once.

Schooling Children Not Proficient in English

Over 6 million schoolchildren in the United States speak a language other than English at home (U.S. Bureau of the Census, 1996). Being able to speak more than one language carries a number of advantages. Beyond the obvious advantage of expanding the number of people in their lives with whom children can communicate, knowledge of another language gives children an understanding of another culture as well and, with that, a better awareness of their own. Bilingualism has also been found to promote children's conceptual understanding and to increase their cognitive flexibility (Diaz, 1983). One might wonder whether these advantages occur at any cost. Are children who are bilingual, for instance, less fluent in either or both of their languages than those who grow up speaking only one? Research suggests that when both languages are spoken in the home while children are growing up, children become as proficient in each of these as do children who grow up speaking only one language (Oller, 1999).

Yet approximately half, or 3.3 million, of all children who speak another language at home are *not* proficient in English at school (Hakuta, 1999). These children come from homes in which English is only infrequently used. In a historic 1974 decision (*Lau v. Nichols*), the Supreme Court ruled that these children are denied equality of treatment even if taught by the same teachers, using the same materials they use for native English-speaking students, unless their schooling also fosters the acquisition of English—since only with the latter is a meaningful edu-

cation accessible to them. Ever since this decision, schools have been faced with the dual task of making sure students who are not native English speakers learn English in addition to the academic content of their courses. It is left to local schools to determine, however, how best to accomplish these dual goals. As a consequence, educating children who are not proficient in English has taken a number of forms.

In one type of program, known as *English as a second language* (ESL), students with limited proficiency in English are taught their academic subjects in the same classrooms as other students, but are given special times of instruction in which they learn English. Thus they are taught English as a subject, just as native English-speaking students might be taught a foreign language, with instruction in vocabulary and grammar. Although this approach addresses the dual concerns of *Lau v. Nichols*, it can be argued that students who are not proficient in English will have difficulty grasping basic concepts through English-based instruction in science or social studies, for example, even though they are also being taught to speak and write in English. A further disadvantage to this approach is that these children may find it more difficult to discuss their schoolwork with their parents than if this work were being taught in a language they share with their parents.

In an alternative to ESL, students are also taught English as a subject, but receive instruction in all their other coursework in their native language. As a consequence, they spend much of

In order to count, children must follow certain rules. They must know, for instance, that you can use each number only once, that numbers must be used in the right order, and that the number of items is indicated by the last number counted. They know, too, that it doesn't matter which item you count first, as long as you count each one only once, using a different number for each ("You're not supposed to count something twice . . . it doesn't make it more") and that it doesn't matter what type of things one is counting because the rules work the same way with any set of objects, from buttons to toes. Once they have these rules down, preschoolers can use counting to do simple arithmetic by about the age of 4 or 5.

Memory

Preschoolers are known for their poor memories. When asked what they did at day care, for instance, they are likely to respond with one-liners such as "We played on the jungle bars" or "I ate some ice cream." Even with prompts such as "Didn't you go on a field trip?" they rarely recall the sequence of activities that filled the day. Similarly, one can send them to the closet for a pair of boots only to find them, much later, playing with an old toy they discovered there. And forget about using them as couriers or message-bearers. Dad has no more than an

their school day in classes that are separate from those being taught in English. This approach is called *bilingual education*, or bilingual-bicultural education. It can be argued that children are in a better position to master basic concepts when these are taught in the language in which they think. It is also argued that it takes a certain amount of time for children to learn a language and that, until they do so, they will fall behind in their basic coursework. This approach also has the advantage of making it easier for the parents of these children to help them with their schoolwork. Those critical of this approach argue that continued instruction in their native language only further delays the acquisition of English, which can be learned more rapidly the younger children are. An additional disadvantage to this approach is that it segregates children who are not proficient in English in separate classrooms, effectively creating two school cultures.

A third approach offers instruction to all students in English, adjusting this instruction to make it easier for those who are not English-proficient to understand. Thus all students are instructed together in the same classrooms. This approach is termed *immersion*, or sheltered instruction. Immersion has the advantage of not isolating students from different cultural backgrounds from each other, thus promoting socializing among children from each language group. Since children learn language best when using it to communicate in real-life settings, this approach should speed the acquisition of English among those not proficient in it.

Are there data to indicate which of these approaches is more effective? Considerable research exists; however, comparisons among the various approaches are difficult to interpret due to the presence of other variables that are frequently confounded with instructional approaches, such as socioeconomic differences. Thus, ESL and immersion are more frequently offered in schools with somewhat higher socioeconomic status (Hakuta, 1999). Notwithstanding, a review of existing research supports a number of conclusions: (1) there is no intrinsic disadvantage to bilingualism and often very real advantages, (2) it takes children a relatively long time to learn a second language, often as long as 3 to 5 years, and (3) how successful children are in becoming literate in a second language depends strongly on the support they receive at home. Most important, however, the research we have to date suggests that bilingual education is more successful than the other two approaches in achieving the dual objectives laid out in *Lau v. Nichols* (Hakuta, 1999). Children master basic concepts more easily *and* become proficient in English more quickly using this approach.

Kenji Hakuta, a researcher and educator in this field, warns that by focusing on comparative evaluations of approaches such as these we may blind ourselves to a more fundamental problem—the fact that students with limited proficiency in English are more likely to experience poverty than are others. Also, even though research supports bilingual education, students being educated in this manner still perform significantly below national norms, by about 1 standard deviation (see the Research Focus, "Descriptive Statistics," in Chapter 3). For these children to get all they should be getting from their education, we need to address the presence of poverty in their lives.

even chance, for instance, of getting a cup of coffee if a preschooler is sent to ask if he would like one.

One of the best-established truths to development, however, is that memory improves with age. But what, precisely, is responsible for the improvement? Robert Siegler (1998), at Carnegie Mellon University, suggests four possibilities: children's basic memory capacities improve; they are better at using strategies to remember; children develop an awareness, or metacognition, of their memory; and their knowledge base increases, making it easier for them to relate new material to what they already know.

Siegler compares *basic capacities* to the hardware of a computer, likening them to the size of a computer's memory, for instance, or its speed. As Figures 8.3 and 8.4 show, research has found that both speed of processing and the number of items children can hold in short-term memory increase with age (Dempster, 1981; Kail, 1991). However, the observed differences in capacity are most likely due to the greater speed with which older children recognize items, thereby functionally increasing the number of items they can work with in a given amount of time. Memory capacity, on the other hand, is more likely to remain constant with age (Siegler, 1998).

The same cannot be said regarding the use of memory strategies. A **strategy** is any activity that is consciously used to improve one's memory, from verbally

strategy Any activity that is consciously used to improve one's performance or attain a goal.

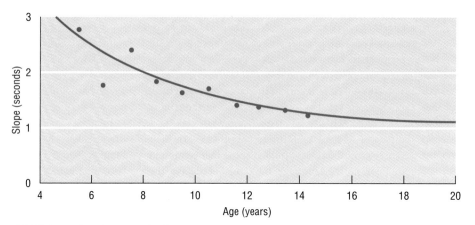

FIGURE 8.3 Age Changes in Speed of Processing Items in Short-Term Memory
Source: R. Kai (1991). Developmental changes in speed of processing during childhood and adolescence. *Psychological Bulletin*, 109, 490–501.

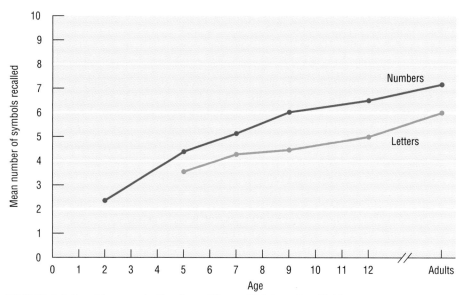

FIGURE 8.4 Age Changes in Number of Items Children Can Hold in Short-Term Memory *Source*: F. N. Dempster (1981). Memory span: Sources of individual and developmental differences. *Psychological Bulletin*, 89, 63–100.

rehearsing the items to be remembered to tying a string on one's finger. In contrast to basic capacities, which are akin to the hardware of a computer, strategies are similar to the particular programs, or software, on a computer. The use of strategies dramatically improves with age, in at least three ways. Older children are more consistent in their use of strategies, use more effective strategies, and are better at generalizing the strategies they use to new situations.

Age differences in the use of rehearsal illustrate the first of these points. **Rehearsal** is a common strategy for holding on to items for a relatively short time, simply by repeating them over and over to oneself. In a classic study, John Flavell, David Beach, and Jack Chinsky (1966) showed children pictures of objects, pointed to several of these, and told the children they would be asked later to remember which ones had been pointed to. Very few of the preschoolers could be heard rehearsing the names of the objects or seen moving their lips. By contrast, most of the 10-year-olds did so. One sees a similar difference in the use of *clustering,* a

rehearsal Repeating items to be memorized; a common strategy for retaining items in short-term memory

TABLE 8.1 Percentage of Children of Different Ages Using Each of Three Strategies for Remembering a Set of Items

	Strategy		
Grade	Repeated Rehearsal	Single Rehearsal	No Rehearsal
Kindergarten	24	56	20
First	63	29	8
Third	78	16	5

Source: K. McGilly & R. S. Siegler. (1989). How children choose among serial recall strategies. *Child Development, 60,* 172–182.

strategy in which one arranges the items to be remembered in categories. Again, younger children are less likely than older ones to rely on such a strategy. Thus, if toys representing a number of categories, such as animals, furniture, and fruit, are scattered on a table and children are told to study them because they will be asked to remember them, older children are likely to rearrange the objects, grouping those from the same category together on the table, whereas younger children are much more likely to simply touch and name them, confusing their recognition of the objects with their later ability to recall them.

Besides being more consistent in their use of strategies, older children use more effective strategies. McGilly and Siegler (1989) videotaped children as they attempted to remember a set of items and found that children of all ages used a number of strategies. The most effective of these, repeated rehearsal, was to say the list of items over and over until asked to recall them. Alternatively, children could repeat the set of items once and then wait (single rehearsal), or they could wait to be asked without rehearsing the items (no rehearsal). The use of repeated rehearsal increased with age and the use of the less effective strategies decreased (Table 8.1).

Older children also are more likely to generalize the use of a strategy to new situations. Why might younger children not be as likely to do so? Even though strategies help children remember, the strategies themselves are not cost-free. They require mental effort, a fact that appears to be particularly true for younger children, who are also less likely to experience as much gain from their use (Siegler, 1998). Thus, younger children are likely to use a strategy only when what is required of memory by the task itself is not too demanding, a fact that is less true of new tasks than of familiar ones.

In addition to strategies such as clustering and rehearsal, adults use external memory cues all the time. We write down phone numbers, mark up calendars, and put things where we will be likely to see them. By school age, children know that such cues help, but it is equally clear from their answers to questions about their use that they do not understand how. For one thing, they do not realize that the cue must be seen in order to be of any help. A note in their pocket is thought to be as effective as one on the breakfast table (Fabricius & Wellman, 1983). In other words, **metamemory,** or knowledge about how memory works, is not well developed.

They also do not appreciate the importance of the timing of the cue, another illustration of the role of metamemory. If they are to remember to bring their homework back to school, a reminder placed on their desk at school (when it's already too late) is seen as just as effective as one by the front door at home. It is assumed that one will remember the cue and, if not, that one will think to search one's memory for it. The cue and the item to be remembered, in other words, are approached as separate memory goals and not related in any means–end way (Fabricius & Wellman, 1983).

metamemory The awareness of one's memory and of those factors that affect it.

Preschoolers don't always remember to deliver notes from home or school, so if it's important, the message should be placed in plain sight.

Thus, given their limited knowledge about memory, young children are less likely to realize they need a strategy in order to remember. Memory itself is not isolated as separate from perceiving or recognizing things. And even later, when they realize strategies would help, they do not use them as effectively as they eventually will. In part, this appears to be because they do not realize how the strategy works. Certainly this seems to be the case with the use of external cues. Young children are as likely to tie a string around someone else's finger as their own.

Similarly, preschoolers are largely unaware that their memory for something can be affected by what they experience subsequently. For instance, in one study, most of the preschoolers who were told a story about a birthday party and questioned as to what might influence their memory about it did not realize that their memories could be affected by suggestions from others, such as a parent or sibling who had not been at the party. Most also did not realize that subsequently experiencing an event similar to the one to be remembered could interfere with their memory for the first (Figure 8.5; O'Sullivan, Howe, & Marche, 1996).

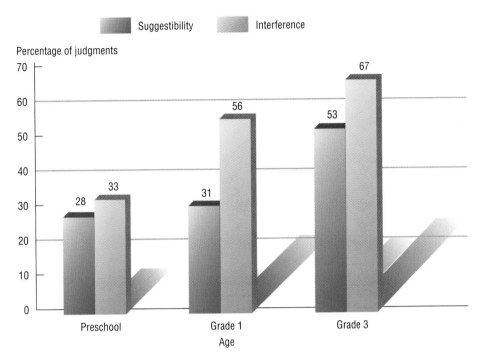

FIGURE 8.5 Age Changes in Children's Realization That Memory Is Affected by Suggestibility and Interference

A final factor contributing to improved memory with age is the development of content knowledge. The more one knows about any area, the easier it is to remember new facts about it. In general, older children can be expected to have more information, or *content knowledge,* than younger ones, enabling them to remember more. In fact, how much one knows about a topic has been found to wash out differences in performance due to factors ordinarily thought to be highly important, such as general intelligence. In one study, children of below-average intelligence who were highly knowledgeable about soccer remembered just as many details from a story about a soccer player's big game as those of above-average intelligence (Schneider, Korkel, & Weinert, 1989). But how can memory for facts, which are specific, be affected by how much one knows in general? Isn't memory a record of particular experiences?

Actually it's a mistake to think of memory as a faithful representation of experience. It is not simply a copy of reality that functions, say, like the tape in a video camera or an answering machine, recording only what is physically present in the signal, never interpreting blurred images or garbled messages to give them more sense. Such a memory would always be accurate; or, when it failed, inaccuracies would merely take the form of systematic losses of information over time. But memory is often inaccurate. And when it is, there are patterns to our "mistakes." We frequently fail to remember things that happened. No surprises here. But we also sometimes "remember" things that did not happen. And in between these extremes, other inconsistencies characterize memory as well. The Research Focus, "The Role of Theory in Research: Children's Memory for Stories," examines differences between children's and adults' memories.

Even though preschoolers' memories are considerably poorer than those of older children or adults (van den Broek, Lorch, & Thurlow, 1996), they make the same types of mistakes as do older individuals. These inaccuracies reflect the way memory is organized by what they know, by a form of content knowledge. Much of this knowledge concerns the recurrent events in their lives, such as getting dressed in the morning, getting ready for day care, or having dinner. Memory for

The Role of Theory in Research: Children's Memory for Stories BY MICHAEL WAPNER

When my daughter Jenny was about 3½ she could take an hour to describe 10 minutes of television. And she was a fast talker even then. And the irony is that even after her very detailed and accurate report, I still didn't know what the program had been about. I did learn about everyone who fell down, wore a funny hat, made a strange noise, hit someone, or was hit by someone. And I got a precise accounting of every animal that appeared on the screen. What I couldn't quite discover, however, was what the story was about.

I tell you this in relation to the issue of children's memory and how it compares to the memory of adults. At age 3½ a child's memory for objects and events can be prodigious, perhaps as good as an adult's. But if you simply take that at face value, you will miss an important difference between child and adult memory. Indeed, even if you do controlled, systematic research on the topic but don't know where to look, you could be misled. Suppose, for instance, you want to research a child's memory for a television program. You might design the research to determine whether children remember "as much" as adults. But if "as much" simply refers to the number of details recalled, no matter how peripheral or central to the story, and you happen to compare a group of kids like Jenny with a group of adults like me, you might conclude that children remember as much as or perhaps even more than adults. But you would have been misled. Or rather, you would have overlooked a crucial dimension of memory on which young children differ considerably from adults.

My point here is that to discover important but subtle dimensions of memory, or of any other aspect of mind or nature, you generally need to already know a good deal about what you are studying. You also need to organize what you already know in a way that directs the questions you ask and how you ask them. Knowledge so organized constitutes a *theory*. And theory-based research is generally the most productive.

An excellent example of theory-based research on children's memory is a study done by van den Broek, Lorch, and Thurlow (1996). These researchers also asked how children's memory of television programs compared to adult memory. But they came to the study with a well-developed theory about what there is to be remembered in a television story and how children might differ from adults. The theory about what there is to be remembered focuses on the *structure* of stories, whether read or televised. Every story can be separated into a series of *events.* These can be thought of as being organized in a network in which certain events lead to certain others. But not every event is equally important to the story. Some events are very central to the story because they are part of a *causal chain* that relates many other

events to each other, from the beginning of the story to the end. If one of these events is omitted, then it leaves a logical or dramatic gap in the story. Other events are quite peripheral and not necessary for the sense of the story. One can rank the centrality of an event by the number of other events it is related to. For instance, in the fairy tale "Cinderella," the mean stepmother dislikes Cinderella and forbids her to go to the ball. Cinderella's fairy godmother comes and arranges things by magic to allow Cinderella to go anyway, but tells Cinderella that she must be home from the ball by midnight, at which time all the magic will be undone. Cinderella goes to the ball, meets the handsome prince, and they fall in love with each other. But at 1 minute to midnight Cinderella rushes away without explaining her precipitous exit. She does, however, drop a glass slipper that the prince uses to trace and find her. The events chronicled so far are central. Each one is part of the logic of the story and is causally connected to many others. To omit one of these (such as the stepmother forbidding Cinderella to go to the ball, the arrival of the fairy godmother, the midnight curfew, and so on) in telling the story would violate the logic of the story. However, the story contains other events that are less central (for example, a pumpkin becomes Cinderella's coach, and mice become the horses in one version of the story). And some events are even more peripheral (the fairy godmother is very beautiful; Cinderella is scrubbing floors when the fairy godmother arrives).

Previous research (van den Broek, 1989) had shown that in recalling the events of a written or told story, the older the child (up to about 8 years), the greater the proportion of central events remembered. The authors reasoned that this developmental difference should hold for the recall of televised stories as well. To test this hypothesis, groups of 4- and 6-year-old children and a group of college students were shown stories from *Sesame Street* and later asked to recall as much of the story as they could. The results showed that the older the subject, the greater the absolute number of events recalled. (Apparently Jenny and I are not typical.) But more important, the results also showed that the older the subject, the greater the recall for events central to the story. The authors observe that what serves us in life is not simply the memory for random events, but rather the ability to recall the causal connections between events. It is the grasp of these connections that allows us to use memory of the past to understand the present and predict the future. Thus, understanding this aspect of memory gives us real insight into the differences between child and adult memory. But without a theory to guide us, we might not even have thought to ask.

recurrent events such as these is thought to be organized in terms of scripts, which help children anticipate, understand, and later reconstruct these daily routines (Schank & Abelson, 1977; Nelson, Fivush, Hudson, & Lucariello, 1983). We saw such scripts at work earlier in the chapter, guiding the pretend play of preschoolers. The scripts themselves are assumed to be organized representations of the events, in that they reflect the relationships among the actions that make them up and are organized in terms of clusters of related components surrounding central events.

Evidence for children's use of scripts can be seen in various aspects of their memory. For instance, if children are told stories about familiar routines, but with the events mentioned out of order, they remember these events in the correct order when recalling the story, just as do adults. Children also mention the various components making up each particular event together, clustering them, in other words. Thus, a script for going to the park might include bringing the dog along as one of the events of the script. When recalling such trips, the activities related to this event are clustered, preschoolers mentioning together such things as getting the dog's leash, fastening it to the collar, and bringing a toy for it to fetch before moving to the activities making up the next event (Price & Goodman, 1990).

Summary

Piaget's Stage of Preoperational Thought

Each stage of thought differs qualitatively from the preceding stage. Preoperational thought is distinguished by the ability to use symbols to represent experience. The use of symbols is characteristic of children's play as well. Symbolic play differs in preschoolers from the form it took in toddlers: It involves more complex sequences of actions, is less dependent on the characteristics of the objects with which they are playing, and is coordinated with the play of other children. Fantasy play among preschoolers is guided by *scripts,* which take the form of schematic representations of familiar routines. In addition to imagination, children's play involves the use of social skills and strategies that reflect the social conventions of their culture.

Preoperational thought derives its name from the lack of *mental operations,* actions older children can carry out in their heads and then reverse. Because of the absence of operations, preschoolers' thought was assumed to suffer from characteristic limitations: (1) *Centration* is the tendency to focus on one aspect of a problem to the exclusion of others. Tests of *conservation* assess a child's ability to see that something actually remains the same despite changes in its appearance. (2) *Intuition* refers to thought that is dominated by the appearance of things. (3) *Egocentrism* reflects a failure to realize that the way something appears to the child is not the way it may look to others. Other investigators have argued that it is the way Piaget's measures are presented to children that causes them to do poorly rather than the particular way children of this age think. When children are tested in ways that make sense to them, they are able to assume the perspective of another and to group objects into subclasses.

Making Wishes and Living with Superheroes

Preschoolers experience more difficulty distinguishing fantasy from reality than older children. With respect to making wishes, young children consider these to involve the use of magic and special powers. The extent to which children offer magical explanations is more a function of their knowledge of the physical causes of events than of age. Similarly, preschoolers also know that fantasy figures are not real, but the distinctions they make are not as clear as they are to older children. Cultural endorsement of such figures most likely contributes to their difficulties in making distinctions.

Distinguishing Appearances from Reality

Even young children can distinguish appearances from reality when questions are embedded within meaningful and familiar contexts. Similarly, children appear to have little difficulty understanding the mental states of others when the measures used to assess their understanding provide them with a familiar context in which questions about others' beliefs become meaningful. In general, preschoolers think best when the situations they are asked to think about are familiar to them. When problems can be related to real-life situations in which goals and intentions are evident, they perform well. One of the most important differences between the thought of younger and older children is not so much the actual form thought takes, but whether it can move beyond familiar experience.

Understanding Pretense and Deception

Most measures of children's understanding of deception involve creating false beliefs in others by moving an object a person believes to have been left in a certain location and assessing whether children will distinguish their knowledge of the object's new location from the false beliefs held by the other person. Three-year-olds fail to distinguish what they know from the beliefs of others unless the task is made meaningful by involving them in plans to deceive the other. Four- and five-year-olds are able on their own to distinguish what they know from what the other person knows.

Awareness of Mental States

Children's symbolic play, in which they talk about their own and others' mental states, helps them distinguish their own thoughts from those of others. Everyday interactions with older siblings and friends also help children understand the mental states of others.

Understanding the Actions of Others

Children first use words referring to their own and others' mental states just before the age of 3. They progress through several stages in understanding others' behavior. Initially, children appear to understand behavior only in terms of feelings (desire phase). Subsequently, they become aware of thoughts as well, but fail to recognize their importance in explaining behavior (desire-belief phase). By the age of 4, they realize that others' beliefs are central to explaining their behavior (belief-desire phase).

Preschoolers have a relatively well developed understanding of thinking: They know that something must be alive to think, that thinking is a mental event that is carried out in one's head, and that thoughts are internal and not available for public inspection.

Failures of Understanding

Preschoolers do not understand that people constantly experience one mental state or another and so do not assume that a person is thinking unless there are observable cues as to this. Preschoolers also have difficulty recognizing what another person is likely to be thinking about, based on contextual cues, perhaps due to their failure to realize that attention is focused. Preschoolers also tend to regard their thoughts as isolated mental events rather than as part of a stream of consciousness.

Questions About Birth and Adoption

Many of children's questions about birth are prompted by the birth of a younger sibling. Because children understand the answers they are given in terms of what they already know, it is helpful to ask what they think before supplying an answer. Many children fail to understand that babies are created rather than having arrived from some other place. Thus answers concerning how people have babies are understand in terms of knowing where to look. Confusion concerning adoption also arises. Preschoolers have difficulty understanding that an adopted child is likely to resemble birth parents in appearance but resemble adoptive parents in beliefs. In general, most preschoolers are not likely to understand adoption even though they may have discussed it with parents.

Information Processing: Acquiring Basic Skills

An information-processing approach focuses on the processes involved in developmental change rather than on the characteristics of stages of thought. These processes include the way information is coded, stored, and retrieved from memory. Even young children use strategies when given problems to solve. Furthermore, children use a number of strategies, and changing from one to the next does not necessarily mean moving from less efficient to more efficient ones.

Both deductive and inductive reasoning are commonly employed by preschoolers. When reasoning breaks down, it is usually because children fail to argue from the premises. By 3, most preschoolers are beginning to count and are aware of the need to follow rules when doing so.

The improvement of memory with age is likely to be due to children's better use of strategies, to improvements in their metamemory, and to an increasingly expanded knowledge base. With age, strategies are used more consistently and effectively and can be generalized more easily to new situations. Metamemory, or knowledge about memory, also improves with age. Finally, the more children know about any area, the easier it is to remember new facts about it. In general, older children have more information, or content knowledge, than younger ones.

Key Terms

centration (p. 300)
conservation (p. 300)
egocentrism (p. 300)

mental operations (p. 299)
metamemory (p. 325)
preoperational thought (p. 296)

rehearsal (p. 324)
scripts (p. 298)
strategy (p. 323)

Early Childhood
Psychosocial Development

I've got a lot of problems," whispers a 4-year-old to his grandmother at bedtime. "It's hard to fall asleep . . . my shoes come off when I run . . . sometimes kids don't want to play with me . . . and I can't catch a ball very well. Don't I have a lot of problems, Grandma? Goodnight."

It's popular to think of early childhood as carefree, when one's biggest problems are learning the alphabet or how to skip rope and when the only things to fear are monsters in dark places. Mothers hurrying children into clothes or through meals often fail to give skipping rope and closet creatures their proper due. And questions such as "Where does el-em-en-o-pee go, Dad?" can receive an impatient answer from fathers who forget they too started with the alphabet. Thank goodness for grandparents, who know the shadows on the wall are real.

The years of early childhood fairly burst with energy and activity. Preschoolers are into everything, inspecting the contents of desk drawers and pants pockets, scrutinizing dead insects, and racing around corners, leaving the rest of the world behind them. Viewed from the outside, their activity looks like random bursts of energy. Looked at from within, the glimmer of a purpose can be seen. Running, climbing, poking, and peering all confirm their awareness of themselves. Like striking a light in the dark, their actions are a means of discovering what they can do and what kind of person they are becoming.

Recognizing the Self

Most children can recognize themselves in photos and mirrors, saying "That's me" or calling out their name by about 18 to 24 months of age. Developmentalists have studied the emergence of *self-recognition* in the laboratory by placing a dot of rouge on an infant's nose and determining the age at which the infant touches its own face when it sees the dot in its reflection in the mirror. Touching one's nose has been taken to mean that children recognize that what is true of one's image must be true of the self. Such behavior has been taken to signify the existence of an objective self-concept (Bertenthal & Fischer, 1978; Lewis & Brooks-Gunn, 1979).

But how similar is this early self-concept to that of adults? Central to adults' understanding of themselves, for instance, is their recognition that despite changes in how they might feel or look from one time to the next, they remain the same person. Do preschoolers have a similar sense of themselves as continuous over time?

Ulric Neisser (1992) argues that they do not, suggesting that initially children experience the self only with respect to the activities in which they are currently engaged. The **ecological self** is the self that is directly perceived through one's actions. This awareness of the self is direct and immediate, based, as it is, on feedback from ongoing activity in an actual surround. It is the awareness of holding something, for instance, as well as of what one is holding, or of kicking one's feet in addition to the ball one is kicking. In addition to this awareness of their present selves, children increasingly remember their past experiences and imagine future possibilities. Neisser refers to this awareness as the **extended self.** Through imagining what they will do and recalling what they have done, children extend the self over time, beyond the immediate moment.

Daniel Povinelli, Keli Landau, and Helen Perilloux (1996) examined the temporal dimensions to preschoolers' self-concept through the use of delayed images. They videotaped 2-, 3-, and 4-year-olds as they played a game and then invited the children to watch on television what they had done just moments before. While they had been playing, a sticker had been covertly placed on the child's

How can you test whether a child recognizes itself in a mirror?

ecological self The self that is directly perceived in terms of one's ongoing actions.

extended self The self that includes not only what one is doing at the present moment but also memories of one's past experiences and imaginings about one's future.

Initially children are aware of the self only in terms of what they are doing at the time.

head. Would children appreciate the causal connections between past and present instances of the self and reach up to touch their heads?

Such an appreciation develops only with age. None of the 2-year-olds, 25% of the 3-year-olds, and 75% of the 4-year-olds reached up for the sticker, even though children of all ages could identify themselves by name as the child in the videotape. These investigators suggest that the emergence of a concept of self that extends over time occurs considerably later than the "on-line" self-concept, or ecological self, that is revealed through live feedback, such as in mirrors. Even though young children realize that the image they are looking at is of themselves, they appear not to understand that the way they experience themselves currently is related to previous states. Only the 4-year-olds in this study were likely to understand that the sticker that had been on their heads several minutes ago must be there now.

Interestingly, even though the younger children labeled the delayed image as themselves, they spoke about it as if it were someone else, saying things such as "it's on *his* head" rather than "*my* head." In fact, the likelihood that children would reach up for the sticker was associated with the pronouns they used to refer to

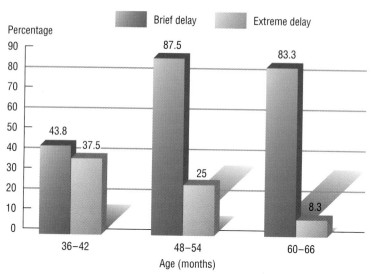

FIGURE 9.1 Percentage of Preschoolers Reaching to Touch a Sticker on Their Heads as a Function of Age and Delay Conditions

themselves in the videotape. Of those who reached up, 83% used the first person to refer to their image, whereas only 3% of those referring to their image in the third person reached for the sticker.

Findings such as these support the distinction between an ecological self and an extended self, suggesting that young children initially think of themselves in terms of their ongoing actions. Information about this aspect of the self is communicated by cues such as contingent movement, like what would be reflected back in a mirror. Delaying the image eliminates this cue, making it difficult for young preschoolers to relate to this image of themselves. As awareness of the extended self develops over time, children should get better at understanding how the self that they presently experience is related to their past experiences. For instance, they should know that the more delayed the image of themselves is, the less reflective that image is likely to be of their present state.

Povinelli and Simon (1998) videotaped preschoolers on two separate occasions, 1 week apart, as they played a game. The videotapings took place in recognizably different rooms. As in the earlier experiment, a sticker had been surreptitiously placed on the child's head during play. Children watched either the video taken just moments ago or the one that had been taken a week ago. In each case, when the video was shown, they were asked, "Can you get that sticker for me?" If awareness of the extended self improves with age, older preschoolers should be less likely to reach up for the sticker when viewing the video from a week ago than when viewing the one taken moments before. Conversely, when watching the recent video, they should be more likely to reach for the sticker than younger children. Both of these expected age differences were found. Thus, the older preschoolers understood that something that had happened just a few minutes ago could still be causally relevant to their present self, but that something that had happened a week ago could not be. The youngest preschoolers, however, did not make this distinction. Figure 9.1 shows the results of this experiment. These trends give support to the development of an extended self, or the awareness, as William James (1890) put it, that "I am the same self I was yesterday" (p. 332).

The conversations children have with their parents contribute to the development of autobiographical memory.

Self-Concept

What might underlie the growth of such a sense of self? Katherine Nelson (1992), at City University of New York, suggests that a new type of memory, which she terms an **autobiographical memory,** emerges at about the age of 4. Autobiographical memories make up an individual's life history. They form the personal narrative that tells the story of oneself. Prior to this age, children may recall particular events, but these do not become part of their life story. Nelson considers language in general, and conversations in particular, to be important for the development of such memory. By the age of 4, children are better able to understand language as a representational system; they are able to step back from the pragmatics of communication and understand language as a way of representing their experiences and communicating these to others. Thus, children begin to use language not simply to communicate their needs or label things around them, but also as a way of representing what they know and what others must know as well. Autobiographical memory represents the same sort of change with respect to memory that one sees in their use of language, the development of an awareness, that is, that these memories are *about* something, namely themselves.

The conversations children have with their parents are assumed to contribute to the development of this memory. Just as Vygotsky (1978) stressed the social context of development, in which children acquire the skills of their culture by working alongside those who are more skilled, children's conversations with parents support the development of an autobiographical memory, both in terms of what is remembered and how it is fit into a personal narrative. Parents provide the narrative structure for this memory by showing children how to make sense of past events.

At what age do childhood memories start for most people?

autobiographical memories
Memories that constitute the personal narrative that tells the story of oneself; emerges at about age 4.

Melissa Welch-Ross (1997), at Georgia State University, assumed that children's ability to participate in these conversations should reflect their developing cognitive capacities (see Chapter 8). Preschoolers were tested for their ability to mentally represent what others know and to coordinate this with their own understanding. Their conversations with their mothers were also recorded. As anticipated, children who had a better understanding of the way in which they and their mothers mentally represented shared experiences participated more actively in conversations about events they had experienced, offering information on their own about these rather than simply responding to what their mothers said. Their participation suggests that they understood that such conversations represented a "meeting of the minds," in which it was necessary for both parties to share information for each to know what the other remembered.

Several distinct conversational styles have been identified in these conversations between parents and children (Reese & Fivush, 1993). Typically, parents either weave past events into a narrative that describes not only the event but also how it relates to the child's other experiences, or they analyze events in terms of general semantic categories rather than the child's experiences. Nelson has noted that children's memories tend to reflect the style in which their personal experiences have been discussed. Parents, in other words, teach their children how to remember things, telling them what is important and which things are related to what other things.

Not only can differences between one parent and the next be expected to influence the nature of parent-child conversations, but so can differences between one culture and the next. One such difference concerns the emphasis cultures give to the individual versus the group. Western cultures have been characterized as emphasizing the personal characteristics that make individuals unique, reflecting a high valuation of personal independence, and Asian cultures as emphasizing the self in relation to others, reflecting the value given to the interdependence that exists among members of a group (Markus & Kitayama, 1991).

Given that parents from different cultural backgrounds might be expected to emphasize somewhat different past experiences in these conversations, what implications might this have? Are differences such as these associated with cultural differences in the way children think of themselves—that is, in the way they construe the self? Do American parents, in other words, foster a construction of the self that is more independent, by encouraging self-expression and telling stories in which the child stands out from others in some way? And do Asian parents foster one that is more interdependent, by discouraging emotional displays or focusing on the self?

Jessica Jungsook Han, Michelle Leichtman, and Qi Wang (1998), at Harvard University, interviewed North American, Korean, and Chinese children, from 4 to 6 years old, asking them about their recent experiences. As expected, American children spoke less about others relative to themselves, talked more about their feelings and thoughts, and gave more details than did the Korean or Chinese children. Consider the responses of two children, one Chinese and one American, when asked to describe what they did at bedtime the evening before:

CHINESE CHILD: "After I washed my face, I asked Dad to tell me a story. Then my mom covered me with the blanket. Then my mom went over there and read magazines. And finally I fell asleep."

INTERVIEWER: What else did you do?

CHINESE CHILD: "Watched TV before going to bed. After watching TV, I went to wash. After washing, I watched again. Just after I finished dinner, my dad asked me to practice writing. After practicing writing, he asked me to play the piano. Just after playing the piano, the TV program began. Then my dad watched TV together with me. After watching TV, I went to sleep."

Personal storytelling about happy occasions is a means of socializing children to their culture.

U.S. CHILD: "I read, did I read last night? No, I played computer, instead of reading, but I liked the book better than the computer."

INTERVIEWER: What else did you do?

U.S. CHILD: "I played with my toys, I think, and then I'll tell you what game I played on the computer. There's a dictionary thing, and there's a word finder, and there's hangman, and other games, and three games, and then there's all different things, and to find a word, you just click on the word finder, and after two or three letters it just finds the word." (p. 708)

These findings show that children acquire the values of their cultures at an early age and that these values shape the way they talk, and presumably think, about themselves.

Peggy Miller, Angela Wiley, Heidi Fung, and Chung-Hue Liang (1997) examined personal storytelling as a means of socializing children into the values of their culture by comparing the narratives told to European American and Chinese children. In particular, they examined mention of past wrongdoings as a way of teaching children and communicating social standards. Although they found the similarities to be greater than the differences, they also found Chinese families to be more likely to mention transgressions as a way of teaching children what was expected of them than were European American families, 35% versus 7% of the stories reflecting transgressions, respectively. Further, when European American parents did mention transgressions, these were typically peripheral to the story line or otherwise marked as nonserious, suggesting these parents did not use past transgressions as a teaching tool. These findings should not be taken to mean that

Box 9.1 *The Use of Personal Storytelling as a Means of Socializing Values*

As the co-narration begins, the grandmother is holding the child in her arms. After the first few words, he gets up and stands by his grandmother.

GRANDMA: Oh, right. This morning when Mom was spanking you, what did you say? You said, "Don't hit me!" Right?

CHILD: Hmn. (nods)

GRANDMA: Then, what did I tell you to say?

CHILD: "I won't push the screen down."

GRANDMA: Oh right. So, what would you say to Mom?

CHILD: I would say to Mom, "Don't have the screen pushed down." (Child moves closer and speaks in a very low tone into Grandma's ear)

GRANDMA: Oh, you would talk to Mom, saying, "Mama, I won't push the screen down."

CHILD: Hmn.

GRANDMA: So, Mom wouldn't hit you.

CHILD: Hmn.

GRANDMA: Right? Hmn. If you asked Mom, "You don't hit me," Mom would have hit you, right?

CHILD: Hmn. (Nods)

GRANDMA: So you would directly say to Mom in this way, "Mom, I won't push the screen down." Then how would Mom have reacted?

CHILD: [Unintelligible]

GRANDMA: What?

CHILD: [Unintelligible]

GRANDMA: Then she wouldn't hit you, right?

CHILD: Hmn. (Nods)

GRANDMA: Oh. So, next time when Mom is going to spank you, which sentence is better for you to say to her?

CHILD: Hmn. Hmn. (Moving close to Grandma's ear) "I won't have [unintelligible] won't have the screen pushed down."

GRANDMA: Oh, right. Now you have choices. You say, "Mom, I won't push the screen down." In that way, Mom won't spank you. So next time when Mom is spanking you, you shouldn't say, "You don't hit me. (High pitch) You don't hit me." (High pitch) You shouldn't say that way.

CHILD: (Laughs)

GRANDMA: You say, "Don't hit me." (Raises her voice) Mom will hit more. Right? Instead, you say to Mom, "I won't push the screen down." What will Mom do to you?

CHILD: Will give me [unintelligible] a tender touch (in Taiwanese).

GRANDMA: What?

CHILD: A tender touch (in Taiwanese).

GRANDMA: A tender touch (in Taiwanese), oh, give you a tender touch (in Taiwanese). OK. (Laughs loudly and holds child in her arms.)

This co-narration ends as it began with the grandmother holding the child in her arms.

Source: Miller, Wiley, Fung, & Liang (1997).

European American parents did not take misbehavior seriously, but rather that they dealt with it in a different way. Similarly, it would be wrong to interpret Chinese families' use of transgressions as being overly critical. The parents found ways to end these stories on a positive note, often giving the child the opportunity to suggest a more appropriate behavior and then praising the child (Box 9.1).

Even with these differences, it should be emphasized that the similarities in the use of personal stories were greater than the differences. In both cultures, most of the stories were about things such as holidays, family outings, or other happy occasions, not about something the child had done wrong.

Age Differences in Self-Concept

The way children think about themselves also changes with their age. Research finds a consistent developmental progression in the way children conceptualize the self. Preschoolers tend to describe themselves in terms of their physical characteristics, such as how tall they are, whether they wear glasses or have freckles; they also mention objective information, such as their age or where they live. As they get older, children increasingly mention aspects of their personality, such as being kind or brave or having a good sense of humor. They are more likely to characterize themselves, in other words, in terms of their psychological makeup. They are also more likely to describe themselves in terms of their relationships and in terms of membership in social groups (Brinthaupt & Lipka, 1985; Livesley & Bromley, 1973).

Richard Ely, Gigliana Melzi, and Luke Hadge, at Boston University, and Allyssa McCabe (1998), at the University of Massachusetts, Lowell, looked at the way children, 4 through 9, conceptualize the self by listening to the way they described themselves in their conversations. These investigators focused on two aspects of personal functioning. Conversations were coded for **agency** when they were about mastery or achievement, such as stories involving some dynamic action, and for **communion** when they were about sharing feelings, friendship, and being together (Bakan, 1966). These two modes of functioning capture both the physical and the psychological dimensions of the self-concept and are more or less balanced in adults (McAdams, Hoffman, Mansfield, & Day, 1996). But we know very little about how children perceive themselves in terms of each of these modes.

These investigators found that children regularly described themselves with respect to both of these modes of functioning, but that activities, rather than feelings and relationships, dominated their descriptions. Although this was true at every age, the frequency with which they mentioned others when talking about themselves increased with age, a finding that is consistent with other research showing that children are more likely to characterize themselves in terms of their social world as they get older. Girls, also, were more likely than boys to mention others and, in general, to mention themes of communion.

Gender and the Self

One of the most important ways in which children come to think of themselves is in terms of their gender. By the time they are 2, most children can identify themselves as a boy or a girl, a process known as **gender labeling.** How much they understand of what this means, however, is another matter. Misunderstandings arise from confusing sex with gender. Sex refers to whether one is biologically female or male and is determined at the moment of conception. **Sex differences** are biologically based. Examples include differences in the reproductive systems

How would a preschooler be likely to describe her older sister? And how would that description most likely differ from the sister's description of herself?

agency An aspect of mature functioning characterized by achievement and mastery; the complement of communion.

communion An aspect of mature functioning characterized by empathy and friendship; the complement of agency.

gender labeling The ability to label oneself as a boy or girl; develops by about age 2.

sex differences Biological and physiological differences distinguishing the sexes.

Between the ages of 3 and 5, children develop notions of which behaviors are appropriate for their sex.

Q Why might clothing such as a Wonder Woman belt or a Superman cape be significant to very young preschoolers?

gender differences Culturally determined differences in masculinity and femininity.

sex constancy The understanding that one's sex remains the same and will not change as a function of how one looks or dresses; also termed *gender constancy.*

gender stereotyping Culturally based expectations of behaviors that are appropriate for each sex.

gender identity Experience of oneself as male or female.

and genitals of females and males or differences in the average height and body proportions of each sex. Gender refers to the distinctions a culture makes in what it considers masculine or feminine. **Gender differences** are socially determined. For example, our culture expects boys to be assertive and noisy and girls to be helpful and understanding. One is *born* female or male, but one is *socialized* to be feminine or masculine.

Initially, most children do not distinguish sex from gender. They do not realize, for instance, that changes in one's appearance will not result in changes in one's sex. Thus, a 3-year-old boy may be afraid to put on a dress, fearing he will become a girl, or a girl may not want to get her hair cut short, thinking that she will turn into a boy. **Sex constancy,** also referred to as gender constancy, is the understanding that one's sex is permanent and will not change as a function of how one looks or dresses. This understanding develops between the ages of 3 and 5. So, too, does **gender stereotyping,** or preschoolers' notions of which behaviors are appropriate for either sex. These stereotypes encompass such things as types of dress, which toys are appropriate to play with, and the occupations children envision for themselves as adults, and they contribute to children's **gender identity,** or experience of themselves as male or female (Lips, 1997).

Children develop gender stereotypes in various ways. Perhaps the simplest is by observing which people do what things. Thus, children can easily sort through pictures of hammers, baby rattles, cooking utensils, and power tools, labeling these as masculine or feminine. Adults' understanding of gender, however, extends beyond objective and concrete examples such as these to what might be called a metaphorical knowledge, or one based on characteristics drawn from other domains of experience and only extended to gender. Examples of this understanding would be to think of girls as "sweet," or of boys as "rough," characteristics borrowed from the domains of taste and touch, respectively. Does this understanding of gender extend to preschoolers as well?

Mary Leinbach, Barbara Hort, and Beverly Fagot (1997) showed children pictures of objects, such as hammers and ironing boards, that were easily stereotyped as masculine or feminine in terms of their usage by males or females, and also pictures of objects embodying characteristics that could only be extended to either

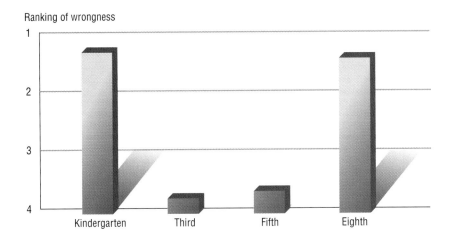

Ranking of wrongness

FIGURE 9.2 Evaluations of Sex-Role Transgressions as a Function of Age

Source: T. Stoddart and E. Turiel (1985). Children's concepts of cross-gender activities. *Child Development,* 56, 1241–1252.

sex metaphorically, such as burlap (rough) and butterflies (soft). Children demonstrated an awareness of gender stereotyping not only for the objects typically used by one sex or the other, but also for those that were only metaphorically associated with either sex. The latter basis for stereotyping was evident even in 4-year-olds, as well as in older children. Thus, burlap, bears, and fir trees were sorted as "mostly a boy kind of thing" whereas cotton, butterflies, and flowers were thought of as "mostly a girl kind of thing."

Even with a metaphoric understanding, preschoolers' gender stereotypes are considerably more rigid than those of older children or adults. Adults understand, for instance, that sex roles are culturally determined and, as such, represent relative rather than absolute standards for behavior. Do young children share this understanding of gender stereotypes? Trish Stoddart and Elliot Turiel (1985) asked children of different ages to evaluate whether sex-role transgressions, such as a boy wearing a barrette or a girl wearing a boy's suit, were wrong and to state why. Preschoolers evaluated transgressions such as these as very wrong and cited concern over maintaining sex constancy as the most frequent reason. In contrast, third- and fifth-graders evaluated sex-role transgressions as only minimally wrong. Eighth-graders, for whom puberty again raises issues of gender, also considered sex-role transgressions to be wrong, but for different reasons, viewing them in terms of their psychological implications rather than possible physical ones (Figure 9.2). Preschoolers' understanding of sex roles as absolute and inflexible makes sense, given their confusion over what might happen were they to violate them. After all, who knows what they might wake up to be were they to wear the wrong clothes to bed at night!

How do children know which behaviors are appropriate for either sex? How do they come to know, in other words, what it means to be a boy or a girl? Once again, different answers have been offered by different schools of thought. We will consider three of these: a social-learning-theory perspective, a psychodynamic perspective, and a developmental constructive perspective.

The Social Learning Approach Social learning theory derives from the environmental model (see Chapter 1). As such, it emphasizes the role of external forces in shaping gender-appropriate behavior. Social learning theorists assume that one's gender role and one's gender identity are learned, just as they assume most other behaviors are (Bandura, 1977). Specifically, children learn gender-appropriate behaviors by *observing* people around them, who serve as *models,* and *imitating* what they do. Not all of the behaviors they imitate, of course, are appropriate for

Hammering like daddy: By imitating their same-sex parent, children acquire both gender-appropriate roles and the skills necessary to fill them.

their sex. Little boys not only do the things they see their fathers, big brothers, and uncles do, but they also may, on occasion, do some of the things Mom and their big sisters do as well, such as put on lipstick or dress up in high heels. Differential reinforcement of behaviors that are appropriate for their gender role makes these more likely to occur, whereas ignoring or even punishing inappropriate behaviors makes these progressively less likely.

Parents play an important part in this learning process, both as the models whom children imitate and as those actively involved in shaping their children's behavior. This does not mean that parents always act intentionally. Parents, in fact, may not know just how differently they actually treat children of either sex. One study, for instance, observed mothers as they interacted with an infant who was dressed up either to look like a boy, in blue pants, or a girl, wearing a pink dress (the infant was actually a boy). These mothers offered the infant different toys when they believed it to be a boy than when they thought it a girl, and smiled more and held the infant more closely when they believed it to be a girl. Yet all of these mothers told the researchers that they would not act differently toward their own sons and daughters (Will, Self, & Datan, 1976).

How do parents influence children's sex-role behavior?

Eric Lindsey, Jacquelyn Mize, and Gregory Pettit (1997), at Auburn University, observed parents as they played with their children, to see whether parents model different types of play for children of either sex. Eleanor Maccoby (1988, 1990), for instance, has noted that boys and girls engage in noticeably different play styles, boys in more rough-and-tumble play and girls more in pretense play. Children of either sex also use different strategies in attempting to influence their peers. Boys are more likely to use direct commands when attempting to get others to do what they want, whereas girls more frequently use polite suggestions (Cramer & Skidd, 1992). What part do parents play in shaping these differences? Lindsey, Mize, and Pettit (1997) found, first, that the play styles of boys and girls differed in the expected ways. They also found that the play patterns of parents differed as well. Fathers engaged in more physical play than did mothers, thus modeling this form of behavior, and mothers similarly modeled, or engaged in, more pretense play than fathers. Children appeared to be sensitive to these differences, as evidenced by the type of play they attempted to engage the parent in. Children of both sexes, for instance, were more likely to engage in pretense play when with mothers than with fathers.

How differently do parents treat daughters and sons? In terms of general socialization, such as in matters of discipline, time spent with their children, and how warm their relationships are, the differences are slight. It is primarily with respect to gender-related behaviors that the differences are more apparent. Thus, parents dress children differently, give them different toys, and frequently ask them to do different chores around the house. Finally, with respect to gender socialization, differences due to both socioeconomic status and ethnicity are evident. Gender stereotyping is more pronounced in lower-income than in middle-income families. Also, African American families are more likely to socialize females to be more androgynous, to be not only caring, but also economically independent, by fostering responsible attitudes toward work (Lips, 1997).

The Psychoanalytic Approach The psychoanalytic approach derives from the organismic model, and so gives greater importance than does social learning theory to biological forces within the individual. Rather than explaining gender differences through the imitation of external models, psychoanalytic theory focuses on the internalization of standards for behavior through a process of **identification.** In identification with the same-sex parent, children internalize, or take on for themselves, all of the behaviors and attitudes of that parent, making it possible for them, in a sense, to carry that parent about with them wherever they go. Identification thus lays the foundation for gender differences and for adult sexuality. The process of identification also resolves one of the central dramas in the young child's life. Freud termed this drama the **Oedipal complex** after the Greek myth of a young man who unknowingly murdered his father and married his mother. Freud believed that every boy falls in love with his mother, and every girl with her father. The resolution to this love triangle, according to Freud, lays the foundation for fundamental differences between the sexes. We shall look at the Oedipal complex in boys first, since Freud framed his theory around the male experience.

During the phallic stage of personality development (see Chapter 1), the libido seeks expression through the genitals. The young boy derives sexual pleasure from masturbating, an activity that imbues his penis with such significance that when he notices a girl without one, he is horrified and assumes she has been mutilated. He also thinks that the same could happen to him if he is not careful. Before you think he is overreacting, consider the reason for his fears. His sexual feelings for his mother have transformed his father into a rival. Castration, he fears, would be a fitting punishment for these emotions. Freud believed the boy's fear, termed *castration anxiety,* to be so great that he represses his sexual desire for his mother. In yielding to his father, he identifies with him, and, in so doing, he takes on the father's values. Thus the boy's fear of castration motivates him to move beyond his incestuous desires, repressing these and identifying with the father. The superego that emerges from this process is strong, since it reflects the power that the boy sees in his father.

The girl falls in love with her father and views her mother as a sexual rival. For her the **Electra complex** revolves around a different set of motives. Instead of anxiety, she experiences longing and inferiority. She sees that she has "come off badly" in comparison with boys and feels inferior because she does not have a penis. She wants her father to give her one, too. Of course, these longings, termed

identification The child's internalization of parental behaviors and attitudes.

Oedipal complex A Freudian concept in which the young boy is sexually attracted to his mother.

Electra complex A Freudian concept in which the young girl is sexually attracted to her father.

Freud believed that every boy falls in love with his mother, and every girl with her father.

penis envy A Freudian concept in which the young girl longs for a penis.

penis envy, cannot be satisfied and are finally replaced by a compensatory wish: that her father give her a baby. Freud writes, "Her Oedipus complex culminates in a desire, which is long retained, to receive a baby from her father as a gift—to bear him a child" (Freud, 1925a/1961, p. 124). Freud believed that the girl's longings for a penis and a child intermingle in the unconscious and prepare her for her future roles of wife and mother.

Notice that the girl never cleanly resolves the Oedipal complex; she retains a lingering longing in the unconscious that imbues her personality with its essential feminine features, one of which is a feeling of inferiority. Freud believed that the female moves from feelings of personal inferiority to contempt for all women. Once she realizes that her lack of a penis is not a personal form of punishment for something she has done, but is shared by all women, "she begins to share the contempt felt by men for a sex which is the lesser in so important a respect" (Freud, 1925b/1961, p. 253).

Freud was ahead of his time in many ways in his acceptance of women. He freely admitted women into his analytic circle and frequently referred patients to women analysts (Tavris & Wade, 1984). However, his theory of the feminine personality is uniquely uncomplimentary. Freud believed females to be masochistic, vain, and jealous. The masochism (deriving pleasure from pain) stems from the frustrated longing for their fathers. The vanity and jealousy he attributed to penis envy. "If she cannot have a penis, she will turn her whole body into an erotic substitute; her feminine identity comes to depend on being sexy, attractive, and adored. Female jealousy is a displaced version of penis envy" (Travis & Wade, 1984, p. 182).

Freud also believed that the female superego is not as strong as that of men; the implication is that females are less moral. Two things account for their weaker superegos. Females are never as highly motivated as males to resolve Oedipal issues, since they literally do not have as much to lose. Also, they identify with a weaker figure than do males; the mother is more nurturant and less threatening and powerful than the father.

Karen Horney, a contemporary of Sigmund Freud, objected to Freud's interpretation of the feminine personality. She countered that he had not properly taken into consideration the male-dominated society in which his patients lived. While women might want the power and privileges that men have, this is a very different matter from Freud's penis envy. Further, women's economic dependence on men creates a psychological dependence and a need to have men validate their self-worth (Horney, 1967).

Horney contended that it is impossible to test Freud's concept of penis envy as long as women do not have the same status in society as men. Though from wealthy families, Freud's female patients lived in a male-dominated society. They were economically dependent first on their fathers and later on their husbands, enjoying few outlets for creativity or productivity. Did they envy a man for his penis? Or did they envy him for his privileged position in society?

Horney also questioned Feud's assertion that masochism is a central feature of the female personality. Freud maintained that since the Oedipal complex is never fully resolved in the girl, she retains a frustrated desire for her father, which becomes associated with later sexual pleasure. Horney pointed out that, although some women may obtain pleasure by sacrificing themselves to the needs of others, so do some men (Tavris & Wade, 1984).

Horney observed that numbers of her male patients expressed envy and fear concerning pregnancy and childbirth. She suggested that men cope with these feelings by reacting with compensatory emotions: Rather than feeling inferior because they are not able to become pregnant, they feel contempt for women for not having a penis. Rather than fearing women's power to give birth, they feel contempt for their weakness.

The Constructive Approach   The constructive approach derives from the organismic model, just as does the psychoanalytic, and similarly stresses forces within the individual in giving shape to behavior. However, important differences exist between these two approaches when it comes to explaining gender differences. The constructive approach assumes that children construct their sexual identities by selectively attending to gender-appropriate behaviors in others, whether these behaviors are evidenced by a parent or another person. Thus, selective perception, and not identification, is the process assumed to be responsible for the development of gender-appropriate behavior. Also, the behavior of any individual, not simply that of a parent, is assumed to be important in the formation of children's gender identities (Martin & Halverson, 1981; Bem, 1981, 1985).

This process of selective perception is guided by **gender schemas;** these are cognitive structures that direct the pickup of information about the self as it relates to one's gender (Bem, 1981). Gender schemas operate as anticipatory schemata (see Chapter 5), creating a readiness to perceive certain types of information, cues that are consistent with one's gender schema and not others. Thus, a young boy whose gender schema for the way boys play includes information about how active and "physical" the play is would be more likely to notice these as elements in climbing on jungle bars, a form of play engaged in more by boys than girls, than as elements in skipping rope, which few boys engage in, even though the latter involves just as much physical activity as the former.

The ability of gender schemas to influence both perception and memory has been dramatically illustrated. Carol Martin and Charles Halverson (1983) showed 5- and 6-year-olds drawings of children performing various activities. The activities were either consistent with their sex role (a girl cooking, a boy boxing) or inconsistent (a boy cooking, a girl boxing). When asked about the pictures a week later, children's memory was more likely to be faulty for those pictures in which the activity was inconsistent with their gender schema. Moreover, the errors they made frequently "corrected" what they had seen; for instance, they remembered a picture of a boy cooking as being that of a girl. Similarly, Bruce Carter and Gary Levy (1988) assessed preschoolers' awareness of gender stereotypes prior to showing them pictures of males and females engaged in activities either consistent or inconsistent with their sex role. As they had expected, they found that children with more firmly established gender schema had more difficulty remembering pictures of activities inconsistent with sex roles and were more likely to make errors in which they "corrected" the sex of the character to fit the activity in the picture they were recalling.

Why might children organize their experiences in terms of gender as opposed to other, equally visible, characteristics? Sandra Bem (1981, 1985) argues that gender has "cognitive primacy" over other social categories because of the importance given it by our society. This is not to say, of course, that children do not organize their experiences according to other categories as well, for they do. However, the extent to which children use gender schemas to process information about themselves or other children most likely depends on the extent to which gender has been emphasized in their socialization.

Bem recommends that parents mention anatomical differences, rather than behavioral ones, when first teaching children about sex differences, since these have the double advantage of being both concrete and precise. She and her husband did so with their preschooler, who, even at a tender age, could identify himself as a boy because he had a penis. Such distinctions, however, do not cover the

gender schemas Cognitive structures that direct the pickup of information about the self as it relates to one's gender.

difficulties children will encounter with friends whose parents have been less objective. Bem (1985), for instance, recounts a conversation their son had with another preschooler when he wore barrettes to nursery school one day:

> Several times that day, another little boy told Jeremy that he, Jeremy, must be a girl because "only girls wear barrettes." After trying to explain to this child that "wearing barrettes doesn't matter" and that "being a boy means having a penis and testicles," Jeremy finally pulled down his pants as a way of making his point more convincingly. The other child was not impressed. He simply said, "Everybody has a penis; only girls wear barrettes." (p. 216)

Ethnicity and the Self

Children's conceptions of themselves also include their ethnicity. The term *ethnicity* has been used to include individuals who differ racially as well as culturally, for several reasons. Both genetic and behavioral variation among individuals of European, African, and Asian descent are greater *within* any racial classification than *between* classifications (Lewontin, 1982; Rowe, Vazsonyi, & Flannery, 1994; Zuckerman, 1990). The *significance* of ethnicity/race can best be understood from a contextual perspective. The community and cultural contexts in which people live and the responses of others to physical features such as skin pigmentation and facial characteristics are what contribute to one's sense of identity (Phinney, 1996).

Ethnicity can influence children's self-concepts in ways not limited to skin color, one's hair, or facial features. Language is one example, as shown in the way Maxine Hong Kingston (1976), who grew up in a Chinese immigrant community in Stockton, California, describes having to talk in school: "It was when I found out I had to talk that school became a misery, that the silence became a misery. I did not speak and felt bad each time that I did not speak. I read aloud in first grade, though, and heard the barest whisper with little squeaks come out of my throat. 'Louder,' said the teacher, who scared the voice away again. The other Chinese girls did not talk either, so I know the silence had to do with being a Chinese girl." ◄

Children who belong to a minority become aware sooner of the racial or ethnic differences that distinguish them than do those who belong to the majority. Majority children may even be unaware that they are also members of a so-called racial group. Thomas Kochman (1987) found that Whites distinguished each other in terms of ethnicity, but not race. They would, for example, refer to themselves as Irish or Polish, never as "White." The terms *minority* and *majority* are relative, of course. Whites are actually in the minority throughout the world, though in the majority in the United States. Similarly, within this country, White children can experience minority status if they live in a community or attend a preschool in which some other group predominates (Phinney, 1996).

But what does it mean to belong to an ethnic group? Jean Phinney (1996), a psychologist at California State University, Los Angeles, points out that ethnicity cannot be thought of simply in terms of labels for groups of people who are neatly distinguished from one another. People using the same label often differ widely from one another, including the ways in which they interpret and use the very terms by which they identify themselves. Rather than sorting people into categories, it is necessary to examine ethnicity with respect to at least three *dimensions* along which individuals vary: their cultural values and attitudes, their sense of

Young children can embrace their native culture by participating in customs and celebrations while the more complex dimensions of ethnicity are still developing.

belonging to the group, and their experience of being a member of a minority. The salience of each of these dimensions can be expected to vary with age.

Although culture, the first dimension of ethnicity, is central to the experiences of children being raised in an ethnic group, there are such large differences in lifestyles and traditions within any group that culture alone is not enough to distinguish members of one group from those of another. The term *Hispanic,* for instance, includes not only Mexican Americans but also people from more than a dozen South American countries, each with its own distinctive culture. *Hispanic* carries a different meaning for each of those cultures. What is important is that individuals belonging to the group are seen by others, and by themselves, as a separate group within society for whom their common heritage continues to be a significant part of their lives. Thus ethnicity is more than ancestry; it almost always involves *culture,* or the socially shared values, beliefs, and norms that determine one's way of life and that are passed on from one generation to the next (Betancourt & Lopez, 1993).

Individuals within an ethnic group differ as well in the degree to which they identify with their group—that is, in their ethnic identity, the second dimension of ethnicity. Ethnic identity itself is multifaceted, including how one labels or identifies oneself as well as one's sense of belonging to a group and the degree to which one values and participates in one's group. Furthermore, one's ethnic identity can be seen to change developmentally, from an initial stage in which

Children are aware of ethnicity at a relatively early age, although ethnic constancy in terms of self-concept isn't yet securely established.

ethnicity is simply taken for granted, through a period of exploration into the significance of belonging to a group, to a secure sense of oneself as a member of that group (Phinney, 1989, 1993).

Being a member of an ethnic group typically brings with it the experience of minority status, the third dimension of ethnicity, although not always. For instance, in Canada, English-speaking and French-speaking people are both members of dominant groups, yet each is a different ethnic group (Phinney & Rotheram, 1987). At this point, the term *minority* deserves closer attention. It might seem, for example, that members of the majority would always outnumber those of a minority. Yet such is not always the case. In certain areas of the United States, people of one group have outnumbered those of another yet were not considered part of the majority. In some counties of Mississippi, the ratio of Blacks to Whites is 3 to 1, yet the latter were considered the majority. It could be argued that the majority status of Whites was determined not by local ratios, but by those for the country as a whole. Yet a historical look at other countries suggests that qualifiers other than sheer numbers are involved in determining majority status. The British, for example, although vastly outnumbered in India, retained their majority status, as did Whites in South Africa (Simpson & Yinger, 1985).

Box 9.2 explores some of the ways that minority parents prepare their children for life in the broader society. Minority status has less to do with numbers per se than it does with the distribution of power within a society, being associated, at least for those of color, with lower status and less power, whether in positions of leadership or, even when education is equated, in annual income (Dovidio & Gaertner, 1986; Huston, McLoyd, & Coll, 1994). Stanley Sue (1991) argues that the very term *minority* connotes the unequal relationships that exist among various groups within a society and that, to fully understand the minority experience, one must understand the ways in which these relationships define patterns of exploitation.

Children are aware of ethnicity at a relatively early age (Ocampo, Knight, & Bernal, 1997; Van Ausdale & Feagin, 1996). Debra Van Ausdale and Joe Feagin (1996) recorded everyday conversations among 58 children, 3, 4, and 5 years old,

Box 9.2 *Racial Socialization—Survival Tactics in a White Society?*

Parents reflect the values of their society and, in doing so, pass them on to their children. Psychologists refer to parents as socialization agents. As "agents" of society, they also communicate the statuses and roles that make up the social order and prepare their children to participate accordingly as adults. So far so good.

So what's the bad part? Minority parents face a special problem when they encounter societal values that can diminish the self-esteem of their children and, if internalized, could prevent them from realizing their potential. How do minority parents prepare their children for entrance into a society that frequently views their group negatively?

In a sense, they become "double agents." In addition to socializing their children into the values of the broader society, minority parents interpret that society's values in ways that shield their children from harm. By explicitly speaking against negative stereotypes, by serving as models themselves, and by exposing their children to cultural experiences that reflect the strengths of their own background, they inculcate feelings of worth and group pride. In Black society, this process is termed *racial socialization.*

The way Black parents perceive society and communicate those perceptions to their children should reflect their own position in it. Yet relatively little is known about the influence of demographic variables on racial socialization. Frequently a single study lacks the scope to address such issues. Tapping into existing databases, often collected from national samples, offers a useful alternative.

What do these databases tell us about racial socialization? Do most Black parents act as double agents to shield their children from harm by the larger society? Michael Thornton, Linda Chatters, Robert Taylor, and Walter Allen (1990), analyzing data from a national survey of African Americans, found that they do. Nearly two thirds of all Black parents engage in some racial socialization. What demographic variables predict racial socialization? These investigators found that sex, age, marital status, and region of the country all predict the likelihood of racial socialization. Mothers are more likely than fathers to prepare their children for the realities of minority status. So, too, are older parents, those who are married (versus never married), and those who are more educated. Regional differences also predict socialization approaches. Black parents living in the Northeast, more so than those in the South, engage in racial socialization.

For most Black parents, race is a salient issue in the socialization process. Most feel the need to prepare their children for the minority experience of living in our society. Yet just like jewelers refining a precious metal, they may find that gold appears beneath the surface dross. The dross? Children learn of racially based restrictions, such as job and housing discrimination. And the gold? They learn that they must work hard, get a good education, and, above all, be proud of who they are.

Source: Thornton, Chatters, Taylor, and Allen (1990).

who were attending an ethnically diverse urban preschool, over an 11-month period of time. During this time, these investigators observed that even the youngest preschoolers referred to themselves and others according to their ethnicity on numerous occasions. On average, ethnicity was mentioned from 1 to 3 times a day. These references included not only an awareness of differences in physical appearance, such as in skin color or facial characteristics, but of cultural differences as well. For instance, one Asian American carried a book around for several days from which she was learning to read in Chinese. Explaining the book to teachers and schoolmates alike, she pointed out that she had already learned a number of characters, adding, "They're called characters, you know." This 5-year-old was well aware that those who were not Chinese, including adults, would not know how to read the characters and might not even know what they were called.

Similarly, children demonstrated an awareness of other cultural differences, such as tastes in food, that distinguished ethnic groups. When one 4-year-old was asked what she brought for lunch, she answered, "I brought food for Chinese people," explaining "Chinese people prefer Chinese food." When one of the teacher's aides asked for a taste, she replied, "Well, you probably won't like it. You're not Chinese" (p. 784). This child could not only distinguish who was and who was not Chinese on the basis of differences in their appearance, but understood as well that such differences were accompanied by cultural differences in preferences and tastes (Van Ausdale & Feagin, 1996).

Of course, misunderstandings concerning ethnicity are also evident among preschoolers. A 4-year-old who was biracial, though she clearly understood that children resemble their parents in terms of their skin color, was uncertain as to how to represent this aspect of ethnicity as part of her identity. We see her confusion as she explains to her friend Sara how to tell the sex of six bunnies she is guarding while their cage is being cleaned. Three of these are white, two of them are black, and the last is spotted black and white.

SARAH: "How many babies are there?"

CORINNE: "Six! Three boys and three girls."

SARAH: "How can you tell if they're boys or girls?"

CORRINE: "Well, my daddy is White, so the white ones are boys. My mommy is Black, so the black ones are girls."

SARAH (counting): "That's only five."

CORRINNE: "Well" (pointing to the spotted bunny) "that one is like me, so it's a girl. See (picking the bunny up), this one is both, like me!" (Van Ausdale & Feagin, 1996, p. 784)

Similarly, confusions were also observed among preschoolers as to the concept of racial constancy. A White 4-year-old, normally very pale, returned from a weekend at the beach with a tan, prompting two friends, one White and one biracial, to wonder whether her skin would continue to get darker until she became an African American. Although the 4-year-old doubted this would occur, she continued to mention the color of her skin and comment on her racial identity for weeks following their discussion (Van Ausdale & Feagin, 1996). Katheryn Ocampo, George Knight, and Martha Bernal (1997) also have found ethnic constancy to be less securely established in 4-year-olds than in older, school-age children.

Clearly, preschoolers form social categories based on ethnicity. But what are the implications of their doing so? Rebecca Bigler, Lecianna Jones, and Debra Lobliner (1997), at the University of Texas at Austin, examined changes in children's intergroup attitudes as a function of the social categories which they had formed. Children 6 to 9 years old were given either yellow or blue shirts to wear in their classrooms. In some classrooms, the color of the children's shirts was used to assign children to various tasks, such as "'yellows' get the art supplies and 'blues' get the reading books," effectively creating two groups. In other classrooms, the color of the shirts bore no relation to the way the class was organized.

At the end of the month, these investigators found that the use of shirt color as a cue to create functional groups had affected the way children perceived each other. Children were more likely to see those assigned to each of the two groups as being more dissimilar when they had been identified by the color of their shirts than when this cue had no functional significance. Perhaps not surprisingly, children perceived those in their own group more positively than they did children in the other group. What is most important about these findings is not so much that children are sensitive to differences among themselves, but that these differences contribute to the way they evaluate others only when they are used as a basis for forming social categories.

Are preschoolers aware of differences in their playmates' ethnic backgrounds?

Liking the Self: Self-Esteem

Bowlby (1982) assumed that children internalize their relationships with attachment figures, forming an *internal working model* of the self based on these relationships (see Chapter 6). The sense of worth that children develop based on their relationships with attachment figures is thought to influence their interactions not only with those persons, but with others as well, serving as a foundation for their working model of the self. Even though the quality of children's attachment relationships is believed to determine their sense of worth, there has been relatively little research into this relationship.

Karine Verschueren, Alfons Marcoen, and Veerle Schoefs (1996), at the University of Louvain in Belgium, explored behavioral correlates of the child's internal working model, assessing quality of attachment through a story completion measure and self-esteem through various measures, including teacher ratings of school adjustment and social competence, and self-reports of perceived competence and social acceptance. As expected, the more positively children viewed themselves, the better adjusted they were. They had better peer relationships, were more confident, more curious, showed more initiative, and were more independent. Also, the more positive the attachment relationship, the more positive children's sense of self, with 72% of those with high self-esteem being securely attached. Of course, one could always argue that it was how well adjusted children were that then determined their feelings of self-worth and not the other way around. With correlational data, in other words, there is always a problem in interpreting the direction of effects. Is it children's sense of themselves, how positively they view themselves, that determines how others will react to them? Or does their adjustment, as reflected in others' reactions to them, affect the way they evaluate themselves? The finding that how positively children perceive themselves, or their sense of self-worth, is positively related to the quality of their relationship with their mother suggests the former, but this relationship, too, is correlational and not definitive.

Emotional Development

Children get increasingly better at understanding emotions throughout the preschool years, both in terms of talking about their feelings, incorporating these into their pretend play, and understanding the emotions of others (Laible & Thompson, 1998; Boone & Cunningham, 1998). At first, though, they are literalists when interpreting the emotional states of others, confusing overt expressions of emotion, or the lack of these, with what a person is likely to be feeling. Ken Rotenberg and Nancy Eisenberg (1997), for instance, found that preschoolers mistakenly assumed

What does it take for preschoolers to realize that their actions are annoying someone else?

that characters who inhibited expressions of emotions actually experienced less emotion. Older children were better at inferring the conditions under which others were likely to experience various emotions.

Relationships within the family should play an important role in preschoolers' understanding of emotions, both in the way these provide opportunities for children to talk about their own and others' feelings and in the way they validate children's own feelings. As a consequence, one might expect the quality of preschoolers' relationships, particularly with respect to attachment figures, to be related to their emotional understanding. Deborah Laible and Ross Thompson (1998), at the University of Nebraska, found support for such a relationship. Preschoolers who were classified as securely attached were better able to describe how someone might feel in a variety of situations and to interpret naturally occurring emotions in other children than were those who were not securely attached. However, quality of attachment predicted emotional understanding only for negative emotions, such as sadness, fear, or anger. When it came to interpreting positive emotions, children who were insecurely attached showed just as much understanding.

Given that relationships fostering secure attachment are ones in which each person is open to the other, they provide the opportunity to experience whatever emotions may arise, whether these be negative or positive. Perhaps more important, these are also relationships in which children feel safe, a feeling that may be necessary for them to explore more dangerous emotions. When parents do discuss emotions with their children, they are more likely to talk about negative than positive ones, since these are the ones that need to be worked out (Dunn, Brown, & Beardsall, 1991).

Children who are in touch with their own feelings are also more empathic. The more children are able to experience and express their own emotions, both positive and negative, the more they are able to share in the emotional experiences of others. William Roberts and Janet Strayer (1996) found that more empathic children were also more prosocial toward others, engaging in such behaviors as sharing, being helpful and cooperative. This relationship was especially true for boys, perhaps because girls are socialized to perform such behaviors whether they empathically relate to the ones they are helping or not. Boys, on the other hand, may experience less pressure to engage in such behaviors, and their doing so may be prompted by their genuine feelings for the other child rather than by social pressure.

Despite advances in emotional understanding, preschoolers' emotional lives are less than calm, and they are still learning ways of managing their emotions. In this respect, play with peers is important. Preschoolers frequently enact emotional situations in their pretend play. In doing so, they gain a better understanding of their feelings, such as the conditions under which they are likely to occur and how to express them in acceptable ways. Play is important as well in that the reactions of peers help preschoolers learn which forms of expression are acceptable and which are not. Even among preschoolers, there are acceptable and unacceptable forms of emotional expression, and peers who engage in the latter are likely to be shunned (Kopp, 1989).

Similarly, mothers are also important in teaching preschoolers acceptable ways of managing emotions. Mothers most frequently do this verbally, talking to their children about their feelings and how they can be expressed. By communicating social standards, parents play an important role in the development of self-regulation. A mother may tell her preschooler, for instance, that it's okay for her to get angry at her sister for breaking a toy, but that it's not okay to hit her sister as a way of expressing this anger. Children also get better with age at talking about their feelings, not only in expressing what they are feeling, but also in under-

Children get increasingly better at understanding the emotions of others.

standing what parents and peers say about the appropriateness of these feelings and in talking about ways of managing them.

Intellectually, preschoolers are at a place where they can understand that belonging to a social group, whether simply their family or a group of friends, means being responsible for their behavior. Emotionally, too, their self-esteem is based not only on how good they feel about what they can do, but also on how others feel about them, on their approval. It is important to keep in mind, though, that their progress in managing their emotions, as in other aspects of development, is uneven; and the 4-year-old who is in control of himself one day can "lose" it the next (Kopp, 1989).

Friendships and Peer Relations

Friendships appear to differ so much with age that one might wonder if there really is anything in common from one age to the next. Do preschoolers enjoy friendships the same way older children do? Do the friendships of either have anything in common with those of adults? And what about infants? Do friendships exist in infancy?

Carolee Howes (1983) studied children's friendships at a number of ages, from infancy through early childhood, over a 1-year period. When defined behaviorally, as doing things together and as mutual preference, Howes found evidence for friendships at all ages, even infancy. Zick Rubin (1980) suggests that friends serve much the same functions at any age: They give us a feeling of belonging, and they contribute to our sense of ourselves.

How children *think* about friends, however, changes with age. These changes, in general, tend to parallel the way they think about themselves, moving from an emphasis on physical characteristics to an emphasis on psychological ones. When asked who makes a good friend, for instance, preschoolers phrase their answers in terms of availability and activity. A friend is someone who "goes to my day care" or who "doesn't start fights." Older children talk about friends in terms of qualities held in common and shared interests, such as "we're both good at soccer" or "we like skating." Similarly, when asked to describe their actual friends, preschoolers talk about their physical characteristics, such as their height or whether they have long hair or wear glasses. Older children show a greater appreciation for psychological characteristics, describing their friends as thoughtful, funny, kind, or strong (Furman & Bierman, 1983; Rubin, 1980).

In a like manner, when asked how to make friends, preschoolers mention direct approaches, such as "go over and play with them." Obstacles to friendship, if thought of at all, are assumed to be physical and never an unwillingness on the part of another child to play with them. As one 4-year-old explained

ADULT: Is it easy or hard to make friends?

CHILD: Hard, because sometimes if you wave to the other person, they might not see you wave, so it's hard to get that friend.

ADULT: What if they see you?

CHILD: Then it's easy. (Selman & Jaquette, as cited in Rubin, 1980)

Older children, in contrast, are aware that people need to discover what they have in common, that this takes time, and that, sometimes, they may find there is very little in common.

By the same token, when asked about their "best" friends, preschoolers phrase their answers in numbers, considering the time they spend with others rather than focusing on feelings that might distinguish one friend from another. A best friend is the one you "spend the most time with." Older children talk of how well a friend knows them, understands and supports them. Qualities such as trust, caring, being glad for one another, and concern for the other are all important aspects to friendship for older children (Rubin, 1980).

Children's views of the nature of friendship itself also change with age, from that of an activity to that of an enduring relationship that transcends the way they may feel at the moment. Preschoolers may end a fight with "you're not my friend," and really mean it, despite the fact that moments or hours later they will be happily playing together again. Older children realize that the friendship is not dependent on momentary feelings and that they will remain friends even though they may be angry with each other at the moment (Furman & Bierman, 1983; Rubin, 1980).

What matters to children about friendship also changes with age. Both affection and support become more important as children grow older. In one study on friendship, only half of the 4- and 5-year-olds who were interviewed even mentioned liking or caring for the other person as important to friendship, but nearly all of the older children did. Young children are concrete in their approach to friends, focusing on what they do together rather than on how they feel. Older children give more emphasis to the emotional and motivational side of friendship. It may be that these trends reflect their growing awareness of their thoughts and feelings and, with this, the knowledge that relationships extend beyond what they are doing at the moment (Furman & Bierman, 1983).

 This knowledge of how a relationship can have implications for future acts or roles is an important shift in how young children perceive the consequences of their actions. Alex Kotlowitz (1991), in his biographical work *There Are No Children Here,* relates the reactions of one child, Lafeyette, who lives in a housing project known as the Horner, to his friend's desire to play alongside gang members:

On this early summer day six of Horner's four thousand children vied to use one of the neighborhood's few good courts. They arched jump shots into the opening created by the crossbars of a faded yellow-and-blue jungle gym. . . .

"Hey, Laf, let's play," James urged his friend. James loved basketball. . . . James, who was short for his age, dreamed of playing professional basketball.

"I don't wanna play ball with them," Lafeyette said, referring to the children by the jungle gym. "They might try to make me join a gang."

About a week earlier, members of one of the local gangs had asked Lafeyette to stand security, and it had made him skittish. His mother told the teenage members she would call the police if they kept after Lafeyette. "I'd die first before I let them take one of my sons," she said.

. . . Lafeyette and James constantly worried that they might be pulled into gangs. Lafeyette knew what might happen: "When you first join you think it's good. They'll buy you what you want. You have to do anything they tell you to do. If they tell you to kill somebody, you have to do that." James figured the only way to make it out of Horner was "to try to make as little friends as possible."

So while a group of young boys shrieked in delight as the basketball ricocheted through the jungle gym's opening, Lafeyette, James, and a few other boys perched idly on the metal benches in front of their building. (pp. 30–31) ◄

Some children have difficulty reading a social situation and knowing when and how to join a group.

Social Competence   What children usually do is play. Simple as this may appear to be, some children are better at playing than others. Play, in other words, requires a certain amount of skill. Research has isolated several important components of social competence (Dodge, Pettit, McClaskey, & Brown, 1986). The first component, *assessing the situation,* is simply to see what's going on, to accurately "read" the social situation, so that one can adapt one's behavior accordingly. In a sense, joining others in play may involve some of the same skills adults use in entering fast-moving traffic. One has to judge the speed of the ongoing activity, get up to that speed oneself, and then move into the thick of things. Pulling onto a freeway at 30 miles an hour requires everyone else to slow down to your speed: It doesn't work.

When preschoolers "pull into the fast lane" with a remark such as "What are you doing?" they're asking others to stop for them, an unwelcome request if they are enjoying themselves. Entry remarks that call attention away from the ongoing activity are likely to be rebuffed. Similarly, remarks about oneself are usually unsuccessful ways of getting a group's attention. Instead, fitting into a group appears to be a matter of figuring out what the group is doing. Children who are better at this are more popular. Simply put, one needs to be able to know what the group is doing in order to join in.

How do socially competent children enter a group of children playing?

Figuring out what is going on, however, is not a matter of simply seeing what others are doing. Recall that the constructive approach taken in this text assumes that individuals read meaning into situations, interpreting them in terms of their own expectations. As a consequence, factors related to one's personality enter into the equation as well. Mary Lynne Courtney and Robert Cohen (1996), at the University of Memphis, showed a videotape to school-age boys who had been rated by their classmates for aggressiveness (see the Research Focus, "An Experiment," in Chapter 1). The tape of two boys playing tag showed one boy falling down after being tagged by the other. Some of the boys had been told the two were good friends (benign prior information); others had been told they did not like each other (hostile prior information); and still others had been told nothing (neutral condition). Boys who were more aggressive perceived the videotaped sequence differently than did those who were less aggressive. The difference was most noticeable when they had the least information about the situation (neutral condition), suggesting that aggressive boys are more vigilant in ambiguous situations.

In general, more aggressive children are likely to attribute hostile intentions to others more frequently than less aggressive ones (Crick & Dodge, 1996; Waldman, 1996).

Children's perceptions of others' intentions are related to their early experiences within the family, experiences that appear to affect the way they process social information. Specifically, their perceptions are related to the way their own intentions are perceived by their parents. Gregory Pettit, Kenneth Dodge, and Melissa Brown (1988) found that preschoolers whose mothers were likely to perceive their children's actions as motivated by hostility when provoked by them were not as socially competent as those whose mothers attributed benign intentions to them. The former children could not think of as many solutions to problems, such as making new friends or getting someone to give them what they wanted, as did the latter. Research such as this points to the importance of parents' values and expectations in shaping children's expectations about their social worlds and, in turn, affecting their social competence.

How accurately preschoolers can predict and understand the emotional reactions of others is directly related to how well liked they are. Susanne Denham, Marcia McKinley, Elizabeth Couchoud, and Robert Holt (1990), at George Mason University, found that children who couldn't say how someone would feel in a given situation were more likely to be disliked by their peers. As with most skills, there are noticeable and relatively stable individual differences from one child to the next. Likability, in other words, is fairly well differentiated among 3- to 5-year-olds.

The second dimension of social competence is *responding appropriately* to others' behavior. Children who are popular are distinguished not as much by their own initiation of encounters as by their positive response to the initiations of others. In fact, popular children approach others infrequently; but they *are* better at keeping things going, and other children appear to have a better time with them (Dodge, 1983). Mothers have been found to contribute to children's social competence by serving as "social coaches," both making suggestions for future behavior and giving feedback on what children have already done. For instance, children who are popular have been found to have mothers who give better advice on how to join a group of children playing together and who are more likely to use feedback as a way of fostering more appropriate behavior than are mothers of unpopular children (Russell & Finnie, 1990).

Jacquelyn Mize and Gregory Pettit (1997) showed videotapes of conflict situations to mothers and their children and observed the ways in which mothers "coached" their children concerning the sources and possible solutions to the conflicts they were viewing. Children whose mothers interpreted the source of the conflicts as unintentional rather than hostile and who suggested positive solutions, such as "I don't think he meant to do that. You can build it again, right?" were more socially skilled and were liked better by their peers. The relationship between maternal practices and children's reactions appears to hold across cultures (Zahn-Waxler, Friedman, Cole, Mizuta, & Hiruma, 1996).

Children's play differs not only as a function of their social competence, but also as a function of their gender. Peer interactions become segregated by sex by the age of 3. A frequently noted gender difference is that boys are more likely to play in groups and girls to play in dyads, or pairs. Joyce Benenson, Nicholas Apostoleris, and Jodi Parnass (1997), at McGill University, examined the development of dyadic and group play by forming play groups of five to six children and observing them as they interacted. Rather than coding play as *either* dyadic or group play, they coded instances of both types of play as these occurred. Thus a child could be interacting with one other child (coded as a dyad) while participating in an ongoing group activity (coded as group play) and coded for each type of play.

When play behavior was coded in this way, the percentage of time spent in dyadic interactions did not differ as a function of sex. Dyadic interactions, however, when they did occur, were maintained for a longer period of time by girls than they were by boys. Whether this difference reflects greater social skills among girls, as has been found to be true for popular children, or whether it reflects gender preferences for one type of play versus another remains unclear. Although the amount of time spent in group play among 4-year-olds did not differ for boys and girls, by the age of 6, boys were more likely than girls to play in groups.

Whether playing with one or several children, preschoolers are more open and relaxed when they are with their friends than with others. They smile, laugh, and talk more; are more likely to say what they want and why; and affirm each other more, answering one another and picking up on each other's play. They are also better at resolving conflicts when these arise (Hartup, 1996). Richard Fabes, Nancy Eisenberg, Melanie Smith, and Bridget Murphy (1996), at Arizona State University, found that preschoolers get just as angry when playing with friends as when playing with peers whom they don't like as well, but that what causes them to get angry differs. With friends, they are most likely to get angry at what might be called relationship issues, such as being rejected or violating the conditions of play—when a child doesn't play by the rules, for instance. In contrast, physical acts, such as being pushed or having a toy knocked over, were the most common causes of anger with less-liked peers.

Children are also more generous in interpreting the motives of those they like, being less likely to see their behavior as intentionally provocative (Fabes et al., 1996). This "generosity" again illustrates the constructive nature of perception. Fabes and his associates found, for instance, that just as with the aggressive boys studied by Courtney and Cohen (1996), the assumptions children made concerning the intentions of others affected the way they perceived the others' behavior. A child who has just been pushed, for example, would be more likely to perceive this behavior as hostile when pushed by someone who is not well liked than when pushed by a friend. The very same behavior by a friend would more likely be interpreted as an invitation to rough-house or as simply clumsy.

Parenting

Most parents are not prepared for the sheer number of things to be done at once, all at once, all the time. Conversations, for example, are rarely held with just one other person—not, at least, when there's more than one child in the family. As soon as one child starts talking, another joins in. Reminders not to interrupt or requests that something be repeated frequently don't help, since it's not always clear who has interrupted whom or what one has missed. All of this typically takes place while the parent is doing something else, such as making lunches before having breakfast or telling a child where to find a misplaced shoe. Parenting, most would say? This had better not be one more thing to think about.

In fact, it usually isn't. Parenting, like life, is what one does while waiting for something else to happen. It's helping a child find the pet mouse before the cat does or listening to a joke your son has just told. People learn how to parent not from reading books or taking a course, although both of these can be helpful, but from the way they were parented. In this sense, parenting is more a matter of who one is than what one does, passed on from one generation to the next much like eye color or body build.

TABLE 9.1 Parenting Style and Social Competence

Parenting Style	Characteristics	Resulting Social Behavior in Child
Authoritative	Demanding, encourages independence; responsive, warm, and nurturing; disciplines with explanation; maintains open dialogue	Social competence and responsibility
Authoritarian	Demanding; consistent in enforcing standards; restrictive, controlling	Ineffective social interaction; inactive
Indulgent	Responsive, warm, and nurturing; undemanding; uses punishment inconsistently and infrequently; exercises little control	Social competence, well-adjusted; peer oriented; misconduct
Neglectful	Unresponsive, little warmth or nurturance; undemanding, sets few limits and provides little supervision	Poor orientation to work and school; behavior problems

Source: D. Baumrind. (1989). Rearing competent children. In W. Damon (Ed.), *New directions for child development: Adolescent health and human behavior* (pp. 349–378). San Francisco: Jossey-Bass.

Diana Baumrind (1967, 1971, 1996), at the University of California, Berkeley, has distinguished four styles of parenting in terms of differences in parental responsiveness and demandingness (shown in Table 9.1). *Responsiveness* refers to how sensitive, supportive, and involved parents are, and *demandingness* to the degree to which parents hold high expectations for their children's behavior and supervise their activities.

Authoritative parents are both responsive and demanding. They are warm and nurturant, listen openly to their children's ideas and plans, yet are willing to assert their own authority and do so in a way that consistently enforces their standards. These parents stress self-reliance and independence, maintain an open dialogue with their children, and give reasons when they discipline. **Authoritarian parents** are equally demanding but less responsive than authoritative ones. They, too, are consistent in enforcing their standards but, perhaps because they value obedience over self-reliance, are less open and responsive to the other's perspective. Instead, they expect their children to do as they are told and not to question. Rather than backing up their discipline with reasons, they are more likely to use force. **Indulgent parents** are responsive to their children, as are authoritative parents; however, they are not demanding. These parents are warm and nurturant, but make few demands for responsible behavior, punish infrequently and inconsistently, and exercise little control or power over their children's activities. **Neglectful parents** are neither responsive nor demanding. These parents provide little nurturance or supervision, are cold and uninvolved, and set few limits, letting their children do whatever they choose. Several studies have found that the quality of parenting is strongly influenced by the kind of social support the parents have (see the Research Focus, "Questionnaires: Social Support and the Quality of Parenting" on page 362).

Both authoritarian and authoritative parents provide strong models, but in different ways. Authoritarian parents attempt to control their children; authoritative ones to guide them. In line with this difference, the latter place greater value on autonomy and self-discipline and the former on obedience and respect for

How is an authoritative parent likely to differ from an authoritarian parent when confronting a child who has done something wrong?

authoritative parenting A style of parenting that stresses self-reliance and independence; parents are consistent, maintain an open dialogue, and give reasons when disciplining.

authoritarian parenting A style of parenting that stresses obedience, respect for authority, and traditional values.

indulgent parenting A style of parenting characterized by warmth and nurturance but little supervision.

neglectful parenting A style of parenting characterized by little warmth, nurturing, or supervision.

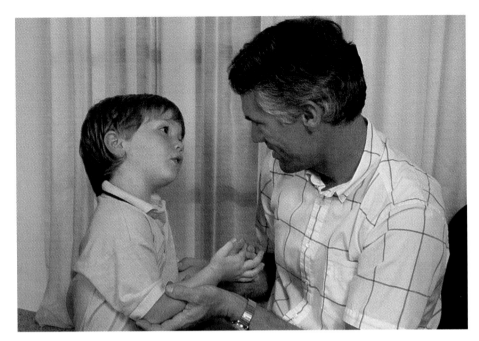

Authoritative parents are warm and nurturant and listen openly to their children's ideas and plans but are also willing to assert their own authority in a way consistent with their standards.

authority. Both types of parents define limits and set standards. Authoritative parents, however, are more willing to listen to reasons and arguments, tending to draw the line around issues rather than set absolute standards.

Authoritarian parents are more likely to use physical punishment than are authoritative ones. The use of harsher forms of discipline has been associated with increased hostility and aggression in children (Hart, Nelson, Robinson, Olsen, & McNeilly-Choque, 1998; Rothbaum & Weisz, 1994). Research finding such a relationship, however, has been based almost exclusively on the study of European American families. Little is known concerning the use of physical discipline in other ethnic groups. Kirby Deater-Deckard, Kenneth Dodge, John Bates, and Gregory Pettit (1996) compared the use of physical discipline by African American and European American mothers in a longitudinal study that followed children from kindergarten through the third grade. Disciplinary practices were assessed through interviews with both mothers and children, and levels of aggression were established through teacher and peer ratings.

These investigators found the relationship between physical discipline and children's aggression to be different in African American than in European American families. Only in the latter was the use of harsher discipline related to children's aggression. Findings such as these suggest that children's perceptions of punishment may differ across ethnic groups. Similar differences have been found for parental attitudes. Among European American parents, for instance, the use of physical punishment is associated with parent-centered child-rearing attitudes rather than child-centered ones. The latter, in contrast, are associated with the use of reasoning and nonphysical discipline. Research with African American mothers, however, finds no such relationship between child-rearing attitudes and the use of physical punishment (Kelley, Power, & Wimbush, 1992).

Similar cultural differences have been found among Chinese and North American mothers. Chinese mothers have been found to be not only more protective and more concerned, but also more punishment-oriented than the latter. These differences in child-rearing attitudes and practices were found to be associated with different behavioral outcomes in children (Chen et al., 1998). With North American

Research Focus

Questionnaires: Social Support and the Quality of Parenting BY MICHAEL WAPNER

Teenage mothers who live with their parents have been found to punish their children less (King & Fullard, 1982). It's also the case that mothers who have more friends parent more competently (Corse, Schmid, & Trickett, 1990), that mothers who have supportive friends are more emotionally responsive to their children (Crnic, Greenberg, Ragozin, Robinson, & Basham, 1983), and that parents who live in friendly communities mistreat their children less (Garbarino & Sherman, 1980).

What are we to make of findings such as these? In general, it appears that the quality of parenting that children receive depends a lot on the kind of social support their parents receive. In the worst case, parents who are isolated, lonely, alienated from family, and distant from friends tend to suffer from psychological distress, low self-esteem, and poor parenting skills. And their children pay for it. Frequently this worst-case scenario is the result of poverty (Golding & Baezconde-Garbanati, 1990). However, not all differences in social networks among families can be attributed to socioeconomic factors. The traditions of different cultures also give rise to different kinds of interpersonal structures. For instance, some cultures value the maintenance of close ties and cooperation among members of the extended family. Other cultures value autonomy and independence more. Thus, loose or abbreviated social networks may result for different reasons. We might ask, then, whether parents from different ethnic backgrounds find support in different kinds of social networks? And is the relationship between social support and child rearing the same from one ethnic group to the next?

David MacPhee, Janet Fritz, and Jan Miller-Heyle (1996) investigated this question. They looked at three ethnic groups: Native American, Hispanic, and Euro-American. All participants were residents of Colorado. All were low-income parents with children between 2 and 5 years old who were referred to an early prevention project by a community agency. Thus, all participants lived in poverty or near-poverty and had children below the age of 5 who were considered at risk by some social or mental health agency.

To assess the relationship between the parents' social support and their child-rearing practices, MacPhee and his associates administered a series of questionnaires. Because the degree of literacy among these parents varied considerably, the questionnaires were read to them; however, respondents were still required to respond in writing. Each questionnaire elicited a great deal of information, including (1) the type of relationship, closeness, and function served by up to 20 people with whom the parent had contact; (2) the parent's satisfaction with available social support; (3) child-rearing practices; and (4) the parent's self-esteem.

Questionnaires, along with interviews, are a type of *survey research*. Both elicit a *self-report*. That is, both ask the respondents to give information about themselves. A major strength of questionnaires is the chance they offer to study behavior that could not otherwise be observed. For instance, patterns of parenting and interactions with friends and relatives, the behaviors under consideration here, extend over innumerable times and places. Having parents report on these in a questionnaire offers a convenient alternative to what otherwise would require many hours of direct observation. Obtaining self-report data through questionnaires is also useful when the behavior of interest is potentially embarrassing or perhaps even illegal. In the MacPhee study, parents might have felt easier about acknowledging that they occasionally abused or neglected their children given the relative *anonymity* of the questionnaire, in contrast to the per-

mothers, for instance, behavioral inhibition was positively related to the use of punishment and lack of acceptance. That is, the more punishment mothers used, the more inhibited were their children. With Chinese mothers, however, inhibition was positively related to acceptance and encouragement of achievement, and *negatively* related to punishment and expression of anger. Thus, mothers who used more punishment had children who were *less* inhibited.

Differences such as these in the relation between child-rearing practices and behavioral outcomes can be better understood in the context of each culture's values. In China, behavioral inhibition in children is considered to be socially appropriate and is fostered within the context of an accepting mother-child relationship. In North America, behavioral inhibition is viewed as a sign of immaturity and inferior social skills and is fostered by the same parenting practices that are associated with other less favorable developmental outcomes. Even so, differences such as these should not overshadow the similarities in child-rearing attitudes that were observed in these two cultures. Although mothers differed in the ways men-

362

sonal exposure of an interview. However, even information from questionnaires is often subject to distortion because the respondents prefer to give the *socially desirable* rather than the true or accurate answer.

Another advantage to questionnaires is that most rely on *closed-ended* questions that supply alternative answers from which to choose. Data from these *multiple* or *forced choice* questions are easy to score, in contrast to the data obtained from interviews, which require elaborate preprocessing or coding before being analyzed. Because of this ease of scoring, questionnaires, as we have already seen, can be administered to large numbers of people at relatively little expense.

There are also disadvantages to the use of questionnaires. In general they can be given only to people who can read, thus eliminating their use with very young children or others with limited reading skills. Even when the questions are read to groups of respondents, as they were in the study under discussion, subjects must be able to respond in writing (orally posed questions responded to orally convert a questionnaire to an interview and change the nature of the data considerably). Individuals also often find responding to questionnaires tedious and even boring, especially when, as in the MacPhee study, they are presented with many questions that require considerable thought. Even for subjects who agree to complete a questionnaire, attention and motivation may change appreciably between early and late items. An even more serious disadvantage, however, is that, unlike an interview, the investigator cannot explain or elaborate on questions for subjects who do not understand or who misinterpret them.

What, then, did this study discover about ethnic differences in types of support networks and about the way these related to patterns of parenting? Support networks for Native American parents most frequently included extended family, with very few members of the network being nonfamily. The most supportive networks were likely to involve intense and frequent

contact among all members. For Hispanic parents also, networks most frequently included family, but also included friends. However, for emotional support, Hispanic parents depended most on members of their immediate families. As with Native Americans, networks involved frequent contact among the members. Support networks for Euro-American parents had the greatest number of nonfamily members. These networks were also more diffuse, with less frequent contact among the members. Euro-American parents were likely to rely on family and friends alike for emotional support. It is always possible, of course, that these differences may reflect differences in mobility, community acceptance, and patterns of housing as much as they do tradition and preference.

What about the relationship between social support networks and parenting? To begin with, the investigators had hypothesized that social networks exercise much of their influence on parenting by providing parents with emotional support and thereby raising their feelings of self-esteem and competence, which, in turn, presumably facilitate parenting. The hypothesis was supported to the extent that for all groups, healthy, effective child-rearing practices were more frequently found among parents who reported feeling competent as parents. Of course, with correlational data, no causal direction can be inferred. To the authors' surprise, the data showed only a very weak overall correlation between social support and feelings of self-esteem. When looked at group by group, the data showed a significant correlation between emotional support and self-esteem only for the Native American and Hispanic groups. There was no such relationship for the Euro-American group. Thus, while it can be said that both the presence of appropriate social support and parental self-esteem are correlated with effective parenting, the ways in which they are related may well be different for different ethnic groups. Perhaps the greater emphasis on individual autonomy made the self-esteem of the Euro-American group less dependent on emotional support.

tioned, their rankings of what they considered to be most important in child rearing were highly similar.

Ruth Chao (1994), at the University of California, Los Angeles, argues that parenting styles cannot be separated in any simple way from their cultural contexts. She points out that Chinese American parenting, often referred to by developmentalists as "authoritarian," "controlling," or "strict," nonetheless is very different from the authoritarian style of parenting identified by Baumrind. "Strictness" and "control" simply do not exist as ways of interacting for most Asian parents. For instance, control, instead of taking the form of a unidirectional exercise of power by parents over the child, in Asian cultures is bidirectional, carrying with it an obligation to nurture and support the child. Thus, parents are as much governed by the child's needs as the child is expected to comply with parental expectations.

Compliance with parental directives is particularly important in Asian cultures, not only as a means of getting children to follow the directives of those who

Research into attitudes and practices among parents from different cultures finds much similarity in parenting styles.

are older but, more generally, as a means of teaching them to consider others when making decisions—that is, as a means of fostering interdependence. Hiroko Kobayashi-Winata and Thomas Power (1989) compared the relationship of compliance to child-rearing practices among Japanese and North American parents. They found that providing children with opportunities for engaging in desired behavior was positively related to compliance in both cultures. Similarly, the use of punishment and physical interventions, such as forcibly taking forbidden objects from the child, resulted in poor compliance. Although Japanese parents were somewhat more likely to rely on verbal reprimands and explanations and American parents to supplement these with opportunities for desired behavior and the use of praise and punishment, children's compliance in each culture was related to parenting that could be characterized as authoritative. Generally, research examining attitudes and practices among parents from different cultures finds considerable overlap (Stevenson-Hinde, 1998).

Baumrind sees authoritative parenting as clearly superior to the other styles and considerable research supports her position, at least for European American families (Baumrind, 1996; Pratt, Kerig, Cowan, & Cowan, 1988; Steinberg, Lamborn, Darling, Mounts, & Dornbusch, 1994). She stresses, however, that it is not a simple way to parent, nor is it stress-free. In fact, parenting authoritatively seems to be distinguished by the presence of tensions produced by the need to balance opposing forces: tradition with individualistic innovation, cooperation with autonomous behavior, and tolerance with principled firmness. The benefits are worth the hassles. Authoritative parents, more so than authoritarian, indulgent, or neglectful ones, are likely to have children who are independent, competent, and responsible. These parents have stressed self-reliance and have paved the way for independence by involving their children in decision making from early childhood on. Similarly, setting high standards and following through to see that these are

Meta-Analysis: Noncustodial Fathers

BY MICHAEL WAPNER

It's rough enough when your parents get divorced. But it's rougher when your dad stops coming around. Or is it? Fathers who don't live with their children are called "nonresident" or "noncustodial" fathers. But that doesn't mean they stop being fathers. A father can maintain contact in many ways with the children he no longer lives with. But how much does it matter to the well-being of his children that he does? This is an important question given that about 50% of marriages end in divorce. So what do we know about this matter? Both a lot, and not that much.

There are some socially important questions that we know too little about because there just hasn't been much research on them. And then there are questions that have received a lot of research attention but still do not have a definitive answer. Sometimes when we have the results of many studies, the question under investigation starts to look more complex than it did at the start. The problem then is not that there is too little information, but that we need some method of bringing order to the results of the many studies that we do have. That is the case with research about the relationship between the involvement of nonresident fathers and the well-being of their children. For instance, of 32 studies on the question, 15 found that contact between a child and a nonresident father was positively related to the child's well-being, 7 found a significant negative relationship, and 10 found no relationship at all (Amato, 1993).

In a more extensive examination of the findings on this question, Paul Amato and Joan Gilbreth (1999) compared the results of 63 studies dealing with nonresident fathers and their children's well-being. The technique they used is called *meta-analysis*. It consists of a set of statistical procedures that compare the *size* and the *significance level* (see the Research Focus, "Inferential Statistics," in Chapter 7) of a given relationship across many studies. In their selection of studies for meta-analysis, Amato and Gilbreth chose studies that contained data relevant to four independent variables indicating the father's involvement and three dependent variables indicating the children's well-being. The indicators of the father's involvement were (1) payment of child support, (2) frequency of contact, (3) feelings of closeness, and (4) authoritative parenting. The indicators of child well-being were (1) academic achievement (test scores, grades, teacher's ratings), (2) externalizing problems (delinquency,

misbehavior, aggression), and (3) internalizing problems (depression, anxiety, low self-esteem). However, not every study contained every variable. Nor did every study use the same terms to characterize the variables. And even when the variables were referred to in the same terms, they were not always measured in the same way. Thus the authors had to use considerable judgment about whether the variables were sufficiently similar to pool and compare. For instance, with regard to payment of child support, some studies reported the amount of child support a mother received during some particular period, while other studies simply distinguished fathers who paid from those who didn't.

More complicated was the variable of "authoritative parenting." Different studies reported on different behaviors engaged in by the fathers toward the children, and Amato and Gilbreth had to decide which behaviors constituted authoritative parenting. They ultimately selected listening to children's problems, giving advice, monitoring school performance, helping with homework, and using noncoercive discipline to deal with misbehavior. But they did not include taking children to dinner or to the movies.

So what did the meta-analysis of 63 studies find? Interestingly, Amato and Gilbreth found that although fathers' payment of child support was positively associated with their children's well-being, frequency of contact was not. However, feelings of closeness and authoritative parenting were positively related to academic success and negatively related to children's externalizing and internalizing problems. In fact, authoritative parenting was the most consistent predictor of child outcomes. So what conclusions can we draw? First, the payment of child support is important. Clearly, children living in homes suffering from financial problems are subject to many kinds of pressures, not the least of which come from mothers coping with economic distress. Second, the father's simply maintaining contact with the child is not enough. How often the father sees the child is less important than what happens when they are together. It matters more that the father engage in actual parenting—guidance, discipline, modeling.

Thus, the message from a meta-analysis of many studies is that divorce cannot relieve fathers of the responsibilities of parenting. It only makes it harder.

met are associated with competence and responsibility in children. The Research Focus, "Meta-Analysis: Noncustodial Fathers," looks at the importance of authoritative parenting for noncustodial fathers.

Interestingly, it is not high standards or rigorous demands that lead to rebelliousness in children, but arbitrary ones. Parental strictness, per se, does not appear to be the issue. Parents encounter rebelliousness, it seems, when they are inconsistent, when they break their own rules, and when punishment is meted out arbitrarily. Baumrind stresses the importance of modeling responsible behavior, of practicing what you preach, in other words. Children do what they see others doing, not what they hear others say. Children are also more responsible when parents are warm and not rejecting. Baumrind is careful to point out that she is not advocating unconditional acceptance of whatever the child does. Parents often need to express displeasure and to punish. In doing so, however, it is important to distinguish the *absence* of emotional warmth from the *presence* of emotional rejection. Rejection is harmful; absence of warmth is at times necessary. Similarly, anger is often a reasonable reaction to some behaviors and can be useful in communicating the unacceptability of those behaviors. Again, however, it is important to distinguish between angry remarks and derogatory ones. The latter belittle and disparage children and can undermine their sense of self (Eisenberg, 1996).

Parents are more effective when they are fair. Being consistent, encouraging children to listen, and taking the time to listen to them are all important. When parents do punish, it is important to avoid forms of punishment that raise children's anxiety to such a level that they cannot appreciate the connection between the punishment and what they have done. For children to be able to generalize the consequences of their actions to other situations, they need to know which particular behavior was unacceptable.

Simple enough to say, you might be thinking. But how much does a 3-year-old understand concerning the logic behind parental rules? When a parent gives a child permission to do something, as "In order to do X, you must meet condition Y," does the child actually know which conditions make the behavior permissible? That is, can the child distinguish which actions would be in keeping with the permission rule and which would violate it? Paul Harris and Maria Nunez (1996) studied 3- and 4-year-olds' understanding of such conditional rules. Children heard a story in which a child was given permission to play outside *if* the child put on a coat. Three-year-olds, for most part, as well as four-year-olds recognized the conditional nature of this rule, distinguishing as "naughty" a picture of a child playing outside without a coat from that of a child also not wearing a coat, but playing inside.

Discipline

Mentioned in the right circles, the word *discipline* can create as much confusion as yelling "fire" in a theater. Many parents equate discipline with punishment. Others protest that discipline can break a child's will. Discipline, however, is not the same as punishment; and, instead of breaking a child's will, it can give children a sense of mastery and accomplishment.

What *is* discipline then? According to most dictionaries, discipline can be defined in a number of ways: as a branch of knowledge or learning, as training that develops self-control, as the acceptance of authority, and as treatment that corrects or punishes. Broadly defined, from the child's perspective, discipline involves learning and self-control; and, from the parent's perspective, it involves teaching and correction. When parents discipline, they teach children what is acceptable and what is not acceptable. They set limits, in other words. These limits can create freedoms both for parents and for their children. Setting limits can mean, for one thing, that within those limits children are free to do as they please. Furthermore, disciplined children, who know the rules and are self-controlled, can be trusted to do things without continual supervision. Their parents, in turn, are freed from nagging. Preschoolers, of course, are still learning the self-control that makes these freedoms possible; and until they do, parental supervision and monitoring are vitally important.

Why might it be important for parents to keep the number of rules in the home to a minimum?

The same principles that apply to learning in any situation apply to effective discipline. Four in particular are important. First, it is important for parents to keep directions clear. Rules need to be stated clearly and maintained consistently. Consistency adds to clarity. It is not always clear what a rule is, if it is broken as much as it is kept. This does not mean that parents must be rigid and inflexible in order to communicate a set of standards. There will always be times when rules need to be modified or relaxed. Second, it is important for parents to keep the number of rules to a minimum. Doing so makes it easier to enforce them, while at the same time making it easier for children to learn what is important. Third, parents need to remember that encouragement and rewards are more effective than criticism and punishment. Letting children know, for instance, how pleased one is that they did a chore without being nagged is more effective than criticizing them for not having done it. Fourth, children do best when they earn their responsibilities. For example, they might be allowed to use scissors only when they learn to carry them point down or to have a pet when they show they can manage simple chores without continual reminders.

Parenting and Poverty

The same dimensions of parenting that foster healthy development in all children also serve as protective factors for children who are at risk for developmental problems. Poverty is associated with a number of risks for young children, such as greater family stress, more medical problems, poorer medical care, and, not surprisingly, poorer developmental outcomes. However, not all children who grow up in poverty are equally affected. There are individual differences here as there are in other areas of development. Children who have one or more risk factors present in their lives, but who develop into healthy individuals, are termed **resilient** (Boyce & Jemerin, 1990; Werner, 1989). Protective factors, however, just like risk factors, can be assumed to have a cumulative effect; the more factors that are present, the greater the chances of resiliency.

Robert Bradley and his associates (1994), at the University of Arkansas, looked at factors present in children's home environments that are related to resiliency. These researchers were especially interested in the way in which such contextual factors interacted with the presence of a biological risk factor. Specifically, they looked at resilience among low-income, premature infants (37 weeks or less gestational age), following them into the preschool years. Prematurity in itself is not associated with developmental problems. However, when coupled with an inadequate environment, such as poor caregiving, it is frequently associated with multiple problems.

As expected, resilient children were found to have more protective factors in their home environments than nonresilient children, with at least three such factors being critical for healthy development. Sixty-nine percent of the 3-year-olds who were identified as resilient, for instance, had three or more protective factors present, whereas 64% of nonresilient children had two or less. In all, children with three or more protective factors in their home environments were nearly 9 times more likely to be resilient at 1 year of age and approximately 3 times more likely at 3 years of age.

These findings strongly suggest that it is the cumulative effect of protective factors, rather than the presence or absence of any one critical factor, that is impor-

resilient Able to recover readily from illness, change, or misfortune.

Building Social Capital

The term *capital* is commonly used to refer to a person's wealth, as measured in terms of such things as money or property. Capital provides a developmental "edge" for children, since it is associated with numerous advantages, such as better schools and safer neighborhoods. Wealth comes in a number of forms, however, and a significant one for children is the presence of supportive relationships within the family and in the community. This type of wealth is referred to as social capital. Children who are developmentally "at risk" due to factors such as poverty or parental substance abuse but who have reserves of social capital on which they and their families can draw are more resilient than those who lack such reserves (Klebanov, Brooks-Gunn, McCarton, & McCormick, 1998; Runyan et al., 1998). This type of capital is to be found not only in children's homes, but also in their neighborhoods, and is associated with differences in developmental test scores and cognitive functioning, both in children who are school-age and even in the preschool years (Klebanov et al., 1998).

How can we as a nation increase the social capital available to children and their parents? One approach is to build the potential for such capital into the neighborhoods in which children live. Presently, many of the children most in need of social capital live in neighborhoods that themselves are bereft of the conditions that could foster their personal growth, conditions such as safe streets, parks and libraries, and neighborhood businesses. Ironically, this circumstance has resulted in part from some of the very policies designed to help families in need. Policies governing public housing are a case in point. Such policies typically cluster public housing in large projects, rather than scattering it throughout the community, at the same time establishing income limits that preclude middle-income families from living in the same area (Garbarino, 1999).

When the proportion of middle-income families making up a neighborhood falls below a certain point, known as a "tipping point," neighborhoods have been found to undergo a relatively rapid decline (Wilson, 1993). Public policies that limit public housing to families whose incomes fall below a certain level virtually ensure the eventual decline of these housing projects through the inclusion of a built-in tipping point. In *There Are No Children Here* (1991), Alex Kotlowitz describes such a process in the Henry Horner neighborhood, a public housing development that sprawled across 34 urban acres in Chicago:

> The neighborhood slowly decayed, as had many urban communities like Horner over the past two decades. First, the middle-class whites fled to the suburbs. Then the middle-class blacks left for safer neighborhoods. Then businesses moved, some to the suburbs, others to the South. Over the past ten years, the city had lost a third of its manufacturing jobs and there were few jobs left for those who lived in Henry Horner. Unemployment was officially estimated at 19%; unofficially, it was probably much higher. (pp. 10–11)

In order to maintain communities that are rich in social capital, we need a healthy mix of families from a range of income levels. Opening public housing to families of varying income levels is one way of increasing a community's social capital and of creating supportive community environments. In fact, Chicago is not only tearing down its decayed high-rise public housing units but is also replacing them with "low-rise housing buffered by playgrounds and lawns"—housing that will include units for working- and middle-class families (Downey & McCormick, 2000, p. 37).

tant for healthy development. The caregiving conditions that were found to serve as protective factors were parental responsiveness; parental acceptance; and having adequate living space, safe play conditions, and a variety of stimulating things to play with. Such factors are related to social capital, the topic of the Social Policy Focus, "Building Social Capital." These conditions, by the way, are the same as those that promote healthy development in all children, presumably because they promote feelings of efficacy and self-esteem. In other words, children feel competent and good about themselves when they are able to discover what they can do and to have their achievements shared and celebrated by those who matter most to them. Being able to play in safety, having interesting things to play with, and having their explorations affirmed by a responsive and accepting parent not only help children develop necessary skills but also contribute positively to a sense of themselves. The presence of caregiving conditions such as these assumes a certain level of organization and stability within the home, in terms of both the actual living space and the quality of children's relationships.

 ## Summary

Recognizing the Self

Self-recognition, as measured by an infant's touching its own face when it sees a dot of rouge in its reflection, emerges between 18 to 24 months of age. This behavior has been taken to signify the existence of an objective self-concept. Unlike adults, however, preschoolers lack a sense of themselves as continuous over time. Initially, children's sense of self is limited to the ecological self, the self that is directly perceived in terms of their ongoing activities. The self becomes extended over time, in the extended self, as children remember past experiences and imagine future possibilities.

Self-Concept

The emergence of an autobiographical memory at about the age of 4 appears to underlie the growth of the extended self. Autobiographical memories are those that make up an individual's life history. Prior to this age, children are apt to recall particular events, but these do not become part of their life story. Developments in language in early childhood are assumed to contribute to the development of this memory. Parents also teach children how to remember things, telling them what is important and which things are related to what other things. Children's self-concepts reflect cultural differences in the way the self is construed.

Age Differences in Self-Concept

A child's self-concept changes systematically with age. Preschoolers tend to describe themselves in terms of their physical characteristics. Beginning by abut age 5 or 6 children are more likely to characterize themselves in terms of their psychological makeup and their relationships.

Gender and the Self

Children are able to correctly label themselves as to gender by the age of 2 but fail to distinguish sex differences, which are biologically based, from gender differences, which are socially determined. An understanding of sex constancy, the understanding that one's sex is permanent and will not change as a function of how one looks or dresses, develops between the ages of 3 and 5. Gender stereotyping, beliefs concerning which behaviors are appropriate for either sex, also develops between the ages of 3 and 5 and contributes to gender identity, or the experience of oneself as male or female.

Three theoretical explanations for the development of sex roles were considered. Social learning theory assumes that one's gender role and gender identity are learned by observing and imitating the behavior of others, such as parents and brothers and sisters, who serve as models. Differential reinforcement of behaviors that are appropriate for one's gender role makes these more likely to occur. Parents are assumed to be important, both as models and as those who shape, through differential reinforcement, their children's behavior.

Freud's psychoanalytic theory focuses on the internalization of standards for behavior through the process of identification, in which children internalize the behaviors and attitudes of the same-sex parent. Identification is involved in the resolution of the Oedipal complex in boys and the Electra complex in girls. Freud assumed that females never completely resolve this complex, but develop feelings of inferiority; he also thought that females have weaker superegos.

The constructive approach assumes that children construct their sexual identities by selectively attending to gender-appropriate behaviors in others. The process of selective perception is guided by gender schemas, cognitive structures that direct the pickup of information about the self as it relates to gender. Gender schemas operate as anticipatory schemata, creating a readiness to perceive certain types of information, cues that are consistent with one's gender schema.

Ethnicity and the Self

Children are aware of ethnicity at a relatively early age and refer to themselves and others according to their ethnicity. These references include an awareness of differences not only in physical appearance, but in cultural behaviors as well. The concept of racial constancy, that one's ethnicity does not change with age or circumstances, develops later. Children's awareness of differences among themselves contributes to the way they evaluate others only when differences are used as a basis for forming social categories.

Liking the Self: Self-Esteem

Bowlby assumed that children form an internal working model of the self based on their relationships with attachment figures. The quality of these early attachment relationships appears to contribute to children's self-esteem. Children with high self-esteem are better adjusted and have better peer relationships. They also are more confident and curious, show more initiative, and are more independent.

Emotional Development

With age, preschoolers become better able to talk about their feelings, incorporate them into their pretend play, and understand the emotions of others. However, they easily confuse overt expressions of emotion with what a person is likely to be feeling; older children are better at inferring the conditions under which others are likely to experience different emotions. There is some evidence suggesting that children's ability to explore their own emotions is related to the quality of their relationships with attachment figures. Despite increases in emotional understanding, preschoolers are still learning ways of managing their emotions; parents help by communicating social standards.

Friendships and Peer Relations

Friends give children a feeling of belonging and contribute to their sense of themselves. There are developmental progressions in the way children think of their friends; they move from an emphasis on physical characteristics to an emphasis on psychological ones. Children's views of the nature of friendship change with age from seeing it as an activity to seeing it as an enduring relationship that transcends the way they may feel at the moment. What children value in their friendships also changes with age, with affection and support becoming more important with age.

Several skills contribute to social competence. Children must be able to assess a social situation in order to determine what is taking place so they can adapt their behavior accordingly, and they must be able to respond appropriately to others' behavior. Mothers contribute to children's social competence by serving as social coaches, suggesting future behavior and giving feedback on what children have done.

Peer interactions become segregated by sex by the age of 3. Although the percentage of time spent in dyadic interactions as opposed to group play does not differ as a function of sex among preschoolers, dyadic interactions are maintained for a longer period of time by girls than they are by boys. By the age of 6, boys are more likely than girls to play in groups. Children are more open and relaxed when they are with their friends than with others, are better at resolving conflicts when they arise, and are more generous in interpreting the motives of those they like, being less likely to see their behavior as intentionally provocative.

Parenting

Four styles of parenting can be distinguished in terms of differences in parental responsiveness and demandingness. *Responsiveness* refers to how sensitive, supportive, and involved parents are, and *demandingness* to the degree to which parents hold high expectations for their children's behavior and supervise their activities. Authoritative parents are both responsive and demanding. Authoritarian parents are also demanding but less responsive than authoritative ones. Indulgent parents are responsive to their children, as are authoritative parents; however, they are not demanding. Neglectful parents are neither responsive nor demanding. Although parenting practices have been found to differ with ethnicity, attitudes and practices among parents from different cultures show considerable overlap.

Discipline can give children a sense of mastery and accomplishment. Discipline involves learning and self-control for children and involves teaching and correction for parents. For discipline to be effective, it is important that rules be clearly stated and consistently maintained and that the number of rules be kept to a minimum. It is also important that encouragement and rewards rather than criticism and punishment be used, and that children earn the responsibilities they request.

Poverty is associated with increased numbers of risks for children. Children who have risk factors present in their lives but develop into healthy individuals are termed resilient. The greater the number of protective factors in a child's life, such as a supportive family, church, or school, the greater the likelihood of resiliency.

Key Terms

agency (p. 341)
authoritarian parents (p. 360)
authoritative parents (p. 360)
autobiographical memory (p. 337)
communion (p. 341)
ecological self (p. 334)
Electra complex (p. 345)

extended self (p. 334)
gender differences (p. 342)
gender identity (p. 342)
gender labeling (p. 341)
gender schemas (p. 347)
gender stereotyping (p. 342)
identification (p. 345)

indulgent parents (p. 360)
neglectful parents (p. 360)
Oedipal complex (p. 345)
penis envy (p. 346)
resilient (p. 367)
sex constancy (p. 342)
sex differences (p. 341)

chapterten

Middle Childhood
Physical Development

I was running down the Penn Avenue sidewalk, revving up for an act of faith." So Annie Dillard describes the time one afternoon when she tried to fly, simply for the joy of attempting something that would challenge everything she brought to it, despite knowing it to be impossible. "I ran the sidewalk full tilt. I waved my arms ever higher and faster; blood balled in my fingertips. I knew I was foolish. I knew I was too old really to believe in this. . . .

"I crossed Homewood and ran up the block. The joy multiplied even as I ran—I ran never actually quite leaving the ground—and multiplied still as I felt my stride begin to fumble and my knees begin to quiver and stall . . . even as I slowed bumping to a walk. I was all but splitting, all but shooting sparks. Blood coursed free inside my lungs and bones, a light-shot stream like air. I couldn't feel the pavement at all" (Dillard, 1987, pp. 107–109). ◄

The middle years of childhood are filled with exuberant activity—skateboarding and roller blading, bicycling and skipping rope, soccer games and sandlot baseball, shooting baskets, and, of course, running with the hope of flying. Mixed in with these unearthly glories is the more pedestrian jumble of schoolwork, chores, and down-to-earth matters such as looking after one's kid sister and remembering one's lunch money for school.

Physical growth and continuing brain maturation contribute to these developments, as do the press of changing expectations and the pleasures to be found in their accomplishment. We will look at changes in height, weight, and body proportions during the school years and at the developing skills that characterize middle childhood before considering the underlying maturation that supports their development. Finally, we will look at the contexts for growth that are provided by families, schools, and communities. The emerging skills of middle childhood depend not only on physical growth and maturation but also on the presence of a supportive environment for their development.

Developmental Profiles

By the age of 6, children are relatively self-sufficient. They can get themselves dressed in the morning, fix a snack when hungry, help with chores around the house, find their way around the neighborhood, look after a younger sibling, and walk to school or the bus stop by themselves. At school they can work alone on projects that challenge their developing skills as well as participate with others in organized activities.

Life is not without its problems, however. And many of the problems 6-year-olds experience can be traced to what some would call "growing pains." Molars start to come in; ear infections are more common than at any time since they were toddlers; those who will need glasses may first experience difficulty at this time; and arm and leg muscles frequently ache as muscles stretch to fit growing limbs. Six-year-olds are also adjusting to school. Still somewhat impulsive, they approach their world in a hands-on fashion, touching and feeling things, rather than appraising them at a distance. Sitting quietly can be difficult. Children in a first-grade classroom are constantly in motion, walking about, fidgeting in their seats, and whispering and talking (Mitchell, 1990).

By 7, children are quieter and more settled. Their actions are controlled and purposeful, and there is a tidy air about them as they move about. This new sense of control may reflect their increasing ability to order their lives in time and space, according to the constraints of clocks and calendars, enabling them not only to find their way about but also to know where they should be at different points in the day and to get there reasonably on time. At school, they move around less,

Seven-year-olds have a new sense of control, which may reflect their growing ability to order their lives in time and space.

and when they do, it is with some clear purpose. They are able to sit quietly for longer periods of time, but can still jump out of their seats at odd moments.

Older children, 8 through 10, move easily in their worlds, with an air of competence, self-possession, and independence. They have not yet begun to experience the stresses of pubertal growth and are over any earlier growing pains. There is an air of practical realism about them. They know they are capable and enjoy being trusted with freedoms and responsibilities. They can manage things around the house when necessary, such as getting younger siblings ready for school or fixing meals when a parent is sick, as well as the more familiar routines that fall within their own domains. They are bigger than many of the other children they find themselves with, such as at school or around the neighborhood, and enjoy being looked up to. Although as yet untouched by puberty, their gatherings are usually segregated by sex, with those of either sex showing a certain interest, albeit motivated more by curiosity than desire, in each other. At school, they are relatively composed and restrained, show more concentration when working, and are generally more businesslike in their approach to what they are doing (Mitchell, 1990).

Discretionary Time: Being on Their Own

The years from 8 through 10 are the ones best remembered from childhood, when children grow up, so to speak. Children spend increasing amounts of time on their own in these years, whether by themselves or with friends, away from the watchful eyes of adults. Even when an adult is present, the presence is more nominal than literal. It is not unusual for an adult to be in the house and for children to be off somewhere in the neighborhood, at a friend's house, a playground, or someplace in between. Supervision takes the form, on the one hand, of *having access* to an adult should one be needed, and on the other, of *being accessible* to an adult, such that someone responsible knows where children are and who they are with (Belle, 1994).

What kind of adult supervision is appropriate for grade school children?

Even then, there's a certain amount of slippage between where they might be at any time and where they are thought to be, mainly for older children, and mostly on weekends and vacations. Summer days, especially, can stretch on endlessly, punctuated only by hunger and boredom or the random occurrence of a truly exciting find. Gerald Haslam (1988) describes such days in his short story "The Horned Toad," in which he has just brought home such a find:

> "Expectoran su sangre!" exclaimed Great-grandma when I showed her the small horned toad I had removed from my breast pocket. I turned toward my mother who translated: "They spit blood."
>
> "De los ojos," Grandma added. "From their eyes," mother explained, herself uncomfortable in the presence of the small beast.

Haslam describes how he and other neighborhood kids would spend their free time playing on a vacant lot across the street, at the edge of the California desert, the lot on which he had found the horned toad:

> Despite the abundance of open land, plus the constant lure of the river where desolation and verdancy met, most kids relied on the vacant lot as their primary playground. Even with its bullheads and stinging insects, we played everything from football to kick-the-can on it. The lot actually resembled my father's head, bare in the middle but full of growth around the edges: weeds, stickers, cactuses, and a few bushes. We played our games on its sandy center, and conducted such sports as ant fights and lizard hunts on its brushy perimeter. (pp. 139–140) ◄

Such unstructured activities are common in middle childhood and play an important role in development. Giving children time in which they are responsible for themselves, doing such things as getting across streets safely, not getting lost, organizing a game with friends, knowing which things are relatively safe to play at and which are not, and finding their way back home at the expected hour, is important in building independence and responsibility. In other words, continual and close supervision in middle childhood is not necessarily the best form of care.

Finding the right balance between adult supervision and expectations for responsible autonomy, however, is the trick for most parents. Children need time to be on their own. But they also need the structured support and emotional warmth that parents and other caregivers provide. How are these to be balanced, and what form does such a balance take? Brenda Bryant (1994) notes that this balance combines two forms of support. The first of these is having a caring adult either present or immediately accessible, not only as an emotional base but also to offer practical help in coping with immediate problems, such as minor accidents or emergencies. The second form of support comes from the way parents socialize children to be competent and autonomous when they are on their own. (The Research Focus, "Basic Versus Applied Research: After-School Activities," looks at issues of supervision and autonomy in various forms of after-school care.)

Baumrind's (1971, 1996) authoritative parenting (see Chapter 9), in which children are empowered through choices that are coupled with parental measures to ensure responsible decision making, illustrates the second form of support. The two defining dimensions running through authoritative parenting are warmth and demandingness, with the latter reflecting expectations for competent autonomy. Paradoxically, it is autonomy, and not dependence, that is fostered by parental warmth and acceptance. Parents who can accept their children's feelings, emotionally supporting their children, for instance, as they experience and talk about feelings, enable children to think through their feelings in more complex ways. This, in turn, enables children to solve their own problems more effectively.

How do children benefit from spending time in unstructured activities by themselves or with friends?

Parental warmth and acceptance during childhood fosters confidence and autonomy in children.

After-School Hours: Latchkey and Supervised Care

Not only summer vacation, but also after-school hours can include long stretches of unsupervised time for many children. Approximately 2½ million children spend a substantial amount of time after school without adult supervision (Cain & Hofferth, 1989). Most of these children get out of school at 3:00, with parents returning from work several hours later. In the absence of grandparents, older siblings, or other family members, these children spend the time alone or with friends. Children who have no adult to supervise them after school have been referred to as "latchkey" children.

Deborah Belle (1994), in reviewing research on latchkey children, notes that the single point that most clearly emerges from this research is the variability in children's responses to self-care. No single statement can be made, in other words, about the effects of self-care on children. It should be kept in mind that children experience unsupervised time in a variety of ways. Furthermore, children who spend part of the day looking after themselves are not necessarily left to fend for themselves. Many of these families appear to make good use of the community resources available to them while parents are at work. Thus, it has been found that children looking after themselves are almost twice as likely as those who are supervised to attend clubs after school, participate in sports, or have after-school lessons. Many also regularly spend time at friends' houses after school (Steinberg & Riley, 1991, as cited in Belle, 1994).

A number of the findings from such research are surprising. For instance, Vandell and Corasaniti (1988) compared the effects of self-care, home care with a mother present, home care with a sitter present, and care in after-school programs for third-graders. Using reports from the children, their parents, teachers, and friends, they found no differences on a variety of measures between self-care children and those supervised by their mothers. Unexpectedly, though, children who attended after-school centers or who were at home with a sitter were perceived more negatively by peers than were self-care children or those at home with their mothers. Those who attended centers also did more poorly academically. It is possible that the children who attended centers or were watched by a sitter differed

Basic Versus Applied Research:
After-School Activities

Tanesha had heard people talking about time stopping, always when they referred to something momentous in their lives. For her, time stopped 5 days a week, Monday through Friday, at the same time each day—40 minutes before school let out. That was when they started their last subject for the day, geography. "How could Mrs. Pfannen make this stuff so dull?" she wondered. She would have loved to go to most of the places they had studied. Just thinking about some of them made her happy. "Those islands, what were they called?" she wondered, as her eyes slid over the dirty snow caked outside her classroom window. The book had said the sand was as soft as silk. Imagine how it would feel, in between your toes, and the water as blue as flowers. She'd paint a beach today, she decided, and put herself in it, soon as she got to her after-school program. Tanesha, like most of her classmates, attended an after-school program at her elementary school.

How do most children spend their time each day once they leave school? Relatively little research exists in this area. That which does finds that boys and girls have somewhat different experiences. Boys are supervised less closely than girls their age and get about the neighborhood more. They also spend more of their time in sports and watching television. Girls spend somewhat more time doing homework than do boys and more time doing chores around the house (Posner & Vandell, 1999; Timmer, Eccles, & O'Brien, 1985).

The question of where and with whom children spend this time is of more than academic interest, in that increasing numbers of schoolchildren have parents whose work prevents them from being at home at the end of the school day. Jill Posner and

Deborah Vandell (1999) were interested in identifying which child and family factors were associated with the types of after-school activities children experience and in determining the developmental implications of these experiences. These investigators followed a group of urban third-graders growing up in Milwaukee for 2½ years, through the fourth and fifth grades, using telephone interviews to determine the types of activities in which they were engaged in their after-school hours.

These investigators had designed a program of applied research, aimed at answering pressing questions concerning after-school experiences. Research can be classified as either basic research or applied research. Those doing basic research are interested in getting answers to key questions concerning basic developmental processes. Frequently, these questions are generated by developmental theories and address general issues in development. Those doing applied research are interested in obtaining answers to specific, practical problems. Both types of research are important, and together they advance our understanding of development. The findings of basic research, for instance, frequently serve to direct and stimulate applied research questions. Applied research on the effects of day care, for example, has been guided by Mary Ainsworth's basic research on attachment (see Chapter 6). Similarly, findings from applied research often stimulate a closer examination of basic research findings. Most recently, legislators overseeing research-granting agencies have questioned the value of basic research and pressed for more socially relevant research. However, it is difficult to anticipate when findings about basic processes can be put to practical use. Skinner, for instance, devoted years to

initially in some way from the others, perhaps by being less mature. This difference may have been the reason parents felt they needed supervised care.

Fourth- and sixth-graders who looked after themselves also were found to feel just as good about themselves, in terms of self-worth and self-esteem, as other children (Berman, Winkleby, Chesterman, & Boyce, 1992). However, those who were looked after by older siblings suffered in this respect, feeling less competent than children who looked after themselves or those who were supervised by an adult. Once again, findings such as these may be unexpected, but make a certain sense, after the fact. Children, for instance, are frequently more severe with each other than are adults, both in their judgments of the acceptability of various behaviors and in the way they communicate these. Thus the care children receive from older siblings may be harsher than that from an adult. Children may also internalize reprimands differently, depending on whom these come from. Being told they have done something wrong by an older sibling, with whom they expect to share a similar outlook on many things, may cause children to doubt themselves more than would the very same words from an adult. Since children are less likely to expect to share the views of an adult than someone closer their age, they may be less apt to doubt their competence when reprimanded by an adult, even though told in much the same way.

programmatic research on operant conditioning with rats and pigeons for which there were no immediately practical uses. However, as we have seen in this chapter, a very real problem faced by a number of schoolchildren, bed-wetting, has been helped by the principles Skinner discovered in his basic research with laboratory animals (Cozby, 1997).

The research of Posner and Vandell identified four types of after-school arrangements. The first of these involved *formal programs*, such as an extended-school program (3 P.M. to 5 P.M.), sponsored by the school district, in which children could participate in two of three activities each day: academic ones such as computers or creative writing, recreational ones such as basketball or art, and tutorial ones such as help with homework. The other three arrangements were *informal neighbor or relative care, self-care,* and *parental care.* Children were contacted periodically during the course of the study to determine where they had spent their time after school, who else was present, and the kinds of activities in which they had engaged. Their answers were coded based on categories arrived at from previous research (see the Research Focus, "Coding," in Chapter 12). Since these investigators were interested in the developmental implications of after-school activities, they obtained measures of academic, social, and emotional adjustment as well.

With respect to the question "How do children spend their time after school?" they found gender differences in the types of activities children experienced. Girls spent more time in academic activities and socializing, and boys spent more time participating in coached sports. Boys also spent more time playing video games and watching television. Few family variables were found to be related to the types of activities in which children engaged, with the exception that White children from single-parent households had somewhat less supervision, spending more time outside in unstructured activities than did those from two-parent households. Age was also related to the types of activities children experienced. Between the third and fifth grades, the time spent in unstructured outside activities decreased by half, and the time spent socializing, such as just talking, doubled. In general, children who were in formal after-school programs spent more of their time doing academic and extracurricular types of things. Children who experienced informal care spent more time watching television and socializing.

These investigators also found an association between enrichment activities and adjustment in schoolchildren. Children who experienced more enrichment activities, whether participating in extracurricular activities or socializing with friends, benefited emotionally from these experiences. Among the African American children in this study, these activities were also found to be positively related to grades in school and work habits. White children's grades in school were also related to their after-school activities, with those spending more time in unstructured outside activities getting poorer grades. Unfortunately, perhaps, it looks as if the days in which children could freely wander about their neighborhoods, meeting friends and spending time by themselves without adult supervision, may be behind us—at least in many urban settings.

Findings such as these offer practical suggestions concerning after-school care, as one would expect from an applied research project. However, they also raise questions that can stimulate basic research, such as why seemingly similar after-school experiences were associated with different outcomes in African American children than in White children. In research, coming up with a good answer often means coming up with another question as well.

Once again, it is important to keep in mind that it is not simply what one person says to another, but the way one *hears* what the other has said that matters. The very same words that make for good-natured banter among friends could be heard as a stinging rebuke if spoken by someone else. In ordinary conversation, as in so many other aspects of our lives, we construct the events to which we respond, hearing what we expect to hear, given the context in which something has been said. In the short story "The Body," Stephen King (1998) illustrates the way the remarks of others can be given a meaning quite apart from any literal interpretation of the words that have been said. Listen to the rough banter of four friends, hanging out in a tree house and playing cards. Their tough talk serves to solidify their friendship, affirming that the tough image each projects is accepted by the others:

"So what are you pissing and moaning about, Vern-O?" Teddy asked.
"I knock," Chris said.
"What?" Teddy screamed, immediately forgetting all about Vern. "You friggin liar! You ain't got no pat hand. I didn't deal you no pat hand."
Chris smirked. "Make your draw, shitheap."
Teddy reached for the top card on the pile of Bikes. Chris reached for

the Winstons on the ledge behind him. I bent over to pick up my detective magazine.

Vern Tessio said: "You guys want to go see a dead body?"

Everybody stopped. (p. 299) ◄

These same epithets, said by anyone other than a close friend, would be heard as a challenge to their identity rather than an affirmation of the way they wanted to be seen by each other.

The time children spend with each other in unstructured play, whether in supervised or unsupervised settings contributes to their development in untold ways. Yet one of the findings to come out of research assessing the effects of different types of care was that children had relatively little time to spend with their friends after school (Belle, 1994). This was true for all children, irrespective of the type of after-school arrangements they had. Those who had activities after school, for instance, said their friends were likely to be in different activities. Similarly, those in self-care often said their friends' parents wouldn't let them visit other children unless one of the parents was at home.

Belle and her associates (1994) also found considerable variability in the amount of time children spent by themselves, without an adult present. Many of the children typically never experienced unsupervised care whereas others were left to care for themselves for several hours each day. Most of the children who were allowed to look after themselves were allowed to go out of the house and also to have friends over. These investigators also found a range of reactions among children experiencing self-care, from tremendously enjoying their independence to very much wanting a parent around. However, none of these measures showed differences in children's experience of social support, such as having someone to talk to when needed or simply receiving emotional support, among the various after-school arrangements. Thus, self-care children were just as likely to feel supported as were those in various forms of supervised care. Also, children's *dis*satisfaction with the types of support they experienced was not found to be a function of any of the various types of after-school care.

The satisfaction elementary school children experience in supervised programs should reflect many of the same variables found to be important in preschool programs. Robert Rosenthal and Deborah Vandell (1996) found this indeed to be so, with smaller student-staff ratios, smaller overall programs, and more highly trained staff improving the quality of after-school child care programs for elementary school children just as they do for preschool programs. These variables appear to contribute to the success of such programs by increasing their flexibility, something that becomes particularly important with elementary school children for whom most of the hours during the day have been tightly structured. The things children mentioned as most important for them in supervised after-school care were the sense of emotional support they received from staff; their experience of autonomy and privacy, such as in being able to do what they wanted when they were there, including being by themselves at times; and the chance to be with others their age. These three aspects of programs accounted for more than 55% of the variance in children's satisfaction with them.

Belle (1994) warns, however, that one cannot assume that what is experienced as supportive by one child will necessarily be experienced that way by another. As we saw earlier with respect to the dialogue among Stephen King's friends in the tree house, the meaning that one takes from what another says or does cannot be separated from the context in which this occurs. Thus, some children might feel supported by being placed in a small, friendly after-school child care program, whereas other children could feel undermined by having to be in such a pro-

What qualities should an after-school program have to make it attractive to grade school children?

Many school-age children participate in team sports after school where they learn the importance of fair play and teamwork as well as develop physical skills.

gram, taking it as a sign that they were not considered old enough or sufficiently responsible to look after themselves. Similarly, some children will feel affirmed by after-school self-care arrangements, taking this as a sign that their parents consider them to be trustworthy, and others might take the same arrangement as a sign that their parents are not involved in their lives or would rather be anywhere but with them.

Mentoring

An effective alternative to supervised after-school child care programs is to be found in mentoring programs. These programs involve children in one-on-one interactions with someone who is both older and wiser and, equally as important, who develops a caring relationship with them. Such programs have been found to be highly effective in promoting healthy development in at-risk children and adolescents (see the Research Focus, "Randomized Versus Quasi-Experimental Designs: What's in a Name? Communication Across the Ages"). Children with mentors not only develop healthier personal habits, but their schoolwork also improves, and they develop more positive attitudes toward life in general and their own futures in particular.

Getting Around the Neighborhood: Children as Pedestrians

Children increasingly move in a world of their own in middle childhood. Their lives are organized around school, not only the time they actually spend at school but also the time it takes getting there and back, the time they spend on homework, and, increasingly with age, the activities that take place there, such as pageants and plays, practices and recitals, and team sports. They spend these hours in their own society, away from home and parents, in the company of each other and of adults their parents know only by name. Many walk to and from school, further increasing the reach of their independence.

Randomized Versus Quasi-Experimental Designs: What's in a Name? Communication Across the Ages

Joey was beginning to like his name. He liked the soft way it sounded when Mrs. Thomas spoke to him, even though this was usually when they were talking about his homework. Funny, a year ago he would never have thought of doing homework. Or going to a museum with his class, or even to school basketball games. But he did now, and his mom did too, every now and then, when Mrs. Thomas called her. For that matter, a year ago he would never have thought he'd even know anyone as old as Mrs. Thomas. She must be at least 60, he thought, as he watched her coming into the room with a pencil and another piece of pie.

Joey lives in a low-income, high-crime neighborhood in Philadelphia. His sixth-grade class is part of an intergenerational mentoring program in which older members of the community, such as Mrs. Thomas, volunteer time with students, doing things such as helping with homework or school projects, going to games or cultural events, and taking part in community service activities. The purpose of the program is to increase the protective factors in the lives of high-risk children. By working with these students, mentors serve as friends and role models, as well as advocates and challengers, helping to build the self-esteem, confidence, and skills they need to stay drug-free.

In addition to mentoring, this unique program includes three additional components. It also involves students in community service, offers classroom-based instruction in life skills, and includes a workshop for parents. The community service aspect of the program enables these students to see how they can help others, giving them a sense of personal and social responsibility and contributing to their self-esteem. In contrast, instruction in real-life skills takes place in the classroom, teaching skills applicable to students' real-life problems within their families, with friends, and with peer pressure. Finally, the workshop for parents helps them develop more effective parenting skills and more positive ways of interacting within the family. Essential to the success of the program are the teachers and school personnel who have been trained in its implementation and evaluation.

Programs like this are expensive—not only in money, but also in a community's investment of its limited reserves of passion and hope. How might one determine whether an intergenerational mentoring program such as this is effective? Leonard LoSciuto, Amy Rajala, Tara Townsend, and Andrea Taylor (1996), at Temple University, employed a *randomized pretest-posttest control group design*. Three sixth-grade classes per school were randomly selected from all of the sixth-grade classes in schools that were willing to participate in the study (almost all of them). Within each school, each class was randomly assigned to one of three conditions:

1. Students received the complete program of mentoring, community service, instruction in life skills, and parent workshops.
2. Students received everything but mentoring.
3. Students received no intervention at all. They were the control condition.

At the beginning of the academic year, prior to beginning the intervention program, students were pretested on a variety of measures assessing their knowledge, attitudes, and behavior related to the program goals. All students were tested again, with a series of posttests, at the end of the academic year. This type of design, because it employs random assignment of subjects to conditions and the use of a separate control comparison (see the Research Focus, "An Experiment," in Chapter 1), in addition to comparing pretest with posttest performance, has high internal validity (see the Research Focus, "Internal and External Validity," in Chapter 14), enabling the investigators to conclude that the changes they observe are actually due to the program and not to some other factor.

Because the students are randomly assigned to conditions, and each student has the same chance as any other of being assigned to each group, one can be reasonably certain that individuals in the three groups do not differ in any systematic way at the outset of the program. Additionally, pretesting students before they begin the intervention program makes it possible to determine whether equivalence has, in fact, been achieved.

This independence, for the most part, is rightfully earned. Children become increasingly knowledgeable concerning their surroundings and rapidly improve in their judgment concerning what is likely to be safe or unsafe in these years. Their very improvement, however, means that the youngest among them are likely to make more than their share of poor decisions. Some of these decisions carry a fair degree of risk. Children are 4 times more likely than adults, for instance, to be injured as pedestrians. Given that they are less likely than adults to be near traffic, this difference has developmental significance. Children younger than 9,

Pretesting offers other advantages as well. Pretests allow investigators to assess the extent to which individuals *change* over time. Thus, if some students are responsive to the treatment, whereas others are not, pretesting may suggest clues that can be followed up in subsequent research as to why some are more responsive than others. Pretesting is also useful when subjects drop out of the program, as is likely with lengthy programs. Loss of subjects in this manner is known as *subject mortality* and is a potential source of bias if it is systematically related to the experimental conditions. For instance, poorer students might be least responsive to the demands of mentoring and community service and most likely to drop out, leaving proportionately more of the better students in the intervention group. In this way, even interventions that have no effect might appear to result in improved performance. By inspecting the pretests of students who drop out, however, one can determine whether these subjects differed from the ones who remained in the program. Pretesting has its disadvantages as well. One potential disadvantage is that it can *sensitize* subjects to the purpose of the investigation, making it possible for them to figure out what is expected of them and potentially affecting the way they respond to the experimental treatment.

Many intervention programs are not able to randomly assign subjects to experimental and control conditions. Research that relies only on comparisons of pretest and posttest performance is termed *quasi-experimental.* A number of problems exist with quasi-experimental designs. Because there is no control condition, we don't know how to interpret the findings. Suppose, for instance, one finds that posttest scores are no better than pretest scores. Can we conclude that the program is ineffective? Not necessarily. It's always possible that performance could have declined during that time, and that only because of the program did scores remain the same. Similarly, increases in performance on the posttest do not lend themselves to a simple interpretation. Several potential *confounds* exist. These can be due to maturation, testing, history, instrument decay, or statistical regression.

Maturation reflects any systematic changes that occur over time. These can be long-term, such as the developmental changes in intelligence discussed in Chapters 4 and 10, or short-term, such as changes due to fatigue, boredom, or practice. *Testing* reflects any changes that might occur due to familiarity with the tests. Since pretests usually involve the same type of question as posttests and frequently measure knowledge about the same subject matter, testing effects are likely. *History* refers to events that occur during the time between testings that can affect the behavior being measured. Television might run a series of public service spots featuring famous athletes who warn kids against the use of drugs at the same time as the intervention program. *Instrument decay* reflects changes in the instruments being used to make measurements. Such changes are especially likely when the instruments are people themselves, whose judgments of various behaviors provide the measures that are being recorded; we might expect people to become more practiced over time or in other ways to have their standards change.

Statistical regression can occur when students are selected for a program because they are atypical, because their scores are either especially low or high. When they are retested, as they are on the posttest, most scores will change somewhat simply because the two tests are not perfectly correlated (no two tests ever are). Students who are selected because of especially low scores will look like they have improved due to the program. In actuality, because they were at the bottom of the distribution, their scores could *only* go up. Of course, by the same token, students with especially high scores on a pretest would show a drop in performance on the posttest. In each case, scores "drift" or regress toward the mean of the distribution, since that is where most scores are to be found.

None of these confounds, however, threaten the validity of LoSciuto's research. What, then, can we say about the effectiveness of this intervention program? These investigators found that students who received all four components of the program were likely to do best. They were more likely to react appropriately when they were offered drugs; were absent from school less; and had more positive attitudes toward school, community service, and their own futures. There is also some indication that mentoring resulted in increased feelings of self-worth and well-being and reduced sadness and loneliness.

for instance, are not good at identifying which places are safe when crossing the road. As long as there isn't a car in sight, they assume that one place is as safe as another, irrespective of whether they are standing at the brow of a hill or at a bend in the road (Ampofo-Boateng et al., 1993).

When grade school children were taken to a number of intersections and asked to point to the route they would follow in crossing them, most of the 5-year-olds indicated ways to cross that were either very dangerous or moderately so. Seven-year-olds were better, but were still likely to choose an unsafe route

At what age can children usually be trusted to cross streets safely?

FIGURE 10.1 Percentage of Routes Falling into Safe and Unsafe Categories by Age *Source:* K. Ampofo-Boteng, J. A. Thompson, R. Grieve, T. Pitcairns, D. N. Lee, and J. D. Demetre. "A developmental and training study of children's ability to find safe routes to cross the road," *British Journal of Developmental Psychology*, March 1993, Vol. II, Part I, pp. 31–46.

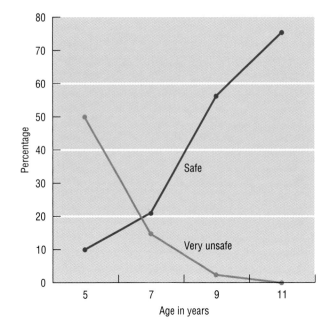

FIGURE 10.2 Sample Routes from Very Unsafe (1) to Safe (4)

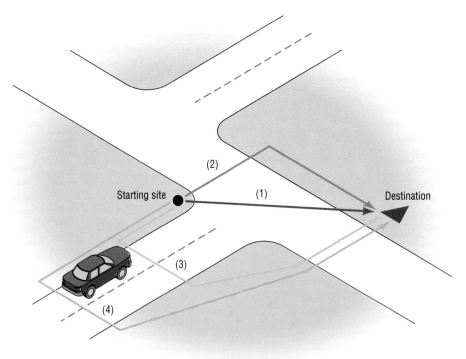

across a complicated intersection. Only 9- and 10-year-olds were likely to choose a safe route across (Ampofo-Boateng et al., 1993). Figure 10.1 shows the results of this experiment.

It should be pointed out that these were familiar crossings to all of the children, since the intersections were within walking distance from their schools. Even so, the younger children were not aware of the dangers present in these situations, such as trying to cross an intersection where traffic comes from several different directions, as shown in Figure 10.2. In fact, many of the 5-year-olds indicated the

Walking home from school with friends can give children a sense of independence. However, younger children have difficulty knowing when or where it's safe to cross the road.

best way to cross such an intersection would be to walk directly to the other side, which would require walking *diagonally* across the intersection. Selection of a safer route would have meant adopting a strategy that would take them away from where they wanted to go, a difficult solution for the youngest children to envision. Although 7-year-olds realized the dangers of such a solution, they were still unaware of other dangers, such as crossing between parked cars. Even when they did realize the dangers and suggested moving to a new place to cross, they frequently chose one equally as dangerous (Ampofo-Boateng et al., 1993).

New Responsibilities

Barbara Rogoff (1996) notes that in most cultures children between the ages of 5 and 7 are entrusted with increasing responsibilities. Not only are they expected to do such things as care for younger children, tend animals, or do chores around the house, they are also expected to act in more adultlike ways, to be well-mannered, for instance, or to remember to do the things they have been told to do. We expect this of them not simply because we believe they have better social skills or better memories than younger children, but because we assume they share with adults an understanding for *why* certain things are important.

Rogoff argues that the behaviors one sees developing in children at this age are not solely, or even primarily, a function of developments occurring within the children themselves, but result as much from the expectations of their communities for different types of behavior. She points out that in the United States, for instance, we expect that children cannot handle sharp knives until at least the age

The skilled behaviors that young children develop depend as much on the expectations of their community as on their own physical and cognitive development.

of 5 without seriously endangering themselves. However, Efe toddlers living in Zaire are able to use a machete by themselves to cut fruit, without injuring themselves, and Fore infants in New Guinea are trusted to handle knives by the time they can walk and do so carefully (Rogoff, 1996). Similarly, Asian children (Miller, Wiley, Fung, & Liang, 1997) are expected to act with sufficient restraint for the family to keep fragile objects around without fear of their being broken or damaged.

Rogoff points out that the adults in these communities are not being irresponsible, as some might assume, by allowing young children to handle sharp implements or by leaving precious but delicate objects about the house. Rather, they are providing children with the skills they will need in their culture. Such provisions, however, cannot be imported in any simple way from one culture to the next. Fragile objects can be left in their places, for instance, because Asian children are socialized in ways that make them at least as attuned, if not more so, to the needs and desires of others (seeing a delicate vase on a table) than to their own needs (picking it up). Rogoff notes that these very same parents would view many of the things North American children are allowed to do as equally dangerous for their age, such as sleeping by themselves or growing up in isolated nuclear families, removed from grandparents, aunts, and uncles.

Rogoff suggests that rather than attempting to chart development in terms of which behaviors can first be seen to occur at any age, researchers look at the activities in which children already participate, focusing on how their roles in these activities change with age. These activities include not just the child, but also those with whom the child is interacting, the materials they are working with, and the traditions that guide what they are doing. Rogoff speaks of this participation as either *guided participation,* when focusing on the interpersonal aspect of the activity, or as *participatory appropriation,* when focusing on the individual. The concept of participation makes explicit the notion that the activity involves others and that children do not develop in isolation from those around them or apart from the cultural traditions that give their roles meaning.

One such role, which shows clear developmental changes during middle childhood, is that of doing chores. Six- or seven-year-olds, for instance, are expected to help with things when they are asked to. By the age of 7, for instance, 63% of a large urban sample of low-socioeconomic-status children reported that they regularly performed several household chores, such as dusting or vacuuming, running errands, and babysitting (Entwisle, Alexander, Olson, & Ross, 1999). These investigators found that the number of chores increased substantially with age. Furthermore, older children are expected to carry out tasks on their own, without having to be asked.

By about the age of 9, clear gender patterns exist in children's chores, with girls' chores more frequently involving work inside the house and those of boys involving work outside the house. Thus, over 80% of boys versus 50% of girls report having to take the trash out (Entwisle et al., 1999). And by 9 or 10, they are expected to carry out tasks on their own, without having to be asked. In *Gryphon* (1999), Charles Baxter gives us a picture of a young boy at the first of these stages, as he arrives home from school after another day with a substitute teacher:

> I kissed my mother. She was standing in front of the stove. "How was your day?" she asked.
>
> "Fine."
>
> "Did you have Miss Ferenczi again?"
>
> "Yeah."
>
> "Well?"
>
> "She was fine, Mom." I asked, "Can I go to my room?"
>
> "No," she said, "not until you've gone out to the vegetable garden and picked me a few tomatoes." She glanced at the sky. "I think it's going to rain. Skedaddle and do it now. Then you come back inside and watch your brother." . . .
>
> "Do you feel all right?"
>
> "I'm fine," I said, and went out to pick the tomatoes. (p. 918) ◄

Attitudes toward work and leisure show surprising continuity through large segments of the life span. Many of the attitudes adults hold toward work, for instance, can first be seen by the time children enter adolescence. Adults who are asked to report how they feel about what they are doing while they are working are likely to indicate they would rather be doing something else. Yet these same individuals acknowledge that work, more than leisure, contributes significantly to their sense of self and frequently is more deeply satisfying (Csikszentmihalyi, 1997).

In a similar fashion, 10- and 11-year-olds report activities they label as work as being less pleasurable than those they label as play, even though they acknowledge that the former more frequently contribute to feelings of high self-esteem. Adolescents as well, when asked to indicate how they feel while they are working, report they are less happy than if doing something else even though their feelings of self-esteem are higher when they are working than at other times, and they are likely to regard what they are doing as important (Csikszentmihalyi, 1997).

Physical Growth

By the age of 6, children stand about 3½ feet tall and weigh about 45 to 50 pounds. Growth is steady in middle childhood, though slower than in early childhood, with children adding between 2 to 3 inches in height each year and gaining

The pattern of growth changes in middle childhood. The school-age child on the left has longer legs relative to the rest of her body and a slimmer look than does the preschooler.

Q The lower part of the body grows faster during middle childhood than it did in early childhood. How might this change in physical growth affect children's activities?

secular trends The differences in size, both in height and in weight, that occur from one generation to the next.

approximately 5 pounds in weight. Even though the numbers of inches and pounds they add are about the same as those gained by preschoolers, the increases in height and weight are *proportionately* less given the relative difference in their sizes. Thus, the rate of growth slows in middle childhood (Hagerman, 1999).

The pattern of growth also changes. The lower part of the body grows faster during middle childhood, whereas in early childhood, the upper body grew at a faster rate. As a consequence, school-age children have longer legs relative to the rest of their bodies and a slimmer look than do preschoolers. This pattern of growth is a continuation of the cephalocaudal trend evidenced earlier in development, in which skeletal growth proceeds downward from the region of the head.

Smooth growth curves such as those appearing in Figure 10.3 can be deceptive, because they suggest that growth occurs evenly over time. When frequent measurements are taken at regular intervals, however, growth is found to occur in spurts, each spurt separated by longer periods in which growth is much slower. On average, these spurts in growth occur at the ages of 6½, 8½, and 10 years in girls, and approximately half a year later, at 7, 9, and 10½ in boys (Butler, McKie, & Ratcliffe, 1990; Johnson, Veldhuis, & Lampl, 1996). Similar research in which measurements of an adolescent's height were taken on a nearly daily basis over a year's time also found evidence of growth spurts rather than gradual increases (Lampl & Johnson, 1993).

Considerable variability in growth exists not only from one time to the next in any given child, but also from one child to the next. Differences in height and weight between any two classmates, in fact, can be as great as those between children separated in age by as much as 4 years. Individual differences such as these tend to increase with age throughout middle childhood, especially with respect to weight (Hagerman, 1999).

Gender differences in height and weight remain insignificant in middle childhood. In fact, it is frequently difficult to distinguish one sex from the other at a distance, given similar forms of dress and the length of their hair. Girls' shoulders are just as wide as boys', and boys' hips are no slimmer than girls'. Nor does size differ appreciably, although boys have a slight edge in height. However, even this changes midway through the school years. After the age of 9, girls are slightly taller than boys, as the early hormonal changes accompanying puberty affect their rate of growth. On average, girls will begin puberty 2 years earlier than boys (Mitchell, 1990).

Because the lower portion of the body is growing faster, children's center of gravity changes as well, moving downward. This change enables them to maintain their balance better when actively moving about, and having longer legs means they can run faster. They also have increased strength and endurance. Lung capacity increases in middle childhood, and muscles are stronger. In all, children are longer-limbed, better coordinated, faster, and stronger than they were before.

As a group, children today are somewhat taller than they were generations ago. Differences in size from one generation to the next are referred to as **secular trends** in growth. Recently, there have also been secular increases in weight. The number of children who are overweight, or are in the 85th percentile of weight for their height, has approximately doubled in the last 25 years (Freedman, Srinivasan, Valdez, Williamson, & Berenson, 1997). This increase is most noticeable among older children, those approaching or already in adolescence; however, a similar trend has been observed among 4- and 5-year-olds. Although there are no gender differences in obesity among older children, among 4- and 5-year-olds, obesity is more prevalent among girls (Freedman et al., 1997). Because this trend has occurred over such a relatively short period of time, it most likely is the result of environmental factors, such as diet or physical activity, rather than genetic ones.

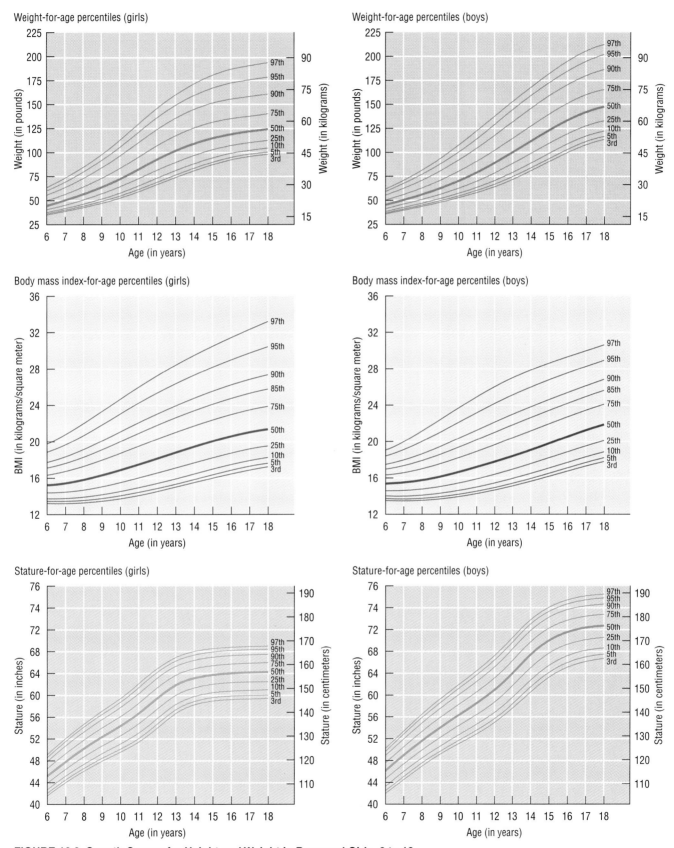

FIGURE 10.3 Growth Curves for Height and Weight in Boys and Girls, 6 to 18

One of the most obvious aspects of physical development in middle childhood is increased coordination.

Skilled Behavior

With each year, children become more accomplished at various activities that require motor skills—such as running, jumping, and maintaining their balance while moving. Stamina and strength also increase year by year, enabling school-children to play actively for longer periods of time without tiring. One of the more obvious aspects of physical development is the increased coordination one sees, both in tasks involving fine motor skills, such as handwriting or drawing, and in those involving larger muscle groups, such as running, biking, skipping rope, and playing ball.

Fine Motor Skills

Children's control over small body movements, such as those involving the fingers and hands, increases steadily in middle childhood. One sees this control not only in the way they hold a pencil or cut with scissors (Figure 10.4) but also in other activities requiring manual dexterity, such as fitting together the pieces of model airplanes and ships, outfitting Barbie, and mastering the fingering on a musical instrument (Pehoski, Henderson, & Tickle-Degnen, 1996, 1997). Most children can print all the letters of the alphabet by the first grade, but find uppercase letters easier than lowercase ones, since the former involve more straight lines and fewer curves. Cursive writing, for the same reason, is more difficult than printing, and children usually do not master this until the third grade. Also, as their motor skills improve, their lettering becomes smaller and more regular.

Gross Motor Skills

Our house is at the end of the road at the top of a slight hill, and children in the neighborhood congregate in the turnaround to play. One day there were several groups, one kicking a soccer ball around and another, older group on skateboards.

Palmar-supinate
1–2 yrs

Pencil or crayon is held by fisted hand; forearm slightly supinated; wrist slightly flexed; shoulder motion produces movement of pencil.

Digital-pronate
2–3 yrs

Pencil or crayon is held by fingers and thumb; forearm pronated; wrist ulnarly deviated; pencil controlled by shoulder movement.

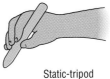

Static-tripod
3+ yrs

Pencil held proximally between thumb and radial two fingers; minimal wrist mobility; pencil controlled by shoulder movement.

Dynamic-tripod
4+ yrs

Pencil is held distally through thumb opposition to the index and long fingers, with the ring and small fingers stabilizing in flexion; small movements at the metacarpophalangeal and interphalangeal joints control the pencil; stabilization occurs at the shoulder, elbow, forearm, and wrist.

FIGURE 10.4 Changes with Age in the Way Children Hold a Pencil
Source: A. F. Vansant. (1995). "Development of posture," Functional Movement Across the Life Span by D. Cech and S. Martin, pp. 275–294.

A 5-year-old had just taken his second swinging kick before connecting with the ball, which looped sideways to his 7-year-old sister, who deftly sent it spinning to her right by catching the ball with the side of one foot, never breaking the gait in her run. One of the 11-year-olds on a skateboard, violating all the rules of soccer, scooped the ball up in his hands while leaning low over the side of his board, and flipped it back to the 5-year-old, maintaining perfect balance throughout. Such incidental displays of grace illustrate the increasing coordination and skill evidenced by children as they age. Their hand-eye coordination improves steadily, as does their agility and balance, enabling them to catch balls on the run, place a well-directed kick at a soccer ball, or maintain their balance while leaning over their center of gravity on a moving skateboard.

Certainly, practice at these various skills leads to improvements with age; however, continuing maturation of the brain is also responsible.

Brain Maturation

In terms of size, brain growth is largely completed in the school years. By the age of 9, for instance, the brain has reached 95% of its adult size. This growth is characterized by two interrelated processes, cell proliferation and cell pruning. **Cell proliferation** consists of the overproduction of both neurons and their interconnections, whereas **cell pruning** involves the selective elimination of excess cells and the cutting back of connections. These complementary processes carry a distinct biological advantage, enabling neural development to be "fine-tuned" by experience. Cell proliferation enables the organism to remain maximally open to experience, with those interconnections that are frequently used being retained and those infrequently used being pruned, or eliminated. Thus, early experiences contribute to the architecture of neuronal connections (Thatcher, 1997).

Each of these growth processes follows a different time course. Cell proliferation takes place through the first several years of life, whereas cell pruning continues, ever more slowly, throughout childhood (Caviness, Kennedy, Bates, & Makris, 1997). Interconnections between neurons, however, increase through middle childhood. This increase occurs with the continued growth of those parts of the neuron that enable it to communicate with other cells. Thus, one sees an increase in the number of tiny filaments, or dendrites, that branch out from the nerve body and receive impulses from neighboring neurons. One also sees growth in the length of the axon leading out from the cell body to other nerve cells, and

cell proliferation A brain growth process that consists of the overproduction of both neurons and their interconnections.

cell pruning A brain growth process that consists of the selective elimination of excess cells and the cutting back of connections.

FIGURE 10.5 Structure of a Neuron, Showing the Dendrites, Cell Body, Axon, and Myelin Sheath

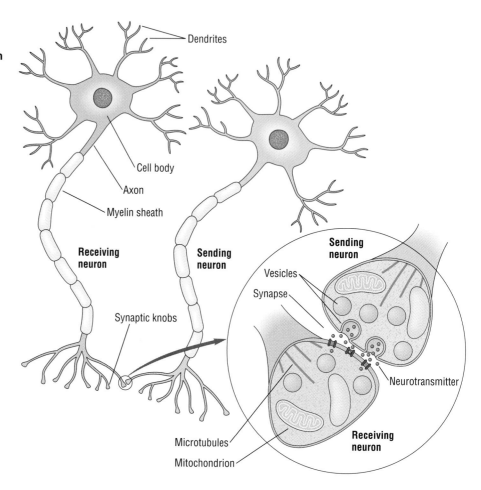

in the development of a fatty sheath, known as myelin, along the length of the axon. Both dendritic branching and the length of the axon affect the number of synapses, or connections, one cell makes with another, whereas myelination, which also continues throughout middle childhood, enables neurons to conduct impulses more rapidly (Eden & Zeffiro, 1997; Figure 10.5).

The brain's metabolism changes markedly at different ages throughout childhood, presumably reflecting the differing energy demands of these growth processes. Harry Chugani (1997), at Wayne State University School of Medicine, used positron emission tomography (PET) to study the rate of metabolism of glucose, the primary energy source for neural activity. Chugani found that between the ages of 4 and 10, the rate at which glucose is metabolized is more than double that of adults in certain areas of the brain, such as the frontal lobes. The number of synapses, or interconnections of one cell with another, for instance, is greater in the frontal cortex of children through middle childhood than in adults (Chugani, 1997; Eden & Zeffiro, 1997).

Changes in the brain's energy needs, or metabolism of glucose, are also indicative of the degree of neural plasticity that exists within the brain, with peaks in metabolism coinciding with maximum plasticity. **Plasticity** refers to the degree to which one area of the brain can assume the functions governed by another area following injury to the latter. Plasticity is greatest during the phase of overproduction of neural connections and diminishes with the occurrence of cell pruning, in which these are cut back, declining at about the age of 8 to 10. This is also the

plasticity The degree to which one area of the brain can assume the functions governed by another area following injury to the latter.

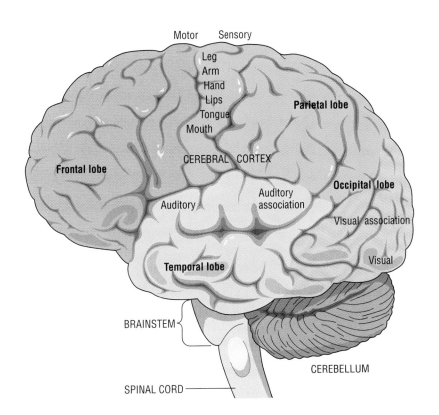

FIGURE 10.6 A Schematic Drawing of the Brain

age at which overall rates of metabolism of glucose decline (Chugani, 1997). Paralleling a decrease in plasticity is the progressive **lateralization** of the brain, in which the two halves of the cortex become increasingly specialized for different functions. The left hemisphere is more involved in analytical and sequential tasks and the right in holistic and integrative ones.

The frontal lobes (Figure 10.6) also undergo development during middle childhood (Luciana & Nelson, 1998). These play an important role in attention, planning, and self-awareness. They do so through their role in integrating the activities of other areas within the brain. For such integration to be possible, however, connections must be established between the frontal lobes and these other areas (Case, 1992).

Robert Thatcher (1994, 1997), using data obtained through neuroimaging techniques with individuals ranging in age from infancy through early adulthood, has found evidence for the progressive establishment of such connections during middle childhood. Thatcher found that, initially, connections appear to be established across relatively short distances, between the frontal lobes and other areas of the brain. Later, connections are formed across longer distances. The cognitive correlate to these changes is an increase in the flexibility of thought, enabling children to do such things as hold more things in mind at once and to shift their attention from one aspect of a problem to another, rather than perseverating in outworn strategies. The short-distance connections appear to create new functional units which, together with the establishment of longer-distance connections among these, increases the flexibility in the executive functioning of the frontal lobes. Figure 10.7 shows the correspondence between Thatcher's measures of cortical activity and performance on various tasks assessing attentional capacity. See the Social Policy Focus, "'D' Is for Disorder: Medicating Young Children," for a discussion of medicating young children who have problems with attention.

lateralization The process of specialization of the two halves of the cortex.

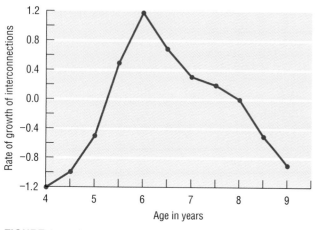

FIGURE 10.7 Correspondence Between Attentional Capacity and the Establishment of Interconnections Linking the Frontal Lobes with Other Cortical Areas *Source:* From "The role of the frontal lobes in the regulation of cognitive development," *Brain and Cognition,* Vol. 20, 51–73 (1992) by R. Case.

What bedtime fears might cause children to feel that they are not as old as they would like to see themselves?

Developmental Asynchronies

Continued growth and maturation enable children to function in ever more competent and adultlike ways throughout middle childhood. Development, however, rarely follows a smooth course, and growth in one area is not necessarily paralleled by comparable mastery in others. The resulting disparities, or asynchronies in development, can occasionally throw children off balance, leaving them to feel quite grown up in certain respects and a child in others. Growing up is a relative term, of course, and the child one was at earlier points in life remains somewhere still inside at any age. Sandra Cisneros (1993) captures this understanding in *Woman Hollering Creek,* as she describes the thoughts of a young girl who has just turned 11:

> What they don't understand about birthdays and what they never tell you is that when you're eleven, you're also ten, and nine, and eight, and seven, and six, and five, and four, and three, and two, and one. And when you wake up on your eleventh birthday you expect to feel eleven, but you don't. You open your eyes and everything's just like yesterday, only it's today. And you don't feel eleven at all. You feel like you're still ten. And you are—underneath the year that makes you eleven.
>
> Like some days you might say something stupid, and that's the part of you that's still ten. Or maybe some days you might need to sit on your mama's lap because you're scared, and that's the part of you that's five. . . .
>
> Because the way you grow old is kind of like an onion or like the rings inside a tree trunk or like my little wooden dolls that fit one inside the other, each year inside the next one. That's how being eleven years old is. ◄

Nowhere are the discrepancies of middle childhood more obvious for some children than when it comes to bedtime. Sleep-related problems can take a number of forms. Perhaps the most obvious is simply a child's resistance to going to bed. Other problems, however, involve difficulty falling asleep, fear of the dark, waking in the night, nightmares, enuresis, and sleepwalking.

The most common complaint of parents during these years is children's resistance to going to bed. Over a quarter of parents surveyed in one study reported this difficulty (Blader, Koplewicz, Abikoff, & Foley, 1997). Although most children who resist going to bed appear to do so for behavioral reasons—that is, reasons that are related to the establishment of bedtime routines—a smaller percentage appear to do so because of other problems, such as having difficulty falling asleep,

"D" Is for "Disorder": Medicating Young Children

BY MICHAEL WAPNER

There have always been children who are more easily distracted than their age-mates, who are less able or willing to concentrate on what they are not interested in, who are restless and fidget when they must sit still, who are disorganized, who overlook details, who speak out of turn, who interrupt. How well these children fare depends on the severity of these problems, on whether they have compensating talents, and on how forgiving the environment is. Frequently they do poorly in school and are difficult for their families and friends. They may also be quite unhappy.

Although there have always been such children, today such a child is likely to be diagnosed as having a specific disorder and given a form of medication that is closely related to amphetamine and cocaine. The diagnosis is Attention-Deficit Disorder (ADD) or Attention-Deficit Hyperactivity Disorder (ADHD). The medication is Ritalin.

Twenty-five years ago no one had ever heard of ADD or ADHD. Now it is the most commonly diagnosed behavioral disorder among American children, afflicting about 3½ million youngsters, or about 5% of those under 18 (Cantwell, 1996). Twenty years ago most authorities believed the disorder disappeared after adolescence. Now they estimate that two thirds of childhood cases persist through adulthood. Fifteen years ago prescribing stimulant medication such as Ritalin to elementary school children was considered very aggressive treatment. Now Ritalin and other stimulants are routinely prescribed for school-children and even for as many as 150,000 children between the ages of 2 and 4 (Zito et al., 2000).

Not all the experts are in agreement that these children suffer from an actual disorder that requires medication. David Keirsey (1999), a psychologist, argues

> There's nothing wrong with these children. Their inborn temperament prevents these concrete, fun loving and impulsive children from adapting to the school. Some day, in the not so distant future the school may come to realize that not all children can be scheduled and routinized, that children, like adults, are fundamentally different in this regard. Perhaps then the school might adapt itself to those children that do not fit its curriculum or its methods of instruction.

There are several reasons that some experts doubt that what is called ADD or ADHD is a form of illness. For one thing, the symptoms of ADD (distractibility, impulsiveness) and ADHD (ADD plus fidgetiness) are commonly found, although perhaps to a lesser degree, among many children, particularly boys. Second, individuals with ADD are often quite able to pay attention if the task is one that particularly interests them. Third, although many causes have been suggested (genetic "error," prenatal injury, neurotransmitter imbalance, brain damage, developmen-

tal deficit), no underlying pathology has yet been discovered. Thus, the diagnosis of ADD and ADHD is often ambiguous, depending on identifying a minimum number of symptoms of sufficient seriousness. Also adding to skepticism among the experts is the suspicion that secondary, nonmedical factors may enter into this diagnosis. Among these are the following. If ADD is an illness, then (1) parents may be spared the responsibility for their child's "bad behavior," (2) teachers needn't blame themselves for being unable to maintain interest and order in the classroom, (3) physicians can prescribe psychoactive drugs without worrying that they are using medication to change personality, (4) all involved can seek help in a pill, (5) pharmaceutical companies may market their drugs as appropriate for these "illnesses," (6) doctors can be reimbursed by insurance companies, (7) sufferers can receive special help and benefits under laws protecting children with disabilities (McHugh, 1999).

As already mentioned, some of the skeptics argue that children diagnosed with ADD and ADHD really have the types of personality that happen not to function well in the regimented contexts of schools and offices. Some writers speak of ADD as characteristic of a hunter's mentality (Hartmann, 1995), sometimes as a metaphor and sometimes actually suggesting that shifting attention, responsiveness to small changes in the environment, and the tendency to act without long consideration all reflect true evolutionary adaptations to a time and place where humans hunted and gathered to live. It is, of course, recognized that what is adaptive in one environment may become a liability in another. Sickle-cell anemia, for instance, protects the bearer from malaria. But where malaria is not a problem, sickle-cell anemia is a painful, debilitating handicap with no redeeming value.

Suppose it is true that what psychologists call ADD and ADHD are more appropriately considered a type of personality or an adaptation to an obsolete way of life. What does that signify for the treatment of children who do not fit into the structure of current public schools and the demands of contemporary adult life? Does it preclude treatment as an illness, including treatment with medication? After all, children who do not "fit" the schools they must attend will suffer frustration and feelings of failure and inadequacy whatever the cause, unless something is done. Of course, given adequate funds and sufficient motivation, some schools might be redesigned to better serve the temperament of these modern young hunters. And perhaps society can benefit from their particular kind of energy and quirky vigilance. Some say that the disorganized Benjamin Franklin and the impulsive Winston Churchill, had they been children in a contemporary school, might well have been diagnosed as having ADD. On the other hand, under current circumstances, it may be necessary to ameliorate the personal suffering and the classroom disruption of impulsive, inattentive, out-of-control youngsters even if, strictly speaking, they are not ill.

Sleep-related problems are common in middle childhood, including resistance to going to bed, difficulty falling asleep, or staying asleep.

having fears, and waking during the night. Approximately 10% of the children in one study experienced difficulty falling asleep, with over half taking from half an hour to an hour to fall asleep. The number of children who woke in the night was considerably less, 6.5%, but given that half of these children had difficulty falling back to sleep in less than an hour, with another quarter taking from 1 to 2 hours, the problem can be serious (Blader et al., 1997).

In *An American Childhood*, Annie Dillard (1987) describes her unwillingness as a child to go to bed because she believed something came into her room at night. She describes it as taking the form of a light that flattened itself against the open door to her room and slid in:

> I could see the blue wall turn pale where it raced over it, and see the maple headboard of Amy's bed glow. . . . Every night before it got to me it gave up. It hit my wall's corner and couldn't get past. It shrank completely into itself and vanished like a cobra down a hole. I heard the rising roar it made when it died or left. I still couldn't breathe. I knew . . . that it could return again alive that same night. (p. 21)

She soon realized that the phantom light was cast by the headlights of passing cars, distorted by the panes in her window and her imagination. But knowing this did not immediately prevent her from responding emotionally to the movement of what appeared to be a visible presence in her room. She describes overcoming her fear through reason: "I could be connected to the outer world by reason, if I chose, or I could yield to what amounted to a narrative fiction, to a tale of terror whispered to me by the blood in my ears, a show in light projected on the room's blue walls. As time passed, I learned to amuse myself in bed in the darkened room by entering the fiction deliberately and replacing it by reason deliberately" (pp. 22–23). ◄

Some sleep-related problems, however, do not yield to reason. Enuresis is one of these. **Enuresis,** or bed-wetting, is a relatively common problem in middle childhood, affecting as many as 10% of 7-year-olds and even higher percentages of younger children (Gontard, Eiberg, Hollmann, Rittig, & Lehmkuhl, 1998). Children are considered to be enuretic if, by the age of 5 or older, they continue to wet the bed several or more times a month.

enuresis Bed-wetting.

Enuresis has a strong genetic component. The presence of the disorder in children has been linked to sites along three different chromosomes (Gontard et al., 1998). Not surprisingly, 75% of enuretic children have a close relative who was also enuretic (American Psychiatric Association [APA], 1985). It has been found that children who are enuretic produce less of an antidiuretic hormone, known as ADH, when they sleep. Normally, levels of ADH increase during sleep. The presence of this hormone decreases the production of urine, thus preventing the bladder from filling while one sleeps (Nørgaard, Pedersen, & Djurhuus, 1985).

It may also be the case that enuretic children find it more difficult to wake to the sensation of a full bladder. Approximately the same number of children as those who are enuretic wake during the night to go to the bathroom. Both may share a common problem of producing too much urine; however, only the latter fail to wake in time. A common treatment for enuresis, in fact, is organized around getting children to wake up to the sensations produced by a full bladder (Hjälmas, 1998).

Rather than thinking of enuresis as symptomatic of psychological problems, it is more accurate to think of it as a sleep-related disorder that has a strong physical base and is the *cause* of psychological problems, especially those related to self-esteem. While enuresis persists, it is a source of shame to most children and can erode their self-esteem. As soon as the problem is corrected, self-esteem has been found to improve (Gontard et al., 1998; Hjälmas, 1998).

Most families, however, do not seek treatment for this problem. Furthermore, many of those who do are told by their doctors that their children will "grow out of it" (Dobson, 1989). It is true that enuresis decreases with age; approximately 15% to 20% of 5-year-olds experience this problem, whereas 10% of 7-year-olds, and even fewer (5%) 10-year-olds are affected. However, these percentages are sizable, given that most children who are enuretic experience shame and embarrassment and that enuresis is a highly treatable disorder (Bath, 1998; Gontard et al., 1998; Skoog, 1998).

Treatment can take a number of forms. Those that are most frequently prescribed by physicians are pharmacological, involving the use of various drugs (Skoog, 1998). Although these have been shown to be effective, they have a higher relapse rate than do nonpharmacological procedures involving behavior modification. The latter are directed toward getting children to wake up when they experience a full bladder, rather than chemically controlling the amount of urine produced (Hjälmas, 1998). These procedures are based on classical conditioning (see Chapter 1), using an alarm system that goes off when the child first starts to wet the bed. A special pad, attached to an alarm, is placed under the sheet. Any moisture on the pad completes a circuit and causes the alarm to go off. The alarm serves as an unconditional stimulus (UCS), in other words, which wakes the child (UCR). Since the sensations of a full bladder (CS) regularly precede waking to the alarm, the child soon wakes to these as well (CR). Waking to these internal cues is a conditioned, or learned, response.

Behavior modification takes somewhat longer than pharmacological interventions to achieve results, requiring up to several months for successful treatment, whereas the latter can begin to achieve results in several days or weeks. Behavior modification, however, does not carry the risk of side effects from the use of various drugs; and children are, as mentioned earlier, less likely to relapse once treatment is discontinued. The use of behavior modification together with pharmacotherapy has proven to be even more effective than either approach alone for some children (Bradbury & Meadow, 1995; Skoog, 1998).

In general, sleep-related disturbances, such as resistance to going to bed or difficulty falling asleep, are as likely to reflect routines surrounding bedtime and

One in five children lives in poverty. Neighborhood resources, such as safe streets and caring neighbors, have an especially large impact on children who are economically disadvantaged.

conditions in the home as they are to reflect factors unique to the child. Children who resist going to bed have been found not only to have less regular bedtimes, but also to be less likely to have parents who showed physical affection, such as a kiss or a hug, as part of their bedtime routines than children whose parents did show affection. Bedtime resistance has also been found to be significantly lower (7% versus 28%) among children whose parents said prayers with them (Blader et al., 1997).

Children who receive physical assurances of their parents' love and who feel secure and protected while they sleep find bedtime less problematic. Despite obvious increases in maturity, school-age children are still relatively concrete in their approach to the world, and physical expressions of love and protection are important. Similarly, when children wake at night, it is helpful for parents to reassure them that everything is okay, offer another kiss goodnight, and tuck them into bed again. Such ministrations have not been found to delay falling back to sleep, whereas others, such as getting into bed with them, have been found to do so (Blader et al., 1997).

Physical Development and Poverty

The face of poverty in the United States has changed over the last two decades. It is no longer the face of the wrinkled elderly, but that of children. Many Americans are unaware of the extent to which poverty affects the lives of children in this country. Over 40% of those who live below the poverty line in the United States are under the age of 18. Approximately 15 million children, or 1 out of every 5, live in poverty (Brooks-Gunn & Duncan, 1997; Corcoran & Chaudry, 1997). Jeanne Brooks-Gunn and Greg Duncan (1997) point out that children must depend on others to meet their needs; they are poor through no fault of their own. Rather, they move into and out of poverty with the rise and fall of their families' fortunes.

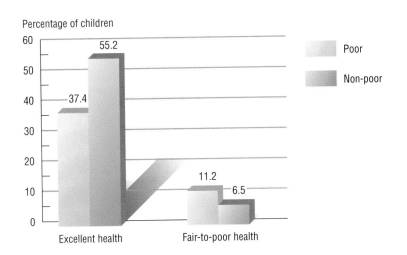

FIGURE 10.8 **The Percentage of Poor and Nonpoor Children in Excellent Health and Fair-to-Poor Health**

Poverty is unequally distributed among children. Those who are most likely to be poor are those who live in single-parent or large families, those who are members of racial or ethnic minorities, and those whose parents have little education. Children living with single-parent mothers, for instance, are over 5 times as likely to be living below the poverty line as are those in two-parent families. Similarly, African American and Latino children are over 2½ times as likely as are Euro-American children to be poor (Corcoran & Chaudry, 1997).

The effects of poverty permeate the lives of these children, from how much food they have to eat and where they will live, to the safety of their neighborhoods and how good their schools will be, to what kind of health care they receive. However, even more important than *whether* children experience poverty is the *duration* over which they experience it. The effects of poverty are approximately twice as great when the poverty is long-term, lasting for 10 years or more, than when it is experienced for a single year or two. This difference has been found to be independent of factors such as family structure, mother's education or age, or the health of the children (Korenman, Miller, & Sjaastad, 1995). Fifteen percent of children who have ever been poor have experienced long-term poverty (Corcoran & Chaudry, 1997).

The effects of poverty can follow children from birth through adulthood. With respect to physical development, poverty can affect both growth itself and general health. Poor children are likely to weigh less at birth and are more likely to have their growth stunted during childhood. Even though relatively few poor children do not actually have enough to eat, poverty is nonetheless associated with significant nutritional deficits, resulting in a greater likelihood of poor children being short for their age, or evidencing *growth stunting*. Their health, as well, can be affected. Children who are poor are significantly less likely, by two thirds, to be in excellent health than other children and nearly twice as likely to be in fair or poor health (Brooks-Gunn & Duncan, 1997; Figure 10.8).

Since children who live in poverty often have less food to eat, how are they likely to be affected?

Preventive and Interventive Programs

A number of federal programs have been found to be effective in reducing the harmful effects of poverty as these relate to physical growth and health. These programs are directed toward improving nutrition, health care, and housing. Included under the former are the Food Stamp Program, a special supplemental program for women with infants and small children (WIC), and school nutrition programs. Medicaid is directed toward health care, and a federal housing program makes up the latter.

School-based nutrition programs supply a significant portion of some children's food.

Nutrition   Even though most children consume nutritious diets, the same cannot be said for the poor. Children living in poverty receive on average less than 70% of the recommended daily allowance for many, if not most, nutrients. Research suggests that participation in the Food Stamp Program has improved the dietary status for these children, especially with respect to calcium, iron, and vitamin C (Devaney, Ellwood, & Love, 1997). Similarly, WIC, which not only provides vouchers for supplemental food, but also educates women about nutrition and health care, has been found to be especially effective in combating iron-deficiency anemia and in promoting immunizations.

A school-based nutrition program, the National School Lunch Program and the School Breakfast Program, is available to low-income children on a daily basis. These meals are frequently a significant portion of what some children get to eat on any day and thus are an important supply of nutrients. The School Lunch Program, for instance, is designed to supply one third of the required daily allowance (RDA) for a number of nutrients, and the School Breakfast Program to supply one fourth of the RDA. Among other foods provided, each meal must include milk and a fruit or a vegetable. As of 1996, this program has also been required to reduce the fat content in school meals (Devaney et al., 1997).

How effective are school-based nutritional programs? Nearly all public schools participate in the school lunch program, making it available to over 90% of schoolchildren. Over half of those for whom it is available participate on any day. Participation varies with family income, with nearly 80% of children who can receive free meals participating, 75% of those eligible for reduced-price meals doing so, and just under half of all others participating choosing to buy their lunches at school rather than bringing them from home. The school breakfast program is available to considerably fewer students, just over half of those who are school age. It is more likely to be in place in those schools whose students are predominantly from lower-income homes. Children are sensitive to the stigma associated with poverty and may choose not to participate to avoid this. Others simply don't like the food. Even so, children who participate in these programs get more of the nutrients they need (Devaney et al., 1997). Box 10.1 lists nutritious

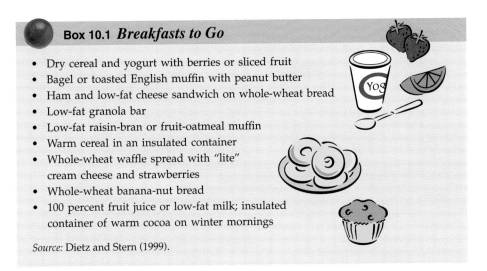

Box 10.1 *Breakfasts to Go*

- Dry cereal and yogurt with berries or sliced fruit
- Bagel or toasted English muffin with peanut butter
- Ham and low-fat cheese sandwich on whole-wheat bread
- Low-fat granola bar
- Low-fat raisin-bran or fruit-oatmeal muffin
- Warm cereal in an insulated container
- Whole-wheat waffle spread with "lite" cream cheese and strawberries
- Whole-wheat banana-nut bread
- 100 percent fruit juice or low-fat milk; insulated container of warm cocoa on winter mornings

Source: Dietz and Stern (1999).

breakfasts that children can carry with them—for those who don't have time to eat at home.

Receiving help, even when it is needed, can be a cause for shame among some children. Dick Gregory (1964) writes of such an experience at school when a collection was taken in class one day for the families of children in need. His family was one of them. He lived in a single-parent home with his mother, sisters, and brothers. He had money in his pocket that he had earned on his own and wanted to impress one of his classmates, a girl on whom he had a crush:

> The teacher opened her book and started calling out names alphabetically.
> "Helene Tucker?"
> "My Daddy said he'd give two dollars and fifty cents."
> "That's very nice, Helene. Very, very nice indeed."
> That made me feel pretty good. It wouldn't take too much to top that. I had almost three dollars in dimes and quarters in my pocket. I stuck my hand in my pocket and held onto the money, waiting for her to call my name. But the teacher closed her book after she called everybody else in the class.
> I stood up and raised my hand.
> "What is it now?"
> "You forgot me."
> She turned toward the blackboard. "I don't have time to be playing with you, Richard."
> "My Daddy said he'd . . ."
> "Sit down, Richard, you're disturbing the class."
> "My Daddy said he'd give . . . fifteen dollars."
> She turned around and looked mad. "We are collecting this money for you and your kind, Richard Gregory. If your Daddy can give fifteen dollars you have no business being on relief."
> "I got it right now, I got it right now, my Daddy gave it to me to turn in today, my Daddy, said . . ." (pp. 184–185)

But he had no father, and the teacher knew that, and soon everyone else did as well. Still standing, he started to cry, further adding to his humiliation. He later reflected, "It seemed like the whole world had been inside that classroom, everyone had heard what the teacher had said, everyone had turned around and felt sorry for me" (p. 185). ◄

About 9 to 11 million children have no health insurance, meaning they are less likely to get medical care when they need it or regular check-ups and immunizations.

Even with programs such as the School Breakfast Program, some 12% of schoolchildren do not eat breakfast before going to school. The number of students failing to do so, however, does not appear to differ as a function of the availability of such programs. In a natural experiment, test scores before children began to participate in the school breakfast program were compared with their scores after being in the program for several months; the comparison showed that test performance had improved. Students in the program were also absent from school less and tardy less (Meyers, Simpson, & Weitzman, 1989). Even so, more research is needed on the effectiveness of these programs in meeting the dietary needs of school-age children and on ways of increasing participation in such programs by those most in need of them.

Health Care   Medicaid extends health care coverage to low-income children by providing them with health insurance. This program provides children with preventive care, such as periodic visits to a health care provider and immunizations, as well as treatment of injuries and illnesses. Although not all low-income children are eligible and standards of eligibility vary from one state to the next, new federal mandates concerning eligibility have increased the number of children whose health needs can be met under this program. Even so, anywhere from 9 million to 11 million children remain uninsured. Of these, 25% most likely are eligible but are simply not enrolled (Devaney et al., 1997).

How effective is Medicaid? Children enrolled in this program have more access to health care services than do children with no insurance. However, they still do not receive the same benefits as those who are privately insured. Additionally, they appear to be less likely to make use of the services available to them. For instance, children insured through Medicaid see a physician less frequently during the year than do those who are privately insured. Given that the health of poor children in general is not as good as that of those who aren't poor, this difference means they are less likely to get medical care when they need it. Children under Medicaid are also less likely to receive all their immunizations than those who are privately insured and are less likely to see a dentist.

Underutilization of programs such as Medicaid reflects a variety of factors. Low-income parents may experience difficulty, for instance, in getting children to health care facilities, given work constraints, poor transportation, and the need for child care for siblings. Part of the problem, too, may be that clinics are not available in low-income and rural areas (Delaney et al., 1997).

Housing   In addition to nutritional programs and health care, assistance with housing is also available to low-income families. This federal program is designed to reduce the cost of housing to 30% of a family's net income. Although providing a place to live meets a fundamental need, federally subsidized housing is not an entitlement program, in which anyone who meets the eligibility requirements will receive benefits. Thus, when funds run out, families must wait. The wait can be long, up to 19 months for public housing and 31 months for subsidized rent, in the form of vouchers, for existing units. A large percentage of those waiting is made up of very low income families with children. By providing vouchers for existing housing, housing programs attempt to avoid isolating poor families from the mainstream of society by concentrating them in public housing projects, which tend to be characterized by higher rates of crime, joblessness, substance abuse, and poorer neighborhood schools. Vouchers, together with counseling on how to search for housing and programs that screen potential tenants, can be used to help low-income families move out of poor neighborhoods.

It is important to keep in mind that the very government measures that were so successful in reducing the rate of poverty among the elderly, from 35% to 11%, offer hope for our children as well. Similar measures can reduce poverty among them.

Summary

Developmental Profiles

In middle childhood, children become increasingly self-sufficient; they are able to find their way around the neighborhood, look after younger siblings, help out with chores, and get themselves to and from school.

Discretionary Time: Being on Their Own

In middle childhood, children begin to spend more time on their own. Unstructured activities can play an important role in development, giving children time in which they are responsible for themselves. Structured support from parents, in the form of providing an emotional base and socializing children to be autonomous, contributes to children's growing competence. These two forms of support parallel the two defining characteristics of authoritative parenting, warmth and demandingness.

After-School Hours: Latchkey and Supervised Care

Approximately 2½ million children are latchkey children, with no adult supervision after school until parents return from work. Children respond to self-care in a variety of ways; in general, few differences are found between self-care children and those supervised by a parent on a variety of measures, including children's experience of social support. With respect to supervised care, most important to children are the sense of being emotionally supported by staff, having a choice in how they will spend their time, and being able to be with others their age. An effective alternative to supervised after-school programs are mentoring programs that involve children in one-on-one interactions with someone with whom they can develop a caring relationship.

Getting Around the Neighborhood

Many children walk to and from school and around their neighborhoods after school. Children are 4 times more likely than adults to be injured as pedestrians; they have difficulty identifying safe routes for crossing intersections and roads even when these routes are familiar to them. Children make increasingly better decisions with respect to pedestrian safety with age.

New Responsibilities

Children are entrusted with increasing responsibilities in most cultures between the ages of 5 and 7. The new behaviors children develop reflect the expectations of their communities as much as they do developments within the children themselves. Children's roles change from being expected to help when asked to being expected to carry out tasks on their own without being asked.

Physical Growth

Growth slows in early childhood; children gain between 2 and 3 inches in height and approximately 5 pounds each year. The lower part of the body grows at a faster rate than the upper body, as a continuation of the cephalocaudal trend. Growth occurs in spurts rather than gradually; these occur at the ages of 6½, 8½, and 10 years in girls and approximately half a year later, at 7, 9, and 10½ in boys. Strength, endurance, and coordination increase as well. Secular trends in growth are evident in that children are somewhat taller and heavier today than in previous generations. The number of children who are overweight has doubled in the last 25 years.

Skilled Behavior

Coordination improves with age both in tasks involving fine motor skills and in those involving large-muscle groups. Most children can print all the letters of the alphabet by the first grade and master cursive writing by the third grade. With respect to gross motor skills, hand-eye coordination improves steadily, as does agility and balance.

Brain Maturation

By the age of 9, the brain has reached 95% of its adult size. Brain growth is characterized by two interrelated processes. Cell proliferation, which takes place through the first several years of life, consists of the overproduction of neurons and interconnections; and cell pruning, which continues throughout childhood, consists of the selective elimination of excess cells and the cutting back of connections. These two processes enable neural development to be fine-tuned by experience, with interconnections that are frequently used being retained and those infrequently used being pruned. Brain metabolism changes throughout childhood, presumably reflecting the differing energy demands of these growth processes.

Plasticity, or the degree to which one area of the brain can assume the functions governed by another following an injury, decreases with age. Paralleling a decrease in plasticity is a progressive lateralization of the brain, in which the two halves of the cortex become specialized for different functions. The frontal lobes also develop, contributing to increases in attention, planning, and self-awareness.

Developmental Asynchronies

Many school-age children experience sleep-related problems, which can take the form of difficulty falling asleep, fear of the dark, waking in the night, and enuresis. Enuresis, or bed-wetting, is a relatively common problem in middle childhood, affecting as many as 10% of 7-year-olds and even higher percentages of younger children. Enuresis has a strong genetic component; 75% of children who are enuretic have a close relative who was also enuretic. Children who are enuretic produce less of the hormone that is responsible for decreased production of urine during sleep, and they may also find it harder to wake to the sensation of a full bladder. Even though most families do not seek treatment, enuresis is a highly treatable disorder.

Physical Development and Poverty

Approximately 15 million children, or 1 out of every 5, live in poverty. Those who are most likely to be poor are those who live in single-parent or large families, who are members of racial or ethnic minorities, and whose parents have little education. Poverty can affect both physical growth and general health. Poor children are more likely to weigh less at birth, to suffer significant nutritional deficits, and to have their growth stunted during childhood; they are nearly twice as likely to be in fair or poor health as other children.

Preventive and Interventive Programs

A number of federal programs are effective in reducing the harmful effects of poverty. With respect to nutrition, these include the Food Stamp Program, a supplemental program for women and infants and small children (WIC), and school nutrition programs. The Food Stamp Program has improved the dietary status of children primarily with respect to calcium, iron, and vitamin C. WIC has been found to be effective in combating iron-deficiency anemia and in promoting immunizations. Nearly 80% of children eligible for school-based nutrition programs participate in these. These programs provide a significant portion of what many children eat on any day and are an important source of nutrients. Medicaid, by extending health insurance to low-income children, provides for preventive care, such as immunizations, as well as treatment of injuries and illnesses. In addition to nutritional programs and health care, assistance with housing is also available to low-income families.

Key Terms

cell proliferation (p. 391)
cell pruning (p. 391)

enuresis (p. 396)
lateralization (p. 393)

plasticity (p. 392)
secular trends (p. 388)

chapter eleven

Middle Childhood
Cognitive Development

A foot in two worlds: that's what it's like to be on the short side of 10. Kids this age are sure that with a bit more time, say a year or two, they could have everything figured out. Like school and sex and what life is really all about. After all, multiplication tables weren't that bad; they discovered where babies really came from; and they finally got it straight about Wonder Woman, Spiderman, and Santa Claus. Too bad in a way. Sometimes it's hard knowing everything. Can't even get anyone to tickle them anymore, except when others forget how grown up they really are.

Quite grown up, in many ways. In the middle years children hone skills they will keep a lifetime. They master the Internet, make legitimate double plays in Little League, win spelling bees, and do homework that can make their parents scratch their brows. Yet with it all, Band-Aids still work better with a hug, and tickling is too good just for the little kids.

Part of what makes children so grown up in these years is the way they think. They appreciate the complexities of time, of tomorrows that turn into today and todays that become yesterday. They are beginning to use strategies to remember things from one day to the next, they can order experience by classes and categories, and their reasoning becomes more logical and less intuitive. Even their sense of humor changes. We will examine several explanations for these developments, before moving to a consideration of the practical side of intellectual development, that of schooling.

Perhaps the single most important factor contributing to the changing world of middle childhood is school. School represents an abrupt change from the life children have been used to, even for those who attended preschool. With time no longer their own, children must follow new rules, form new relationships, and be away from home for a significant portion of the day. Some children adapt to these changes more easily than others. We will look at factors that affect adjustment to school, as well as at the skills children develop there.

The success children have in navigating changes such as these depends in large measure on the support they receive from others—from families, teachers, and friends—and the communities in which they live. We will examine these sources of support at the conclusion of the chapter.

Piaget's Stage of Concrete Operational Thought

Perhaps because of his background as a biologist, Piaget's theory of intellectual development shows the influence of Darwin's theory of evolution. Piaget approached human intelligence, in other words, with questions a biologist might ask if discovering a new organism. How does this creature adapt to its surroundings? What does it do that allows it to survive? How is it changed by the processes that maintain it? Piaget viewed intelligence as a means of adapting to one's environment, in which only those forms of thought that promoted adaptation survived with increasing age. He assumed adaptation to take place through the complementary processes of assimilation and accommodation (see Chapter 1). These processes actively shape the individual's exchanges with the world at every age and are responsible for the growth of thought.

Piaget traced the intellectual developments of middle childhood to the emergence of **mental operations,** internalized actions that children could perform in their heads and that were presumed to develop with the maturation of centers and pathways within the brain (see Chapter 10). Piaget believed that mental operations evolved out of the action schemes of infancy and early childhood. Once these became internalized, they enabled children to carry out in their heads what

mental operations Piaget's term for actions that can be carried out in one's head and then reversed or undone.

Mass (continuous substance)

Two identical balls of playdough are presented. The child agrees that they have equal amounts of dough.

One ball is rolled into the shape of a snake.

Conserving child recognizes that each object contains the same amount of dough (average age, 6–7).

FIGURE 11.1 A Demonstration of Conservation, Using Two Balls of Clay *Source:* From Life-Span Human Development, 1st edition by C. Sigelman and D. Schaffer.

previously they could do only with their hands (Piaget & Inhelder, 1969). You can see what infants are thinking, in other words, by watching what they are doing. But you have to ask school-age children what they are thinking and then wonder if they have really told you. The Research Focus "Between-Subjects Design: Tolerance" looks at how children distinguish among thought, speech, and action.

Piaget considered reversibility to be an important quality to mental operations. By this he meant that children could not only imagine performing some action but could also think of reversing, or undoing, that action to get back to the point from which thought had started. This mental "two-step," one step forward and one back again, enables children to consider the same problem from several perspectives, greatly increasing the flexibility of their thought. Such flexibility can be seen in perhaps the best known of Piaget's many measures of intellectual functioning. Children are shown two identical glasses, each filled with the same amount of liquid, and watch as the liquid from one of these is poured into a tall, narrow glass, where it rises to a higher level. Piaget then asks whether the amount of liquid in the narrow glass is the same as that remaining in the other, wider glass. School-age children, who can mentally reverse what they have just watched and imagine pouring the liquid back into the wider glass, understand that the liquid would again come to the same level as before. Preschoolers, who lack this flexibility, can only answer on the basis of how the liquid appears in each of the containers.

Operations have a second quality that, like reversibility, makes thought more flexible. Each operation belongs to a set of operations, making it possible to see how the effects of one are related to those of another. Think, for a moment, what it means for children to understand the concept of "six." They know, for example, that six pencils, six erasers, and six pennies are alike in that all are "six things." They can also imagine moving the pencils, erasers, and pennies into groups of 3s, or 2s. A mental operation such as this allows children to appreciate relationships between the class of "six things" and other classes, such as classes of "two things" and "three things." They realize not only that 6 is larger than 3, but also that 6 is the same as two 3s, and so on. Being able to relate one operation to another, to see how one thing relates to another, enables children to impose a new order on experience instead of taking it as a given. Thinking, as a result, becomes more logical.

This logic takes a number of forms. Unlike preschoolers, school-age children understand that if a ball of clay is rolled into the shape of a snake the amount of clay is unchanged, an understanding that Piaget referred to as conservation. (Figure 11.1). Children's achievement of conservation rests on several principles. The first of these, already mentioned, is the principle of *reversibility.* This is the understanding that one could roll the snake back into a ball, thereby reversing or nullifying the effects of the first operation. This understanding, that the amount of clay in the two must be the same because one can reverse, or undo, the effects of the first action, is related to a second principle, the *identity* principle. Children also realize that the clay making up the snake is the same clay that was in the ball, that the substance of each, in other words, is unchanged despite changes in the

How might mental operations enable a child to understand that a tall, narrow glass contains the same amount of liquid as a low, wide one?

Children who have entered the stage of mental operations can follow a recipe and understand how to transform raw ingredients into cookies.

Between-Subjects Design: Tolerance

BY MICHAEL WAPNER

The scene was repeated every few days for several weeks. But each time it was worse. First came the voices, raised in anger and argument. Then came pickets with their signs of protest. Then the store windows were broken. Then there were fistfights and the police came. People were arrested. The broken windows were boarded up and the store was closed.

The owner of the store was a Vietnamese immigrant. So were the protesters. All had come to this small community in Southern California to escape the oppression, violence, and death of the war in Vietnam and its aftermath. What precipitated the confrontation was that the store owner had displayed a picture of Ho Chi Minh in the window—a picture of the same "Uncle Ho" whose victorious forces had 25 years before overrun South Vietnam and driven out so many South Vietnamese, along with all their American allies.

One letter to the newspaper criticized the protesters harshly and observed that immigrants to the United States must learn that in a democracy "we are tolerant of the views of others, even when we strongly disagree." Another letter argued that it was a provocative affront to display the picture of the very man who was responsible for the death or imprisonment of family members of the residents of this community and that the store owner should have expected just what he got. A third letter pointed out that many who rejected the demonstrators' intolerance as un-American would have sung another tune had the picture been of Adolf Hitler.

Without tolerance we would always be at each other's throats. Every difference would be a provocation. On the other hand, indiscriminate tolerance invites chaos. Surely we must speak up and even act when we observe behavior of which we disapprove. But these examples are extremes. Tolerance need not be an all-or-nothing matter. One is not simply tolerant or intolerant. Distinctions must be made. Is the display of an "objectionable" picture free speech or the creation of a hostile environment? Do hateful thoughts lead to hateful words and then hateful deeds? And if so, where does one draw the line? Shall we allow words but suppress deeds? Or if words incite deeds, perhaps we should control speech also? And what about thought . . . ? And what about motives? For example, suppose you believe, as most of us do, that doctors cure illness and that it's a good thing they do. Is your tolerance for parents who refuse their sick child medical attention because they believe it is of no benefit (a factual disagreement) different than it is for parents who accept that medicine might help but reject it for religious reasons (a values disagreement)?

When viewed in these more complex terms, "tolerance" becomes a social-cognitive phenomenon. It depends both on the value system one has developed and on one's cognitive capacity to distinguish among thought, belief, and action, among error, evil, and disagreement. Consequently, it should not be surprising, as we shall see below, that the boundaries of tolerance follow a developmental course (Enright and Lapsley, 1981).

Wainryb, Shaw, and Maianu (1998) designed a study to examine the way tolerance for disagreement differs with age. Two of the questions they asked were (1) Does age affect the way subjects distinguish among objectionable beliefs, speech, and actions? and (2) Does tolerance at different ages depend on whether the disagreement is over facts or values? To investigate

appearance of either. A third principle, that of *compensation*, is the realization that changes along one dimension, such as length, are compensated for by changes along a second dimension, that of width. Although the snake is longer than the ball, it is not as wide, and the differences in width make up for those in length.

The dawning of operations burns through the mists of childhood thought like the morning sun. Ideas emerge from shadow, etched crisply in logic. New skills follow as the day follows night. At school, mathematical concepts such as place value emerge from addition of single-digit numbers. In social studies, it's possible to understand that one's state is larger than a city and smaller than the nation. At home, stamp albums, baseball cards, and doll collections reflect a new ability to mentally order one's world.

Piaget assumed that because these intellectual changes are biologically based, younger children lack the capacity to think the way school-age children do. Other developmentalists (Donaldson, 1978; Siegler, 1996a) point out that younger children frequently show these forms of thought, although more often they do not. Why, then, might they not? We turn to an information-processing approach for an analysis of factors influencing children's approaches to problems.

these issues they compared students at four grade levels: first grade (mean age 7.3), fourth grade (mean age 10.4), seventh grade (mean age 13.6), and college undergraduates (mean age 20.1). All participants were presented with short stories describing a person engaged in a practice which was harmful or unfair and of which all participants disapproved. One of the stories, for instance, was about a teacher who criticizes and insults her students when they make mistakes. The investigators made sure that all subjects disapproved of the behavior described in the story. For half the participants the behavior of the character in the story was based on deviant values (that is, "It is okay to be mean to children"). For the other half the character's behavior issued from deviant factual beliefs (that is, criticism and insult are the best way to educate children).

Randomly assigning half the subjects a value disagreement and the other half a factual disagreement constitutes a *between-subjects design*. In this type of design, each subject experiences only one condition of the independent variable. This is in contrast to a *within-subjects design* where each subject receives all conditions of the independent variable. A major advantage of the between-subjects design is that investigators need not worry that subjects' responses will reflect the effects of a previous condition that may still be present. In other words, what if subjects responding to the factual disagreement condition had just been exposed to the value disagreement condition? Could we safely assume that these subjects would be able to separate their reactions to each situation? In a between-subjects design, one need not worry about such matters. Also, because subjects can be assigned at random to conditions, investigators can be reasonably confident that groups do not initially differ until they impose different treatments. Both assumptions involve the issue of internal validity (see the Research Focus, "Internal and External Validity," in Chapter 14). To the extent that guarantees exist in experimental research, between-subject designs offer high guarantees of internal validity.

After reading the stories, subjects were questioned regarding their tolerance for the story character's *belief* (Is it all right for the character to believe X?), *speech* (Should the character be prevented from expressing X?), and *action* (Should the character be allowed to do X?).

One of the most salient, but not very surprising, findings is that the distinction between thought, speech, and action becomes more important with increasing age. A majority of all ages tolerated differences of belief (although 40% of first-graders were intolerant even of that). When it came to contrary speech, a large majority of first-graders and half of fourth-graders expressed intolerance. All age groups refused to tolerate actions with which they disagreed, if the actions were harmful. Interestingly, it was only with respect to speech that it mattered whether the disagreement was factual or over values, and then only slightly. The relative intolerance of the younger subjects for both belief and speech becomes more understandable when we look at the reasons they gave. The older the child, the clearer he or she was about the distinctions between thought, speech, and action. First-graders think that to think something leads necessarily to doing it. Older subjects were not so likely to make that equation. Of course, because younger children are not as able as older ones to inhibit behavior, an idea, once thought, is more likely to be manifest in action. So for them thought, speech, and action are indeed closely related.

These results raise an interesting possibility. Could it be the case that adults who have trouble with impulse control will tend to be intolerant of the ideas of others with which they disagree? Not being able to separate thought, speech, and action in oneself may cause one to distrust the thoughts of others. It would make an interesting experiment.

An Information-Processing Approach to Cognitive Development

Information-processing theorists view thinking as the processing of information and approach its study by looking at how information is encoded or represented in children's minds, and at the processes involved in its transformation and use. Robert Siegler (1998), summarizing two fundamental characteristics of cognition, points out that thinking is both limited and flexible. Simply put, we are limited in just how much we can attend to at any point in time, and we are very good at adapting the way we think to the demands of the task or the moment. With age, children develop increasingly efficient processes for overcoming these cognitive limitations.

Three of these processes are automatization, encoding, and the use of strategies. **Automatization** refers to increases, with continued experience, in the efficiency with which children can engage in various mental activities, such that these require less of their attention, thereby placing fewer demands on attention and memory (Siegler, 1998). For instance, school-age children can recognize words at

automatization Increases, with continued experience, in the efficiency with which children can engage in various mental activities.

411

The ability to categorize underlies the collecting enthusiasm typical of middle childhood, making it possible for these boys to organize players according to their teams, positions, and scoring/assist records.

a glance that younger children have to sound out letter by letter. Differences in the ease of pronouncing words also reflect automatization.

Encoding refers to the formation of mental representations for one's experience. The specific features of a situation that children notice, or encode, change with age. Older children are better at recognizing which features are most important as well as at processing these more efficiently. They are also able to focus on more features of a problem at once, whereas preschoolers typically limit their attention to a single feature. Siegler (1996a) points out that it is not simply what children of either age think to notice on their own, but also how much they can profit from instructions to solve problems in new ways. And this is related to what they have encoded.

Siegler (1976) has studied differences in the way children encode features of a problem through the use of a simple balance. Pegs are positioned at equal distances along each of the two arms so that weights can be added without slipping off. Children are asked to predict whether the arms will be balanced, or whether one will tip down, when various combinations of weights are placed at different distances along each arm (Figure 11.2). The amount of weight on either arm is a joint product of both the number of the weights that have been added and the distance of each from the center. Thus, to solve such a problem children must attend to both the number and the distance of the weights.

A common initial solution is to look only at the number of weights, without taking into consideration their distance from the center of the balance. When 8-year-olds were given feedback that distance was also important, they were able to adjust the way they approached the problem, whereas the same feedback didn't help the 5-year-olds. Siegler (1996a) reasoned that perhaps this was because the 5-year-olds were not looking at, or encoding, the relevant aspects of the problem as they were given feedback. He could see, for instance, that the 8-year-olds not only looked up and down at the number of weights added to any arm, but also back and forth at their distance from the balance point. Five-year-olds, by

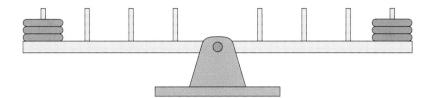

FIGURE 11.2 Siegler's Balance Problem *Source:* R. S. Siegler (1976). Three aspects of cognitive development. Cognitive Psychology, 8, 481–520.

contrast, only looked up and down. When 5-year-olds were taught to encode distance as well as weight, they were then able to profit from feedback and solve problems that required attending to two dimensions for their solution. The difference between the younger and older subjects was that the younger ones needed to be shown to look for a second dimension, whereas older ones did this spontaneously.

Why might older children be likely to encode more information in problems such as this? Siegler (1996a) cites three possible factors. The first relates to increases in the ease with which they can process new information, due to processes such as automatization, even when faced with an unfamiliar task. Younger children, by way of contrast, need to narrow their focus when faced with problems that tax their processing ability, such as those that are unfamiliar. In doing so, they are likely to focus on whatever stands out as the most perceptually salient dimension. By attending to less, younger children thereby reduce the amount of information they must process and remember.

Siegler also suggests that children's beliefs, or worldviews, can contribute to the solutions they adopt. Older children are less likely than younger ones to believe that simple comparisons, such as which arm of a balance will tip down, or in which glass liquid will rise to a higher level, are explained by equally simple differences. Thus, they are prompted to look for more than the first difference that catches their attention. They also encode information differently, scanning the features of objects more systematically than younger children, with the result that they are less likely to be influenced by a particularly noticeable, but misleading, dimension, such as the height of the weights on any peg or the water level in a glass.

Finally, school-age children enjoy not only greater automaticity and are more likely to spontaneously notice, or encode, multiple aspects to a problem, but they are also likely to use more efficient strategies when solving problems. A strategy is simply any activity that is deliberately used to improve one's performance at a task. Even simple strategies, such as using one's fingers when counting (see later section on arithmetic), can be effective when an answer does not immediately come to mind. Children of any age have available a number of strategies, or differing approaches, to a problem (Alibali, 1999; Canobi, Reeve, & Pattison, 1998). Siegler (1996b) points out that these strategies coexist over an extended period of time in each child's life. It is this diversity, in fact, that creates the necessity of selecting among various approaches, with the result that the more adaptive ones eventually come to characterize more mature forms of thought. Development for Siegler, then, takes the form of changes in the frequency with which *existing* strategies are used, as well as of the appearance of new ones (Figure 11.3). Thus, just as Darwin identified competition among the various species as resulting in evolutionary change, Siegler sees the same process accounting for cognitive change.

One of the areas in which the use of strategies shows obvious improvement in middle childhood is that of memory. We turn to a consideration of this topic next.

Why might older children be better at solving Siegler's balance problem than younger ones?

FIGURE 11.3 Cognitive Development as the Use of More Efficient Strategies

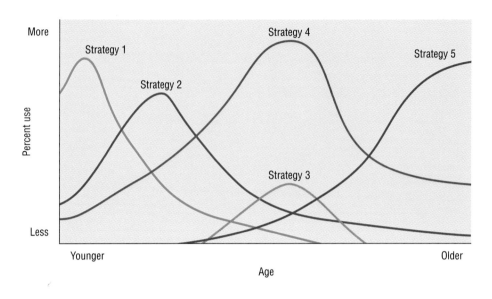

Memory

Have you ever asked a person to repeat something, only to find you know what that person said before hearing it again? How many times have you found yourself repeating a phone number you have just looked up until you can reach the phone and dial it? And have you ever noticed that you know what you *don't* know in addition to what you *do* know?

Rather than existing as a single system, memory exists as a number of interrelated systems, each with different characteristics. **Sensory memory** is very brief, lasting for half a second or less. This is the memory that allows you to reconstruct that lost snippet of conversation you asked someone to repeat, before hearing it again. There are no real age differences in sensory memory, 8-year-olds, for instance, doing as well as adults on tasks measuring this.

A second memory system is that of **short-term memory,** also known as working memory. This is the memory we rely on when dealing with information immediately surrounding us, such as holding a phone number in mind before dialing it. Short-term memory is limited in what it can hold, or work on, at any time to about seven items, give or take a few. This limitation is relatively constant over a wide range of items, being as true for small items such as numbers and letters, as larger ones such as words or even sentences. As long as the item exists as a single unit, or "chunk," it matters little whether it is made up of one letter or five. "Zebra" is as easy to remember as "z."

Short-term memory is also limited in duration, holding information for only 15 to 20 seconds. For information to be kept alive longer than this, it must be rehearsed, or repeated over and over, as one does with a phone number before dialing (see Chapter 8). Older children can hold on to more information in their working memories than can younger ones. It is not clear precisely why they can. Perhaps this difference reflects age changes in the actual capacity of memory, or perhaps it reflects processing differences. With respect to the latter, older children are able to rehearse items more rapidly than younger children, as pronunciation improves with age, thereby enabling them to keep a larger number of items alive in memory.

Long-term memory lasts from a minute to a lifetime. Because of the vastness of this memory, differences in capacity are essentially irrelevant. Information is semantically encoded, or stored according to meaning, in long-term memory. To

When a child who is trying to memorize a phone number repeats it over continuously, which memory system is likely to be involved?

sensory memory A very brief form of memory, lasting for less than a second, that is used during the processing of information.

short-term memory The form of memory used for immediate tasks; its capacity is about seven items at one time; also known as *working memory.*

long-term memory The form of memory in which information is semantically encoded, or stored according to meaning, for later retrieval.

As children grow older, they can retain more information in their short-term and long-term memories than preschoolers can and therefore are capable of memorizing lines for a play.

hold on to long-term information, one must relate it to things one already knows. Even though long-term memory has no time or capacity limitations, there is no guarantee that one will always be able to use the information that is encoded in it. Retrieving information is the biggest problem. Imagine misplacing a book in a large city's public library. How likely are you to recover the book if you can't remember which part of the library you were in when you put it down? The book is likely still there, but you can't retrieve it without using the system by which it was coded.

We also find age differences in long-term memory, a number of which reflect speed of processing—in this case, how quickly children can reach and retrieve information as it is needed. Age differences also include knowledge about one's memory. School-age children know more than do preschoolers about their memories, and they use their knowledge to monitor what they do. This knowledge is called *metamemory.* Older children know, for instance, that they are likely to forget things. They also know that they will be more likely to forget the more time has passed. Thus, when 6- and 8-year-olds were asked how much of something they would remember either 1 day or 1 week later, most 8-year-olds knew they were likely to remember less after a week than after a day. However, none of the 6-year-olds predicted this (Howe, O'Sullivan, & Marche, as cited in O'Sullivan, Howe, & Marche, 1996).

Julia O'Sullivan, Mark L. Howe, and Tammy Marche (1996) studied the development of metamemory by telling children (preschoolers, first- and third-graders) a story in which the characters tried to remember what had happened at a party

Why might young children be likely to believe that their memories are faithful representations of their experiences?

the day before. Children were asked how successful the characters would be and whether their memories would be affected by what others might tell them or by what they experienced subsequently. The researchers found systematic increases in metamemory with age. Preschoolers, for instance, believed that their memories faithfully represented reality and would not be affected by such things as suggestibility and interference. By the first grade, however, children become aware that memory can be influenced by having experienced something similar to what they are trying to remember. But not until the third grade do children become aware of the way their own memories can be influenced by the failings of someone else's memory—that is, their suggestibility to false memories.

Metamemory should develop hand in hand with children's more general awareness of their minds (see Chapter 8). Adults, for instance, are able to monitor their thoughts and describe these to others. The years of middle childhood appear to be particularly important in the development of such an awareness. John Flavell, Frances Green, and Eleanor Flavell (1995) looked at changes with age in children's ability to introspect, or look in on their own mental activity. They showed children "impossible" events, such as a scarf changing color as it was pulled through someone's hand and, after a few moments, asked them whether they had just been thinking about anything. If the children said they had, they asked them to describe their thoughts.

Nearly 70% of the time, 5-year-olds said they had not been thinking of anything. When they did mention something, it was twice as likely to be about something other than what they had just seen. Sixty-three percent of the 7- and 8-year-olds, on the other hand, said they had been thinking about what they had just seen. Note, however, that even at these ages, over a third of the times they were asked, they reported not having thought of anything. Thus even second- and third-graders seemed relatively unaware of their thoughts, not being that good at reporting the contents of the thoughts they had had even moments before. However, even 5-year-olds can accurately report other types of mental activity, such as mentally rotating a figure to determine whether it is the same as an upright one, suggesting that metamemory, just like other aspects of cognition, does not develop at the same pace across all domains (Estes, 1998).

Children also appear to be aware at an earlier age of those aspects of their mental activity over which they have control than they are of those aspects over which they do not have control (Kipp & Pope, 1997). Adults, for instance, realize that people often find it difficult to prevent themselves from thinking about things they don't want to consider. But at what age do children begin to realize that they are not the masters of their own minds? Flavell, Green, and Flavell (1998) traced the development of children's understanding of what they termed "mental uncontrollability" by telling children, adolescents, and adults a story about a person who sees something that is likely to trigger an unwelcome thought (getting a shot in a doctor's office) and asking them how successful the person would be in *not* thinking about that.

Adolescents and adults agreed that it would be very difficult not to think of getting the shot. Five-year-olds, on the other hand, indicated that people could keep themselves from thinking about such things if they wanted to. By the age of 9, children admitted the existence of unwelcome thoughts. They were also aware by this age of other aspects of mental life over which they had no control, such as not being able to stop for any appreciable amount of time the stream of consciousness that characterizes thought. These investigators conclude that most of our understanding of the uncontrollability of our own minds develops in middle childhood. Children's understanding of the limitations to their minds is important

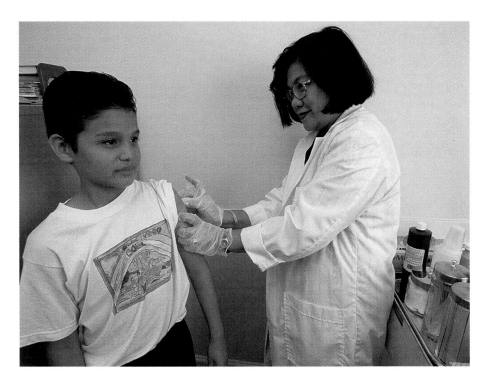

By the age of 9, children realize that they cannot always control unwelcome thoughts, such as fear of getting a shot at the doctor's office.

because it leads to a more careful monitoring of what they are thinking about and consequently leads to checking up on, or monitoring, themselves.

Limitations of Thought in Middle Childhood

Although children's thought is flexible in middle childhood, it is limited as well. Children do not think easily about things they cannot see. Their thought is not abstract. Children think of things that are absent only through simple extensions of their thoughts about what is present. Thought, in other words, is still prompted by the here and now.

Because school-age children tend to focus on aspects to a problem that can be seen, they tend to miss alternatives they could reach only by turning something around in their minds. Failure to speculate about other possible solutions frequently means they fasten on thoughts with finality. David Elkind (1978b) points out that school-age children frequently mistake their assumptions for facts, erroneously assuming that their first answer is the only answer and not looking for alternatives. Adults and adolescents check their assumptions out, rejecting them if they are not supported by facts.

Elkind says children operate according to **assumptive realities,** assumptions that they make on the basis of limited information. One assumptive reality, common during the school years, is what Elkind calls "cognitive conceit," or children's belief that they are clever, whereas adults are not. In contrast to preschoolers who believe that their parents know everything they know (see Chapter 8 for a discussion of egocentrism), school-age children realize they know things their parents don't know. On the basis of this, they jump to the conclusion that their parents must be ignorant and know nothing. Elkind wonders, in fact, whether cognitive conceit contributes to children's frequent reluctance to grow up. He points to numerous stories in which children outwit adults—Tom Sawyer

assumptive realities Assumptions made on the basis of limited information.

What children find funny changes with age.

outfoxing Aunt Polly, Nancy Drew solving mysteries for which her father hadn't a clue, and Peter Pan fooling Mr. And Mrs. Darling (even the *dog* knew what was going on).

Sometimes logic like this can only be taken with a grain of salt or a pinch of humor. Children develop a sense of the ludicrous in these years. Their appreciation of humor, just like their intellectual functioning in general, shows a developmental trend, which we will consider next.

Why are stories such as Peter Pan, Tom Sawyer, and Nancy Drew so appealing to school-age children?

Humor: A Sense of the Ridiculous

What makes a situation funny? Jokes that can turn an 8-year-old into jelly with giggling may only get a yawn from an adolescent. Paul McGhee (1979) identifies at least three ingredients to any humorous situation, each of which can be expected to change with age.

The first element in humor is what might be called the incongruous. We laugh, or smile, at things that violate our expectations. School-age children are able to appreciate incongruities that go over the heads of younger children. Many of these incongruities are provided by the multiple meanings some words have, which form the basis for many of the jokes and riddles children enjoy at this age. School-age children find this type of joke particularly funny, appreciating the ambiguity arising from the several possible meanings of a word, whereas preschoolers, failing to catch more than one meaning to the word, miss the joke. Consider the joke, "Order! Order in the court!" "I'll have a ham and cheese on rye, your honor."

A second ingredient to humor is the emotional release it affords. Humor provides a way of coping with situations and feelings that cause us to feel anxious by poking fun at them (Freud, 1961). Because different situations are problematic for children of different ages, the things that children find funny should also change with age. Preschoolers, for instance, are concerned with issues of bodily control, especially as these reflect elimination. Consequently, much of their humor could be characterized as "bathroom" humor. School-age children, on the other hand, are concerned with issues of mastery, as reflected in the riddles that characterize so much of humor in middle childhood. In a sense, riddles can be viewed as a microcosm of the schoolchild's experiences of being questioned and needing to have the right answers, but not always being sure what makes these right. However, the one who asks the riddle is the one who knows the answer, putting that person in control of the situation. This makes for a pleasant reversal of who is in control of knowledge.

A final component to humor is intellectual (see the Research Focus, "Generative Interview: An Astronomical Joke"). Concepts that are recently mastered are sufficiently challenging to be humorous. A joke about a man who orders a whole pizza for dinner and, when asked whether he wants it cut into six or eight pieces, responds "You'd better make it six, I could never eat eight!" is particularly funny to school-age children. Children who have just mastered conservation enjoy a joke where the same quantity cut into eight pieces could be thought to be more than it would be as six pieces (McGhee, 1979).

The content of much of children's humor during these years reflects their growing concerns over mastery and the development of new skills. An important component of intellectual development in middle childhood is the acquisition of the skills that will equip them for life in the larger culture. We turn next to a consideration of school and the mastery of basic skills such as arithmetic and reading.

The World of School

Perhaps no single transition is greater in children's lives, other than the birth of a sibling or the breakup of a family, than going off to school. School-age children spend most of their hours each day away from home, surrounded by other children, sitting still for longer periods of time than they are initially comfortable with, and bending their minds to tasks they have not chosen for themselves. And yet most children eagerly rise to all of this.

For some children, this transition can be harder than for others. In school, children not only learn to master basic skills such as reading and writing, but also take their first steps toward becoming members of a larger society, one that awaits them outside the intimate confines of their homes. To the extent that this society, as mirrored in their schooling, does not reflect the comfort and safety they have known within the privacy of their families, the step is a difficult one to take. In *Hunger of Memory*, Richard Rodriguez (1982) writes of his reluctance to take this step, by adopting English, the public language used in school:

> Without question, it would have pleased me to hear my teachers address me in Spanish when I entered the classroom. I would have felt much less afraid. I would have trusted them and responded with ease. But I would have delayed—for how long postponed?—having to learn the language of public society. I would have evaded—and for how long could I have afforded to delay?—learning the great lesson of school, that I had a public identity.
>
> Fortunately, my teachers were unsentimental about their responsibility. What they understood was that I needed to speak a public language. So their voices would search me out, asking me questions. Each time I'd hear them, I'd look up in surprise to see a nun's face frowning at me. I'd mumble, not really meaning to answer. The nun would persist, "Richard, stand up. Don't look at the floor. Speak up. Speak to the entire class, not just to

Generative Interview: An Astronomical Joke

BY MICHAEL WAPNER

Here's a joke.

A famous astronomer is giving a public lecture. When he is finished regaling his very impressed audience with the latest findings on black holes, white dwarfs, and quarks, he asks for questions. Immediately a small, gray-haired man jumps up and furiously waves his hand for recognition. The astronomer calls on him.

"I want a straight answer and no evasions," challenges the little man.

"I'll do my best," replies the famous scientist, just a touch patronizingly.

"O.K. then. What holds up the earth?"

Obviously pleased with himself for asking so fundamental a question, the man from the audience smiles knowingly at the people around him as he awaits his answer.

The scientist, having in his years of public lectures encountered flat-earthers, UFO abductees, and telepaths in direct thought contact with Mars, is not much surprised by the question. He attempts to get around it without offending.

"Well, you see, there is a problem with the way the question is put. Strictly speaking nothing holds up . . ."

"Enough!" breaks in the little man, triumph in his voice and on his face. "I knew you would try to wiggle out. All you academic smarties dodge the hard ones. As a matter of fact, I know the answer to my own question. It's a turtle. A turtle holds up the earth."

The scientist, condescension growing with impatience, responds, "And what holds up the turtle?"

The little man, gracious on the edge of victory: "Another turtle, of course."

The scientist, now in full sarcasm, "And what, pray tell, holds up that . . . ?"

The little man, not waiting for the end of the challenge, pounces for the *coup de grâce.* "I got you now. It's another turtle. And then another turtle under that one. In fact, it's turtles all the way down!"

However funny we find this story (and I hope you find it as funny as I did the first few times I heard it), there is more than humor here. Overlooking for the moment his turtle explanation, the little man's conceptual problem is quite understandable and not at all unusual. All of us, even small children, know that the earth is round and moves in empty space around the sun. We have heard and read about it over and over. We have even seen pictures, taken from space, of the round earth. But it is one thing to know this as a isolated fact. It is a deeper and more difficult thing to internalize the astronomical frame of reference into which this fact fits and still more difficult to reason on the basis of this broader frame of reference. The man in the audience is having just this difficulty. He knows, as an isolated fact, that the earth is an object in space. But his frame of reference has not caught up with that fact. He wants to know how the earth remains in space without falling. It is his, as it is everyone else's, common experience that heavy, unsupported objects fall. And the direction in which they fall is down. But everyone's common experience is from an earthbound perspective, in which earth is not itself an object but the "floor of the world." When we take an astronomical perspective, then we no longer speak of "falling" and there is no meaning to the term *down.* The man in the audience has confused these two perspectives.

Stella Vosniadou (1994; Vosniadou & Brewer, 1992) was particularly interested in how children and adolescents deal with this same problem, with how they reconcile what they have heard about the roundness of earth with their more deeply internalized earthbound perspective. To investigate this question she used what she terms a *generative* interview. A generative interview is one in which the interviewer does not stop with the

me!" But I couldn't believe that the English language was mine to use. (In part, I did not want to believe it.) I continued to mumble. I resisted the teacher's demands. (Did I somehow suspect that once I learned public language my pleasing family life would be changed?) Silent, waiting for the bell to sound, I remained dazed, diffident, afraid. ◄

Arithmetic

The expression "It's as simple as two plus two" is a common way of saying that something couldn't be easier. Yet learning basic arithmetic, such as addition and subtraction, is not necessarily easy at first. In fact, children frequently resort to the use of one or more strategies to help them arrive at the right answer. Robert Siegler

answers to factual questions, but gives the subject problems that probe the reasoning behind the factual answers. Consider the following interview with Jamie, a third-grader:

E: What is the shape of the earth?

J: Round.

E: Can you draw a picture of the earth?

J: (Child draws a circle to depict the earth.)

E: If you walked for many days in a straight line, where would you end up?

J: Probably in another planet.

E: Could you ever reach the end or the edge of the earth?

J: Yes, if you walked long enough.

E: Could you fall off that end?

J: Yes, probably.

Clearly, had the interviewer stopped when Jamie said the earth was round, she would have left with a seriously mistaken understanding of Jamie's view of the earth. If one can "reach the end of the earth by walking long enough" and then "probably" fall off, one is not walking on the surface of an earth that is "round" as astronomers understand that term.

By posing astutely chosen questions, (which are more like problems to be solved than questions to be answered), Vosniadou and Brewer are able to infer the cognitive model of earth the child must have constructed.

You may have noticed that the *generative interview* owes a great deal to the *clinical interview* of Jean Piaget. Piaget also posed "diagnostic" questions that allowed him to infer the way children think. The generative, or clinical, interview is to be contrasted with the *survey interview*. This latter form is designed to elicit *facts* or *opinions* of which the respondent is consciously aware. The generative interview, on the other hand, focuses more deeply, on the cognitive structures that lie beneath conscious facts and opinions. To conduct a generative interview, the interviewer must be much more skilled, since each question must build on the child's last response and thus cannot be totally scripted beforehand. The standardized protocol of a survey interview is much too rigid to serve a generative function. On the other hand, the necessity to ask somewhat different questions of different subjects in the generative interview makes standardization, and hence data interpretation, more complicated. There is also a greater danger, in a generative interview, of the questions suggesting and hence contaminating the responses, since the material elicited is more complex and hence more vulnerable to suggestive influence.

In spite of these dangers, the generative interview is wonderfully productive of insights on children's cognitive models. Here is Matthew, a first-grader:

E: If you walked and walked for many days, where would you end up?

M: If we walk for a very long time we might end up at the end of the earth.

E: Would you ever reach the edge of the earth?

M: I don't think so.

E: Say we kept on walking and walking and we had plenty of food with us?

M: Probably.

E: Could you fall off the edge of the earth?

M: No, because if we were outside the earth we could probably fall off, but if we were inside the earth we couldn't fall off.

Matthew has done pretty well in imagining the earth to be round. Where his cognitive model seems to disagree with conventional science is that he has us living *inside* the sphere. That's why we don't fall off.

and Mitchell Robinson (1982) studied the strategies children used by giving them problems in which they were asked to add two numbers, neither of which exceeded the number of fingers on each hand. One of the first things they noticed was that children typically had available to them a number of different strategies. Sometimes children would raise the number of fingers that corresponded to each number of items to be counted, counting the fingers that were raised (counting fingers strategy). Or they might raise that number of fingers but without any appearance of counting them (fingers strategy). At other times, children would count, without using any fingers (counting strategy). And sometimes they appeared to do nothing, simply retrieving the answer directly (retrieval strategy).

These strategies were clearly different, both in their accuracy and in the time it took to use them. The use of retrieval, for instance, was much faster than the

TABLE 11.1 Speed, Accuracy, and Frequency of Use of Strategies for Counting by Preschoolers

Strategy	Seconds	Accuracy	% Trials Used
Counting fingers	14.0	87	15
Fingers	6.6	89	13
Counting	9.0	54	8
Retrieval	4.0	66	64

Source: R. S. Siegler & M. Robinson. (1982). The development of numerical understandings. In H. W. Reese & L. P. Lipsitt (Eds.), *Advances in child development and behavior* (Vol. 16). New York: Academic Press.

One of the first strategies children use when doing math is counting with their fingers—and it works.

other strategies, but not nearly as accurate (Table 11.1). Also, children did not necessarily use the same strategy each time they solved the same problem. When given the same problem on different weeks, children used a different strategy 34% of the time. And the change was not necessarily because they moved to a more sophisticated strategy.

In addition to differences within any individual child such as these, there are large cultural differences both in the efficiency of the strategies that children use and in their general mathematical skills (Geary, Bow-Thomas, Fan, & Siegler, 1993, 1996). American children tend to place near the bottom of rankings comparing students from different countries (Youth Indicators, 1996; Figure 11.4). Such disparities have been explained in the past in terms of cultural expectations for achievement and differences in instruction. However, the language children speak also contributes to their relative ease in acquiring certain mathematical skills. A comparison of schoolchildren from China and the United States, for instance, found marked differences in the strategies they used when doing addition problems. When not immediately able to think of an answer, Chinese students preferred to verbally count, whereas American students were more likely to count on their fingers. The reliance on verbal counting as a strategy by Chinese children reflects the more rapid rate at which numbers can be pronounced in Chinese (Geary et al., 1996).

Many Asian languages confer a second, and more important, advantage when doing simple math problems. The names for numbers communicate information about the place value of the numbers. Children in the United States have difficulty understanding the concept of place value well into the second and even the third grades. Asian children find this concept considerably easier to grasp (Kamii, 1991). When one looks at the names given to numbers in Chinese and English, for instance, one sees the relative advantages of the former. Thus, the word for "11" in Chinese is translated as "ten one," and for "12" as "ten two."

Children must understand the concept of *place value*, that the value of a number changes depending on its place within a double-digit number, to know what they are doing when they add two-digit numbers. Adults have come, through long usage, to take this understanding as a given. This concept remains a mystery, however, to many schoolchildren even though they come up with reasonably good scores on tests of addition or subtraction of double-digit numbers.

Mieko Kamii (1991) demonstrated the types of misunderstandings American schoolchildren have by asking them to count out the number of items in a pile of 25 poker chips and to write down their answer. Then children were asked about the values of the "2" and the "5" in their answer. Kamii describes one second-grader who, when asked about the 5, answered that it stood for five chips, which

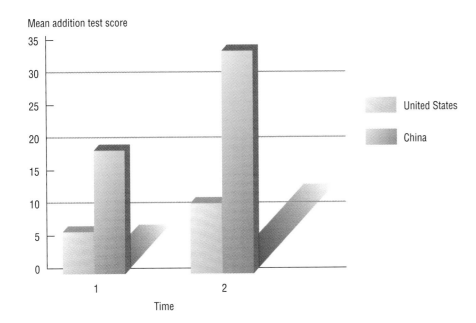

Mean addition test score

Time

FIGURE 11.4 Performance in Addition by Chinese and U.S. Kindergarten Children near the Beginning (time 1) and End (time 2) of the School Year. *Source:* D. C. Geary, C. C. Bow-Thomas, L. Fan, and R. S. Siegler. (1996). Development of arithmetical competencies in Chinese and American children: Influence of age, language, and schooling. *Child Development, 67,* 2022–2044.

he then counted out, but when asked about the 2, responded that it stood for the two piles he had just created. Another second-grader answered that the "5" stood for five chips and the "2" for two chips, and the two-digit number for all 25 of them. Even though third graders did better in mentioning such things as "tens" and "ones," their failure to understand the meaning of what they were saying became evident when they were given two numbers to add, such as 18 and 13, in which they had to "carry" the "1." When asked to show the number of chips the "1" stood for, they were likely to indicate 1 chip, not 10.

Over and above such things as the advantages communicated by language are differences in how mathematics is taught. This latter difference is perhaps of paramount importance in contributing to cultural differences in mathematics achievement (Stigler & Stevenson, 1991). James Stigler and Harold Stevenson have compared the way mathematics is taught to American and Asian students and summarize a number of differences. In Asian classrooms, students spend more time interacting with each other and the teacher than they do working alone at their desks. Lessons also typically begin with a concrete problem, enabling children to become active participants in a process of discovery, rather than passive recipients of information. Finally, up to 8 times as much time is devoted to reviewing and summarizing what they have learned than in American classrooms. Let's take a look at one of the examples Stigler and Stevenson give; this is a fifth-grade class in Japan, a typical lesson:

> The teacher walks in carrying a large paper bag full of clinking glass. Entering the classroom with a large paper bag is highly unusual, and by the time she has placed the bag on her desk the students are regarding her with rapt attention. What's in the bag? She begins to pull items out of the bag, placing them, one-by-one, on her desk. She removes a pitcher and a vase. A beer bottle evokes laughter and surprise. She soon has six containers lined up on her desk. The children continue to watch intently, glancing back and forth at each other as they seek to understand the purpose of this display.
>
> The teacher, looking thoughtfully at the containers, poses a question: "I wonder which one would hold the most water?" (p. 14)

Active lessons with concrete items and problems to work on with classmates have been shown to be more successful in students' comprehension of math concepts than are lessons where students work out problems alone on paper.

Why is it effective to teach mathematics in elementary school using real-life problems?

After getting a number of different answers, she asks how they can discover which answer is correct. The class agrees on a way of measuring each and is divided into familiar working groups, each assigned to measure one of the containers. Students move about the classroom, each group carrying out the procedures agreed on by the class and recording their observations in a notebook. When they are finished, the teacher stands at the blackboard and asks a child from each group to report what that group has found:

> She has written the names of the containers in a column on the left and a scale from 1 to 6 along the bottom. Pitcher, 4.5 cups; vase, 3 cups; beer bottle, 1.5 cups; and so on. As each group makes its report, the teacher draws a bar representing the amount, in cups, the container holds.
>
> Finally, the teacher returns to the question she posed at the beginning of the lesson: Which container holds the most water? She reviews how they were able to solve the problem and points out that the answer is now contained in the bar graph on the board. She then arranges the containers on the table in order according to how much they hold and writes a rank order on each container, from 1 to 6. She ends the class with a brief review of what they have done. No definitions of ordinate and abscissa, no discussion of how to make a graph preceded the example—these all became obvious in the course of the lesson, and only at the end did the teacher mention the terms that describe the horizontal and vertical axes of the graph they had made. (pp. 14–15)

Stigler and Stevenson liken such lessons to a good story. They are organized around a central drama and capture students' interest. Like a story, they have a beginning in which a problem is introduced, a middle that is characterized by a search for a solution, and an end in which the problem is mastered. They also, like good stories, maintain children's interest and capture their imaginations. Fur-

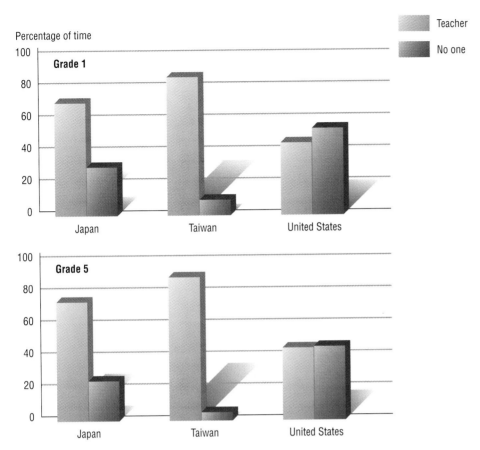

Percentage of time

Grade 1

Grade 5

- ▨ Teacher
- ▨ No one

FIGURE 11.5 Percentage of Time Students in Japan, Taiwan, and the United States Spend in Teacher-Led Instruction Versus Instruction Led by No One *Source:* J. W. Stigler and H. W. Stevenson. (1991). How Asian teachers polish each lesson to perfection. *American Educator,* (Spring) 12–20, 43–47.

thermore, lessons are not interrupted by extraneous activities that would break students' interest or lessen the experience of discovery and mastery at their conclusion. Nearly 50% of American fifth-grade math lessons, for instance, experienced some interruption, whereas fewer than 10% of classes were interrupted in Asian classrooms.

Finally, the amount of time devoted to actual instruction is greater in Asian classrooms. American lessons are more likely to have students working on problems at their seats, with the teacher walking around answering questions. Teacher-led instruction accounts for only 46% of class time in U.S. classrooms, in contrast to 90% of class time in Taiwan and 74% in Japan (Figure 11.5). Put another way, there was no one guiding the instructional period for only 9% of the time in Taiwan and 26% in Japan, but this was true for 51% of the time in American classrooms, leaving U.S. children to work by themselves for relatively long periods of time during which they may have had difficulty focusing on their work or understanding how it was relevant (Stigler & Stevenson, 1991).

Reading

In addition to learning mathematical mysteries, such as the place value of numbers and how to add or subtract, schoolchildren learn the mysteries of reading, of breathing sound into letters on a page, and of discovering the meaning behind these. Most are prepared to begin this adventure by the time they reach school. Before ever beginning school, most children can already recognize many letters if they are printed in uppercase, and they engage in pretend reading, telling a story while holding and looking at a book (Worden & Boettcher, 1990).

Learning to read involves a number of skills. At the most elementary level, children must be able to visually scan a word to identify individual letters. Laboratory research in which children are asked to search for a target letter among nontarget letters has found that the speed and accuracy with which they are able to detect the letter they are looking for is also related to their reading efficiency. Those who perform well at such a search task are better readers, reading at a rate that is 1½ times that of those who perform less well (Casco, Tressoldi, & Dellantonio, 1998).

Children need to know not only the names of the letters in a word, but also the sounds these letters make. This knowledge enables them to decode the sounds that make up a word. One of the difficulties children face, however, is that each letter can have more than one sound. There are only 26 letters in the alphabet, but over 50 different sounds, or **phonemes,** for which these can stand. The word "hot," for instance, has three phonemes, "huh," "ah," and "teh," one for each letter. However, the word "hope" also has three phonemes, "huh," "oh," and "peh," even though it contains four letters. Furthermore, the "o" in "hope" makes a different sound than does the "o" in "hot." Hidden within the scramble of letters and phonemes to be found even among these two words is a key that helps children unlock some of the mysteries of the sounds letters make. The key, that words ending in "e" give a different sound to the vowel within them, is itself something additional they must learn. And, just like Alice, many have difficulty grasping hold of this key as they experience the vagaries of vowels that can grow shorter or longer with seemingly no rhyme or reason.

Children use their knowledge of the name of the letter when learning the sound it will make, "mapping" the sound in the name onto the corresponding phoneme (Treiman, Tincoff, Rodriguez, Mouzaki, & Francis, 1998). For some letters, this approach works well. For others it can lead to errors, such as mistaking the letter "y" ("wai") as standing for the sound of a "w." An important difference among letters is whether the sound they make occurs in the name of the letter. Also important is whether this sound occurs at the beginning of the letter's name (b, c, d, g, j, k, p, t, v, and z) or at the end (f, l, m, n, r, s, and x). For a few letters, such as "h," "q," "w," and "y," the sound is absent altogether. Even though children can name one type of letter as accurately as another, they find it considerably easier to identify the sound a letter will make when it occurs at the beginning of the letter's name than at the end, and both types of letters make it easier to "map" the corresponding phoneme than when the sound is absent from the letter's name altogether.

Phonological skills, or the ability to sound out words, are fundamental to learning how to read (Ball, 1997). However, children also rely on context when faced with unfamiliar and phonologically ambiguous words, such as "beige," "diesel," or "canoe." In general, children who have better reading skills are better both at phonologically decoding new words (Booth, Perfetti, & MacWhinney, 1999) and at using context more effectively in recognizing new words (Nation & Snowling, 1998).

These differences among readers increase with age, with better readers becoming even better with time and poorer readers becoming relatively worse. In reading, as in other aspects of life, those who have get even more, and those who have not, fall even further behind. A 3-year longitudinal study of schoolchildren in the Netherlands suggests that the increasing differences between skilled and nonskilled readers largely reflect differences in their word-recognition skills, which

phonemes The smallest distinguishable units of sound in a language.

This first-grader is learning to read. Research comparing the basic-skills approach to teaching reading with the whole language approach find each to be equally effective.

are related, at least in part, to their ease in sounding out words rather than to differences in reading comprehension (Bast & Reitsma, 1998).

Given that sounding out a word contributes so importantly to reading skills, is it best, then, to teach reading by beginning with phonics, in which children are drilled in recognizing individual letters and the sounds of each, in order to master the rules for translating letters into sounds? Such an approach, known as a **basic-skills approach**, starts with letters and sounds before moving to simple unambiguous words, making sure that children can sound these out before moving on to more complicated material. An alternative approach, known as the **whole-language approach**, teaches reading by exposing children to the varied contexts in which reading is important, through stories, ingredients to recipes, video titles, grocery lists, and the like. This approach attempts to engage children's interest, thereby motivating them to attempt to read and so discover the basic principles. Research comparing these approaches has not found one to be consistently superior to the other (Stahl, McKenna, & Pagnucco, 1994).

basic-skills approach An approach to teaching reading that starts with teaching children the sounds of individual letters and how to sound out words.

whole-language approach An approach to teaching reading that starts by exposing children to contexts where reading is important in order to engage their interest so that they will be motivated to attempt to read and discover the basic principles of reading.

Culture and Gender in the Classroom: Education for All

Using materials that capture interest and fire imagination is a goal of education for all students. However, some schools still use materials that exclude half their students from the most exciting adventures.

Gender Stereotypes in Teaching Materials   From Tom Sawyer to Harry Potter, most of the characters children read about in classics or see in films are males. School materials also take their readers to high adventure most readily if they are males. These trends begin in elementary school and continue into high school.

Visual Materials   Several studies of children's textbooks have found that males are pictured more often than females and shown in more adventurous roles. Although female characters appear as often as male characters, they still appear in fewer occupations and need rescuing more frequently (Purcell & Stewart, 1990; Smith & Rhodes, 1994). Furthermore, nearly twice as many of the authors are females as are male, but a male character has the central role in the story by a margin of 3 to 1 (Narahara, 1998).

Even so, these comparisons represent a giant step away from the sexism that characterized school materials 25 years ago. A similar survey conducted in 1972 found the same trends but differences that were even more exaggerated (Women on Words and Images, 1975). For instance, Gail Goss (1994), after reviewing 45 children's books, noted the recent emergence of female adventurers and rescuers and of males who care for the house and the children.

About 90% of students' time in school is spent with various types of educational materials such as books, films, or class handouts. Surveys indicate that most school materials have been sex-biased and that the use of stereotyped materials influences students' attitudes (Tittle, 1986). Even though many states have introduced regulations to ensure that the portrayal of females and males in textbooks is balanced, some schools cannot buy new books until the old ones need replacing.

Materials that show women and men in nontraditional roles or filling roles in proportion to their actual numbers in the work force lead to greater flexibility in gender-role attitudes among students. These findings are consistent across dozens of studies. Students who read about females who are doctors or postal carriers and males who are telephone operators or day care directors are less gender-typed in their approach to occupations in general and in their personal interest in these professions (Switzer, 1990).

Language   A second form of bias occurs through the gender characteristics of language itself. English, all too frequently, either ignores females or treats them as exceptions. **Male generic language** uses the pronoun *he* to refer to an individual of either sex and uses words such as *man* or *mankind* to refer to all people. When individuals are identified as female, it is often to call attention to the fact that they are *not* male, such as in terms like *woman doctor* or *sculptress*. These usages suggest not only that doctors and sculptors ordinarily are males, but that when they are females, they are different enough from "regular" doctors and sculptors to require different labels (Lips, 1997).

A formidable array of research shows that male generic language causes people to think of males, not of people in general (Fisk, 1985; Henley, 1989; Hyde, 1984; Switzer, 1990). In one study, seventh-graders completed a story about a student's first day in class. Some students read a story referring to the new student as "he"; others read stories in which the student could be of either sex. When the subject was referred to as "he," all the males and 80% of the females wrote stories

male generic language Use of the pronoun *he* to refer to an individual of either sex and use of words such as *man* or *mankind* to refer to all people.

describing the student as a male. When "he or she" or "they" were used, significantly fewer students referred to the new student as a male. Those most affected by the use of inclusive language ("he and she" or "they") were females; whereas 80% wrote stories in which the subject, when referred to as "he," was a male, 21% and 12% wrote about a male when the subject was referred to as "he or she" or "they," respectively (Switzer, 1990). When we realize that teachers are just as susceptible to the influence of male generic language as students, the implications of these findings assume even larger proportions.

Male generic language also affects children's judgments of how competent a woman is in different types of jobs. When students are asked to consider how well a woman might perform a fictional job (for example, a "wudgemaker"), their evaluations are influenced by the sex of the pronouns used to describe the characters performing the job. Women are thought to be least competent for the job when the wudgemaker is referred to as "he" and most competent when referred to as "she" (Hyde, 1984). Referring to doctors, mechanics, scientists, or artists as "he" has clear implications not only for girls' ability to see themselves in those professions, but also for all students' evaluation of the relative competence of the men and women in those occupations (Lips, 1999).

Multicultural Education

LaRue glanced briefly at his group as Mr. Brooks, his teacher, finished giving the assignment: to study the activity of gases. That shouldn't be too difficult, he thought. But what would he do for his part? He had to think of common examples illustrating the properties of gases. Paulo had an easy part to present to the group; all he had to do was describe their chemical properties. Becky's part would be interesting: identifying the gases that are present in different substances. He could imagine the fun Yinpeng would have with that one. He liked his group. They worked well together, and it was more interesting than working on their own. But what could he contribute? Then he remembered the canned drinks he had put in the freezer—the juices had burst open but the soda hadn't. Of course, gases constrict and liquids expand when cold.

LaRue's class is organized as a **jigsaw classroom.** Students work in small groups that are balanced for ethnic background and ability. Each student in the group contributes a different part of the lesson. The parts fit together, much like the pieces of a jigsaw puzzle: One needs each part to get the whole picture. This approach to classroom learning fosters cooperation among students and promotes better relations among children from different ethnic and racial backgrounds (J. Banks, 1993).

Even in classes that foster cooperative and friendly relations, minority children often face problems that don't exist for those from the dominant culture. They do not always share the cultural perspective, for instance, that is assumed by much of their class material; many textbooks reflect a Eurocentric bias in their portrayal of minorities, often omitting their contributions or presenting them negatively (Garcia, 1993; Hu-DeHart, 1993). Seeing things from a different point of view can make otherwise easy material difficult to understand. Does the westward expansion have the same implications for Native Americans, Hispanics, and African Americans as it does for European American students (Seixas, 1993)? Probably not. Classes that introduce *multicultural perspectives* surmount this difficulty. Asking students to describe the experiences of the pioneers, the American Indians, and the Mexicans turns this problem into an advantage. The introduction of a multicultural perspective enriches all students' understanding of the issues surrounding westward expansion (C. Banks, 1993; Howard, 1993).

jigsaw classroom A classroom organized into small, ethnically balanced working groups in which each student contributes a different part of the lesson.

In "jigsaw classrooms," students work in small groups balanced for ethnic background and ability.

In the classroom, unfamiliar patterns of communication complicate learning for some minority students. The simple matter of asking questions is a case in point for many African American students. Teachers ask questions in very different ways than do adults in the community (Brice-Heath, 1982). Teachers use questions to stimulate classroom discussions and to focus ongoing behavior. It's common to ask about things the class has already discussed. Outside the classroom, adults are likely to ask questions only when they want information they do *not* have. They rarely use questions as a way of discussing issues or of channeling ongoing behavior into more desirable forms (as a teacher might, by asking a question of a student who is talking with a classmate to get that student to pay attention). Consequently, students may misunderstand questions regarding material the class has already covered ("What is she asking for? We've gone over that"). Effective intervention depends on discovering differences such as these. The solution in this instance is for everyone—teachers, parents, and students—to be made aware of the different rules that regulate language in class and at home (Slaughter-DeFoe, Nakagawa, Takanishi, & Johnson, 1990).

Other problems arise from lack of familiarity in using Standard English, the language used in the classroom. Some minority students—such as Hawaiians, Native Americans, and Eskimos—can understand Standard English well enough, but still not be at ease speaking it in front of classmates if they speak a dialect at home. Using different languages at home and in school limits opportunities to practice the way ESL students need to speak at school and can cause them to be silent for fear of embarrassing themselves. Many bilingual children, such as Richard Rodriguez (1982), whom we encountered at the beginning of the chapter, speak of their difficulty in overcoming the conflict, discomfort, and ultimately, the sense of loss occasioned by the use of one language at home and another at school:

One Saturday morning I entered the kitchen where my parents were talking, but I did not realize that they were talking in Spanish until, the moment they saw me, their voices changed and they began speaking English. The gringo sounds they uttered startled me. Pushed me away. In that moment of trivial misunderstanding and profound insight, I felt my throat twisted by unsounded grief. I simply turned and left the room. But I had no place to escape to where I could grieve in Spanish. My brother and sisters were speaking English in another part of the house.

Again and again in the days following, as I grew increasingly angry, I was obliged to hear my mother and father encouraging me: "Speak to us *en inglés.*" Only then did I determine to learn classroom English. Thus, sometime afterward it happened: One day in school, I raised my hand to volunteer an answer to a question. I spoke out in a loud voice and I did not think it remarkable when the entire class understood. That day I moved very far from being the disadvantaged child I had been only days earlier. Taken hold at last was the belief, the calming assurance, that I *belonged* in public. ◄

Even written schoolwork becomes problematic for students who have difficulty translating the ideas they frame easily in the intimate language of their home into Standard English. Additional complications arise when corresponding terms are not available in the two languages (Feldman, Stone, & Renderer, 1990).

Overcoming the Differences   The increasing ethnic diversity of our society makes it progressively difficult to characterize students in terms of simple behavioral and motivational profiles. Recognizing the distinctive approaches that characterize different ethnic groups can be a start and can be used to advantage in the classroom. Research on ethnic groups reveals distinct differences along four dimensions of personal interaction: group versus individual orientations, active versus passive coping styles, attitudes toward authority, and expressive versus restrained mannerisms.

Group Versus Individual Orientations   Some cultures, such as Asian and Hispanic cultures, stress affiliation, interdependence, and cooperation. Other cultures, such as northern European, stress individual achievement, independence, and competition. Within the United States ethnic differences emerge along this dimension. Chinese, Hispanic, and African American children, for instance, are more group-oriented than those from the dominant culture (Rotheram & Phinney, 1987). These children are more attentive to the feelings and expectations of others than their White counterparts are. A Hispanic or an African American child may pay as much attention to the feelings of others as to the demands of the task at hand, an orientation many teachers may not understand or appreciate. However, in learning situations that require students to work together, this orientation will serve these students as well inside the classroom as outside it (Rotheram & Phinney, 1987).

Active Versus Passive Coping Styles   Cultures characterized by active coping styles stress the importance of controlling one's environment and being productive. Those with passive styles place more emphasis on being than on doing. The sense of the present is greater in the latter and of the future in the former. These differences—like those of group versus individual orientation—can translate into either strengths or weaknesses in the classroom. Children with a take-charge attitude may find it difficult to wait for others, or to take enough time to explore all the issues. The strength of this approach is the way that it fosters achievement.

The strengths of the passive approach are the freedom it gives students to turn themselves over to the moment and learn what it can teach them. The disadvantages to this coping style are most apparent in classrooms structured according to active coping strategies. Children from cultures with a passive coping style are not as likely to ask for help or materials, and, if teachers and classmates assume that no help is needed unless asked for, these students will not receive the help they need to keep up (Rotheram & Phinney, 1983).

Attitudes Toward Authority   Clear ethnic differences exist for this dimension as well. Hispanic and Asian American children, for instance, are likely to have been raised in authoritarian homes (see Chapter 9) and taught to be respectful and not to question those in authority. Certain Native American and many White children have been socialized to make decisions for themselves and are less accepting of authority (Rotheram & Phinney, 1987). It should not be surprising that some students want to be told what to do and do their best work under those conditions, whereas others want to make decisions for themselves and do not fare well with authoritarian teachers.

Expressive Versus Restrained Mannerisms   Interactions in some cultures are informal and open and in others are ritualized and private. The former is more characteristic of Black and White children, the latter of Asian American children. Black children express their feelings even more openly than Whites; theirs is a high-intensity culture, in which feelings are given more open expression. An Asian American student might easily misread a Black student's expressions of anger as aggression or a White student might regard an Asian American's reaction to an incident as timid simply because each is not familiar with the other's culture.

Children are not very accurate in predicting how those from another culture will react. Differences along each of these dimensions underscore the importance of developing cross-ethnic awareness among students as well as teachers.

Many minority children have difficulty predicting their own experiences as they move from home, to school, to community. Urie Bronfenbrenner (1979) describes the experiences that make up one's reality in terms of overlapping spheres of influence. At the most immediate level, the *microsystem,* are one's first-hand experiences—interactions at home, in the classroom, and with friends. The *mesosystem* arises from interactions among one's different microsystems. Minority children frequently experience problems with interactions involving the mesosystem. They may see their parents distrust the system or teachers communicate less respect for their parents than for those of other students.

Children experience the *exosystem* at the level of their communities. Available housing and the types of schools they attend reflect decisions made at the community level but influence their lives directly. The *macrosystem,* which consists of the underlying social and political climate, is even further removed from children's daily experiences, yet it impinges on their realities in very real ways. Laws concerning compulsory education, the mainstreaming of students with special needs, and the separation of grades into elementary, junior high, and high schools all illustrate the direct ways the macrosystem can affect the lives of schoolchildren. A less observable, but no less real, effect of the macrosystem is experienced in the form of beliefs, biases, and stereotypes. The values of the macrosystem can be at odds with those of the home microsystem for children from some minority groups (Spencer, 1985).

John Ogbu (1981, 1992) offers a disturbing analysis of the plight of many minority students. He notes that educational programs have assumed that the problems many minorities experience at school (poor attendance, high dropout rates, low achievement) should be addressed at the level of the microsystem—by improving the home environment or enriching educational experiences. Ogbu suggests that the problem is generated at the macrosystem level and can only be solved by changes introduced at that level. He attributes poor academic performance and high dropout rates among minorities to a "job ceiling," or discrimination in job opportunities, and to their perception that members of their own families have not been rewarded for their achievements.

If all children progressed through the same *social mobility system,* one in which mobility, or social class, reflects their abilities, then the most effective method of intervention for minorities who are failing would be at the microsystem level, reaching into the home or classroom to bring their abilities and skills up to the level of the others. But *do* all members of our society move through the same mobility system? Is there more than one system, similar to that of academic tracking, once students reach high school, but with respect to economic rather than educational opportunities?

If there is more than one mobility system, what factors other than ability and skill determine the system in which individuals participate? Notice that if we have more than one social mobility system, social class is an *effect* rather than a cause, and minority problems must be addressed at another level. Social status among minorities, argues Ogbu, reflects the realities of a job ceiling: a consistent set of social and economic obstacles preventing equal selection based on ability imposed on certain minorities at birth—that is, a society stratified by ethnic and racial castes as well as by class. The problems of minority groups can be resolved only at the macrosystem level, by addressing social ills such as prejudice and discrimination.

Children at the Edge

Two other groups of students have special needs and frequently find themselves out of step with the rest of the class. These children come from all backgrounds. They are the gifted and those with learning disabilities.

Gifted Children   In 1925, Lewis Terman of Stanford University defined the gifted as those who place among the top 2% on a test of intelligence. Seventy years later, the most common criterion for placing students in special educational programs is still a score on an intelligence test: 130 or higher (Horowitz & O'Brien, 1986). The following descriptions come close to what the average person is likely to think of as gifted: the super-smart, the ones who ace school, the kids behind the books.

In 1981 Congress passed the Education Consolidation and Improvement Act, which defines giftedness more broadly. The gifted and talented are those "who give evidence of high performance capability in areas such as intellectual, creative, artistic, leadership capacity, or specific academic fields, and who require services or activities not ordinarily provided by the school in order to fully develop such capabilities" (Sec. 582).

Howard Gardner (1983) also includes more than traditional measures of intelligence in defining giftedness. Gardner considers seven domains of intelligence: musical, bodily-kinesthetic, logical-mathematical, linguistic, spatial, interpersonal, and intrapersonal. Children can be creative in any of these different domains, and, for Gardner, creativity is the highest form of functioning. Creativity and giftedness, however, are not neatly related. Many gifted individuals are also highly creative, but many are not. Also, many creative people are not intellectually gifted.

Some characteristics of giftedness, such as being bored or restless, are often not seen as signs of intelligence.

Q   Why might it be difficult to identify gifted children by their performance in the classroom?

Identifying the Gifted   Perhaps because intelligence reflects our personalities, gifted students fail to fit any stereotype. It is easy to identify those who have large vocabularies or who top out on standard tests of achievement. But what about the ones who never see things the way others do, have zany senses of humor or vivid imaginations, those who get bored easily or who, when they can't do things perfectly, fail to do them at all? Gifted children are likely to fit any of these descriptions as well.

Barbara Clark (1988), an educator at California State University, Los Angeles, offers the characteristics listed in Box 11.1 as indices of cognitive giftedness. Many of these characteristics would not be taken as signs of unusual talent or intelligence by most of us. Some, in fact, seem to signal just the opposite.

Do gifted children apply their intelligence to advantage in areas of their lives other than academic ones? Research offers a tentative yes. Various studies have found the gifted to be more mature, to have better social skills, and to be more self-confident, responsible, and self-controlled than age-mates of average intelligence (Hogan & Weiss, 1974; Hogan, 1980). Terman (1925) even noted that his gifted children were slightly more likely to be physically superior to average children, to be heavier at birth, to walk earlier as infants, grow taller, and generally have fewer physical defects. So much for the negative stereotypes of the gifted as bookworms and wimps.

Being gifted does not offer immunity to social and emotional setbacks. In fact, it may make them harder to take. Social injustices can be especially difficult for those concerned with social or political problems, and slights can easily be exaggerated by those who react to life intensely and with passion.

Educating the Gifted   Educational programs follow one of two alternatives: enrichment or acceleration. The goal of *enrichment* is to provide gifted students with more opportunities and experiences than they would normally get, without moving them to a higher grade. An example would be offering special courses in literature, math, science, or the arts, along with the normal course of studies.

Box 11.1 *Some Characteristics of a Gifted Student*

Asks many questions
Has much information on many topics
Adopts a questioning attitude
Becomes unusually upset at injustices
Is interested in social or political problems
Has better reasons than you do for not doing what you want done
Refuses to drill on repetitive tasks
Becomes impatient when can't do an assignment perfectly
Is a loner
Is bored and frequently has nothing to do
Completes part of an assignment and leaves it unfinished for something else
Continues to work on an assignment when the rest of the class moves on
to something else
Is restless
Daydreams
Understands easily
Likes to solve problems
Has own ideas as to how things should be done
Talks a lot
Enjoys debate
Enjoys abstract ideas

Source: Clark (1988).

Acceleration allows gifted students to advance beyond their grade level at a faster than normal rate—that is, to skip grades (Horowitz & O'Brien, 1986). Advocates of enrichment point to the social and emotional needs of gifted students, arguing that these are best met by keeping them with others their age. Although many gifted children are socially and emotionally more advanced than their peers, this argument is especially compelling for late maturers, especially boys.

On the other hand, failure to advance the highly gifted can present as many problems as acceleration. Students who experience little or no intellectual challenge in their classes and feel they are simply "marking time" can face intellectual stagnation, loneliness, and apathy—difficulties as serious as any introduced by moving ahead of their age-mages (Horowitz & O'Brien, 1986).

Children with Learning Disabilities   For some students, marking time takes a very different form. They, too, have difficulty maintaining interest in their classes but for reasons very different from those of gifted students. These students have experienced difficulty in school almost from the beginning. Many live with the bewildering sense that something is wrong, though they can't say what. Most feel stupid, though they are not. These children have a learning disability.

Having a learning disability is not to be confused with intelligence. Learning-disabled children are just as intelligent as other children and perform as well as their classmates on tasks that do not require them to process information in particular ways. Thus one type of learning disability might take the form of a child having difficulty understanding instructions when these are stated orally to the class as a whole, but not when they appear in writing at the top of her worksheet.

Conversely, another learning-disabled child might be unable to distinguish b's from p's and d's on a printed page, making reading difficult, but be able to comprehend a story that is read to him as well as any of his classmates.

 John Dixon (1997), research director for the American Shakespeare Theater, describes his experiences as a gifted child who also had a learning disability:

> It was a combination of mystification and depression that set in when Mrs. Wilson struggled at introducing me to reading in the first grade. As I looked around at my classmates, their ease at turning written words into the correct spoken words seemed to make them coconspirators. They possessed a secret wisdom to which I was not privy. Mrs. Wilson looked upon them with eyes of pleasure. They were her teacher's delight, her measure of success. She looked upon me with eyes of forlorn patience. I was the stumbling block in her attempt to deliver a class full of readers to the second grade teachers. I remember sitting bent low at my school desk, eyes downward, hoping not to be noticed as I bumbled over Dick and Jane. . . .
>
> Throughout these eight years there was an interesting discrepancy. Although my reading never changed from a slow to halting pace, I nevertheless loved reading. Sometimes I would spend every minute possible devouring whole sets of books from the library bookcase in the back of the classroom; slowly, ruminatingly, but devouring. There was no way my reading could be rushed. Deep twinges of anguish accompanied speed reading drills. I would pretend to be reading faster than I could because I didn't want to be the last student to raise his hand to indicate being finished. Most of all I hated reading tests. If I didn't rush through tests much faster than I could possibly comprehend the material, I would find myself far from the end of the test when the time was called. Yet there were times when I spent all the time I could reading. Books were the entry way to the larger world. The ideas in books were marvelous even if my reading mechanics were tortuous. The ideas in books came to be an important focus of my life, and I would learn to put up with the difficulty for the sake of learning. (pp. 174–175) ◄

Estimates of the number of school-age students with learning disabilities range from 2% to over 30%, depending on how learning disabilities are defined (Lovitt, 1989). Of those with learning disabilities, approximately 33% will eventually graduate with a diploma. Another 5% will graduate through certification, but 19% of all learning-disabled students will drop out of school (U.S. Department of Education, 1988).

Defining Learning Disabilities   Who are these students, and what special problems do they face? Only recently have experts achieved some consensus in answering these questions. Their answers focus on three defining features of learning disabilities: (1) a discrepancy between expected and actual performance, (2) difficulty with academic tasks that cannot be traced to emotional problems or sensory impairment, and (3) presumed neurological dysfunction.

First, learning-disabled students show a *discrepancy between expected and actual performance*. Students with a learning disability are of average or above-average intelligence but don't perform at the level one would expect based on their intelligence, frequently falling behind their peers in academic skills. Second, their *difficulty with academic tasks* cannot be traced to emotional or sensory dysfunction. They may experience difficulty in one or more specific areas (for example, reading or math) or in the general skills needed for many areas, such as being able to pay attention or to monitor their performance (such as remembering which subroutines they have completed in a math problem in order to begin the next). They do not have a learning disability if the source of the difficulty is an emotional problem, problems at home, or a sensory impairment, such as a hearing loss. Finally, students with a learning disability are presumed to have some *neurological dysfunction*, because they are of at least average intelligence and their difficulties are not primarily the result of sensory, emotional, or cultural causes (Lovitt, 1989).

Addressing Problems Learning-disabled children face problems both inside and outside the classroom. In the classroom, programs can range from difficulty paying attention or following class discussions to failure to turn in written assignments. Learning-disabled students have difficulty keeping up with classmates. In addition, most learning-disabled students have poorer study habits, are less likely to do their homework, and, when it comes to demonstrating what they *have* learned, have poorer test-taking skills. Frequently, nonattendance, incomplete assignments, and failure to turn in homework contribute to their failure in a course as much as their scores on tests do (Lovitt, 1989).

The problems of learning-disabled children don't end when they leave the classroom. As a group, they have poorer social skills than other students. They are less likely to pick up on another's mood and respond appropriately and are less aware of the effect their behavior has on others. Subtle cues can go right by them. The same problems that make it difficult for them to understand what their teachers are saying in class can affect their interactions with friends. They may miss nuances of conversation and respond inappropriately or miss rule changes in a game and feel they've been taken advantage of when the old rules no longer apply. Frequently they prefer the company of those who are younger, just because they are more compliant.

The learning-disabled are less likely to be involved in extracurricular activities than other students (Spreen, 1988). Perhaps this fact reflects their general disenchantment with school. Or it may reflect a poorer self-image and expectations of failure in these activities as well. Increasing learning-disabled students' involvement in extracurricular activities such as teams, clubs, and music and drama productions might be one of the most important ways of increasing their participation and their motivation to stay in school (Lovitt, 1989).

Schooling the Learning Disabled *Mainstreaming* places learning-disabled children in regular classes in which teachers attempt to accommodate their special needs. Perhaps because so little can be done to meet the special needs of the learning-disabled in most classrooms, mainstreaming can introduce special problems of attendance. A growing number of schools that mainstream learning-disabled students provide a *special education consultant* who meets with regular teachers to discuss ways of managing the needs of these students. This procedure allows students to attend classes with their peers while receiving materials designed by someone who has specialized in learning disorders.

The other extreme from mainstreaming places learning-disabled students in *special education classes*. The obvious advantages of such an approach are small classes in which materials can be personalized to the needs of students and a teacher who is experienced in the special needs of the learning-disabled. Disadvantages are that association with nondisabled students who might serve as positive role models is limited, and teachers may not hold the learning-disabled to the same standards that are required of other students (Lovitt, 1989).

Children who are mastery oriented enjoy situations that challenge them.

Success, Failure, and Patterns of Achievement   The attitude children take toward their successes and failures is an important determinant of future success. It's not so much whether they fail or succeed—all children experience their share of both; the important thing is what they attribute their failure or success to that determines whether they will persist and eventually achieve. Research distinguishes two quite different patterns of achievement behavior: one defined by a focus on the task and what it takes to master it (a *task-mastery orientation*) and the other by a focus on one's performance or ability (a *performance-ability orientation*). The first approach is adaptive; the second is not (Dweck, 1989).

Children who are task, or mastery, oriented enjoy situations that challenge them, and they work at them even when they are difficult. They even take pride in how much effort they have to put into mastering something new. Children who are performance, or ability, oriented avoid challenging situations and show little persistence in the face of difficulty. They view any effort they must expend negatively, because having to try hard puts their ability in question. If at first they don't succeed, they find something else to do (Burhans & Dweck, 1995; Dweck, 1989).

Performance-oriented students tend not to pursue challenging material unless they're sure they will succeed. They choose situations that will not reveal what they regard as their lack of ability. These students are likely to prefer tasks that are either very easy or very difficult; failure at the first is unlikely, and failure at the second cannot be taken as a measure of their ability. Even above-average students who are performance-oriented will avoid situations that involve risk in preference to those they can perform effortlessly, thereby making them feel smart. In doing so, however, they miss situations that promote further understanding (Dweck, 1986).

The difference between students who stick it out and those who give up is basically one of attitude, which researchers term *attribution of outcome.* Children who persist when they experience failure tend to attribute the outcome of their actions to their efforts. Believing they haven't tried hard enough, they increase their efforts. They are task-oriented (Dweck & Reppucci, 1973; Heyman & Dweck, 1998).

Those who are disrupted by failure, frequently to the point of giving up, are performance-oriented. Because they interpret failure to mean that they lack the ability for what they have attempted, they defensively withdraw in the face of it. To believe that failure means that one lacks ability is also to believe that trying harder isn't going to help. Rather than trying harder, these students explain their failure as bad luck or the task's being too difficult. For them, having to try too hard is dangerous; it's just another way of calling their ability into question.

Claudia Mueller and Carol Dweck (1998) point out that praising children's intelligence when they do well by telling them they are smart may cause them to focus more on their performance than on what they are working on. These investigators gave fifth-graders problems to complete, after which they were told they had done very well. Some were praised for their intelligence ("You must be smart at these problems"), some for their effort ("You must have worked hard at these problems"), and those in a control condition were given no additional feedback. All were then given a choice as to whether they wanted to continue with problems they could "learn a lot from" even though they might not "look so smart" (learning goal) or with those that were "pretty easy" in which they could expect to "do well" (performance goal).

They found that children's choice of what type of problem to continue with was definitely affected by the type of praise they received. Two-thirds of those who had been praised for their intelligence chose to work on problems on which they could expect to do similarly well. In contrast, over 90% of those who had been praised for working hard at the first set of problems chose to work with ones

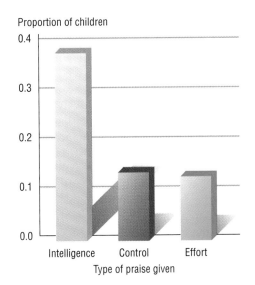

Proportion of children

FIGURE 11.6 Proportion of Children Misrepresenting Their Success on Problems After Being Praised for Their Intelligence or Their Effort or Receiving No Feedback. *Source:* C. S. Mueller and C. S. Dweck. (1998). Praise for intelligence can undermine children's motivation and performance. *Journal of Personality and Social Psychology, 75,* 33–52.

from which they could learn something. Approximately equal numbers of children in the control condition chose either of the two types of problems.

In order to discover whether praise also affects how children interpret failure experiences, all children were told they had done worse on the second set of problems. It was found that those who initially had been praised for being smart were more likely to attribute their subsequent failure to lack of ability, whereas those who had been praised for working hard were more likely to attribute this to lack of effort. Finally, when children were asked to describe for another child how well they had done on these problems, those who received praise for their ability were more likely to misrepresent how well they had done, nearly 40% lying about the number of problems they had actually solved (Figure 11.6). In contrast, only 13% of those praised for how hard they had worked misrepresented their performance, a number close to that for children who received no feedback (14%).

The Contexts of Development: Supportive and Responsive Environments

Children's pleasure in learning, understanding what their successes and failures communicate about themselves, and their persistence at challenging tasks are as much a product of their experiences at home as they are of those in the classroom. Supportive parenting has been found to be positively related to children's intellectual development as well as to their social and emotional well-being. Supportive parents are characterized by their warmth and firmness in their interactions with children, their use of reasoning when disciplining, and their involvement in the various aspects of their children's lives (Baumrind, 1967, 1989).

Supportive parenting, additionally, is related to children's overall adjustment to school. Gregory Pettit, John Bates, and Kenneth Dodge (1997) found academic performance among kindergarten children to be related to parental warmth and involvement and, among the same children when they reached the sixth grade, to parental involvement and the use of reasoning. In addition, supportive parenting acted as a protective factor for children who might otherwise be at risk for school adjustment, such that the relation between supportive parenting and adjustment in the sixth grade was strongest for children from low-income and single-parent families.

Cognitively stimulating home environments motivate children academically.

Adele Gottfried, James Fleming, and Allen Gottfried (1998) followed a group of largely middle-class, European American children from 8 to 13, examining the relation between home environments and students' intrinsic academic motivation. They found, as might be expected, that children who grow up in homes that are cognitively stimulating are more likely to find academic pursuits intrinsically interesting. Furthermore, growing up in a cognitively stimulating home environment had an impact on academic intrinsic motivation in ways that could not be explained simply in terms of differences in family income level. This is not to say that family income level is not important, but that its effects are filtered through the more immediate environment of interactions within the family and the transmission of family values. This environment not only fosters curiosity and exploration, but also promotes the development of competencies.

Parents who otherwise might not offer sufficiently optimal environments can be shown ways of making these more stimulating. Terry Cronan, Sonia Cruz, Rosa Arriago, and Andrew Sarlom (1996) tutored parents of Head Start children in effective ways of reading to their children. Children were randomly assigned to either a high- or low-intervention program or to a no-intervention control. Parents of children in the first group attended 18 sessions in which a tutor met individually with them and their child and showed them effective ways of reading to their children. Parents were also shown how to teach basic concepts, such as naming colors and shapes, and told the importance of asking their children questions and of talking to them. Tutors met with families on an average of once a week. Parents of children in the low-intervention group received similar instruction, but only for three sessions.

These investigators found that parents in the high-intervention group not only read to their children more often, but also were more likely to build this into a ritual, such as having a regular time or place for reading. These parents were also more likely to use the library, checking out books to read together with their children and by themselves, and were more likely as well to bring their children to the library than were those in the control condition. Children whose parents were given the intensive training showed improved language skills and improved conceptual development. Intervention programs such as this one are important, because they help to create a more responsive environment for children by building in patterns of interaction, such as reading together, sharing more activities, and, in general, talking more with each other.

Other attempts at intervention have focused on day care programs. Participation in day care during the first 3 years of life has been found to serve as a protective factor for at-risk children whose home environments are otherwise impoverished. Children who are enrolled in early day care programs do better once they reach school than those not enrolled, showing improvement in both mathematics and reading skills. Reading skills, especially, are affected by early intervention, with children who are enrolled by the age of 2 showing the strongest effects. Day care has not been found to affect all children the same way. Children from impoverished environments have been found to especially benefit from day care if enrolled early in such programs, before reaching the age of 1, perhaps because their responsiveness to their environment is increased (Burchinal, Campbell, Bryant, Wasik, & Ramey, 1997). Enrollment this early has an opposite effect on children from more optimal home environments (Caughy, DiPietro, & Strobino, 1994).

Although participation in preschool programs such as Head Start has been found to contribute to children's cognitive development and to their success in school (Barnett, 1992, 1995; Neisser et al., 1996), exposure to such programs cannot protect children from the effects of poverty indefinitely. One of the recommendations to come out of research on early childhood intervention programs is

Parental involvement in children's education has a strong positive effect on children's school performance.

that intervention be extended into the school years, such that its effects can better take root in children's and families' lives (National Head Start Association, 1990). Being able to continue in a program for the first several years of schooling, as opposed to ending with kindergarten, may be an important source of stability, by providing continuity not only in a learning environment, but also in a social environment, preserving supportive relationships with peers and teachers. Such programs may also be effective in involving parents in their children's schooling.

Arthur Reynolds and Judy Temple (1998) compared school achievement between children who participated in an extended intervention program, lasting from preschool to the second or third grade, and children whose participation ended when they were in kindergarten. They found that extended intervention significantly improves the effectiveness of early-intervention programs. This is not to say that preschool and kindergarten programs are not effective, because they are. However, enrollment in an extended intervention program through the second and third grades for children who had previously been enrolled in preschool and kindergarten programs significantly increased the benefits of the earlier intervention. Furthermore, these benefits persisted through the seventh grade and held up even when other important factors, such as family background variables, parents' attitudes toward education, and level of achievement among children at the completion of kindergarten, were controlled.

The parents of children in extended intervention also become more involved in their children's schooling, participating more in the activities of the school, volunteering in the classroom and interacting more with other parents (Reynolds & Temple, 1998). In general, parental attitudes of children enrolled in early intervention programs are quite positive; they express optimism about their children's education and affirm their belief in the importance of doing well in school (Galper, Wigfield, & Seefeldt, 1997).

The importance of parents' involvement in their children's education cannot be stressed too much. James Comer (1985, 1988), at Yale University, has created a program in which parents, along with teachers, administrators, and staff, are responsible for administering the activities of the school. This program addresses

Educational Equality and School Choice

BY MICHAEL WAPNER

One unhappy reality of American public education is that not every school provides quality instruction. As measured by achievement test scores, likelihood of finishing high school, and the proportion of graduates entering and completing college, there are wide gulfs between the best and poorest public schools (Godwin, Kemerer, Martinez, & Ruderman, 1998).

A second unhappy reality is that despite legislation against intentional segregation and the widespread busing of students to achieve desegregation, schools still show great disparities in racial and ethnic populations. Approximately two thirds of African American students and nearly three fourths of Hispanic students who attend public schools go to schools in which the student body is predominately minority. For over a third of these students, 90% of the students in the schools they attend are members of an ethnic minority group (Godwin et al., 1998; Orfield, 1993).

At the intersection of these two unhappy realities lies a third. Schools with the highest concentration of minority students are among those that provide education of the lowest quality. High among the variables that influence the quality of learning in a school are the social class and ethnic composition of its student body (Bryk, Lee, & Holland, 1993). These two variables are tightly linked. A student in an intensely segregated minority school is 14 times as likely to be in a high-poverty school as is a student in a school where black or Latino students make up less than 10% of the student body (Orfield, 1993). Thus, race is linked to poverty, both are linked to segregation, and segregation is linked to poor schools and educational failure (Orfield, 1993).

One strategy for breaking the pattern of separation and underachievement would be to broaden the selection of schools that minority students can attend—to dilute the concentration of poor minority students in particular schools, to place students at risk for low achievement among higher-achieving students in better schools, and, as a very desirable bonus, to increase the cultural diversity of the student body. There are a number of ways this might be achieved but, in addition to questions regarding educational effectiveness, every one of them raises knotty economic, political, social, and ethical issues.

Busing

Since the Supreme Court struck down the "separate but equal" formula that had rationalized school segregation and educational inequality, one of the most frequently employed mechanisms for achieving school integration has been transporting groups of students by bus. However, busing often generates hard feelings in the community. It often requires enforcement by the courts and even police, it does not allow for student or parental choice, and it is expensive.

Changing Residence

The greatest determinant of school choice is housing. Everything else being equal, children go to the schools that are closest to where they live. Unfortunately, where people live depends overwhelmingly on what they can afford. Poor people are forced to "choose" low-cost housing, frequently in ethnically segregated neighborhoods where the schools are poor.

Magnet Schools

Specializing in some particular academic area (science, arts, and the like), magnet schools accept qualified students from throughout a school district or, sometimes, from neighboring school districts. In large urban districts, about 20% of high

the social and developmental, as well as the educational, needs of students. Comer believes, for instance, that social skills and ties to the community are as important as academic subjects, especially for lower-income students, who often lack these assets. In two inner-city schools using Comer's model, student performance so improved that the schools tied for third and fourth place in the district, with the students testing up to a year above the average for their grade. Attendance also improved dramatically, and behavior problems practically disappeared.

It is easy to understand why such a program could work: teaching becomes more relevant when academic subjects are translated into the daily concerns of students and their families. In turn, what is learned in the classroom receives the support of parents who are committed to educational programs they help plan. The Social Policy Focus, "Educational Equality and School Choice," examines various attempts to provide inner-city students with better educational opportunities.

school students are likely to attend magnet schools. Outcome studies have shown that magnet schools have a positive effect on student performance (Godwin et al., 1998). However, these schools frequently skim the best students from the local schools, thus leaving the latter even worse off than before.

Open Enrollment

Another mechanism for achieving desegregation and greater equality of education is to give students and their parents the freedom to enroll in any school they choose rather than to restrict them to single school districts. While this principle seems good in theory, its effect is frequently to *increase* rather than decrease ethnic and economic segregation (Wells, 1996). The more affluent and knowledgeable families in a school district are more likely to be able to afford transportation costs and to know the relative qualities of the various schools. Thus, as with magnet schools, open enrollment tends to skim the least at-risk students, leaving local schools even more economically and educationally disadvantaged.

School Vouchers

A voucher system gives families a certain amount of money (usually some percentage of the cost to educate a child in the local public schools) to send their children to private schools. The basic idea behind this system, clearly, is to open education to the forces of the marketplace. Presumably, parents will patronize those schools that provide the best education for their children. This competition will force schools to improve—or lose enrollment, which will ultimately force them to close. Studies of the use of vouchers in Great Britain, France, the Netherlands, and Chile suggest that when vouchers are made available to families at all socioeconomic levels, more affluent families are more likely to use the vouchers to send their children to private schools. The result is even greater economic and ethnic segregation in the schools (Ambler, 1994; Pary, 1996).

In the United States, the Milwaukee Parental Choice Program has systematic outcome data available. This program provided vouchers only to low-income families; 95% of the participating students were either African American or Latino. The results are mixed but promising. Witte and colleagues (1994) found no difference in test scores between students using their vouchers to go to private schools and a random sample of students in the public schools. But other studies found that voucher students who remain in private schools show significantly greater improvement than students who applied to but could not enroll in private schools because of space limitations (Godwin et al., 1998).

The private schools involved in the Milwaukee study were all nonreligious. Current interpretations of constitutional restrictions preclude the use of publicly funded vouchers in religious schools. Interestingly, among private institutions, it is Catholic schools that appear to bring out the greatest educational achievement with poor, minority students—better test scores and higher percentages graduating from high school and from college (Witte, 1996; Bryk et al., 1993).

So, what can we conclude? The bottom line is that schools do not exist in a vacuum. They reflect the social, cultural, economic, and political conditions under which the students, their families, teachers, and friends live. Thus, well-intentioned programs for improving the educational opportunities for low-income children cannot succeed without breaking the vicious cycles which these conditions converge to create. Poor people get poor educations. Poorly educated people live in poverty. Whom you go to school with influences how much you learn. But how much you know determines whom you go to school with. A democracy must provide its citizens with equal opportunity for education. But without education one cannot take advantage of educational opportunities. The one good thing about circles, however, is that there are many places to enter and many from which to exit.

Summary

Piaget's Stage of Concrete Operational Thought

Piaget traced the intellectual developments of middle childhood to the emergence of mental operations, internalized actions that children can perform in their heads. Mental operations are reversible, enabling children to imagine both performing an action and reversing that action to get back to the point from which they had started. Each operation belongs to a set of operations, making it

possible to see how the effects of one are related to those of another. Being able to reverse an operation carried out in one's head and to relate one operation to another causes thinking to become more logical.

School-age children, when given tests of conservation, are capable of understanding that an object can remain the same despite having changed in appearance. Conservation reflects three processes: (1) reversibility, or the understanding that one could nullify the effects of the operation that resulted in the changed appearance, (2) identity, or the realization that the substance in each of the two states has not changed, and (3) compensation, the realization that changes along one dimension are compensated for by changes along a second dimension.

An Information-Processing Approach to Cognitive Development

Information-processing theorists view thinking as the processing of information and approach its study by looking at how information is encoded, or mentally represented, and at the processes involved in its transformation and use. With age, children develop more efficient ways of processing information. Automatization refers to increases with age in the efficiency with which children engage in various mental activities such that these require less of their attention. Encoding also changes with age such that older children are better able to recognize which features are important. Encoding appears to become more efficient with age due to increases in the ease of processing new information, to more systematic searches for relevant information, and to the use of more efficient strategies when solving problems.

Memory

Memory exists as several interrelated systems, each with different characteristics. Sensory memory, which lasts for no more than half a second, does not reveal age differences. Short-term memory is limited in both capacity, to approximately seven items, and duration, to no more than 15 to 20 seconds. For information to be held longer than this, it must be rehearsed, or continuously repeated. Age differences exist in the number of items children can hold in short-term memory. Long-term memory is unlimited both in capacity and duration. Age differences in long-term memory are evident primarily in information retrieval. With age, children can retrieve information more rapidly and develop greater awareness of their memory known as metamemory, which enables them to monitor what they are doing and increases the likelihood of using strategies for remembering.

Limitations of Thought in Middle Childhood

Thought in middle childhood is not abstract; thus, it is difficult for children to think of things they cannot see. Because children focus on visible aspects of a problem, they fail to speculate about other, less immediately evident solutions. Consequently, they frequently operate according to assumptions that they make on the basis of limited information.

Humor: A Sense of the Ridiculous

Three ingredients to humorous situations have been identified; each of these changes with age. The perception of incongruity, or violations of one's expectancies, increases in middle childhood due to children's ability to appreciate multiple meanings of words. This component of humor forms the basis for many of their jokes and riddles. Emotional release is a second component of humor; because different situations are problematic for children of different ages, the things that children find funny will also change with age. The third component of humor is intellectual. Concepts that are recently mastered are sufficiently challenging to be humorous.

The World of School

The intellectual developments that occur in middle childhood ready children for school. Even so, many of the basic tasks they must master are difficult and require the use of strategies. Children typically have available for their use a number of strategies that differ in their efficiency. Changes in strategies do not necessarily reflect movement to more sophisticated approaches. In arithmetic, children from different cultures differ in the efficiency of the strategies they use and in their general mathematical skills. Language has been found to contribute to both their choice of strategies and their understanding of basic mathematical concepts such as place value. Differences in how mathematics is taught also contribute to achievement.

Learning to read involves a number of skills. Children must be able to identify individual letters and must know the sounds these letters make. This knowledge enables them to decode the sounds that make up a word. Children use their knowledge of the name of the letter when learning the sound it will make, mapping the sound in the name onto the corresponding phoneme. Children also rely on context when sounding out unfamiliar or phonologically ambiguous words. Reading has been taught through either of two basic methods. The basic-skills approach starts with letters and sounds before moving to words, whereas the whole-word approach teaches by exposing children to contexts that facilitate the discovery of principles.

Culture and Gender in the Classroom

Some gender-role stereotyping still exists in teaching materials. In textbooks, males are still pictured more frequently than females, appear in more diverse occupations, and need rescuing less frequently. But these differences represent tremendous improvements over the materials in use a generation ago.

The use of male generic language represents another form of bias. Using the masculine pronoun generically predisposes students and their teachers to think of males, not of individuals in general. Their evaluations of the competence of students of either sex for different types of work are thereby skewed.

Jigsaw classrooms, where students work in small groups, each contributing a different part of the lesson, foster cooperation and promote better relations among students from different ethnic backgrounds. Presenting material from several cultural perspectives is helpful to minority students who may not always share the perspective assumed in the textbook or other materials used.

Communication problems arise for some minority students when language is used differently at school and at home. Four distinctive approaches characterize different ethnic and racial groups: group versus individual orientations, active versus passive coping styles, attitudes toward authority, and expressive versus restrained mannerisms. Intervention programs that heighten teacher and student awareness of these differences improve the quality of multicultural education.

Most intervention programs have focused on problems minority students may experience at the level of the microsystem—that is, in the home and the classroom. Problems of poorer achievement may have to be addressed at the level of the macrosystem.

Children at the Edge

Children who score 130 or above on an intelligence test or who have creative, artistic, leadership, or other special talents are defined as gifted. Gifted children fail to fit any stereotype. Educational programs for the gifted can offer enrichment, providing them with more experiences than they would ordinarily get, or acceleration, allowing them to advance beyond their grade level.

Children with learning disabilities are of average or above-average intelligence and show a discrepancy between expected and actual performance. They have difficulty in academic tasks that presumably can be traced to a neurological dysfunction. Learning-disabled students fall at least two grade levels behind classmates and their difficulties cannot be traced to emotional or sensory dysfunction. Social skills are also affected for many.

Mainstreaming places learning-disabled students in regular classes. A consulting special education teacher may advise regular teachers on the special needs of these students. At the other extreme, learning-disabled students may be placed in special classes with specially trained teachers. Each of these educational options has different advantages.

Success, Failure, and Patterns of Achievement

Achievement motivation patterns distinguish schoolchildren. Task-oriented children focus on the task and work to increase their mastery. Performance-oriented children focus on their performance and use it as a measure of their ability. Task-oriented children are less likely to be disrupted by initial failure, believing it to result from a lack of sufficient effort rather than inability. Performance-oriented children are likely to withdraw in the face of failure and attribute it to an external cause rather than their own lack of effort. Praising children's intelligence when they do well may cause them to focus more on their performance than on what they are working on. Conversely, praising children for working hard appears to cause them to focus on the effort they must put into a task in order to succeed.

The Contexts of Development: Supportive and Responsive Environments

Supportive parenting, which takes the form of parental warmth, involvement, firmness, and use of reasoning when disciplining, is positively related to children's intellectual development, adjustment to school, and intrinsic academic motivation. Parents who otherwise might not offer optimal environments can be shown ways of making these more stimulating. Participation in extended day care programs, lasting from preschool to the second or third grade, offers another effective form of intervention. One of the benefits of such programs is the increased involvement of parents in their children's education.

Key Terms

assumptive realities (p. 417)
automatization (p. 411)
basic-skills approach (p. 427)
encoding (p. 412)

jigsaw classroom (p. 429)
long-term memory (p. 414)
male generic language (p. 428)
mental operations (p. 408)

phonemes (p. 426)
sensory memory (p. 414)
short-term memory (p. 414)
whole-language approach (p. 427)

Middle Childhood
Psychosocial Development

Bye, Dad! Charlie's mom is here to take us to practice. See you at the talent show tonight—get a seat where I can see you this time, okay?"

"Sure thing," he muses, reviewing the evening—pick Jessie up from basketball tryouts, bring home some take-out for diner, and work up that report for tomorrow. "Front row center," he calls back.

Perhaps never faster than in middle childhood does time rush by. As one wise uncle said, "The years go faster than the days." They do in fact, compressed by school and homework, soccer games and basketball practice, and, of course, household chores and talent shows.

These are rich years, filled with growth and change. Children are not only physically stronger and intellectually more adultlike than they were just a few years ago, but they are also beginning to master activities they could only dream about earlier. They will spend hours for instance, practicing rim shots, doing scales on a clarinet, and completing complex projects for school, such as constructing an igloo from sugar cubes, complete with an explanation of how one can stay warm inside a house made from ice. In mastering these accomplishments children learn not only the particular skills involved but also, in each case, something about themselves. They discover what they can do when they really try. They also discover that their earlier fantasies of extraordinary feats are no longer as satisfying as their actual, if less than perfect, accomplishments.

The Self

Erikson (1968) spoke of this new satisfaction as a sense of **industry.** By *industry* he meant the sense of accomplishment that comes from being able to make things and that comes with doing things well. Children come to know themselves

In middle childhood, children are especially ready to apprentice themselves as learners.

industry (versus inferiority)
Erikson's term for the sense of accomplishment that comes from being able to make things and that comes with doing things well.

through the things they can do, through their skills. Erikson believed that children are especially ready to apprentice themselves as learners when they reach middle childhood. They want to be big by sharing in the activities of those whom they regard as big. They willingly work alongside parents and teachers, watching what they do and attempting the same themselves. Accomplishment comes only with perseverance and discipline, however, and Erikson points out that a sense of inferiority can develop in children who are not willing, or able, to persist at the things they attempt until mastery is achieved.

Children become more reflective during the school years as well. In combination with their newly developing skills, this reflection lays a foundation for changes in the ways in which they think of themselves, of their self-concept.

Self-Concept

How do children think of themselves? What are they most likely to say, for instance, if asked to describe themselves? Listen to what two children have to say. We will first hear from Lisa, who is 8, and then from her 4-year-old brother Jason. Lisa says this of herself:

> I'm in third grade this year, and pretty popular, at least with the girls. That's because I'm nice and helpful and can keep secrets. Most of the boys at school are pretty yukky. I don't feel that way about my little brother Jason, although he does get on my nerves. I love him but at the same time, he also does things that make me mad. But I control my temper, I'd be ashamed of myself if I didn't. At school, I'm feeling pretty smart in certain subjects, Language Arts and Social Studies. I got A's in these subjects on my last report card and was really proud of myself. But I'm feeling pretty dumb in Arithmetic and Science, particularly when I see how well the other kids are doing. Even though I'm not doing well in those subjects, I still like myself as a person, because Arithmetic and Science just aren't that important to me. How I look and how popular I am are more important. (Harter, 1996, p. 208)

Jason, who is still a preschooler, also has quite a bit to say about himself:

> My name is Jason and I live in a big house with my mother and father and sister, Lisa. I have a kitty that's orange and a television in my own room. I know all of my A, B, C's. listen: A, B, C, D, E, F, G, H, J, L, K, O, M, P, Q, X, Z. I can run faster than anyone! I like pizza and I have a nice teacher. I can count up to 100, want to hear me? I love my dog, Skipper. I can climb to the top of the jungle gym, I'm not scared! Just happy. You can't be happy and scared, no way! I have brown hair and I go to pre-school. I'm really strong. I can lift this chair, watch me! (p. 208)

These self-descriptions illustrate several characteristic differences between the way older and younger children think of the self. Older children, for instance, describe themselves in terms of general traits. Thus, Lisa says of herself that she is smart and gives examples of school subjects in which she has done well, mentioning that she got A's on her report card. Younger children, in contrast, describe themselves in terms of specific behaviors. Jason, for instance, talks about how well he can climb a jungle gym, not how good he is at sports in general.

Older children are likely to describe themselves interpersonally, in terms of their relationships with others, whereas younger children are more likely to describe themselves in terms of their preferences and possessions. Lisa, for instance, talks about how she is with others and how she feels toward them,

As children grow older, self-perceptions of both strengths and weaknesses become more realistic.

School-age children are able to describe themselves in terms of contradictions and inconsistencies, whereas younger children cannot. What explanation might Piaget offer to explain this difference?

Older children have been found to compare their present performance at a task with how well they have done before, whereas younger children do not. How might we expect children's perceptions of themselves to change based on this difference?

describing herself as popular, telling us what she thinks of boys, and using such relational terms as "helpful" and being able to "keep secrets." Jason, on the other hand, tells us that he likes pizza and that he has a cat, a dog, and his own television.

Self-characterizations also become more complex with age, tolerating contradictions and inconsistencies, whereas those of younger children remain relatively simple, describing themselves and others as either all good or all bad in any particular domain. Jason argues, for instance, that one cannot be both "happy *and* scared," whereas Lisa recognizes that she can be smart in one subject and "pretty dumb" in another. As a consequence, preschoolers tend to have a positive bias when describing themselves, whereas older children tend to be more self-critical. Jason describes himself in glowing positive terms, saying he knows all of his ABCs, can run faster than anyone, and is really strong. Older children admit to weaknesses as well as strengths. Lisa feels "pretty smart" in some subjects but not that smart in others. Similarly, she considers herself popular, but only with other girls.

With respect to this latter point, children's self-perceptions tend to become more realistic with age, their initial optimism declining as their appraisal of their strengths and weaknesses becomes more realistic (Marsh, Craven, & Debus, 1998). But on what basis do children make these evaluations? Do they compare their performance with what they have done in the past, or do they evaluate themselves in comparison with others?

Ruth Butler (1998) gave children the task of tracing a path from one point to another and told them either that they had done better or worse than another child or better or worse than they had done on a previous attempt. Irrespective of age, she found that children appraised themselves more positively when they were told they had done better than another child as opposed to having done worse. However, only older children used information from their previous performance in appraising themselves. This latter finding is to be expected given young children's difficulty in recognizing the continuity of the self over time (Povinelli et al., 1996; Povinelli & Simon, 1998), suggesting that comparisons with previous attempts would not provide a meaningful basis for self-appraisal for younger children (see Chapter 9).

Self-appraisal can also be seen in the expression of socially derived emotions, such as pride and shame (see Chapter 9). Harter notes that children's experience of these is dependent on the existence of an internalized standard, such as that provided by parental values, against which children evaluate the self. One might expect that prior to the internalization of such a standard, parents would actually have to be present for children to experience such feelings about themselves, whereas once parental values are internalized, children should experience such emotions even when others are not present.

Harter (1996) examined this possibility by telling children a story in which a child took something after being told not to and then was either discovered or not. When children were asked how the child and the parent would feel in either case, preschoolers talked only about the child being scared or worried if discovered and not about being ashamed. Although 6- and 7-year-olds mentioned being ashamed, this was only if the child had been caught. Only 7- and 8-year-olds said the child would feel shame even though no one might have seen what had been done.

The way children think of the self reflects their culture as well as their age. Maxine Hong Kingston (1976), a novelist and poet, illustrates this point when writing of the difficulty she experienced as a schoolgirl, growing up with Cantonese as her first language, when she tried to understand the way the words for "I" and "you," words used to describe the self versus others, were written in English:

> It was when I found out I had to talk that school became a misery, that the silence became a misery. I did not speak and felt bad each time that I did not speak. I read aloud in first grade, though, and heard the barest whisper with little squeaks come out of my throat....
>
> Reading out loud was easier than speaking because we did not have to make up what to say, but I stopped often, and the teacher would think I'd gone quiet again. I could not understand "I." The Chinese "I" has seven strokes, intricacies. How could the American "I," assuredly wearing a hat like the Chinese, have only three strokes, the middle so straight? Was it out of politeness that this writer left off the strokes the way a Chinese has to write her own name small and crooked? No, it was not politeness; "I" is a capital and "you" is lower-case. I stared at that middle line and waited so long for its black center to resolve into tight strokes and dots that I forgot to pronounce it. ◄

The problem she experienced in reading English had very little to do with the mechanics of reading itself, of knowing which symbols stood for which sounds. Rather, it had to do with the sense to give to these symbols. And this sense was intimately tied to the sense of self she had acquired as a Chinese American, one that reflected her culture's value of modesty, as well as civility and respect for others.

Self-Esteem

If the self-concept is what one takes to be true about the self, then self-esteem is how good one feels about this. A boy who might describe himself as smart, witty, a leader, loyal to his friends, and not very athletic does not stop there. He evaluates each of these qualities. "So I'm a wit, but is that as good as being athletic? Is

Children's friendships affect not only the way they think of themselves but also what they expect from relationships in general.

Why are children's relationships with their parents so important for their self-esteem?

it really okay to be as social as I am, or should I be more concerned with my studies? Am I loyal enough with my friends? And what about the times they do things I can't support?" The way he answers questions such as these contributes to how he feels about himself, to his feelings of self-worth. Self-esteem refers to children's overall positive or negative evaluation of themselves.

Relationships with parents provide the foundation for self-esteem. When parents are loving, children feel lovable and develop feelings of self-worth. These feelings become established early in life. Infants quickly learn whether the world in which they live will meet their needs; when those around them are responsive, they develop a sense of trust. The establishment of trust in these first, basic relationships permeates all later ones. Self-esteem in children then, as well as their more general self-perceptions, will reflect their interactions with parents (Bowlby, 1969, Erikson, 1968).

When do most children first begin to evaluate themselves in terms of their overall worth? Harter (1996) first finds evidence of an overall evaluation of the self in terms of self-worth at about the age of 8. She is quick to point out, however, that the absence of such evaluative remarks in younger children cannot be taken to mean that they do not differ with respect to how good they feel about themselves; rather, they simply do not articulate these feelings in relation to a self. Instead, one sees differences reflected in such things as their confidence in being able to do things versus their reluctance to show what they can do.

Constructing the Self with Others

Children's friendships affect not only the way they think of themselves, but also what they come to expect from relationships in general. Because of the egalitarian nature of their relationships with friends, as opposed to those they have with parents, children come to appreciate the importance of taking others' ideas into consideration. The reciprocity that characterizes friendships fosters an awareness in children of the obligations that one person has toward the other. This interde-

What quality primarily distinguishes children's friendships from their relationships with their parents?

pendence, in fact, is what distinguishes their relationships with friends from those they have with others (Youniss, 1994).

James Youniss (1994), at Catholic University, extends the constructivist position elaborated at earlier points throughout this text to include the social construction of reality through interaction with others. Thus, for Youniss, the basic unit in which knowledge is constructed is the interaction that takes place between children. Youniss notes that when children are together, they respond to each other's ideas, creating a shared meaning, each child putting forth his or her own understanding and reacting in turn to the way others receive it. In other words, children do not simply want to understand what is going on or how something makes sense, they want to share that understanding with someone else. In this way, the reality to which each responds is co-constructed, in that each child works toward the end of creating an understanding that is shared by the other. We see an example of such an interactive exchange between several boys in grade school as they attempt to give meaning to the somewhat unusual behavior of a substitute teacher who has just appeared in their classroom. Charles Baxter (1999), a novelist and short-story writer, describes the scene as follows:

> Therefore it was a surprise when a woman we had never seen came into the class the next day carrying a purple purse, a checkerboard lunchbox, and a few books. She put the books on one side of Mr. Hibler's desk and the lunchbox on the other, next to the Voice of Music phonograph. Three of us in the back of the room were playing with Heever, the chameleon that lived in a terrarium and on one of the plastic drapes, when she walked in.
>
> She clapped her hands at us. "Little boys," she said, "why are you bent over together like that?" She didn't wait for us to answer. "Are you tormenting an animal? Put it back. Please sit down at your desks. I want no cabals this time of the day." We just stared at her. "Boys," she repeated, "I asked you to sit down."
>
> I put the chameleon in his terrarium and felt my way to my desk, never taking my eyes off the woman.... Her fine light hair had been done up in what I would learn years later was called a chignon, and she wore gold-rimmed glasses whose lenses seemed to have the faintest blue tint. Harold Knardahl, who sat across from me, whispered, "Mars," and I nodded slowly, savoring the imminent weirdness of the day. (p. 909) ◄

This example illustrates, as well, the cooperative nature of children's interactions. Youniss regards cooperation as an essential feature of the social construction of reality. Friends implicitly agree, in other words, to be guided by the perceptions and promptings of each other. The alternative is to take one another's remarks as an occasion to offer a countering remark of one's own, resulting in a "stalemate" as both defend their own positions. Instead, friends agree to jointly order reality, understanding that in doing so they can rely on each other to validate their perceptions. "Yes," these boys were agreeing, "this is going to be a weird day."

Friendships are important as well in constructing the self, contributing to the way children come to see themselves. Friends provide feedback not only about the activities that they co-construct, but also about themselves as they engage in these. The shared meanings that friends arrive at, in other words, involve the ways in which they come to see themselves as well as the way they see their world. Children whose opinions are not listened to at home, for instance, may discover they have something to say when their friends come to them for help with problems. Similarly, children who are used to being protected by an older sister or brother may see themselves as able to stand up for others when their friends look to them for support. Friends also help each other sort through feelings, letting each other know that the way they feel is normal and shared by others. As one young girl put it, a friend is "someone who helps you understand how you feel" (Youniss, 1994).

Such feelings are not always positive, nor do friends always contribute to children's understanding of themselves through the experiences they share. Sometimes the awareness children gain of themselves is even more powerful when they have been left out or left behind. Nora Ephron (1972), an essayist and screenwriter, describes such an experience:

> I am eleven years old, about to enter the seventh grade, and Diana and I have not seen each other all summer. . . . We are meeting, as we often do, on the street midway between our two houses and we will walk back to Diana's and eat junk and talk about what has happened to each of us that summer. I am walking down Walden Drive in my jeans and my father's shirt hanging out and my old red loafers with the socks falling into them and coming toward me is . . . I take a deep breath . . . a young woman. Diana. Her hair is curled and she has a waist and hips and a bust and she is wearing a straight skirt, an article of clothing I have been repeatedly told I will be unable to wear until I have the hips to hold it up. My jaw drops, and suddenly I am crying, crying hysterically, can't catch my breath sobbing. My best friend has betrayed me. She has gone ahead without me and done it. She has shaped up. ◄

Because friends contribute in such important ways to children's sense of themselves, having even a single good friend should be especially important for children whose sense of self-esteem cannot be derived from their relationships with their parents. We know, for instance, that maltreated children have less positive self-concepts than do other children (Okun, Parker, & Levendosky, 1994) and, when maltreated in early childhood, have lower self-esteem (Bolger, Patterson, & Kupersmidt, 1998). Is it reasonable to expect, then, that self-esteem would be higher among maltreated children who have a close friendship with at least one other child than among those who do not?

Kerry Bolger, Charlotte Patterson, and Janis Kupersmidt (1998) reasoned that it would be. Friendships can provide the emotional security children need in order to explore their worlds, just as healthy relationships with parents have been found to provide a secure base for children who have not been maltreated (see Chapter 6). Also, children learn appropriate social skills through interactions with friends, skills that maltreated children are less likely to acquire in their interactions at home. These investigators conducted a longitudinal study in which they followed a group of maltreated children and a matched control group of nonmaltreated children over a 3-year period. They found that having a good friend was particularly important for chronically maltreated children, such friendships being associated with greater increases in self-esteem over time than for their nonmaltreated peers.

Friendships

Who are children most likely to have as friends? By the time they reach middle childhood, friends are almost exclusively of the same sex (Kovacs, Parker, & Hoffman, 1996; Oswald, Krappmann, Uhlendorff, & Weiss, 1994). In fact, school-age children rarely interact with peers of the opposite sex and, on the occasions when they do, follow a strict code of unspoken rules. Such rules maintain that these contacts must be accidental or, if intentional, must appear to be unfriendly and dismissive; and under no circumstances must they occur unless accompanied by someone of one's own sex (Sroufe, Bennett, Englund, Urban, & Shulman, 1993).

In addition to being of the same sex, friends are likely to be similar in race, socioeconomic background, and grade in school, and to have the same social status with peers. None of these similarities, however, is as important as that of being of the same sex (George & Hartmann, 1996; Hartup, 1992). Finally, friends are likely to share similar perceptions of others (Haselager, Hartup, van Lieshout, & Riksen-Walraven, 1998).

What contributes to the quality of children's relationships? When interviewed about their friends, children are most likely to talk about the assistance they receive from each other, whether through offers of encouragement, helping each other out, or sharing confidences. Of course, fooling around together and having fun are also important (Oswald et al., 1994). Hans Oswald and his associates (1994) found that children described upwards of eight or nine important relationships when asked to describe their friends. These friendships were remarkably individual, with very different patterns of qualities characterizing the relationships children had with their different friends. Important to all, however, was the assistance they could count on from each other. It is all too easy to overlook the very real difficulties children experience on a day-to-day basis and the importance to them of being able to rely on each other for support. It is no less difficult for an 8-year-old to stand up to a playground bully or to work problems at the blackboard than it is for parents to resolve a dispute with a neighbor or to fill out their tax returns. In each case, having the support of a friend can make all the difference.

In middle childhood, children's friends are almost always of the same sex.

Peer Relations

Children's social status, or their relative popularity with peers, is fairly stable, showing little change throughout the grade school years (Downey, Lebolt, Rincon, & Freitas, 1998; George & Hartmann, 1996). By using measures in which children are asked to name those they most and least like to play with, researchers have been able to identify a number of such statuses. What behaviors, especially, distinguish children of one status from those of another?

Popular children behave very much like average ones in many ways. Both are cooperative, good at taking turns, and play well with others. Both, in other words, engage in many prosocial behaviors and relatively few antisocial ones. In addition, popular children tend to set the norms for their group, reminding others of the rules and giving suggestions. Perhaps because they have better social skills, they are able to maintain their play with other children for longer periods of time, and others appear to have more fun when they are with them (Dodge, 1983; Coie & Kupersmidt, 1983). The children, in other words, engage in the types of supportive behaviors that Oswald and his associates found children to value in their relationships with others.

This happy picture does not hold for all children. Children whom others indicate they least like to play with are classified as rejected. Also, some children are not mentioned by any of their classmates, either as being liked or disliked. These children are classified as neglected. Since most of this research has been conducted with boys, we will specifically refer to the children in these studies as boys.

Rejected boys tend to be very active and often aggressive when they play with others, taunting and teasing as well as being physically aggressive. They are more likely than other children to exclude others when playing, and they engage in more inappropriate behavior, such as grabbing something away from someone or standing on a table. Unlike popular boys, they have difficulty sustaining an activity, even when it involves play. They are also at greater risk for adjustment

Popular children seem to instinctively know how to enter an ongoing group; other children may need help building social skills.

How helpful is it to encourage a child who is always off by him- or herself, watching others play, to simply go over and start to play with others?

problems as adolescents and adults. Neglected boys spend most of their time in solitary play. This, however, does not appear to be out of preference, since they initially make numerous social overtures to others. Their behavior, just like that of rejected boys, is at times inappropriate; however, it does not take an aggressive form. Unlike rejected boys, they are not at risk for later adjustment problems. They hold down jobs and live comfortably with themselves as adults despite the stringent criteria defining this status in childhood; that is, these boys have no friends (Dodge, 1983).

John Coie and Janis Kupersmidt (1983) formed play groups of boys who did not know each other, in order to study the emergence of social status among their peers. These investigators initially determined boys' social status among their classmates and, based on this, formed play groups consisting of rejected, popular, neglected, and average boys. The play groups met for 1 hour a week. These investigators found that social status became established quickly. By the 3rd week, after only 3 hours of playing together, a boy's status in his group corresponded to his status at school. Findings such as these indicate that the successes or the failures children experience with their peers are not simply accidental, but reflect very genuine social skills. Coie and Kupersmidt also found, however, that neglected boys frequently benefited from being among a new group of peers, suggesting that children's reputations as well as their skills affect their social status.

The studies of Dodge and Coie and Kupersmidt have implications for intervention programs. It isn't enough simply to encourage children who are having problems in making friends to interact with others more. These children have already tried to do so and failed. Instead, intervention needs to focus on building social skills. Reputation may also be more important than previously thought, in that the same behaviors in popular and rejected children are responded to differ-

Conflict Resolution in the School System

BY ANDREA HAYES

It is clear that national concerns over school safety have risen to a high level. Traditionally, our approach to solving the problems of interpersonal conflicts and school violence has been crime-focused; such problems are seen as resulting from the behavior of chronically disruptive, or "bad," kids. These students are suspended, transferred to alternative schools (filled with other youths on probation), and effectively isolated from nonproblematic, "successful" students (Dupper, 1995). This approach, though effective with respect to the immediate, or precipitating, problem, can result in the early marginalization of youth, as well as foster the assumption that crime-focused legislation (such as tougher laws, stricter sentencing, and trying children as adults) is the only response. With our juvenile and adult prison systems currently overcrowded, we are in a position to reevaluate this approach and to ask whether isolating these youths has solved the problem of violent conflicts at school (Irwin & Austin, 1997).

Have our beliefs about the cause of violence been too narrow? Some social scientists believe that they have. In spite of well-intentioned interventions and tougher laws, the juvenile arrest rate for aggravated assault and murder rose more than 50% from 1987 to 1996. Furthermore, homicide rates among youth in small towns and rural communities increased by 38% in 1997 (Garbarino, 1999). We can no longer hide behind the assumption that violence happens only among ethnic groups in the inner city. In the school environment alone, a national survey of high school students found that 8% were threatened or injured with a weapon, 16% participated in a physical fight, and 34% had their personal property stolen or deliberately damaged (Centers for Disease Control, 1996c).

Comprehensive, multifaceted, environmental approaches to resolving conflicts in the school environment are receiving attention. These approaches change a school's *culture* by teaching students, parents, teachers, and the community skills for building personal responsibility and resolving conflict in a nonviolent way. One such program, called the Bullying Prevention Program (Olweus, Limber, & Mihalic, 1999), attempts to reduce the opportunities and rewards for bullying behavior by involving the students themselves through anonymous questionnaires, discussion groups, and peer-based supervisory roles. The classrooms are a place for regular conflict-resolution discussions, empathy development, and teacher enforcement of prosocial behavior. Parents are considered an invaluable resource and involved in all levels of the program. The Bullying Prevention Program has reduced the frequency of bully/victim student and teacher reports by 50%. Students also report significant reductions in vandalism, theft, and truancy.

A second program, Building the Peace: The Resolving Conflict Creatively Program (RCCP), offers a national model for conflict resolution (DeJong, 1999). RCCP focuses on creating *school* change through public policy at the school administration level. It requires administration buy-in and philosophical alignment. Teachers can then promote an appreciation of diversity and shared decision making among students and can facilitate the recognition of common purposes. Students *daily* practice skills in communication, cooperation, bias awareness, mediation, and conflict resolution. Parents are taught to help implement new skills at home to resolve family conflict as well. Studies among different school sites around the country have indicated that students experience less violence in the classroom, the student dropout rate decreases significantly, and teachers report more positive classroom climates and observe students using conflict resolution skills spontaneously around campus (DeJong, 1999). Why rely on metal detectors that cost $100,000 annually to create safe school environments? A program like RCCP costs $33.00 per student per year while teaching lifetime interpersonal skills *and* creating a safer school environment. Punishment or prevention? Which seems the wiser choice?

ently, children reacting more positively to popular boys, even when they are aggressive, than to others. Although it is certainly possible that children's reactions may be due to subtle differences in the behaviors themselves, it is also possible that children are reacting not just to the momentary exchange, but also to a history of interactions. The Social Policy Focus, "Conflict Resolution in the School System," looks at some comprehensive conflict resolution programs aimed at changing a school's culture.

Research on entry behaviors finds that popular children are better at entering ongoing groups. They seem to try to determine the frame of reference of the groups, what the others are doing, and then share in this. Unpopular children appear to divert attention to themselves. Rather than fit themselves into the group, they ask the group to shift gears to include them. They are more likely to ask what others are doing, to disagree as a way of inserting themselves into an activity, to talk about themselves, or to state their feelings. Each of these only draws other children's attention away from the activity that interests them and is likely to be ignored or rebuffed (see Chapter 9) (Putallaz, 1983; Putallaz & Gottman, 1981).

Although it is relatively easy to imagine friendships among children who are cooperative, take turns, and play well with others, it is less easy to imagine the types of friendships that children have who are aggressive. Before considering these, however, we need to distinguish two forms of aggression. **Overt aggression** involves physical acts such as hitting, punching, and kicking. **Relational aggression,** on the other hand, involves acts aimed at manipulating the relationship, such as divulging secrets or spreading lies. The former is more characteristic of boys and the latter of girls, although children of either sex can be seen to engage in both forms of aggression (Grotpeter & Crick, 1996 as cited in Crick & Grotpeter, 1995).

To determine how the friends of aggressive children fare, Jennifer Grotpeter and Nicki Crick (1996) identified children as either relationally aggressive, overtly aggressive, or nonaggressive, and asked children in each group and their friends to describe the qualities of their friendships. Are children who are aggressive with peers aggressive in their friendships as well? The answer, it seems, is both a yes and a no. These investigators found that although relationally aggressive children enjoyed many of the qualities to friendships that characterize those of nonaggressive children, such as intimacy, caring, and companionship, they nonetheless engaged in the same forms of relational aggression with friends that distinguished their interactions with their peers. Thus, for example, they rarely disclosed much about themselves even though their friends reported relatively high amounts of self-disclosure, putting the former in a position to control the friendship through threatening to tell the other's secrets. So, yes, children who show this form of aggression with peers are likely to do the same thing in their friendships.

In contrast to the friendships of relationally aggressive children, those of overtly aggressive children are characterized by an *absence* of aggression. Instead, these children were found to direct their aggression toward those outside the relationship, enlisting the support of their friends in the aggression as well. This was true whether their friends were initially aggressive or not. Thus, children who form friendships with either type of aggressive child run certain risks, either of being the object of relational aggression themselves or of being drawn into aggressive interactions with others. On a final note, Grotpeter and Crick observe that children's friendships, just like those of adults, are a complex mix of positive and negative qualities, a point that is especially true for aggressive children and those who befriend them.

A significant number of children, approximately 10%, are bullied at school. Furthermore, pretty much the same children get picked on from one time to the next. Victimization, just like aggression, is a relatively stable characteristic of children. Children identified by their classmates as victims are the same ones to be identified a year later as most likely to be bullied. Those who are likely to be victimized are children who cry easily, have poor social skills, and are submissive when attacked, thereby rewarding their aggressors. However, having a friend decreases the likelihood of being victimized, as well as buffering the effects of this when it does occur (Hodges, Boivin, Vitaro, & Bukowski, 1999).

Not all bullied children are submissive. Some victims are actually aggressive, being easily provoked by others and reacting angrily, their outbursts apparently targeting them for retaliation. Their aggression differs from that of bullies, however, taking the form of unwitting emotional outbursts rather than being used intentionally to dominate others. These victims, who more typically are boys, are more likely to have been physically abused and treated harshly when growing up. In fact, David Schwartz, Kenneth Dodge, Gregory Pettit and John Bates (1997) found that 29% of boys who had been physically harmed became aggressive vic-

overt aggression Hostility expressed in physical acts such as hitting, punching, and kicking.

relational aggression Hostility expressed in acts manipulating the relationship, such as divulging secrets or spreading lies.

The likelihood of cross-ethnic friendships is affected by the stability of ethnic balance in the school and the degree of integration in the neighborhood.

tims, in comparison to only 6% of unharmed boys. Bullies, although also likely to have been exposed to adult aggression, are not as likely to have experienced harm themselves.

Cross-Ethnic Friendships

Although children are most likely to form friendships with others who share their ethnic background, cross-ethnic friendships are likely to occur when children from different backgrounds are classmates. Mary Jane Rotheram and Jean Phinney (1983), examining cross-ethnic friendships in kindergarten and third grade, found no difference in acceptance of others from different backgrounds as a function of grade level. However, they did find differences among schools. They noted that in some schools, there were relatively few cross-ethnic friendships and little acceptance of peers from a different ethnic background in general. These investigators suggest that the racial tensions noted in these classrooms may be due to rapid changes in the ethnic balance in the schools, a phenomenon that characterizes many urban schools today. In Los Angeles, where this study was conducted, a familiar pattern is for a primarily African American school with African American teachers to become more than 50% Hispanic within the span of several years. Each of the classrooms where they observed racial tensions were in schools that had experienced a rapid change in ethnic balance. Classrooms in schools that had been integrated for some time and were stable in their ethnic balance showed a high level of acceptance and friendship.

Neighborhood conditions also affect the likelihood of cross-ethnic friendships. Most children who attend ethnically mixed schools report having at least one close friend at school from another ethnic background, but fewer than one third of these see the friend outside school. Those who do are more likely to live in ethnically mixed neighborhoods and are also less likely to be European American. African American children are almost twice as likely as European Americans to maintain school friendships with those from other groups outside of school; however, they have more close neighborhood friends in general than do European American children (DuBois & Hirsch, 1990).

Cross-ethnic friendships face special challenges, not the least of which are differences in the enculturation experiences of children from different backgrounds. **Enculturation** is the acquisition of the norms of one's ethnic group. It differs from *acculturation,* which is the acquisition of the norms of the larger society. The norms of one's group shape children's expectations and reactions to others. The Mexican American culture, for example, stresses group affiliation, interdependence, and cooperation. The African American culture, in contrast, places greater emphasis on individualism and independence. Mexican American children have been brought up in homes with clear hierarchical family relationships and are expected to accept and show respect for authority figures. African American children grow up in more egalitarian homes that permit questioning of authority (Rotheram & Phinney, 1987). We might expect these enculturation experiences to affect the way children from either culture react to social situations, and they do.

Mary Jane Rotheram-Borus and Jean Phinney (1990) showed videotapes of social encounters to African American and Mexican American children and adolescents. The videotapes were of everyday scenes. In one, a student asked a peer for lunch money; in another, a student witnessed a fight; and in another, a student needed materials that another had in order to complete a class assignment.

Clear ethnic differences emerged in reactions to these scenes. The responses of Mexican American children reflected the emphasis their culture places on the group. They were more likely, for example, to say that a peer should share lunch money with someone who had lost it, even when the latter was someone they disliked. They also expected others to anticipate their needs (as they would the needs of others) and would wait for others to notice what those needs were. In response to the video in which two peers were working at the same table and the supplies that both needed were beyond the reach of one and close to the other, Mexican American children saw no problem with the situation, expecting the other person to hand over the supplies. African American children indicated they would be upset and were likely to reach over and get what they needed for themselves. A small difference? Not really. These are just the types of situations that create misunderstandings and lead to hurt feelings among friends.

Another sequence showed a boy being rejected for a team. African American students reported they would get angry or leave; not one of them said they would feel badly. Two thirds of the Mexican American children said they would feel hurt, but almost none of them would leave, and relatively few said they would be angry. These differences translate easily into the failures of understanding that test friendships. Consider an example in which Eddie, a Hispanic, tries out for soccer, but gets cut early in the tryouts. He doesn't seem especially angry and doesn't say much about it. His friend Joe, who is African American, thinks Eddie must not care and offers no consolation. Eddie, who has been waiting for his friend to say something, doesn't understand Joe's ostensibly callous attitude and begins to question whether he's really his friend. Joe, assuming that Eddie would react as he would if he minded being cut (by being angry, not silently hurt) has no way to anticipate his friend's growing resentment toward him.

Families in Transition

enculturation Acquiring the norms of one's social group.

Several major social trends affect the lives of increasing numbers of children. More children today experience divorce, single parenting, and stepparenting, and more live in homes in which both parents are wage earners than ever before.

Changing Family Structures

Divorce Children today are more likely to experience divorce than were their parents or grandparents. Approximately half of all children will experience the divorce of their parents and live for about 5 years in a single-parent family (Hetherington & Clingempeel, 1992). What impact does divorce have on children? Simple answers don't exist. Its impact will vary for each child, based on a host of conditions: the family situation prior to the divorce, the child's coping skills, the degree of family conflict, the child's age and gender, the availability of social supports such as friends and extended family, the amount of time spent with the non-custodial parent, the quality of the relationship with the custodial parent, parental monitoring of activities, whether the divorce involves economic hardship, moving to a new neighborhood or new school, and so on. E. Mavis Hetherington, a developmentalist who has followed numerous families through divorce, remarks that one of the most notable things she has observed is the tremendous diversity in the responses of parents and children (Hetherington, 1989; Hetherington, Hagan, & Anderson, 1989).

What are some of the changes that divorce brings about in children's lives?

Even relatively amicable divorces can be emotionally charged and stressful events. As a consequence, developmentalists have not been surprised to find a number of negative effects associated with its occurrence. Children from divorced homes have been found to differ in measures of self-concept, self-esteem, social competence, happiness, and maturity (Hetherington & Clingempeel, 1992; Wallerstein, 1989; Wallerstein, Corbin, & Lewis, 1988).

Perhaps because these findings support popular stereotypes of children from divorced homes, developmentalists have been relatively slow to look beneath surface statistics to determine what factors other than *not* living with a father in the home (the usual custodial arrangement) might be contributing. Studies that have followed children of divorce over time have discovered a number of conditions contributing to stress, not the least of which is divorce's effects on the parents (Hetherington & Clingempeel, 1992; Hetherington, Cox, & Cox, 1982). Recently divorced mothers, for example, report more depression than do mothers in intact families. Difficulties in adjusting among their children can be traced, in part, to the mothers' reactions to the divorce (Forehand, Thomas, Wierson, Brody, & Fauber, 1990; Hetherington & Clingempeel, 1992). Divorce can be highly damaging to a parent's self-esteem and sense of worth. Many leave a divorce with a sense of failure, not just in the relationship, but as individuals. Most experience depression and increased tension as they adjust to their changed life circumstances. Parents can become preoccupied with their own problems and consequently less responsive to the needs of children who are also adjusting to the divorce.

Perhaps not surprisingly, parenting is less effective initially following a divorce. Fathers become more permissive, perhaps reluctant to spoil their available time on a dispute over discipline, and mothers become more inconsistent, at times ignoring infractions and other times reacting more severely. Each of these changes adds to the level of stress (Hetherington & Clingempeel, 1992; Hetherington, Cox, & Cox, 1982).

Life evens out within a 2- to 3-year period following the divorce. Parents and children regain much of their earlier emotional stability, and each is better able to "be there" for the other.

Because divorce is more common today than in previous generations, children are less likely to experience any stigma associated with it. Many of their friends have gone through a similar experience, and natural support groups exist in which children can air their feelings and gain perspective on their situation.

Even so, children and adolescents whose parents are divorced are less likely than peers from intact homes to adopt mature coping strategies, especially when they feel threatened. This is true even though they may recognize that the strategies they use—such as escape, avoidance, confrontation, or self-blame—are not particularly effective. They are also more vulnerable to stress, in that they are not as likely to see themselves as potentially controlling the situation or managing a successful outcome. Perhaps experiencing a divorce, which is an event beyond their control, makes these children less likely to feel in control of other stressful situations. Or it might be that the degree of control they perceive themselves to have in a situation is related to their self-esteem, which is lower in these children (Irion, Coon, & Blanchard-Fields, 1988).

Marital conflict rather than divorce per se contributes heavily to the stress children experience. Conflict most likely affects children by affecting the quality of parent-child relationships (Fauber, Forehand, Thomas, & Wierson, 1990). Children are more likely to experience problems when their parents divorce relatively late rather than earlier, most likely because they have been exposed to more years of marital conflict (Needle, Su, & Doherty, 1990; Smith, 1990). A 3-year longitudinal study of over 1,000 seventh-, ninth-, and eleventh-graders found that conflict within the family, not divorce, was associated with negative effects such as depression, anxiety, and physical symptoms. Children from intact homes with high levels of conflict showed lower levels of well-being than those in low-conflict divorced homes on all measures that were used (Mechanic & Hansell, 1989). A full 25% of the children and adolescents reported that their parents' divorce was a positive change. Other studies find even higher agreement among children and adolescents on the preferability of divorce to their previous conflict-ridden lives (McLaughlin & Whitfield, 1984).

Exposure to conflict need not always be negative; sometimes it is the only way of working through differences. But how sensitive are children to cues, such as conciliatory or angry tones of voice, versus the actual content of what is said in resolving conflict? Kelly Shifflett-Simpson and Mark Cummings (1996), at West Virginia University, had 5- to 7-year-olds and 9- to 12-year-olds watch videotaped arguments between a couple, systematically varying the endings in terms of emotional tone and content. Thus, an argument might end in a sarcastic apology ("I'm *so* sorry I wasn't more sensitive to your needs," said in a negative tone of voice) or a genuine one (the same words spoken in a positive tone of voice). Adolescents are better at discerning what is actually taking place than are children, reacting emotionally to both the content and the emotional tone of the argument. Children, on the other hand, are more literal, responding simply to the verbal content of the message.

Single-Parent Families   Most of the children who live in single-parent families do so because of divorce; most of them live with their mothers (Buchanan, Macoby, & Dornbusch, 1992). One of the most noticeable differences between these children and those from intact homes is their economic well-being. Approximately half of all families headed by a single female parent live below the poverty level, compared to only 10% of two-parent families (McLanahan & Booth, 1989). For many children, this income level is a dramatic change. One year following a divorce, a single mother's income is likely to have dropped to 67% of the total household income before divorce, whereas the father's income is likely only to drop to 90%. The initially lower earning capacity of most women, along with frequent lack of child support and little state support, contributes to this pattern. On average, single mothers working part-time earn approximately 30% of what married fathers earn, and mothers employed full-time earn 60% as much (McLanahan

A parent's remarriage is usually more difficult for adolescents than for younger children, who are better able to form a genuine attachment to a stepparent.

& Booth, 1989). Economic hardship can contribute to children's distress in intact families as well. In this case, however, it does so primarily by undermining the marital relationship that then affects the way each partner relates to the children (Ge et al., 1992).

Remarriage and Stepparents   Parents who divorce are likely to remarry and to introduce a stepparent into their children's lives. Close to 20% of children under the age of 18 live with a stepparent, who in most cases is a stepfather. Remarriage usually occurs soon on the heels of the divorce, typically within 3 years. Many stepparents bring a stepsibling or two (residential or weekend) in the process. For many children, this series of events comes on top of the changes introduced by moving to a new residence, changing schools, and making new friends. Fewer changes would still be enough to disrupt anyone's equilibrium. Yet many families weather the stresses of these new relationships, and some even thrive (Giles-Sims & Crosbie-Burnett, 1989; Glick, 1989).

One sees differences in adjustments to divorce and remarriage as a function both of children's gender and their age. Following divorce, boys exhibit more problems than girls. However, following remarriage, girls exhibit more problems. Boys' relationships with their mothers following divorce tend to be somewhat negative and coercive, whereas those of girls tend to be closer and more positive. The introduction of a stepfather may be more of a threat to girls' relationships with their mothers than to boys', because boys have less to lose in the first place and may have something to gain by the appearance of a warm and supportive older male.

Marital transitions, whether divorce or remarriage, are difficult for children of all ages. However, remarriage appears to be most difficult for early adolescents, for a number of reasons. Younger children appear to be better able to form genuine emotional attachments to stepparents. Also, early adolescents may have had to shoulder adult responsibilities while living with a single parent and, while welcoming more discretionary time, may resent any threats to their autonomy by the introduction of a stepparent. Finally, early adolescents' concerns with their own sexual feelings may compound their reactions to a parent's new sexual relationship.

We don't have much information about the conditions that facilitate or hinder healthy stepfamily relations (Giles-Sims & Crosbie-Burnett, 1989; Hetherington & Clingempeel, 1992). Yet some general statements can be made. Perhaps the first is to underscore the importance of **role clarity,** the understanding among family members regarding each person's role and how it affects the others (Giles-Sims & Crosbie-Burnett, 1989; Visher & Visher, 1989). The most successful families establish clear guidelines for interactions. Families with the most ambiguity in roles are those with a stepmother and at least one child in common (Pasley & Ihenger-Tallman, 1989). The difficulties facing stepmothers are especially acute, because they are likely to oversee the management of the household, a role that can bring them into direct conflict with stepchildren who may resent their presence. For families experiencing problems, support groups and counseling can help establish guidelines for daily living, such as who supervises homework, who disciplines, buys clothes, cleans up, and so on. Mundane matters can easily become explosive unless defused with professional help (Visher & Visher, 1989).

In research comparing children in nondivorced families, divorced single-mother families, and remarried families, Mavis Hetherington and Glenn Clingempeel (1992) found that when differences among the three types of families emerged, they favored children in nondivorced families. Significant numbers of children living in divorced single-mother families evidenced problems in adjustment both at home and at school for up to 4 or even 6 years following the divorce. Children also had difficulty adjusting to their parent's remarriage, showing more problem behavior than children from nondivorced families. Two years after remarrying, however, mothers' relationships with their children differed little from those of never-divorced mothers. However, relationships between stepparents and stepchildren frequently, though not always, remained problematic.

Children and Their Families

Even when the family structure remains stable, children's relationships with parents change in middle childhood. At the most immediate level, children and parents simply spend less time together. As we have seen (Chapter 10), children have more discretionary time in middle childhood to spend on their own or with friends. They also spend more hours a day in school than do younger children, and many spend additional hours after school in activities such as clubs or sports, band practice or play rehearsals—or they simply spend time at a friend's house.

In order to study changes such as these, Reed Larson, Maryse Richards, Giovanni Moneta, Grayson Holmbeck, and Elena Duckett (1996) had children and adolescents wear pagers for a week, asking them to record what they were doing and how they were feeling when beeped at random intervals during the day and evening. Larson and his associates noted dramatic changes with age, as well as important continuities, in the ways children interacted with their families. Fifth-graders, for instance, spend about 35% of their waking hours with their families. By the time children are in the twelfth grade, however, this figure is down to about 14%. Despite the dramatic reduction with age in the amount of time children and parents spend together, children still spend the same amount of time alone with each of their parents when they become adolescents as they did in middle childhood and just as much time as before talking with them.

Not only the time parents and children spend together, but also the way they interact changes. Parents spend less time in hands-on caretaking activities and more in monitoring activities at a distance, keeping track of where children are when they're not at home and whom they are with. Irrespective of distance, how-

role clarity An understanding among family members about each one's role.

ever, communication within the family becomes increasingly important as children and parents begin to redefine their roles relative to each other when children become more independent with age.

Central to any effective communication is one's acceptance of the other person. Frequently, there isn't any need to offer help or give advice; all that's needed is simply to listen. Parents' comments are usually motivated by good intentions: They only want to help their children learn new skills ("Here's how you should do that") or to prevent them from making unnecessary mistakes. ("Watch out, that could spill.") However, such comments communicate nonacceptance, letting the child know that the parent's way is better. Active listening offers an alternative.

Listening to Children: Active Listening   **Active listening** is a way of drawing children out and helping them explore their feelings by feeding their message back to them. In the process, you find out if you have understood what they said. Consider the following example:

ALLEN: Do I have to get up? [He has just been told it's nearly time to leave for a baseball game.]

FATHER: You don't feel like playing baseball today?

ALLEN: I'll miss messing around with my friends.

FATHER: You'd rather mess around with your friends than play baseball?

ALLEN: Yes. We have fun together.

FATHER: It's not fun to play baseball?

ALLEN: No. Sometimes the other guys razz me when I don't get a hit.

FATHER: You don't like being teased?

ALLEN: It makes me feel like I'm not a very good player.

FATHER: You'd like to be good at baseball?

ALLEN: Yes, I felt terrific that day I got that base hit.

FATHER: Would you like to practice before the game?

ALLEN: Hey, Dad, that'd be great. I'll get dressed.

Notice how Allen is able to discover how he really feels when his father actively listens. Notice, too, that his father does not offer a solution, give advice, or do anything other than feed back what his son is saying.

An essential ingredient to active listening is communicating acceptance to the other person. The paradox in accepting people as they are is that as they feel accepted, they are free to change. Many parents, and children for that matter, communicate nonacceptance, believing that if you want someone to change, you must let the other person know what needs improvement. Telling children, or parents, that they need to improve communicates that they are not all right the way they are. This communication puts the person on the defensive—and closes off the conversation.

Active listening takes time. Each must be willing to let the other feel his or her way through a problem. If you don't have the time, it is important to say so and arrange some other time to talk. Parents must also genuinely want to let the child find a solution to the problem and not use active listening merely as a way to get her or him to do what they think should be done. They must accept the problem as the child presents it and accept the child's feelings about it. Parroting words without reflecting feelings is not active listening. You need to feed back all of the message, and feelings are an important part of it.

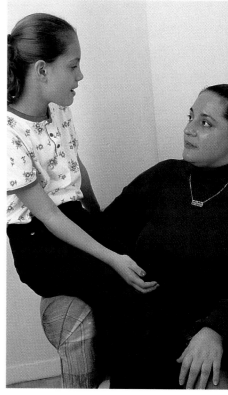

As parents and children begin to redefine their roles toward each other, "active listening" keeps conversations open, and helps them discover how they feel about these changes.

Why does active listening usually make children more willing to talk with their parents?

active listening A way of listening that reflects the message and feelings back to the speaker.

Talking to Children: You-Messages and I-Messages   Let's turn the situation around and look at how parents can talk so that children will listen to them. The simplest approach would be to let children know how they feel, but parents rarely do that. Instead, they are likely to tell children what to do ("Pick up your clothes"), warn them what will happen if they don't ("If I have to tell you one more time, you've lost your clothes allowance"), moralize ("You should contribute your share of the work around the house"), or make a suggestion ("Why don't you put your clothes in the hamper when you take them off?"). Each of these approaches is usually met with resistance. After all, who likes being told what to do, warned, or made to feel wrong?

The parental comments in the preceding paragraph are examples of **you-messages.** They communicate that parents do not expect children to be helpful unless they are told to be. And by offering a solution without letting children help in defining the problem, such remarks subtly communicate that parents don't think children can help or are willing to find a solution.

An **I-message** tells children how their actions make others feel. Children can hear such messages as a fact about the parent, not as an evaluation of themselves, and thus they have little need to be defensive. A parent who says "I can't hear what she's saying to me when you interrupt" communicates a different message than one who says "It's rude of you to interrupt." I-messages let children know how their behavior affects others. These messages also communicate to children that parents trust them to find a solution and put the responsibility for change with the recipient. Because I-messages do not accuse, suggest, or warn, they are easier for children to hear.

Family Conflict and Changing Domains of Authority   Perhaps at no time are their changing roles more evident than when parents and children discuss their perceptions of family conflicts. Judith Smetana and Rusti Berent (1993), at the University of Rochester, asked seventh-, ninth-, and eleventh-graders and their mothers to respond to vignettes describing typical conflicts that occur at home, such as those involving household chores, keeping one's room clean, or personal appearance. Each conflict was presented both from the parent's perspective and the child's, by giving justifications each might use in appealing to the other. (Table 12.1 shows the different perspectives.)

Perhaps not surprisingly, given their responsibility for maintaining family ways, mothers considered conventional justifications to be more adequate in resolving conflict than did children. Children, on the other hand, saw this type of reasoning as a source of conflict. This was especially true of mid-adolescent ninth-graders, for whom family conflict is likely to have reached a peak as gains in autonomy are won by questioning parental authority.

Mothers also considered appeals to authority and threats of punishment to be more effective in getting their children to comply with their wishes than did the children, a difference that increased with the children's age. Children and adolescents, on the other hand, appealed to practical considerations, perhaps because such arguments are less likely to be challenged by parents. Smetana has found that, although children may believe their position can be justified by appeals to personal jurisdiction ("It's my room and I can keep it as I like"), they will use pragmatic reasons ("It doesn't matter if it's messy; I can find whatever I need") when arguing with a parent. Parents are not as likely as children to view the behaviors in question as rightfully within the child's purview (Smetana, Braeges, & Yau, 1991).

Children's appeals to social convention in resolving family conflict are likely to generate more conflict than they settle, usually because the conventions referred to are those of their peers, perhaps already a sore point for many parents.

you-message A message communicating what you think of another person.

I-message A message that tells the listener how his or her actions make one feel.

TABLE 12.1 Differences in the Parent's and the Child's Attempts to Resolve Conflict

The examples below are responses to a typical conflict: Mother wants Anne to wear something else, but Anne doesn't want to.

	Type of Justification	Example
Parent	Conventional	Reference to behavior standards, arbitrarily arrived at by family members; e.g., "I'd be embarrassed if any of my friends saw you looking like that."
	Pragmatic	Consideration of practical needs or consequences; e.g., "You'll catch a cold."
	Authoritarian	Reference to authority and punishment; e.g., "I'm your parent, and I say you can't dress like that."
Child	Conventional	Reference to standards of behavior shared with peers; e.g., "My friends would think I'm weird."
	Pragmatic	Consideration of practical needs or consequences; e.g., "I'm comfortable in these clothes."
	Personal	Portraying the issue as one of maintaining personal jurisdiction in an area; e.g., "The way I dress is an expression of me and my personality."

Source: J. G. Smetana & R. Berent. (1993). Adolescents' and mothers' evaluations of justifications for disputes. *Journal of Adolescent Research, 8,* 252–273.

The complexity derives from the fact that different domains of authority exist within the family. Only in some domains is there a shift in parental authority as children grow older. In others, parents continue to be perceived as having a legitimate say, both by themselves and by their children. Conflict arises over which issues lie within which domains: Children and parents, in other words, don't always see things eye to eye (Smetana & Asquith, 1994).

Judith Smetana and Pamela Asquith (1994) asked sixth- through tenth-graders and their parents to indicate the legitimacy of parental authority concerning various hypothetical issues, shown in Box 12.1. Almost all children and parents agreed that parents have the authority, even the obligation, to set rules concerning *moral issues,* in which a person's actions can affect the well-being of another. Similarly, most children and parents considered *conventional issues* to be the legitimate province of parental decision making, although parents saw themselves as having more authority here than did children. These perceptions, by the way, did not change with age, suggesting that parents are seen as rightfully the ones to establish and maintain the social as well as the moral order and children as the ones seeking greater autonomy within this.

There was similar agreement between children and parents about *personal issues,* both believing that children should have the say concerning these. When disagreements arose, they were most likely to concern *friendship issues, multifaceted issues* (involving both personal and conventional concerns), and *prudential issues,* which involved children's well-being or possible harm. Children, for instance, believed their friendships to be matters of personal choice, whereas parents considered these to more legitimately fall within their domain, feeling obligated to step in when they disapproved of certain friends. Similarly, even though parents and children agreed that parents had the authority and were even obligated to set down rules concerning prudential issues, disagreements arose over which specific issues fell within this domain, with parents seeing themselves as having more authority to govern children's behavior than children did. The large differences in parents' and children's perceptions of these issues indicate where the struggle for increasing independence is fought—not on moral or even conventional grounds, but on what constitutes children's personal prerogatives.

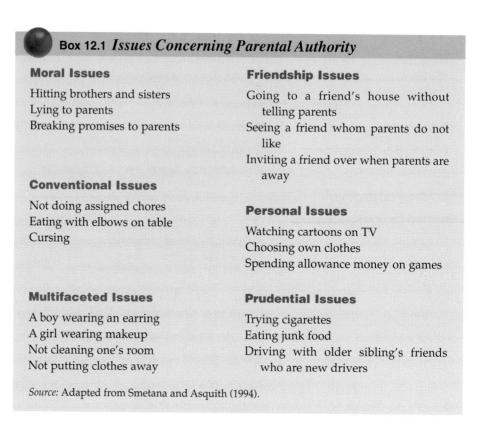

Box 12.1 *Issues Concerning Parental Authority*

Moral Issues

Hitting brothers and sisters
Lying to parents
Breaking promises to parents

Conventional Issues

Not doing assigned chores
Eating with elbows on table
Cursing

Multifaceted Issues

A boy wearing an earring
A girl wearing makeup
Not cleaning one's room
Not putting clothes away

Friendship Issues

Going to a friend's house without telling parents
Seeing a friend whom parents do not like
Inviting a friend over when parents are away

Personal Issues

Watching cartoons on TV
Choosing own clothes
Spending allowance money on games

Prudential Issues

Trying cigarettes
Eating junk food
Driving with older sibling's friends who are new drivers

Source: Adapted from Smetana and Asquith (1994).

In general, for both children and parents, the realm of issues considered to be properly the domain of children increased with age, with more items being considered personal as children got older, thus expanding the sphere of their independence (Bosma et al., 1996; Smetana & Asquith, 1994). Smetana and Asquith point out, however, that this sphere remains narrower for parents than for their children, the former continuing to see themselves as legitimately setting rules governing children's bodies, physical appearance, and choice of friends. Issues of parental authority and children's rights are considered in the Research Focus, "Coding: 'Hey, I'm 10, and I Got a Right to See My Friends!'"

Samuel Vuchinich, Joseph Angelelli, and Antone Gatherum (1996), at Oregon State University, followed 63 families in a 2-year longitudinal study of family problem solving, making their first observations when the children were in the fourth grade. These investigators found that the struggle for increasing independence, or autonomy, begins in preadolescence, even before the ages observed by Smetana and Asquith. Families were videotaped as they discussed an issue that had been a problem in the family during the past month. As preadolescents got older, from 9½ to 11½ years, problem solving became less effective, with family members finding it more difficult to reach a solution or even take the other's perspective. With age, preadolescents became more negative. Fathers, especially, appear to react negatively to this, mothers being more the "peacemaker." Consistent with the findings of Smetana and Asquith, difficulties in communicating were not so much a matter of *what* was being discussed, mundane issues generating as much difficulty as significant ones, as was the age of the child.

In general, however, it is not children, but their parents who are responsible for changes in the emotional climate within the family. Reed Larson and David Almeida (1999) point out that this climate changes as emotions are transmitted from one person to another through daily interactions. In fact, one can actually follow the path of an emotion as it moves through a family. A parent, for instance,

Research Focus

Coding: "Hey, I'm 10, and I Got a Right to See My Friends!"

"What do you mean I can't have friends over after school? I've got rights around here too, you know!" Terry shouted as he slammed his bedroom door inches from his mother's face.

"You come out here this minute and we'll talk about those rights, mister!" his mother fumed.

"You have the right to be taken care of," she continued as Terry appeared in the doorway, "and that means I need to know something about the company you keep. And while we're on the issue of rights, I have the right to be addressed with respect by you, no matter how you feel about what I've just said."

"If you were here when I got home, you'd know who my friends were," Terry answered his mother sullenly. "You know how I hate being alone after school."

"Some days that can't be helped. If a meeting runs late, I can't just get up and walk out. And with Nana only a phone call away, you always have someone to call on if you need help."

Terry and his mother had both mentioned his rights, but were they talking about the same thing? What *are* the rights of children? And how do children think of these rights? For that matter, what do we as adults understand these rights to be?

Until relatively recently, considerations of children's rights focused almost exclusively on their right to be cared for and protected. More recently, those working with children, such as social service providers, legislators, and the courts, have also taken into consideration children's right to exercise some control over decisions affecting their lives (Hart, 1991). Terry was talking about the latter, what some call *self-determination rights;* his mother was talking about the former, or *nurturance rights.* But how do children understand each of these types of rights?

Martin Ruck, Rona Abramovitch, and Daniel Keating (1998) presented children (8 to 16) with hypothetical vignettes describing situations in which a child's right to either nurturance or self-determination conflicted with the desires of a parent or a teacher, and they asked the children to describe in their own words what the story character should do and why. This approach involves the use of *free-response data* or *descriptive data.* When researchers begin to investigate an area in which relatively little is known they will frequently simply observe what people do in natural settings, or, when this is impossible given the sensitive nature of the behavior, they will listen to what people have to tell them. Open-ended questions such as those used by Ruck, Abramovitch, and Keating are useful when one wants to know what people are thinking (Cozby, 1997). Another advantage to descriptive responses is that they generate a rich source of data, useful in formulating future research questions. An additional advantage is the increased *external validity* of the research or the likelihood that the answers one gets are representative of the way people actually think.

There are disadvantages to the use of descriptive free responses as well. Perhaps the most formidable of these is the need to *code*, or classify, the specific answers that people give into broader classes of answers. Instead of attempting to work with everything people say, for instance, one looks at categories of answers. This approach makes it easier to detect relationships. Patterns emerge showing the frequency of different types of answers for different people, such as those given by older versus younger children. How does one arrive at the codes to be used in analyzing descriptive responses? One might simply decide in advance to look for certain types of answers, given what other investigators have found. One might also look at the actual answers that are given by a sample of the respondents, grouping specific answers into larger categories based on similarities in their meaning. These investigators had two independent raters code each of the response protocols; each rater was ignorant of the age of the respondent whose answers he or she was reading. The use of more than one coder makes it possible to determine the *reliability* with which answers are coded, or the degree to which the two raters working independently of each other agree in their coding.

The use of free-response or descriptive data is a time-intensive procedure. Raters must be trained to identify responses accurately, and this takes time. The actual scoring of the data also takes more time. In a sense, one enters a stream of behavior with a net—ready to catch (code) certain specimens of interest—but there is little way of speeding up the rate at which the behaviors flow by.

These investigators found that for younger children self-determination rights were not nearly as salient as were nurturance rights, as one might expect given the frequency with which young children need to be cared for and helped and the relative infrequency with which they get to participate in decisions about themselves. By the age of 14, however, adolescents were just as aware of their rights of self-determination as they were of nurturance rights. The salience of self-determination rights for adolescents most probably reflects their perception of themselves as able to fend for themselves in a variety of situations as well as their increasing need for autonomy.

might come home after work tense and irritable and yell at a child, who then fights with a sibling.

Research on such **emotional transmission** reveals a number of characteristic patterns. First, negative emotions are more easily transmitted than are others. It is easier to pass on anger, anxiety, or depression, for instance, than joy or peacefulness; or as Larson and Almeida put it, "negative emotions may trump positive ones." In general, however, families with greater psychological resources are less likely to experience the transmission of negative emotions than those with fewer resources.

Second, some members of the family are more likely than others to transmit emotions. The flow of emotions from one person to another is often unidirectional rather than reciprocal. Specifically, the emotions of men are more likely to affect their wives and children than vice versa. It is unclear whether this pattern reflects individuals' relative power within the family or, with respect to women, a greater sensitivity to the emotional states of others and also greater responsiveness to these. Emotions are also more likely to flow from parents to children than vice versa (Larson & Gillman, 1999). However, when they do, these are more likely to be the father's emotions than the mother's. This is not to say that mothers do not pass on their emotional states at the moment to their children, but that they are just less likely to do so.

Many of the negative emotions fathers pass on can be traced to stresses they experience at work. Mothers seem to be better at keeping these from spilling over into the emotional life of the family and may even become more responsive to their children when stressed at work. Marital tensions, on the other hand, are likely to be transmitted by mothers and fathers alike (Almeida, Wethington, & Chandler, 1999; Repetti, 1993).

Finally, it is common for an emotion that is passed from one person to assume a different form in the next person. Thus, the transmission of anger on the part of a parent may result not in anger in the child, but in anxiety. In this way, the effects of "secondhand" emotions on children can include physiological symptoms and patterns of behavior as well as emotional states. Thus, children can experience nervous stomachs or headaches, form "defensive alliances" within the family, or simply experience anxiety.

The way children react to the emotions of others depends in large measure on the way in which they interpret these emotions. Children actively construct, or make sense of, the emotional states of others just as they do other aspects of their world. Simply because an emotion is expressed does not mean that it will be experienced in the same way by different individuals. Geraldine Downey, Valerie Purdie, and Rebecca Shaffer-Neitz (1999) compared anger transmission from mother to child in mothers who experienced chronic pain and those who did not. They found that anger in the latter was likely to result in consequent anger in the child, but not in children in families in which the mother experienced chronic pain. Children of mothers with chronic pain simply did not interpret the anger the same way as they would were it not for the pain—that is, as a statement about themselves.

Families and Ethnicity

Over the past two decades, the number of ethnic families in the United States has increased dramatically. Twenty percent of all children under the age of 17 belong to an ethnic minority. By the year 2010 one third of all those in school will be Asian American, African American, Hispanic, Native American, or a member of some other minority. Ethnicity is an important factor contributing to the impact

---

Why are emotions more likely to be transmitted from men to their wives and children than vice versa?

---

emotional transmission Transference of emotions from one person to another, especially in a family, through daily interactions.

of the family on development. The organization of the family system often takes typically different forms in families with differing cultural backgrounds.

Family roles and relationships in minority-culture families are likely to differ from those typical in the dominant culture.

Asian American Families   Less than 4% of children in the United States are Asian and Pacific Islander American (Federal Interagency Forum, 1997), and most of them are of Chinese and Japanese backgrounds, although Vietnamese, Korean, and Filipino groups are growing in number. Asian traditions emphasize the importance of the group rather than the individual, and Asian American children feel strong loyalties to their families. Chinese Americans, as adults, continue to see their parents frequently, 2 to 3 times a week (Ying, 1994). Roles in Asian American families are more rigidly defined than in Western families, and relationships are vertically, or hierarchically, arranged, with the father in a position of authority at the top. Family relationships reflect the roles of members more than in individualistic, Western cultures. An aspect of the children's role is to care for their parents. This sense of responsibility to the family characterizes Asian American children (Huang & Yin, 1989; Nagata, 1989). Socialization practices emphasize duty, maintaining control over one's emotions and thoughts, and obedience to authority figures within the family (Nagata, 1989). Even with proportionately higher educational achievements, more Asian and Pacific Islander two-parent families (12.4%) experience poverty than do European American families (4.7%); however, the reverse is true for female-headed families. This difference might be attributable to the fact that the earnings of Asian and Pacific Islander males are 87% of those of European American males, whereas the earnings of Asian and Pacific Islander females are generally comparable to those of European American females (Day, 1996).

African American Families   Approximately 15% of children in the United States are African American (Federal Interagency Forum, 1997). Family roles are more flexible and are less gender-specific than in the dominant culture; parents assume responsibilities within the household according to work hours and type of task rather than according to gender-based roles. Parents also show less differentiation in the roles and tasks they assign to children of either sex (Gibbs, 1989). Support from extended family members is also more common than in majority families (Levitt, Guacci-Franco, & Levitt, 1993). The median income of African American families with children is approximately 67% that of European American families, and usually both parents must be employed for families to have middle-class status (Baugher & Lamison-White, 1996).

Hispanic Families   Nearly 14% of U.S. children are Hispanic. Most of these are Mexican American, although large numbers come from Puerto Rican, Cuban, and South and Central American backgrounds (Federal Interagency Forum, 1997). For children from Spanish-speaking homes, the sense of being between two cultures is especially strong. Traditionally, Hispanic families are patriarchal, with fathers making the decisions and supporting the family (Webster, 1994), and mothers caring for children and the home. These roles have changed as more Hispanic women find work outside the home. Employment is associated with higher status for the wife and greater decision making in the family (Herrera & DelCampo, 1995). Children are socialized into well-differentiated gender roles (Casas, Wagenheim, Banchero, & Mendoza-Romero, 1994; Ramirez, 1989). As do African American families, Hispanic families enjoy greater extended family support than do majority families (Levitt, Guacci-Franco, & Levitt, 1993). And, as with Asian and Pacific Islander and with African American families, more Hispanic families (27%) experience poverty than do non-Hispanic families (11%) (Baugher & Lamison-White, 1996).

Native American Families   Native Americans include Indians, Eskimos, Aleuts, Alaska Natives, and Metis, or people of mixed ancestry (LaFromboise & Low, 1989). One percent of children are Native Americans. Over 500 different native entities are recognized by the federal government. Each has its own customs and traditions, and over 200 Native American languages are spoken today (LaFromboise & Low, 1989).

Native American children frequently experience a cultural shock when they begin school. Many speak another language and have been raised with cultural values that run counter to those of the dominant culture. Often parents can be of little assistance, because they have not successfully assimilated themselves (LaFromboise & Low, 1989).

Siblings

Another aspect of the family system that affects children's development is its size. Children growing up with sisters and brothers experience a different family life, and are affected differently by it, than do those without siblings. Most children find that, despite the conflicts that inevitably arise, they develop close bonds of affection with siblings. Gene Brody, Zolinda Stoneman, and Kelly McCoy (1994), at the University of Georgia, followed 70 families over a 4-year period, assessing the quality of sibling relationships. In general, siblings reported that their relationships with each other improved over time. However, as siblings reached early adolescence, they reported relationships with other children in the family as being more negative, a finding that corroborates that of Larson and associates (1996),

Older siblings are models for younger ones. This young boy wants to be just like his older brother.

who also found adolescents' emotional experiences, when they were with their families, to become more negative by junior high.

The quality of the relationships siblings enjoy with each other is moderated, in part, by the relationships their parents have with other children in the family. This is especially true for their parents' relationships with the older child (Brody, Stoneman, & McCoy, 1994). Gene Brody, Zolinda Stoneman, and Kenneth Gauger (1996) found this "spillover" effect to be especially noticeable when the temperament of the older sibling was "difficult." The quality of each parent's relationship with the older child is only marginally associated with sibling relationships when the older sibling's temperament is "easy," but dramatically so when it is "difficult." Good parental relationships with difficult children appear to buffer those children's relationships with their siblings, perhaps through building better interpersonal skills, or by affecting self-regulatory skills, or simply by creating the expectation that relationships can be rewarding. Considering only relationships among the siblings themselves, the temperament of the older child rather than that of the younger is most important in determining the quality of the relationship, because older children are better able to dominate a relationship, influencing the form their interactions will take.

Older siblings are models for younger ones. Through their interactions with parents and others, they illustrate expected forms of behavior and family standards.

Their achievements influence younger siblings' aspirations and interests. A girl's interest in sports, for example, will be influenced by having an older sister on the varsity field hockey team. She sees the interest her parents take in her sister's activities and the pride her sister has in her team role. The girl takes it for granted that girls participate in sports and intends to try out for the swimming team herself when she reaches junior high.

Siblings provide friendship and company for each other. Because they are closer in age to each other than to a parent, they are often more in touch with the problems each faces and can frequently offer better advice than a parent. An older brother can advise a boy that the problems he is having at a new school will soon end. He knows, because that was his experience a year ago when he was the new boy at school. A parent would be less likely to have this information.

 Siblings often describe their relationship as a mixture of rivalry and love. Here is how two girls talked about their relationships with their older brothers. Nilmarie, age 9, says, "My brother is sixteen and he treats me like a baby. He calls me shrimp and I hate that. And he's always torturing me . . . like there's this huge sofa and everybody in the house loves sitting on the sofa. So when my brother sits on the sofa, I say, 'Mom wants you in the kitchen.' So he goes to the kitchen and I stretch out on the sofa. Then he comes back and throws me on the floor." Anna, who is 10, responds by saying that her 18-year-old brother is even worse, holding her upside down until her face turns blue, and sums it up by saying, "I'm telling you, big brothers are trouble." But then, after a reflective moment, Anna adds, "last month we took him to college, and I just had to go back into the car because I was crying. Because he was going to stay there for five months." When asked if she were going to miss him, Anna nodded, surprised at her own reaction, "I was sobbing. I couldn't believe it. I mean, that's the brother that I fight with the most, that I kick, who beats me up. And there I am crying" (Samalin, 2000, pp. 73–74).◄

A Developing Morality

The development of moral reasoning undergoes a number of significant changes in middle childhood. Children internalize the standards of their communities and begin to use these in evaluating their own and others' behavior. They also begin to take intentions into consideration rather than judging actions simply in terms of their consequences, such as whether they were punished or praised. Finally, they begin to examine values that they once unthinkingly accepted and to formulate their own principles for evaluating the acceptability of various behaviors. What is responsible for these developmental changes? The answers will differ depending on who we turn to. We will consider four explanations of moral development in the section that follows: social-cognitive theory, which derives from the environmental model, and the theories of Kohlberg, Gilligan, and Freud, all of which reflect the assumptions of the organismic model.

Social-Cognitive Theory and Moral Development

Why do children internalize the standards of their communities? Why do they take intentions into consideration and examine their values? Social-cognitive theorists look to principles of learning for explanations.

Internalizing Standards   Those who adopt the social-cognitive approach assume that rewards and punishments regulate behavior. These incentives are initially effective in young children only when other people, such as parents and teachers, are around to administer them. As children imitate adult models, they also tell themselves when they have been good or bad, administering their own rewards and punishments (Mischel & Mischel, 1976).

Community standards determine which behaviors are to be rewarded and which ones punished. In learning the consequences of their behavior, children also acquire the standards of the group. These internalized controls tend to be concrete at first. Children learn specific actions and their consequences; they learn to say thank you, for example, or not to interrupt. In time they also acquire the principles behind these actions. Being polite, for instance, can take the form of a thank you or considering others' feelings by not interrupting. Thus, social-cognitive theory offers an explanation for internalizing the standards of one's community.

Considering Intentions   How does social-cognitive theory explain age-related changes in moral thought? Children at first do not take the intentions of others into consideration; they judge actions in terms of their consequences. This literal focus is one of the facts that any theory of moral development must address. Social-cognitive theorists point out that the experiences of children make this type of reasoning likely. Adults rarely use reasoning with young children, often simply relying on physical restraints. Because physical rewards and punishments are common with young children, they are more likely to attend to the rewards or punishments that follow what they do than to the reasons that directed their actions (Mischel & Mischel, 1976).

Parental reactions to damage and messes probably contribute to children's literal focus. Most parents become more upset over big messes than small ones, even though both can be equally unintentional. Consider a child who, keeping out of his mother's way as she fixes dinner, attempts to pour himself a glass of milk. His grip slips as he positions the milk carton, and he watches, transfixed, as a stream of milk sends the cup scudding, flooding the countertop with milk. Is this mother likely to comment on his thoughtfulness at not disturbing her? Probably not. This child, like most, will be scolded for making a mess. It makes sense that children fail to understand that intentions can enter into one's evaluation of a situation when their intentions are so imperfectly considered.

Questioning Values   Social-cognitive theory also explains the questioning of values that occurs as children get older. Parents and teachers expect older children and adolescents to start thinking for themselves, to evaluate ideas on their merit instead of accepting the endorsement of authorities. Social-cognitive theorists argue that we subtly reward older children and adolescents for questioning the very ideas we taught them to uncritically accept as younger children. Similarly, learning experiences explain the relativistic form of thought that emerges in many adolescents as they near their 20s. Exposure to new values challenges them to consider their own set of values as only one of a number of possible belief systems.

How does social-cognitive theory explain the questioning of values that occurs in older children and adolescents?

Acting Morally   How likely are children to act in ways that reflect their moral understanding? In part, it depends on the incentives. *Incentives* are the rewards and punishments for acting in particular ways. For instance, if children believed they would be rewarded for doing certain things, or if they could be sure nothing bad would happen to them if they acted irresponsibly, they might be more likely to act in either of these ways.

Factors other than incentives also effect the likelihood of action. Children are more likely to imitate the actions of prestigious people than of those whom they don't regard as important. Models who are nurturant are also more likely to be imitated, perhaps because we like them more than less-nurturant people and want to be like them. Models who are similar to us in one or more ways are also likely to be imitated, again perhaps because we can imagine being like them (Mischel & Mischel, 1976).

Critique of Social-Cognitive Theory   How well does this approach explain particular forms of moral behavior? We can look at how well it explains a very practical form of behavior: cheating at school.

Cheating   Cheating in most students is motivated by the fear of failing or the need for approval. However, whether students with those motives will actually cheat is influenced by situational variables such as the normative behavior of classmates, incentives either for being honest or for cheating, the amount of risk involved, and characteristics of models for honesty and dishonesty.

Both personality and situational variables are related to cheating. In one experiment, schoolchildren worked at unsolvable problems that could be finished only if they cheated. Some worked for a tangible prize and others just for recognition. The likelihood of cheating was related both to the students' personalities and to the incentives they were working for. Both self-esteem and need for approval predicted cheating. Students with high self-esteem and low approval needs were least likely to cheat. Those with equally high self-esteem but high need for approval were as likely to cheat as those with low self-esteem. Regardless of personal motives, students working for a tangible prize were more likely to cheat (Lobel & Levanon, 1988). Cultural differences have also been found in what students consider to be cheating. Even so, similarities seem to be greater than differences, with all students, irrespective of their nationality, understanding that cheating involves, in one way or another, a shirking of their responsibilities to their studies (Evans, Craig, & Mietzel, 1993; Waugh, Godfrey, Evans, & Craig, 1995).

Little mention has been made about conscience in this discussion. Social-cognitive theory suggests that many internalized controls are not necessarily related to moral values or to conscience; they simply reflect conditioning. Children become helpful or law-abiding in order to avoid the anxiety they associate with doing otherwise. Conscience, when it does apply to behavior, is merely the set of standards one internalizes with the learning process (Seiber, 1980). For social-cognitive theorists, there is no inner voice other than the echo of the voices around them.

Kohlberg and Moral Development: Morality as Justice

What makes one moral? Is it simply that one internalizes the standards of one's community? Is it ever possible for individuals to function at a higher level than the society in which they live? Where does a sense of justice come from if it is not present in the social order? Lawrence Kohlberg's theory of moral reasoning addresses these questions.

Kohlberg's (1976, 1984) theory bases its assumptions about moral development on the organismic model, stressing the importance of the inner forces that organize development. The most important of these forces is a sense of justice, which underlies the highest forms of moral thought.

Kohlberg's theory traces moral reasoning over a number of discrete stages. Movement from one stage to the next is prompted by the need to resolve conflict. This conflict arises when one realizes that others view things differently. Children gain insight into the perspectives of others through increases in role-taking skills. As they become able to put themselves in the place of another, they can see things as that person does. Cognitive maturity—the ability to think about and balance the competing demands produced by examining several perspectives—also contributes to moral development. Kohlberg (1976, 1984) assumes that children's level of cognitive development places limits on the sophistication of moral thinking.

Kohlberg traces moral development over three levels of moral reasoning, with two stages at each level. The levels reflect the stance individuals take in relation to the standards of their community. Not all standards reflect moral issues. Some standards exist as laws, others simply as conventions or customary ways of behaving. It is the law, for example, that one not take another person's life; it is customary that one not giggle when hearing of another's death. Both of these reflect a common value—the sacredness of life. But only when individuals reach the postconventional level of moral reasoning do they distinguish social convention, whether codified as laws or customs, from the values these conventions reflect. And only then, according to Kohlberg, can they distinguish conventional concerns from moral ones.

Preconventional Moral Reasoning Children at the level of **preconventional moral reasoning** want only to satisfy their needs and not get punished while doing so. They have not as yet internalized the standards of their community, even though they know what these standards are. They abide by the rules only when someone else is around. The rule enforcers, and not the rules, constrain their actions. In the absence of the former, anything goes as long as you don't get caught (Kohlberg, 1984).

Stage 1: Obedience Children at this stage assume that everyone else sees things as they do, not realizing that their view of a situation is just one of several possible perspectives. Consequently, they experience little or no conflict in their interactions with others. Their actions reflect only a need to satisfy their own desires, without getting punished for doing so. Stage 1 morality is not reflective; children do not take motives and intentions into consideration (they do not understand others' feelings and points of view easily). They judge behavior simply in terms of its consequences. Actions that are rewarded must have been good; those that were punished, bad.

Stage 2: Instrumental, or Considering Intentions As children become better able to put themselves in the place of another person, they can see things as the other person would. Adopting the other's perspective gives them two points of view, and, in turn, the likelihood that they will experience conflict. Which perspective is right? They can understand the reasons for the other person's actions and know that the other can understand theirs—that each of them can consider the intentions of the other. Children who reason at this level don't have to rely on others' reactions to evaluate behavior. They can look at the motives behind an action. Even though fairness is central to reasoning at this stage, morality is still preconventional because children consider only the actions and intentions of those they are with and not the rules or laws of the group, whether the school or community.

Conventional Moral Reasoning: Internalizing Standards Children at the level of **conventional moral reasoning** want to live up to the standards of their group and are not motivated simply by the desire to avoid punishment. These standards have become their own and are no longer simply other people's rules.

preconventional moral reasoning Kohlberg's first level of moral reasoning, characterized by the absence of internalized standards.

conventional moral reasoning Kohlberg's second level of moral reasoning, in which moral thinking is guided by internalized social standards.

In the course of moral development, adolescents come to see themselves not only as members of the community but also as able to challenge community decisions that they feel are wrong. These high school students are attending a school board meeting to protest the dropping of a class.

Stage 3: Conformist, or "Good Boy, Nice Girl"   The self-reflection that comes with formal thought makes it possible for children, when they move into adolescence, to see themselves as they imagine others would. This third-person perspective forms the basis for taking the norms of their group, in the form of concern with what others think of them, into consideration. This concern about the opinions of others adds a new dimension to morality: the need to live up to the expectations of others. Kohlberg (1984) believes that Stage 3 reasoning is dominant during adolescence and is even common in adulthood. The prevalence of Stage 3 reasoning helps to explain adolescents' sensitivity to the approval of peers. Rather than thinking through a situation in terms of the claims of those involved, adolescents are likely to be swayed by the opinions of their friends. See the Research Focus, "The Dependent Variable: When Is a Stereotype Simply a Good Guess, and When Is It Bad Judgment?"

Stage 4: Social Accord, or "Law and Order"   As the ability to think more abstractly increases, adolescents begin to see themselves as members of an invisible but nonetheless real community. As such, they realize the need to evaluate actions by the community's standards. Kohlberg believes that reasoning at the fourth stage is frequently the highest that most people reach. Although Stage 4 reasoning is usually adequate for most situations, it breaks down when laws conflict with human values. When this occurs, individuals must develop a way to see their society in relation to the needs of others.

Postconventional Moral Reasoning: Questioning Values   Only at the level of **postconventional moral reasoning** does Kohlberg believe that individuals develop genuine inner controls over behavior; the principles by which they live are self-derived standards rather than the conventions of their community. Motives, as well, reflect a sense of obligation to live within a code that is determined by one's principles. Thus, Kohlberg distinguishes levels of moral development in terms of both a progressive internalization of standards for behavior and motives for living according to these standards (Hoffman, 1980; Kohlberg, 1984).

postconventional moral reasoning
Kohlberg's third level of moral reasoning, in which moral thinking is guided by self-derived principles.

Stage 5: Social Contract   Kohlberg believes that individuals move into Stage 5 only when they have been exposed to other value systems, usually in late adolescence.

The Dependent Variable: When Is a Stereotype Simply a Good Guess, and When Is It Bad Judgment?

We all know that it's wrong to react to others on the basis of stereotypes. Yet how often do we do so? Stereotypes lead us to expect one type of behavior or another in individuals, based simply on their group membership. Adolescents live in a world of well-defined social groups, each of which is associated with characteristic behaviors. "Jocks," for instance, are thought of as noisy and rowdy, "preppies" as well-to-do and college bound, and "techies" as spending more time with their computers than with peers. How likely are adolescents to make judgments about the behavior of other adolescents, in the absence of any other information, based on stereotypes such as these?

Stacey Horn, Melanie Killen, and Charles Stangor (1999) wanted to know as well. These investigators were interested in the way high school students would evaluate the appropriateness of punishing other students, in the absence of supporting evidence, when the actions of which they were accused were either consistent or inconsistent with stereotypes for their groups. Would adolescents' decision making, in other words, be affected by commonly held stereotypes about members of other groups?

Stacey Horn and her associates asked ninth-graders to read a scenario in which some students had too much to drink at a dance and committed an act of vandalism. The students subsequently were told by the student council that they must pay for the damages despite the absence of evidence indicating they were responsible. The students were described either as "jocks" (football players) or as "techies" (computer club members), and the vandalism they committed was either damaging the sound equipment at the party or breaking into the school computer system. Thus, the action could be consistent with students' stereotypes (for example, computer club members who broke into the computer system) or inconsistent (for example, football players who broke into the computer system). After reading the scenario, students were asked to evaluate the action of the student council, to give the reasons on which they based their evaluation, and then to indicate whether they believed the student council's behavior was justified.

Why did these investigators use more than one measure of stereotyping? If the measures don't all show the same relationships, how are we to evaluate which one is more accurate? The answer is that different measures pick up different aspects of behavior. Three criteria distinguish accurate measures: reliability, validity, and sensitivity.

The first consideration with any measure of behavior, or *dependent variable,* is its *reliability.* It should yield the same value for a person each time. If a student takes an intelligence test, for instance, and retakes it in 3 weeks, one expects the score to be about the same on both occasions. Differences in IQ from one testing to the next reflect factors other than intelligence—that is, *error.* Reliable measures have little error. Second, measures must have *validity.* They must measure what they are designed to measure. Some of the very first intelligence tests were highly reliable but not very valid. Some, for instance, measured how rapidly people could tap their fingers, something that can be measured with little error but that turns out to have little to do with actual intelligence. Third, *sensitivity* is a characteristic of good measures: They are able to detect even small differences where these exist. Current measures of intelligence do more than sort individuals into categories of, say, bright, average, and dull. They offer numerous distinctions within each.

Returning to adolescents' stereotypes and their decision making, let's consider what Horn and her associates found. They discovered that adolescents evaluated the actions of the student council as wrong, indicating that it would be unfair to punish a group simply because the type of damage that had been done fit the stereotype of the group. However, they also found that the types of reasons adolescents brought to bear in supporting this position differed depending on whether the actions were consistent with their stereotypes of either group. When their stereotypes were confirmed, they were less likely to bring moral arguments to bear, leading to fewer concerns about fairness in the absence of supporting evidence. Only by using several response measures could the investigators sort out these differing relationships.

Individuals who come to respect others' ways of life find it difficult to continue seeing their own as more valid. Once individuals recognize that their society's conventions are in some sense arbitrary, they are forced to look beyond the conventions themselves to the function they serve. When they do, they discover that laws derive their importance because they represent agreements among people who live together, not because they are right in and of themselves. Members of a society enter into a contract with others in the society in which they agree to live within its laws, forgoing some individual freedoms, for the mutual benefit of all.

Stage 6: Universal Principles   This stage provides individuals with yet another perspective: seeing past the mutual agreements shared by members of a society to the values these agreements reflect. The social contracts we enter into reflect underlying values such as truth, justice, honor, and the value of life itself. The step that individuals take in order to gain a perspective on their society removes them from the claims of time and circumstance. Kohlberg (1984) asserts that all societies throughout history have recognized these values—that they are, in fact, universal ethical principles. Those who reason at this final stage understand that social conventions are imperfect reflections of these values and, consequently, individuals must look beyond conventions, and even laws, to their own principles when arriving at moral decisions.

Critique of Kohlberg's Theory   Elliot Turiel (1983), a psychologist at the University of California, Berkeley, maintains that even very young children distinguish moral rules from conventional ones. Conventional rules reflect accepted ways of doing things. As these change, so do the rules. Standards of dress and speech reflect these flexible relationships. Rules relating moral concerns to behavior, however, are inflexible. Moral rules reflect a concern for the well-being of others and do not change with climates of opinion.

Charles Helwig, Carolyn Hildebrandt, and Elliot Turiel (1995) interviewed first-, third-, and fifth-graders and found that nearly all the children agreed that moral acts such as pushing someone down would not be all right even in the context of a game that legitimized such actions. The youngest children, however, were less clear about acts leading to psychological harm, such as name-calling as part of a game. Similarly, Larry Nucci, Cleanice Camino, and Clary Sapiro (1996), interviewing 9- and 15-year-olds in Brazil, found that children as well as adolescents distinguished moral from conventional issues, agreeing that if there were no rules against doing so, it would be all right not to wear a school uniform, but not to hit or steal. Thus, even children distinguish moral from conventional concerns.

Although even very young children distinguish moral acts from conventional ones on the basis of whether they involve harm, it is unclear whether this is because they have isolated harm itself as the issue of concern or because such actions are typically punished. Philip Zelazo, Charles Helwig, & Anna Lau (1996) told children stories in which an action that typically is harmful, such as hitting, has positive consequences. Thus, children were told a story in which parents who had gone on a trip brought back a strange animal that "gets hurt and cries" when petted and "feels good and smiles" when it is hit. The question of interest is whether children, when asked whether it was good or bad to hit the animal, would base their judgments on indications of whether harm had occurred (outcomes such as crying or smiling) or rely on known sanctions against hitting.

They found that at every age, from 3 through 5, children based their judgments as to whether an action was acceptable on whether the character appeared to have been harmed—that is, on the outcome of the action. Since this was true for both types of stories, these findings indicate that even young children take the welfare of another into consideration rather than relying on social sanctions against specific actions such as hitting. They also found that, with age, the complexity of children's judgments increased. Thus, the youngest preschoolers tended to base their evaluations on a single consideration, such as the outcome of the action *or* the intentions of the character, whereas by the age of 5, children could consider both when evaluating actions.

Lying and Truth Telling   Not only do children distinguish moral issues from conventional concerns at an earlier age than Kohlberg assumed they could, but they also take intentions into consideration when evaluating the acceptability of various behaviors. One such behavior is lying versus truth telling.

Piaget (1965) was one of the first to look at children's understanding of what it means to lie. Adults consider people to have lied when they have misrepresented what they know to be so in order to deceive someone. Simply failing to report something accurately in the absence of intentional deception is not considered lying. Piaget found that, in making judgments about lying, children relied more heavily on whether a child had been believed than on whether that child had intended to deceive someone. Later research has found that children consider intention at a much earlier age than Piaget believed possible (Peterson, 1995; Wimmer, Gruber, & Perner, 1984).

In most cases, intentional deception involves an attempt to get away with something. However, what if misrepresentations of the truth, even though intentional, were motivated not by a desire to get away with something, but by respect for one's cultural values? Thus, children raised in collectivist cultures that emphasize not only honesty but also modesty as ways of promoting social harmony might consider it acceptable to lie about their achievements if asked to acknowledge these publicly. In comparison, children raised in individualistic cultures, in which behaviors that aggrandize the self are not considered wrong, should evaluate lying about a good deed as less acceptable.

Kang Lee, Catherine Cameron, Fen Xu, Genyao Fu, and Julie Board (1997) compared Canadian and Chinese children's evaluations of the goodness or badness of telling the truth or lying under different circumstances. Canadian children can be expected to reflect their culture's value of individualism and pride in personal accomplishments. Chinese children can be expected to reflect their culture's emphasis on collectivism and modesty in order to maintain social harmony. Thus, in China, doing a good deed is valued, but admitting to having done so violates cultural values of modesty and humility. These values raise the interesting question of how Chinese children would evaluate telling the truth versus lying about having done a good deed. A comparison of Chinese and Canadian children should show the effect of culture, whereas a similar comparison concerning lying about misdeeds would not be expected to find any differences.

Seven-, 9, and 11-year-olds evaluated stories about children as "naughty" or "good" in which the children had done a good deed or committed a misdeed and either told the truth about what they had done or lied. They found that Canadian children evaluated telling the truth equally positively at each age, whereas Chinese children's evaluations of telling the truth became less positive with age, increasingly reflecting the culture's value of modesty. Thus, 8% of 7-year-olds, 28% of 9-year-olds, and 48% of 11-year-olds evaluated telling the truth negatively. When asked why, they were likely to say the child was trying to get the teacher's praise, something that is actively discouraged in schools.

With respect to lying about doing a good deed, Canadian children considered telling a lie to be wrong, though older children tended less so than younger ones. Only the youngest Chinese children, however, considered it wrong to lie about a good deed. Older children evaluated this positively, as reflecting a value of modesty and humility. With respect to telling the truth about committing a misdeed, however, Canadian and Chinese children did not differ. Both evaluated telling the truth positively.

With respect to questioning values, long before children can read bumper stickers telling them to "Question Authority!" they do so. Even young children have been found to question the legitimacy of directives from authority figures such as parents and teachers when these could result in harm to others or are patently unfair. That is, children distinguish moral issues from conventional, or

In collectivist cultures where humility is highly valued, not speaking about one's accomplishments is regarded more positively than in individualist cultures where personal achievement is highly valued.

authority-based, ones at an early age (Laupa & Turiel, 1986). They also distinguish how much a person knows about a situation when evaluating who should be listened to, even when the more knowledgeable person is a child rather than an adult (Laupa, 1991).

But to what extent are children able to make such distinctions when the moral dimensions are less clear-cut, as when they are separated from issues of physical harm? And to what extent are judgments such as these affected by one's culture? Most Asian cultures, for instance, regard respect for one's elders and deference to those in positions of authority as virtues, elevating these above mere convention.

Korean children in first, third, and fifth grades listened to stories about moral dilemmas in which a child was told to do something that was morally right or not right, such as trying to find the person who had lost some money or keeping the money. Children indicated it was better to listen to those who encouraged the child to do the (morally) right thing, even when these directions ran counter to directions given by a person in authority, such as a principal or teacher. Thus, even in instances where no physical harm is involved, children distinguish moral issues from obedience to authority figures. This distinction is especially compelling in that it is made by children raised in a culture in which deference to those in authority is regarded as virtuous (Kim, 1998).

Kohlberg's theory, despite contradictory findings such as the above, enjoys wide support. His theory has an intrinsic elegance. Each of the six stages is a logical extension of the preceding one, and the progression is systematically related to new role-taking skills and cognitive maturity. But there may be another reason to account for the popularity of this theory. Kohlberg has given us a sympathetic view of human nature. He accounts for our ability to control our behavior in terms of the development of an inner sense of justice, rather than the carrot-and-stick approach of social-cognitive theory.

Carol Gilligan questions whether justice is the highest arbiter of moral issues. She finds that an ethic of care, rather than a morality of justice, is more characteristic of females. She points out that Kohlberg developed his theory based on interviews with males. Like many developmentalists before him, Kohlberg equated the male perspective with development in general (see Chapter 1).

Gilligan: An Ethic of Care

Carol Gilligan (1982, 1988a, 1988b, 1989a, 1989b), of Harvard University, offers a fresh perspective on moral development, one that balances male-oriented theories such as Kohlberg's and Freud's with insights gained from interviews with females. Gilligan finds that most females think of morality more personally than males do; they adopt an **ethic of care.** They speak of morality in terms of their responsibilities to others rather than as the rights of individuals. Their moral decisions are based on compassion as well as reason, and they stress care for others as well as fairness.

Gilligan traces these approaches to differences in the way females and males define themselves in relation to others. Whereas males tend to view themselves as separate from others, females see themselves in terms of their relationships with others. These themes of separation and connectedness translate into different approaches to morality. The assumption that one is separate from others highlights the need for rules to regulate the actions of each person with respect to the other; the assumption that one is connected to others emphasizes the responsibility each has to the other (Gilligan, 1982).

Gender differences also exist in the way individuals think of responsibility. Males tend to think of responsibility as *not* doing something that would infringe

ethic of care Gilligan's description of a morality based on responsiveness to and care for others.

on the rights of others, such as not hurting them. Females think of responsibility in terms of *meeting* the needs of others—that is, as something to be done. Both males and females are concerned with not hurting others, yet each sex thinks of this in a different way. Gilligan points out that, given differences such as these, attempts to chart moral development as a single sequence are bound to give us only half the picture.

Gilligan traces moral development in females through three levels, each of which reflects a different resolution to the conflict between responsibility to self and responsibility to others. Movement from one level to the next occurs in two transitional periods. At the first level, the primary concern is with oneself. Transition to the next level occurs when one sees caring only for oneself as selfish and at odds with responsibility to others. At the second level, females equate morality with goodness and self-sacrifice, or caring for others. Transition to the third level occurs when they experience problems in their relationships that result from excluding themselves from their own care. At the third level, they equate morality with care for both themselves and others.

Level 1: Caring for Self (Survival)   The primary concerns at this level of moral development are pragmatic: What's best for me? Actions are guided by self-interest. Gilligan notes that the issue of "rightness" is considered only when several of one's needs are in conflict and force the individual to consider which need is more important. Otherwise there is little conflict over making the right decision.

Why might individuals function at this level? Gilligan believes that a preoccupation with one's needs reflects feelings of helplessness and powerlessness. These feelings have their origin in being emotionally cut off, or *disconnected*, from others. The females she interviewed who were at this level had frequently been hurt by others and often chose to hold themselves apart from others rather than experience further pain. Feeling alone and cut off from others, they were left with the sense that they had to look to their own needs, because no one else would (Gilligan, 1982).

This first level is similar to Kohlberg's preconventional level of moral reasoning. In neither level do individuals consider others except for their possible reactions to what they do—-that is, except as potential consequences for their actions. Conflict is also absent in both levels and self-interest, rather than the need to make the right decision, dictates what one does.

Transition: From Selfishness to Responsibility   Individuals begin to move beyond the first level when they experience a discrepancy between the way they are and the way they feel they ought to be, between self-concern and responsible concern for others.

Level 2: Caring for Others (Goodness)   Gilligan assumes that females move to a second level of moral development when they internalize social conventions. The progression is similar to that described by Kohlberg for movement from preconventional to conventional reasoning. Gilligan (1982) notes that, in the first level,

> morality is a matter of sanctions imposed by a society of which one is more subject than citizen, [and in the second] moral judgment relies on shared norms and expectations. The woman at this point validates her claim to social membership through the adoption of societal values. Consensual judgment about goodness becomes the overriding concern as survival is now seen to depend on acceptance by others. (p. 79)

Transition: From Conformity to Choice   The equation of morality with conventional feminine goodness is a step toward repairing the failed relationships that led to a preoccupation with the self at the first level. But this equation creates a second imbalance that itself is in need of repair. Conventional images of feminine goodness center on the care of others. They also involve self-sacrifice. Females at the second level of morality purchase membership in the larger community at the cost of caring for themselves. The price of membership is costly and introduces tensions that, for some, will prompt movement to the third level. These individuals realize that excluding themselves from their own care creates as many problems as excluding others had done previously; in other words, goodness results in as much hurt as selfishness (Gilligan, 1986). This realization is an important step in moving to an ethic of care that includes themselves as well as others. Gilligan, like Kohlberg before her, believes that many females do not take this step and do not develop beyond conventional forms of thought.

Level 3: Caring for Self and Others (Truth)   To move into the third level, females must move beyond the conventional wisdom that tells them to put the needs of others above their own. In doing so, they must reformulate their definition of care to include themselves as well as others. As females reconsider their relationships with others, they once again must consider their own needs. Questions such as "Is this selfish?" again arise. Because these occur in the context of relationships with others, they also prompt a reexamination of the concept of responsibility.

When one moves beyond conventional forms of wisdom, one finds there is no one to turn to for answers but oneself. Females at this level cannot rely on what others might think; they must exercise their own judgment. This judgment requires that they be honest with themselves. Being responsible for themselves, as well as for others, means they must know what their needs actually are. As Gilligan (1982) asserts, "The criterion for judgment thus shifts from goodness to truth when the morality of action is assessed not on the basis of its appearance in the eyes of others, but in terms of the realities of its intention and consequence" (p. 83). The bottom line is simple: To care for oneself, one must first be honest with oneself and acknowledge the reasons behind one's actions.

Individuals at this level adopt an inclusive perspective that gives equal weight to their responsibility to themselves and to others. Care extends to all. To exclude the self would introduce pain that could otherwise be avoided, and their commitment to minimizing pain requires a new balance of concern for self with responsibility for others.

Although Gilligan and Kohlberg document developmental sequences that parallel each other in many respects, a critical difference separates these two accounts. Kohlberg believes that his sequence is a path universally trodden by all individuals as they move into adulthood. He assumes that this sequence takes the form it does because it reflects developments in cognitive maturity that have a strong biological component (see the discussion of Piaget in Chapter 1). Gilligan is not equally convinced that the sequence she documents in adolescent girls and young women is developmentally necessary. She does not believe the sequence to be "rooted in childhood," as does Kohlberg. She suggests, instead, that it is a response to a crisis and that the crisis is adolescence itself (Gilligan, 1989a).

Gilligan proposes that leaving childhood is problematic for girls in ways that it is not for boys. The problem lies with the culture each enters. Adolescence introduces the expectation that children will assume the conventions of their society, whether these be adult gender roles, the knowledge that forms the basis of cultural wisdom, or behaviors that fit prescribed definitions of "goodness" and "rightness." Why should this expectation present more problems for girls?

Gilligan's answer is powerful. The most visible figures populating the landscape of adulthood are males—whether plumbers, politicians, poets, or philosophers—and their collective experiences form its norms. Girls risk losing themselves as they relax the intimate bonds of childhood to embrace a larger world of experience. Gilligan (1989b) writes

> As the river of a girl's life flows into the sea of Western culture, she is in danger of drowning or disappearing. To take on the problem of her appearance, which is the problem of her development, and to connect her life with history on a cultural scale, she must enter—and by entering disrupt—a tradition in which "human" has for the most part meant male. Thus a struggle often breaks out in girls' lives at the edge of adolescence. (p. 4)

The problem is pervasive because it is woven into the very fabric of cultural thought. Even formal education, Gilligan suggests, presents a challenge to female identity: "In learning to think in the terms of the disciplines and thus to bring her thoughts and feelings into line with the traditions of Western culture, . . . she also learn[s] to dismiss her own experience" (p. 2).

Gilligan (1989a) traces the crisis of connection for girls to their ability to find a "voice" with which to speak and a context in which they will be heard. The culture they are entering has not been equally responsive to the voices of women and men, "or at least has not been up to the present. The wind of tradition blowing through women is a chill wind, because it brings a message of exclusion. . . . The message to women is: keep quiet and notice the absence of women and say nothing" (p. 26).

Critique of Gilligan's Theory   Gilligan has suggested that individuals are likely to function at Level 1 when they have been hurt by others, causing them to be preoccupied with their own needs. As a consequence, one might expect that children who have been maltreated would evaluate moral transgressions differently than those who had not been maltreated. Surprisingly, however, when such comparisons have been made, maltreated children do not differ from others in their evaluations of hypothetical moral situations (Smetana, Kelly, & Twentyman, 1984). One might still find differences, however, if they were evaluating actual transgressions.

Judith Smetana and her associates (1999) looked for such differences, comparing maltreated and nonmaltreated children's evaluations of actual transgressions in their classrooms, such as hitting or name-calling, as well as hypothetical transgressions. As might be expected, actual transgressions were judged to be more serious than hypothetical situations. However, maltreated children did not differ from those who were not maltreated in how seriously they evaluated moral transgressions (either hypothetical or actual) or in their reasons for why actions were permissible or wrong. Thus, their own maltreatment did not blunt their moral sensitivities. However, they did differ in their emotional reactions to mistreatment. Among those who had been abused, the ones who expressed most sadness also evaluated actual transgressions as more serious, thought they should be punished more severely, and were more likely to mention the intrinsic harmfulness of these actions. These findings suggest that the way children perceive and evaluate social relations is constructed from their own experiences and that those who have been physically harmed are, if anything, even more sensitive to the intrinsic harm to others in moral transgressions.

What evidence is there for gender differences in moral concerns? D. Kay Johnston (1988) asked 11- and 15-year-olds to generate solutions to two of Aesop's fables involving moral issues. Specifically, she wanted to know whether gender differences exist in the spontaneous use of justice and care orientations and whether both orientations are available to adolescents of each sex. Boys were much more likely to spontaneously adopt a justice than a care approach to both of the fables. Girls, however, were fairly evenly divided in their adoption of either approach. Judgments about the best solution showed that boys still strongly preferred (three to one) a justice solution to one of the fables; girls strongly favored a care solution as best to both of the fables.

Judy Daniels, Michael D'Andrea, and Ronald Heck (1995) replicated Johnston's experiment with adolescents in Hawaii and found no difference in the solutions spontaneously offered by girls and boys. Furthermore, when asked for the best solution to the dilemmas, all adolescents offered a care approach. Differences between their findings and those of Johnston might reflect cultural differences or simply changes in gender roles with time. In individualistic cultures such as the mainland United States, the rights of individuals tend to be emphasized, whereas in traditionally collectivistic cultures such as Hawaii, the good of the collective, or group, is emphasized (Markus & Kitayama, 1991).

It is also possible that differences between these studies may be due to changing gender roles (Sochting, Skoe, & Marcia, 1994). Rosemary Jadack and her associates (1995) found that females and males differed little in the extent to which they adopted a care or a justice orientation in reasoning about real-life types of dilemmas. In fact, individuals of either sex frequently used reasoning characteristic of both approaches, suggesting that these are not competing perspectives. Similarly, Gillian Wark and Dennis Krebs (1996) found that, although females did mention more care-based reasons than males, the difference was small and occurred only when they were reasoning about certain types of problems.

Gilligan views the developmental sequence that she catalogues as complementing that of Kohlberg, not as an alternative (Gilligan & Attanucci, 1988). She points out, however, that the care orientation would have been missed had she and others not studied females as systematically as Kohlberg studied males.

Freud: Morality and the Superego

Freud's theory of moral development derives from his more general theory of personality development. Like other organismic theorists, Freud looked to sources within the organism to explain certain developmental changes. Freud assumed that the strong biological forces he identified must be balanced by equally strong social constraints that develop only with age.

Freud believed that responsibility for moral behavior resides with the **superego**, the last of the three facets of the personality to develop (see Chapter 9). The superego embraces the cultural standards of right and wrong that make up the *conscience*. Prior to the development of the conscience (at about age 5), Freud assumed that children are governed only by the desire to win parental affections and the fear of being rejected for wrongdoing. Like social-cognitive theorists and Kohlberg, Freud believed that an internalized code or ethic is not present in early childhood.

Freud (1925b/1961) assumed that the libido—the life force within each individual—seeks genital expression in childhood, and that the object of the child's sexual desires is the very person who is closest in so many other ways. For the boy, this is the mother; for the girl, it will become the father. Sexual desire for the parent of the opposite sex makes the parent of the same sex a rival. The emotional triangle that results creates unbearable anxiety in the child. Freud believed that children repress their sexual desires to reduce the anxiety they experience and

superego The aspect of personality in Freudian theory that represents the internalized standards and values of society.

identify with the same-sex parent. **Identification** is the process by which the child internalizes or appropriates the values and behaviors of the parent. These values form the superego and serve as the basis for an internalized set of standards for behavior.

Freud assumed the situation differed for male and female children. Freud reasoned that girls are not as motivated as boys to resolve Oedipal tensions, because they have already suffered an incalculable loss: They were not born with a penis. Rather than fearing castration (castration anxiety), they long for a penis (penis envy). Because girls literally have less to lose than boys, they do not experience the same anxiety that motivates boys to identify with the same-sex parent. Also, the figure with whom the girl identifies, the mother, is not as powerful or threatening as the father. As a consequence, Freud believed that girls' superegos are not as strong or as demanding as those of boys.

The final step in moral development occurs in adolescence when puberty threatens the surface tranquility achieved through repression and identification. New sexual desires assail the fragile bulwark the child has erected against Oedipal turmoil. Freud assumed that adolescents' only defense against the onslaught of their own sexuality and the incestuous threat this poses is to emotionally distance themselves from their parents. In doing so, they have to toss out the parental figures they had internalized in childhood. Adolescence becomes a time for reworking the parental standards that have been uncritically accepted as part of these figures (Josselson, 1980, 1987).

Critique of Freud's Theory   Freud's theory of personality development and his assumptions about moral development are widely accepted. His theory influences vast numbers of clinical practitioners and is taught in college courses around the world. Many of his concepts—such as the unconscious, projection, and repression—have entered the popular vocabulary. Nevertheless, the bulk of support for this theory comes from clinical evidence based on small numbers of individuals and is often heavily interpreted (Hoffman, 1980).

Carol Travis and Carole Wade (1984) point to the absence of systematic, objective support for Freud's twin concepts of castration anxiety and penis envy, concepts that are central to his explanation of moral development in males and females, respectively. Regarding the concept of penis envy, they note that females as well as males value the male role more highly, but point out that males have enjoyed more power, greater opportunities, and more privileges than females. Do females envy males for their penis? Or do they desire the social advantages that go with having one?

Freud believed that the absence of castration anxiety in females and the presence, in its stead, of penis envy resulted in a weaker superego in females and differences in their moral behavior.

These assumptions concerning the basis for gender differences in moral behavior have not received empirical support. Research on the internalization of moral standards does not find males to have stronger superegos than females. Nor do differences in behavior, when they occur, favor males. They are, if anything, as likely to favor females (Ford, Wentzel, Wood, Stevens, & Siesfeld, 1989; Lobel & Levanon, 1988).

Research has similarly failed to support other of Freud's assumptions related to the development of morality. For instance, adolescence is not a period of emotional turmoil for most teenagers. Also, large surveys of normal adolescents do not find they are preoccupied with sex or with controlling their impulses. Nor do most adolescents have weak egos, nor have they cut emotional ties with their parents (see Chapter 9).

identification The child's uncritical incorporation of parental ways and beliefs.

Internalizing Standards   How does Freud explain the facts that other theories of moral development have addressed? Like social-cognitive theorists (as well as Kohlberg and Gilligan for conventional standards of morality), Freud assumes that individuals acquire their values and their sense of right and wrong by internalizing society's norms. The conditions that prompt children to internalize parental standards differ for each theory, however. Freud traces internalization to resolution of the Oedipal complex and identification with the parent of the same sex. Social-cognitive theory speaks of the child's ability to reinforce itself, rather than having to receive praise or punishment at the hands of others. Both theories must address the central problem with internalization as an explanation for moral conduct: If one's culture is the ultimate source of moral authority in an individual's life, how does a person ever reach a level higher than that which characterizes the society? Gilligan and Kohlberg both view the internalization of social conventions as an intermediate step in moral development. Gilligan believes that females take this step when they experience a discrepancy between their self-concern and concern for others. Kohlberg traces this step to increases in cognitive maturity.

Considering Intentions   For Freud, the emergence of the superego explains the child's shift from evaluating behavior in terms of its consequences to the motives that underlie it. Social-cognitive theorists, in contrast, explain this shift in terms of the social-learning experiences of the child, but frequently fail to take into consideration the child's own motives and intentions or the expectation that adolescents will begin to think for themselves. Kohlberg attributes this shift to new levels of cognitive maturity and role-taking skills. Gilligan's analysis of morality begins with individuals who have already made this transition.

Questioning Values   And how might Freud explain the flexibility that characterizes the moral thought that develops in some with late adolescence? Rather than refer to changing social expectations, increasing cognitive maturity, or the need to repair relationships, psychoanalytic thought attributes flexibility in moral judgments to the work of the ego in balancing the demands of the id and superego. Individuals who remain relatively inflexible are those dominated by a threatening superego. The ability to evaluate a situation, to develop coping strategies, and to delay gratification of one's impulses are all functions of the ego and characterize mature moral functioning.

Children's Religious Beliefs

Do children think of God the same way adults do? Or does one find evidence of developmental changes in their understanding of God just as one does in their moral understanding? James Fowler (1981, 1991) suggests that such evidence exists. He has identified stages of religious belief that parallel the stages of moral development discussed earlier.

Schoolchildren's views of God, for instance, reflect the concrete nature of the way they think in general. To them, God is someone with a human form who sits celestially enthroned above them. They accept the teachings and stories of their religion literally and do not question them, other than to try to fit them into their current ways of understanding, such as wondering how God can be everywhere at the same time (Fowler, 1981).

Similarly, the ability to think in more abstract ways that comes with adolescence transforms children's religious beliefs. More abstract qualities of God, such

Children go through different stages of religious belief. This boy, at his bar mitzvah, may later question some of the dogma he has learned in preparation for this important Jewish rite.

as compassion, righteousness, and mercy, can be appreciated; and more sophisticated reasoning about religious practices is possible (Helwig, 1995). Adolescents also begin to question their religious beliefs, just as they question other values that they had previously taken for granted. For instance, adolescents are likely to wonder, "If God is all-powerful, why is there suffering and evil in the world?" The answers they arrive at reflect an increasingly personalized faith, much as Kohlberg's and Gilligan's final stages of morality reflect commitment to personally-arrived-at principles.

One of the first components to children's religious identity, just as with gender or ethnicity, consists in labeling, or identifying themselves in terms of a particular religious denomination. When children are asked what these labels mean, one sees evidence of a clear developmental trend to their understanding. In a series of studies, David Elkind (1961, 1962, 1963) asked Catholic, Jewish, and Protestant children how they could tell whether a person was of the same religion that they were. Irrespective of the particular religion, children's understanding of what distinguished one religion from another underwent the same developmental sequence. The youngest children, 5- to 6-year-olds, had not as yet distinguished what it meant to belong to a particular religion. For instance, when asked "What is a Protestant?" they were likely simply to answer "a person."

By middle childhood, however, children identified members of religious groups in terms of concrete behaviors and characteristics. Thus, one who is Catholic might be identified as someone who goes to Mass every Sunday, or one who is Jewish as a person who goes to temple and attends Hebrew School. Such an understanding, as Elkind points out, highlights the differences between religions. That is, if one is going to temple, one cannot also be attending Mass. One is either one religion or the other, and the two are noticeably different.

At a third stage, however, which children reach as they enter adolescence, they begin to appreciate the commonalities to different religions, understanding that one can worship God irrespective of whether one does this in a temple or a church. In this stage, children identify their religion in terms of abstract beliefs.

Thus, Jewish children might describe someone of their faith as "a person who believes in one God and doesn't believe in the New Testament," or a Protestant might describe another Protestant as "a person who believes in God and Christ and is loving to other people" (Elkind, 1961, 1962, 1963).

How important, one might ask *is* religion to children's sense of themselves? When asked to describe themselves, in other words, how likely are children to mention their religion? Rachel Royle, Martyn Barrett, and Eithne Buchanan-Barrow (1998) had children of various religions and nationalities, all of whom lived in London, sort cards into either of two boxes, one labeled "Me" and the other "Not Me." Each card identified some aspect of a single identity component, such as a child's gender, ethnicity, language, age, or religion. Once children had finished this initial sort, they were asked to go through the "Me" cards again and select the one that was most descriptive of themselves. This card was removed and they selected the next most descriptive card, continuing in this way until each of the terms had been ranked in terms of importance.

Religion emerged as a significant aspect of identity, being among those most likely to be selected as "Me." Furthermore, its importance to children's sense of themselves increased with age. Perhaps predictably, younger children (4–6 years) were more likely to identify themselves in terms of their gender. Middle children (7–8 years), on the other hand, were more likely to do so in terms of their nationality. But for older children (9–11), religion was more important, being mentioned more frequently than their sex, age, or nationality. Even so, some religions contributed to children's identity more heavily than did others, possibly reflecting the minority status they conferred. A similar trend has been found for ethnicity, in which individuals who are members of a minority are more aware of their ethnicity than are those belonging to the majority, the latter frequently not even having a sense of their own ethnicity (Phinney, 1989). So, too, with religion. For Muslims living in London, religion was more salient than it was for Christians.

When children think of religion, how do they think of God? Bradley Hertel and Michael Donahue (1995) analyzed the responses of fifth- through ninth-graders to nine descriptors of God. Two dimensions emerged. One described God in terms of love, and the second described God in terms of authority. Items related to the first of these, for instance, described God as loving someone irrespective of what that person had done, whereas those related to the second described God in terms of rules and punishing wrongdoers. Of these two dimensions, the image of God that predominated among these youth was overwhelmingly that of a loving God. This was true, by the way, for their parents as well.

Summary

The Self

In middle childhood, children develop a sense of industry, through which they come to know themselves by their accomplishments. They are ready to apprentice themselves as learners and willingly work alongside parents and teachers. A sense of inferiority can develop in those who do not persist at the things they attempt until mastery is achieved. Increases in reflectiveness, in combination with newly developing skills, lay a foundation for changes in their self-concept.

Self-Concept

Children's self-concept refers to the set of beliefs children hold about themselves. There are characteristic differences between the way older and younger children think of the self. Older children describe themselves in terms of general traits; younger children describe themselves in terms of specific behaviors. Older children describe themselves in terms of their relationships with others; younger children describe themselves in terms of their preferences and possessions. Older children's self-characterizations are more complex and tolerate inconsistencies, whereas those of younger children remain simple. Finally, children's self-concepts tend to become more realistic with age.

Self-Esteem

Self-esteem refers to children's overall positive or negative evaluation of themselves. Relationships with parents provide the foundation for self-esteem. When parents are loving, children feel lovable and develop feelings of self-worth. Children appear to first evaluate themselves in terms of overall self-worth at about the age of 8; prior to this, children differ in how they feel about themselves but do not articulate these feelings in relation to their concept of self.

Friendships

Friends are usually of the same sex, race, socioeconomic background, and grade in school, and they have the same social status with peers. The assistance children receive from each other as well as the fun they have together contribute to the quality of their relationships. Children are likely to have as many as eight or nine important friendships; different patterns of qualities characterize the relationships children have with different friends.

Peer Relations

Children's social status is fairly stable throughout the grade school years. A number of statuses can be distinguished in terms of their interactive styles. Both popular and average children are cooperative, take turns, and play well with others. Popular children tend to set the norms for their group and are able to maintain play with others for longer periods of time; others appear to have more fun when playing with them. Rejected children are more aggressive than others, both physically and verbally, are more likely to exclude others when playing, and engage in more inappropriate behavior. Neglected children, who spend most of their time in solitary play, also engage in inappropriate behavior but are not aggressive. Since these statuses appear to reflect genuine differences in skills, intervention programs need to focus on skill building.

Children who form friendships with aggressive children run the risk either of being the object of relational aggression or of being drawn into aggressive interactions with others. Victimization, just like aggression, is a relatively stable characteristic of children. Those who are likely to be victimized are children who cry easily, have poor social skills, and are submissive when attacked.

Cross-Ethnic Friendships

Interracial and interethnic friendships form when children live in integrated neighborhoods and attend integrated schools. Interracial friendships face challenges posed by different enculturation experiences. Children of different backgrounds can perceive and react to the same situation differently; misinterpretations and hurt feelings can result.

Families in Transition

Nearly half of all children will experience divorce. The impact of divorce depends on conditions in the child's life, such as age, gender, amount of marital conflict, support from family and friends, and economic stability. The effectiveness of parenting drops in the first several years following divorce, and both parental self-esteem and children's coping strategies suffer. Marital conflict, rather than divorce itself, contributes heavily to the stress children experience, but exposure to conflict need not always be negative.

Most children in single-parent families live with their mothers. Daughters fare better in single-parent families than do sons. With remarriage, daughters experience more problems than before, whereas sons experience fewer. Stepparents, usually stepfathers, report that most difficulties center on issues of authority and discipline. Role clarity facilitates interaction in stepparent families.

Children and Their Families

Even when the family structure remains stable, children's relationships with parents change in middle childhood; children and parents simply spend less time together. Not only the time parents and children spend together, but also the way they interact, changes. Parents spend less time in hands-on caretaking activities and more in monitoring activities at a distance, keeping track of where children are and whom they are with.

Several domains of authority exist within a family, and parental authority shifts in only some of them. Conflicts arise when parents and children do not agree about which issues should remain under parental authority and for how long.

The emotional climate within the family changes as emotions are transmitted from one person to another. Research on emotional transmission reveals a number of patterns. First, negative emotions are more easily transmitted than positive ones. Second, the emotions of men are more likely to affect their wives and children than vice versa. Third, emotions are more likely to flow from parents to children than from children to parents; and fourth, it is common for an emotion that is passed from one person to assume a different form in the next person.

Social-Cognitive Theory and Moral Development

Social-cognitive theory assumes that children eventually internalize controls that initially are effective only when enforced by others. In doing so, children acquire their community's standards. Age-related changes in moral thought are explained by referring to the experiences that make different forms of thought most likely at different ages. Research on variables predicting cheating supports social-cognitive theory.

Kohlberg and Moral Development: Morality as Justice

At the preconventional level of moral reasoning, individuals lack internalized standards of right and wrong; their motives are only to satisfy their needs without getting into trouble. At the conventional level of moral reasoning, individuals have internalized the standards of their community and are motivated to live according to the standards of their group. At the postconventional level of moral reasoning, individuals live according to self-derived principles rather than the conventions of their community.

Higher levels of reasoning increase with age. Although some studies find that many individuals reason at adjacent stages about different situations, critics of Kohlberg's theory argue that individuals can usually distinguish conventional from moral issues even as children.

Gilligan: An Ethic of Care

Gilligan asserts that most females think of morality more personally than do males. She finds that an ethic of care characterizes females' approach to moral decisions; this ethic emphasizes compassion and a sense of responsibility to others in contrast to the justice orientation of Kohlberg, which emphasizes reliance on reasoning and moral standards.

Gilligan traces gender differences in moral reasoning to differences in ways of viewing the self. Females define themselves in relation to others; from this comes a sense of responsibility of each to the other. Males define themselves as separate from others; the assumption of separateness highlights the need for rules to regulate the actions of each with respect to the other.

Gilligan traces moral development in females through three levels, each reflecting a different resolution to their conflict between responsibilities to themselves and to others. In Level 1 the primary concern is care for oneself. Females soon see this as selfish and move to Level 2, in which they equate morality with care of others. Only as they encounter problems that result from excluding themselves as legitimate recipients of their own care do females move on to Level 3, in which they equate morality with care both of themselves and of others.

Research finds that while a care orientation is not necessarily the approach adopted by all females it is somewhat more characteristic of females than males. Studies find that both females and males share concerns about justice and care and that individuals frequently use both orientations in thinking through a dilemma.

Freud: Morality and the Superego

Freud placed the responsibility for moral behavior in the superego, an aspect of the personality that embraces cultural standards of right and wrong. The superego develops when the young child identifies with the same-sex parent. Freud assumed the superego of females to be weaker than that of males because they are not as motivated to resolve Oedipal tensions and they identify with a less-threatening parental figure.

Despite the usefulness of Freud's theory to clinicians, his assumptions concerning gender differences in moral development have not been supported by research.

Children's Religious Beliefs

Schoolchildren's views of God reflect the concrete nature of the way they think in general. They accept the teachings and stories of their religion literally and do not question them. With age, intellectual changes make it possible for older children and adolescents to view God in new ways and to question beliefs they once accepted uncritically. As with identity status, processes of exploration and commitment determine the form beliefs will take. Religion remains important in children's lives across changes in age. One of the first components to children's religious identity, just as with gender or ethnicity, consists in labeling, or identifying themselves in terms of a particular religious denomination. By middle childhood, children identify members of religious groups in terms of distinctive behaviors and characteristics. By adolescence, they are able to appreciate the commonalities to different religions. Across all ages, children are most likely to describe God in terms of love.

Key Terms

active listening (p. 465)
conventional moral reasoning
    (p. 477)
emotional transmission (p. 470)
enculturation (p. 460)
ethic of care (p. 482)

identification (p. 487)
I-message (p. 466)
industry (p. 448)
overt aggression (p. 458)
postconventional moral reasoning
    (p. 478)

preconventional moral reasoning
    (p. 477)
relational aggression (p. 458)
role clarity (p. 464)
superego (p. 486)
you-message (p. 466)

chapterthirteen

Adolescence
Physical Development

*S*he checked herself in the mirror again. Maybe she'd wear the new shirt. Or maybe she'd put the bag it came in over her head, and go to school that way. Glasses . . . braces . . . and two more pimples! Wonder what Helen of Troy had looked like at 13? She had probably been cute—and short. This face wouldn't get a rowboat off the beach. And she was taller than everyone in her class—including the teacher. Being different was lonely at times. Sometimes she felt left out altogether.

Feeling left out and being rushed into changes too quickly are common for adolescents. Although both of these things happen to all teenagers, the process of change is faster for some than for others. In the space of a few years, adolescents exchange the bodies of children for those of adults—complete with a full set of emotions and fancy accessories. But none of the equipment is road-tested as yet. And for most adolescents, it seems someone else must still have the owner's manual.

This chapter maps the journey into maturity. The first stop takes us deep within the body, to the headquarters of an elaborate communications network, the endocrine system. This network of glands and hormones plays a significant role in regulating the changes of puberty. A finely tuned feedback system triggers the onset of puberty and then shuts it down, much as a thermostat signals a furnace to click on and off once the temperature reaches a preset level. This biological thermostat regulates delicate changes within the body that transform immature sexual organs into those capable of sexual reproduction. The endocrine system is also responsible for everything from a remarkable growth in height to the nose becoming disproportionately large for one's face. (Although it stays this way only briefly, it can leave a lasting dread of what surprises the body might bring next.)

The second stop checks out the remarkable changes that take place in height, weight, and body contours. Puberty involves a surge of growth that brings adolescents eye to eye and nose to nose with their parents. Adolescents add inches in a single year at the peak of their growth. Sex differences become noticeable with changing body proportions and gains in weight; girls add more subcutaneous fat than boys do, and boys add more muscle mass than girls. Not all adolescents grow the same amount or at the same rate. Nor do they start at the same age; some will begin years ahead of others. And, to the confusion of all, different parts of the body mature at different rates. Yet trends exist, and we will review them.

Changes as significant as those of puberty can have far-reaching psychological and social effects, and these effects are discussed in the third part of the chapter. The changes themselves may not be as important as when they take place for a particular individual. Staying the same when all one's friends are changing can be every bit as stressful as going through the changes. The timing of puberty is important, along with its end results. Early and late maturers face different challenges.

Sexual decision making brings adolescents several steps closer to adulthood. These steps can be problematic for a number of reasons. Adolescents must integrate their sexuality into a sense of self. Most receive little guidance in this task, and many lack the information needed to make responsible decisions. Even when they are informed, many adolescents find it difficult to make decisions responsibly due to their own emotional and intellectual immaturity.

Some adolescents will limit their experiences to necking; others will go further. Each decision involves others. We examine adolescents' sexual attitudes about masturbation, petting, oral-genital sex, and sexual intercourse.

Sex means different things to different people. To a lover, it is the stuff of dreams. To a biologist, it is a means of reproduction. Adolescents are better lovers than biologists, and only a few consistently take care not to reproduce. The chapter ends with a consideration of contraception use and programs aimed at helping adolescents make sexual decisions.

TABLE 13.1 Endocrine Glands and Hormones Regulating Pubertal Change		
Glands	**Hormones**	**Target or Function**
Pituitary	Gonadotrophic hormones: Luteinizing hormone (LH) Follicle-stimulating hormone (FSH)	Stimulates gonads to produce sex hormones; menstrual cycle (females)
	Adrenocorticotrophic hormone (ACTH)	Stimulates adrenals to release androgens
	Growth hormone	Growth
	Thyroid-stimulating hormone (TSH)	Stimulates thyroid to release thyroxine
Adrenals	Androgens	Body hair
Thyroid	Thyroxine	Growth spurt
Gonads		Development of reproductive system and secondary sex characteristics
Ovaries	Estrogens	
Testes	Androgens	

The Endocrine System

The **endocrine system** consists of glands within the body that produce hormones and structures in the central nervous system that regulate their activity. It is part of a larger feedback system that controls the timing of puberty. The production of **hormones,** chemical messengers that travel through the bloodstream, increases during late childhood. A dramatic rise in sex hormones (androgens in males and estrogens in females) and in the hormones that govern their release occurs in early adolescence. The action of these hormones is part of a complex chain of events that triggers the onset of puberty (Kulin, 1991a). Table 13.1 lists the major glands of the endocrine system affecting puberty and the hormones each one secretes. Figure 13.1 shows where the glands are located in the body.

The Timing of Puberty

The timing of puberty is intimately connected to centers within the brain tucked beneath the cortex (the "gray matter"), a few inches behind the bridge of the nose. The most important center in puberty is the hypothalamus. The **hypothalamus** has sometimes been called the body's master clock, because it serves as a control center for biological rhythms, including those of puberty. The **pituitary,** an endocrine gland, hangs from the hypothalamus by a slender stalk (the infundibulum). The pituitary has two lobes, or sections. The one closer to the nose is the anterior (front) lobe. The one farther is the posterior (back) lobe.

The hypothalamus is actually very small, just one three-hundredths of the brain's total size. Yet it is involved in many aspects of bodily functioning and plays a central role in regulating the events of puberty. Most of what we know about the hypothalamus comes from experiments with laboratory rats. For example, if the blood supply from the hypothalamus to the pituitary is cut off, a rat's reproductive organs soon begin to wither and the animal becomes sterile (Restak, 1984). But what is this important substance carried in the blood?

Research has shown that the hypothalamus secretes a hormone called gonadotropin-releasing hormone (GnRH), which tells the anterior pituitary to manufacture gonadotrophic hormones, which act directly on the gonads. The **gonads** are the sex glands—the ovaries in females and the testes in males. Two

endocrine system The system of the body that includes the glands that produce hormones and those parts of the nervous system that activate, inhibit, and control hormone production.

hormones Chemical messengers that are secreted directly into the bloodstream and are regulated by the endocrine system.

hypothalamus A center within the brain that regulates hormonal activity and regulatory activities such as eating, drinking, and body temperature.

pituitary An endocrine gland located beneath the hypothalamus that is part of a feedback system regulating the hormonal control of puberty.

gonads The sex glands; the ovaries in females and the testes in males.

FIGURE 13.1 The Major Endocrine Glands Involved in Puberty

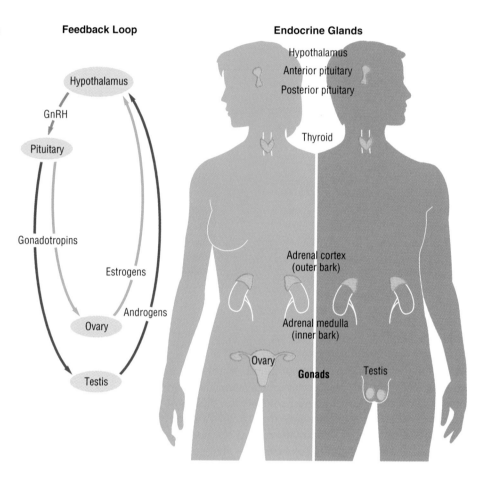

gonadotrophic hormones—luteinizing hormone (LH) and follicle-stimulating hormone (FSH)—stimulate the glands to produce their own sex hormones, estrogens in females and androgens in males. The whole system acts sort of like a row of dominoes. Knocking the first one over trips the second, which affects the third, and so on. In the laboratory rats, when the blood supply from the hypothalamus failed to reach the anterior pituitary, the anterior pituitary stopped producing the hormones that stimulate the gonads. When the gonads were no longer stimulated, they shut down and withered, reverting to an earlier state (Restak, 1984).

The hypothalamus functions like a clock by measuring out its signals in rhythmic pulses. A single pulse of GnRH normally reaches the anterior pituitary each hour. The timing of these pulses is critical. If the pulses decrease to one every several hours or even increase, the mechanism breaks down and the anterior pituitary fails to release its gonadotropins into the bloodstream, with the result that the gonads will not develop (Knobil, 1980; Kulin, 1991a).

Both LH and FSH circulate through the bloodstream in low levels during childhood. Levels of each increase prior to puberty, starting at about age 8 or 9 in girls.

A Feedback System   The level at which hormones circulate in the bloodstream is controlled by a delicate feedback system involving the hypothalamus, the anterior pituitary, and the gonads, as shown in Figure 13.1. A feedback system sends information from one point in a sequence back to an earlier point, thereby regulating later activity. A gonadostat, much like the thermostat controlling the heat in your home, is located in the hypothalamus. Instead of sensing temperature, it senses the presence of circulating hormones. When the levels drop too low, the hypo-

Although young adolescent boys may be self-conscious about their bodies if the signs of puberty are late in coming, young adolescent girls are more likely to feel self-conscious if they start to mature physically before most of their peers.

thalamus signals the anterior pituitary to increase production of gonadotrophic hormones, which in turn stimulate the gonads to produce more sex hormones. As levels of sex hormones increase, the hypothalamus decreases its signals to the anterior pituitary.

During childhood, the gonadostat is set at a low level. This makes the feedback system especially sensitive to circulating hormones. Even small amounts prompt the hypothalamus to cut back its signals to the pituitary. This low setpoint keeps the prepubertal level of circulating hormones low. Late in the prepubertal period, the hypothalamic gonadostat is reset, allowing the levels of circulating hormones to increase (Kulin, 1991a).

The Physical Changes of Puberty

Puberty brings about the physical differences that distinguish females and males. Differences in the reproductive system itself, such as growth of the ovaries in females and the testes in males, constitute **primary sex characteristics.** Other changes, such as the growth of pubic hair, the development of breasts in females and facial hair in males, represent **secondary sex characteristics.** Not all of these changes occur at once, of course, and not all are viewed as equally important by adolescents. The changes that occasion most fascination, such as menstruation in girls or facial hair in boys, are not usually the first to occur, although the timing of these changes varies considerably (Petersen, Crockett, Richards, & Boxer, 1988).

The sequence of changes varies less than their timing. One adolescent can be almost fully matured before another has begun to develop, yet each will experience the events of puberty in roughly the same order (Tanner, 1974).

primary sex characteristics Sex differences in the reproductive system that develop during puberty.

secondary sex characteristics Differences between females and males in body structure and appearance, other than differences in the reproductive system; include differences in skeletal structure, hair distribution, and skin texture.

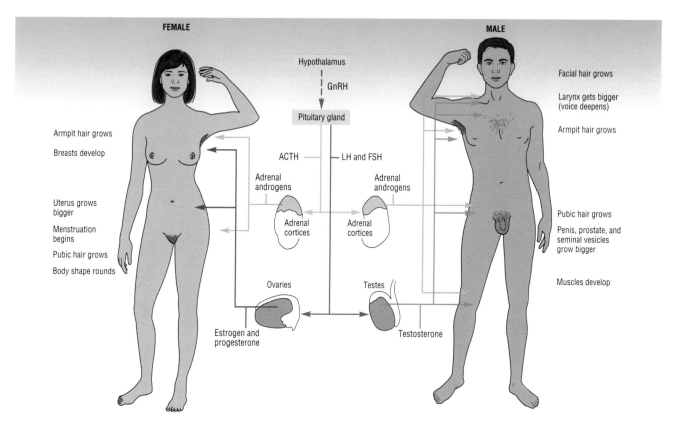

FIGURE 13.2 Effects of Hormones on Physical Development and Sexual Maturation at Puberty

Source: Paul M. Insel and Walton T. Roth, *Core Concepts in Health,* Sixth Edition, Mayfield.

The changes of puberty are easiest to follow if we chart them separately for each sex (Figure 13.2). Girls are generally 2 years ahead of boys. We will start with them first, as nature has done. A fictitious adolescent named Sarah will serve as our model.

Recollections of an Adolescent Girl

Sarah reports that the first change she noticed was in her breasts. She was in the fifth grade at the time, not quite 11 years old. It was such a small change that she almost didn't notice it at first. A slight mound had appeared just below each nipple. Sometime later the skin around the nipple darkened slightly. She couldn't see any difference when she was dressed, but by the time school let out for the summer, she felt a bit self-conscious in a bathing suit.

Sarah remembers the day she discovered a few wisps of pubic hair. It seemed as if they had appeared overnight. Actually, they had been growing for quite some time, but she hadn't noticed because they were unpigmented and very soft. Other changes were occurring within Sarah that she would never see. Her uterus and ovaries were enlarging and developing as the level of hormones circulating through her bloodstream increased.

She didn't notice anything else until the sixth grade. By then it became obvious how much faster she was growing, compared to before. By winter vacation, most of her fall back-to-school clothes were too short, and she was taller than most of the boys in her class. She spent a lot of time that vacation shopping for clothes. By the end of the sixth grade, she had grown several inches since the previous year.

Just before spring vacation, when she was in the seventh grade and 12 years old, Sarah had her first menstrual period. She had known for a while that it could

Hormones contribute to more than the physical changes of puberty. Exuberant, inexperienced, and self-centered thinking, especially in young boys, can lead to risk-taking behavior. This boy knows his behavior is risky, but he does not seem to understand that he could be seriously hurt.

happen at any time. A number of her classmates had begun menstruating this year, as had one or two the year before. She knew girls in the ninth grade who had not begun to menstruate. Her mother told her that a girl could start as early as 10 or as late as 16.

She stopped growing as quickly as she had started—a relief, because she'd started to identify with the giants in children's stories. She had also begun using an underarm deodorant and was shaving under her arms. Actually, she remembered thinking she looked pretty mature. Her figure had begun to fill out, and no one asked her age at PG-13 movies.

Recollections of an Adolescent Boy

Alfred will talk about his experiences of puberty. He, too, is a fictitious adolescent and just as typical for boys as Sarah is for girls. Alfred recalls being very impatient for something to happen. With mixed emotions, he first noticed a change in his scrotum. It was slightly larger and a bit darker than it had been. This was in the seventh grade, just after he had turned 12. Very shortly after, wisps of pubic hair appeared at the base of his penis. Despite these early signs of his manhood, his penis remained the same size. He remembers having some problems with acne once he started the seventh grade. Other changes had begun within his body, but Alfred remained unaware of them. His testes were growing and secreting more androgen than before, and his seminal vesicles and prostate were developing. Maturation of the testes would be necessary for the ejaculation of seminal fluid, the wet dreams he had heard so much about.

TABLE 13.2 Summary of the Changes of Puberty and Their Sequence		
Characteristic	**Age of First appearance (Years)**	**Major Hormonal Influence**
Girls		
1. Growth of breasts	8–13	Pituitary growth hormone, estrogen, progesterone, thyroxine
2. Growth of pubic hair	8–14	Adrenal androgens
3. Body growth	9½–14½	Pituitary growth hormone, adrenal androgens, estrogen
4. Menarche	10–16½	Hypothalamic releasing factors, FSH, LH, estrogen, progesterone
5. Underarm hair	About 2 years after pubic hair	Adrenal androgens
6. Oil- and sweat-producing glands (acne occurs when glands are clogged)	About the same time as underarm hair	Adrenal androgens
Boys		
1. Growth of testes, scrotal sac	10–13½	Pituitary growth hormone, testosterone
2. Growth of pubic hair	10–15	Testosterone
3. Body growth	10½–16	Pituitary growth hormone, testosterone
4. Growth of penis	11–14½	Testosterone
5. Change in voice (growth of larynx)	About the same time as penis growth	Testosterone
6. Facial and underarm hair	About 2 years after pubic hair appears	Testosterone
7. Oil- and sweat-producing glands, acne	About the same time as underarm hair	Testosterone

Source: B. Goldstein. (1976). *Introduction to human sexuality* (p. 80). Belmont, CA: Star.

By the end of the seventh grade, he had started to grow. It had begun slowly at first, but during the eighth grade, he grew 3 inches in a single year. His parents complained they couldn't keep him in clothes: As soon as they bought new ones, he outgrew them. During the eighth grade he noticed, too, that his penis had started to grow longer. What a relief. He remembers dreading gym class; he couldn't face the showers. A few of the guys in there looked as mature as his father. Of course, others still looked like kids.

Alfred recalls continuing to grow a lot in the ninth grade. By then he was 14 and his voice was starting to change. He experienced his first ejaculation at about this time, too. He had the sexiest dream with it. His pubic hair was now thick and curly, and he had started to get some axillary (underarm) hair. He was still growing but says he started to slow down a bit after the ninth grade. He still didn't have any hair on his face. He was 15 before he noticed a few hairs growing in over his upper lip. His mom called it peach fuzz. He didn't have a real beard until he was 16. By then he also had a fair amount of hair on his body. Alfred says he didn't actually stop growing until his early twenties. He also developed more hair on his chest, back, and stomach all through his late teens.

The typical sequence of these events appears in Table 13.2, along with their age ranges. Sarah and Alfred are typical adolescents. However, other adolescents

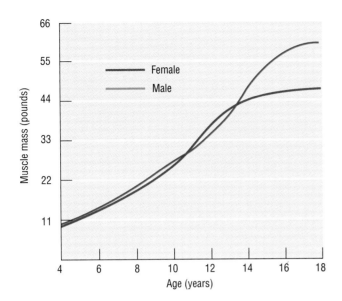
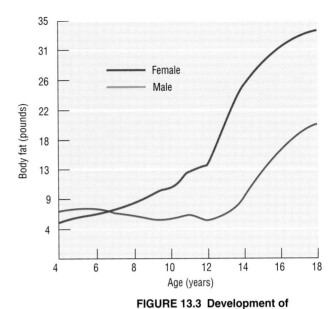

FIGURE 13.3 Development of Muscle Mass and Body Fat for Females and Males *Source:* Adapted from D. B. Check (1974). Body composition, hormones, nutrition, and adolescent growth. In M. M. Grumbach, G. D. Grave and F. E. Moyer, eds. *Control of the Onset of Puberty.* New York: Wiley.

can pass through these changes at different ages, or even in different sequences, and still be just as normal. You can see that for some events, such as menstruation in girls or body growth in boys, some adolescents can be as much as 6 years ahead of others and each will be within a range considered normal for development. With differences like these, the exception is almost the norm.

The Growth Spurt

The **growth spurt,** an aspect of pubertal growth, differs for girls and boys.

Females   Girls experience a period of rapid growth in height starting at about age 11 and lasting about 2½ years. For some girls it can be as brief as 1½ years, and for others it can last up to 4 years. Girls gain about 8 to 10 inches in height from the start of the growth spurt until they have finished growing. The most rapid growth occurs before **menarche,** the beginning of the menstrual cycle (Malina, 1990).

Body proportions begin to change even earlier. About 1½ years before the growth spurt, girls' legs start to grow faster than their bodies, giving them a long, leggy look. Most of the early gain in height is due to a lengthening of the legs. The shoulders also widen before the actual growth spurt. Somewhat later, during puberty itself, the hips widen. These growth patterns give young adolescent girls a characteristic look: relatively long legs, slender bodies, wide shoulders, and narrow hips—our present standard of beauty. Puberty changes all this (Faust, 1983).

Males   The growth spurt can begin anywhere from age 10½ to age 16 in boys. Boys grow for a longer time than girls, reaching their peak rate in growth 2 years later than girls reach theirs. The average height of boys prior to the height spurt is 58 inches. They add another 12 or 13 inches during the growth spurt. Most of this increase is due to a lengthening of the trunk, because the legs began to grow earlier.

Striking sex differences begin to appear in muscle mass and body fat. Figure 13.3 shows the dramatic increase in muscle mass that accompanies the height spurt in males, and the corresponding increase in body fat for females (Petersen, Crockett, Richards, & Boxer, 1988). In addition to obvious differences in muscle

growth spurt A period of rapid growth that occurs during puberty.

menarche The occurrence of a girl's first menstrual period.

In addition to obvious differences in muscle mass, males develop larger hearts and lungs and higher systolic blood pressure and carry more oxygen in their blood than females do. These differences may reflect the increase in males' activity levels and the decrease in females' during adolescence.

mass, males also develop larger hearts and lungs; they have higher systolic blood pressure, can carry more oxygen in their blood, and can dispose of the chemical by-products of exercise more efficiently than females. They also have more red blood cells. These differences, although genuine sex differences, can reflect differences as well in activity levels between females and males that become more pronounced during adolescence. The most obvious change, however, is in the shape of the body itself: In males, the shoulders widen relative to the hips (Petersen & Taylor, 1980).

The Reproductive System

Changes in the reproductive system, a second aspect of pubertal growth, are not so obvious to others but are one of the most significant aspects of adolescence.

Females   During puberty, the uterus, ovaries, and vagina (Figure 13.4) all increase in size. The **uterus** is a muscular sac shaped like an upside-down pear, enclosed at the neck by the **cervix,** which opens into the vagina. The length of the uterus doubles during puberty, growing to about 3 inches at maturity (McCary & McCary, 1982).

The **ovaries,** which house the **ova,** or eggs, begin to grow at a slightly faster rate at about the age of 8. Somewhat later, they also begin to produce more estrogens. Other hormones stimulate the follicles, individual chambers housing each egg, to develop.

The **Fallopian tubes** feed into either side of the uterus from the ovaries. Each tube is approximately 4 inches long, and is lined with tiny hairs called cilia that move in a sweeping motion and set up currents within the fluid in the tubes. These currents catch the mature egg as it is released from the ovary and sweep it

uterus A muscular enclosure at the top of the vagina that holds the fetus during pregnancy.

cervix The opening to the uterus.

ovaries Structures within the female reproductive system flanking the uterus that house the ova and produce female sex hormones.

ovum (plural, ova) The female sex cell, or gamete.

Fallopian tubes The tubes that feed into either side of the uterus from the ovaries; also called *oviducts.*

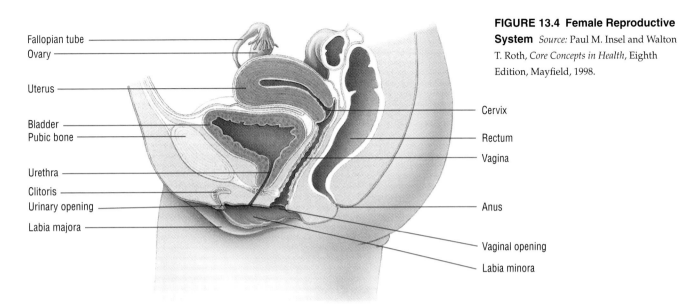

FIGURE 13.4 Female Reproductive System *Source:* Paul M. Insel and Walton T. Roth, *Core Concepts in Health*, Eighth Edition, Mayfield, 1998.

Labels (left): Fallopian tube, Ovary, Uterus, Bladder, Pubic bone, Urethra, Clitoris, Urinary opening, Labia majora

Labels (right): Cervix, Rectum, Vagina, Anus, Vaginal opening, Labia minora

into the oviduct, where it is carried to the uterus. If live sperm are present to fertilize the egg, fertilization will take place at the top of the oviduct. If no sperm are present, the egg passes outside the body along with the lining of the uterus, which is prepared monthly for a fertilized egg.

The **vagina** is a muscular tube leading to the uterus. During puberty it lengthens to its adult length of 4 to 6 inches and becomes more flexible, developing a thick lining. Two glands on either side of the vaginal opening, Bartholin's glands, also develop during puberty. These secrete a lubricant during sexual arousal.

Many girls mistakenly think of the vagina as a hollow tube leading to an even larger space inside. This misunderstanding can cause some teenage girls to be fearful of losing tampons in some vast, unknown space within. In actuality, the vagina is closed off at the inner end by a tight, muscular gate, the cervix. Menstrual fluids or semen can pass through, but the cervix must be dilated (opened) for anything larger to pass.

The **clitoris,** not the vagina, is the primary source of sexual stimulation. The clitoris is similar to the penis in that both have a glans, a shaft, and a prepuce. The glans is supplied by an extensive network of nerve endings, making it the most sensitive part of the clitoris. Hidden beneath the skin and connected to the glans is the shaft. Numerous blood vessels, which develop during puberty, feed into the shaft. During arousal, these become engorged with blood, causing the clitoris to become erect. A thin covering of skin, the prepuce, covers the glans.

Males   The epididymis, vas deferens, seminal vesicles, prostate gland, and Cowper's gland form the internal male sex organs (Figure 13.5). The **epididymis** is a long, oval mass sitting near the top of each testis that receives the sperm produced by the testis. The epididymis leads into the **vas deferens,** a long, coiled tube that carries the sperm to the **seminal vesicles** where they are stored. Tiny hairlike cilia line the walls of the epididymis and the vas deferens, just as they do the Fallopian tubes in females, and move the immature sperm on their way to the seminal vesicles.

vagina The muscular tube in females leading from the labia at its opening to the uterus.

clitoris That part of the external genitals in females that is the primary source of sexual stimulation.

epididymis A mass of coiled tubes near the top of each testis that receives the sperm produced by the testes.

vas deferens Long, coiled tube that carries sperm to the seminal vesicles, where they are stored.

seminal vesicles Structures within the male reproductive system in which sperm are stored.

FIGURE 13.5 Male Reproductive System *Source:* Paul M. Insel and Walton T. Roth, *Core Concepts in Health*, Eighth Edition, Mayfield, 1998.

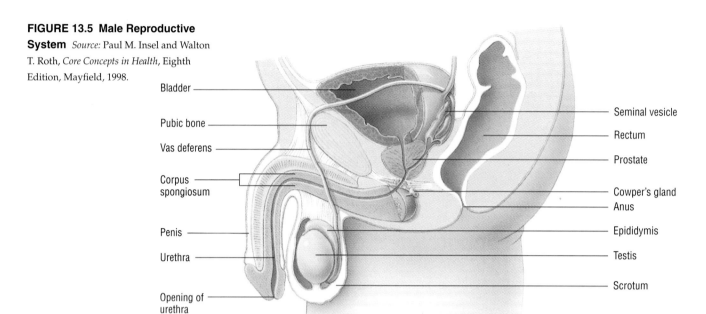

Both the seminal vesicles and the **prostate gland** produce **semen,** a milky white fluid in which the **sperm** are suspended. This fluid is ejaculated during an orgasm. The prostate gland begins to develop at around 11 years of age, at about the time the testes begin to develop. Sperm can be found in the urine of boys by about the age of 14 (Kulin, 1991b). A single ejaculate of approximately 3.5cc contains upward of 200,000,000 sperm. A mature male will produce several hundred million sperm each hour (Gilbert, 1994).

The **Cowper's glands** begin to mature at about the same time as the prostate. These glands secrete a lubricating fluid that facilitates passage of the sperm through the urethra and also protects them from the acidic environment of the urethra. This fluid appears at the opening of the glans of the penis during sexual arousal and frequently contains some sperm. Intercourse, even with no ejaculation, can result in pregnancy just from the presence of sperm in the lubricating fluid (McCary & McCary, 1982).

At puberty, the same hormones that stimulate the ovaries to develop and produce estrogen stimulate the testes to develop and produce testosterone and to produce sperm.

Sperm are carried through the epididymis to the vas deferens, the tube leading to the seminal vesicles. Mature sperm are discharged in an ejaculate, or they gradually lose vitality and are reabsorbed by the body.

The **penis,** like the clitoris in females, is the primary source of sexual stimulation. It has three major parts: the glans, the shaft, and the prepuce. The glans, or rounded head of the penis, is the most sensitive, as it is richly supplied with nerve endings. The shaft of the penis is filled with spongy pads of erectile tissue surrounding the **urethra,** the canal for urine and semen. An extensive network of blood vessels feeds into these tissues. During sexual arousal, blood fills cavities within the tissues, causing the penis to become hard and erect. In a nonaroused state, the penis is soft and flaccid. Erections occur throughout infancy and childhood. They can be triggered by many forms of stimulation, such as washing, needing to urinate, tight clothing, or masturbation. The frequency of spontaneous erections without ejaculation increases once the penis starts to grow (Levitt, 1981).

prostate gland A structure at the base of the urethra in males that is involved in producing sperm.

semen A milky white fluid in which sperm are suspended.

sperm The male sex cell, or gamete.

Cowper's glands Glands in males that secrete a lubricating fluid that facilitates passage of sperm through the urethra.

penis The part of the external genitals in males that is the primary source of sexual stimulation.

urethra The urinary canal, leading from the bladder to the urethral opening.

The penis doubles in length and thickness during puberty, growing to about 3 to 4 inches. Adolescent boys frequently express concerns about the size of their penis. These concerns almost surely reflect the considerable variability in size that exists from one boy to the next, and the mistaken belief that the size of the penis is related to masculinity and sexual prowess.

The prepuce, sometimes called the foreskin, is a thin fold of skin that covers the glans of the penis. The prepuce is frequently removed surgically, usually right after birth, in a procedure known as **circumcision.** Circumcision is widely practiced in the United States for hygienic purposes as well as for religious reasons. A thick secretion known as **smegma** collects around the glans under the prepuce of males who are not circumcised, and care has to be taken to pull back the prepuce to expose the glans during washing to prevent germs from accumulating and possibly causing infection. Although female circumcision bears the same name, the procedure is in no way comparable. In this procedure, appropriately termed **female genital mutilation,** the clitoris of the young girl is cut out, usually without benefit of anesthesia or sterile conditions, and frequently the outer labia are sewn together, leaving only a small opening for the passage of urine. The procedure is comparable to cutting off the penis. It robs the female of the source of sexual pleasure and makes even simple acts, such as walking, sitting, or urinating, difficult. This procedure is practiced on millions of girls in non-Western nations today and has recently entered the United States with those emigrating from these nations.

The **scrotum** is the sac that hangs just beneath the penis and houses the **testes,** the two glands that produce sperm and testosterone. The testes start to grow at about age 11 and more than double in length during puberty. One of the first changes of puberty for boys is an increase in the size of the scrotum, as the testes within begin to grow. The testes themselves are about the same size, but the left testis frequently appears larger, perhaps because it hangs a bit lower than the right.

The scrotal sac protects the testes from harm. One might argue that they would be even safer if tucked securely inside the body, as indeed they would. However, the temperature within the body is a few degrees too high for the optimal production of sperm. The range of temperatures ideal for the breeding of sperm is relatively narrow. The scrotal sac accommodates to temperature fluctuations by contracting or relaxing, adjusting the distance of the testes from the warmth of the body cavity. Adolescent males may notice that the scrotum contracts in the cold, drawing the testes closer to the body. In hot weather, or after a hot shower, it hangs lower, keeping the testes farther from the body.

Menarche

Menarche is the term for a girl's first menstrual period. The average age for reaching menarche is presently about 12½ in the United States (Brooks-Gunn & Warren, 1985). Reaching a certain proportion of body fat appears to trigger menarche. The chronological age for menarche varies considerably from one girl to the next, but each achieves about the same percentage of body fat just prior to menarche (Frisch, 1991). Most likely genetic factors play a significant role in determining these conditions (Pickles et al., 1998). Aside from the estrogen produced by the ovaries, estrogen is converted from androgens in fatty tissues (Frisch, 1991). Additional support for the importance of body fat to menarche comes from girls who are athletes or dancers. These girls have proportionately less fat for their total weight—and they also tend to have delayed menarche and irregular periods (Frisch, 1991).

circumcision Surgical removal of the prepuce covering the glans of the penis.

smegma A thick secretion that collects around the glans in males and under the prepuce.

female genital mutilation Removal of the clitoris, the primary source of sexual stimulation in females, and of the inner labia, and sewing shut most of the outer labia (sometimes inaccurately referred to as *female circumcision*).

scrotum The sac that hangs just beneath the penis and houses the testes.

testes Structures within the male reproductive system contained in the scrotum that produce sperm and male sex hormones.

Reactions to spermarche are generally positive; boys feel excited and grown-up and suddenly drawn to pictures of naked women.

Most girls have mixed feelings about menarche. They look forward to it so they can be like others, but they also express negative feelings, such as embarrassment and concerns about discomfort (Moore, 1995). Many girls are reluctant to discuss their menstrual experiences right away. After telling their mothers, most wait several months before talking with friends (Brooks-Gunn & Ruble, 1982).

Spermarche

Spermarche, a boy's first ejaculation of seminal fluid, usually occurs early in his teens, by about 13 (Stein & Reiser, 1994). For some, it will occur spontaneously in a **nocturnal emission** (also known as a wet dream); for others, through masturbation or intercourse. Relatively few boys are likely to have anyone explain all this to them. Peers and books or magazines are the most likely sources of information, boys learning more about menarche than about ejaculation in their health classes. Despite the relative lack of preparation, most boys are not alarmed, although most do admit to being surprised. Generally, reactions are positive, boys reporting feeling excited, grown up, and glad (Gaddis & Brooks-Gunn, 1985; Stein & Reiser, 1994).

Boys are not likely to discuss their experience with friends or with their fathers. This reaction to ejaculation contrasts sharply with that of girls to menarche, most of whom tell their mothers immediately and share their new status with friends several months later (Ruble & Brooks-Gunn, 1982; Stein & Reiser, 1994). The difference may reflect the closer association of first ejaculation with masturbation for boys. Neither boys nor girls seem to discuss masturbation. For girls, the lack of any association of menarche with masturbation may account for their greater willingness to discuss it. Or it may be that they have had discussion modeled for them by their mothers, because most are prepared for menarche, whereas most boys have not been prepared for first ejaculation by their fathers (Gaddis & Brooks-Gunn, 1985).

Most adolescent boys receive considerably less information than girls about the reproductive nature of pubertal changes. Few fathers explain nocturnal emis-

spermarche A boy's first ejaculation of seminal fluid.

nocturnal emission A spontaneous ejaculation of seminal fluid during sleep; sometimes called a wet dream.

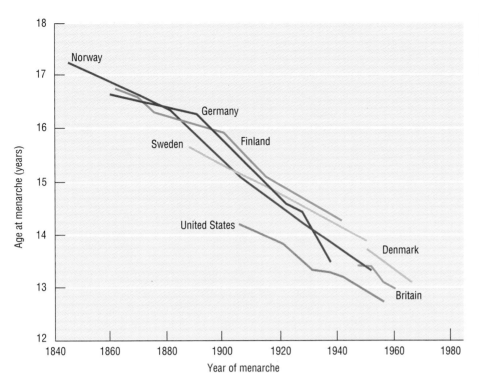

FIGURE 13.6 Trends in the Age of Menarche *Source:* J. M. Tanner, "Earlier maturation in man." *Scientific American,* January, 1968, p. 26.

sions to their sons, and neither parent is likely to explain menstruation. A survey of college males found that many had gotten much of their information about menstruation as young adults from female friends, once the security of early adulthood permitted such discussions (Brooks-Gunn & Ruble, 1986).

Why are boys less likely to discuss their first ejaculation than girls are to discuss their first menstruation?

The Secular Trend

Quite a bit of evidence indicates that puberty begins earlier today than it did in the past. This downward shift in age is called the **secular trend.** Figure 13.6 shows a striking drop in age at menarche over a period of 130 years for a number of countries. The greatest changes occurred from the mid-1800s to the mid-1900s. Age at menarche has dropped by about 3 to 4 months every 10 years (Tanner, 1991).

Adolescents not only begin puberty earlier than in previous generations, but they also grow faster. We have only scanty records from earlier centuries, but the pieces fit a predictable pattern. In the 19th century in Britain, females reached their adult height at about 21. Adolescent girls stop growing today by 16 to 18, and boys by 20 to 21, some 4 years sooner than a century ago (Frisch, 1983). Adolescents also grow to be larger than they once did, girls growing half an inch to an inch taller than their mothers and weighing about 2 pounds more. For boys these differences can be even greater.

The Psychological and Social Implications of Puberty

Even experiences as close to a biological ground zero as those of puberty do not necessarily have the same significance from one adolescent to the next. Adolescents continually interpret the biological frontiers they are crossing, reading the reactions of friends and family for the meaning of the changes they

secular trend The earlier onset of puberty, faster growth, and larger size reached by adolescents today than in the past.

FIGURE 13.7 Frequency with Which Family Members Feel Gradations of Happiness and Unhappiness

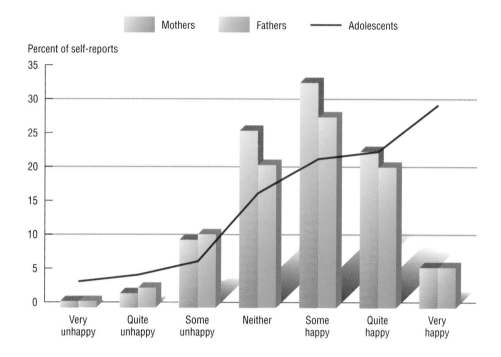

FIGURE 13.7 Frequency with Which Family Members Feel Gradations of Happiness and Unhappiness

are going through. Nor are they alone in doing so. Their parents, siblings, friends, and teachers also read significance into the biological script unfolding before them. Not surprisingly, puberty affects adolescents' closest relationships in intimate ways.

Reed Larson and Maryse Richards (1994) were able to document the details of adolescents' lives by having them wear beepers and paging them at random intervals throughout the day and evening, when they would report on their activities and feelings. These investigators remind us of what we too easily forget about our own lives—that even the simplest activities that make up a day, things such as having breakfast or hassling over kitchen responsibilities, are often suffused with emotion. They also remind us that such activities, when they involve more than one member of the family, are rarely experienced in the same way by each of them, that there are as many realities to be experienced as individuals to experience them. This reminder should strike a familiar note at this point, illustrating one of the central assumptions of the constructive approach taken in this text. Namely, that we continually interpret our experiences, putting events together in ways that make sense to us, constructing the reality to which we eventually respond.

Heightened Emotionality

Larson and Richards point out that tensions are greatest in early adolescence, when puberty tips the psychosocial balance established throughout childhood. As adolescents' bodies assume more adult proportions, those around them, particularly parents and teachers, expect them to behave in more adult ways as well. Crowding in on the heels of puberty are additional stressors such as starting middle school or junior high, navigating problematic relationships with peers, redefining relationships with parents, and, for many, facing increasing pressures to experiment with sex and drugs. Because of the secular trend, adolescents as young as

10 or 11 begin to face these pressures of puberty, often before either they or their parents are ready for them (Larson & Richards, 1994).

How do early adolescents react to these changes? A common stereotype is that, with puberty, adolescents become moody, their emotions swinging from one extreme to another with little predictability. Larson and Richards indeed found some support for heightened emotionality in adolescence. Figure 13.7 shows that adolescents more frequently report experiencing extreme states than do their parents. They also report a wider range of emotions. In addition to simply feeling happy, for instance, adolescents report feeling great, free, cheerful, proud, accepted, in love, friendly, and kindly. They also report a wider gamut of negative feelings, describing themselves as unsure, lonely, awkward, ignored, and nervous, or, as Larson and Richards (1994) put it, "a whole array of painful feelings that remind us adults why we never want to be adolescents again" (p. 83). Even though they feel self-conscious and embarrassed 2 to 3 times as often as their parents, they are also bored more often, perhaps because they feel less in control and less invested in the moment, often saying they would rather be doing something else. Furthermore, despite the advantage of youth, adolescents are more likely to say they feel tired, weak, and have little energy. These differing inner realities, as well as the more visible differences of their exterior lives, virtually ensure that misunderstandings with parents will arise.

When adolescents and their parents were asked to wear beepers so they could be paged at random intervals throughout the day, what did investigators discover concerning the emotions experienced by each?

Relationships with Parents

Good relationships with parents can provide a powerful buffer against the stresses of life. Adolescents who see their parents as warm and loving, for instance, experience fewer emotional or behavioral problems (Wagner, Cohen, & Brook, 1996). Emotional harmony within the home may even affect the rate of physical development. In research following girls and their families from childhood into adolescence, warm and supportive relationships with parents, especially with fathers, were predictive of later, rather than earlier, pubertal development (Ellis, McFadyen-Ketchum, Dodge, Pettit, & Bates, 1999). For most adolescents, however, closeness with parents temporarily decreases and conflict increases with the onset of puberty (Laursen, Coy, & Collins, 1998). Adolescents begin to demand a greater role in family decision making and more freedom in areas that their parents still believe require parental oversight, such as the adolescents' well-being. The Social Policy Focus, "Abortion and Judicial Review: Rights of Parents Versus Adolescents," looks at the question of adolescent decision making in terms of the issue of abortion. For their part, parents may see that the ways they have always parented are no longer appropriate, yet they have no ready substitutes for outmoded forms of discipline and guidance. The resulting scuffles, though often uncomfortable, lay the groundwork for renegotiated relationships. With few exceptions, however, studies of these changes have involved White middle-class families.

Brooke Molina and Laurie Chassin (1996) compared parent-adolescent relationships in Hispanic and non-Hispanic families. These investigators found increased conflict and decreased closeness with pubertal onset only in White adolescent boys. For Hispanic boys, just the opposite occurred, with puberty actually bringing parents and sons closer together. Hispanic boys reported less conflict and greater emotional support from their parents once they began puberty. This increased closeness may reflect the value Hispanic families place on the traditional male role. Supporting this interpretation, Hispanic girls did not experience a comparable improvement in their relationships with parents.

Abortion and Judicial Review: Rights of Parents Versus Adolescents BY ANDREA HAYES

The debate over legalized abortion that began almost 30 years ago with *Roe v. Wade* (1973) has so divided the nation that it is sometimes referred to as "the new civil war" (Beckman & Harvey, 1998). Within this tumult are individuals such as Becky Bell, an adolescent who died after an abortion she obtained illegally in order to avoid telling her parents.

Although adult women have the right to choose, the Supreme Court lets each state impose restrictions on the rights of female adolescents. Currently, most states have adopted the policy that females under 18 must notify a parent and obtain parental consent for the procedure. If the minor refuses to do so, she has the option of requesting a judicial review in which the court decides whether to lift the restriction.

Part of the rationale for this approach is the belief that abortion often leads to psychological and medical complications for adolescent girls. Research in the 1970s seemed to support this position, but more recent studies have not confirmed earlier findings. Instead of psychological or emotional harm, female adolescents who undergo an abortion frequently report reduced anxiety and a greater sense of personal control (Adler, Smith, & Tschann, 1998). Medically as well, undergoing an abortion presents fewer risks to the adolescent than does pregnancy and childbirth.

A second rationale for restrictions is based on the assumption that adolescents may not be intellectually and emotionally competent to make decisions regarding an abortion. Koocher and DeMaso (1990) define such competence in terms of the ability to understand the information that needs to be considered, use reasoning to reach a decision, and appreciate the consequences of that decision. Is this assumption correct?

Although there seems to be little difference between adolescents' and adults' decision-making abilities, the prefrontal cortex, the brain's control panel for planning and judgment, continues to develop through adolescence, not reaching maturity until adulthood. It is possible, in other words, that adolescents might be able to understand all the facts about pregnancy and abortion but still not be able to anticipate the outcomes of their actions or make good judgments. If that is the case, should public policy require adolescents to obtain parental approval for an abortion?

In reality, most pregnant adolescents do consult with their parents or with another trusted adult (Beckman & Harvey, 1998). Out of 1,500 adolescents, 75% voluntarily told a parent about their pregnancy, a figure suggesting that a parental consent law may be superfluous. Consent laws may even be harmful if adolescents, out of fear of parental reactions, end up seeking illegal or self-induced abortions. Which value should social policy affirm: the child's right to privacy and self-determination or the responsibility of parents for the well-being of their minor child?

The Timing of Change: Early and Late Maturers

Differences in the timing of pubertal change from one adolescent to the next, or within any adolescent, are collectively known as **asynchrony.** Asynchrony simply means that all changes do not occur at the same time. For adolescents who believe changes should occur together, the fact that they haven't, or that they occurred together but at the wrong time, can have enormous implications. Many changes receive cultural as well as personal interpretation. These interpretations affect the way adolescents feel and think about themselves. Change can be difficult enough when all goes according to schedule, but when adolescents develop faster or slower than their friends and classmates, or at obviously uneven rates within their own lives, differences can be hard to ignore.

It is common for adolescents to experience asynchrony today. In fact, our society seems to foster adolescent asynchrony. Most adolescents are biologically and intellectually mature by their mid- to late teens, yet many remain emotionally and socially dependent on parents while they obtain the education they need to succeed in an increasingly technological society. Little information exists on the possible effects of these asynchronies on personality development. Certainly, we need more research on this important topic because it affects the lives of millions of adolescents and their parents.

Early- and Late-Maturing Boys Early research found that boys who matured early appeared more adult and more attractive to their peers and to adults than

asynchrony Differences in the timing of pubertal changes within an adolescent, or from one adolescent to the next.

Differences in the timing of pubertal changes from one to the next can be great, giving early maturers such as the boy on the left a distinct edge when disagreements arise.

boys who matured later. Early-maturing boys were also more popular and achieved more recognition in activities ranging from captain of the football team to class president. Personality measures showed further differences between early- and late-maturing boys. Early maturers were more self-confident and less dependent. The late maturers often appeared more rebellious and more concerned with rejection. Some differences persisted into adulthood. These, too, favored the early maturers, who by then were men in their 30s (Jones, 1957, 1958, 1965; Jones & Bayley, 1950; Jones & Mussen, 1958; Mussen & Jones, 1957).

Other investigators report similar findings, suggesting that early maturation offers distinct advantages and that late maturation may even handicap boys in relatively permanent ways. These beliefs have received little challenge, despite the fact that in some studies only a few of the comparisons between early and late maturers are statistically significant, and even these do not support the notion of a handicap.

Later research has challenged these pictures of early- and late-maturing boys (Peskin, 1967, 1973). Peskin suggests that early maturation may have some disadvantages. Recall that adults and peers react to early-maturing boys as adults much sooner than they do to late maturers. Early-maturing boys may feel pressured into prematurely committing themselves to goals and life choices in order to live up to the expectations of others, whereas their late-maturing cohorts have more opportunity to explore personal alternatives. Perhaps late maturers can

Q Early maturation carries a number of advantages for boys, but this developmental pattern is not cost-free. What disadvantage may early-maturing boys experience?

better reflect on their feelings, both positive and negative, maybe leading to greater insight as well as a heightened awareness of negative feelings—for example, the rejection and rebellion frequently found in later maturers in earlier studies.

The work of John Clausen (1975) gives us yet another way to interpret differences between early- and late-maturing males. Clausen suggests that the importance of early maturation may be greater among working-class boys, but that more general differences in body type, height, and intelligence better predict personality differences than timing per se. He suggests, for instance, that adults as well as peers tend to look to boys with muscular bodies (mesomorphs) as leaders, and are more likely to perceive boys who are especially thin (ectomorphs) as timid and less assured.

Just how important is rate of maturation or body type to personality development? Efforts to disentangle the effects of such factors are complicated by the fact that the significance of physical characteristics can change even within a culture from one ethnic group to another or from one generation to another. An attribute such as body type may not be equally valued by all segments of society. The stereotype of the computer hacker may be as popular to one group as that of the varsity linebacker is to another.

Early- and Late-Maturing Girls   Clear gender differences exist in the effects of timing. Early-maturing girls do not share the advantages of early-maturing boys (Brooks-Gunn, 1991). Many are self-conscious about their adult bodies and lack the poise of late-maturing girls. Their height, menarcheal status, and developing breasts can be sources of embarrassment among classmates who have the bodies of children. The picture brightens with junior high. Early-maturing girls are no longer set apart by their adult bodies. They enjoy a new prestige and, with this, frequent popularity. Socioeconomic status appears to be important in mediating the effects of timing for girls as well. Early maturation is a more positive experience for middle-class girls than for working-class girls (Clausen, 1975).

Several factors contribute to the difficulties generally experienced by early-maturing girls. For one thing, early-maturing girls are less likely to be prepared for pubertal changes than late maturers because most will begin to menstruate before they learn of menstruation either from their mothers or in a health class. They are also less likely to have close friends with whom they feel comfortable discussing the changes they are experiencing. In general, early maturers have more negative attitudes concerning menstruation, poorer body image, and more eating problems. The latter may be due to being somewhat heavier in a culture that values thinness (Brooks-Gunn, 1991; Tschann, Adler, Irwin, & Millstein, 1994).

Body Image

Among boys, early maturers have more positive body images. Just the opposite is true among girls: Late maturers feel more positive about their bodies and more attractive than early maturers do. As we have seen, how satisfied adolescents are with their bodies depends a lot on how others react to them. Adolescents' self-images reflect the attitudes of others or their perceptions of these attitudes, as well as their own evaluations of how attractive a particular trait may be. Body images are reflected by social mirrors and always capture comparisons with others.

These images can get pretty distorted at times, especially in adolescence, when bodies change in so many ways. In early adolescence, physical changes contribute heavily to adolescents' senses of themselves. Adolescents' self-images are strongly tied to their body images; this is true for both sexes. Furthermore, just how satisfied adolescents are with their bodies roughly predicts their levels of self-esteem, especially for girls. Superficial or not, this relationship reflects something of a social reality, because peer acceptance is related to body type (Stiles, Gibbons, Hardardottir, & Schnellmann, 1987; Tobin-Richards, Boxer, & Petersen, 1983).

This preoccupation with peer acceptance and one's body image can result in extreme efforts to try to fit a macho image of masculinity, even if it means taking illegal and harmful anabolic steroids. A 15-year-old boy, identified only as D. H. (Hanauer, 2000), describes how powerful an influence the need to fit in can be:

> I was one of only three sophomores to get a varsity letter in football. At five-foot-nine and 174 pounds, I was muscularly inferior to the guys on the same athletic level and quite conscious of the fact. So, when I heard about this wonderful drug called steroids from a teammate, I didn't think twice about asking to buy some. I could hardly wait to take them and start getting bigger.
>
> Within only a week, everything about me started to change. I was transforming mentally and physically. My attention span became almost non-existent. Along with becoming extremely aggressive, I began to abandon nearly all academic and family responsibilities. In almost no time, I became flustered and agitated with simple everyday activities. My narcissistic ways brought me to engage in verbal as well as physical fights with family, friends, teachers, but mostly strangers.
>
> My parents grew sick and tired of all the trouble I began to get in. They were scared of me. ◄

In general, boys have more positive body images than girls (Benedikt, Wertheim, & Love, 1998; Savage & Scott, 1996). Girls tend to be critical of the way they look, believing themselves to be heavier than they are and wanting to be thinner (Field et al., 1999; Rosenblum & Lewis, 1999). Boys, on the other hand, are content with their appearance, wanting, if anything, only to be somewhat more muscular. Girls' tendency to overestimate their weight declines after mid-adolescent; however, their dissatisfaction with their bodies continues to increase through late adolescence (Phelps et al., 1993). See the Research Focus, "Longitudinal Designs: Body Image and Gender."

Fitting a new body image into a sense of self is an important developmental task of early adolescence, and more girls experience difficulty than boys. In a longitudinal study of over 600 adolescents, Roberta Simmons and Dale Blyth (1987) found consistent gender differences in body image and self-esteem during early and mid-adolescence. Girls are less satisfied with their weight and their general body type and consider themselves less attractive than do boys. These differences appear as early as the sixth grade and persist into the tenth. Perhaps not surprisingly, girls have lower self-esteem than boys at each of these grades and are more self-conscious. Girls not only evaluate their looks more negatively than boys, but they also place more value on personal appearance than do boys (Wood, Becker, & Thompson, 1996).

Important ethnic differences exist among adolescent girls in terms of body image—African American girls view their bodies quite differently than European American girls do. A team of researchers at the University of Arizona, studying junior high and high school students, found that although 9 out of 10 European American girls are dissatisfied with their body weight, 7 out of 10 African American girls are satisfied. Additionally, whereas 62% of European American girls said they had been on a diet within the past year, a comparable percentage of African American girls, many of whom also had dieted, nonetheless believed it to be

Between the ages of 10 and 14, girls are usually taller than boys of the same age. Because girls reach physical maturity earlier than boys, social interactions between them can be awkward at times.

Longitudinal Designs: Body Image and Gender

Jesse, 18, popped several more chips in his mouth as his sister Virginia, 15, looked on disapprovingly. "How can you eat so many of those?" she asked. "Don't you know how many calories there are in a bag of chips?"

"Don't know, and don't care" Jesse replied, crumpling up the empty bag and making a bank shot into the corner wastebasket. "We can't all be as thin as you are, skinny Ginnie," he teased. Nor do I need to be, thought Jesse, noting uncritically the slight roll of flesh visible through his T-shirt and ruing only that he hadn't more chips. No, he certainly didn't understand why his sister and her friends were continually concerned with their bodies, even disliking parts of themselves as much as they did. When had that begun? They were only 15.

Are Jesse's sister and her friends unusual for adolescents their age? Gianine Rosenblum and Michael Lewis (1999) examined the development of body image in adolescents of both sexes as a function of two factors: their weight and their physical attractiveness. Weight has been found to be an important determinant of adult women's satisfaction with their bodies (Cash & Henry, 1995), more so than for adult men, and might be expected to contribute to gender differences in body image as these develop in adolescents. Similarly, physical attractiveness, because of the way it contributes to social feedback about one's appearance, could be expected to shape body image. Furthermore, each of these factors might be expected to become particularly salient in adolescence, due to the dramatic bodily changes introduced by puberty, thus influencing adolescents' developing body image. Since pubertal changes are associated with an actual gain in body weight, these investigators expected

that girls' body image would decrease with age, whereas boys' body image would not. They also expected that physical attractiveness would be positively correlated with body image (see the Research Focus, "Correlational Research: Hangin' Out on a Friday Night," in Chapter 15).

In order to chart these changes, they followed a group of adolescents over a 5-year period, obtaining measurements of body weight, physical attractiveness, and body image at three different ages: 13, 15, and 18. Body weight was assessed through self-report measures. With respect to physical attractiveness, both photographs and videotapes of the adolescents were rated by two independent observers. Finally, body image was assessed through the use of a short questionnaire, in which adolescents indicated their satisfaction with various parts of their bodies.

These investigators used a *longitudinal design*. In this type of research, one studies a single *cohort*, a group of individuals all the same age, and takes several measurements, each at different ages. Rosenblum and Lewis selected three *times of measurement*, assessing adolescents' body weight, physical attractiveness, and body image at each of three ages.

By following the same individuals over time, we can see patterns to development that we might otherwise miss. And because we are comparing the adolescents with themselves at each age, we minimize the problem of having equivalent samples. Are there any problems with this type of research? Unfortunately, the answer is yes. To understand what these problems are, we must define three terms: age changes, time of measurement differences, and confounding.

Q What important difference exists in the way European American and African American girls view their bodies?

better to be somewhat overweight than underweight (Parker et al., 1995). Table 13.3 summarizes the results of this body satisfaction survey.

Are the pounds adolescents add simply excess fat from the Big Macs, Whoppers, fries, and shakes they consume, or are they the muscle and subcutaneous fat that will transform their bodies into those of adults?

Eating Disorders

Some adolescents mistake the natural changes of maturation for unwanted fat and diet to regain their former shapes. Others, perhaps unsure whether they are ready for adulthood, attempt to delay its appearance by literally starving themselves. Still others turn to food when stressed and become obese.

Dieting

Dieting is not an eating disorder, and most adolescents who lose weight do so in healthy ways, such as by eating fewer snacks and decreasing their intake of fat

Age changes are the biological and experiential changes that always accompany aging. They occur in all cultures and at all points in history. We assume that age changes have a biological basis (although we are not always able to identify them) and should therefore be universal; that is, they should occur in all people no matter what their social or cultural background. A good example of an age change is the neural development that continues into adolescence and underlies the development of abstract thought, enabling adolescents to be aware of the ways in which they are perceived by others.

Time of measurement differences reflect social conditions, currents of opinion, and historical events that are present when we make our observations and that can affect attitudes and behavior. When we study age changes by repeatedly observing the same group of individuals over time, we can mistake time of measurement changes for age changes. It's always possible, for example, that changing standards of beauty could affect raters' or adolescents' evaluations of attractiveness from one point in time to the next.

Confounding occurs when observations reflect systematic differences in more than one variable, with the result that we cannot separate the effects of one from those of the other. Longitudinal research frequently confounds age changes with time of measurement differences, making it impossible to conclusively separate the effects of age from those due to time of measurement. Do changes in body image reflect differences due to age or to changing standards of beauty?

Longitudinal research can suffer from other problems as well. It is difficult to keep in touch with individuals over the years. Maintaining elaborate records, and the staff required for this bookkeeping, can be expensive. Longitudinal research is also time-consuming. We must wait while individuals age. And there is no guarantee that we will outlive them. A more serious problem than any of these is the nearly inevitable loss of subjects over time. People move away, die, or for other reasons are not available for study. This loss is called *subject mortality* and is almost always systematically related to age. In other words, the individuals who remain in the study are not necessarily representative of those their age in the general population, because the less healthy and otherwise less fortunate are the first to leave the sample. (Perhaps adolescents with poor body images do not want to be reminded of this and drop out of the study.)

With these cautions in mind, let's go back to Rosenblum and Lewis's study and see what they found about the development of body image in adolescents. As these investigators had expected, girls' body image worsened with age; conversely, the body image of boys improved. These trends developed relatively rapidly, with no difference in body image being evident at 13 years of age, but a distinct difference appearing by the age of 15.

In contrast to the expected relationship between age and body image, body weight was not consistently related to body image for either sex. Nor was physical attractiveness related to body image in any simple way. Early in adolescence, the expected relationship was observed. That is, adolescents who were rated as being more attractive had more positive body images. By late adolescence, however, this relationship had disappeared. However, when Rosenblum and Lewis looked at the relationship between an adolescent's attractiveness in *early* adolescence and that adolescent's body image in *late* adolescence, they found these to be related, suggesting that one's body image develops in early adolescence and remains unchanged thereafter.

(French, Perry, Leon, & Fulkerson, 1995). Even so, many girls believe they are too fat, even when they are not, and place themselves on diets (Ledoux, Choquet, & Manfredi, 1993; Phelps et al., 1993). One study of ninth-graders found that 25% of the girls were currently on diets, and 75% reported having been on a diet at some prior time. Many skipped breakfast and ate salads as their main meal. All knew which foods were high in calories and stayed away from them. Boys were untroubled about their weight; 80% said they had never tried to lose any weight (Leon, Perry, Mangelsdorf, & Tell, 1989).

Cultural messages on the importance of being thin are clear: To be considered attractive, females need to be thin. For instance, nearly three quarters of the female characters on television are actually underweight; most of the males, however, are of average weight (Fouts & Burggraf, 1999; Silverstein, Perdue, Peterson, & Kelly, 1986). Those most susceptible to this message, and most likely to experience eating problems, are girls who were early maturers who are less likely to be thin than late maturers (Smolak, Levine, & Gralen, 1993; Swarr & Richards, 1996).

Television is not unique in communicating to females the importance of being thin. Silverstein and associates (1986) sampled advertisements in popular women's and men's magazines for messages about body shape. Ads for diet products in

TABLE 13.3 Body Satisfaction Among African American and European American Adolescent Girls	
African American Girls	**European American Girls**
70% express satisfaction with their bodies.	90% express dissatisfaction with their bodies.
64% believe it is better to be somewhat overweight than somewhat underweight.	62% report dieting within the past year.

Source: S. Parker, M. Nichter, M. Nichter, N. Vuckovic, C. Sims, & C. Ritenbaugh. (1995). Body image and weight concern among Afro American and White adolescent females: Differences that make a difference. *Human Organization, 54,* 103–115.

women's magazines outnumbered those in men's magazines 60 to 1. Despite the clear message to stay thin, women's magazines contained over 1,000 advertisements for food; 10 appeared in all the men's magazines.

Adolescent females today face a standard of beauty that is considerably thinner than in the past. Models of feminine beauty—whether actresses, performers, or individuals advertising products—are thin indeed, compared to their curvaceous counterparts of generations past. The flapper era of the 1920s was the only other time during this century when popular images represented women as thin as they are at present. Developmentalists note with some alarm that eating disorders became epidemic among young women then and warn that, with respect to eating disorders, history may be repeating itself.

The line between dieting when one actually needs to lose weight and having an eating disorder is not always clear. In part, this vagueness stems from our relationship with food: For many, food is used to meet a number of needs, physical hunger being only one. As one young college student recounts

> My perspective is: I am heavier than everybody else. [sighs] I'm not anorexic or bulimic, but I definitely have a bad relationship with food.
>
> I never enjoy food; there's always the guilt. Guilt, guilt, guilt. If I eat too much today, then I won't eat tomorrow at all. I weigh myself every single day without fail, and if I gain a pound it affects my mood the whole day. I tie food to emotions. . . .
>
> My roommates were the ones that said . . . "We're calling your parents if you don't (get help)." Finally my roommate made the appointment. I said, "Fine, I'll go once"—and I went three times. But oh my God, to this day I'm still denying the fact that I have an eating disorder. Or I see it as, "Lots of people have eating disorders; mine isn't serious." (Lewis, 1996, p. 102) ◄

Bulimia and Anorexia

Both bulimia and anorexia are more common among females than males (Tobias, 1988). **Bulimia** is characterized by binge eating: consuming large amounts of food in a short time, usually in less than 2 hours. Binges are usually accompanied by the fear that one cannot stop oneself and are followed by self-deprecating thoughts. They tend to be done in secret and usually end only because of abdominal pain or falling asleep.

Anorexia is a disorder in which individuals severely limit their intake of food, dieting to the point of actual starvation. Actual starvation has mental and emotional effects, as well as physical ones, and anorexics can be apathetic and irrita-

bulimia An eating disorder characterized by binging and then purging; most common in females.

anorexia An eating disorder characterized by severely limiting the intake of food; most common in females.

ble. Due to the loss of body fat, anorexics frequently become amenorrheic, ceasing to have menstrual periods.

Most bulimics are aware that their eating patterns are abnormal, and most make continued attempts to lose weight through highly restrictive diets, self-induced vomiting, and use of laxatives or diuretics. Anorexics deny that they have any problem and reject help (American Psychiatric Association, 1994).

Both disorders are more common among adolescents from European American, middle-class, upwardly mobile homes, who are typically good girls seeking approval and love by pleasing others. Both disorders require professional intervention. Each is a serious threat to health and reflects underlying emotional problems that need treatment (Tobias, 1988).

Eating Disorders and Family Conflict Amy Swarr and Maryse Richards (1996) followed a sample of adolescent girls over a 2-year period and found that adolescents who enjoyed close positive relationships with their parents had healthier attitudes both toward their weight and toward eating. Eating disorders, when they occur, hide deeper, underlying problems in which family experiences play an important role. Four characteristics of families that lead to the expression of psychological problems as physical symptoms frequently characterize the families of anorexics and bulimics (Minuchin, Rosman, & Baker, 1978; Tobias, 1988). *Enmeshment* exists when boundaries between family members are not clear. In enmeshed families, everyone is involved in everyone else's life, making it difficult to be independent or autonomous. *Overprotective* families show an inappropriate concern for the welfare of family members. Families characterized by *rigidity* have a need to maintain the status quo and are unable to face change. These qualities make adolescence, a time of many changes, especially difficult. Finally, families in which there is *inadequate conflict resolution* avoid conflict, with the result that differences are never cleanly resolved and members continue to impinge on each other. An eating disorder may be the only way in which adolescents from such families can gain a sense of maintaining control over their lives (Tobias, 1988). The Research Focus, "Bias and Blind Controls: Eating Disorders," describes another study of the families of girls with eating disorders.

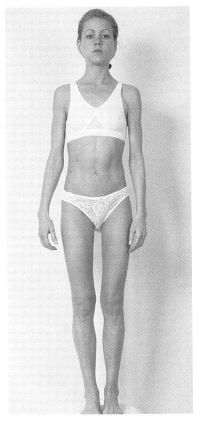

Anorexics severely limit their intake of food; some lose up to 25% of their body weight. However, they usually have a distorted body image; even though they look dangerously emaciated to friends and family, to themselves, they still do not feel thin enough.

Obesity

Physical appearance is perhaps never more important than during adolescence. Body image contributes significantly to self-image for most adolescents. Those who are obese tend to have less-positive self-images and lower self-esteem than adolescents of average weight (Miller & Downey, 1999). **Obesity,** defined as weighing more than 30% above one's ideal body weight, reflects excessive weight for one's height and is expressed in terms of one's **body mass index (BMI),** or one's weight in kilograms divided by the square of one's height in meters. To convert pounds and inches to kilograms and meters, multiply weight by .45 and height by .0254. Individuals of normal weight have a BMI of 19 to 24.9; overweight individuals have a BMI of 25 to 29.9; obese individuals have a BMI of 30 or more (Hwang, 1999). Figure 13.8 on page 521 shows the thresholds for obesity at various heights. The prevalence of obesity has risen steadily in the United States over the past decade, affecting individuals of all ages (Mokdad et al., 1999). A number of factors are most likely responsible for this trend, among the more important being changes in eating habits and in patterns of physical activity (CDC, 1999; Troiano & Flegal, 1998). With respect to eating habits, a greater reliance on fast foods, which are higher in fats and sugars and lower in dietary fiber, and a ten-

Even though adolescents suffering from anorexia and bulimia differ markedly in the amount of food they consume, both are likely to come from families evidencing similar problematic relationships. What characteristics of families are common to both eating disorders?

obesity A condition in which one weighs more than 30% above one's ideal body weight.

body mass index (BMI) Weight in kilograms divided by the square of a person's height.

Bias and Blind Controls: Eating Disorders

"You always shut yourself off in your room," her mother said, somewhat angrily.

"I just want to be left alone," she pleaded, the hint of a whine in her voice. The teenager was 17, and her dark eyes communicated a sulky resentment.

The research assistant on the other side of the one-way mirror quickly coded the girl's response: "asserting," "appeasing," "separating," and "interdependent."

"Some message!" he thought, as he watched the family in front of him.

The girl was trim, neither overweight nor underweight. He couldn't tell from her appearance which type of disorder she suffered from; he only knew that this project was about adolescents with eating disorders. For all he knew, she could be part of the control group.

Why keep this graduate student in the dark about the families he is observing? Why not assume that the more he knows, the better he'll understand and more accurately record their behavior? Investigators have found from painful experience that their expectations all too often influence what they see—sometimes even causing them to read things into a person's behavior that just aren't there. Their expectancies can *bias*, or systematically alter, the results of the study.

Whenever investigators know the condition of which a subject is part, they can bias the outcome of the research either by unconsciously treating subjects in that condition differently or by interpreting—that is, scoring—their behavior differently. If, for example, this graduate student believed that the parents of girls with a certain type of eating disorder were harsh and demanding, he might read hostility into their remarks even when it wasn't there or perhaps be less friendly with them when introducing them to the experiment. The latter difference might lead to tensions in family interactions that otherwise would not be present, thus unintentionally confirming initial expectations.

Investigators can eliminate experimenter bias by conducting the experiment "blind." In a *single-blind control* procedure, such as the one above, the investigator is unaware of the condition of which each subject is part; expectations cannot contribute to any of the observed differences. A single-blind control is adequate in many experiments. Some, however, require a *double-blind control*, in which both the subjects as well as the experimenter are ignorant of which condition each subject is in. Double-blind controls are frequently used in drug studies in which it is necessary to control for the patients' as well as the doctor's expectations that they will get better if they take an experimental medication. In double-blind drug studies, *all* subjects are given a pill, but half receive a *placebo*, or sugar pill.

Let's get back to the other side of the one-way mirror. Do families of girls with different eating disorders interact in characteristically different ways? Laura Humphrey (1989) observed 74 adolescent girls with their parents. Sixteen were *anorexic*, 16 were *bulimic*, 18 were both *bulimic and anorexic*, and 24 were normal controls. All of those in the first three categories were patients who had been hospitalized long enough so that one could not distinguish the anorexics by their appearance.

Parents of anorexics were both more nurturing and comforting *and* more ignoring and neglecting than were those of bulimics or controls. The anorexic girls were the most submissive of the group when they were with their parents. Bulimics and their parents were more likely to engage in mutual grumbling and blaming and to exchange disparaging remarks. Interactions of normal controls and their parents were characterized more by helping, protecting, trusting, and simple enjoyment of each other.

These findings underscore the importance of treating the family as a whole, as well as working individually with the adolescent when treating eating disorders. Most eating disorders are associated with a pattern of disturbed family interactions.

---

dency to snack more frequently throughout the day have led to an increase in the average daily energy intake. This increase has gone hand in hand with a decrease in physical activity, or in the amount of energy actually expended. As a consequence, the resulting excess energy is stored as fat (Koplan & Dietz, 1999).

Perhaps the biggest difference between obese adolescents and those of average weight is in how active they are, not how much they eat. Obese adolescents are considerably less active than their peers of average weight. A low level of activity can contribute as much to obesity as excess eating. Once again, separating cause from effect is difficult. Are obese adolescents less active because of their weight; that is, are they less likely than their peers to be chosen for the team or

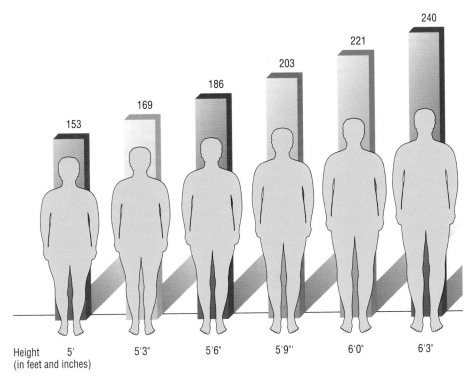

FIGURE 13.8 Thresholds for Obese Weight (in pounds for various heights)

Height 5'   5'3"   5'6"   5'9"   6'0"   6'3"
(in feet and inches)

to be good at sports? Or do adolescents who are inactive simply run a greater risk of becoming obese (Lucas, 1988)?

The relationship between obesity and inactivity highlights the importance of exercise in weight reduction programs. Exercise increases the body's metabolism, allowing the body to burn excess calories more rapidly; in moderate amounts, exercise also depresses appetite.

Adolescents attempting to lose weight often have unrealistic expectations. Many view their weight as central to all their problems and expect that once they lose weight, their problems will be solved—they will become popular, make the team, and so forth. When their problems do not roll away with the pounds, adolescents can become frustrated and fall off their diets. The most successful programs are multifaceted. The success of a weight control program for adolescents almost always depends on successfully integrating the family into the treatment program. As with bulimia and anorexia, obesity is often a symptom of underlying conflicts within the family.

Making Sexual Decisions

Puberty brings new sexual feelings and emotions, and the natural need to integrate these into a sense of oneself. Doing so can be difficult, especially because many of these feelings have been labeled in childhood as "forbidden" or "bad." Adolescents cannot simply add new sexual feelings to an old self. They must revise that self so that what they add fits. In other words, adolescents cannot continue to see themselves as children and simply add sexual feelings and behaviors to this self-image. "Sexy children" is a contradiction in terms in most societies—to be sexual is to be adult. To integrate sexuality into their sense of themselves,

Young adolescence is the age when many teens start making sexual decisions.

In what ways might adolescents' experience of conflict regarding their sexuality affect their sexual decision making?

adolescents must take a big step toward adulthood—and away from childhood. For many, this step is a hard one to take, not so much for what they are stepping into as for what they are leaving behind.

Not surprisingly, adolescents frequently experience conflict when contemplating their own sexuality. Conflict isn't necessarily bad, but it can interfere with responsible sexual decision making, often leading to avoidance and denial. Translated into the terminology of sexual decision making, adolescents who experience conflict may deny that they are assuming a stance that is any different from that which they have always taken. Rather than consciously thinking through the consequences of becoming actively sexual, these adolescents will engage in sex without planning to do so—and without doing so responsibly (Table 13.4).

The lack of consistent adult guidance makes the transition to adult forms of sexual behavior even more difficult. The transition itself occurs in several steps, but, unlike the first steps of toddlers, these are not taken with a parent's guidance and support. Adolescents usually cross this terrain guided by someone their own age. They rarely, for instance, cite parents as their principal source of information, being much more likely to mention a sibling (Ansuini, Fiddler-Woite, & Woite, 1996). As a consequence, sexual decision making reflects considerable misinformation.

Unlike many attitudes, those surrounding sex are not likely to be openly discussed, especially with parents. In itself, that may not be surprising, but adolescents also find it hard to talk openly about sex with friends and even with sexual partners. Those who do talk with their parents are not as likely to begin their sexual experiences early or to engage in high-risk behavior once they have begun

TABLE 13.4 Percentage of High School Students Who Have Had Sexual Intercourse

	Ever Had Sexual Intercourse	Have Had Four or More Sex Partners	Currently Sexually Active*
Sex			
Female	52.1	14.4	40.4
Male	54.0	20.9	35.5
Grade			
9	36.9	12.9	23.6
10	48.0	15.6	33.7
11	58.6	19.0	42.4
12	66.4	22.9	49.7
Race or Ethnicity			
White	48.9	14.2	34.8
Black	73.4	35.6	54.2
Hispanic	57.6	17.6	39.3

*Of those who had ever had sexual intercourse, the percentage who had had intercourse during the 3 months preceding the survey.

Source: Centers for Disease Control (1996, September 27). CDC surveillance summaries. *Morbidity and Mortality Weekly Report, 45,* no. SS-4.

(Baumeister, Flores, & Marin, 1995). Similarly those who can talk openly with their sexual partners engage in sex more responsibly (Darling & Hicks, 1982; Leland & Barth, 1993).

Contraception Use

One might think that early sexual activity among adolescents would be accompanied by an equal sophistication concerning contraception, but data suggest this is not the case. More than a million adolescent girls become pregnant every year. Most of them do so unintentionally. Yet adolescents can select from a wide range of birth control measures. The most effective of these all but eliminate the possibility of pregnancy. Why aren't they effective for teenagers? The answer, it seems, is that most sexually active teenagers do not systematically use contraceptives.

Only 27% of sexually active 13- to 18-year-olds say they always use some form of birth control (Benda & DiBlasio, 1994). Sporadic use of birth control, however, is higher. In a national survey of high school students, over 54% of the sexually active respondents reported they or their partner had used a condom during their most recent sexual encounter, and 17.4% said they or their partner had used birth control pills during their most recent encounter (CDC, 1996a). Those least likely to use a condom are early adolescents and those who do not believe that responsibility for contraception is shared (Pleck, Sonenstein, & Ku, 1990). Males who have a close relationship with their sexual partners are more likely to use a condom. Condom use may be a transitional behavior; couples who are going steady or engaged are more likely to use a female method. Even so, condoms remain important as protection from sexually transmitted diseases, even when other forms of contraception are used.

It is important to know why contraceptive use is at best sporadic for most adolescents. A number of possible reasons exist. Three of the more likely are lack of information, inability to accept one's sexuality, and cognitive-emotional immaturity.

Lack of Information   Most adolescents are surprisingly misinformed about their own reproductive capabilities. Some surveys have shown that as many as two thirds of adolescent girls believe it isn't necessary for them to take any precautions because they are too young to get pregnant or because they have not had intercourse enough times to become pregnant. An equal number of adolescents appear to be so anxious about their sexual activities that they are not able to deal with the associated issues in any practical way (Strong & DeVault, 1997).

What is the relationship between what adolescents know about reproduction and how likely they are to use some form of contraception? Findings here are inconclusive. Much research suggests that the more adolescents know about the risk of pregnancy, the more likely they are to use a contraceptive (Hayes, 1987). Other findings suggest that knowledge and behavior are unrelated. Pleck, Sonenstein, and Swain (1988), for example, found that 18% of adolescent males with no sex education used a condom—the same percentage as those who *did* have sex education. Perhaps the reason that sex education does not increase condom use is that using a condom correctly requires a certain amount of skill, which if not acquired beforehand, is not likely to be mastered in the heat of the moment. Most sex education programs do not offer students experience in gaining skill in condom use (Barth, Fetro, Leland, & Volkan, 1992).

Most adolescents also do not receive any information about reproduction or contraception from their parents. Nor are most likely to disclose their concerns to their parents. How likely adolescents are to talk to their parents depends on the quality of the relationship they have with them (Papini, Farmer, Clark, & Snell, 1988), as well as their levels of self-esteem and individuation (Papini, Snell, Belk, & Clark, 1988). This last point suggests that young adolescents especially will not bring their sexual concerns to their parents because they are still in the early stages of the process of individuation.

One study of communication between adolescents and parents found that adolescents are least likely to talk with parents about sexual concerns once they have decided to become sexually active and most likely to talk to parents only when their attitudes are not well formed (Papini, Farmer, Clark, & Snell, 1988). Adolescents appear to talk to parents as a way of clarifying their own attitudes, but once they have done so, they disclose little to their parents or to their friends. This study suggests that once adolescents become sexually active, they are even less likely to get the information they need from parents. Once sexually active, they are guided only by their peers, who are likely to be blatantly misinformed, and some by a need to deny their own sexuality.

Inability to Accept One's Sexuality   First sexual encounters can occasion considerable conflict in many adolescents, especially in girls. A number of reasons exist for this conflict. Sexual behavior is closely tied to moral issues, which are not likely to be openly examined and discussed. In some homes sexual matters are cloaked with secrecy, and discussions of sexual concerns are infrequent or absent entirely. Many adolescents, even those who are sexually active, simply are uncomfortable discussing their sexuality. Adolescent girls who *can* accept and talk about their own sexual behavior are more likely to use contraceptives effectively.

Cause for conflict among many adolescent girls can be found in current stereotypes of femininity and masculinity. Compare these components of the feminine stereotype—yielding, shy, sensitive to the needs of others, childlike, and compassionate—with those of the masculine stereotype—makes decisions easily, is self-reliant, independent, assertive, and willing to take risks. Who is most likely to make decisions, be self-reliant, or assertively insist on the use of a condom?

Although many males prefer not to use a condom, many females may have difficulty insisting they do, and other females may fail to use a contraceptive because it simply isn't feminine to plan to have sex or to take precautions against getting pregnant.

Cognitive-Emotional Immaturity   One of the hallmarks of cognitive development is the ability to think about things that have not been experienced. Thought that is limited by experience is limited to what has happened before. Most adolescents are just entering a form of thought in which they can consider events that may only exist as possibilities for them. Most have never been pregnant before either.

Despite the emergence of new mental skills that enable adolescents to imagine things they have never experienced, things that exist only as abstractions or possibilities, these skills appear at different times for different individuals. Some adolescents may be facing sexual decisions while still approaching daily problems in a concrete fashion, their thinking limited to what is immediate and currently apparent (see Chapter 14). Thus a 13-year-old girl flattered by the attentions of an older boy may not have the cognitive maturity, in the pressure of the moment, to consider distant consequences. The concrete problem is, "What will make him like me now?" Pregnancy and disease belong to the world of tomorrow, and tomorrow is but dimly represented in concrete thought.

Even among those adolescents who can think more abstractly, the absence of practical experience and accurate information can make imagined consequences hard to evaluate. Many adolescents are able to conceive of problems intellectually yet feel personally immune to them. To these individuals disease and pregnancy are possible but not real, and it's hard to take dangers seriously if they believe such things only happen to others.

How might contraceptive use be related to adolescents' intellectual development?

Early adolescents tend to think that other people are as interested in what they are thinking and doing as they are themselves (Elkind, 1967; Lapsley, FitzGerald, Rice, & Jackson, 1989). In doing so they create an imaginary audience. Imagining that others are aware of their feelings or activities can mean that their private fantasies about sex risk becoming public knowledge. The imaginary audience can also give adolescents the feeling that they are special (the personal fable). Why else would everyone be so aware of what they are feeling and doing? Being special carries the implication that what happens to others will not happen to you. Thus many girls believe they will not get pregnant even though their friends do. As one 18-year-old said,

> Like when I'm having sex, I don't really connect it with getting pregnant cause I've never been pregnant, you know, and a lot of my friends have but I just can't picture it happening to me. And, like you really don't connect it, you know, until once you've been pregnant. Because when it's never happened you say "Why should it happen?" or, "It's never happened yet," you know. You always look at the other person and say, "It happened to them, but it'll never happen to me." And I . . . I don't really kinda put it together. I don't . . . you just don't worry about it. You don't believe it can happen to you. (Sorsenson, 1973, p. 324)

Teenage pregnancies will almost surely continue to be a major problem until courses in sex education integrate facts about the biology of reproduction with approaches that make sense to the adolescents involved. Specifically, they must address the attitudes that adolescents and their parents have about being sexual. We also need to consider sexual decision making in light of what we know about

What should be taught in this sex education class? Sexual anatomy? Sexual functioning? Contraceptive methods? Although most adults—and most adolescents—favor sex education in the schools, the content of such programs is controversial, especially if they are perceived to condone or encourage teenage sexuality.

adolescents' ability to understand things that may, at the moment, exist for them only as possibilities.

Sex Education: What Adolescents Need to Know

Nearly 90% of adults favor sex education in the schools (Harris, 1988), as do most adolescents themselves. Almost 90% of large school districts offer some form of sex education (Kenny, Guardado, & Brown, 1989). The goals of the programs differ. Nearly all provide information designed to prepare adolescents to make informed sexual decisions; most also teach material about the reproductive system as a means of achieving this goal. Few that are offered in junior high cover contraceptive techniques, perhaps assuming that doing so would communicate approval of teenage sexuality. However, this information, not that about reproduction per se, is related to the likelihood that adolescents will use some form of contraception (Scott-Jones & Turner, 1988). Most programs focus on information and provide little opportunity for students to interact with the information in ways that would make it most meaningful to them.

The information covered by many courses may be so technical, textbookish, and abstract that teenagers fail to make the connection between what they are learning and their own bodies—or at the very least what they need to know and do in order to practice effective contraception. One 16-year-old girl recalled, "We had to memorize the parts of the body—the Fallopian tubes . . . and how all that is connected. Which was a big help, let me tell you. I didn't know what I needed to know, but that wasn't it" (Aitken & Chaplin, 1990, p. 24).

The Effectiveness of School Programs   More programs are involving parents, with the assumption that doing so will improve communication within the family. Some train students to listen to peers and to help them find information. These programs assume that teenagers are more comfortable discussing sexual matters with each other than with adults. Which approaches work best? Information on the effectiveness of programs is limited and not always consistent. Involving parents may improve communication between adolescents and their parents, but such an approach appears to be most effective with younger children. Peer counseling programs appear to be effective, but primarily by raising the awareness of adolescent counselors to sexual issues rather than by reaching other students (Hayes, 1987).

Do sex education programs that include information on contraception make it more likely that adolescents in these programs will engage in sexual activity? Evidence suggests they do not and that teenagers who are already engaging in sex are likely to have intercourse somewhat less often and also are more likely to use condoms (Barth, Fetro, Leland, & Volkan, 1992). Although some studies have found no relationship between contraception use and sex education courses (Kirby, 1984, as cited in Hayes, 1987; Pleck, Sonenstein, & Swain, 1988), others have. Pregnancy prevention intervention programs, for instance, can be highly effective in altering adolescents' contraception use. Adolescents in one such program who were at risk of becoming pregnant due to low income and family background factors were more than twice as likely to effectively use contraceptives as age-mates who were not enrolled in such a program (Levinson, Wan, & Beamer, 1998).

An important factor contributing to the success of a program almost surely is the degree to which it allows adolescents to actually practice the skills they will need either to abstain or to successfully use contraception. Richard Barth, Joyce Fetro, Nancy Leland, and Kevan Volkan (1992) incorporated homework assignments, such as talking with parents or pricing birth control methods, and classroom role-playing of sexual encounters in a program covering both abstinence and birth control. Although adolescents completing the program were no less likely to engage in sexual intercourse, they were more likely to use birth control.

A number of programs stressing abstinence have reported some success in changing adolescents' attitudes, with more adolescents who took such a program believing that their sexual urges were controllable and that there were good reasons to wait until marriage before engaging in sex (Eisenman, 1994). The success of sex education programs stressing abstinence, however, is significantly affected by how committed teachers are to the objectives of such programs (de Gaston, Jensen, Weed, & Tanas, 1994).

Programs that teach adolescents assertiveness and decision-making skills offer an attractive supplement to information-based programs. These programs approach sexual decision making by building interpersonal and problem-solving skills. Sex *is* problematic for most adolescents, and it is highly interpersonal. Many adolescents feel pressured into sexual encounters that they would otherwise avoid or postpone if they felt comfortable stating how they felt. These pressures affect adolescents of both sexes. Adolescent males frequently feel pressured into making sexual overtures simply because they assume it's expected of them or that everybody else is having sex. One of the ways in which sex education programs can be effective is to correct perceptions such as these (Barth et al., 1992).

The few data we have on assertiveness and decision-making programs suggest that they are effective. Program-solving and communication skills improve, as does knowledge of reproduction. Data suggest that contraception use also improves among adolescents enrolled in such programs. Only small numbers of adolescents have been involved, and more research is needed.

What elements appear to be key to the success of school programs on sex education?

Summary

The Endocrine System

The endocrine system consists of glands within the body that produce hormones and of structures within the central nervous system that regulate their activity.

Endocrine activity is regulated by a feedback system that controls the timing of puberty. The hypothalamus and the anterior pituitary are the brain centers most closely related to the timing of pubertal events. The hypothalamus secretes a hormone that stimulates the anterior pituitary to produce hormones that act directly on the gonads. These in turn produce the sex hormones—estrogens in females and androgens in males. The hypothalamus is sensitive to levels of circulating hormones and adjusts its signals to the anterior pituitary whenever these get too high or too low.

The Physical Changes of Puberty

Puberty ushers in a growth spurt and maturation of the reproductive system. Primary sex characteristics involve changes in the reproductive system itself; other changes, such as the appearance of pubic hair, represent secondary sex characteristics. Considerable variability exists from one adolescent to the next in the timing and, to a lesser degree, the sequence of these changes.

In girls, the appearance of pubic hair is one of the first visible signs of change. Breasts begin to develop at about the same time. The uterus, vagina, labia, and clitoris all develop simultaneously with the breasts. The ovaries also grow as the ova within mature.

Boys begin puberty an average of 2 years later than girls. The first sign of change is an enlargement of the scrotum, followed by the appearance of pubic hair. The penis starts to grow a year later. Internal organs—the testes, seminal vesicles, Cowper's glands, and prostrate gland—also mature, and levels of circulating testosterone increase markedly during puberty. The height spurt precedes a change in voice and the appearance of facial and underarm hair.

Girls experience a period of rapid growth and add subcutaneous fat before reaching menarche, the onset of menstrual periods that occurs midway through puberty. Most girls reach menarche in their 12th year. The menstrual cycle is regulated by a feedback loop involving the ovaries, the anterior pituitary, and the hypothalamus. When levels of estrogen reach a peak at midcycle, ovulation occurs. Most adolescent girls have irregular cycles at first, many of which do not involve the release of an ovum.

In boys, the presence of testosterone and other hormones stimulates the testes to produce sperm. Both the seminal vesicles and the prostate gland produce semen, the fluid in which sperm are suspended. Most boys experience spermarche, the first ejaculation of seminal fluid, by mid-adolescence.

Puberty begins earlier today than in past generations. Adolescents also grow faster and grow to be larger than in the past, a trend known as the secular trend. Improved nutrition is a likely cause of the secular trend.

The Psychological and Social Implications of Puberty

The significance of puberty is different for each adolescent, depending on how the adolescent interprets the changes he or she is going through and how friends and relatives react to those changes. Adolescents react to these changes with a heightened emotionality. Tensions are common between adolescents and parents and lead to renegotiated relationships.

Biological, intellectual, emotional, and social maturation occur at different times during adolescence, and rates of maturation are also different from one adolescent to the next. Both early and late maturation seem to affect how adolescents see themselves and how others see them. In particular, adolescents' self-image is tied to their body image. Females generally have less-positive body images than males and experience more eating disorders.

Eating Disorders

Most adolescents do not have eating disorders; however, problem eating behaviors are fairly common. A majority of adolescent females have been or are on diets. Standards for female attractiveness show thinner models today than in past generations.

Bulimia and anorexia are closely related eating disorders. Bulimia is characterized by binge eating alternated with purging through self-induced vomiting, laxatives, or diuretics. Anorexia is an eating disorder in which food intake is severely limited to the point of self-starvation. Both disorders are more common among females than males and are more likely to occur in adolescents who come from families characterized by enmeshment, overprotectiveness, rigidity, and inadequate conflict resolution.

Obesity is defined as weighing more than 30% above one's ideal body weight. The prevalence of obesity has risen in the United States over the past decade. This trend most likely reflects changes in both eating habits and in patterns of physical activity. The average daily intake of calories has increased, primarily through a greater reliance on fast foods and a tendency to snack more throughout the day. This increase has been accompanied by a decrease in physical activity. Effective treatments for obesity include exercise and involve the family.

Making Sexual Decisions

Adolescents must revise their self-concepts to include new sexual feelings and behaviors. This process is problematic for those who experience conflict in leaving their childhood behind them. Changing social attitudes and values are reflected in the sexual decisions adolescents make.

Contraception Use

Most adolescents do not systematically use contraceptives because they lack adequate information. Many also do not practice responsible sex because they are unable to accept their own sexuality. Many more engage in unprotected sex due to their cognitive and emotional immaturity.

Sex Education

Most adolescents do not talk to their parents about their sexual concerns. Sex education programs in the schools are a common source of information for many adolescents. Although most programs are effective in communicating information, they may not be equally effective in changing behavior.

Key Terms

anorexia (p. 518)
asynchrony (p. 512)
body mass index (BMI) (p. 519)
bulimia (p. 518)
cervix (p. 504)
circumcision (p. 507)
clitoris (p. 505)
Cowper's glands (p. 506)
endocrine system (p. 497)
epididymis (p. 505)
Fallopian tubes (p. 504)
female genital mutilation (p. 507)
gonads (p. 497)

growth spurt (p. 503)
hormones (p. 497)
hypothalamus (p. 497)
menarche (p. 503)
nocturnal emission (p. 508)
obesity (p. 519)
ovaries (p. 504)
ovum (p. 504)
penis (p. 506)
pituitary (p. 497)
primary sex characteristics (p. 499)
prostate gland (p. 506)
scrotum (p. 507)

secondary sex characteristics (p. 499)
secular trend (p. 509)
semen (p. 506)
seminal vesicles (p. 505)
smegma (p. 507)
sperm (p. 506)
spermarche (p. 508)
testes (p. 507)
urethra (p. 506)
uterus (p. 504)
vagina (p. 505)
vas deferens (p. 505)

chapterfourteen

Adolescence
Cognitive Development

Yaun-Pin—Pete, to his friends—read alternatives "b" and "c" again. He knew this material. He had distinguished his family with good marks in this very subject before coming to this country. Yet he couldn't understand the question. The two choices seemed the same to him. He could feel the heat rising in his face as the words danced and mocked him. Blindly, he marked "c" and moved on. The bell would ring soon. So much depended on him. He would have to study his English again tonight after he and his father closed the shop. No time for hanging out, for videogames or the sitcoms his friends watched each night. No wonder they thought he was a loner. Sometimes he thought he was crazy. How could he explain one world to the other? Or to himself?

Sehti's mind wandered as she stared at the quiz. She was still angry that she hadn't been able to study more last night. She'd had to help her mother with dinner. Why had her uncle and aunt picked that night to visit? And why couldn't her brothers have helped? They didn't have half the homework she had, and they never had to help. Her mother said it was women's work, that she should leave her brothers alone. The bell—oh, no! She quickly marked alternative "b." Why couldn't she concentrate?

Joe looked at the quiz: 15 questions. He knew the answers to all of them—all but number 11. Actually, it was the way the question was worded. He could make an argument for either "b" or "c." Joe loved junior high. Math, social studies, drama, English lit—each left him more excited than the last. By the end of the day, he was filled with ideas, ideas he framed easily in words that he spoke with quiet confidence. The bell! He chose "b" and wondered how successful he'd be in convincing Mr. Allen of his reasoning if his teacher had keyed "c" as correct.

You have just met three students, each competent, each standing on the threshold of a new world of thought and experience. All adolescents embark on the journey these three are beginning. Not all travel the same distance. Yuan-Pin, Sehti, and Joe probably will not either. They aren't likely to get the same grade on this quiz or to do equally well in junior high. Is this unfair? Differences in their grades will not necessarily reflect their capabilities. Yuan-Pin is still learning English; he doesn't have a chance to show what he knows. Sehti's concentration is scattered by conflicting demands at home and at school. Intellectual performance almost always reflects more than what one knows. Motives, interests, and even expectations held by others can affect performance.

Early adolescents face intellectual changes that are every bit as profound as the biological changes discussed in the last chapter. These changes usher in adult forms of thought, just as the latter usher in adult bodies. Adolescents can plan for the future, imagine the impossible, catch multiple meanings to words and situations, understand nuance, follow a philosophical discussion, and respond to a simple question with an answer that would make the captain of a debating team proud. We will look at the nature of these changes and at explanations that have been offered for them. We will also consider conditions that affect intellectual performance in adolescents like Yuan-Pin, Sehti, and Joe.

Piaget offers a constructive developmental analysis of intellectual development. Adolescence marks the last of his four stages. For Piaget, the ability to imagine the possible, rather than thinking only of the actual, is the most important quality of mature thought. With this step, thought becomes abstract. It also becomes logical and systematic. Adolescents can think of problems in terms of the variables that define them, isolating first one and then the other, until they come up with all possible combinations.

Some developmentalists believe that what Piaget identified as new forms of thought may only reflect continuous growth in abilities already present. Because these abilities are known to increase with age, one could explain Piaget's formal thought in terms of age changes in general intelligence. This approach, known as a psychometric approach, focuses on the abilities that underlie general intelligence and on how these are measured.

We will look at how intelligence tests are constructed, what they measure, and some of the problems they introduce when not interpreted correctly. The greatest strength of intelligence tests is in predicting academic success. This strength is also a weakness. The paradox arises from our inability to distinguish what success reflects: the general abilities presumed to be tapped by the tests or the degree of familiarity with the culture required to understand the questions? Just as Yuan-Pin experienced difficulty on his math quiz, he would have difficulty with many of the items on an intelligence test.

Throughout the chapter, we will look at the practical side to intellectual development in adolescence: Adolescents can study new things in school, support their ideas with adult arguments, experience new emotions, think about themselves in new ways, plan for their futures, and understand the complexities of social relations in more subtle ways.

How Adolescents Think

Thought takes interesting turns in early adolescence and carries teenagers places children don't easily go. Adolescents can think about things that don't exist and may never exist. They can think about what is possible as well as what actually is. Thinking becomes highly systematic and logical. This is not to say that adolescents are always logical and that children never are, or that children never consider possibilities as well as realities, or that adolescents always reason in the abstract. It is, rather, that adolescents do so more often and with greater ease. Each of these characteristics of adolescent thought—thinking abstractly, thinking hypothetically, and thinking logically—is discussed in the sections that follow.

How does adolescents' ability to think abstractly enable them to answer questions such as "How is a camel like a shark?"

Thinking Abstractly

"How is a horse like a goldfish?" If you ask adolescents this question, they are likely to come up with any number of answers. They might say, "Well, a horse and a fish are both animals," or "Both have to eat to live," or "Both take in oxygen and give off carbon dioxide." Children are more likely to stare you down. You can almost hear them think, "That was a stupid question!" In any event, they are not likely to think of any similarities. Why is their response so different from that of adolescents?

Because this adolescent can consider possibilities as well as what is actually in front of him, this game my appear quite different than it does to his younger sisters.

FIGURE 14.1 Classification of Thoughts by Adolescents and Children *Source:* From J. M. Hunt, *Intelligence and Experience,* Ronald Press, 1960.

Science Project

Ms. Jones has asked her seventh-grade class to consider the following problem: Imagine that scientists have just discovered a new planet. A research team has been given the task of determining all possible life forms that may exist on this planet. A space probe has returned with data suggesting that life could exist either in bodies of water (aquatic) or on land (terrestrial). The team suspects that life on this planet, as on ours, could be either vertebrate or invertebrate. What are all the possible forms that life might take?

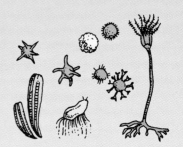

Children think of four types by combining the four separate forms: terrestrial vertebrates, aquatic vertebrates, terrestrial invertebrates, and aquatic invertebrates. Adolescents come up with twelve more possibilities. They think not only to combine the separate forms of life but also to combine the combinations! The original four combinations, plus the separate life forms, give them a total of sixteen possibilities. One of these is the possibility of no life at all.

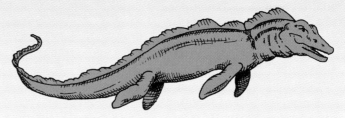

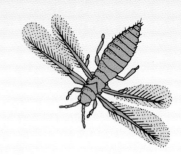

1. Terrestrial vertebrates (TV)
2. Aquatic vertebrates (AV)
3. Terrestrial invertebrates (TI)
4. Aquatic invertebrates (AI)
5. Only vertebrates (TV and AV)
6. Only invertebrates (TI and AI)
7. Only terrestrial animals (TV and TI)
8. Only aquatic animals (AV and AI)
9. TV and AI
10. AV and TI
11. TV, AV, and TI
12. TV, AV, and AI
13. TV, TI, and AI
14. AV, TI, and AI
15. TV, AV, TI, and AI
16. No animals at all

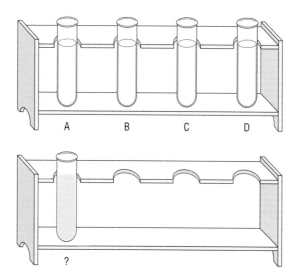

FIGURE 14.2 A Problem Involving Chemical Solutions That Requires Hypothetical Thinking to Solve
Source: From the growth of logical thinking: From childhood to adolescence, by Jean Piaget and Barbel Inhelder.

In one measure of hypothetical thinking, adolescents see a rack of four test tubes, each containing a clear liquid. A second rack holds a single test tube with a clear yellow liquid. The problem is to find the combination of colorless liquids that produces the yellow color. Adolescents can think of all the possible (i.e., hypothetical) combinations, whereas children simply combine the chemicals.

Children tend to think of things in terms of their physical properties. With horses and goldfish, this approach doesn't take them very far. If you had asked how a horse was like a dog, they would have had no problem: Both have four legs. They could tell you how a horse is like a cow: Both are large and eat grass. But as long as their thoughts are bound by the physical characteristics of things, fish remain worlds removed from horses. Adolescents can think of things as members of classes and can even think of ways to classify those classes (Drumm & Jackson, 1996). An adolescent can say, for example, "Both are animals, and animals can be either aquatic or terrestrial." Figure 14.1 shows an example of the type of science project adolescents can solve because they can think in terms of classes.

Thinking Hypothetically

Thinking abstractly is related to another characteristic of adolescent thought: hypothetical thinking. Adolescents can turn a problem around in their minds and come up with all the possible variations it might take (Figure 14.2). Only then do they start to work, testing each possibility to find the one that applies in that situation. Being able to imagine what is possible, instead of thinking only of what is real, allows adolescents to think hypothetically.

Children, in contrast, focus on the actual, perceptible elements of a situation and rarely speculate about possibilities they cannot generate by actually doing something. They are more likely to jump in and do something with no plan of attack. Even if they succeed in solving the problem, they are not likely to have kept a record of what they did. John Flavell, a psychologist at Stanford University who has written widely on cognitive development, remarks that the schoolchild's "speculations about other possibilities—that is, about other potential, as yet undetected realities—occur only with difficulty and as a last resort. An ivory-tower theorist the elementary school child is not" (Flavell, Miller, & Miller, 1993).

Models of atomic structures and other abstract concepts are meaningful only to students who have reached a level of cognitive development that enables them to use symbolic representations to evaluate the logical consistency of ideas.

Thinking Logically

As thought becomes abstract, adolescents are able to test different ideas against one another to establish their truth. They become aware of the logical relations that exist among ideas and can use logical consistency to determine whether a statement is true or false. Children check their ideas against hard facts; so do adolescents, but logical consistency is equally compelling for them.

The difference is dramatically illustrated in a simple experiment. Adolescents and children are shown poker chips and asked to judge whether statements about the chips are true or false. Sometimes the chips are hidden in the experimenter's hand; at other times they are clearly visible. The experimenter has just picked up a green chip and holds it in clear view. He says, "The chip in my hand is either green or it's not green." Both the adolescent and the child agree that the statement is true. Next the experimenter holds up a chip that is hidden in his hand and says, "The chip in my hand is either red or it's not red." The adolescent knows the statement must be true and agrees. The child says, "I can't tell," and asks to see the chip. Children evaluate statements such as these by comparing them to what they can see, not realizing that they could still evaluate their truth based on their logical properties. Adolescents know that thoughts can be checked against themselves for logical consistency (Osherson & Markman, 1975).

One might assume, at this point, that all adolescents think and solve problems alike. But thinking, like every other aspect of development, is highly individual. Tremendous differences exist among early adolescents in the rate at which they acquire new reasoning abilities, and many adolescents do not reason in these ways even by the end of junior high (Martorano, 1977). Instead, thinking improves with age throughout adolescence (Arnett & Taber, 1994).

How does the capacity for abstract thought change the way adolescents establish whether something is true?

Early adolescents are in transition from concrete to formal operational thought and so still need concrete activities in school.

Piaget's Stage of Formal Operations

Development, for Piaget, is a gradual freeing of thought from experience. Once thought becomes removed from the limitations of immediate experience, one is able to consider possibilities that do not exist and perhaps never will. We have seen how this quality characterizes adolescent thought. Piaget believed that it takes approximately 11 years to develop.

Formal operational thought begins at about age 11. In a sense it is simply an extension of the concrete operations children have used all along in sorting and classifying the objects around them. In another sense it is an extension that quite literally opens up new worlds of possibilities for adolescents. The extension is a simple one: Adolescents can extend their earlier operations on classes of *objects* to classes of *classes*. The adolescent mind can include itself in the things it considers. Adolescents can think about their thinking.

The ability to think about thought allows adolescents to arrive at possibilities they could never reach otherwise. We can see this quality of formal thought at work in one of Piaget's tasks, a game in which balls are shot onto a gameboard with a spring launcher. The balls differ in size and in the smoothness of their surfaces. Eventually each stops rolling, the larger and rougher ones first. Piaget asks adolescents to explain why they stop. At first adolescents identify wind resistance and friction as important. But they soon realize something else: that the balls would roll forever if neither of these were present. This conclusion can be reached only through thought, because the conditions under which the event would occur are never actually present (Flavell, Miller, & Miller, 1993; Ginsburg & Opper, 1988).

Few developmentalists object to the way Piaget described thought at any age; the differences he noted are clear. Not as clear is what accounts for these differences. Piaget attributed changes with age to the emergence of stages, each one distinct and different from the last, each abruptly ushering in a new form of thought when new mental structures mature, and each making its appearance in all individuals despite differences in their backgrounds.

formal operational thought
Piaget's fourth stage of intellectual development, assumed to characterize adolescence and adulthood, during which mental operations are extended to include thoughts in addition to concrete objects.

FIGURE 14.3 Logical Thinking About a Concrete Problem *Source:* From P. C. Watson and P. N. Johnson-Laird, *Psychology of Reasoning: Structure and Content.*

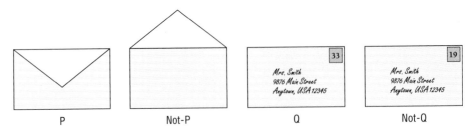

Imagine that you are a postal worker sorting letters. You know that sealed letters must have a 33-cent stamp. Among the letters that appear above, select just those you would need to turn over to determine whether they break this rule. The answer appears at the end of the chapter.

Contextual Effects and Formal Thinking

Does intellectual development progress at the same rate and take the same form independent of the larger context in which adolescents find themselves? Quite a lot of evidence suggests that it does not. Perhaps the first place in which to look for contextual influences on cognitive development is school.

Piaget believed that the changes he chronicled were not simply due to learning, but became possible only with the biological maturation of underlying mental structures. Yet Lavee Artman and Sorel Cahan (1993), working with large numbers of fourth-, fifth-, and sixth-graders, found that schooling contributed more to their success on certain Piagetian-type problems than did age.

The assumptions we bring to a problem, irrespective of how it may be presented to us, also affect the type of logic we bring to bear in solving a problem. These assumptions are formed through daily experiences with everyday objects. Consider the problem illustrated in Figure 14.3. People are told to pretend they are postal workers sorting letters. Their job is to determine whether the following rule has been broken: "If a letter is sealed, it has a 33-cent stamp on it" (that is, If there is a P, then there is a Q). Subjects are told to select just those letters they would have to turn over to determine whether they broke the rule. Even adults have difficulty with problems of this type—with or without formal thought. The most frequent mistake is to pick P and Q even though Q gives no information about whether the rule is broken. One has the tendency to check to see whether, if P is not present, Q is not either. However, the initial premise says nothing about what happens when P is *not* present; it only states what should be the case when it *is* present (Wason & Johnson-Laird, 1972).

Perhaps reasoning is less than optimal in problems such as the above simply because of their difficulty. Yet when adults are asked simple, even though misleading, questions designed to test conservation of weight, many still fail to reason in even a concrete operational way. Gerald Winer and Chadd McGlone (1993) asked individuals questions such as "When do you weigh more, when you are standing up or lying down (moving or being still; running or walking)?" Approximately 70% of those who, moments before, had correctly answered a more obvious misleading question gave at least one wrong answer to the weight question, suggesting that their failure could not be explained simply on the basis of acquiescing to an absurd situation. Rather, when faced with a situation that is initially confusing, even adults at times fall back on more intuitive forms of thinking, a tendency that becomes even more likely when considering the weight of their own body versus that of some other object (Winer, Craig, & Weinbaum, 1992).

Although research indicates that thinking changes dramatically with adolescence, it is equally clear that individual differences are large and that even adolescents who use formal logic do not apply it in all situations. Some critics of Piaget's constructive developmental approach suggest that measures of formal reasoning actually reflect the more general abilities that contribute to intelligence

These adolescents contradict Piaget's assumption that once formal thought emerges, individuals think logically all the time. Even though these young women are certainly aware of the health risks of smoking, their behavior does not reflect their ability to reason logically or to envision the long-term consequences of their actions.

at all ages (Keating, 1980). This argument brings us to a second approach to intellectual development, one that comes out of the intellectual testing movement.

A Psychometric Approach to Intelligence

Robert Sternberg, a psychologist at Yale University, tells an amusing story that illustrates some of the difficulties in measuring intelligence using the psychometric approach. A team of psychologists tested people from a Third World country with some of the tasks typically included on standard tests of intelligence. One of the tasks involved sorting pictures. In Western cultures, the most intelligent approach to this task is to sort categorically, to put a picture of a robin under that of a bird, and so on. Cross-cultural comparisons such as this one frequently find that people from Third World nations are not as "intelligent" as those from Western countries.

The people in this study were no exception. Instead of sorting the pictures categorically, they sorted them functionally. For example, they placed the picture of the robin with that of a worm, explaining that robins eat worms. No amount of encouragement or hinting from the research team could get them to sort categorically. Finally, in exasperation, one of the psychologists told them to sort the pictures the way someone who *wasn't* intelligent would do it. Each person executed a perfect categorical sort. These people were clearly intelligent enough to sort categorically. They just thought that it wasn't a smart way to sort (Baron & Sternberg, 1987).

Does practicing the guitar develop intelligence? The answer depends on whether intelligence is a single innate capacity or one of several specific abilities, such as musicality or numerical ability.

Intelligence: What Is It?

Why might intelligence be expected to increase more over time among individuals living in highly industrialized, technological societies than among those living in nonindustrialized societies?

Intelligence is a term that most of us use almost daily. Out of sheer familiarity, one might think it would be easy to define. But it is not. In fact, even experts in the field have come up with widely differing views of what it is. Yet most agree that intelligence allows us to profit from our experiences and adapt to our surroundings, and that it frequently involves abstract reasoning.

Differences among the experts as to the nature of intelligence are primarily between the "lumpers" and the "splitters," those who view intelligence as a single, general capacity versus those who view it as numerous specific abilities (Mayr, 1982).

The measures that we have—intelligence tests—are simply collections of questions that reflect the information and abilities of the average person in our society. Depending on which questions are included, people with different experiences will do either better or worse on the tests.

Figure 14.4 shows the percentage of individuals falling in each of seven classifications of intelligence. These percentages reflect the performance of nearly 2,000 people tested during the most recent standardization of the WAIS-R (Wechsler Adult Intelligence Scale-Revised), the most widely used intelligence scale for adults and adolescents 16 years old and older. The **WAIS-R** is constructed so that the intelligence quotient for the average person at any age will be 100. Notice that performance is distributed relatively evenly above and below the average score; scores ranging from 90 to 109 are considered average. The figure shows the percentages of individuals falling at different points from the mean IQ of 100. Approximately two thirds of all adults score between 85 and 115. Ninety-five percent score between 70 and 130, and over 99% score between 55 and 145 (Wechsler, 1981).

Widely-used scales for children and early adolescents are the Wechsler Preschool and Primary Scale of Intelligence-Revised (WPPSI-R), for ages 3–7, the Wechsler Intelligence Scale for Children-Third Edition (WISC-III), for ages 6–16,

intelligence The ability to profit from experience and adapt to one's surroundings; measured by intelligence tests.

WAIS-R An intelligence scale for adults that is individually administered.

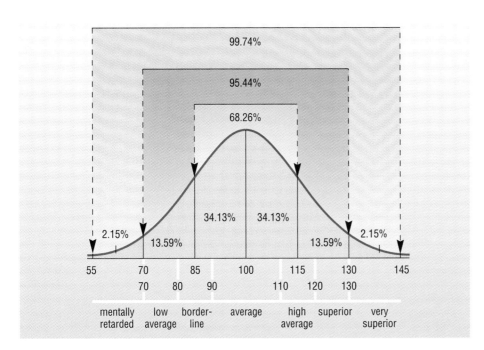

FIGURE 14.4 Percentage of Individuals and Intelligence Classifications at Different Points from the Mean IQ of 100 *Source:* From Ronald J. Cohen and Mark E. Swerdlik, *Psychological Testing and Assessment,* Fourth Edition, Mayfield, 1999.

and the Stanford-Binet Intelligence Scale: Fourth Edition (SB:FE), which has been standardized for use with children as young as 2 years of age (Cohen, Swerdlik, & Phillips, 1996).

Intelligence itself seems to be increasing over time, with mean scores on various intelligence tests showing a gain of about 3 IQ points per decade for the past 60 years (Flynn, 1984). A number of explanations for this increase have been offered, from better nutrition and education to the need of individuals to adapt to an increasingly complex modern environment. A comparison of the performance of adolescents on a variety of Piagetian tasks known to correlate with performance on conventional intelligence tests finds a similar increase over a 30-year period (Flieller, 1999).

A Closer Look: The WAIS-R

One way of understanding intelligence is to take a look at what is measured by an intelligence test. We will use WAIS-R as our example, because it is appropriate for adolescents as well as adults and is one of the most commonly used measures of intelligence. The WAIS-R includes 11 subtests, grouped into Verbal and Performance Scales (described in Box 14.1). Despite these different scales, David Wechsler was a "lumper." Each scale contributes to an overall IQ score. His inclusion of a performance scale was an attempt to correct the heavy reliance of other measures on verbal items.

Rather than ask questions that reflect academic knowledge, such as "What is the distance between the earth and the sun?" Wechsler asked questions that reflect general information. Questions on the Information subtest, for instance, tap the type of information average people are expected to acquire on their own. Examples of such questions are "What is the distance between London and San Francisco?" and "How tall is the average American man?" (Wechsler, 1981).

Notice that members of some groups are more likely to have the information required to answer these questions than others are. Sehti, one of the adolescents

Box 14.1 *Sample Subtests on the WAIS-R*

Verbal Scale

1. Information
   Individuals are asked questions that tap their knowledge of common events, places, and people.
   • "What is steam made of?"
2. Digit Span
   Individuals hear a series of digits, which they must repeat back verbatim.
   • 6—1—9—4—7—3
3. Vocabulary
   Individuals are given words to define.
   • winter
   • repair
4. Arithmetic
   Individuals are given arithmetic problems to solve mentally.
5. Comprehension
   Individuals must answer questions concerning everyday problems that tap practical knowledge and judgment, such as what one should do if one found a stamped and sealed envelope on the sidewalk.

Performance Scale

7. Picture Completion
   Individuals look at pictures of common objects in order to identify an important aspect of each one that is missing.

8. Picture Arrangement
   Subjects look at a set of cards printed with pictures. They must arrange the pictures so they tell a story. [Figure 14.5 illustrates this type of task.]

in the introduction to this chapter, might be more familiar with the height of men in another culture than with that of men in the United States, for example. And Yuan-Pin might be able to estimate the distance between Peking and Bombay more accurately than the distance between London and San Francisco. In addition to information that is general knowledge in a culture, one also must be familiar with cultural expressions and even with a cultural sense of humor. One must know, for example, that "the apple of one's eye" is not the same as "the pear of one's ear" and that our culture pokes fun at men and women in different ways than others. The henpecked husband is humorous in our culture, but not in all.

Questions are arranged in each subtest in order of increasing difficulty. A question is considered to be good if the frequency with which it is correctly answered increases with the intellectual level of those answering it. Not all questions discriminate equally well among all levels of ability. Some, for instance, nicely distinguish at the lower levels ("How many months are there in a year?")

Q Why might one expect performance on intelligence tests to differ with ethnicity?

9. Block Design
   Individuals must replicate geometric patterns using cubes of two colors.

 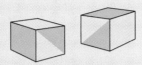

10. Object Assembly
    Individuals must assemble puzzles of common objects to form a meaningful picture.

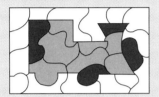 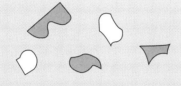

11. Digit Symbol
    Individuals are shown a row of boxes, each with a symbol that corresponds to a digit in a box beneath. Using this key, they must fill in the symbols corresponding to the digits to reflect the code above.

1	7	6	1	5	3	6
—	∧	0	—			

Source: The Psychological Corporation (1997).

but not at higher levels. Other questions distinguish at higher levels ("What is the Koran?") but not at lower levels, being missed by nearly all individuals below a certain level of intelligence. It is interesting that as our culture includes more individuals from different ethnic and religious backgrounds, questions such as this last one may lose their discriminating power at the higher level, as they reflect a broader base of knowledge among the population in general.

Are There Differences in Intelligence with Social Class and Ethnicity?

Imagine the following scene of a teenager taking the Picture Arrangement subtest of the WAIS-R. She is Asian American. The examiner places a set of four cartoon drawings on the table in front of her and tells her to arrange them so that they tell a story (Figure 14.5). One drawing shows a man fishing by a river. A second

FIGURE 14.5 Example of a Type of Item in the Picture Arrangement Subtest of the WAIS-R

shows a woman pointing at a garden while the man looks on. The third shows the man digging and discovering a worm, and the fourth shows him getting out the gardening tools. The girl tries first one arrangement, then another. None seems right to her. Finally the time runs out. You are puzzled. Why was this difficult for her? You quickly arrange the pictures mentally in this order: the second, the fourth, the third, the first. The story? The man has been told by his wife to garden, gets out the tools, discovers a worm as he works, and, reminded of more pleasant pursuits, goes off fishing. It's easy for most North Americans—unless they happen to be of Asian descent. Asian wives don't give chores to their husbands. This girl knew that, and the pictures made no sense to her (Wechsler, 1981).

Performance on measures such as the one above reflect not only a person's ability but also the extent to which that person's background is similar to that of the dominant culture. If one belongs to certain minorities, one is not as likely to do as well as someone from the dominant culture. Differences exist even among individuals within the same culture but from different social classes. Adolescents from lower-income homes can score as much as 15 to 20 points below their age-mates from the middle class. Ethnic and racial differences can be equally as large, and the latter have prompted considerable debate.

Thomas Sowell (1978), a behavioral scientist at Stanford University, points out that the performance of minorities today closely resembles that of other minorities in the early 1900s, whether of European or non-European descent, before they assimilated into the culture. Sowell focuses on African Americans, highlighting three distinct patterns that characterize their performance. He notes first that they do most poorly on the most abstract items on the tests. Investigators have concluded from this pattern that lower performance is genetically based, because abstract items should not reflect information specific to a culture. Sowell notes that European American ethnic groups experienced a similar difficulty with abstract items when they immigrated to this country. Yet when members of these same ethnic groups were tested several generations later, they performed no differently from the population in general on the same items.

Sowell identifies a second pattern in the test performance of African Americans: a decline in the intelligence of children as they age. Again, this decline occurred among children of European immigrants. Third, Sowell compares the performance of African American women with that of women from European American ethnic groups when they first immigrated. All scored higher than the men in their ethnic groups. This pattern exists even though intelligence does not differ appreciably between men and women for the population in general. Gen-

Will standardized performance tests fully reveal this young woman's abilities? Many researchers believe that such tests may be weighted with questions based on experiences of the dominant culture and that the scores from such tests may not accurately represent the capabilities of adolescents from nondominant cultures.

der differences in intellectual functioning among early immigrants show the same pattern: higher scores for women. Recent comparisons with Mexican Americans and Puerto Ricans also show the same trend.

Sowell suggests that degree of assimilation, not racial or ethnic differences, best predicts a group's level of functioning on measures of intelligence. Those groups that are upwardly mobile—one of our best indices of assimilation—show marked increases in intelligence from one generation to the next. Groups that assimilate more slowly do not show an equivalent increase with time.

One last set of differences deserves our attention before we leave this approach to intelligence. These differences concern the sexes. It is only natural to ask whether males and females differ in their intellectual functioning.

Are There Gender Differences in Intelligence?

Does intelligence differ in females and males? Popular belief holds that it does. We hear, for instance, that males are more logical and females more intuitive, that males are better at numbers and females at language. Some differences have been noted, but they are not large nor are they always the ones stereotypes would lead us to expect (Lips, 1997).

Before we look more closely, keep in mind that there are no gender differences in overall intelligence. In fact, intelligence tests are constructed so that there will not be. Questions that are answered more accurately by females are balanced by other questions that favor males. There is also no evidence linking intellectual functioning to specific biological factors, such as prenatal hormones or the presence of the X or Y chromosome, that would differ for either sex (Lips, 1997).

Several specific gender differences exist. The first of these is verbal ability. Females do somewhat better on measures of verbal reasoning and fluency, comprehending written passages, and understanding logical relations (Li, Sano, & Merwin, 1996). This difference first appears in infancy as children learn to speak.

Are males more logical and females more intuitive? Are males better at numbers and females better at language? Does any difference matter between males and females, or between any two individuals regardless of sex, when it comes to mastering the computer?

Boys soon catch up, and the difference disappears by about age 3. Performance during the grade school years shows no differences. By early adolescence, girls again perform better on measures of verbal ability. This difference persists throughout the remainder of adolescence and adulthood. Despite the consistency of the findings from one study to the next, the difference attributable to gender is always quite small, accounting for less than 1% of the variability between scores (Hyde, 1981).

Gender differences in spatial ability also exist. Males do better on tests that require one to mentally manipulate things or remember a visual figure in order to find it in a more complex figure (Schaie & Willis, 1993). Most research has found this difference to be small, accounting for less than 5% of the variability among individuals. A comparison of males' and females' spatial abilities found some measures to account for 15% of the variability among individuals of either sex (Krasnoff, 1989). However, none of the published differences are large enough to explain the preponderance of males in professions that might tap these abilities, such as engineering or architecture (Hyde, 1981).

A third gender difference favors males: math. Differences do not appear until early adolescence; then boys begin to do better than girls on measures of quantitative ability. The overall difference, once again, is small, accounting for 1% to 5% of the variability among adolescents. Despite the slight advantage held by boys, girls may still get better grades in math at school. Some studies have found that among the most able students in mathematics, those with the higher scores are more likely to be boys. Their findings are dramatic, yet they should be interpreted with caution. Comparisons at the very highest levels of ability often involved only small numbers of adolescents (Benbow & Stanley, 1980, 1982, 1983). Carol Dweck (1986) interprets these differences to reflect gender differences in motivational patterns that occur when adolescents encounter new and initially confusing material (see Chapter 12). Schaie and Willis (1993) report differences in adulthood, although only on some measures.

Gender differences in adolescents' motivational patterns about math are not completely their own; teachers, peers, and parents also influence students' attitudes, regardless of their ability to learn math. Curtis Sittenfeld's essay "Your Life as a Girl" (1995) describes how one girl's interest in math was affected:

> In the spring, you get moved from the higher to the lower math class, because you have a C-plus average. At first, you don't mind because in the lower math you have the best grade in your class. Your teacher, Mr. Willet, asks for the answers to problems he's working out on the chalkboard, and he's pleased when you respond. But sometimes he doesn't call on you, even when you're the only one raising your hand, and he says in a humorless voice: "Well, we all know Anna has the answer. Let's see if anyone else does." On the comments sent home to your parents, Mr. Willet writes that though he appreciates your hard work, he wishes you'd give other students a chance to speak. He says that you're intimidating them. ◄

Being good at math is expected more of adolescent males than adolescent females in this culture. Differences in mathematical ability emerge in adolescence, when individuals become aware of cultural sex roles. Also, gender differences disappear when prior mathematical experience is controlled. Of course, it is possible that by limiting comparisons to samples of girls who have had as much mathematical experience as boys, one is drawing samples that are not representative of girls in general. Even so, the overall difference between males and females is so small as to be negligible, and certainly does not allow one to predict success or failure in mathematics courses in school or, later, in a mathematics-related profession on the basis of gender. One authority on gender differences pointedly asks

> Has it been our intent to divide the population into the pinks and the blues and to develop one set of cognitive skills in the pinks and another set in the blues? If this is not our intent, the educational and social practices that have occurred "naturally" will need reexamination. (Sherman, 1978, p. 66)

Thought and the Adolescent

Pseudostupidity

Many of the intellectual advances of early adolescent thought have their down side. The ability to hold a problem in mind and consider it from all possible perspectives occasionally leads teenagers to make things more complicated than they actually are. David Elkind (1978b), a psychologist who writes extensively on thinking in childhood and adolescence, suggests that frequently teenagers fail to see the obvious not because the task is too hard for them, but because they have made a simple task more complicated than it actually is. He refers to this tendency as **pseudostupidity.** While a teenager is mentally ticking off all the oddball but nonetheless possible alternatives, someone else usually comes up with the obvious. Teenagers can feel stupid, asking themselves, "Why didn't I think of that?"

Early adolescents also frequently read complex motives into situations where none exist. A simple request such as, "Would you hand me the paper on your way out?" can be viewed with skeptical eyes. The teenager may wonder, "Is this just another attempt to control?" To avoid being controlled, the adolescent may consider refusing, but may also suspect that the need to refuse is merely another response to control. Neither able to comply nor to refuse, the teenager shoots back

pseudostupidity The inability to see the obvious by making a simple task more complicated than it is; believed to derive from the ability to think hypothetically and consider a problem from all possible perspectives.

Adolescents assume that everyone is as preoccupied with them as they are with themselves. This self-focused perception often leads to extreme self-consciousness and an intense need for privacy as well as a feeling of being unique and special.

an angry remark to the effect that the news isn't worth the ink it takes to print it and storms out, leaving the parent to wonder what would have been done with something as loaded as "How was your day?"

An Imaginary Audience

In what way can being able to think abstractly create problems for adolescents?

One of the hallmarks of adolescent thought is the ability to think in the abstract, and nothing is more abstract than thought itself. Adolescents can think about thinking, not only their own thoughts but also those of others. This ability can bring its own problems. Elkind (1967, 1985) assumes that this ability underlies a new form of egocentrism in early adolescence. Early adolescents frequently lose perspective as to what concerns them and what concerns others. Because so many of their concerns focus on themselves, they can have the feeling that others, too, are thinking about them. Elkind refers to this loss of perspective as the **imaginary audience.** Adolescents can have the feeling that every eye is on them and every thought is about them. The imaginary audience may explain adolescents' exaggerated feelings of self-consciousness, as well as their intense need for privacy.

Very few of us command the type of attention that adolescents feel they capture. Those who do are special; they are political figures, athletes, entertainment personalities, or in some other way notable. The imaginary audience gives adolescents this same feeling of specialness. Elkind (1978b) calls this feeling the

imaginary audience The illusion of being the focus of attention; assumed to be due both to adolescents' ability to think about thought in others and to their confusing the concerns of others with their preoccupation with themselves.

personal fable. It is a belief that we are different and special and that what happens to others won't happen to us. Elkind reminds us that this story we tell ourselves isn't true.

The personal fable can have some very personal consequences for adolescents. One is a confusion over what they have in common with others and what is genuinely unique to themselves. Confusions such as this lead to the belief that no one else can understand their feelings, because they are the only ones to have ever felt this way. It's not unusual, for example, for early adolescents to tell their parents that they couldn't possibly understand how it feels to be in love.

Another consequence is a mistaken assumption that everyone else shares their concerns. Jim may feel that his nose is too big for the rest of his face and not want to go anywhere because he's afraid he'll be kidded about it. In fact, no one else notices his nose or particularly cares what size it is. Convincing him of this, however, may be next to impossible. Adolescents caught in this form of the personal fable are not dissuaded by reasoning. Elkind suggests agreeing with them. If one were to agree with Jim that his nose was too big, he might end up defending himself.

Elkind (1978b) suggests that the personal fable explains many of the tragic cases of adolescents who appear to be self-destructive. Their behavior may not be motivated as much by a desire to destroy themselves as by their belief that what they see happening to others won't happen to them—that because they are unique, they are invulnerable to the events that touch others' lives.

The capacity of adolescents to catch glimpses of themselves in the eyes of others may be important to gaining a more accurate sense of themselves. Erikson (1968) speaks of identity formation as a process by which adolescents come to see themselves as individuals and at the same time as members of a social group. Even while assessing their individual worth, adolescents use the standards and norms shared by members of their social group. How they see themselves will reflect the way they measure up in the eyes of others. The ability of adolescents to examine their thoughts and to imagine the thoughts of others underlies a new awareness of their own separateness from others and of what they have in common with others through shared values and behaviors.

The transition for adolescents from one kind of thinking to a more complex kind is not always smooth or predictable, as is evident from the recollections of one junior high school teacher:

> One day I brought six candy bars into class for a lesson on the distribution of goods. I put the candy bars on the desk and told the class they were welcome to have them and should agree on how to divide them. For the rest of the period and part of the next, alternatives were presented and discussed. . . . proposals were made including equal division, grades, fighting, working, bidding, and drawing lots. None, by the way, suggested that I as teacher decide. Finally, drawing lots was agreed upon as the best method. As I moved the candy bars to another spot in the room, the elected class chairman grabbed at one. I asked him why, since all had agreed to the division by lots. He said he wanted one. I held out the bars and he took one, opened it, and proceeded to eat it. The universal reaction of the class was silent confusion. (Martin, 1986, p. 231) ◄

The silent confusion among these early adolescents bears witness to more than the simple defiance of a group decision. By taking the candy bar, their classmate challenged, in a fundamental way, the unspoken assumptions underlying the process of identity formation—that each of these adolescents was not only

personal fable The feeling of being different and special; thought to derive from the imaginary audience.

Factorial Designs: Perceiving an Ambiguous Situation

Dylan was the picture of cool as he sat facing the interviewer, one arm casually thrown over the back of the chair and his long legs stretched out in front of him. Despite his demeanor, he felt on edge. The interviewer had suggested that it might be helpful to have a friend present during the interview and had asked Dylan to choose someone from his class. A research assistant had been sent to bring his friend to the interview. As Dylan looked up, the assistant appeared in the doorway and said that his friend wouldn't come. "Some friend," thought Dylan, reacting with anger to what he perceived as an intentional slight.

Not all adolescents would react as Dylan did. Some would simply assume their friends would have wanted to come if they could, but weren't able to leave the class. What might account for differences among adolescents in the way ambiguous social situations such as this are perceived? And how might such differences affect them and their friendships?

Attachment theory (Bowlby, 1982) proposes that individuals form working models of relationships, in the form of expectations, based on their earliest experiences of acceptance or rejection. These expectations, in the case of rejection, promote a readiness to perceive the actions of others negatively, whereas expectations of acceptance promote more charitable interpretations. Geraldine Downey, Amy Lebolt, Claudia Rincon, and Antonio Freitas (1998) were interested in whether adolescents who defensively expect to be rejected are more likely than are others to be upset by ambiguous situations such as the one

described above and whether their reactions actually create problems with friends.

On the basis of a rejection-sensitivity questionnaire, they distinguished two groups of early adolescents (mean age = 12.2 yrs): those who were high in expectations of rejection and those who were low in rejection expectations. Adolescents from these two groups were randomly assigned to either an experimental or a control condition that differed in how ambiguous the rejection was. Those in the experimental condition were told their friend would not join them, but were given no explanation for the friend's refusal. Those in the control condition were also told their friend would not join them, but were informed this was because the teacher would not allow their friend to leave. After hearing that their friend would not join them, all adolescents completed a measure indicating how much distress they felt.

These investigators used a factorial design that included two variables: rejection sensitivity (high or low) and ambiguity of the rejection (experimental or control). In a *factorial design,* two or more independent variables, or factors, are completely *crossed* so that each level of one variable is combined with each level of all the other variables. This design appears in schematic form in Figure A. Factorial designs provide information about the effect of each independent variable alone, called a *main effect,* and information about the effect of a variable when another variable is present, called an *interaction.*

uniquely an individual, with needs and wants, but also a member of a larger group. In doing what they could not allow themselves to do, take a candy bar for themselves, this student devalued them both as individuals and as members of the group from which they derived their collective identity.

New Emotions

How one feels depends on the interpretations one gives to experience. "Did that person just brush me off, or simply fail to notice that I was going to say something?" Depending on which interpretation one gives, the encounter can occasion either feelings of irritation or no feelings in particular. (See the Research Focus, "Factorial Designs: Perceiving an Ambiguous Situation.") Intellectual development in adolescence makes it possible for teenagers to react emotionally in new ways. Children focus on the immediate elements of the situation: To a compliment they react with pleasure; to a present, with happiness. Adolescents do all this and more.

Adolescents can consider what a situation might mean as well as the way it appears. By being able to turn something around in their minds, they can assign more than the obvious meaning to social encounters. Adolescents do not always complicate life in this way, but they do so more than children and also more than most adults. A compliment can be the occasion for anger if seen as an attempt to

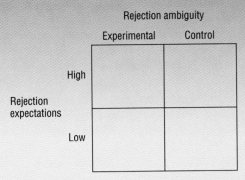

Figure A *A factorial design to determine correlation of rejection expectations and ambiguity.*

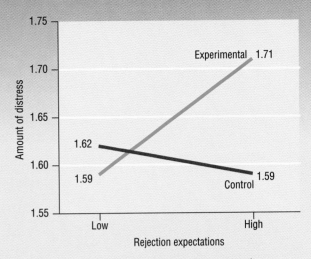

Figure B *Distress as a function of rejection expectations and rejection ambiguity.* Source: G. Downey, A. Lebolt, C. Rincon and A. L. Freitas (1998).

An interaction exists when the effect of a variable changes when a second variable is present. We might find, for instance, that neither type of adolescent would experience much distress under the low-ambiguity condition (control), but that those with high rejection expectations would experience more distress than those with low expectations when the reason for the refusal was ambiguous (experimental). The existence of an interaction means that we must qualify what we say about a variable. Are adolescents with high rejection expectations more likely than those with low expectations to be distressed by a friend's refusal to join them? It depends. If they are given no reason for the refusal, then they are. But if they are told why, then they are not.

Downey and her associates found the interaction they had expected (Figure B). Adolescents with high rejection expectations experienced more distress only in the ambiguous situation, in which they presumably interpreted the refusal as intentionally hostile. A longitudinal follow-up 1 year later revealed that differences in rejection sensitivity predicted the amount of conflict adolescents experienced with peers and the extent to which they had difficulties with their teachers. Thus, adolescents who expected to be rejected were more likely to perceive situations as rejection and to react defensively and angrily, leading to interpersonal difficulties with both their friends and their teachers.

win a favor. Or a present can cause depression if seen as an emotional bribe. Adolescents also experience emotions that are relatively foreign to children; they get high on themselves, moody, depressed, or elated (Hirsch, Paolitto, & Reimer, 1979). Unlike children, adolescents relate their feelings to their experience of themselves as well as to the events that may prompt the feelings, adding an extra level of magnification to their view of the world.

Arguing

The ability of adolescents to consider the possibilities in any situation affects more than their emotions. An immediate consequence is that adolescents can argue better than children can. To carry out an argument, whether in a debating class at school or with a parent in the kitchen, one must come up with ideas for or against something. Adolescents are not limited, as are children, to testing their ideas against facts; they can test them against other ideas. (Remember the experiment with the green and red poker chips?) This new ability makes it possible for adolescents to argue for or against an idea regardless of whether they actually believe in it. The test of the argument is whether it has an inner logic. Children are limited to arguing either for things they believe in or against those they do not. The only test they can apply is to compare what they say with how things really are for them—how they feel or what they believe.

One evening during a discussion, parents may suddenly realize that their adolescent's arguments are better constructed and more difficult to refute. Her improved ability at argumentation may at times be frustrating, but it is also a sign that she is learning to manage her emotions.

Because of their literal approach, children cannot consider that a statement could mean something other than it says it does: It's simply taken at face value. A father's complaint, "If we had no dandelions, this would be a fine lawn" will bring a response of "But we have lots of dandelions, Dad," or "I like our lawn." Adolescents can consider statements about things that are contrary to the way they presently are or about things that don't exist. They can imagine a lawn that is free of dandelions, or even a lawn of *nothing but* dandelions. Perhaps this ability to divorce thought from fact, to think in ideals, even when these are counter to fact, provides the basis for the new ability of adolescents to plan and to gain new perspectives on themselves, their families, and their friends.

Doubt and Skepticism

Prior to the development of formal thought, children believe that knowledge comes simply with exposure to the facts, never considering that factual information can be interpreted in more than one way. As a consequence, differences of opinion are treated as one person being wrong and the other one right. With formal thought, adolescents realize that what they have regarded as truth is simply one fix on reality and that other equally compelling interpretations are possible. The result can be a profound skepticism in which they come to doubt the possibility of ever knowing anything in this "newly created world of wholesale uncertainty" (Boyes & Chandler, 1992).

Adolescents in the Classroom

High school courses in mathematics, science, and literature require increasingly abstract and logical thought. Adolescents taking algebra, for instance, must solve problems in which they let x equal 5, or y equal -14. They know better than to assume that x really *is* 5 or y really *is* -14 (Bjorklund, 1989). Literature courses ask them to discuss the nuances of motives and meaning in characters who live only in the pages of their books. In physical science, they must make observations, generate explanations for these, then systematically test each one out, controlling for extraneous conditions as they do.

Inductive Reasoning

These problems are the sort Piaget claimed require formal thinking, where both inductive and deductive reasoning come into play. **Inductive reasoning** takes one from the particular to the general, from specific events to the class to which these belong—that is, to an explanation. For instance, to find that water in a closed container boils at several degrees below the point at which it boils in an uncovered container is a single observation resulting in a single fact—interesting, perhaps, but of limited value to science or the student. The logical thought process that enables a student to extrapolate from this single fact to a general rule (that there is an inverse relationship between the pressure exerted on a liquid and its boiling point) is an example of inductive reasoning.

Similarly, the adolescent who must write an essay analyzing why Hamlet was so slow to avenge his father's murder is also confronted with a task of induction. Shakespeare describes specific events in the life of Hamlet—conversations, thoughts, actions. To explain Hamlet's motives, the student must use induction to arrive at his character, to the source (class) of likely actions and the rules of their occurrence. The events Shakespeare actually shows us are analogous to the individual observations of a chemistry experiment such as the one above, and the step from these particulars to a general personality is as much an act of induction as is formulating the rule relating pressure on a liquid to its boiling point.

Deductive Reasoning

Deductive reasoning works the other way, going from the general to the particular; when reasoning deductively, one might check a hypothesis by seeing what happens when conditions change. Thus, starting with the rule that the boiling point of water drops by a certain amount with every increase of pressure, one can deduce (predict) any particular boiling point for any given pressure. Likewise, given the diagnosis of Hamlet as indecisive but impulsive (the general personality or rule from which spring all his actions), one can predict (deduce) that left to himself Hamlet will have difficulty formulating a plan of action, but once provoked, will act quickly and rashly.

The ability to think logically, abstractly, and hypothetically increases with age throughout adolescence, as does the speed at which adolescents process information (Hale, 1990; Overton, Ward, Noveck, Black, & O'Brien, 1987; Ward & Overton, 1990). Even on simple deductive tasks, we see a definite developmental progression in reasoning. Ward and Overton (1990) gave sixth-, ninth-, and twelfth-graders propositions such as the ones in Box 14.2. Propositions that made sense were solved more readily than nonsensical ones (Figure 14.6). However, for younger adolescents, even familiar and sensible content does not help. Figure 14.6

inductive reasoning Reasoning from the particular to the general.

deductive reasoning Reasoning from the general to the particular.

Box 14.2 *Deductive Reasoning: Sensible and Nonsensical Propositions*

Propositions that make sense (in which the first statement is relevant to the second):

If a person is drinking beer, then the person is 21 years of age.

If a person is driving a motor vehicle, then the person is 16 years of age.

If you are caught running in the halls, then you will be punished.

If a student strikes a teacher, then the student is suspended.

Propositions that make little sense (little relevance of the first statement to the second):

If a person is drinking beer, then the person goes to church.

If a person is driving a motor vehicle, then the person is a schoolteacher.

If you are caught running in the halls, then you are wearing sneakers.

If a student strikes a teacher, then the alarm goes off.

Source: Adapted from Ward and Overton (1990).

shows that sixth-graders found sensible (high-relevant) propositions to be nearly as difficult as those with little relevance.

Changing Sleep Patterns and Concentration on Schoolwork

Perhaps the biggest challenge facing adolescents in the classroom, at least in their early morning classes, is staying awake and concentrating on the material. Sleep rhythms change with the onset of puberty, making it difficult for many adolescents to fall asleep at night (Szymczak, Jasinska, Pawlak, & Zwierzykowska, 1993; Wolfson, 1996). Due to reductions in the actual amount of REM sleep they receive, these adolescents can find it especially difficult to wake up in the morning. Problems introduced by changing sleep patterns are further complicated by the fact that many school districts schedule classes to begin at an even earlier hour for adolescents than for younger schoolchildren. Sleepiness decreases as the morning progresses, with adolescents becoming more alert as the day wears on (Thorpy, Korman, Spielman, & Glovinsky, 1988).

Minority Adolescents in the Classroom

Minority adolescents face an additional challenge: to find a way to reconcile the often contradictory perspectives presented at school with their own life experiences. Comedian Dick Gregory once remarked that he and his friends used to root for the Indians against the cavalry, because they didn't think it was fair for textbooks to characterize the cavalry's winning as a great victory and the Indians' winning as a massacre. Many minority adolescents would agree. For them, life experiences frequently run counter to what they must learn at school. Will *Tom Sawyer* or *Huckleberry Finn* be read with the same interpretation, or with sensitivity to the same issues, by African American, Asian American, or Native American adolescents as by European American adolescents? Which students' experiences are more likely to be reflected by their teachers?

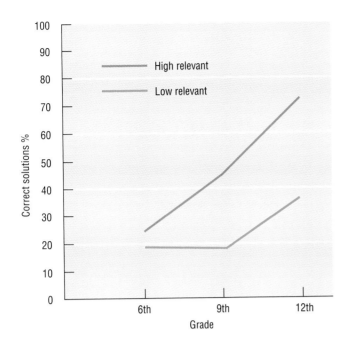

FIGURE 14.6 Deductive Reasoning for Sensible and Nonsensical Propositions

Similarly, carpetbaggers have traditionally been portrayed as low-life opportunists who turned the chaos following the Civil War to personal advantage. Yet if one believes that members of the White majority at that time, or the present, have opportunistically taken advantage of minorities, this portrayal does not raise meaningful distinctions, or at least does not evoke the same sensitivities as it would for those whose views reflect the dominant culture.

Consider the westward expansion on the North American continent. Numerous treaty violations with Native Americans led to the eventual decimation of these people. The internment of Japanese Americans during World War II violated all their civil rights. How are these events covered in most U.S. history books? Do textbooks, or teachers, simply adopt the dominant cultural perspective, and if they do, can we expect minorities to understand the facts presented in class as easily as students for whom these facts present no cultural conflict?

Textbooks used in courses such as history and literature frequently present a narrative account that evolves from a single frame of reference—a European American perspective. Many teachers uncritically adopt this same perspective. Students who do not share this view of history, as many minorities do not, will fail to experience these courses as "making sense." Yet teachers and textbooks are the authoritative sources, and students who cannot remember the facts as presented will be seen as problems.

Can Adolescents Think like Scientists?

Early adolescents can marshal facts to support or oppose principles, generate a realm of possible alternatives for any situation, think in abstractions, and test their thoughts against an inner logic. These abilities set them apart from children. They also make new forms of learning possible in the classroom. Adolescents' systematic approach to problems, for one thing, lends itself especially well to science.

Much of the excitement of science involves discovery. Often the first discovery is the nature of the problem itself. Alexander Fleming, for example, documents

High school courses demand a greater degree of abstract and logical thinking than do classes in elementary and junior high school. In science classes, for instance, students must make observations, explain them, and test their explanations.

the discovery of penicillin by telling of a mold that had formed in one of his petri dishes. He noticed that the bacteria surrounding the mold had died. Instead of cleaning out the dish and starting a new culture, Fleming was puzzled (that is, he had discovered a problem). Why had only the bacteria around the mold died?

One could identify other, less interesting, problems, such as, "What did I do wrong?" Perhaps Fleming did, too, but he chose to move on to why the bacteria surrounding the mold had died. What Fleming saw illustrates the first step in solving a problem. One must analyze a situation to discover its salient features (what a scientist would call the relevant variables). Only when these have been isolated can a strategy be formulated. Given a strategy, one can begin to test each of the features to see which produce a solution. Finally, one must be able to reach conclusions based on these tests (Ginsburg & Opper, 1988).

Notice that the success of the whole endeavor rests on the ability to think the situation through before starting to work on it. Adolescents can do this. They can identify each of the possible variables and then generate combinations. Remember that a characteristic of adolescent thought is to think in terms of possibilities. In doing so, they are also generating a strategy, because each possibility must be tested.

A strategy makes for a systematic approach to problems. Adolescents know, for instance, that they must hold all of the conditions constant except the one they are testing. Only then can they be sure their test reflects the possibility they have in mind instead of some other. They know, too, that frequently an effect can result from more than one combination of conditions. Even though they may discover that the bacteria die under one particular combination of conditions, they will continue with their tests, exhausting all the possibilities.

The reasoning process just described is fine for adolescents who have reached formal thought. But many adolescents have not. Science teachers may need to combine abstract approaches that illustrate isolating variables with concrete examples to bring their points home to thinkers who do not use formal thought. The example in Box 14.3 of a discussion in a science class illustrates this point. Notice how the discussion revolves around common objects such as a Frisbee, a shoe-box lid, and the cover to a tin can. Even concrete thinkers can wrap their minds around these examples.

Study Skills and Knowing What You Don't Know

One of the factors contributing to better learning is that adolescents, more so than children, are aware of what they don't know and adjust the way they study to accommodate for the gaps in their knowledge. Children, on the other hand, often fail to realize when they have not learned what they have been studying. Campione and Brown (1978) observed fifth-graders through college students as they studied material in a textbook. Younger students focused on the same information each time they reviewed the material, whereas older students, realizing what they had missed, directed their attention to that material on subsequent readings. The development with age of metacognitive skills, and the consequent use of strategies, underlies this improvement.

Students who fail to monitor their performance can be taught to do so. Poor readers who were shown how to assess their reading comprehension by noting what they have missed climbed from the 20th percentile to the 56th percentile (Palinscar & Brown, 1984).

Similarly, Hiller Spires, Joan Gallini, and Jan Riggsbee (1992) found that fourth-graders who were taught to attend to cues such as chapter headings and other pedagogical tools or to focus on cues embedded in the passages themselves (such as "in comparison to" or "on the other hand") improved in their comprehension.

Metaphors and Meaning: When Is a Ship a State?

Children interpret remarks literally; adolescents can understand multiple levels of meaning. When asked to interpret an expression such as "His bark is louder than his bite," for example, children might answer that "You can't hear a dog bite" or that "Some dogs bark loudly." Adolescents can understand the expression to mean that some individuals bluff their way through situations. Their ability to understand figurative uses of language makes many types of literature accessible that previously were not.

Adolescents can also appreciate *metaphor;* a metaphor makes an implicit comparison between ideas or objects to show some hidden similarity. They understand that when politicians refer to a government as a "ship of state," they are communicating that the fate of all citizens is bound together, just like the fate of passengers and crew on a ship at sea. Similarly, the phrase "evening of life" communicates that life is drawing to an end, just like the day at the approach of evening. Early adolescents easily understand expressions such as these; children do not (Geller, 1985).

Box 14.3 *Science in the Classroom: Analysis of a Frisbee*

The teacher in this science class has told students to bring in something that flies. One student brought in a Frisbee.

TEACHER: Okay, let's consider some explanations now. Why is the Frisbee built this way? Look back at our list of structural features on the blackboard and see if you can explain one of them. Why is the Frisbee designed the way it is? I'd like to see almost everyone's hand up with one idea.

STUDENT 1: Well, it's round so you can spin it.

TEACHER: Okay. How many other people were thinking something like that? Now let's take this a little bit further. Could you spin it if it weren't round?

STUDENT 1: No. Well, I guess you could. But it wouldn't work very well.

TEACHER: How come? What would go wrong?

STUDENT 1: It would flop around; it wouldn't sail smoothly.

TEACHER: Can you give another model case of that?

STUDENT 1: Well, I can't think of anything.

TEACHER: Can anyone think of an example of something shaped like a Frisbee a little bit, but not round? What has a rim like a Frisbee but isn't round?

STUDENT 2: Maybe the lid of a shoe box. You know, it's shaped like a rectangle but it has sides like a Frisbee.

TEACHER: And what would happen if you spun it like a Frisbee?

STUDENT 2: Well, it wouldn't go very far.

TEACHER: Why not?

STUDENT 2: I don't know. I guess it's not so heavy. The air slows it down maybe.

TEACHER: Good. Anyone else have some ideas about why it slows down?

STUDENT 3: It doesn't spin well because the sides of the box lid hit the air.

TEACHER: Good point. When it's not round, the sides hit the air and slow it down. That's a reason for a Frisbee being round. But that leads to another question: Why is spin so important? [No one raises a hand.] Let me ask the question this way, and again I'd like almost everyone to think of an answer. What happens if you throw a Frisbee without spinning it, versus throwing the Frisbee with a spin? [Most hands go up.]

STUDENT 4: It flops if you don't spin it. So I guess the spinning keeps it straight.

TEACHER: How many other people had a similar answer? [Several raise their hands.] Anyone have a different answer?

STUDENT 5: It's like a gyroscope that we studied last week.

TEACHER: That's very good. How many others noticed that connection? [Two or three hands go up.] Could you explain?

STUDENT 5: Well, we learned that the gyroscope effect keeps something in the same position, so it doesn't tilt or wobble. So the gyroscope effect keeps the Frisbee from toppling over.

Early adolescents also begin to understand irony, sarcasm, and satire. Their ability to think in terms of hypothetical situations as distinct from actual ones makes an understanding of these concepts possible. Being able to consider the perspective of another and anticipate the other's intended effects by their remarks almost surely contributes to this new appreciation. Adolescents can appreciate the irony in passages from works such as *Pilgrim at Tinker Creek,* in which Annie Dillard (1974) writes the following:

TEACHER: Very good. So a Frisbee is round so it can spin fast without slowing down when its edges hit the air. And it needs to spin to keep it from tumbling. What about some other feature on the structure list? Who has an explanation for something else? . . .

STUDENT 6: It's rounded on top. I mean it isn't perfectly flat. That maybe helps it to fly.

TEACHER: A very interesting idea. Anyone else have that one? So a Frisbee is a kind of spinning wing. The spinning keeps it straight and the wing shape helps it to stay up. How much does that shape help it to stay up, though? [No answer.] Can anyone think of other things you can throw somewhat like a Frisbee? Maybe we can see whether they fly just as well.

STUDENT 7: A discus.

STUDENT 8: A tin-can lid. You can throw those by spinning them.

TEACHER: Interesting examples. I wonder if we can see whether the rounded shape of a Frisbee really gives it more lift than something that's flat.

STUDENT 9: But a discus is pretty heavy; so are tin-can lids.

TEACHER: That's a good point. When you worry about a difference like that, you're worrying about what scientists call control of variables. That means that when you're making a comparison, you want it to be fair. If you're comparing how much the rounded top helps, you don't want the comparison messed up by other differences, like weight. So a discus is a good idea but, thinking about it, we see it's too heavy. Is there any way we could make a fairer comparison? Could we test the Frisbee against itself somehow?

STUDENT 10: How about cutting off the rim?

TEACHER: Could be. A good idea. You're thinking up ways to compare it with itself. Let's think if it's a fair comparison.

STUDENT 10: I guess not. Cutting off the rim would make it lighter.

TEACHER: Well, that's a point. Can we test it against itself without making it lighter?

STUDENT 11: How about throwing it upside down? If the rounded top really helps it to stay up, it shouldn't fly as well upside down.

TEACHER: That's a good idea. Is it a fair comparison?

STUDENT 11: Sure, because it weighs the same right-side up and upside down.

TEACHER: Okay, so we have a good idea for controlling the variables. It's a fair test because everything is the same except what we're interested in—the rounded top. We have a Frisbee here, so let's try the experiment.

Source: Perkins (1987).

Somewhere, and I can't find where, I read about an Eskimo hunter who asked the local missionary priest, "If I did not know about God and sin, would I go to hell?" "No," said the priest, "not if you did not know." "Then why," asked the Eskimo earnestly, "did you tell me?" ◄

The ability of adolescents to appreciate the irony in this story may be especially acute. They, like the Eskimo, face a challenge to change because of what they know.

Secondary Schools Today

The growth of secondary education in this country during the past century has been nothing short of phenomenal. Over the past 100 years, this society has progressed from fewer than 5% of the population completing high school to 86% with either a diploma or equivalent degree (U.S. Bureau of the Census, 1999). Quite a success story. Yet the successes of secondary education have been punctuated by crises as well.

As more students attend high school, the diversity of the student population has increased. The increasing ethnic diversity of our society is also a source of differences among students (Youth Indicators, 1996). Teachers must reach students of widely differing cultural backgrounds, some of whom have limited knowledge of English or of the dominant culture. In years past, the less successful would not have remained in school. Many schools face the need to instruct students from two dozen or more cultural backgrounds.

Secondary schools face another crisis: a dramatic increase in the number of students attending school and the need for more teachers and schools to accommodate them. School enrollment declined steadily from the early 1970s through the mid-1980s, as birth rates declined. Beginning in 1985, however, enrollment in kindergarten through the eighth grade began to increase. The number of students in elementary and secondary schools is expected to exceed the record previously set by the baby boomers, with enrollment continuing to increase beyond the year 2000 (Youth Indicators, 1996).

Academic Tracking

One of the biggest problems facing high schools is the tremendous diversity of their students. Generations ago, only those who were academically oriented completed high school. Others found jobs and got married. High school was for those with a special interest in and capacity for learning. Today, all possible interests, gradations of ability, and goals are present. Can we expect all students to take the same courses? Will some learn so quickly that teachers must move ahead before others have mastered the material? Will slower learners hold the class back? And what about different interests? Should we require all students to take the same courses? If so, what should these be? Can we expect everyone to have an equal interest in math? Auto mechanics? English literature?

Academic tracking is a common solution to problems created by the diverse interests and abilities of students. **Academic tracking** is the practice of offering students several programs of study, with assignment to a particular program based on prior achievement, stated goals, and the evaluations of counselors.

Most high schools offer at least two tracks—college preparatory and noncollege—and many offer other options. Students in different tracks frequently do not take classes together even for the same course. When the same course, such as basic math or English, is required in both tracks, students from different tracks take different sections. Educators assume that multiple tracks allow students to work at different paces and teachers to adjust the content of the courses to match differing interests. These assumptions make tracking seem a reasonable approach for teaching students with different abilities and interests.

However, tracking may in fact contribute to the problems it was designed to correct. Adolescents from minority groups and low-income families are still more likely to be in noncollege than in college tracks (Page, 1990; Youth Indicators, 1996). Of the students in noncollege tracks, more lose interest in school and drop

academic tracking The assignment of students to one of several courses of study in high school on the basis of criteria such as academic interests and goals, past achievement, and ability.

The tremendous diversity of students in high school classes is a problem for teachers because they must find a level to teach that matches students' capacities and interests.

out than do those in college preparatory tracks. Can assignment to a lower track contribute to a sense of alienation and failure among students? Research suggests that it does (Snow, 1986).

Analysis of a national sample of over 10,000 high school students reveals that those students assigned to a lower track do more poorly and are less likely to graduate from high school (Gamoran & Mare, 1989). These investigators used achievement scores in mathematics and the probability of graduating as indices of student success. Most of the difference in mathematics achievement between students assigned to college and noncollege tracks was accounted for by pre-existing differences. At first glance, these data would appear to support the belief that students assigned to each track differ primarily in ability. However, 20% of

How might assignment to a lower academic track affect a student's performance in school?

the difference could be traced to the assignment to tracks. A difference this size is more than the increase in math achievement scores gained by an average student between his or her sophomore and senior years. It is also larger than the difference between the scores of students in noncollege tracks and the scores of high school dropouts. Tracking has an even greater effect on the probability of staying in school than it does on math scores. Over 50% of the difference in graduation rates between students in college and noncollege tracks could be explained by their track assignment (Gamoran & Mare, 1989).

These and similar data strongly suggest that the practice of tracking adversely affects students who are assigned to lower tracks (Oakes, 1985). Tracking makes it more likely that these students will work toward lower goals, proceed at a slower pace, have fewer opportunities to learn, and achieve less than students in higher tracks (Raudenbush, Rowan, & Cheong, 1993). More class time goes to discipline and less to instruction. Even the quality of teaching differs, in addition to what is taught (Page, 1990). The Research Focus, "Internal and External Validity: 'Tuning Out' Powerless Adults," looks at communication styles among teachers.

Educators are examining alternatives to tracking for dealing with diverse student populations. Students of different ability levels can be placed together in small working groups. This approach, known as cooperative learning, gives students recognition for both their individual performance and that of the group. Power relationships subtly shift, placing the responsibility for learning on students rather than the teacher (C. Banks, 1993). Cooperative learning increases achievement in many students and has eased tensions in multicultural classrooms (Slavin, 1985).

Another powerful alternative is the involvement of parents in the educational process. Parents can be involved in a number of ways: instructing students in the classroom, helping them at home, participating in school governance, and becoming involved in community service. James Comer and his colleagues (1985, 1988, 1996), at Yale University, have created a program in which parents, along with teachers, administrators, and staff, are responsible for administering the activities of the school. This program addresses the social and developmental, as well as the educational, needs of students. Comer believes, for instance, that social skills and ties to the community are as important as academic subjects, especially for lower-income students, who often lack these assets. In two inner-city schools using Comer's model, student performance so improved that the schools tied for third and fourth place in the district, with the students testing up to a year above the average for their grade. Attendance also improved dramatically, and behavior problems practically disappeared.

It is easy to understand why such a program could work: Teaching becomes more relevant when academic subjects are translated into the daily concerns of students and their families. In turn, what is learned in the classroom receives the support of parents who are committed to educational programs they help plan.

Despite their proven success, alternatives such as cooperative learning and Comer's model will not be beneficial unless teachers and staff are trained to use them effectively. Cooperative learning, for example, is a relatively complex technique to implement, requiring in-service training. Similarly, parental involvement can be cumbersome and can even increase conflict if parents' and teachers' views of education conflict (C. Banks, 1993).

Another alternative combines assignment to noncollege tracks with actual work experience for which students receive academic credit. This approach also addresses the financial difficulties many low-income students face. The Social Policy Focus, "Job Training for Youth—When Social Policy Fails," explores the issue

Internal and External Validity: "Tuning Out" Powerless Adults

Cass found himself gazing about the room as Mrs. Butler went over the worksheet once again. Why couldn't he focus when she explained things to the class? She never seemed to look at him, he thought, or anyone else when she talked to them. She was describing the steps in long division now, pausing hesitantly as she spoke and smiling, every now and then, at no one in particular. After telling the class to turn to the next page, she turned in Cass's direction and snapped, "If you can't pay attention over there, Mr. Cassidy, you'll find yourself doing this worksheet during recess!" and then added, just as sweetly, "Just kidding, Cass," with another ingratiating smile.

Mrs. Butler's classroom manner is characteristic of adults who, though in positions of authority over children, nonetheless feel relatively powerless when interacting with them. Their apprehensive feelings are revealed in their ambiguous communication styles, by characteristics such as halting speech, ingratiating smiles, and softly worded but negative messages. Ambiguous communication, by definition, is not easy to interpret, and one might wonder how children respond when such communication is directed at them. Cass, recall, found his attention wandering in Mrs. Butler's classroom.

Daphne Bugental, Judith Lyon, Eta Lin, Emily McGrath, and Alfred Bimbela (1999) suggest that because ambiguous messages make it difficult for children to predict the speaker's intentions or behavior, children may experience a certain amount of confusion and distress. This, in turn, may prompt them to cope with these feelings by withdrawing their attention. In other words, ambiguous communication styles can prompt children to "tune out" powerless adults. In doing so, however, children's ability to process other information, such as instructions for doing long division in this case, may also be affected.

These investigators examined children's attention to messages given by women who were selected as being either relatively powerless or powerful, based on the way they interacted with children. The messages took the form of videotaped instructions given by each type of "teacher." Children's attention was measured physiologically, as changes in heart rate and skin conductance. After watching the videotaped instructions, children were also asked to complete several tasks, one of which involved mental arithmetic. As expected, these investigators found that children attended less to powerless teachers than to powerful ones. They also made more errors in mental arithmetic after listening to less powerful teachers.

These investigators had wanted to determine how children would respond to naturally occurring, or unstaged, communi-cational styles differing in ambiguity. Thus, they selected speakers who already spoke in either of these ways. When children responded differently to these speakers, Bugental and her associates were able to say that communicational ambiguity, as this occurs in spontaneous and naturally occurring interactions, affects the way children respond. Research that can be generalized to naturally occurring situations, to situations and people outside an investigator's laboratory, is said to have *external validity*.

A second type of validity is *internal validity*. Does research allow investigators to rule out competing explanations for their findings and to attribute the differences they observe only to the variables of interest? To the extent this is true, research is said to have internal validity. Most things in life are not free, however, and this is true with respect to research as well. The conditions that are necessary for the establishment of internal validity are frequently at odds with those necessary for external validity. One "pays" for external validity, that is, by sacrificing internal validity and vice versa. Let's see how this might work.

By selecting speakers who naturally spoke in one way or the other, Bugental and her associates maximized the external validity of their research. These investigators were aware, however, that in doing so they were jeopardizing its internal validity. Speakers who differ in one respect are likely to differ in other respects as well. And *these* differences, rather than communicational ambiguity per se, might have accounted for the way children reacted to the two types of messages. Simply put, there could be more than one possible explanation for the findings they obtained. When research fails to provide an unambiguous answer to the question it was designed to address, we say that it lacks internal validity.

To address this possibility, Bugental and her associates conducted an actual experiment in which they trained a number of "teachers" to give either ambiguous or nonambiguous messages. Since the same individuals gave both types of messages, these investigators could be sure that children were responding only to differences in message ambiguity and not to characteristics of the speaker. The results of the second experiment corroborated those of the first: Namely, children are less attentive to powerless forms of speech characterized by communicational ambiguity. Furthermore, communicational ambiguity has negative consequences for their performance, in that they make more errors on tasks after being instructed by powerless "teachers."

Job Training for Youth—When Social Policy Fails

BY ANDREA HAYES

"Give a man a fish, and you've given him a meal. Teach a man to fish, and he'll have food for a lifetime."

For the past century, social policy attempts to deal with poverty and joblessness have wavered between "giving fish" and "teaching to fish." At the turn of the twentieth century the strategy thought most effective was to "teach to fish" by creating public training institutions such as vocational schools. Since the 1960s, however, a new discussion has begun. Is *training* truly the most effective tool, or is *work itself*? This question is immediately relevant to the many youth who today face a problematic future. Most students assume that school is designed to prepare them for their future, including the job or career they will choose, as well as the skills needed for college. For those planning to join the work force immediately after high school, this assumption is false. The content of most classes has little to do with the skills necessary for the job they will acquire.

In the 1980s the Reagan administration developed the Job Training Partnership Act (JTPA), a policy directed at solving this dilemma. The goal of this program was to provide work habits and job-specific skills to noncollege-bound youth, who would then be placed in an actual work setting. Despite these admirable goals, JTPA has failed on a number of levels. Most of the employment positions have involved temporary summer jobs offering, at best, 12 weeks of actual work. More generally, most JTPA recipients receive training and counseling only; a very small percentage progress to an actual job.

Rather than wait for social policy to meet the immediate needs of inner-city youth, one man has recently created hope and a future for many. Striking a balance between "giving a fish" and "teaching to fish," Father Greg Boyle, a Catholic priest serving in the 16-square-mile area of Boyle Heights in East Los Angeles, provides solid job opportunities to Latino youth (Fremon, 1995). Father Greg, or "G-dog" as the youth affectionately call him, runs the community's "Jobs for a Future" program, which he developed to address the area's youth unemployment problem. The program includes "Homeboy Industries," a silkscreen print shop, and "Homeboy Bakeries," two businesses that provide a service to the community and are completely run by youth (Fremon, 1995).

In addition to fulfilling his duties as a priest and guiding the youth in job acquisition, Father Greg spends much of his time speaking publicly about his ministry. The personal stories of economic disadvantage and the oppressive reality of gang life have moved many listeners to offer employment at their own businesses. At other times Father Greg has paid some of the youth's salaries himself, just to get them in the workplace. Due to the program's renown, as well as Father Greg's charismatic personality, state legislators and politicians have sought him for counsel on public policy. Father Greg is an excellent example of how the gaps left by social policy can often be filled by grassroots organizing. Sometimes, all it takes is one person to generate the energy.

of job training programs. Innovative use of computers is a promising alternative for students who are "light-sensitive"—that is, who get most of their information through visual media such as television or the Internet and spend little time reading (Solomon, 1990).

Academic Achievement

Laurence Steinberg, Bradford Brown, and Sanford Dornbusch (1996) studied over 20,000 adolescents, talking as well with parents and teachers, in an effort to discover why some adolescents succeed in school and others do not. These investigators worked with an ethnically diverse sample, with nearly 40% of the adolescents from African American, Asian American, and Hispanic families, approximately the percentage that will soon characterize the general U.S. population. A number of their findings are alarming; others are equally encouraging.

One of the more disturbing findings is that many high school students are disengaged from school and simply are not serious about their studies. This disengagement is not limited to students who are struggling to succeed academically. One talented student, commenting on the classroom atmosphere in his school, had this to say, "People aren't comfortable in school, so they never learn the joy of putting everything they've got into learning. . . . There's really no room for being honest. . . . Everything in there is awkward." When asked what would make students comfortable, this student talked about relationships, reminiscing about a wilderness first aid course in which the instructor started by greeting each of the students, offering them fresh coffee and juice, and making sure they were relaxed before moving on to the course itself. Relating this to his experiences in high school, he reflected, "We don't even introduce ourselves. Teachers just say 'Okay, you're in physics'" (Hersch, 1998, pp. 222–223). ◄ Teachers echo these researchers' concerns. In a national survey of secondary school teachers, 38% indicated student apathy as a serious problem, 36% said students came to school unprepared to learn, and 34.5% noted a lack of parental involvement (U.S. Department of Education, 1996).

Steinberg and his colleagues suggest that the problems in secondary education are due not so much to what is taking place in the classroom as to what is going on outside the classroom—at home, with friends, and in the community. This is not to say that the quality of schooling does not matter—it does. But it does point to the importance of the larger context in contributing to the influence schools can have. What contextual factors might be supporting this disengagement from school?

One factor appears to be students' beliefs about how important it is for them to do well in school in order to be successful once they graduate. Steinberg and his associates found that although students believe that future success is related to graduating from high school, they do not relate success to how well they did in their classes. In other words, they believe that having a *diploma* is important, rather than what they have learned. Given this belief, it is not surprising that many put so little work into their classes. In motivational terms, many students appear to be motivated more by the need to avoid failing, or the fear of not graduating, than by the need to get something out of their classes.

How might one change this motivational pattern? Several answers were suggested, interestingly, by differences in achievement among adolescents from different ethnic backgrounds. Specifically, Asian American adolescents consistently outperformed European American adolescents, who performed better than African American or Hispanic adolescents. These differences existed even after other factors that are known to relate to academic success, such as family income or parental education, had been controlled for. In fact, ethnicity was more importantly related to academic achievement than any other factor, including affluence. As Steinberg points out, mention of ethnic differences in academic achievement is a sensitive subject, leading as it does to questions of differences in native ability. A more probable explanation than native ability, however, is that Asian American students simply work harder and have more adaptive attitudes toward school. In fact, Steinberg quips, if they really were superior, they would not put in twice as many hours on homework as other students.

So what is it that contributes to the academic success of Asian American students? We mentioned one factor—effort. They spend more time on schoolwork than their peers. Differences in their beliefs, however, are also important. Steinberg and his associates found that students from different ethnic backgrounds differed little in their beliefs about school success, about the importance of getting a good education, but they did differ in their beliefs about failing in school. When asked, for instance, if they thought that not doing well in school would interfere with their ability to get a good job, striking differences emerged. Asian American students, more so than any others, believed that not doing well would hurt their chances for later success. Steinberg points out that it is excessive optimism, not

What factors contribute to Asian American students' success in school?

pessimism, that is the problem for many African American and Hispanic students: They do not believe that doing poorly in their classes will affect their later success (Steinberg, Brown, & Dornbusch, 1996).

What are the encouraging findings from this research? Perhaps the most important is the power for change that lies within the reach of parents. Most parents value education and want their adolescents to succeed in school. However, not all ways of parenting are equally effective in promoting academic achievement. The most effective parents are accepting (versus rejecting), are firm (versus lenient), and encourage autonomy in their children (versus controlling them). This type of parenting is known as *authoritative parenting* (see Chapter 9). Authoritative parenting, in addition to promoting competence, maturity, and academic success, can also offset negative peer influences (Mounts & Steinberg, 1995). Parental expectations, and adolescents' perceptions of these, contribute significantly to academic achievement in students differing widely in background and ability. In combination with other factors—such as prior achievement, effort, family income, and gender—parental involvement, parental communication, and parental expectations have been found to account for over 70% of the variance in academic achievement (Patrikakou, 1996). The good news is that parents can learn to parent authoritatively.

A final encouraging note is that when parents become engaged in their children's schooling, their children become engaged as well, and academic achievement improves (Comer, 1985, 1996).

Answer to the problem in Figure 14.3: P and Not-Q.

Summary

How Adolescents Think

Three advances characterize adolescent thought: (1) Thought becomes more abstract; adolescents can think of things in terms of class membership and can classify the classes. (2) Thought becomes hypothetical; adolescents can think of things that are only possible but not real. (3) Thought becomes more logical; adolescents can test one thought against another. These changes in the way adolescents think are prompted by the biological maturation of the brain.

A Psychometric Approach to Intelligence

Common measures of intelligence reflect the knowledge and abilities of the average person in our society. Most intelligence tests reflect one's familiarity with the culture. Racial and ethnic differences in intelligence exist and may reflect different rates of assimilation into the dominant culture. Gender differences in intelligence may also reflect different socialization experiences.

Thought and the Adolescent

Adolescents frequently make problems more complex than they are and feel stupid when someone else comes up with the obvious solution. Elkind refers to this tendency as pseudostupidity. Elkind believes that the ability of adolescents to think about thinking leads them to create an imaginary audience in which they feel themselves to be the center of everyone's attention. More sophisticated forms of thought affect adolescents' emotions and their ability to argue for what they believe in. Changes in considering another person's perspective may explain the concept of the imaginary audience.

Adolescents in the Classroom

Adolescents' ability to think hypothetically makes it possible for them to study science, and their ability to appreciate multiple levels of meaning broadens their understanding of literature. They can understand irony, sarcasm, satire, and metaphor.

Secondary Schools Today

Academic tracking is a common solution to diverse interests and abilities among students. But tracking itself contributes to differences in achievement and dropout rates between those assigned to college and noncollege tracks.

Powerful alternatives to tracking include forming small cooperative learning groups in the classroom and involving parents in the educational process. Work-study programs and computer-assisted instruction (CAI) offer additional alternatives.

Key Terms

academic tracking (p. 560)

deductive reasoning (p. 553)

formal operational thought (p. 537)

imaginary audience (p. 548)

inductive reasoning (p. 553)

intelligence (p. 540)

personal fable (p. 549)

pseudostupidity (p. 547)

WAIS-R (p. 540)

chapterfifteen

Adolescence
Psychosocial Development

Annie is 13 and standing in the dark on her aunt's doorstep. It's 2:30 in the morning. Only blocks away, Annie's frantic mother has called the police to say that her daughter has run away. That morning Annie's mother, looking for the medical card she had given Annie to use, found two joints in Annie's purse. When she confronted Annie about them, Annie screamed that her mother was spying on her, grabbed the purse and said that she was leaving for good. Annie's mother stood in the doorway and said they had to talk, but Annie pushed past her and nearly knocked her over. Later, when the police, Annie's mother, and Annie all converge in her aunt's living room, Annie tells them she ran away because her mother is cold, selfish, demanding, and doesn't love her. Annie's mother describes Annie as bright and sweet, but immature, irresponsible, and thoughtless. Each has nothing to say that will reach the other.

If asked to describe herself, Annie's mother would never use words such as *cold* or *selfish*, nor would she say that she didn't love her daughter. Nor would Annie describe herself as immature or thoughtless. How can the two of them see things so differently? What has gone wrong? How much of their difficulty is because of Annie? How much is because of her mother? And how much is because Annie is 13?

Eddie, 12, is sitting in his room waiting for his father to open the door. His little sister went running to get him after she saw all the hair in the bathroom and found her mother crying in the kitchen. It hadn't been all that good around the house lately. Things came to a head, literally, when Eddie shaved both sides of his head, leaving a swath down the middle, which he dyed green and spiked with hair gel. His mother said she had never seen anything like that. Who knows what his father will say. Or do. Eddie tells himself he doesn't care. He has never felt so alone in all his life.

How is it possible for Eddie to feel alone with his family all around him? And what possessed him to give himself a green Mohawk?

A Constructive Interpretation of Relationships

In giving meaning to their experiences, adolescents actively construct the events to which they respond, putting together a reality that makes sense, given the way they perceive their world. One's worldview changes, as we have seen, in adolescence. In the preceding chapter, we examined these changes in terms of adolescents' intellectual grasp on reality. In this chapter, we will consider changes in the meaning adolescents make of themselves. In particular, we will look at how their meaning of self changes in relation to their families.

What prompts these changes? Why are relationships with parents renegotiated in adolescence and not, say, in middle childhood or early adulthood? Puberty gives us one answer. The biological changes discussed in Chapter 13 have important implications for the way adolescents and their parents interact. Among European American adolescents in our culture, puberty ushers in increased conflict and decreased closeness with parents. As adolescents develop the bodies and feelings of mature adults, their and their parents' expectations change. Adolescents, for their part, expect to be treated in more adult ways, to be given more autonomy and a greater say in family decision making. Parents, in turn, expect adolescents to be more responsible and to act in more adult ways. Conflict frequently results.

These trends are not universal, and the importance of the way a culture interprets, or constructs, biological events such as puberty cannot be overemphasized. Puberty, for instance, is associated with very different changes among Hispanic adolescents, at least for boys, for whom relationships with parents actually improve (Molina & Chassin, 1996).

Another factor contributing to a renegotiation of relationships in early adolescence is the way adolescents begin to think. The intellectual changes discussed in the preceding chapter give adolescents new perspectives from which to view themselves and their relationships with others. Adolescents can no longer see themselves as they always have. What sense, then, are they to make of themselves? And how does a constructive perspective help us understand adolescents such as Annie and Eddie?

Despite other differences between them, both Annie and Eddie have one thing in common. Both have organized their meaning of the self in terms of their relationships with their parents. If asked to talk about herself, Annie would likely say something such as, "The problem's not me so much as it is my mother. She doesn't really care about me and wants to control me." Annie has a hard time separating her feelings from how she sees her mother, her *self* from the *other*. One could say that she simply is not being honest. But the truth is, she is being honest. This is the way things are for her. In order for her to relate differently to her mother, she must be able to see *herself* differently. She must be able to distinguish her needs and feelings of the moment from her larger sense of who she is, from her sense of self. Robert Kegan (1982) characterizes this differentiation as, "'I' no longer *am* my needs . . . I *have* them." This distinction brings with it the possibility of not only coordinating her needs but also coordinating them with the needs of others, ushering in the potential for mutuality. In recognizing the needs of her mother as well as her own and the obligations of each toward the other, she will have stepped out of the role of a child with a parent, into a relationship characterized by greater mutuality.

And what about Eddie? How are we to understand his feelings of loneliness? The differentiation that eventually leads to greater mutuality in relationships with parents takes years to achieve. Eddie didn't have years to spend on differentiation that afternoon. He knew he wasn't a child, like his sister, but he was not sure what it was that made him different from children her age or, for that matter, different from adults such as his parents. He didn't want to be seen as a kid anymore, nor did he want to be like his parents. At 12, scissors and paint, cutting and pasting, promised a quick fix to an identity. Why, then, was he feeling so lonely? Eddie had lost something. He had lost the self he had known himself to be, and he had not put together a way of being to step into when he stepped out of the other.

In life, one frequently finds oneself in the middle of something without knowing exactly what it is one is doing or precisely what one wants to get out of it—not at all a new experience for adolescents as they attempt to understand themselves in new ways. Change at any age doesn't come easily, and the more people who are involved, the more difficult it is; for as adolescents define themselves in new ways, so, too, must those around them, most notably their parents.

Why *is* it so hard to forge a new meaning for the self in adolescence? In part, it is because adolescents must gain hold of a new way of being. But they must do something else as well. They must also let go of, or be willing to lose, the self they have always known. Just how easy or difficult it is for adolescents to gain a new sense of themselves and let go of the old one will depend on the type of support they receive from the environment in which this process takes place—their relationships with their parents. The first section of this chapter examines the way adolescents put together their experiences within the family to give a new sense of self.

A messy room and a busy phone may be signs of a young adolescent moving toward autonomy rather than of innate sloppiness or irresponsibility.

Autonomy and Individuation

The drama of gaining a sense of themselves unfolds on a well-known stage: at home as adolescents interact with parents, pressing for greater autonomy. In winning new responsibilities, they discover strengths that are uniquely theirs and that distinguish them from their parents, a process known as individuation.

Autonomy

One of the major issues confronting early adolescents is to become more autonomous. **Autonomy** involves independence and being responsible for one's actions. Adolescents press for greater inclusion in decisions; they ask to be treated as more adult. The number of decisions they make by themselves increases with age from early to late adolescence, whereas those shared with parents or made by parents alone decrease with age. These trends are more pronounced for males than females (Dornbusch, Ritter, Mont-Reynaud, & Chen, 1990).

Bids for greater autonomy might be expected to occasion some conflict with parents, and they do. Most conflicts are over household routines, such as picking up after oneself, doing homework, and chores. And most of these involve mothers, because they are more immediately involved in maintaining the household than are fathers (Steinberg, 1987, 1989). Parenting style, especially that of mothers, is particularly important for girls' autonomy. For boys, age is the single most important determinant of increasing independence (Bartle, Anderson, & Sabatelli, 1989).

Autonomy is a much larger issue for younger adolescents than for older ones. Arehart and Smith (1990) found that concern with questions of autonomy

autonomy Being independent and responsible for one's actions.

accounted for nearly half of the variability among early adolescents' answers to a measure of psychosocial maturity. By the end of high school, autonomy issues have been resolved and new issues appear.

Parents can either facilitate or hinder the growth of autonomy (Pardeck & Pardeck, 1990). As adolescents vie for a say in and eventual control over the decisions that affect them, some conflict with parents may be inevitable. Not all parents react in similar ways to these demands. Some are able to turn over increasing responsibility to their children; others, threatened by bids for greater autonomy, react negatively. See the Research Focus, "Nonprobability Sampling: Adolescent-Parent Conflict." The less conflict in the family, the greater the adolescent's movement toward psychosocial maturity (Gavazzi & Sabatelli, 1990). Not all of the difficulty comes from parents. Adolescents contribute their share as well.

Individuation: The Developmental Process

In order to achieve autonomy, adolescents must go through a psychic house-cleaning known as individuation. They must undo one of their major accomplishments as children; they must disassemble and rebuild the psychological structure they have lived in through childhood. They do this by examining their feelings, attitudes, and beliefs, in order to discover which are really theirs and which are their parents'. Because children uncritically assume for themselves their parents' attitudes and ways, this examination process is a necessary step for early adolescents. It may be that the only way children can feel strong enough to step out on their own and explore the world for themselves is to carry some of their parents' strengths along with them. However, the very internalizations that promote autonomy in childhood are the ones that adolescents must get beyond in order to grow, and this process is termed **individuation** (Josselson, 1980, 1988).

Adolescents accomplish this growth in ordinary ways—by making decisions for themselves and by living with the consequences of these decisions. The major decision all adolescents face is who is going to make the decisions, but because decisions take many different forms, this point is easily missed. Adolescents find themselves arguing about who they can go out with, how tight is too tight for jeans, how late they can stay up, when they do their homework, or who gets to say what courses they can take in school. Much of the process is repetitive. Decisions made one day must be renegotiated the next, as the same issues continue to come up in different forms.

Perhaps the process is repetitive because it involves learning in a real-life situation instead of in a classroom. In the classroom, principles are stated explicitly, frequently apart from any context, and adolescents must relate these principles to real-life situations. Just the opposite occurs when learning outside the classroom. Outside their classes, adolescents learn by doing and by experiencing the consequences. No one is there to help identify which principles operate in that situation. As a result, it is often difficult to separate the elements that remain constant across situations from the situations themselves. Are adolescents really arguing about how loud their music can be or about who gets to decide how loud is too loud?

There is another reason why adolescents tend to repeat the decision-making process. Frequently what they learn from their decisions has very personal consequences, which they may not be ready to accept. Discovering how to solve an algebraic equation has little bearing on life outside math class; algebra is "safe" knowledge. But discovering that you are the only one who can make decisions

What positive function do arguments with parents serve in adolescence?

individuation The process of distinguishing one's attitudes and beliefs from those of one's parents.

Nonprobability Sampling: Adolescent-Parent Conflict

When conflict arises between parents and adolescents, it's usually not over the big things in life, but over the little ones, such as whether chores have been done or the music is too loud. One might think, as a result, that such disagreements are of little consequence to adolescents or their parents, creating only momentary "blips" on the big screen of life. But such is far from the case. Developmentalists regard such squabbles as significant for several reasons. If for no other reason, they would be of interest because they are a natural part of everyday intimate relationships. Perhaps of even greater interest, however, is the developmental significance they hold. These minor skirmishes appear to be responsible for "democratizing" adolescent-parent relationships, changing these from the unilateral relationships that characterize childhood to the more egalitarian ones of late adolescence as adolescents push for greater autonomy.

When parents have been asked how they interpret such conflicts, they tend to regard them as conventional matters and see themselves as enforcing agreed-on norms. Adolescents are more likely to see these conflicts as ways of widening their jurisdiction over what they regard to be personal matters. Thus, what an adolescent chooses to wear to a family gathering (let's say she has chosen to wear jeans "stylishly" torn at the knee and cuff and a top that leaves her midriff bare) may be seen by her mother as a violation of all the conventions of dress and decorum that she holds dear, whereas to the adolescent, it may be seen simply as a personal fashion choice that is her prerogative to make (Smetana & Asquith 1994).

Most of the research on such conflicts has studied middle-class, European American families. We know relatively little, however, as to whether this research is representative of conflict among minority adolescents and their parents. It may be, for instance, that the value placed on family harmony and respect of elders, as in African American and Asian American cultures, may minimize or postpone struggles for autonomy among adolescents from these cultural backgrounds.

Judith Smetana and Cheryl Gaines (1999) examined such conflicts between African American pre- and early adolescents and their parents by using a within-ethnic-group design in which all participants were African American. In order to obtain sufficient numbers of African American adolescents and their parents, these investigators used haphazard sampling to constitute their sample. This particular approach to sampling, also known as convenience sampling, obtains participants from wherever they can be found, rather than attempting to draw them at random from a defined population. Smetana and Gaines recruited their participants from African American churches and social organizations, and they also asked those who had already participated for the names of other African American families they knew.

Haphazard sampling is a form of *nonprobability sampling*, a sampling procedure commonly used in psychological research. In nonprobability sampling, the probability of any member of the population being drawn is not known. In probability sampling, in contrast, each member of the population has the same chance of being drawn as any other member, thus the larger the sample, the more it can be assumed to resemble the population from which it was drawn (Cozby, 1997).

When one wants to make statements about, or describe, the population from which a sample has been drawn, it is important to use probability sampling. However, when one is primarily interested in discovering the relationships among the variables in a research study, nonprobability sampling is most typically used. Most psychological research is based on nonprobability sampling procedures. The majority of participants in psychological research, for instance, are students in introductory psychology classes, a most convenient sample for university-based research. Similarly, if one is interested in a particular group of individuals, such as African American families, it is more efficient, in terms of time and cost, to obtain research participants by contacting social groups and organizations to which they are likely to belong, than by attempting to randomly sample individuals of that background from the general population.

What did these investigators find? Conflicts occurred relatively frequently and were typically mild, just as with European American adolescents and parents. Similarly, African American parents and adolescents were found to justify their positions in ways similar to those found for European American parents and adolescents. Parents tended to justify themselves by referring to conventional issues, such as those defined by role relationships, shared expectations, and group norms. Adolescents tended to justify their side of the argument by reasoning that these were matters of personal choice. Thus, in a disagreement over keeping one's room clean, a parent might say, "I think it's important for him to see that everybody participates in the household tasks. Because if he didn't have to do it, somebody else has to, and generally it's me." The adolescent, though likely to agree that it is important for everyone to help out around the house, is equally likely to claim that his room is his own personal space and that no one need clean it but himself. Thus, disagreements between African American adolescents and parents appear to reflect the same developmental processes as those for European American adolescents. When it comes to disagreeing with one's parents, some things don't vary that much.

for yourself, and that there is no one to blame or praise but yourself, is something else again. Understanding is rarely just an intellectual matter; it also reflects one's emotions and beliefs, and some things can be understood only when one is prepared to let go of old beliefs. Sometimes adolescents, or adults for that matter, cannot allow themselves to understand until they can live with the consequences of that understanding. They may prefer to live with isolated actions, not seeing how one fits with another to form a larger picture (M. L. Wapner, 1980, personal communication).

Even though the daily decisions adolescents make often seem trivial, the process itself never is; it is a way of separating themselves as individuals. The process is also frequently lonely. Rejecting parental attitudes and values can often leave adolescents with an empty feeling; they've discarded old ways before developing new ones of their own. Ruthellen Josselson (1980) suggests that emotions help adolescents with this transition. The very intensity of their emotions lets them know there is still someone inside. This function may account for some of the emotional intensity of early adolescence. Older adolescents have become surer of their decisions, and much of the earlier emotional overkill drops out. By late adolescence most have disentangled their needs and ideas from those of their parents and have a sense of being in charge of their lives. They no longer need emotion to fill a psychic void or to convince themselves, or others, that they are in control.

Throughout the individuation process, adolescents attempt to preserve a sense of sameness of their inner selves and of what they mean to others. The identities that emerge must be continuous with their past and also allow them to project themselves into the future. Adolescents who successfully sort through their own and their parents' attitudes and beliefs can maintain a comfortable closeness with their parents, without fearing a loss of their own individuality. This closeness is an important source of continuity in their lives. Adolescents do not need to discard old relationships or adopt completely new lifestyles in order to be their own person (Mazor & Enright, 1988). Individuation involves both a growing independence from parents, such as in managing daily events or needing less support, and positive feelings about one's independence. The latter, at least for late adolescents, appears to be a better index of individuation than the more concrete changes, as it can predict such things as easier adjustment to college (Rice, Cole, & Lapsley, 1990).

The conditions that foster healthy development at one age within the life span should be similar to those promoting development at other ages as well. This appears to be true with respect to the conditions that promote individuation. Adolescents whose parents are emotionally open and supportive are those who feel free to explore life possibilities. Similarly, Ainsworth (1973, 1993) found that infants whose caregivers are sensitive and responsive are more curious and more likely to explore their surroundings. Individuation, like attachment, reflects a healthy balance between a growing independence and continued closeness with parents. To the extent this balance is maintained, adolescents are able to assume increasing responsibility for their own individuality without fearing that doing so will distance them from their parents.

When adolescents' own need for emotional closeness threatens their independence or when their need for autonomy hampers emotional closeness with parents, healthy development should be affected. Ernest Hodges, Regina Finnegan, and David Perry (1999) found that early adolescents' relationships with parents that reflected both connectedness and independence predicted healthier patterns of adjustment over time than those in which these relationships were skewed.

Individuation is the process of distin-guishing one's own attitudes and beliefs from those of one's parents. Adolescents who successfully complete this process can maintain a comfort-able closeness with their parents and not fear they will lose their newly fledged identity.

Family Interaction and Adolescents' Individuation

Harold Grotevant and Catherine Cooper (1986), developmentalists at the University of Minnesota and the University of California, Santa Cruz, identified dimensions of family interaction that contribute to the development of individuation. They used a deceptively simple approach to study family interactions: They asked families to make plans for an imaginary vacation, and analyzed the communication patterns that developed within the family. They looked for patterns that evidenced two qualities they believed to be critical for the development of individuation: individuality and connectedness. **Individuality** is the ability to have and express one's own ideas (*self-assertion*) and to say how one differs from others (*separateness*). **Connectedness** reflects one's openness to others' opinions (*permeability*) and one's respect for their ideas (*mutuality*). These investigators looked for statements that illustrate each of these four factors.

Adolescents in an individuated relationship have a clear sense of themselves as distinct from other people yet feel emotionally connected with them. They have their own ideas, which they can express, and are open to the ideas of the person they are with. In a sense, individuation allows them to respect each person as an individual—including themselves. Equally important, individuated relationships allow adolescents to experience their connectedness with another person and still see how they are different. Research on individuation suggests that adolescents who achieve high levels of individuation can remain close to their parents without feeling a loss of their own distinctiveness. The research also supports the view that parent-adolescent relationships continue to be close as they move toward greater mutuality (Mazor & Enright, 1988; White, Speisman, & Costos, 1983).

Adolescents do not have to have an individuated relationship with both parents. A single relationship in which there are moderate to high degrees of separateness and permeability makes individuation possible. Adolescents who achieve the highest levels of individuation, however, are likely to come from families in

individuality A quality of family interactions thought to be important for individuation, reflecting the ability to express one's ideas and say how one differs from others.

connectedness A quality of family interactions thought to be important for individuation; it reflects openness to and respect for others' opinions.

which members delight in examining their differences yet experience connectedness with each other.

Adolescents low in individuation typically have families who avoid disagreeing with each other and are so responsive to others' opinions that they cannot form a differing opinion of their own. Families with few disagreements communicate one important message to their members: that it is important to agree. Adolescents from these families must express the family point of view in order to voice anything at all. Doing so reassures others that they agree with them. As an extreme example, when the mother in one family asked where they should go on their vacation, each member responded by repeating the father's suggestion of going back to Spain. When asked for more suggestions by her father, the adolescent daughter could not elaborate and fumbled an "I don't know," indicating her father should offer more suggestions. It was hard for this adolescent to explore issues outside her family's belief system, even when these only involved choices for an imaginary family vacation (Grotevant & Cooper, 1986). Adolescents who can experience their separateness from other members of the family are freer to develop their own point of view. Even so, their explorations take place in an emotional context of connectedness, which provides the security that allows them to examine ideas.

To develop a point of view, adolescents must be able to see how their ideas differ from those of others. Interactions that focus on differences and similarities provide important developmental experiences; they can also involve conflict. Conflict itself isn't necessarily bad. In the context of clarifying a position, it can help adolescents gain a sense of what they believe. For adolescents to have their ideas challenged without experiencing this as criticism, a supportive family atmosphere is important (Powers, Hauser, Schwartz, Noam, & Jacobson, 1983; Shulman, Seiffge-Krenke, & Samat, 1987). In fact, adolescents' experience of support is generally unrelated to conflicts with parents (Barrera, Chassin, & Rogosch, 1993).

> What characteristics of family interactions are related to the development of individuation?

Identity: The Normative Crisis of Adolescence

Perhaps no term is more closely associated with the writing and thinking of Erik Erikson (see Chapter 1) than *identity*. Erikson was, above all else, a clinician whose concepts reflected real-life experiences. In writing about the personality, Erikson noted that "old troubles" return when we are tired or otherwise defenseless, simply because we are what we *were* as well as what we might want to become or presently may be (Coles, 1970; Erikson, 1954).

Erikson believed that, like his patients, adolescents have to confront "old troubles" in arriving at an identity. Consider Erikson's (1968) description of Jill, a young woman he knew:

> I had known Jill before her puberty, when she was rather obese and showed many "oral" traits of voracity and dependency while she also was a tomboy and bitterly envious of her brothers and in rivalry with them. But she was intelligent and always had an air about her (as did her mother) which seemed to promise that things would turn out all right. And, indeed, she straightened out and up, became very attractive, an easy leader in any group, and, to many, a model of young girlhood. As a clinician, I watched and wondered what she would do with that voraciousness and with the rivalry which she had displayed earlier. Could it be that such things are simply absorbed in fortuitous growth?

Identity is built out of the continuity of experience over time. This teen's love of animals has prompted her to volunteer at a veterinary clinic to help her decide if she wants to study veterinary medicine.

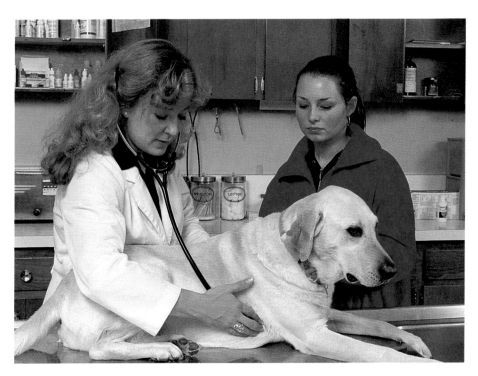

Then one autumn in her late teens, Jill did not return to college from the ranch out West where she had spent the summer. She had asked her parents to let her stay. Simply out of liberality and confidence, they granted her this moratorium and returned East.

That winter Jill specialized in taking care of newborn colts, and would get up at any time during a winter night to bottle-feed the most needy animals. Having apparently acquired a certain satisfaction within herself, as well as astonished recognition from the cowboys, she returned home and reassumed her place. I felt that she had found and hung on to an opportunity to do actively and for others what she had once demonstrated by overeating: she had learned to feed needy young mouths. But she did so in a context which, in turning passive into active, also turned a former symptom into a social act.

One might say that she turned "maternal" but it was a maternalism such as cowboys must and do display; and, of course, she did it all in jeans. This brought recognition "from man to man" as well as from man to woman, and beyond that the confirmation of her optimism, that is, her feeling that something could be done that felt like her, was useful and worthwhile, and was in line with an ideological trend where it still made immediate practical sense. (pp. 130–131) ◄

Jill fashioned her identity, as Erikson said we all do, out of old cloth, but she tailored it to the needs of the present. She translated what she *was*—an energetic, intelligent, but envious and dependent child—into a mature personality, capable of responding to her own and others' needs.

Identity Defined

Identity, as Erikson used the term, refers to the sense of self that we achieve through examining and committing ourselves to the roles and pursuits that define

One signal of an adolescent's developing sense of self is involvement in a cause—whether against governmental action or for the preservation of an endangered species. Ideology, or commitment to principle, is the name Erik Erikson gave to this domain of identity formation.

an adult in our society. Identity gives us a sense of who we are, of knowing what is "me" and what is "not me." As Jill's story demonstrated, the "me" includes more than the present. Identity allows us to experience a continuity of self over time. We can relate what we have done in the past to what we hope to do in the future, to our ambitions and dreams. Finally, our perception of self includes how others see us, the importance they attach to our values and accomplishments (Patterson, Sochting, & Marcia, 1992).

> How did Erikson think of the concept of identity?

Jill's story illustrates these aspects of identity. Her new maturity grew out of familiar issues, her "old troubles," that she approached in new ways. Because the "me" that she had been as a child was still recognizable in her more adult concerns, there was a continuity to her experience over time. Lastly, her perception of herself, her confidence and self-esteem, resulted not only from becoming skilled in something she valued, but also from receiving the recognition of the society in which she achieved this, the cowboys she had worked with.

In defining identity, Erikson considered three domains to be of paramount importance: sexuality as expressed in an adult gender role; occupation; and ideology, or religious and political beliefs.

The Process of Identity Consolidation   Prior to adolescence, children's identities reflect a simple **identification** with parents: They uncritically take on the behaviors and ways of their mothers and fathers. Adolescents move beyond the identity organizations they had as children by synthesizing elements of their earlier identity into a new whole, one that bears the personal stamp of their own interests, values, and choices. This process is termed **identity formation,** and involves individuation. Individuation gives adolescents a set of attitudes and ways of acting that are genuinely their own; however, they must still put these together into a working whole that reflects an inner sense of self. Although the process begins in early adolescence, adolescents do not consolidate these changes until late adolescence or even early adulthood when choices about jobs, college, and relationships force identity issues to a head. Identity, for Erikson, derives from, as well as

identification A child's uncritical incorporation of parental ways and beliefs.

identity formation In adolescence, a synthesizing of elements of one's earlier identity into a new whole; involves individuation.

directs, the adolescent's commitment to occupational, religious, political, and gender roles and values.

Adolescents who achieve a personal identity appreciate their uniqueness even while realizing all they have in common with others. Experience in making decisions for themselves has given them feedback about their strong and weak points, and they are less dependent on others' judgments in evaluating themselves. They can also become intimate with others without fear of blurring their personal boundaries.

Variations on a Theme of Identity

Although Erikson was the first to describe and elaborate the concept of identity as a normative crisis in adolescence, James Marcia has been largely responsible for generating research on identity formation, primarily by constructing a measure of ego identity, which has made it possible to empirically test many implications of Erikson's writings.

Identity Statuses   Most of the work we do on our identity takes place in adolescence. However, as Marcia notes with a touch of humor, if identity formation were necessary by the end of adolescence, many of us would never become adults. His point is that achieving a personal identity is not an easy process. Adolescents must be willing to take risks and live with uncertainty.

Some of the uncertainty comes from exploring possibilities and options in life that differ from those chosen by one's parents. Most adolescents expect this exploration to be risky. Few adolescents, however, expect the risks that occur when they must make commitments based on their exploration. Adolescents form their identities both by taking on new ways of being *and* by excluding others. It is every bit as important to commit themselves to a definite course of action and let go of their fantasies as it is to challenge the familiar by exploring possibilities never even considered by their parents or families. Marcia (1980) refers to these two dimensions of the identity process as exploration and commitment.

Marcia distinguishes four ways by which adolescents arrive at the roles and values that define their identities. Each of these ways, or identity statuses, is defined in terms of the dimensions of commitment and exploration. Adolescents who are committed to life options arrive at them either by exploring and searching for what fits them best or by forgoing exploration and letting themselves be guided by their parents' values. The first alternative results in the ego reorganization that Erikson characterized as identity formation; the second leaves parental identifications unchallenged and unchanged. Adolescents who have searched for life options that fit them best are termed **identity achieved;** those who adopt their parents' values without question are termed **identity foreclosed** (Kroger, 1996; Marcia, 1980).

Similarly, two paths lead to noncommitment. Some adolescents begin to evaluate life options but don't close off certain possibilities because the decisions seem too momentous to risk making a mistake; as a result, they remain uncommitted to any path. These adolescents are in **moratorium.** Others remain uncommitted for the opposite reason: failure to see the importance of choosing one option over any other. They are termed **identity diffused.** Even though adolescents in moratorium begin to question parental ways, like foreclosed adolescents they ultimately do not challenge parental identifications: They can't risk making a wrong choice. Identity-diffused adolescents fail to challenge earlier identifications because they lack the sense of urgency that would prompt them to make decisions that would distinguish them as individuals.

What two processes does James Marcia regard as responsible for distinguishing differences among identity statuses?

identity achievement The resolution of conflict over identity through the personal formulation of adult gender roles, occupational goals, and religious and political commitments.

identity foreclosure A resolution of the problem of identity through the assumption of traditional, conventional, or parentally chosen goals and values without the experience of crisis or conflict concerning identity issues.

moratorium The experience of conflict over the issues of identity formation prior to the establishment of firm goals and long-term commitments.

identity diffusion A failure to develop a strong sense of self coupled with a failure to experience much discomfort or conflict over the issues of identity resolution.

Most, if not all, of these football players probably dream of sports scholarships or even going pro. But, as they go through the process of identity formation, they will gradually let go of such fantasies and commit themselves to more realistic futures.

Adolescents who open themselves to new possibilities, whether personal beliefs or vocational options, tend to be more tolerant of individual differences and allow others the same freedom for self-definition. Conversely, foreclosed adolescents, who fail to question their lifestyles or to explore religious beliefs or career options, tend to be more authoritarian, living by the rules and believing that others should too. They hold up the conventional standards they apply to themselves to others.

The process of reorganizing earlier identifications continues into late adolescence—and beyond. Sally Archer (1989a, 1989b) found that among the adolescents she interviewed, relatively few were in either the moratorium or identity-achieved status by the twelfth grade. Self-definition in areas of occupational choice, religious and political beliefs, and gender roles continues into early adulthood (Kroger, 1988).

Given that we expect adolescents to become more mature with age, to do things such as think for themselves and plan for the future, there is an implicit developmental trend in these statuses. In both moratorium and identity achievement, for instance, adolescents can be seen to engage in thoughtful decision making concerning the direction their lives might take. Identity-achieved adolescents, in addition, pursue their plans, allowing themselves to be defined by their choices. In contrast, there is little evidence of reflective decision making in the foreclosure and diffusion statuses. Although foreclosed adolescents are committed to the goals and beliefs they are pursuing, these do not result from personal exploration, but from holding tight to what they have received from others. Finally,

James Marcia's theory of identity statuses suggests that some of these young men are considering a military career because of a family military tradition, that others are motivated by a personal commitment to serve their country, and that still others see military service as a way to postpone deciding what they ultimately want to do with their life.

identity-diffused adolescents neither explore nor commit themselves to roles that will define them as adults.

Jane Kroger (1996; Kroger & Greene, 1996), at the University of Tromso in Norway, points out that a certain amount of movement from one status to another is to be expected. This movement is not always in the "developmentally correct" direction, however. Developmentalists use the term **regression** to refer to movement from a more complex, differentiated state to one that is less so, a move that decreases the adaptiveness of behavior. Kroger (1996) distinguishes several forms of regression with respect to identity statuses. *Regression of disequilibrium* can occur when the way in which an adolescent has made sense of the world is challenged, such as by one's experiences at college or by entering a new situation where new rules apply. This type of regression is a healthy regrouping, one that is most likely to take place in adolescents who are open to their experiences and can tolerate a certain amount of uncertainty. In contrast to this relatively adaptive response to conflict, *regression of rigidification* is a closing off or narrowing of one's perspectives after having begun to explore options. Not only do personality variables, such as a tolerance for ambiguity, influence the form regression can take in the face of conflict, but so do the options that are realistically available to adolescents. A young girl growing up in a small town in which the only women she knows are her mother, her aunt, several teachers, a beautician, and the clerk at the market may dream of going off to college and becoming a social worker, but she may not be able to hold on to her vision, or even be sure that she wants to (Nurmi, Poole, & Kalakoski, 1996).

Even within a status, not all adolescents appear to have addressed the individuation process in similar ways. For instance, although a commitment to life-defining pursuits or values is absent in identity-diffused adolescents, some adolescents ("true diffusions") will remain uncommitted, whereas others ("passive

regression Movement from a more complex, differentiated state to one that is less so, with decreases in the adaptiveness of behavior.

moratoriums") appear likely to enter a period of exploration. Kroger (1995) has suggested that a distinction can be made within the foreclosure status as well, with individuals differing in their openness to change. Those who are willing to accept new challenges, "developmental" foreclosures, eventually move into the moratorium status, and those who are closed, "firm" foreclosures, remain as foreclosures. Kroger, in a 2-year longitudinal study, looked for personality differences underlying these two approaches, specifically in adolescents' willingness to experience the anxiety that accompanies the separation from internalized parental figures, underlying personal growth. As anticipated, a greater need for nurturance and security when initially interviewed predicted that "firm" foreclosures would remain in that identity status.

Do adolescents simultaneously address identity issues in each of the different domains? That is, do they consider occupational, ideological, and sexual alternatives at the same point in time? Or do different domains become salient at different points in an adolescent's life (Archer, 1989a)? Can a 17-year-old male be identity-achieved in his occupational plans ("I'll work in construction with my uncle"), but foreclosed in his gender role ("I want my wife to stay home with the kids the way Mom did"), diffused in his political beliefs ("I don't see the point in getting too worked up over political issues; after all, what can one person do?"), and in moratorium about his religious beliefs ("I don't think of God the way I did as a kid, but I can't dismiss the idea that God is interested in me personally")?

In a 2-year follow-up study of late adolescents, Jane Kroger (1988) found that only half the adolescents she studied had a common status in any two domains; another 9% had no domains in common. These data suggest that identity is not "a unitary structure, but . . . a sequence of distinct psychosocial resolutions involved in the definition of self" (p. 60). Kroger's findings are comparable to those of other investigators in suggesting that adolescents do not work simultaneously on all identity domains (Archer, 1989a; Kroger, 1986; Rogow, Marcia, & Slugowski, 1983).

Identity: Gender and Ethnicity

Adolescents find answers to the question "Who am I?" by examining the societal roles they see around them, roles they will soon assume. Erikson considered the most central of these roles to be that of a future occupation. Following close on the heels of this decision come decisions about political and religious beliefs, and the expression of an adult gender role (Erikson, 1968).

Gender Differences in Identity Formation

Occupation, political stance, and ideology—all of these characterized males more than females at the time Erikson formulated his concept of identity. Thirty years ago, relatively few females wrestled with issues of occupation and ideology. *Was Erikson writing primarily about males? If so, how did he think females formulated an identity?*

Erikson did, in fact, believe that the process of identity formulation differed for males and females—in content, timing, and sequence (Patterson, Sochting, & Marcia, 1992). With respect to the content of identity, he considered interpersonal issues, rather than vocational and ideological ones, to be central for females. He also thought the timing of identity resolution is different for males and females, with females keeping their identity options partially open, rather than resolving them as males do, so that they might better complement a potential mate. Erikson also believed that females resolve identity and intimacy issues more or less concurrently, whereas males resolve these issues sequentially (Patterson, Sochting, & Marcia, 1992).

Why would male and female adolescents go about so fundamental a process in different ways? In partial answer, Erikson (1968) referred to a "profound difference . . . between the sexes in the experience of the ground plan of the human body" that "predisposes" adolescent males and females to work out their identities in different ways. He believed that women find "their identities in the care suggested in their bodies and in the needs of their issue, and seem to have taken it for granted that the outer world space belongs to the men" (p. 274). According to Erikson, males achieve their identities by exploring this outer world and finding pursuits and beliefs to which they can commit themselves—an occupation and an ideology.

Erikson (1968) asserted that a female finds her identity "whatever her work career" when she "commits herself to the love of a stranger and to the care to be given to his and her offspring" (p. 265). When asked by young women whether they can attain an identity before they marry, Erikson answered that "much of a young woman's identity is already defined in her kind of attractiveness and in the selective nature of her search for the man (or men) by whom she wishes to be sought" (p. 283). He argued that she may postpone identity closure with education or a career, but that "womanhood arrives when attractiveness and experience have succeeded in selecting what is to be admitted to the welcome of the inner space 'for keeps'" (p. 283).

Was Erikson right? Do sex differences such as the "ground plan of the human body"—for example, a female's sense of "inner space" (the womb)—primarily shape the process by which one achieves an identity? Do we see the same pattern of concerns and commitments among adolescents today as Erikson saw a generation ago? A number of studies supply us with answers to these questions.

Research on Gender Differences   Early research on Marcia's identity statuses found differences in the adaptiveness of different statuses for either sex (Bourne, 1978a, 1978b; Marcia, 1980). Later research, however, found few differences among male and female adolescents in identity development. In three separate studies, Sally Archer (1989a) interviewed nearly 300 adolescents in the sixth, eighth, tenth, and twelfth grades, using a semistructured interview similar to the one developed by Marcia. With few exceptions, she found equivalent numbers of males and females in each of the identity statuses. When gender differences occurred, males were more likely than females to be in the foreclosure status.

Was Erikson right in assuming that the content of identity differs for males and females? Archer (1989a) examined whether different content domains have greater salience for adolescents of one sex than the other by looking separately at vocational choice, religious beliefs, political ideologies, and gender roles. Few differences appeared within any of the domains. When they did, males were more likely to be foreclosed and females to be diffused in their political beliefs, and females were more likely than males to be identity achieved or in moratorium concerning family roles. Overall, Archer (1989) concluded from her research that

> the minimal finding of gender differences in the processes, domains, or timing of identity activity in these three studies suggests that the traditional theoretical assumptions . . . should be discarded, or at least reconsidered. . . . Taken together the findings from these studies . . . suggest a similar epigenetic underpinning to the formative period of identity development for males and females. (p. 136)

For some young people, travel is a way to learn more about themselves and the world. For others, however, it is a way to put off making life decisions.

Do females keep identity options partially open, as Erikson suggested, resulting in differences in the timing of development? The answer to this question is yes—and no. That is, at least two courses appear to be open to females when it comes to resolving identity issues. One involves a process of self-searching and introspection and is typical of females with continuous careers. It is, in other words, the same process followed by Marcia's identity-achieved and moratorium individuals. The other is the more traditional course described by Erikson, in which females define themselves interpersonally through their husbands and children, gaining a sense of their importance and value largely through their relations with others.

O'Connell (1976) distinguishes the first of these two courses as personal identity and the second as reflected identity. Females who pursue personal identities undergo the most progress in identity development in late adolescence, as do most males. In other words, they do not differ in the timing of their development. Females with reflected identities, however, describe themselves in terms of relational roles until their children start school, and only then begin to develop a personal identity. Contrary to Erikson's assumptions then, a woman's identity does not await confirmation by having children. Instead, having to care for young children appears to require women to postpone work on their personal identity (Patterson, Sochting, & Marcia, 1992).

The sequencing of identity formation appears to be more stepwise for males, with identity serving as a foundation for later intimate relationships. For females, issues of intimacy and identity are more apt to be resolved concurrently (Patterson, Sochting, & Marcia, 1992). Research by Ruthellen Josselson (1988, 1992), based on narrative accounts of women's lives, reveals the importance that relationships have in giving women a sense of themselves. Josselson's interviews indicate that, rather than defining their identities primarily in terms of individual goals and principles, women also include issues of relatedness and responsibility to others. On the basis of this research, Serena Patterson, Ingrid Sochting, and James Marcia

(1992) suggest that, in addition to exploration and commitment, a third dimension, relatedness, is important in defining identity statuses for females.

Is this suggestion contrary to Archer's conclusion that the process of identity formation is more similar than different between adolescents of either sex? Archer (1992) offers a tentative resolution to this apparent contradiction. She points to a remarkable tunnel vision that she noticed in her interviews with adolescents when it came to seeing the implications that commitments in one domain have for another domain. For instance, an adolescent boy might describe his vocational plans in detail as well as his plans for marriage and children, and yet not connect the two. Thus, potential conflicts, such as who would care for the children if his wife also chose a career or whose career would determine where they would live, simply are not anticipated. Those interviewed by Archer who were most likely to make connections between domains were late adolescent females. A sense of relatedness for females, an awareness of themselves in relation to others, may prompt them to integrate identity domains.

Relatedness may also play a more central role in defining the process of exploration in females than in males. For example, a sense of relatedness may cause females to give greater thought to the implications of adopting one lifestyle over another or of setting aside traditional beliefs, each of which would be a potential outcome of exploration. Mary Belenky and her associates, for instance, cite the concern of young college women that, by taking an intellectual stand, they might isolate themselves from others (Belenky, Clinchy, Goldberger, & Tarule, 1986). The very decision to go to college or pursue a career is, for some women, a repudiation of their family's ways, especially for minority females from traditional backgrounds.

In such cases, relationship implications set limits to exploration. However, it is equally possible that the limits may prompt more creative approaches to identity formation given the greater complexities that they introduce to the task for females (Archer, 1985). Patterson, Sochting, and Marcia (1992), in summarizing the findings of Archer and others on this point, note that females face a need to balance competing occupational and interpersonal commitments, involving them in "meta-decisions" across domains. In contrast, males can resolve these more easily as separate issues than females can.

Taken together, the research on gender differences reveals that the *process* of identity formation is comparable for adolescents of either sex. Adolescents who allow themselves to question, explore, and experience the uncertainty of not knowing—to experience a period of crisis—mature in this process. However, the particular content that adolescents address in finding their own way can differ for either gender. Thus similarities in process do not rule out other gender differences.

Contributions of Ethnicity to Identity Development

Because our sense of self reflects an awareness of how others see us, cultural values as well as individual experiences contribute to the development of identity. What happens when the larger society fails to validate these sources of identity? Thirty years ago, Erikson (1968) noted that minorities whose groups are devalued by society risk internalizing the negative views of society and can develop negative identities.

Only relatively recently have social scientists begun to systematically examine the psychological implications of ethnicity and minority status as these contribute to an **ethnic identity** (Phinney, 1990, 1996). Yet the developments that underlie an identity search in majority adolescents are likely to contribute to an awareness of one's ethnicity in minority adolescents. Social networks widen in

ethnic identity An awareness of belonging to an ethnic group that shapes one's thoughts, feelings, and behavior.

adolescence, frequently including those from other backgrounds. Intellectual capacities develop, making it possible to view the self from a third-person perspective, heightening one's sense of self. Broader intellectual horizons make it likely that adolescents will recognize the existence of racial and ethnic overtones in local and national issues. All of these factors argue for ethnicity's being a salient factor in adolescent identity development.

The boundaries that define one's group provide members with a feeling of belonging. When boundaries are clear, they allow adolescents to distinguish between their own and other groups and result in stronger ethnic identity. Some boundaries are maintained from within by the group; others are imposed on the group by the dominant culture. Internal boundaries come about through identifying with others in one's group. Adolescents adopt the values, attitudes, and perspectives of their group. Interactions with those outside the group provide a second type of boundary, through which minority adolescents experience the social opportunities and constraints that exist for members of their group—the relative status and value given them by others. The status of one's group within society is an important component of ethnic identity (Phinney, 1996).

Adolescents' consciousness of their ethnic identity varies with the situations they are in. Rosenthal and Hrynevich (1985) found that adolescents experience a strong ethnic identity when they are with their family or speaking their parents' native language, but feel part of the dominant culture when with others from that culture, such as when they are at school. They also found that the strength of the inner boundary of the ethnic group relates to adolescents' pride in their ethnic identity. Their measure of this strength was the institutional completeness of the community, the extent to which it provides its own schools, markets, churches, and other institutions. This finding may explain why African Americans in segregated schools frequently have higher self-esteem than those in integrated schools (Powell, 1985).

In the process of acculturation, external behaviors of minority adolescents frequently become less distinct from those of the majority culture, whereas attitudes and values remain unchanged. Doreen Rosenthal and Shirley Feldman (1992) suggest that some components of ethnic identity may be more resistant to change than others because they are more central. Minority adolescents whose behavior closely resembles that of peers from the dominant culture might still have strong ethnic identities in other respects.

These investigators compared first- and second-generation Chinese American and Chinese Australian adolescents on several measures of ethnic identity. As expected, they found that, despite differences in knowledge about their culture and in observable behavior between first- and second-generation minorities, the core aspects to their ethnic identities differed little; both first- and second-generation adolescents ascribed the same importance to their ethnic group membership and evaluated their ethnicity equally positively.

William Cross, at Cornell University, distinguishes several steps to the process of forming an ethnic identity. In the *pre-encounter* stage, individuals identify with the dominant culture. They notice differences between themselves and the dominant culture but do not consider them important. The second stage of identity formation, which happens only for minority adolescents, is the *encounter*. Cross traces the emergence of this stage to one or more vivid incidents in which adolescents experience discrimination. These experiences precipitate an awareness of membership in their ethnic group. This stage is a turning point in the development of an ethnic identity in which minority adolescents turn from the ways and values of the dominant culture and take on those of their ethnic group (Cross, 1980, 1987).

In the third stage of ethnic identity formation, adolescents immerse themselves in the ways of their ethnic or racial group. Here, three young Native Americans prepare to participate in a pow-wow.

In the stage that follows, which Cross called the *immersion* stage, adolescents immerse themselves in the ways of their ethnic group, developing a high degree of awareness and valuation of those ways, along with a devaluation of those of the dominant culture. This stage is frequently characterized by social activism or even militancy. Finally, in the *internalization* stage, adolescents become able to appreciate themselves and others as individuals and to recognize differences that don't always correspond to group membership. Attitudes toward others reflect personal characteristics rather than group membership, as in the previous stage. Ethnic identity is less strident, and attitudes toward the dominant culture are less negative (Cross, 1980, 1987). Deborah Plummer (1995, 1996), at Cleveland State University, assessed racial identity attitudes among African American adolescents and found that 14 to 18-year-olds largely endorsed internalization attitudes, having healthy racial identities.

This progression parallels a number of other developmental progressions in which development moves from a focus on the self to a focus on the group, to respect for the individual (Aboud, 1987).

Do minority adolescents first internalize the values of the dominant culture and then question these values as they experience their implications before they adopt the values of the minority culture? For ethnic identity—just as for identity achievement in general—a crisis in which one questions the values one had previously accepted may be central to further development. Gordon Parks (1990), an African American photographer, describes such an incident from his boyhood:

I was only 12 when [a] cousin of mine, Princetta Maxwell, a fair girl with light red hair, came from Kansas City to spend the summer at our house. One day she and I ran, hand in hand, toward the white section of town to meet my mother, who worked there as a domestic. Suddenly three white boys blocked our path. I gripped my cousin's hand and we tried going around them, but they spread out before us.

"Where you going with that nigger, blondie?" one snarled to my cousin.

We stopped. The youngest one eased behind me and dropped to his hands and knees, and the other two shoved me backward. Pain shot through my head as it bumped against the sidewalk, and I could hear Princetta screaming as she ran back toward home for help. I caught spit in my face and a kick in the neck. I jumped up and started swinging, only to be beaten down again. Then came a kick in the mouth. Grabbing a foot, I upended its owner, scrambled up and started swinging again. Then suddenly there was help—from another white boy. Waldo Wade was in there swinging his fists alongside mine. The three cowards, outnumbered by the lesser count of two, turned tail and ran.

Waldo's left eye began puffing up as we walked along nursing our bruises. "How'd it all start?" he finally asked.

"They thought Princetta was white." "Idiots," he answered. "Hell, I know'd she was a nigger all the time." Waldo and I had trapped and fished together all our lives, but only through the delicacy of the situation did I resist busting him in his jaw.

That fight was sort of a turning point. (p. 4) ◄

Stages of Ethnic Identity Development   Jean Phinney, a psychologist at California State University, Los Angeles, points out that the progression toward an ethnic identity parallels differences among Marcia's (1988) identity statuses. Although Marcia did not initially think of the statuses developmentally, most research suggests that identity achievement is the most mature resolution and diffusion the least, with foreclosure and moratorium as intermediate steps (Josselson, 1982; Orlofsky & Frank, 1986). Phinney (1989, 1993) has proposed a stage model of ethnic identity development that parallels Marcia's analysis of identity.

Three distinct stages to ethnic identity development emerge. Just as with Marcia's identity statuses, it is possible for minority adolescents to avoid exploring the implications of their ethnicity and to remain committed to the values of the dominant culture. Adolescents with an **unexamined ethnic identity** have simply internalized the values and attitudes of the dominant culture, in a way similar to that of foreclosed adolescents, and have little understanding of issues related to their ethnicity. Those in an **ethnic identity search,** or moratorium stage, are involved in exploring the meaning of their ethnicity and may experience a growing conflict between the values of the dominant culture and those of their ethnic group. Adolescents with an **achieved ethnic identity** have a clear sense of their ethnicity that reflects feelings of belonging and emotional identification. They have little defensiveness and show confidence in their ethnicity (Phinney, 1989; Phinney & Rosenthal, 1992). Although different procedures and the use of somewhat different definitions make it difficult to compare findings from one study of ethnic identity development to the next, research suggests that psychosocial adjustment is associated with an achieved, or internalized, ethnic identity (Phinney & Kohatsu, 1997; Speight, Vera, & Derrickson, 1996).

unexamined ethnic identity The initial stage in ethnic identity formation; a lack of awareness of the issues related to one's ethnicity; a simple internalization of the values of the dominant culture.

ethnic identity search The intermediate state in ethnic identity formation; exploration of the meaning of one's ethnicity.

achieved ethnic identity The final stage in ethnic identity formation; a clear sense of one's ethnicity that reflects feelings of belonging to and emotional identification with one's group.

TABLE 15.1 Percentage of Minority Adolescents in Stages of Ethnic Identity Formation

	Unexamined	Search (Moratorium)	Achieved
Asian American	57.1%	21.4%	21.4%
Blacks	56.5	21.7	21.7
Hispanics	52.1	26.9	21.7
Total	55.7%	22.9%	21.3%

Source: Adapted from J. Phinney. (1989). Stages of ethnic identity development in minority group adolescents. *Journal of Early Adolescence, 9,* 34–49.

Phinney (1989) interviewed tenth-graders from different ethnic backgrounds regarding ethnic identity issues. These adolescents were Asian Americans, Blacks, Hispanics, and Whites. The interviews contained questions that tapped their exploration of and commitment to their ethnicity. An exploratory question was "Do you ever talk with your parents or other adults about your ethnic background or what it means to be———?" Commitment was tapped by questions such as "Some people find these questions about their background pretty confusing and are not sure what they really think about it, but others are pretty clear about their culture and what it means to them. Which is true of you?" Adolescents also completed measures of ego identity, self-evaluation, sense of mastery, social and peer relations, and family relations.

As Phinney expected, stages of ethnic identity development correlated positively with the measure of ego identity. Similar correlations existed for measures of a sense of mastery and peer and family interactions. These findings suggest that the stages are indeed developmental, although we can't say that they increase with age. Slightly less than 50% of the minority adolescents had explored the implications of their minority status by the tenth grade. Even though a direct comparison is not possible because different samples are involved, this percentage is still higher than that for eighth-graders found in a previous study (Phinney & Tarver, 1988).

The stages themselves were independent of any particular minority. As shown in Table 15.1, just about the same percentage of adolescents from the three minorities was in each of the three stages of ethnic identity formation. This latter finding suggests that adolescents from different minorities have the same need to come to terms with the personal implications of minority membership. The important element appears not to be the particular minority group the adolescent is from, but the adolescent's stage of development of an ethnic identity. The one exception to this finding comes from White adolescents, who had no sense of their own ethnicity and saw themselves only as "American." Phinney notes that this ethnocentric attitude is out of touch with our increasingly pluralistic society in which minorities constitute about one third of those between the ages of 15 and 25.

Somewhat different issues are important for different ethnic groups. Asian American adolescents were more likely to express concerns related to academic achievement, such as quotas for universities that might exclude them. Black males expressed concern about job discrimination and negative images of Black adolescents, and Black females mentioned standards of beauty that did not include them, such as long, flowing hair and "creamy" skin. Hispanic adolescents reported most concern with prejudice (Phinney, 1989). Despite these concerns, relatively few minority adolescents appear to have internalized negative attitudes toward their

group. Only 20% mentioned negative attitudes during the interview, and these were distributed evenly across identity statuses (Phinney, 1989).

Whereas young children derive much of their sense of self-worth from their parents, and adults from their work and their children, adolescents receive validation primarily from their friends.

Friendships During Adolescence

Friends are important at any age, but especially in adolescence when so many things are new. Friends are emotional supports to whom adolescents turn with their concerns, triumphs, secrets, and plans. In larger numbers, they are socialization agents, guiding adolescents into new, more adult roles. And one on one, they are mirrors into whom adolescents look to glimpse the future within.

Adolescents gain a sense of who they are and what their lives are about through seemingly small and insignificant daily encounters with friends and members of their families (Erikson, 1968). They try out new aspects of themselves in the relative safety of close relationships. As a consequence, adolescents are often just as interested in what they discover about themselves as in what they find out about each other. This is especially true for friendships during early adolescence. See the Research Focus, "Correlational Research: Hangin' Out on a Friday Night," for a discussion of adolescent friendships and identity formation.

Adolescents experiment with new behaviors as they face a pressing need to discover what is acceptable and what is not. They know, for example, that they cannot be as dependent as before, but neither are they totally self-reliant. And what about their emotions? Sentimentality is "uncool," but do they have to put a cap on all emotion? Friends provide essential feedback. Adolescents try on new behaviors much as they do clothes on a shopping spree. Which ones fit? Which make them look better? Friends become mirrors in which they can see themselves

Correlational Research: Hangin' Out on a Friday Night

It's Friday night and a group of 17-year-olds is sitting around the television, talking, channel surfing, and working their way through a bag of chips. Periodically, one of them will call the others' attention to something on the screen or mention some event that happened that week at school, but as the evening wears on, the conversation gets more serious. They talk about being friends, about what they've been through together, and what lies ahead for each of them.

Despite their casual appearance, adolescents have a lot on their minds. Mixed in with studying for tests, picking up the latest CD, or hanging out on a Friday night, are their concerns about the future—their futures. One of the major tasks facing adolescents is that of identity formation, gaining a sense of themselves that reflects what they value and want to be and, in turn, is valued by those whom they respect. One might suspect, as a consequence, that adolescents' aspirations would be related to those of their friends. But are they? Are other factors involved? And how might one go about finding answers to questions such as these?

One would first need to measure both adolescents' and their friends' aspirations, as well as any other factors one thinks might be related. Then one could look for relationships among these variables. When changes along one variable correspond to changes along another, the variables are said to be *correlated*. *Correlation coefficients* are statistics that reflect the degree of relationship between variables. Scatterplots show this relationship pictorially. In the figure, the scatterplot on the left illustrates no relationship ($r = 0$); the one on the right shows a strong relationship ($r = +1.00$). One could have an equally strong relationship but in the opposite direction ($r = −1.00$); that is, variables can be either positively or negatively correlated. In the first case, increases along one variable match increases along the other. In the second case,

increases along one are accompanied by decreases along the other. Let's look at how one team of investigators used this approach to determine whether adolescents' future aspirations are related to various characteristics of their friends, such as their friends' ambitions, beliefs, and use of drugs.

Judith Stein and Michael Newcomb (1999) gave seventh-through ninth-graders a measure of their future aspirations (positive future aspirations), asking them how well they were doing in school, what their educational aspirations were, and what their ambitions were. They also questioned them about their friends (conventional friends). Specifically, they asked how much they talked with their friends about their homework, what grades their friends got, whether their friends planned to go to college, and what their parents thought of their friends. In addition, they assessed how conventional the adolescents' attitudes were, asking about law abidance, liberalism, and religiosity (social conformity). Finally, they assessed their use of drugs (drug use).

Are adolescents' future aspirations related to characteristics of their friends? Absolutely. Stein and Newcomb found that adolescents' future aspirations correlated positively with having conventional friends and with greater social conformity. Conversely, high future aspirations correlated negatively with drug use.

This research is further distinguished by the fact that these investigators followed these same adolescents into adulthood, testing them again 13 years later when they were young adults and then again 20 years later when they reached middle adulthood. Tracing the paths of these adolescents into adulthood revealed that those who had positive goals for themselves in adolescence (positive future aspirations) showed more efficacy and agency as young adults. Further, both efficacy and agency in early adulthood predicted greater fulfillment and satisfaction with life in middle adulthood.

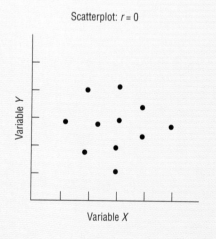

Scatterplot: $r = 0$

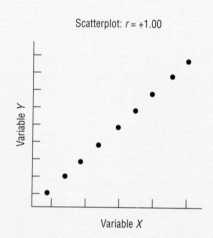

Scatterplot: $r = +1.00$

as they imagine they must look to others. The ability of adolescents to consider the thoughts of others gives early friendships this special reflective quality (Berndt, 1982; Elkind, 1980; Frankel, 1990).

Changes in Friendships with Age

Friendships change with age, taking on themes that characterize the concerns of each age group. Preadolescents want to be understood and accepted by others; adolescents want to understand themselves—and different processes facilitate both of these concerns. Gossip helps preadolescents establish norms and avoid being rejected; self-disclosure helps adolescents define themselves. Friendships reflect these themes in characteristic patterns of interacting.

Understanding is an important component to friendships. How does concern with understanding change from preadolescence to adolescence within friendships?

Preadolescence Preadolescents spend a lot of time comparing themselves to others. In fact, being accepted by others is one of their central concerns. Peer reactions figure heavily in determining preadolescents' levels of self-esteem and self-definition. The cognitive changes discussed in Chapter 14, especially being able to assume the perspective of another, contribute to their awareness of the importance of socially appropriate behavior and the need for "impression management." Fear of rejection and ridicule, and jockeying for position in friendships, characterize relationships among this age group (Parker & Gottman, 1989). In fact, Keller and Wood (1989) found that most of the preadolescents they interviewed mentioned trust as the most important issue in their friendships.

Insecurity regarding one's social position is perhaps best reflected in a characteristic mode of interaction: gossiping. Gossiping is important to preadolescents with good reason: It discloses the attitudes and beliefs that are central to the peer group (Parker & Gottman, 1989). This function is vital when we realize that these behaviors are the basis for being accepted or rejected by the group. Listen in on the following conversation as two friends discuss telling lies, something friends are not supposed to do with each other:

DARI: Barb said that her mom gave her $300 to buy a dress and shoes for the dance, and that the dress, the yellow one she showed us, remember? Well, that dress cost over $200.

TRACEY: That yellow dress she took out of the closet? It was ripped. I saw it!

DARI: Yeah. Under the arm. I saw it too.

TRACEY: That wasn't a new dress. There was a stain on it.

DARI: She told us she bought it for $200. But I think her sister gave it to her, the one who's married.

TRACEY: Yeah. She gives her a lot of clothes.

Notice that in gossiping about Barb, Dari and Tracey affirm the norms of the group; that is, friends don't lie to each other. They also communicate to each other that they adhere to these norms.

Mutual disclosure and affirmation of group norms through gossip allows preadolescents to reaffirm their membership in the group. This is especially important because preadolescents are often insecure about their social status and their general acceptability. Much of the energy that goes into friendship is devoted to solidifying their position and protecting themselves against rejection (Parker & Gottman, 1989).

Gossip serves another important function. It allows preadolescents to explore peer attitudes in areas where they lack clear norms, without actually committing themselves to a position. Because many of the behaviors in question are not common among their peers, gossip frequently involves well-known older adolescents, as in the following example, or even popular figures such as rock musicians and movie stars:

BRIAN: They say Dale [captain of the varsity football team] uses steroids every football season.

ANDY: A lot of athletes do. It helps them build up muscle.

BRIAN: Steroids are really drugs, you know.

ANDY: You think the coach knows?

BRIAN: Nah. How could he and still let Dale do it? He might lose his job.

ANDY: Yeah.

Neither Brian nor Andy directly stated an opinion about using steroids or drugs in general. Yet by the end of the conversation, they had established that athletes who use them have to hide that fact from others and consequently it must be wrong to use them. As demonstrated in this example, gossiping is a low-risk way of determining the attitudes of one's peer group. Neither boy had to reveal a view of his own in order to discover the position taken by the other. Their conversation affords them a way of sampling the reactions and attitudes of peers regarding behaviors that are not yet common to their group (Parker & Gottman, 1989).

Preadolescents are still learning which emotions are appropriate for them and what rules exist for displaying these. By monitoring feedback from peers in social situations, they gain invaluable information regarding each of these aspects of social competence. Even so, their rules for emotional expression are rough at first. Perhaps their most salient guideline is to avoid sentimentality at all costs, especially when with one's friends. The rule of thumb is to be rational, cool, and in control.

Adolescence   Adolescents' friendships reflect different concerns, which at this stage take the form of defining who they are and what they are going to be in life. Friends get together to discuss the mix of experiences offered up each day. The remarks of classmates, teachers, and parents and the successes and failures of the day are expressed, taken apart, analyzed, and reanalyzed. Friends provide the support—and sometimes the challenge—that adolescents need in order to meet the new and untried, as the following conversation illustrates (Parker & Gottman, 1989):

JAMES: So we're watching the game last night and my dad says, "You need to think about your future." Like, I don't know what I want to do but it doesn't really bother me. [Laughs.]

SAM: [Returns laughter.]

JAMES: [Laughs again.] It's my life and it bothers my dad more than me that I haven't got my future planned.

SAM: My dad's the same. I tell him: "I know I'll be doing *something*."

JAMES: Right, *something*! [Laughs nervously.]

SAM: "*Que sera*," you know?

Exploring uncharted territories in one's life is never easy, as the nervous laughs of the two adolescents above suggest. Yet adolescents are peculiarly well equipped for the task. In many ways, they have reached the pinnacle of thought and can think easily in the abstract, reasoning about the possibilities in their lives

Although girls generally find it easier than boys to share their innermost thoughts, disclosure to a close friend is one of the most important ways that all older adolescents learn about themselves.

and those of their friends. Rather than seeing themselves as limited to their present circumstances, they can see their present realities as reflecting a limited sample of the many possible alternatives that exist. Parker and Gottman (1989) note that adolescents are uniquely qualified to help each other through indecisions such as these and do so with genuine concern, even seeing this as one of the obligations of friendship.

They take this obligation seriously. When adolescents are with their friends, they are most likely to talk about themselves rather than gossip about others. Just as gossip serves the very real needs of preadolescents—affirming group norms and group membership—self-disclosure serves the needs of adolescents. It is one of the primary means by which they discover themselves. **Self-disclosure** is an intimate sharing or exchange of thoughts, feelings, and otherwise undisclosed aspects of the self with another person. It takes a very different form in adolescence than in childhood or preadolescence. Adolescents respond to disclosures with an honest, almost confrontational examination of the issues raised. They accept these offerings of the self in the spirit in which they are given—as problems to be addressed and solved—whereas self-disclosures among preadolescents are more likely to evoke feelings of solidarity, such as "Me, too" (Parker & Gottman, 1989).

Adolescent friendships reflect considerable emotional development beyond those of preadolescents. Adolescents begin to master the rules for emotional display and feeling that so mystify preadolescents. Adolescents are comfortable expressing a range of emotions, which preadolescents would likely deny. They have moved beyond cool to compassion or any of the many other emotions that might be called for in a situation. They understand that actions can be motivated by several emotions. What remains to define is an understanding of the potential impact of emotion on their relationships. Many of their conversations are about losing control of an emotion—exploding at someone or just "blowing it"—and the effects this can have (Parker & Gottman, 1989).

self-disclosure The sharing or exchange of personal information; considered a primary basis for the development of intimacy.

Friendship Patterns

What do adolescents want from their friends? Emotional support, intimacy, and advice. They get these in somewhat different ways depending on their sex. The major activity in girls' friendships is talking. Girls develop close friendships primarily by sharing their feelings. Self-disclosure contributes to emotional closeness in boys as well, but they also develop emotional closeness through sharing experiences, such as sports and other activities (Camarena, Sarigiani, & Petersen, 1990; Frankel, 1990).

Same-sex friendships become more intimate and affectionate with age and become increasingly important as sources of emotional support. Whereas parents are the primary source of support for children, mid-adolescents are as likely to confide in their same-sex friends as in their parents, and late adolescents indicate that friends are more important in this respect than are parents (Furman & Buhrmester, 1992; Levitt, Guacci-Franco, & Levitt, 1993). Not surprisingly, adolescents spend a lot more time with friends than they did as children.

The number of friends also increases in adolescence, especially for girls. The percentage of these friends whom mothers know (40%) remains about the same as in childhood; however, because the circle of friends widens in adolescence, the actual number of friends whom mothers do not know increases substantially (Feiring & Lewis, 1993).

Interethnic Friendships   Generally, adolescents are likely to have friends who live in the same neighborhood, go to the same school, and share other things in common—including ethnic background. Of those who live in ethnically mixed neighborhoods and have classes together, a number form friendships with those from other groups. Adolescents report these friendships to be close, although they do not see these friends with the same frequency outside of school as they do friends of the same ethnic group (DuBois & Hirsch, 1990; Hallinan & Teixeira, 1987).

Several conditions affect the formation of friendships between adolescents from different ethnic backgrounds. Classroom climates have been found to affect the sociability of European American adolescents toward African American peers. Classrooms where students work together, such as those in which teachers assign students to small working groups, have more interethnic friendships.

In general, it appears that the more positively adolescents regard their own ethnic group, the more positive are their attitudes toward those who belong to other groups. Jean Phinney, Debra Ferguson, and Jerry Tate (1997) found this relationship to be mediated by adolescents' ethnic identity. Adolescents who were secure in their own ethnicity, in other words, were likely to regard other members of their group positively. These positive in-group attitudes, in turn, were related to more positive attitudes toward classmates who were members of other groups. These investigators also found that each of the ethnic minorities they studied tended to perceive their own group more favorably than the other groups. They point out that this bias, commonly referred to as ethnocentrism, rather than contributing to negative attitudes toward other groups, actually appeared to support the development of positive intergroup attitudes.

How favorably adolescents viewed students from other ethnic minorities is also related to how much contact they have with them outside of school (Phinney, Ferguson, & Tate, 1997).

The Peer Group

A Malayan proverb counsels that one should trumpet in a herd of elephants, crow in the company of cocks, and bleat in a flock of goats. This pretty much sums up the behavior of adolescents with their peers. The peer group is one of the most important socializing forces in the lives of adolescents, regulating the pace as well as the particulars of the socialization process. Adolescents who fall behind their friends in social skills are dropped from the group, just as are those who move ahead too quickly. Similarly, those whose tastes and attitudes fail to match the group's are likely to be considered nerdy, geeks, or just "out of it." The cost of bleating when others are crowing can be high.

The peer group assumes special importance in adolescence for a number of reasons. Adolescents are moving toward greater autonomy and independence, and peers provide much needed emotional and social support. Adolescents also learn many social skills with peers that they would not learn from parents or teachers. Peers reward each other with potent reinforcers: acceptance, popularity, and status (Muuss, 1990).

Types of Social Groups   Friendships differ in how exclusive they are, with adolescents frequently having a number of close friends in common. Small groups of such friends are known as **cliques.** A clique can be as large as ten or as small as three, but whatever the size, its members spend much, if not most, of their available time together. These friends are usually the same sex and age, are in the same class in school, share the same ethnic background, and live relatively close to each other. Best friends are also likely to be similar in many of their behaviors, attitudes, and aspects of their identity (Akers, Jones, & Coyl, 1998). Nearly always, one's best friend is in the same clique (Ennett & Bauman, 1996; Urberg, Degirmencioglu, Tolson, & Halliday-Scher, 1995). Similarities in the composition of boys' and girls' cliques are striking. Aaron Hogue and Laurence Steinberg (1995), at Temple University, asked over 6,000 high school students to name their closest friends at school. Sixty-five percent of boys' cliques and 63% of girls' cliques were made up exclusively of same-sex friends, and 85% of boys' and 86% of girls' cliques had no more than one friend of the opposite sex.

Susan Ennett and Karl Bauman (1996), in a study of peer relationships among ninth-graders at five different schools, found that even though cliques are the most common type of social grouping, somewhat less than half of the students (44%) belonged to a clique. What about the other half? Two other types of peer relationships, liaisons and isolates, were also common, each making up about 30% of the students. **Liaisons** are adolescents who are socially active and have friends in a number of cliques but do not themselves belong to any one of these. These students serve the important function of bringing together groups of adolescents who otherwise would have few channels of communication—in a sense, plugging these cliques into the larger social network within the school. **Isolates,** on the other hand, have few friends, either within a clique or outside it, having few links to other adolescents in the social network. (Figure 15.1 illustrates these peer relationships.)

In addition to small groups of friends, larger groups also exist. A **crowd** is larger than a clique and more impersonal. Crowds usually number about 20. Not all the members of a crowd are close friends, but each is someone adolescents feel relatively comfortable with. Crowds usually consist of several of the friends in one's clique along with adolescents from several other cliques. For about half of the adolescents, their best friend is also in the same crowd. It is relatively unlikely for an adolescent to be a member of a crowd without belonging to one of these cliques; however, many adolescents belong to a clique and not to a crowd (Urberg, Degirmencioglu, Tolson, & Halliday-Scher, 1995).

The functions of cliques and crowds differ. Crowd events provide the settings in which adolescents try out new social skills. Clique activities provide feedback about the success of these skills and advice when skills fall short. If the crowd has a single purpose, it is to help adolescents move from same-sex to mixed-sex

What are adolescents likely to do when they are with their crowd that they are not likely to do when they are with their clique?

clique A peer group made up of one's best friends, usually including no more than five or six members.

liaison A term for adolescents who have friends in several cliques but who do not themselves belong to any one clique.

isolate A term for adolescents who have few friends, either within a clique or outside it, and who have few links to other adolescents in the social network.

crowd A peer group, averaging 20 members and formed from several cliques of the same age group.

FIGURE 15.1 Adolescent Friendship Patterns: Cliques, Liaisons, and Isolates *Source:* S. T. Ennett and R. E. Bauman. (1996). Adolescent social networks: School, demographic, and logitudinal considerations. *Journal of Adolescent Research*, 11, 194–215.

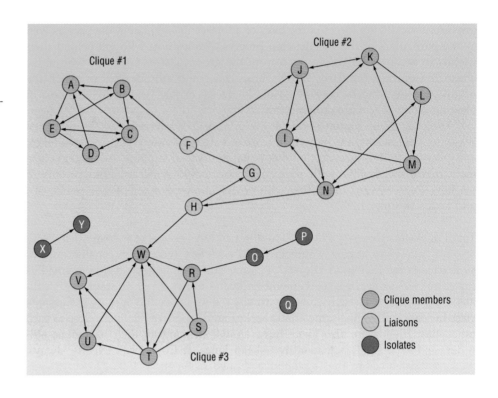

interactions. Many adolescents need all the help they can get. Susan Toth (1986) describes how complicated this process can be when adolescents first start to date:

> Just when I was approaching sixteen, I found Peter Stone. Or did he find me? . . . I was afraid I would never have a real boyfriend, never go parking, never know true love. So when Peter Stone asked his friend Ted to ask Ted's girlfriend Emily who asked me if I would ever neck with anyone, I held my breath until Emily told me she had said to Ted to tell Peter that maybe I would. (p. 158)

Awkward as such maneuvers are, the outcomes are frequently successful. Toth continues

> On my sixteenth birthday, Peter gave me a small cross on a chain. All the guys had decided that year to give their girlfriends crosses on chains, even though none of them was especially religious. It was a perfect gift, they thought, intimate without being soppy. Everyone's cross cost about ten dollars, a lot of money, because it was real sterling silver. Long after Peter and I stopped seeing each other, I kept my cross around my neck, not taking it off even when I was in the bathtub. Like my two wooden dolls from years before, I clung to that cross as a superstitious token. It meant that someone I had once cared for had cared for me in return. Once I had had a boyfriend. (p. 164) ◄

Adolescents spend most of their time talking about crowd activities when they are with members of their clique, either planning the next event or rehashing the last one, gathering valuable information from such "pregame" and "postgame" analyses. The feedback comes from specialists—other adolescents who know just how difficult a social maneuver can be and who can recommend something that has worked for them in similar situations.

At crowd events, such as high school football games, where various cliques mingle, adolescents can practice new social skills and new roles with new people.

If clique activities are coaching sessions, crowd events are the game itself. Adolescents enter the field ready to try out new social moves. Reflecting their specialized nature, crowd and clique activities take place at different times during the week. Crowd events, just like actual games, occur on weekends, and clique activities, like other coaching sessions, take place throughout the week.

Developmental changes occur in the structure of peer groups just as they do with friendships. Both cliques and crowds evolve as adolescents face different issues; so does the importance of being in a group. Belonging to groups is most important to early and middle adolescents, and less so for preadolescents, for whom they are not yet needed, or late adolescents, who no longer need them (Gavin & Fuhrman, 1989). Late adolescents are comfortable with others of the opposite sex, and the crowd disintegrates into loosely grouped cliques of couples who are "going together." Cliques also become less important with age. The number of adolescents belonging to a clique declines from the sixth to the twelfth grade; however, the membership of a clique tends to be stable over time.

The Problems of Youth

Adolescents face many pressures. Some have more than their share. Most adolescents will cope in one fashion or another; relatively few will fail to cope. Box 15.1 discusses a tragedy where warning signs were overlooked and two teens went over the edge. In this section we will address the problems of those for whom coping has become the ultimate test: the severely depressed and the suicidal.

Box 15.1 *Columbine: The Imaginary Audience and a Real Stage* WITH MICHAEL WAPNER

The columbine is a flower. But for too many of us the word no longer evokes images of blossoms. Instead, it is associated with images of the dead and dying, of students and teachers screaming and crying, cowering under desks, fleeing for their lives. We have other names that evoke images of violent death—Dallas, Waco, Oklahoma City. But Columbine doesn't belong to that group. Columbine is different. It is the name of a school, and the images it evokes—of both killers and killed—are those of adolescents, children. Tragically, Columbine has come to stand for a new collection of events—shootings in which students murder other students at school.

In one sense, the image of school as a place of violent death is all out of proportion. Less than 1% of homicides involving school-age children occur in or near school (National School Safety Center, 1998). However, 1% is an alarming figure given the circumstances that have given rise to it. Schools are supposed to be safe havens, not places of violent death. Since 1992, from 20 to 55 students a year have been killed in school shootings (National School Safety Center, 1998).

How can we begin to understand this rash of deadly violence? Can we even group into a single category the events at Columbine High School in Littleton, Colorado, and at schools at West Paducah, Kentucky, at Jonesboro, Arkansas, and Springfield, Oregon? A number of elements are certainly common to all, but they seem few indeed, perhaps because of their very ordinariness. The killers were all males; all were teenagers, as were almost all of their victims; all carried out their deadly acts at school; and all used guns to do it. Also common to these events was what was missing, the conditions or characteristics one might expect to find in the lives of violent youth. In none of these cases do we find uncaring or incompetent parents, substance abuse, domestic violence, poverty, or a crime-infested environment. Columbine, like the other shootings, defies easy answers to our questions.

It is clear, then, that we are unlikely to find a single cause for the events that took place at Columbine. James Garbarino (1999), at Cornell University, argues such a point. Consider just one environmental context, that of the family. Garbarino points out that parenting is only one of many influences in a child's life and interacts with many other influences, such as the child's own temperament, the changing developmental challenges faced by a child at different points in life, and the larger culture into which that child steps. Loving, authoritative parenting, for instance, may be sufficient at one point in development, such as the early years of childhood, but may not be enough to counter pressures introduced by the demands of school, the influence of peers, or the larger youth culture when the child reaches adolescence. Garbarino notes that this is especially true for children who by temperament are less easygoing, more negative in their moods, or less flexible in adapting to change.

Temperament can similarly interact with another environment, that of school. Examples of friendly, nurturing support among students are everywhere to be found in schools—but so are bullying, teasing, name-calling, and petty exclusiveness. Unfortunately, boys who already feel resentful and unaccepted are much more likely to experience the latter. And, if you are expecting to be hurt, there is no place like a schoolyard or cafeteria to have those expectations fulfilled. Adolescents with extremely sensitive temperaments, either violently excessive or coldly deficient, do not easily form friendships or achieve a sense of belonging, making it even more difficult for them to buffer themselves from rejection. But there are contexts in which such boys may come together—in clubs organized around hate (e.g., neo-Nazi or racist groups), violence (e.g., guns, martial arts), or provocative deviance (e.g., outrageous dress). Or they may join with just one or two other youths with similar outlooks. This affiliation of two or three resentful, marginal young men who may encourage each other to act out their violent fantasies is particularly dangerous.

A few bumper stickers may say that the best revenge is living well. But that's not what Rambo says. And that's not what thousands of movies, television programs, and video games say. Culture is the medium that gives form to the expression of feelings. Marginal, hypervigilant young men have plenty of feelings. And when the forms provided by the culture feature automatic weapons and high explosives to "blow away" your antagonist, the mix

Depression

Emotions color experience and give meaning to life. For most individuals they are anchored in reality, tethered to the situations that prompt them. Some individuals are pulled past reality to an inner world of thoughts and feelings that bear little resemblance to the situations that occasion them. These individuals suffer from **affective disorders,** disturbances that affect their mood. Mood is an enduring emotional state that varies along a continuum of depression to elation (American

affective disorders Disorders whose primary symptoms reflect a disturbance of mood, such as depression.

is monstrous. Adolescents are steeped in violence, not only in the commercial images of films, television, and song lyrics, but also in the reality of their lives, from verbal and physical skirmishes at school to everyday speech peppered with expletives to nightly statistics on the evening news.

The United States leads other nations in homicides to a staggering degree. Of all the factors contributing to the lethal nature of violence in this nation, in all likelihood the most important of these is the accessibility of firearms. Nearly half the tenth-grade males in one large survey indicated they could get a gun if they wanted to; this figure is even higher for inner-city youth (*Digest of Education Statistics*, 1993). Individuals are not necessarily more aggressive in the United States than in other countries, but they do have readier access to guns, a difference that is often lethal. A comparison of two demographically similar cities, Seattle and Vancouver, conducted over 6 years, offers strong support for the position that accessibility of firearms is related to the greater incidence of homicide in the United States. Seattle had virtually no restrictions governing gun possession and use, whereas Vancouver had many. Despite similar rates of conviction for violent crime in each of the cities, rates of homicide were nearly twice as high in Seattle (Sloan et al., 1988).

A final set of factors to consider in the Columbine shootings involves the developments that take place in adolescence itself. In particular, cognitive development enables adolescents to react not only intellectually, but also emotionally in new ways. Adolescents' ability to interpret the actions of others enables them to assign more than the obvious meaning to any social encounter. Further, their heightened awareness of themselves makes it likely that they will relate these actions to themselves. As a consequence, adolescents are more likely to experience emotions such as moodiness, depression, or resentfulness than are children or adults.

In the case of Columbine, the motivation seems to have been not just retaliation, but also a desire for celebrity. Why, some have asked, if Dylan Klebold and Eric Harris were enraged at the athletes who taunted them, didn't they place their bombs in the locker room?

FBI agent Mark Holstlaw suggests instead that "They wanted to be famous. And they are. They're infamous." This particular shooting may have been influenced by the media, but not in the way typically assumed, which presumes the media to be the cause of the violence. Instead, knowing that the media would be drawn to their violence, Klebold and Harris may have used the media in an attempt to become celebrities, even going so far as to imagine that famous directors would fight for the chance to make a movie of their story.

If true, this concern with celebrity reflects another quality of adolescent thinking—the tendency to act for an imaginary audience. Adolescents' capacity for abstract thought enables them to think not only about their own thoughts but about the thoughts of others as well. David Elkind suggests that adolescents frequently lack perspective about what concerns them and what concerns others, leading them to believe that everyone else is as interested in them as they are and that others are continually noticing them. The imaginary audience gives adolescents exaggerated feelings of self-consciousness and self-importance.

We have considered a number of factors—type of parenting, temperament, violence in the culture, accessibility of guns, and characteristics of adolescent thought—that may have contributed to the events at Columbine. Yet none of these, either separately or in some complex mix, explains why these adolescents acted as they did while other adolescents, sharing many of their experiences and backgrounds, did not. We frequently think we understand youth violence, at least with respect to those instances in which adolescents come from bad homes or otherwise bad environments. Yet even "predictable" violence such as this leaves us with few explanations when we are asked to consider the many nonviolent youth from those very same homes and neighborhoods who lead caring, disciplined, and considerate lives. The actions of these latter youth are unrecorded, their names absent from police blotters or reports on the evening news. Contributing factors offer no more complete explanation, in other words, for violence that fits the mold than for violence that breaks it. In each case, one is left to explain why a handful of adolescents acted as they did, while others did not.

Psychiatric Association, 1994). Individuals who suffer from affective disorders live much of their lives at the extremes of this continuum.

Three Depressive Disorders From time to time everyone feels sad. Those who live with **depression** feel a crushing weight of hopelessness and despair. They may have any of three major forms of depression. Adolescents with *major depressive disorder* experience severe periods of depression lasting several weeks or more. These

depression An affective disorder that may take any of three major forms, all of which are characterized by a disturbance of mood; the three forms are major depressive disorder, dysthymia, and adjustment disorder with depressed mood.

Adolescents who live in gang-ridden neighborhoods experience a high degree of stress. Some try to cope by looking for solutions to the problem; others try to minimize the emotional damage by joining a gang themselves or by emotionally withdrawing.

are accompanied by some or all of the following symptoms: difficulty concentrating, loss of pleasure, slowed speech and movements, and vegetative signs such as sleepiness, loss of appetite, and weight changes. Adolescents suffering from *dysthymia* have a less severe form of depression but one that generally lasts much longer. The third form, *adjustment disorder with depressed mood,* is brought on by stress and is relatively brief (Petersen et al., 1993).

Feelings of sadness, loneliness, and despair become common by mid-adolescence. Nearly half of all adolescents report experiencing some of the symptoms that characterize depression—sadness, crying spells, pessimism, and feelings of unworthiness. Even so, the prevalence of major depressive disorder among adolescents is considerably lower—about 10%—with three quarters of those affected being female (McFarlane, Bellissimo, Norman, & Lange, 1994).

Adolescents who suffer from depression share with adult depressives feelings of low self-esteem, pervasive sadness, hopelessness, and helplessness (Craighead & Green, 1989). A self-defeating cycle exists in which low self-esteem contributes to depression, which in turn fuels negative feelings about the self (Rosenberg, Schooler, & Schoenbach, 1989). More females than males experience depression. A change in the sex ratio of those suffering from depression occurs during puberty (Rutter, 1986). This change could reflect hormonal influences or may reflect identification with culturally defined gender roles. The female gender role includes more socially undesirable characteristics than does the male gender role. This difference could easily affect the self-esteem of adolescent females as they identify with the culturally defined role. Craighead and Green (1989) found differences in self-esteem to account for approximately half of the variability in depression among normal adolescents.

Masked Depression Depression is often masked in early adolescence. Several symptoms signal *masked depression,* the most frequent being fatigue, poor concentration, and hypochondriasis (excessive concern with illness or health). Continual fatigue can reflect inner struggles with feelings that adolescents cannot put to rest or talk about with others. Similarly, difficulties in concentration can result from concerns they do not yet feel secure enough to articulate, and preoccupations with their health, or a seeming lack of it, may reflect fears of inadequacy or incompetence.

Each of these symptoms can be mistakenly interpreted as a natural part of adolescence. Fatigue is expected, given the accelerated growth of puberty and the demands of school, friends, and family. Similarly, poor concentration can easily be mistaken for problems with schoolwork ranging from boredom to being overwhelmed, and excessive concern with one's body is natural, given thchanges that take place during puberty. Treatments that take into consideration the underlying source of an adolescent's depression will be more effective in combating these symptoms than those that are directed at the symptoms themselves: the fatigue, poor concentration, or excessive concern with health (Weiner, 1980).

Irving Weiner (1980) suggests that adolescents may not be able to admit feelings of inadequacy and still accomplish the developmental tasks they face—achieving emotional independence, finding a sense of self, developing sexual relationships, and so on. Any one of these would be difficult under the best of conditions and can be impossible with feelings of inadequacy. Early adolescents may also be more caught up in *doing* things than in reflecting about them. In either case, depression, or attempts to keep it at bay, are likely to at first assume a physical form in early adolescence.

Suicide

An alarming number of adolescents report thinking about suicide. In a national survey of high school students in 1995, 24% said that they had thought seriously about attempting suicide at some point during the past year, 18% indicating they had even made specific plans (CDC, 1996c). By comparison, the percentage who actually attempt suicide is relatively low, 8.7%, and still fewer actually commit suicide.

Warning Signs Although every case of suicide is unique, a number of common warning signs exist. These include sudden changes in behavior, changes in patterns of sleeping or eating, loss of interest in usual activities or withdrawal from others, experiencing a humiliating event, feelings of guilt or hopelessness, an inability to concentrate, talk of suicide, or giving away one's most important possessions (Blumenthal & Kupfer, 1988). The presence of any one of these is a cause for concern; the presence of several is a clear signal that an adolescent is in danger (Figure 15.2).

What signs indicate that an adolescent may be thinking about suicide?

Counseling and Prevention In some adolescents, suicidal behavior may be a desperate attempt to effect a change in someone they love, such as an alcoholic parent, rather than a true wish to die, as is more likely in older suicide victims (Weiner, 1980). Tragically, the intellectual changes that make it possible for adolescents to reflect on their lives also make it possible for them to imagine the reactions of others to their deaths. Elkind (1978b) warns that the personal fable, the belief that one is different from others and somehow invulnerable to the dangers others face, may prevent adolescents from realizing the consequences of their

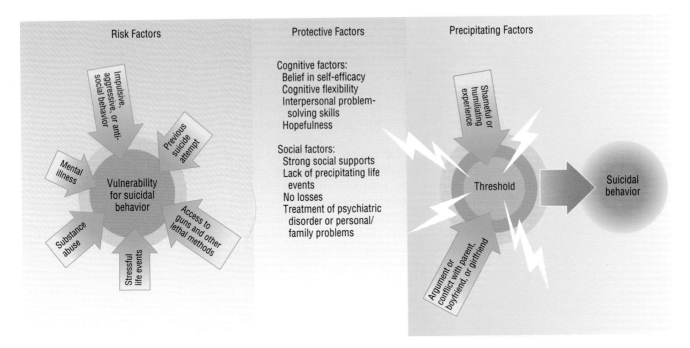

FIGURE 15.2 Factors Contributing to Suicide *Source:* Adapted from S. J. Blumenthal & D. J. Kupfer. (1988). Overview of early detection and treatment strategies for suicidal behavior in young people. *Journal of Youth and Adolescence, 17,* 1–23.

actions—that they will not be around to see how much others actually cared for them.

Communicating with Suicidal Adolescents Weiner (1980) stresses the pivotal place of communication in the lives of suicidal adolescents. Adolescents who are genuinely listened to following an attempt are less likely to engage in further suicidal behavior. Conversely, callous or angry reactions or even indifference from those they love can prompt further suicidal attempts. Caring, open, and supportive efforts to address problems on the part of those closest to the adolescent are vital. Yet important as these efforts are, they should never replace professional help.

Frequently suicidal adolescents communicate with their peers. Frequently, too, peers are uninformed concerning warning signs of suicidal intent. Only half of one sample of adolescents knew, for instance, that remarks about wanting to die, seeming worried, or having problems in school or with a relationship might be related to suicidal behavior. Fewer than 20% knew that adolescents who are suicidal are likely to threaten that they will kill themselves. Even more alarming was the finding that over 40% of these adolescents believed that such behaviors were *not* likely to be related to suicide (Norton, Durlak, & Richards, 1989).

What advice is there to give to those who fear that an adolescent close to them may be suicidal? Suicidal adolescents communicate their pain to those to whom they are closest. It is important to pick up on these signals. One should not be afraid to openly ask the adolescent if she or he has thought of self-destructive behavior. Listening to what the adolescent has to say can be painful, but it is vitally important. Attempting to deny the reality of the adolescent's pain through false assurances that everything will be okay only communicates that one has not heard the pain or the hopelessness. Serious thoughts of suicide require professional attention. Loving concern, though important in its own right, is not a substitute. Professional help should be obtained immediately.

Often, suicidal teens will communicate with their peers about thoughts of suicide. It's important to listen and suggest professional help to adolescents in emotional pain.

Prevention Programs   The most effective programs help suicidal adolescents face truths in their lives and have these work for them. Sometimes the truth can be as simple as learning how to say something and then make it happen. The approaches that work best are brief, crisis-oriented, and give adolescents skills they can apply in their ongoing relationships (Kerfoot, Harrington, & Dyer, 1995).

To be effective, programs must reach the adolescents who need them. Many adolescents who attempt suicide do not show up for therapy, or they drop out before they complete it. One study found that 20% did not keep any of the appointments they made, another 19% dropped out during the initial assessment sessions, and nearly 33% more discontinued the program before they finished (Trautman & Rotheram, 1986). Given the chaotic home lives of many of these adolescents, completing anything, even breakfast, can be an accomplishment. One program found it helpful to give adolescents who had been hospitalized for a suicide attempt a token that would give them readmission to the hospital on a "no questions asked" basis, should circumstances become intolerable (Cotgrove, Zirinksy, Black, & Weston, 1995).

The most effective treatments are highly structured programs that train adolescents in skills they can apply at home and in school. Most also teach adolescents to attribute their successes to their own efforts; they aim at getting them to a place where they can say, "I did that and I did it well."

Usually counselors help adolescents identify problem areas and generate alternative solutions. When adolescents can think of alternative solutions to conflicts and predict the effects of acting one way or another, they can cope more effectively. Even if the other person reacts negatively, being able to predict a response puts adolescents less "at the effect of" the other person. If adolescents can also anticipate their own feelings about negative reactions, they are in an even better place to control these feelings. In a sense, conflict management is a bit like surfing: You need to stay just behind the crest of the wave to keep it from crashing down on you.

Family Therapy   Because many suicide attempts are precipitated by conflict with a parent, treatment that includes the family will almost always be the most effective. This type of therapy shifts the focus from the adolescent to family interactions that preceded the suicide attempt. Improving communication within the family is usually an important element to intervention programs (Kerfoot, Harrington, & Dyer, 1995).

The Strengths of Youth: Caring and Prosocial Behavior

Daniel Hart, at Rutgers University, and Suzanne Fegley, at Temple University (1995), were interested in how adolescents who are distinguished by remarkable caring and prosocial behavior understand their world and themselves. These investigators studied a group of urban minority adolescents, African American and Hispanic, in an economically distressed Northeastern city. These adolescents were remarkable in one way or another for their involvement in such things as volunteer work or unusual family responsibilities. (The sample was arrived at by contacting social agencies, church leaders, schools, and youth groups.) A comparison group of adolescents was matched for age, gender, ethnicity, and neighborhood. The latter adolescents were also well adjusted, attended school regularly, and many of them were also involved in volunteer activities, but not to the same degree. All adolescents were interviewed and completed a number of personality measures.

These investigators found, as anticipated, that the caring adolescents understood themselves quite differently than did the comparison adolescents. They were more likely to describe themselves in terms of their values and ideals. Also, their parents contributed more heavily to their sense of themselves than was the case for the comparisons, for whom best friends contributed most heavily. Differences between the caring and comparison adolescents, however, did not appear to be due to any single factor, such as overall maturity or sophistication of thought. The former did not, for instance, use more advanced moral reasoning or have more complex or sophisticated perceptions of others. Also, because these adolescents were not followed over time, one cannot say for sure whether the ways in which these remarkable teenagers saw themselves were responsible for the care they extended to others or whether their involvement in the care of others drew them away from friends, thus causing them to see themselves less in terms of their peers and more in terms of idealized figures.

P. Lindsay Chase-Lansdale, Lauren Wakschlag, and Jeanne Brooks-Gunn (1995) point to the importance of the family for the development of caring. The experience of being loved appears to be essential if one is to develop as a caring person. The research on attachment, beginning in infancy but extending throughout the life span (Ainsworth, 1985; Ainsworth, Blehar, Waters, & Wall, 1978; Bowlby, 1982), underscores the importance of the caregivers' sensitivity to the child's needs and of responsiveness in meeting these for healthy development. Children cared for in this way not only develop a sense of trust in their world but come to believe that others are trustworthy and, perhaps most important of all, come to believe that *they* are worthy of being cared for in this way (Erikson, 1968).

Not all adolescents are born into homes in which they will receive this type of care from their parents. What sort of chances do such adolescents have of developing into competent, caring adults? The research of Emily Werner and her colleagues (Werner, 1989; Werner & Smith, 1982, 1992) indicates that the chances are good—as long as there is at least one caring person in that young person's life, someone such as a grandparent, an aunt or uncle, or a sibling to love him or her.

Protective Factors in Adolescence

Adolescents are supported, or "held," by many protective factors in their environment. Each of these factors—whether aspects of their homes, schools, or communities—helps adolescents to redefine themselves, to change the way they know themselves, so that the self they bring to their encounters with others will be one that is capable of mutuality and one that can continue to grow.

Families

Among the most important supports in adolescents' lives are their relationships within the family, especially with parents. These relationships can be characterized in terms of two broad dimensions: *responsiveness*, which involves care and support; and *demandingness*, or discipline and monitoring of adolescents' activities (see Chapter 9). Both of these dimensions of families has been found to be related to healthy development.

Longitudinal research confirms the contribution of responsiveness. Kristin Moore and Dana Glei (1995) followed a nationally representative sample of children from the ages of 7 through 11 to the ages of 18 to 22, interviewing both children and parents. These investigators found that adolescents who experienced fewer family disruptions, such as marital conflict or divorce, and who had warm and emotionally satisfying relationships with their parents in childhood were more likely to have a greater sense of well-being in adolescence and to avoid serious risk taking, such as dropping out, using cigarettes or other drugs, or engaging in delinquent behavior. Similar findings from an even larger study of over 30,000 adolescents confirm the importance of caring and a feeling of connectedness within the family as significant protective factors contributing to the well-being of adolescents, even when other family variables such as socioeconomic status and single- versus two-parent family structure were controlled for (Resnick, Harris, & Blum, 1993).

Robin Jarrett (1995), at Loyola University, summarizes a number of family characteristics—illustrating the dimensions of responsiveness and demandingness—that enhance the development of youth. Although these strategies are ones that have been found effective specifically in counteracting the eroding effects of poverty among African American families, their wisdom cuts across income level and ethnicity, making them applicable in varying degrees to all families.

One of the first characteristics to emerge from the welter of research reviewed by Jarrett, a characteristic illustrating the dimension of responsiveness, involved the use of supportive adult network structures. These networks took the form of additional adults who could be called on to provide care. Adults, such as grandparents, godparents, or neighbors, provided resources that otherwise would not be available to these adolescents. The following excerpt illustrates this type of support:

> [Aunt] Ann . . . paid for [Ben's] class ring, his senior pictures, and his cap and gown. Ann did not see this as unusual behavior as it was exactly what Jean [her sister] had done for her a long time ago. She also pointed out that she had been helping to pay nominal school fees for Jean's children for several years. (Zollar, 1985, p. 79, as cited in Jarrett, 1995)

Being expected to help with family needs, such as caring for younger siblings, gives adolescents a sense of competence, an important factor in healthy development.

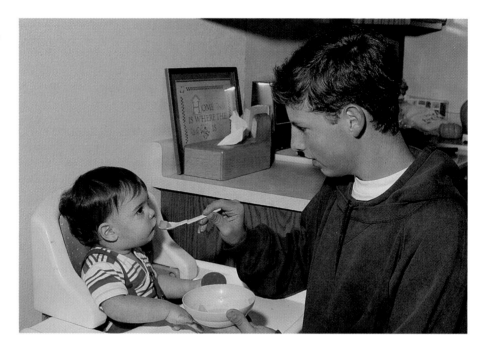

These successful families also made use of supportive institutions within the community, such as churches and schools. Churches were found not only to undergird these families spiritually but also to offer activities for youth in which they could form friendships and develop new skills. Church beliefs also foster self-respect, personal discipline, and a concern for others (Jarrett, 1995; Moore & Glei, 1995). Parental use of schools similarly took a number of forms. Parents collaborated with school personnel, attending parent-teacher meetings, serving on committees, and maintaining close contact with their children's teachers. But parents were also willing to confront school personnel in order to ensure that their children received the attention they needed. As one mother explained, "This lady tells me that the principal doesn't have time to look at everybody's case. So I told that lady, 'that may be the case but this is one that he's going to look at.' . . . I was going to the Board of Education and everywhere I could think of to see that Marie could go ahead and graduate" (Clark, 1983, p. 41, as cited in Jarrett, 1995).

The strategies identified by Jarrett also illustrate the second dimension of family interaction: demandingness. For instance, Jarrett found parents to monitor their adolescents' activities and friendships, setting limits on whom they could associate with, what they could do, and when they were to get home. "Chaperonage" figured centrally in this monitoring, beginning in childhood as parents accompanied their children as they went into the neighborhood and taking a particularly inventive form in adolescence by having a younger sibling tag along on dates and other activities. Other research, as well, finds that adolescents whose parents monitor their activities by asking where they are going and who they will be with have fewer problem behaviors (Blyth & Leffert, 1995; Buchanan, Maccoby, & Dornbusch, 1992).

Demandingness was also evident in parental expectations that adolescents assume responsibility for helping with the family's needs, whether economic or domestic. Thus adolescents might be expected to have a part-time job to contribute to the family budget, do chores around the house, or help with younger siblings or an elderly grandparent. Such responsibilities not only contribute to family cohesion but also foster individual competencies and give a feeling of mastery (Jarrett, 1995).

Earlier in the text, we discussed several aspects to family interactions that contribute to healthy personality development, specifically, to the development of individuation in adolescence. Harold Grotevant and Catherine Cooper (1986) identified two such dimensions of interaction: *connectedness* and *individuality.* The first of these reflects the degree of emotional support within the family, support that takes the form of openness to others' opinions (permeability) and respect for their ideas (mutuality). The dimension of connectedness is similar to the dimension of responsiveness. The second dimension—individuality—reflects the ability to function as an individual within this supportive context, to see how one differs from others and to express one's own ideas. There is a paradox to these findings—namely, that it is necessary to be held in order to be set free. Or, said another way, it is necessary to be supported by one's family in order to find oneself as an individual.

In a sense, these findings should not come as a surprise. Mary Ainsworth (1993; Ainsworth, Blehai, Walters, & Wall, 1978) observed much the same thing in her studies of attachment in infants and toddlers. Infants whose mothers were sensitive and responsive to their needs—qualities, by the way, that are similar to the permeability and mutuality that constitute connectedness—were those who as toddlers were the most independent and curious. These were the ones who would be likely to disappear around a corner to explore, knowing that Mom or Dad would be there in a moment if they should call out. That, after all, is what they had learned: that it's safe to venture out on your own, because your parents will be there when you need them. To be held, or supported, by one's family does not create dependency in children. It frees them to develop as individuals.

Communities

Dale Blyth and Nancy Leffert (1995), at the Search Institute in Minneapolis, compared over 100 communities in terms of the experiences of the adolescents living in them, to discover the ways in which communities support their youth. They defined the health of these communities in terms of the relative absence of problem behaviors in their youth. They found that although the communities were quite similar in terms of their demographic makeup, they differed considerably in the number of problem behaviors engaged in by youth and in the support their youth experienced.

The healthiest communities were those in which adolescents were more likely to be "plugged in" to institutions within the community. Adolescents in these communities experienced their schools as caring and supportive, were more likely to attend religious services, and to participate in activities within the community. According to Blyth and Leffert, the strong relationship between active participation in religious and other community-based activities and the overall health of the community suggests that such extracurricular activities "may not be *extras*" after all. Their observation mirrors Robin Jarrett's finding about the ways that successful families use institutions within their communities.

Blyth and Leffert note, too, that the adolescents who profit most from living in healthy communities are the ones who are most in need of support and who have the fewest personal resources. Even though similar findings have emerged from comparisons of adolescents from widely differing types of communities, such as inner-city versus suburban youth, Blyth and Leffert point out that they also

Attending church and having spiritual values are among the protective factors that help adolescents weather the stresses of growing up.

hold true for communities that, on the surface, have few visible differences. The Social Policy Focus, "Shooting Deaths Among Children," looks at communities as protective factors from another perspective, that of access to guns.

Personal Strengths: Temperament, Competence, and Religion

The personal qualities that adolescents possess also serve as protective factors, qualities such as temperament and outlook on life, intelligence, competence, attitudes about self-efficacy, and religious beliefs. Adolescents with easy temperaments—that is, those who react positively to new situations and who are sociable and moderate in their activity level—are more likely to ride out the stresses of daily living. Not only does their positive approach equip them to deal with problems better, but their engaging ways also endear them to others, thus enabling them to recruit the support they need. Possessing at least average intelligence, being able to communicate well with others, and believing that they are in control of, rather than simple reacting to, the circumstances affecting their life (known also as having an internal locus of control) also serve as important protective factors (Chase-Lansdale, Wakschlag, & Brooks-Gunn, 1995; Lau & Lau, 1996; Werner, 1989).

Religious beliefs also are an important factor contributing to healthy development (Brody, Stoneman, & Flor, 1996; Donahue & Benson, 1995). For instance, Loyd Wright, Christopher Frost, and Stephen Wisecarver (1993) found that adolescents who attend church frequently and for whom their religion gives their life meaning are also the least likely to suffer from depression. Similarly, Kristin Moore and Dana Glei (1995) found that greater religiosity contributes to a sense of well-being in adolescents, and Jarrett (1995), reviewing numerous research studies, found attendance at church and spiritual values to contribute to healthy development, even in the face of the multiple risks associated with poverty. Emily

Shooting Deaths Among Children

The rate of firearm deaths among children in the United States is almost 12 times higher than is the *combined* rate of such deaths in over two dozen other industrialized nations. In a single year, firearms were responsible for the deaths of no children in Japan, 19 children in Great Britain, 57 children in Germany, 109 in France, 153 in Canada, and 5,285 in the United States (Krug, Dahlberg, & Powell, 1996). An even greater number of children, approximately 4 times the number killed, were likely to suffer gunshot wounds in the same period of time (Christoffel, Spivak, & Witwer, 2000).

Most of these shooting deaths are accidental. Among young children, for instance, accidental gunshot deaths are likely to occur when a child happens to find a loaded gun and plays with it. The trigger resistance in most handguns is so slight that even a preschooler can fire a gun, and some guns will even fire when dropped (Center to Prevent Handgun Violence, 2000). Among adolescents, gunshot deaths also result from criminal and gang-related activities. Additionally, guns account for the majority of deaths due to suicide among adolescents in the United States. The increase in the rate at which adolescents commit suicide by shooting themselves has risen 3 times faster than the rates for other methods. This increase has paralleled the increased availability of guns to teenagers, both in their own homes (Brent et al., 1988; U.S. Department of Justice, 1995) and in society in general (Garland & Zigler, 1993).

Figures such as these prompt questions. What can be done to make firearms less accessible to children and adolescents?

And what can be done to make firearms safer? Various states have instituted child access prevention (CAP) laws that make the owner of the gun responsible for injuries incurred when it is used by another person, such as a child. Such laws are designed to increase the likelihood that those owning guns will exercise greater caution in keeping them out of the hands of children. And, in fact, accidental gunshot deaths among children decreased 23% following passage of CAP laws in the dozen states in which such laws were in place by 1997. Child access prevention laws, however, have not been passed in most states.

Similarly, laws raising the age for handgun ownership to 21 should further reduce gunshot deaths and injuries. More crimes are committed by late adolescents than by any other age group. Even though the Brady Law now makes it illegal for individuals below the age of 21 to purchase a handgun from a licensed dealer, they are still able to legally purchase handguns from private individuals. And in a majority of states it is still legal for adolescents to own long guns such as rifles—and assault weapons. Other pieces of legislation that have proven effective in reducing gunshot deaths are "one-gun-a-month" laws. Such laws prevent the mass sale of guns. When such laws were passed in Virginia and Maryland, juvenile homicides in Washington, D.C., decreased by 63% (Justice Policy Institute, 1997).

Finally, guns themselves can be made safer through the use of trigger locks and through sensing devices on "smart guns" that require identification of some characteristic of the owner's hand for the gun to be fired.

Werner and Ruth Smith (1982, 1992) also noted the importance of a strong religious faith to the healthy development of resilient individuals from infancy to middle adulthood.

Love

Finally, one cannot overestimate the importance of being loved. Even though this is a truth we all live with, it is encouraging to see it find empirical support. Chase-Lansdale, Wakschlag, and Brooks-Gunn (1995) emphasize that just one caring relationship in an adolescent's life can make the difference between developing in a healthy or unhealthy way, even in the face of family conflict, poverty, parental psychopathology, and other formidable factors. Similarly, Emily Werner and Ruth Smith (1982, 1992) found that the essential ingredient to healthy development in each of the individuals they studied, who were at risk for one or more reasons, was a "basic, trusting relationship" with someone who cared for them.

Perhaps Urie Bronfenbrenner (1990) summed it all up best when he said what adolescents need most is someone who finds them "somehow special, especially wonderful, and especially precious" (p. 31).

Summary

A Constructive Interpretation of Relationships

The process of defining oneself, differentiating aspects of the self from others, leads to a renegotiation of the parent-child relationship during adolescence. This relationship is a focus of development during this period of life because of the biological changes of puberty and the changes in the way adolescents think and process information.

Autonomy and Individuation

Adolescents become more autonomous as they become more independent and responsible for their actions. Frequently these changes bring conflict with parents over household routines, more frequently with mothers than fathers. Parenting style, especially of mothers, is related to girls' autonomy; age is the best predictor of increased autonomy for boys.

Increased individuation accompanies autonomy as adolescents sort through values and views to discover which ones reflect the way they think. This discovery involves making decisions for themselves and living with the consequences of these.

Individuation gives adolescents a set of attitudes and ways of acting that are genuinely their own; however, they must still put these together into a working whole that reflects an inner sense of self. Family characteristics of individuality and connectedness facilitate the process of identity achievement. Individuality refers to having and expressing ideas of one's own and being able to say how one differs from others. Connectedness reflects one's openness to others' opinions and respect for their ideas. These qualities of family life help adolescents explore options while feeling emotionally supported even when family disagreements arise.

Identity

Achieving an identity is a central task facing adolescents. Identity gives one a coherent, purposeful sense of self.

There are several ways adolescents arrive at the roles and values that define their identities. Some paths, involving either a personal search or an adherence to old beliefs, lead to commitments. Conversely, other paths can lead to noncommitment—some adolescents not being able to choose among alternatives for fear of closing off important options, and others failing to see the importance of choos-

ing. These paths lead to four identity statuses: identity achievement, identity foreclosure, moratorium, and identity diffusion. Adolescents may move from one status to another, depending on their willingness to accept new challenges and to experience anxiety.

Even though Erikson believed the search for identity to be a central task facing all adolescents, he assumed that females and males approach it differently. The task for males involves making choices and commitments about an occupation, a set of beliefs, and their sex role. Erikson believed females arrive at their identity by committing themselves to a future mate.

Research shows that gender differences in identity development are minimal. The process and timing of development suggest more similarities than differences.

Ethnic identity development progresses through several stages. Adolescents with an unexamined ethnic identity internalize the values and attitudes of the dominant culture. Those in an ethnic identity search are exploring the meaning of their ethnicity, and those with an achieved ethnic identity have a clear sense of their ethnicity and emotionally identify with their ethnic group. These stages correlate with ego identity statuses. Some bicultural adolescents see themselves equally as members of their ethnic group and of the dominant culture; for others, however, one identity or the other predominates according to the situation.

Friendships During Adolescence

Adolescents experiment with new behaviors with their friends and, in doing so, discover new things about themselves. Friends are important sources of self-esteem during adolescence.

Friendships change with age. Those of preadolescents reflect a concern with being accepted. Preadolescents use gossip as a way of affirming group norms and their membership in the group. Adolescent friendships reflect a concern with self-discovery; self-disclosure becomes important to this process.

Friendship Patterns

Patterns of friendship differ with the age and sex of adolescents. Early adolescent girls' friendships focus on the activities that bring friends together. Friendships in mid-adolescence for girls are concerned with the personal qualities of friends more than before. Girls want friends they can confide in and trust. Friendships in late adolescence focus more on personalities. Intimacy continues to grow and more friends are of the opposite sex.

Boys' friendships in early adolescence are also centered on shared activities. By middle adolescence, their friendships are as closely emotionally as girls' friendships but involve less discussion of feelings.

Despite gender differences in close friendships, peer interactions show many of the same patterns for either sex. Most friendships are with peers of the same race.

Adolescents of both sexes experience greater pressure to grow up faster than adolescents of previous generations.

Interracial and interethnic friendships form when adolescents live in integrated neighborhoods and attend integrated schools. Classroom climates affect the formation of cross-race friendships, which are likely to develop when students are assigned to small groups to work together in a noncompetitive atmosphere. Interracial friendships face challenges posted by different enculturation experiences. Adolescents of different backgrounds may perceive and react to the same situation differently; misinterpretations and hurt feelings can result.

The Peer Group

The peer group regulates the pace of socialization. Adolescents who either fall too far behind or move too far ahead of their friends are dropped from the group.

The most common type of peer group is the clique, a small group of friends. Adolescents not in cliques may be liaisons, who are socially active and have friends in several cliques, or isolates, who have only a few individual friends and are not part of the social network.

Crowds are groups of about 20. Adolescents try out new social skills at crowd events, the most important of which involve the opposite sex. The crowd is primarily important in helping adolescents move from same-sex to opposite-sex relationships, whereas clique activities provide feedback about the success of new social skills.

Cliques and crowds change in importance as adolescents age. They are most important in mid-adolescence and become less so as adolescents begin to form couples who are "going together."

Depression

Depression is an affective disorder that can take a number of forms. Adolescents with major depressive disorder suffer episodes of debilitating depression that can last for several weeks or more. Those with dysthymia experience less

severe but longer-lasting symptoms. Those with adjustment disorder with depressed mood experience brief bouts of depression brought on by stress. Adolescents who suffer from depression have feelings of low self-esteem, sadness, hopelessness, and helplessness. Depression can be masked by physical symptoms in early adolescence.

Suicide

The rate of suicide among adolescents has nearly tripled over the past 3 decades. Males are more likely than females to complete a suicide. Suicide is the third most common cause of death among those 15 to 19 years old.

Warning signs include sudden changes in behavior, changes in sleeping or eating patterns, loss of interest in usual activities or withdrawal from others, experiencing a humiliating event, feelings of guilt or hopelessness, inability to concentrate, talk of suicide, or giving away important possessions.

Factors that place adolescents at risk of suicide are mental illness, substance abuse, life stresses and chaotic family lives, biochemical imbalances, availability of lethal means, and prior suicide attempts.

The most effective treatment programs work with the family as well as the suicidal adolescent.

Beyond Coping: Caring and Prosocial Behavior

Prosocial adolescents are more likely than their peers to describe themselves in terms of their values and ideals, and their sense of themselves is more likely to come from their parents than from their peers. The experience of being loved, of having their needs met by someone important in their life, appears to be essential for adolescents to develop into caring adults.

Protective Factors in Adolescence

From their families and their communities, adolescents need a combination of care (responsiveness) and discipline (demandingness). Responsiveness can be expressed not only by immediate family members but also by adult network structures and by community institutions. Demandingness is expressed through monitoring adolescents' activities and expecting them to help out with the family's needs. Family interactions that promote both connectedness and individuality also contribute to healthy personality development.

Communities having the fewest problem behaviors among their youth are those where the adolescents experience their schools as caring and supportive and are likely to attend religious services and participate in other community activities. In addition to characteristics of the family and the community, the personal qualities of adolescents themselves are also protective factors. Their temperament, intelligence, competence, sense of self-efficacy, and religious beliefs can help protect them against the stresses of daily life. Research into protective factors in adolescence shows that just one caring relationship in an adolescent's life can make the difference between developing in a healthy or an unhealthy way.

Key Terms

achieved ethnic identity (p. 589)
affective disorders (p. 600)
autonomy (p. 572)
clique (p. 597)
connectedness (p. 576)
crowd (p. 597)
depression (p. 601)
ethnic identity (p. 586)

ethnic identity search (p. 589)
identification (p. 579)
identity achievement (p. 580)
identity diffusion (p. 580)
identity foreclosure (p. 580)
identity formation (p. 579)
individuality (p. 576)
individuation (p. 573)

isolate (p. 597)
liaison (p. 597)
moratorium (p. 580)
regression (p. 582)
self-disclosure (p. 595)
unexamined ethnic identity (p. 589)

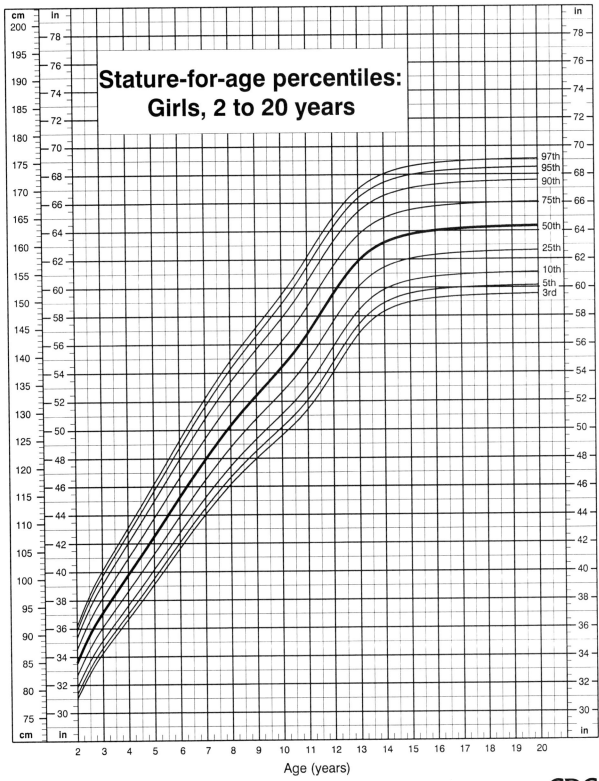

**Stature-for-age percentiles:
Girls, 2 to 20 years**

Age (years)

SOURCE: Developed by the National Center for Health Statistics in collaboration with
the National Center for Chronic Disease Prevention and Health Promotion (2000).

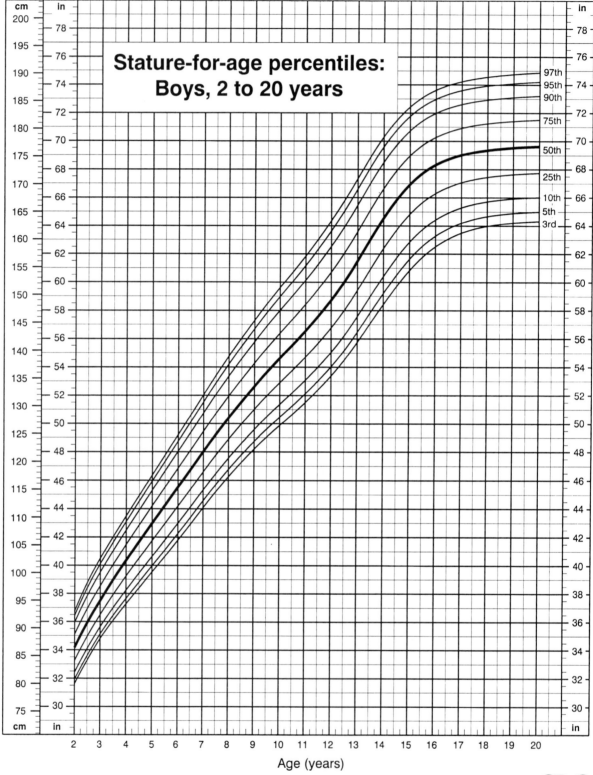

Stature-for-age percentiles:
Boys, 2 to 20 years

Age (years)

SOURCE: Developed by the National Center for Health Statistics in collaboration with
the National Center for Chronic Disease Prevention and Health Promotion (2000).

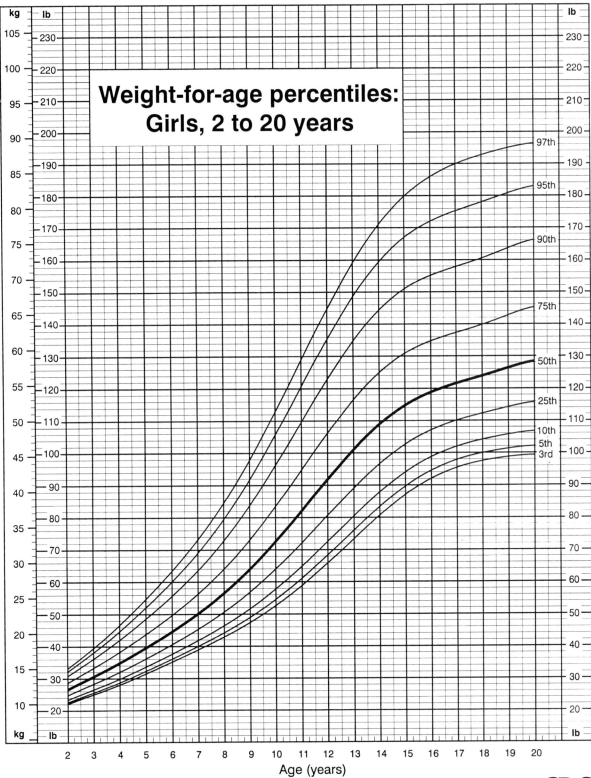

Weight-for-age percentiles: Girls, 2 to 20 years

Age (years)

SOURCE: Developed by the National Center for Health Statistics in collaboration with
the National Center for Chronic Disease Prevention and Health Promotion (2000).

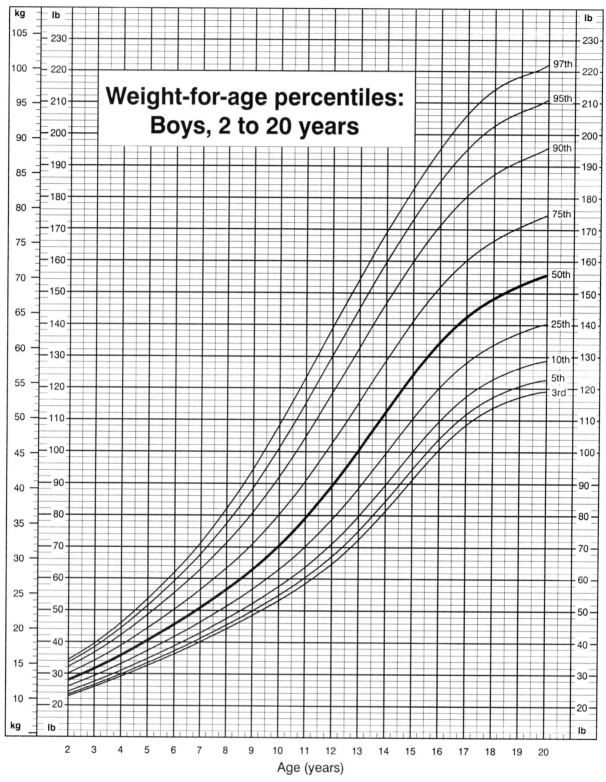

Weight-for-age percentiles: Boys, 2 to 20 years

Age (years)

SOURCE: Developed by the National Center for Health Statistics in collaboration with the National Center for Chronic Disease Prevention and Health Promotion (2000).

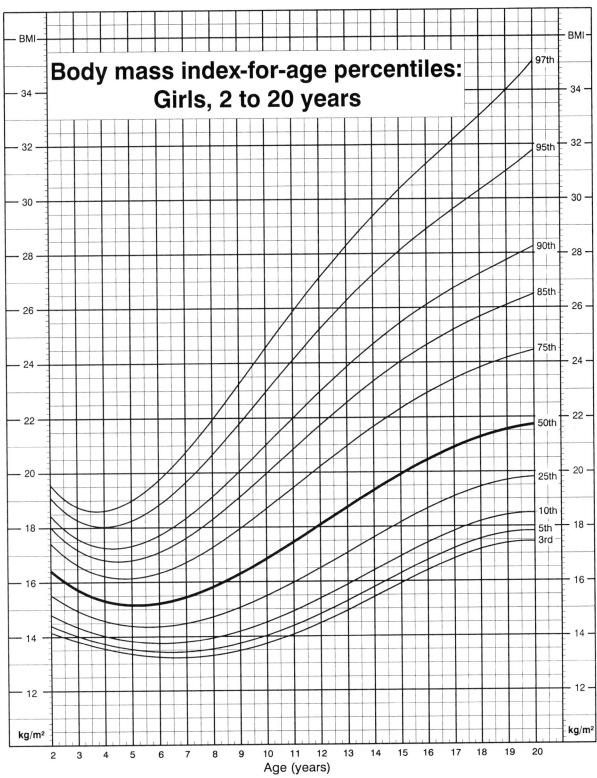

Body mass index-for-age percentiles: Girls, 2 to 20 years

SOURCE: Developed by the National Center for Health Statistics in collaboration with
the National Center for Chronic Disease Prevention and Health Promotion (2000).

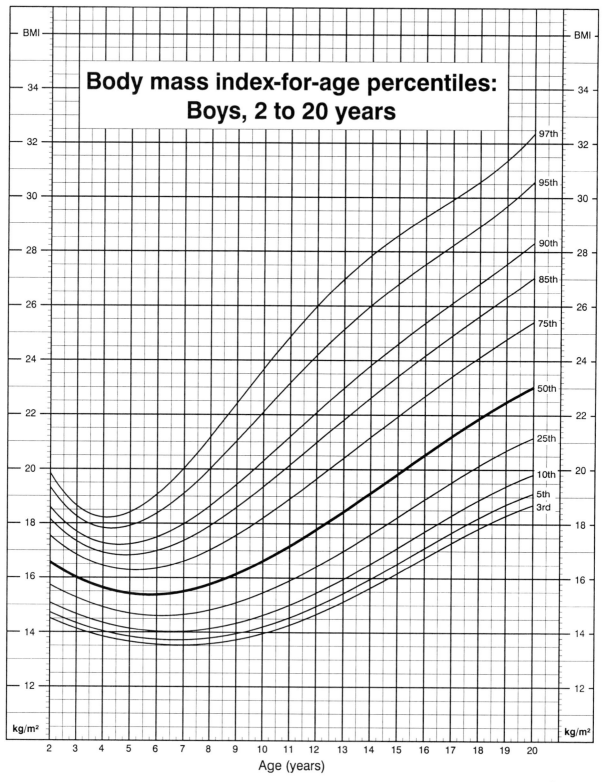

Body mass index-for-age percentiles: Boys, 2 to 20 years

SOURCE: Developed by the National Center for Health Statistics in collaboration with the National Center for Chronic Disease Prevention and Health Promotion (2000).

Glossary

academic tracking   The assignment of students to one of several courses of study in high school on the basis of criteria such as academic interests and goals, past achievement, and ability.

accommodation   Piaget's term for the process by which individuals alter cognitive structures to fit new experiences or events.

achieved ethnic identity   The final stage in ethnic identity formation; a clear sense of one's ethnicity that reflects feelings of belonging to and emotional identification with one's group.

acrosomal reaction   The release of the enzymes by the acrosome as a result of capacitation.

acrosome   The cap on the head of the sperm containing enzymes that digest the outer surface of the ovum.

activators   Proteins that facilitate the copying of DNA segments by picking up messages at regulatory sites along the DNA track and relaying them to coactivators.

active listening   A way of listening that reflects the message and feelings back to the speaker.

active sleep   A sleep state characterized by frequent body movement; also known as REM sleep because of the presence of rapid eye movements.

active wakefulness   A waking state characterized by frequent and vigorous movement.

affective disorders   Disorders whose primary symptoms reflect a disturbance of mood, such as depression.

afferent, or sensory, pathway   A series of neurons carrying impulses from the periphery (skin, muscles, joints, and internal organs) to the central nervous system.

agency   An aspect of mature functioning characterized by achievement and mastery; the complement of communion.

alleles   The complementary forms of a gene located at the same site on the autosomes that determine the expression of a particular trait.

allocentric representation   Representing the location of objects in relation to an abstract frame of reference, such as a map.

amniotic sac   A transparent, watertight membrane that develops around the embryo and is filled with amniotic fluid.

anorexia   An eating disorder characterized by severely limiting the intake of food; most common in females.

Apgar scale   A method of rating the physical state of a newborn in terms of appearance or color, heart rate, reflex irritability, muscle tone, and respiration.

ascending infections   Infections transmitted during birth; the most common are the herpes viruses and gonorrhea.

assimilation   Piaget's term for the process by which individuals fit new information into their present ways of understanding.

assumptive realities   Assumptions made on the basis of limited information.

asynchrony   Differences in the timing of pubertal changes within an adolescent, or from one adolescent to the next.

attachment   The affectional bonds that infants form with those who care for them; the ways in which infants organize their behavior around these caregivers, using them as a base from which to explore and to which to return for safety when stressed.

authoritarian parenting   A style of parenting that stresses obedience, respect for authority, and traditional values.

authoritative parenting   A style of parenting that stresses self-reliance and independence; parents are consistent, maintain an open dialogue, and give reasons when disciplining.

autobiographical memories   Memories that constitute the personal narrative that tells the story of oneself; emerges at about age 4.

automatization   Increases, with continued experience, in the efficiency with which children can engage in various mental activities.

autonomy   Being independent and responsible for one's actions.

autosomes   The 22 matching pairs of chromosomes that, together with the sex chromosomes of the 23rd pair, are found in the cell nucleus.

axioms   The unquestioned assumptions that form the basis of a theory.

axon   A long filament extending from a nerve cell, through which neural impulses are transmitted.

babbling   The production of vowel and consonant sounds by infants in the 2nd to 3rd month.

basal factors   Factors that communicate directly with RNA polymerase.

basic-skills approach   An approach to teaching reading that starts with teaching children the sounds of individual letters and how to sound out words.

bimanual coordination   The ability to use both hands simultaneously but to do different things, such as holding a paper with one hand and cutting with scissors with the other.

blastocyst   A thin-walled hollow sphere resulting from the differentiation of morula cells into the trophoblast and the inner cell mass.

body mass index (BMI)   Weight in kilograms divided by the square of a person's height in meters.

bootstrapping   A strategy children use to learn names for things through their knowledge of word classes and syntactic cues.

brain stem   The area at the base of the brain that contains the midbrain, the pons, and the medulla oblongata and controls basic functions such as breathing and heart rate.

bulimia   An eating disorder characterized by bingeing and then purging; most common in females.

capacitation   A change in the outer membrane of the sperm, triggered by chemicals in the female reproductive tract, that allows the acrosome's enzymes to be released.

cell proliferation   A brain growth process that consists of the overproduction of both neurons and their interconnections.

cell pruning   A brain growth process that consists of the selective elimination of excess cells and the cutting back of connections.

central nervous system   The brain and the spinal cord.

centration   Piaget's term for the tendency to focus on one aspect of an object to the exclusion of others; characterizes preoperational thinking.

cephalocaudal growth trend   The developmental pattern in which growth begins in the region of the head and proceeds downward.

cerebellum   A large structure located behind the cerebral cortex that coordinates sensory input and muscle responses.

cervix   The opening to the uterus.

chromosomes   Microscopic filaments within a cell nucleus carrying genetic information and composed of DNA and protein.

circumcision   Surgical removal of the prepuce covering the glans of the penis.

cleavage   The form of cell division initiated by fertilization; unlike ordinary mitosis, the cells do not double in size before dividing.

clique   A peer group made up of one's best friends, usually including no more than five or six members.

clitoris   That part of the external genitals in females that is the primary source of sexual stimulation.

coactivators   Molecules that integrate signals from activators and repressors and send them on to basal factors.

communion   An aspect of mature functioning characterized by empathy and friendship; the complement of agency.

conditional response (CR)   In respondent conditioning, the reflex learned in response to a new stimulus.

conditional stimulus (CS)   In respondent conditioning, the new environmental stimulus used to elicit a conditional, or reflexive, response.

connectedness   A quality of family interactions thought to be important for individuation; it reflects openness to and respect for others' opinions.

conscience   That part of the personality that is concerned with issues of right and wrong.

conservation   The realization that something remains the same despite changes in its appearance.

constructive approach   The theoretical perspective that individuals' expectations color their experiences of the world; that each individual constructs a particular reality from experience.

continuity-discontinuity issue   The question of whether the same set of developmental laws applies to all stages of the life cycle and to all species (continuity assumption) or whether different laws apply to different stages and different species (discontinuity assumption).

conventional moral reasoning   Kohlberg's second level of moral reasoning, in which moral thinking is guided by internalized social standards.

corpus luteum   The ruptured ovarian follicle formed by the release of an ovum; important source of progesterone early in pregnancy.

Cowper's glands   Glands in males that secrete a lubricating fluid that facilitates passage of sperm through the urethra.

crossing over   During meiosis, the exchange of corresponding genes in homologous chromosomes; one of the sources of genetic diversity.

crowd   A peer group, averaging 20 members and formed from several cliques of the same age group.

cytomegalovirus   A member of the herpes family that has become the most common form of fetal viral infection.

deductive reasoning   Reasoning from the general to the particular.

defining features   Characteristics that identify items as members of a category.

dendrites   Fibers extending from a neuron that receive input from neighboring neurons.

depression   An affective disorder that may take any of three major forms, all of which are characterized by a disturbance of mood; the three forms are major depressive disorder, dysthymia, and adjustment disorder with depressed mood.

development   The orderly set of changes that occur over the life span.

differentiation   A developmental trend characterized by a progression from the general to the specific.

difficult infants   Infants who tend to be negative in mood, irregular in their biological functioning (such as in patterns of sleeping and waking and becoming hungry), and slow to adapt to changes; a temperament type identified by Thomas and Chess.

dizygotic twins   Twins who develop from two separate ova, fertilized at the same time by different sperm.

DNA   Deoxyribonucleic acid, the double-stranded molecule in chromosomes that encodes genetic information.

dominant allele   The gene of an allele pair that produces a particular trait.

donor insemination   A fertility procedure in which sperm from a donor are injected into the birth mother's uterus at the time of ovulation.

Down syndrome   A chromosomal disorder caused by an extra 21st chromosome (trisomy 21); characterized by distinctive facial features, slow motor development, and some degree of mental retardation.

drowsiness   A state of either falling asleep or waking up when the body is relaxed, breathing is regular, and the eyes have a dreamy stare.

easy infants   Infants who tend to be cheerful and playful, regular in their biological functioning (such as in patterns of sleeping and waking and becoming hungry), and able to adapt easily to changes; a temperament type identified by Thomas and Chess.

ecological self   The self that is directly perceived in terms of one's ongoing actions.

ectoderm   The outer layer of the inner cell mass, which will develop into the outer layer of skin, the nervous system, and the sensory organs.

efferent, or motor, pathway   A series of neurons carrying impulses from the central nervous system to the periphery (skin, muscles, joints, and internal organs).

egg and sperm donation   A fertility procedure in which donor sperm are used to fertilize donor ova, and the resulting embryo is inserted into the birth mother's uterus.

egg donation   A fertility procedure in which an ovum removed from a donor woman is fertilized with the father's sperm, and the resulting embryo is inserted into the birth mother's uterus.

ego   In psychoanalytic theory, the executive aspect of the personality that attempts to satisfy impulses in socially acceptable ways.

egocentric representation   Representing the location of objects in relation to oneself; typical of young children's subjective understanding of space.

egocentrism   The failure to realize that one's perspective is not shared by others.

Electra complex   A Freudian concept in which the young girl is sexually attracted to her father.

emotional transmission   Transference of emotions from one person to another, especially in a family, through daily interactions.

encoding   The formation of mental representations for one's experience.

enculturation   Acquiring the norms of one's social group.

endocrine system   The system of the body that includes the glands that produce hormones and those parts of the nervous system that activate, inhibit, and control hormone production.

endoderm   The inner layer of the inner cell mass, which will develop into the digestive and respiratory tracts and internal glands and organs.

endometrium   The inner lining of the uterus.

enuresis   Bed-wetting.

epididymis   A mass of coiled tubes near the top of each testis that receives the sperm produced by the testes.

epigenesis   At each stage of development, the emergence of new complexities that cannot be predicted from, or reduced to, earlier forms.

epigenetic principle   Erikson's assumption that an internal plan governs the timing or period of ascendance for each new development.

epiphyseal growth plates   In a child, areas near the ends of a bone that produce new cells.

episiotomy   An incision made in the mother's vaginal opening to prevent tearing of the tissue during delivery.

equilibration   Piaget's term for the balance between assimilation and accommodation that is responsible for the growth of thought.

estrogens   Sex hormones produced primarily by the ovaries.

ethic of care   Gilligan's description of a morality based on responsiveness to and care for others.

ethnic identity   An awareness of belonging to an ethnic group that shapes one's thoughts, feelings, and behavior.

ethnic identity search   The intermediate state in ethnic identity formation; exploration of the meaning of one's ethnicity.

ethnographic field study   Observational research conducted in natural settings that facilitates the study of the unique contributions of the social groups to which individuals belong.

experience-dependent mechanisms   Neural processes that enable the organism to establish new connections between neurons when exposed to unique experiences.

experience-expectant mechanisms   Neural processes, such as those specialized for language use or for pattern detection, that enable the organism to respond to common environmental stimuli.

extended self   The self that includes not only what one is doing at the present moment but also memories of one's past experiences and imaginings about one's future.

factor analysis   A statistical procedure designed to identify underlying dimensions, or factors, that account for the relationship among several variables.

Fallopian tubes   The tubes that feed into either side of the uterus from the ovaries; also called oviducts.

fast mapping   Children's ability to map the meaning of a new word onto a referent after hearing the word used in context just once.

female genital mutilation Removal of the clitoris, the primary source of sexual stimulation in females, and of the inner labia, and sewing shut most of the outer labia (sometimes inaccurately referred to as female circumcision).

fetal alcohol effects (FAE) A pattern of disabilities related to, but less severe than, fetal alcohol syndrome.

fetal alcohol syndrome (FAS) A pattern of disabilities, including mental retardation, low birthweight, heart defects, and atypical facial features, resulting from consumption of alcohol during pregnancy.

flow The experience of becoming totally absorbed in a challenging activity.

fontanels In an infant, gaps between the bony plates of the skull.

formal operational thought Piaget's fourth stage of intellectual development, assumed to characterize adolescence and adulthood, during which mental operations are extended to include thoughts in addition to concrete objects.

gametes Sperm and ova, which, when mature, have 23 individual instead of 23 pairs of chromosomes.

gastrulation The formation of three layers of embryonic cells: the ectoderm, the mesoderm, and the endoderm.

gender differences Culturally determined differences in masculinity and femininity.

gender identity Experience of oneself as male or female.

gender labeling The ability to label oneself as a boy or girl; develops by about age 2.

gender schemas Cognitive structures that direct the pickup of information about the self as it relates to one's gender.

gender stereotyping Culturally based expectations of behaviors that are appropriate for each sex.

genes Short segments of the DNA strand, responsible for transmission of particular traits; thousands of genes are carried within each chromosome.

genotype The total set of genes inherited at conception.

glial cells Cells that support and nourish neurons and produce myelin.

gonads The sex glands; the ovaries in females and the testes in males.

gonorrhea A sexually transmitted bacterial infection that can be transmitted to an infant during birth and can lead to blindness; damage can be averted with preventive measures at birth.

grasp reflex Spontaneously grasping an object pressed against the palm of the hand.

growth The result of metabolic processes in which proteins are broken down and used to make new cells.

growth spurt A period of rapid growth that occurs during puberty.

guided participation Rogoff's term for the shared activity of a novice and one who is more skilled, in which both participate to decrease the distance between their respective contributions to the activity; an extension of Vygotsky's zone of proximal development that assumes a more active role for the learner.

habituation Decreased responsiveness to a stimulus with repeated exposure to it.

hand dominance The superiority of one hand to the other for doing such things as throwing a ball, writing, or using a fork; occurs at the time of brain lateralization.

hand preference The tendency to use one hand instead of the other to do such things as throw a ball, write, or use a fork, even when marked superiority is not apparent with the preferred hand.

hedgehog genes Genes that direct the manufacture of morphogens.

hepatitis B A virus that can cause liver failure, jaundice, and fever in infected infants.

herpes A viral infection that can be transmitted during birth; can damage the central nervous system.

holophrase A single word used to represent a phrase or sentence; typical of the first stage of language acquisition.

hormones Chemical messengers that are secreted directly into the bloodstream and are regulated by the endocrine system.

human immunodeficiency virus (HIV) Can be transmitted by an infected mother to her fetus; the risk of transmission can be reduced with drug therapy.

hypothalamus A center within the brain that regulates hormonal activity and regulatory activities such as eating, drinking, and body temperature.

id In psychoanalytic theory, the aspect of the personality that demands immediate gratification of biological impulses; operates according to the pleasure principle.

identification The child's uncritical internalization of parental behaviors and attitudes.

identity achievement The resolution of conflict over identity through the personal formulation of adult gender roles, occupational goals, and religious and political commitments.

identity diffusion A failure to develop a strong sense of self coupled with a failure to experience much discomfort or conflict over the issues of identity resolution.

identity foreclosure A resolution of the problem of identity through the assumption of traditional, conventional, or parentally chosen goals and values without the experience of crisis or conflict concerning identity issues.

identity formation In adolescence, a synthesizing of elements of one's earlier identity into a new whole; involves individuation.

imaginary audience The illusion of being the focus of attention; assumed to be due both to adolescents' ability to think about thought in others and to their confusing the concerns of others with their preoccupation with themselves.

I-message A message that tells the listener how his or her actions make one feel.

individuality A quality of family interactions thought to be important for individuation, reflecting the ability to express one's ideas and say how one differs from others.

individuation The process of distinguishing one's attitudes and beliefs from those of one's parents.

inductive reasoning Reasoning from the particular to the general.

indulgent parenting A style of parenting characterized by warmth and nurturance but little supervision.

industry versus inferiority Erikson's term for the sense of accomplishment that comes from being able to make things and that comes with doing things well.

in-hand manipulation The ability to move an object around in one hand without the help of the other hand, such as moving a crayon from the palm of the hand to the fingertips.

initiative The term used by Erik Erikson for a child's sense of purposefulness and effectiveness.

inner cell mass The group of cells in the blastocyst from which the embryo is formed.

intelligence The ability to profit from experience and adapt to one's surroundings; measured by intelligence tests.

intentionality model Lois Bloom's model of language development, which assumes that the impetus for language development is the growth of the child's mind rather than the conversational skills of the adult.

in vitro fertilization A fertility procedure in which ova are taken from the birth mother and fertilized in a laboratory with sperm from the father.

isolate A term for adolescents who have few friends, either within a clique or outside it, and who have few links to other adolescents in the social network.

jargon babbling Babbling that reproduces the intonation, rhythmic structure, and pitch of speech.

jigsaw classroom A classroom organized into small, ethnically balanced working groups in which each student contributes a different part of the lesson.

Klinefelter's syndrome A genetic disorder in males caused by an extra X chromosome; symptoms include small testes, insufficient production of testosterone, and infertility.

landmark representation Representing the location of objects in relation to environmental landmarks.

lanugo Fine, downy hair that covers the skin of the fetus.

lateralization The process of specialization of the two halves of the cortex.

laws Relationships that are derived from axioms and that can be proven to be true or false.

liaison   A term for adolescents who have friends in several cliques but who do not themselves belong to any one clique.

libido   In psychoanalytic theory, the psychic energy that is expressed through different zones of the body and motivates much of behavior.

long-term memory   The form of memory in which information is semantically encoded, or stored according to meaning, for later retrieval.

low birthweight   Weight of less than 5½ pounds, or 2,500 g, at birth.

male generic language   Use of the pronoun he to refer to an individual of either sex and use of words such as man or mankind to refer to all people.

maltreatment   Nonaccidental and avoidable harm done to children, whether from abuse or neglect.

mean length of utterance (MLU)   The average number of morphemes in a child's sentences.

meiosis   The process of cell division in which sex cells mature, reducing the number of chromosomes from 23 pairs to 23 individual chromosomes.

membrane depolarization   The neutralization of the surface polarity of the ovum after a sperm succeeds in fusing with the ovum's membrane; this change bars entrance by other sperm.

menarche   The occurrence of a girl's first menstrual period.

mental operations   Piaget's term for actions that can be carried out in one's head and then reversed or undone.

mesoderm   The middle layer of the inner cell mass; it will develop into the muscles, bones, and circulatory, excretory, and reproductive systems.

messenger RNA (mRNA)   The form of ribonucleic acid (RNA) that carries genetic codes from the DNA in the cell nucleus to the sites of protein synthesis in the cytoplasm.

metamemory   The awareness of one's memory and of those factors that affect it.

mitosis   The process of cell division in which body cells replicate; the chromosomes of each new cell are identical to those of the parent cell.

model   A set of assumptions about reality and human nature from which theories proceed.

monozygotic twins   Twins who develop from the same fertilized ovum, or zygote.

moratorium   The experience of conflict over the issues of identity formation prior to the establishment of firm goals and long-term commitments.

Moro reflex   A reflex in infants in response to a sudden loss of support or loud noise, in which they arch their back, throw their arms out, and quickly bring them in.

morphemes   The units of language that communicate meaning.

morphogens   Proteins that tag different embryonic cells for different functions.

morula   A solid cluster of cells resulting from the cleavage of a fertilized ovum.

multiple regression   A statistical technique designed to investigate the relationship between a set of predictor variables and an outcome variable.

multiply determined   Of characteristics that are the result of many contributing factors.

myelin   A fatty substance that coats axons and increases the speed of conduction of nerve impulses.

nature-nurture controversy   The controversy concerning whether heredity (nature) or the environment (nurture) is primarily responsible for development.

negative reinforcement   An event that increases the frequency of the behavior on which its removal is made contingent.

neglectful parenting   A style of parenting characterized by little warmth, nurturing, or supervision.

neurons   Brain cells responsible for the conduction of nerve impulses.

neurotransmitters   Chemicals released into the synapse that mediate the transmission of impulses.

nocturnal emission   A spontaneous ejaculation of seminal fluid during sleep; sometimes called a wet dream.

normally distributed   Frequency distributions in which most scores cluster around the middle, or the mean, in the shape of a bell curve.

nucleotides   Subunits of DNA consisting of a sugar molecule, a phosphate molecule, and a nitrogenous base.

obesity   A condition in which one weighs more than 30% above one's ideal body weight.

observational learning   In social-cognitive theory, learning by observing what others do and imitating what one sees.

Oedipal complex   A Freudian concept in which the young boy is sexually attracted to his mother.

operant conditioning   A simple form of learning in which the probability of a behavior is affected by its consequences.

outer cell mass   The outer layer of cells (the trophoblast) of the blastocyst that will develop into tissues supporting the developing organism.

ovaries   Structures within the female reproductive system flanking the uterus that house the ova and produce female sex hormones.

overextension   A child's use of a word to refer not only to all members of the group that the word labels for adults but also to other referents.

overt aggression   Hostility expressed in physical acts such as hitting, punching, and kicking.

overweight   A condition in which children are at or above the 85th percentile of weight for their height.

ovum (plural, ova)   The female sex cell, or gamete.

penis   The part of the external genitals in males that is the primary source of sexual stimulation.

penis envy   A Freudian concept in which the young girl longs for a penis.

peripheral nervous system   That part of the nervous system that connects the sensory receptors and muscles and glands and internal organs to the central nervous system.

personal fable   The feeling of being different and special; thought to derive from the imaginary audience.

phenotype   The observable or measurable characteristics of an organism, resulting from the interaction between the genotype and the environment.

phonemes   The smallest distinguishable units of sound in a language.

pituitary   An endocrine gland located beneath the hypothalamus that is part of a feedback system regulating the hormonal control of puberty.

placenta   A spongy mass of tissue attached to the uterine lining and connected to the embryo by the umbilical cord from which the fetus receives oxygen and nutrients and through which waste products are excreted.

plasticity   The degree to which one area of the brain can assume the functions governed by another area following injury to the latter.

positive reinforcement   An event that increases the frequency of the behavior on which its occurrence is made contingent.

postconventional moral reasoning   Kohlberg's third level of moral reasoning, in which moral thinking is guided by self-derived principles.

preconventional moral reasoning   Kohlberg's first level of moral reasoning, characterized by the absence of internalized standards.

preoperational thought   Piaget's second stage of intellectual development, thought to characterize toddlerhood and early childhood, during which experience is represented symbolically.

preterm   Infants born more than 3 weeks before the due date.

primary circular reactions   Substage 2 of Piaget's sensorimotor stage in which infants (1–4 months) repeat a physical behavior involving their own body.

primary motor cortex   The area of the cortex responsible for governing voluntary movement of discrete muscles.

primary sex characteristics   Sex differences in the reproductive system that develop during puberty.

prostate gland   A structure at the base of the urethra in males that is involved in producing sperm.

protective factors   Factors that counter risk factors and reduce the probability of undesirable developmental results.

proximity seeking   An infant's attempts to stay close to the mother and follow after her, asking to be picked up or attempting to crawl into her lap; a behavior seen during the clear-cut attachment phase.

proximodistal growth trend The developmental pattern in which growth progresses outward from the center of the body to the extremities.

pseudostupidity The inability to see the obvious by making a simple task more complicated than it is; believed to derive from the ability to think hypothetically and consider a problem from all possible perspectives.

quiet sleep A sleep state characterized by relative inactivity except for brief startles; there are no rapid eye movements (REM); also known as NREM (non-REM) sleep.

quiet wakefulness A waking state in which an infant is relaxed and attentive and moves its body little.

rapid eye movements (REM) Rapid movements of the eyes beneath closed lids during certain sleep stages.

recessive allele The gene of an allele pair that governs the expression of a trait only in the presence of another recessive allele.

reductionism The explanation of complex behaviors by reducing them to their simpler components.

reflective abstraction Piaget's term for the process in which features of actions become abstracted, turning the actions into thought.

regression Movement from a more complex, differentiated state to one that is less so, with decreases in the adaptiveness of behavior.

regulatory genes Genes in the DNA strand that regulate which genes are copied.

rehearsal Repeating items to be memorized; a common strategy for retaining items in short-term memory

reinforcement An event that, when it is made contingent on behavior, increases the frequency of that behavior.

relational aggression Hostility expressed in acts manipulating the relationship, such as divulging secrets or spreading lies.

REM smiles Early smiles in infants prompted by changes in brain-wave activity in the brain stem.

repression A defense mechanism that operates by relegating distressful thoughts and feelings to the unconscious.

repressors Proteins that inhibit the copying of DNA segments by picking up messages at regulatory sites along the DNA track and relaying them to coactivators.

resilient Able to recover readily from illness, change, or misfortune.

respondent conditioning A simple form of learning in which an involuntary reflex is brought under the control of another environmental stimulus.

risk factors Factors associated with an increased rate of undesirable behavior or disease.

RNA polymerase An enzyme that copies DNA into messenger RNA during the transcription process.

role clarity An understanding among family members about each one's role.

rooting reflex Turning the head and starting to suck in response to a brush on the cheek; an adaptive reflex in infants.

rubella German measles; once a common cause of birth defects in the United States.

"rules" for scanning Patterns of scanning used by infants to actively search for things in their visual field.

scaffolding model A model of language development that assumes that the impetus for language development is adults' initiation of conversation and providing of a scaffold, or structure, to support the emergence of new language forms.

schemas Piaget's term for the mental structures through which the child represents experience through actions.

scripts Schematic representations of familiar routines used by young children to organize and recall everyday events.

scrotum The sac that hangs just beneath the penis and houses the testes.

secondary circular reactions Substage 3 of Piaget's sensorimotor stage in which infants (4–8 months) repeat behaviors affecting objects outside their body.

secondary motor cortex The area of the cortex responsible for voluntary patterned movements of groups of muscles.

secondary sex characteristics Differences between females and males in body structure and appearance, other than differences in the reproductive system; include differences in skeletal structure, hair distribution, and skin texture.

secular trend The earlier onset of puberty, faster growth, and the differences in size, both in height and in weight reached by adolescents today than in the past.

secure base The use of the caregiver by infants as a base from which to venture forth to explore and to periodically return for comfort and reassurance.

self-disclosure The sharing or exchange of personal information; considered a primary basis for the development of intimacy.

semen A milky white fluid in which sperm are suspended.

seminal vesicles Structures within the male reproductive system in which sperm are stored.

sensitivity The ability to accurately "read" an infant's signals; a behavior related to the attachment relationship.

sensorimotor stage Piaget's first stage of intellectual development, during which sensory experiences are coordinated with motor behaviors.

sensory memory A very brief form of memory, lasting for less than a second, that is used during the processing of information.

separation anxiety The evident distress infants experience when the mother or other caregiver is out of sight; a behavior seen during the clear-cut attachment phase.

sex chromosomes The 23rd pair of chromosomes that determine the sex of the child; females have two X chromosomes, and males have one X and one Y chromosome.

sex constancy The understanding that one's sex remains the same and will not change as a function of how one looks or dresses; also termed gender constancy.

sex differences Biological and physiological differences distinguishing the sexes.

short-term memory The form of memory used for immediate tasks; its capacity is about seven items at one time; also known as working memory.

slow-to-warm infants Infants who have low activity levels, give mild reactions, are slow to adapt to changes,

tend to withdraw from new situations, and react to situations in a mild way; a temperament type identified by Thomas and Chess.

small for gestational age (SGA) Low-birthweight infants who weigh less than 90% of the infants of the same gestational age.

smegma A thick secretion that collects around the glans in males and under the prepuce.

social capital The relationships, both within the family and the community, that contribute to resiliency in children.

social referencing Checking with a caregiver or other familiar figure for cues about how to respond to a new or ambiguous event.

social smiling Smiling in response to what is taking place around one; expression of emotion that begins between 4 and 6 weeks.

sperm The male sex cell, or gamete.

spermarche A boy's first ejaculation of seminal fluid.

stage A level of development that is assumed to be qualitatively different from the earlier level from which it evolves. Stages are assumed to occur in a fixed sequence and to occur universally within a species.

standard deviation A standardized unit that expresses the average variability among scores.

strange situation A procedure used by Mary Ainsworth to assess differences in attachment security: The mother sits with the infant in a comfortable room until a stranger enters; she and the stranger talk a while and she leaves when the infant is not looking, leaving the infant alone with the stranger.

strategy Any activity that is consciously used to improve one's performance or attain a goal.

structural genes Genes in the DNA strand that provide the codes for the construction of new proteins.

sucking reflex Sucking in response to a touch on the mouth; an adaptive reflex in infants.

sudden infant death syndrome (SIDS) Also called crib death, the principal cause of death in infants from the 1st month to the 1st year of life; smoking during pregnancy increases the risk.

superego   In psychoanalytic theory, the aspect of the personality that represents the internalized standards and values of society and emerges when the child identifies with the parent of its own sex.

surfactant   A substance that lines the air pockets in the lungs.

surrogate birth mother   A woman who becomes pregnant usually by artificial insemination or surgical implantation of a fertilized egg for the purpose of carrying the fetus for another woman.

syphilis   A sexually transmitted bacterial infection that can cause damage to the central nervous system and to developing organs and bones; easily treated with antibiotics.

temperament   Underlying predispositions contributing to an infant's activity level, emotionality, and sociability.

teratogens   Agents that interfere with normal prenatal development.

tertiary circular reactions   Substage 5 of Piaget's sensorimotor stage in which infants (12–18 months) begin to experiment with different ways of accomplishing something; the beginning of problem solving.

testes   Structures within the male reproductive system contained in the scrotum that produce sperm and male sex hormones.

testosterone   A sex hormone produced by the testes.

theory   A set of testable statements derived from the axioms of a model.

toxoplasmosis   A parasitic disease, often transmitted in cat feces, that can cause birth defects if the mother is infected during the first trimester.

transfer RNA (tRNA)   The form of ribonucleic acid (RNA) that carries amino acids to the cytoplasm, where proteins are assembled according to the genetic code carried by the messenger RNA.

transition   The phase of labor when uterine contractions reach a peak and the cervix is nearly completely dilated.

transplacental infections   Infections of the fetus due to organisms that initially infect the mother and then cross the placenta.

trophoblast   The outer layer of blastocyst cells from which develop the tissues that support the developing organism.

Turner's syndrome   A rare genetic disorder in females caused by the absence of one X chromosome; characterized by a distinctive physical appearance (such as webbing of the neck and drooping eyelids) and failure of the ovaries to develop.

umbilical cord   The cord connecting the embryo to the placenta through which oxygenated blood and nutrients are carried to the organism, and waste products are removed.

unconditional response (UCR)   In respondent conditioning, the reflexive response to a particular stimulus.

unconditional stimulus (UCS)   In respondent conditioning, the stimulus that triggers a reflexive, or unconditional, response.

underextension   A child's use of a word to refer to only some but not all of the instances for which it is used by adults.

unexamined ethnic identity   The initial stage in ethnic identity formation; a lack of awareness of the issues related to one's ethnicity; a simple internalization of the values of the dominant culture.

urethra   The urinary canal, leading from the bladder to the urethral opening.

uterus   A muscular enclosure at the top of the vagina that holds the fetus during pregnancy.

vagina   The muscular tube in females leading from the labia at its opening to the uterus.

vas deferens   Long coiled tube that carries sperm to the seminal vesicles, where they are stored.

vernix   A protective white, greasy coating that covers the skin of the fetus.

visual acuity   Ability to see fine detail.

vocabulary explosion   The rapid addition of new words to a toddler's vocabulary; usually occurs late in the 2nd year.

WAIS-R An intelligence scale for adults that is individually administered.

whole-language approach An approach to teaching reading that starts by exposing children to contexts where reading is important in order to engage their interest so that they will be motivated to attempt to read and discover the basic principles of reading.

XYY syndrome A genetic disorder in males caused by an extra Y chromosome; symptoms may include above-average stature, speech delays, learning disabilities, some degree of mental retardation, and behavior disturbance; also known as polysome Y syndrome.

yolk sac A sac outside the body of the embryo that produces blood cells until the embryo's liver, spleen, and bone marrow are sufficiently developed to take over this function.

you-message A message communicating what you think of another person.

zona reaction A release of granular particles and enzymes beneath the ovum's outer membrane, triggered by the sperm's fusion with the ovum's membrane, that affects the membrane's ability to bind with sperm.

zone of proximal development Vygotsky's term for the closeness between a person's current performance and what it might optimally be; readiness to learn something new.

zygote A single cell resulting from the union of the ovum and sperm at conception.

References

Aboud, F. E. (1987). The development of ethnic self-identification and attitudes. In J. S. Phinney & M. J. Rotheram (Eds.), *Children's ethnic socialization.* Beverly Hills, CA: Sage.

Acredolo, L. P. (1978). The development of spatial orientation in infancy. *Developmental Psychology, 14,* 224–234.

Acredolo, L. P., & Hake, J. L. (1982). Infant perception. In B. J. Wolman (Ed.), *Handbook of developmental psychology.* Englewood Cliffs, NJ: Prentice-Hall.

Adler, N., Smith, L., & Tschann, J. (1998). Abortion among adolescents. In L. Beckman & S. Harvey (Eds.), *The new Civil War.* Washington, DC: American Psychological Association.

Ahlsten, G., Cnattinguis, S., & Lindmark, G. (1993). Cessation of smoking during pregnancy improves fetal growth and reduces infant morbidity in the neonatal period: A population-based prospective study. *Acta Paediatrica, 82,* 177–181.

Aiken, L. R. (1987). *Assessment of intellectual functioning.* Boston: Allyn & Bacon.

Ainsworth, M. D. S. (1973). The development of infant-mother attachment. In B. M. Caldwell & H. N. Ricciuti (Eds.), *Review of child development research* (Vol. 3). Chicago: University of Chicago Press.

Ainsworth, M. D. S. (1985). Attachments across the lifespan. *Bulletin of the New York Academy of Medicine, 61,* 791–812.

Ainsworth, M. D. S. (1993). Attachment as related to mother-infant interaction. In C. Rovee-Collier & L. P. Lipsett (Eds.), *Advances in infancy research* (Vol. 8). Norwood, NJ: Ablex.

Ainsworth, M. D. S., & Bell, S. M. (1969). Some contemporary patterns of mother-infant interaction in the feeding situation. In A. Ambrose (Ed.), *Stimulation in early infancy.* New York: Academic Press.

Ainsworth, M. D. S., Blehar, M. C., Waters, E., & Wall, S. (1978). *Patterns of attachment: A psychological study of the strange situation.* Hillsdale, NJ: Erlbaum.

Ainsworth, M. D. S., & Marvin, R. S. (1995). On the shaping of attachment theory and research: An interview with Mary D. S. Ainsworth (Fall 1994). In E. Waters, B. E. Vaughn, G. Posada, & K. Kondo-Ikemura (Eds.), Caregiving, cultural, and cognitive perspectives on secure-base behavior and working models: New growing points of attachment theory and research. *Monographs of the Society for Research in Child Development,* Serial No. 244, 60, Nos. 2–3.

Aitken, D., & Chaplin, J. (1990). Sex miseducation. *Family Therapy Networker, 14,* 24–25.

Akers, J. F., Jones, R. M., & Coyl, D. D. (1998). Adolescent friendship pairs: Similarities in identity status development, behaviors, attitudes, and intentions. *Journal of Adolescent Research, 13,* 178–201.

Alibali, M. W. (1999). How children change their minds: Strategy change can be gradual or abrupt. *Developmental Psychology, 35,* 127–145.

Allen, K. E., & Marotz, L. (1989). *Developmental profiles: Birth to six.* Albany, NY: Delmar.

Almeida, D. M., Wethington, E., & Chandler, A. L. (1999). Daily transmission of tensions between marital dyads and parent-child dyads. *Journal of Marriage and the Family, 61,* 49–61.

Als, H. (1995). The preterm infant: A model for the study of fetal brain expectation. In J. P. Lecanuet, W. P. Fifer, N. A. Krasnegor, & W. P. Smotherman (Eds.), *Fetal development: A psychobiological perspective* (pp. 439–471). Hillsdale, NJ: Erlbaum.

Amato, P. R. (1993). Children's adjustment to divorce: Theories, hypotheses and empirical support. *Journal of Marriage and the Family, 55,* 23–38.

Amato, P. R., & Gilbreth, J. G. (1999). Nonresident fathers and children's well-being: A meta-analysis. *Journal of Marriage and the Family, 61,* 557–573.

Ambler, J. S. (1994). Who benefits from school choice: Some evidence from Europe. *Journal of Policy Analysis and Management, 13,* 454–476.

American Psychiatric Association. (1985). Functional enuresis. In *Diagnostic and statistical manual of mental disorders III-R.* Washington, DC: Author.

American Psychiatric Association. (1994). *Diagnostic and statistical manual of mental disorders* (4th ed.). Washington, DC: Author.

Ampofo-Boateng, K., Thomson, J. A., Grieve, R., Pitcairn, T., Lee, D. N., & Demetre, J. D. (1993). A developmental and training study of children's ability to find safe routes to cross the road. *British Journal of Developmental Psychology, 11,* 31–45.

Ansuini, C. G., Fiddler-Woite, J., & Woite, R. S. (1996). The source, accuracy, and impact of initial sexuality information on lifetime wellness. *Adolescence, 31,* 283–289.

Archer, S. L. (1985). Career and/or family: The identity process for adolescent girls. *Youth and Society, 16,* 289–314.

Archer, S. L. (1989a). Gender differences in identity development: Issues of process, domain, and timing. *Journal of Adolescence, 12,* 117–138.

Archer, S. L. (1989b). The status of identity: Reflections on the need for intervention. *Journal of Adolescence, 12,* 345–359.

Archer, S. L. (1992). A feminist's approach to identity research. In G. R. Adams, T. P. Gullotta, & R. Montemayor (Eds.), *Adolescent identity formation.* Newbury Park, CA: Sage.

Arduini, D., Rizzo, G., & Romanini, C. (1995). Fetal behavioral states and behavioral transitions in normal and compromised fetuses. In J. P. Lecanuet, W. P. Fifer, N. A. Krasnegor, & W. P. Smotherman (Eds.), *Fetal development: A psychobiological perspective* (pp. 83–99). Hillsdale, NJ: Erlbaum.

Arehart, D. M., & Smith, P. H. (1990). Identity in adolescence: Influences of dysfunction and psychosocial task issues. *Journal of Youth and Adolescence, 19,* 36–72.

Arey, L. B. (1954). *Developmental anatomy.* Philadelphia: W. B. Saunders.

Armstrong, D. F., Stokoe, W. C., & Wilcox, S. E. (1995). *Gesture and the nature of language.* Cambridge: Cambridge University Press.

Arnett, J. J., & Taber, S. (1994). Adolescence terminable and interminable: When does adolescence end? *Journal of Youth and Adolescence, 23,* 517–537.

Artman, L., & Cahan, S. (1993). Schooling and the development of transitive inference. *Developmental Psychology, 29,* 753–759.

Asher, S. R. (1983). Social competence and peer status: Recent advances and future directions. *Child Development, 54,* 1427–1434.

Asher, S. R., Markell, R. A., & Hymel, S. (1981). Identifying children at risk in peer relations: A critique of the rate-of-interaction approach to assessment. *Child Development, 52,* 1239–1245.

Bahrick, L. E., Walker, A. S., & Neisser, U. (1981). Selective looking by infants. *Cognitive Psychology, 13,* 877-890.

Baillargeon, R. (1987). Object permanence in 3½- and 4½-month-old infants. *Developmental Psychology, 23,* 655–664.

Bakan, D. (1966). *The duality of human existence: Isolation and communion in Western man.* Boston: Beacon Press.

Baldwin, D. A., Markman, E. M., Bill, B., Desjardins, N., Irwin, J. M., & Tidball, G. (1996). Infants' reliance on a social criterion for establishing word-object relations. *Child Development, 67,* 3135–3153.

Ball, E. W. (1997). Phonological awareness: Implications for whole language and emergent literacy programs. *Topics in Language Disorders, 17,* 14–26.

Bandura, A. (1977). *Social learning theory.* Englewood Cliffs, NJ: Prentice-Hall.

Bandura, A. (1980). Self-referent thought: A developmental analysis of self-efficacy. In J. H. Flavell & L. D. Ross (Eds.), *Cognitive social development: Frontiers and possible futures.* New York: Cambridge University Press.

Bandura, A., Ross, D., & Ross, S. A. (1963). Imitation of film-mediated aggressive models. *Journal of Abnormal and Social Psychology, 66,* 3–11.

Banks, C. A. McG. (1993). Restructuring schools for equity: What we have learned in two decades. *Phi Delta Kappan, 75,* 42–48.

Banks, J. A. (1993). Multicultural education: Development, dimensions, and challenges. *Phi Delta Kappan, 75,* 22–28.

Bardwick, J. M., & Douvan, E. (1971). Ambivalence: The socialization of women. In V. Gornick & B. K. Moran (Eds.), *Women in sexist society.* New York: Basic Books.

Barkley, R. A. (1990). *Attention deficit hyperactivity disorder: A handbook for diagnosis and treatment.* New York: Guilford Press.

Barnard, K. E., Morisset, C. E., & Spieker, S. (1993). Preventive interventions: Enhancing parent-infant relationships. In C. H. Zeanah, Jr. (Ed.), *Handbook of infant development.* New York: Guilford Press.

Barnett, W. S. (1992). Benefits of compensatory preschool education. *Journal of Human Resources, 27,* 279–312.

Barnett, W. S. (1995). Long-term effects of early childhood programs on cognitive and school outcomes. *The Future of Children, 5,* 25–50.

Baron, J. B., & Sternberg R. J. (1987). *Teaching thinking skills: Theory and practice.* New York: Freeman.

Barrera, M., Jr., Chassin, L., & Rogosch, F. (1993). Effects of social support and conflict on adolescent children of alcoholic and nonalcoholic fathers. *Journal of Personality and Social Psychology, 64,* 602–612.

Barrett, K. C. (1995). A functionalist approach to shame and guilt. In J. P. Tangney & K. W. Fischer, (Eds.), *Self-conscious emotions: The psychology of shame, guilt, embarrassment, and pride* (pp. 25–63). New York: Guilford Press.

Barrett, K. C., Zahn-Waxler, C., & Cole, P. M. (1993). Avoiders vs. amenders: Implications for the investigation of guilt and shame during toddlerhood? *Cognition and Emotion, 7,* 481–505.

Barrett, M. (1995). Early lexical development. In P. Fletcher & B. MacWhinney (Eds.), *The handbook of child language* (pp. 362–392). Oxford: Blackwell.

Barth, R. P., Fetro, J. V., Leland, N., & Volkan, K. (1992). Preventing adolescent pregnancy with social and cognitive skills. *Journal of Adolescent Research, 7,* 208–232.

Bartle, S. E., Anderson, S. A., & Sabatelli, R. M. (1989). A model of parenting style, adolescent individuation and adolescent self-esteem: Preliminary findings. *Journal of Adolescent Research, 4,* 283–298.

Bartsch, K. (1996). Between desires and beliefs: Young children's action predictions. *Child Development, 67,* 1671–1685.

Bartsch, K., & Wellman, H. M. (1995). *Children talk about the mind.* New York: Oxford University Press.

Bast, J., & Reitsma, P. (1998). Analyzing the development of individual differences in terms of Matthew effects in reading: Results from a Dutch longitudinal study. *Developmental Psychology, 34,* 1373–1399.

Bates, E., Camaioni, L., & Volterra, V. (1975). The acquisition of performatives prior to speech. *Merrill Palmer Quarterly, 2,* 205–226.

Bath, J. (1998). Dealing with nocturnal enuresis in children. *Community Nurse, 4,* 15–16.

Bauer, P. J., & Mandler, J. M. (1989). Taxonomies and triads: Conceptual organization in one- to two-year-olds. *Cognitive Psychology, 21,* 156–184.

Baugher, E., & Lamison-White, L. (1996). *Poverty in the United States: 1995* (U.S. Bureau of the Census Current population reports, Series P60-194). Washington, DC: U.S. Government Printing Office.

Baumeister, L. M., Flores, E., & Marin, B. V. (1995). Sex information given to Latina adolescents by parents. *Health Education Research, 10,* 233–239.

Baumrind, D. (1967). Child care practices anteceding three patterns of preschool behavior. *Genetic Psychology Monographs, 75,* 43–88.

Baumrind, D. (1971). Current patterns of parental authority. *Developmental Psychology Monographs, 4,* 1–103.

Baumrind, D. (1989). Rearing competent children. In W. Damon (Ed.), *Child development today and tomorrow* (pp. 349–378). San Francisco: Jossey-Bass.

Baumrind, D. (1991). Effective parenting during the early adolescent transition. In P. A. Cowan & E. M. Hetherington (Eds.), *Family transitions* (pp. 111–164). Hillsdale, NJ: Erlbaum.

Baumrind, D. (1993). The average expectable environment is not good enough: A response to Scarr. *Child Development, 64,* 1199–1217.

Baumrind, D. (1996). The discipline controversy revisited. *Family Relations, 45,* 405–414.

Baxter, C. (1999). Gryphon. In J. A. Stanford (Ed.), *Responding to literature* (3rd ed., pp. 908–920). Mountain View, CA: Mayfield. (Reprinted from *Through the safety net,* by C. Baxter, 1985, New York: Viking)

Beardsley, T. (1991). Smart genes. *Scientific American, 265,* 86–95.

Beckman, L., & Harvey, S. (1998). *The new Civil War: The psychology, culture, and politics of abortion.* Washington, DC: American Psychological Association.

Belenky, M. F., Clinchy, B. M., Goldberger, N. R., & Tarule, J. M. (1986). *Women's ways of knowing.* New York: Basic Books.

Belkin, L. (1999, July 25). "Getting the girl." *The New York Times Magazine,* 26–31, 38, 54.

Bell, R. Q. (1968). A reinterpretation of the direction of effects in studies of socialization. *Psychological Review, 75,* 81–85.

Belle, D. (1994). Social support issues for "latchkey" and supervised children. In F. Nestmann & K. Hurrelmann (Eds.), *Social networks and social support in childhood and adolescence* (pp. 293–304). New York: Walter de Gruyter.

Belsky, J. (1984). The determinants of parenting: A process model. *Child Development, 55,* 83–96.

Belsky, J. (1986). Infant day care: A cause for concern? *Zero to Three, 6,* 1–7.

Belsky, J. (1990). Parental and nonparental care and chidren's socio-emotional development: A decade in review. *Journal of Marriage and the Family, 52,* 885–903.

Belsky, J. (1996). Parent, infant, and social-contextual antecedents of father-son attachment security. *Developmental Psychology, 32,* 905–913.

Belsky, J., Campbell, S. B., Cohn, J. F., & Moore, G. (1996). Instability of infant-parent attachment security. *Developmental Psychology, 32,* 921–924.

Bem, S. L. (1981). Gender schema theory: A cognitive account of sex-typing. *Psychological Review, 88,* 354–364.

Bem, S. L. (1985). Androgyny and gender schema theory: A conceptual and empirical integration. In T. B. Sonderegger (Ed.), *Nebraska symposium on motivation, 1984: Psychology and gender* (pp. 179–226). Lincoln: University of Nebraska Press.

Benbow, C. P., & Stanley, J. C. (1980). Sex differences in mathematical ability: Fact or artifact? *Science, 210,* 1262–1264.

Benbow, C. P., & Stanley, J. C. (1982). Consequences in high school and college of sex differences in mathematical reasoning ability: A longitudinal perspective. *American Educational Research Journal, 19,* 598–622.

Benbow, C. P., & Stanley, J. C. (1983). Sex differences in mathematical reasoning ability: More facts. *Science, 222,* 1029–1031.

Benda, B. B., & DiBlasio, F. A. (1994). An integration of theory: Adolescent sexual contacts. *Journal of Youth and Adolescence, 23,* 403–420.

Bendersky, M., Alessandri, S. M., Sullivan, M. W., & Lewis, M. (1995). Measuring the effects of prenatal cocaine exposure. In M. Lewis & M. Bendersky (Eds.), *Mothers, babies, and cocaine: The role of toxins in development* (pp. 163–178). Hillsdale, NJ: Erlbaum.

Benedikt, R., Wertheim, E. H., & Lave, A. (1998). Eating attitudes and weight-loss attempts in female adolescents and their mothers. *Journal of Youth and Adolescence, 27,* 43–57.

Benenson, J. F., Apostoleris, N. H., & Parnass, J. (1997). Age and sex differences in dyadic and group interaction. *Developmental Psychology, 33,* 538–543.

Benoit, D., & Parker, K. C. H. (1994). Stability and transmission of attachment across three generations. *Child Development, 65,* 1444–1456.

Berezin, J. (1990). *The complete guide to choosing child care.* New York: Random House.

Berman, B. D., Winkleby, M., Chesterman, E., & Boyce, W. T. (1992). After-school child care and self-esteem in school-age children. *Pediatrics, 89,* 654–659.

Berndt, T. J. (1982). The features and effects of friendships in early adolescence. *Child Development, 53,* 1447–1461.

Bernstein, A., & Cowan, P. (1975). Children's concepts of how people get babies. *Child Development, 46,* 77–91.

Bertenthal, B. I., Campos, J. J., & Barrett, K. (1984). Self-produced locomotion: An organizer of emotional, cognitive, and social development in infancy. In R. Emde & R. Harmon. *Continuities and discontinuities in development* (pp. 174–210). New York: Plenum Press.

Bertenthal, B. I., & Fischer, K. W. (1978). Development of self-recognition in the infant. *Developmental Psychology, 14,* 44–50.

Best, C. T. (1988). The emergence of cerebral asymmetries in early human development: A literature review and a neuroembryological model. In D. L. Molfese & S. J. Segalowitz (Eds.), *Brain lateralization in children: Developmental implications* (pp. 5–34). New York: Guilford Press.

Betancourt, H., & Lopez, S. R. (1993). The study of culture, ethnicity, and race in American psychology. *American Psychologist, 48,* 629–637.

Bigler, R. S., Jones, L. C., & Lobliner, D. B. (1997). Social categorization and the formation of intergroup attitudes in children. *Child Development, 68,* 530–543.

Birch, L. L. (1980). Effects of poor models' food choices and eating behaviors on preschoolers' food preferences. *Child Development, 51,* 489–496.

Birch, L. L., & Deysher, M. (1986). Caloric compensation and sensory specific satiety: Evidence for self-regulation of food intake by young children. *Learning & Motivation, 16,* 341–355.

Birch, L. L., & Fisher, J. O. (1998). Development of eating behaviors among children and adolescents. *Pediatrics, 101,* 539–549.

Birch, L. L., Johnson, S. L., Andresen, G., Peters, J. C., & Schulte, M. C. (1991). The variability of young children's energy intake. *New England Journal of Medicine, 324,* 232–235.

Birch, L. L., McPhee, L., Shoba, B. C., Steinberg, L., &

Krehbiel, R. (1987). "Clean up your plate": Effects of child feeding practices on the conditioning of meal size. *Learning & Motivation, 18,* 301–317.

Bjorklund, D. F. (1989). *Children's thinking.* Pacific Grove, CA: Brooks/Cole.

Blader, J. C., Koplewicz, H. S., Abikoff, H., & Foley, C. (1997). Sleep problems of elementary school children. *Archive of Pediatric Adolescent Medicine, 151,* 473–480.

Bledsoe, E. (1996). "Out of a jam." From *Chicken soup for the soul: Home delivery.* An e-mail service from M. V. Hansen.

Bloom, L., Margulis, C., Tinker, E., & Fujita, N. (1996). Early conversations and word learning: Contributions from child and adult. *Child Development, 67,* 3154–3175.

Blumberg, M. S., & Lucas, D .E. (1996). A developmental and component analysis of active sleep. *Developmental Psychobiology, 29,* 1–22.

Blumenthal, S. J., & Kupfer, D. J. (1988). Overview of early detection and treatment strategies for suicidal behavior in young people. *Journal of Youth and Adolescence, 17,* 1–23.

Blyth, D. A., & Leffert, N. (1995). Communities as contexts for adolescent development: An empirical analysis. *Journal of Adolescent Research, 10,* 64–87.

Bolger, K. E., Patterson, C. J., & Kupersmidt, J. B. (1998). Peer relationships and self-esteem among children who have been maltreated. *Child Development, 69,* 1171–1191.

Bolton, I. M. (1989). Perspectives of youth on preventive intervention strategies. *Report of the Secretary's Task Force on Youth Suicide* (Vol. 3). Washington, DC: U.S. Government Printing Office.

Boone, R. T., & Cunningham, J. G. (1998). Children's decoding of emotion in expressive body movement: The development of cue attunement. *Developmental Psychology, 34,* 1007–1016.

Booth, J. R., Perfetti, C. A., MacWhinney, B. (1999). Quick, automatic, and general activation of orthographic and phonological representations in young readers. *Developmental Psychology, 35,* 3–19.

Bornstein, M. H., Haynes, O. M., O'Reilly, A. W., & Painter, K. M. (1996). Solitary and collaborative pretense play in early childhood: Sources of individual variation in the development of representational competence. *Child Development, 67,* 2910–2929.

Bosma, H. A., Jackson, S. E., Zijsling, D. H., Zani, B., Cicognani, E., Xerri, M. L., Honess, T. M., & Charman, L. (1996). Who has the final say? Decisions on adolescent behavior within the family. *Journal of Adolescence, 19,* 277–291.

Bouchard, C., Malina, R. M., & Perusse, L. (1997). *Genetics of fitness and physical performance.* Auckland, New Zealand: Human Kinetics.

Bourne, E. (1978a). The state of research on ego identity: A review and appraisal. Part I. *Journal of Youth and Adolescence, 7,* 223–257.

Bourne, E. (1978b). The state of research on ego identity: A review and appraisal. Part II. *Journal of Youth and Adolescence, 7*, 371–392.

Bower, T. G. R. (1982). *Development in infancy* (2nd ed.). San Francisco: W. H. Freeman.

Bower, T. G. R., Broughton, J. M., & Moore, M. K. (1971). The development of the object concept as manifested by changes in the tracking behavior of infants between 7 and 20 weeks of age. *Journal of Experimental Child Psychology, 11*, 182–193.

Bowlby, J. (1982). *Attachment: Attachment and loss* (Vol. 1). New York: Basic Books.

Boyce, W. T., & Jemerin, J. M. (1990). Psychobiological differences in childhood stress response: I. Patterns of illness and susceptibility. *Developmental and Behavioral Pediatrics, 11*, 86–93.

Boyes, M. C., & Chandler, M. (1992). Cognitive development, epistemic doubt, and identity formation in adolescence. *Journal of Youth and Adolescence, 21*, 277–304.

Bradbury, M. G., & Meadow, S. R. (1995). Combined treatment with enuresis alarm and desmopressin for nocturnal enuresis. *Acta Paediatrica, 84*, 1014–1018.

Bradley, R. H., Whiteside, L., Mundfrom, D. J., Casey, P. H., Kelleher, K. J., & Pope, S. K. (1994). Early indications of resilience and their relation to experiences in the home environments of low birthweight, premature children living in poverty. *Child Development, 65*, 346–360.

Braine, M. D. S. (1963). The ontogeny of English phrase structure: The first phase. *Language, 39*, 3–13.

Brazelton, T. B., & Cramer, B. G. (2000). Caring for a premature infant. In D. N. Sattler, G. P. Kramer, V. Shabatay, & D. A. Bernstein (Eds.), *Child development in context; Voices and perspectives* (pp. 16–20). Boston: Houghton Mifflin.

Brent, D. A., Perper, J. A., Goldstein, C. E., Kolko, D. J., Allan, M. J., Allman, C. J., & Zelenak, J. P. (1988). Risk factors for adolescent suicide: A comparison of adolescent suicide victims with suicidal in-patients. *Archives of General Psychiatry, 45*, 581–588.

Brice-Heath, S. (1982). Questioning at home and at school: A comparative study. In G. Spindler (Ed.), *The school achievement of minority children: New perspectives*. Hillsdale, NJ: Erlbaum.

Brinthaupt, T. M., & Lipka, R. P. (1985). Developmental differences in self-concept and self-esteem among kindergarten through twelfth grade students. *Child Study Journal, 15*, 207–221.

Brodinsky, D. M., Singer, L. M., & Braff, A. M. (1984). Children's understanding of adoption. *Child Development, 55*, 869–878.

Brody, G. H., Stoneman, Z., & Flor, D. (1996). Parental religiosity, family processes, and youth competence in rural, two-parent African American families. *Developmental Psychology, 32*, 696–706.

Brody, G. H., Stoneman, Z., & Gauger, K. (1996). Parent-child relationships, family problem-solving behavior, and sibling relationship quality: The moderating role of sibling temperaments. *Child Development, 67*, 1289–1300.

Brody, G. H., Stoneman, Z., & McCoy, J. K. (1994). Forecasting sibling relationships in early adolescence from child temperaments and family processes in middle childhood. *Child Development, 65*, 771–784.

Bronfenbrenner, U. (1979). *The ecology of human development*. Cambridge, MA: Harvard University Press.

Bronfenbrenner, U. (1990). Discovering what families need. In D. Blankenhorn, S. Bayme, & J. B. Elshtain (Eds.), *Rebuilding the nest* (pp. 27–38). Milwaukee, WI: Family Service American.

Bronson, G. W. (1974). The postnatal growth of visual capacity. *Child Development, 45*, 873–890.

Bronson, G. W. (1982). *The scanning patterns of human infants: Implications for visual learning*. Norwood, NJ: Ablex.

Bronson, G. W. (1994). Infants' transitions toward adult-like scanning. *Child Development, 65*, 1243–1261.

Brooks-Gunn, J. (1991). Consequences of maturational timing variations in adolescent girls. In R. M. Lerner, A. C. Petersen, & J. Brooks-Gunn (Eds.), *Encyclopedia of adolescence* (Vol. 2, pp. 614–618). New York: Garland.

Brooks-Gunn, J., & Duncan, G. J., (1997). The effects of poverty on children. *Children and Poverty, 7*, 55–71.

Brooks-Gunn, J., & Ruble, D. N. (1982). The development of menstrual-related beliefs and behaviors during early adolescence. *Child Development, 53*, 1557–1566.

Brooks-Gunn, J., & Ruble, D. N. (1986). Men's and women's attitudes and beliefs about the menstrual cycle. *Sex Roles, 14*, 287–299.

Brooks-Gunn, J., & Warren, M. P. (1985). Measuring physical status and timing in early adolescence: A developmental perspective. *Journal of Youth and Adolescence, 14*, 163–189.

Brown, J. L., & Pollitt, E. (1996). Malnutrition, poverty, and intellectual development. *Scientific American, 274*(2), 38–43.

Brown, J. R., Donelan-McCall, N., & Dunn, J. (1996). Why talk about mental states? The significance of children's conversations with friends, siblings, and mothers. *Child Development, 67*, 836–849.

Brown, R. (1957). Linguistic determinism and the part of speech. *Journal of Abnormal and Social Psychology, 55*, 1–5.

Brown, R. (1958). How shall a thing be called? *Psychological Review, 65*, 14–21.

Brown, R. (1965). *Social psychology*. New York: Free Press.

Brown, R. (1973). *A first language: The early stages*. London: Allen & Unwin.

Bruner, J. S. (1983). *Child's talk: Learning to use language.* Oxford: Oxford University Press.

Brunquell, D., Crichton, & L., Egeland, B. (1981). Maternal personality and attitude in disturbances of child rearing. *American Journal of Orthopsychiatry, 51,* 680–690.

Bryant, B. K. (1994). How does social support function in childhood? In F. Nestmann & K. Hurrelmann (Eds.), *Social networks and social support in childhood and adolescence* (pp. 23–36). New York: Walter de Gruyter.

Bryk, A. S., Lee, V., & Holland, P. B. (1993). *Catholic schools and the common good.* Cambridge, MA: Harvard University Press.

Buchanan, C. M., Maccoby, E. E., & Dornbusch, S. M. (1992). Adolescents and their families after divorce: Three residential arrangements compared. *Journal of Research on Adolescence, 2,* 261–291.

Bugental, D. B., Lyon, J. E., Lin, E. K., McGrath, E. P., & Bimbela, A. (1999). Children "tune out" in response to the ambiguous communication style of powerless adults. *Child Development, 70,* 214–230.

Burchinal, M. R., Campbell, F. A., Bryant, D. M., Wasik, B. H., & Ramey, C. T. (1997). Early intervention and mediating processes in cognitive performance of children of low-income African American families. *Child Development, 68,* 935–954.

Burchinal, M. R., Ramey, S. L., Reid, M. K., & Jaccard, J. (1995). Early child care experiences and their association with family and child characteristics during middle childhood. *Early Childhood Research Quarterly, 10,* 33–61.

Burhans, K. K., & Dweck, C. S. (1995). Helplessness in early childhood: The role of contingent worth. *Child Development, 66,* 1719–1738.

Butler, G. E., McKie, M., & Ratcliffe, S. G. (1990). The cyclical nature of prepubertal growth. *Annals of Human Biology, 17,* 177–190.

Butler, R. (1998). Age trends in the use of social and temporal comparison for self-evaluation: Examination of a novel developmental hypothesis. *Child Development, 69,* 1054–1073.

Cain, K. M., & Dweck, C. S. (1995). The relation between motivational patterns and achievement cognitions through the elementary school years. *Merrill-Palmer Quarterly, 41,* 25–52.

Cain, V. S., & Hofferth, S. L. (1989). Parental choice of self-care for school-age children. *Journal of Marriage and the Family, 51,* 65–77.

Camarena, P. M., Sarigiani, P. A., & Petersen, A. C. (1990). Gender-specific pathways to intimacy in early adolescence. *Journal of Youth and Adolescence, 19,* 19–32.

Campbell, F. A., Helms, R., Sparling, J. J., & Ramey, C. T. (1998). Early childhood programs and success in school: The Abecedarian study. In W. S. Barnett et al. (Eds.), *Early care and education for children in poverty: Promises, programs, and long-term results.* Albany: State University of New York Press.

Campione, J. C., & Brown, A. L. (1978). Toward a theory of intelligence: Contributions from research with retarded children. *Intelligence, 2,* 279–304.

Canobi, K. H., Reeve, R. A., & Pattison, P. E. (1998). The role of conceptual understanding in children's addition problem solving. *Developmental Psychology, 34,* 882–891.

Cantwell, D. P. (1996). Attention deficit disorder: A review of the past 10 years. *Journal of the American Academy of Child and Adolescent Psychiatry, 35,* 978–987.

Carey, S. (1978). The child as word learner. In M. Halle, J. Bresnan, & G. A. Miller (Eds.), *Linguistic theory and psychological reality* (pp. 264–293). Cambridge, MA: MIT Press.

Carter, D. B., & Levy, G. D. (1988). Cognitive aspects of early sex-role development: The influence of gender schemas on preschoolers' memories and preferences for sex-typed toys and activities. *Child Development, 59,* 782–792.

Casas, J. M., Wagenheim, B. R., Banchero, R., & Mendoza-Romero, J. (1994). Hispanic masculinity: Myth or psychological schema meriting clinical consideration? *Hispanic Journal of Behavioral Sciences, 16,* 315–331.

Casco, C., Tressoldi, P. E., & Dellantonio, A. (1998). Visual selective attention and reading efficiency are related in children. *Cortex, 34,* 531–546.

Case, R. (1992). The role of the frontal lobes in the regulation of cognitive development. *Brain and Cognition, 20,* 51–73.

Cash, T. F., & Henry, P. E. (1995). Women's body images: The results of a national survey in the USA. *Sex Roles, 33,* 19–28.

Caughy, M. O., DiPietro, J. A., & Strobino, D. M. (1994). Day-care participation as a protective factor in the cognitive development of low-income children. *Child Development, 65,* 457–471.

Caviness, V. S., Jr., Kennedy, D. N., Bates, J. F., & Makris, N. (1997). The developing human brain: A morphometric profile (pp. 3–14). In R. W. Thatcher, G. R. Lyon, J. Rumsey, & N. Krasnegor (Eds.), *Developmental neuroimaging: Mapping the development of brain and behavior.* San Diego: Academic Press.

Cech, D., & Martin, S. (1995). *Functional movement development across the life span.* Philadelphia: W. B. Saunders.

Center to Prevent Handgun Violence. (2000). *The school shootings . . . and beyond.* Retrieved March 8, 2000, from the World Wide Web: http://www.handguncontrol.org/chldgns.htm

Centers for Disease Control and Prevention. (1993). Recommendations of the International Task Force for Disease Eradication. *Morbidity and Mortality Weekly Report, 42,* 17.

Centers for Disease Control and Prevention. (1995a). Monthly immunization table. *Morbidity and Mortality Weekly Report, 44*(43), 823.

Centers for Disease Control and Prevention. (1995b). Symptoms of substance dependence associated with use of cigarettes, alcohol, and illicit drugs—United States, 1991–1992. *Morbidity and Mortality Weekly Reports, 44*(44), 830–831; 838–839.

Centers for Disease Control and Prevention. (1995c). Update: AIDS among women—United States, 1994. *Morbidity and Mortality Weekly Report, 44*(5), 81–84.

Centers for Disease Control and Prevention. (1995d). Vaccination coverage levels among children aged 19–35 months—United States, April–June 1994. *Morbidity and Mortality Weekly Report, 44*(20), 396–398.

Centers for Disease Control and Prevention. (1996a). CDC surveillance summaries, September 27, 1996. *Morbidity and Mortality Weekly Report, 45* (No. SS-4).

Centers for Disease Control and Prevention. (1996b). Youth risk behavior surveillance—United States, 1995. *Morbidity and Mortality Weekly Report, 45* (No. SS-4), 1–86.

Centers for Disease Control and Prevention. (1999). Prevalence of sedentary leisure-time behavior among adults in the United States. Retrieved October 4, 1999, from the World Wide Web: http://www.cdc.gov/nchswww/products/pubs/pubd/hestats/3and4/sedentary.htm

Centers for Disease Control and Prevention. (2000, Winter). Preventing obesity among children. *Chronic Disease Notes & Reports, 13*, 1–4.

Chandler, M. (1997). Rescuing magical thinking from the jaws of social determinism. *Child Development, 68*, 1021–1023.

Chandler, M. J., & Hala, S. M. (1994). The role of personal involvement in the assessment of early false-belief skills. In C. Lewis & P. Mitchell (Eds.), *Origins of an understanding of mind* (pp. 403–426). Hove: Erlbaum.

Changeux, J. P., & Danchin, A. (1976). Selective stabilisation of developing synapses as a mechanism for the specification of neuronal networks. *Nature, 264*, 705–712.

Chao, R. K. (1994). Beyond parental control and authoritarian parenting style: Understanding Chinese parenting through the cultural notion of training. *Child Development, 65*, 1111–1119.

Charpak, N., Ruiz-Pelaez, J. G., Figueroa de C., Z., & Charpak, Y. (1997). Kangaroo mother versus traditional care for newborn infants less than 2000 grams: A randomized, controlled trial. *Pediatrics, 100*, 682–688.

Chase-Lansdale, P. L., Gordon, R., Brooks-Gunn, J., & Klebanov, P. K. (1997). Neighborhood and family influences on the intellectual and behavioral competence of preschool and early school-age children. In J. Brooks-Gunn, G. Duncan, & J. L. Aber (Eds.), *Neighborhood poverty: Context and consequences for development* (pp. 79–118). New York: Russell Sage.

Chase-Lansdale, P. L., Wakschlag, L. S., & Brooks-Gunn, J. (1995). A psychological perspective on the development of caring in children and youth: The role of the family. *Journal of Adolescence, 18*, 515–556.

Chasnoff, I. J., Landress, H. J., & Barrett, M. E. (1990). The prevalence of illicit-drug or alcohol use during pregnancy and discrepancies in mandatory reporting in Pinellas County, Florida. *New England Journal of Medicine, 32*, 1202–1206.

Chen, X., Hastings, P. D., Rubin, K. H., Chen H., Cen, G., & Stewart, S. L. (1998). Child-rearing attitudes and behavioral inhibition in Chinese and Canadian toddlers: A cross-cultural study. *Developmental Psychology, 34*, 677–686.

Child Care Aware. (1999). Ways to measure quality. Retrieved August 27, 1999, from the World Wide Web: http://www.naccrra.net/childcareaware/quality.htm

Children's Defense Fund. (1994). *The state of America's children: Yearbook 1994.* Washington, DC: Author.

Chiu, M. L., Feldman, S. S., & Rosenthal, D. A. (1992). The influence of immigration on parental behavior and adolescent distress in Chinese families residing in two Western nations. *Journal of Research on Adolescence, 2*, 205–239.

Chodorow, N. (1978). *The reproduction of mothering.* Berkeley: University of California Press.

Chomsky, N. (1957). *Syntactic structures.* The Hague: Mouton.

Chomsky, N. (1965). *Aspects of the theory of syntax.* Cambridge, Mass: MIT Press.

Christoffel, K. K., & Arisa, A. (1998). Commentary. *Pediatrics, 101*, 103–105.

Christoffel, K. K., Spivak, H., & Witwer, M. (2000). Youth violence prevention: The physician's role. *MS JAMA, 283*, 1202-1203.

Chugani, H. T. (1997). Neuroimaging of developmental nonlinearity and developmental pathologies (pp. 187–196). In R. W. Thatcher, G. R. Lyon, J. Rumsey, & N. Krasnegor (Eds.), *Developmental neuroimaging: Mapping the development of brain and behavior.* San Diego: Academic Press.

Church, J. (1961). *Language and the discovery of reality.* New York: Random House.

Cicchetti, D., & Lynch, M. (1995). Failures in the expectable environment and their impact on individual development: The case of child maltreatment. In D. Cicchetti & D. J. Cohen (Eds.), *Developmental psychopathology* (Vol. 2, pp. 32–71). New York: Wiley.

Cicchetti, D., & Rizley, R. (1981). Developmental perspectives on the etiology, intergenerational transmission and sequelae of child maltreatment. In *New directions for child development* (Vol. 11, pp. 31–56). San Francisco: Jossey-Bass.

Cisneros, S. (1993). *Woman hollering creek, and other stories.* New York: Random House.

Clark, B. (1988). *Growing up gifted* (3rd ed.). New York: Macmillan.

Clark, E. V. (1995). Later lexical development and word formation. In P. Fletcher & P. MacWhinney (Eds.), *The handbook of child language* (pp. 393–412). Oxford : Blackwell.

Clark, R., Hyde, J. S., Essex, M. J., & Klein, M. H. (1997). Length of maternity leave and quality of mother-infant interactions. *Child Development, 68,* 364–383.

Clausen, J. A. (1975). The social meaning of differential physical and sexual maturation. In S. E. Dragastin & G. H. Elder (Eds.), *Adolescence in the life cycle.* New York: Wiley.

Codori, A. M., Hanson, R., & Brandt, J. (1994). Self-selection in predictive testing for Huntington's disease. *American Journal of Medical Genetics, 54,* 167–173.

Cogswell, M. E. Scanlon, K. S., Fein, S. B., & Schieve, L. A. (1999). Medically advised, mother's personal target, and actual weight gain during pregnancy. *Obstetrics and Gynecology, 94,* 616–622.

Cohen, R. J., Swerdlik, M. E., & Phillips, S. M. (1996). *Psychological testing and assessment* (3rd ed.). Mountain View, CA: Mayfield.

Cohen, W. R. (1995). Maternal-fetal conflicts: Ethical and policy issues. In A. Goldworth, W. Silverman, D. K. Stevenson, E. W. D. Young, & R. Rivers (Eds.), *Ethics and perinatology* (pp. 10–28). New York: Oxford University Press.

Cohler, B. J., Stott, F. M., & Musick, J. S. (1995). Adversity, vulnerability, and resilience: Cultural and developmental perspectives. In D. Cicchetti & D. J. Cohen (Eds.), *Developmental psychopathology* (Vol. 2, pp. 753–800). New York: Wiley.

Coie, J. D., & Kupersmidt, J. B. (1983). A behavioral analysis of emerging social status in boys' groups. *Child Development, 54,* 1400–1416.

Cole, P. M., & Newcombe, N. (1983). Interference effects of verbal and imaginal strategies for resisting distraction on children's verbal and visual recognition memory. *Child Development, 54*(1), 42–50.

Coleman, J. S. (1988). Social capital in the creation of human capital. *American Journal of Sociology, 94,* 95–120.

Coles, R. (1970). *Erik Erikson: The growth of his work.* Boston: Little, Brown.

Coley, R., & Chase-Lansdale, P. (1999). Stability and change in paternal involvement among urban African American fathers. *Journal of Family Psychology, 13*(3), 416–435.

Comer, J. P. (1985). The Yale–New Haven Primary Prevention Project: A follow-up study. *Journal of the American Academy of Child Psychiatry, 24,* 154–160.

Comer, J. P. (1988). Educating poor minority children. *Scientific American, 259,* 42–48.

Comer, J. P., Haynes, N. M., Joyner, E. T., & Ben-Avie, M. (Eds.). (1996). *Rallying the whole village: The Comer process for reforming education.* New York: Teachers College Press.

Condon, W., & Sanders, L. (1974). Synchrony demonstrated between movements of the neonate and adult speech. *Child Development, 45,* 456–462.

Condry, J. C., & Ross, D. F. (1985). Sex and aggression: The influence of gender label on the perception of aggression in children. *Child Development, 56,* 225-238.

Cooper, R. P., & Aslin, R. N. (1990). Preference for infant directed speech in the first month after birth. *Child Development, 61,* 1584–1595.

Corcoran, M. E., & Chaudry, A. (1997). The dynamics of childhood poverty. *Children and Poverty, 7,* 40–54.

Corse, S. J., Schmid, K., & Trickett, P. K. (1990). Social network characteristics of mothers in abusing and nonabusing families and their relationships to parenting beliefs. *Journal of Community Psychology, 18,* 44–59.

Cotgrove, A., Zirinksy, L., Black, D., & Weston, D. (1995). Secondary prevention of attempted suicide in adolescence. *Journal of Adolescence, 18,* 569–577.

Coulton, C. J., Korbin, J. E., & Su, M. (1999). Neighborhoods and child maltreatment: A multi-level study. *Child Abuse & Neglect, 23,* 1019–1040.

Courage, M. L., & Adams, R. J. (1990). Visual acuity assessment from birth to three years using the acuity card procedures: Cross-sectional and longitudinal samples. *Optometry and Vision Science, 67,* 713–718.

Courtney, M. L., & Cohen, R. (1996). Behavior segmentation by boys as a function of aggressiveness and prior information. *Child Development, 67,* 1034–1047.

Coustan, D. R. (1995a). Fetal physiology. In D. R. Coustan, R. V. Haning, Jr., & D. B. Singer (Eds.), *Human reproduction: Growth and development* (pp. 139–160). New York: Little, Brown.

Coustan, D. R. (1995b). Maternal physiology. In D. R. Coustan, R. V. Haning, Jr., & D. B. Singer (Eds.), *Human reproduction: Growth and development* (pp. 161–181). New York: Little, Brown.

Cozby, P. C. (1997). *Methods in behavioral research* (6th ed.). Mountain View, CA: Mayfield.

Craighead, L. W., & Green, B, J. (1989). Relationship between depressed mood and sex-typed personality characteristics in adolescents. *Journal of Youth and Adolescence, 18,* 467–474.

Cramer, P., & Skidd, J. E. (1992). Correlates of self-worth in preschoolers: The role of gender-stereotyped styles of behavior. *Sex Roles, 26,* 369–390.

Crane, J. (1991). The epidemic theory of ghettos and neighborhood effects on dropping out and teenage childbearing. *American Journal of Sociology, 96,* 1126–1159.

Cratty, B. J. (1986). *Perceptual and motor development in infants and children* (3rd ed.). Englewood Cliffs, NJ: Prentice-Hall.

Crick, N. R., & Dodge, K. A. (1996). Social information-processing mechanisms in reactive and proactive aggression. *Child Development, 67,* 993–1002.

Crick, N. R., & Grotpeter, J. K. (1995). Relational aggression, gender, and social-psychological adjustment. *Child Development, 66,* 710–722.

Crnic, K. A., Greenberg, M. T., Ragozin, A., Robinson, N., & Basham, R. (1983). Effects of stress and social support on mothers and premature and full-term babies. *Child Development, 54,* 209–217.

Cronan, T. A., Cruz, S. G., Arriago, R. I., & Sarlom A. J. (1996). The effects of a community-based literacy program on young children's language and conceptual development. *American Journal of Community Psychology, 24,* 251–272.

Cross, W. E., Jr. (1980). Models of psychological nigrescence: A literature review. In R. L. Jones (Ed.), *Black psychology.* New York: Harper & Row.

Cross, W. E., Jr. (1987). A two-factor theory of black identity: Implications for the study of identity development in minority children. In J. S. Phinney & M. J. Rotheram (Eds.), *Children's ethnic socialization.* Beverly Hills: Sage.

Csikszentmihalyi, M. (1990). *Flow: The psychology of optimal experience.* New York: Harper & Row.

Csikszentmihalyi, M. (1997). *Finding flow.* New York: Basic Books.

Dahl, M., Tybjærg-Hansen, A., Wittrup, H., Lange, P., & Nordestgaard, B. (1998). Cystic fibrosis F508 heterozygotes, smoking and reproduction: Studies of 9141 individuals from a general population sample. *Genomics, 50(1),* 89–96.

Daniels, J., D'Andrea, M., & Heck, R. (1995). Moral development and Hawaiian youths: Does gender make a difference? *Journal of Counseling and Development, 74,* 90–93.

Darling, C. A., & Hicks, M. W. (1982). Parental influence on adolescent sexuality: Implications for parents as educators. *Journal of Youth and Adolescence, 11,* 231–245.

Davidson, E. H. (1990) How embryos work: A comparative view of diverse modes of cell fate specification. *Development, 108,* 365–389.

Dawson, G., & Fischer, K. W. (1994). *Human behavior and the developing brain.* New York: Guilford Press.

Day, J. C. (1996). *Population projections of the United States by age, sex, race, and Hispanic origin: 1995 to 2050* (U.S. Bureau of the Census Current Population Reports No. P25-1130). Washington, DC: U.S. Government Printing Office.

Deater-Deckard, K., Dodge, K. A., Bates, J. E., & Pettit, G. S. (1996). Physical discipline among African American and European American mothers: Links to children's externalizing behaviors. *Developmental Psychology, 32,* 1065–1072.

DeCasper, A. J., & Fifer, W. P. (1980). Of human bonding: Newborns prefer their mothers' voices. *Science, 208,* 1174–1176.

DeCasper, A. J., & Spence, M. J. (1986). Prenatal newborns' perception of speech sounds. *Infant Behavior and Development, 9,* 135–150.

de Gaston, J. F., Jensen, L., Weed, S. E., & Tanas, R. (1994). Teacher philosophy and program implementation and the impact on sex education outcomes. *Journal of Research and Development in Education, 27,* 265–270.

Dejin-Karlsson, E., Hanson, B. S., Oestergren, P. E., Sjoeberg, N-O., & Marsal, K. (1998). Does passive smoking in early pregnancy increase the risk of small-for-gestational age infants? *American Journal of Public Health, 88,* 1523–1527.

DeJong, W. (1999). Building the peace: The resolving conflict creatively program. *National Institute of Justice, Program Focus,* 2–16.

Dempster, F. N. (1981). Memory span: Sources of individual and developmental differences. *Psychological Bulletin, 89,* 63–100.

Denham, S. A., McKinley, M., Couchoud, E. A., & Holt, R. (1990). Emotional and behavioral predictors of preschool peer ratings. *Child Development, 61,* 1145–1152.

Devaney, B. L., Ellwood, M. R., & Love, J. M. (1997). Programs that mitigate the effects of poverty on children. *Children and Poverty, 7,* 88–112.

de Vries, J. I. P. (1992). The first trimester. In J. I. P. de Vries (Ed.), *Fetal behavior: Developmental and perinatal aspects* (pp. 3–16). New York: Oxford University Press.

Dewey, J. (1896). The concept of the reflex arc in psychology. *Psychological Bulletin, 3,* 357–370.

Diaz, R. M. (1983). Thought and two languages: The impact of bilingualism on cognitive development. *Review of Research in Education, 10,* 23–54.

Dietz, W. H., & Gortmaker, S. L. (1985). Do we fatten our children at the television set: Obesity and television viewing in children and adolescents. *Pediatrics, 75,* 807–812.

Dietz, W. H., & Stern, L. (Eds.). (1999). *American Academy of Pediatrics: Guide to your child's nutrition.* New York: Villard Books.

Dillard, A. (1974). *Pilgrim at Tinker Creek.* New York: Harper's Magazine Press.

Dillard, A. (1987). *An American childhood.* San Francisco: Harper & Row.

Dixon, J. P. (1997). The spatial child. In D. N. Sattler & V. Shabatay (Eds.), *Psychology in context: Voices and perspectives* (pp. 173–176). Boston: Houghton Mifflin.

Dobson, P. (1989). Easing childhood shame. *Nursing Times, 85,* 79–80.

Dodge, K. A. (1983). Behavioral antecedents of peer social status. *Child Development, 54(6),* 1386–1399.

Dodge, K. A., Pettit, G. S., McClaskey, C., & Brown, M. (1986). Social competence in children. *Monographs of the Society for Research in Child Development, 51* (2, Serial No. 213).

Doherty, W. J., Kouneski, E. F., & Erickson, M. F. (1998). Responsible fathering: An overview and conceptual framework. *Journal of Marriage and the Family, 60,* 277–292.

Donahue, M. J., & Benson, P. L. (1995). Religion and the well-being of adolescents. *Journal of Social Issues, 51,* 145–160.

Donaldson, M. (1978). *Children's minds.* New York: Norton.

Dornbusch, S. M., Ritter, P. L., Mont-Reynaud, R., & Chen, Z. (1990). Family decision making and academic performance in a diverse high school population. *Journal of Adolescent Research, 5,* 143–160.

Dorris, M. (1989). *The broken cord.* New York: Harper & Row.

Dovidio, J., & Gaertner, S. (1986). *Prejudice, discrimination, and racism.* Orlando, FL: Academic Press.

Downey, G., Lebolt, A., Rincon, C., & Freitas, A. L. (1998). Rejection sensitivity and children's interpersonal difficulties. *Child Development, 69,* 1074–1091.

Downey, G., Purdie, V., & Schaffer-Neitz, R. (1999). Anger transmission from mother to child: A comparison of mothers in chronic pain and well mothers. *Journal of Marriage and the Family, 61,* 62–73.

Downey, S., & McCormick, J. (2000, May 15). Razing the vertical ghettos. *Newsweek,* pp. 36–37.

Drumm, P., & Jackson, D. W. (1996). Developmental changes in questioning strategies during adolescence. *Journal of Adolescent Research, 11,* 285–305.

Dubois, D. L., & Hirsch, B. J. (1990). School and neighborhood friendship patterns of Blacks and Whites in early adolescence. *Child Development, 61,* 524–536.

Duke-Duncan, P. (1991). Body image. In R. M. Lerner, A. C. Petersen, & J. Brooks-Gunn (Eds.). *Encyclopedia of adolescence* (Vol. 2, pp. 90–94). New York: Garland.

Dunn, J., Brown, J., & Beardsall, L. (1991). Family talk about feeling states and children's later understanding of others' emotions. *Developmental Psychology, 27,* 448–455.

Dupper, D. (1995). Moving beyond a crime-focused perspective of school violence. *Social Work in Education, 17*(2), 71–72.

Dweck, C. S. (1986). Motivational processes affecting learning. *American Psychologist, 41,* 1040–1048.

Dweck, C. S. (1989). Motivation. In A. Lesgold & R. Glaser (Eds.), *Foundations for a psychology of education.* Hillsdale, NJ: Erlbaum.

Dweck, C. S., & Repucci, N. D. (1973). Learned helplessness and reinforcement responsibility in children. *Journal of Personality and Special Psychology, 25,* 109–116.

Early, L. A., Bhatt, R. S., & Rovee-Collier, C. (1995). Developmental changes in the contextual control of recognition. *Developmental Psychobiology, 28,* 27–43.

Ecklund-Flores, L., & Turkewitz, G. (1996). Asymmetric headturning to speech and nonspeech in human newborns. *Developmental Psychobiology, 29,* 205–217.

Eden, G. F., & Zeffiro, T. A. (1997). PET and MRI in the detection of task-related brain activity: Implications for the study of brain development (pp. 77–90). In R. W. Thatcher, G. R. Lyon, J. Rumsey, & N. Krasnegor (Eds.), *Developmental neuroimaging: Mapping the development of brain and behavior.* San Diego: Academic Press.

Eimas, P. D., & Quinn, P.C. (1994). Studies on the formation of perceptually based basic-level categories in young infants. *Child Development, 65,* 903–917.

Eisenberg, N. (1996). Meta-emotion and socialization of emotion in the family—a topic whose time has come: Comment on Gottman et al. (1996). *Journal of Family Psychology, 10,* 269–276.

Eisenman, R. (1994). Conservative sexual values: Effects of an abstinence program on student attitudes. *Journal of Sex Education and Therapy, 20,* 75–78.

Ekman, P. (1984). Expressions and the nature of emotion. In P. Ekman & K. Scherer (Eds.), *Approaches to emotion.* Hillsdale, NJ: Erlbaum.

Ekman, P. (1994). Strong evidence for universals in facial expressions: A reply to Russell's mistaken critique. *Psychological Bulletin, 115,* 268–287.

Elkind, D. (1961). The child's conception of his religious denomination I: The Jewish child. *Journal of Genetic Psychology, 99,* 209–225.

Elkind, D. (1962). The child's conception of his religious denomination II: The Catholic child. *Journal of Genetic Psychology, 101,* 185–193.

Elkind, D. (1963). The child's conception of his religious denomination III: The Protestant child. *Journal of Genetic Psychology, 103,* 291–304.

Elkind, D. (1967). Egocentrism in adolescence. *Child Development, 38,* 1025–1034.

Elkind, D. (1978a). *The child's reality: Three developmental themes.* Hillsdale, NJ: Erlbaum.

Elkind, D. (1978b). *A sympathetic understanding of the child: Birth to sixteen* (2nd ed.). Boston: Allyn & Bacon.

Elkind, D. (1980). Strategic interactions in early adolescence. In J. Adelson (Ed.), *Handbook of adolescence.* New York: Wiley.

Elkind, D. (1985). Egocentrism redux: Reply to D. Lapsley and M. Murphy's *Developmental Review* paper. *Developmental Review, 5,* 218–226.

Ellis, B. J., McFadyen-Ketchum, S., Dodge, K. A., Pettit, G. S., & Bates, J. E. (1999). Quality of early relationships and individual differences in the timing of pubertal maturation in girls: A longitudinal test of an evolutionary model. *Journal of Personality and Social Psychology, 77,* 387–401.

Ely, R., Melzi, G., Hadge, L., & McCabe, A. (1998). Being brave, being nice: Themes of agency and communion in children's narratives. *Journal of Personality, 66,* 257–284.

Emde, R. N., & Harmon, R. J. (1972). Endogenous and exogenous smiling systems in early infancy. *Journal of the American Academy of Child Psychiatry, 11,* 77–100.

Emde, R. N., Plomin, R., Robinson, J, Corley, R., DeFries, J., Fulker, D. W., Reznick, J. S., Campos, J., Kagan, J., & Zahn-Waxler, C. (1992). Temperament, emotion, and cognition at fourteen months: The MacArthur longitudinal twin study. *Child Development, 63,* 1437–1455.

Emde, R. N., & Robinson, J. (1979). The first two months: Recent research in developmental psychobiology and the changing view of the newborn. In J. Noshpitz & J. Call (Eds.), *Basic handbook of child psychiatry*. New York: Basic Books.

Engle, P. L., Gorman, K. S., Martorell, R., & Pollitt, E. (1992). The ORIENTE study: Infant and preschool psychological development. *Food & Nutrition Bulletin, 14*, 201–214.

Ennett, S. T., & Bauman, K. E. (1996). Adolescent social networks: School, demographic, and longitudinal considerations. *Journal of Adolescent Research, 11*, 194–215.

Enright, R. D., & Lapsley, D. K. (1981). Judging others who hold opposite beliefs: The development of belief-discrepancy reasoning. *Child Development, 52*, 1053–1063.

Ensher, G. L., & Clark, D. A. (1994). Newborns at risk: *Medical care and psychoeducational interventions* (2nd ed.). Gaithersburg, MD: Aspen.

Entwisle, D. R., Alexander, K. L., Olson, L. S., & Ross, K. (1999). Paid work in early adolescence: Developmental and ethnic patterns. *Journal of Early Adolescence, 19*, 363–388.

Ephron, N. (1972). *Crazy salad: Some things about women.* New York: Knopf.

Erdrich. L. (1996). *The blue jay's dance.* New York: Harper-Perennial.

Erikson, E. H. (1954). Problems of infancy and early childhood. In G. Murphy & A. J. Bachrach (Eds.), *An outline of abnormal psychology*. New York: Modern Library.

Erikson, E. H. (1959). Identity and the life cycle: Selected papers. *Psychological Issues Monograph* (1, Series 1). New York: International Universities Press.

Erikson, E. H. (1963). *Childhood and society* (2nd ed.). New York: Norton.

Erikson, E. H. (1968). *Identity, youth and crisis.* New York: Norton.

Eskanazi, B., & Bergman, J. J. (1995). Passive and active maternal smoking during pregnancy, as measured by serum cotinine, and postnatal smoke exposure. I. Effects on physical growth at age 5 years. *American Journal of Epidemiology, 142*, 10–18.

Estes, D. (1998). Young children's awareness of their mental activity: The case of mental rotation. *Child Development, 69*, 1345–1360.

Estes, T. K. (1998). From birth to conception: Open or closed. *European Journal of Obstetrics, Gynecology, and Reproductive Biology, 78*, 169–177.

Evans, E. D., Craig, D., & Mietzel, G. (1993). Adolescents' cognitions and attributions for academic cheating: A cross-national study. *Journal of Psychology, 127*, 585–602.

Executive Summary. (1999, October). *The Carolina Abecedarian Project.* Chapel Hill, NC: Frank Porter Graham Child Development Center, University of North Carolina at Chapel Hill. Retrieved October 22, 1999, from the World Wide Web: http://www.fpg.unc.edu/~abc/embargoed/executive_summary.htm

Eysenck, H. J., & Eysenck, M. W. (1985). *Personality and individual differences: A natural science approach.* New York: Plenum.

Fabes, R. A., Eisenberg, N., Smith, M. C., & Murphy, B. C. (1996). Getting angry at peers: Associations with liking of the provocateur. *Child Development, 67*, 942–956.

Fabricius, W. V., & Wellman, H. M. (1983). Children's understanding of retrieval cue utilization. *Developmental Psychology, 19*, 15–21.

Farver, J. A., & Shin, Y. L. (1997). Social pretend play in Korean- and Anglo-American preschoolers. *Child Development, 68*, 544–556.

Fauber, R., Forehand, R., Thomas, A. M., & Wierson, M. (1990). A mediational model of the impact of marital conflict on adolescent adjustment in intact and divorced families. *Child Development, 61*, 1112–1123.

Faust, M. S. (1983). Alternative constructions of adolescent growth. In J. Brooks-Gunn & A. C. Petersen (Eds.), *Girls at puberty*. New York: Plenum.

Federal Interagency Forum on Child and Family Statistics. (1997). *America's children: Key national indicators of well-being.* Washington, DC: U.S. Government Printing Office.

Feiring, C., & Lewis, M. (1993). Do mothers know their teenagers' friends? Implications for individuation in early adolescence. *Journal of Youth and Adolescence, 22*, 337–354.

Feldman, C. F., Stone, A., & Renderer, B. (1990). Stage, transfer, and academic achievement in dialect-speaking Hawaiian adolescents. *Child Development, 61*, 472–484.

Feldman, S. S., Mont-Reynaud, R., & Rosenthal, D. A. (1992). When East moves West: The acculturation of values of Chinese adolescents in the U.S. and Australia. *Journal of Research on Adolescence, 2*, 147–173.

Fenson, L., Dale, P. S., Reznick, J. S., Bates, E., Thal, D., Bates, E., Hartung, J., Pethick, S., & Reilly, J. (1993). *The MacArthur communicative development inventories: User's guide and technical manual.* San Diego: Singular Publishing Group.

Fernald, A. (1985). Four-month-old infants prefer to listen to motherese. *Infant Behavior and Development, 8*, 181–195.

Fernald, A. (1993). Approval and disapproval: Infant responsiveness to vocal affect in familiar and unfamiliar languages. *Child Development, 64*, 657–674.

Field, A. E., Camargo, C. A., Taylor, C. B., Berkey, C. S., Frazier, L., & Gillman, M. W. (1999). Overweight, weight concerns, and bulimic behaviors among girls and boys. *Journal of the American Academy of Child and Adolescent Psychiatry, 38*, 754–760.

Field, T. M., Schanberg, S. M., Scafidi, F., Bauer, C. R., Vega-Lahr, N., Garcia, R., Nystrom, J., & Kuhn, C. M. (1986). Effects of tactile/kinesthetic stimulation on preterm neonates. *Pediatrics, 77*, 654-658.

Filer, L. J., Jr. (1995). Iron deficiency. In F. Lifshitz (Ed.), *Childhood nutrition* (pp. 53–60). Ann Arbor, MI: CRC Press.

Fillmore, C. J. (1982). A descriptive framework for spatial deixis. In R. Jarvella & W. Klein (Eds.), *Speech, place, and action: Studies in deixis and related topics.* New York: Wiley.

Finkelhor, D. (1990). Early and long-term effects of child sexual abuse: An update. *Professional Psychology: Research and Practice, 21,* 325–330.

Fisher, C., & Tokura, H. (1996). Acoustic cues to grammatical structure in infant-directed speech: Cross-linguistic evidence. *Child Development, 67,* 3192–3218.

Fisher, J. O., & Birch, L. L. (1996). Maternal restriction of young girls' food access is related to intake of those foods in an unrestricted setting. *FASEB Journal, 10,* A225.

Fisk, W. R. (1985). Responses to "neutral" pronoun presentations and the development of sex-biased responding. *Developmental Psychology, 21,* 481–485.

Flavell, J. H., Beach, D. R., & Chinsky, J. M. (1966). Spontaneous verbal rehearsal in a memory task as a function of age. *Child Development, 37,* 283–299.

Flavell, J. H., Flavell, E. R., & Green, F. L. (1983). Development of the appearance-reality distinction. *Cognitive Psychology, 15,* 95–120.

Flavell, J. H., Flavell, E. R., Green, F. L., & Korfmacher, J. E. (1990). Do young children think of television images as pictures or real objects? *Journal of Broadcasting & Electronic Media, 34,* 399–419.

Flavell, J. H., Green, F. L., & Flavell, E. R. (1993). Children's understanding of the stream of consciousness. *Child Development, 64,* 387–398.

Flavell, J. H., Green, F. L., & Flavell, E. R. (1995). Young children's knowledge about thinking. *Monographs of the Society for Research in Child Development, 60*(1, Serial No. 243).

Flavell, J. H., Green, F. L., & Flavell, E. R. (1998). The mind has a mind of its own: Developing knowledge about mental uncontrollability. *Cognitive Development, 13,* 127–138.

Flavell, J. H., Miller, P. H., & Miller, S. A. (1993). *Cognitive development* (3rd ed.). Englewood Cliffs, NJ: Prentice-Hall.

Fleming, P. J., Blair, P. S., Bacon, C., et al. (1996). Environment of infants during sleep and risk of the sudden infant death syndrome: Results from 1993–1995 case-control study for confidential inquiry into stillbirths and deaths in infancy. *British Medical Journal, 313,* 191–195.

Flieller, A. (1999). Comparison of the development of formal thought in adolescent cohorts aged 10 to 15 years (1967–1996 and 1972–1993). *Developmental Psychology, 35,* 1048–1058.

Flynn, J. R. (1984). The mean IQ of Americans: Massive gains 1932–1978. *Psychological Bulletin, 95,* 29–51.

Ford, M. E., Wentzel, K. R., Wood, D., Stevens, E., & Siesfeld, G. A. (1989). Processes associated with integrative social competence: Emotional and contextual influences on adolescent social responsibility. *Journal of Adolescent Research, 4,* 405–425.

Forehand, R., Thomas, A. M., Wierson, M., Brody, G., & Fauber, R. (1990). Role of maternal functioning and parenting skills in adolescent functioning following parental divorce. *Journal of Abnormal Psychology, 99,* 278–283.

Fouts, G., & Burggraf, K. (1999). Television situation comedies: Female body images and verbal reinforcements. *Sex Roles, 40,* 473–481.

Fowler, J. W. (1981). *Stages of faith: The psychology of human development and the question for meaning.* San Francisco: Harper & Row.

Fowler, J. W. (1991). Stages in faith consciousness. *New Directions for Child Development, 52,* 27–45.

Frankel, K. A. (1990). Girls' perceptions of peer relationship support and stress. *Journal of Early Adolescence, 10,* 69–88.

Freedman, D. G., & Freedman, M. (1969). Behavioral differences between Chinese-American and American newborns. *Nature, 224,* 1227.

Freedman, D. S., Srinivasan, S. R., Valdez, R. A., Williamson, D. F., & Berenson, G. S. (1997). Secular increases in relative weight and adiposity among children over two decades: The Bogalusa heart study. *Pediatrics, 99,* 420–426.

Fremon, C. (1995). *Father Greg and the homeboys.* New York: Hyperion.

French, S. A., Perry, C. L., Leon, G. R., & Fulkerson, J. A. (1995). Dieting behaviors and weight change history in female adolescents. *Health Psychology, 14,* 548–555.

Freud, A. (1937). *The ego and the mechanisms of defense.* London: Hogarth Press.

Freud, S. (1961). *Collected works, standard edition.* London: Hogarth Press.

Freud, S. (1961). New introductory lectures in psychoanalysis. In J. Strachey (Ed.), *The standard edition of the complete psychological works of Sigmund Freud.* New York: Norton. (Originally published 1933.)

Freud, S. (1961). Some psychical consequences of the anatomical distinction between the sexes. In J. Strachey (Ed.), *The standard edition of the complete psychological works of Sigmund Freud* (Vol. 19). London: Hogarth Press. (Original work published 1925b.)

Freud, S. (1961). The dissolution of the Oedipal complex. In J. Strachey (Ed.), *The standard edition of the complete psychological works of Sigmund Freud* (Vol.19). London: Hogarth Press. (Original work published 1925a.)

Freud, S. (1964). The neuro-psychoses of defense. In J. Strachey (Trans. and Ed.), *The standard edition of the complete psychological works of Sigmund Freud* (Vol. 3, pp. 45–61). London: Hogarth Press. (Original work published 1894.)

Frick, J. E., & Columbo, J. (1996). Individual differences in infant visual attention: Recognition of degraded visual forms by four-month-olds. *Child Development, 67,* 188–204.

Fried, P. A., O'Connell, C. M., & Watkinson, M. A. (1992). 60- and 72-month follow-up of children prenatally exposed to marijuana, cigarettes, and alcohol: Cognitive and language assessment. *Developmental and Behavioral Pediatrics, 13,* 383–391.

Fried, P. A., & Watkinson, B. (1990). 36- and 48-month neurobehavioral follow-up of children prenatally exposed to marijuana, cigarettes, and alcohol. *Journal of Developmental and Behavioral Pediatrics, 11,* 49–58.

Fried, V. M., Makuc, D. M., & Rooks, R. N. (1998). Ambulatory health care visits by children: Principal diagnosis and place of visit. *Vital Health Statistics, 13*(137).

Friedler, G. (1988). Effects on future generations of paternal exposure to alcohol and other drugs. *Alcohol Health & Research World, 12,* 126–129.

Friedler, G. (1996). Paternal exposures: Impact on reproductive and developmental outcome: An overview. *Pharmacology, Biochemistry and Behavior, 55*(4), 691–700.

Friedman, W. J. (1999, April 16). *Arrows of time in infancy: The representation of temporal invariances.* Electronic poster presented at the meetings of the Society for Research in Child Development. Albuquerque, NM.

Friedman, W. J. (1997, November 20). *The development of infants' perception of temporally undirected events.* Paper presented at the Fifth Annual Workshop on Object Perception and Memory, Philadelphia.

Frisch, R. E. (1983). Fatness, puberty, and fertility: The effects of nutrition and physical training on menarche and ovulation. In J. Brooks-Gunn & A. C. Petersen (Eds.), *Girls at puberty.* New York: Plenum.

Frisch, R. E. (1991). Puberty and body fat. In R. M. Lerner, A. C. Petersen, & J. Brooks-Gunn (Eds.), *Encyclopedia of adolescence* (Vol. 2, pp. 884–892). New York: Garland

Frye, D., Rawling, P., Moore, C., & Myers, I. (1983). Object-person discrimination and communication at 3 and 10 months. *Developmental Psychology, 19,* 303–309.

Furman, W., & Bierman, K. L. (1983). Developmental changes in young children's conceptions of friendship. *Child Development, 54*(3), 549–556.

Furman, W., & Buhrmester, D. (1992). Age and sex differences in perceptions of networks of personal relationships. *Child Development, 63,* 103–115.

Gaddis, A., & Brooks-Gunn, J. (1985). The male experience of pubertal change. *Journal of Youth and Adolescence, 14,* 61–69.

Galper, A., Wigfield, A., & Seefeldt, C. (1997). Head Start parents' beliefs about their children's abilities, task values, and performances on different activities. *Child Development, 68,* 897–907.

Gamoran, A., & Mare, R. D. (1989). Secondary school tracking and educational inequality: Compensation, reinforcement, or neutrality? *American Journal of Sociology, 94,* 1146–1183.

Garbarino, J. (1999). *Lost boys.* New York: Free Press.

Garbarino, J., & Sherman, D. (1980). High-risk neighborhoods and high-risk families: The human ecology of child maltreatment. *Child Development, 51,* 188–198.

Garcia, J. (1993). The changing image of ethnic groups in textbooks. *Phi Delta Kappan, 75,* 29–35.

Gardner, H. (1983). *Frames of mind.* New York: Basic Books.

Gardner, J. M. M., Grantham-McGregor, S. M., Chang, S. M., Himes, J. H., & Powell, C. A. (1995). Activity and behavioral development in stunted and nonstunted children and response to nutritional supplementation. *Child Development, 66,* 1785–1797.

Garfinkel, I., Miller, C., McLanahan, S., & Hanson, T. (1998). *Deadbeat dads or inept states: A comparison of child support enforcement systems.* New York: Russell Sage.

Garland, A. F., & Zigler, E. (1993). Adolescent suicide prevention: Current research and social policy implications. *American Psychologist, 48,* 169–182.

Garnica, O. (1977). Some prosodic and paralinguistic features of speech to young children. In D. E. Snow & C. A. Ferguson (Eds.), *Talking to children: Language input and acquisition.* Cambridge: Cambridge University Press.

Garrett, P., Ng'andu, N., & Ferron, J. (1994). Poverty experiences of young children and the quality of their home environments. *Child Development, 65,* 331–345.

Gavazzi, S. M., & Sabatelli, R. M. (1990). Family system dynamics, the individuation process, and psychosocial development. *Journal of Adolescent Research, 5,* 500–519.

Gavin, L. A., & Fuhrman, W. (1989). Age differences in adolescents' perceptions of their peer groups. *Developmental Psychology, 25,* 827–834.

Ge, X., Conger, R. D., Lorenz, F. O., Elder, G. H., Montague, R. B., & Simons, R. L. (1992). Linking family economic hardship to adolescent distress. *Journal of Research on Adolescence, 2,* 351–378.

Geary, D. C., Bow-Thomas, C. C., Fan, L., & Siegler, R. S. (1993). Even before formal instruction, Chinese children outperform American children in mental addition. *Cognitive Development, 8,* 517–529.

Geary, D. C., Bow-Thomas, C. C., Fan, L., & Siegler, R. S. (1996). Development of arithmetical competencies in Chinese and American children: Influence of age, language, and schooling. *Child Development, 67,* 2022–2044.

Geller, L. G. (1985). *Word play and language learning for children.* Urbana, IL: National Council of Teachers of English.

George, T. P., & Hartmann, D. P. (1996). Friendship networks of unpopular, average, and popular children. *Child Development, 67,* 2301–2316.

Gershkof-Stowe, Thal, D. J., Smith, L. B., & Namy, L. L. (1997). Categorization and its developmental relation to early language. *Child Development, 68,* 843-859.

Gesell, A. (1940). *The first five years of life: The preschool years.* New York: Harper.

Gewirtz, J. L. (1976). The attachment acquisition process as evidenced in the maternal conditioning of cued infant responding (particularly crying). *Human Development, 19,* 143–155.

Giardino, A. P., Christian, C. W., & Giardino, E. R. (1997). *A practical guide to the evaluation of child physical abuse and neglect.* Thousand Oaks, CA: Sage.

Gibbs, J. T. (1989). Black American adolescents. In J. T. Gibbs, L. N. Huang, & associates (Eds.), *Children of color.* San Francisco: Jossey-Bass.

Gibson, J. J. (1966). *The senses considered as perceptual systems.* Boston: Houghton Mifflin.

Gilbert, S. F. (1994). *Developmental biology* (4th ed.). Sunderland, MA: Sinauer Associates.

Giles-Sims, J., & Crosbie-Burnett, M. (1989). Stepfamily research: Implications for policy, clinical interventions, and further research. *Family Relations, 38,* 19–23.

Gilligan, C. (1982). *In a different voice: Psychological theory and women's development.* Cambridge, MA: Harvard University Press.

Gilligan, C. (1986). Exit-voice dilemmas in adolescent development. In A. Foxley, M. S. McPherson, & G. O'Donnell (Eds.). *Development, democracy, and the art of trespassing: Essays in honor of Albert O. Hirschman.* Notre Dame, IN: University of Notre Dame Press.

Gilligan, C. (1988a). Adolescent development reconsidered. In C. Gilligan, J. V. Ward, J. M. Taylor, & B. Bardige (Eds.), *Mapping the moral domain.* Cambridge, MA: Harvard University Press.

Gilligan, C. (1988b). Exit-voice dilemmas in adolescent development. In C. Gilligan, J. V. Ward, J. M. Taylor, & B. Bardige (Eds.), *Mapping the moral domain.* Cambridge, MA: Harvard University Press.

Gilligan, C. (1989a). Preface: Teaching Shakespeare's sister. In C. Gilligan, N. P. Lyons, & T. J. Hanmer (Eds.), *Making connections: The relational worlds of adolescent girls at Emma Willard School.* Cambridge, MA: Harvard University Press.

Gilligan, C. (1989b). Prologue. In C. Gilligan, N. P. Lyons, & T. J. Hanmer (Eds.), *Making connections: The relational worlds of adolescent girls at Emma Willard School.* Cambridge, MA: Harvard University Press.

Gilligan, C., & Attanucci, J. (1988). Two moral orientations: Gender differences and similarities. *Merrill-Palmer Quarterly, 34,* 223–237.

Ginsburg, H., & Opper, S. (1988). *Piaget's theory of intellectual development.* (3rd ed.). Englewood Cliffs, NJ: Prentice-Hall.

Glezerman, M. (1993). Artificial insemination. In V. Insler & B. Lunenfeld (Eds.), *Infertility: Male and female* (2nd ed.). New York: Churchill Livingstone.

Glick, P. C. (1989). Remarried families, stepfamilies, and stepchildren: A brief demographic profile. *Family Relations, 38,* 24–27.

Globus, A., Rosenzweig, E. L., Bennett, E. L., & Diamond, M. C. (1973). Effects of differential experience on dendritic spine counts in rat cerebral cortex. *Journal of Comparative and Physiological Psychology, 82,* 175–181.

Godwin, K. A., Kemerer, F., Martinez, V., & Ruderman, R. (1998). Liberal equity in education: A comparison of choice options. *Social Science Quarterly, 79,* 502–522.

Golding, J. M., & Baezconde-Garbanati, L. A. (1990). Ethnicity, culture, and social resources. *American Journal of Community Psychology, 18,* 465–486.

Goldman-Rakic, P. S. (1987). Development of cortical circuitry and cognitive function. *Child Development, 58,* 601–622.

Goldsmith, D. F., & Rogoff, B. (1997). Mothers' and toddlers' coordinated joint focus of attention: Variations with maternal dysphoric symptoms. *Developmental Psychology, 33,* 113–119.

Goldsmith, H. H., Buss, K. A., & Lemery, K. S. (1997). Toddler and childhood temperament: Expanded content, stronger genetic evidence, new evidence for the importance of environment. *Developmental Psychology, 33,* 891–905.

Goldsmith, H. H., Buss, A. H., Plomin, R., Rothbart, M. K., Thomas, A., Chess, S., Hinde, R. A., & McCall, R. B. (1987). Roundtable: What is temperament? Four approaches. *Child Development, 58,* 505–529.

Golinkoff, R. M., Jacquet, R. C., Hirsh-Pasek, K., & Nandakumar, R. (1996). Lexical principles may underlie the learning of verbs. *Child Development, 67,* 3101–3119.

Golombok, S., Cook, R., Bish, A., & Murray, C. (1995). Families created by the new reproductive technologies: Quality of parenting and social and emotional development of the children. *Child Development, 66,* 285–298.

Gomes-Schwartz, B., Horowitz, J., & Cardarelli, A. (1990). *Child sexual abuse: The initial effects.* Newbury Park, CA: Sage.

Gontard, von A., Eiberg, H., Hollmann, E., Rittig, S., & Lehmkuhl, G. (1998). Molecular genetics of nocturnal enuresis: Clinical and genetic heterogeneity. *Acta Paediatrica, 87,* 571–578.

Gorman, K. S., & Pollitt, E. (1992). Relationship between weight and body proportionality at birth, growth during the first year of life, and cognitive development at 36, 48, and 60 months. *Infant Behavior and Development, 15,* 279–296.

Goss, G. (1996, February). *Weaving girls into the curriculum.* Paper presented at the annual meeting of the American Association for Colleges for Teachers Education, Chicago.

Gottfried, A. E., Fleming, J. S., & Gottfried, A. W. (1998). Role of cognitively stimulating home environment in children's academic intrinsic motivation: A longitudinal study. *Child Development, 69,* 1448–1460.

Grandjean, A. C. (1988). Eating versus inactivity. In K. Clark, R. Parr, & W. Castelli (Eds.), *Evaluation and management of eating disorders*. Champaign, IL: Life Enhancement.

Greenberg, M. T., Lengua, L. J., Coie, J. D., Pinderhughes, E. E., Bierman, K., Dodge, K. A., Lochman, J. E., & McMahon, R. J. (1999). Predicting development of school outcomes using a multiple-risk model: Four American communities. *Developmental Psychology, 35*, 403–417.

Greenfield, P. M., & Smith, J. H. (1976). *The structure of communication in early language development.* New York: Academic Press.

Greenough, W. T., Black, J. E., & Wallace, C. S. (1987). Experience and brain development. *Child Development, 58*, 539–559.

Gregory, D., with Lipsyte, R. (1964). *Nigger: An autobiography.* New York: Dutton.

Groome, L., Bentz, L., & Singh, K. (1995). Behavioral state organization in normal human term fetuses: The relationship between periods of undefined state and other characteristics of state control. *Sleep, 18*(2), 77–81.

Grotevant, H. D., & Cooper, C. R. (1986). Individuation in family relationships. *Human Development, 29*, 82–100.

Grotpeter, J. K., & Crick, N. R. (1996). Relational aggression, overt aggression, and friendship. *Child Development, 67*, 2328–2338.

Gunnar, M. R., Brodersen, L., Nachmias, M., Buss, K., & Rigatuso, J. (1996). Stress reactivity and attachment security. *Developmental Psychobiology, 29*, 191–204.

Guntheroth, W. G. (1995). *Crib death: The sudden infant death syndrome* (3rd ed.). Armonk, NY: Futura.

Gustafson, G. E., & Harris, K. L. (1990). Women's responses to young infants' cries. *Developmental Psychology, 26*, 144–152.

Hagerman, R. J. (1999). Growth and development. In W. W. Hay, Jr., A. R. Hayward, M. J. Levin, & J. M. Sondheimer (Eds.). *Current pediatric diagnosis & treatment* (pp. 1–18). Stamford, CT: Appleton & Lange.

Haith, M. M. (1980). *Rules that infants look by.* Hillsdale, NJ: Erlbaum.

Haith, M. M. (1993). Future-oriented processes in infancy: The case of visual expectations. In C. Granrud (Ed.), *Visual perception and cognition in infancy* (pp. 235–264). Hillsdale, NJ: Erlbaum.

Haith, M. M., Bergman, T., & Moore, M. J. (1977). Eye contact and face scanning in early infancy. *Science, 198*, 853–855.

Haith, M. M., Hazan, C., & Goodman, G. S. (1988). Expectation and anticipation of dynamic visual events by 3.5-month-old babies. *Child Development, 59*, 467–479.

Haith, M. M., Wentworth, N., & Canfield, R. L. (1993). The formation of expectations in early infancy. In C. Rovee-Collier & L. P. Lipsitt (Eds.), *Advances in infancy research* (Vol. 8). Norwood, NJ: Ablex.

Hakuta, K. (1999). The debate on bilingual education. *Developmental and Behavioral Pediatrics, 20*, 36–37.

Hala, S., & Chandler, M. (1996). The role of strategic planning in accessing false-belief understanding. *Child Development, 67*, 2948–2966.

Hale, S. (1990). A global developmental trend in cognitive processing speed. *Child Development, 61*, 653–663.

Hall, C. S. (1954). *A primer of Freudian psychology.* Cleveland: World.

Hallinan, M. T., & Teixeira, R. A. (1987). Opportunities and constraints: Black-White differences in the formation of interracial relationships. *Child Development, 58*, 1358–1371.

Han, F. J., Leichtman, M. D., & Wang, Q. (1998). Autobiographical memory in Korean, Chinese, and American children. *Developmental Psychology, 34*, 701–713.

Hanauer, D. (D. H.) (2000). Dying to be bigger. In D. N. Sattler, G. P. Kramer, V. Shabatay, & D. A. Bernstein (Eds.), *Child development in context: Voices and perspectives* (pp. 102–105). Boston: Houghton Mifflin.

Hanna, E. Z., Faden, V. B., & Dufour, M. C. (1997). The effects of substance use during gestation on birth outcome, infant and maternal health. *Journal of Substance Abuse, 9*, 111–125.

Harlow, H. F., & Zimmerman, R. (1959). Affectional responses in the infant monkey. *Science, 130*, 421–432.

Harper, L. V., & Sanders, K. M. (1975). The effect of adults' eating on young children's acceptance of unfamiliar foods. *Journal of Experimental Child Psychology, 20*, 206–214.

Harper, M. J. K. (1988). Gamete and zygote transport. In E. Knobil & J. Neill (Eds.), *The physiology of reproduction* (pp. 103-134). New York: Raven.

Harris, L. (1988). *Public attitudes toward teenage pregnancy, sex education, and birth control.* New York: Planned Parenthood of America.

Harris, P. L. (1997). The last of the magicians? Children, scientists, and the invocation of hidden causal powers. *Child Development, 68*, 1018–1020.

F, P. L., & Nunez, M. (1996). Understanding of permission rules by preschool children. *Child Development, 67*, 1572–1591.

Harsha, D. W. (1995). The benefits of physical activity in childhood. *American Journal of Medical Science, 310*, S109–S113.

Hart, C. H., Nelson, D. A., Robinson, C. C., Olsen, S. F., & McNeilly–Choque, M. K. (1998). Overt and relational aggression in Russian nursery-school-age children: Parenting style and marital linkages. *Developmental Psychology, 34*, 687–697.

Hart, D., & Fegley, S. (1995). Prosocial behavior and caring in adolescence: Relations to self-understanding and social judgment. *Child Development, 66*, 1346–1359.

Hart, S. N. (1991). From property to person status: Historical perspective on children's rights. *American Psychologist, 46,* 53–59.

Harter, S. (1996). Developmental changes in self-understanding across the 5 to 7 shift. In A. J. Sameroff & M. M. Haith (Eds.), *The five to seven year shift* (pp. 207–236). Chicago: University of Chicago Press.

Hartmann, T. (1995). *ADD success stories.* Grass Valley, CA: Underwood Books.

Hartup, W. W. (1992). Conflict and friendship relations. In C. U. Shantz & W. W. Hartup (Eds.), *Conflict in child and adolescent development* (pp. 186–215). New York: Cambridge University Press.

Hartup, W. W. (1996). The company they keep: Friendships and their developmental significance. *Child Development, 67,* 1–13.

Haselager, G. J. T., Hartup, W. W., van Lieshout, C. F. M., & Riksen-Walraven, J. M. A. (1998). Similarities between friends and nonfriends in middle childhood. *Child Development, 69,* 1198–1208.

Haslam, G. (1988). The horned toad. In G. Soto (Ed.), *California childhood* (pp. 138–145). Berkeley, CA: Creative Arts.

Hauser-Cram, P. (1996). Mastery motivation in toddlers with developmental disabilities. *Child Development, 67,* 236–248.

Hayes, C. D. (Ed.). (1987). *Risking the future: Adolescent sexuality, pregnancy, and childbearing.* (Vol. 1). Washington, DC: National Academy Press.

Heemskerk, J., & DiNardo, S. (1994). *Drosophila hedgehog* acts as a morphogen in cellular patterning. *Cell, 76,* 449–460.

Hegi, U. (1995). *Salt dancers.* New York: Simon & Schuster.

Helburn, S., Culkin, M. L., Morris, J., Mocan, N., Howes, C., Phillipsen, L., Bryant, D., Clifford, R., Cryer, D., Peisner, Feinberg, E., Burchinal, M., Kagan, L. L., & Rustici, J. (1995). *Cost, quality, and child outcomes in child-care centers.* Public report. Denver: Economics Department, University of Colorado.

Held, R., & Hein, A. (1963). Movement-produced stimulation and the development of visually guided behaviors. *Journal of Comparative and Physiological Psychology, 56,* 872–876.

Helwig, C. C. (1995). Adolescents' and young adults' conceptions of civil liberties: Freedom of speech and religion. *Child Development, 66*(1), 152–166.

Helwig, C. C., Hildebrandt, C., & Turiel, E. (1995). Children's judgments about psychological harm in social context. *Child Development, 66,* 1680–1693.

Henderson-Smart, D. J., Ponsonby, A-L., & Murphy, E. (1998). Reducing the risk of sudden-infant-death syndrome: A review of the scientific literature. *Journal of Paediatric Child Health, 34,* 213-219.

Henley, N. (1989). Molehill or mountain? What we do know and don't know about sex bias in language. In M. Craw-ford & M. Gentry (Eds.), *Gender and thought.* New York: Springer-Verlag.

Hepper, D. G. (1992). Fetal psychology: An embryonic science. In J. G. Nijhuis (Ed.), *Fetal behaviour: Developmental and perinatal aspects* (pp. 129–156). New York: Oxford University Press.

Hermer, L., & Spelke, E. S. (1994). A geometric process for spatial reorientation in young children. *Nature, 370,* 57–59.

Herrera, R. S., & DelCampo, R. L. (1995). Beyond the superwoman syndrome: Work satisfaction and family functioning among working-class, Mexican-American women. *Hispanic Journal of Behavioral Sciences, 17,* 49–60.

Hersch, P. (1998). *A tribe apart; A journey into the heart of American adolescence.* New York: Fawcett Columbine.

Hertel, B. R., & Donahue, M. J. (1995). Parental influences on God images among children: Testing Durkheim's metaphoric parallelism. *Journal for the Scientific Study of Religion, 34,* 186–199.

Hervada, A. R., & Hervada-Page, M. (1995). Infant nutrition: The first two years. In F. Lifshitz (Ed.), *Childhood nutrition* (pp. 43–60). Ann Arbor, MI: CRC Press.

Hetherington, E. M. (1989). Coping with family transitions: Winners, losers, and survivors. *Child Development, 60,* 1–14.

Hetherington, E. M., & Clingempeel, W. G. (1992). Coping with marital transitions: A family systems perspective. *Monographs of the Society for Research in Child Development, 57*(2–3, Serial No. 227).

Hetherington, E. M., Cox, M., & Cox, R. (1982). Effects of divorce on children and parents. In M. E. Lamb (Ed.), *Nontraditional families.* Hillsdale, NJ: Erlbaum.

Hetherington, E. M., Hagan, M. S., & Anderson, E. R. (1989). Marital transitions: A child's perspective. *American Psychologist, 44,* 303–312.

Heyman, G. D., & Dweck, C. S. (1998). Children's thinking about traits: Implications for judgments of the self and others. *Child Development, 64,* 391–403.

Heymann, S. J., & Earle, A. (1999). The impact of welfare reform on parents' ability to care for their children's health. *American Journal of Public Health, 89,* 502–505.

Hill, J. O., & Trowbridge, F. L. (1998). Childhood obesity: Future directions and research priorities. *Pediatrics, 101,* 570–574.

Hirsch, R. H., Paolitto, D. P., & Reimer, J. (1979). *Promoting moral growth: From Piaget to Kohlberg.* New York: Longman.

Hjälmas, K. (1998). Nocturnal enuresis: Basic facts and new horizons. *European Urology, 33,* 53–57.

Hodges, E. V. E., Boivin, M., Vitaro, F., & Bukowski, W. M. (1999). The power of friendship: Protection against an escalating cycle of peer victimization. *Developmental Psychology, 35,* 94–101.

Hodges, E. V. E., Finnegan, R. A., & Perry, D. G. (1999). Skewed autonomy-relatedness in preadolescents' conceptions of their relationships with mother, father, and best friend. *Developmental Psychology, 35,* 737–748.

Hoffman, H. J., Damus, K., Hillman, L., & Krongrad, E. (1988). Risk factors for SIDS: Results of the NICHD SIDS cooperative epidemiological study. *Annal New York Academy of Sciences, 533,* 13–30.

Hoffman, M. (1991). How parents make their mark on genes. *Science, 252,* 1250–1251.

Hoffman, M. L. (1980). Moral development in adolescence. In J. Adelson (Ed.), *Handbook of adolescent psychology.* New York: Wiley.

Hogan, R. (1980). The gifted adolescent. In J. Adelson (Ed.), *Handbook of adolescence.* New York: Wiley.

Hogan, R., & Weiss, D. (1974). Personality correlates of superior academic achievement. *Journal of Counseling Psychology, 21,* 144–149.

Hogue, A., & Steinberg, L. (1995). Homophily of internalized distress in adolescent peer groups. *Developmental Psychology, 31,* 897–906.

Holt, J. (1969). *How children learn.* New York: Pitman.

Hooker, D. (1952). *The prenatal origin of behavior.* University of Kansas Press.

Horn, S., Killen, M., & Stangor, C. (1999). The influence of group stereotypes on adolescents' moral reasoning. *Journal of Early Adolescence, 19,* 98–113.

Horney, K. (1937). *The neurotic personality of our time.* New York: Norton

Horney, K. (1967). *Feminine psychology.* New York: Norton.

Hornik, R., Risenhoover, N., & Gunnar, M. (1987). The effects of maternal positive, neutral and negative affective communications on infant responses to new toys. *Child Development, 58,* 937–944.

Horowitz, F. D., & O'Brien, M. (1986). Gifted and talented children. *American Psychologist, 41,* 1147–1152.

Horta, B. L., Victora, C. G., Menezes, A. M., Halpern, R., & Barros, F. C. (1997). Low birthweight, preterm births, and intrauterine growth retardation in relation to maternal smoking. *Paediatr Perinat Epidemiol, 11,* 140–151.

Howard, G. R. (1993). Whites in multicultural education: Rethinking our role. *Phi Delta Kappan, 75,* 36–41.

Howes, C. (1983). Patterns of friendship. *Child Development, 54,* 1041–1053.

Howes, P., & Cicchetti, D. (1993). A family/relational perspective on maltreating families: Parallel processes across systems and social policy implications. In D. Cicchetti & S. L. Toth (Eds.), *Child abuse, child development, and social policy* (pp. 399–438). Norwood, NJ: Ablex.

Huang, L. N., & Yin, Y. (1989). Chinese American children and adolescents. In J. T. Gibbs, L. N. Huang, & associates (Eds.), *Children of color.* San Francisco: Jossey-Bass.

Hu-DeHart, E. (1993). The history, development, and future of ethnic studies. *Phi Delta Kappan, 75,* 50–54.

Hudspeth, W. J., & Pribram, K. H. (1992). Psychophysiological indices of cerebral maturation. *International Journal of Psychophysiology, 12,* 19–29.

Humphrey, G. K., & Humphrey, D .E. (1985). The use of binaural sensory aids by blind infants and children: Theoretical and applied issues. In F. Morrison & C. Lord (Eds.), *Applied developmental psychology* (Vol. 2). New York: Academic Press.

Humphrey, L. L. (1989). Observed family interactions among subtypes of eating disorders using structural analysis of social behavior. *Journal of Consulting and Clinical Psychology, 57,* 206–214.

Hunt, L., Fleming, P., & Golding, J., the ALSPAC Study Team. (in press). Does the supine sleeping position have any adverse effects on the child? I: Health in the first six months. *Pediatrics.*

Hur, Y., & Bourchard, T. J. (1995). Genetic influences on perceptions of childhood family environment: A reared apart twin study. *Child Development, 66,* 330-345.

Huston, A. C., McLoyd, V. C., & Coll, C. G. (1994). Children and poverty: Issues in contemporary research. *Child Development, 65,* 275-282.

Hwang, M. Y. (1999). Are you obese? *Journal of the American Medical Association, 282,* 1596.

Hyde, J. S. (1981). How large are cognitive gender differences? A meta-analysis using $w2$ and d. *American Psychologist, 36,* 892–901.

Hyde, J. S. (1984). Children's understanding of sexist language. *Developmental Psychology, 20,* 697–706.

Idjradinata, P., & Pollitt, E. (1993). Reversal of developmental delays in iron-deficient anaemic infants treated with iron. *Lancet, 341,* 1–4.

Irion, J. C., Coon, R. C., & Blanchard-Fields, F. (1988). The influence of divorce on coping in adolescence. *Journal of Youth and Adolescence, 17,* 135–145.

Irwin, J., & Austin, J. (1997). *It's about time: America's imprisonment binge.* Belmont, CA: Wadsworth.

Isabella, R. A. (1994). Origins of maternal role satisfaction and its influences upon maternal interactive behavior and infant-mother attachment. *Infant Behavior and Development, 17,* 381–388.

Iverson, J. M., & Goldin-Meadow, S. (1997). What's communication got to do with it? Gesture in children blind from birth. *Developmental Psychology, 33,* 458–467.

Izard, C. E. (1983). Emotions in personality and culture. *Ethos, 11,* 305–312.

Izard, C. E. (1994). Innate and universal facial expressions: Evidence from developmental and cross-cultural research. *Psychological Bulletin, 115,* 288–299.

Izard, C. E., & Maletesta, C. Z. (1987). Perspectives on emotional development I. In J. D. Osofsky (Ed.), *Handbook of infant development* (2nd ed.). New York: Wiley.

Jackson, J. F. (1993). Human behavioral genetics, Scarr's theory, and her views on interventions: A critical review and commentary on their implications for African American children. *Child Development, 64*, 1318–1332.

Jadack, R. A., Hyde, J. S., Moore, C. F., & Keller, M. L. (1995). Moral reasoning about sexually transmitted diseases. *Child Development, 66*, 167–177.

James, W. T. (1890). *The principles of psychology*. New York: Holt.

Jansen, R. P. S. (1978). Fallopian tube isthmic mucus and ovum transport. *Science, 201*, 349–351.

Jansen, R. P. S. (1984). Endocrine response in the fallopian tube. *Endocrine Review, 5*, 525–551.

Jarrett, R. L. (1995). Growing up poor: The family experiences of socially mobile youth in low-income African American neighborhoods. *Journal of Adolescent Research, 10*, 111–134.

Jensen, A. R. (1969). How much can we boost IQ and scholastic achievement? *Harvard Educational Review, 39*, 1–123.

Jensen, A. R. (1985). The nature of the Black-White difference on various psychometric tests: Spearman's hypothesis. *Behavioral and Brain Sciences, 8*, 193–263.

Joffe, M., & Ludwig, S. (1988). Stairway injuries in children. *Pediatrics, 82*, 457–461.

John, E. M., Savitz, D. A., & Sandler, D. P. (1991). Prenatal exposure to parents' smoking and childhood cancer. *American Journal of Epidemiology, 133*, 123–132.

Johnson, M. H. (1995). The inhibition of automatic saccades in early infancy. *Developmental Psychobiology, 28*, 281–291.

Johnson, M. L., Veldhuis, J. D., & Lampl, M. (1996). Is growth saltatory? The usefulness and limitations of frequency distributions in analyzing pulsatile data. *Endocrinology, 137*, 5197–5204.

Johnson, R. L., Laufer, E., Riddle, R. D., & Tabin, C. (1994). Ectopic expression of *Sonic hedgehog* alters dorsal-ventral patterning of somites. *Cell, 79*(7), 1165–1173.

Johnson, S. C., & Solomon, G. E. A. (1997). Why dogs have puppies and cats have kittens: The role of birth in young children's understanding of biological origins. *Child Development, 68*, 404–419.

Johnson, S. L., & Birch, L. L. (1994). Parents' and children's adiposity and eating style. *Pediatrics, 94*, 653–661.

Johnson, S. P., & Aslin, R. N. (1995). Perception of object unity in 2–month-old infants. *Developmental Psychology, 31*, 739–745.

Johnson, S. P., & Nanez, J. E. (1995). Young infants' perception of object unity in two-dimensional displays. *Infant Behavior and Development, 18*, 133–143.

Johnson, W., Emde, R. N., Pannebecker, B., Stenberg, C., & Davis, M. (1982). Maternal perception of infant emotion from birth through 18 months. *Infant Behavior and Development, 5*, 313–322.

Johnston, D. K. (1988). Adolescents' solutions to dilemmas in fables: Two moral orientations—two problem-solving strategies. In C. Gilligan, J. V. Ward, J. M. Taylor, & B. Bardige (Eds.), *Mapping the moral domain*. Cambridge, MA: Harvard University Press.

Jones, M. C. (1957). The late careers of boys who were early- or late-maturing. *Child Development, 28*, 113–128.

Jones, M. C. (1958). A study of socialization patterns at the high school level. *Journal of Genetic Psychology, 93*, 87–111.

Jones, M. C. (1965). Psychological correlates of somatic development. *Child Development, 36*, 899–911.

Jones, M. C., & Bayley, N. (1950). Physical maturing among boys as related to behavior. *Journal of Educational Psychology, 41*, 129–148.

Jones, M. C., & Mussen, P. H. (1958). Self-conceptions, motivations, and attitudes of early- and late-maturing girls. *Child Development, 29*, 491–501.

Joos, S. K., Pollitt, E., & Mueller, W. H. (1982). The Bacon Chow Study: Effects of maternal nutritional supplementation on infant mental and motor development. *Food & Nutrition Bulletin, 4*, 1–4.

Josselson, R. L. (1980). Ego development in adolescence. In J. Adelson (Ed.), *Handbook of adolescent psychology*. New York: Wiley.

Josselson, R. L. (1982). Personality structure and identity status in women as viewed through early memories. *Journal of Youth and Adolescence, 11*, 293–299.

Josselson, R. L. (1987). *Finding herself: Pathways to identity development in women*. San Francisco: Jossey-Bass.

Josselson, R. L. (1988). The embedded self: I and thou revisited. In D. K. Lapsley & F. C. Power (Eds.), *Self, ego, and identity*. New York: Springer-Verlag.

Josselson, R. L. (1992). *The space between us*. San Francisco: Jossey-Bass.

Jusczyk, P. W., Hirsh-Pasek, K., Kemler Nelson, D. G., Kennedy, L. J., Woodward, A., & Piwoz, J. (1992). Perception of acoustic correlates of major phrasal units by young infants. *Cognitive Psychology, 24*, 252–293.

Jusczyk, P. W., Johnson, S. P., Spelke, E. S., & Kennedy, L. J. (1999). Synchronous change and perception of object unity: Evidence from adults and infants. *Cognition, 71*, 257–288.

Just, E. E. (1919). The fertilization reaction in *Echinarachinus parma*. *Biological Bulletin, 36*, 1–10.

Justice Policy Institute. (1997, Fall). *Crime and justice trends in the District of Columbia*. Prepared by the National Council on Crime and Delinquency. Washington, DC: Office of Grants Management and Development, District of Columbia Government.

Kagan, J. (1981). *The second year*. Cambridge, MA: Harvard University Press.

Kagan, J. (1996). Three pleasing ideas. *American Psychologist, 51*, 901–908.

Kagan, J. (1997). Temperament and the reactions to unfamiliarity. *Child Development, 68*, 139–143.

Kagan, J., Arcus, D., Snidman, N., Feng, W. Y., Hendler, J., & Greene, S. (1994). Reactivity in infants: A cross-national comparison. *Developmental Psychology, 30*, 342–345.

Kagan, J., & Snidman, N. (1991). Temperamental factors in human development. *American Psychologist, 46*, 856–862.

Kail, R. (1991). Developmental changes in speed of processing during childhood and adolescence. *Psychological Bulletin, 109*, 490–501.

Kamii, M. (1991). Why Big Bird can't teach calculus: The case of place value and cognitive development in the middle years. In N. Lauter-Klatell (Ed.), *Readings in child development* (pp. 100–104). Mountain View, CA: Mayfield.

Kaufman, C., Grunebaum, H., Cohler, B., & Gamer, E. (1979). Superkids: Competent children of schizophrenic mothers. *American Journal of Psychiatry, 136*, 1398–1402.

Keating, D. P. (1980). Thinking processes in adolescence. In J. Adelson (Ed.), *Handbook of adolescent psychology.* New York: Wiley.

Keen, S. (1970). Reflections on a peach-seed monkey. In *To a dancing God* (pp. 100–101). New York: Harper & Row.

Kegan, R. (1982). *The evolving self: Problem and process in human development.* Cambridge, MA: Harvard University Press.

Kegan, R. (1994). *In over our heads.* Cambridge, MA: Harvard University Press.

Keirsey, D. (1999, January 25). The great A.D.D. hoax. Retrieved March 3, 2000, from the World Wide Web: http://keirsey.com/addhoax.html

Keith, L. G., & Luke, B. (1993). Multiple gestation. In F. R. Witter & L. G. Keith (Eds.). *Textbook of prematurity: Antecedents, treatment, and outcome* (pp. 115–126). Boston: Little, Brown.

Keller, M., & Wood, P. (1989). Development of friendship reasoning: A study of interindividual differences in intraindividual change. *Developmental Psychology, 25*, 820–826.

Kelley, M. L., Power, T. G., & Wimbush, D. D. (1992). Determinants of disciplinary practices in low-income Black mothers. *Child Development, 63*, 573–582.

Kenen, R. (1993). *Reproductive hazards in the workplace.* New York: Haworth Press.

Kennell, J., Klaus, M., McGrath, S., Robertson, S., & Hinkley, C. (1991). Continuous emotional support during labor in a U.S. hospital. *Journal of the American Medical Association, 265*, 2197–2201.

Kenny, A. M., Guardado, S., & Brown, L. (1989). Sex education and AIDS education in the schools: What states and large school districts are doing. *Family Planning Perspective, 21*, 56–64.

Kent, R. D., & Miolo, G. (1995). Phonetic abilities in the first year of life. In P. Fletcher & P. MacWhinney (Eds.), *The handbook of child language* (pp. 301–334). Oxford: Blackwell.

Kerfoot, M., Harrington, R., & Dyer, E. (1995). Brief home-based intervention with young suicide attempters and the families. *Journal of Adolescence, 18*, 557–568.

Kim, J. M. (1998). Korean children's concepts of adult and peer authority and moral reasoning. *Developmental Psychology, 34*, 947–955.

King, S. (1998). The body. In *Apt pupil* (pp. 293–436). New York: Signet.

King, T., & Fullard, W. (1982). Teenage mothers and their infants: New findings on the home environment. *Journal of Adolescence, 5*, 333–346.

Kingston, M. H. (1976). *Woman warrior: Memoirs of a girlhood among ghosts.* New York: Knopf.

Kipp, K., & Pope, S. (1997). The development of cognitive inhibition in streams-of-consciousness and directed speech. *Cognitive Development, 12*, 239–260.

Kirby, D. (1984). *Sexuality education: An evaluation of programs and their effect.* Santa Cruz, CA: Network Publications.

Klebanov, P. K., Brooks-Gunn, J., McCarton, C., & McCormick, M. C. (1998). The contribution of neighborhood and family income to developmental test scores over the first three years of life. *Child Development, 69*, 1420–1436.

Klesges, R. C., Shelton, M. L., & Klesges, L. M. (1993). Effects of television on metabolic rate: Potential implications for childhood obesity. *Pediatrics, 91*, 281–286.

Klonoff-Cohen, H. S., Edelstein, S. L., Lefkowitz, E. S., Srinivasen, I. P., Kaegi, D., Chang, J. C., & Wiley, K. J. (1995). The effect of passive smoking and tobacco exposure through breast milk on sudden infant death syndrome. *Journal of the American Medical Association, 273*, 795–798.

Knobil, E. (1980). The neuroendocrine control of the menstrual cycle. *Recent Progress in Hormone Research, 36*, 53–88.

Ko, Y. H., & Pedersen, P. L. (1997). Frontiers in research on cystic fibrosis: Understanding its molecular and chemical basis and relationship to the pathogenesis of the disease. *Journal of Bioenergetics and Biomembranes, 19*, 417–427.

Kobayashi-Winata, H., & Power, T. G. (1989). Child rearing and compliance: Japanese and American families in Houston. *Journal of Cross-Cultural Psychology, 20*, 333–356.

Kochanska, G., Casey, R. J., & Fukumoto, A. (1995). Toddlers' sensitivity to standard violations. *Child Development, 66*, 643–656.

Kochanska, G., Murray, K., & Coy, K. C. (1997). Inhibitory control as a contributor to conscience in childhood: From toddler to early school age. *Child Development, 68*, 263–277.

Kochman, T. (1987). The ethnic component in Black language and culture. In M. J. Rotheram & J. S. Phinney (Eds.), *Children's ethnic socialization: Pluralism and development* (pp. 219–238). Beverly Hills: Sage.

Kohl, H. W., III, & Hobbs, K. E. (1998). Development of physical activity behaviors among children and adolescents. *Pediatrics, 101,* 549–554.

Kohlberg, L. (1976). Moral stages and moralization: The cognitive developmental approach. In T. Lickona (Ed.), *Moral development and behavior.* New York: Holt, Rinehart & Winston.

Kohlberg, L. (1984). *The psychology of moral development.* New York: Harper & Row.

Kohlberg, L., & Kramer, R. (1969). Continuities and discontinuities in childhood and adult moral development. *Human Development, 12,* 93–120.

Kohler, I. (1962). Experiments with goggles. *Scientific American, 206,* 62–86.

Kontos, S., Howes, C., Shinn, M., & Galinsky, E. (1995). *Quality in family child care and relative care.* New York: Teachers College Press.

Koocher, G. P., & DeMaso, D. (1990). Children's competence to consent to medical procedures. *Pediatrician, 17,* 68–73.

Koplan, J. P., & Dietz, W. H. (1999). Caloric imbalance and public health policy. *Journal of the American Medical Association, 282,* 1579–1581.

Kopp, C. B. (1989). Regulation of distress and negative emotions: A developmental view. *Developmental Psychology, 25,* 343–354.

Korbin, J., & Coulton, C. (1995). *Neighborhood impact on child abuse and neglect: Final report on Grant # 90CA-1494.* Washington, DC: National Center on Child Abuse and Neglect.

Korenman, S., Miller, J. E., & Sjaastad, J. E. (1995). Long-term poverty and child development in the United States: Results from the NLSY. *Children and Youth Services Review, 17*(1–2), 127–155.

Kotlowitz, A. (1991). *There are no children here.* New York: Anchor/Doubleday.

Kovacs, D. M., Parker, J. G., & Hoffman, L. W. (1996). Behavioral, affective, and social correlates of involvement in cross-sex friendship in elementary school. *Child Development, 67,* 2269–2286.

Krasnoff, A. G. (1989). Early sex-linked activities and interests related to spatial abilities. *Personal and Individual Differences, 10,* 81–85.

Krebs-Smith, S. M., Cook, A., Subar, A. F., Cleveland, L., Friday, J., & Kahle, L. L. (1996). Fruit and vegetable intakes of children and adolescents in the United States. *Archives of Pediatric Adolescent Medicine, 150,* 81–86.

Kroger, J. (1986). The relative importance of identity status interview components: A replication and extension. *Journal of Adolescence, 9,* 337–354.

Kroger, J. (1988). A longitudinal study of ego identity status interview domains. *Journal of Adolescence, 11,* 49–64.

Kroger, J. (1995). The differentiation of "firm" and "developmental" foreclosure identity statuses: A longitudinal study. *Journal of Adolescent Research, 10,* 317–337.

Kroger, J. (1996). Identity, regression, and development. *Journal of Adolescence, 19,* 203–222.

Kroger, J., & Greene, K. E. (1996). Events associated with identity status change. *Journal of Adolescence, 19,* 477–490.

Krug, E. G., Dahlberg, L. L., & Powell, K. E. (1996). Childhood homicide, suicide, and firearm deaths: An international comparison. *World Health Statistics Quarterly, 49,* 230-235.

Kuhl, P. K., Andruski, J. E., Chistovich, I. A., Chistovich, L. A., Kozhevnikova, E. V., Ryskina, V. L., Stolyarova, E. I., Sundberg, U., & Lacerda. F. (1997). Cross–language analysis of phonetic units in language addressed to infants. *Science, 277,* 684–686.

Kuhn, T. S. (1962). *The structure of scientific revolutions.* Chicago: University of Chicago Press.

Kulin, H. E. (1991a). Puberty, hypothalamic-pituitary changes of. In R. M. Lerner, A. C. Petersen, & J. Brooks-Gunn (Eds.), *Encyclopedia of adolescence* (Vol. 2, pp. 900–907). New York: Garland.

Kulin, H. E. (1991b). Puberty, endocrine changes at. In R. M. Lerner, A. C. Petersen, & J. Brooks-Gunn (Eds.), *Encyclopedia of adolescence* (Vol. 2, pp. 897–899). New York: Garland.

LaFromboise, T. D., & Low, K. G. (1989). American Indian children and adolescents. In J. T. Gibbs, L. N. Huang, & associates (Eds.), *Children of color.* San Francisco: Jossey-Bass.

Lagattuta, K. H., Wellman, H. M., & Flavell, J. H. (1997). Preschoolers' understanding of the link between thinking and feeling: Cognitive cueing and emotional change. *Child Development, 68,* 1081–1104.

Laible, D. J., & Thompson, R. A. (1998). Attachment and emotional understanding in preschool children. *Developmental Psychology, 34,* 1038–1045.

Lakoff, G. (1987). *Women, fire and dangerous things.* Chicago: University of Chicago Press.

Lamb, M. E. (1977). The development of mother-infant and father-infant attachments in the second year of life. *Developmental Psychology, 13,* 637–648.

Lamb, M. E. (1981). The development of father-infant relationships. In M. E. Lamb (Ed.), *The role of the father in child development* (2nd ed., pp. 459–488). New York: Wiley.

Lamott, A. (1993). *Operating instructions: A journal of my son's first year.* San Francisco: Pantheon Books.

Lampinen, J. M., & Smith, V. L. (1995). The incredible (and sometimes credulous) child witness: Child eyewitnesses' sensitivity to source credibility cues. *Journal of Applied Psychology, 80,* 621–627.

Lampl, M., & Johnson, M. L. (1993). A case study of daily growth during adolescence: A single spurt or changes in the dynamics of saltatory growth? *Annals of Human Biology, 20,* 595–603.

Landau, S., Lorch, E. P., & Milich. (1992). Visual attention to and comprehension of television in attention-deficit hyperactivity disordered and normal boys. *Child Development, 63,* 928–937.

Lannfelt, L., Axelman, K., Lilius, L., & Basun, H. (1995). Genetic counseling in a Swedish Alzheimer family with amyloid precursor protein mutation (letter). *American Journal of Human Genetics, 56,* 332–335.

Lapsley, D. K., FitzGerald, D. P., Rice, K. G., & Jackson, S. (1989). Separation-individuation and the "new look" at the imaginary audience and personal fable: A test of an integrative model. *Journal of Adolescent Research, 4,* 483–505.

Larson, R. W., & Almeida, D. M. (1999). Emotional transmission in the daily lives of families: A new paradigm for studying family process. *Journal of Marriage and the Family, 61,* **5**–20.

Larson, R. W., & Gillman, S. (1999). Transmission of emotions in the daily interactions of single-mother families. *Journal of Marriage and the Family, 61*(1), 21–37.

Larson, R. W., Richards, M. H., Moneta, G., Holmbeck, G., & Duckett, E. (1996). Changes in adolescents' daily interactions with their families from ages 10 to 18: Disengagement and transformation. *Developmental Psychology, 32,* 744–754.

Larson, R., & Richards, M. H. (1994). *Divergent realities.* New York: Basic Books.

Lau, S., & Lau, W. (1996). Outlook on life: How adolescents and children view the life-style of parents, adults and self. *Journal of Adolescence, 19,* 293–296.

Laupa, M. (1991). Children's reasoning about three authority attributes: Adult status, knowledge, and social position. *Developmental Psychology, 27,* 321–329.

Laupa, M., & Turiel, E. (1986). Children's concepts of adult and peer authority. *Child Development, 57,* 405–412.

Laursen, R., Coy, K. C., & Collins, W. A. (1998). Reconsidering changes in parent-child conflict across adolescence: A meta-analysis. *Child Development, 69,* 817–832.

Lawrence, R. A. (1994). *Breastfeeding: A guide for the medical profession.* St. Louis: Mosby.

Lecours, A. R. (1982). Correlates of developmental behavior in brain maturation. In T. Bever (Ed.), *Regressions in mental development.* Hillsdale, NJ: Erlbaum.

Ledoux, S., Choquet, M., & Manfredi, R. (1993). Associated factors for self-reported binge eating among male and female adolescents. *Journal of Adolescence, 15,* 75–91.

Lee, K., Cameron, C.A., Xu, F., Fu, G., & Board, J. (1997). Chinese and Canadian children's evaluations of lying and truth telling: Similarities and differences in the context of pro- and antisocial behaviors. *Child Development, 68,* 924–934.

Leger, J., Limoni, C., & Czernichow, P. (1997). Prediction of the outcome of growth at 2 years of age in neonates with intra-uterine growth retardation. *Early Human Development, 48,* 211–223.

Leinbach, M. D., Hort, B. E., & Fagot, B. (1997). Bears are for boys: Metaphorical associations in young children's gender stereotypes. *Cognitive Development, 12,* 107–130.

Leland, N. L., & Barth, R. P. (1993). Characteristics of adolescents who have attempted to avoid HIV and who have communicated with parents about sex. *Journal of Adolescent Research, 8,* 58–76.

Leon, G. R., Perry, C. L., Mangelsdorf, C., & Tell, G. J. (1989). Adolescent nutritional and psychological patterns and risk for the development of an eating disorder. *Journal of Youth and Adolescence, 18,* 273–282.

Lerner, R. M. (1976). *Concepts and theories of human development.* Menlo Park, CA: Addison-Wesley.

Lerner, R. M. (1986). *Concepts and theories of human development* (2nd ed.). New York: Random House.

Leslie, A. M. (1982). The perception of causality in infants. *Perception, 11,* 173–186.

Leslie, A. M. (1986). The necessity of illusion: Perception and thought in infancy. In L. Weiskrantz (Ed.), *Thought without language* (pp. 185–210). Oxford: Clarendon.

Lester, B. M., Boukydis, C. F., & Zachariah, C. (1992). No language by a cry. In H. Papousek, J. Jurgens, & M. Papousek (Eds.), *Nonverbal vocal communications: Comparative and developmental approaches.* New York: Cambridge University Press.

Lester, B. M., Freier, K., & LaGasse, L. (1995). Prenatal cocaine exposure and child outcome: What do we really know? In M. Lewis & M. Bendersky (Eds.). *Mothers, babies, and cocaine: The role of toxins in development* (pp. 19–40). Hillsdale, NJ: Erlbaum.

Lever, J. (1976). Sex differences in the games children play. *Social Problems, 23,* 478–487.

Lever, J. (1978). Sex differences in the complexity of children's play and games. *American Sociological Review, 43,* 471–483.

Levine, L. E. (1983). Mine: Self-definition in 2-year-old boys. *Developmental Psychology, 19,* 544–549.

Levinson, R. A., Wan, C. K., & Beamer, L. J. (1998). The contraceptive self-efficacy scale: Analysis in four samples. *Journal of Youth and Adolescence, 27,* 773–793.

Levitt, M. J., Guacci-Franco, N., & Levitt, J. L. (1993). Convoys of social support in childhood and early adolescence: Structure and function. *Developmental Psychology, 29,* 811–818.

Levitt, R. A. (1981). *Physiological psychology.* New York: Holt, Rinehart & Winston.

Lewis, C., Freeman, N. H., Kyriakidou, C., Maridaki-Kassotaki, K., & Berridge, D. M. (1996). Social influences on false belief access: Specific sibling influences or general apprenticeship? *Child Development, 67,* 2930–2947.

Lewis, M. (1993). The emergence of emotions. In M. Lewis & J. Havilland (Eds.), *Handbook of emotions* (pp. 223–235). New York: Guilford Press.

Lewis, M. (1995). Embarrassment: The emotion of self-exposure and evaluation. In J. P. Tangney & K. W. Fischer (Eds.),. *Self-conscious emotions: The psychology of shame, guilt, embarrassment, and pride* (pp. 198–218). New York: Guilford Press.

Lewis, M., & Brooks-Gunn, J. (1979). *Social cognition and the acquisition of self.* New York: Plenum.

Lewis, M., & Michaelson, L. (1983). From emotional state to emotional expression: Emotional development from a person-environment perspective. In D. Magnusson & V. L. Allen (Eds.), *Human development: An interactional perspective* (pp. 261–275). New York: Academic Press.

Lewis, M., Ramsay, D. S., & Kawakami, K. (1993). Differences between Japanese infants and Causasian American infants in behavioral and cortisol response to inoculation. *Child Development, 64,* 1722–1731.

Lewis, S. (1996). *A totally alien life-form—Teenagers.* New York: New Press.

Lewkowicz, D. J. (1996). Infants' response to the audible and visible properties of the human face: 1. Role of lexical-syntactic content, temporal synchrony, gender, and manner of speech. *Developmental Psychology, 32,* 347–366.

Lewontin, R. (1982). *Human diversity.* New York: Scientific American Books.

Li, X., Sano, H., & Merwin, J. C. (1996). Perception and reasoning abilities among American, Japanese, and Chinese adolescents. *Journal of Adolescent Research, 11,* 173–193.

Lillard, A. S. (1993). Young children's conceptualization of pretense: Action or mental representational state? *Child Development, 64,* 372–386.

Lillard, A. S. (1996). Body or mind: Children's categorizing of pretense. *Child Development, 67,* 1717–1734.

Lindsey, E. W., Mize, J., & Pettit, G. S. (1997). Differential play patterns of mothers and fathers of sons and daughters: Implications for children's gender role development. *Sex Roles, 37,* 643–661.

Lips, H. M. (1997). *Sex and gender: An introduction* (3rd ed.). Mountain View, CA: Mayfield.

Little, R. E., & Sing, E. F. (1987). Father's drinking and infant birth weight: Report of an association. *Teratology, 36,* 59–65.

Livesley, W. J., & Bromley, D. B. (1973). *Person perception in childhood and adolescence.* London: Wiley.

Lobel, T., & Levanon, I. (1988). Self-esteem, need for approval, and cheating behavior in children. *Journal of Educational Psychology, 80,* 122–123.

Longo, F. J. (1987). *Fertilization.* New York: Chapman and Hall.

LoSciuto, L., Rajala, A. K., Townsend, T. N., & Taylor, A. S. (1996). An outcome evaluation of Across Ages: An intergenerational mentoring approach to drug prevention. *Journal of Adolescent Research, 11,* 116–129.

Lou, H. C., Hansen, D., Nordentoft, M., Pryds, O., Jensen, F.,

Nim, J., & Hemmingsen, R. (1994). Prenatal stressors of human life affect fetal brain development. *Developmental Medicine and Child Neurology, 36,* 826–832.

Lovitt, T. C. (1989). *Introduction to learning disabilities.* Boston: Allyn & Bacon.

Lucas, B. (1988). Family patterns and their relationship to obesity. In K. C. Clark, R. B. Parr, & W. P. Castelli (Eds.), *Evaluation and management of eating disorders.* Champaign, IL: Life Enhancement.

Luciana, M., & Nelson, C.A. (1998). The functional emergence of prefrontally-guided working memory systems in four- to eight-year-old children. *Neuropsychologia, 36,* 273–293.

Lund, R. D., & Chang, F. F. (1986). The normal and abnormal development of the mammalian visual system. In W. T. Greenough & J. M. Juraska (Eds.), *Developmental neuropsychobiology* (pp. 95–118). San Diego: Academic Press.

Lynch, S. R. (2000). The potential impact of iron supplementation during adolescence on iron status in pregnancy. *Journal of Nutrition, 130,* 448S–451S.

Maccoby, E. E. (1984). Socialization and developmental change. *Child Development, 55*(2), 317–328.

Maccoby, E. E. (1988). Gender as a social category. *Developmental Psychology, 26,* 755–765.

Maccoby, E. E. (1990). Gender and relationships. *American Psychologist, 45,* 513–520.

MacFarlane, J. (1975). Olfaction in the development of social preferences in the human neonate. In *Parent-infant interaction* (Ciba Foundation Symposium No. 33, pp. 103–117). Amsterdam: Elsevier.

Macfie, J., Toth, S. L., Rogosch, F. A., Robinson, J-A., Emde, R. N., & Cicchetti, D. (1999). Effect of maltreatment on preschoolers' narrative representations of responses to relieve distress and of role reversal. *Developmental Psychology, 35,* 460–465.

MacPhee, D., Fritz, J., & Miller-Heyl, J. (1996). Ethnic variations in personal social networks and parenting. *Child Development, 67,* 3278–3295.

Maletesta, C. Z., Culver, C., Tesman, J. R., & Shepard, B. (1989). The development of emotional expression during the first two years of life. *Monographs of the Society for Research in Child Development, 54* (Serial No. 219).

Malina, R. M. (1990). Physical growth and performance during the transitional years (9–16). In R. Montemayor, G. R. Adams, & T. P. Gullotta (Eds.), *From childhood to adolescence.* Newbury Park, CA: Sage.

Malina, R. M., & Bouchard, C. (1991). *Growth, maturation, and physical activity.* Champaign, IL: Human Kinetics Books.

Malloy, M. H., Kleinman, J. C., Land, G. H., & Schramm, W. F. (1988). The association of maternal smoking with age and cause of infant death. *American Journal of Epidemiology, 128,* 46–55.

Mandler, J. M. (1990). A new perspective on cognitive development in infancy. *American Scientist, 78,* 236–243.

Mandler, J. M. (1992). How to build a baby: II. Conceptual primitives. *Psychological Review, 99,* 587–604.

Mandler, J. M., Bauer, P. J., & McDonough, L. (1991). Separating the sheep from the goats: Differentiating global categories. *Cognitive Psychology, 23,* 263–298.

Mangelsdorf, S. C., Shapiro, J. R., & Marzolf, D. (1995). Developmental and temperamental differences in emotion regulation in infancy. *Child Development, 66,* 1817–1828.

Marcia, J. E. (1980). Identity in adolescence. In J. Adelson (Ed.), *Handbook of adolescent psychology.* New York: Wiley.

Marcia, J. E. (1988). Common processes underlying ego identity, cognitive/moral development, and individuation. In D. K. Lapsley & F. C. Power (Eds.), *Self, ego, and identity: Integrative approaches.* New York: Springer-Verlag.

Marcus, M., Silbergeld, E., Mattison, D., & the Research Needs Working Group. (1993). A reproductive hazards research agenda for the 1990s. *Environmental Health Perspectives Supplements, 101,* 175–180.

Marieb, E. N. (1992). *Human anatomy and physiology* (2nd ed.). Redwood City, CA: Benjamin/Cummings.

Markus, H. R., & Kitayama, S. (1991). Culture and the self: Implications for cognition, emotion, and motivation. *Psychological Review, 98,* 224–253.

Marsh, H. W., Craven, R., & Debus, R. (1998). Structure, stability and development of young children's self-concepts: A multicohort-multioccasion study. *Child Development, 69,* 1030–1053.

Martin, C. L., & Halverson, C. F. (1981). A schematic processing model of sex typing and stereotyping in children. *Child Development, 52,* 1119–1134.

Martin, C. L., & Halverson, C. F. (1983). The effects of sex-typing schemas on young children's memory. *Child Development, 61,* 1427–1439.

Martin, E. C. (1986). Being in junior high. In D. Cavitch (Ed.), *Life studies: A thematic reader* (2nd ed.). New York: St. Martin's.

Martorano, S. C. (1977). A developmental analysis of performance on Piaget's formal operations tasks. *Developmental Psychology, 13,* 666–672.

Mascolo, M. F., & Fischer, K. W. (1995). Developmental transformations in appraisals for pride, shame, and guilt. In J. P. Tangney & K. W. Fischer (Eds.), *Self-conscious emotions: The psychology of shame, guilt, embarrassment, and pride* (pp. 64–113). New York: Guilford Press.

Maugh, T. (1999, October 22). Study finds major benefits from quality day care. *Los Angeles Times,* pp. A3, A38.

Maurer, D., & Maurer, C. (1988). *The world of the newborn.* New York: Basic Books.

Mayes, L. C., & Bornstein, M. H. (1995). Developmental dilemmas for cocaine-abusing parents and their children. In M. Lewis & M. Bendersky (Eds.), *Mothers, babies, and cocaine: The role of toxins in development* (pp. 251–272). Hillsdale, NJ: Erlbaum.

Mayr, E. (1982). *Growth of biological thought: Diversity, evolution, and inheritance.* Cambridge, MA: Harvard University Press.

Mazor, A., & Enright, R. D. (1988). The development of the individuation process from a social-cognitive perspective. *Journal of Adolescence, 11,* 29–47.

McAdams, D. P., Hoffman, B. J., Mansfield, E. D., & Day, R. (1996). Themes of agency and communion in significant autobiographical scenes. *Journal of Personality, 64,* 339–377.

McCartney, K., Scarr, S., Phillips, D., & Grajek, S. (1985). Day care as intervention: Comparisons of varying quality programs. *Journal of Applied Developmental Psychology, 6,* 247–260.

McCary, J. L., & McCary, S. P. (1982). *McCary's human sexuality* (4th ed.). Belmont, CA: Wadsworth.

McCormick, L. K., Bartholomew, L. K., Lewis, M. J., Brown, M. W., & Hanson, I. C. (1997). Parental perceptions of barriers to childhood immunization: Results of focus groups conducted in an urban population. *Health Education Research, 12,* 355–362.

McFarlane, A. H., Bellissimo, A., Norman, G. R., & Lange, P. (1994). Adolescent depression in a school-based community sample: Preliminary findings on contributing social factors. *Journal of Youth and Adolescence, 23,* 601–620.

McGhee, P. E. (1979). *Humor: Its origin and development.* San Francisco: Freeman.

McGilly, K., & Siegler, R. S. (1989). How children choose among serial recall strategies. *Child Development, 60,* 172–182.

McHugh, P. R. (1999). How psychiatry lost its way. *Commentary, 108*(5), 32.

McLanahan, S. S., & Booth, K. (1989). Mother-only families: Problems, prospects, and politics. *Journal of Marriage and the Family, 51,* 557–580.

McLaughlin, D., & Whitfield, R. (1984). Adolescents and their experience of parental divorce. *Journal of Adolescence, 7,* 155–170.

McNeill, D. (1970). *The acquisition of language: The study of developmental psycholinguistics.* New York: Harper & Row.

Mechanic, D., & Hansell, S. (1989). Divorce, family conflict, and adolescents' well-being. *Journal of Health and Social Behavior, 30,* 105–116.

Meeks Gardner, J. M., Grantham-McGregor, S. M., Chang, S. M., Himes, J. H., & Powell, C. A. (1995). Activity and behavioral development in stunted and nonstunted children and response to nutritional supplementation. *Child Development, 66,* 1785–1797.

Meltzoff, A. N., & Borton, R. W. (1979). Intermodal matching by human neonates. *Nature, 282,* 403–404.

Menken, J., Trussell, J., & Larsen, U. (1986). Age and infertility. *Science, 233,* 1389–1394.

Menn, L., & Stoel-Gammon, C. (1995). Phonological development. In P. Fletcher & P. MacWhinney (Eds.), *The handbook of child language* (pp. 335–359). Oxford : Blackwell.

Menticoglou, S. M., Manning, F., Harman, C., & Morrison, I. (1995). Perinatal outcome in relation to second-stage duration. *American Journal of Obstetrics and Gynecology, 173,* 906–912.

Merriman, W. E., Evey-Burkey, J. A., Marazita, J. M., & Jarvis, L .H. (1996). Young two-year-olds' tendency to map novel verbs onto novel actions. *Journal of Experimental Child Psychology, 63,* 466–498.

Merriman, W. E., & Stevenson, C. M. (1997). Restricting a familiar name in response to learning a new one: Evidence for the mutual exclusivity bias in young two-year-olds. *Child Development, 68,* 211–228.

Mervis, C. B. (1987). Child-basic object categories and early development. In U. Neisser (Ed.), *Concepts and conceptual development* (pp. 201–235). Cambridge: Cambridge University Press.

Meryash, D. L. (1995). *Genetics.* In D. R. Coustan, R. V. Haning, Jr., & D. B. Singer (Eds.), *Human reproduction: Growth and development.* New York: Little, Brown.

Meyers, A. F., Simpson, A. E., Weitzman, M., et al. (1989). School breakfast program and school performance. *American Journal of Diseases of Children, 143,* 1234–1239.

Miller, C. T., & Downey, K. T. (1999). A meta-analysis of heavyweight and self-esteem. *Personality and Social Psychology Review, 3,* 68–84.

Miller, D. T., Weinstein, S. M., & Karniol, R. (1978). Effects of age and self-verbalization on children's ability to delay gratification. *Developmental Psychology, 14,* 569–570.

Miller, G. (1989). Foreword. In J. T. Gibbs, L. N. Huang, & associates (Eds.), *Children of color.* San Francisco: Jossey-Bass.

Miller, G. A., Galenter, E., & Pribram, K. H. (1960). *Plans and the structure of behavior.* New York: Holt, Rinehart & Winston.

Miller, J. (Ed.). (1973). *Psychoanalysis and women.* New York: Brunner/Mazel.

Miller, J. (1976). *Toward a new psychology of women.* Boston: Beacon Press.

Miller, L. A., Shaikh, T., Stanton, C., Montgomery, A., Rickard, R., Keefer, S., & Hoffman, R. (1995). Surveillance for fetal alcohol syndrome in Colorado. *Public Health Reports, 110,* 690–697.

Miller, P. J., Wiley, A. R., Fung, H., & Liang, C. (1997). Personal storytelling as a medium of socialization in Chinese and American families. *Child Development, 68,* 557–568.

Minuchin, S., Rosman, B., & Baker, L. (1978). *Psychosomatic families: Anorexia nervosa in context.* Cambridge, MA: Harvard University Press.

Mischel, H. N., & Mischel, W. (1983). The development of children's knowledge of self-control strategies. *Child Development, 54,* 603–619.

Mischel, W. & Mischel, H. N. (1976). A cognitive social-learning approach to morality and self-regulation. In T. Lickona (Ed.), *Moral development and behavior: Theory, research, and social issues.* New York: Holt, Rinehart & Winston.

Mischel, W., & Rodriguez, M. L. (1993). Psychological distance in self-imposed delay of gratification. In R. R. Cocking, K. A. Renninger, et al. (Eds.), *The development of meaning of psychological distance* (pp. 109–121). Hillsdale, NJ: Erlbaum.

Mischel, W., Shoda, Y., & Rodriguez, M. L. (1992). Delay of gratification in children. In G. Loewenstein, J. Elster, et al. (Eds.), *Choice over time* (pp. 147–164). New York: Russell Sage.

Mitchell, E. A., Scragg, R., Stewart, A. W., Becroft, D. M. O., Taylor, B. J., Ford, R. P. K., Hassall, I. B., Barry, D. M. J., Allen, E. M., & Roberts, A. P. (1991). Results from the first year of the New Zealand cot death study. *New Zealand Medical Journal, 104,* 71–76.

Mitchell, E. A., Touhy, P. G., Brunts, J. M., Thompson, J. M. D., Clements, M. S., Stewart, A. W., Ford, R. P. K., & Taylor, B. J. (1997). Risk factors for sudden infant death syndrome following the prevention campaign in New Zealand. *Pediatrics, 100,* 835–840.

Mitchell, J. J. (1990). *Human growth and development: The childhood years.* Calgary, Alberta: Detselig Enterprises.

Mix, K. S., Levine, S. C., & Huttenlocher, J. (1997). Numerical abstraction in infants: Another look. *Developmental Psychology, 33,* 423–428.

Mize, J., & Pettit, G. S. (1997). Mothers' social coaching, mother-child relationship style, and children's peer competence: Is the medium the message? *Child Development, 68,* 312–332.

Mokdad, A. H., Serdula, M. K., Dietz, W. H., Bowman, B. A., Marks, J. S., & Koplan, J. P. (1999). The spread of the obesity epidemic in the United States, 1991–1998. *Journal of the American Medical Association, 282,* 1519–1522.

Molina, B. S. G., & Chassin, L. (1996). The parent-adolescent relationship at puberty: Hispanic ethnicity and parent alcoholism as moderators. *Developmental Psychology, 32,* 675–686.

Moon, C., Cooper, R .P., & Fifer, W. P. (1993). Two-day-olds prefer their native language. *Infant Behavior and Development, 16,* 495–500.

Moore, K. A., & Glei, D. (1995). Taking the plunge: An examination of positive youth development. *Journal of Adolescent Research, 10,* 15–40.

Moore, K. L, & Persaud, T. V. N. (1993). *Before we are born* (4th ed.). Philadelphia: Saunders.

Moore, S. M. (1995). Girls' understanding and social constructions of menarche. *Journal of Adolescence, 18,* 87–104.

Morrison, T. (1973). *Sula.* New York: Plume.

Mounts, N. S., & Steinberg, L. (1995). An ecological analysis of peer influence on adolescent grade point average and drug use. *Developmental Psychology, 31,* 915–922.

Mueller, C. M., & Dweck, C. S. (1998). Praise for intelligence can undermine children's motivation and performance. *Journal of Personality and Social Psychology, 75,* 33–52.

Mumme, D. L., Fernald, A., & Herrera, C. (1996). Infants' responses to facial and vocal emotional signals in a social referencing paradigm. *Child Development, 67,* 3219–3237.

Munoz, K. A., Drebs-Smith, S. M., Ballard-Barbach, R., & Cleveland, L. E. (1997). Food intakes of U.S. children and adolescents compared with recommendations. *Pediatrics, 100,* 323–329.

Munroe, R. (1955). *Schools of psychoanalytic thought.* New York: Dryden Press.

Muscati, S. K., Koski, K. G., & Gray-Donald, K. (1996). Increased energy intake in pregnant smokers does not prevent human fetal growth retardation. *Journal of Nutrition, 126,* 2984–2989.

Musick, J., Stott, F., Spencer, K. K., Goldman, J., & Cohler, B. (1987). Maternal factors related to vulnerability and resiliency in young children at risk. In E. J. Anthony & J. J. Cohler (Eds.), *The invulnerable child* (pp. 229–252). New York: Guilford.

Mussen, P. H., & Jones, M. C. (1957). Self-conceptions, motivations, and interpersonal attitudes of late- and early-maturing boys. *Child Development, 28,* 243–256.

Muuss, R. E. (1990). *Adolescent behavior and society* (4th ed.). New York: Random House.

Nagata, D. K. (1989). Japanese American children and adolescents. In J. T. Gibbs, L. N. Huang, & associates (Eds.), *Children of color.* San Francisco: Jossey-Bass.

Narahara, M. (1998). *Gender bias in children's picture books: A look at teachers' choice of literature.* Unpublished master's thesis, University of California, Long Beach, Long Beach, California.

Nation, K., & Snowling, M. J. (1998). Individual differences in contextual facilitation: Evidence from dyslexia and poor reading comprehension. *Child Development, 69,* 996–1011.

National Center for Health Statistics. (1968–1991). *Vital statistics of the United States: Vol. 2. Mortality—Part A* [for 1966–1988]. Washington, DC: U.S. Government Printing Office.

National Center for Health Statistics. (1999). *Healthy people 2000 review, 1998–99.* Hyattsville, MD: Public Health Service.

National Head Start Association. (1990). *Head Start: The nation's pride, a nation's challenge.* Alexandria, VA: Author.

Needle, R. H., Su, S. S., & Doherty, W. J. (1990). Divorce, remarriage, and adolescent substance use: A prospective longitudinal study. *Journal of Marriage and the Family, 52,* 157–169.

Neisser, U. (1967). *Cognitive psychology.* New York: Appleton-Century-Crofts.

Neisser, U. (1976). *Cognition and reality.* San Francisco: Freeman.

Neisser, U. (1992). The development of consciousness and the acquisition of self. In F. S. Kessel, P. M. Cole, & D. L. Johnson (Eds.), *Self and consciousness: Multiple perspectives* (pp. 1–18). Hillsdale, NJ: Erlbaum.

Neisser, U., Boodoo, G., Bouchard, T. J., Boykin, A. W., Brody, N., Ceci, S. J., Halpern, D. F., Loehlink, J. C., Perloff, R., Steinberg, R., & Urbina, S. (1996). Intelligence: Knowns and unknowns. *American Psychologist, 51,* 77–101.

Nelson, K. (1992). Emergence of autobiographical memory at age 4. *Human Development, 35,* 172–177.

Nelson, K., Fivush, R., Hudson, J., & Lucariello, J. (1983). Scripts and the development of memory. In M. T. H. Chi (Ed.), *Trends in memory development: Contributions to human development* (Vol. 9, pp. 52–70). Basel, Switzerland: Karger.

Ness, R. B., Grisso, J. A., Hirschinger, N., Markovic, N., Shaw, L. M., Day, N. L., & Kline, J. (1999). Cocaine and tobacco use and the risk of spontaneous abortion. *New England Journal of Medicine, 340,* 333–339.

Netley, C. T. (1986). Summary overview of behavioral development in individuals with neonatally identified X and Y aneuploidy. *Birth Defects, 22,* 293–306

Newacheck, P. W., Hughes, D. C., & Stoddard, J. J. (1996). Children's access to primary care: Differences by race, income, and insurance status. *Pediatrics, 97,* 26–32.

Newman, D. L., Caspi, A., Moffitt, T. E., & Silva, P. A. (1997). Antecedents of adult interpersonal functioning: Effects of individual differences in age 3 temperament. *Developmental Psychology, 33,* 206–217.

NICHD Early Child Care Research Network. (1998). Relations between family predictors and child outcomes: Are they weaker for children in child care? *Developmental Psychology, 34,* 1119–1128.

Nicholls, R. D. (1993). Genomic imprinting and uniparental disomy in Angelman and Prader-Willi syndromes. *American Journal of Medical Genetics, 46,* 16–25.

Nicklas, T. A., Webber, L. S., Srinivasan, S. R., & Berenson, G. S. (1993). Secular trends in dietary intakes and cardiovascular risk factors of 10-year-old children: The Bogalusa Heart Study. *American Journal of Clinical Nutrition, 57,* 930–937.

Nieto, A., Matorras, R., Serra, M., Valenzuela, P., & Molera, J. (1994). Multivariate analysis of determinants of fetal growth retardation. *Eur J. Obstet Gynecol Reprod Biol, 53,* 107–113.

Nijhuis, J. (1995). Physiological and clinical consequences in relation to the development of fetal behavior and fetal behavioral states. In J.-P. Lecanuet, W. P. Fifer, N. A. Krasnegor, & W. P. Smotherman (Eds.), *Fetal development: A psychobiological perspective* (pp. 67–82). Hillsdale, NJ: Erlbaum.

Nilsson, L., & Hamberger, L. (1990). *A child is born.* New York: Delacorte.

Nørgaard, J. P., Pedersen, E. B., & Djurhuus, J. C. (1985). Diurnal anti-diuretic hormone levels in enuretics. *Journal of Urology, 134,* 1029–1031.

Norton, E. M., Durlak, J. A., & Richards, M. H. (1989). Peer knowledge of and reactions to adolescent suicide. *Journal of Youth and Adolescence, 18,* 427–437.

Nowakowski, R. S. (1987). Basic concepts of CNS development. *Child Development, 58,* 568–595.

Nucci, L., Camino, C., & Sapiro, C. M. (1996). Social class effects on northeastern Brazilian children's conceptions of areas of personal choice and social regulation. *Child Development, 67,* 1223–1242.

Nurmi, J.-E., Poole, M. E., & Kalakoski, V. (1996). Age differences in adolescent identity exploration and commitment in urban and rural environments. *Journal of Adolescence, 19,* 443–452.

O'Connell, A. N. (1976). The relationship between life-style and identity synthesis and re-synthesis in traditional, neotraditional, and nontraditional women. *Journal of Personality, 44,* 675–688.

O'Shea, P. A. (1995). The fetus as patient: Prenatal diagnosis and treatment. In D. R. Coustan, R. V. Haning, Jr., & D. B. Singer (Eds.). *Human reproduction: Growth and development* (pp. 247–264). New York: Little, Brown.

O'Sullivan, J. T., & Howe, M. L. (1995). Metamemory and memory construction. *Consciousness and Cognition: An International Journal, 4*(1), 104–110.

O'Sullivan, J. T., Howe, M. L., & Marche, T. A. (1996). Children's beliefs about long-term retention. *Child Development, 67,* 2989–3009.

Oakes, J. (1985). *Keeping track: How schools structure inequality.* New Haven, CT: Yale University Press.

Oakley, G. P., Jr. (1997). Doubling the number of women consuming vitamin supplement pills containing folic acid: An urgently needed birth defect prevention complement to the folic acid fortification of cereal grains. *Reproductive Toxicology, 11,* 579–581.

Ocampo, K. A., Knight, G. P., & Bernal, M. E. (1997). The development of cognitive abilities and social identities in children: The case of ethnic identity. *International Journal of Behavioral Development, 21,* 479–500.

Ogbu, J. U. (1981). Black education: A cultural-ecological perspective. In H. P. McAdoo (Ed.), *Black families.* Beverly Hills: Sage.

Ogbu, J. U. (1992). Understanding cultural diversity and learning. *Educational Researcher, 21,* 5–14.

Ogden, C. L., Troiano, R. P., Briefel, R. R., Kuczmarski, R. J., Flegal, K. M., & Johnson, C. L. (1997). Prevalence of overweight among preschool children in the United States, 1971 through 1994. *Pediatrics, 99*(4), E1.

Okun, A., Parker, J. G., & Levendosky, A. A. (1994). Distinct and interactive contributions of physical abuse, socioeconomic disadvantage and negative life events to children's social, cognitive, and affective adjustment. *Development and Psychopathology, 6,* 77–98.

Oller, D. K. (1999, August). *Bilingual infants show neither advantages nor disadvantages over monolingual infants.* Paper presented at the meeting of the Society for Research in Child Development, Kansas City.

Olsen, J. (1992). Cigarette smoking in pregnancy and fetal growth. Does the type of tobacco play a role? *International Journal of Epidemiology, 21,* 279–284.

Olshan, A. F., & Faustman, E. M. (1993). Male-mediated developmental toxicity. In *Annual Review of Public Health, 14,* 159–181.

Olshan, A. F., Teschke, K., & Baird, P. A. (1990). Birth defects among offspring of firemen. *American Journal of Epidemiology, 131,* 312–321.

Olson, H. C., Grant, T. M., Martin, J. C., & Streissguth, A. P. (1995). A cohort study of prenatal cocaine exposure: Addressing methodological concerns. In M. Lewis & M. Bendersky (Eds.), *Mothers, babies, and cocaine: The role of toxins in development* (pp. 129–162). Hillsdale, NJ: Erlbaum.

Olweus, D., Limber, S., & Mihalic, S. (1999). *Blueprints for violence prevention. Book 9: Bullying prevention program.* Boulder, CO: Center for the Study and Prevention of Violence.

Orfield, G. A. (1993). *The growth of segregation in American schools: Changing patterns of segregation and poverty since 1968.* Alexandria, VA: National School Boards Association.

Orlofsky, J., & Frank, M. (1986). Personality structure as viewed through early memories and identity status in college men and women. *Journal of Personality and Social Psychology, 5,* 580–586.

Osherson, D. N., & Markman, E. M. (1975). Language and the ability to evaluate contradictions and tautologies. *Cognition, 3,* 213–226.

Oswald, H., Krappmann, L., Uhlendorff, H., & Weiss, K. (1994). Social relationships and support among peers during middle childhood. In F. Nestmann & K. Hurrelmann (Eds.), *Social networks and social support in childhood and adolescence* (pp. 171–189). New York: Walter de Gruyter.

Overton, W. F., Ward, S. L., Noveck, I. A., Black, J., & O'Brien, D. P. (1987). Form and content in the development of deductive reasoning. *Developmental Psychology, 23,* 22–30.

Oyen, N., Markestad, T., Skjaerven, R., Irgens, L. M., Helweg-Larsen, K., Alm, B., Norvenius, G., & Wennergren, G. (1997). Combined effects of sleeping position and prenatal risk factors in sudden infant death syndrome: The Nordic epidemiological SIDS study. *Pediatrics, 100,* 613–621.

Padden, C., & Humphries, T. (1989). *Deaf in America: Voices from a culture.* Cambridge, MA: Harvard University Press.

Page, D. C., Fisher, E. M., McGillivray, B., & Brown, L. G. (1990). Additional deletion in sex-determining region of human Y chromosome resolves paradox of X, = (Y;22) female. *Nature, 346,* 279–281.

Page, R. N. (1990). Games of chance: The lower-track curriculum in a college-preparatory high school. *Curriculum Inquiry, 20,* 249–281.

Paley, V. G. (1997). Mollie is three. In D. N. Sattler & V. Shabatay (Eds.), *Psychology in context: Voices and perspectives* (pp. 139–143). Boston: Houghton Mifflin.

Palinscar, A. S., & Brown, A. L. (1984). Reciprocal teaching of comprehension-monitoring activities. *Cognition and Instruction, 1,* 117–175.

Papini, D. R., Farmer, F. L., Clark, S. M., & Snell, W. E., Jr. (1988). An evaluation of adolescent patterns of sexual self-disclosure to parents and friends. *Journal of Adolescent Research, 3,* 387–401.

Papini, D. R., Snell, W. E., Belk, S. S., & Clark, S. (1988, April). *Developmental correlates of women's and men's sexual self-disclosures.* Paper presented at the meeting of the Southwestern Psychological Association, Tulsa, OK.

Pardeck, J. A., & Pardeck, J. L. (1990). Family factors related to adolescent autonomy. *Adolescence, 25,* 31–319.

Parker, J. G., & Gottman, J. M. (1989). Social and emotional development in a relational context. In T. J. Berndt & G. W. Ladd (Eds.), *Peer relationships in child development.* New York: Wiley.

Parker, S., Nichter, M., Nichter, N., Vuckovic, N., Sims, C., & Ritenbaugh, C. (1995). Body image and weight concerns among Afro American and White adolescent females: Differences that make a difference. *Human Organization, 54,* 103–115.

Parks, G. (1990). *Voices in the mirror: An autobiography.* New York: Doubleday.

Parry, T. R. (1996). Will pursuit of higher quality sacrifice equal opportunity in education? An analysis of the education voucher system in Chile. *Social Science Quarterly, 77,* 821–841.

Pasley, B. K., & Ihenger-Tallman, M. (1989). Boundary ambiguity in remarriage: Does ambiguity differentiate degree of marital adjustment and integration? *Family Relations, 38,* 46–52.

Patrikakou, E. N. (1996). Investigating the academic achievements of adolescents with learning disabilities: A structural modeling approach. *Journal of Educational Psychology, 88,* 435–450.

Patterson, S. J., Sochting, I., & Marcia, J. E. (1992). The inner space and beyond: Women and identity. In G. R. Adams, T. P. Gullotta, & R. Montemayor (Eds.), *Adolescent identity formation.* Newbury Park, CA: Sage.

Pavlov, I. P. (1927). *Conditioned reflexes.* London: Oxford University Press.

Peck, S. (1995). *All-American boy: A memoir.* Los Angeles: Alyson.

Pederson, D. R., & Moran, G. (1995). A categorical description of infant-mother relationships in the home and its relation to Q-sort measures of infant-mother interaction. In E. Waters, B. E. Vaughn, G. Posada, & K. Kondo-Ikemura (Eds.). Caregiving, cultural, and cognitive perspectives on secure-base behavior and working models: New growing points of attachment theory and research. *Monographs of the Society for Research in Child Development, 60* (2–3, Serial No. 244).

Pegg, J. E., Werker, J. F., & McLeod, P. J. (1992). Preference for infant-directed over adult-directed speech: Evidence from 7-week-old infants. *Infant Behavior and Development, 15,* 325–345.

Pehoski, C., Henderson, A., & Tickle-Degnen, L. (1996). In-hand manipulation in young children: Rotation of an object in the fingers. *American Journal of Occupational Therapy, 51,* 544–552.

Pehoski, C., Henderson, A., & Tickle-Degnen, L. (1997). In-hand manipulation in young children: Translation movements. *American Journal of Occupational Therapy, 51,* 719–728.

Perkins, D. N. (1987). Knowledge as design: Teaching thinking through content. In J. B. Baron & R. J. Sternberg (Eds.), *Teaching thinking skills: Theory and practice.* New York: Freeman.

Peskin, H. (1967). Pubertal onset and ego functioning. *Journal of Abnormal Psychology, 72,* 1–15.

Peskin, H. (1973). Influence of the developmental schedule of puberty on learning and ego development. *Journal of Youth and Adolescence, 2,* 273–290.

Peskin, J. (1996). Guise and guile: Children's understanding of narratives in which the purpose of pretense is deception. *Child Development, 67,* 1735–1751.

Petersen, A. C., Compas, B. E., Brooks-Gunn, J., Stemmler, M., Ey, S., & Grant, K. (1993). Depression in adolescence. *American Psychologist, 48,* 155–168.

Petersen, A. C., Crockett, L., Richards, M., & Boxer, A. (1988). A self-report measure of pubertal status: Reliability, validity, and initial norms. *Journal of Youth and Adolescence, 17,* 117–134.

Petersen, A. C., & Taylor, B. (1980). The biological approach to adolescence. In J, Adelson (Ed.), *Handbook of adolescent psychology.* New York: Wiley.

Peterson, C. C. (1995). The role of perceived intention to deceive in children's and adults' concepts of lying. *British Journal of Developmental Psychology, 13,* 237–260.

Pettit, G. S., Bates, J. E., & Dodge, K. A. (1997). Supportive parenting, ecological context, and children's adjustment: A seven-year longitudinal study. *Child Development, 68,* 908–923.

Pettit, G. S., Dodge, K. A., & Brown, M. M. (1988). Early family experience, social problem solving patterns, and children's social competence. *Child Development, 59,* 107–120.

Phelps, K. E., & Woolley, J. D. (1994). The form and function of young children's magical beliefs. *Developmental Psychology, 30,* 385–394.

Phelps, L., Johnston, S. S., Jimenez, D. P., Wilczenski, F. L., Andrea, R. K., & Healy, R. W. (1993). Figure preference, body dissatisfaction, and body distortion in adolescence. *Journal of Adolescent Research, 8,* 297–310.

Phillips, D. A., Voran, M., Kisker, E., Howes, C., & Whitebook, M. (1994). Child care for children in poverty: Opportunity or inequity? *Child Development, 65,* 472–492.

Phillips, D. M., & Dryden, G. L. (1991). Comparative morphology of mammalian gametes. In B. S. Dunbar & M. G. O'Rand (Eds.). *A comparative overview of mammalian fertilization.* New York: Plenum Press.

Phinney, J. S. (1989). Stages of ethnic identity development in minority group adolescents. *Journal of Early Adolescence, 9,* 34–49.

Phinney, J. S. (1990). Ethnic identity in adolescents and adults: Review of research. *Psychological Bulletin, 108,* 499–514.

Phinney, J. S. (1993). A three-stage model of ethnic identity development. In M. Bernal & G. Knight (Eds.), *Ethnic identity: Formation and transmission among Hispanics and other minorities* (pp. 61–79). Albany: State University of New York Press.

Phinney, J. S. (1996). When we talk about American ethnic groups, what do we mean? *American Psychologist, 51,* 918–927.

Phinney, J. S., Ferguson, D. L., & Tate, J. D. (1997). Intergroup attitudes among ethnic minority adolescents: A causal model. *Child Development, 68,* 955–969.

Phinney, J. S., & Kohatsu, E. (1997). Ethnic and racial identity development and mental health. In J. Schulenberg, J. Maggs, & K. Hurrelmann (Eds.), *Health risks and developmental transitions during adolescence* (pp. 420–443). New York: Cambridge University Press.

Phinney, J. S., & Rosenthal, D. A. (1992). Ethnic identity in adolescence: Process, context, and outcome. In G. Adams, R. Montemayor, & T. Gullotta (Eds.), *Advances in adolescent development* (Vol. 4). Newbury Park, CA: Sage.

Phinney, J. S., & Rotheram, M. J. (1987). Childen's ethnic socialization: Themes and implications. In M. J. Rotheram & J. S. Phinney (Eds.), *Children's ethnic socialization: Pluralism and development.* Beverly Hills: Sage.

Phinney, J. S., & Tarver, S. (1988). Ethnic identity search and commitment in Black and White eighth graders. *Journal of Early Adolescence, 8,* 265–277.

Piaget, J. (1952). *The origins of intelligence in children.* New York: International Universities Press.

Piaget, J. (1954). *The construction of reality in the child.* New York: Basic Books.

Piaget, J. (1965). *The moral judgment of the child.* New York: Free Press.

Piaget, J. (1971). *Biology and knowledge.* Chicago: University of Chicago Press.

Piaget, J., & Inhelder, B. (1969). *The psychology of the child.* New York: Basic Books.

Pickles, A., Pickering, K., Simonoff, E., Silberg, J., Meyer, J., & Maes, H. (1998). Genetic "clocks" and "soft" events: A twin model for pubertal development and other recalled sequences of developmental milestones, transitions, or ages at onset. *Behavior Genetics, 28,* 243–253.

Pipp-Siegel, S., & Foltz, C. (1997). Toddlers' acquisition of self/other knowledge: Ecological and interpersonal aspects of self and other. *Child Development, 68,* 69–79.

Pleck, J. H., Sonenstein, F. L., & Ku, L. C. (1990). Contraceptive attitudes and intention to use condoms in sexually experienced and inexperienced adolescent males. *Journal of Family Issues, 11,* 294–312.

Pleck, J. H., Sonenstein, F. L., & Swain, S. O. (1988). Adolescent males' sexual behavior and contraceptive use: Implications for male responsibility. *Journal of Adolescent Research, 3,* 275–284.

Plomin, R., & Daniels, D. (1987). Why are children in the same family so different from one another? *Behavioral and Brain Sciences, 10,* 1–60.

Plomin, R., DeFries, J. C., & Fulker, D. W. (1988). *Nature and nurture during infancy and early childhood.* Cambridge, MA: Cambridge University Press.

Plomin, R., DeFries, J. C., & McClearn, G. E. (1990). *Behavioral genetics: A primer* (2nd ed.). New York: Freeman.

Plomin, R., Reiss, D., Hetherington, E. M., & Howe, G. W. (1994). Nature and nurture: Genetic contributions to measures of the family environment. *Developmental Psychology, 30,* 32–43.

Plummer, D. L. (1995). Patterns of racial identity development of African American adolescent males and females. *Journal of Black Psychology, 21,* 168–180.

Plummer, D. L. (1996). Black racial identity attitudes and stages of the life span: An exploratory investigation. *Journal of Black Psychology, 22,* 169–181.

Pollitt, E. (1994). Poverty and child development: Relevance of research in developing countries to the United States. *Child Development, 65,* 283–295.

Pollitt, E., Golub, M., Gorman, K., Grantham-McGregor, S., Levitsky, D., Schurch, B., Strupp, B., & Wachs, T. (1996). A reconceptualization of the effects of undernutrition on children's biological, psychosocial, and behavioral development. *Social Policy Report, 10*(5), 1–22.

Pollock, S., & Gilligan, C. (1982). Images of violence in Thematic Apperception Test stories. *Journal of Personality and Social Psychology, 42,* 159–167.

Porter, R .H., Makin, J. W., Davis, L. B., & Christensen, K. M. (1992). An assessment of the salient olfactory environment of formula-fed infants. *Physiology & Behavior, 50,* 907–911.

Posada, G., Gao, Y., Wu, F., Posada, R., Tascon, M., Schoelmerich, A., Savi, A., Kondo-Ikemura, K., Haaland, W., & Synnevaag, B. (1995). The secure-base phenomenon across cultures: Children's behavior, mothers' preferences, and experts' concepts. In E. Waters, B. E. Vaughn, G. Posada, & K. Kondo-Ikemura (Eds.), Caregiving, cultural, and cognitive perspectives on secure-base behavior and working models: New growing points of attachment theory and research. *Monographs of the Society for Research in Child Development,* 60 (2–3, Serial No. 244).

Posner, J. K., & Vandell, D. L. (1999). After-school activities and the development of low-income urban children: A longitudinal study. *Developmental Psychology, 35,* 868–879.

Povinelli, D. J., Landau, K. R., & Perillous, H. K . (1996). Self-recognition in young children using delayed versus live feedback: Evidence of a developmental asynchrony. *Child Development, 67,* 1540–1554.

Povinelli, D. J., & Simon, B. B. (1998). Young children's understanding of briefly versus extremely delayed images of the self: Emergence of the autobiographical stance. *Developmental Psychology, 34,* 188–194.

Powell, G. J. (1985). Self-concepts among Afro-American students in racially isolated minority schools: Some regional differences. *Journal of the American Academy of Child Psychiatry, 24,* 142–149.

Powers, S. I., Hauser, S. T., Schwartz, J. M., Noam, G. G., & Jacobson, A. M. (1983). Adolescent ego development and family interaction: A structural-developmental perspective. In H. D. Grotevant & C. R. Cooper (Eds.), *Adolescent development in the family.* San Francisco: Jossey-Bass.

Pratt, M. W., Kerig, P., Cowan, P. A., & Cowan, C. P. (1988). Mothers and fathers teaching 3-year-olds: Authoritative parenting and adult scaffolding of young children's learning. *Developmental Psychology, 24,* 832–839.

Price, D. W. W., & Goodman, G. S. (1990). Visiting the wizard: Children's memory for a recurring event. *Child Development, 61,* 664–680.

Prislin, R., Dyer, J. A., Blakely, C. H., & Johnson, C. D. (1998). Immunization status and sociodemographic characteristics: The mediating role of beliefs, attitudes, and perceived control. *American Journal of Public Health, 88,* 1821–1826.

Pungello, E. P., & Kurtz-Costes, B. (1999). Why and how working women choose child care; A review with a focus on infancy. *Developmental Review, 19,* 31–96.

Purcell, P., & Stewart, L. (1990). Dick and Jane in 1989. *Sex Roles, 22,* 177–185.

Putallaz, M. (1983). Predicting children's sociometric status from their behavior. *Child Development, 54*(6), 1417–1426.

Putallaz, M., & Gottman, J. M. (1981). An interactional model of children's entry into peer groups. *Child Development, 52,* 986–994.

Quinn, P. C., & Eimas, P. D. (1996). Perceptual cues that permit categorical differentiation of animal species by infants. *Journal of Experimental Child Psychology, 63,* 189–211.

Ramirez, O. (1989). Mexican American children and adolescents. In J. T. Gibbs, L. N. Huang, & associates (Eds.), *Children of color.* San Francisco: Jossey-Bass.

Raudenbush, S. W., Rowan, B., & Cheong, Y. F. (1993). Higher order instructional goals in secondary schools: Class, teacher, and school influences. *American Educational Research Journal, 30,* 523–553.

Ray, W., & Ravizza, R. (1985). *Methods toward a science of behavior and experience* (2nd ed.). Belmont, CA: Wadsworth.

Reese, E., & Fivush, R. (1993). Parental styles of talking about the past. *Developmental Psychology, 29,* 596–606.

Reese, H. W., & Overton, W. F. (1970). Models of development and theories of development. In L. R. Goulet & P. B. Baltes (Eds.), *Life-span developmental psychology: Research and theory.* New York: Academic Press.

Reiss, A. L., Abrams, M. T., Singer, H. S., Ross, J. L., & Denckla, M. B. (1996). Brain development, gender and IQ in children: A volumetric imaging study. *Brain, 119,* 1763–1774.

Repacholi, B. M., & Gopnik, A. (1997). Early reasoning about desires: Evidence from 14- and 18-month-olds. *Developmental Psychology, 33,* 12–21.

Repetti, R. L. (1993). Short-term effects of occupational stressors on daily mood and health conditions. *Health Psychology, 12,* 125–131.

Repetti, R. L., & Wood, J. (1997). Families accommodating to chronic stress: Unintended and unnoticed processes. In B. H. Gottlieb (Ed.), *Coping with chronic stress* (pp. 191–220). New York: Plenum.

Report of the Secretary's Task Force on Youth Suicide (1989). *Vol. 1: Overview and recommendations* (DHHS Publication No. ADM 89-1621). Washington, DC: U.S. Government Printing Office.

Resnick, M., Harris, L., & Blum, R. (1993). The impact of caring and connectedness on adolescent health and well-being. *Journal of Pediatrics and Child Health, 29* (Suppl. 1), 3–9.

Restak, R. (1984, November). Master Clock of the brain and body. *Science Digest,* 54–104.

Reynolds, A. J., & Temple, J. A. (1998). Extended early childhood intervention and school achievement: Age thirteen findings from the Chicago longitudinal study. *Child Development, 69,* 231–246.

Rice, C., Koinis, D., Sullivan, K., Flusberg, H. T., & Winner, E. (1997). When 3-year-olds pass the appearance-reality test. *Developmental Psychology, 33*, 54–61.

Rice, K. G., Cole, D. A., & Lapsley, D. K. (1990). Separation-individuation, family cohesion, and adjustment to college: measurement validation and test of a theoretical model. *Journal of Counseling Psychology, 37*, 195–202.

Rieser, J. (1979). Spatial orientation of six-month-old infants. *Child Development, 50*, 1078–1087.

Rivara, F. P., & Grossman, D.C. (1996). Prevention of traumatic deaths to children in the United States: How far have we come and where do we need to go? *Pediatrics, 97*, 791–797.

Roberts, L. (1991) Does egg beckon sperm when the time is right? *Science, 252*, 214.

Roberts, W., & Strayer, J. (1996). Empathy, emotional expressiveness, and prosocial behavior. *Child Development, 67*, 449–470.

Robinson, J. A., McKenzie, B. E., & Day, R. H. (1996). Anticipatory reaching by infants and adults: The effect of object features and apertures in opaque and transparent screens. *Child Development, 67*, 2641–2656.

Rochat, P., & Morgan, R. (1995). Spatial determinants in the perception of self-produced leg movements by 3- to 5-month-old infants. *Developmental Psychology, 31*, 626–636.

Rockefeller, J. D. (1998, Fall). [Interview]. *Georgetown Public Policy Review.*

Rodriguez, R. (1982). *Hunger of memory: The education of Richard Rodriguez.* Boston: Godine.

Roggman, L. A., Langlois, J. H., Hubbs-Tait, L., & Rieser-Danner, L. A. (1994). Infant day-care, attachment, and the "file drawer problem." *Child Development, 65*, 1429–1443.

Rogoff, B. (1990). *Apprenticeship in thinking.* New York: Oxford University Press.

Rogoff, B. (1996). Developmental transitions in children's participation in sociocultural activities. In A. J. Sameroff & M. M. Haith (Eds). *The five to seven year shift* (pp. 273–294). Chicago: University of Chicago Press.

Rogow, A. M., Marcia, J. E., & Slugowski, B. R. (1983). The relative importance of identity status interview components. *Journal of Youth and Adolescence, 12*, 387–400.

Roquer, J. M., Figueras, J., Botet, F., & Jimenez, R. (1995). Influence on fetal growth of exposure to tobacco smoke during pregnancy. *Acta Paediatrica, 84*, 118–121.

Rosa, F. W., Wilk, A. L., & Kelsey, F. O. (1986). Teratogen update: Vitamin A congeners. *Teratology, 33*, 355–364.

Rosch, E., & Mervis, C. B. (1975). Family resemblances: Studies in the internal structure of categories. *Cognitive Psychology, 8*, 382–439.

Rosen, C. S., Schwebel, D. C., & Singer, J. L. (1997). Preschoolers' attributions of mental states in pretense.

Child Development, 68, 1133–1142.

Rosenberg, M., Schooler, C., & Schoenbach, C. (1989). Self-esteem and adolescent problems: Modeling reciprocal effects. *American Sociological Review, 54*, 1004–1018.

Rosenblum, G. D., & Lewis, M. (1999). The relations among body image, physical attractiveness, and body mass in adolescence. *Child Development, 70*, 50–64.

Rosenthal, D. A., & Feldman, S. S. (1992). The nature and stability of ethnic identity in Chinese youth: Effects of length of residence in two cultural contexts. *Journal of Cross-Cultural Psychology, 23*, 213–227.

Rosenthal, D. A., & Hrynevich, C. (1985). Ethnicity and ethnic identity: A comparative study of Greek-, Italian-, and Anglo-Australian adolescents. *International Journal of Psychology, 20*, 723–742.

Rosenthal, E. (1990, February 4). When a pregnant woman drinks. *The New York Times Magazine, 30*, 49, 61.

Rosenthal, R., & Vandell, D. L. (1996). Quality of care at school-aged child-care programs: Regulatable features, observed experiences, child perspectives, and parent perspectives. *Child Development, 67*, 2434–2445.

Rosenzweig, M. R. (1984). Experience, memory, and the brain. *American Psychologist, 39*, 365–376.

Rosenzweig, M. R., Bennett, E. L., & Diamond, M. C. (1972). Brain changes in response to experience. *The nature and nurture of behavior: Developmental psychobiology.* New York: Freeman.

Rotenberg, K. J., & Eisenberg, N. (1997). Developmental differences in the understanding of and reaction to others' inhibition of emotional expression. *Developmental Psychology, 33*, 526–537.

Rothbart, M. K. (1986). Longitudinal observation of infant temperament. *Developmental Psychology, 22*, 356–365.

Rothbart, M. K., & Ahadi, S. A. (1994). Temperament and the development of personality. *Journal of Abnormal Psychology, 103*, 55–66.

Rothbaum, F., & Weisz, J. R. (1994). Parental caregiving and child externalizing behavior in nonclinical samples: A meta-analysis. *Psychological Bulletin, 116*, 55–74.

Rotheram, M. J., & Phinney, J. S. (1983). *Intercultural attitudes and behaviors of children.* Paper presented at the meeting of the Society for Intercultural Evaluation, Training and Research, San Gimignano, Italy.

F, M. J., & Phinney, J. S. (1987). Ethnic behavior patterns as an aspect of identity. In J. Phinney & M. Rotheram (Eds.), *Children's ethnic socialization: Pluralism and development.* Beverly Hills: Sage.

Rotheram-Borus, M. J., & Phinney, J. S. (1990). Patterns of social expectations among black and Mexican-American children. *Child Development, 61*, 542–556.

Rowe, D. C., Vazsonyi, A. T., & Flannery, D. J. (1994). No more than skin deep: Ethnic and racial similarities in developmental process. *Psychological Review, 101*, 396–413.

Royle, R., Barrett, M., & Buchanan-Barrow, E. (1998, July). *"Religion is the opiate of the masses" (Marx, 1876): An investigation of the salience of religion for children.* Paper presented at the XVth Biennial Meeting of the International Society for the Study of Behavioural Development, Berne, Switzerland.

Rubin, D. H., Krasnilnikoff, P. A., Leventhal, J. M., Weile, B., & Berget, A. (1986). Effect of passive smoking on birthweight. *Lancet, 2,* 415–417.

Rubin, J., Provenzano, F., & Luria, Z. (1974). The eye of the beholder: Parents' views on sex of newborns. *American Journal of Orthopsychiatry, 44,* 512–519.

Rubin, Z. (1980). *Children's friendships.* Cambridge, MA: Harvard University Press.

Ruble, D. N., & Brooks-Gunn, J. (1982). The experience of menarche. *Child Development, 53,* 1557–1566.

Ruck, M. D., Abramovitch, R., & Keating, D. P. (1998). Children's and adolescents' understanding of rights: Balancing nurturance and self-determination. *Child Development, 64,* 404–417.

Runyan, D. K., Hunter, W. M., Socolar, R. R. S., Amaya-Jackson, L., English, D., Landsverk, J., Dubowitz, H., Browne, D. H., Bangdiwala, S. I., & Mathew, R. M. (1998). Children who prosper in unfavorable environments: The relationship to social capital. *Pediatrics, 101,* 12–18.

Russell, A., & Finnie, V. (1990). Preschool children's social status and maternal instructions to assist group entry. *Developmental Psychology, 26,* 603–611.

Rutter, M. (1986). The developmental psychopathology of depression. In M. Rutter, C. E. Isard, & P. B. Read. (Eds.), *Depression in young people.* New York: Guilford Press.

Sadler, T. W. (1990). *Langman's medical embryology* (6th ed.). Baltimore: Williams & Wilkins.

Sahni, R., Schulze, K. F., Stefanski, M., Myers, M. M., & Fifer, W. P. (1995). Methodological issues in coding sleep states in immature infants. *Developmental Psychobiology, 28,* 85–101.

Salkovskis, P. M. & Rimes, K. A. (1997). Predictive genetic testing: Psychological factors. *Journal of Psychosomatic Research, 43,* 477–487.

Saltz, E., Campbell, S., & Skotko, D. (1983). Verbal control of behavior: The effects of shouting. *Developmental Psychology, 19*(3), 461–464.

Samalin, N. (with Whitney, C.). (2000). Sibling rivalry, sibling love. In D. N. Sattler, G. P. Kramer, V. Shabatay, & D. A. Bernstein (Eds.), *Child development in context* (pp. 70–75). Boston: Houghton Mifflin.

Sansavini, A., Bertoncini, J., & Giovanelli, G. (1997). Newborns discriminate the rhythm of multisyllabic stressed words. *Developmental Psychology, 33,* 3–11.

Savage, M. P., & Scott, L. B. (1996). Physical activity and rural middle school adolescents. *Journal of Youth and Adolescence, 27,* 245–253.

Savitz, D. A., & Chen, J. (1990). Parental occupation and childhood cancer: Review of epidemiologic studies. *Environmental Health Perspectives, 88,* 325–337.

Savitz, D. A., Schwingl, P. J., & Keels, M. A. (1991). Influence of paternal age, smoking and alcohol consumption on congenital anomalies. *Teratology, 44,* 429–440.

Savitz, D. A., Whelan, E. A., & Kleckner, R. C. (1989). Effect of parents' occupational exposures on risk of stillbirth, preterm delivery, and small-for-gestational-age infants. *American Journal of Epidemiology, 129,* 1201–1217.

Savitz, D. A., Zhang, J., Schwingl, P., & John, E. M. (1992). Association of paternal alcohol use with gestational age and birth weight. *Teratology, 46,* 465–471.

Scarr, S. (1992). Developmental theories for the 1990s: Development and individual differences. *Child Development, 63,* 1–19.

Scarr, S. (1993). Biological and cultural diversity: The legacy of Darwin for development. *Child Development, 64,* 1333–1353.

Scarr, S., & Weinberg, R. A. (1983). The Minnesota adoption studies: Malleability and genetic differences. *Child Development, 34,* 260–267.

Schaal, B., Orgeur, P., & Rognon, C. (1995). Odor sensing in the human fetus: Anatomical, functional, and chemoecological bases. In J. P. Lecanuet & W. P. Fifer (Eds.), *Fetal development: A psychobiological perspective.* Hillsdale, NJ: Erlbaum.

Schaie, K. W., & Willis, S. L. (1993). Age difference patterns in psychometric intelligence in adulthood: Generalizability within and across ability domains. *Psychology and Aging, 8,* 44–55.

Schanck, R., & Abelson, R. P. (1977). *Scripts, plans, goals, and understanding.* Hillsdale, NJ: Erlbaum.

Schneider, W., Korkel, J., & Weinert, F. E. (1989). Domain-specific knowledge and memory performance: A comparison of high- and low-aptitude children. *Journal of Educational Psychology, 81,* 306–312.

Scholer, S. J., Mitchel, E. F., Jr., & Ray, W. A. (1997). Predictors of injury mortality in early childhood. *Pediatrics, 100,* 342–347.

Schuckit, M. A., & Schuckit, J. J. (1989). Substance use and abuse: A risk factor in youth suicide. In *Report of the Secretary's Task Force on Youth Suicide. Vol. 2.* Washington, DC: U.S. Government Printing Office.

Schwartz, D., Dodge, K. A., Pettit, G. S., & Bates, J. E. (1997). The early socialization of aggressive victims of bullying. *Child Development, 68,* 665–675.

Schwartz, J. C., Schrager, J. B., & Lyons, A. E. (1983). Delay of gratification by preschoolers: Evidence for the validity of the choice paradigm. *Child Development, 54,* 620–625.

Scott-Jones, D., & Turner, S. L. (1988). Sex education, contraceptive and reproductive knowledge, and contraceptive use among black adolescent females. *Journal of Adolescent Research, 3,* 171–187.

Sedlak, A. J., & Broadhurst, D. D. (1996). *Third national incidence study of child abuse and neglect.* U.S. Department of Health and Human Services. Washington, DC: U.S. Government Printing Office.

Seiber, J. E. (1980). A social learning approach to morality. In M. Windmiller, N. Lambert, & E. Turiel (Eds.), *Moral development and socialization.* Boston: Allyn & Bacon.

Seifer R., & Schiller M., (1995). In E. Waters, B. E. Vaughn, G. Posada, & K. Kondo-Ikemura (Eds.), Caregiving, cultural, and cognitive perspectives on secure-base behavior and working models: New growing points of attachment theory and research. *Monographs of the Society for Research in Child Development,* Serial No. 244, 60, Nos. 2–3.

Seifer, R., Sameroff, A. J., Barrett, L.C., & Krafchuk, E. (1994). Infant temperament measured by multiple observations and mother report. *Child Development, 65,* 1478–1490.

Seixas, P. (1993). Historical understanding among adolescents in a multicultural setting. *Curriculum Inquiry, 23,* 301–327.

Shaw, G. M., O'Malley, C. D., Wasserman, C. R., Tolarova, M. M., & Lammer, E. J. (1995). Maternal periconceptional use of multivitamins and reduced risk for conotruncal heart defects and limb deficiencies among offspring. *American Journal of Medical Genetics, 59,* 536–545.

Sherman, J. A. (1978). *Sex-related cognitive differences: An essay on theory and evidence.* Springfield, IL: Thomas.

Shifflett-Simpson, K., & Cummings, E. M. (1996). Mixed message resolution and children's responses to interadult conflict. *Child Development, 67,* 437–448.

Short-DeGraff, M. (1988). Sensory and perceptual development and behavioral organization (pp. 337–410). In M. Short-DeGraf (Ed), *Human development for occupational and physical therapists.* Baltimore: Williams & Wilkins.

Shulman, S., Seiffge-Krenke, I., & Samat, J. (1987). Adolescent coping style as a function of perceived family climate. *Journal of Adolescent Research, 2,* 367–381.

Siegler, R. S. (1976). Three aspects of cognitive development. *Cognitive Psychology, 8,* 481–520.

Siegler, R. S. (1991). *Children's thinking* (2nd ed.). Englewood Cliffs, NJ: Prentice-Hall.

Siegler, R. S. (1996a). Unidimensional thinking, multidimensional thinking, and characteristic tendencies of thought. In A. J. Sameroff & M. M. Haith (Eds.), *The five to seven year shift: The age of reason and responsibility* (pp. 63–84). Chicago: University of Chicago Press.

Siegler, R. S. (1996b). *Emerging minds: The process of change in children's thinking.* New York: Oxford University Press.

Siegler, R. S. (1998). *Children's thinking* (3rd ed.). Upper Saddle River, NJ: Prentice-Hall.

Siegler, R. S., & Robinson, M. (1982). The development of numerical understandings. In H. W. Reese & L. P. Lipsitt (Eds.), *Advances in child development and behavior* (Vol. 16). New York: Academic Press.

Silverstein, B., Perdue, L., Peterson, B., & Kelly, E. (1986). The role of the mass media in promoting a thin standard of bodily attractiveness for women. *Sex Roles, 14,* 519–532.

Simmons, R. G., & Blyth, D. A. (1987). *Moving into adolescence.* New York: Aldine de Gruyter.

Simpson, G. E. & Yinger, J. M. (1985). *Racial and cultural minorities* (5th Edition). New York; Plenum Press.

Simpson, J. L. (1995). Pregnancy and the timing of intercourse. *New England Journal of Medicine, 333,* 1563–1565.

Sinclair, A. H., et al. (1990). A gene from the human sex-determining region encodes a protein with homology to a conserved DNA-binding motif. *Nature, 346,* 240–244.

Singer, D. B. (1995). Human embryogenesis. In D. R. Coustan, R. V. Haning, Jr., & D. B. Singer (Eds.), *Human reproduction: Growth and development* (pp. 27–37). New York: Little, Brown.

Singer, D. G., & Singer, J. L. (1990). *The house of make-believe.* Cambridge, MA: Harvard University Press.

Sitskoorn, M. M., & Smitsman, A. W. (1995). Infants' perception of dynamic relations between objects: Passing through or support? *Developmental Psychology, 31,* 437–447.

Sittenfeld, C. (1995). Your life as a girl. In B. Findlen (Ed.), *Listen up: Voices from the next feminist generation* (pp. 36–44). Seattle: Seal Press.

Skinner, B. F. (1938). *The behavior of organisms: An experimental analysis.* New York: Appleton-Century-Crofts.

Skinner, B. F. (1953). *Science and human behavior.* New York: Macmillan.

Skinner, B. F. (1961). *Cumulative record* (Rev. ed.). New York: Appleton-Century-Crofts.

Skoog, S. J. (1998). Editorial: Behavior modification in the treatment of enuresis. *Journal of Urology, 160,* 861–862.

Slaughter, V., & Gopnik, A. (1996). Conceptual coherence in the child's theory of mind: Training children to understand belief. *Child Development, 67,* 2967–2988.

Slaughter-Defoe, D. T., Nakagawa, K., Takanishi, R., & Johnson, D. J. (1990). Toward cultural/ecological perspectives on schooling and achievement in African- and Asian-American children. *Child Development, 61,* 363–383.

Slavin, R. E. (1985). Cooperative learning: Applying contact theory in desegregated schools. *Journal of Social Issues, 31,* 45–62.

Sloane, J., Kellerman, A., Reay, D., Ferris, J., Kospesell, T., Rivara, F., Rice, C., Gray, L., & LoGerfo, J. (1988). Handgun regulation, crime, assaults, and homicides. *New England Journal of Medicine, 319,* 1256–1262.

Smetana, J. G., & Asquith, P. (1994). Adolescents' and parents' conceptions of parental authority and personal autonomy. *Child Development, 65,* 1147–1162.

Smetana, J. G., & Berent, R. (1993). Adolescents' and mothers' evaluations of justification for disputes. *Journal of Adolescent Research, 8,* 252–273.

Smetana, J. G., Braeges, J. L., & Yau, J. (1991). Doing what you say and saying what you do: Reasoning about adolescent-parent conflict in interviews and interactions. *Journal of Adolescent Research, 6,* 276–295.

Smetana, J. G., & Gaines, C. (1999). Adolescent-parent conflict in middle-class African American families. *Child Development, 70,* 1447–1463.

Smetana, J. G., Kelly, M., & Twentyman, C. T. (1984). Abused, neglected, and nonmaltreated children's conceptions of moral and conventional transgressions. *Child Development, 55,* 277–287.

Smetana, J. G., Toth, S. L., Cicchetti, D., Bruce, J., Kane, P., & Daddis, C. (1999). Maltreated and nonmaltreated preschoolers' conceptions of hypothetical and actual moral transgressions. *Developmental Psychology, 35,* 269–281.

Smith, J. A., & Epstein, L. H. (1991). Behavioral economic analysis of food choice in obese children. *Appetite, 17,* 91–95.

Smith, J. C. (1994). Hedgehog, the floor plate, and the zone of polarizing activity. *Cell, 76,* 193–196.

Smith, L., & Rhodes, J. (1994, April). *Exploring female representation in current adolescent literature.* Paper presented at the annual meeting of the American Educational Research Association, New Orleans.

Smith, T. E. (1990). Parental separation and the academic self-concepts of adolescents: An effort to solve the puzzle of separation effects. *Journal of Marriage and the Family, 52,* 107–118.

Smolak, L., Levine, M. P., & Gralen, S. (1993). The impact of puberty and dating on eating problems among middle school girls. *Journal of Youth and Adolescence, 22,* 355–368.

Snow, C. E. (1995). Issues in the study of input: Finetuning, universality, individual and developmental differences, and necessary causes. In P. Fletcher & B. MacWhinney (Eds.), *The handbook of child language* (pp. 180–193). Oxford: Blackwell.

Snow, R. E. (1986). Individual differences and the design of educational programs. *American Psychologist, 41,* 1029–1039.

Sochting, I., Skoe, E. E., & Marcia, J. E. (1994). Care-oriented moral reasoning and prosocial behavior: A question of gender or sex role orientation. *Sex Roles, 31,* 131–147.

Sokolov, E. M. (1963). Higher nervous functions: The orienting reflex. *Annual Review of Physiology, 25,* 545–580.

Solomon, G. (1990). Using technology to reach at-risk students. *Electronic Learning, 9,* 14–15.

Solomon, G. E. A., Johnson, S. C., Zaitchik, D., & Carey, S. (1996). Like father, like son: Young children's understanding of how and why offspring resemble their parents. *Child Development, 67,* 151–171.

Sorel, N. C. (1984). *Ever since Eve: Personal reflections on childbirth.* New York: Oxford University Press.

Sorenson, R. C. (1973). *Adolescent sexuality in contemporary America: Personal values and sexual behavior, ages thirteen to nineteen.* New York: World.

Sowell, T. (1978). Race and IQ reconsidered. In T. Sowell (Ed.), *American ethnic groups.* Washington, DC: Urban Institute.

Speight, S. L., Vera, E. M., & Derrickson, K. B. (1996). Racial self-designation, racial identity, and self-esteem revisited. *Journal of Black Psychology, 22,* 37–52.

Spelke, E. S. (1988). Where perceiving ends and thinking begins: The apprehension of objects in infancy. In A. Yonas (Ed.), *Perceptual development in infancy: The Minnesota Symposia on Child Psychology,* Vol. 20. Hillsdale, NJ: Erlbaum.

Spencer, M. B. (1985). Racial variations in achievement prediction: The school as a conduit for macrostructural cultural tension. In H. McAdoo & J. McAdoo (Eds.), *Black children: Social, educational, and parental environments.* Beverly Hills: Sage.

Spires, H. A., Gallini, J., & Riggsbee, J. (1992). Effects of schema-based and text structure-based cues on expository prove comprehension in fourth graders. *Journal of Experimental Education, 60,* 307–320.

Spreen, O. (1988). *Learning disabled children growing up.* New York: Oxford University Press.

Springer, K. (1996). Young children's understanding of a biological basis for parent-offspring relations. *Child Development, 67,* 2841–2856.

Sroufe, L. A., Bennett, C., Englund, M., Urban, J., & Shulman, S. (1993). The significance of gender boundaries in preadolescence: Contemporary correlates and antecedents of boundary violations and maintenance. *Child Development, 64,* 455–466.

Stahl, S. A., McKenna, M. C., & Pagnucco, J. R. (1994). The effects of whole-language instruction: An update and a reappraisal. *Educational Psychologist, 29,* 175–185.

Starkey, P., Spelke, E. S., & Gelman, R. (1990). Numerical abstraction by human infants. *Cognition, 36,* 97–128.

Stein, J. A., & Newcomb, M. D. (1999). Adult outcomes of adolescent conventional and agentic orientations: A 20-year longitudinal study. *Journal of Early Adolescence, 19,* 39–65.

Stein, J. H., & Reiser, L. W. (1994). A study of white middle-class adolescent boys' responses to "semenarche" (the first ejaculation). *Journal of Youth and Adolescence, 23,* 373–384.

Stein, Z., Susser, M., Saenger, G., & Marolla, F. (1975). *Famine and development: The Dutch hunger winter of 1944–1945*. Oxford: Oxford University Press.

Steinberg, L. (1987). The impact of puberty on family relations: Effects of pubertal status and pubertal timing. *Developmental Psychology, 23*, 451–460.

Steinberg, L. (1989). Reciprocal relationship between parent-child distance and pubertal maturation. *Developmental Psychology, 24*, 122–128.

Steinberg, L., Brown, B. B., & Dornbusch, S. M. (1996). *Beyond the classroom*. New York: Simon & Schuster.

Steinberg, L., Lamborn, S. D., Darling, N., Mounts, N. S., & Dornbusch, S. M. (1994). Over–time changes in adjustment and competence among adolescents from authoritative, authoritarian, indulgent, and neglectful families. *Child Development, 65*, 754–770.

Stevenson-Hinde, J. (1998). Parenting in different cultures: Time to focus. *Developmental Psychology, 34*, 698–700.

Stigler, J. W., & Stevenson, H. W. (1991, Spring). How Asian teachers polish each lesson to perfection. *American Educator, 12–20*, 43–47.

Stiles, D. A., Gibbons, J. L., Hardardottir, S., & Schnellmann, J. (1987). The ideal man or woman as described by young adolescents in Iceland and the United States. *Sex Roles, 17*, 313–320.

Stipek, D. (1995). The development of pride and shame in toddlers. In J. P. Tangney & K. W. Fischer (Eds.), *Self-conscious emotions: The psychology of shame, guilt, embarrassment, and pride* (pp. 237–254). New York: Guilford Press.

Stipek, D., Recchia, S., & McClintic, S. (1992). Self-evaluation in young children. *Monographs of the Society for Research in Child Development, 57* (Serial No. 226).

Stoddart, T., & Turiel, E. (1985). Children's concepts of cross-gender activities. *Child Development, 56*, 1241–1252.

Straus, M. A., & Gelles, R. J. (1986). Societal change in family violence from 1975 to 1985 as revealed by two national surveys. *Journal of Marriage and the Family, 48*, 465–479.

Streissguth, A. P. (1994). A long-term perspective of FAS. *Alcohol Health & Research World, 18*, 74–81.

Streri, A., & Spelke, E. S. (1988). Haptic perception of objects in infancy. *Cognitive Psychology, 20*, 1–23.

Strong, B., & DeVault, C. (1999). *Human sexuality* (3rd ed.). Mountain View, CA: Mayfield.

Sue, S. (1991). Ethnicity and culture in psychological research and practice. In J. Goodchilds (Ed.), *Psychological perspectives on human diversity in America* (pp. 51–85). Washington, DC: American Psychological Association.

Super, C. M., Herrera, M. G., & Mora, J. O. (1990). Long-term effects of food supplementation and psychosocial intervention on the physical growth of Colombian infants at risk of malnutrition. *Child Development, 61*, 29–49.

Swanston, H. Y., Tebbutt, J. S., O'Toole, B. I., & Oates, R. K. (1997). Sexually abused children 5 years after presentation: A case-control study. *Pediatrics, 100*, 600–608.

Swarr, A. E., & Richards, M. H. (1996). Longitudinal effects of adolescent girls' pubertal development, perceptions of pubertal timing, and parental relations on eating problems. *Developmental Psychology, 32*, 636–646.

Switzer, J. Y. (1990). The impact of generic word choices: An empirical investigation of age- and sex-related differences. *Sex Roles, 22*, 69–82.

Szymczak, J. T., Jasinska, M., Pawlak, E., & Zwierzykowska, M. (1993). Annual and weekly changes in the sleep wake rhythm of school children. *Sleep, 16*, 433–435.

Tanaka, J. W., & Taylor, M. (1991). Object categories and expertise: Is the basic level in the eye of the beholder? *Cognitive Psychology, 23*, 457–482.

Tanner, J. M. (1974). Sequence and tempo in the somatic changes in puberty. In M. M. Grumbach, G. D. Grave, & F. E. Mayer (Eds.), *Control of the onset of puberty*. New York: Wiley.

Tanner, J. M. (1978). *Foetus into man: Physical growth from conception to maturity*. Cambridge, MA: Harvard University Press.

Tanner, J. M. (1991). Menarche, secular trend in age of. In R. M. Lerner, A. C. Petersen, & J. Brooks-Gunn (Eds.), *Encyclopedia of adolescence* (Vol. 2, pp. 637–641). New York: Garland.

Tavris, C., & Wade, C. (1984). *The longest war: Sex differences in perspective* (2nd ed.). San Diego: Harcourt Brace Jovanovich.

Taylor, M., & Carlson, S. M. (1997). The relation between individual differences in fantasy and theory of mind. *Child Development, 68*, 436–455.

Terman, L. M. (1925). *Genetic studies of genius. Vol. 1: Mental and physical traits of a thousand gifted children*. Stanford, CA: Stanford University Press.

Thatcher, R. W. (1994). Cyclic cortical reorganization. In G. Dawson & K. W. Fischer (Eds.), *Human behavior and the developing brain*. New York: Guilford.

Thatcher, R. W. (1997). Neuroimaging of cyclic cortical reorganization during human development. In R. W. Thatcher, G. R. Lyon, J. Rumsey, & N. Krasnegor (Eds.), *Developmental neuroimaging: Mapping the development of brain and behavior* (pp. 91–106). San Diego: Academic Press.

Thelen, E. (1995). Motor development. *American Psychologist, 50*, 79–95.

Thelen, E., & Fisher, D. (1982). Newborn stepping: An explanation for a "disappearing reflex." *Developmental Psychology, 18*, 760–775.

Thomas, A., & Chess, S. (1977). *Temperament and development*. New York: Brunner/Mazel.

Thomas, A., Chess, S., & Birch, H .G. (1963). *Behavioral individuality in early childhood*. New York: New York University Press.

Thomas, J. R., & French, K. E. (1985). Gender differences across age in motor performance: A meta-analysis. *Psychological Bulletin, 98*, 260–282.

Thomas, R. M. (1979). *Contemporary theories of child development*. Belmont, CA: Wadsworth.

Thompson, J. S., & Thompson, M. W. (1986). *Genetics in medicine* (4th ed.). Philadelphia: Saunders.

Thornton, M. C., Chatters, L. M., Taylor, R. J., & Allen, W. R. (1990). Sociodemographic and environmental correlates of racial socialization by Black parents. *Child Development, 61*, 401–409.

Thorpy, M. J., Korman, E., Spielman, A. J., Glovinsky, P. B. (1988). Delayed sleep phase syndrome in adolescents. *Journal of Adolescent Health Care, 9*, 22–27.

Tickle, C., Summerbell, D., & Wolpert, L. (1975). Positional signaling and specification of digits in chick limb morphogenesis. *Nature, 254*, 199–202.

Timmer, S. G., Eccles, J., & O'Brien, K. O. (1985). How children use time. In F. T. Juster & F. P. Stafford (Eds.), *Time, goods, and well-being* (pp. 353–381). Ann Arbor: University of Michigan.

Tittle, C. K. (1986). Gender research and education. *American Psychologist, 41*, 1161–1168.

Tjian, R. (1995). Molecular machines that control genes. *Scientific American, 272*, 54–61.

Tobias, A. L. (1988). Bulimia: An overview. In K. Clark, R. Parr, & W. Castelli (Eds.), *Evaluation and management of eating disorders*. Champaign, IL: Life Enhancement Publications.

Tobin-Richards, M. H., Boxer, A. M., & Petersen, A. C. (1983). The psychological significance of pubertal change: Sex differences in perceptions of self during early adolescence. In J. Brooks-Gunn & A. C. Petersen (Eds.), *Girls at puberty*. New York: Plenum Press.

Toth, S. A. (1986). The boyfriend. In *Life studies: A thematic reader* (2nd ed.). New York: St. Martin's.

Trautman, P. D., & Rotheram, M. J. (1986). Specific treatment modalities for adolescent suicide attempters. In *Report of the Secretary's Task Force. Vol. 3*. Washington, DC: U. S. Government Printing Office. Reported in Trautman, P. D. (1989).

Treiman, R., Tincoff, R., Rodriguez, K., Mouzaki, A., & Francis, D. J. (1998). The foundations of literacy: Learning the sounds of letters. *Child Development, 69*, 1524–1540.

Troiano, R. P., & Flegal, K. M. (1998). Overweight children and adolescents: Description, epidemiology, and demographics. *Pediatrics, 101*, 497–504.

Tschann, J. M., Adler, N. E., Irwin, C. E., & Millstein, S. G., et al. (1994). Initiation of substance use in early adolescence: The roles of pubertal timing and emotional distress. *Health Psychology, 13*, 326–333.

Tudor, T. (1980). *The Tasha Tudor book of fairy tales*. New York: Platt & Munk.

Turiel, E. (1983). *The development of social knowledge: Morality and convention*. Cambridge, England: Cambridge University Press.

UNICEF. (1993). *The state of the world's children, 1993*. New York: Oxford University Press.

Urberg, K. A., Degirmencioglu, S. M., Tolson, J. M., & Halliday-Scher, K. (1995). The structure of adolescent peer networks. *Developmental Psychology, 31*, 540–547.

U.S. Bureau of the Census. (1992). *Current population reports, Series P-25, No. 1104a, Projections of the population of the United States by age, sex, and race: 1983–2080*. Washington, DC: U.S. Government Printing Office.

U.S. Bureau of the Census. (1996). *Statistical abstract of the United States, 1996* (116th ed.). Washington, DC: U.S. Government Printing Office.

U.S. Bureau of Labor Statistics. (1995). *Employment status of women: By marital status and presence and age of children: 1960–1994* (Bulletin 2340). Washington DC: U.S. Department of Labor, Bureau of Labor Statistics.

U.S. Bureau of Labor Statistics. (1999).*Employment characteristics of families in 1998*. Washington DC: U.S. Department of Labor, Bureau of Labor Statistics.

U.S. Department of Education. (1996a). *Digest of educational statistics 1996, NCES 96-133*. Washington, DC: U.S. Government Printing Office.

U.S. Department of Education. (1996b). *Eighteenth annual report to Congress on the implementation of the Individuals with Disabilities Education Act*. Washington, DC: OSERS.

U.S. Department of Health and Human Services, Children's Bureau. (1998). *Child maltreatment 1996: Reports from the states to the National Child Abuse and Neglect Data System*. Washington, DC: U.S. Government Printing Office.

U.S. Department of Justice. (1995). *Justice sourcebook, 1995*. Washington, DC: Bureau of Justice Statistics.

Van Ausdale, D., & Feagin, J. R. (1996). Using racial and ethnic concepts: The critical case of very young children. *American Sociological Review, 61*, 779–793.

Vandell, D. L., & Corasaniti, M. A. (1988). The relation between third graders' after-school care and social, academic, and emotional functioning. *Child Development, 59*, 868-875.

van den Boom, D. C. (1989). Neonatal irritability and the development of attachment. In G. A. Kohnstamm, J. E. Bates, & M. K. Rothbart (Eds.), *Temperament in childhood* (pp. 299–318). New York: Wiley.

van den Boom, D. C. (1994). The influence of temperament and mothering on attachment and exploration: An experimental manipulation of sensitive responsiveness among lower-class mothers with irritable infants. *Child Development, 65*, 1457–1477.

van den Boom, D. C. (1995). Do first-year intervention effects endure? Follow-up during toddlerhood of a sample of Dutch irritable infants. *Child Development, 66*, 1798–1816.

van den Broek, P. W. (1989). Causal reasoning and inference making in judging the importance of story statements. *Child Development, 60*, 286–297.

van den Broek, P. W., Lorch, E. P., & Thurlow, R. (1996). Children's and adults' memory for television stories: The role of causal factors, story-grammar categories, and hierarchical level. *Child Development, 67*, 3010–3028.

Van de Walle, G., & Spelke, E. S. (1996). Spatiotemporal integration and object perception in infancy: Perceiving unity versus form. *Child Development, 67*, 2621–2640.

Van Gool, W. A., & Mirmiran, M. (1986). Effects of aging and housing in an enriched environment on sleep-wake patterns in rats. *Sleep, 9*(2), 335–347.

Vansant, A. F. (1995). Development of posture. In D. Cech & S. Martin (Eds.), *Functional movement development across the life span.* (pp. 275–294). Philadelphia: Saunders.

Verschueren, K., Marcoen, A., & Schoefs, V. (1996). The internal working model of the self, attachment, and competence in five-year-olds. *Child Development, 67*, 2493–2511.

Viano, D. C. (1995). Restraint effectiveness, availability, and use in fatal crashes: Implications to injury control. *Journal of Trauma, 38*, 538–546.

Vikan, A., & Clausen, S. E. (1993). Freud, Piaget, or neither? Beliefs in controlling others by wishful thinking and magical behavior in young children. *Journal of Genetic Psychology, 154*, 297–314.

Visher, E. B., & Visher, J. S. (1989). Parenting coalitions after remarriage: Dynamics and therapeutic guidelines. *Family Relations, 38*, 65–70.

von Gontard, A., Eiberg, H., Hollmann, E., Rittig, S., & Lehmkuhl, G. (1998). Molecular genetics of nocturnal enuresis: Clinical and genetic heterogeneity. *Acta Paediatrica, 87*(5), 571–578.

von Hofsten, C. (1982). Eye-hand coordination in newborns. *Developmental Psychology, 18*, 450–461.

Vosniadou, S. (1994). Universal and culture-specific properties of children's mental models of the earth. In L. A. Hirschfeld & S. A. Gelman (Eds.), *Mapping the mind: Domain specificity in cognition and culture* (pp. 412–430). New York: Cambridge University Press.

Vosniadou, S., & Brewer, W. F. (1992). Mental models of the earth: A study of conceptual change in childhood. *Cognitive Psychology, 24*, 535–585.

Vuchinich, S., Angelelli, J., & Gatherum, A. (1996). Context and development in family problem solving with preadolescent children. *Child Development, 67*, 1276–1288.

Vygotsky, L. S. (1978). *Mind in society: The development of higher psychological processes.* Cambridge, MA: Harvard University Press.

Wagner, B. M., Cohen, P., & Brook, J. S. (1996). Parent/

adolescent relationships: Moderators of the effects of stressful life events. *Journal of Adolescent Research, 11*, 347–374.

Wainryb, C., Shaw, L. A., & Maianu, C. (1998). Tolerance and intolerance: Children's and adolescents' judgments of dissenting beliefs, speech, persons, and conduct. *Child Development, 69*(6), 1541–1555.

Waldman, I. D. (1996). Aggressive boys' hostile perceptual and response biases: The role of attention and impulsivity. *Child Development, 67*, 1015–1033.

Wallerstein, J. S. (1989). *Second change.* New York: Ticknor & Fields.

Wallerstein, J. S., Corbin, S. B., & Lewis, J. M. (1988). Children of divorce: A ten-year study. In E. M. Hetherington & J. D. Arasteh (Eds.), *Impact of divorce, single-parenting, and stepparenting on children.* Hillsdale, NJ: Erlbaum.

Ward, S. L., & Overton, W. F. (1990). Semantic familiarity, relevance, and the development of deductive reasoning. *Developmental Psychology, 26*, 488–493.

Wark, G. R., & Krebs, D. L. (1996). Gender and dilemma differences in real-life moral judgment. *Developmental Psychology, 32*, 220–230.

Wason, P. C., & Johnson-Laird, P. N. (1972). *Psychology of reasoning: Structure and content.* Cambridge, MA: Harvard University Press.

Wasserman, P. M. (1988) The mammalian ovum. In E. Knobil & J. Neill (Eds.), *The physiology of reproduction* (pp. 69–102). New York: Raven.

Waters, E. (1978). The reliability and stability of individual differences in infant-mother attachment. *Child Development, 49*, 483–494.

Waters, E., Vaughn, B. E., Posada, G., Kondo-Ikemura, K. (Eds.). (1995). Caregiving, cultural, and cognitive perspectives on secure-base behavior and working models: New growing points of attachment theory and research. *Monographs of the Society for Research in Child Development, 60* (2–3, Serial No. 244).

Watson, D., Clark, L. A., & Harkness, A. R. (1994). Structures of personality and their relevance to psychopathology. *Journal of Abnormal Psychology, 103*, 18–31.

Watson, J. D. (1968). *The double helix: A personal account of the discovery of the structure of DNA.* New York: Atheneum.

Waugh, R. F., Godfrey, J. R., Evans, E. D., & Craig, D. (1995). Measuring students' perceptions about cheating in six countries. *Australian Journal of Psychology, 47*, 73–80.

Webster, C. (1994). Effects of Hispanic ethnic identification on marital roles in the purchase decision process. *Journal of Consumer Research, 21*, 319–331.

Wechsler, D. (1981). *WAIS-R Manual: Weschler Adult Intelligence Scale – Revised.* San Antonio, TX: Psychological Corporation.

Weiner, I. B. (1980). Psychopathology in adolescence. In J. Adelson (Ed.), *Handbook of adolescent psychology.* New York: Wiley.

Welch-Ross, M. K. (1997). Mother-child participation in conversation about the past: Relationships to preschoolers' theory of mind. *Developmental Psychology, 33,* 618–629.

Wells, A. S. (1996). African-American students' view of school choice. In B. Fuller & R. Elmore (Eds.), *Who chooses? Who loses? Culture, institutions, and the unequal effects of choice.* New York: Teachers College Press.

Werner, E. (1989). High-risk children in young adulthood: A longitudinal study from birth to 32 years. *American Journal of Orthopsychiatry, 59,* 72–81.

Werner, E. (1994). Overcoming the odds. *Developmental and Behavioral Pediatrics, 15,* 131–136.

Werner, E., & Smith, R. (1982). *Vulnerable but invincible: A longitudinal study of resilient children and youth.* New York: McGraw-Hill.

Werner, E., & Smith, R. (1992). *Overcoming the odds: High risk children from birth to adulthood.* Ithaca, NY: Cornell University Press.

Wertz, D. C., Fletcher, J. C., & Berg, K. (1995). *Guidelines on ethical issues in medical genetics and the provision of genetic services.* Geneva: World Health Organization.

White, K. L., Speisman, J. C., & Costos, D. (1983). Young adults and their parents: Individuation to mutuality. In H. D. Grotevant & C. R. Cooper (Eds.), *Adolescent development in the family.* San Francisco: Jossey-Bass.

Wilcox, A. J., Weinberg, C. R., & Baird, D. D. (1995). Timing of sexual intercourse in relation to ovulation. *New England Journal of Medicine, 333,* 1517–1521.

Wilder, P. A. (1995). Muscle development and function. In D. Cech & S. Martin (Eds.), *Functional movement development across the life span* (pp. 137–157). Philadelphia: Saunders.

Wiley, A. R., Rose, A. J., Burger, L. K., & Miller, P. J. (1998). Constructing autonomous selves through narrative practices: A comparative study of working-class and middle-class families. *Child Development, 69,* 833–847.

Will, J., Self, P., & Datan, N. (1976). Maternal behavior and perceived sex of infant. *American Journal of Orthopsychiatry, 46,* 135–139.

Williams, M. (1983). *The velveteen rabbit.* New York: Knopf.

Wilson, R. S., & Matheny, A. P., Jr. (1986). Behavior-genetics research in infant temperament: The Louisville Twin Study. In R. Plomin & J. Dunn (Eds.), *The study of temperament: Changes, continuities and challenges* (pp. 81–98). Hillsdale, NJ: Erlbaum.

Wilson, W. J. (1993). *The ghetto underclass: Social science perspectives.* Newbury Park, CA: Sage.

Wimmer, H., Gruber, S., & Perner, J. (1984). Young children's conception of lying: Lexical realism—moral subjectivism. *Journal of Experimental Child Psychology, 37,* 1–30.

Winer, G. A., Craig, R. K., & Weinbaum, E. (1992). Adults' failure on misleading weight-conservation tests: A developmental analysis. *Developmental Psychology, 28,* 109–120.

Winer, G. A., & McGlone, C. (1993). On the uncertainty of conservation: Responses to misleading conservation questions. *Developmental Psychology, 29,* 760–769.

Wise, P., Chavkin, W., & Romero, D. (1999). Assessing the effects of welfare reform policies on reproductive and infant health. *American Journal of Public Health, 89,* 1514–1521.

Witte, J. F. (1996). School choice and student performance. In H. F. Ladd (Ed.), *Holding schools accountable: Performance-based reform in education.* Washington, DC: Brookings Institution.

Witte, J. F., Thorn, A. C. A., Pritchard, K., & Claibourn, M. (1994). *Fourth-year report: Milwaukee parental choice program.* Madison, WI: Robert LaFollette Institute of Public Affairs.

Witter, F. R., & Keith, L. G. (1993). *Textbook of prematurity: Antecedents, treatment, & outcome.* Boston: Little, Brown.

Wolf, W. S., & Campbell, C. C. (1993). Food pattern, diet quality, and related characteristics of school children in New York State. *Journal of the American Dietetic Association, 93,* 1280–1284.

Wolfson, A. R. (1996). Sleeping patterns of children and adolescents: Developmental trends, disruptions, and adaptations. *Child & Adolescent Psychiatric Clinics of North America, 5,* 549–568.

Women on Words and Images. ((1975). *Dick and Jane as victims: Sex stereotyping in children's readers* (Expanded ed.). Princeton, NJ: Author.

Wood, K. C., Becker, J. A., & Thompson, J. K. (1996). Body image dissatisfaction in preadolescent children. *Journal of Applied Developmental Psychology, 17,* 85–100.

Woolley, J. D. (1997). Thinking about fantasy: Are children fundamentally different thinkers and believers from adults? *Child Development, 68,* 991–1011.

Worden, P. E., & Boettcher, W. (1990). Young children's acquisition of alphabet knowledge. *Journal of Reading Behavior, 22,* 277–295.

Wright, L. S., Frost, C. J., & Wisecarver, S. J. (1993). Church attendance, meaningfulness of religion, and depressive symptomatology among adolescents. *Journal of Youth and Adolescence, 22,* 559–568.

Wrobel, G. M., Ayers-Lopez, S., Grotevant, H. D., McRoy, R. G., & Friedrick, M. (1996). Openness in adoption and the level of child participation. *Child Development, 67,* 2358–2374.

Wynn, K. (1992). Addition and subtraction by human infants. *Nature, 358,* 749–750.

Wynn, K. (1995). Infants possess a system of numerical knowledge. *Current Directions in Psychological Science, 4,* 172–177.

Wynn, K. (1996). Infants' individuation and enumeration of actions. *Psychological Science, 7,* 164–169

Yau, J., & Smetana, J. G. (1993). Chinese-American adolescents' reasoning about cultural conflicts. *Journal of Adolescent Research, 8,* 419–438.

Ying, Y. (1994). Chinese American adults' relationship with their parents. *International Journal of Social Psychology, 40,* 35–45.

Yip, R., Parvanta, I., Scanlon, K., Borland, E. W., Russell, C. M., & Trowbridge, F. L. (1992). Pediatric Nutrition Surveillance System—United States, 1980–1991. *Morbidity and Mortality Weekly Report, 41,* 1–24.

Yoder, J. D., & Kahn, A. S. (1993). Working toward an inclusive psychology of women. *American Psychologist, 48,* 846–850.

Youniss, J. (1994). Children's friendship and peer culture: Implications for theories of networks and support. In F. Nestmann & K. Hurrelmann (Eds.), *Social networks and social support in childhood and adolescence* (pp. 75–88). New York: Walter de Gruyter.

Youth Indicators. (1996). *Trends in the well-being of American youth.* Washington, DC: U.S. Government Printing Office.

Zahn-Waxler, C., Friedman, R. J., Cole, P. M., Mizuta, I., & Hiruma, N. (1996). Japanese and United States preschool children's responses to conflict and distress. *Child Development, 67,* 2462–2477.

Zelazo, P. D., Helwig, C. C., & Lau, A. (1996). Intention, act, and outcome in behavioral prediction and moral judgment. *Child Development, 67,* 2478–2492.

Zeskind, P. S., Klein, L., & Marshall, T. R. (1992). Adults' perceptions of experimental modifications of durations of pauses and expiratory sounds in infant crying. *Developmental Psychology, 28,* 1153–1162.

Zhang, J., Savitz, D. A., Schwingl, P. J., & Cai, W. (1992). *International Journal of Epidemiology, 21,* 273–278.

Zito, J. M., Safer, D. J., dosReis, S., Gardner, J. F., Boles, M., & Lynch, F. (2000). Trends in the prescribing of psychotropic medications to preschoolers. *Journal of the American Medical Association, 283,* 1025–1030.

Zollar, A. C. (1985). *A member of the family: Strategies for Black family continuity.* Chicago: Nelson-Hall.

Zuckerman, B. (1988). Marijuana and cigarette smoking during pregnancy. In I. J. Chasnoff (Ed.), *Drugs, alcohol, pregnancy, and parenting* (pp. 73–89). Hingham, MA: Kluwer Academic.

Zuckerman, M. (1990). Some dubious premises in research and theory on racial differences. *American Psychologist, 45,* 1297–1303.

Credits

Photo Credits

Contents p. vii, © Amy C. Etra/Photo Edit; p. viii, © Petit Format/Nestle/PhotoResearchers, Inc.; p. ix, © Mark Richards/PhotoEdit; p. x, © Laura Dwight/PhotoEdit; p. xi, © Michael Newman/PhotoEdit; p. xii, © Jose Carrillo/PhotoEdit; p. xiii, © Tom McCarthy/PhotoEdit; p. xiv, © Myrleen Cate/PhotoEdit; p. xv, © Dwayne Newton/PhotoEdit; p. xvi, © Shmuel Thaler, Jeroboam; p. xvii, © Jeff Greenberg/PhotoEdit; p. xviii, © David Young-Wolff/PhotoEdit; p. xix, © Tony Freeman/PhotoEdit **Chapter 1** p. 0, © Jonathan Meyers/FPG International; p. 2, © Myrleen Ferguson/PhotoEdit; p. 5, © Wm. Cochrane/Impact Visuals; p. 10, © Elizabeth Crews; p. 11, © Neil Ricklen/PhotoEdit; p. 12, © Amy C. Etra/PhotoEdit; p. 14, © Elizabeth Crews; p. 18, © AP/Wide World Photos; p. 25, Courtesy Professor Albert Bandura/Stanford University; p. 26, © Corbis; p. 27, © Ted Streshinsky/Corbis; p. 29, © Rachel E. Chodorow-Reich; p. 31, © Farrell Grehan/Corbis; p. 34, © David Young-Wolff/PhotoEdit; p. 36, © Jerry Bauer/Courtesy Carol Gilligan; p. 40, © Louis Goldman/Photo Researchers, Inc. **Chapter 2** p. 45, © Tom Levy/Photo 20–20; p. 49, Courtesy Carnegie Institution of Washington; p. 52, © Dr. Dennis Kunkel/Phototake; p. 56, © David M. Phillips/Science Source/Photo Researchers, Inc.; p. 57, Courtesy Marine Biological Laboratory; p. 67, © Jose Carrillo/PhotoEdit; p. 69, © SPL/Custom Medical Stock Photo; p. 73, © Joel Gordon **Chapter 3** p. 80, © Lee White/Corbis; p. 84L, Photo Lennart Nilsson/Albert Bonniers Forlag. *A Child is Born.* Dell Publishing Company; p. 84R, Photo Lennart Nilsson/Albert Bonniers Forlag. *A Child is Born.* Dell Publishing Company; p. 86, © Custom Medical Stock Photo; p. 87L, Photo Lennart Nilsson/Albert Bonniers Forlag. *A Child is Born.* Dell Publishing Company; p. 87R, © Petit Format/Nestle/Photo Researchers, Inc.; p. 90, Photo Lennart Nilsson/Albert Bonniers Forlag. *A Child is Born.* Dell Publishing Company; p. 95, Photo Lennart Nilsson/Albert Bonniers Forlag. *A Child is Born.* Dell Publishing Company; p. 99, © Index Stock Imagery; p. 105, © Spencer Grant/PhotoEdit; p. 106, © David Young-Wolff/PhotoEdit; p. 107L, Courtesy of Victor W. Swayze, MD, Associate Professor, University of Iowa, College of Medicine, and staff psychiatrist, Veterans Affairs Medical Center, Iowa City, IA; p. 107R, © Peter Berndt, M.D., P.A./Custom Medical Stock Photo; p. 116, © David Young-Wolff/PhotoEdit; p. 118, © Mark Richards/PhotoEdit; p. 121, © Jonathan Nourok/PhotoEdit **Chapter 4** p. 130, © David Young-Wolff/PhotoEdit; p. 133, © Myrleen Cate/PhotoEdit; p. 138TL, © Elizabeth Crews; p. 138TR, © Elizabeth Crews; p. 138BL, © Elizabeth Crews; p. 138BR, © Elizabeth Crews; p. 139, Courtesy Fels Research Institute; p. 143, © Myrleen Ferguson/PhotoEdit; p. 144, © Michael Newman/PhotoEdit; p. 147, © Amy C. Etra/PhotoEdit; p. 149, © Michael Newman/PhotoEdit; p. 153TL, © Elizabeth Crews; p. 153TR, © Elizabeth Crews; p. 153ML, © Michael Newman/PhotoEdit; p. 153MR, © Laura Dwight/PhotoEdit; p. 153BL, © Elizabeth Crews; p. 159, © Elizabeth Crews; p. 161, © Shmuel Thaler/Jeroboam **Chapter 5** p. 168, © David Young-Wolff/PhotoEdit; p. 170, © Laura Dwight/PhotoEdit; p. 174, © Elizabeth Crews; p. 176, © Elizabeth Crews; p. 185, © Michael Newman/PhotoEdit; p. 186, © Myrleen Cate/PhotoEdit; p. 189, © Mary M. Steinbacher/PhotoEdit; p. 192, © Amy C. Etra/PhotoEdit; p. 194, © Elizabeth Crews; p. 196, © Spencer Grant/PhotoEdit; p. 200, © Michael Newman/PhotoEdit; p. 202, © Michael Newman/PhotoEdit; p. 205, © D. Greco/The Image Works, Inc.; p. 209, © Index Stock Imagery **Chapter 6** p. 212, © Myrleen Cate/PhotoEdit; p. 214, © Myrleen Cate/PhotoEdit; p. 215, © Myrleen Cate/PhotoEdit; p. 216, Courtesy Harlow Primate Lab, University of Wisconsin, Madison; p. 217, © Mary Kate Denny/PhotoEdit; p. 220, © Michael Newman/PhotoEdit; p. 223, © Elizabeth Crews; p. 228, © Mark Richards/PhotoEdit; p. 229, © Tony Freeman/PhotoEdit; p. 231, © Logan Wallace/The Image Works; p. 235, © Index Stock Imagery; p. 237, © Elizabeth Crews; p. 241, © Myrleen Cate/PhotoEdit; p. 242, © Michael Newman/PhotoEdit; p. 243, © Elizabeth Crews **Chapter 7** p. 248, © Myrleen Cate/PhotoEdit; p. 250, © Myrleen Cate/PhotoEdit; p. 252, © Jose Carrillo/PhotoEdit; p. 254, © Clark Jones/Impact Visuals; p. 255, © Tony Freeman/PhotoEdit; p. 256, © Rachel Epstein/PhotoEdit; p. 262, © Elizabeth Crews; p. 263, © Elizabeth Crews; p. 265, © Mary Kate Denny/PhotoEdit; p. 269, © Spencer Grant/PhotoEdit; p. 273, © Mark Richards/PhotoEdit; p. 275, © Stephanie Rausser/FPG International; p. 280, © Cindy Charles/PhotoEdit; p. 288, © David Young-Wolff/PhotoEdit; p. 289, © Elizabeth Crews **Chapter 8** p. 294, © Laura Dwight/PhotoEdit; p. 298, © Elizabeth Crews; p. 299, © M. Bernsau/The Image Works; p. 301, © Michael Siluk/Jeroboam; p. 303, © Tom Prettyman/PhotoEdit; p. 305, © Barbara Stitzer/PhotoEdit; p. 311, © David Young-Wolff/PhotoEdit; p. 315, © Felicia Martinez/PhotoEdit; p. 318, © Laura Dwight/PhotoEdit; p. 319, © William Cochrane/Impact Visuals; p. 321, © Elizabeth Crews; p. 326, © Myrleen Cate/PhotoEdit **Chapter 9** p. 332, © Joel Gordon; p. 335, © Michael Newman/PhotoEdit; p. 337, © Elizabeth Crews; p. 339, © David Young-Wolff/PhotoEdit; p. 342, © Elizabeth Crews; p. 344, © Tony Freeman/PhotoEdit; p. 346, © Michael Newman/PhotoEdit; p. 349, © Phil Lauro/Index Stock Imagery; p. 350, © Tom McCarthy/PhotoEdit; p. 355, © Mary Kate Denny/PhotoEdit; p. 357, © Elizabeth Crews; p. 361, © Myrleen Cate/PhotoEdit; p. 364, © Elizabeth Crews **Chapter 10** p. 372, © Shmuel Thaler/Jeroboam; p. 375, © Elizabeth Crews; p. 377, © Rudi Von Briel/PhotoEdit; p. 381, © Rachel Epstein/PhotoEdit; p. 385, © R. Hutchings/PhotoEdit; p. 386, © Phil Schermeister/Corbis; p. 388, © Michael Newman/PhotoEdit; p. 390, © Elizabeth Crews; p. 396, © David Young-Wolff/PhotoEdit; p. 398, © A. Lichtenstein/The Image Works; p. 400, © Michael Newman/PhotoEdit; p. 402, © Zuzana Killam/Jacksonville Journal-Courier/The Image

Care Resource and Referral Agencies (NACCRRA), Washington, D.C. Fig. 6.2 From D. L. Newman, A. Caspi, T. E. Moffitt and P. A. Silva, 1997, "Antecedents of Adult Interpersonal Functioning: Effects of Individual Differences in Age 3 Temperament," *Developmental Psychology*, 33, p. 213. Copyright © 1997 by the American Psychological Association. Adapted with permission. Fig. 6.3 From M. R. Gunnar, L. Brodersen, M. Nachmias, K. Buss and J. Rigatuso, "Stress Reactivity and Attachment Security," *Developmental Psychobiology*, Vol. 29, pp. 191-204. Reprinted by permission of John Wiley & Sons, Inc. T 6.1 From D. Stipek, S. Recchia and S. McClintic, 1992, "Self-Evaluation in Young Children," *Monographs of the Society for Research in Child Development*, Vol. 57, 1, Serial No. 226. With permission from Society for Research in Child Development. **Chapter 7** Box 7.1, 7.2 From K. E. Allen and L. Marotz, 1989, *Developmental Profiles: Birth to 6*, First Edition. Reprinted with permission of Delmar, a division of Thomson Learning. Fax 800 730-2215. T 7.1, 7.2, 7.4, 7.5 From *American Academy of Pediatrics: Guide to Child's Nutrition* by W. H. Dietz and L. Stern. Copyright © 1999 by W. H. Dietz and L. Stern. Reprinted by permission of Villard Books, a Division of Random House, Inc. Box 7.4 From *A Practical Guide to the Evaluation of Child Physical Abuse and Neglect* by A. P. Giardino, C. W. Christian, and E. R. Giardino, 1997. Reprinted by permission of Sage Publications, Inc. **Chapter 8** Fig. 8.2 From C. S. Rosen, D. C. Schwebel and J. L. Singer, 1997, "Preschoolers' Attributions of Mental States in Pretense," *Child Development*, Vol. 68, 1133-1142. With permission from Society for Research in Child Development. Fig. 8.3 From R. Kai, 1991, "Developmental Changes in Speed of Processing During Childhood and Adolescence," *Psychological Bulletin*, Vol. 109, 490-501. Copyright © 1991 by the American Psychological Association. Reprinted with permission. Fig. 8.4 From F. N. Dempster, 1981, "Memory Span: Sources of Individual and Developmental Differences," *Psychological Bulletin*, Vol. 89, pp. 63-100. Copyright © 1981 by the American Psychological Association. Reprinted with permission. T 8.1 From K. McGilly and R. S. Siegler, 1989, "How Childen Choose Among Serial Recall Strategies," *Child Development*, Vol. 60, pp. 172-182. With permission from Society for Research in Child Development. **Chapter 9** Box 9.1 From P. J. Miller, A. R. Wiley, H. Fung and C. Liang, 1997, "Personal Storytelling as a Medium of Socialization in Chinese and American Families," *Child Development*, Vol. 68, 557-568. With permission from Society

for Research in Child Development. Fig. 9.2 From T. Stoddart and E. Turiel, 1985, "Children's Concepts of Cross-Gender Activities," *Child Development*, Vol. 56, pp. 1241-1252. With permission from Society for Research in Child Development. T 9.1 From D. Baumrind, 1989, "Rearing Competent Children," in W. Damon, ed., *New Directions for Child Development: Adolescent Health and Human Behavior*, pp. 349-378. Reprinted by permission of Jossey-Bass, Inc., a subsidiary of John Wiley & Sons, Inc. P. 368 Graph in Social Policy Box from *Journal of Applied Psychology*, 1995, Vol. 80, pp. 621-627. **Chapter 10** Fig. 10.2 From K. Ampofo-Boateng, J. A. Thompson, R. Grieve, T. Pitcairns, D. N. Lee and J. D. Demetre, "A Developmental and Training Study of Children's Ability To Find Safe Routes To Cross the Road," *British Journal of Developmental Psychology*, March 1993, Vol. 11, Part 1, pp. 31-46. Copyright © 1993 British Journal of Developmental Psychology. Reproduced with permission of the publisher. P. 387 From "Gryphon" in *Through the Safety Net* by Charles Baxter, p. 909. With permission from Darhansoff and Verill Literary Agency. Fig. 10.4 From A. F. Vansant, 1995, "Development of Posture," *Functional Movement Across the Life Span* by D. Cech and S. Martin, pp. 275-294. With permission from W. B. Saunders. Fig. 10.7 From "The role of the Frontal Lobes in the Regulation of Cognitive Development," *Brain and Cognition*, Vol. 20, pp. 51-73, 1992 by R. Case. Copyright © 1992 by Academic Press. Reproduced by permission of the publisher. Box 10.1 From *American Academy of Pediatrics: Guide to Your Child's Nutrition* by W. H. Dietz and L. Stern. Copyright © 1999 by W. H. Dietz and L. Stern. Reprinted by permission of Villard Books, a Division of Random House, Inc. **Chapter 11** Fig. 11.1 From *Life-Span Human Development*, First Edition by C. Sigelman and D. Shaffer. Copyright © 1991 by Wadsworth. Reprinted with permission of Wadsworth, a division of Thomson Learning. Fax 800 730-2215. Fig. 11.2 From R. S. Siegler, 1976, "Three Aspects of Cognitive Development," *Cognitive Psychology*, Vol. 8, pp. 481-520. Copyright © 1976 by Academic Press. Reproduced by permission of the publisher. Fig. 11.3 From R. S. Siegler, *Children's Thinking*, Third Edition. Copyright © 1997 Prentice-Hall, Inc. Reprinted by permission of Prentice-Hall, Inc., Upper Saddle River, NJ. Fig. 11.4 From D. C. Geary, C. C. Bow-Thomas, L. Fan and R. S. Siegler, 1996. "Development of Arithmetical Competencies in Chinese and American Children's Influence of Age, Language, and Schooling," *Child Development*, Vol. 67, pp. 2022-2044. With permission from Society for Research in

Child Development. Fig. 11.5 From J. W. Stigler and H. W. Stevenson, 1991, "How Asian Teachers Polish Each Lesson to Perfection," *American Educator* (Spring), pp. 12-20, 43-47. Reprinted with permission from the Spring 1991 issue of the American Educator, the quarterly journal of the American Federation of Teachers. P. 436 From *The Spatial Child* by John Dixon, pp. 174-175. Courtesy of Charles C. Thomas, Publisher, Ltd., Springfield, Illinois. Fig. 11.6 From C. S. Mueller and C. S. Dweck, 1998. "Praise for Intelligence Can Undermine Children's Motivation and Performance," *Journal of Personality and Social Psychology*, Vol. 75, pp. 33-52. Copyright © 1998 by the American Psychological Association. Reprinted with permission. **Chapter 12** P. 455 From "Gryphon" in *Through the Safety Net* by Charles Baxter, p. 918. With permission from Darhansoff and Verill Literary Agency. T 12.1 From J. G. Smetana and R. Berent, 1983, "Adolescents' and Mothers' Evaluation of Justifications for Disputes," *Journal of Adolescent Research*, vol. 8, pp. 252-273. Reprinted by permission of Sage Publications, Inc. Box 12.1 Adapted from J. G. Smetana and P. Asquith, 1994, "Adolescents' and Parents' Conceptions of Parental Authority and Personal Autonomy," *Child Development*, Vol. 65, pp. 1147-1162. With permission from Society for Research in Child Development. **Chapter 13** Table 13.2 From B. Goldstein, 1976, *Introduction to Human Sexuality*, 1976, p. 80, Star Publishing Company, Belmont, CA. Used with permission from the publisher. Fig. 13.3 Adapted from D. B. Cheek, 1974, "Body Composition, Hormones, Nutrition, and Adolescent Growth," in M. M. Grumbach, G. D. Grave and F. E. Mayer, eds., *Control of the Onset of Puberty*. Reprinted by permission of John Wiley & Sons, Inc. Fig. 13.6 From J. M. Tanner, "Earlier Maturation in Man," *Scientific American*, January 1968, p. 26. Copyright © 1968 by Scientific American, Inc. All rights reserved. **Chapter 14** Fig. 14.1 From J. M. Hunt, *Intelligence and Experience*, Ronald Press, 1960. Used with permission of John Wiley & Sons, Inc. Fig. 14.2 From *The Growth of Logical Thinking: From Childhood to Adolescence* by Jean Piaget and Barbel Inhelder. Copyright © 1958 by Basic Books, Inc. Reprinted by permission of Basic Books, a member of Perseus Books, L. L. C. Fig. 14.3 Reprinted by permission of the publisher from *Psychology of Reasoning: Structure and Content* by P. C. Watson and P. N. Johnson-Laird, Cambridge, Mass.: Harvard University Press. Copyright © 1972 by P. C. Watson and P. N. Johnson-Laird. Box 14.1 WAIS subtests credit to come P. 553 Graph in Research Focus Box from G. Downey, A. Lebolt, C. Rincon and A. L. Freitas, 1988, "Rejection, Sensitivity and Children's Interpersonal Difficulties," *Child Development,* Vol. 69, pp. 1074, 1091. With permission from Society for Research in Child Development. Box 14.2 Adapted from S. L. Ward and W. F. Overton, 1990, "Semantic Familiarity, Relevance, and the Development of Deductive Reasoning," *Developmental Psychology*, Vol. 26, pp. 488–493. Copyright © 1990 by the American Psychological Association. Adapted with permission. Box 14.3 From D. N. Perkins, 1987, "Knowledge as Design: Teaching Thinking Through Content," in *Teaching Thinking Skills: Theory and Practice* by J. B. Baron and R. J. Sternberg. With permission from David Perkins. **Chapter 15** Pp. 577–578 From *Identity: Youth and Crisis* by Erik H. Erikson. Copyright © 1968 by W. W. Norton & Company, Inc. Used by permission of W. W. Norton & Company, Inc. P. 588 From *Voices in the Mirror* by Gordon Parks. Copyright © 1990 by Gordon Parks. Used by permission of Doubleday, a division of Random House, Inc. Fig. 15.1 From S. T. Ennett and K. E. Bauman, 1996, "Adolescent Social Networks: School, Demographic, and Longitudinal Considerations," *Journal of Adolescent Research*, vol. 11, pp. 194–215. Reprinted by permission of Sage Publications, Inc. Fig. 15.2 Adapted from S. J. Blumenthal and D. J. Kupfer, 1986, "Generalizable Treatment Strategies for Suicidal Behavior" in *Psychobiology of Suicidal Behavior, Annals of the New York Academy of Sciences, Volume 487*, edited by J. J. Mann and M. Stanley, New York Academy of Sciences, New York, 1986, pp. 327–340. Used with permission.

Author Index

Subject Index

Peter Merseburger · Grenzgänger

Peter Merseburger

GRENZGÄNGER

Innenansichten der anderen
deutschen Republik

C. Bertelsmann

1. Auflage

© 1988 C. Bertelsmann Verlag GmbH, München
Lektorat: Dr. Erich Rößler
Satz: Mühlberger, Augsburg
Druck und Bindung: Mohndruck Gütersloh
ISBN 3-570-04746-6
Printed in Germany

Für Sabine –
mitgegangen, mitgefangen von der
deutschen Frage

Inhalt

Vorwort

Was hier vorgelegt wird, ist kein Versuch, die »Eingeborenen«
der DDR zu entdecken, zu beschreiben oder gar systematisch
zu katalogisieren wie das – mitsamt colorierten Kupferstichen
– einst der süddeutsche Prinz zu Wied mit den nordamerika-
nischen Indianern tat. Zwar mag richtig sein, daß einige Bundesbürger, durch angestrengte Weltläufigkeit und Reisen in
die entlegensten Winkel der Erde abgestumpft, inzwischen die
eher triste realsozialistische Szene Magdeburgs oder Eisen-
hüttenstadts als exotischen Lustreiz empfinden, das Zurück-
gebliebensein gegenüber manchen Entwicklungen im Westen
als beschauliche Fahrt in Bilder aus der deutschen Vergangenheit. Wer fünf Jahre nicht nur von Berufs wegen genau hinge-
schaut hat und bemüht war, hinter die Fassade der offiziellen
Parolen und der Angepaßtheit zu schauen, kann derlei Exotik
nicht sehr spaßig finden. Er kann allerdings auch nicht jene
romantische Haltung teilen, die Unterschiede der politischen
Systeme verwischt und das Deutsche über alle anderen Werte
stellt, als gebe es einen neuen deutschen Sonderweg zwischen
den Lagern und den Supermächten. Die DDR versteht sich als
alternativer Gesellschaftsentwurf zu einer kapitalistischen
Ordnung auf deutschem Boden, der fest ins sozialistische Lager eingebunden ist. In einem Jahr feiert sie den 40. Jahrestag
ihrer Gründung, wie die Bundesrepublik. Sie existiert damit
bald so lange wie das wilhelminische Reich, das im Ersten
Weltkrieg endete, sie hat bereits heute die dreifache Lebens-
dauer der Weimarer Republik und die des »tausendjährigen
Reichs«, das im Zweiten Weltkrieg unterging. Wie weit greift

nach so langer Zeit der Herrschaftsanspruch einer marxistisch-leninistischen Partei, wie sehr prägt der reale Sozialismus das Bewußtsein der Bürger, die in ihm aufwachsen und leben müssen? Wie viele sind überzeugt, wie viele hoffen auf grundsätzliche Veränderung, wer paßt sich an und heult nur mit den Wölfen? Wie groß sind die Freiräume für Selbstverwirklichung und wo endet die Möglichkeit einer auch kritischen Mitwirkung innerhalb des Systems? Schließlich: Wie fügt dieses ungeliebte Kind der deutschen Teilung, entstanden aus dem Octroi einer von der sowjetischen Besatzungsmacht gestützten kommunistischen Gruppierung, sich in die gemeinsame Geschichte der Deutschen ein – versucht es einfach, sich davon zu stehlen, oder ist es ein Stück jener Tradition, die eine Vielfalt von Staaten als deutsches Schicksal und den Nationalstaat, die Regel der großen anderen Völker, als zeitlich knapp befristete Ausnahme kennt? Waren die deutschen Kommunisten nicht einmal als Verfechter der Einheit angetreten? Wie halten sie es also mit der Nation?

Ich hatte die Chance, solchen Fragen nachzugehen. Dieses Buch erhebt keinen Anspruch auf eine umfassende Darstellung und Analyse. Es handelt von einer DDR, die neben vielen Schwächen auch eindeutige Erfolge aufzuweisen hat und sich in einer schwierigen Umbruchphase befindet. Nach der Politik des Dialogs mit dem Westen ist nun der Dialog nach innen gefragt, den die Spitzen von Partei und Staat mit einer Jugend führen müssen, die nicht länger brav offiziellen Parolen folgt, sondern sie kritisch hinterfragt und Freiheiten im Rahmen der eigenen Verfassung fordert. Noch ist nicht abzusehen, ob die Führung sich dieser Herausforderung stellen will oder weiter der repressiven Praxis vertraut, alle, die aufmucken zu verhaften und über die Grenzen abzuschieben – als lästiges Störpotential. Mit der Biermann-Ausweisung gelang es ihr, sich eine innenpolitische Atempause von fast zehn Jahren zu verschaffen. Derlei Ruhephasen dürften nach der Abschiebung Stephan Krawczyks, Freya Kliers und Ralf Hirschs nun kürzer bemessen sein, da die Zahl der Engagierten, die auf Reformen dringen und im Lande bleiben wollen, wächst. Was hier vorgelegt wird, ist ein Angebot, an Erlebtem teilzuhaben und es im nötigen Kontext zu sehen. Der Leser, der sich einlassen will auf die DDR, wie das der Autor tat, ist also eingeladen.

1. Berlin, Heinrich-Heine-Straße

Wer dem Grenzübergang näher kommt, sieht zunächst den Mann im Turm. Hoch thront er über Mauer und Einfahrt. Manchmal trinkt er Kaffee oder beißt in seine *Bemme*; gelegentlich träumt er vor sich hin oder er liest. Oft spielt er das Spiel der Grenzer aller Seiten und aller Länder: Das Fernglas-Abtast-Spiel. Mit Zeiss-Jena-geschärftem Weitblick übt er den optischen Schlagabtausch mit den Wächtern des anderen Bündnis- und Gesellschaftssystems, wie östliche Sprachregelung umständlich aber genau vermerkt; oder er schaut verstohlen zu, was sich hinter einem Fenster jener Welt abspielt, die, beherrscht vom Klassenfeind, wie die Ideologen ihn lehrten, fremd und unerreichbar bleibt. Dabei ist Kreuzberg nur einen Schritt über die Grenzlinie entfernt.

Wer ist der Mann im Turm? Ein Überzeugter, ein Hundertprozentiger? Ein mit allen Wassern der Agitation gewaschener, in der Wolle gefärbter Beschützer des real existierenden Sozialismus? Oder einer, der sein Amt nicht als Berufung versteht, sondern als Job, der gutes Gehalt, Chancen zu schnellem Aufstieg und eine grenznah gelegene Komfortwohnung zu schätzen weiß? Nicht in Frage steht seine preußische Korrektheit. Nur selten muß ich durch ein knappes Lichtsignal auf mich aufmerksam machen. Meist reagiert er ohne Mahnung und drückt den Knopf. Der Schlagbaum hebt sich, die Ampel schaltet auf grün. Die Slalomfahrt in eine Zwischenwelt beginnt, die eher einer Festung gleicht als einem Übergang.

Einige tausend Male habe ich in diesen Jahren die Grenze

passiert, die beide Halbstädte trennt. Nahezu tägliche Übung macht vieles zur Routine, aber sie schärft auch den Blick. Nirgendwo sonst habe ich viele meiner westlichen Landsleute sich so beflissen und servil gerieren sehen. Sie öffnen den Kofferraum ihres Mercedes, die Motorhaube ihres BMW und reißen die Wagenschläge auf, als könnte deutlich demonstrierter Eifer die Kontrolleure milde und gnädig stimmen – Zöllner, denen sie sich sonst turmhoch überlegen fühlen. Nur die Jüngeren reagieren verhaltener, gelassener; bei ihnen haben, scheint es, Jahrzehnte Einübung in Demokratie und Training des aufrechten Gangs dann doch in die Tiefe gewirkt. Bei den Älteren liegt der Verdacht nahe, daß viele, wären sie in der anderen deutschen Republik aufgewachsen und dort geblieben, heute zu jenen Grenzwächtern zählten, die gehalten sind, Fluchtversuche mit der Waffe zu verhindern und im Zweifel dies auch tun. Hier die verängstigten Westbürger, dort die penibel, unbeirrt und mit nahezu altpreußischer Sturheit ihres Amtes waltenden Ost-Beamten, zusammen bieten sie das allzu vertraute, gesamtdeutsche Bild von Unterwerfung und autoritärer Obrigkeit.

Gewiß, der Festungscharakter der Grenze wirkt einschüchternd. Allein der harte, metallene Knall, mit dem einer der vielen Schlagbäume des inneren Grenzbereichs in die Verriegelung fällt, kann empfindlichen Gemütern einen Schrecken einjagen. Hunde, vom Zwinger zu den Lastwagen geführt, müssen auf Leitern klettern, um die Ware zu beschnüffeln. An anderen Grenzen sind sie auf Sprengstoff und Heroin abgerichtet, an dieser auf Menschen. Made in Germany galt einmal als Inbegriff deutscher Solidität und Wertarbeit. Mit dem Bau der sichersten, häßlichsten und brutalsten Grenze der Welt hat die DDR diesen Begriff aufs Schlimmste pervertiert; aber auch dabei gibt sie sich betont deutsch. Ich denke an die Stiefmütterchen, mit denen die Betonhindernisse der Slalom-Einfahrt bepflanzt sind – ein fast schon rührend lächerlicher Versuch, dem scheußlich Abnormen scheinbar normale Züge zu verleihen. Dabei lehrt er nur, wie nahe Brutalität und Sentimentalität im deutschen Wesen beieinander wohnen.

Natürlich steckt in dieser westdeutschen Beflissenheit vor

ostdeutschen Grenzbeamten Angst vor dem anderen System, das auch nach anderthalb Jahrzehnten deutsch-deutscher Entspannungspolitik noch fremd und abweisend wirkt. Nicht nur die oft einschüchternde DDR-Grenzroutine, auch die westlichen Medien haben diese tief im westdeutschen Gemüt wurzelnde Furcht immer wieder bestärkt. Sie haben auch jene Mauer in unseren Köpfen befestigen helfen, welche die Bürger der anderen deutschen Republik wie selbstverständlich durch den Mißbrauch des Wortes deutsch ausgrenzt. Wenn die Tagesschau über deutsch-sowjetische Spannungen berichtet, sind natürlich nur die Beziehungen zwischen der Bundesrepublik und der UdSSR gemeint; wenn vom Niedergang der deutschen Werftindustrie die Rede ist, hat der Sprecher die Werften an Weser und Elbe, nicht die von Rostock und Stralsund im Sinn, denn deren Auftragsbücher sind durch sowjetische Großaufträge voll, auf Jahre hinaus; der triumphierend vermeldete Sieg einer deutschen Mannschaft ist in aller Regel der eines Teams aus der Bundesrepublik. Ein überheblicher Sprachgebrauch, der die Hallsteindoktrin der 50er Jahre in die Umgangssprache der 80er hinübergerettet hat und der kontraproduktiv wirkt. Schließlich liegt den Alleinvertretern doch angeblich das ganze Deutschland am Herzen. Doch diese Art Alleinvertretung reduziert es um ein gutes Drittel auf das Territorium der Bundesrepublik.

Eine Grenzempfehlung des Ministerrats der Deutschen Demokratischen Republik garantiert den in der DDR akkreditierten Journalisten bevorzugte Abfertigung beim Zoll und erspart lästige Prozeduren, die man an westlichen Grenzen kaum kennt: Der Kofferraum muß nicht geöffnet werden, Zeitungen und Bücher werden nicht als ideologische Konterbande konfisziert, sondern können als Arbeitsmaterial mitgeführt werden; der Tank wird nicht umständlich mit Meß-Stäben auf Umbauten (da könnte ja etwas oder gar einer versteckt sein!) ausgelotet. Das Hin und Her zwischen den Halbstädten, das in Wahrheit eine zwischen zwei politischen Welten ist, wurde Routine, und doch haftete ihr stets etwas Schmerzliches an. Da blieb der furchteinflößende Anblick der

Sperranlagen, den auch bunte Graffiti auf der westlichen Seite nicht mildern können. Und da bleibt das allgegenwärtige DDR-Mißtrauen gegen die eigenen Bürger, das mit Beton, Stacheldraht und elektronischen Alarmanlagen zur scheußlich-abstoßenden Form gerann. Schaltet der Mann im Turm auf grün und hebt sich die erste Schranke, rollt der Wagen auf eine Reihe mit Erde gefüllter, einen Meter hoher Stahlkästen zu – das erste Hindernis nach der Einfahrt vom Westen her. Wenn im Frühjahr hier zwei Gärtner Blumen pflanzen, stehen zwei Offiziere der Grenztruppen neben ihnen, die Pistolen locker im Halfter. Für die Bepflanzer dieser eisernen Blumenkästen liegt jene andere Hälfte der Stadt, die sich in ihrer Fernsehwerbung als eine Glitzerwelt des Wohlstands, des Überflusses und einer ungeahnten Freiheit der Konsumwahl präsentiert, nur wenige Schritte entfernt und doch unerreichbar weit. Das letzte Loch in der Mauer wird nur durch eine Schranke blockiert, die sich mühelos überspringen oder unterlaufen ließe. So nahe am Gegner, vertraut die Sicherheit ausschließlich Uniformierten mit silbergeflochtenen Schulterstücken – Rängen vom Major an aufwärts. Einmal beobachtete ich bei der Einfahrt einen Arbeiter im blauen Kittel, der den Boden der Grenzstation hinter der ersten, Richtung Kreuzberg stehenden Schranke fegte. Zwei Offiziere der Grenztruppen hatten sich in seiner Nähe postiert und ließen kein Auge von ihm. Das Bild erinnerte an Filmszenen von Häftlingen bei der Arbeit außerhalb der Strafanstalt, nur das Zahlenverhältnis von Aufsehern und Gefangenen wollte nicht stimmen. Ein anderes Mal bot sich ein eher komischer Anblick. Offenbar klemmte die Automatik der vordersten Schranke. Zwei Monteure in blauen Overalls bemühten sich fachmännisch, drei wohlbeleibte ältere Herren in Uniform schauten interessiert zu und bildeten einen Sicherheits-Schirm unmittelbar vor dem Grenzstreifen, vornübergebeugt, das defekte Hebewerk beäugend. So streckten sich mir zur Begrüßung drei stattliche Popos entgegen. Kein Zweifel: Die höheren Chargen haben sämtlich einen Hang zur Korpulenz, und die Arbeiter, die angeblich die Herren sind in der anderen deut-

16

schen Republik, gelten an der Front zum Klassenfeind als Sicherheitsrisiko. Die Schranke, die sie reparieren, soll für sie geschlossen bleiben.

Im zurückgelegenen Teil der Festung Heinrich-Heine-Straße genügen dann zwei Unteroffiziere mit umgehängten Kalaschnikows. Regelmäßig ziehen sie als Wache auf, wenn Elektriker die Neonleuchten des überdachten Zollgeländes auswechseln oder die Ampeln reparieren, die schließlich freie Fahrt in jenen »ersten Arbeiter- und Bauernstaat auf deutschem Boden« signalisieren, der sich gern als Hort der Geborgenheit und »Staat der wahren Menschlichkeit« empfiehlt. Doch vor dem Eintritt liegen abgründige Sperren des Mißtrauens. Dreimal erfolgen Paß- und Gesichtskontrollen; die sie vornehmen, sind fast durchweg Offiziere vom Leutnant an aufwärts. Für DDR-Verhältnisse hochbezahlte Hauptleute verrichten Handlangerdienste, weil man sie geringeren Chargen nicht anzuvertrauen wagt.

Tägliche Übung schärft den Blick nicht nur für das Bedrohliche und Häßliche der Grenze, sondern auch für das »Murkelige«, das zum Charakter der DDR gehört wie die schwarzrotgoldene Fahne mit Hammer, Zirkel und Ährenkranz auf dem Amtssitz des Staatsratsvorsitzenden am Marx-Engels-Platz. DDR-Gründervater Walter Ulbricht war einst Tischler von Beruf, doch der Paß wird durch die Klappe eines Holzkastens in die Kontrollbaracke gereicht, die kein Zimmermann oder Tischlerlehrling als Gesellenstück abzuliefern wagte. Die Schilder an den Grenzbaracken haben den Charme eines galizischen Grenzbahnhofs der Jahrhundertwende, wie er für den Film über den k.u.k. Oberst Redl eigens hergerichtet werden mußte. Wer zu Fuß die Grenze überqueren will, dem wird umständlich per Hand eine eiserne Drahttür aufgeschlossen; den Weg aus dem Westen bis zu dieser Pforte säumen Draht-Laufgitter, die an Viehfarmen im amerikanischen Westen erinnern. Der Blick durch das Fenster, hinter dem Pässe geprüft, Visagebühren kassiert oder Zählkarten gestempelt werden, fällt auf die Lieblingszierde vieler DDR-Büros – auf gelbgrün gefleckte, gummibaumartige Hängepflanzen, die, stufenförmig auf Gestellen angeordnet, das Bild der »Nummer 1« garnieren. So nennen DDR-Funktionäre vertraut-despektierlich ihren Partei- und Staatschef. Der prangt auf knallblauem Hintergrund, den er von seinem Besuch in Griechenland mitgebracht haben muß, denn solcher Himmel wölbt sich nie über dem Braunkohle-Niflheim, an dessen wenig einladender Pforte ich immer wieder Einlaß begehrte. Bemüht milde, doch ein wenig verkniffen lächelnd, schaut Honecker dem Grenzbeamten über die Schulter. Der befragt inzwischen seinen Computer, ob dem Besucher auch Eintritt gewährt wird in das Land, das Charles de Gaulle mit seinem untrüglichen Sinn für Historie so gern als la Prusse et la Saxe titulierte.

Nach nur zwei Wochen Aufenthalt in der DDR gehörte ihr spezifischer Geruch für mich zu den unveränderlichen Kennzeichen des Arbeiter- und Bauernstaates. Mit verbundenen Augen vom Mars kommend über der Erde abgesetzt, hätte ich die glückliche Landung im realexistierenden Sozialismus zwischen Elbe und Oder umgehend am intensiven Braunkohledunst und an den Abgasen der Zweitaktmotoren orten können. Diese Auspuffwolken enthalten gefährlich viel unverbrannte Ölrückstände, die an schönen Sommerwochenenden, wenn sich die Trabi- und Wartburgschlangen von den märkischen Seen über den Autobahnzubringer Schönefeld heimwärts quälen, in dichten Schwaden die Luft der Hauptstadt verpesten. Andere Quellen der unverkennbaren Duftnote Marke DDR sind Lysol und ein Linoleum-Reinigungsmittel, deren Geruch, mit Kohl- und Bratendünsten vermischt, penetrant durch jedes Hochhaus zieht. Doch die DDR läßt sich nicht nur erriechen, sondern auch erschmecken: In einer kalten, nebligen Winternacht im Zentrum von Weimar, wo fast jeder seinen Ofen noch mit Briketts heizt, zergeht der Braunkohleruß buchstäblich auf der Zunge.

Ganz so Unrecht hatte de Gaulle natürlich nicht, wenn er die DDR schlicht in der Nachfolge von Preußen und Sachsen sah. Zwar vergaß er Mecklenburg, den landschaftlich schönsten, von der andernorts systematisch betriebenen Naturzerstörung weitgehend verschonten Teil der DDR. Doch in

Mecklenburg kommt ohnehin alles 100 Jahre später, sagt das Sprichwort. Nur zwanzig Jahre nach dem großen Franzosen führen westdeutsche Politik-Wissenschaftler den in der anderen deutschen Republik geschaffenen, wenn auch bescheidenen Wohlstand auf eine Kombination sächsischer und preußischer Tugenden zurück: Auf sächsischen Gewerbefleiß und preußische Disziplin.

In meinem Tagebuch, in dem ich den ersten Eindruck der Wiederbegegnung mit dem Monstrum Mauer nach Jahren in Amerika festgehalten habe, finde ich den Eintrag: »Die Grenzer sind korrekt, steif und angestrengt um Höflichkeit bemüht, aber die bleibt hölzern. Das preußische dominiert eindeutig, der Glaubensfarbe Rot zum Trotz.« Später, wann immer ich vor Schalter 2 auf die Rückgabe von Paß und Zählkarte warte, wird dieser erste Eindruck korrigiert. Bei den Kontrolleuren überwiegt die obersächsische Dialektfarbe, die so garnicht zackig klingt. Gut die Hälfte der DDR-Bewohner stammt aus den südlichen Bezirken, in denen man sächselt wie einst Luther und Bach, Wagner und Nietzsche. Ich sehe Offiziere der Grenztruppen auf dem Weg zum vorgeschobenen Wachtturm über der Mauereinfahrt, in der Linken Aktentasche und Stullenpaket, mit der Rechten einen Kaffeetopf balancierend. Die durch und durch unkriegerische, eher an Bahn- oder Postbeamte erinnernde Szene wiederholt sich häufig und will so recht nicht zum tradierten Feindbild von den blutrünstigen Parteisoldaten passen, die aus ideologischer Verblendung oder gar aus lauter Lust am Morden auf die eigenen Bürger wie »auf Hasen« schießen. Doch war mir Hannah Ahrendts Satz von der Banalität des Bösen stets gewärtig, und es stimmte ja auch: Pflichtgemäß würden die braven Familienväter morgen auf Flüchtende schießen, wenn auch in Zeiten der deutsch-deutschen Entspannung seltener gezielt und eher zur Abschreckung geschossen wird. Nach solchen bescheidenen Verhaltensänderungen scheint sich der Fortschritt an dieser häßlichen Grenze zwischen Deutschen zu bemessen. Und doch wäre es falsch, ihn für gering zu erachten. Der Rückblick zeigt, daß sich an der Grenze gerade in den letzten Jahren manches zum Besseren gewandelt hat. Aber das setzte Umdenken auf beiden Seiten voraus, das manch einem gewiß nicht leicht gefallen ist.

Als am 10. April 1983 der Transitreisende Rudolf Burkert bei der Einvernahme in einer Zollbaracke des Grenzübergangs Drewitz tot zusammenbrach, spach ein führender westdeutscher Politiker von Mord an der Grenze. Die DDR reagierte empört. Zu spät zwar, um die westliche Aufgeregtheit zu vermeiden, aber dann doch penibel, wiesen ihre Experten nach, was westliche Gerichtsmediziner nach einer Obduktion der Leiche schließlich bestätigten: Daß der Transitreisende nicht brutal zusammengeschlagen, sondern Opfer eines Herzinfarktes geworden war. Für am Kopf festgestellte Verletzungen gab es danach eine völlig natürliche Erklärung. Burkert war, als die Herzattacke einsetzte, in sich zusammengesackt und beim Sturz auf den Heizkörper aufgeschlagen. Die emotionale Debatte, die in westdeutschen Blättern um den tragischen Tod im Zwischendeutschland der Kontrollstation damals entbrannte, belegte eindrucksvoll, daß alte Erfahrungen von schikanösen Wartezeiten und raffinierten Durchsuchungspraktiken im kollektiven Gedächtnis der Westdeutschen, vor allem der Westberliner gespeichert sind. In Form handfester Vorurteile und Schreckensbilder brechen sie sich beim geringsten Anlaß Bahn, frei nach dem Motto: Denen da drüben trauen wir doch nur das Schlimmste zu.

Die traurige Geschichte des Kraftfahrers Burkert aus Asendorf in Niedersachsen war der erste gravierende Grenzzwischenfall, über den ich in den Jahren in Ostberlin zu berichten hatte, und er ist bis heute ein Paradebeispiel dafür, daß diese Grenze eben keine normale ist wie jede andere, auch wenn das die DDR noch so unermüdlich behauptet – dazu ist sie als Markierungslinie zwischen zwei Staaten viel zu emotional besetzt, und zwar nicht nur im Westen. Geht es um das eigene Grenzregime, zeigt man im Osten eine hochneurotische Sensibilität, die sich aus dem Nachholbedarf an Souveränität, an Anerkennung erklären mag, die der Westen über zwei Jahrzehnte verweigerte. Nur so läßt sich verstehen, daß eine schludrige Unterlassung des Ostens und eine überzogene Pressereaktion im Westen zu einer deutsch-deutschen Krise eskalierten, die schließlich zur – ersten – Absage des ursprünglich schon für Sommer oder Herbst 1983 geplanten Honecker-Besuchs in der Bundesrepublik führte. Hätten die DDR-Behörden gleich einen Gerichtsmediziner bestellt und die Gesichtsverletzungen an der Leiche Burkerts hinreichend erklärt, hätte die Staatsanwaltschaft im westdeutschen Verden wohl keinen unnötigen Verdacht geschöpft; dann wären auch Spekulationen der westlichen Massenpresse über Faustschläge in der Zollbaracke unterblieben – Tatarennachrichten, die Bonns früherer Ständiger Vertreter in der DDR, Günter Gaus, auf den Plan riefen. Er warnte vor einer regelrechten Massenhysterie.

Die DDR-Presse und Moskauer Blätter schrieben von einer westdeutschen Hetz- und Verleumdungskampagne, von einem Rückfall in den Kalten Krieg und dem Versuch, die Beziehungen zwischen beiden deutschen Staaten durch Unterhöhlung des Transitabkommens »weit zurückzuwerfen«. Der Obduktionsbefund wies aus, daß ein Zungenbeinhorn beim Aufschlagen des Kopfes gebrochen war, was einige westliche Zeitungen als Beleg für »Folterungen« durch DDR-Zöllner werteten. Die DDR trat dem in einer Fernsehsondersendung mit einer Interview-Expertise des international renommierten Gerichtsmediziners Prokop entgegen, eines Österreichers, der in Ost-Berlin forensische Medizin lehrt. Er hatte den Unfallort besichtigt, mit den Zollbeamten gesprochen und nannte diese »gute, ruhige, sachliche Leute« – ein Wort, auf das zurückzukommen ist. Der Bruch eines Zungenbeinhorns, Unterkopfblutungen und Schleimhautrisse an der Lippe bezeichnete Prokop als ganz normal – jedenfalls dann, wenn ein Mensch durch plötzliches Herzversagen »zu ebener Erde umfällt«. Da gebe es eindeutige, charakteristische Zeichen: »Abschürfungen und Platzwunden,... unterhalb der Hutkrempe«.

Kaum schien der Fall Burkert vom Tisch, sorgte eine Meldung des DDR-amtlichen Allgemeinen Deutschen Nachrichtendienstes ADN vom 27. August dafür, daß die deutsch-deutsche Grenze als hochsensibles Thema auf der Tagesordnung von Bonn und Ostberlin blieb. Danach war der 68jährige Rentner Heinz Moldenhauer aus dem hessischen Philippsthal während einer »eingehenden Belehrung« durch DDR-Zollorgane nach einem Ohnmachtsanfall am Grenzübergang Wartha auf der Rückreise verstorben. Zwar zeigte sich, daß die DDR erste Lehren aus dem Fall Burkert gezogen hatte. War in Drewitz eine gerichtsmedizinische Untersuchung durch DDR-Experten versäumt worden, ließ die DDR den Leichnam Moldenhauers noch in der Nacht in der Medizinischen Akademie Erfurt obduzieren. Zumindest der Befund, »Herzversagen infolge schwerer Herzgefäßverkalkung bei Herzvergrößerung und alten Herzinfarkten«, wurde im Westen diesmal nicht angezweifelt, zumal ein Beamter der Bonner Ständigen Vertretung bei der DDR Gelegenheit hatte, umgehend mit dem Erfurter Ordinarius für Gerichtliche Medizin zu sprechen. Das war neu im Umgang miteinander. Die DDR-Spitze sah offenbar die Gefahr, daß dieser weitere Herztod in einer ihrer Grenzstationen sich zur ernsten Belastung der deutsch-deutschen Beziehungen auszuwachsen drohte. Deshalb war sie um äußerste Korrektheit bemüht. Aber die Wogen der Entrüstung schlugen im Westen dennoch hoch.

Was die SED »Ohnmachtsanfall« mit Todesfolge nach einer eingehenden Belehrung nannte, bezeichnete der deutschlandpolitische Sprecher der CDU/CSU-Bundestags-Fraktion, Lintner, als das Ergebnis massiver Einschüchterung und »systemimmanenter Unmenschlichkeit«; harmlose Besucher würden aus völlig nichtigem Anlaß in Angst und Schrecken versetzt. Heinrich Windelen, damals Bundesminister für innerdeutsche Beziehungen, hatte schon nach dem Fall Burkert erklärt, das Verhalten der DDR-Organe sei mit gutnachbarlichen Beziehungen nicht vereinbar; nun glaubte er sich bestätigt. Und der damalige CSU-Generalsekretär Wiesheu packte die Gelegenheit gleich beim Schopf: »Die große politische Wende«, forderte er, »habe vor allem auch die Wende in der Deutschlandpolitik und damit die Wende für Deutschland« zu umfassen. Das war ein deutlicher Versuch, aus diesen Zwischenfällen politisches Kapital zu schlagen. Helmut Kohl, seit Herbst 1982 Bundeskanzler, gerade erst im März mit überzeugender Mehrheit in Bundestagswahlen im Amt bestätigt worden, brütete in Bonn über dem Entwurf seiner zweiten Regierungserklärung. In der ersten, nach dem Abgang Helmut Schmidts, hatte er die Kontinuität der Deutschland- und der Ostpolitik versprochen. Doch auf dem rechten Flügel der eigenen Partei, bei den Stahlhelmern um Alfred Dregger und bei der bayrischen Schwesterpartei wuchs der Widerstand gegen die Fortführung einer Politik, die eindeutig die Handschrift der Sozialliberalen Koalition trug und von der CDU/CSU, als sie noch die Bänke der Opposition drückte, bis aufs Messer bekämpft worden war.

Schrille Töne kamen aber nicht nur von der Bonner Rechten, sie drangen auch aus dem großen grauen Haus, wie Ostberliner Volksmund das Gebäude nennt, das einst die Reichsbank Hjalmar Schachts beherbergte und heute der SED als Sitz ihres Zentralkomitees dient. In einer Stellungnahme, mit der er der westdeutschen Pressekampagne entgegentreten wollte, überzog Erich Honecker nun selbst, als er bundesdeutsche und Westberliner Autofahrer beschuldigte, sie glaubten, ermutigt durch unverantwortliche Berichte in »einschlägig bekannten westdeutschen Medien«, die Gesetze und Rechtsvorschriften der DDR mißachten zu können. Er sprach von Spionage und »subversiven Aktionen« gegen die DDR, für die »kriminelle Banden« die Transitwege mißbrauchten und hatte dabei zweifellos kommerzielle Fluchthilfe-Organisationen im Sinn. Unter den geringeren Delikten erwähnte er Alkohol am Steuer (in der DDR gilt die 0-Promillegrenze), Geschwindigkeitsüberschreitungen und »pöbelhafte Angriffe« gegen DDR-Volkspolizisten. Das alles war gedacht, sich schützend vor die eigenen Beamten und Funktionäre zu stellen und zugleich vor Mißbrauch und Belastungen des Transitabkommens zu warnen. Übrigens funktioniert dieses Abkommen, wie selbst kritische Kommentatoren im Westen zugeben, weitaus besser, als die Bonner CDU-Opposition beim Abschluß des Vertrages zwischen Bonn und Ostberlin 1971 es je für möglich gehalten hatte. Die »pöbelhaften Angriffe«, die Honecker beklagte, mochten ihre Ursache in den drakonischen Geldstrafen haben, mit denen Volkspolizei ausschließlich valutaträchtige Westreisende belegt, um der DDR-Staatskasse Devisen zuzuführen. Das zweierlei Maß bei der Ahndung von Geschwindigkeitssünden fordert Proteste geradezu heraus. Ansonsten unterstrich die Liste seiner Beschwerden nur den singulären Charakter, der die Beziehungen zwischen beiden deutschen Staaten im internationalen Vergleich auszeichnet, weil beide erst in allerjüngster Geschichte aus der Erbmasse eines gemeinsam deutschen Reichs hervorgegangen sind.

Dabei ist unbestritten, daß die Transitwege nach Berlin aus der Sicht der SED ein Sicherheitsrisiko darstellen, das besondere Überwachungsmaßnahmen rechtfertigt; aber nicht wenige dieser Risiken sind von der DDR selbst verschuldet. Wenn beispielsweise DDR-Bürger ihre westdeutschen Verwandten nicht treffen dürfen, weil die eigene Regierung solche Begegnungen einem Kontaktverbot unterwirft, das vielen davon Betroffenen unverständlich erscheint, werden eben Parkplätze und Raststätten an der Transitautobahn genützt, dennoch zueinanderzukommen und die aufgezwungene Sperre zu unterlaufen. So fand schließlich auch der Fall Rudolf Burkert seine Erklärung. Am 10. April 1983 hatte er auf der Raststätte »Magdeburger Börde« dem Ehemann seiner Cousine, die als DDR-Staatsbedienstete keine Beziehungen mit Bundesbürgern unterhalten darf, eine Damenarmbanduhr, ein Paar Stereolautsprecher und einige Auto-Sitzgurte übergeben. Der Große Bruder wacht immer und überall, sagt das Sprichwort, und es bewies wieder einmal seine Gültigkeit. Ein Spitzel von der Staatssicherheit hatte die Transaktion beobachtet und Burkerts Autonummer nach Drewitz gemeldet. Dort auf dem Weg nach Berlin angekommen, wurde er nach der offiziellen Darstellung der DDR um 13 Uhr einer Befragung unterzogen, in deren Verlauf er dann gegen 14.40 Uhr »unvermittelt von seinem Sitz fiel«.

Nach dem Transitabkommen hatten die DDR-Behörden zweifellos das Recht, den Transitreisenden Burkert zu verhören, denn mit der Übergabe von Gegenständen – geschätzter Wert: 3000 DM – hatte er gegen die Bestimmungen verstoßen. Die Erregung, die auch eine korrekt geführte Befragung hervorruft, kann bei entsprechender Prädisposition durchaus zu einem Herzinfarkt führen; aber unbeantwortet blieb bis heute die Frage, warum das Verhör in der Drewitzer Zollbaracke, das ja nur der Aufklärung eines Bagatellfalles diente, über eine Stunde währte.

Dem Rentner Heinz Moldenhauer aus Philippsthal wurde eine Lappalie zum Verhängnis, als er, von einem Tagesausflug in die DDR zurückkehrend, an der Grenzstation Wartha eintraf: Die auf der Zollerklärung angegebenen Geldbeträge stimmten mit der mitgeführten Summe nicht überein. Offenbar hatte er seine Geldbörse öffnen, Scheine und Münzen vorzählen müssen, eine an anderen Grenzen unbekannte, kleinkarierte Art der Zollkontrolle, die das Verbot der Ausfuhr von DDR-Mark in den Westen verhindern soll. Denkbar ein Irrtum, der dem immerhin bald 70jährigen beim Ausfüllen des Formulars unterlaufen war; denkbar auch, daß er Ostgeld, unzulänglich versteckt, im Auftrag von Verwandten mitführte, um es im Westen zu tauschen und dafür ersehnte Westware zu schicken; möglich weiterhin, daß er Westgeld, dessen Besitz DDR-Bürgern ja nicht untersagt ist, mitnehmen sollte, etwa um Ersatzteile für einen geschenkten, uralten Volkswagen zu besorgen oder um es für Bekannte, die einen Ausreiseantrag laufen hatten, auf ein Konto zu legen. Aus der Sicht von DDR-Bürgern sind das Freundschaftsdienste, die ein »Wessi« den »Ossis« wie selbstverständlich schuldet. Daß sie als Zollvergehen geahndet werden, ist für viele Bundesbürger, die Urlaub im westlichen Ausland machen, schwer nachzuvollziehen. Zwischen Ländern mit frei konvertierbarer Währung sind derlei Delikte unbekannt. Da haben dann die wenigsten Verständnis, daß sie ausgerechnet an einer Grenze legitim sein sollen, die durch ein Volk geht und immer noch Familien trennt.

Warum breite ich diese alten Geschichten so ausführlich aus? Findet sich, wer so kritisch diese Grenze beschreibt, nicht automatisch in der Gesellschaft von Reaktionären und Kalten Kriegern wieder, mit denen er sonst nichts zu tun haben will? Die beste Antwort ist eine Gegenfrage. Wollen einige Linke und Liberale, die aus lauter Sorge um Frieden und Entspannung die Dinge nicht mehr beim Namen nennen, vielleicht nur ihre Ruhe haben vor der lästigen deutschen Frage? Sehen sie bewußt weg, weil sie die Illusion nötig haben, die DDR sei besser als sie ist, damit sie sich mit dem Status quo arrangieren können – auf Dauer und ohne schlechtes Gewissen?

Als »gute, ruhige und sachliche Leute«, als Männer »mit Herz und Gemüt« charakterisierte der österreichische Gerichtsmediziner Prokop die Zollbeamten, die Rudolf Burkert in Drewitz in ihre Grenzbaracke gebeten hatten. Diese Worte kamen mir in Erinnerung, als ich sah, wie einer der blaugrau uniformierten Mitarbeiter des DDR-Zolls am Grenzübergang Heinestraße einen Wagen aus der Warteschlange herauswinkte, den Fahrer aufforderte, sämtliche Gepäckstücke in eine Baracke zu schleppen und mit dem zum Filzen Auserwählten längere Zeit verschwand. Würde er sich hinter verschlossenen Türen so korrekt wie draußen verhalten? Schafft allein die Tatache, daß sich ein Reisender dieser besonderen Durchleuchtung unterziehen muß jene »Situation der Angst und Spannung«, von der Franz Josef Strauß nach dem Herztod in der Drewitzer Baracke gesagt hatte, daß sie unerträglich sei? Strauß hatte seinerzeit polternd von Mord gesprochen und die DDR bezichtigt, sie verstoße durch den Ausbau der »Schandgrenze, die deutsches Land auf 1393 Kilometer Länge brutal durchschneidet«, gegen den Geist von Helsinki, denn sie stelle »Abschottung über alle Entspannungsbeschlüsse«. Später korrigierte er sich leicht, ohne sich in der Sache zurückzunehmen: »Ich habe immer gewußt, daß es sich nicht um Mord im strafrechtlichen Sinn des Wortes handelt, aber nach meiner Überzeugung liegt vorsätzliche Körperverletzung mit Todesfolge vor.«

Diese scharfe öffentliche Kritik am DDR-Grenzregime hin-

derte Erich Honecker freilich nicht, mit dem in den DDR-
Medien über Jahrzehnte als »Fürst der Finsternis« porträtier-
ten Bayern ins Geschäft zu kommen – nicht nur über einen
Kredit in Milliardenhöhe, sondern auch über den Umgangston an der DDR-Grenze. Strauß schildert das so: »Kurze Zeit
nach dieser scharfen Kritik kam es zu einem Gespräch mit
einem hohen Beamten der DDR, der offensichtlich von seinem Chef beauftragt war. Im Mittelpunkt dieses Gespräches
standen die Verhältnisse an der Grenze, die nach meiner Meinung gründlich geändert werden mußten... Beim zweiten
Gespräch, das kurze Zeit darauf erfolgte, wurde ich gefragt, ob
sich an der Grenze etwas geändert hätte. Auf Grund der uns
vorliegenden Meldungen, auch der bayrischen Grenzpolizei,
konnte ich, wie ich es bereits mehrmals in der Öffentlichkeit
getan habe, bestätigen, daß hier eine Wende zum Erfreulichen
eingetreten sei.« Strauß zitierte die »Süddeutsche Zeitung«:
»Es heißt dort, daß ein Sprecher des Bayrischen Grenzpolizei-
präsidiums in München erklärt habe, die Grenzkontrollen der
DDR seien nun schon seit etwa sechs Wochen freundlicher
und großzügiger. Das gesamte Verhalten der DDR-Beamten
sei lockerer und viel freundlicher geworden. Man müsse an-
nehmen, daß hier von höchster Stelle entsprechende Anweisung gegeben worden sei. Ein drittes Gespräch dann über das
Thema Kredit fand wieder einige Zeit später statt.«

Nicht nur der Form halber machte auch Strauß eine klare
Trennung zwischen dem von ihm eingefädelten Milliarden-
kredit und dem veränderten, gelockerten, freundlicheren Verhalten der DDR-Grenzbeamten, das ab Juni 1983 schwerlich
zu übersehen war. Die DDR achtet nun einmal peinlich darauf, nicht als käuflich oder erpreßbar zu erscheinen. Wenn
auch manches valutaträchtige Geschäft in humanitären Fragen die puritanisch-strenge Fassade löchrig aussehen läßt,
kann es doch keinen Zweifel geben, daß sich die SED-Führung
bei zentralen politischen Positionen nichts abhandeln läßt.
Eher ist man bereit, den Gürtel enger zu schnallen, als auch
nur ein Jota der eigenen Überzeugung aufzugeben. Die Wech-
selwirkung zwischen dem Kredit und der von Honecker be-

fohlenen Offensive des Lächelns an der Grenze stellt sich deshalb komplizierter dar. Wenn in einem Zeitraum von zwei Wochen gleich zwei westdeutsche Transitreisende bei Verhören wegen Bagatellverstößen in DDR-Zollbaracken tot zusammenbrechen und die öffentliche Entrüstung in der Bundesrepublik dazu führt, daß der rechte Flügel der neuen Bonner Koalition die angekündigte Kontinuität in der Deutschlandpolitik in Frage stellt, ist dies für das SED-Politbüro Grund genug, die »eingehenden Belehrungen« der eigenen »Organe« zu hinterfragen. Schließlich stand auch Erich Honeckers Politik des Dialogs auf dem Spiel – der Versuch, Friedens- und Gesprächsbereitschaft zwischen beiden deutschen Staaten zu demonstrieren, der Sprachlosigkeit zum Trotz, die damals zwischen den Supermächten herrschte. Um diese Politik abzusichern ist die SED bereit, im Gespräch selbst dem schärfsten politischen Gegner zuzuhören, wenn er erklärt, was diesen Dialog aus seiner Sicht beschwert. Und wenn es machbar ist, werden auch Konsequenzen gezogen. Die Grenzbeamten anzuweisen, sich höflicher und entgegenkommender zu geben und westliche Reisende schneller abzufertigen, war eine Konzession in der Form, nicht in der Substanz. Da wo es ans Eingemachte ging, ans Grenzregime selbst, an den Rechten und Zuständigkeiten der DDR auf den Transitwegen, wurde nicht das Geringste verändert. Übrigens dient diese Maßnahme bis heute dem wohlverstandenen Eigeninteresse der SED, tragen doch freundliche DDR-Grenzer dazu bei, Feindbilder abzubauen und den ersten Schock zu lindern, den der Staat der regierenden deutschen Kommunisten bei der Einfahrt in die Grenzsperranlagen beim Besucher auslöst. Sie kostete nichts und sie brachte viel. Selbst der später erfolgte Abbau der Selbstschußautomaten bedeutete keine Minderung der Sicherheit, denn er wurde durch den Ausbau der elektronischen Überwachung im tiefgestaffelten Vorfeld wettgemacht.

Der entscheidende Gewinn aber war, daß die »Operation Lächeln« das entsprechende Klima schuf, das es der neuen Koalition in Bonn ermöglichte, dem von der DDR seit Herbst 1982 gewünschten Kredit zuzustimmen. Daß diese Milliarde ausgerechnet durch Franz Josef Strauß vermittelt wurde, erwies sich bald als unschätzbare Dreingabe, denn dadurch wurde der wichtigste Gegner der sozialliberalen Ostpolitik, der ein halbes Jahr zuvor noch die Wende in der Deutschlandpolitik gefordert hatte, in die Politik der Kontinuität, zu der sich Kohl und Genscher verpflichteten, eingebunden. Der mächtige Chef der CSU, so ein Kommentar aus dem »großen grauen Haus«, saß nun mit im Boot, eine ernstzunehmende Opposition gegen die neue alte Ostpolitik war damit in Bonn nicht mehr zu erwarten. Da war es dann kein Wunder, daß Erich Honecker den Bayern wie einen Staatsgast behandelte, als dieser zum ersten Mal die DDR besuchte. Nicht genug damit, daß der SED-Chef Franz Josef Strauß an der Staatsgrenze durch seinen Kreditunterhändler Schalck-Golodkowski – er ist Staatssekretär im DDR-Außenministerium – persönlich begrüßen ließ, ihm eine dunkelblaue DDR-Staatskarosse der Marke Volvo zur Verfügung stellte und gleich die ganze Familie Strauß zum Mittagessen in sein Jagdschloß Hubertusstock lud. Strauß durfte, anders als Helmut Schmidt, der 1981 auf Hubertusstock am Werbellinsee mit Honecker konferierte, auf seiner Reise in Erfurt und Dresden ein »Bad in der Menge« nehmen, Hände schütteln und Petitionen empfangen. Schließlich wurde dem Bayern die besondere Gunst gewährt, von Erfurt mit dem eigens aus München eingeflogenen Privatflugzeug zurück in die bayrische Heimat zu starten, Strauß selbst am Steuerknüppel und via diretissima, wie seine Umgebung stolz verlauten ließ – auf direktem Wege also, beinahe Luftlinie. Einen solchen Flug von Deutschland nach Deutschland hatte es nach 1945 noch nie gegeben. Ganz andere Bilder sind vom Besuch Helmut Schmidts in der Barlach-Stadt Güstrow in Erinnerung geblieben. Schmidt, der als Barlachverehrer gekommen war, wurde von Polizeikordons und Spalieren der Kunstlederjacken von der Sicherheit empfangen. Angst vor den spontanen Gefühlen der eigenen Bürger trieb die DDR dazu, sich von ihrer häßlichsten, der militaristischen Seite zu zeigen. Doch zugegeben: Schmidt war bei der Masse der Deutschen in der anderen Republik ungleich beliebter als

Strauß, die Gefahr einer spontanen Massenkundgebung für den westdeutschen Kanzler, nach dem Muster der »Willy, Willy«-Rufe beim Brandt-Stoph-Treffen in Erfurt, mithin höher zu veranschlagen als bei dem »Privatreisenden«, der aus Bayern gekommen war. Ideologie hin, Marxismus-Leninismus her, die DDR-Führung hatte einmal mehr bewiesen, daß sich die deutschen Kommunisten ebenso exzellent auf Realpolitik verstehen wie der populistische Konservative aus München. Zwar hatten Honecker und Strauß anschließend einige Vermittlungsschwierigkeiten gegenüber der jeweiligen Basis. Viele treuegläubige SED-Mitglieder rieben sich erstaunt die Augen, als sie auf der Titelseite des parteiamtlichen »Neuen Deutschland« »ihren Erich« in trautem tête à tête mit dem »Fürsten der Finsternis« abgebildet sahen; und am rechten Rand der CSU artikulierte sich Unverständnis. Doch der Deal war perfekt. Strauß, einst Anwalt eines Kurswechsels der Bonner Politik gegenüber Ostberlin, hatte die eigene deutschlandpolitische Wende vollzogen. Zur Erklärung berief er sich in einer Pressekonferenz auf die Maxime Konrad Adenauers: Im Grundsatz unnachgiebig, in anderen Fragen pragmatisch zu handeln. Was die Wahl seiner Mittel betreffe, sei er halt flexibler geworden. Die SED-Spitze verzichtete auf eine eigene Kommentierung und zitierte stattdessen aus dem westdeutschen Blätterwald, was aus ihrer Sicht die richtige Deutung für die eigene Bevölkerung war: Daß Honecker auf einen langen Zeitraum mit einer von der CDU geführten Bundesregierung in Bonn rechne und daß die DDR in der kritischen Phase der Raketenstationierung den Kontakt auch zu entschiedenen politischen Gegnern suche.

Als Honecker dann schließlich die Bundesrepublik besuchte, empfangen mit DDR-Hymne und militärischem Zeremoniell, war es der bayrische Ministerpräsident Strauß, der den DDR-Staatsgast mit der stattlichsten Polizeieskorte ehrte. Zuvor hatte Honecker im saarländischen Neuenkirchen etwas bis dahin für die regierenden deutschen Kommunisten Unvorstellbares getan: Er hatte eingeräumt, daß die Grenzen »nicht so sind, wie sie sein sollten«. Doch zu Jubel war deshalb kein

Anlaß, denn den gegenwärtigen Zustand fand er »nur allzu verständlich«, weil beide Staaten fest in gegensätzlichen Bündnissystemen verankert seien. Was er an Besserung in Aussicht stellte, klang vage: Vielleicht werde im Zuge beiderseitiger friedlicher Zusammenarbeit einmal der Tag kommen, »an dem Grenzen uns nicht trennen, sondern Grenzen uns vereinen, so wie uns die Grenze zwischen der Deutschen Demokratischen Republik und der Volksrepublik Polen vereint«. Reisen von Polen in die DDR und umgekehrt unterliegen dem Paß- und Visumzwang. Vielleicht wollte Honecker den Bonnern mit diesem Vergleich auch zu verstehen geben, daß die Bundesrepublik zuvor ihre Position in der Staatsbürgerschaftsfrage zu ändern habe. Immerhin: Die Nummer 1 hatte sich zum Grenzregime eingelassen, das der SED als Symbol der Souveränität ihres Staates als so sakrosankt gilt, daß sich jede Diskussion mit anderen darüber bislang von selbst verbot.

Greifbar dagegen waren die Ergebnisse des Straußschen Milliardenhandels, die ich bald am Grenzübergang Heinestraße beobachten konnte. Zwar änderte sich nichts an der üblichen Routine. Für die Masse der Reisenden hieß es weiter »Motorhaube hoch« und »Kofferraum auf«, wie bisher wurden bei der Einreise Westzeitungen beschlagnahmt, bei der Ausreise Gepäckstücke nach Antiquitäten und Wertsachen durchwühlt. Vor allem blieb es beim gewohnten Anblick, den DDR-Zöllner bieten, wenn sie halb ins Auto kriechen, um den Rücksitz auf versteckte Personen oder Schmuggelgut zu untersuchen – da stellt die sozialistische Obrigkeit, fast schon provozierend, nur ihr Hinterteil zur Schau. Aber der Umgangston war entspannter, die hölzernen Marionetten hatten sich in Menschen verwandelt, die nun auch mal einen Scherz über das Wetter wagten. Wurde die häßliche Grenze, die niemals zu akzeptieren die westdeutschen Politiker nach dem 13. August 1961 fast unisono geschworen hatten, dadurch ein Stück selbstverständlicher? Manchmal stellte ich mir vor, man hätte in Warschau versucht, ein solches Bauwerk quer durch die Stadt zu errichten. Die Polen werden uns ja in Sonntagsreden und

nationalgesonnenen Leitartikeln häufig als Vorbild beschwo-
ren, weil sie, geteilt und besetzt, über 150 Jahre zäh und
unbeirrt am Ziel der nationalen Freiheit festgehalten haben.
Andrzej Szczypiorski, ein Pole, schrieb nach einem Besuch
Berlins: »Es bedurfte deutscher Geduld, deutscher Disziplin,
Achtung vor dem Recht und Mangel an Phantasie, damit die
Mauer so viele Jahre überdauerte, damit diese geistige Absur-
dität akzeptiert wurde. Ich stellte mir eine Mauer vor, die
Warschaus Straßen trennt, und zuckte die Achseln. In Warschau wäre das einfach unmöglich.« Hätten die Polen eine
solche Mauer also schon am ersten Tag, als die Kampfgruppen
aufmarschierten und Pioniere Drähte spannten, durch einen
Volksaufstand auf beiden Seiten hinweggefegt? Haben wir
Deutschen uns unserer Schafsgeduld zu schämen, mit der wir
uns in diese brutale Teilung fügen? Oder ist unsere Passivität
zu rühmen, weil wir, nach den Verheerungen, die der deutsche Exzeß in Nationalismus im letzten Kriege angerichtet
hat, eine durch Schuld bestimmte Einsicht entwickelt haben,
uns in die Teilung zu schicken – um des Friedens willen?

Auch der erste Kanzler der Bundesrepublik war nicht bereit, die Mauer hinzunehmen. Doch als ihn die schlimme
Nachricht aus Berlin erreichte, führte Konrad Adenauer un-
gerührt seinen Wahlkampf weiter. Er mied den Anblick dieser
Großbaustelle, die eine Kernthese seines politischen Programms – daß Westintegration, Mitgliedschaft der Bundesrepublik in der NATO und eine Politik der Stärke die Wiedervereinigung bringen würde – als die Lebenslüge der 50er Jahre
entlarvte. Zur Begründung führte er später an, er habe die
Stimmung in Berlin nicht unnötig anheizen wollen. Weil ihr
die demokratische Legitimation fehle, hatte er sich auch stets
geweigert, die andere deutsche Republik anzuerkennen, die
als Antwort auf die Gründung der Bundesrepublik entstanden
war. Nicht ein Jahr würde die DDR überstehen, orakelte ein
westdeutscher Leitartikler; noch vor ihrem ersten Jahrestag,
dem 7. Oktober 1950, werde dieses »Ulbricht-Regime« wegen
der Ablehnung durch die eigenen Bürger in sich zusammenbrechen. Auch wenn das übertrieben formuliert war, der Te-

nor entsprach einer im Westen weit verbreiteten Überzeugung, daß die Lebenserwartung der östlichen Gegengründung gering zu veranschlagen sei. Da wurde nicht nur die Macht und Entschlossenheit der Sowjetunion unterschätzt, die unter schweren Opfern errungene geostrategische Position im Herzen Europas niemals aufs Spiel zu setzen. Auch der Kampfgeist, das Können und das Durchsetzungsvermögen deutscher Kommunisten wurden zu gering erachtet, die 1945 im sowjetisch besetzten Teil Deutschlands angetreten waren, auf den Trümmern der alten eine neue und, wie sie fest glaubten, bessere Gesellschaftsordnung zu errichten. Gestützt auf die sowjetische Militäradministration regierten sie ohne demokratische Diskussion und gegen die Mehrheit der eigenen Bevölkerung, aber ihre Indoktrinations- und Umerziehungsdiktatur schuf heranwachsende Kader von Überzeugten und Treuen im Glauben, auf die sie sich bald verlassen konnten. Im Westen mißverstand man Wilhelm Pieck und Walter Ulbricht oft als bloße Kollaborateure der Besatzungsmacht. Es war Nikita Chruschtschow, der auf bekannt drastische Weise diese Fehleinschätzung korrigierte. Der bundesdeutschen Delegation, die 1955 mit Adenauer nach Moskau gekommen war, sagte er: »An der Entstehung des Marxismus-Leninismus sind auch Sie, die Deutschen ›schuld‹. Marx und Engels sind doch in Deutschland geboren. Sie haben den Brei angerührt, also löffeln Sie ihn aus.« Gegenüber einer wenige Tage nach Adenauer angereisten DDR-Delegation gebrauchte er eine knappere und griffigere Formel: »Die Deutschen haben das Bett des Marxismus gemacht, und jetzt liegen sie darin.«

In der Tat: Mußte für einen Mann wie Chruschtschow, der im Marxismus die beste aller deutschen Traditionen sah, nicht selbstverständlich sein, daß auch im Lande von Karl Marx mit dem Aufbau des Sozialismus begonnen wurde? Fragt sich nur, was »Charlie M.« beim Anblick dieser Grenze gedacht hätte – nicht nur, weil er und sein Freund »Frederick« engagierte Großdeutsche waren, die schon die Teilung der Deutschen durch Preußen und Österreich als nationales Unglück beklagten. Ins Bett des realexistierenden Sozialismus hätten sich

Karl Marx und Friedrich Engels gewiß nicht legen mögen, dazu waren sie, die ihr Leben lang gegen Zensoren und für Meinungsfreiheit kämpften, viel zu westeuropäisch geprägt.

Grenzgänger-Routine ließ nach und nach eine gewisse Vertrautheit aufkommen mit den Torwächtern der DDR, die sich als »Krönung der bisherigen deutschen Geschichte« versteht. Unter der Mannschaft in der Heinrich-Heine-Straße gab es über die Jahre nur wenig Veränderungen. Auch wenn kaum mehr als die nötigsten Worte gewechselt wurden, man lernte einander kennen, wobei der Grenzer stets im Vorteil war: Er wußte Namen und Daten, ich blieb auf Rangabzeichen angewiesen und suchte, in Gesichtern zu lesen. Doch wie anders Gesichter ohne die dazugehörige Uniform aussehen, erfuhr ich während eines FDJ-Jugendfestivals in Berlin. Im Lustgarten, vor der prachtvollen Kulisse von Schinkels Altem Museum, stieß ich zwischen Würstchenbuden und Bierzelten auf einen vermeintlich alten Bekannten im zivilen Freizeithemd, ging auf ihn zu und sagte: »Ihren Namen habe ich leider nicht im Kopf, aber wir kennen uns doch aus Halle.« »Irrtum«, erwiderte der Angesprochene und lachte etwas verklemmt; »wir sehen uns fast täglich an der Grenze.« Sprach's und machte auf dem Absatz kehrt. Private Westkontakte sind Zollbeamten und Grenzsoldaten untersagt.

Die älteren Grenzoffiziere kann man sich gut im Meisterkittel am Fließband, als Brigadiere oder als biedere Handwerker vorstellen. Es sind Männer der Aufbaugeneration meist proletarischer Herkunft und mit fundierter politischer Überzeugung, die man als Freiwillige für den Schutz des Sozialismus gewann. Erst in jüngster Zeit dienen, wenn auch besonders gesiebte Wehrpflichtige in den Grenztruppen, die der frühere DDR-Verteidigungsminister Heinz Hoffmann einmal als die »Garde« der Nationalen Volksarmee bezeichnete. Daß man einander inzwischen gut kannte, gaben die Älteren durch einen freundlich-rauhen Kumpelton zu erkennen, doch blieben sie dabei jederzeit um eine angestrengte Sachlichkeit bemüht. Wenn ich auch sicher war, daß sie abends vor dem Westfernsehen saßen und damit auch unsere kritische DDR-

Berichterstattung verfolgten, verkniffen sie sich doch jeden Kommentar. Nur einmal, nach einer Reportage über Zusammenstöße zwischen Rockfans und Volkspolizei Pfingsten 1986 Unter den Linden, durchbrach ein rundlicher Hauptmann das Schweigeritual und meinte: »Na, gestern mal ordentlich auf den Putz gehauen, was?« Doch klang das eher launig denn vorwurfsvoll.

Gemessen an den biederen Grenzern der älteren Generation wirken die jüngeren souveräner, lockerer und auch gewandter. Das ist kein Wunder, denn die DDR investiert viel in ihre Elite der Zuverlässigen. Jeder angehende Offizier der Grenztruppen muß seine Ausbildung mit einem Studium an der Offiziers-Hochschule Rosa Luxemburg in Suhl abschließen. Wer dort zum Leutnant befördert wird, hat automatisch das Diplom eines Gesellschaftswissenschaftlers in der Tasche. Sie blicken neugieriger und forschender, die Grenzer der jüngeren Generation, manchmal blitzt sogar ein Funke von Ironie in ihren Augen auf, und der eine oder andere signalisiert auf die merkwürdigste Weise, daß er Anteil am Leben von uns Grenzgängern nimmt. »Ihr Mann ist aber noch nicht durch«, sagte ein blutjunger Fähnrich einmal zu meiner Frau, als sie in Richtung Ostberlin über die Grenze fuhr. Eine Viertelstunde später ließ mich derselbe Scherzbold wissen: »Ihr Frauchen ist schon zu Hause!« Ich frage mich noch heute: War ich in seinen Augen nun das Hundchen oder das Herrchen? Auf jeden Fall hieß es: Husch, heim ins Körbchen – dies blieb der Gipfel an Vertrautheit in fünf Jahren Grenzgängerdasein.

2. Zwischen Überzeugung und Anpassung: Leben im realen Sozialismus

»Wir haben nun einmal das Pech, hier zu leben. Wer nicht mit den Wölfen heult, der wird getreten.« Dieser Satz erklärt, warum viele DDR-Bürger sich in einem ungeliebten Staat einrichten, und er bestätigt ein im Westen weitverbreitetes Klischee über das Leben im realen Sozialismus zwischen Elbe und Oder. Er stimmt für die, die so denken, und das mögen nicht wenige sein; daß sie eine klare Mehrheit bilden, scheint mir jedoch zweifelhaft.

Der ihn äußerte, ein Kürschnermeister, der im Vogtland ein privates Pelzgeschäft betreibt, war stolzer Besitzer eines Schnauferls vom Typ Elite S 18, Baujahr 1925 und nahm an der 13. Veteranenrallye der DDR in Dresden teil. Sein Elite-Auto brachte Kunde aus jener sagenhaften Zeit, da man in Sachsen nicht technisch veraltete Trabis, sondern prachtvolle Karossen baute, »sächsische Edelfabrikate«, wie die Hersteller in Brand-Erbisdorf bei Dresden ihre Produkte priesen, die den Mercedes-Automobilen der Schwaben ebenbürtig waren. Noch mancher Schnauferlbesitzer in Sachsen erinnert sich voller Stolz, daß in einem solchen »Elite« Reichspräsident Hindenburg einmal eine Parade der Reichswehr abgenommen hat.

Die in der anderen deutschen Republik alte Autos als Hobby pflegen, sind ein kleiner, für DDR-Verhältnisse besonders feiner Verein. Es sind ihrer nicht mehr als 1700, sie leben verstreut in der ganzen Republik, und doch kennt fast jeder jeden. Ihre Rallyes gleichen deshalb großen Familienfesten. Kraftfahrzeugmeister und Schlosser, aber auch private Handwerker der verschiedensten Branchen sind nicht zufällig überproportional vertreten. Die meisten rekonstruieren ihre Schnauferl selbst; doch wer sich in der DDR den Luxus leisten kann, den Aufbau eines Dixie vom Jahrgang 1928 oder eines ob seiner Stromlinie und des Art-Déco-Designs vielbewunderten Adler Typ 10 (genannt Autobahn) als Auftrag zu vergeben, der muß über begehrte Ware verfügen, mit der seltene Ersatzteile zu ertauschen oder Freizeitmechaniker zu locken sind.

Die Schnauferlbesitzer sind im Allgemeinen Deutschen Motor Verein, dem ADAC der DDR, organisiert, ihr Sport blieb von Politik, die sonst alles durchdringt, weitgehend verschont. Sie bilden, wenn man so will, eine Sportnische, und die Mechaniker und Handwerker, LPG-Bauern und Akademiker, die sich in ihr zusammengefunden haben, äußern nicht selten ketzerische Gedanken. »Einige heucheln, einige haben eine Meinung, die meisten machen es fürs Geld«, beschied mich der Fahrer eines 1930 in Stralsund gebauten Stöver. Es war seine Antwort auf die Frage, die mich die ganzen Jahre in der DDR beschäftigte und die ich mir und anderen immer wieder aufs neue stellte, ohne zu einem schlüssigen Ergebnis zu gelangen: Wie viele derer, die sich für die SED oder für den Aufbau des realen Sozialismus engagieren, sind hundertprozentig überzeugt, bereit, auch in schwierigen Zeiten ohne Zögern und Zaudern für die Sache einzustehen? Bei den meisten Funktionären der älteren Generation, die noch die Spätphase der Weimarer Republik erlebten und die Hitlerzeit im KZ oder in der Emigration durchlitten, widerlegten die Opfer, die sie brachten, alle Zweifel. Doch die jüngeren machten nicht Jahre des politischen Kampfes und der Verfolgung durch, sie kennen ihren sozialistischen Staat und die Partei ausschließlich in der Rolle eines Inhabers der politischen Macht. Wie weit läßt sich Mitgliedschaft, die auch Machtteilhabe bedeutet, da von der Karriere trennen, für die das Parteibuch oft die unerläßliche Voraussetzung ist? Einigen wollte mein Schnauferlbesitzer »eine Meinung«, also politische Überzeugung zugestehen, etwa ebenso vielen unterstellte er, daß sie um der Karriere willen zu Gesinnungsheuchlern geworden seien. Von den meisten glaubte er, sie seien Anpasser, wie es sie in jeder Gesellschaft gibt, Menschen, die vorgegebene politisch-gesellschaftliche Rahmenbedingungen nicht hinterfragten, sondern akzeptierten, um das für sie persönlich Beste daraus zu machen. War Hermann Tröger, Brigadier im Braunkohle-Tagebau Nochten im Senftenberger Revier, einer von ihnen?

»Ich kann mich eigentlich nicht beklagen«, gab mir der Brigadier in einem Interview zu Protokoll. »Ich habe eine schöne Wohnung und außerdem einen Freizeitbungalow. Ich hab 'nen Betrieb, für den ich schon jahrelang arbeite; ich verdiene gutes Geld und bin eigentlich ganz zufrieden. Mag sein, daß es Menschen gibt, die besser leben, aber ich fühle mich eigentlich wohl.« Als ich ihn traf, war Tröger Schichtleiter von 40 bis 45 Bergleuten und Technikern einer Brigade, wie man solche Schichtkollektive in der DDR nennt, und für den reibungslosen Betrieb eines 600 Meter langen, 70 Meter hohen, 24 000 Tonnen schweren Förderbrückenverbandes verantwortlich. Die drei Bagger dieses Verbandes schaufeln rund um die Uhr in 24 Stunden bis zu 350 000 Tonnen Abraum über der Braunkohle frei, die in 40 bis 90 Metern Tiefe liegt. Trögers Aufgabe war, von seiner Kommandozentrale auf der Brücke die Fahrweise seines technischen, auf 900 Rädern laufenden Ungetüms festzulegen, die maximale Leistung zu fahren, die geologischen Gegebenheiten zu berücksichtigen und bei extremen Wetterbedingungen wie Gewitterstürmen oder starkem Frost stets auf die Standsicherheit zu achten. Das bedeutete eine Menge Verantwortung, denn ein solcher Förderbrückenverband stellt einen Investitionswert von 250 Millionen Mark dar. Da ohne Kohle fast nichts läuft in der DDR-Wirtschaft, hängt viel von dem fachmännischen Können und der Zuverlässigkeit solcher Brigadiere ab. Als zum Jahreswechsel 1978/79 das Wetter in wenigen Minuten umschlug und Regen sich bei einbrechender Kälte bis zu 20 Grad minus plötzlich in Schnee und Eis verwandelte, gingen nicht nur in der Lausitz und im Bezirk Cottbus die Lichter aus. Der Großtagebau Nochten ist Hauptlieferant des Kraftwerks Boxberg, des größten Wärmekraftwerks Europas, das auf Braunkohle-basis betrieben wird. Mit 3600 Megawatt liefert es 16 Prozent des DDR-Strombedarfs und verbraucht in 24 Stunden 85 000 Tonnen Rohbraunkohle.

Tröger, notierte ich im Herbst 1983, wohnt in Schleife oder Slepe, einem Dorf im Bezirk Cottbus, wo man, wie das zweisprachige Ortsschild am Eingang verkündet, die Sprache der sorbischen Minderheit ein wenig künstlich am Leben erhält. Er zählt zu jenen, die sich eingerichtet haben in der anderen deutschen Republik und dem gemächlichen, oft beschaulichen Tempo des »sozialistischen Gangs« die angenehmen Seiten abgewinnen. Er hat keine Sorge um den Arbeitsplatz, er fühlt sich nicht durch täglichen Konkurrenzkampf ausgelaugt und er weiß, daß mehr Stufen auf der Leiter des Aufstiegs zu nehmen, für ihn kaum lohnen würde. In der Lohntüte hat er 1300 Mark netto im Monat, seine Frau verdient halbtags mit. Für die Miete seiner Zweieinhalb-Zimmer-Werkswohnung in einem Neubau zahlt er 34 Mark im Monat, und wie viele Bürger der DDR nennt er eine Datsche sein eigen, von der er etwas vollmundig als seinem Bungalow spricht. Sie liegt an einem Baggersee, und wann immer das Wetter schön ist und seine Zeit es erlaubt, erholt sich der Brigadier aus dem Tagebau Nochten hier mit Frau Martha und Sohn René. Tröger, dem klassischen Heimwerker, ist die Datsche nicht nur Stolz, sondern auch Hobby. Fünf Jahre hat er an ihr gebastelt und gebaut. Das Grundstück wurde für 23 Mark pro Jahr auf 99 Jahre gepachtet. Für den ersten neuen Trabant, den er vor drei Jahren ausgeliefert bekam, legte er, inklusive Extras, rund 10 000 Mark auf den Tisch. Um die zehn- bis zwölfjährige Wartezeit bis zur Lieferung des nächsten Neuwagens abzukürzen, hat sich seine Frau in die Bestell- und Warteliste eingetragen, so daß die Trögers damit rechnen können, alle fünf bis sechs Jahre einen neuen Wagen zu erhalten.

Da der sozialistische Staat treue Dienste mit einer Flut von Auszeichnungen lohnt, gleicht Trögers Bergmannsuniform der Ordensbrust eines sowjetischen Generals. Gleich fünfmal erhielt der Brigadier den Ehrentitel »Aktivist der sozialistischen Arbeit«, einmal sogar den eines »verdienten Aktivi-

sten«, der pro Jahr nicht mehr als 500 oder 600 Produktions-
arbeitern in der ganzen Republik zuerkannt wird und mit
einer Geldprämie von 1000 Mark verbunden ist. Ebenfalls
mehrfach errang er den Titel »Kollektiv der sozialistischen
Arbeit« (verbunden mit einer Anerkennungszahlung an das
Kollektiv), der zwar nur einmal verliehen, aber im Rahmen
des »sozialistischen Wettbewerbs« verteidigt und durch besondere Leistungen Jahr für Jahr bestätigt werden kann. Die
Inflation von Orden, Ehrenzeichen und Verdienstmedaillen,
die sowjetischem Vorbild entlehnt ist und inzwischen jeden
Berufszweig überschwemmt, führte zu Titeln, die für westliche Leser den Reiz unfreiwilliger Komik haben. Da gibt es
neben dem »Verdienten Mitarbeiter der Staatssicherheit«
(Prämie: 5000 Mark) auch »verdiente Züchter«, »verdiente
Erfinder«, »verdiente Tierärzte«, »verdiente Eisenbahner«,
»verdiente Mitarbeiter des Finanzwesens«; ja selbst wer es
nur zur Putzfrau oder zum Hausmeister bringt, hat Aussicht,
als »verdienter Werktätiger des Bereichs der haus- und kom-
munalwirtschaftlichen Dienstleistungen« eine Spange für die
Brust und 5000 Mark für Sparbuch oder Portemonnaie zu
erhalten. Aus der Sicht des politischen Systems, das mit solchen Auszeichnungen besondere ökonomische, soziale oder
politische Leistungen honoriert, nehmen die Ausgezeichneten
eine herausgehobene Stellung ein und verfügen über besonderes Sozialprestige. Als Tröger mir die einzelnen Medaillen
und Schnallen erklärte, die an seiner Uniformjacke prangten,
klang deutlich Stolz in seiner Stimme mit. »Hier geht es weiter mit Auszeichnungen der Kampfgruppe für treue Dienste,
10 und 15 Jahre«, erläuterte er, »das ist die Verdienstmedaille
der Kohleindustrie, und als letzte Auszeichnung habe ich den
Orden ›Banner der Arbeit‹ erhalten.« Den gibt es laut Verlei-
hungsurkunde für »hervorragende und langjährige Leistungen bei der Stärkung und Festigung der DDR, insbesondere
für hohe Arbeitsergebnisse in der Volkswirtschaft«. Tröger
selbst interpretierte seinen Beitrag zur »Stärkung« seines
Staates eher bescheiden und ohne jeden Schwulst: »Ich hab'
mir bisher immer Mühe gegeben und mein Bestmögliches

getan. Der Vorschlag für diesen Orden kommt vom Abteilungsleiter, der Kombinatsdirektor und die Gewerkschaften müssen ihn bestätigen.« Wie Tröger es schilderte, wird im Osten freilich häufig prämiert, was sich im Westen von selbst versteht. Da hätte eher mit Entlassung zu rechnen, wer nicht über die Tugenden verfügt, die in der DDR für den Titel »Aktivist der sozialistischen Arbeit« qualifizieren. Den kriegt man nämlich, so der Brigadier aus Schleife, »wenn man gewissenhaft und ordnungsgemäß seine Arbeit macht, ständig Arbeitsschutz und Sicherheit dabei beachtet und Disziplin und Sauberkeit im Betrieb einhält«. Da klingt dann die Klage des DDR-Wirtschaftswissenschaftlers Jürgen Kuczynski verständlich, der in einer Diskussion einmal bemerkte: »Jeder nach seinen Fähigkeiten und Leistungen ist ein altes Prinzip im Sozialismus, aber es wird bei uns nur zur Hälfte durchgeführt. Wenn jemand etwas Gutes leistet, kriegt er eine Prämie. Aber davon, daß bei schlechter Leistung die Gehälter gesenkt werden oder die Löhne, wie es selbstverständlich nach diesem Prinzip sein muß, ist bei uns nicht die Rede.«

Der vielfach ausgezeichnete Brigadier Tröger versteht etwas von seinem Fach und hätte seinen Weg auch bei uns gemacht, mit weniger Medaillen zwar, aber mit höherem Realeinkommen – vorausgesetzt, man hätte seinen Arbeitsplatz nicht wegrationalisiert. Bei uns wäre er vielleicht Besitzer eines Reihenhauses, seine Stimme bei Wahlen gäbe er am liebsten Männern vom Schlage eines Helmut Schmidt oder auch eines Norbert Blüm; statt eines Trabant führe er einen Golf oder einen Opel; und gelegentlich würde er im Urlaub mit seiner Familie und dem Wohnwagen in den Süden fahren. Als ich ihn auf das in der DDR stets heikle Thema Reisen ansprach und nach Traumzielen fragte, die für ihn unerreichbar bleiben würden, bekannte er durchaus Lust auf Palmen und südliche Meere, aber er tat dies geschickt und systemkonform: »Durch das Fernsehen bekommt man sehr viel zu sehen heutzutage, und selbstverständlich ist es schön, wenn man dort selber mal hinfahren kann, das streite ich auf keinen Fall ab.« Für die Verlockung durch den Duft der großen weiten Welt fand er eine Chiffre, die ich später noch öfter hören sollte; sie vermeidet jeden Konflikt mit Partei und Staat und drückt doch Sehnsucht nach exotischen Stränden aus: »Mein größter Wunsch«, sagte Tröger, »ist es, mit dem Schiff einmal nach Kuba zu fahren.« Einmal durfte der vielfach ausgezeichnete Brigadier in die Bundesrepublik reisen, denn er zählte zu dem kleinen Zuschauerkontingent, das die DDR 1972 zu den Olympischen Spielen in München schickte. Sein wichtigster Eindruck: »Völlig neu für uns waren die Sex-Geschäfte, so was kannten wir bei uns ja gar nicht.« Und er bekannte: »München war schön, das muß ich sagen, und daß der Handel dort anders dasteht als bei uns, kann man nicht abstreiten.«

Natürlich durfte ein Mann wie Tröger nur nach München reisen, weil er als einer der Zuverlässigen galt. Nicht besonders früh, erst mit 32 Jahren, fünf Jahre nach dem Bau der Mauer, trat er in die Sozialistische Einheitspartei ein. Er hält dort keine bemerkenswerte Position, aber er zählt sich halt dazu. Er ist kein Eiferer, er bekennt sich gelassen und unverklemmt, und er räumt auch Mängel ein, die dem realen Sozialismus anhaften, auch und gerade weil er erklärt, er sei von »seiner« Gesellschaftsordnung überzeugt: »Wir haben große Lücken im Handel, da ist noch viel zu tun in Sachen Versorgung und Warensteuerung. Es gibt eigentlich fast alles bei uns, aber dort gibt es das, und woanders jenes, und es ist immer mit viel Rumfahrerei verbunden. Das ist ein Mangel bei uns.«

Gewiß hätten wir diesen verdienten Brigadier nicht an seinem Arbeitsplatz, in der Werkswohnung und auf seiner Datsche drehen und interviewen dürfen, wenn der für die Genehmigung letztlich zuständige Abteilungsleiter für Agitation und Propaganda im ZK der SED sich Trögers nicht absolut sicher gewesen wäre. Ebenso sicher haben jene DDR-Bürger recht, die an derart verhaltener Kritik am Versorgungssystem in der DDR, wie Tröger sie äußerte, monieren, daß sie besser auf die Parteiversammlung passe, und selbst da habe man oft harschere, deftigere Töne vernommen. Immerhin sprach unser Bagger- und Abraumförderbrückenführer von der DDR

nicht als einem »blühenden sozialistischen Garten«, wie
FDGB-Chef und Politbüro-Mitglied Harry Tisch auf dem XI.
Parteitag der SED, der die Schöpferkraft der Werktätigen fast
in den Himmel hob: »Wenn einer meint, na ja, aber in diesem
oder jenem Beet wächst mal nicht alles gleich gut oder man
könnte noch buntere Blumen pflanzen – dann sagen wir: Aber
bitteschön, nichts dagegen, angepackt, damit es *noch schöner*
wird. Aber wir antworten auch: Auf unser Werk sind wir
stolz, daran lassen wir niemanden rütteln.« Das Parteiproto-
koll verzeichnete an dieser Stelle »starken Beifall«. (Hervor-
hebung vom Autor.)

Tischs kernige Sätze waren an keinen Geringeren als Michail Gorbatschow gerichtet, der, den Knopf für die Übersetz-
zung im Ohr, als Ehrengast die SED-Heerschau im Palast der
Republik auf dem Podium aufmerksam verfolgte. Dem Prediger der radikalen Reformen in Moskau, der dem sowjetischen
Wirtschaftsschlendrian den Kampf ansagte, um die ökonomische Basis der Sowjetunion zu erneuern, ohne die sie über die
nächsten Jahrzehnte den Rang einer Weltmacht schwerlich
behaupten kann, wurde auf diesem Parteitag gleich mehrfach
bedeutet, daß die DDR derlei Roßkuren nicht nötig hat. Weil
ihre Kombinate in der Tat effizienter wirtschaften als die jedes
anderen sozialistischen Bruderlands, beließ es die SED dabei,
dem Ruf nach radikalen Reformen ein wenig selbstgefällig die
Parole von der »Vervollkommnung des Erreichten« entgegen-
zusetzen. Doch das Motto Tischs – wir lassen uns unsere
Leistungen und Erfolge von niemandem kaputtreden – traf
eine Grundstimmung, die nicht nur unter Parteitagsdelegier-
ten weit verbreitet war. Die Zeiten, in denen die DDR in die
Reihe der wirtschaftlich Lahmen und Fußkranken gehörte,
sind längst vorbei, auch wenn mancher Bürger in Magdeburg
oder Erfurt, der immerzu westliche Fernsehwerbung sieht,
das so recht nicht verstehen wird. Ich vergesse nicht den ver-
wunderten Ton und das Erstaunen im Blick, mit dem mir ein
protestantischer Pfarrer, frisch von einem Kongreß mit Vertretern der Ökumene und damit auch aus der Dritten Welt
zurück, erzählte, er habe lernen müssen, daß »seine« DDR zu

den reichsten Ländern der Erde gehöre. Da kommt es auch, aber nicht nur auf den Blickwinkel an. Erfolgreich darf sich der DDR-Bürger vor allem fühlen, wenn er nach Osten schaut, denn im eigenen Lager hat er den bei weitem höchsten Lebensstandard, und das Gefälle gegenüber der östlichen Vormacht ist besonders groß. Auf den, der aus Kiew oder aus Kasachstan nach Ostberlin, Leipzig oder Erfurt kommt, wirkt die DDR wie ein westliches Paradies. Sowjetische Soldaten staunen über das reiche Warenangebot. Fast jeder zweite Haushalt in der DDR besitzt ein Automobil, in der Sowjetunion ist es nur einer von zehn. Das Handbook of Economic Statistics des amerikanischen CIA führt Indikatoren auf, nach denen sich der Lebensstandard bemißt. Bei allen fünf liegt die DDR weit vor der Sowjetunion: Pro Kopf produziert sie mehr Getreide (690 gegenüber 620 Kilogramm) und mehr Fleisch (115 gegenüber 61 Kilo); sie verbraucht mehr Energie (40 gegenüber 33 barrels Öl), hat mehr Automobile (168 gegenüber nur 33 je tausend Einwohner) und verfügt über die höhere durchschnittliche Lebenserwartung (72 gegenüber 70 Jahre). Im Vergleich mit den anderen Bruderländern wird sie nur von Rumänien, Bulgarien und Ungarn in der Pro-Kopf-Produktion von Getreide übertroffen; die Ungarn allein produzieren mehr Fleisch, liegen jedoch wie alle übrigen RGW-Staaten bei den anderen Indikatoren deutlich unter DDR-Niveau. Wer den Daten des CIA mißtrauen sollte, mag zu anderen Quellen greifen und wird doch kein wesentlich anderes Bild der Lage finden. In einer Osteuropa-Studie der New Yorker »L. W. International Financial Research Inc.« über das Sozialprodukt Pro-Kopf im Ostblock führt die DDR mit 9800 Dollar mit Abstand vor der Tschechoslowakei (8278 Dollar) und Ungarn (7220 Dollar). Abschiednehmen muß die DDR allerdings von der liebgewordenen und deshalb immer wieder gern von ihr aufgegriffenen Behauptung, sie nehme auf der Weltrangliste der Industrienationen den 10. oder 11. Platz ein. Solche Berechnungen sind, zugegeben, nicht einfach zu erstellen, weil die statistischen Daten von Ost und West sich nicht in allen Details vergleichen lassen. In einer vom »Deutschen Institut für Wirtschaftsforschung« in Berlin als besonders verläßlich bezeichneten Studie der italienischen Banca Nationale del Lavoro über die National- und Pro-Kopf-Einkommen der 200 Länder der Erde findet die DDR sich mit ihrem Bruttosozialprodukt auf Platz 17 (die Bundesrepublik auf Platz 4), also immerhin unter den ersten 20 Ländern, und, die riesige Sowjetunion auf Platz 3 ausgenommen, an der Spitze der sozialistischen Länder Osteuropas. Beim Sozialprodukt pro Kopf steht sie knapp hinter Großbritannien und deutlich vor Italien auf Platz 16 (die Bundesrepublik auf Platz 7); die Sowjetunion hält nach Ungarn und vor Griechenland nur die 29. Position. Cum grano salis gibt dies ein einigermaßen verläßliches Bild.

Eine Studie der Weltbank wollte einmal errechnet haben, daß der Lebensstandard in der DDR dem in Großbritannien vergleichbar sei und bezog sich dabei auf das Sozialprodukt pro Kopf, bei dem beide Staaten statistisch etwa gleichauf lagen. Aber die Indices dafür sind nicht unbedingt auf den Lebensstandard zu übertragen, denn es kommt entscheidend darauf an, wie das erwirtschaftete Sozialprodukt verwendet wird, ob für Investitionen, den privaten oder den öffentlichen Verbrauch. Auch ist eine frei konvertible Währung, die Importe aus und Reisen in fast alle Länder der Welt möglich macht, ein kaum zu unterschätzender Faktor bei der Bemessung des Lebensstandards, und er hat wahrlich nichts mit dem Sozialprodukt pro Kopf zu tun. Es sind die Unterschiede im System, die korrekte Vergleiche zwischen Ost und West so schwierig machen.

So verblüffte das »Neue Deutschland« seine Leser im Mai 1986 mit dem Bericht über die Untersuchung eines Westberliner Instituts, den es mit der Zeile »Kaufkraft der Mark in der DDR höher als in der BRD« überschrieb und damit den Schluß nahelegte, der Michel-Ost könne sich mehr leisten als der Michel-West. Am selben Tag berichtete die »Frankfurter Allgemeine Zeitung« über die nämliche Untersuchung, jedoch unter der Überschrift: »DDR-Einkommen halb so hoch.« Beide Behauptungen schienen ganz offensichtlich einander diametral zu widersprechen, und doch trafen beide zu. Jede Zeitung hatte sich das ihr Angenehme für die Überschrift herausgepickt. In einer Untersuchung über Kaufkraft, Einkommen und Lebensstandard in der DDR war das Deutsche Institut für Wirtschaftsforschung zu dem Schluß gekommen, daß eine Mark der DDR 24 Prozent mehr Kaufkraft besaß als eine D-Mark. Freilich stimmte diese Berechnung, nach der Bundesbürger für vergleichbare Waren und Dienstleistungen etwa ein Viertel mehr zu zahlen hatten, nur, wenn man die Verbrauchsstruktur eines Vierpersonenhaushalts in der DDR zugrunde legte. Ging man dagegen von bundesdeutschen Konsumgewohnheiten aus, dann hatte die DDR-Mark für eine Arbeitnehmerfamilie mit mittlerem Einkommen eine Kaufkraft von nur 89 Prozent der D-Mark. Für den gleichen Warenkorb waren bei dieser Annahme also in der DDR elf Prozent mehr zu bezahlen als in der Bundesrepublik. Die umfangreiche Untersuchung machte deutlich, wie kompliziert es ist, die Einkommens- und Preisentwicklung in beiden deutschen Staaten zu vergleichen, denn in der DDR werden die Preise für Mieten, Strom, Gas, Grundnahrungsmittel und öffentliche Verkehrsmittel durch hohe staatliche Subventionen, extrem niedrig gehalten; dafür kostet Kaffee das vierfache, und bei vielen Elektroartikeln, Textilien und Schuhen erreicht die Kaufkraft der DDR-Mark nur 40 Prozent der D-Mark. Vor allem für Waren besserer Qualität muß man in der anderen Republik sehr viel tiefer in die Tasche greifen. Bei Nahrungsmitteln haben die DDR-Bürger den Stand der Bundesrepublik weitgehend erreicht, beim Verzehr von Fleisch sogar überboten, aber dabei bleibt zu bedenken: in der DDR ißt man weniger Rind-, kaum Kalb- und vor allem fettes Schweinefleisch. Viele Obst- und Gemüsesorten, in der Bundesrepublik selbstverständlich und fast das ganze Jahr über im Angebot, sind in der DDR überhaupt nicht oder nur in der Saison erhältlich. Beim Verbrauch harter Alkoholika hat sich Michel-Ost dagegen eindeutig auf Platz zwei der Weltrangliste vorgetrunken: Das statistische Jahrbuch der DDR wies einen Anstieg des Schnaps- und Branntweinverbrauchs in der Zeit von

1960 bis 1985 von 3,5 auf über 15 Liter pro Kopf aus. Aber ein Waschvollautomat kostet den DDR-Bürger dreimal mehr als den Michel-West, und für einen Farbfernseher muß der DDR-Bürger rund 845 Stunden, sein Kollege im Westen nur 96 Stunden arbeiten. So kam das Institut zu dem Schluß, daß die durchschnittlichen Netto-Einkommen der Arbeitnehmer- und Rentnerfamilien, gemessen in der jeweiligen Währung, in der Bundesrepublik doppelt so hoch sind wie in der DDR. Der Einkommensrückstand in der anderen deutschen Republik beträgt mithin rund 50 Prozent.

Allerdings bleibt zu fragen, ob sich Lebensstandard und Lebensqualität ausschließlich nach der Kaufkraft berechnen lassen. Bezieht man nämlich Lebens- und Arbeitsbedingungen mit ein, kommt Psychologie ins Spiel, die das Bild verändern kann. Inwieweit wird die Tatsache, daß Farbfernseher in der DDR um ein Vielfaches teurer sind, dann durch Lehrstellen für Jugendliche aufgewogen, die, im Gegensatz zur Bundesrepublik, ausreichend vorhanden sind? Oder läßt sich die teure vollautomatische Waschmaschine gegen die staatliche Finanzierung von Studium und Stipendien aufrechnen, die sich in der DDR auf 12 420 Mark pro Jahr und Student beläuft und diesem eine völlig kostenlose, akademische Ausbildung sichert? Und keine Statistik sagt aus, was es bedeutet, in einer Gesellschaft zu leben, die keine Absturz- und Existenzängste kennt, keine Arbeitslosigkeit im westlichen Sinn, keine Furcht, zum sozialen Außenseiter zu werden, zum untauglich Gestempelten, der für immer in die »Neue Armut« absinkt. Um der Korrektheit willen sei freilich angemerkt, daß die Rentenbemessung im realen Sozialismus einen Makel darstellt, der sich dem der westlichen Arbeitslosigkeit durchaus vergleichen läßt. Die Durchschnittsrente beläuft sich auf 40 Prozent des Durchschnittseinkommens. Mit rund 400 Mark im Monat führen jene, die nach dem Krieg die Grundlagen für den neuen Arbeiter- und Bauernstaat schufen, eine ärmliche, oft würdelose Existenz. Die Durchschnittsrenten im Westen liegen mit rund 1500 DM immerhin bei 70 Prozent des Durchschnittseinkommens.

Daß nahezu alle DDR-Bürger die soziale Sicherheit zu schätzen wissen, die man ihnen bietet, ist eine Sache; ob sie deshalb an die Überlegenheit des Sozialismus glauben, welche die Partei ihnen predigt, eine völlig andere. Vor allem die jungen Menschen in der anderen Republik haben gelernt, zwischen den Vorzügen und Nachteilen beider Systeme sorgfältig abzuwägen. »Mit unserem mikrigen Betrieb könnten wir bei Euch nicht mithalten«, sagte ein Lehrling, »aber ob ich bei Euch leben möchte, weiß ich nicht, da braucht man zuviel Ellenbogen.« »Die persönliche Freiheit, die einem in der Bundesrepublik gegeben wird«, meinte eine angehende Krankenschwester, »ist doch größer. Und auf der anderen Seite ist es in der DDR wieder besser. Man ist doch irgendwie festgebunden an seinem Arbeitsplatz und damit sicher im ganzen Gefüge drin.« Jüngere DDR-Bürger gaben sich vor der Kamera lockerer, souveräner und offener als die meist vorsichtigen Älteren, die entscheidend vom Stalinismus geprägt wurden. So gab mir ein junger Zimmergeselle zu Protokoll: »Hier ist zum Beispiel gut, daß wir einen Lehrplatz kriegen, wenn wir aus der Schule kommen. Überhaupt die soziale Sicherheit. Was natürlich hier nicht so doll ist, das ist die allgemeine Versorgung. Wir haben zwar auch Gemüse und Lebensmittel, aber nicht in dem Überfluß wie in der Bundesrepublik. Da gibt es sogar im Winter Erdbeeren und sowas. Also, die sieht man hier gerade mal, wenn Hochsaison ist, und dann muß man anstehen. Aber ansonsten... Ich kann mir kein Leben in der Bundesrepublik vorstellen. Wir sehen das ja nur im Fernsehen. Wenn ich jetzt die Chance hätte, in der Bundesrepublik zu leben oder in der DDR, müßte ich ganz ehrlich sagen, das kann ich gar nicht entscheiden.«

Was für die Bundesrepublik im Rückblick die goldenen sechziger Jahre waren, das sind für die DDR die goldenen siebziger – Jahre des schnellen wirtschaftlichen Wachstums, das sich für die Bürger deutlich spürbar niederschlug in höherem Konsum. Mitte der 70er Jahre, als die DDR durch hohe Westverschuldung in eine schwierige außenwirtschaftliche Phase eintrat, schwächte sich die Zunahme des Verbrauchs ab, die erste Hälfte der 8oer Jahre war dann von Stagnation, wenn nicht von einem leichten Rückgang des Lebensstandards gekennzeichnet, wie Versorgungskrisen in den Wintern 1981 und 1982 unübersehbar signalisierten. Zwar setzte Mitte der 8oer Jahre wieder ein, wenn auch nur sanfter, Aufwärtstrend ein. Langlebige und gefragte Konsumgüter, zum Beispiel Tiefkühltruhen, sind seither leichter erhältlich. Doch wenn es um den täglichen Konsum geht, dann meinen die Hausfrauen in der anderen Republik beim Einkauf in den großen HO-Läden und Kaufhallen nicht, daß es wieder aufwärts gehe. Im Gegenteil: Sie spüren die Folgen einer Politik der Kaufkraftabschöpfung, welche die offizielle Behauptung der SED, im realen Sozialismus gebe es keine Inflation, schlicht der Lüge überführt. Da werden nämlich, ganz in Nachahmung sonst so verwerflicher kapitalistischer Praktiken, Produkte, die früher billig zu haben waren, einfach aus dem Sortiment genommen, um wenig später leicht verändert und anders verpackt wieder im Laden zu erscheinen – zu Preisen, welche die Verbesserung der Waren bei weitem übersteigen. Und da wird das Billigangebot in den normalen Kaufhallen gezielt so ausgedünnt, daß der Käufer, der sich mit den drei einfachsten Wurstsorten nicht zufrieden gibt, in den teuren Delikat-Laden gehen muß, wo Schinken oft um das Doppelte oder Dreifache teurer im Angebot ist als früher – freilich, dort findet er ihn auch.

Pünktlich zum Weihnachtsgeschäft 1984 wurde gegenüber dem Ostberliner Kaufhaus Centrum am Alexanderplatz eine neue Ladenzeile mit Spezialitätengeschäften eröffnet, für die der Berliner Volksmund sogleich den Namen »Neu-Delhi« prägte. Zwar gab es da auch Gewürze aus dem Orient, aber mit Indien hatte der Namen nichts gemein. Er war auf die »Exquisit«- und »Delikat«-Läden gemünzt, in die inzwischen alles abwandert, was die DDR an hochwertigen Konsumgütern produziert oder importiert. Natürlich bot »Neu-Delhi« auch Westwaren feil, etwa Rinder- oder Hühnerbrühe für 9 oder 9,50 Mark, eine Preisgestaltung, die den Kurs der DDR-Mark dem von der SED so gern als »Schwindelkurs« bezeichneten der westlichen Wechselstuben annäherte. Im Westen war die nämliche Rinderbrühe schon für 2,95 DM zu haben. Eine Packung Pralinen einer gängigen westdeutschen Marke kostete gegenüber dem Kaufhaus Centrum in Ostberlin 19,50 Mark, im Kaufhaus des Westens nur 6 DM. Betrug der Umrechnungskurs einer DM bei diesem Beispiel schon 3,25 Mark der DDR, liegt er bei qualitativ hochwertigen Textilien und Schuhen in den Exquisitläden oft bei eins zu vier oder gar eins zu fünf.

In Gesellschaften ohne Meinungsfreiheit haben Witze eine Art Ventilfunktion. Ein DDR-Witz, der damals kursierte, fragte: »In welchem Zeitalter leben wir? Sie wissen, die Partei behauptet, nach Feudalismus, Absolutismus und Kapitalismus leben wir im entwickelten Sozialismus. Aber das stimmt nicht mehr; wir haben eine weitere Stufe erklommen und sind im Delikatismus angelangt. Und was, bitte, ist Delikatismus? Er steht für das Zeitalter des Übergangs vom Sozialismus zum Kommunismus, in dem man den Bürgern schon das Geld aus der Tasche zieht, das sie im Kommunismus angeblich nicht mehr brauchen.«

Drei andere Witze werfen ein Licht auf das Verhältnis zur östlichen Vormacht, denn in ihnen kommt eine gewisse Arroganz der DDR-Bürger gegenüber den Russen zum Ausdruck, ein Hochmut, in dem sich ein Stück von dem Stolz auf die eigene Leistung verbirgt, die sich der FDGB-Chef Harry Tisch von niemandem kaputtreden lassen wollte. Der erste erzählt von Iwan Iwanowitsch, der zur Parteiversammlung geht, dort aufsteht, um das Wort bittet und den Genossen sagt: »Ich weiß, daß wir es unerhört schwer haben. Die Imperialisten haben uns eingekreist, der Westen boykottiert den Handel und will uns in die Knie zwingen. Genossen, ich weiß; aber ich esse nun einmal für mein Leben gerne Borscht. Meine Frau ist in Moskau von Laden zu Laden gegangen, aber nirgendwo gab es Kohl. Genossen, können wir nicht wenigstens Kohl für den Borscht produzieren?« Darauf entzieht ihm der Vorsitzende das Wort mit der Bemerkung: »Du solltest nicht vergessen, für solche Sätze wärest Du vor 25 Jahren noch erschossen worden.« Bedrückt geht Iwan Iwanowitsch nach

Hause und sagt zu seiner Frau: »Irina, stell Dir vor, es ist alles noch schlimmer, als ich angenommen habe, jetzt gibt es nicht einmal mehr Patronen.«

Der zweite handelt von einem großen sowjetischen Erfolg, denn angeblich ist es sowjetischen Biologen gelungen, erstmals eine Kreuzung zwischen Erdbeere und Kürbis zu züchten. Und wie, wird gefragt, sieht die Frucht aus, die am Ende so vieler Mühen steht? »Sie hat die Größe einer Erdbeere und den Geschmack eines Kürbis.«

Der dritte fragt, wie der Sozialismus siegen wird. Die Antwort: »Mit polnischem Fleiß, sowjetischer Gründlichkeit und mongolischer Mikroelektronik.«

Ob die Verachtung des großen Bruders, von der solche Witze künden, einmal in Respekt umschlagen wird, wenn der Reformkurs Gorbatschows erste vorzeigbare Erfolge bringt, bleibt abzuwarten. Die Gewißheit, daß man »den Freunden«, wie man die Sowjets mit einem kräftigen Schuß Ironie oft nennt, eindeutig überlegen ist, sitzt tief, sie wird von Überzeugten wie Gegnern des Systems geteilt, und die Basis, auf der sie ruht, ist der bescheidene, aber gesicherte Wohlstand, den beide, Regimeanhänger und Regimekritiker, unter schwierigen Bedingungen über Jahrzehnte gemeinsam geschaffen haben. Wenn die DDR unter den Ländern des Ostblocks sich zu wirtschaftlichen Musterknaben mauserte, hat das auch mit Fleiß, Sparsamkeit und Disziplin zu tun, mit den klassischen Tugenden also, die man den Deutschen gerne nachsagt. Wirtschaftswissenschaftler sprechen in diesem Zusammenhang eher nüchtern von einem Startvorteil, den die DDR zu nutzen wußte, denn sie wies nach dem Krieg unter den Ländern des späteren RGW den höchsten Industrialisierungsgrad auf, verfügte über einen guten Stamm qualifizierter Facharbeiter und über moderne Produktionsanlagen. Und noch vor der Gründung der DDR gelang es der Führung, jene straffe Disziplinierung, ja Militarisierung der Arbeit, wie sie von den Nationalsozialisten über die Rüstung und durch die Proklamierung des totalen Krieges organisiert worden war, mit neuen Parolen und Inhalten versehen, fortzuführen und in ihren Dienst zu stellen. Daß eine anderen sozialistischen Ländern überlegene Mentalität und Einstellung zur Arbeit den Erfolg der DDR-Wirtschaft innerhalb des Ostblocks mit ausmacht, ist schlechterdings nicht zu bestreiten. Freilich zeigt der folgende Witz, daß sich die Bürger der anderen Republik über die Relativität der eigenen Anstrengungen sehr wohl im klaren sind: Da reist eine japanische Gewerkschaftsdelegation durch die DDR, besichtigt einen Betrieb und sagt anschließend den Vertretern des FDGB: »Bitte versteht, liebe Kollegen, daß wir uns eurem Bummelstreik nicht anschließen können, wir gehören eben einer anderen Gewerkschaft an.« Was soviel signalisiert wie: Im Rahmen unseres immobilen, konkurrenzfeindlichen Systems der Planwirtschaft sind wir gut, ohne diese Bedingungen könnten wir noch viel, viel besser sein.

Solchen relativierenden Einsichten zum Trotz ist der Stolz auf das Geschaffene weit verbreitet, und westliche Besucher, die Zweifel an der Berechtigung dazu hegen, sollten zum Überseehafen nach Rostock fahren und eine Hafenrundfahrt buchen, die sich bei DDR-Ostsee-Urlaubern großer Beliebtheit erfreut. Wo 1957 noch die Lämmer weideten, hat die DDR ihr Tor zur Welt buchstäblich aus dem Marschboden gestampft. Seine Hafenanlagen erstrecken sich über ein Areal von 17,5 Quadratkilometern und schlagen inzwischen um die 20 Millionen Tonnen Güter jährlich um. Rostock ist damit heute Lissabon oder Antwerpen vergleichbar, die auf jahrhundertealte Überseetradition zurückblicken können. Unter den rund 6000 Schiffen aus 50 Nationen, die in einem Jahr hier festmachen, führt mit Abstand die Flagge der Sowjetunion, des größten Handelspartners der DDR. »Für alle, die daran mitarbeiteten, war es die Aufgabe unseres Lebens«, sagte mir Kapitän Gerd Peters, vom Kombinat Seeverkehr und Hafenwirtschaft, das den Überseehafen und die DDR-Handelsflotte betreibt, und er hatte dabei nicht nur den imposanten Hafen mit 9,8 Kilometern Kaianlagen zum Löschen und Laden im Sinn. Im Schiffahrtsmuseum Rostock ist das Modell des einzigen Handelsschiffs zu sehen, das der DDR aus der gesamt-

deutschen Erbmasse verblieben war. Nur weil es nicht see-
tüchtig war, als die Russen kamen, setzte seine Besatzung sich
nicht wie die der anderen Dampfer in den Häfen Stralsund,
Wismar und Rostock über die Ostsee nach Schleswig-Holstein
ab. Die DDR ließ das Schiff auf der Neptun-Werft general-
überholen, taufte es auf den Namen »Vorwärts« und stellte es
1950 als erstes unter eigener Flagge in Dienst. Damit war der
Grundstein zu einer eigenen Handelsflotte gelegt, die 1985
dann schon stolze 171 Schiffe zählte. Nach der Tonnage liegt
die sozialistische Seefahrt der DDR unter den Schiffahrtsna-
tionen inzwischen auf Platz 37 nach den Polen.

Der neue Hafen mußte gebaut werden, weil Wismar, der
einzige Tiefwasserhafen, über den die DDR bei ihrer Gründung verfügte, nur maximal 2 bis 3 Tonnen umschlagen
kann. Inzwischen ist Rostock nicht nur das ostdeutsche Tor
zur Welt, sondern mit Neptun- und Warnow-Werft auch das
Zentrum des DDR-Schiffbaus, der keine Werftkrise kennt.
Über 70 Schiffe laufen hier Jahr für Jahr vom Stapel, davon
zwei Drittel für sowjetische Auftraggeber, und die Kapazität
ist auf Jahre ausgebucht. Kapitän Gerd Peters, der unser
ARD-Team bei Dreharbeiten für eine Reportage über den
Überseehafen an der Warnow begleitete, verfügt über elegan-
te Umgangsformen und Weltläufigkeit, die noch immer rar
sind im Arbeiter- und Bauernstaat, und er zählt zu denen
unter den heute 50- bis 60jährigen, die an ihrer Grundüberzeugung, dies sei die richtige Partei und der richtige Staat, nie
irre wurden. Als ich wissen wollte, ob er stolz sei auf Hafen
und Flotte, die nach dem Krieg praktisch aus dem Nichts entstanden, sagt er ohne Umschweife: »Ja, sehr sogar, das ist ein
Stück meiner Aufbauleistung, der Arbeit meiner ganzen Generation.« Der Mann vom Jahrgang 1934 fuhr gute 17 Jahre
als Kapitän zur See. Auf die Frage, ob es neben der christlichen Seefahrt inzwischen auch eine sozialistische gebe, antwortete er: »Ja, das kann man so sagen, denn in mancher
Beziehung unterscheiden wir uns doch, vor allem im inneren
Schiffsbetrieb, von den Schiffen kapitalistischer Großreede-
reien.« Auf den Frachtern der DDR hat der Kapitän zwar das

Kommando, aber nicht allein das Sagen, denn Partei, Gewerkschaft und FDJ sind mit an Bord. Vor ihren Organisationen muß der Kapitän während der Fahrt Rechenschaft ablegen über seine Arbeit und das Besatzungskollektiv informieren und motivieren. »Das kostet ihn mehr Überzeugungskraft und mehr persönlichen Einsatz als den Kapitän, sagen wir eines englischen Schiffes, das eine Besatzung aus Pakistani oder Hongkong-Chinesen an Bord hat, denn da fällt das alles weg«, meinte Peters. »Muß ein Kapitän Mitglied der SED sein«, fragte ich. Seine Antwort: »Er ist es. Und zwar nicht erst, wenn er Kapitän ist, sondern man entscheidet sich ja für die Mitgliedschaft in unserer Partei recht früh, weil man durch die Partei erzogen wird.«

Die Deutsche Seereederei betreibt zur Zeit 26 Liniendienste, die Auslastung ihrer Flotte liegt wegen Dumpingpreisen, die die westliche Konkurrenz beklagt, deutlich über dem internationalen Durchschnitt. Aber daß Politik immer mitfährt an Bord, daß Fracht für Mitglieder und Freunde des sozialistischen Lagers besonderen Stellenwert genießt, zeigt ein Blick in das Traditionskabinett des Rostocker Schiffahrtsmuseums. In solchen »Kabinetten« bewahrt man in der DDR Auszeichnungen im sozialistischen Wettbewerb, Traditionswimpel von Partei- und Gewerkschaftsgruppen auf, in Rostock auch die Fahrtbücher und Fotoalben der FDJ-Bordkollektive oder Souvenirs, die an besondere Leistungen erinnern. So wird in einem Schaukasten das Einlaufen des DDR-Frachters »Frieden« in den 1973 von den Amerikanern verminten Hafen von Haiphong in Wort und Bild als »Blockadedurchbruch« und als »Ruhmestat« der Besatzung gefeiert. Ein Bombensplitter, nach einem amerikanischen Angriff auf Haiphong auf dem Deck des im übrigen völlig unversehrten Frachters gefunden und nun hier zur Schau gestellt, hat alle Weihen einer sozialistischen Reliquie. Schiffstagebücher, in denen die verschiedenen Besatzungen ihre Eindrücke aus fernen Ländern festgehalten haben, belegen, daß Partei, FDJ und Gewerkschaft an Bord den DDR-Seeleuten unentwegt das sozialistische Gewissen schärfen, das ihnen schon während ihrer Ausbildung eingebleut wurde. Wichtige Teile der Freizeit, das zeigt schon flüchtiges Durchblättern der Fotoalben, werden kollektiv verplant, etwa mit einem Besuch des Grabes von Karl Marx auf dem Londoner Highgate-Friedhof, sobald das Schiff im Hafen an der Themse festgemacht hat. Stetige Kontrolle durch das Kollektiv mag dafür sorgen, daß nur wenige DDR-Seeleute vom Landgang nicht zurückkommen. »Die Männer all meiner Besatzungen«, sagte Kapitän Peters, »die in den 17 Jahren, die ich zur See gefahren bin, das Weite suchten, kann ich an den Fingern einer Hand abzählen.« Natürlich wollte ich von ihm wissen, ob er Probleme mit der deutschen Identität erlebt, in fremden Häfen stets als DDR-Kapitän oder als Deutscher behandelt worden sei. In Westeuropa, erfuhr ich, wurde er immer korrekt und ordnungsgemäß als Kapitän der DDR empfangen. In fernen Ländern aber, »zum Beispiel in Hongkong, oder auch gelegentlich in Mexiko und mittelamerikanischen Ländern, die über die Besonderheit des Umgangs der beiden deutschen Staaten miteinander nicht so genau informiert waren, dort hat man nicht so differenziert.« Da wurde Peters auch mal mit einem Kapitän aus der Bundesrepublik verwechselt. »Unangenehm«, meinte der welterfahrene DDR-Mann lächelnd, »war das nicht, weil das natürlich keine Nachteile mit sich bringt. Aber wir legen schon Wert darauf, überall als Handelsschiff der DDR angesehen zu werden und haben das dann unseren Gastgebern oder auch Maklern und Hafenbehörden gegenüber möglichst freundlich zur Kenntnis gebracht.«

Der normale DDR-Bürger neidet den Angehörigen der sozialistischen Seefahrt die Freizügigkeit, die sie genießen, auch wenn den Landgang in den exotischen Ländern noch die Partei oder die FDJ organisiert. Rostock, dieses Tor zur Welt, das der ganze Stolz der Aufbaugeneration des Kapitän Peters ist, bleibt für die meisten ein unpassierbares Nadelöhr. Auf einer Barkasse während einer Hafenrundfahrt fragte ich einige Ostseeurlauber, was sie beim Anblick der vielen Schiffe aus fernen Ländern dachten. »Mal 'ne richtige Kreuzfahrt«, sagte der eine, »das bringt einen schon auf Ideen.« »Ja, aber leider ist es ja nicht möglich, dahin zu fahren, wohin man möchte«, erklärte ein Chemiearbeiter aus Bitterfeld, ohne jede Furcht vor der Kamera. Er wußte, daß ihm diese Äußerung Ärger bringen konnte, aber hatte ihn einkalkuliert. »Ja, sendet das ruhig, die oben müssen endlich wissen, wie wir denken«, tuschelte er mir zu, als wir von Bord gingen. Ein anderer sagte: »Reisen ist schön; einmal nach Kuba hatten wir uns vorgenommen, aber ich glaube nicht, daß das irgendwann klappen wird.« Kubareisen bleiben wenigen Zuverlässigen, Verdienten und Auserwählten vorbehalten. Aber da war sie wieder, jene systemkonforme Chiffre für Reiselust und Exotik, die auch der Brigadier Tröger gebrauchte und die, weil sie das »Bruderland Zuckerinsel« zum Traumziel erklärt, jeden Konflikt mit der Partei vermeiden hilft.

Vom Duft der großen weiten Welt, wie er sich für DDR-Bürger mangels anderer Möglichkeiten meist an den Küsten des Schwarzen Meeres und in den südlichen und südöstlichen Sowjetrepubliken einfangen läßt, kündete im Wohnzimmer von Helge Häger ein Samowar aus Samarkand. Ohne Frauen wie sie stünde die andere deutsche Republik heute schlechter da, denn Helge Häger zählt zu den Fleißigen und Nimmermüden. Mein Kürschnermeister aus dem Vogtland würde sie weder den Heuchlern zurechnen noch gar denen, die es »fürs Geld machen«, er gestünde ihr ohne Zögern »eine Meinung« zu. Ich lernte die sozialistische Karrierefrau im Frühjahr 1984 kennen, als sie schon vier Jahre »Herr« war, wie man so sagt, über die 51 000 Werktätigen des Braunkohlekombinats Bitterfeld. Von ihrem Verwaltungssitz aus dirigierte die Genossin Generaldirektor ein stattliches Imperium, bestehend aus 19 Tagebauen, 26 Heizkraftwerken, 24 Brikettfabriken und einem Montanwachswerk. Allein daß eine Frau in der rauhen Welt des Bergbaus und der dampfenden schwelenden Brikettpressen ihren Weg nach oben macht, fordert schon Respekt, doch meine Achtung vor Helge Häger wuchs in den zwei Tagen, in denen wir ihren Arbeitsalltag mit der Kamera einzufangen suchten: Der begann pünktlich um 6 Uhr in der

Frühe, wenn die Generaldirektorin über Lautsprecher den Rapport entgegennahm, der über den Stand der Produktion Auskunft gibt. Unser erster Drehtag fiel auf einen Montag, und was uns blechern entgegenschallte, war eine Mischung aus aufgeblasenem Parteichinesisch und bürokratischem Produktionskauderwelsch. »Glückauf, Genossen«, dröhnte der Mann vom Rapport –, »in allen Kombinatsbetrieben wurden die am Wochenende an uns gestellten Aufgaben und Forderungen mit hoher Disziplin und Verantwortung realisiert. In der materiellen Produktion konnte dabei in allen Bereichen die Planauflage in stabiler Kontinuität und zielgerichtet übererfüllt werden...« Das schepperte und klirrte bombastisch daher, war ganz offensichtlich für den Besuch des West-Fernsehens mehrfach geprobt und sollte doch nur soviel heißen wie: Keine besonderen Vorkommnisse, das Kombinat liegt gut im Plan – eine Formel, die der vortragende Direktor in der anschließenden Sitzung mit den wichtigsten Kombinatsmitarbeitern dann auch verwendete. Helge Häger leitete diese Morgenkonferenz der Direktoren routiniert; sie zeigte, daß sie über die Tugend des Zuhörenkönnens verfügt und doch genau weiß, was sie will. Klar und bestimmt erteilte sie am Ende einer sachlichen Diskussion ihre Weisungen. Wir folgten der Genossin Generaldirektor in einen Tagebau, in dem sie, mit Gummischuhen und Schutzhelm versehen, einen der großen Abraumförderverbände erklomm. An den Schalthebeln der Baggerführer und im Leitstand des Brückenfahrers wollte sie erkunden, wie sich die Förderleistung steigern ließe. Die Arbeit der Kumpels im Tagebau ist hart, in unserer westlichen Vorstellung ist der Bergbau deshalb ein klassischer Männerberuf. Die deutsche Sprache kennt den Bergmann, die Bergfrau gibt es nicht. Und doch wirkte Frau Häger auf dieser Brücke in der Mondlandschaft des riesigen Tagebaus nicht fremd oder fehl am Platz, sondern so, als ob sie wie selbstverständlich hierher gehörte, und die Kumpel schienen sie als kompetenten Chef zu respektieren.

Helge Häger hörte es nicht gern, aber sie war nun einmal ein sozialistischer Paradefall, und ein doppelter dazu – erstens für die Gleichberechtigung der Frau in der Berufswelt der DDR, welche die Partei durch eine soziale Infrastruktur der Kinderkrippen und Ganztagskindergärten gezielt fördert; und zweitens für die Möglichkeit, als einfacher Arbeiter an die Spitze eines ganzen Kombinats aufzusteigen. Denn die Generaldirektorin des Braunkohlekombinats Bitterfeld, Jahrgang 1939, stammt aus einer Bergmannsfamilie im Mansfeldischen, wo ihr Vater Kupferschürfer war. Sie hat damit eine lupenreine proletarische Herkunft, die einer Karriere im Arbeiter- und Bauernstaat noch nie schädlich gewesen ist, ganz im Gegenteil; doch das Wort »Karriere« schätzt sie nicht. Sie möchte nicht als »Karrieristin« gelten, ihr Weg nach oben stellt sich ihr als völlig normale Entwicklung dar. Auf die Frage, ob dieser Weg für eine Frau im Bergbau einfach oder schwer gewesen ist, gab sie zur Antwort: »Er war schön. Ich habe Betriebsschlosser in einem Braunkohlewerk gelernt, also in einem Kollektiv von Bergarbeitern angefangen und wurde dort als Schlossermädchen akzeptiert. Ich habe den Facharbeiter gemacht, bin dann auf die Fachhochschule gegangen und habe mit dem Ingenieur abgeschlossen. Karriere ist das eigentlich nicht. Ich hab' erst die Praxis kennengelernt, danach die Theorie studiert und bin beim Bergbau geblieben. Es hat mir immer Freude gemacht, bei den Arbeitern zu sein. Die Tradition der Bergleute ist sehr schön.«

Nein, Helge Häger wollte partout nichts Besonderes sein. Bergbau, meinte sie mit der ihr eigenen, fast schon übertreibenden Bescheidenheit, sei längst nicht mehr allein Sache der rauhen Männerwelt, denn in ihrem Kombinat liege der Anteil der Frauen unter den Werktätigen bei etwa 26 Prozent. »Frauen, die Facharbeiter sind, die qualifiziert sind, die Fachschulstudium haben, auch Frauen, die große Geräte fahren, E-Loks oder Abraum- und Förderbrücken. Also, die Frau ist im Bergbau nicht selten, sie ist da, und natürlich auch in leitenden Funktionen. Ich bin nichts Außergewöhnliches. Nebenan, im Chemiekombinat Wolffen/Film ist auch eine Frau Generaldirektor.«

Nun stimmt zwar, daß in der DDR heute gut ein Drittel

aller leitenden Funktionen von Frauen ausgeübt werden, aber eine Karriere wie die Helge Hägers zählt noch immer zu den großen Ausnahmen. Unter 40 Ministern der DDR-Regierung gab es, als ich Helge Häger interviewte, nur eine Frau, Margot Honecker, und die stimmberechtigten Mitglieder des SED-Politbüros waren ein reiner Männerverein. Bei allem Respekt vor der beeindruckenden Sachkompetenz, dem Organisationstalent und dem Durchsetzungsvermögen, die dem »Schlossermädchen« eigen sind, wäre ihr Aufstieg allerdings nicht möglich gewesen, zählte sie nicht zu den ganz Treuen im sozialistischen Glauben. Sie trat früh der SED bei, bekennt sich zu »ihrer« DDR – »ich konnte mich in diesem Staat entwickeln, das ist das Schöne, und natürlich habe ich mich immer politisch für ihn engagiert« –, sie ist Volkskammerabgeordnete der SED und führt daheim ein Leben in einer wahrhaft sozialistischen Musterfamilie: Der Mann im Hauptberuf Parteisekretär einer SED-Betriebsgruppe, der einzige Sohn »jederzeit gefechtsbereit für Frieden und Sozialismus« als Berufsunteroffizier der Nationalen Volksarmee.

Der Lebenszuschnitt der Hägers ist bescheiden. Die Generaldirektorin, eine eher unauffällige Erscheinung, die man sich genausogut in der Dienstkleidung einer Straßenbahnfahrerin oder als Abteilungsleiterin in einem Kaufhaus vorstellen kann, bewohnt mit ihrem Mann eine Vierzimmerwohnung im zweiten Stock eines Mehrfamilienhauses in Bitterfeld, jener Chemie-Stadt, die von Schwefelabgasen geräuchert und vom Braunkohlestaub eingeschwärzt, den unangefochtenen Ruf genießt, die häßlichste der ganzen DDR zu sein. Für die komfortable, aber keineswegs luxuriöse, mit nüchternen modernen Möbeln eingerichtete Wohnung zahlt Genossin Generaldirektor 106 Mark Miete pro Monat. Sonntags geht sie mit ihrem Mann Werner und mit Enkel Sven gern am Ufer eines Stausees spazieren, der aus einem alten Tagebau entstanden ist. Beruflich reiste sie schon einmal in die Bundesrepublik, aber Urlaub machen die sozialistischen Mustermenschen Häger am liebsten in der Sowjetunion: »Wir fahren in jedem Jahr ein-, zweimal dahin, dort ist ein so großes Feld, da kann

60

man jedes Klima kennenlernen.« Nein, eigentlich gäbe es nichts zu berichten über Helge Häger, die ebenso resolut wie kleinbürgerlich brav und bieder wirkt und so gar nichts Spektakuläres an sich hat, wäre da nicht ihre in der Bundesrepublik kaum vorstellbare Karriere, der Aufstieg von der einfachen Betriebsschlosserin an die Spitze eines Kombinats mit 70 Einzelbetrieben und 51 000 Mitarbeitern.

Nicht Heuchler und solche, die es »fürs Geld tun«, sondern Männer mit »einer Meinung« sind ohne Zweifel auch Erich Müller und Wolfgang Biermann, die Erich Honecker in seinen Lebenserinnerungen neben Werner Frohn als Kampfgefährten hervorhebt, deren wirtschaftspolitischen Rat er schätzt. In seiner Arbeit spüre er oft, schrieb der Generalsekretär, welche »gesellschaftliche Kraft« von den Kombinaten, den Werktätigen und ihren Leitern ausgehe. Werner Frohn ist Herr über das Petrolchemische Kombinat Schwedt, das in der Nähe der polnischen Grenze am Endpunkt der Pipeline »Freundschaft« liegt, über die sowjetisches Erdöl in die DDR gepumpt wird und das die Produktion fast der Hälfte des in der DDR hergestellten Benzins besorgt. Wolfgang Biermann dirigiert das Industriekombinat Zeiss-Jena, von seiner Struktur her vielleicht das komplizierteste der DDR, aber eines der wenigen, die mit einem Teil ihrer Produktion – in Jena vor allem hochwertige optische Geräte und Meßinstrumente – auf dem Weltmarkt mithalten können. Und Erich Müller regiert das größte geschlossene Industrieareal der DDR, die »VEB Leuna-Werke Walter Ulbricht«, ein Kombinat, das sich, sieben Kilometer lang und zwei Kilometer breit, südlich von Halle erstreckt.
  Die Karrieren der drei verliefen nach einem Muster, das zeigt, wo die SED in den 70er Jahren die Elite ihrer Wirtschaftsmanager rekrutierte und durch welche Schule sie sie gehen ließ: Werner Frohn, Jahrgang 1929, stammt aus ärmlichen Verhältnissen. Seine Mutter arbeitete bei Bitterfeld in einem Betrieb des I.G.-Farben-Konzerns. Als Flakhelfer geriet er Ende des Krieges in russische Gefangenschaft und trat, aus dem Lager Brandenburg entlassen, nach langen Gesprächen

mit dem Bruder seiner Mutter, einem überzeugten Altkommunisten, in die SED ein. Er besuchte die Landesverwaltungsschule, verließ sie mit dem Abschluß eines »Stadtinspektors« und wurde von der SED, die seine Begabung schätzte, nach kurzer Tätigkeit in der Parteikreisleitung von Bitterfeld zum Studium geschickt. Als promovierter Industrieökonom der Spezialrichtung Chemische Technologie brachte er es im Chemiekombinat Bitterfeld bald zum stellvertretenden Generaldirektor und wurde 1970 als neuer Chef des Petrolchemischen Kombinats nach Schwedt in Marsch gesetzt.

Wolfgang Biermann, Jahrgang 1927, ist Sohn eines Buchdruckers in Leipzig. Er lernte Maschinenschlosser, bildete sich zum Maschinenbau-Ingenieur weiter und studierte später »so nebenbei«, wie er sagt, Ökonomie. Als Leiter des Werkzeugmaschinen-Kombinats »7. Oktober« in Berlin promovierte er mit einer Arbeit über »Die Entwicklung der sozialistischen Industriekombinate der DDR« und wurde im Herbst 1975, als das Zeiss-Kombinat den Anschluß an die moderne Technologie nicht mehr schaffte und unübersehbar kriselte, als starker Mann nach Jena geschickt. Zur SED war Biermann, der die beiden letzten Kriegsjahre als Soldat erlebte und kurz vor Torschluß noch der NSDAP beitrat, nach dem 17. Juni 1953 gestoßen, ein »Akt demonstrativer Solidarität mit der Partei der Arbeiterklasse«, wie er später sagte. Auch Erich Müller, ein Voigtländer des Jahrgangs 1921, war zunächst Maschinenschlosser. Bei Kriegsende diente er als Torpedomechaniker der Luftwaffe in Nordnorwegen, und freimütig bekannte er, daß er in diesen Jahren »noch nicht genügend Verstand hatte«, sich schon für den Sozialismus zu engagieren. Heimgekehrt, arbeitete er wieder als Schlosser, trat unter Einfluß von Verwandten 1946 der KPD bei, studierte Ökonomie – »das war schon nicht leicht, da haben's jüngere Jahrgänge mit höherer Qualifizierung besser, ich hatte doch nur Volksschulabschluß« – und war danach in einer Gewerkschaftszentrale tätig. Als ich ihn 1985 in Leuna in seinem Büro interviewte, stand er schon 17 Jahre an der Spitze dieses Kombinates. Alle drei, Frohn, Biermann und Müller, kommen aus proletarisch-kleinbürgerlichem Milieu; alle drei verfügen unstreitig über Qualitäten, die sie befähigt hätten, auch in einer bürgerlichen Demokratie mit kapitalistischer Wirtschaftsordnung berufliche Erfolge zu erzielen.

Werner Frohn hätte es mit Hilfe des zweiten Bildungsweges sicher zum Oberstadtdirektor gebracht, Wolfgang Biermann vielleicht zum Gewerkschaftsboß oder SPD-Minister und Erich Müller zum Arbeitsdirektor in einem Mitbestimmungs-Unternehmen. Doch alle drei sind festen Glaubens, daß ihr Aufstieg in die »Kommandozentrale« gewaltiger Betriebe nur in der realsozialistischen DDR möglich war. »Ich verdanke dieser Gesellschaft alles, was ich geworden bin«, gab mir Biermann 1986 in Jena in einem Interview zu Protokoll, »ich habe eben alles mitgemacht, aus einer Arbeiterfamilie, über den Maschinenschlosser bis zu dem, was ich heute bin«. Und er fügte hinzu: »Daß ich mich für meine Partei und den Sozialismus engagiere, ist nicht eine Frage der Dankbarkeit, aber man soll eben nicht vergessen, wo man herkommt und was man früher einmal war.« Auch Erich Müller meinte, eher ginge das sprichwörtliche Kamel durchs Nadelöhr, als daß er es in der Bundesrepublik zum Vorstandsvorsitzenden eines Konzerns oder Chefmanager eines Großunternehmens gebracht hätte: »Ich glaub's nicht«, sagte er, »ich kann mir vorstellen, daß dort eine privilegierte Schicht berufen ist, an eine Konzernspitze zu treten, und die wird sicher nicht aus der Arbeiterschaft hervorgehen.« Müller über die Bedingungen seines Erfolges: »Die Partei hat mich zur Schule geschickt, hat mich studieren lassen, dazu kommen Einsichten, die das Leben mitbringt; das ist mein Werdegang, so ist er bestimmt.«

Wer die Autobahn von Berlin in Richtung Süden fährt, sieht an einem klaren Tag vor Sonnenuntergang zwischen Schkeuditzer Kreuz und der Abfahrt Bad Dürrenberg am Horizont zur Rechten eine gewaltige, aus zahllosen Kühltürmen und Schornsteinen dampfende, schwelende und qualmende Industriekulisse – Erich Müllers Reich. Ohne Leuna läge die Industrie in der DDR brach, denn hier entstehen nicht nur

Plastik, Harze und die Ausgangsprodukte für synthetische Fasern, von hier kommen auch die Katalysatoren, ohne die vier Fünftel aller chemischen Verarbeitungsprozesse in der DDR nicht laufen würden. Aus heutiger Sicht hat Leuna in der jüngsten deutschen Geschichte fatale Dienste geleistet. Im Ersten Weltkrieg wurde es gebaut, um die deutschen Armeen mit Sprengstoff zu versorgen. Die britische Blockade hatte das »Reich« von der für die Munitionsherstellung wichtigen Salpeterzufuhr abgeschnitten. Leuna, die Kernzelle der Chemischen Industrie Mitteldeutschlands, schuf nach der Entdeckung der Ammoniaksynthese für Natursalpeter nun einen chemischen Ersatz. Und erstmals wurde in Leuna auch jenes Verfahren erprobt und in großem Stil angewendet, ohne das die deutschen Blitzkrieg-Verbände zu Beginn des Zweiten Weltkriegs nicht weit hätten rollen können: Kohlehydrierung, Gewinnung von Benzin und Treibstoffen auf Kohlebasis. Leuna gehörte einst zum I.G.-Farben-Konzern; und wenn das Werk heute den Namen des DDR-Gründungsvaters Walter Ulbrich trägt, dann als Zeichen des Triumphs und Sieges, den die regierenden deutschen Kommunisten über die verhaßten »Monopolherren« im Klassenkampf errangen, als sie die Anlagen entschädigungslos enteigneten.

Seither soll der Begriff »Volkseigener Betrieb« im neuen Leunatitel suggerieren, daß das Werk im Besitz des Volkes sei oder gar den Arbeitern gehöre, obschon diese nicht den geringsten Einfluß auf Art oder Umfang der Produktion nehmen können. Die angeblichen Eigentümer haben vor allem Pflichten und wenig Rechte, eine Tatsache, die dadurch, daß »einer von ihnen«, ein ehemaliger Maschinenschlosser, nun den früheren I.G.-Farben-Betrieb dirigiert, nicht einmal notdürftig verdeckt wird. Daß es den neuen »Eigentümern« am rechten Bewußtsein mangelt, machte Professor Hans Luft im Dezember 1985 in der »Zeitschrift für Philosophie« deutlich. »Volkseigentum und genossenschaftliches Eigentum« stand da zu lesen, »habe die Spaltung in Nichteigentümer und Eigentümer im Sozialismus beseitigt«, doch habe sich die »individuelle Verantwortung für das sozialistische Eigentum an den Produktionsmitteln nicht automatisch« entwickelt. Zu deutsch hieß das, die Arbeiter verhalten sich nicht wie Eigentümer, die sie angeblich sind, leisten zu wenig und widmen Unterhalt und Pflege des Maschinenparks nur einen Bruchteil der Aufmerksamkeit, die sie für den eigenen Trabi erübrigen. Das rechte »Eigentümerverhalten« manifestiere sich nämlich in »fleißiger, initiativereicher Arbeit, wobei viele Werktätige verschiedenster Berufe, in dem Bewußtsein, für sich selbst zu arbeiten, oft mehr tun als ihre Pflicht«. Um das Manko wettzumachen, empfahl der Autor, »die ständige bewußte Herstellung der Übereinstimmung von gesellschaftlichen und persönlichen Interessen«, was soviel bedeutet wie eine wirksame Mischung aus Agitation und Leistungsprämien.

Daß der Betrieb Gewinn abwirft, daß er konkurrenzfähig bleibt, daß Investitionen mit Blick auf die Zukunft geplant werden, darin sei sich verantwortliches Management in Ost und West gleich, erklärte mir Wolfgang Biermann in Jena. Den entscheidenden Unterschied sieht er darin, daß der erwirtschaftete Gewinn eines Unternehmens nicht in private Taschen fließt. Doch über die Verwendung solcher Gewinne entscheiden nicht jene, die ihn erwirtschaftet haben, weder die Werktätigen noch die Manager, sondern die Spitze der Partei, was das Fehlen des rechten sozialistischen Eigentumsbewußtseins an der Basis hinreichend erklärt. »Es gilt als Bürgerpflicht bei uns«, so Erich Müller im Interview, »den Plan zu erfüllen, besser, überzuerfüllen.« Aber die Planvorgaben werden oben diktiert.

Der renommierte DDR-Ökonom Harry Maier, der sich 1986 in den Westen absetzte, weil die Staatssicherheit ihn zum Ausspähen und Aushorchen westlicher Kollegen verpflichten wollte, nennt das eine »Kommandowirtschaft«, die auf dem autoritären Konzept einer in zwei Gruppen gespaltenen Gesellschaft beruhe: »Eine kleine Gruppe gibt die ökonomischen Leistungsziele vor, und die große Mehrheit arbeitet mit Fleiß und Hingabe an deren Erfüllung. Marx würde sich im Grabe umdrehen.«

Wenn es überhaupt so etwas wie Mitbestimmung und Diskussion über den richtigen Weg in der DDR-Wirtschaft gibt, dann nur auf dem Umweg über die SED; und in dieser Partei mit über zwei Millionen Mitgliedern – »mindestens eine Million davon sind Heuchler und Karrieristen«, so meint Kürschnermeister aus dem Vogtland – ist die Diskussion über die »Kommandos« oder Weichenstellungen auf den Kreis der »Erlauchten« beschränkt, jener rund zweihundert Mitglieder des SED-Zentralkomitees, in dem Frohn, Biermann und Müller Sitz und Stimme haben. Daß die Kommandos der Zentrale nach unten »durchgestellt« werden, wie man das in der DDR gern nennt, dafür sorgen – Motto: »Wo ein Genosse ist, da ist die Partei« – die führenden Mitarbeiter jedes Kombinats. Als wir in Leuna eine Sitzung Erich Müllers mit seinen Direktoren drehten, gab es keinen, der nicht das Abzeichen der Partei im linken Knopfloch trug. Nicht anders bei der Besprechung, die Wolfgang Biermann in Jena leitete. Ich fragte den Zeiss-Chef nach der Rolle, welche die Partei in seinem Betrieb spiele. »Wir haben nie ein Hehl daraus gemacht, daß die Sozialistische Einheitspartei Deutschlands die führende Partei der DDR ist«, antwortete Biermann und riet mir, das »theoretisch vom Marxismus-Leninismus her« zu sehen. Die Partei sei nun einmal »Beauftragte der Arbeiterklasse und der Werktätigen«, darauf gründe sie ihren Führungsanspruch. Deshalb sei es »kein Geheimnis, daß in den Leitungsfunktionen des Kombinats nur Parteimitglieder« sitzen.

Die SED hat die Monopolherren ausgeschaltet, aber in jüngster Zeit Monopolkonzerne, die bundesdeutsches Kartellrecht verbieten würde, neu geschaffen. Ein Kombinat in der DDR stellt nämlich nichts anderes dar als einen Riesenkonzern, der alle in der DDR vorhandenen Industriebetriebe einer bestimmten Wirtschaftsbranche zusammenfaßt und von der Grundlagenforschung und den Rohstoffen über die Produktion bis zum Absatz in einem geschlossenen Kreislauf in sich vereint. Der Erfinder dieser Konzeption ist Günter Mittag, Mitglied des Politbüros und Wirtschaftschef der SED. Wolfgang Biermann war Mittags Testpilot, der bei der Kombinatsbildung immer forsch an der Spitze marschierte. So hört alles, was in der DDR auch nur entfernt mit Optik zu tun hat, auf sein Kommando. Als ich den »verdienten Techniker des Volkes« im Frühjahr 1986 in Jena sprach, umfaßte sein Kombinat bereits 24 weithin über die DDR verstreute Einzelbetriebe, die Produktionspalette reichte vom Haushaltsglas und vom simplen Brillengestell über Planetarien und Spiegelteleskope bis zum modernen Lasermeß-System. Ob diese Konzentration höhere Effektivität garantiert, bleibt zweifelhaft, denn da wurde auch mancher sanierungsbedürftige Betrieb angegliedert. Die Tendenz vergleichbarer westlicher Großunternehmen ist eher gegenläufig. Sie neigen dazu, unrentable Fertigungszweige abzustoßen. Zwar braucht das Biermann-Kombinat bei einigen Spitzenprodukten keinen Vergleich zu scheuen, aber bei der Arbeitsproduktivität liegt es weit hinter der westdeutschen Zeiss-Stiftung in Heidenheim.

Wie ganz Deutschland, wurde auch die Carl-Zeiss-Stiftung nach dem Krieg geteilt. Als die Amerikaner, die Thüringen vor den Sowjets besetzt hatten, sich in ihre Besatzungszone zurückzogen, nahmen sie die Spitze der Firma mit 126 leitenden Angestellten mit, die schon bald in Oberkochem die Herstellung optischer Geräte wieder aufnahmen. Nach langem Streit einigten sich Zeiss-Ost und Zeiss-West, daß die Firma in Heidenheim den Qualitätsnamen Zeiss exklusiv in der Bundesrepublik und den wichtigsten westlichen Ländern führen, in der DDR und dem Ostblock aber nur als »Opton Feintechnik GmbH« auftreten darf. Umgekehrt hat das DDR-Kombinat mit dem alten Firmensitz Jena das ausschließliche Recht auf die Nutzung des Namens Zeiss im ganzen Ostblock und firmiert im Westen als »Jenoptik GmbH«. In einigen Ländern der Dritten Welt sind beide Firmen unter dem Namen Zeiss vertreten.

Allerdings sprechen die Direktoren von Zeiss-West mit Respekt von Wolfgang Biermann und bescheinigen ihm, daß die Konkurrenz härter geworden sei, seit er das Kombinat mit strenger Hand regiert. Er wiederum räumt ein: »Das sind schon Leute bei Zeiss-Oberkochem, die etwas von ihrem Fach verstehen und Gebiete haben, wo sie die Spitzenposition halten.« Fünftausend von den knapp 50 000 Mitarbeitern des Kombinats, darunter Computer-Experten, Mathematiker, Informatiker und Physiker, arbeiten in der Forschungsabteilung von Zeiss-Jena an technisch-wissenschaftlichen Problemlösungen. Ihre Anstrengungen gelten vor allem der Lichtleitertechnik und der Mikroelektronik. Im Konzept der DDR-Planwirtschaft stellt die in den Kombinaten betriebene zielorientierte Forschung einen »organischen Verbund von Wissenschaft und Produktion dar, von dem man sich Schubkraft für Innovationen verspricht. Wenn die Innovationsrate der DDR-Wirtschaft dennoch seit Jahren erheblich unter der des Westens liegt, dann machen westliche Experten ausgerechnet jene Kombinate dafür verantwortlich, die der ganze Stolz Günter Mittags sind. Ihre Monopolstruktur verführe nämlich zur Trägheit. Solange nicht mehrere Betriebe mit vergleichbaren Produkten gegeneinander konkurrieren, sondern die Erzeugung bei einem riesigen Kombinat konzentriert bleibt, wird sich das Tempo der Erneuerung kaum beschleunigen lassen. Intern diskutieren Wirtschaftswissenschaftler in der DDR seit langem offen über die Möglichkeiten einer sozialistischen Marktwirtschaft, doch solange der Zentralist Günter Mittag, ein ehemaliger Eisenbahner, das Sagen hat, haben ihre ketzerischen Überlegungen keine Chance und vor allem keine Öffentlichkeit. Sie werden nicht einmal in Fachpublikationen gedruckt.

Sehr viel früher als die Sowjetunion und lange vor Gorbatschow hat die DDR die Umstellung von der extensiven auf die intensive Wirtschaft vollzogen, was konkret heißt, daß die Betriebe durch Einsparung von Material und Energie und durch die bessere Auslastung der zum Teil überalterten Maschinen und Anlagen sparsamer produzieren. In Leuna beispielsweise ist es durch eine Umstellung der Technologie gelungen, aus nur 5 Millionen Tonnen Erdöl dieselbe Menge Benzin, Heizöl, Diesel- und Schwere Öle zu gewinnen, wie zuvor aus 8 Millionen. Erich Müller bekundete stolz darauf, »daß unsere Leute das gekonnt haben«, und hatte dabei die 2500 Mitarbeiter der Forschungsabteilung seines Kombinats im Auge. Als Triebkraft für die höchste Ausnutzung des Erdöls nannte er »die Angst vor der Kohle«, eine Chiffre, die für ein Grund-Dilemma der ganzen DDR-Wirtschaft steht, das sich auf absehbare Zeit nicht lösen läßt. Einerseits nämlich weiß die DDR-Führung genau, daß der vermehrte Rückgriff auf die Braunkohle sie wegen der damit einhergehenden schweren Schädigung der Umwelt langfristig unerhört teuer zu stehen kommt. Andererseits hat sie, seit die Sowjetunion ihre Öllieferungen kürzte, keine andere Wahl, als die einzige heimische Energiequelle verstärkt auszubeuten. Dabei gingen allein die Kosten der Umstellung vieler mit Öl betriebener Anlagen auf Braunkohle, die seit 1980 vorgenommen wurde, schon in die Milliarden, so daß für die kostspielige Technik, die den erhöhten Schadstoffausstoß eindämmen könnte, keine Mittel verfügbar sind. Auch die Leuna-Werke brauchen für einen Teil ihrer Fertigung Braunkohle-Schwelkoks. Zu den Produktionsrekorden, die keine Statistik im sozialistischen Wettbewerb meldet, zählen deshalb 100 000 Tonnen Schwefeldioxyd pro Jahr, mit denen sie die Luft verpesten.

Erich Müller wußte genau, welche Gefahren für die Umwelt von seinem Kombinat ausgehen. Er hatte sich im Westen über die verschiedenen Methoden der Entschwefelung sachkundig gemacht. Die wirklich effektiven Anlagen erforderten jedoch aus seiner Sicht »einen riesigen materiellen Aufwand« und waren ihm »einfach zu teuer«. Er wollte deshalb lieber auf ein perfektes Verfahren warten, das es ermöglicht, die entweichenden schwefligen Gase zu binden, damit der darin enthaltene Schwefel wieder für die Produktion von Kunstfasern verwendet werden kann: »Das Werk braucht Elementarschwefel, wenn ich ihn wieder einfangen kann, dann habe ich einen Rohstoff.« Ein solcher geschlossener Kreislauf der Entschwefelung käme dem Ei des Kolumbus gleich. Doch bis ein solches Verfahren entwickelt und von der DDR obendrein finanziert werden kann, dürfte mindestens ein weiteres Jahrzehnt verstrichen sein. Der Gesamtausstoß an Schwefeldioxyd in der DDR stieg in den letzten Jahren von 3,5 auf 4 Millionen Tonnen pro Jahr, die Kosten für Entschwefelungsanlagen, welche die Schadstoff-Emissionen auch nur um 1 Million Tonnen pro Jahr senken könnten, werden von Experten auf 20 Milliarden (West-)Mark geschätzt, ein Betrag, der für DDR-Ökonomen geradezu unvorstellbar ist, übersteigt er doch bei weitem die Mittel, welche der gesamten Energiewirtschaft in der DDR für Investitionen zur Verfügung stehen. Wenn die DDR in der Lage wäre, eine solche Anstrengung zu verkraften, argumentieren westliche Experten, dann hätte sie den verstärkten Rückgriff auf die Braunkohle gar nicht nötig gehabt. Es wäre billiger für sie gewesen, Öl auf dem Weltmarkt zu kaufen und die teure Umstellung der Industrie und Heizkraftwerke auf Kohle von Anfang an zu vermeiden.

Erich Honecker selbst bezifferte Mitte der 80er Jahre den Rückstand der DDR gegenüber der Bundesrepublik auf dem Gebiet der Arbeitsproduktivität auf 30 Prozent, westliche Wirtschaftsfachleute schätzen ihn weit höher ein, und der Abstand, darin sind sich Ökonomen in Ost und West einig, ist in den letzten Jahren nicht geringer, sondern eher größer geworden. Gemessen an der Sowjetunion mag die andere deutsche Republik zwar relativ erfolgreich sein, aber ihre Wettbewerbsfähigkeit auf dem Weltmarkt ist rückläufig. Harry Maier attestiert dem »zentralisierten System, in dem keine kritische Meinung geduldet wird«, sinkende Exportkraft, die auf technologischen Rückstand vor allem bei der Mikroelektronik, einen Mangel an Innovationen und auf eine Verschlechterung der »terms of trade«, zurückzuführen sei. Die DDR sei stolz auf ihre straff gelenkten Riesenkombinate, doch ein Mann wie Gorbatschow, der sich ursprünglich durch sie beeindruckt zeigte, sehe die DDR heute nicht als ein Modell, an dem sich seine Reformpolitik orientieren könnte. Der sowjetische Parteichef habe vielmehr die Rolle der kleinen Betriebe als Motor des Fortschritts erkannt. »Nicht die Kombinate, sondern die Restbestände an privatem Handwerk, Handwerksgenossenschaften sowie privaten Gaststätten und Dienstleistungsbetrieben interessieren die sowjetischen Reformer in der DDR.«

Einen solchen Rest, und zweifellos einen beachtlichen, den westlichen Medien zu präsentieren sich die DDR-Obrigkeit nicht scheut, studierte ich im Herbst 1985 in Berlin-Schöneweide. Die Trabant-Vertragswerkstatt des Kraftfahrzeugmeisters Gerhard Graubaum begann morgens um halb sechs mit der Arbeit, aber die meisten Kunden kamen laut knatternd mit ihren Trabis schon gegen fünf Uhr auf den Hof gefahren. »Gerhard Graubaum«, sagte eine Kundin, »hat eine Werkstatt, die man sich suchen kann; da wird wirklich noch korrekt gearbeitet. Wer hier Stammkunde sein kann, der darf sich glücklich schätzen.« Daß die Dienstleistungen mit der zunehmenden Motorisierung in der DDR nicht Schritt halten, bezeugen oft hundert Meter lange Wartburg- und Trabi-Schlangen vor den Minol-Tankstellen, die sich auf dem Höhepunkt der Urlaubs- und Reisesaison auf den Abbiegerspuren der Autobahn bilden. Auch bei den Werkstätten heißt es anstehen und warten. Wer bei Gerhard Graubaum einen Termin für eine Inspektion erhalten wollte, mußte sich 4 bis 6 Wochen vorher anmelden. Ein Firmenchef in der DDR, der so kostbares Gut wie rare, begehrte Werkstattstunden zu verwalten und zuzuteilen hat, kann Freundlichkeit, ja Fügsamkeit erwarten. Der selbstsichere und resolute Gerhard Graubaum, ein Berliner des Jahrgangs 1935, war sich dieser Position bewußt. Er nahm grundsätzlich nur Fahrzeuge in »sauberem und gewaschenem Zustand« an: »Wenn ich zum Zahnarzt oder zum Schuhmacher gehe, putze ich ja auch vorher die Zähne oder die Schuhe.« So streng sind die Sitten, wenn nicht der Kunde, sondern der Verkäufer König ist.

Fast jeder zweite in der DDR zugelassene PKW war 1987 ein Trabant, gefertigt von den IFA-Werken in Zwickau – ein lautes, von einem luftgekühlten 26 PS-Zweitaktmotor getriebenen Gefährt, das dem DDR-Volksmund zufolge nur deshalb nicht in schwarz geliefert wird, weil es mit einem Brikett verwechselt werden könnte. Es gibt viele Witze über den Trabi, der trotz seiner vorsintflutlichen Technik das Ziel vieler Träume und Wünsche darstellt, weil es für den kleinen Mann zwischen Elbe und Oder letztlich doch erreichbar bleibt. Für den DDR-Normalverbraucher mit einem statistischen Durchschnittseinkommen von 1000 Mark im Monat ist der Wagen – der Preis beträgt, unerläßliche Extras inklusive, 10 500 Mark – einigermaßen erschwinglich und ohne großen Aufwand zu unterhalten. Der Trabi gilt als unkompliziert, robust und pflegeleicht. Immer gut für einen Trabiwitz ist der 10-Markschein der DDR, der auf der einen Seite eine junge Chemikerin in einem Industrielabor, auf der anderen Seite Clara Zetkin in unverkennbar reifen Jahren zeigt. Ein Taxifahrer in Leipzig, der mir eine solche Note mit dem Wechselgeld herausgab, deutete erst auf die Seite mit der jungen Frau und sagte: »So sieht man aus, wenn man bei uns einen Trabant bestellt«, drehte den Schein um, tippte auf Clara Zetkin: »und so grau ist man, wenn er endlich geliefert wird.« Von der im Westen unvorstellbar langen Wartezeit von 10 bis 13 Jahren handelt ein Witz über einen amerikanischen Millionär, den selbst Funktionäre genüßlich erzählen. Der Amerikaner sammelt mit Leidenschaft kostbare Automobile. Als er von den Lieferzeiten für den Trabant erfährt, ordert er sofort, denn er glaubt, eine besondere Rarität zu erwerben. Weil er in Valuta zahlt, wird der Trabi jedoch umgehend geliefert. So erzählt der Millionär seinen Freunden: »Ihr könnt Euch gar nicht denken, welch tollen Service diese East-Germans haben. Ich bestellte ein Auto, das erst in 10 Jahren geliefert wird; doch vorweg haben sie ein Spielzeugmodell aus Pappe geschickt. Und stellt Euch vor: Es fährt!« Es ist ein Witz mit doppeltem Boden: Zwar nicht aus Pappe, doch aus einem Duroplast genannten Kunststoff ist die Außenhaut der Karosse gefertigt, welche die Hersteller in ihren – in der DDR wahrlich überflüssigen – Werbeprospekten deshalb pompös als »verwitterungsstabil« anpreisen. Und tatsächlich entfällt für DDR-Bürger, die über zahlungskräftige und spendierfreudige West-Verwandtschaft verfügen, die jahrelange Wartezeit: Gegen harte Valuta liefert die DDR-Firma Gemex über ihre Filialen in Kopenhagen und Zürich Trabis innerhalb der DDR nicht nur sofort, sondern obendrein zum halben Preis.

Am Beispiel Trabant lassen sich auch andere Merkwürdigkeiten studieren, typisch für Märkte, auf denen der Mangel diktiert. Wagen, die acht Jahre gelaufen sind, bringen beim Wiederverkauf oft mehr als den Anschaffungspreis ein. So braucht ein DDR-Ehepaar, das einmal einen fabrikneuen Wagen erhalten hat, im Grunde nie wieder ein neues Auto zu bezahlen, vorausgesetzt, es ist gewitzt genug, die vorhandenen Möglichkeiten auszuschöpfen. Dann nämlich haben sich die »Bestellkünstler« abwechselnd so geschickt in die Listen eingetragen, daß die Wartezeit halbiert und für einen der beiden jeweils nach fünf oder sechs Jahren ein neuer Wagen fällig wird, dessen Anschaffungspreis sich bequem aus dem Erlös für das alte Auto decken läßt. Da nur volljährige DDR-Bürger einen Trabant, Wartburg oder Lada bestellen dürfen, haben vor allem die späten Teens und frühen Twens eine Durststrecke zu überstehen. Sie versuchen sie mit Motorrädern zu überbrücken (die Zahl der zugelassenen Krafträder in der DDR liegt deutlich über der in der Bundesrepublik), besonders aber mit Gebrauchtwagen, die meist weit über 100 000 Kilometer gelaufen und nicht selten das Ergebnis emsiger Bastelarbeit sind. In der Werkstatt von Gerhard Graubaum wurde grundsätzlich kein Trabi, auch der älteste nicht, verschrottet, sondern bis zum letzten ausgeschlachtet. Über die holprigen Straßen der DDR rollt so mancher Kleinwagen, der aus Einzelteilen dutzender ausgeweideter Trabis rund um das Stahlskelett einer uralten Zwickauer Winzigkarosse neu aufgebaut worden ist. Die lange Wartezeit treibt die seltsamsten Blüten auf dem Schwarzen Markt. Geschäftstüchtige Neuwagenbesitzer können bei schnellem privaten Weiterverkauf mühelos Gewinne von 10 000 Mark kassieren. Das knappe Warenangebot in der DDR hat zu einem Kaufkraftüberhang geführt, der es vielen DDR-Bürgern ermöglicht, für fast neue Gebrauchtwagen den doppelten Neupreis zu zahlen.

Wenn das Wort Familienbetrieb seine Berechtigung hat, dann in den letzten privaten Wirtschaftsoasen des realen Sozialismus. In der Werkstatt, die Gerhard Graubaum von seinem Vater übernommen und ausgebaut hat, arbeiteten sechs Graubaums aus drei Generationen einträchtig nebeneinander.

Die älteste des Clans, Großmutter Jenny, Jahrgang 1914, stand als Putzfrau beim Sohn in Lohn und Brot und besserte sich die Rente auf. Seine Frau Rita besorgte die Buchhaltung, die Söhne Henri und Rolf waren als Schlosser, Schwiegertochter Angelika als Sekretärin beschäftigt. Private Handwerksbetriebe, die maximal zehn Angestellte beschäftigen dürfen, bieten persönlichen und politischen Freiraum. Bei den Graubaums spürte man nichts von der offiziellen Ideologie, die mit ihren Agitprop-Losungen sonst die ganze Arbeitswelt der DDR durchsetzt. Da gab es keine Parteisekretäre und keine »Brigade der Deutsch-Sowjetischen Freundschaft«, da forderte keine Gewerkschaft zu Sonderschichten für den Frieden, den Jahrestag der Republik oder den sozialistischen Wettbewerb auf, keine Betriebskampfgruppe verpflichtete zum Ausrücken ins Wochenendmanöver. Da, zumal unter Familienangehörigen, auch die Arbeitszeiten flexibler gehandhabt werden, verfügen solche politikfreien Zonen über besondere Anziehungskraft für jene, die Erfolg und Bestätigung nicht im Rahmen der gesetzten sozialen und politischen Normen suchen und auf Titel und Auszeichnungen wie »Bester Produktionsarbeiter« oder »Held der sozialistischen Arbeit« verzichten können. Das erklärt, warum private Handwerksbetriebe, die ihre Mitarbeiter meist nicht so gut entlohnen dürfen wie staatliche Firmen, nie um Arbeitskräfte verlegen sind.

»Mit Fug und Recht kann ich sagen, daß ich mit dem, was ich erreicht habe, zufrieden sein kann«, erzählt Graubaum im Interview vor der Kamera. »Ich kann gut leben, ich kann mir gewisse Dinge leisten und kann nicht sagen, daß ich mich benachteiligt fühle. Inzwischen habe ich auch den Eindruck, daß ich diesen Betrieb und alles, was ich erarbeitet habe, an die Söhne weitergeben kann.« Diese neue Sicherheit ist auf einen Kurswechsel des SED-Politbüros zurückzuführen, das seit 1984 die Existenz und selbst die Neugründung privater Handwerksbetriebe fördert, weil es erkannt hat, daß anders der chronischen Misere auf dem Dienstleistungssektor nicht beizukommen ist. Da werden nicht nur spottbillige Kredite mit langen Laufzeiten und lächerlich geringen Tilgungsraten zur Verfügung gestellt, da wird neuerlich auch auf Maßnahmen verzichtet, die einst mit dem ausschließlichen Ziel in Kraft gesetzt wurden, die Reste des privaten Sektors in der DDR klein zu halten, zurückzustutzen und zum Zusammenschluß zu Produktionsgenossenschaften zu zwingen. So durfte Graubaum seit 1985 Lehrlinge ausbilden, was ihm bis dahin untersagt war, weil die Doktrin die Ausbildung Staats- und Genossenschaftsbetrieben vorbehielt, in denen die erzieherische Einwirkung der Partei gesichert war.

Graubaum repariert Trabis, aber privat fährt er einen der begehrten Volvos, welche die DDR-Führung Ende der 70er Jahre zusammen mit 10 000 Golf, 10 000 Mazda und 5000 Citroën importierte, um den Ausfall fest zugesagter polnischer und sowjetischer PKW-Lieferungen auszugleichen. Ein importierter Volvo kostete 42 000 Mark und war für den Durchschnittsbürger der anderen Republik (Netto-Jahreseinkommen 12 000 Mark) wahrlich unerschwinglich. Da die meisten in Berlin zugelassen wurden und ihre Nummernschilder ausgerechnet die Kennzeichen IBM erhielten, deutete der Volksmund dies prompt als »Ich bin Millionär«. Mit einem Nettoeinkommen von 40 000 Mark im Jahr stand Graubaum sich mindestens so gut wie ein Generaldirektor von Leuna, Zeiss-Jena oder Schwedt. Auch im Sozialismus hat Handwerk eben goldenen Boden. Die DDR nennt sich Arbeiter- und Bauernstaat, aber käme es auf den höchsterreichbaren pesönlichen Wohlstand an, hieße sie besser Staat der Handwerker und Bauern. Nur Handwerker können sich einen jener VW-Kombi (Preis: 58 000 Mark) leisten, den die DDR importiert, seit das lange erhoffte große Geschäft mit VW abgeschlossen wurde. Danach lieferte VW alte Fließbänder für umweltfreundliche, wassergekühlte Benzinmotoren in die DDR, die anstelle der umweltverpestenden Zweitaktmotoren in die Wartburg-Serie eingebaut werden. Die Bezahlung erfolgt, typisch für solche deutsch-deutschen Geschäfte, die ohne Valuta abgewickelt werden, durch Lieferung eines Teils der in der DDR gefertigten VW-Motoren an Salzgitter, und damit wird auch der Import einiger VW-Kombi in die DDR finanziert.

Am Wochenende trifft sich der Graubaum-Clan auf einer Datsche 30 Kilometer nordöstlich von Berlin an einem märkischen See. Das 3000 qm große Ufergrundstück kostet nicht einmal 100 Mark Pacht im Jahr. Haus und Nebengebäude mit insgesamt 80 qm Wohnfläche hat der Handwerksmeister mit Söhnen und Freunden selbst gezimmert und eingerichtet. Der Lebensstandard der Graubaums stellt die Spitze dessen dar, was ein DDR-Bürger erreichen kann, ohne seine Seele an Partei und Staat zu verkaufen. Nur wenige Künstler, Schriftsteller und Wissenschaftler sind in der Lage, mehr materiellen Wohlstand zu erwirtschaften. Ihr Beruf läßt sie zwar weltläufiger sein, denn Reisen in das sogenannte NSW (Nichtsozialistische Wirtschafts-Gebiet) werden vielen von ihnen schon deshalb ermöglicht, weil die DDR seit ihrer Anerkennung durch die westliche Staatenwelt auf kulturelle Selbstdarstellung bedacht ist. Doch der Preis dafür ist allemal in Wort, Schrift und Bild bewiesene Loyalität gegenüber dem sozialistischen Staat und der marxistisch-leninistischen Partei.

»Gerhard Graubaum«, sagte ich in einem Portrait über den erfolgreichsten privaten KFZ-Meister Ostberlins, das 1985 gesendet wurde, »ist ein selfmademan, erfolgreich innerhalb der Grenzen, die die DDR privaten Betrieben gezogen hat – und die liegen bei maximal zehn Angestellten. Außer der Freiheit zu reisen, wohin er will, oder zu lesen, was nicht von Partei und Staat verordnet ist, fehlt ihm eigentlich nichts. Freilich weiß er, daß er ohne harten persönlichen Einsatz so weit nicht gekommen wäre.«

»In einem Staatsbetrieb«, meinte Graubaum, »will keiner die Norm durch höhere Leistung verschlechtern. Das macht einen entscheidenden Unterschied. Und keiner denkt auch nur dran, seinen Arbeitsplatz sauber zu machen.« Die Einsicht, daß solch persönlicher Einsatz, welcher der Gesellschaft nützt, Früchte tragen muß für den, der ihn leistet, hat der realsozialistische Staat, wenn auch zu spät, gezeigt. Doch so mancher Altgenosse erblickt darin noch immer eine Sünde wider den kommunistischen Glauben, für den er in der Weimarer Republik gekämpft, unter Hitler gelitten und nach dem Krieg schwierige Aufbaujahre mit durchgestanden hat.

»Es gibt auch Dinge, die mißbraucht werden«, steht in der »Lebensgeschichte des Chemiearbeiters Gustav R., Jahrgang 1902«, zu lesen, die von Wolfgang Herzberg aufgezeichnet und von der Zeitschrift »Neue Deutsche Literatur« im Juli 1985 veröffentlicht wurde. Es ist die Geschichte eines gelernten Bergarbeiters aus Schlesien, der nach dem Ersten Weltkrieg auf Wanderschaft ging, im Rheinland über den Roten-Frontkämpfer-Bund zur KPD stieß und in der Hitlerzeit einige Monate im Zuchthaus saß. Nach 1945 avancierte er zum Parteisekretär und wurde als Aktivist in einem Glühlampenwerk ausgezeichnet. »Der Mensch muß ja auch mal zum Idealisten erzogen werden, ein edler Mensch werden, aber viele sind noch schwerere Materialisten«, meint dieser Altkommunist, der das Unverständnis vieler alter Genossen gegenüber den Notwendigkeiten des realen Sozialismus verkörpert. Die DDR handelt nach dem Motto: »Jedem nach seinen Fähigkeiten, jedem nach seinen Leistungen«, das als spezifisches Merkmal der sozialistischen Gesellschaftsformation gilt. (Übrigens geht diese Formel auf eine Vorstellung von Karl Marx zurück, der in der Kritik des Gothaer Programms das Prinzip der angemessenen Verteilung des Arbeitsertrags in jener ersten Phase der kommunistischen Gesellschaft erörterte, die noch mit den Merkmalen »der alten Gesellschaft« behaftet ist). Die DDR rechtfertigt mit diesem Grundsatz eine erhebliche Differenzierung der Einkommen. Soziale Gleichheit in Produktion, Distribution und Konsumption wird damit praktisch auf den Anbruch des kommunistischen Zeitalters verschoben, in dem einmal das Prinzip »Jedem nach seinen Bedürfnissen« gelten soll. Im Kern mag dies ein durchaus vernünftiger und pragmatischer Gedanke sein, doch verhindern der Nepotismus der Partei, die Vorherrschaft der Bürokratie und die Zwänge der Planwirtschaft das Entstehen einer echten Leistungsgesellschaft schon im Ansatz. Und Altkommunisten wie der Chemiearbeiter Gustav R. empfinden das relativ große Einkommensgefälle, das durch Verzicht auf die von der neuen Offenbarung verheißene Gleichheit aller – wenn auch, theoretisch, nur für eine Übergangszeit zugelassen wird – schlicht als Verrat an der Idee und als Skandal. »Wie kann man das besser machen?«, fragt Gustav R. »Erst, wenn's allen gut geht, dann sind wir im Kommunismus. Aber allen geht's ja noch nicht gut. Es reißt ziemlich bei uns ein, man macht da noch gewaltige Unterschiede. Die Erziehung zum WIR, die geht nicht so schnell vorwärts. Es gibt noch zu viele ICH-Menschen, das sind eben Materialisten, die kriegen nicht genug... Wenn ich zum Beispiel son Handwerker nehme. Das stimmt ja, der wird manchmal Millionär. Das ist meiner Ansicht nach doch nicht richtig. Ich meine, er kann doch nicht mehr Kapitalist werden, Ausbeuter kann er nicht mehr werden, das ist ja untersagt, aber er schafft sich doch einen Reichtum an. Wenn er den Reichtum zu wohltätigen Zwecken verwenden würde, aber das macht er nicht. Solche Leute so zu entwickeln, dazu ist der Sozialismus nicht da, sondern für die armen Menschen.«

Weil der reale Sozialismus à la DDR und Ostblock das Los für die Armen nicht wirksam verbessern kann, ohne die Produzenten, ganz gleich ob Arbeiter oder Bauern, Handwerker oder Manager, durch ein gestaffeltes Prämiensystem zu höherer Leistung anzuhalten, murren einige der ganz Treuen im Glauben. Zugleich aber konterkariert ein Zuviel an Rücksicht auf die heiligen Prinzipien, gegen die nach Meinung der »Treuen« verstoßen wird, die ganze Zielsetzung dieser Politik. Das wurde mir am Beispiel eines Kunstgewerbebetriebs in Seiffen im Erzgebirge klar. Dort besuchte ich Werner Füchtner, einen blonden Hünen mit der brummigen, wortkargen Gemütlichkeit eines Teddybären. Anders als erwartet, sprach er nicht sächsisch, sondern eher mit süddeutschem Akzent. Die Dialektgrenzen überlappen sich im Süden der DDR. Im thüringischen Meiningen und im sächsischen Seiffen klingen schon fränkische Töne an. Füchtner gehörte bereits zur vierten Generation seiner Familie, die Nußknacker mit blauen oder roten Mänteln und schwarzen Schaftstiefeln produziert, in der DDR eine vom Staat geschätzte Ware, die auf Westmärkten harte Valuta bringt. Und er war voller Stolz, daß er für die Haare seiner Nußknackerkönige nicht *Plaste*, wie der volkseigene VEB-Kunsthandwerk in Seiffen, sondern echtes Kaninchenfell verwenden konnte. Wie die Trabantwerkstatt Gerhard Graubaums war auch sein Kunstgewerbebetrieb ein Familienunternehmen. Die sieben Mitarbeiter, die er beschäftigte, zählten sämtlich zur Verwandtschaft. So werkelten seine Frau, zwei Söhne, seine Schwester, eine Cousine, ein Schwager und eine Stieftochter in der Firma, die im Erdgeschoß seines Wohnhauses am Ortsrand untergebracht war. Pro Woche wurden hier 80 bis 90 Nußknacker und rund 100 Räuchermänner produziert. Der erste Füchtner, Wilhelm, hatte mit dem Drechseln von Nußknackern 1870 begonnen, aber erst Werner Füchtners Vater Kurt erkor sich nach dem Zweiten Weltkrieg die Winter-Heimarbeit zum Haupt- und Dauerberuf. Er war Zimmermann und Besitzer eines kleinen Bauunternehmens. Offenbar scheute er den Zwang, einer Produktionsgenossenschaft beizutreten und zog die Freiheit eines kleinen, aber unabhängigen Nußknackerfabrikanten vor. Wie Gerhard Graubaum hatte sich auch Werner Füchtner keiner der Blockparteien angeschlossen, auch nicht der NDPD, der viele Handwerker angehören, um damit den Nachweis zu erbringen, daß sie sich dem sozialistischen Staat nicht verweigern. Das Lohnniveau in den staatlichen Betrieben des VEB-Kunstgewerbe Seiffen lag aus Prinzip stets um mindestens eine halbe Mark pro Stunde über dem, was Private wie Füchtner ihren Mitarbeitern zahlen durften. Der Staat fühlt sich ja schon qua Ideologie verpflichtet, die vorhandenen Arbeitskräfte vorrangig dem öffentlichen Sektor zuzuführen, nicht jenen kapitalistischen Residuen, geduldeten privaten Kleinbetrieben, die nach der reinen Lehre wenn nicht noch in diesem, dann spätestens irgendwann im nächsten Jahrhundert mit Ausbruch des wahren Kommunismus zum Aussterben verurteilt sind. Trotz des Lohngefälles gegenüber den Volkseigenen Betrieben aber arbeitete Füchtners »Belegschaft« lieber bei ihm. Es war wie bei den Graubaums: Jeder, der bei dem Füchtner-Chef in Lohn und Brot stand, war eifrig und fleißig dabei, aber die Arbeitszeit wurde nicht stur, sondern flexibel gehandhabt. Wer einmal ein paar Stunden wegbleiben wollte, holte die Fehlzeiten später auf. Mutter Füchtner kochte mittags für die anverwandten Mitarbeiter typisch sächsisches: Kartoffelsuppe mit Majoran, Quarkkeulchen mit Apfelmus oder Kartoffeln mit Fleisch. Nicht eine der offiziellen Parolen fand sich in der Füchtner-Werkstatt, dafür eine Tabelle der Fußballweltmeisterschaft, die damals ausgetragen wurde. Und da kämpfte nicht etwa die Mannschaft der Bundesrepublik, da spielte »Deutschland« gegen Marokko auf. Gedanklich lebten die Mitarbeiter dieser privaten Oase im realen Sozialismus in der Welt des Westens, die wenige Kilometer südlich von Seifen begann.

War Füchtner alleiniger Eigentümer seines Betriebs, und führte er ihn völlig selbständig, so gehörte er doch einer Einkaufs- und Liefergenossenschaft an, die ihm die Abnahme seiner gesamten Produktion, gleich ob Nußknacker oder Räuchermann, garantierte und seine Ware weitervertrieb. Mithin war dem privaten Kleinunternehmer geschäftliches Risiko völlig unbekannt. Andererseits gab es für ihn auch keinerlei Anreiz, mehr zu produzieren. »Bei Ihnen drüben«, sagte mir der Nußknackerfabrikant, »hätte sich mein Betrieb völlig anders entwickelt.« Da schien ein wenig Sehnsucht nach anderen als den realsozialistischen Verhältnissen mitzuschwingen, mit denen er sich nolens volens arrangiert hatte. Dieses Arrangement, das nahezu alle Handwerker in der anderen deutschen Republik befolgen, bedeutet vor allem: Möglichst klein und so unauffällig wie möglich zu bleiben. Natürlich hat sich der realsozialistische Staat seinen Teil dabei gedacht, als er dieses Verhalten förderte. Ein bißchen Kapitalismus an der Basis, so die Logik, die dahinter steckt, fördert Dienstleistungen, die gefragt und im Rahmen der bürokratischen Planwirtschaft nicht anders zu bekommen sind. Aber zuviel davon verstößt gegen die ideologische Doktrin, an die man sich gebunden weiß, und führt obendrein zu so lästigen Fragen wie denen des Chemiearbeiters Gustav R., ob da etwa das Entstehen einer neuen Klasse von Kleinkapitalisten geduldet oder gefördert werde. Und solche Sorgen der ganz Treuen im sozialistischen Glauben führen wiederum dazu, daß viele private Handwerker dem Frieden mit dem sozialistischen Staat auf die Dauer doch nicht ganz trauen, auch wenn sie heute wieder einmal gefördert werden. »Wer kann schon versichern, daß es übermorgen nicht wieder ganz anders kommt«, meinte der Kürschnermeister aus dem Vogtland während der Veteranen-Rallye in Dresden. Das Mißtrauen des Staates gegen zuviel Unternehmergeist und der von den Parteiideologen immer wieder aufs neue genährte Verdacht der kleinen Privaten, irgendwann ginge es ihnen vielleicht doch wieder ans Leder, bedingt letztlich Stagnation. Füchtner jedenfalls hat seinen Warenausstoß seit Jahren nicht erhöht, sondern produziert immer die gleiche Menge seiner erzgebirglerischen Heimatkunst-Figuren und hat ein für DDR-Verhältnisse gutes Auskommen dabei. Verdiente er mehr, wüßte er nicht einmal, wie er den höheren Gewinn anlegen sollte. Reisen mit seiner Familie in die Länder, die ihn locken, sind ihm verwehrt, und das Geld, das er auf der Bank hat, ist im Ausland ohnehin nichts wert. So folgt er dem Motto »small is beautiful« à la DDR und erwirtschaftet ein persönliches Optimum, das weit unter dem wirtschaftlich möglichen Maximum bleibt. Ob Michail Gorbatschow solches im Sinn hat, wenn er sich für die Reste der Privatwirtschaft in der DDR interessiert?

3. Von Neubauwut und dem Umgang mit dem kulturellen Erbe

Es gibt eine kleine Schar Privilegierter, die keine Funktionäre sind, nicht in Partei- oder Regierungsgeschäften reisen und doch einen Paß mit dem nötigen Visum besitzen, der Gehen und (Zurück-)Kommen nach Lust und Laune möglich macht. Schauspieler und Regisseure, Maler und Wissenschaftler, meist Angehörige der Ostberliner Akademie der Künste und der Wissenschaften, zählen zu dieser winzigen, in der DDR viel beneideten »die-dürfen-jederzeit-raus«-Minderheit, in der sich nicht nur der SED willfährige, sondern auch rundum kritische Geister finden wie der Dramatiker Heiner Müller, oder gar unbotmäßige, wenn sie schon Rang und Namen haben, wie der Schriftsteller Stefan Heym. Was er empfindet, wenn er vom Grenzübergang Friedrichstraße mit der S-Bahn zum Bahnhof Zoo auf die andere Seite der Mauer fährt, beschrieb der Ostberliner Grenzgänger Heiner Müller als einen Unterschied von »Zivilisationen und Epochen«, vor allem aber von Zeit: »Man fährt da wirklich durch eine Zeitmauer.«

Wenn Heiner Müller das sagt, zielt er natürlich auf mehr als oberflächlichen Augenschein, der einige westliche Besucher Ostberlins, teils ehrlich entzückt, glauben läßt, der Fahrstuhl der Geschichte habe sie in die 50er Jahre zurückgebracht. (»Die müssen ja nicht hier leben«, kommentierte ein Ostberliner bissig diese naive Entdeckerfreude). Für Müller stellt sich das eher umgekehrt dar. Für ihn ist die Bundesrepublik, ihren modernistisch glitzernden Fassaden zum Trotz, eine Warengesellschaft ohne Zukunft: Der Westen befindet sich gegenüber dem realen Sozialismus in der Position einer

Nachhut, weil dieser, so häßlich, ärmlich und bürokratisch deformiert er sich auch heute noch präsentieren mag, wenigstens über die Utopie als Programm und damit über eine Besserungs- oder Entwicklungschance, über den Ansatz zu einer alternativen Gesellschaft verfügt. Doch auch für den, der nicht an die Dialektik des Sprungs vom Reich der Notwendigkeit in das Reich der Freiheit glaubt, der da einmal kommen soll, trifft das Wort von der Zeitmauer treffend genau jenen Unterschied von Zeit und Zeitgefühl, der in der anderen Republik überall, besonders deutlich aber abseits der Autobahn in der Provinz zu spüren ist. Oft scheint die Zeit wie eingefroren auf den Stand der dreißiger oder vierziger Jahre. Für viele ältere Westdeutsche macht dies Reisen zum Nostalgieerlebnis, denn urplötzlich werden Bilder aus der Jugendzeit lebendig. Da führen noch schöne, alte Chausseen über Land, deren Ahorn- und Apfelbäume nicht dem wachsenden Verkehr geopfert wurden. Wo Landschaft besonders reizvoll ist und Freizeitwert besitzt – das Elbtal zwischen Meißen und der tschechischen Grenze, die Ostseeküste bei Warnemünde –, wurde sie nicht zersiedelt. Gehörte sie zum nichtsozialistischen Ausland, wie offizieller DDR-Jargon alles bezeichnet, was westlich von Werra und Elbe liegt, wären die lieblichen Hänge des Thüringer Waldes längst übersät mit Ferienhäusern und Eigenheimen. Doch um Rudolstadt oder Meiningen, Saalfeld oder Ilmenau schaut sich die Landschaft wie vor 40 Jahren an, und in den engen, verwinkelten Gassen von Fachwerk-Städten wie Quedlinburg, Wernigerode oder Mühlhausen hat der Kommerz die alten Fassaden nicht zerstört. So meint mancher, in der DDR ein Stück deutscher Identität zu finden, wie es sie im Westen nicht mehr gibt, eine Art lebendiges Geschichtsmuseum, das Deutschland zeigt, wie es vor der Amerikanisierung des westdeutschen Lebensstils auch in der heutigen Bundesrepublik einmal ausgesehen hat.

Aber Verklärung ist nicht angebracht. Wirkte im Westen ein vorwiegend kommerziell motivierter Modernisierungsdrang zerstörerisch, war es im Osten staatlich dirigierte Neubauwut. In Anlehnung an das imperiale Modell Moskau entstanden in Berlin riesige innerstädtische Magistralen wie die Karl-Marx-Allee oder weiträumige Freiflächen wie der Alexanderplatz – gut für Massendemonstrationen und gewaltige Aufmärsche am 1. Mai, doch der einzelne fühlt sich verloren und unbehaust. Der historische Fischerkiez auf der südlichen Spreeinsel, einst ein Teil des alten Cölln und somit die Keimzelle des späteren Berlin, hätte durchaus gerettet werden können. Im Zuge einer »Neuplanung ohne Ressentiment« riß man ihn ab und setzte 21geschossige, architektonisch mediokre »Punkthäuser« an seine Stelle. Um den Jahrzehnte später erkannten Fehler, so gut es eben ging, wettzumachen, zogen die sozialistischen Planer zur 750-Jahr-Feier hundert Meter entfernt um die alte Nikolai-Kirche eine künstliche Altstadt hoch. Die Fassaden von alten Bürgerhäusern und historischen Kneipen wie Zilles »Zum Nußbaum« und die »Gerichtslaube«, die früher hier nie gestanden hatten, wurden nach alten Fotos rekonstruiert und zu einem sozialistischen Disneyland fürs Berliner Gemüt zusammengebacken, das auch durch überaus verschwenderischen Einsatz von schmiedeeiserner Zier nicht an Authentizität gewinnt. Mochte die Sprengung des Berliner Schlosses als »Zwingburg der Reaktion« wenige Jahre nach dem Krieg als programmatische Tat noch verständlich sein, kommt der Abriß der alten Leipziger Universitätskirche 1968 dagegen einem barbarischen Akt gegen überkommenes Kulturgut gleich. Wie ein gigantischer architektonischer Mißgriff beherrscht nun das Hochhaus der Karl-Marx-Universität in Form eines Buches die Messestadt, – und ist doch als Wahrzeichen des siegreichen Sozialismus gedacht.

Der sozialistische Neuaufbau war von einer verständlichen und tiefen Abneigung gegen Zilles »Milljöh«, gegen Mietskasernen und Hinterhöfe geprägt, die als verhaßtes Erbe des Kapitalismus galten. An ihre Stelle sollten nach einer Formulierung aus der Ulbrichtzeit »sozialistische Wohnpaläste« nach dem Vorbild der Stalin-Allee treten, die das erste städtebauliche Leitbild der DDR-Architekten nach dem Kriege widerspiegelt. »Vertausendfachen Sie die großzügige Ausstattung der

Straßen, den technischen Komfort der Häuser, die schönen Ladengeschäfte, Sozialeinrichtungen und Gaststätten und Sie gewinnen eine ungefähre Vorstellung von dem beglückenden Leben in den sozialistischen Wohnvierteln der Zukunft«, hieß es in einem Artikel aus diesen Jahren. Zwar hatten sich die führenden Meister des Bauhauses, das knapp 100 Kilometer von Berlin entfernt in Dessau auf dem heutigen Territorium der DDR steht, als Sozialisten gefühlt, doch die von ihnen entwickelte funktionale Bauweise wurde von der SED in den fünfziger Jahren als »brutaler, verlogener ›Weltstil‹ amerikanischer Prägung« abgelehnt. In bewußter Frontstellung gegen den »bürgerlichen Kosmopolitismus« hielt man deshalb an der Blockrandbebauung von Straßen und Plätzen fest, übernahm sowjetische Vorbilder und schrieb eine nationale und regionale Bauweise fort, die im Westen als stalinistischer Zuckerbäckerstil belächelt wurde. Aber wer die vielverspottete Stalin-Allee heute mit dem vergleicht, was sozialistische Architekten und Stadtplaner vollbrachten, seit die DDR die ästhetischen Vorbehalte gegen die Moderne aufgab, zum Großmontagebau von Fertigplatten und zur »aufgelockerten Bebauung mit Punkt- und Scheibenhäusern« überging, der empfindet sie wie ein Pflaster auf das geschundene Gemüt.

Sicher hat dieser Eindruck auch damit zu tun, daß der stalinistische Schnörkelstil plötzlich Anflüge von zeitgenössischem Chic gewinnt, denn manches von den Stilelementen und den städtebaulichen Leitbildern der früheren Stalin- und heutigen Karl-Marx-Allee findet eine Entsprechung in der postmodernen Architektur. Wichtiger aber ist, daß die DDR in dem Bemühen, das Wohnungsproblem möglichst schnell und billig zu lösen, beinahe hemmungslos die Sünden des kapitalistischen Massenwohnungsbaus wiederholt, als habe es die Erfahrungen eines Märkischen Viertels nie gegeben. Als besonders abschreckendes Beispiel muß bis heute Halle-Neustadt gelten, ein in den 60er Jahren aus dem Boden gestampftes Neubauviertel für mehr als 100 000 Menschen, vom Volksmund »Arbeiterschließfach« genannt, das ein Bild geradezu rigoroser Monotonie bietet und eindrücklich vor Augen führt, mit welchen Anfangsschwierigkeiten Städteplaner und Architekten bei der Anwendung der industriellen Bauweise zu kämpfen hatten. Zwar spricht das äußere Bild der modernen Hochhausbauten in Berlin-Marzahn oder Groß-Klein bei Rostock dafür, daß die schlimmsten Kinderkrankheiten seit Anfang der 80er Jahre überwunden sind. Die seelenlose Eintönigkeit schlecht und unregelmäßig verfugter grauer Betonkies-Fertigplatten ist einer Plattenvielfalt gewichen, die gelegentlich schon ans Spielerische grenzt, etwa, wenn rings um den ehemaligen Gendarmenmarkt in Ostberlin Neubauten mit historisierenden Fassaden verschiedener Stilepochen verkleidet wurden, die sämtlich aus Beton gegossen sind. Eindrucksvoll belegen solche Leistungen, wie gut man die neue Technik inzwischen meistern lernte. Auch haben die meisten DDR-Bürger ihre fernbeheizten Wohnzellen in den großen Scheibenhäusern am Rande der Städte angenommen, schon weil diese den unschätzbaren Vorteil haben, daß ihre Bewohner keine Briketts schleppen müssen, was in den ofenbeheizten, sanitär schlecht ausgestatteten Altbauten üblich ist. Daß der individuelle Geschmack sich inmitten dieser monotonen Wohnlandschaft aus Beton, wenn auch oft auf kitschige Weise, zu behaupten sucht, lehrt ein Blick auf die Balkone, auf denen man nicht selten alte Wagenräder, Kutscherlampen und großblumige Tapeten entdeckt. Doch gibt es immer wieder Klagen über schlechte Innenverarbeitung vor allem bei den sogenannten Naßzellen, die auf die schlechte Qualität des verarbeiteten Materials zurückzuführen ist. »Der Sozialismus ist arm«, sagte mir einmal ein Staatssekretär, der als Leiter eines wichtigen Festkomitees in einer für diese Sonderaufgabe mehr schlecht als recht hergerichteten Baracke residierte. Daß die DDR, anders als die Bundesrepublik, die durch Kredite schnell den Anschluß an westliche Qualitätsstandards fand, noch bis heute unter Materialnot leidet, zeigt ein Blick auf kläglich gefertigte Plastik-Armaturen in Küchen und Bädern selbst in Vorzeige-Objekten wie den Wohnblocks in der Leipziger Straße in Ostberlin, in denen Diplomaten und westliche Korrespondenten wohnen. Dort wurden Wasserrohre aus rosten-

dem Stahl verlegt, was den Wasserverbrauch in die Höhe
treibt, denn oft genug war erst die vierte Badewannenfüllung
nicht mehr tief rotbraun verfärbt. Und nicht selten habe ich
mich bei einem Besuch in einem der neuen Hochhäuser über
krumme Treppengeländer, schiefe Stufen oder miserabel ver-
putzte Wände gewundert, Ergebnisse jener Kranideologie,
nach der allein die hochgezogenen Kubikmeter umbauten
Raums zählen. Über derlei Pfusch, erzählte mir der Bewohner
eines Neubaus in Ostberlin, hätten sich zwei in seinem Haus
eingezogene altgediente Genossen mehrmals beschwert. Als
nach Monaten immer noch nichts geschah, gaben sie verär-
gert ihre Parteibücher zurück.

Im Selbstverständnis der DDR ist der moderne Wohnungs-
bau das Kernstück des sozialpolitischen Programms. Bis 1990,
so legt das SED-Programm von 1976 fest, soll die Wohnungs-
frage gelöst und damit »ein altes Ziel der revolutionären Arbeiterbewegung« verwirklicht werden. Konkret heißt dies,
daß in den Jahren von 1976 bis 1990 insgesamt 2,8 bis 3
Millionen Wohnungen neugebaut oder saniert werden sollen,
eine gewaltige Anstrengung, deren Kosten sich auf 200 Milliarden Mark belaufen und mit der Erich Honecker sein persönliches Prestige verknüpft hat. »Seht, Großes ist voll-
bracht«, prangte auf einem Plakat, das symbolisch die verschiedenen Etappen des Städtebaus in der DDR, vom restau-
rierten Bürgerhaus bis zu den riesigen Wohnscheiben, zeigte,
und am 35. Jahrestag der DDR an allen Litfaß-Säulen klebte.
Die Führung ist stolz auf diesen Kraftakt, der sich, jedenfalls
vom Volumen her, sehen lassen kann, und reagiert auf Kritik
deshalb äußerst sensibel.

So geriet im Mai 1983 der DEFA-Film »Insel der Schwäne« in
die Schußlinie des »Neuen Deutschland«, weil er die Geschichte
eines Jungen erzählt, der aus einer ländlichen Idylle am See in
die moderne Großstadt umziehen muß. Da es ihn ausgerechnet nach Marzahn verschlägt, wird er von verständlichem
Heimweh nach dem freien Landleben, nach Natur und den
Schwänen geplagt. In der neuen Umwelt dient eine Baugrube
als Spielplatz, doch eines Tages kommt der Bagger und walzt

sie zu. Als eine neue Spielfläche aus Beton entsteht, proben die Kinder den Aufstand. An der Bekanntmachungstafel bringen sie ein Plakat mit der Forderung an: »Wir wollen Wiesen und keinen Beton.« Ein Kritiker des LDPD-Blattes »Der Morgen« nannte »Insel der Schwäne« einen »herausragenden DEFA-Film von sorgsamer Machart« und »intensiv ansprechenden Vorgängen«, doch die führende SED-Zeitung beklagte eine verstellte Sicht auf die Wirklichkeit im realen Sozialismus: »Wieviel Borniertheit«, so der Kritiker des »Neuen Deutschland«, »gehört eigentlich dazu, einen Film über Jugendliche zu machen und dabei jene Leistung, die von ungezählten jungen Menschen mitvollbracht worden ist – moderne, neue Wohnviertel – als eine furchterregende, niederdrückende Betonwelt abzuwerten?« Dabei rieb sich das Parteiblatt an einer längst durch die Zensur gemilderte Fassung, denn Regisseur Hermann Zschoche und Drehbuchautor Ulrich Plenzdorf hatten einige Szenen ganz streichen, andere ins Positive wenden müssen, ehe der Film nach heftigen Kämpfen endlich freigegeben werden konnte.

Kritik an den neuroseträchtigen, die Suizidrate fördernden Wohnverhältnissen in den großen Neubauvierteln klingt in manchen Werken zeitgenössischer Autoren an, besonders deutlich in Brigitte Reimanns »Franziska Linkerhand«, aber auch in Christoph Heins Novelle »Der fremde Freund« (in der Bundesrepublik unter dem Titel »Drachenblut« erschienen). Doch der da geschilderten, oft schon pathologischen Selbstentfremdung gewinnen DDR-Soziologen in einer Art fröhlicher Gleichmacherei bewußt positive Seiten ab. Sie preisen die »Homogenität« der neuen »Lebensweise« in den riesigen Wohnsilos, weil durch sie in allen Teilen der Republik die gleichen Lebensbedingungen geschaffen und die verbliebenen Klassenunterschiede etwa zwischen Arbeitern und Angehörigen der Intelligenz weiter abgeschliffen werden.

Der Bau von Halle-Neustadt, dem eher abschreckenden Beispiel für die erste Anwendung der industriellen Bauweise in großem Stil, band die im Bezirk vorhandenen Kapazitäten und Ressourcen, so daß den Preis die alte Stadt Halle bezahlen mußte. Deren Altbausubstanz blieb mit Ausnahme einer neu geschaffenen Fußgängerzone über Jahrzehnte dem Verfall preisgegeben. Von aggressiver Leuna-Luft und schwefligen Braunkohlenschwaden eingeschwärzt, bot sie den Anblick eines riesigen, anthrazitgrauen, verwitterten Fossils. In kleinerem Maßstab und keineswegs überall mit eklatanten Mängeln behaftet, findet sich ein Halle-Neustadt am Rande fast jeder mittleren Stadt in der DDR, denn Neubauten hatten nun einmal lange Zeit absoluten Vorrang. Draußen in der Provinz allerdings ist ihre Höhe schon aus Gründen der Billigkeit meist auf fünf oder sechs Geschosse begrenzt, weil damit der Einbau von Fahrstühlen entfällt. Die Bewohner solcher »Sechsgeschosser«, die Bierkästen und Kartoffelsäcke nach oben schleppen müssen, leiden unter dieser Sparmaßnahme, doch der Besucher Quedlinburgs, das vor 1000 Jahren einmal Zentrum des Reiches war, empfindet sie eher als angenehm. Niedrige Neubauten zerstören die alte Stadtsilhouette nicht. So sind in Quedlinburg Schloß und Dom, auf einem Sandsteinfelsen hoch über der Stadt gelegen, das beherrschende Wahrzeichen der Stadt geblieben, und der Blick vom Schloßberg schweift noch immer über eine weitgehend intakte »mittelalterliche Dachlandschaft«, die kein häßlich-moderner Eternit- oder Kunststoffziegel entstellt. Nach dem Willen der DDR-Denkmalpflege, die 1981 fast die gesamte Altstadt zum Flächendenkmal erklärte, soll sie erhalten bleiben, obschon dies auf die Dauer schwerfallen dürfte. Die Produktion der halbrunden, wellenförmig über- und ineinandergreifenden, von den Experten »Mönche und Nonnen« genannten Dachziegel war in keinem Plan vorgesehen. Für Reparaturen nutzte man bei Abrißarbeiten sichergestelltes Material.

In Quedlinburg findet sich der sagenumwobene Platz, auf dem Sachsenherzog Heinrich einst die deutsche Königskrone angetragen wurde. Wenn die rührende Geschichte stimmt, dann muß der Finkenherd, an dem Heinrich gesessen hat, damals anders ausgesehen haben – voller Gebüsch und von Felsbrocken umgeben. Die kleinen, verwinkelten, altersschiefen Fachwerkhäuser, die ihn heute säumen, wurden mit viel Kosten und Mühen auf neue Fundamente gestellt und von Grund auf erneuert. Quedlinburg steckt voller Historie, die für die spätere deutsche Nation entscheidende Weichen stellte, denn hier begann die deutsche Expansion nach Osten. Im Schloß residierten die Kaiserinnen Adelheid und Theophano, Friedrich Barbarossa feierte hier 1154 das Osterfest; im romanischen Dom finden sich Adler an den Kapitellen, die lombardischen Vorbildern nachempfunden sind; zwischen seinen Säulen tagte unter den Sachsenkaisern der Reichstag, unter seinem Dach schloß Otto I. 973 Frieden mit den Ungarn, seine Krypta ist die Grabkirche Heinrichs, des ersten Königs der Deutschen. Das Kruzifix im Chor, eine Arbeit aus Freiburg an der Unstrut aus dem 15. Jahrhundert, fand seinen Platz dort erst, als der Nazispuk vorüber war. Weil Heinrich I. die deutsche Macht nach Osten weitete, hatten Himmler und Rosenberg seinen 1000. Todestag 1936 dazu mißbraucht, die alte Basilika in eine heidnische Kultstätte für eine neue Ostkolonisation zu verwandeln. SS-Männer wurden nun im Dom auf das Schwert Himmlers vereidigt. Baldur von Schirach weihte hier die Fahne der Hitlerjugend.

Wer das Schloßmuseum besichtigt, dem stellt sich die Geschichte der Ottonen heute kritisch dar. In den marxistisch aufbereiteten Schautafeln markiert Heinrich den Beginn der Jahrhunderte währenden Raubkriege des deutschen Adels, der im Osten blutige Unterdrückung und grausame Herrschaft praktiziert habe. Dabei wird eine slawophile Grundeinstellung der DDR-Geschichtsschreibung deutlich, welche von Marx und Engels, die sich beide über den Panslawismus lustig machten, so kaum geteilt worden wäre. Es klingt wie ein Tribut an die sozialistisch-slawischen Brudernationen, wenn der große Slawenaufstand, der die deutsche Herrschaft vorübergehend in Mecklenburg und Brandenburg zurückwarf, ausdrücklich gefeiert wird, weil er den Ostslawen letztlich die Gründung und Festigung selbständiger Staaten ermöglicht habe.

Am Fuße des Schloßberges stößt der Besucher auf ein Paradestück sozialistischer Erbepflege. Die DDR hat das Geburtshaus Klopstocks, des Autors des »Messias«, der die deutsche Literatur um antike Versmaße bereicherte, in ein Museum verwandelt. Klopstock, wohl der größte Sohn Quedlinburgs, war ein religiöser Patriot mit progressiven Neigungen, die von den Museologen natürlich besonders herausgestellt werden. So wird eine Urkunde mit der Unterschrift Dantons gezeigt, die Klopstock, der den amerikanischen Unabhängigkeitskrieg besang und die Französische Revolution begrüßte, zum Ehrenbürger der französischen Republik ernennt. Daß Klopstock auch eine vaterländische Gefühlswoge auslöste, die spätestens mit Wagner zum Problem wurde, ist nicht vermerkt.

Wer jenem Zeitunterschied nachspüren will, der Reisen in die DDR zu Expeditionen in ein vergangenes Deutschland macht, sollte nach Quedlinburg fahren, denn dort läßt sich studieren, wie der Effekt zustande kommt, der alte Städte auf nostalgische Weise »deutscher« erscheinen läßt. Er ist vor allem auf eine Politik jahrzehntelangen Nichtstuns zurückzuführen. Fast 30 Jahre lang, von 1945 bis 1975, wurden die meisten Fachwerkhäuser im altsächsischen Stil, die so typisch sind für Quedlinburg, weder neu gestrichen noch gar instandgesetzt. Als 1975 die ersten Restaurierungsarbeiten begannen, diskutierte man noch, ob nicht die Hälfte des gesamten Altstadtkerns einfach abzureißen sei. Wer überhaupt nichts tut, kann freilich auch nichts Falsches bauen. Weil die Bautätigkeit sich ausschließlich auf das neue Wohnviertel am Stadtrand konzentrierte, blieb das Grundmuster der alten Ackerbürgerstadt erhalten und wurde nicht, wie in vergleichbaren westdeutschen Städten, mit Betonneubauten für Warenhäuser und modernen Großgaragen durchsetzt. Auch fehlen die aufdringliche, grelle Werbung und die modernisierten, gläsernen Ladenfronten, die in manch einer zur Fußgängerzone umgewandelten westlichen Altstadt zum Kauf verlocken sollen. So hat, was in den alten Städten der DDR noch zu sehen ist, meist ursprünglicheren Charakter, und die DDR-Denkmalpfleger mühen sich redlich, ihn für künftige Generationen zu bewahren.

Warenhäuser und Kaufhallen im Zentrum Quedlinburgs wollen sie deshalb auch künftig verhindern.

Alle Häuser ihres »Flächendenkmals« zu restaurieren, dürfte Millionen und Abermillionen kosten und Jahrzehnte in Anspruch nehmen; und doch legen sie inzwischen strengste Maßstäbe an: Polnische Restauratoren, die seit dem Wiederaufbau Danzigs weltweiten Ruhm genießen, wurden auch in die Stadt zu Füßen des Harzes um Hilfe gebeten. Von einem Haus mit reich geschnitzten Fachwerkbalken, in dem heute der Kulturbund tagt, ließen sie nur die Außenwände stehen, innen zogen sie Decken aus Stahlbeton ein und brachten die alten Balken danach wieder als Zierrat an. Solche Methoden sind den Puristen der DDR-Denkmalpflege heute nicht mehr gut genug, und so rekonstruiert die kleine Gruppe polnischer Experten in Quedlinburg inzwischen originalgetreu.

Von den 30 000 Einwohnern Quedlinburgs arbeiten viele in einem Werk für Meß- und Regeltechnik und in der Möbelindustrie, gut 3000 sind in den volkseigenen Betrieben der Saat- und Pflanzenzucht beschäftigt, die seit alters her einen guten Ruf weit über die Grenzen der Stadt hinaus genießt.

Wer die Bürger der Stadt vor dem Harz fragt, ob sie den Rettungsversuchen der Restauratoren eine Chance geben, stößt auf weitverbreitete Skepsis. Zwar wird anerkannt, daß in den letzten Jahren viel getan wurde, aber der Tenor der Antworten, die ich bei einer genehmigten Umfrage vor der Kamera sammelte, lief auf: »Zu wenig und zu spät« hinaus, und es steht zu befürchten, daß die Bürger gegen die Denkmalpfleger recht behalten werden. Die Gegend um den Markt und die wichtigsten Straßenzüge würden sich bewahren lassen, meinten die Quedlinburger; der Rest des ehrgeizigen Programms sei zum Scheitern verurteilt, weil es an Kapazitäten, Restauratoren und den nötigen Materialien fehle – kurz: Weil den Bemühungen um die Altstadtsanierung ökonomische Grenzen gezogen seien.

Nicht viel anders lauteten die Antworten, die ich im thüringischen Mühlhausen bekam, wo die ökonomischen Grenzen noch enger gezogen sind, denn zum Flächendenkmal wurde die tausendjährige Stadt an der Pforte zum Eichsfeld nicht erklärt. Vom Dreißigjährigen Krieg blieb Mühlhausen verschont wie von den Bomben der Alliierten. Mit vielen stattlichen Türmen und zwei Kilometern Stadtmauer, die gut erhalten sind, so notierte ich während einer Drehreise Anfang Mai 1987, bietet die Stadt das Bild einer unnachahmlichen Mischung aus Mittelalter und realem Sozialismus à la DDR. Da quälen sich Trabis durch enge Fachwerkgassen und Offiziere der sowjetischen Garnison stechen mit ihren riesigen Tellermützen beim Einkaufsbummel in der Fußgängerzone ins Auge. So manche Schaufensterdekoration bringt den Betrachter zurück in die 50er Jahre, und ein Laden der LPG Thomas Müntzer stellt das Gemüseangebot zur Schau, das der DDR-Norm außerhalb der Sommermonate entspricht: Außer Rot- und Weißkohl, ein paar alten Möhren, Äpfeln und traurig verpackten Konserven ist fast nichts im Angebot. Neben Würstchenbuden gibt es für 44 000 Einwohner ganze 22 Gaststätten und Restaurants, eine Broilerbar, wie man in der DDR einen Hähnchengrill nennt, inbegriffen. »Der Nachbar«, gegenüber der alten Allerheiligenkirche, liebevoll neu auf alt eingerichtet, bietet als nahezu einzige Ausnahme neben einer Vielfalt an Gerichten auch eine gepflegte Atmosphäre.

Das Dienstleistungsgewerbe liegt, wie fast überall in der DDR, sichtbar darnieder: In einem Schaufenster, dessen alter Holzrahmen dringend einen neuen Anstrich braucht, entdecke ich das Qualitätszeichen »Vorbildlicher Reparaturbetrieb des Handwerks«. In der Auslage sind, in kümmerlicher Anordnung flach auf den mit bedrucktem braunen Papier ausgelegten Fensterboden plaziert, verschiedene Einlegesohlen, ein paar Damenschuh-Absätze, etliche Gummisohlen und zwei Klebstofftuben zu sehen. Einige Häuser weiter, im Fenster eines Elektro-Reparaturbetriebs schreckt ein handgemaltes Pappschild mit der Nachricht ab: »Zur Zeit keine Annahme!« Immer wieder finde ich bestätigt, daß eine Wirtschaft, die den Wettbewerb als marktregulierende Kraft nicht kennt und nur mit Mühe die notwendigsten Bedürfnisse befriedigen kann, auch für die Sinne, vor allem für das Auge, nichts zu bieten hat. Gibt es im Westen im Zeichen der Überproduktion ein Zuviel an lockender Werbung und zählt die Verpackung inzwischen oft mehr als der Inhalt, ist im Osten nicht der Absatz, sondern immer noch die Produktion das Problem. Das führt dann dazu, daß Waren mit unsachgemäßer Verpackung, armseliger Aufmachung und »murkeligem« Design mühelos Käufer finden. Was fehlt, sind gute Qualität, gefällige Aufmachung und Dienst am Kunden. Das heutige Niveau bei Service-Leistungen liegt oft erheblich unter dem Standard der Vorkriegsjahre.

Künstlerisch mag diese ärmliche Selbstdarstellung der DDR-Planwirtschaft auf manchen anregend wirken, doch der normale HO-Käufer wird wenig Verständnis haben, wenn er jenes große Lager-Regal betrachten könnte, in dem Joseph Beuys typische DDR-Produkte stapelte – Kunsthonig in Pappbechern, Tempo-Erbsen oder Lubos-Heilerde. In »Wirtschaftswerte« (1980), diesem Stück arte povera dominierte, wie ein Kritiker schrieb, die »glanzlose Gebrauchsästhetik der Behelfsverpackung«. Für Beuys war der realsozialistische DDR-Alltag offenbar eine Fundgrube für Stoffe und Materialien, er sammelte DDR-Wundschnellverbände und graue technische Filze aus Zittau, die er mit seinem Stempel versah. Sein Regal wollte er alles andere denn ironisch verstanden wissen. Im Behelfsmäßigen, Primitiven, Handgefalteten sah er nicht nur eine weit zurückgebliebene, sondern eine in der Tendenz ökologische Produktionsweise, was er durch das betonte Zurschaustellen von DDR-Konserven in der Form altertümlicher Mehrweg-Einweckgläser unterstreichen wollte. Doch wer jeden Tag in einer DDR-Kaufhalle Besorgungen machen muß, den wird diese Ästhetik der Armut kaum erfreuen; überdies ist die DDR bemüht, ihren Rückstand an Hochglanzverpackung, der Beuys so animierte, abzubauen.

Versuche, durch sozialistischen Wettbewerb in den Griff zu bekommen, was im Westen der Markt, die Konkurrenz und der materielle Anreiz besorgen, sind zwar nicht effizient, aber zeigen gelegentlich rührende Züge, etwa, wenn ein gerahmtes

Schild im Schaufenster dem Käufer verkündet, der Kurzwarenladen, vor dem er steht, sei eine »Verkaufsstelle der vorbildlichen Verkaufskultur«. Geschmückt ist die Auszeichnung, die das Arbeitskollektiv im sozialistischen Wettbewerb errang, mit zwei Gummibäumen, Stolz fast jeder deutschen Mutti vor einem halben Jahrhundert. Nicht minder rührend oft die Namen, die man in der DDR-Provinz für Cafés, Läden oder Frisierstuben bereit hält. »Charmant« nennt sich ein Fußpflegesalon im sächsischen Radebeul, »Süße Ecke« ein HO-Café in Eisenach, »Adrett« ein Textilladen im Vogtland, »Flott« ein Frisierkunst-Etablissement im Märkischen. »Köstlich und Gesund« heißt der Fischladen im Herzen Wernigerodes, und die Weinhandlung nebenan firmiert unter »Süß und Süffig«, was dem Geschmack der meisten DDR-Bürger entspricht und ziemlich genau den Charakter eines Rotweins nicht näher bezeichneten Ursprungs trifft, der das Etikett »Romanze in Rouge« trägt.

Natürlich hat auch Mühlhausen sein kleines Halle-Neustadt vor der Tür. Fast 12 000 Wohnungen wurden bis Mitte 1987 in industrieller Bauweise für die 44 000 Einwohner am Stadtrand neu erstellt. Aber vierzig Prozent der alten Häuser im Stadtkern, sagte mir der Stadtbaudirektor, müssen abgerissen werden. Sie sind so heruntergewirtschaftet, daß eine Grunderneuerung nicht lohnt. Nun wurde gewiß auch in der Bundesrepublik so manches Altstadtproblem mittels Kahlschlagsanierung gelöst. Doch der jedem Besucher sichtbare Verfall der alten Stadt Mühlhausen hat Gründe, die im System zu suchen sind.

Daß ein jeder sich durch redliche Arbeit ernähre, daß keiner von den Zinsen oder Erträgen leben soll, die er aus Kapitalvermögen oder aus Haus- und Grundbesitz bezieht, ist ein hehrer gesellschaftspolitischer Leitsatz. In der Praxis kollidiert er mit der Tatsache, daß sich noch immer über 50 Prozent aller Häuser in der DDR in privatem Besitz befinden. Da die Mieten für Altbauwohnungen, dem Leitsatz entsprechend, auf das Niveau von 1938 eingefroren sind, bringen sie meist nicht die

Mittel ein, die für eine ordentliche Instandhaltung aufgewendet werden müssen. Auch entfällt jeder Anreiz für den Eigentümer, eine Modernisierung vorzunehmen. Wenn nur die Hälfte aller Wohnungen in der DDR mit Bad oder Dusche und mit Innentoilette ausgestattet sind – die Vergleichszahl in der Bundesrepublik liegt bei über 90 Prozent –, dann ist dafür die staatliche Politik verantwortlich, die jede private Initiative der Eigentümer abtötet, weil die Partei privates Hauseigentum eigentlich nicht will. Da Eigenheime sowie Häuser und Gebäude privater Handwerksbetriebe von diesem ideologischen Eigentumsvorbehalt ausdrücklich ausgenommen sind, gilt er im Grunde nur für Mietshäuser. Vor der Konsequenz jedoch, die Enteignung und Überführung in kommunalen oder staatlichen Besitz geheißen hätte, schreckt die SED zurück. Dabei mag einmal die Überlegung eine Rolle gespielt haben, Staat und Kommunen nicht die Lasten für Instandhaltung und Modernisierung in Milliardenhöhe aufzubürden, zum andern die Furcht, von den Mietern, die mehrheitlich Arbeiter sind, nun direkt für den schlechten Zustand der Wohnungen verantwortlich gemacht zu werden. Die SED entschloß sich deshalb für eine ambivalente Politik, welche die Mietshäuser in privatem Besitz beließ, aber den Eigentümern jede Rendite vorenthielt. In der Praxis lief dies auf eine schleichende Enteignung hinaus. Häuser, deren Eigentümer in den Westen gegangen sind, wurden einer kommunalen Treuhandverwaltung unterstellt; Hausbesitzer, die in der DDR blieben, werden durch die »volkseigenen kommunalen Wohnungsverwaltungen«, über die allein Reparaturarbeiten an privaten Mietshäusern ausgeführt werden, praktisch entmündigt. »Es lohnt sich nicht, in der DDR ein Haus zu besitzen«, sagen deshalb schon Besitzer von Zwei- oder Dreifamilienhäusern, auch wenn sie eine Etage selbst bewohnen. Die billigen Mieten können nicht darüber hinwegtäuschen, daß die Zeche für diese verfehlte Politik, die zum Verfall der Altbausubstanz führte, letztlich doch die Mieter zahlen. Jahrzehnte ließ man sie in herabgewirtschafteten Wohnungen hausen, deren sanitäre Ausstattung oft dem kläglichen Niveau der Jahrhundertwende entsprach. Als die ersten Baubrigaden vor einigen Jahren mit ihren Taktstraßen in das traditionelle Ostberliner Arbeiterviertel Prenzlauer Berg einrückten und mit der Sanierung der alten Mietskasernen begannen, war kostbare Zeit vertan. Über die Jahrzehnte stetig betriebene Instandhaltung und eine kontinuierliche Modernisierung – Schritt für Schritt, hätte die Wohnqualität für die Werktätigen sehr viel früher verbessert und die Volkswirtschaft der DDR nicht entfernt so viel gekostet wie der aufwendige Versuch, in beinahe letzter Minute zu sanieren und zu retten, was an Altbauten noch zu retten ist.

»Es kommt alles zu spät«, »Es geht alles kaputt«, »Wenn man gleich etwas getan hätte, wären die Kosten nicht so immens hoch«, lauteten die Kommentare, die Mühlhauser Bürger vor der Kamera wagten, aber einige waren auch zuversichtlich: »Wir haben 1989 vor uns, bis dahin wird sich hier sicher viel verändern«. Derlei Hoffnung gründete in der Gewißheit, daß Mühlhausen in der Gestalt Thomas Müntzers, des revolutionären Bauernführers, über einen Volksheiligen verfügt, den die Obrigkeit verehrt. Für anfallende Jubiläen historischer Personen, die ins nationale Erbe Eingang fanden oder gar die progressive Tradition des deutschen Volkes verkörpern, werden von Staat und Partei ohne Zögern die Mittel bereitgestellt, um die Städte für die mit großem Aufwand vorbereiteten Geburtstagsfeiern ansehnlich herauszuputzen. Daß die Mühlhauser ihre Hoffnung zu Recht in den 1989 anstehenden 500. Geburtstag ihres Volksheiligen Müntzer setzen, lehrt die Erfahrung mit seinem großen Gegenspieler Martin Luther. Die Bürger der Luther-Städte Eisleben und Wittenberg freuen sich noch heute ihrer zum 500. Geburtstag des Reformators der Deutschen 1983 neu getünchten Fassaden und beklagen nur, daß der Anstrich wegen der schlechten Qualität der verwendeten Farbe nicht bis zum nächsten Jubiläum halten wird.

Die DDR pflegt das progressive Erbe des deutschen Bauernkrieges, dessen unumstrittener Führer im Thüringer Raum Thomas Müntzer war, ein Prediger, der sich in der Tradition alttestamentarischer Propheten berufen glaubte, den Gottes-staat auf Erden mit dem Schwert Gideons zu errichten. Müntzers Gottes-Reich trug urkommunistische Züge; alles sollte allen gehören, vor allem das den Fürsten entwundene Schwert dem gemeinen Volk. In der Sicht der SED-Ideologen hat der Kampf dieses revolutionären Gottesmannes, der an der Spitze eines Haufens von 6000 Bauern gegen die Fürsten zu Felde zog und unterlag, durch die Errichtung der sozialistischen DDR letztlich doch ein siegreiches Ende gefunden.

»Ein tiefes Verhältnis zur Geschichte stärkt die Verbundenheit der Bürger mit ihrem sozialistischen Vaterland und erhöht ihren Stolz auf die Errungenschaften der sozialistischen Revolution.« In großen Lettern empfängt dieser Satz Erich Honeckers die Besucher der Zentralen Gedenkstätte »Deutscher Bauernkrieg«, die in einer einschiffigen gotischen Kirche am alten Kornmarkt untergebracht ist. Unter ihrem Dach versammelten sich einst Barfüßer-Mönche zur Heiligen Messe; im Frühjahr 1525, in den Wochen des Aufstands, wurden hier Glocken eingeschmolzen und Geschütze gegossen. Unter den pädagogisch geschickt erläuterten Exponaten trifft man freilich auf wenig originale Stücke, die von dem religiösen Schwärmer stammen, der im Gegensatz zu Luther nicht nur der Schrift – verächtlich sprach er vom »Buchstabenglauben von Wittenberg« –, sondern auch der göttlichen Eingebung folgte und sich für einen Erwählten hielt. Dieser Mangel erklärt sich aus der Rache der Sieger. Auf ihr Geheiß wurden alle Spuren getilgt, die an so Unerhörtes wie bewaffnete Rebellion gegen gottgewollte Herrschaft je erinnern konnten. Nicht einmal die Gräber Müntzers und seines Mitstreiters, des Pfarrers Heinrich Pfeiffer, der von der Kanzel der Allerheiligenkirche gegen Adel und Pfaffen wetterte, sind bekannt.

Alljährlich im Mai marschiert eine Ehrenformation des NVA-Regiments »Thomas Müntzer« mit klingendem Spiel zum Mühlhauser Frauentor. Die Volksarmisten ehren den Revolutionär, dessen Name ihre Einheit trägt, am Jahrestag der Schlacht von Frankenhausen, vor einem Müntzer-Denkmal mit einer feierlichen Kranzniederlegung. Die lokalen

Spitzen von Partei und Staat, der Parteisekretär, der Bürgermeister, eine Abordnung der FDJ und Vertreter der Massenorganisationen nehmen an der Feierstunde teil, doch der Ort, an dem dies geschieht, ist beliebig gewählt, man hätte die Büste Müntzers auch an jedem anderen malerischen Flecken vor der Stadtmauer aufstellen können. »Es ließen auch die Fürsten«, so berichtet eine alte Chronik, die sich im Stadtarchiv befindet, »Müntzern und Pfeiffern richten mit dem Schwert und danach spießen. Müntzer setzten sie an den reißenden Berg, Pfeiffer aber an die Wegescheide bei der Schadebergswarte, als man nach Bollstedt gehet.« Nach der Hinrichtung vor den Toren des »Ketzernestes« wurde also der Kopf vom Rumpf der Rebellen getrennt und auf Spießen zwecks Abschreckung zur Schau gestellt, bis man die Überreste Tage später an unbekanntem Ort verscharrte.

Für die Gedenkstätte am Kornmarkt ließen Müntzers späte Erben die Fahne des Predigers, der den »Streit Gottes streiten« und die »gottlosen Bösewichte« mit dem Schwert ausrotten wollte, nach-wirken. Auf 30 Ellen Seide zeigt sie einen Regenbogen auf weißem Grund und den Spruch »Verbum domini manet in eternum« (das Wort Gottes währet ewiglich), der sie zum Zeichen eines ewigen Bundes Gottes machte. Diese Fahne wehte über dem Haufen der 6000 Bauern auf dem Schlachtberg in Frankenhausen zu Füßen des Kyffhäusers, wo es zur entscheidenden Auseinandersetzung mit den Fürsten kam. Doch gab es dort eher ein Gemetzel als eine Schlacht, denn der Schwärmer Müntzer hatte seinen Bauern Unverwundbarkeit durch Gottes Hilfe versprochen. Die Kugeln der Fürsten, der »großen, dicken, feisten Pausbacken«, die ihr Leben »mit tierischem Fressen und Saufen« zubrachten, sollten der Schar der Gerechten nichts anhaben können. Als die ersten Treffer in die Wagenburg einschlugen, als Blut floß und die Täuschung zerbrach, liefen die Bauern in Panik davon und wurden einfach niedergemacht. Fünftausend tote Aufständische aber nur sechs gefallene Fürstenknechte zählte man nach dem Treffen. Blutrinne heißt noch heute das kleine Tal, das vom Schlachtberg zur Stadt herunterführt. Müntzer floh nach Frankenhausen und versteckte sich auf einem Dachboden, bis er entdeckt und abgeführt wurde – wahrlich kein heldenhafter Abgang für einen, der sich in der Nachfolge von Gideon und David sah. Immerhin hatte der eine die Midianiter, der andere Goliath besiegt.

Zu historischem Rang verhalf Müntzer vor allem die Kontroverse mit Luther, der den selbsternannten Gottesknecht mit dem Schwert einen Mordpropheten und Satan nannte und seinen Kurfürsten Friedrich den Weisen zum Krieg wider die von Müntzer geführte »räuberische und mörderische Rotte der Bauern« Thüringens ermunterte. Müntzer gab's zurück und schimpfte Luther das »geistlose, sanftlebende Fleisch zu Wittenberg«, einen »Doktor Lügner«, einen »einfältigen Mann« und »lästerlichen Mönch«, der ein »neuer Christus« sein wollte. In Thüringen wie in Sachsen gab es keine Leibeigenschaft, die von Müntzer zum Aufstand aufgerufenen Bauern kämpften vor allem für das Recht auf freie Weide, freie Jagd und freies Holz. Sein Reich Gottes auf Erden gründete Müntzer nicht mit Bauern, sondern mit Hilfe armer Bürger im gotischen Rathaus der Freien Reichsstadt Mühlhausen, die zu seiner Zeit mit 7000 Einwohnern größer war als Leipzig oder Dresden. Dort zeigt ein Bild, nach dem Krieg von der DDR in Auftrag gegeben, den Prediger im Disput mit den Patriziern im Rat der Stadt, als Anwalt der Plebejer, der auf seine Weise eine christliche Demokratie, eine Volksherrschaft unter dem Wort Gottes errichten will. In der historischen Ratsstube, in der diese Auseinandersetzung einst stattfand, haben DDR-Denkmalspfleger Fresken aus der Müntzerzeit freigelegt. Als Originalton einer Führung durch den Leiter der Zentral-Gedenkstätte »Deutscher Bauernkrieg«, Obermuseumsrat Dr. Rolf Barthel, habe ich notiert: »Hier tagte der Ewige Rat (das Vollzugsorgan der Mühlhauser Revolution), der von Müntzer wesentlich beeinflußt wurde, und er faßte Beschlüsse, die für jene Zeit utopisch bleiben mußten und erst in unserer Deutschen Demokratischen Republik verwirklicht wurden.« Auf die Frage, welche Beschlüsse er konkret im Auge habe, antwortete der Obermuseumsrat, ein Mitglied der

SED: »Ich denke an die Tatsache, daß Land des Deutschen Ritterordens aufgeteilt und den Ärmsten der Stadt zur Verfügung gestellt wurde, ich denke aber auch an den Beschluß, Saatgut und Lebensmittel an die Ärmsten zu verteilen.« Da kam mir ein Kirchenhistoriker in den Sinn, der die marxistische Interpretation Müntzers als Metaphern betrachtete, in denen sich vor allem »die vorausgesetzte eigene revolutionäre Metaphysik« ausdrückt. Müntzer und die Reformation interessieren danach weniger als Geschichte denn als »Formel für die Selbstauslegung der eigenen Weltanschauung«. Das ist, zugegeben, eine überspitzte These, aber wird sie nicht durch einen Satz bestätigt, in dem behauptet wird, die Bauernkriege hätten »durch die Agrarpolitik der DDR« ihre »Aktualität eingebüßt«? Platter, agitatorischer läßt sich sozialistische Traditions- und Erbepflege schlechterdings kaum betreiben. Damit soll nichts gegen den Versuch gesagt sein, revolutionäre und demokratische Traditionen der deutschen Geschichte zu pflegen, auch wenn es sich dabei ehrlicherweise nur um die Darstellung von Niederlagen handeln kann. Gibt es in der östlichen deutschen Republik solche Versuche im Übermaß, herrscht in der westlichen ein Defizit. Die Mahnung Gustav Heinemanns an die westdeutschen Historiker, sich auf die freiheitlichen Entwicklungsstränge in unserer Geschichte zu konzentrieren, scheint leider noch immer aktuell.

Im Rahmen der marxistischen Geschichtsschreibung wird die Bedeutung Thomas Müntzers sichtlich übertrieben. Über den engeren Raum Thüringens hinaus hat der Schwarmgeist und Chiliast keine Resonanz gefunden, aber vielleicht ist die Tatsache, daß seine Wirkungsstätten sämtlich auf dem Territorium der DDR liegen, ein geographischer Schlüssel für das Verständnis der Überdimensionierung seiner Figur: Erbepflege läßt sich so geschickt mit der Förderung des Heimatgedankens verbinden.

Überbewertung ja oder nein, den historischen Gemäuern, die zu Müntzer-Gedenkstätten umgewandelt sind, bekommt sie gut. Die Kornmarktkirche und das Rathaus, die geschichtlichen Orte der Mühlhauser Revolution, zeigen sich in einem

Zustand, den man allen Resten der einst mächtigen Freien Reichsstadt nur wünschen kann. Die dafür sorgen, entdeckt der Besucher Mühlhausens bei seinem Spaziergang unterhalb der Stadtmauer in der Nähe des Rabenturms inmitten einer malerischen Idylle, die an mittelalterliche Bauhütten denken läßt: Da bearbeiten junge Handwerker auf altväterliche Art den Stein und hauen dicke Quader mit Hammer und Meißel zurecht. Sie sind Angestellte des VEB Denkmalpflege Erfurt, der in Mühlhausen eine, wie es im hölzern-bürokratischen DDR-Stil heißt, »territoriale Außenstelle« unterhält. Nicht nur für Bauarbeiter, die des seelenlosen Montierens vorfabrizierter Betonplatten überdrüssig sind, bietet dieser volkseigene Betrieb der Denkmalpflege interessante Arbeitsmöglichkeiten. Im Bezirk Erfurt beschäftigt er Handwerker von 25 verschiedenen Gewerken, darunter Tischler, Maurer und Zimmerleute, Steinmetze, Holz- und Steinbildhauer und Möbelrestauratoren, und in vielen dieser Handwerksberufe bildet er inzwischen selbst Lehrlinge zu Gesellen und Meistern heran. Die Berufe sind gefragt, wie mir der Leiter der Mühlhauser Werkstätten versicherte: »Denkmalpflege genießt hohe gesellschaftliche Anerkennung, und die jungen Menschen haben Spaß an der Arbeit, denn später können sie einmal mit Stolz sagen: Das haben wir mitgeschaffen.«

Im Gegensatz zu dem sozialistischen Disneyland, das in Ostberlin rings um die Nikolaikirche entstand, wollen die Leute dieser Werkstätten weder romantische Kulissen noch Potemkinsche Dörfer schaffen. Ihr Programm heißt, soviel wie nur irgendmöglich von der Originalsubstanz zu erhalten, da nur von ihr »emotionale und intellektuelle Wirkungen« ausgehen. So ist es für sie ein Gebot der Redlichkeit, daß ersetzte Bauelemente, etwa neu eingezogene Fachwerkbalken, deutlich gekennzeichnet werden. Der Betrachter soll erkennen können, was zur Stützung des Alten an Neuem hinzugefügt wurde. Dank ihrer Arbeit kann auch St. Marien, die imposante, fünfschiffige gotische Hallenkirche, in der Müntzer den Aufstand predigte, heute für Konzerte und Vorträge genutzt werden. In dieser nach dem Erfurter Dom größten

Kirche des westlichen Thüringens, versammelten sich die Bürger Mühlhausens 1525, um mit Mehrheit den Rat der Patrizier ab- und den Ewigen Rat einzusetzen, unter ihrem Dach pflanzte Thomas Müntzer wenige Wochen vor der Niederlage von Frankenhausen die Regenbogenfahne der Aufständischen neben der Kanzel auf. Eine Tafel im alten Pfarrhaus gegenüber von St. Marien vermeldet, daß dort der revolutionäre Bauernführer wohnte – daß er Pfarrer war, steht auf ihr nicht verzeichnet. St. Marien gehört heute dem Staat, der sie in eine »Thomas-Müntzer-Gedenkstätte« verwandelt hat. Die Glocken im mächtigen Turm sind noch die alten, die schon zu Müntzers Zeiten zum Gottesdienst oder zur revolutionären Versammlung riefen. Damit die Läutmaschinerie nicht rostet, läßt die atheistische Obrigkeit sie Freitagnachmittags bewegen. Für Mühlhausen, diese unnachahmliche Mischung aus Mittelalter und realem Sozialismus, läuten sie das Wochenende ein. Thomas Müntzer, meint der heutige Pfarrer der Mariengemeinde, der weder über die Kirche noch über die Glocken verfügen kann, würde sich im Grab umdrehen, wenn er wüßte, daß sie nicht mehr zum Gottesdienst läuten: »Müntzers Waffe war die Schrift« – eine Tatsache, die in der von Marxisten-Leninisten regierten DDR gelegentlich in Vergessenheit zu geraten scheint.

4. Der Alltag der neuen Konventionen

»Ich kann mit diesem Staat keine Übereinkunft schließen, ohne mich selbst zu verleugnen.« Der das sagte, hatte unangemeldet an der Wohnungstür in der Leipziger Straße geklingelt und Einlaß verlangt. Er war einer von vielen, die Westkontakte suchten und Hilfe für einen Ausreiseantrag erhofften. Westliche Diplomaten und Korrespondenten dienten als Anlaufstellen für jene kleine Schar Entschlossener, die dem realen Sozialismus entrinnen wollten, weil sie die ständige Bevormundung durch die Partei nicht länger ertragen konnten. Von der größeren Zahl Ausreisewilliger, die vor allem vom Warenüberfluß des westlichen Werbefernsehens angelockt wurden, unterschied sie eine erhebliche Bereitschaft zum Risiko. Denn das Hochhaus in der Leipziger Straße war überwiegend von westlichen Ausländern, meist Angehörigen von Botschaften oder Handelsvertretungen, bewohnt. Ein DDR-Bürger, der hier an eine Tür pochte, wußte, daß die Wände aus »russisch Beton« gefertigt waren, wie der Volksmund sagt. Das Wort steht für eine besondere Mischung aus je einem Drittel Zement, Sand und Mikrophonen. Jeder Satz, der in einer solchen Wohnung gesprochen wurde, konnte abgehört und dem Besucher zum Verhängnis werden. Der Wohnblock war von Volkspolizei bewacht, die Identität von DDR-Bürgern, die sich unbotmäßig äußerten, ließ sich leicht feststellen. Und, Paragraph 219 des DDR-Strafgesetzbuches drohte für Kontaktaufnahme zu Vertretern westlicher Institutionen, als die wir allesamt, gleich ob Diplomaten oder akkreditierte Journalisten, betrachtet wurden, bis zu fünf Jahren

Gefängnis an. Der mir völlig Unbekannte, der da an einem Spätnachmittag Mitte Januar 1983 plötzlich vor der Tür stand, zeichnete sich also durch Courage aus. Bald stellte sich heraus, daß er über den Mut derer verfügte, die nichts mehr zu verlieren haben. »Viele können zu einer Übereinkunft kommen und sich eine Nische zimmern. Sie wollen Aufstieg und bescheidenen Wohlstand«, sagte mein ungebetener Gast. »Aber ich bin von materiellen Dingen unabhängig. Und ich kann hier nicht leben, weil mir diese Gesellschaft keinen Freiraum läßt.« Dabei stammte er aus jenem Milieu, aus dem die SED bevorzugt ihre Funktionäre und Parteimitglieder rekrutiert. Der Vater war Arbeiter, ein Werkzeugmacher, die Mutter Kindergärtnerin. Mein Besucher nannte sich Andreas, kam aus einer mittleren Kleinstadt im Sächsischen, war 26 Jahre alt und gewiß nicht der Typ, der von sich aus die Konfrontation sucht. Zwar mochte er den Dienst in der Volksarmee nicht, aber er hatte ihn auch nicht verweigert, sondern die 18 Monate einfach »abgerissen« – lustlos wie die meisten, merkte er an. »Es war halt vertane Zeit.« Seine Familie hatte dem Regime nicht immer kritisch gegenübergestanden, ganz im Gegenteil: Um den »Aufbau des Sozialismus gegen Provokateure, Diversanten und Agenten des Klassenfeindes zu schützen«, hatte sich der Vater einst freiwillig zur Grenzpolizei gemeldet. Doch die Kluft zwischen den Idealen, für die er auf dem Kamm des Thüringer Waldes Wache schob, und dem sozialistischen Alltag wurde nicht geringer, sie wuchs und wuchs. »Angewidert von der Praxis«, erzählte Andreas, »zog er sich zurück. Vor drei Jahren ist er dann aus der Partei ausgetreten.« Seinem Bruder, einem Wärmetechniker, der sich im Fernstudium zum Ingenieur qualifizieren wollte, wurde nach einer kritischen Äußerung über den Einmarsch der Sowjets in die ČSSR die Verteidigung seiner Abschlußarbeit untersagt. Andreas selbst, Medizinstudent, hatte am Ende des 4. Studienjahres im Fach Marxismus-Leninismus (M-L) die Note 5 erhalten; damit war auch ihm der Weg zum Examen verbaut.

Daß er die politische Pflicht-Hürde für jeden erfolgreichen

Studienabschluß nicht nahm, hatte nichts mit intellektuellen Defekten zu tun, sondern mit einem inneren Widerstreben, einer psychologischen Sperre, die mir nach der ganzen Familiengeschichte verständlich schien. Gegen die offiziellen Gebetsmühlen eines sinnentleerten Marxismus-Leninismus-Rituals hatte er sich hinter seiner Medizin verschanzt. »Mein Ziel ist, Menschen zu helfen. Und ich konnte nur bei größter Isolierung, Konzentration und Abschirmung nach außen meine Leistung erbringen. Ich konzentrierte mich auf Medizin.« Der M-L-Dozent gab freilich den Kampf um die abtrünnige Seele nicht so schnell auf. »Er schickte mich zu Nervenärzten und Psychologen«, berichtete Andreas. »Er behauptete, den Marxismus-Leninismus abzulehnen sei entweder gleichbedeutend mit fehlender Intelligenz oder Haß gegen den sozialistischen Staat, mit willentlichem Versagen oder Geisteskrankheit.« Der sperrige Student stellte schließlich einen Ausreiseantrag und wurde umgehend exmatrikuliert. Seine Schwester, eine Fachhochschul-Dozentin in Berlin, sagte sich in aller Form vom Bruder los. Sie wollte ihre weitere Karriere nicht gefährden. Seine Adresse hat er mir nicht geben wollen, und so habe ich Andreas nie wieder gesehen.

Er war vor allem gekommen, um sich mitzuteilen. »Die im Westen« sollten wissen, was Menschen wie ihm im realen Sozialismus widerfuhr, wenn sie sich den politischen Zwängen nicht beugen wollten. Daß er nicht zu den vielen Heuchlern im Lande und nicht zu den Schlitzohren zählte, die sich äußerlich anpassen, um sich desto besser durchzumogeln, hatte er überzeugend dargelegt. Seine Haltung forderte Hochachtung und Respekt. Aber bei aller Entschiedenheit machte er auf mich einen erregten oder verwirrten Eindruck, was möglicherweise der Situation zuzuschreiben war, in der er sich befand. Denn alles, was er mir in meinen vier Wänden aus russischem Beton erzählte, darauf hatte ich ihn natürlich aufmerksam gemacht, war geeignet, seine Lage weiter zu erschweren. War er ein Michael Kohlhaas? Braucht, wer nicht die von der Partei vorgeschriebenen Pfade wandelt und dabei das schützende Dach der Kirche (die allein, wenn auch begrenzten, Freiraum bieten kann) nicht über sich weiß, einen Mut zum Abwegigen und zum Eigensinn, der in den Augen der ins System Integrierten schon leicht verrückte Züge trägt? Was immer auch rätselhaft bleiben mochte an diesem 26jährigen Medizinstudenten, soviel war doch klar: Er war nicht von jener Schizophrenie befallen, die in den Köpfen vieler DDR-Bürger nistet und sich darin äußert, daß man nach außen beflissen der politischen Konvention folgt und in der Familie und unter guten Freunden gänzlich anders redet – so wie man wirklich denkt. Wenn diese Gespaltenheit die Norm war, dann zeigte Andreas in der Tat bedenkliche anormale Züge. Doch was war die Norm und wie schwer wog die Konvention?

»Ja, wir erziehen Lügner und Heuchler«, bekannte ein LPG-Bauer aus dem Mecklenburgischen, »aber es geht nun einmal nicht anders. Wenn die Kinder es zu etwas bringen sollen, müssen sie sich anpassen und schreiben, was der Lehrer von ihnen erwartet. Das heißt ja nicht, daß sie den politischen Unfug auch glauben müssen.« Ich traf ihn während der Neustädter Pferdetage, die von den Pferdenarren der anderen deutschen Republik als ihr großes Volksfest gefeiert werden. Selbst aus den südlichen Bezirken zieht es Züchter und Reitsportler zum Turnierplatz an der Dosse, nördlich von Berlin. An drei Sonntagen im September veranstaltet die »volkseigene Pferdezuchtdirektion Mitte« diese Leistungsschau in einem ehemals königlich-preußischen Gestüt, das Friedrich Wilhelm II. 1788 gegründet hatte, um seine Kavallerie mit Pferden zu versorgen. An vielen Stallungen war noch das alte Brandzeichen zu sehen – ein Pfeil mit einer Schlange, das vom Pferdeideal der damaligen Züchter kündete: Schnell wie die Pfeile und wendig wie die Schlangen hatten die Wallache für Preußens Gloria zu sein. Heute züchtet man eher Behäbiges, das »edle Warmblutpferd der DDR«, wie es offiziell heißt. Es ist ein »vielseitiges, zuverlässiges Sport-, Reit- und Gebrauchspferd«, ein Exportschlager und Valutabringer, wegen seines niedrigen Preises im Westen inzwischen selbst in Kanada und den USA gefragt.

Westliche Besucher der Neustädter Pferdetage haben wenig Sensationen zu erwarten. Eine Hengstparade in der einen deutschen Republik ist der in der anderen zum Verwechseln ähnlich. Kanoniere der Grande Armée und preußische Dragoner, Kreuzritter, arabische Krieger und römische Quadrigen zogen auf dem Turnierplatz auf. Natürlich fehlte im Neustädter Parade-Repertoire auch das Einzelgespann des Neubauern nicht, der durch die Bodenreform einige Hektar Land bekam, um wenig später zur Mitgliedschaft in einer LPG gezwungen zu werden. Das freilich wurde über Lautsprecher nicht angesagt. Doch in der Pferdezucht herrscht Tradition, die Regeln für die Dressur sind international, die üblichen politischen Sprechblasen wirken da eher wie lästige Pflichtübungen – etwa, wenn die Zuschauer zum Auftakt der großen Pferdegaudi zunächst im Namen der SED-Betriebs-Parteiorganisation und danach erst von der Direktion »aufs herzlichste begrüßt« werden. Nirgendwo schienen mir der marxistisch-leninistische Firnis, mit dem die SED den ganzen DDR-Alltag überzieht, so dünn, die parteilichen Floskeln so hohl, die politische Konvention so aufgesetzt wie hier.

Unter den Zuschauern fanden sich viele private Pferdehalter, von denen es in der DDR mehr gibt, als man im Westen annimmt. Rund ein Drittel von knapp 90 000 Pferden sind in Privatbesitz. Ärzte, Künstler und Professoren haben Pferde in den Dörfern am Rande der großen Städte stehen, doch die meisten gehören Genossenschaftsbauern, die nun einmal über die besten Voraussetzungen für die private Pferdehaltung verfügen. Sie nutzen unbestellbare Restflächen ihrer LPG's, zusätzlich die paar Morgen Acker- und Weideland, die ihnen für ihren privaten Bedarf zustehen, und sie haben Ställe in alten Hofgebäuden, die noch immer ihnen gehören. Da lockt das Aufziehen einiger eigener Pferde als lukrativer Nebenverdienst. An den Bauern und Pferdeliebhabern jedenfalls, die ich in Neustadt sprach, schienen die offiziellen Parolen abzuprallen. Einige waren der Bauernpartei beigetreten, um lästigen »gesellschaftlichen Organisationsdruck« abzuschütteln. Die meisten hatten sich Bedingungen, die von der SED diktiert wurden und die sie nicht ändern konnten, angepaßt und gewannen der genossenschaftlichen Organisation der Landwirtschaft inzwischen auch Vorzüge ab. Sie ließe ihnen ausreichend Freizeit, ihrem privaten Hobby, der Pferdezucht und dem Reitsport nachzugehen. So kommt es, daß Spitzenleistungen im Reiten in der anderen deutschen Republik zwar relativ selten sind, aber die Reiterei, anders als im Westen, nicht die Sache wenig gut Betuchter, sondern ein Breitensport auf dem flachen Lande ist.

Läßt sich, so notierte ich in meinem Tagebuch, diese Neustädter Erfahrung als ein Beispiel dafür nehmen, daß man mit der politischen Konvention ganz gut leben kann, wenn man mit ihr so umzugehen versteht wie (nicht nur) die Bewohner einer rheinischen Kleinstadt mit ihrer Zugehörigkeit zur katholischen Konfession? Man geht beileibe nicht immer um des Glaubens willen zur Messe, sondern weil es unerhört wäre, nicht zu gehen; weil sich der Kirche fernzuhalten, sich von der Gemeinde abzusondern, Nachteile brächte, das Dabeisein und Gesehenwerden dagegen hilfreich ist, wenn es darum geht, Stolpersteine auf dem Weg zur Karriere und gesellschaftlichem Ansehen aus dem Weg zu räumen.

Die Erfahrung von Neustadt wurde bei Bad Doberan an der Ostseeküste bestätigt. Es war ein kalter, trüber Novembermorgen, als die Bläser das Signal zur Treibjagd gaben. In diesem Revier gingen einst die Herzöge von Mecklenburg auf die Pirsch. Wir waren gekommen, um das Portrait einer sozialistischen Jagdgesellschaft zu drehen. Ihr Vorsitzender, ein Forstmeister, der aus Ostpreußen stammte und als junger Offizier der Wehrmacht gegen die Rote Armee gekämpft hatte, trug demonstrativ das Parteiabzeichen der SED am grünen Försterrock. »Jagd und Politik sind eng miteinander verknüpft«, behauptete er, »denn nur, wenn ich fest auf dem Boden unseres Staates, unserer Politik stehe, bin ich in der Lage, auch ordnungsgemäß die Jagd auszuüben und durchzuführen. Deshalb sind Jagd und Politik eine Einheit, und in dieser Form wird auch bei uns verfahren.« Dieser Jagdvorsitzende leistete entschieden ein ideologisches Übersoll, vielleicht, weil er vor westlichen Kameras stand. Er klopfte die Leerformeln eines sozialistischen Jägerlateins. Tatsächlich nämlich, das stellte sich bei näherem Hinsehen sehr schnell heraus, sind Hege, Pflege und jagdliches Brauchtum im realen Sozialismus der DDR und in der bürgerlich-demokratischen Bundesrepublik weitgehend gleich. Ein schwacher Bock wird in Mecklenburg nicht anders »angesprochen« als im Holsteinischen, die Kriterien für einen Hegeabschuß, wie die Jäger sagen, sind in Bad Doberan nicht anders als in Springe am Deister; im Sozialismus wie im Kapitalismus wirken die alten steinzeitlichen Jagdrituale gleich mächtig fort. Doch war das Klischee, das sich in westlichen Köpfen eingenistet hatte und besagt, die Jagd in der DDR sei ein Privileg der Spitzen von Partei und Staat, offensichtlich korrekturbedürftig. Sicher stimmt, daß in manchen Jagdgesellschaften rund um Berlin Armeegeneräle und Offiziere der Staatssicherheit das Sagen haben; aber die ich in den Wäldern an der Ostseeküste auf Dam- und Rotwild lauern oder auf fette Keiler knallen sah, waren Förster und Genossenschaftsbauern, Ärzte und Handwerker, Redakteure und Maschinenschlosser – ganz »normale« Bürger der DDR. Anders als in der Bundesrepublik, ist die Jagd unabhängig vom Eigentums- oder Nutzungsrecht an Grund und Boden. Die Leitung des Jagdwesens obliegt dem Ministerium für Land- und Forstwirtschaft. Wildbestand und Abschußpläne werden durch Verträge zwischen den Jagdgesellschaften und den Forstbetrieben geregelt. Besitzer von Jagdrevieren oder Verpächter, die für das Jagdrecht stolze Summen fordern, zumal wenn Dam- oder Rotwild in den Wäldern steht, gibt es folglich nicht. Laut Gesetz gehört das Wild dem Volk, weshalb die Jagdkollektive ihre »Strecke« als Beitrag zur Versorgung der Bevölkerung abzuliefern haben. Die Jäger kassieren dafür eine Abschußprämie und dürfen die Trophäe behalten. Nach dem Statut der Jagdgesellschaften haben sie auch das Recht, ein Stück Wild zum Vorzugspreis zurückzukaufen.

Offen blieb die Frage, ob jeder an der Jagd interessierte Bürger auch Zugang zu einer der knapp 900 DDR-Jagdgesell-

schaften hat. Immerhin standen am Anfang des »sozialistischen Jagdwesens« in der DDR einmal Jagdkommandos der
Volkspolizei, denen nur politisch besonders Zuverlässige angehören konnten. Sorge und Mißtrauen, die Waffen könnten
in die Hände politischer Gegner gelangen, waren in den ersten
Nachkriegsjahren groß. Und als 1953 die ersten Jagdkollektive
gegründet wurden, blieben sie zunächst fest in die »Gesellschaft für Sport und Technik« integriert, die, von erprobten
Genossen geleitet, im Auftrag von Partei und Staat die paramilitärische Ausbildung pflegt. Erst 1962 fühlte sich die DDR
souverän genug, unabhängige Jagdgenossenschaften zuzulas-
sen, deren Leitung freilich in den Händen treuer SED-Mitglieder liegt. Gestandene Jäger haben inzwischen ihre privaten Waffen daheim im Schrank, doch die meisten leihen sich
ihre Büchse noch immer für jeweils sieben Tage aus den Arse-
nalen ihrer Vereine aus.

Das Jagdgesetz der DDR beschränkt die Teilnehmer an der
Jagd zwar ausdrücklich auf solche Personen, die an der Festigung und dem Schutz des Arbeiter- und Bauernstaates mit-
wirken. In der Praxis aber läuft das meist darauf hinaus, daß
jagen darf, wer im Beruf seinen Mann steht – der Arbeitsplatz
ist schließlich immer auch ein Kampfplatz für den Frieden –
und von dem sicher ist, daß er politisch nicht wider den Stachel löckt. Daran gemessen erweist sich so mancher Spruch
von Jagd und Politik als hohl. Es bedurfte keines ideologischen
Übereifers nach dem Muster des Vorsitzenden, um Mitglied
der Jagdgesellschaft von Bad Doberan zu werden; es reichte
aus, nicht gegen den Strom zu schwimmen. Drei Wochen
nach der Treibjagd gab es dann den traditionellen Jägerball mit
einem üppigen Büffet und Tanz. Er war kleinbürgerlich-
deutsch im Stil und sah, nimmt man die modische Qualität
der Kleidung einmal aus, vergleichbaren gesellschaftlichen
Höhepunkten im Leben einer westdeutschen Kleinstadt zum
Verwechseln ähnlich. Meist, so notierte ich in meinem Tagebuch, trägt die Konvention der Kleinbürger auch im realen
Sozialismus den Sieg über die neue, die politische, davon.

Es gibt freilich auch den Fall, daß die aufgesetzte politische Konvention zu einer neuen gesellschaftlichen wurde und heute von nahezu allen angenommen ist. Das beste Beispiel dafür bietet die Jugendweihe, die aus einer alten Tradition der sozialistischen Jugendbewegung stammt. In einer überwiegend volkskirchlichen Umwelt stellte sie einst den Versuch dar, der katholischen Kommunion, vor allem aber der protestantischen Konfirmation einen ebenbürtigen atheistischen Initiationsritus für die Aufnahme Jugendlicher in die Welt der Erwachsenen entgegenzustellen. Als wir im Frühjahr 1986 die Jugendweihe von 31 Jungen und Mädchen in Britz im Bezirk Frankfurt an der Oder drehten, hatte der alte Ritus einer atheistischen Minderheit sich längst zur pseudosakralen Feierstunde des realen Sozialismus gemausert, der sich keiner der 14jährigen Schüler der Gemeinde entzog. Mit Eltern und Verwandten waren sie in die große Turnhalle gekommen, um in ihren neuen Sonntagskleidern per Urkunde und Handschlag aus Kindern in »würdige Bürger des sozialistischen Staates« verwandelt zu werden. Dem ging ein feierliches Gelöbnis voraus, in dem sie sich im Chor unter anderem verpflichteten,

— für die »große und edle Sache des Sozialismus zu arbeiten und zu kämpfen«,
— als »treue Söhne und Töchter« des Arbeiter- und Bauernstaates »Meister ihres Fachs zu werden«, all »ihr Wissen und Können für die Verwirklichung unserer humanistischen Ideale einzusetzen« sowie
— als »wahre Patrioten« die »Freundschaft mit der Sowjetunion zu vertiefen«, im »Geiste des proletarischen Internationalismus zu kämpfen« und »den Sozialismus gegen jeden imperialistischen Angriff zu verteidigen«.

Ihr »Ja, das geloben wir«, klang fast wie ein Soldateneid. Die Lieder und Gedichte, die in der Turnhalle von Britz für die Schüler der Klasse 8a und 8b gesungen und rezitiert wurden, hatten so eindeutig agitatorischen Charakter wie die Reden. Eine Blondine im Kleinen Schwarzen und Möchtegern-Mon-roe-Look, eine von der Berliner Staatsoper ausgeliehene Sopranistin, sang:

Glückliche Enkel des Roten Oktober,
wir sind befreundet, wir sind befreit,
in unseren Herzen Erfahrung der Väter,
stürmen wir vorwärts in unsere Zeit.
Partei, deine jungen Genossen
tragen die rote Fahne voran...

Junge Pioniere erklommen die Bühne und verkündeten Leitsprüche fürs Leben, die von Patriarchen des Sozialismus, Gründern der DDR oder Kämpfern der Arbeiterklasse stammten. Als besonders banale Beispiele notierte ich Wilhelm Piecks Satz: »Dein Wissen wird erst dann zum festen Fundament für Deine Arbeit, wenn Du es ständig in der Praxis anwendest«. Und ein Motto Ernst Thälmanns, das ebenso wie das Piecks, auch von jedem braven Hausvater hätte stammen können: »Auf welche Straße des Lebens Du auch in der Zukunft gehen wirst, Vorbedingung für Dein Verhalten ist Dein Charakter.« Der Festredner, ein Professor der Forstwirtschaft und Mitglied der SED, entwarf ein simplistisches, manichäisches Bild der Welt, das keinen Zweifel daran ließ, wie sicher die Heimat der 31 Schüler in Britz im Lager des Guten und des Lichts verwurzelt war. In dem herrschte Anstand, Sauberkeit, Vollbeschäftigung und das unermüdliche Streben nach Frieden; in der Welt des Bösen und der Finsternis würden Rauschgiftsucht und Verbrechen gezüchtet, hunderttausenden Jugendlichen die Lehrstellen verweigert, atomare Aufrüstung betrieben und Kriege vorbereitet. »Im Zweiten Weltkrieg versanken Städte in Schutt und Asche, in Hiroshima und Nagasaki verbrannten Männer, Frauen, Greise, Kinder, Tiere, Pflanzen, alles Leben. Das heute in die Staatspolitik einer Regierung einzukalkulieren, ist verbrecherisch. Welch ein Glück, daß es neben solchen finsteren Kräften auch eine mächtige Gemeinschaft sozialistischer Staaten gibt. Ihr Kern ist die Sowjetunion, und wir sind mit diesem Land freundschaftlich verbunden. Welch ein Glück für uns und die ganze Menschheit, daß humane, kluge, sachliche Politiker an der Spitze unserer sozialistischen Staaten stehen.«

Zur Vorbereitung auf ihre Jugendweihe hatten die 31 Schülerinnen und Schüler in Britz die üblichen zehn Jugendstunden absolviert, die helfen sollen, den Sinn des Gelöbnisses »richtig zu begreifen«. Eine Stunde dieses sozialistischen Konfirmationsunterrichts galt dem Thema »Freundschaft zum Lande Lenins – Herzenssache unseres Volkes«. Im Leitheft für die Jugendstunden, herausgegeben vom Zentralausschuß für die Jugendweihe der DDR, wurde dazu angemerkt: »Freundschaft zu Sowjetmenschen, wer von Euch hätte dazu nicht persönliche Erfahrungen gesammelt: Begegnungen mit sowjetischen Pionieren oder Komsomolzen, mit Sowjetsoldaten, Brieffreundschaften. Seht Euch im Heimatkreis um, wo überall deutsch-sowjetische Freundschaft spürbar ist. Bekennt Euch zu dieser Freundschaft, schützt sie gegen alle Angriffe und Verleumdungen. Eignet Euch gute Kenntnisse in der Sprache unserer Freunde an.« Eine andere Stunde stand unter dem Motto: »Unser sozialistisches Vaterland«, das nach diesem Leitfaden »durch vorbildliches Lernen, durch schöpferische, ehrliche und disziplinierte Arbeit« selbstverständlich zu stärken war. Formell ist der Zentralausschuß, der die Richtlinien für diese Art Indoktrination herausgibt, eine unabhängige, weder der SED noch der FDJ zugehörige Institution, aber die Jugendstunden werden im Rahmen eines FDJ-Lehrjahres absolviert. Daß die Jugendweihe selbst als »spezifischer Beitrag zur Erziehung junger Revolutionäre« gilt, wird in der DDR wahrlich nicht als Geheimnis gehütet. Es ist vielfach in anderem Kontext nachzulesen. Eine dritte Jugendstunde, der sich die Teenager unterziehen mußten, stand unter dem Leitwort »Wir erfüllen das revolutionäre Vermächtnis«. Sie sollte die Jugendlichen mit dem progressiven Erbe, mit den Kämpfen der Arbeiterbewegung und mit dem antifaschistischen Widerstand bekannt machen. Wie das in der Praxis geschieht, dafür mag der Arbeiterfunktionär Werner Starke in Sachsenhausen als Beispiel dienen. Ich beobachtete ihn im März 1986, als er Teilnehmern solcher FDJ-Jugendstunden über das Leben im Lager erzählte, in dem ihn die Nazis jahrelang gefangen gehalten hatten. Er war ein einfacher, aber intelligenter, knorriger Typ, geprägt durch das Arbeitermilieu, aus dem er stammte, durch Jahre der Verfolgung und des illegalen Kampfes. Anders als viele der wendigen, glatten und anpasserischen Obmänner des SED-Regimes in den zentralen Verwaltungsstuben verfügte dieser Funktionär der alten Schule über Haltung und Charakter, die Respekt erheischten. Getreu dem Motto »Wissen ist Macht«, so erzählte er voller Stolz den 14jährigen, die er durch das Lager führte, habe er Goethe und Schiller im Zuchthaus gelesen. Es fiel zwar schwer, sich diesen Werner Starke auf gewienertem, diffizilen diplomatischen Parkett vorzustellen, aber daß ein Mann wie er nach dem Krieg und nach Gründung der DDR es im diplomatischen Dienst der anderen Republik zu Position und Ansehen brachte, gefiel mir schon, als er davon berichtete. Ich wünschte mir auch, es gehörte zum Pflichtpensum einer jeden westdeutschen Schulklasse, einmal durch eine solche Stätte des Folterns und der Barbarei geführt zu werden. Mein Respekt wuchs, und ich war schon dabei, für Werner Starke Sympathie zu empfinden, als der alte Feuerkopf plötzlich aus einem Gedicht Armin Stolpers zitierte. »Was ist heute revolutionär?«, hatte dieser Poet vom politischen Dienst als Frage gereimt und umgehend selbst die Antwort im richtigen Versmaß gegeben: »Hammer, Zirkel und Gewehr«. Doch daß ich der Anfechtung widerstand, den verdienten Respekt für unseren Jugendstunden-Führer in Sympathie umzuwandeln, hatte noch einen anderen Grund. Um den jungen Teilnehmern der Führung durch Sachsenhausen zu demonstrieren, daß politische Angeklagte von der Nazijustiz wie Rechtlose behandelt wurden, holte er einen Haftbefehl aus der damaligen Zeit aus der Tasche und sagte: »Stellt Euch vor, die Anklageschrift konnten wir vor dem Prozeß nur einmal einsehen, behalten und mit in die Zelle nehmen durften wir sie nicht.« Seine Behauptung war unstreitig korrekt. Sie belegt eine Praxis, die in jedem rechtsstaatlichen Verfahren undenkbar ist, weil sie die Verteidigung erheblich behindert. Die jungen Menschen zeigten sich beeindruckt. Doch mir fiel während Starkes Schilderung ein Gespräch mit einem DDR-Rechtsanwalt ein, der zwei junge Feinoptiker aus Jena, beide Mitglieder der unabhängigen Friedensbewegung, verteidigt hatte. Sie standen wegen selbstgefertigter Handzettel vor Gericht, in denen sie sich unter anderem jener Äquidistanz zu den Großmächten schuldig machten, welche die Vormacht des Westens so heftig bei den Grünen in der Bundesrepublik beklagt. So wurde auf einem der illegalen Flugblätter nicht nur Freiheit für das Volk El Salvadors, sondern auch für das Polens gefordert. Eine andere Losung lautete: »Amis raus aus Lateinamerika, Sowjets raus aus Afghanistan.« Als weit schlimmer bewerteten die DDR-Anklagebehörden jedoch die Parolen, die sie »pseudopazifistisch« nannten, etwa die Forderung: »Boykott der Wehrkunde – Friedenskunde ist wichtig«, und eine in ganzen sechs Exemplaren verbreitete Handzeichnung, auf der Panzer gezeigt wurden, die sich in Gießkannen verwandelten. Die Anklageschrift sah in den pazifistischen Parolen Schutzbehauptungen, eine Art Deckmantel, der vorsätzliche Angriffe gegen die staatliche Ordnung der DDR verbergen sollte. Das Urteil, am 8. August 1984 verkündet, lautete auf Freiheitsstrafe von vier, beziehungsweise drei Jahren. Als mir mein Gewährsmann von diesen Fällen erzählte, führte er lebhaft Klage, daß die Strafprozeßordnung der DDR bei solchen politischen Delikten die Aushändigung der Anklageschrift und selbst des Urteils an die Betroffenen und ihren Rechtsbeistand untersagt. Es gibt in der DDR nur das Recht auf Einsicht der Akten: Weil er nicht einmal eine Kopie anfertigen durfte, war dieser Anwalt gezwungen, die wichtigsten Punkte der Anklage und der belastenden Zeugenaussagen handschriftlich zu notieren. Wußte Werner Starke, der gestandene Antifaschist vom Jahrgang 1910 etwa nicht, daß die politische Justiz der DDR Praktiken kennt, die er an der nationalsozialistischen Willkürjustiz, deren Opfer er einmal war, mit vollem Recht kritisierte?

Konventionen lassen sich natürlich auch erzwingen. Formell ist die Teilnahme an der Jugendweihe freiwillig, in der Praxis liegt sie bei 98 Prozent eines Jahrgangs, ein Ergebnis, das ursprünglich durch massiven gesellschaftlichen Druck zustande kam. Nichtteilnahme gilt als Zeichen gesellschaftlicher Unzuverlässigkeit und verlegt nicht selten den Weg zu Oberschule und akademischer Bildung. Als katholische Jugendliche, die aus Prinzip der atheistischen Jugendweihe ferngeblieben waren, bei der Zulassung zum Studium trotz guter Noten benachteiligt wurden, protestierten die katholischen Bischöfe der DDR. In der Antwort, die ihnen das Ministerium für Volksbildung zukommen ließ, hieß es sinngemäß, ein wichtiges Kriterium bei der Auswahl der Besten für das Studium sei das Bekenntnis zum sozialistischen Staat. »Dazu zählt auch die Jugendweihe«, wurden die Bischöfe wörtlich belehrt, »durch die sich die Schüler umfassend auf das Leben als sozialistische Staatsbürger ... vorbereiten.« Was das im Einzelfall bedeuten kann, schildert die Schriftstellerin Gabriele Eckart in einem ihrer »Protokolle aus der DDR« (»So sehe ick die Sache«). Da wird von dem Elektronikfacharbeiter Thomas erzählt, der in Mathematik und Physik immer eine Eins hatte und »nach seinen Leistungen eigentlich zur Oberschule hätte gehen oder eine Lehrstelle mit Abitur bekommen müssen«. Doch er wurde nicht zur erweiterten Oberschule zugelassen. »Vielleicht«, heißt es in diesem Protokoll, »hat das deshalb nicht geklappt, weil er nicht an der Jugendweihe teilnahm.« Weil die Kirchen die über die Jugendweihe vermittelte Weltanschauung mit der christlichen Botschaft für prinzipiell unvereinbar hielten, stellten sie ihre Gläubigen in den 50er Jahren vor die Alternative, entweder an der Konfirmation (bzw. Kommunion) oder an der Jugendweihe teilzunehmen. Sie bezogen damit eine Position, die sie zu sicheren Verlierern machte. Angesichts der drohenden schweren Benachteiligung ihrer Kinder in Schule, Ausbildung und Beruf wuchs der Druck der Eltern auf die Bischöfe, an die Stelle eines unzumutbaren Entweder-Oder ein geregeltes Nebeneinander zu setzen. So halten die evangelischen Kirchen in der Theorie zwar weiterhin an der Unvereinbarkeit fest, doch in der Praxis schließen Jugendweihe und Konfirmation einander seit langem nicht mehr aus. Nur auf einer Schamfrist, die zwischen dem Vollzug beider Rituale verstreichen soll, bestehen sie noch. So konnte, wer im Frühjahr 1987 das pseudosakrale Gelübde für den real-existierenden Sozialismus ablegte, in der Regel erst 1988 mit der kirchlichen Einsegnung rechnen, falls er sie dann noch wünschen sollte. Im Gegensatz zu der konstant hohen Beteiligung an der Jugendweihe gehen die Zahlen bei den Konfirmanden ständig zurück.

An Pathos war wahrlich kein Mangel in der großen Turnhalle in Britz. Die schwarzgewandete Sopranistin sang: »Strahlende Sonne ist unser Begleiter / hell ist der Himmel, blau ist das Meer / ihr habt gekämpft und die Macht uns erobert / wir aber geben sie nie wieder her. « Brav saßen die Ururenkel des Roten Oktober in der ersten Reihe und blickten zu dem Festredner auf, der ihnen mit sonorer, bedeutungsschwerer Stimme kundtat, daß sie »feierlich in die große Gemeinschaft des werktätigen Volkes« aufgenommen würden, »das unter Führung der Arbeiterklasse und ihrer revolutionären Partei die entwickelte sozialistische Gesellschaft in der Deutschen Demokratischen Republik errichtet«. Ganz das Produkt einer auf Leistung und Gehorsam ausgerichteten Erziehung, wirkten sie so ernst und diszipliniert, als seien sie darauf gedrillt worden, an ihrem großen Tag wie die Miniaturausgaben von Erwachsenen aufzutreten. Dieser Festakt, daran war kein Zweifel erlaubt, markierte den Höhepunkt einer jahrelang über die Jungen Pioniere, die FDJ und die Schule betriebenen massiven Indoktrination. Ich konnte mir nur schwer vorstellen, daß sämtliche Eltern und die zahlreich erschienenen Anverwandten mit dem politischen Inhalt des Dargebotenen nahtlos übereinstimmten, und doch entdeckte ich keine Zeichen des Unmuts oder der Skepsis auf den Gesichtern. »Ein paar Gläubige sind natürlich darunter, aber der Prozentsatz ist nicht erheblich«, versicherte mir nach der Feier ein Graphiker aus Britz. Er war mir von einem Pfarrer in Berlin als kritischer Geist genannt worden, gefeit gegen die offizielle Indoktrination, aber auch frei von blindem Haß auf das System.

»Erstens hat sich die Jugendweihe durchgesetzt, weil Kinder

keine Außenseiter sein wollen«, erklärte er. »Sie wird in der
Schule propagiert, vor allem aber in der FDJ, in der fast alle
Mitglieder sind. Und zweitens haben Eltern natürlich den
Wunsch, daß ihre Söhne und Töchter im Leben ohne große
Schwierigkeiten vorankommen.« Aber er warnte davor, aus
derlei Anpassung und Mitläuferei den Schluß zu ziehen, daß
auch der ideologische Gehalt solcher bombastischen Feiern
azeptiert werde: »Bei den meisten geht das zum einen Ohr
rein und zum andern wieder raus.« Seine Meinung fand ich in
vielen anderen Gesprächen bestätigt. Danach hat die Jugendweihe in der DDR in der Tat den Stellenwert, den früher die
Einsegnung genoß. Sie ist eine Art säkulare Konfirmations-
feier, die heute gängige Form, einen neuen Lebensabschnitt
zu beginnen. Die politische Predigt wird von den meisten
hingenommen wie in der Volkskirche der Chorgesang und das
Wort von der Kanzel. Entscheidend ist das Fest in der Familie,
und für die 14jährigen zählen vor allem die Geschenke.

Wie alle Vergleiche, hinkt natürlich auch der mit der Volkskirche. Christliche Tradition ist über mehr als tausend Jahre
im Volke verwurzelt, die realsozialistische Konvention das
Ergebnis einer Octroi der jüngsten Geschichte. Eine winzige
Minderheit, die sich von der Arbeiterklasse beauftragt glaubt
und vorgibt, in deren Interesse zu handeln, zwang sie der
breiten Mehrheit auf. Gerade deshalb bleibt es erstaunlich, wie leicht und schnell der volkskirchliche Initiationsritus der Konfirmation sich in der DDR gegen den säkular-mar-
xistischen der Jugendweihe austauschen ließ. Wer eine Erklärung wünscht, erforscht besser Ursachen für die Schwächen der volkskirchlichen Tradition, statt auf die Überzeugungskraft des neuen, staatlich propagierten Glaubens zu
setzen.

»Wir igeln uns ein, wir haben einen kleinen Kreis von Freunden und Bekannten, in dem sind wir offen, denn da kann einer
sich auf den anderen verlassen.« So beschrieb ein Handwerker
aus dem Sächsischen sein Leben in der Doppelwelt, die für
viele DDR-Bürger so typisch ist. Da gibt es zunächst die von

der Partei und ihren Parolen geprägte Außenwelt mit Arbeitsplatz, Berufskollegen und den Anforderungen der realsozialistischen Konvention. Man genügt ihr und leistet Lippendienste, um nicht unangenehm aufzufallen. Und da ist die Binnenwelt der Familie und der guten Freunde in der Verstellung nicht nötig ist. Vorausgesetzt, sie entstammen einem Elternhaus, das in den zwölf Jahren der Hitlerherrschaft von dem damals grassierenden Massenwahn nicht infiziert war, erinnert ältere Bürger der permanente Druck zu politisch konformem Verhalten in der DDR-Außenwelt an die eigene Jugend in der Nazizeit. Der sächsische Landesbischof Hempel hatte den Mut, die peinliche Parallele öffentlich zu benennen: »Ich erinnere mich an eine Kindheitserfahrung«, berichtete er den Synodalen des evangelischen Kirchenbundes der DDR in Potsdam. »Ich kam in das Zimmer meiner Eltern, abends, und sie sagten: ›Junge, gehe sofort raus, wir haben etwas wichtiges zu besprechen‹.« So etwas auf dem Territorium der DDR offen auszusprechen, stellte immerhin ein Wagnis dar. Der Bischof kleidete seine Schelte deshalb in einen vorsichtig formulierten Appell an seine kommunistische Obrigkeit, der wachsenden Unzufriedenheit vieler DDR-Bürger durch eine »Neuentwicklung der Kultur des Umgangs miteinander« auch bei heiklen oder kontroversen Themen zu begegnen. Obschon bedingungslos in der Sache, erhielt die Kritik durch diesen Kontext, die konstruktive Tendenz, die nötig ist, damit die Parteiführung sie überhaupt zur Kenntnis nimmt. Das realsozialistische Klima der Auseinandersetzung duldet ja Kritik nur, insoweit sie klar der Förderung der von der Partei gesetzten Ziele oder der Verbesserung der Methoden dient, die zum Erreichen dieser Ziele führen sollen. Wo die Grenzen solcher Kritik selbst für einen Mann der Kirche verlaufen, der Sanktionen von Partei und Staat nicht zu fürchten braucht, machte die Art deutlich, wie der Landesbischof von Sachsen den in der DDR zugelassenen Stil der öffentlichen Auseinandersetzung umschrieb. »Es ist in der sozialistischen Gesellschaft unseres Landes schwer, über Schwachheit zu reden, und zwar über die eigene Schwachheit als auch über die gemeinsame Schwachheit. Das Reden über die Schwachheit wird verwechselt mit klassenfeindlicher Agitation.« Noch in der Formulierung »gemeinsame Schwachheit« steckt ein Bekenntnis zum sozialistischen Staat; erst, nachdem dieses, wenn auch in christlichem Predigtstil verpackt, abgelegt ist, kann die offene Attacke erfolgen, die besagt: Wer Kritik übt, wird zum Klassenfeind erklärt.

Der Bischof ohne Furcht und Tadel äußerte dies im Verlauf einer Debatte über die Ursache der Ausreisewelle in der DDR, die im Frühsommer 1984 einen neuen Höhepunkt erreichte. Zwar hatte es stets einige zehntausend DDR-Bürger gegeben, die ihren Frieden mit dem System nicht machen wollten. Zäh und beharrlich hatten viele einzelne oder ganze Familien oft über Jahre gekämpft, Schikanen ertragen und Demütigungen in Kauf genommen, um endlich die ersehnte Ausreise in den Westen durchzusetzen. Viele waren von einer geradezu grimmigen Unbedingtheit, die freilich taktisches Verhalten nicht ausschloß. List ist ja nicht nur ein taugliches, sondern auch legitimes Mittel des einzelnen gegen einen Leviathan von Staat, der seine Bürger ständig bevormundet, überwacht und durch einseitig gesteuerte Information unerträglich gängelt. Daß die Zahl der Ausreisewünsche im Winter 1983 und Frühjahr 1984 sprunghaft anstieg, hatte mit der politischen Großwetterlage zu tun, auf die die Bevölkerung der DDR von jeher besonders sensibel reagiert. Die Entschlossenheit der neuen Regierung Kohl, am Nato-Doppelbeschluß festzuhalten und Pershing-II-Raketen auf westdeutschem Boden zu stationieren, beantwortete Erich Honecker mit der Drohung einer »neuen Eiszeit«. Sie werde das Verhältnis zwischen beiden deutschen Staaten erheblich belasten, signalisierte der SED-Chef damit und sprach zugleich vom »westlichen Raketenzaun«, über den hinweg man schwerlich gutnachbarlich verkehren könne. Daß Honecker nach der Stationierung dann sein ganzes Prestige im eigenen Bündnis in die Waagschale warf, um den Dialog über die deutsch-deutsche Grenze dennoch weiterzuführen – Motto: »Zehnmal miteinander reden ist besser als einmal aufeinander zu schießen« –, daß er oft unverhüllten Rügen aus Moskau trotzend, unbeirrt an seiner Politik der Vernunft und des Gesprächs festhielt, ließ sich damals nicht absehen. Das Wort von der Eiszeit jedenfalls löste eine Torschlußpanik aus, vergleichbar nur mit dem großen Exodus zur Zeit des Berlin-Ultimatums von Nikita Chruschtschow, der schließlich zum Bau der Berliner Mauer führte. Jetzt oder nie hieß plötzlich die Parole vieler Ausreisewilliger. Und wem die örtlichen Behörden, wie dies damals häufig und in rüder Form geschah, die Annahme der Ausreiseanträge verweigerten, der suchte nicht selten Rat, Beistand oder gar Zuflucht in den westlichen Botschaften in der DDR.

5. »Wahre« und andere Menschenrechte

Mit der Ankündigung einer neuen Eiszeit nach der Aufstellung der Pershing begannen die Besetzerdramen um die Ständige Vertretung Bonns in Ostberlin und die bundesdeutsche Botschaft in Prag. Der Massenansturm sogenannter Asylanten deckte eine Praxis der Zusammenarbeit zwischen DDR-Behörden und westlichen Diplomaten auf, die bei strenger Geheimhaltung über Jahre mit Erfolg ausgeübt worden war. Seit Bonn und die drei Westmächte nach Abschluß des Grundlagenvertrages Beziehungen zur DDR unterhielten, hatten immer wieder ihres sozialistischen Vaterlandes überdrüssige DDR-Bürger in westlichen Missionen vorgesprochen. Zwar suchten Volkspolizisten derlei Kontaktaufnahme durch rigorose Ausweiskontrollen zu verhindern. Doch Ausreisewillige, denen es einmal gelungen war, ins Missionsgebäude vorzudringen, weigerten sich häufig, es zu verlassen. Sie bestanden auf einer verbindlichen Zusage der DDR, straffrei auszugehen und die Genehmigung zur Ausreise aus der DDR erhalten. In aller Stille hatten sich Westdiplomaten und DDR-Vertreter auf einen Modus geeinigt, der solche Fälle lösen half. Den Schutz- und Beistandsuchenden einfach die Tür zu weisen, hätte die Amerikaner als Verfechter der Menchenrechte, die Bundesdeutschen mit Blick auf das Grundgesetz, das nur eine deutsche Staatsangehörigkeit und damit auch die von der DDR vehement bestrittene Obhutspflicht für alle Deutschen kennt, in Schwierigkeiten gebracht. Umgekehrt war die SED-Spitze daran interessiert, vor der eigenen Öffentlichkeit nicht publik werden zu lassen, daß Westbotschaften Fluchtburgen darstellen, in denen man sich, wenn auch befristet, dem Zugriff der DDR-Sicherheitsorgane entziehen kann – Inseln des Beistands, in denen zumindest Rat und praktische Hilfe für die Ausreise erhältlich sind.

Das sorgsam gehütete Arrangement der Interessen platzte mit lautem Knall, als sechs DDR-Bürger im Januar 1984 in die US-Botschaft in Ostberlin eindrangen, um ihre Ausreise zu erzwingen. Einigen in der DDR akkreditierten westlichen Journalisten hatten sie zuvor einen offenen Brief an Präsident Reagan zugespielt, in dem sie politische Entmündigung und Mangel an demokratischen Freiheiten als Motiv für ihre Aktion benannten. »Auf Grund unserer inneren Überzeugung«, hieß es in dem Schreiben, das der US-Botschafter nach Washington weiterzuleiten versprach, »ist uns ein Leben in der DDR unmöglich geworden.« Zwei der Botschaftsbesetzer hatten wegen versuchter Republikflucht bereits mehrere Monate Haft verbüßt.

Als die erste Meldung über die ARD-Hörfunksender lief, sahen sich nicht nur die Amerikaner in einer schwierigen Situation. Formell gibt es die Anerkennung eines Asylrechts nur zwischen lateinamerikanischen Staaten; Europäer, Amerikaner und Sowjetrussen weigern sich prinzipiell, Asylsuchende in ihren Missionen zu beherbergen. Zwei Tage lang schien das Schicksal der sechs völlig ungewiß. Amerikanische Botschaftsangestellte versicherten, sie seien entschlossen, die Eindringlinge abzuschieben. Doch die sechs in der Botschaft zeigten sich völlig unbeeindruckt, als die Amerikaner demonstrativ einige Marineinfanteristen aus Westberlin zur Verstärkung holten. Gegen Versuche, sie mit Gewalt vor die Tür zu setzen, kündigten sie passiven Widerstand an. Intensiv wurde hinter hermetisch verschlossenen Türen verhandelt. Wie würden die Amerikaner letztlich entscheiden? Es gab da zwar einen Präzedenzfall, aber er spielte in Moskau und hatte, weil die breite sowjetische Öffentlichkeit nie von ihm erfuhr, eine andere Qualität. Fünf Jahre lebte eine siebenköpfige Familie aus Sibirien im Souterrain der US-Botschaft in der Sowjetunion. Es war ihr gelungen, an den Posten vor der Botschaft vorbei in die Konsularabteilung vorzudringen. Da sowjetische Gesetze jede eigenmächtige Kontaktaufnahme von Sowjetbürgern mit fremden Botschaften unter Strafe stellt, forderten die Amerikaner eine Garantie von den sowjetischen Behörden, daß die Asylbewerber nach dem Verlassen der Botschaft weder verhaftet noch verfolgt würden. Erst als die Sowjets dies endlich zusicherten und auch die Ausreisegenehmigung in Aussicht stellten, ließen die Amerikaner die Familie aus Sibirien ziehen. Auf eine Kurzformel gebracht, lautete die amerikanische Politik: Einerseits kann Asyl nicht gewährt werden, andererseits darf die Ausweisung aus der Botschaft nicht einer Überstellung an die Behörden zum Zweck der Verhaftung und Strafverfolgung gleichkommen. Das Strafgesetzbuch droht für »ungesetzliche Verbindungsaufnahme« zu Organisationen, Einrichtungen oder Personen, die sich eine gegen die »staatliche Ordnung der DDR gerichtete Tätigkeit zum Ziel setzen«, Freiheitsstrafen bis zu fünf Jahren an. Ob westliche Botschaften zu solchen Organisationen zählen, wird von Fall zu Fall entschieden.

Für die DDR schien eine Lösung nach dem sowjetisch-amerikanischen Modell nicht nur schwierig, weil zwei der jungen DDR-Bürger Söhne von Offizieren des Staatssicherheitsdienstes waren. Anders als die sowjetische Regierung mußte die SED-Führung auch befürchten, daß das Beispiel wegen der breiten Publizität Schule machen würde. Dennoch entschloß sie sich zu schnellem, pragmatischem und vernünftigem Handeln: Die sechs wurden formell ausgebürgert und über die Grenze abgeschoben.

Natürlich blieb nicht aus, daß die spektakuläre Aktion vielfach Nachahmung fand. So meldete die DDR-Presse Ende Februar 1984, daß Willi Stoph, Politbüromitglied, Vorsitzender des Ministerrats und nach Erich Honecker der zweite Mann im Staat, mit »den Handlungen einer Familie Berg«, die gegenwärtig »Gast« der bundesdeutschen Botschaft in Prag sei, nicht das geringste zu tun habe. Nach langem Schweigen und auf die nachgerade DDR-typische verschlungene und verquere Weise bestätigte dieses vermeintliche Dementi nur die Berichte westdeutscher Zeitungen, nach denen eine Nichte Stophs zu einer Gruppe von DDR-Bürgern gehörte, die über die »Besetzung« der Bonner Botschaft in der CSSR ihre Ausreise aus der DDR durchsetzen wollten. Denn ein Hans Dieter Berg, stand da zu lesen, sei mit einer Ingrid, geb. Stoph verheiratet. Doch wurde dieser Hans Dieter Berg nicht nur als Wanderer zwischen zwei Welten ins Zwielicht gerückt, durch den Hinweis, er sei in seiner Jugend straffällig geworden, wurden zugleich alle möglichen Botschaftsbesetzer unter kriminellen Verdacht gestellt. Frei nach dem Motto »ein schwarzes Schaf kommt in den besten Familien vor«, hatte sich die DDR-Führung mit dieser Erklärung schützend vor ihren Regierungschef gestellt. Aber daß sie ihr sonst so beharrliches Schweigen zum Ausreisethema damit brach – ihre eigenen Medien hatten die sechs in der US-Botschaft mit keinem Wort und keiner Zeile bedacht –, zeigte nur, wie sehr ihr die offene Debatte der Problematik im Westen inzwischen unter die Haut ging. Die Berichterstattung in westlichen Zeitungen wurde als »Verleumdungskampagne« bezeichnet, betrieben von Kräften, die eine Belastung des deutsch-deutschen Verhältnisses wünschten.

Nun hatte es anfänglich auch bei westlichen Diplomaten in Ostberlin den Vorwurf gegeben, die Meldungen über die Aktion der sechs in der US-Botschaft wären besser unterblieben, weil Öffentlichkeit der Abwicklung der äußerst sensiblen humanitären Geschäfte zwischen Ost und West nur schaden könne. Im Prinzip war und ist dieser Einwand richtig. In Zehntausenden von Einzelfällen hat sich die Regel bewährt, daß Unterstützung, die DDR-Bürger aus dem Westen zuteil werden soll, um so wirksamer ist, je unauffälliger die westlichen Helfer und ihre östlichen Partner dabei zu Werke gehen. Im Falle der sechs ist der Vorwurf freilich unbegründet. Die breite Publizität, die ihre Verzweiflungstat erhielt, ja auch die Tatsache, daß sich immer mehr Nachahmungstäter in der bundesdeutschen Botschaft in Prag und Bonns Ständiger Vertretung in Ostberlin einfanden, hat entscheidend dazu beigetragen, der DDR-Führung endlich die Größenordnung des

Ausreiseproblems ins Bewußtsein zu rücken. Selbst das SED-Politbüro erkannte nun, daß die sechs in der amerikanischen Botschaft nur die Spitze eines Eisbergs darstellten. Jedenfalls wurde bald darauf das Ventil für die Ausreise großzügig geöffnet. Über 20 000 Antragsteller durften innerhalb weniger Monate die DDR verlassen, darunter viele der SED Unbequeme, Dissidenten oder radikale Gegner des realen Sozialismus. Doch erwies sich alsbald, daß das Problem mit dieser überstürzten Maßnahme, die in manchen Fällen einer Abschiebung unerwünschter Regimekritiker gleichkam, noch lange nicht erledigt war.

Kaum waren die Schleusen wieder geschlossen, begann das Drama der Botschaftsbesetzungen von neuem. Zunächst versuchte die DDR, durch massiven Einsatz von Sicherheitskräften rund um Bonns Ständige Vertretung die eigenen Bürger von jedem Versuch abzuschrecken, hier vorzusprechen. Der Amtssitz von Staatssekretär Bräutigam glich zeitweilig einer belagerten Festung: Ein gutes Dutzend uniformierte DDR-Beamte, verstärkt durch zahlreiche zivile Mitarbeiter des Staatssicherheitsdienstes fingen DDR-Bürger schon im Vorfeld ab, führten Ausweiskontrollen durch und forderten sie auf, die gegenüberliegende Straßenseite zu benutzen. Der Besuchsverkehr in der Bonner DDR-Mission schrumpfte innerhalb weniger Monate auf ein Fünftel des früheren Umfangs. Wer dennoch durchkam, dem drohte nicht selten die Festnahme, sobald er das Gebäude in der Hannoverschen Straße wieder verließ. Bräutigams Mitarbeiter waren gewiß nicht darauf erpicht, möglichst viele ausreisewillige DDR-Bürger zu empfangen und Wünsche für Beistand und Hilfe entgegenzunehmen, die sie nach Lage der Dinge nicht erfüllen konnten. Einerseits bewahrte sie der Aufmarsch der Staatsgewalt vor ungebetenen Quartiergästen, andererseits stellte er eine Behinderung der normalen Arbeit der Vertretung dar, die mit den üblichen diplomatischen Sitten schwerlich in Einklang stand und deshalb nicht hinzunehmen war. Als Bräutigam darüber öffentlich Klage führte, entschloß sich die DDR zu einer Politik des »stop and go«. So, wie sie vorübergehend die

Schleusen für die Ausreise geöffnet und dann wieder geschlossen hatte, zog sie nun plötzlich die Masse der Bewacher ab und gab den Zugang zur Vertretung frei. Es war ein Katz- und Mausspiel zwischen zwei Staaten, das den Deutschen so schnell keiner nachmachen kann. Anfang Mai 1984, in einem Tagesschau-Beitrag zum 10. Jahrestag der Eröffnung der Ständigen Vertretung in Ostberlin, hatte Staatssekretär Hans-Otto Bräutigam über die Behinderung des Besuchsverkehrs öffentlich Klage geführt. Acht Wochen später war er zum Herbergsvater von 45 DDR-Bürgern geworden, die im 5. Stock der Vertretung hausten. Das Umschwenken von stop zum go zeigte nun die von der DDR erhoffte Wirkung. Im Vorraum der Bonner Vertretung drängten sich die Hilfesuchenden, und der Hausherr, der des Ansturms nicht mehr Herr werden konnte, mußte handeln wie der Manager eines ausgebuchten Hotels, der das Schild »besetzt« an die Tür heftet. In Abstimmung mit der Bonner Zentrale wurde die Vertretung für den Besuchsverkehr geschlossen. Im Gegensatz zur früher gängigen Praxis hatte sich die DDR diesmal taub gestellt, als Bräutigam um die Entsendung von DDR-Anwälten als Vermittler bat. War in früheren Fällen ein Mann wie Wolfgang Vogel gekommen, um den DDR-Bürgern zu versichern, daß ihnen nach Verlassen der Ständigen Vertretung weder Strafe noch Benachteiligung drohe und ihre Anträge auf Ausreise wohlwollend geprüft würden, blieben solche Überredungsversuche diesmal aus. Deprimiert sprach Bräutigam von einem traurigen Tiefpunkt seiner Karriere. Der Besucherverkehr wurde erst nach einem Umbau wieder aufgenommen. Für DDR-Bürger war nun ein besonderer Raum geschaffen worden, der zwar direkt von außen zugänglich blieb, aber von dem keine Tür für sie nach innen führte. Bonn hatte durch die Umbaumaßnahmen guten Willen bekundet und mittels Ziegelsteinen und Panzerglas bekräftigt, was es nach außen ohnehin unermüdlich versichert hatte: Daß ausschließlich die Behörden der DDR für Ausreisewünsche zuständig sind und die Ständige Vertretung dafür die falsche Adresse ist. Es lag nun an der DDR, das Ihre zu tun, um die

Ursachen für die Botschaftsbesetzungen auszuräumen. Viele derer, die in den diplomatischen Missionen Zuflucht suchten, waren schließlich von bitterer Enttäuschung geprägt und kamen oft genug als von Verzweiflung Getriebene. Die »unteren Organe«, wie die örtlichen Behörden auf DDRisch heißen, hatten häufig schon die bloße Annahme ihrer Ausreiseanträge verweigert oder sie ohne Angabe von Gründen wiederholt abschlägig beschieden.

Die DDR handelte, aber sie konnte sich nur zu einer halben Entscheidung durchringen. Eine Anweisung von der Spitze an die für die Ausreise zuständigen Behörden für Inneres bei den Städten, Kreisen und Bezirken sorgte dafür, daß Antragsteller nicht länger unflätig beschimpft oder als »Verräter am Sozialismus« wie Aussätzige behandelt wurden. Ihre Anträge wurden nun mit der Versicherung entgegengenommen, daß sie geprüft und bearbeitet würden. Das war ein Schritt in die richtige Richtung, und er linderte den Druck, der oft für die Kontaktaufnahme mit westlichen Missionen ausschlaggebend gewesen war. Eine Lösung des Problems brachte er nicht. Auch die Lockerung der Reisebestimmungen, die plötzlich Zehntausende von jüngeren Menschen erstmals einen Besuch im Westen ermöglichte und von der sich die DDR-Führung viel erhofft hatte, erwies sich letztlich als Bumerang. Zwar kommen die meisten, die da fahren dürfen, wieder zurück. Aber viele von ihnen stellen nach der Heimkehr umgehend einen Ausreiseantrag für die ganze Familie. »Die SED hat uns um unser Leben betrogen«, war der Kommentar eines Bekannten nach der ersten Begegnung mit einer Gesellschaft, die Waren im Überfluß feilhält. Künstler, Intellektuelle und Pastoren reagierten auf andere Reize. »Ich kaufte mir auf dem Bahnhof den ›Spiegel‹, den ›Stern‹, die ›Zeit‹ und zwei Tageszeitungen verschiedener Couleur, setzte mich ins Abteil und begann zu lesen. Sie können sich nicht vorstellen, was für ein tolles Gefühl das für mich war. Ich meine nicht nur die ungeahnte Vielfalt oder die große Auswahl, die ich plötzlich hatte. Ich war frei, dies im Zug öffentlich auszubreiten, und es gab keinen von der Sicherheit, der mir über die Schulter schaute und mich am Lesen hindern konnte.« So der Bericht eines protestantischen Theologen nach seiner ersten Reise in den Westen. »Reise und Ausreise sind eine Art Geburtsmakel, mit dem wir geschlagen sind«, sagte ein hoher Funktionär einmal zu mir. »Wie immer wir es wenden und was immer wir tun, es gibt keine Patentlösung, die uns helfen kann.«

Der Entschluß, die Heimat zu verlassen, einen sicheren Arbeitsplatz, Wohnung und materielle Habe gegen eine unsichere Existenz im Westen einzutauschen, wird von den meisten nicht von heute auf morgen getroffen, sondern ist das Ergebnis langwierigen Haderns mit der realsozialistischen Umwelt. Die Hoffnung auf eine Verbesserung der persönlichen Lage, der Reisemöglichkeiten oder auf Minderung des Konformitätsdrucks läßt viele über Jahre selbst unter Umständen ausharren, die sie längst als verabscheuungswürdig empfinden. So gibt es ein latentes Potential von Ausreisewilligen in der DDR, das Männer der evangelischen Kirche mit 50 bis 80 000 beziffern und das zahlenmäßig stabil bleibt. Die Zwänge und Ärmlichkeiten des realen Sozialismus sorgen dafür, daß jedem Ausgereisten ein Ausreisewilliger nachwächst. Der entscheidende Schritt, der einen latent Ausreisewilligen in einen Antragsteller verwandelt, erfolgt oft unter dem Eindruck persönlicher Demütigungen durch einen Funktionär. Als eine der Quellen für die Enttäuschung und die wachsende Verbitterung nannte Landesbischof Hempel das »Umspringen des Staates« mit seinen Bürgern: »Auf der mittleren und auf der örtlichen Ebene ... werden Bürger oft hart oder formal behandelt.« Auch die Benachteiligungen aus politischen Gründen oder die Erfahrung der Rechtlosigkeit in einem System, das keine Verwaltungsgerichtsbarkeit kennt, wirken als mobilisierende Faktoren, die latente Ausreisewünsche plötzlich in akute verwandeln. Wer sich gegen die Allmacht der Bürokratie wehren will, ist in der DDR auf das Petitions- und Eingaberecht verwiesen und bleibt mithin ewig auf die Rolle des Bittstellers beschränkt. Bei vielen Auflagen in der DDR, notierte Gabriele Eckart, »kränkt es die Menschen am meisten, daß fast keinerlei Verbot begründet war«. Viele Engagierte versuchten, »an dem erstarrten Land etwas zu ändern oder Mißstände auch nur ins Gespräch zu bringen«, wurden dafür aber »vom Staat nur vor den Kopf gestoßen«. In Treue zur Partei erzogen und als aufstrebende Jungpoetin viele Jahre von der FDJ gefördert, machte die Schriftstellerin einen »langjährigen, schwierigen Übergang von blindem Glauben an den Staat zu kritischem Denken« durch, der mit einem Ausreiseantrag einen vorläufigen Höhepunkt erreichte. Nach einem langen Nervenkrieg gegen sie zog sie ihn wieder zurück und schloß einen brüchigen Frieden mit dem Staat, dem früher einmal ihre volle Loyalität gehört hatte. Heute lebt sie im Westen, will aber ihre DDR-Staatsangehörigkeit nicht aufgeben. In Tonbandprotokollen aus dem »Havelobst« hatte sie authentische Biographien, Erlebnisse, Urteile und Ansichten von Obstbauern aus Werder bei Potsdam zusammengetragen. Ihr Buch handelte von den Erfolgen, aber auch den Mühen und Schwierigkeiten nicht nur der ersten Aufbaujahre; der Verlag »Der Morgen« hatte es deshalb als besonderen Beitrag zum 35. Jahrestag der DDR gedacht. Unprätentiös im Ansatz, ganz auf Faktisches, Selbsterlebtes abgestellt, gewährten diese Lebensberichte Einblick in ein geballtes, ungeschöntes Stück realsozialistischen Alltags auf dem flachen Land. Doch der Vorabdruck dreier Protokolle in DDR-Monatsschriften erregte das Aufsehen westlicher Medien, denn da war nicht nur Kritisches zu Intershops und Delikat-Läden enthalten, die befragten DDR-Bürger klagten über Reisebeschränkungen, mangelndes Vertrauen der Führung zu ihrer Basis oder prangerten die schädlichen Folgen der DDR-Landwirtschaftspolitik für die Umwelt an. Da ist beispielsweise Fritz, der moderne Wanderimker. In 5-Tonnen-LKW-Hängern fährt er mit seinen Bienenvölkern kreuz und quer durch die DDR und muß jeweils rechtzeitig bei der einen oder anderen Monokultur zur Stelle sein, damit seine Bienen ausschwärmen und mittels Bestäubung einen guten Ernteertrag sichern. So pendelt er zwischen Mecklenburg und Potsdam, wann immer die Apfelintensivplantagen bei Werder oder die riesigen Rapsfelder

Mecklenburgs, auf denen 70 Prozent des gesamten Rapsanbaus der DDR erfolgt, der Bestäubung durch seine Bienenvölker bedürftig waren. Wie die meisten Bauern, die in diesem Buch zu Wort kommen, ist auch Fritz kein Gegner des Systems, doch benennt er mit der Insider-Kenntnis und der Direktheit des Fachmanns Umweltsünden, über die in Reportagen im »Neuen Deutschland« selbstverständlich kein Wort verloren wird. Monokulturen, sagt Fritz, erfordern intensiven Pflanzenschutz. »In Amerika züchtet man Antiinsekten, die die Pflanzenschädlinge auffressen. Bei uns geht das nicht. Die Insekten würden schon den Winter nicht überstehen. Also brauchen wir das Gift. Aber man hätte darauf achten müssen, als man die großen Apfelplantagen hier gepflanzt hat, daß um die Dörfer eine Schutzzone bleibt, damit die Gifte nicht in den Ort getragen werden. Es gibt zwar ein Gesetz, das vorschreibt, bis zu welcher Windgeschwindigkeit ein Hubschrauber fliegen und diese Mittel sprühen darf, aber das muß ja alles in zwei, drei Tagen passieren, wenn der Schädling soweit ist. Also wird oft trotz Wind geflogen, das Gift kommt auf die Futterflächen oder auf Seen, dann sterben die Fische und uns Imkern die Bienen... Tote Bienen sind der erste Anzeiger für Schadstoffe in der Luft, wie der Hahnenfuß auf einer Wiese anzeigt, daß der Boden übersäuert ist. Wir müßten für diese Dinge mehr tun, das sollte uns unsere Gesundheit wert sein.«

Und da ist Hans, langjähriger Vorsitzender einer Genossenschaft, die den industriemäßigen Anbau von Äpfeln betreibt. Immer, wenn er von einer Reise in andere sozialistische Staaten nach Werder zurückkommt, hat er das Gefühl: »Hier gefällt es mir doch am besten.« Er sagt aber auch: »Mich belastet, daß ich nicht reisen darf, wohin ich will.« In der DDR hatte er eine Frau aus Afrika kennengelernt und wurde von ihrem Vater nach Kenia eingeladen. »Ich habe alles mögliche versucht, um dahin fahren zu können, aber nichts erreicht«, hieß es in seinem Protokoll. »Das ist etwas, was einen bedrücken kann. Man müßte sich doch an allen fünf Fingern abzählen können, daß ich mit meinen 59 Jahren und meiner gesicherten Existenz hier, daß ich da nicht denken kann... Ist das Mißtrauen größer als das Vertrauen?«

Natürlich zitierten die westlichen Medien solche Sätze genüßlich, denn was war besser geeignet, die von der SED immer wieder beschworene Einheit von Führung und Volk als das in totalitären Staaten übliche Wunschdenken an der Spitze zu entlarven. Immerhin schien nun endlich in einem in der DDR erschienenen Dokument bewiesen, was im Westen stets behauptet worden war: Daß selbst die treuesten Mitstreiter beim »Aufbau des Sozialismus« nicht immun waren gegen den gefährlichen Virus der Reisekrankheit, der die ganze Gesellschaft der DDR befallen hatte. Um so betroffener zeigten sich die Kultur-Apparatschiks vom Zentralkomitee der SED. Prompt setzten sie ihre ganze Machtfülle ein, nicht nur, um das Erscheinen des im Verlagskatalog bereits angekündigten Buches zu untersagen. Über die örtlichen Parteifunktionäre übten sie zudem Druck auf die von der Autorin Interviewten aus, ihre Zustimmung zur Veröffentlichung zurückzuziehen: Als Grund sollten sie die unzulängliche Wiedergabe ihrer Meinungen anführen, denn Wichtiges sei der Kürzung zum Opfer gefallen. Es gab auch Repressalien. Einem der interviewten Bauern, der leidenschaftlich gern auf die Jagd ging, beschlagnahmte die Polizei sein Jagdgewehr.

In der Tat waren, wie in der von Gabriele Eckart angewendeten neuen dokumentarischen Literaturform üblich, lange autobiographische Tonbandgespräche mit den Bauern und Bäuerinnen aus dem Havelobst auf die wichtigsten Aussagen komprimiert worden. Die gestaltende Funktion einer Autorin beschränkt sich bei dieser Art Literatur darauf, auszuwählen, zuzuordnen und zusammenzufassen. Als ob sie den Vorwurf mangelnder Authentizität vorausgeahnt hätte, mit dem die Parteiführung nun ihr ganzes Buch unglaubwürdig machen wollte, hatte sie jedes Protokoll den Interviewten vor der Veröffentlichung vorgelegt und um Korrekturen gebeten. Was schließlich in Druck gehen sollte, hatte mithin das Einverständnis der Betroffenen. Die meisten zeigten sich gegenüber den Sendboten der Partei auch standhaft und zogen die Autorisierung nicht zurück. Wenn einige der autorisierten Passagen in den Verlagsfahnen des Buches fehlten, dann hatte diesen Mangel vor allem die SED-Kulturbürokratie selbst verschuldet. Der SED unbequeme Passagen mußten noch vor der Druckgenehmigung gestrichen werden. Nichtsdestoweniger benutzte die SED auf zahllosen Parteiversammlungen ausgerechnet die von ihr selbst angeordneten Kürzungen als Beweis für Fälschungen und Verzerrungen durch die Autorin. »Wenn die Texte, die neu gedruckt werden sollten, mit den autorisierten Texten nicht identisch sind, so nur deshalb, weil ich über 60 Seiten streichen mußte, damit das Buch die Druckgenehmigung erhielt. Es fehlen also brisante Stellen«, schrieb Gabriele Eckardt in einem Brief, in dem sie ihre Ausreise beantragte. »Wenn daraus nun gemacht wird, ich hätte verzerrt und verfälscht, ja sogar mit staatsfeindlicher Absicht, so ist dies eine Beleidigung, die ich als Schriftsteller nicht hinnehmen kann.« Als das Unangenehmste an den vielen Demütigungen, die sie nach diesem Brief – wie die meisten Antragsteller – hinnehmen mußte, empfand sie die Tatsache, daß die allmächtige Bürokratie für solche miesen Praktiken auch noch »mit großem Pathos die ganze Menschheitsutopie« mit Beschlag belegt. Und wie viele berief sie sich in den Gesprächen über die Ausreise auf die Menschenrechtskonvention der Vereinten Nationen, die das Recht auf Auswanderung und den Wechsel der Staatsbürgerschaft kennt und von der DDR unterzeichnet worden ist.

Was die Menschenrechte angeht, gibt es jüngere Dokumente als die UN-Konvention, etwa die Schlußakte von Helsinki, auf die Ausreisewillige sich ebenfalls berufen können. Freilich enthalten die in diesem Zusammenhang wichtigen Passagen eine Synopse der Menschenrechts-Vorstellungen beider Lager, was es der DDR erheblich leichter macht, an sie adressierte Vorwürfe von Menschenrechtsverletzungen mit Gegenanschuldigungen zu kontern. Wenn es in der Bundesrepublik zwei Millionen Arbeitslose gibt, dann stellt dies aus der Sicht der DDR natürlich eine erhebliche Verletzung der sozialökonomischen Menschenrechte dar.

Wie es im realsozialistischen Völkerrecht um das Recht der
Ausreise und Emigration steht, ist im Lehrbuch »Staatsrecht
der DDR« nachzulesen, das 1977 in Ostberlin erschien. »Die
Auswanderung ist ein typisches Produkt der Krisenwirtschaft
kapitalistischer Staaten, die den Werktätigen häufig nicht einmal das Existenzminimum sichern können«, heißt es da wörtlich. »Deshalb übernehmen die Werktätigen vielfach in einem
anderen Ausbeuterstaat selbst die niedrigsten Arbeiten zu politisch und sozial diskriminierenden Bedingungen. Die entsprechende Menschenrechtskonvention (der UN – d. V.) ermöglicht die Auswanderung, überläßt es jedoch der souveränen Regelung der Staaten, ihre Voraussetzungen zu bestimmen, und verweist dabei vor allem auf die Verantwortung für
den Schutz der nationalen Sicherheit, der öffentlichen Ordnung, ›Gesundheit und Moral oder der Rechte und Freiheiten
anderer‹ (Art. 12). Diese Kriterien sind für die DDR maßge-
bend. Sie kann davon ausgehen, daß die sozialistischen Ge-
sellschaftsverhältnisse den Menschen erstmals beständig soziale Sicherheit, freie und ungehinderte Persönlichkeitsentfal-
tung gewährleisten. In der DDR gibt es keine soziale Basis für
ein Grundrecht auf Auswanderung.« Damit nicht genug, wird
sogar etwas wie ein Sorgerecht proklamiert, um mögliche
Auswanderungswillige vor etwaigen Menschenrechtsverletzungen aus sozialistischer Sicht, die ihnen im Land ihrer
Träume widerfahren könnten, vorsorglich zu bewahren: »Die
politische und moralische Verantwortung für jeden Bürger
gebietet der sozialistischen Staatsmacht, die Klassenauseinandersetzung zwischen Sozialismus und Imperialismus auch bei
Entscheidungen über Auswanderungsanträge zu berücksichtigen. Sie stellt in Rechnung, daß die Auswanderung in einen
imperialistischen Staat bedeutet, Menschen einem System
auszuliefern, das sie ausbeutet und zwingt, einer aggressiven
Politik zu dienen, die ihre Existenz gefährdet und sich gegen
den Sozialismus richtet.« Wenn es eines Beweises bedürfte,
daß diese Sätze aus dem Lehrbuch nach Helsinki das Handeln,
die Politik und die Argumentation auf der Seite der DDR
bestimmen, dann erbrachte ihn die Anhörung von DDR-Ver-

tretern vor der UN-Menschenrechtskommission im Herbst 1984 in Genf. Da wurde unter Berufung auf den in der UN-Konvention aufgeführten »Schutz der nationalen Sicherheit und der öffentlichen Ordnung« zugegeben, daß die Ausreisefreiheit auch aus wirtschaftlichen Gründen eingeschränkt bleiben müsse. Wenn die Bürger einfach »wegrennen«, so die DDR-Experten, sei es eben legitim, dieses Problem unter dem Gesichtspunkt der »Ordre Public« zu behandeln. Und was Mauer, Stacheldraht und Schüsse an der Grenze anging, beriefen sie sich in Genf über die »Ordre Public« hinaus auf das Prinzip der Unverletzlichkeit der Grenzen.

Die Auseinandersetzung mit Marxisten-Leninisten über die Menschenrechte ist auch schwierig, weil sich schon Karl Marx verächtlich über sie geäußert hatte. Er sah die klassischen bürgerlichen Rechte der Französischen Revolution – Liberté, Egalité und Fraternité – sozial an die Bourgeoisie gebunden, die sie dem Feudalismus abrang, weil sie sie zur Mehrung ihres Privateigentums benötigte. So betrachtet, dienten die Menschenrechte vor allem der Marktfreiheit und sicherten Selbstbestimmung nur dem Bürgertum, das sie den Proletariern verweigerte. Im Grunde hielt es Marx mit den Anhängern Babeufs: »Was nutzen uns die Menschenrechte, wenn der Brotpreis steigt?« Kein Geringerer als der DDR-Wirtschaftshistoriker Jürgen Kuczynski hat darauf hingewiesen, daß weder Marx noch Engels Menschenrechte für den Sozialismus kennen. Zwar möge es im Sozialismus noch »Reste von Klassen (bzw. Restklassen und Schichten) und den Interessen dieser Klassen entsprechend handelnde Menschen geben«, argumentierte der Senior der DDR-Nationalökonomie in einer 1978 vorgelegten Arbeit über »Menschenrechte und Klassenrecht«, doch kommt er zu dem Schluß: »In der klassenlosen Gesellschaft ... sind sie keine Rechte mehr, um deren Anspruch man kämpfen muß, zumal ihnen auch keine Pflichten, sondern nur noch Bedürfnisse entsprechen.« Und es ist gewiß nicht ohne Pikanterie, wenn Historiker des Marxismus darauf hinweisen, daß das in der Menschenrechtsauseinandersetzung zwischen beiden großen Lagern gerade von den Realsozialisten so gern und viel beschworene Menschenrecht auf Arbeit, bei dem sich der Westen als Sünder erweist, vom Erzvater der Lehre persönlich als Widersinn bezeichnet wurde, denn es gelte ja gerade die Lohnarbeit abzuschaffen, die mit dem Recht auf Arbeit gefordert werde. Im übrigen sind Grundrechte, weil das Recht nach Marx bereits im Sozialismus abgestorben ist, als einklagbare Sache nach dem Sieg des Proletariats schlechterdings nicht vorstellbar, wie Karl Brunner in einer Studie über Marx und die Grundrechte in der DDR anmerkt.

Es lohnt sich schon deshalb, einige Augenblicke bei der Entwicklung der marxistischen Position gegenüber den Menschenrechten zu verweilen, weil Helsinki nun einmal ein Synonym für den Entspannungsprozeß in Europa ist und der Westen dazu neigt, alle in ihn gesetzte Hoffnungen am Fortschritt auf dem Gebiet der Menschenrechte zu messen. Umgekehrt wertet der Osten Helsinki vor allem als Festschreibung der durch den Krieg entstandenen Nachkriegsgrenzen in Europa, als Siegel des Westens auf die deutsche Teilung und die Gleichschaltung der Länder Osteuropas. Die Bundesrepublik, die sich ja als Rechtsnachfolger des Reichs verstand und die Option eines einigen Deutschland aufrechterhielt – ob ganz oder teilweise in den Grenzen von 1937, ließ Bonn bewußt offen – lief mit ihrer bisherigen Politik ins Leere. Denn ein Friedensvertrag, der die existierenden Grenzen anerkennt, erübrigte sich jetzt aus Moskauer Sicht. Zwar stand dem Prinzip der Anerkennung der Souveränität aller Unterzeichnerstaaten (zu ihnen gehörten die beiden deutschen Republiken), ihrer territorialen Integrität und der Unverletzlichkeit der Grenzen auch im Schlußdokument von Helsinki die Respektierung des Rechts auf friedlichen Wandel gegenüber. Es beinhaltet die Möglichkeit, Grenzen ohne Gewalt, auf der Basis gegenseitigen Einvernehmens, neu zu ziehen. Doch hindert dies die Agitpropzentralen in Ostberlin, Warschau, Prag und Moskau nicht, jedes im Westen für die friedliche Überwindung der deutschen Teilung vorgebrachte Wort als revanchistischen Akt zu dennunzieren.

Dem prinzipiellen marxistischen Einwand gegen das westliche Menschenrechtsverständnis, daß es nämlich Selbstbestimmung nur für den besitzenden Teil der Gesellschaft sichert, entspricht der These, daß die Entwicklung der Persönlichkeit nur in Gemeinschaft mit anderen möglich ist. Weil nach marxistischer Lehre die volle Emanzipation des Menschen erst in der klassenlosen Gesellschaft erfolgt und diese nur durch den Sieg der Arbeiterklasse geschaffen werden kann, ist die westliche Forderung nach liberalen Menschenrechten und individuellen Freiheiten nichts anderes als Heuchelei. Sie soll die Herrschaft weniger Privilegierter verschleiern und zugleich verewigen helfen. Der Anspruch aller Menschen auf Freiheit und volle Entfaltung ihrer Persönlichkeit kann nur nach der Revolution, nach der Abschaffung des Eigentums an den Produktionsmitteln Wirklichkeit werden. Und in einer Zeit des Übergangs, in der die Revolution gesichert und der Weg in den Kommunismus beschritten werden soll, ist es, der orthodoxen marxistisch-leninistischen Lehre folgend, Sache der Partei als der Avantgarde des Proletariats, dafür zu sorgen, daß die Bourgeoisie niemals ihre Kräfte zum konterrevolutionären Gegenschlag sammeln kann. Diese Zielsetzung wiederum rechtfertigt dann nicht nur die Diktatur des Apparats über den Geist und die Seelen von Millionen Menschen, mit ihr werden auch die Entmündigung der Bürger, die Aufhebung der Pressefreiheit, die Zensur von Film, Literatur und Theater und die Abschaffung von Versammlungs-, Koalitions- und Organisationsfreiheit begründet – eine Erziehungsdiktatur stalinschen oder orwellschen Ausmaßes. Dem Endziel werden all jene bürgerlichen Freiheiten geopfert, ohne die kommunistische Parteien sich unter der Herrschaft der Bourgeoisie nie hätten formieren können. Und als nahezu mystische Legitimation gilt jener legendäre Sprung in das »Reich der Freiheit«, der bevorsteht und das Reich der (grimmen, scheußlichen, oft blutigen) Notwendigkeiten auf den Trümmerhaufen der Vorgeschichte der Menschheit verweist. Die wahre Geschichte des freien, emanzipierten Menschen hebt nun erst an. Nach dieser Logik repräsentieren die Klassenanliegen des Proletariats nicht nur die Wünsche und Ziele der gesamten Menschheit, ihr zufolge sichert die Diktatur des Proletariats letztlich die vollen Menschenrechte – wenn auch in einem Reich, das dereinst erst kommen soll. In der Vision von Marx bringt die Verwirklichung des Sozialismus ja nicht nur die Emanzipation der Massen und das Ende aller bisherigen Geschichte, die utopische Entwicklung wird auch durch das Erscheinen des »neuen Menschen« gekrönt, der erstmals unabhängig ist von Zwängen, der ganz nach seinen Bedürfnissen lebt und mithin erstmals rundum völlig Freiheit genießt.

Daß die realsozialistischen Verfassungen keine angeborenen, unveräußerlichen und allein aus der Würde des Menschen sich herleitenden Menschenrechte kennen, die über der staatlichen Rechtsordnung stehen, ist nach alledem einleuchtend. Doch seit es Stalin 1936 mit Blick nach dem Westen aus propagandistischen Gründen ratsam schien, einen Katalog sozialistischer Grundrechte in die neue Verfassung der Sowjetunion aufzunehmen, enthalten sie sämtliche Bürgerrechte, deren Geltungsgrundlage freilich immer das staatlich gesetzte Recht bleibt. Im Gegensatz zur westlichen Menschenrechts-Konzeption stehen die sozialistischen Grundrechte also unter Staatsvorbehalt. Es sind zwar persönliche Rechte, aber niemals Rechte gegen den Staat; und da sie zusammen mit den Grundpflichten eine untrennbare Einheit bilden, wird stillschweigend davon ausgegangen, daß von diesen Grundrechten nur zum Wohle des sozialistischen Staates Gebrauch zu machen ist. »Das sind eben Grundgesetze und Grundrechte einer Gesellschaftsordnung und nicht Rechte der Menschen, Menschenrechte«, macht Jürgen Kuczynski unmißverständlich klar. Da im DDR-Alltag die Partei bestimmt, was dem Wohl der sozialistischen Gesellschaft dient, bedeutet das zum Beispiel: Das Recht auf Auswanderung, das in der ersten, an Weimar angelehnten DDR-Verfassung noch enthalten war, schrumpfte in der heute geltenden sozialistischen Verfassung auf das Recht auf Freizügigkeit innerhalb der Grenzen der DDR. Natürlich verstößt die DDR mit dieser restriktiven Auslegung gegen Verpflichtungen, die sie mit der Unterzeichnung der beiden UN-Menschenrechts-Konventionen beim

UN-Beitritt 1973 und der Unterschrift unter die KSZE-Akte 1975 eingegangen ist. Auch in Artikel 2 des Grundlagenvertrages hatte Ostberlin versprochen, die Menschenrechte zu wahren.

In der ideologischen Ost-West-Auseinandersetzung, die nach Helsinki den Entspannungsprozeß begleitete, nutzte der Westen deshalb die Menschenrechte für die Offensive, während der Osten zunächst abwiegelte. So behaupteten DDR-Völkerrechtler, die UN-Menschenrechts-Pakte begründeten Rechte und Pflichten nur für Staaten, nicht jedoch für einzelne; ihre Verwirklichung sei deshalb ausschließlich Sache souveräner Staaten. Und wenn ein Unterzeichnerstaat einen anderen konkreter Menschenrechtsverletzungen bezichtige, dann stelle das eine Einmischung in innere Angelegenheiten dar, die nach dem Völkerrecht verboten sei.

Doch bald ging die DDR zum ideologischen Gegenangriff über, in dem sie von der »Einheit der Menschenrechte« sprach, die sie als »politische, ökonomische, soziale und kulturelle Rechte« definierte, die umfassend nur im Sozialismus verwirklicht seien. »In der bisherigen Menschheitsentwicklung«, schrieb Harald Schiwa in der SED-Zeitschrift »Einheit« 1986, »hat keine Gesellschaftsordnung so *massenhaft* und *sozial unbeschränkt* die Persönlichkeitsentwicklung gefördert wie der Sozialismus. Für unsere Gesellschaft ist die Individualitätsentwicklung außerordentlich bedeutsam, weil sie die individuelle Selbstverwirklichung des einzelnen mit der massenhaften Persönlichkeitsentwicklung verbindet.« Menschenrechte, so Schiwa weiter, würden im realen Sozialismus »auf einer qualitativ neuen geschichtlichen Stufe« verwirklicht, da sie »unvereinbar mit Individualismus und Egoismus« sind. Es handelt sich nämlich um »Mitmenschenrechte, weil sie kollektives Handeln zur Erreichung persönlich und gesellschaftlich bedeutsamer Ziele fördern«. Und zu den »wesentlichen Merkmalen der neuen Qualität der Menschenrechtsverwirklichung in der sozialistischen Gesellschaft gehört, daß sie ein unvergleichlich höheres Maß an Sicherheit für den einzelnen gewährleistet als vorsozialistische Gesellschaftsordnungen«.

So waren aus den einst von Stalin eingeführten sozialistischen Grundrechten nun doch wieder Menschenrechte geworden, auch wenn sie das sozialistische Lager deutlich vom liberalen Menschenrechtsverständnis abgesetzt wissen will. Wie alle Staaten des Ostblocks legt die DDR die Priorität auf die »sozialen« Menschenrechte, die das Recht auf Arbeit und Bildung, Gesundheitsversorgung und Erholung einschließen, und sie darf sich dabei auf den Sozialrechtspakt der Vereinten Nationen aus dem Jahr 1966 berufen. Nun bestreitet der Westen in der Auseinandersetzung mit dem östlichen Menschenrechtskonzept nicht die sozialen, ökonomischen und kulturellen Rechte, die der Osten für vorrangig hält. Er stellt nur die klassischen, die liberalen Menschenrechte obenan. Ein für diese Auseinandersetzung typischer Schlagabtausch zwischen Ost und West fand im November 1985 im Rahmen des »Bergedorfer Gesprächskreises« in der Godesberger Redoute in Bonn statt. Da machte Professor Eberhard Poppe, Völkerrechtler aus Halle, entschieden darauf aufmerksam, daß der KSZE-Schlußakte keineswegs die westliche Menschenrechtskonzeption zugrunde liegt. »Der Sinn der Menschenrechte, dem Individuum Freiheit, Würde und Entfaltung zu garantieren und den einzelnen zu schützen, wird nicht allein mit Meinungs-, Informations-, Gewissens- und Glaubensfreiheit erfüllt, so unverzichtbar diese Rechte sind. Ebenso unverzichtbar aber ist das Recht auf Arbeit und einen Arbeitsplatz, auf Bildung entsprechend den Fähigkeiten des Individuums... Um es ganz offen zu sagen: Wer anhaltende Massenarbeitslosigkeit duldet, Zehntausende von Jugendlichen ohne Ausbildung und sinnvolle Lebensziele läßt, begeht Menschenrechtsverletzungen, die das Leben der Betroffenen für immer deformieren können«, sagte Poppe und bezichtigte alle der Einäugigkeit, die Menschenrechte nur nach der westlichen Konzeption definieren wollen. Botschafter Eckehard Eickhoff vom Auswärtigen Amt griff den Vorwurf auf: »Ich bin mir sehr wohl bewußt, daß uns da entgegengehalten wird: Wie steht es bei euch mit dem Recht auf Arbeit angesichts der Arbeitslosigkeit in den westlichen Ländern? Wie ist das in Übereinstimmung zu bringen mit den Menschenrechtspakten der

Vereinten Nationen, zu denen ihr euch bekannt und in denen ausdrücklich das Recht auf Arbeit aufgeführt ist?« Er gab auch die Antwort: »Die westlichen Staaten«, führte er aus, »haben eine Güterabwägung vorgenommen, sie wollen die großen Einschränkungen der persönlichen Entscheidungsfreiheit, die mit einer vollen Regulierung des Arbeitsmarktes verbunden wären, nicht in Kauf nehmen. Der einzelne soll die Möglichkeit der freien Entscheidung im Berufsleben behalten. Dafür bieten wir ihm soziale Sicherungen an, die ihm auch als Arbeitslosem einen der Menschenwürde entsprechenden Lebensstandard erhalten.« Joseph Rovan von der Universität Paris unterstrich zunächst die westliche Position: »Es ist ungemein leicht, das zu verwischen, was uns als zentral erscheint, nämlich die Möglichkeit für einen jeden einzelnen, das auszudrücken, was ihm am Herzen liegt . . . Wenn zum Beispiel die Manifestation dieses Willens zur freien Äußerung in der Sowjetunion, in Polen und in anderen Staaten Osteuropas aufgrund von juristischen Interpretationen mit Qualifikationen kriminalisiert werden, die mit dem, was wir unter Menschenrechten verstehen, nichts mehr zu tun haben.« Doch später suchte der Professor aus Paris eine Brücke zu schlagen zwischen den »kollektiven Menschenrechten«, die der Professor aus Halle auf die Oktoberrevolution zurückgeführt wissen wollte, und den Menschenrechten der Amerikanischen und Französischen Revolution. »Wir können uns also fragen«, merkte Rovan an, »ob die Schwierigkeit, uns zu verständigen, nicht zumindest theoretisch so gelöst werden könnte, daß wir gegenseitig anerkennen, die eine Bewegung ist ohne die andere unvollkommen. Das gilt aber für beiden Seiten. Ein Fortschritt auf dem einen Wege, zum Beispiel zu dem der neuen kollektiven Menschenrechte, würde dann nicht ohne die Verwirklichung der anderen, der individuellen, persönlichen Rechte möglich sein. Niemand könnte also sagen, wir machen erst das eine und dann das andere.«

Wer den umfassenden Menschenrechtsbegriff akzeptiert, den die Vereinten Nationen entwickelten und der der Schlußakte von Helsinki zugrunde liegt, sieht als Ergebnis dieses

Schlagabtauschs Sünder im Osten wie im Westen. Doch gibt es einen kleinen, für die politische Praxis entscheidenden Unterschied: Die Unterschrift unter einen Katalog von Menschenrechten, die in der DDR-Verfassung nicht verankert und vor keinem DDR-Gericht einzuklagen sind, macht der DDR-Führung ungleich mehr zu schaffen als der Bundesregierung vorerst noch das Recht auf Arbeit, zu dem sich Bonn durch Unterzeichnung der UN-Konvention bekannte. Übrigens ist dieses Recht weder im Grundgesetz enthalten noch vor dem Bundesarbeitsgericht einklagbar – so wenig wie das Recht auf Auswanderung in der DDR.

Geschickt berufen sich vor allem Vertreter der DDR-Kirchen auf die Schlußakte von Helsinki. Im politischen Selbstverständnis der DDR stellt sie ja einen wahren Meilenstein auf dem Weg der internationalen Anerkennung ihrer »territorialen Integrität« dar und gilt als bisher wichtigstes Ergebnis der Entspannungspolitik. Offensichtlich in Einklang mit der Politik der Partei- und Staatsführung fällt es da leicht, den Helsinki-Prozeß demonstrativ zu loben, und dem Tenor der Zustimmung fordernde Töne beizumischen. Wie man Helsinki für mehr Freiraum bei den individuellen Rechten in Anspruch nimmt, demonstrierte der »Außenminister« des DDR-Kirchenbunds, Oberkonsistorialpräsident Manfred Stolpe auf dem Greifswalder Kirchentag im Juni 1985. Deutlich sprach er sich für die Entspannungspolitik im Sinne der Schlußakte von Helsinki aus und unterstrich, daß viele der kollektiven Menschenrechte in der DDR verwirklicht seien – bedeutende soziale und kulturelle Rechte. »Unschätzbare Errungenschaften«, nannte sie der Kirchenmann in Anlehnung an das gängige leninistische Pathos, deren Wert erst der zu spüren bekomme, der sie »leichtfertig durch Auswanderung« verliere. Deshalb sei es wichtig, die »noch vorhandenen Defizite« bei den individuellen Rechten und Möglichkeiten »schrittweise abzubauen«.

Aus der Sicht der SED waren solche DDR-öffentlichen Hinweise auf eine zumindest teilweise defizitäre Menschenrechts-bilanz ärgerlich. Umsichtig vorgetragen, blieben sie der Form nach unangreifbar. Um nicht in der Defensive zu verharren, entschloß sich die Parteiführung deshalb zur Flucht nach vorn. Ab Mitte 1985 häuften sich Elendsreportagen aus den Zentren der kapitalistischen Welt in der »Aktuellen Kamera«, und das »Neue Deutschland« führte die Menschenrechts-Auseinandersetzung plötzlich selbstbewußt und offensiv. So wurde eine Analyse der UNO-Wirtschaftskommission aus Genf, derzufolge mehr als 100 000 Bürger der Bundesrepublik obdachlos waren, mit der Schlagzeile »Verletzung der Menschenrechte in der BRD« versehen. Als Gründe für die Obdachlosigkeit wurden Dauerarbeitslosigkeit, überhöhte Mieten und Spekulationen auf dem Wohnungsmarkt angegeben. Und im Februar 1986 behauptete das Blatt dann unter der nicht weniger spektakulären Unterschrift »Wichtige Menschenrechte in der BRD nicht garantiert«, nicht nur, daß mehr als 10 000 Bundesbürger, vom Radikalenerlaß betroffen, Berufsverbot erhalten hätten: »Für Millionen ohne Arbeit und Wohnung«, wurde ein westdeutscher DKP-Funktionär an prominenter Stelle zitiert, seien »freie Entfaltung der Persönlichkeit, Recht auf Leben und körperliche Unversehrtheit, Gleichheit vor dem Gesetz und Meinungsfreiheit angesichts ihrer trostlosen Situation nichts als Phrasen«.

Davon deutlich abgesetzt, hieß es in einem Leitartikel vom 25. November 1986: »In unserem sozialistischen Land bestimmen soziale Sicherheit und zuverlässige Perspektiven das Leben und motivieren das Handeln der Menschen, während sich ganz im Gegensatz dazu, die Zahl der Arbeitslosen in den 24 am meisten entwickelten kapitalistischen Ländern seit 1970 auf nunmehr 31 Millionen verdreifacht hat. Das Gerede über die Menschenrechte, mit dem Politiker des Westens immer wieder aufwarten, ist keinen Pfifferling wert, wie die Realität zeigt. Menschenrechte werden da verwirklicht, wo die Ausbeutung des Menschen durch den Menschen abgeschafft ist, wo das Recht auf Arbeit, auf einen Arbeitsplatz garantiert wird, wo das Volk seine schöpferischen Kräfte, Talente und Fähigkeiten zum eigenen Wohl entfalten kann, wie in unserer

Deutschen Demokratischen Republik.« Selbst »General Winter« wurde in die Menschenrechtsoffensive der DDR eingespannt. Um die Jahreswende 1986/87 fielen vorübergehend Teile der Stromversorgung der DDR aus. Beinahe gleichzeitig gingen schockierende Bilder von Obdachlosen um die Welt, die in westlichen Metropolen in U-Bahnstationen oder zwischen Kisten und Matratzen Zuflucht vor der unbarmherzigen Kälte suchten. Die Bilder entsprachen Tatsachen. Auf eindrucksvolle Weise belegten sie, wie wenig sich die Überflußgesellschaften des Westens um jene kümmern, die durch die Maschen des sozialen Netzes fallen und den Bodensatz einer modernen Unterklasse bilden.

»Wenn auch bei uns der Winter nicht geringe Schwierigkeiten brachte«, diese Mißstände gäbe es im realen Sozialismus nicht, schrieb das »Neue Deutschland« in einem Leitartikel und fragte: »Wird nicht den Obdachlosen elementares Menschenrecht verweigert? Wie viele von ihnen sind schon so lange arbeitslos, daß sie ihre Wohnung aufgeben mußten, daß die ›neue Armut‹ sie in den Würgegriff nahm?« In anderen Jahreszeiten falle es vielleicht weniger auf, aber im Grunde habe der Frost »nur ein kaltherziges System bloßgestellt«, in der Menschlichkeit und Menschenrechte zu nichtssagenden Worthülsen degradiert worden seien.

Demgegenüber wurde die DDR einmal mehr als Hort der Geborgenheit gepriesen, als »ein Staat des Friedens und der sozialen Sicherheit«; wer ihn verläßt, soll bleiben, wo der Pfeffer wächst. Das jedenfalls war das Motto vieler Leserstimmen, die das Parteiblatt im Frühjahr 1985 veröffentlicht hatte, nachdem in großer Aufmachung über die Rückkehrwünsche ausgereister DDR-Bürger berichtet worden war. »Über 20 000 Ehemalige wollen zurück«, hatten die DDR-Medien gemeldet und aus Briefen Ausgereister zitiert, die in der westlichen Ellenbogengesellschaft nur schwer Fuß fassen konnten. Da das Drama in der Prager Botschaft der Bundesrepublik erst vor wenigen Wochen zu Ende gegangen war, konnte über die Adressaten dieser Kampagne nicht der geringste Zweifel bestehen: Zielgruppe war das latente Potential der Ausreisewilligen, denen die Konsequenzen einer möglichen Abwanderung in die Bundesrepublik in den abschreckendsten Farben geschildert werden sollte. Als Medium bediente sich die Parteiführung jener Schar vom Westen Enttäuschter, deren genaue Zahl schwer zu schätzen ist, auch wenn kein Zweifel daran besteht, daß ein guter Teil der aus der DDR Ausgereisten mit erheblichen Integrationsschwierigkeiten zu kämpfen hat, wenn das Land ihrer Träume sie mit unerwartet bitteren Realitäten konfrontiert.

Die Gründe, die aus den an den Staatsratsvorsitzenden, den Ministerrat oder an das ZK der SED gerichteten Schreiben wiedergegeben wurden, klangen durchaus glaubwürdig. Da fühlte sich der eine im Westen als »Fremder in einer fremden Welt«, ein anderer war erschrocken über die »soziale Unsicherheit in der BRD«, oder nannte »falsche Vorstellungen vom Leben dort«. Andere sahen »keine berufliche Perspektive« für sich, »keine Zukunft für die Kinder« oder hatten sich ein falsches Bild vom »realen Kapitalismus« gemacht. Und die 47jährige Angestellte Margarete Kröber aus Bergisch-Gladbach wollte schlicht in die DDR zurück, um »einen DDR-Bürger zu heiraten«. Reporter des Deutschlandfunks gingen einigen Fällen nach, fanden die Angaben oft bestätigt und ihre Reportage unverhofft im »Neuen Deutschland« nachgedruckt. Der Kraftfahrer Reinhard Oehme aus Vellmar in Hessen war einer der im SED-Blatt genannten. Dem Deutschlandfunk-Reporter Schwan gab er zu Protokoll, daß er nach seiner Übersiedlung zunächst in seinem alten Beruf als Bohrwerksdreher in einem kleinen Betrieb gearbeitet habe, aber daß die sozialen Bedingungen »in keiner Weise« seinen »Erwartungen entsprachen«. Von der Rücksiedelung in die DDR erhoffte er sich, »da ja immer so viel von Menschenrechten gesprochen wird«, die Einlösung des Menschenrechts Nr. 1, daß nämlich »der Anspruch und die Pflicht auf Arbeit besteht«. Auf die Frage, ob er die Gedanken- und die Reisefreiheit im Westen nicht dennoch vermissen werde, räumte er ein: »Ja, das ist mein Problem.« Er sei mit der Erwartung in den Westen gekommen, durch Arbeit Geld zu verdienen »und an der sogenannten Freiheit teilhaben zu können. Aber unter den gegebenen Umständen, wie Sie sie ja täglich im Fernsehen sehen können, muß man ja abschätzen können, daß . . . auf lange Sicht keine Möglichkeit besteht, Gebrauch davon zu machen.« Auch wenn sich die DDR-Agitatoren aus den Original-Tönen verständlicherweise die Rosinen herausgepickt hatten, die ihnen in ihr Konzept paßten – das alles klang sachlich, ungeschönt und plausibel.

Daß unter den Ausgereisten sich nicht wenige Illusionen über den Westen gemacht hatten, war schon immer klar. Als sich jedoch unter dem Eindruck der DDR-Kampagne der Bundestagsausschuß für innerdeutsche Beziehungen in einer Anhörung mit der »Lage der Übersiedler aus der DDR« befaßte, wurden Fakten bekannt, die so manche Integrationsschwierigkeit in neuem Licht erscheinen ließ. Viele Übersiedler, heißt es im stenographischen Bericht der 41. Ausschuß-Sitzung vom 12. Juni 1985, »haben oft einen jahrelangen Kampf mit den Behörden drüben geführt, denen sie ausgeliefert waren. Jetzt endlich sind sie frei. Das, was auf sie zukommt, ist nüchterne, knochenharte Bürokratie.« Die Kritik zielte auf das Bundes-Notaufnahmeverfahren, das alle Ausgereisten entweder in Berlin oder in Gießen durchlaufen und das die Sachverständige Karin Wagner vom Christlichen Jugenddorfwerk »undurchschaubar und bedrohlich« nannte. »Zu diesem Urteil«, so erklärte sie vor dem Ausschuß, »bin ich gekommen, nachdem ich sehr viele DDR-Zuwanderer in unserer Beratungsstelle in Berlin gefragt habe und eigentlich immer wieder kam: Ja, wo wir jetzt gewesen sind, wer uns befragt hat und wozu das dient, können wir eigentlich gar nicht mehr sagen. Dazu war das alles viel zu viel. – Gerade die Befragung durch die Alliierten ist etwas, was man nicht unterschätzen sollte. . . . Es gibt eine ganze Menge DDR-Zuwanderer, die ziemlich kaputt da herauskommt. Ich habe sehr häufig von Zuwanderern das Urteil gehört: Da fühlt man sich ja nicht besser als drüben. Ein solches Urteil in den ersten Tagen fördert sicher nicht die Bereitschaft zur Integration.« Einige Sachverständige monierten den »Getto-Charakter« der Übergangswohnheime, in denen die Ausgereisten untergebracht werden und sprachen von einem Schock, den die hohen Mietpreise selbst der Sozialwohnungen verursachen. Andere wiesen auf die mangelnde Kenntnis vieler Deutscher im Westen über die Verhältnisse in der DDR hin, die den Ausgereisten oft ein »Gefühl des Nichtverstandenwerdens« vermittle. Professor Volker Ronge von der Universität Wuppertal nannte als das »eigentliche Problem«, daß die ehemaligen DDR-Bürger einer »monistischen Bürokratie« ausgeliefert waren, von der ihr Leben zentral geregelt worden sei und der »hier im Westen eine sehr gespaltene, differenzierte Bürokratie« gegenüberstehe. Wenn der Professor damit die Tatsache umschrieb, daß die Deutschen aus der DDR, von der sie stets bevormundet wurden, sich nun schwer taten, Eigeninitiative zu entwickeln, um vor westdeutschen Amtsvorstehern nicht als Bittsteller, sondern als Fordernde aufzutreten, die Rechte geltend machten, dann trifft dies zu. Sich im planwirtschaftlichen System mit seinen Zwängen, aber auch seinen Vorteilen zu bewegen – darin kannten sie sich alle aus. Sich aber auf dem freien Markt aus eigenem Antrieb um Wohnung und Arbeitsplatz zu kümmern, fiel vielen schwer. Auch mit dem Wort von der »Abwärtsmobilität«, das er in die Anhörung einbrachte, traf der Professor den Nagel auf den Kopf. Der soziologische Begriff steht für »berufliches Einsteigen auf einer niedrigeren Ebene, als sie der Ausbildung entspricht«, was vor allem für viele Akademiker unter den Ausgereisten eine schmerzliche Erfahrung ist. Die Aktiven unter den Übersiedlern, deren Zahl Ronge auf insgesamt zwei Drittel schätzt, seien bereit gewesen, Arbeit anzunehmen, für die sie überqualifiziert waren. Doch hätten viele sich inzwischen fortentwickeln können, »teilweise sogar innerhalb der Betriebe, in die sie eingestiegen sind«. Ronge sprach auch das Mißtrauen an, mit dem die einheimische Bevölkerung besondere »integrationspolitische Unternehmungen« betrachtet: »Je mehr besondere Behandlungen zugunsten dieser Teilgruppe der Übersiedler eingefordert werden, um so mehr Probleme schafft man sich in der Öffentlichkeit. Wenn es beispielsweise darauf hinausläuft, daß ein Jugendlicher seinen Berufswunsch erfüllt bekommen soll, dann wird sich die einheimische Bevölkerung natürlich fragen, wo das eigentlich hier der Fall ist.«

Die wichtigste Ursache für die Schwierigkeiten vieler Übersiedler wurde vom Vertreter der Bundesanstalt für Arbeit in Nürnberg benannt: »Das Haupthindernis, das sich gegenwärtig der Integration entgegenstellt, ist die ungünstige Arbeitsmarktlage.« Doch die schockierendste Erkenntnis auf dieser 41. Sitzung des Innerdeutschen Ausschusses der 10. Wahlperiode war, daß ein Zehntel der 100 000 Obdachlosen in der Bundesrepublik sich aus DDR-Übersiedlern rekrutierte – jeder zehnte Obdachlose eine gescheiterte Existenz bei dem Versuch, von dem einen Deutschland in das andere auszuwandern! Wie ein Schlaglicht rückt diese Nachricht die Tatsache ins Bewußtsein, daß zu den vielen Chancen der Freiheit auch die gehört, im Westen einfach kaputt und vor die Hunde zu gehen.

Daß es der DDR im Zuge der Rückkehr-Kampagne beileibe nicht darum ging, möglichst viele der verloren gegangenen Töchter und Söhne verzeihend in die sozialistischen Arme zu schließen, wurde durch die Auswahl der veröffentlichten Leserzuschriften überdeutlich. Die Illusionen dieser »Ehemaligen« über das Leben im kapitalistischen Alltag seien zerplatzt wie Seifenblasen, hieß es beinahe schadenfroh im Vorspann, den die Redaktion des »Neuen Deutschland« den Briefen vorangestellt hatte. »Sie haben sich vom Klassenfeind blenden lassen«, meinte die Näherin Franka Archmutat aus der Brigade »Völkerfreundschaft« im VEB Berlins Damenmoden. »Für Wanderer zwischen zwei Welten«, so der Rentner Heinz Petzold aus Cottbus, »sollte es bei uns keinen Platz geben«. Meisterin Jutta Schädle im VEB Herrenbekleidung »Fortschritt« Berlin schrieb: »Die DDR ist kein Wartesaal, in dem man kommen und gehen kann, wie es einem beliebt.« Und Angelika Noack, Lehrausbilder im Forster VEB Web- und Strickwaren, verurteilte: »Sie haben ihr Vaterland verraten und es vor Presse und Fernsehen der BRD schlecht gemacht. Was wollen sie dann wieder in unserem ›unfreien‹ Land?« In der verqueren Art, die für derlei DDR-Aufklärung typisch ist, wollte das »unfreie Land« potentielle Wiederholungstäter warnen. Motto: Denkt lieber dreimal nach, ob ihr drüben wirklich euer Glück machen könnt, denn die Gefahr, auf die Nase zu fallen, ist groß. Und wer dort scheitert, ist auch hier nicht mehr erwünscht. Da war kein Platz für eine differenzierte Betrachtung oder gar für Menschlichkeit.

Der Vorgang belegte, wie schwer sich die SED mit der Ausreiseproblematik tat, auch nachdem sie die Schleuse vorübergehend geöffnet hatte. Die 20 000, die sie mit einem Schlag hatte ziehen lassen, wollte sie vor der eigenen Öffentlichkeit nun mit 20 000 Rückkehrwünschen verrechnen, die zudem mit Hilfe einer bestellten vox populi rüde zurückgewiesen wurden. Was ein solches Schicksal zwischen Ost und West im Einzelfall bedeuten konnte, zeigte der Fall eines 52jährigen Übersiedlers, der zwei erwachsene Söhne und eine Schwester im Süden der DDR zurückgelassen hatte, um in Norddeutschland zu einer Frau zu ziehen, mit der er zusammenleben wollte. »Sie war der einzige Grund, der ihn veranlaßte, in der DDR um Ausreise nachzukommen. Doch die Bindung kam nicht zustande«, so ein Bericht des Westberliner »Tagesspiegel« 1987. »Die neue Umgebung war ihm fremd. Wahrscheinlich empfand er auch sie so abweisend, wie es die Frau war, wegen der er gekommen war.« Die DDR lehnte seine Bitte auf Rückkehr ab. Offenbar hielt sie ihn für einen Sozialfall. Jedenfalls zählte sie ihn nicht zu jener Kategorie, von der die SED-Funktionärszeitschrift »Was und Wie« behauptet hatte: »Wenn sicher ist, daß der Betreffende einen wertvollen Beitrag zur Stärkung der DDR leistet, wird der Antrag genehmigt.« Drei Jahre nach der Übersiedlung in die Bundesrepublik nahm sich der Mann, dem die DDR das Recht auf Heimat verweigerte, das Leben.

»Ein Mensch, der seine Heimat verlassen will, egal warum, sollte diese Gelegenheit haben, auch mit Rückfahrkarte«, schrieb mir ein Ausgereister, den ich im Sächsischen kennengelernt hatte und der im Westen nach ersten euphorischen Erfahrungen mit der neuen Freiheit eine tiefe persönliche Krise durchgemacht hatte. »Jeder wird sich irgendwann die Antworten auf die Richtigkeiten seines Tuns geben müssen, und warum soll man nicht einen Fehler eingestehen und daraus lernen? Auch für andere Menschen kann so eine ehrliche Erfahrung sehr wichtig sein.« Sich solch ehrlichen Erfahrungen und einfachen menschlichen Einsichten zu stellen, ist die SED nicht nur durch den Hochmut der Macht gehindert. Sie glaubt sich offenbar zu schwach dafür.

Als er noch in der DDR lebte, glaubte Manfred Krug, daß den Deutschen in Ost und West die gleichen, unverwechselbaren Charakteristika anhafteten. Man brauchte, dachte er damals, die Bevölkerungen nur komplett gegeneinander auszutauschen, und nach sechs Wochen würden sich alle benehmen, wie von den etablierten Obrigkeiten im Osten oder Westen erwünscht: Frühere DDR-Bewohner wie Bürger der Bundesrepublik und umgekehrt. Heute denkt er anders. Eher würden *Wessis* sich im Osten daran gewöhnen, daß Partei und Staat ihr Leben bis ins Detail regulieren, meinte der inzwischen in den Westen übergesiedelte Schauspieler in einer Talkshow, als *Ossis* damit zurechtkommen, daß ihnen keiner mehr vorschreibt, wie sie alles zu machen hätten. In der Tat haben die unterschiedlichen Sozialisationsbedingungen in beiden deutschen Staaten die Menschen insoweit geprägt, daß differierende sozialpsychologische Verhaltensmuster entstanden sind. Das betrifft nicht so sehr den Geschmack der breiten Massen bei der Mode oder der Unterhaltung, denn da sorgen die in der DDR empfangenen elektronischen Westmedien allabendlich für östliche Anpassung. Biedere, volkstümliche Sendungen wie »Zum Blauen Bock«, ausgestrahlt vom Hessischen Rundfunk, und der »Krug zum grünen Kranz«, gesendet von Berlin-Adlershof, sind einander zum Verwechseln ähnlich. Die Derbheit der Witze, über die da gelacht, die seichte Musik, zu deren Klängen nicht selten geschunkelt wird, bezeugen, daß die Einheit der Nation geradezu prächtig funktioniert, wenn es gilt, den deutschen Hang zu spießiger, biederer Gemütlichkeit zu demonstrieren. Das ist anders, wenn es um die tägliche Freiheit geht.

»Im Osten«, schrieb mir ein aus Dresden ausgereister Freund nach seinem ersten Jahr West-Erfahrung, »hatte ich den Glauben an meine Fähigkeit, fast alles in den Griff zu bekommen. Nur, was dort schwierig und deshalb eine Herausforderung war, bereitet hier nicht die geringste Mühe. Hier wird das Freisein zum Problem.« Ein Student erzählte mir einmal, wie schwer er sich getan hat, nach vier Semestern Plan-Studium in Jena plötzlich an einer hiesigen Universität sein Studium frei gestalten zu können, beziehungsweise zu müssen. Der Umgang mit dieser Freiheit ist schwer und erfordert anscheinend das gleiche Training wie in einer Sportart, in der man erfolgreich sein will. »Diese Erfahrung«, schrieb der Freund weiter, »kann ich bestätigen. Auch ich muß lernen, mit dieser Welt umgehen zu können, denn zu viele Reaktionen und Routinehandlungen sitzen auch heute noch fest in mir. Bestes Beispiel ist der Einkauf. Das vielfältige Angebot mit den unterschiedlichen Preisen macht mir heute noch zu schaffen, ebenso, manche Käufe nicht aus der Notwendigkeit, sondern aus der Überlegung heraus zu tätigen, wer weiß, ob sich diese Gelegenheit wieder bietet – typisch DDR-isch, nicht?« Auch den Unterschied zwischen sozialen und freien, Warm- und Kaltmieten zu begreifen, und das bei schwankenden Ölpreisen, fällt einem Ex-DDRler anfänglich schwer.

Wolf Biermann schrieb nach langen Jahren im Westen für Eva-Maria Hagen, inzwischen auch schon einige Zeit der realsozialistischen Heimat entfremdet, das Lied: »Ich bin ja 'ne Deutsche und darf hier sein – ich bleib' trotzdem die aus'm Osten.« Auf verschiedenste Weise ist für viele der Ausgereisten das Kapitel DDR innerlich lange nicht abgeschlossen, auch wenn die einen sich schnell, die anderen unter langen Qualen der ungewohnten Ordnung anzupassen lernen. Bei nahezu allen Ausgereisten trifft man auf einen offenbar mit der DDR-Muttermilch eingesogene, tiefverwurzelte egalitäre Grundüberzeugung. Angesichts vieler ungewohnter, oft krasser sozialer Unterschiede im Westen verlockt das selbst jene, die voller Haß auf das Regime gegangen sind, zu Kommentaren mit dem Tenor: »Das zumindest hat es im Osten nicht gegeben.« »Ich habe viele Menschen kennengelernt, denen die Probleme des täglichen Lebens, auf andere Art als im Osten, ganz schön zu schaffen machen, und mich selbst bedrückt der hohe Aufwand an Geld für einen alleinstehenden Menschen für Miete und Versicherung«, schrieb der Freund aus Dresden. »Mein Verständnis für die Menschen am Rande der Gesellschaft ist inzwischen sehr gewachsen, denn ich habe festgestellt, wie schnell jeder dahin kommen kann.« Der Wechsel von dem einen in das andere Gesellschaftssystem legt das Vergleichen nahe und schärft den kritischen Sinn. Bei vielen bewirkt der Wechsel eine tiefe Verunsicherung. In der DDR wußten die Ausgereisten noch genau zwischen Freund und Feind zu unterscheiden, eine Fähigkeit, die selbst in bedrohlichen Situationen ein Gefühl von innerer Sicherheit vermittelte.

Daß viele ihr unsichtbares Kreuz mit der DDR noch lange Zeit im Westen mit sich herumschleppen, trifft vor allem für die Intellektuellen zu. Das schlaue Taktieren und Finassieren, mit dem sie sich im Osten bescheidene Freiräume gegen die großen Apparate erkämpften, die List als Waffe des Widerstands gegen die Allmacht der Partei, dienten ja nicht nur der Selbstbehauptung, sondern auch der Selbstbestätigung. Im Westen, wo fast alles erlaubt ist, sind solche Techniken selten gefragt. Ein Schriftsteller, Dramatiker oder Theaterregisseur konnte sich im Osten schon deshalb größerer Wirkung sicher sein, weil Literatur und Theater einen Teil der kritischen Funktion übernommen haben, welche der Presse in der DDR wahrzunehmen untersagt ist. Das läßt Theaterstücke und Neuerscheinungen oft zum Politikum werden, und so erklärt sich manche Behinderung im Osten schlicht mit der großen Bedeutung, die jedem geschriebenen Wort im scholastischen System der SED zukommt. »Alles, was man im Osten schreibt, ist sehr wichtig, oder die Gesellschaft glaubt, daß es wichtig ist. Man hat es hier schwer, etwas zu publizieren«, sagte Heiner Müller in einem Interview. »In der Bundesrepublik hat man keine Schwierigkeit, publiziert zu werden, außer, wenn es sich um etwas handelt, das mit Terrorismus zu tun hat. Das ist das westdeutsche Tabu.« Weil im Osten Informationsfreiheit unterdrückt wird, ist nicht nur die Ausdrucksebene viel stärker, das Publikum weiß auch, was zwischen den Worten geschieht, meint Müller. »Die Leute im Westen tun das nicht. Für sie ist da nur ein leerer Raum.« Kurzum: Kunst, Literatur und Theater in einer geschlossenen Gesellschaft mit Zensur haben größere Relevanz als in der freien Gesellschaft des Westens, die den einzelnen mit einer wahren Flut von Information überschwemmt, die auf Ausgereiste zunächst desorientierend wirkt. So vermissen DDR-Künstler im Westen, so paradox das klingen mag, gelegentlich die Reibungsflächen, die ihnen die DDR-Kulturbürokratie bot. An ihnen konnten sie ihre Fähigkeiten, ihren Mut und auch die Findigkeit erproben, die nötig sind, die Grenzen des Erlaubten, wenn auch in winzigen Schritten, auszudehnen. Gelang es ihnen, war ihnen der Dank und der Applaus eines geschulten Publikums gewiß. Im Westen vermissen sie, selbst wenn sie Aufmerksamkeit finden, oft die Wirkung und klagen, das Ergebnis ihrer Anstrengung sei zu schnell verpufft. Einige ausgereiste Intellektuelle sind stark vom Marxismus geprägt und haben den Glauben an die Utopie nicht verloren. Sie träumen den Traum von einem freiheitlichen Marxismus, schließen sich im Westen den Alternativen an oder führen ein Leben am Rande der Gesellschaft. Als Beispiel dafür mag Rudolf Bahro gelten, der von innen her, als Intimkenner des Apparats, die vielleicht treffendste und vernichtendste Kritik der SED-Parteiwirtschaft geschrieben hat. Im Westen ging er zunächst zu den Grünen. Inzwischen führt er das Leben eines kuriosen, skurrilen, aber bedeutungslosen Gurus.

Als im Jahr 1986 ein DDR-Ökonom, der in einer für Deutschland politisch entscheidenden Zeit dem DDR-Ministerrat zugearbeitet hatte, aus der DDR ausreiste, ließ er Freunde in einflußreichen Positionen des Apparats zurück, die seinen Weggang bedauerten. Einer von ihnen arbeitete als Professor in einem der Thinktanks der SED, die der politischen Führung durch Erstellen von Analysen und Expertisen Entscheidungshilfe leisten. Er bezeichnete den langjährigen Mitstreiter und

Genossen als einen jener »Moralisten, Gläubigen und Bedingungslosen, die von Politik besessen sind«. Auf eine Art, meinte der Professor, seien er und seine Freunde im Institut natürlich auch von Politik besessen. »Es kommt doch darauf an zu verändern, und sei es auch nur millimeterweise. Doch wer hier weggeht, verändert gar nichts, nicht einmal einen halben Millimeter. Unser Freund«, fuhr er fort, »hat sich doch der Politik verschrieben, also will er etwas ändern. Aber bei Ihnen drüben wird er gar nichts bewirken. Und wenn doch, dann wahrscheinlich das Gegenteil dessen, was er für richtig hält, weil das erfahrungsgemäß die Mechanismen sind, denen sich Dissidenten nicht entziehen können.« Das Gespräch bei trockenem Meißener Wein war für mich nicht nur aufschlußreich, weil es völlig frei blieb von der Verklemmtheit und der üblen Nachrede, mit der SED-Offizielle üblicherweise reagieren, sobald die Unterhaltung auf einen der ihren kommt, der das Land verlassen hat. Dabei war weniger wichtig, ob seine Einschätzung der Wirkungsmöglichkeiten des ausgereisten Freundes stimmte, auch wenn die Mechanismen für viele Fälle zutreffend beschrieben schienen. So mancher politische Kopf unter den Ausgereisten denkt demokratisch links, wird jedoch wegen seiner ätzenden Kritik am SED-Regime von der ganz auf Entspannung eingeschworenen SPD nur als Störenfried empfunden. Verständnis und weit geöffnete Arme findet er dann da, wo er sie ursprünglich weder gesucht noch erwartet hatte: Bei den Rechtskonservativen. Wichtiger schien mir die Art, in der mein Gegenüber den Sündenfall seines alten Kampfgefährten einordnete – als Verzicht auf Politik, die, anklingend an Max Webers Wort vom gründlichen, langsamen Bohren dicker Bretter nur in winzigen Schritten meßbare Erfolge bringen kann. Diese Äußerung war typisch für die Haltung jener im SED-Apparat, die allen Widersprüchen und Rückschlägen zum Trotz der Sache des Sozialismus die Treue halten. Da gibt es neben Opportunisten und Karrieremachern – denen mit dem »hündischen Parteisekretär-Blick, das Kreuz im rechten Winkel abgeknickt« (Manfred Krug) – eben auch Überzeugte im Glauben. Es sind Realisten, die um die Scheußlichkeit fast jedes Kompromisses wissen, den sie tagtäglich schließen müssen; es sind Dialektiker, die eine Tagesentscheidung in historischer Perspektive sehen, und es sind Taktiker, die sich dem hehren Endziel, das die alltägliche Misere des realexistierenden Sozialismus überstrahlt, in den verschlungensten Winkelzügen nähern. Millimeter für Millimeter, wie mein Gesprächspartner versicherte. Um die Mängel und Schwächen des gegenwärtigen DDR-Systems wissen solche SED-Genossen besser Bescheid als ihre ärgsten Widersacher im Westen. Und doch sind sie überzeugt, daß sie langfristig die Folgen einer neuen industriellen Revolution besser meistern und den Wettbewerb der Systeme als Sieger bestehen.

6. Von der Subversivität
der Poesie

Es gibt andere, die dem Sozialismus die Treue halten, im Lande bleiben wollen und sich doch von der SED gelöst haben. Der Liedermacher, den ich im Frühjahr 1986 traf, war aus der Partei ausgetreten, weil er sich vor der Kontrollkommission rechtfertigen sollte. Als er mit den Funktionären aneinandergeriet, warf er sein Parteibuch auf den Tisch: »Das könnt ihr behalten«, sagte er und ging davon. Der Hintergrund der Auseinandersetzung war persönlich. »Das hat wie so vieles überhaupt nichts mit Politik zu tun, ihr im Westen versteht das immer falsch«, sagte der Erfinder und Mitinitiator des »Festivals des politischen Liedes«, einer alljährlichen FDJ-Veranstaltung, die im Rahmen der offiziellen politischen Kultur der DDR hohen Stellenwert genießt. Mein Liedermacher war zusammen mit einer Schauspielerin aufgetreten, die eine enge Beziehung zu einem SED-Bezirkssekretär unterhielt. Von Eifersucht geplagt, hatte der Parteigewaltige, dem man mancherlei Affären nachsagte, seine geballte politische Macht aufgeboten und den vermeintlichen oder tatsächlichen Nebenbuhler schließlich vor eine Art Parteigericht gezerrt. Doch den ekelte das »dreckige Spiel« nur noch an.

Von Haus aus Diplomphilosoph, sah das ehemalige SED-Mitglied die Verhältnisse in seinem Land klar und scharf und ohne jede Beschönigung. Meine Frage, ob er sich selbst als Kommunist betrachte, beantwortete er nach einigem Zögern mit »ja«. Aber er war kein Kommunist der gängigen Sorte, wie die SED sie schätzt. »Wenn etwas falsch gemacht wird, tut mir das weh, vor allem, wenn die Dummheit an die Macht kommt und das Land versaut«, sagte er und beteuerte sofort mit beinahe beschwörendem Unterton: »Ich bin kein Anarchist.« Seine Loslösung von der Partei bezeichnete er als eine »allmähliche Geschichte«. Ende der 60er Jahre habe es eine Entwicklungseuphorie bei den jungen Menschen gegeben. Die ersten Anzeichen eines Bruchs mit der Partei datierte mein Gesprächspartner, der zum Jahrgang 1944 zählt, auf den VIII. Parteitag, der im Juni 1971 die Ära Ulbricht beendete und den Anfang des Konsum- oder Gulaschkommunismus von Erich Honecker markiert. »Hier begannen das Nachäffen des Westens und der Verzicht auf den eigenen Weg«, meinte er. »Seither bietet die SED keinen alternativen Gesellschaftsentwurf an, sondern ist von der Kaufhallenideologie beherrscht. Das alles geht letzten Endes nicht auf, weil in Sachen Konsum der Osten den Westen doch nicht überbieten kann. Käme es dem Osten nur darauf an, sollte er besser gleich kapitalistisch werden.« Mich erinnerte dies an eine Position, wie sie Wolfgang Harich in seinem nur im Westen erschienenen, inzwischen weitgehend vergessenen Buch über einen Kommunismus ohne Wachstum gegenüber der Politik Nikita Chruschtschows bezogen hatte. Die Absage des Liedermachers an Honeckers Kaufhallenideologie entsprach Harichs Kritik an den bombastischen Versprechen Chruschtschows, den Westen bei der Produktion aller wichtigen Konsumgüter zu überholen. Damit, so Harich, habe sich der Osten nicht nur auf einen Wettlauf eingelassen, den er nie gewinnen konnte, sondern alle Startvorteile – zentrale Planung und gesellschaftliche Kontrolle der Produktionsmittel – verspielt, um einen anderen, nicht den ausgetretenen Pfaden des Kapitalismus folgenden, ideologisch »sauberen« Weg weiterer industrieller Entwicklung einzuschlagen. Doch hatte Harichs Kritik damals auch Adressaten in der DDR. Wenn mein Gesprächspartner das »Nachäffen« auf die Ära Honecker begrenzte, übersah er, vielleicht aus Unkenntnis, daß Walter Ulbricht die großspurigen Ankündigungen Chruschtschows für die DDR vollmundig übernommen hatte. So verkündete der V. SED-Parteitag als wirtschaftliche Hauptaufgabe: »Die Volkswirtschaft der

DDR ist innerhalb weniger Jahre so zu entwickeln, daß die Überlegenheit der DDR gegenüber dem Bonner Staat eindeutig bewiesen wird und infolgedessen (bis 1961) der Pro-Kopf-Verbrauch der Bevölkerung mit wichtigen Lebensmitteln und Konsumgütern den Pro-Kopf-Verbrauch in Westdeutschland erreicht und übertrifft.« Freilich hielt Ulbricht im Gegensatz zu Honecker an der Fiktion einer sozialistischen Menschengemeinschaft fest, die eine neue, höhere, nämlich sozialistische Moral ermöglichte. Die Utopie vom neuen Menschen, der da eines Tages kommen werde, war noch immer nicht ausgeträumt – im Gegenteil: Eigentlich hätten sich nur mit Hilfe eines solchen Wundergeschöpfes all die wirtschaftlichen Höchstleistungen vollbringen lassen, die der Gründervater der DDR 1957 in Aussicht stellte. Ulbricht wünschte volle Kaufhallen, ohne den Preis dafür zu entrichten, den der Liedermacher dem Ulbricht nachfolgenden Gulaschkommunisten Honecker ankreidete: die Kaufhallen-Ideologie. Kritik am Nachäffen des Westens findet sich häufig bei jenen Intellektuellen, die der Idee des Sozialismus die Treue halten – dem realexistierenden Modell zum Trotz. Viele von ihnen kritisieren die ökonomische Schizophrenie des Intershop-Systems, in dem westliche »Luxusware« – in der Bundesrepublik sind es normale Güter des täglichen Bedarfs – gegen Westmark verkauft werden. »Die eigentliche Gefahr für uns ist, daß die Westmark auch unser Standard wird«, sagte Heiner Müller in einem Interview, das freilich nur im Westen erschien.

Ein Autor vieler Texte, die noch immer mit voller Brust von FDJ-Chören gesungen werden, hatte sein Parteibuch im Zorn auf den Tisch der Kontrollkommission geknallt und damit den Schnitt mit der SED für sich vollzogen. Für die Partei zählte das nicht. Die Vorhut der Arbeiterklasse erkennt die freie Entscheidung eines einzelnen, ihr nicht länger anzugehören, nicht an. In der Regel besteht sie darauf, daß es nur einen Weg gibt, ihrer Mitgliedschaft ledig zu werden: die Ausstoßung des irrenden, unbotmäßigen Individuums durch das Kollektiv. So wurde der einst hochgeschätzte Verfasser von FDJ-Liederbüchern in aller Form mit der Strafe des Parteiausschlusses belegt, obwohl er nach seiner Meinung längst die Trennung von sich aus vollzogen hatte. Zum Schaden gereichte ihm das nicht. Zwar war er für die DDR-Medien nach dem »Ausschluß« praktisch ein toter Mann, sein Name wurde nicht länger genannt. Da »offizielle Werbung hierzulande meist Negativ-Werbung ist«, wie er voller Spott behauptete, hatte er plötzlich mehr Auftritte in Studentenclubs, Kulturhäusern und auf Betriebsveranstaltungen als je zuvor. »Die zweite Ebene funktioniert hier prächtig, das läuft auf Zuruf und Absprache. Unter der Hand empfiehlt einer den anderen weiter.« Einen Antrag auf Ausreise zu stellen, kam ihm nie in den Sinn. Er wollte die thüringische Heimat nicht missen, die er als Schnittpunkt von Ost und West und Nord und Süd verstand, als einzigartige Kulturlandschaft mit durch Historie gedüngten Boden, weil er sich stets gegenwärtig war, was sich auf ihm ereignet hatte: Reformation und Bauernkrieg, Dreißigjähriger Krieg, Jena und Auerstädt und die Völkerschlacht bei Leipzig. Sein Vater, Dreher und überzeugter Katholik, hatte den Sohn auf eine Klosterschule geschickt. Aus Protest gegen das bigotte Ambiente lernte der spätere Liedermacher Russisch und übersetzte Gedichte sowjetischer Autoren. Möglich, daß inzwischen wieder Frieden herrscht zwischen dem linken Kommunisten und der in seinen Augen opportunistischen Partei: Wenn ja, dann hat gewiß die Partei den ersten Schritt getan. Er schien mir für eine Annäherung aus eigener Initiative zu verbittert, enttäuscht, aber auch zu selbstbewußt – einer von denen, über die das DDR-Sprichwort sagt: »Er hat viele Beulen am Helm, die wenigsten stammen vom Klassenfeind.«

»Ich bin hier hinein geboren, hier habe ich dreißig Jahre gelebt, hier möchte ich etwas verändern.« Der das sagte, arbeitete tagsüber in einem akademischen Beruf und war abends Liedermacher aus Leidenschaft. Auch sein Helm hatte Beulen, verursacht von der Staatsgewalt. Die Lieder, die er in Jugendclubs, vor Studenten und häufig auf kirchlichen Veranstaltungen zur Gitarre vortrug, waren von einer sanften Art, die in den Ohren der Obrigkeit befremdlich klang. Daß er pazifistische Ideen verbreite, war nur einer der Vorwürfe, den die SED-Kulturbürokratie gegen ihn erhob. Manche seiner Songs hatten auch Reizworte wie Schießbefehl, Reiseprivileg und Machtmißbrauch enthalten. Daß er einem Westbesucher eine Kassette mit einigen seiner Lieder mitgab, die vom Zoll konfisziert wurde, brachte ihm 1984 drei Monate Untersuchungshaft ein. »Ungesetzliche Verbindungsaufnahme« lautete die Beschuldigung, die sich auf Paragraph 219 des DDR-Strafgesetzbuches stützte. Es ist einer jener typischen Gummiparagraphen, welche die Staatsgewalt nach Belieben strecken und dehnen kann, denn welche Organisation oder Person eine »gegen die staatliche Ordnung der Deutschen Demokratischen Republik gerichtete Tätigkeit« ausübt und welche Materialien oder Schriften den Interessen der DDR schaden, bedarf von Fall zu Fall der Interpretation, die im Zweifel die Staatssicherheit oder der Staatsanwalt besorgt.

Und weil sie so dehnbar sind, eignen sie sich vortrefflich zur Einschüchterung. So wurden Freunde in einer thüringischen Kleinstadt, die für die deutsche Nationalkultur von etlicher Bedeutung ist, nach einem Treffen mit uns vom Betriebsparteisekretär vorgeladen und befragt, ob sie denn etwa den Paragraphen 219 des DDR-Strafgesetzbuches nicht kennten. Offenbar zählten für den eifernden SED-Amtswalter auch beim DDR-Außenministerium akkreditierte, westliche Journalisten zu den Personen, die sich »eine gegen die DDR gerichtete Tätigkeit zum Ziele setzen«. Das Beispiel ist leider kein Einzelfall.

»Viele DDR-Gesetze«, heißt es nicht zufällig im Jahresbericht 1986 von Amnesty International, »vor allem aber die, welche die Meinungs- und die Versammlungsfreiheit betreffen, sind sehr vage gehalten (*vaguely worded*), und selbst wenn man die Handlungen eines Gefangenen vor der Verhaftung kennt, ist durchaus nicht immer ersichtlich, wegen welcher Taten die Anklage erhoben wurde. Amnesty International ist jedoch der Auffassung, daß diese Gesetze die Ausübung der Rechte auf Meinungs- und Versammlungsfreiheit einschränken und deshalb mit dem internationalen Menschen-rechtsstandard nicht zu vereinbaren sind.« Als Verstoß gegen diesen Standard wertet die Organisation, die sich als weltweites Gewissen und Hüter der Rechte der politischen Gefangenen aller Lager und Systeme versteht, auch die Paragraphen 213 und 214, die »unerlaubten Grenzübertritt« und »Behinderung staatlicher Organe« unter Strafe stellen. Und moniert wird im Jahresbericht 1987 auch der Ausschluß der Öffentlichkeit bei politischen Verfahren in der DDR: »Alle politischen Fälle, über die Amnesty International im Laufe des Jahres 1986 etwas in Erfahrung bringen konnte, wurden hinter verschlossenen Türen verhandelt. Freigelassene Gefangene berichteten unserer Organisation, daß ihre Familien nicht einmal zur Urteilsverkündung zugelassen waren. Während der Besuche von Familienangehörigen war ihnen jede Äußerung über ihren Fall untersagt. Die Familien der Gefangenen waren deshalb über die Gründe der Verhaftung nur unzulänglich informiert. Wenn sie versuchten, das Wenige an Information, über das sie verfügten, ausländischen Organisationen oder Personen zuzuspielen, liefen sie Gefahr, wegen Verstößen gegen die Paragraphen verfolgt zu werden, die das Weitergeben von Informationen verbieten.«

Was das im Einzelfall bedeutet, erzählte mir ein junger Schriftsteller. Er hatte als Student an einer Aktion für den zu Zuchthaus verurteilten Regimekritiker Rudolf Bahro teilgenommen, Flugblätter verteilt, in denen seine Freilassung gefordert wurde und hatte dafür drei Jahre im Gefängnis verbracht. Seine Eltern wurden über den Grund seiner Verurteilung offiziell nie informiert. Nach der Entlassung besaß er weder eine Kopie des Urteils, geschweige denn der Anklageschrift. Als einziger Nachweis diente ein »kleiner Papierstreifen« für die Sozialversicherung, auf dem Antritt und Ende der Haft eingetragen waren – ohne Angabe irgendeines Paragraphen oder eines Gesetzesverstoßes. »Danach«, erzählte der Schriftsteller voller Empörung, »hätte ich genausogut wegen Sittlichkeitsverbrechen hinter schwedischen Gardinen sitzen können.«

Der Liedermacher im Nebenberuf hatte mehr Glück und kam nach drei Monaten Untersuchungshaft frei. Die langen Vernehmungen, die er über sich ergehen lassen mußte, bezeichnete er als »strapaziös, aber erträglich«, und das Essen habe ihm besser geschmeckt als in der Kantine seines Großbetriebs. »Für mich war das eine entscheidende Erfahrung«, berichtete er. Er habe nicht nur gelernt, vorsichtiger zu sein, gewisse Reizworte habe er seither vermieden. Als Beispiel nannte er eine Verszeile, die von den Behörden unverständlicherweise als Provokation empfunden wurde: »dann schwelgen beim großen Gelage / die Fürsten unserer Tage«. So etwas sang er nun nicht mehr. Aber er betonte zugleich: »Durch die Haft bin ich in meinem Anliegen gefestigt worden, öffentlich auszusprechen, was ich für wichtig halte.« Seine Haltung ist exemplarisch für eine kleine, aber wachsende Schar junger DDR-Bürger, die erstaunliche Zivilcourage zeigen – eine Haltung, die Hochachtung und Respekt erheischt. Die zu dieser Schar zählen, stehen dem Regime äußerst kritisch gegenüber, aber sie verwerfen es nicht absolut. Ausreise betrachten sie als eine ultima ratio, von der sie nur Gebrauch machen wollen, wenn die Partei ihnen buchstäblich keine Luft zum Atmen läßt, um ihren persönlichen Freiraum auszuweiten. Die Vor- und Nachteile beider Systeme wägen sie gegeneinander ab, und beim Urteil über die westliche Gesellschaft herrscht eher vorsichtige Skepsis vor. »Man sitzt zwischen Baum und Borke«, sagte einer zu mir. »Hier geht einfach zu vieles nicht, aber drüben ist es kälter. Meine Schwester im Westen wird vom Alltag verwaltet, ihr Leben bestimmt sich durch Ferien-Reisekataloge und Sonderangebote.« Mein Liedermacher war überzeugt, daß man sich im Westen als Persönlichkeit freier entfalten kann. »Aber bei Euch macht man Geschäfte auf der Grundlage fehlgeleiteter Bedürfnisse«, sagte er. Sein Urteil fällte er mit Vorbehalt, denn persönlich hatte er den Westen noch nicht kennengelernt. Doch sein Gefühl sagte ihm, er gehöre in das Land, in dem er geboren wurde, in dem er aufgewachsen ist. »Hier bin ich zu Hause, deshalb will ich lieber hier dafür kämpfen, daß ich mit dem Reisepaß in fremde Länder kann.«

Es gibt andere, die mehr Freiraum für persönliche Entfaltung in der DDR-Gesellschaft schaffen wollen, weil sie überzeugte Kommunisten sind und nicht aufhören, den realen Sozialismus mit der Elle der ursprünglich aufklärerisch-humanitären Vision des jungen Karl Marx zu messen. Und es gibt solche, die sich persönlichen Spielraum erkämpfen, weil sie als Fachleute aufstiegen und als Experten unentbehrlich wurden. Ich denke an den kunstbeflissenen, rundum gebildeten Endfünfziger, der in Leipzig bei Hans Mayer und Ernst Bloch studierte und den Neuanfang nach dem Krieg als Versuch empfunden hatte, an die linksintellektuelle Kultur der 20er Jahre in der Weimarer Republik anzuknüpfen. »Wir lasen Thomas und Heinrich Mann«, erzählte er voller Stolz, »und der gesamte Feuchtwanger wurde zuerst bei uns und sehr lange nicht im Westen verlegt.« Daß Exilschriftsteller wie Anna Seghers, Arnold Zweig und Bert Brecht in die sowjetische Besatzungszone und spätere DDR zurückkehrten, wertete er als Beleg für die These, daß der antifaschistische Neubeginn im Osten die besten Traditionen jenes anderen Deutschland fortschreibe, das im Gegensatz zum konservativ-bürgerlichen nicht schuldig geworden sei. Zwar stieß er nie zur Partei, aber er dachte und fühlte links. Der Westen reizte ihn und seine Kommilitonen damals nicht: »Der kam für uns überhaupt nicht in Frage, da waren die Kräfte der Restauration am Werk. In der DDR herrschte unter den Studenten Aufbruchstimmung. Wir glaubten, daß es bei uns mehr Zukunft gab.« Begabt und vor allem unbelastet, weil einige Jahre zu jung, um als Täter oder Mitläufer in die Verbrechen des Dritten Reichs verstrickt zu werden, erklomm er in jungen Jahren bald eine verantwortliche Position. Die ihm übertragene kulturhistorische Aufgabe gefiel ihm, der Beruf wurde bald zum Hobby, und als das Eis des Kalten Krieges mit dem Tauwetter der Ostverträge brach – »wir waren plötzlich wer, wurden akzeptiert und eingeladen, das war ein unerhört neues Gefühl!« – verschafften Besuche im westlichen Ausland ihm, der zum »DDR-Reisekader« zählte, neue Erlebnishorizonte.

Doch als ich ihn 1986 kennenlernte, traf ich auf einen ernüchterten, zutiefst Verbitterten, der von sich behauptete, er habe jahrelang wie ein Betriebsblinder gelebt, unfähig wahrzunehmen, was außerhalb seiner Berufssphäre vor sich ging. Die ihm nachwachsen würden, hielt er für wenig kompetent, weil das Parteibuch in vielen Fällen die Sachautorität ersetzte. »Wenn das oben links im Knopfloch fehlt, ist die Karriere so manches qualifizierten Mannes in unserem Land schnell erledigt.« Auf das Konto solcher Knopfloch-Karrieristen buchte er nun Anzeichen von Krise und Verfall, die er erst um sich herum wahrnahm, seit es ihm »wie Schuppen von den Augen fiel«. Das leckende Dach eines Theaters von ruhmreicher Tradition neu einzudecken, erzählte er mit allen Anzeichen des Entsetzens, sei unmöglich. Der Bezirksparteisekretär – »kein schlechter Mann« – habe den Schaden inspiziert und festgestellt: »Das schaffen wir nicht. Das erfordert ja die gesamte Dachdeckerkapazität des Bezirks für volle zwei Jahre.« Der Staat, der 1958 angekündigt hatte, den Westen bis 1961 im Pro-Kopf-Verbrauch bei Nahrungsmitteln und den wichtigsten Industriegütern zu überholen, mußte ein Vierteljahrhundert nach dem bombastischen Versprechen immer noch das eine Loch aufreißen, um das andere zu stopfen. »Dieses System«, sagte mein Kunsthistoriker, »kann einfach nicht überleben. Das Ganze ist nur eine Frage von Jahrzehnten.« Ein Teil seiner Bitterkeit mochte daher rühren, daß die Tochter sich mit Ausreisegedanken trug. Betriebsblindheit, so warf er sich jetzt vor, habe ihn und seine Frau dazu gebracht, »sie in eine Welt hineinzuwerfen, die sie nicht für erträglich hält«.

Es gab viele, die bekannten sich nach dem Krieg schnell zur Partei, machten manche Niederungen durch und erlebten nach Jahren der Demütigungen den Höhenrausch, den eine Position mit Einfluß und Macht vermittelt. Und nicht wenige zählten zu jenen, die durch nationalsozialistische Erziehung und Kriegserlebnis geprägt, nun unter dem Eindruck des totalen Zusammenbruchs aller bisherigen Autorität samt der durch sie vermittelten Vorbilder ihre Loyalität um 180 Grad wechselten. Das ging oft so erstaunlich schnell vor sich, daß der Schluß naheliegt, unter der Generation gläubiger Hitler-jungen habe es viele gegeben, die das durch den Sturz ihres früheren Idols entstandene Vakuum umgehend durch den nächsten, den sozialistischen Gott, füllen wollten. Dieser war ja nicht nur von der Gloriole des Sieges umstrahlt und hatte damit nach der von den Nationalsozialisten verbreiteten vulgärdarwinistischen Lehre vom Recht des Stärkeren also legitim triumphiert. Die Sieger aus dem Osten zeigten zudem eine brutale Vitalität, die sie denen aus dem dekadenten Westen überlegen erscheinen ließen. Auch behauptete die neue Ideologie jene Zukunft für sich, die nach der alten der »Jugend des Führers« schon immer gehört hatte. Vielleicht mag dies alles den plötzlichen Schwenk so manches überzeugten oder indoktrinierten Hitlerjungen zu den roten Siegern hin erklären. Selbstkritisch, präzis und schonungslos offen beschreibt Erich Loest, Jahrgang 1926, in seiner Autobiographie »Durch die Erde ein Riß«, wie er selbst den Wandel vom Fähnleinführer mit der grünweißen Schnur und vom Werwolf zum SED-Mitglied, Parteijournalisten und Vorsitzenden des Leipziger Schriftstellerverbandes durchgemacht hat.

»Jetzt bist Du für uns, sagten sie, arbeitest mit uns, was sollen die alten Geschichten. Die Aufnahme in die SED dauerte eine Viertelstunde und war absolut unfeierlich, sie war ein selbstverständlicher Schritt nach anderen, sie kostete keine Überwindung und war ein formeller Akt«, schreibt Loest und fragt: »War er Karrierist? Eines ist gewiß: Nicht mehr lange hin, und er wäre verwundert gefragt worden: Du bist kein Genosse? Aber warum denn nicht? ... Einer, der einer Karriere wegen seine Gesinnung verleugnete, war er nicht. Aber genausowenig war er sich der Tragweite dessen, was er da tat, bewußt: Februar 1945: Wir werden siegen, weil wir den Führer haben. Februar 1946: Nie wieder Politik! Februar 1947: Brüder in eins nun die Hände! Verwirrend genug.« Sein erster Roman hieß »Jungen, die übrig blieben«; er handelte von halben Kindern, die zum Dienst als Flakhelfer eingezogen wurden und als halbe Greise aus dem Krieg zurückkamen. Unter dem Eindruck der Chruschtschow-Rede über die Verbrechen Stalins, welche den neuen, säkularen Glauben so vieler als schrecklichen Irrtum entlarvte, stieß er dann zu jenen Reformgruppen, die das Recht auf freie innerparteiliche Diskussion und die Reinigung des Marxismus von stalinistischer Verfälschung forderten. Er saß dafür viele Jahre im Zuchthaus Bautzen ein. Sein Parteiausschluß elf Jahre später, notiert der unbestechliche Chronist in eigener Sache, »war organisatorisch und seelisch tausendmal aufwendiger« als der schnelle Eintritt 1946.

»Wir kannten keine Demokratie. Rechts hatten wir gehabt und waren damit gescheitert. Nun kam Links an die Reihe.« So schilderte mir einer, der zusammen mit Loest die Anklagebank gedrückt hatte, die Stimmung der ersten Nachkriegsjahre: »Wir haben einfach umgeschaltet. Wir wurden gebraucht, denn ohne unsere Jahrgänge ging das alles nicht. So nahm man uns mit offenen Armen auf.« Zwar war sein Vater einst Kommunist gewesen, doch der Sohn hatte die bündische Jugend dem kommunistischen Turnverein vorgezogen. Als die Wehrmacht den Rekruten des Jahrgangs 1921 rief, zog dieser als völkisch-national Gesonnener ins Feld. Als Leutnant kämpfte er bei den Panzergrenadieren, wurde mehrfach verwundet und glaubte bis tief in das Jahr 1944 hinein an den »Endsieg«. Aus der Gefangenschaft entlassen, stieß er sofort zur KPD und fing nach einem Schnellkursus als Neulehrer in einer Dorfschule am Rande des Harzes an. Bald fiel er als guter Redner und Schreiber auf und wurde zu Höherem in die Hauptstadt berufen: Zunächst Mitarbeiter in der Kulturabteilung der SED, hielt er bis 1956 dann eine führende Position im Schriftstellerverband der DDR. Daß die SED bis Ende der fünfziger Jahre als die Partei der deutschen Einheit firmierte und die Politik Konrad Adenauers als rheinischen Separatismus und Verrat an der Nation anprangerte, mochte vielen heimgekehrten Frontsoldaten das neue linke Engagement erleichtern, immer vorausgesetzt, daß sie nicht schieren opportunistischen Instinkten folgten. Als Mittler wirkten häufig Offiziere, die sich in sowjetischer Gefangenschaft auf marxistisch-leninistische Weise die Augen über den Nationalsozialismus hatten öffnen lassen. Den Redakteur des Leipziger Parteiblattes, der ihn in seine Redaktion holte, beschrieb Erich Loest beispielsweise so: »Der Chef, gelernter Journalist, war NS-Parteimitglied gewesen und als Hauptmann in sowjetische Kriegsgefangenschaft geraten, über das Nationalkomitee Freies Deutschland kam er zur KPD und in diese Funktion.« Und Loests Knastkamerad erzählte mir: »Die nationale Frage stand für uns ganz obenan. Wir verstanden uns als das linke Piemont Deutschlands, als Modell und Keimzelle für ein einiges Deutschland nach sozialistischem Muster.« Die ersten Nachkriegsjahre durchlebte er als einen »Rausch des Aufbaus und des Neubeginns«, bis der Schock der Chruschtschow-Rede auch ihn ernüchterte. An der unter Intellektuellen in der Partei damals beginnenden Reformdiskussion hatte sich anfänglich, wenn auch mit der gebotenen Vorsicht, selbst Kurt Hager beteiligt und die »Seuche des Kommandierens« gegeißelt. Reformkommunistische Vorschläge – »unter dem Einfluß der jugoslawischen Experimente wollten wir die Dezentralisierung der Wirtschaft und die Arbeiterselbstverwaltung der großen Betriebe« – gingen Ulbricht allerdings schnell wider den Strich. Als Anhänger der Gruppe Harich, die einen besonderen »deutschen Weg zum Sozialismus«, die Abschaffung der politischen Geheimpolizei und die Beseitigung der Vorherrschaft des Apparates über die SED-Mitglieder wollte, mußte der in der Wolle gefärbte Leutnant der Panzergrenadiere für seine kommunistischen Reformillusionen vier Jahre in Bautzen büßen. Zwei davon saß er in Einzelhaft. Was mich in den langen Gesprächen, die ich mit ihm führte, am meisten beeindruckte, war eine Szene aus dem Gerichtssaal, die er beschrieb. Er war zunächst als Zeuge im Prozeß gegen Walter Janka geladen, einem Spanienkämpfer, der sich vor dem Zugriff der Nazis nach Mexiko geflüchtet hatte und nun den Ostberliner Aufbauverlag leitete. Wie der Philosophie-Dozent Wolfgang Harich wollte Janka das Tauwetter nach dem XX. Parteitag nutzen, um mit dem Personenkult aufzuräumen und die Partei zu demokratisieren. Mitten im Gerichtssaal, in dem man gegen Janka verhandelte, wurde der Zeuge verhaftet und anschließend selbst vor Gericht gestellt. »Als Zuschauer«, erinnerte er sich, »saßen Johannes R. Becher, Anna Seghers und Helene Weigel auf der Tribüne. Immer wieder nickten sie uns Angeklagten zu, als ob sie uns zum Durchhalten ermuntern wollten.« Der Zuspruch durch Nikken bedeutete, daß die Sache, für die sich Janka, Harich und ihre Mitstreiter zu verantworten hatten, ihre Sympathie genoß. Der überwiegende Teil der Parteiintelligenz hatte ja die Entstalinisierung als Chance begriffen, gegen die Vormacht des bornierten Apparats und gegen seine brutalen, primitiven Führungsmethoden anzugehen. Schon im Juli 1953 hatte Wolfgang Harich in einem Artikel der »Berliner Zeitung« sich gegen undialektische Schönfärberei, für eine »freiheitlichere Atmosphäre« sowie für »mehr konkrete Selbstkritik« ausgesprochen. Brecht sekundierte dieser Attacke im »Neuen Deutschland«, wenn auch wie stets verschlüsselt, mit der Forderung, der sozialistische Realismus müsse »zugleich ein kritischer Realismus sein«. Die Angriffe gegen den Stalinismus und gegen die Person Ulbrichts, die weitgehend mit dem Personenkult gleichgesetzt wurden, häuften sich unter den Intellektuellen in der Partei nach der antistalinistischen Gomulka-Revolte in Polen. Mängel des Systems und Charakterschwächen seiner Spitzenpolitiker wurden jetzt weniger verdeckt diskutiert. Hans Mayer kritisierte die Vorstellung vom Schriftsteller als einem »Ingenieur der menschlichen Seele«, die von Stalin stammte und Schriftsteller zu Psychomanipulatoren im Auftrag der Partei degradierte. Er klagte mehr künstlerische Freiheit ein. SED-Professoren und Studenten forderten das Ende der Einmischung des Parteiapparates in Fragen der Wissenschaft. Kurzum: Die Reformpläne, deretwegen man die Angeklagten vor Gericht gestellt hatte, waren in Hunderten von Intellektuellen-Zirkeln des Landes laut gedacht und mehr oder weniger offen diskutiert worden. Janka und Harich wurden stellvertretend für die Tauwetter-Ideen des progressiven Teils der Parteiintelligenz abgeurteilt. Deshalb nickten Johannes R. Becher, Anna Seghers und Helene Weigel so aufmunternd. »Sie signalisierten ihr heimliches

Einverständnis mit uns Tätern«, schloß der Häftling aus Bautzen seinen bitteren Bericht. »Aber den Mut aufzustehen, sich selbst als Zeugen zu benennen und für uns öffentlich auszusagen, hatten sie nicht.« Dabei handelte es sich um Personen von Rang und Namen, die selbst für einen Walter Ulbricht unangreifbar waren.

Einer vom Jahrgang 1921, der am neuen Glauben nie irre geworden war, irritierte mich in einem langen Gespräch plötzlich mit der Behauptung: »Ohne eine Vision kann und will ich nicht leben.« Auch er hatte im Krieg ausdauernd als Offizier für Hitler gekämpft, auch für ihn war die nationale Frage ein entscheidendes Motiv für den Eintritt in die SED. Das erste Buch, das er später in der DDR als Verleger edieren sollte, enthielt nicht zufällig Gedichte und Lieder Theodor Körners, der in den Freiheitskriegen gegen Napoleon fiel. Er war der Sohn eines pommerschen Landarbeiters, der vor 1933 als Gewerkschaftssekretär für die Rechte der polnischen Schnitter eingetreten war – jener Gastarbeiter, die von den ostelbischen Rittergutsbesitzern über die Grenze gerufen wurden, wenn es galt, die Ernte einzubringen. Das Kriegsende hatte ihn zunächst in die Westzone verschlagen, doch bald ging er nach Leipzig, um Germanistik, Kunstgeschichte und Journalistik zu studieren. Für seine Visionen mußte er nie die Leiden erdulden, die der Altkommunist und »Aufbau«-Verleger Janka durchzustehen hatte. Stetig machte der neue Genosse seinen Weg nach oben. Daß er sich für den Osten entschied, hat ihn, allen materiellen Entbehrungen zum Trotz, nie gereut. Und mit der Zeit erwarb er eine taktische Meisterschaft, den Freiraum für Literatur und Kunst zu erweitern – zäh, unerhört gewitzt, aber systemimmanent. »Im Westen kann man auf den Markt bringen, was immer man will. Verkauft wird es nur durch die richtige Absatzstrategie«, erklärte er mir. »Bei uns im Osten beginnt alles mit der Durchsetzungsstrategie. Es kommt darauf an, die Genehmigung zu erhalten, ein Produkt überhaupt herzustellen. Hat man die Idee einmal durchgepaukt und das nötige Papier dazu, läuft der Verkauf dann wie von selbst.« Tatsächlich wurden ihm die vielen bibliophilen Bücher, die er in seinem Verlag herausbrachte, aus der Hand gerissen. »Wer klug ist, kann fast alles durchsetzen«, behauptete er, vergaß freilich, die nötigen Voraussetzungen zu erwähnen: eine Position mit Einfluß, durch treue Gefolgschaft in kritischen Zeiten erdient. Freilich schmälert das nicht seine Leistung. Er hatte immer Mut und war Manns genug, für Außenseiter einzutreten. Als Beispiel für den Spielraum, den er genoß, nannte er das Buch zweier junger Leipziger Künstler, die auf uralten und für die DDR gerade deshalb revolutionären Pfaden wandelten. Wie vor ihnen Penck, der die DDR verließ, hatten die jungen Leipziger Elementarzeichen und Piktogramme, Chiffren vergangener Kulturen aufgegriffen, und sie machten auch Material zur Kunst: Papiere, aus einem Brei von Brennesseln und Kräutern geschöpft, Ziegenleder, Birkenrinde – aus vielen einzelnen Teilen wurde in einer Art Manufakturbetrieb ein Band in einer Auflage von über 100 Exemplaren hergestellt, eine Mühe, der sich kaum ein westlicher Künstler unterziehen würde. Daß die Hälfte der Auflage gegen Valuta verkauft werden konnte, mochte einen Teil des Geheimnisses beinhalten, das dieses Werk in der DDR möglich machte. Für den Westen war formal so neu nicht, was da entstand, immerhin hatte schon Paul Klee die Reduktion von Kunst auf eine Ursprache versucht. Aber das Erscheinen in der DDR, deren Kunstdoktrin offiziell noch immer dem sozialistischen Realismus und der Figürlichkeit verpflichtet ist, belegte erweiterte Wirkungsmöglichkeiten für Individualität. Das Werk war eher ein Objekt denn ein Kunstbuch, und es steckte ein alternativer Ansatz darin, denn es knüpfte an eine südamerikanische Indianerkultur an, welche die Natur nicht auszubeuten, sondern in Harmonie mit ihrer Umwelt zu leben suchte. Eigentlich hätte der DDR-Kulturbürokratie der kultisch-esoterische Mystizismus, der hier mit dem Erbe eines Naturvolks getrieben wurde, so wenig passen dürfen wie die radikale künstlerische Abstraktion, die der Leipziger Verlag da plötzlich auf den heimischen Markt brachte. Des Rätsels Lösung findet sich in der gehörigen Portion

List, die der ausgefuchste Verleger ins Feld zu führen verstand. Die DDR, erklärte er den verdutzten Funktionären, sei schon immer stolz darauf gewesen, für vom Untergang bedrohte Kulturen einzutreten und trotzte ihnen mit diesem Argument die Druckgenehmigung ab. Obendrein gelang es ihm, in der kulturpolitisch einflußreichen Ostberliner »Weltbühne« eine positive Kritik zu lancieren. Dieses »Novum«, stand da zu lesen, sprenge die »Fesseln der Konvention«, knüpfe an »verschüttete Kulturbegriffe« an und stelle die »letzte große Buchmanufakturarbeit des 20. Jahrhunderts« dar. Alle Achtung. Aber brauchte man wirklich Visionen, um mit Zähigkeit und List einige Millimeter Freiraum zu erweitern? Oder hatte der Verleger Glauben nötig, weil er zu jener Generation Deutscher zählte, denen man in ihrer Jugend eingebleut hatte, sie seien geboren, für »das heilige Deutschland« zu sterben? Ich kam mir plötzlich sehr nüchtern und sehr westlich vor.

Treffend beschreibt Uwe Johnson die in den Nachkriegsjahren bei den jungen Intellektuellen, Künstlern und Schriftstellern der DDR vorherrschende Stimmung (»Versuch eine Mentalität zu erklären«). Die Proklamation der sozialen Neuordnung habe auf jugendliche Gemüter anziehend gewirkt, die Eindeutigkeit des Antifaschismus sei verführerisch gewesen, ja selbst die Brutalität, mit der die deutschen Kommunisten ihre soziale Revolution in Gang setzten, habe ihren Eindruck nicht verfehlt. »Wer das Personal der Justiz, der Schule, der Verwaltung auswechselt, wer da enteignet und verhaftet und verurteilt, der hat den Staat und die Macht dazu. Noch das Irrationale an der neuen Art von Rechtsprechung machte denken oder glauben: dies ist auf ewig. Die Wirklichkeit mochte noch nicht richtig sein: vorhanden war sie.« Ein Stück dieser Stimmung findet sich noch in Christa Wolfs Erzählung »Der geteilte Himmel«, in der die Heldin Rita Seidel sich gegen ihren in den Westen gegangenen Geliebten Manfred und für die neue sozialistische Gesellschaft entscheidet, auch wenn diese noch mit vielen Mängeln und Fehlern behaftet ist. Der Roman von Rita, die als junge Dorfbuchhalterin einer Versicherungsfiliale von einem »Bevollmächtigten für Lehrerwerbung« entdeckt, als künftige Pädagogin für den Staat rekrutiert und zum Studium geschickt wird, erschien 1963, dem Jahr, in dem Walter Ulbricht die Schriftsteller der DDR aufforderte: »Vereint eure Kräfte, um die Schönheit und Wahrheit unserer Wirklichkeit zu gestalten, damit das Wahre und Schöne, das in den menschlichen Beziehungen, auch in den menschlichen Triumphen und Niederlagen, seinen Ausdruck findet! Gebt Zeugnis von der großen Wahrheit, daß das Leben unserer Zeit auch mit seinen inneren und äußeren Konflikten lebenswerter und liebenswerter ist.« Was Rita vom realen Sozialismus während ihres Praktikums in einer Waggonfabrik erfährt, schildert Christa Wolf so schonungslos, daß er gewiß nicht in jener Schönheit erstrahlt, die sich der Parteichef erträumte. Aber gerade dadurch gewann der Roman Wahrhaftigkeit. Da fehlt es vor allem an der Leistungsmotivation der Werktätigen, die DDR-Wirtschaftsexperten auch ein Vierteljahrhundert später noch so schmerzlich vermissen sollten: Da werden Brigadebilanzen geschönt und Normen gedrückt; da wird der reale Aufwand an Arbeitszeit verschleiert und der Betrieb um 3000 Mark geprellt. Eifernde dogmatische Jungfunktionäre reden von der Parteilinie »wie die Katholiken über die unbefleckte Empfängnis«, aber das positive Leitbild des Arbeiters, ein fünfzigjähriger Meister namens Meternagel, wurde zu unrecht geduckt. So aufopfernd kämpft er gegen Dummheit, Unfähigkeit und Schlamperei, daß er am Ende krank an Herz, Kreislauf und Nieren darniederliegt. Doch Christa Wolfs Heldin, die in diese Konflikte und Widersprüche hineingerät, ergreift schon bald Partei für jene, die am Ausbau und der Festigung der neuen Ordnung gegen alle Schwierigkeiten festhalten wollen. Ihr Verlobter Manfred kommt aus einem bürgerlichen Haus. Seine Mutter wird als vorgestrig, sein Vater als ewiger Opportunist und Mitläufer geschildert, der einst in der SA war und nach dem Krieg eines Tages mit dem neuen Parteiabzeichen im Knopfloch erschien. Nicht nur das Aufbegehren gegen die verlogene Moral der Eltern, auch Verachtung für die mangelnde Effizienz im sozialistischen Wissenschaftsbetrieb treibt den Doktoranden der Chemie in den Westen. Der Sozialismus, sagt Manfred, sei geschaffen für östliche Völker, die seien unverdorben durch Individualismus und höhere Zivilisation und könnten »die einfachen Vorzüge der neuen Gesellschaft voll genießen«. Rita dagegen kommt aus kleinen, »den Charakter festigenden Verhältnissen«, die einfache Lehren vermitteln – »gut, böse, richtig, falsch – instinktiv läuft das ab«. Sie folgt dem Verlobten für einige Tage nach Westberlin, doch fühlt sie sich vom westlichen Milieu abgestoßen. »Man ist schlimmer als im Ausland, weil man die eigene Sprache hört. Man ist auf schreckliche Weise in der Fremde.« Leuchtreklamen vom Typ »Neckermann macht's möglich« blieben für sie »geheime Chiffren, unentzifferbar«, die ganze Stadt war »aus einem anderen Stoff als anderswo: Aus einem Stoff fremden Lebens«. Weil sie den Westen als mit verlockenden Waren vollgestopfte Leere empfindet, wählt sie die Herausforderung, welche die Mitarbeit am Aufbau des Sozialismus bedeutet. Zwar fällt ihr die Absage nicht nur wegen des Verzichts auf den Geliebten schwer: »Alles wäre leicht...« läßt Christa Wolf ihre Heldin sagen, »wenn sie dort als ›Kannibalen‹ auf den Straßen herumliefen oder wenn sie hungerten oder wenn ihre Frauen rotgeweinte Augen hätten. Aber sie fühlen sich ja wohl. Sie bemitleiden uns ja. Sie denken: Da muß doch jeder auf den ersten Blick sehen, wer in diesem Land ärmer und wer reicher ist.« Nichtsdestoweniger sucht Rita ihr Glück im Kollektiv, im Aufbruch zu den Ufern einer neuen Ordnung. Es sind zuvorderst die Hoffnungen, für welche diese erst im Entstehen begriffene Gesellschaft steht, mit denen sie sich identifiziert.

Christa Wolfs »Geteilter Himmel« brach in der DDR ein Tabu: Erstmals wurde davon gesprochen, daß einer Grund hat wegzugehen, und erstmals waren die Gründe einigermaßen einleuchtend beschrieben. Doch steckt im DDR-positiven Ende der Erzählung eine ordentliche Portion vom Pathos der ersten Aufbaujahre, auch viel Gläubigkeit, die den Widersprüchen, Mißlichkeiten und Entartungen des realen Sozialismus immerzu trotzen muß. Nicht zufällig spielt ein Angehöriger jener Generation eine Rolle, deren Idealismus die Nazis mißbrauchten – einer von denen, »die nach dem abgetanen System der Faschisten«, so jedenfalls sah es Uwe Johnson, die neue Autorität als die von Haus aus bessere respektierten, schlicht weil sie jetzt eine antifaschistische war. Jener Bevollmächtigte für Lehrerwerbung, der Rita aus der dörflichen Idylle reißt, ein Arbeitersohn, wollte zum Werwolf gehen wie Erich Loest, als der Krieg zu Ende ging. »Damals hatten wir Haß und Verachtung verdient und erwartet«, sagt Schwarzenbach, doch »die Partei war nachsichtig und geduldig mit uns, wenn auch anspruchsvoll«. Für Rita wird er zum Ersatzvater, politischen Erzieher und persönlichen Ratgeber. Im Zweifel verteidigt er die humanitären Ideale des Programms gegen den Absolutheitsanspruch des Apparats. Gegen eifernde Dogmatiker führt er jene revolutionäre Tugend der Geduld ins Feld, deren Vorzüge er in den ersten Nachkriegsjahren an sich selbst erfahren hatte: »Immer noch versuchen manche zu diktieren, statt zu überzeugen. Aber wir brauchen keine Nachplapperer, wir brauchen Sozialisten.«

Im Rückblick mag für das kulturpolitische Binnenklima der DDR der frühen 60er Jahre nicht nur typisch sein, daß die sehr reale Schilderung der Auseinandersetzungen unter den Arbeitern einer Waggonfabrik bei einigen auf Kritik stieß. Das verstand sich beinahe von selbst und konnte doch nicht verhindern, daß der Roman ein Erfolg wurde und Konrad Wolf das meistdiskutierte Werk der damaligen DDR-Literatur verfilmte. Wichtiger war schon der Vorwurf, die Autorin sei der Gefahr der »Gegenüberstellung von Weg und Ziel des Sozialismus« erlegen. Damit war die Tatsache gemeint, daß Christa Wolf den wahrhaft vorbildlichen Erbauer des Sozialismus, Meister Meternagel, als einen Puritaner und Asketen dargestellt hatte, der sein persönliches Wohlergehen auf dem Altar der großen Sache opferte. Persönliches Glück, so beharrten die ideologischen Gralshüter unter den Kritikern, dürfe völlig legitim auch schon in der ersten Aufbauphase –

auf dem Weg zum Sozialismus – genossen werden und sei nicht erst am Ziel aller Anstrengungen einzufordern – an jenem utopisch fernen Tag, an dem sich der Sozialismus einmal vollenden soll. Gerade in den Jahren, in denen die Partei den Massen einen sprunghaften Anstieg des Lebensstandards in Aussicht stellte, schien der Gedanke, der hinter dem Vorwurf an die Adresse der Autorin steckte, einleuchtend: Der »besten Sache der Welt« werden die Arbeiter gleichgültig gegenüberstehen und auf die Dauer in Scharen davonlaufen, wenn sie dafür immer nur hart zu schuften haben und konkrete Verbesserungen ihrer Lage auf den St. Nimmerleinstag verschoben werden. So lobte der Zirkel schreibender Arbeiter des VEB Waggonwagenbau Ammendorf in einem Brief an Christa Wolf zwar die offene Darstellung von Konflikten im Betrieb und half damit, kritische Einwände aus anderer Richtung abzufangen. Aber sie betonten, daß der immerwährende Kampf der Arbeiterklasse für eine bessere Gesellschaft nicht nur Opfer verlange, sondern schon jetzt die individuelle Glückserfüllung gefördert hätte.

Man tut der inzwischen in Ost und West meist geachteten lebenden deutschen Schriftstellerin gewiß keinen Tort an, wenn man in diesem Zusammenhang an einige Fakten ihrer Biographie erinnert. Christa Wolf, Jahrgang 1929, promovierte bei Hans Mayer in Leipzig. Schon als junge Studentin trat sie 1949 in die SED ein. Als Lektorin und Schriftstellerin, die sich offen bekannte, machte sie in der Partei zunächst auch Karriere. Von 1963 bis 1967 war sie Kandidatin des Zentralkomitees der SED. »Wenn wir Partei sagen, sagen wir, wir! und davon lassen wir uns nicht durch irgendwelche Lobhudeleien von irgendeiner Seite abbringen, die das manchmal versucht«, erklärte sie ihren Genossen auf dem 11. Plenum des ZK im Dezember 1965. Sie sei froh, in der DDR zu leben und zu schreiben. Dabei schlug sie sich in ihrem Diskussionsbeitrag dialektisch geschickt und wacker für eine liberale Handhabung der Reisemöglichkeiten: »Wenn man zurückkommt, sagt man: Zu Hause! Und dieses Gefühl ist bei allen Kollegen, die ich kenne und die in Westdeutschland gewesen sind und dort ihren Mann gestanden haben, in den mir bekannten Fällen wirklich der Fall.« Im Westen sei sie jedoch gefragt worden, ob sie als Schriftstellerin nicht auch zu Kritik an der eigenen Gesellschaft verpflichtet sei. Da habe sie geantwortet: »In dem Moment, da ich der Ansicht wäre, daß es richtig und nötig wäre, an den Grundlagen unserer Gesellschaft zu zweifeln, würde ich versuchen, so zu schreiben. Dieser Ansicht bin ich aber nicht. Ganz im Gegenteil, ich bin der Ansicht, daß die sozialistische Gesellschaft nicht nur die Gesellschaft an sich weiterentwickelt, sondern die einzige Gesellschaft ist, die der Literatur und der Kunst eine reife Entwicklung ermöglicht.«

Das wurde immerhin zu einer Zeit gesagt, in der Hans Mayer, Christa Wolfs Doktorvater, Leipzig verlassen hatte und Ernst Bloch in den Westen nachgefolgt war, weil er nicht mitschuldig werden wollte – »durch Ohnmacht oder Zuschauen an einer Vergiftung der Seelen«. Zu einer Zeit, in der Stefan Heym, Wolf Biermann und Robert Havemann als Skeptiker an den Pranger gestellt wurden, befallen von einer Krankheit namens »Zweifelsucht«. Zu einer Zeit auch, in der SED-Kulturpapst Wilhelm Girnus den Lyriker Günter Kunert, der gewagt hatte, ein Gedicht über Kafka zu schreiben, offiziell ermahnte, »zurückzukehren aus den hoffnungslosen, grauen Gefilden von Kafka und Benn in die lebensstarke Welt des umfassenden Aufbaus des Sozialismus«. Und es wurde von Christa Wolf auf jenem für die Kulturpolitik der DDR wahrlich fatalen 11. Plenum gesagt, auf dem Erich Honecker viele Schriftsteller, Dramatiker und Filmkünstler abkanzelte, weil sie den »schöpferischen Charakter der Arbeit der Menschen negieren und dem Sozialismus fremde, schädliche Tendenzen und Auffassungen« verbreiteten. Besonders Heiner Müllers Stück »Der Bau« hatte den Zorn des späteren Parteichefs erregt, weil die DDR-Wirklichkeit darin als »schweres, opferreiches Durchgangsstadium zu einer illusionären, schönen Zukunft« – als »die Fähre zwischen Eiszeit und Kommunismus« geschildert werde. Honecker machte in seiner Rede wider den »spießbürgerlichen Skeptizismus« eine erstaunlich simple Rechnung auf: »Wollen wir die Arbeitsproduktivität und damit den Lebensstandard weiter erhöhen, woran doch alle Bürger der DDR interessiert sind, dann kann man doch nicht nihilistische, ausweglose und moralzersetzende Philosophien in Literatur, Film, Theater, Fernsehen und in Zeitschriften verbreiten.« Und er drohte auch offen allen, die sich der von der Partei geforderten Sinngebungskunst zur Hebung des Leistungswillens der Werktätigen verweigern würden: »Sie irren sich, wenn sie die Arbeitsteilung in unserer Republik so verstehen, daß die Werktätigen die sozialistische Gesellschaft aufopferungsvoll aufbauen und andere daran nicht teilzunehmen brauchen, daß der Staat zahlt und andere das Recht haben, den lebensverneinenden, spießbürgerlichen Skeptizismus als alleinseligmachende Religion zu verkünden.«

Kein Wunder, wenn dieser bedingungslose Glauben an die neue Ordnung und die in ihr enthaltenen Chancen für die freie Entwicklung der Person und der Literatur, von dem die Rede der Kandidatin des ZK auf diesem 11. Plenum durchdrungen war, bald vielerlei Brechungen erfahren sollte. Seit dem Erscheinen ihres Buches »Nachdenken über Christa T.« 1968 jedenfalls ist, allen Auszeichnungen und Nationalpreisen zum Trotz, eine stetig wachsende Distanz zwischen Partei und Schriftstellerin zu verzeichnen. Das Thema des neuen Werks war schon im »Geteilten Himmel« mit der Figur Schwarzenbachs angeklungen, der ja den Menschen gegen das Dogma verteidigt. Nun wird es konsequent, aber mit durchweg pessimistischem Grundtenor aufgegriffen. Denn diese Christa T., die einst mit großem Idealismus und begeistert am Aufbau der besseren Zukunft teilgenommen hat, scheitert letztlich am Widerspruch von Utopie und Wirklichkeit. Schritt für Schritt zieht sie sich aus der Gesellschaft zurück, kapselt sich völlig ab und stirbt. Der Möglichkeit der individuellen Selbstverwirklichung im Sozialismus wird damit eine wahrhaft klägliche Diagnose gestellt. Kulturfunktionäre der Partei vermißten die optimistisch-fröhliche Perspektive.

Eher als mit den unbeschwert Fröhlichen hält Christa Wolf es eben mit den Sensiblen und den Empfindsamen. In ihrem

Buch »Kein Ort. Nirgends« spann sich das Leitmotiv von »Christa T.« fort – in anderer Zeit und mit einem erdachten Dialog zwischen dem Dramatiker Heinrich von Kleist und der Stiftsdame Caroline von Günderode, in dem es um die Lebensfähigkeit in der Gesellschaft nach der Französischen Revolution von 1789 geht. Beide schieden freiwillig aus dem Leben. Im »Neuen Deutschland« wurde Christa Wolf daraufhin bescheinigt, das Menschliche gerate ihr zu einem »isolierten Bezirk«, denn Humanismus und objektive gesellschaftliche Realität fielen bei ihr auseinander. »Die Literatur als Sachwalter der Menschlichkeit entsagt ihrer Bindungen an Politik und Ökonomie.« Völlig unmarxistisch glaube die Autorin offenbar, die Welt lasse sich mit Hilfe der Moral verändern. Das einzig legitime Mittel der Veränderung, so las sich das, ist und bleibt der Klassenkampf, geführt von der Avantgarde der Arbeiterklasse, der Partei. So der irrenden Genossin Christa Wolf ins Stammbuch geschrieben von Professor Klaus Jarmatz, Literaturhistoriker an der Parteihochschule der SED.

Die Kritik fiel noch eindeutiger und heftiger aus, als die Autorin auf dem Höhepunkt der Diskussion um die Nachrüstung ihre »Kassandra« vorlegte, eine moderne Deutung der antiken Seherin, die kommendes Unheil voraussagt, vor tragischen Fehlern warnt, auf die aber keiner hören will. In ihrer Erzählung benutzt Christa Wolf die Figur der Kassandra, um die Blindheit aufzuzeigen, mit der die eigene Welt in den Untergang treibt. Verantwortlich dafür ist nach ihrer Deutung vor allem aggressives Besitzdenken, das im jahrtausendealten, auf Wettbewerb ausgerichteten und maskulin geprägten Verhalten seinen Ursprung hat. Wie schwer sich die Wächter über die Reinheit der Lehre beim Zentralkomitee mit diesem Werk taten, zeigt allein schon der Erscheinungstermin: Der Aufbau-Verlag in Ostberlin hatte »Kassandra« für Sommer 1983 angekündigt, doch zunächst brachte es der westdeutsche Luchterhand Verlag auf den Markt – im Herbst 1983. Erst im Frühjahr 1984 lag »Kassandra« in kleiner Auflage in den DDR-Buchhandlungen aus – mit Streichungen. Sie betrafen nur die vier begleitenden Frankfurter Vorlesungen und waren korrekt durch eckige Klammern ausgewiesen, zwischen denen sich nun gesammelte Leere dehnte. Was dem Rotstift des Zensors zum Opfer gefallen war, zeugte von einer gleichermaßen kritischen Haltung gegenüber beiden Großmächten, über die sich Amerikaner bei bundesdeutschen Linken ärgerten. Es handelte sich meist um pazifistische Passagen.

Erstes Beispiel: Christa Wolf schreibt: »Die Nachrichten beider Seiten bombardieren uns mit der Notwendigkeit von Kriegsvorbereitungen, die auf beiden Seiten Verteidigungsvorbereitungen heißen.« Vom Zensor gestrichen, denn darin steckt eine unerlaubte Gleichsetzung der Systeme, wo doch das des Ostens immerzu das bessere und moralisch überlegene ist.

Zweites Beispiel: Christa Wolf schreibt: »Mit nichts ausgerüstet als dem unbändigen Wunsch, meine Kinder und Enkel leben zu lassen, erscheint mir das vielleicht ganz und gar Aussichtslose vernünftig: Einseitig abzurüsten (ich zögere – trotz der Reagan-Administration? Da ich keinen anderen Ausweg sehe: trotz ihrer!) und damit die andere Seite unter den Druck der Weltöffentlichkeit stellen.« Gestrichen. Die Partei lehrt: Der Friede muß bewaffnet sein.

Drittes Beispiel: Christa Wolf schreibt von der Müdigkeit, sich zu engagieren, und fragt, ob sich dahinter gar »Hoffnungsmüdigkeit« verberge. Ein Satz nur, doch auch er gestrichen. DDR-Bürger, meint die Partei, haben nicht nur nicht müde zu sein, sie sind auch gehalten, nie die Hoffnung fahren zu lassen.

So gab sich die Zensur wieder einmal selbst der Lächerlichkeit preis. Doch schwerer wogen Vorwürfe, die Schriftstellerin mache patriarchalisch-herrschaftliches Denken für den Zustand dieser Welt verantwortlich, die wissend der Katastrophe entgegengehe. Der erste Angriff gegen derart feministische Interpretationsversuche von Geschichte kam von Wilhelm Girnus, kaum daß erste Auszüge als Vorabdruck in der Ostberliner Zeitschrift »Sinn und Form« erschienen waren. Ein solcher Zugriff stehe für unerlaubte Naivität bei der Beurteilung historischer Prozesse. Nicht vom Gegensatz zwischen Mann und Frau, sondern von Klassenkämpfen sei die Geschichte geprägt. Daß »so ein blühender Unsinn in einem sozialistischen Land das Licht der Welt erblickt, das kann doch nicht wahr sein«, meinte Girnus, der lange Jahre selbst als Chefredakteur »Sinn und Form«, die wichtigste kulturpolitische Zeitschrift der DDR, geleitet hatte. Elegant parierte die Autorin den Angriff des pensionierten Altstalinisten. Sie zitierte einen »Klassiker«, dem Girnus den Respekt schlechterdings nicht verweigern konnte. Bei Friedrich Engels nämlich steht zu lesen: »Die erste Klassenunterdrückung (fällt zusammen) mit der des weiblichen Geschlechts durch das männliche.« Der erste Angriff auf den »Feminismus« der Christa Wolf, der von den hoffnungslos Vorgestrigen kam, die kaum mehr Verständnis fanden bei den Lesern, war damit erfolgreich abgeschlagen. Ernsthaftere Auseinandersetzung erforderte eine Kritik in »Sinn und Form«, die im Grundtenor weitaus wohlwollender, in der Art des Hinterfragens freilich auch gescheiter und deshalb herausfordernder war. Da wurde von Hans Kaufmann angemerkt, Christa Wolfs Verhalten zu wissenschaftlichem Denken sei von auffallenden Widersprüchen geprägt. Auf der einen Seite benötige sie Wissenschaft als »Klärbecken der poetischen Arbeit«, auf der anderen erhebe sie schwerwiegende Einwände gegen die Wissenschaft, »die aus der Polemik gegen das Patriarchat« erwüchsen. »Schon früher lasen wir bei Ch. Wolf, das Überwiegen von Rationalität und wissenschaftlich-technischem Fortschrittsdenken, verbunden mit Gefühlsarmut und kultureller Verantwortungslosigkeit, sei Attribut der Männer«, wurde ihr da mit Blick auf ihre Arbeit »Selbstversuch« entgegengehalten. »Beides dehnt sie nun auf die dreitausendjährige europäische Geschichte aus.« Der Kritiker fühlte sich freilich nicht nur dadurch provoziert. Zum Widerspruch sah er sich in erster Linie veranlaßt, weil sie in einigen Passagen der Frankfurter Vorlesungen der Geschichte vorgehalten hatte, »sie sei ungerecht gegen die Frau gewesen und wäre besser anders verlaufen«. Zwar formuliert Kaufmann sehr viel sublimer als Girnus, aber im

Grunde ist er mit ihm in der Sache durchaus einig, wenn er schreibt: »Das Katastrophale und Grausame der historischen Entwicklung – sie gleicht nach einem Wort von Marx jenem scheußlichen Götzen, der den Nektar aus den Schädeln der Erschlagenen trinkt – ist nur insofern moralisch zu betrachten, als dies zum Stachel wird, die Welt zu ändern. Für das Verhältnis der Geschlechter gilt in dieser Hinsicht nichts anderes als für die sonstigen Gebrechen und Verbrechen einer im sozialen Antagonismus sich bewegenden Geschichte.« Das klang unerhört gelehrt, gestelzt und aufgeblasen. Kritiker Kaufmann hatte sich jedoch von vornherein für befangen erklärt, weil die Schuldzuweisung an das männliche Denken, das für die Katastrophen der Menschheit verantwortlich sei, ihn (als Mann) nach dem Verständnis der Autorin für eine ernsthafte Auseinandersetzung mit ihr disqualifiziere.

Das war, wie gesagt, alles sehr viel seriöser vorgetragen als die altväterisch-verbissene Attacke eines Wilhelm Girnus, doch schimmerte in dieser Kritik immer noch reichlich viel Unverständnis für Gedankengänge durch, wie sie in der westlichen Welt seit Jahrzehnten gang und gäbe sind – seien es nun feministische oder psychoanalytische Denkansätze, die im geschlossenen scholastischen System des Marxismus-Leninismus mit einem Tabu belegt sind. Ich werde nicht so schnell vergessen, mit welchem Stolz mir der Verleger des Leipziger Reclam-Verlags ein Taschenbuch mit Auszügen aus den Schriften von Sigmund Freud zeigte: »Dies ist der erste Band, der von Freud in der DDR erscheint!« Für ihn war das ein unerhörtes Erfolgserlebnis, denn er hatte DDR-Lesern bis dahin von den Zensoren des Apparats unterschlagenes Gedankengut, wenn auch bruchstückweise, zugänglich gemacht. Es stimmte ja auch, daß kulturpolitisch damit ein Signal gesetzt war, das auf mehr Öffnung deutete. Leider zeigte ein Blick auf den Klappentext, daß dieses Wagnis durch einen geradezu akrobatischen Trick an Verlogenheit (oder war es nur Schlitzohrigkeit?) sanft abgepuffert werden mußte. Auf der Rückseite des Taschenbuch-Covers stand nämlich zu lesen, daß die Gegner Sigmund Freuds vor allem im konservativen Bürgertum zu Hause waren, weil der Begründer der Psychoanalyse die tradierte bürgerlich-sittliche Wertordnung auf gefährliche Weise hinterfragte. Freuds Lehre, heißt es da wörtlich, wurde »von Konservativen als ›Wiener Geschlechtsphilosophie‹ denunziert«. Der Sache nach mochte das ja stimmen. Nur hatten bürgerliche Verleger Freud publiziert, die kommunistischen Scholastiker ihn als Feind auf den Index gesetzt. Psychoanalyse wird auch heute in der DDR nicht gelehrt. Erst in jüngster Zeit sind Mediziner und Psychiater dazu übergegangen, die psychoanalytische Theorie Freuds zwar kritisch, aber zunehmend differenziert zu behandeln. Das gilt übrigens auch für das Unbewußte. Marxistische Ideologie wollte es bislang nicht wahrhaben und leugnete seine Existenz. Jetzt beginnt man zögernd, sich mit seiner offenbar unleugbaren Kraft und Gewalt auseinanderzusetzen.

»Der Schmelz ist weg vom Planeten, nicht?« – dieser Satz findet sich im jüngsten Werk von Christa Wolf. »Störfall« entstand unter dem Eindruck der Katastrophe von Tschernobyl, und noch entschiedener als in ihrer »Kassandra« löst sich die Autorin hier von jenem Geschichtsverständnis der schematischen Kategorien des Klassenkampfes, das den Funktionären so am Herzen liegt. Da wird nicht nur dem Glauben an den Fortschritt abgeschworen, ohne den man sich Marxismus schwerlich vorstellen kann. Da wird nicht mehr nach der Fehlentwicklung von Klassen, sondern nach der der menschlichen Gattung gefragt: »An welchem Kreuzweg ist womöglich die Evolution bei uns Menschen fehlgelaufen, daß wir Lustbefriedigung an Zerstörungsdrang gekoppelt haben?« Das Buch ist eine Art meditativer Monolog der Autorin, die von der Schreckensmeldung in einem Dorf in Mecklenburg erfährt. In Gedanken spricht sie mit dem Bruder, der sich in der fernen Großstadt einer Gehirntumor-Operation unterziehen muß. Penibel wird der Tagesablauf mitsamt all den fremden Begriffen eines Wissenschaftschinesisch protokolliert, das die Medienmacher mit Gewißheit selbst nicht verstanden, was sie natürlich nicht davon abhielt, ihre ebenso hilf- wie ahnungslosen Zuschauer damit zu überschütten: »15 milli-rem fallout pro Stunde« oder Jod 131 – »ein neuer Name für Gefahr wird in Umlauf gesetzt«. Am Rande sei vermerkt, daß die Nachrichten, auf die Christa Wolf in diesem Monolog Bezug nimmt – etwa der Rat, bei der Gartenarbeit vorsorglich Handschuhe anzuziehen oder eine Empfehlung zum Konsumverzicht, die den Bürgern selbst »die Lust am Schnittsalat und am Spinat« genommen hat – sämtlich aus westlichen Kanälen stammen müssen. Die DDR-Medien betrieben in den ersten Tagen nach Tschernobyl nämlich das genaue Gegenteil von Glasnost. Sie beschwichtigten. »O Himmel, strahlender Azur«, zitiert Christa Wolf aus Brechts »Ballade von den Seeräubern« und denkt zu dem Bruder: »Dieser makellose blaue Himmel entgeht Dir, dieses Sinnbild der Reinheit, auf dem sich heute die bangen Blicke von Millionen treffen.« Sie erzählt auch von der radioaktiven Wolke, die »unserer großen Fernsehfamilie« gehört, als das »Schmuddelkind, sozusagen«. In den Nachrichten der »Aktuellen Kamera« kam es überhaupt nicht vor.

Doch zu den Konsequenzen, welche die Existenz dieses Schmuddelkinds nach Meinung der Autorin geradezu kategorisch zu ziehen gebietet, »gehört als nicht geringster Verzicht der Verzicht auf den Feind«. Und damit reißen dann plötzlich Taue, an denen »unser Lebensnetz an gewissen Halterungen« bisher befestigt war. Denn ein solcher Feind ist natürlich auch der Klassenfeind. Deshalb steckt in dieser Überlegung ein für marxistische Scholastiker wahrlich radikaler Ansatz: Er erklärt den Abbau der tradierten Feindbilder zur Voraussetzung für das Überleben der Menschheit. Schlimmer noch. Wenn auch in Frageform, denkt Christa Wolf diesen Gedanken weiter, indem sie ihn kritisch gegen die Geschichte der radikalen Linken wendet, zu der sie sich auch in dieser Frage noch bekennt: »Waren wir Monster«, fragt die Schriftstellerin, »als wir uns um einer Utopie willen – Gerechtigkeit, Gleichheit, Menschlichkeit für alle –, die wir nicht aufschieben wollten, diejenigen bekämpften, in deren Interesse diese Utopie nicht lag (nicht liegt) und, mit unseren eigenen Zweifeln, diejenigen, die zu bezweifeln wagten, daß der Zweck die Mittel hei-

ligt?« Damit wird das Thema »Stalin und seine Opfer« ange-
schnitten, auf das später in anderem Zusammenhang zurückzukommen ist. Christa Wolf selbst hat sich dazu selten eingelassen, am überzeugendsten vielleicht in ihrer Rede anläßlich
der Annahme des westdeutschen Schillerpreises im Herbst
1983. Da beschwor sie die Erinnerung an einen schwäbischen
Arbeiter und Kommunisten, Friedrich Schlotterbeck, eines Illegalen im Leipzig des Jahres 1933, der unter Hitler im Zuchthaus saß: »Er hat nie die Versuchung verspürt, seine Feinde
zu verteufeln«, sagte die Preisträgerin damals in Stuttgart.
»In Hitler und seinen Mannen hat er nie den Teufel und die
Teufelsbrut gesehen.« Aber sie fügte hinzu: »Er hat sich auch
keinen Götzen geschaffen, von denen die Bewegung nicht frei
blieb, der er angehörte: Auch sie gezeichnet durch die Geschichte der Deutschen, deren Produkt sie ja ist, anfällig zu
Zeiten für irrationale Handlungen, deren eine Frieder Schlotterbeck wiederum, diesmal durch die eigenen Genossen, unter
falschen Anschuldigungen ins Gefängnis brachte.«

Christa Wolf ist heute eine Art Kultfigur für die jüngere
Generation, in beiden deutschen Republiken, geschätzt als
ebenso kritische wie moralische Instanz. Auf bewundernswer-
te Weise hat sie sich freigeschrieben von Dogma und blinder
Gläubigkeit. Auf die ihr eigene beharrliche, analytische, aber
auch sanfte Art, hat sie sich internationale Reputation und
Unabhängigkeit erkämpft, die inzwischen auch die parteiamt-
lich bestellten Zensoren im großen grauen Haus am Werder-
schen Markt respektieren müssen. In vielem wird sie der Partei, der sie noch immer angehört, immer voraus bleiben, in
manchem aber hat der Apparat längst zu ihr aufschließen
müssen. Wenn die SED im Zeichen des »Neuen Denkens« den
Imperialisten im Westen heute einräumt, was vor wenigen
Jahren undenkbar war: Friedensfähigkeit, dann erscheinen die
vom Sekretariat des SED-Zentralkomitees erzwungenen Aus-
lassungen in den Vorlesungen zur »Kassandra« heute als ein
schlechter Witz. Damals wurde moniert, daß Christa Wolf
nicht nur die aggressiven westlichen Imperialisten, sondern
auch die eo ipso friedliche Sowjetmacht des Hangs zur Auf-

und Überrüstung beschuldigte. Spätestens seit der Unterzeichnung des INF-Vertrages durch Gorbatschow und Reagan dürfte sich die Autorin bestätigt fühlen. Da wurde nämlich offenbar, daß die Sowjets weit mehr Raketen verschrotten müssen als die westliche Vor- und Gegenmacht. Parteizensoren, die auf taktische Gebote der Tagespolitik verpflichtet sind, erweisen sich allemal als kurzatmig gegenüber Literatur, die eher Prinzipielles im Sinn hat.

Mit der Zeit hat auch Christa Wolf gelernt, sich zur Wehr zu setzen und zurückzuschlagen. In einem Interview mit der Ostberliner »Wochenpost« monierte sie nach Erscheinen ihrer »Kassandra«: »Es hat aus meiner Sicht bei uns jahrelang eine Anmaßung von Kritik und Theorie gegenüber Schreibenden und ihren Arbeiten gegeben. Es ist aber das eine, darum zu wissen, und etwas anderes, mit schwerwiegenden persönlichen Vorwürfen fertig zu werden. Bei mir hat das dazu geführt, daß ich das eine oder andere Buch weniger geschrieben habe. Und dazu, daß ich mich auf das besann, was ich wirklich will und muß.«

Sicher stritt Christa Wolf nicht so heftig und leidenschaftlich wider Kritiker in Partei und Schriftstellerverband wie etwa Stefan Heym. Der wies Honeckers Kritik an seiner Person auf dem 11. Plenum in einer Rede vor der Vollversammlung des Berliner Schriftstellerverbandes mit Verve zurück und überführte Ulbrichts damaligen Kronprinzen beinahe der arglistigen Täuschung. Honecker hatte sich nämlich auf Briefe Werktätiger berufen, denen zufolge Heym zu den »ständigen negativen Kritikern der Verhältnisse in der DDR« gehöre. Heym wies nach, daß die »Werktätigen« beamtete Funktionäre des Kulturbunds und des Kulturdezernats des Berliner Stadtbezirks Pankow waren. Nach der Ausweisung Biermanns rechnete er, wiederum vor Berliner Schriftstellern, im März 1977 mit dem SED-Chef von Berlin ab, daß die Fetzen flogen: »Kritik ist immer negativ«, hielt er Konrad Naumann entgegen, der sich gern populistisch als Stimme des Volkes gab und immer nach dem Positiven fragte. Energisch verwahrte sich Heym gegen die Lösung ideologisch strittiger Fragen mittels Ausschluß aus dem Verband oder der Partei. Zwei Jahre später, vor dem Plenum der schreibenden Kollegen, machte er dann mit bis dahin unerhörter Deutlichkeit Front gegen die Eingriffe der Funktionäre: »Die Zensurbehörden des Fürsten Metternich wurden wenigstens von dem Schriftsteller Gentz geleitet, einem sehr geistreichen und sehr gescheiten Mann. Und die Zensur der russischen Zaren war immerhin bereit, Karl Marx in Rußland erscheinen zu lassen. Welch kritischer Denker darf hierzulande gedruckt werden?« Er sagte das 1979, natürlich als ein Opfer der Zensur. Ähnlich mutige Töne sollten erst acht Jahre später wieder auf einem Schriftsteller-Plenum zu hören sein, als Günter de Bruyn erklärte: »Die Leser werden bevormundet, die Schreiber entmündigt und manche werden veranlaßt, das Land zu verlassen, was nicht nur ihnen und den Lesern schadet, sondern auch dem Land.« Und Christoph Hein scheute sich nicht, die Zensur als überlebt, nutzlos, paradox, menschenfeindlich und volksfeindlich zu bezeichnen. Das allerdings zu einer Zeit, als es längst möglich war, sich auf das Beispiel Glasnost zu berufen, das Gorbatschow in Moskau gab.

Heyms Roman »Fünf Tage im Juni«, eine kritische, aber der sozialistischen Sache wohlgesonnene Darstellung der Ereignisse des 17. Juni, durfte in der DDR nie erscheinen, und das staatliche Büro für Urheberrechte suchte den unbequemen Schreiber, der unermüdlich die Freiheiten der Französischen Revolution für den Sozialismus anmahnte, wegen angeblicher Devisenvergehen zu kriminalisieren. Die neueren Bücher Heyms sind seither nur noch im Westen erschienen. Daß dieser Autor politischer diskutierte, hat damit zu tun, daß er vom Journalismus kam. Und wenn er weniger als andere bereit war, ein Blatt vor den Mund zu nehmen, dann hat das mit seiner Biographie zu tun. Der jüdische Sozialist emigrierte 1933 und kämpfte im Krieg auf der Seite der Amerikaner gegen Hitlerdeutschland. Als der linientreue Verbands-Vorsitzende Hermann Kant die Schikanen gegen Heym verteidigte, antwortete dieser bissig: »Wer in der falschen Uniform und mit den falschen Abzeichen in ein falsches Lager geriet, sollte lieber nicht gegen die zu Felde ziehen, die damals in der richtigen Uniform auf der richtigen Seite für die richtige Sache kämpften.« Keines der kritischen Werke Heyms, so besonders sein Roman »Collin«, wurde in der DDR verlegt. Collin ist ein erfolgreicher Schriftsteller, Spanienkämpfer und Westemigrant, der des ständigen Anpassungsdrucks überdrüssig wird und im Krankenhaus nun Memoiren schreibt, in denen er nichts verschweigen will.

Der aktive Kampf gegen Hitler garantiert Heym, wie einst Robert Havemann, eine Sonderstellung. Er darf relativ unbehelligt im Osten wohnen, die Grenze passieren und – freilich nur im Westen – publizieren. Heyms letzter Roman, »Schwarzenberg«, beschreibt den Traum eines dritten deutschen Weges zwischen Kommunismus und Kapitalismus am Beispiel einer weder von den Sowjets noch den Amerikanern in den ersten Nachkriegswochen besetzten Exklave im Erzgebirge. Auf einer Pressekonferenz auf der Buchmesse in Leipzig begründete der Chef des Verlags »Der Morgen«, in dem frühere Heym-Werke noch immer erscheinen, warum »Schwarzenberg« der zahlreichen Heym-Gemeinde in der DDR vorenthalten bleibt: »Die Prüfung dieses Romans im Verlag hat leider zu einem negativen Ergebnis geführt. Die Kollegen weisen darauf hin, daß die literarische Qualität dieses Buches sie nicht befriedigt. Hinzu kommt, daß der Autor in diesem Buche... einige Thesen vertritt, insbesondere über die Rolle der USA und der UdSSR nach Ende des Krieges, die der historischen Wahrheit widersprechen.« Er hätte es auch kürzer sagen können: Ihm und der SED paßte die ganze Richtung nicht. Heym freilich läßt sich das nicht anfechten. Als ich die Erlaubnis erhielt, ihn zu seinem 70. Geburtstag in seiner Dachstube in der Rabindranath Tagore-Straße in Berlin-Grünau zu interviewen, erklärte er verschmitzt: »Ich – das weiß jeder – bin für den Sozialismus und meine, daß er unter anderem auch Meinungsfreiheit beinhaltet...« Ich fragte nach: »Also sind Sie nicht für diesen realen Sozialismus, wie er jetzt existiert?« Heym antwortete: »Ich bin für den wirklichen Sozialismus.«

Stefan Heyms harter Ausfall gegen Hermann Kant traf einen, der mit Sprache witzig, gelegentlich deftig zu jonglieren weiß, einen Fabulierer, der stolz ist auf den Aufstieg vom armen Gärtnerssohn und gelernten Elektriker zum Schriftsteller und Träger des Nationalpreises I. Klasse. Ein Werk, das über seinen Weg Aufschluß gab, erschien relativ spät unter dem Titel »Der Aufenthalt«. Der Roman schildert in Anlehnung an Kants Biographie den Reifeprozeß eines deutschen Soldaten in polnischer Kriegsgefangenschaft. Da sitzt der gefangene Wehrmachtsangehörige Mark Niebuhr wegen des Verdachts, ein polnisches Mädchen umgebracht zu haben, zusammen mit SS-Mördern in einem polnischen Gefängnis ein und erfährt durch die Erzählungen seiner Mitgefangenen von deutschen Verbrechern und deutscher Schuld. Ein Zeugnis der »Freundschaft zwischen Volkspolen und der DDR« hatte das »Neue Deutschland« diesen Roman genannt. Die offizielle Biographie Hermann Kants weist aus, daß er sich von 1945 bis 1949 in polnischer Gefangenschaft befand, im Arbeitslager Warschau ein Antifa-Komitee gründete, an einer Antifaschismus-Schule lehrte und nach der Entlassung in die DDR im Jahr 1949 der SED beigetreten ist. Für die Verfilmung des »Aufenthalts« bot die DEFA 1982 ihre Besten auf: Michael Kohlhaase schrieb das Drehbuch, Frank Beyer führte Regie, für die polnischen Untersuchungsoffiziere, welche die Vergangenheit des Verdächtigen Niebuhr durchleuchten, wurden namhafte polnische Schauspieler engagiert. Der Schluß des vorzüglich gemachten Films stellte ganz auf den Gerechtigkeitssinn der polnischen Offiziere ab, die nach langen Verhören die Unschuld des deutschen Soldaten erkennen und das Verfahren gegen ihn einstellen. Auf deutsche Betrachter wirkte er als gelungener, streckenweise ergreifender Beitrag zur Vergangenheitsbewältigung. Als solcher war er sicherlich gedacht, und in dieser Gewißheit hatte die DDR ihn für die Westberliner Filmfestspiele 1983 nominiert. Nach einer Demarche aus Warschau zog ihn Ostberlin in buchstäblich letzter Minute zurück, denn die der DDR brüderlich verbundenen Volkspolen waren der Überzeugung, der Film könnte antipolnische Emotionen wecken.

Kant zeigte sich bestürzt und sprach von einem »grandiosen Mißverständnis«. Der Schluß war, für ein deutsches Publikum einleuchtend, ganz auf die Freilassung von Frank Niebuhr zugespitzt. Gerade auf diese Schlußwendung hatte Regisseur Frank Beyer vertraut und sich deshalb in der ersten Hälfte des Films »harte, schneidende Situationen« erlaubt. Als die Unschuld des Deutschen erwiesen ist, verabschiedet sich der zuständige polnische Offizier mit der kühlen Frage: »Sie erwarten doch nicht, daß wir uns entschuldigen.« Darauf folgt der Abspann. Hermann Kant sagte damals auf meine Frage, ob dieser letzte Satz vielleicht der Grund für die polnische Demarche sei: »Die Situation verbot jede Art von Entschuldigung, zumal ja die Leistung vorliegt. Der Film zeigt sie: Eine Riesenmannschaft von untersuchenden Leuten, um die Unschuld eines einzigen Deutschen aufzuklären.« Zweifellos hatten die Polen übersensibel reagiert, auch wenn ein polnischer Kollege in Ostberlin mir diese Reaktion einigermaßen plausibel erklärte: »Im Film beginnt die Geschichte damit, daß Deutsche in polnischen Gefängnissen sitzen«, sagte er, »historisch war es aber genau umgekehrt: Da wurden zuerst die Polen in deutschen Konzentrationslagern eingesperrt.«

Der Fall wäre kaum der Erwähnung wert, hätte der Autor Kant in dieser Situation nicht etwas getan, was er anderen in seiner Funktion als Präsident des Schriftstellerverbandes als Loyalitätsverstoß ankreidete. Hat nämlich einer »seine Post über das Relais der Gegenseite laufen lassen, wird ihr die Annahme meist verweigert«, schrieb er 1980 in »Sinn und Form« über jene DDR-Autoren, die sich »westlicher Rundfunk- und Fernseheinrichtungen bedienten, um der Welt... ihre kritische Meinung kundzutun«. Nun aber nutzte er selbst unseren ARD-Kanal, um seine Position öffentlich zu verteidigen. In den Medien der DDR war weder das Zurückziehen des Films »Der Aufenthalt« noch die polnische Kritik an diesem Stück DDR-Vergangenheitsbewältigung mit auch nur einem Wort gemeldet worden. Offiziell existierte das Problem für die DDR-Öffentlichkeit wieder einmal nicht, doch natürlich wußten alle über die westlichen Rundfunksender bestens Bescheid. Da die SED offenbar gewillt war, den Fall im eigenen Land totzuschweigen, wurde Kant also selbst ein Opfer der Zensur, die er gegen andere verteidigte. Was lag da näher, als die »Post über das Relais der Gegenseite«, über unseren ARD-Kanal zu schicken – in der Hoffnung freilich, daß die Annahme diesmal nicht verweigert würde.

In demselben Artikel, in dem er die Nutzung westlicher Fernseheinrichtungen geißelte, findet sich ein Satz Kants, der als Maxime gelten darf für die Art, in der er den Schriftstellerverband leitet: »Es ist Klassenkrieg, und ob wir auch aufbegehren, er erfordert unsere Schuldigkeit.« Immer erwies sich Hermann Kant als getreuer Interpret und Exekutor der Parteilinie. Als eine Gruppe von Künstlern, darunter die namhaftesten des Landes – die Schauspieler Manfred Krug und Katharina Thalbach, die Schriftsteller Stephan Hermlin und Stefan Heym, Christa Wolf und Volker Braun – sich gegen die Ausweisung Biermanns in einem Protestbrief an die Parteispitze verwahrten, wurden viele mit seinem Einverständnis gerügt oder mit Ausschluß gestraft. Es gibt nicht den geringsten Zweifel, daß Kants Haltung jenen Aderlaß begünstigte, den die DDR-Literatur durch die Abwanderung Jurek Beckers und Sarah Kirschs, Günter Kunerts und Reiner Kunzes erlitten hat. Weil viele Autoren schreiben, was keine Zeitung drucken darf, werden Schriftsteller zu Identifikationsfiguren für die Kritischen im Lande – gerade deshalb ließ und läßt die SED viele von ihnen ziehen. Die meisten gingen schweren Herzens, aber weil sie nicht mehr veröffentlicht wurden, blieb ihnen keine andere Wahl. Kant verzeichnete solche Abgänge in einem Interview mit der »Frankfurter Rundschau« völlig kühl und gelassen: »Von dem Moment an, wo sich jemand in den Westen abgesetzt hat, habe ich eine ganz andere Haltung zu ihm. Unser Schriftstellerverband braucht sperrige und schwierige Leute. Gründe zum Weglaufen gibt es immer. Aber man darf sich davon nicht überwältigen lassen. Das Weglaufen ist die einfachere Lösung, die schwierigere ist die Selbstbehauptung.« Nicht nur Kants Opfer dürften diese Sätze als Gipfel des Zynismus empfinden. Wie denn, bitte, ist Selbstbehauptung möglich, wenn derselbe Mann, der sperrige Leute fordert, sie aus dem Verband wirft, kaum daß sie schwierig werden?

Die Außenansicht der Dinge legt diese Frage geradezu zwingend nahe. In der Binnensicht Kants stellt sich das natürlich anders dar. Da kämpft auch er bitter und zäh um Freiraum für Literatur und Kritik – freilich hinter verschlossenen Türen, im Gespräch mit den Zuständigen in der Partei, die ihn auf dem letzten Parteitag zum Mitglied des Zentralkomitees wählte. Als der FDJ-Funktionär Hartmut König auf dem Kulturkongreß in Leipzig Mitte der achtziger Jahre die negative Tendenz in Literatur und Malerei anprangerte, »da war es mühselig, die bisherige Linie zu wahren«, beteuerte Kant bei einem Mittagessen. In der Tat zielte die Kulturkampagne der FDJ damals auf eine radikale kulturpolitische Wende: Bühne und Film, bildende Kunst und Literatur sollten auf verbindliche, positive Leitbilder eingeschworen werden. Damals zog sich Hermann Kant vorübergehend aus dem Vorsitz des Schriftstellerverbandes zurück. Es hieß, er sei krank. Das stimmte, aber es war nur die halbe Wahrheit. Sein Rückzug hatte auch mit Politik zu tun. Kaum hatte er sich zurückgemeldet, sprach er betont von der Notwendigkeit der Kritik.

»Das Aufmunternde und Positive, das Aufbauende verlangen so viele von den Genossen«, gab er einmal zu verstehen, »da ist es manchmal schwer, mit dem Argument dagegenzuhalten, daß kritische Darstellung nichts zum Einsturz bringt, sondern Bewußtsein schafft. Viele befürchten, daß ein anarchistisches Stück das Theater zur Versammlung macht, von der Aufruhr ausgeht. Dabei ist das meiste nach Schluß der Vorstellung vergessen – im kalten Trabant oder beim Warten auf die Straßenbahn.« Als ich einmal klagte, uns werde jeder Antrag auf Drehgenehmigung in DDR-Kabaretts abgelehnt, sprach er kritisch von der »übergroßen Vorsicht der Genossen«, die vom Gegner abhängig mache. »Wir wollen nicht, daß die im Westen etwas ausschlachten, wenn wir etwas anprangern oder uns lustig machen. Wir fürchten immerzu, wir machen uns lächerlich. Und wenn wir Kritik untereinander austragen, haben wir Angst, es wird in den westdeutschen Medien hochgespielt. Das ist leider ein erheblicher Mangel an Souveränität.«

Es war nicht lange her, daß die Aufführung von Rainer Kerndls »Georgsberg« im Maxim Gorki-Theater überraschend abgesetzt worden war, als ich Hermann Kant wiedertraf. Kerndl, ein langjähriger Theaterkritiker des »Neuen Deutschland«, gehört zu denen in der DDR, die sich eher vom Westen abschotten wollen, als zu viele Kompromisse mit dem Klassenfeind zu schließen. Konsequent hatte er in seiner volksnahen Klamotte die Intershop-Mentalität der späten Honecker-Jahre aufs Korn genommen und dabei dem Volk aufs Maul geschaut. Da spielt der Bürgermeister einer grenznahen DDR-Kleinstadt in landschaftlich reizvoller Lage mit dem Gedanken, den Georgsberg an einen westlichen Hotelkonzern zu verpachten, damit endlich harte Valuta in die Gemeindekasse komme. Das Stück ist voller bissiger Anspielungen, denn was da geplant wird, existiert ja längst in Wirklichkeit in Form der Interhotels, die Luxus gegen harte D-Mark bieten. »Unser Georgsberg Privatgelände für irgendwelche Leute mit Valuta! Und Du und ich und alle ausgesperrt! Aus einem Stückchen Georgshausen, das dazugehört wie eben der Himmel und die Bäume!« empört sich Kerndls Hauptfigur Sebastian, der nach vielen Jahren in seine Heimat zurückkehrt. Sein alter Schulfreund Lauer aber fragt erstaunt: »Wo hast'n Du gelebt inzwischen? Lyrik! Geh mal die alten Wege. Weit kommst du nicht. Zum Buchenhain? Gesperrt. Da haben Ärzte ihre Datschen. Die Kreuzbergwiesen? Verbaut mit Ferienheimen. Der Finkenteich? Wenn Du da baden willst, heirat' erst eine Handwerkerstochter. Artfremde beißt der Hund. Privatgelände überall.«

So bittere Kritik am realen Sozialismus hatte das Theaterpublikum zwischen Elbe und Oder bisher nur von sowjetischen Autoren gekannt: Die Kerndl-Aufführung im Maxim Gorki-Theater war der Versuch, sowjetischen Stücken wie »Das Nest des Auerhahns« oder »Das Gemälde« von Granin endlich etwas Hausgemachtes an die Seite zu stellen, das sich an Mißständen im eigenen Land rieb. Doch Politbüromitglied Günter Mittag und, wie es hieß, selbst die Nummer 1 erblickten darin einen bösartigen Angriff auf ihre Wirtschaftspolitik. Nach wenigen Aufführungen war das Stück sang- und klanglos vom Spielplan verschwunden. Warum, fragte ich Hermann Kant, versteckt sich die DDR so gern hinter sowjetischer Gegenwartsdramatik? Seine Antwort klang distanziert: »Die Genossen sagen, wir liegen im Gegensatz zur Sowjetunion an der Grenzlinie der Systeme, und die Westmedien strahlen ein; wenn wir über unsere Fehler lachen, lachen die Kapitalisten hämisch mit.«

Es gibt viele, die diesen Hermann Kant angreifen, weil er nach außen immerzu die Parteilinie vertritt. Er fühlt sich damit natürlich verkannt, weil die von Außen seine Binnenwelt nicht kennen. Nach seinem Selbstverständnis ist er ja unermüdlich bestrebt, Freiraum für Kritik zu schaffen, aber eben auf jene unauffällige Weise, die dem Klassenfeind die Möglichkeit zur hämisch grinsender Einmischung nimmt. Ich verstehe den Zorn, den der aus der DDR abgewanderte Romancier Hans Joachim Schädlich (»Versuchte Nähe«) über ihn empfand, als sich Kant zur »Zweiten Berliner Begegnung« als Abgesandter des DDR-Schriftstellerverbandes mit kritischen Autoren aus dem Westen an einen Tisch setzte, um zu diskutieren, wie der Friede zu retten sei. Immerhin habe Kant, schrieb er in der »Zeit« im März 1984, über einen Schriftsteller, der gezwungen war, die DDR zu verlassen, den Satz geäußert: »Kommt Zeit, kommt Unrat.« Das sind in der Tat Worte, die sich bei aller Freude am Wortspiel auch für einen Schriftsteller-Präsidenten von selbst verbieten sollten.

Kant gehört nun einmal zu jenen, die sich nach dem Erlebnis des Zusammenbruchs einer neuen Autorität unterwarfen und die Partei als eine Art kollektives Über-Ich anerkannten. Sie mag taktische, in Einzelfällen tragische Fehler begehen, er steht zu ihr, weil sie im Zweifel immer auf dem rechten Wege ist. Wenn er sich dem Ratschluß des Politbüros unterwirft, das soviel wie das Exekutivkomitee der Avantgarde oder die

Vernunft, das »Hirn der Klasse« darstellt, dann darf er sich auf große Vorbilder berufen. Auf Anna Seghers zum Beispiel, die im November 1966 auf dem Jahreskongreß des Schriftstellerverbandes forderte, daß stets die rechte Perspektive durchzuschimmern habe: »Es muß möglich sein, bei einem Manuskript, bevor Arbeit und Geld hineingesteckt wird..., festzustellen: Ist die Arbeit schädlich, womöglich gar feindlich? Dann darf sie nicht herauskommen. Ist sie jedoch von einem richtigen Standpunkt aus geschrieben und enthält gleichwohl Stellen, die Kritik nötig machen? Solche Arbeiten sollten veröffentlicht und offen diskutiert werden.« War das nun der Ruf nach der Zensur oder der Ruf nach der Kritik? Wenn Kant Geduld fordert, denkt er in Fortschritten und Freiräumen oft in der Größenordnung von winzigen Scheibchen – aber auch ein Mann wie Heiner Müller meint, vieles lasse sich nur millimeterweise diskutieren und bewegen. Viele derer, die Kant des Taktierens auf der jeweils letzten, gerade gültigen Parteilinie bezichtigen, haben oft genug lange selbst mittaktiert. In einer Gesellschaft, der man die marxistisch-leninistische Ideologie als Lehr- und Denkgebäude überstülpt, ist Taktik ein selbstverständliches Mittel für Erfolg, vulgär-darwinistisch gesagt, fürs Überleben. Persönliches Fortkommen erfordert Anpassung, Erweiterung des Freiraums ist fast nie durch offene Opposition, sondern meist nur auf der Basis wohlwollend-kritischen Mitgehens möglich. Der dialektische Materialismus, auf den die Partei als Weltanschauung eingeschworen ist, das Spiel von den Widersprüchen, in denen sich der Fortschritt entfaltet, bedeutet für den sozial-realistischen Alltag: Taktik als Mitte zwischen Anpassung und Widerstand.

»Hermann Kant ist ein verläßlicher Freund seinen Freunden, ein verläßlicher Genosse seinen Genossen, ein verläßlicher Feind unseren Feinden, denen, die der Welt ans Leben wollen, und denen, die ihnen ihre dunklen Worte verleihen.« So zu lesen in »Sinn und Form«, geschrieben von Dieter Schlenstedt zu Kants 60. Geburtstag. Ob er, »der verläßliche Funktionär«, sich über solches Lob gefreut hat?

197

Stephan Hermlin wird im Westen gelegentlich als DDR-Staats-dichter geschmäht. Man tut ihm Unrecht damit, denn er ist einer, der unter schwierigen Bedingungen Mutiges sagt und auf eigenen Gedanken beharrt. Das tut der Tatsache keinen Ab-bruch, daß er dennoch der Partei, der er sich schon als 16jähriger anschloß, treu geblieben ist. Nur hat er nicht, vor allem in letzter Zeit, jede ihrer taktischen Wendungen mitvollzogen: Hermlin ist ein Lyriker, Übersetzer und Schriftsteller aus jüdisch-groß-bürgerlichem Elternhaus. Wenn er heute Widerspruch einlegt, geschieht das selten heftig, schrill oder laut, sondern mit eher sanfter, »provokatorischer Bedenklichkeit«, die auf Sprachstil achtet und bei der sich Pathos und Ironie oft die Waage halten. Auf dem VIII. Schriftstellerkongreß der DDR 1978 in Ostberlin verwahrte er sich gegen eine Formulierung, nach der die Schrift-steller des Landes als eine Mannschaft zu betrachten seien: »Mannschaften im militärischen Sinne stehen unter dem Befehl von Offizieren, und die Mannschaft eines Schiffs hat die Wei-sungen ihres Kapitäns widerspruchslos zu befolgen«, merkte Hermlin an. »Aber der Verfasser des Artikels wollte wohl zum Ausdruck bringen, daß man die Schriftsteller der DDR einzeln genommen einander nicht gegenüberstellen sollte, daß man sie nicht einteilen sollte in schwarze und weiße Schafe – und darin gebe ich ihm durchaus recht. In der Tat haben Schriftsteller, wenn sie denn welche sind, gar nichts mit Schafen gemein. Sie sind Leute, die kaum unter einen Hut zu bringen sind.« Wichti-ger in dieser Rede war freilich sein Hinweis, die Existenz einer Literatur sei nicht deckungsgleich mit der von Staaten. Damit attackierte er eine Lieblingsvorstellung der Partei, nach der die neue sozialistische deutsche Nation, die sich in der DDR gebildet habe, natürlich auch über eine ihr spezifische geistige Zierde verfüge: Über eine »DDR-Nationalliteratur«. Bewußt bekann-te sich Hermlin demgegenüber als »deutscher Schriftsteller« und nannte die deutsche Literatur einen »alten, mächtigen Stamm«, der so leicht nicht abzuschaffen sei. Zwar existiere so etwas wie eine DDR-spezifische Literatur, aber sie gehöre eben zur »deutschen Literatur« wie die der Bundesrepublik, Öster-reichs oder der Schweiz.

Wenn es so etwas gäbe wie Deutsch-Links-Nationale, wäre Hermlin, sich auf die demokratisch-großdeutsche Konzeption von Marx und Engels berufend, vielleicht einer von ihnen? Als ich ihn 1982 fragte, ob noch eine deutsche Nation als grenzüberschreitender Begriff existiere, erhielt ich die Antwort: »Es steht nicht nur für mich, sondern im allgemeinen fest, daß sich Nationen über lange Zeiträume hinweg entwikkeln und daß sie auch nicht von einem Tag zum andern entschwinden.« Und auf die Frage, ob ein Gesamtdeutschland für alle Zukunft auszuschließen sei, sagte er ohne Einschränkung und jedes Zögern: »Nein, ganz sicher nicht. Die Geschichte hat die Eigenschaft, daß sie sehr lang ist.« Damit Hermlin hier kein Unrecht widerfährt, sei ausdrücklich angemerkt, daß er an anderer Stelle etwa bekannte: »Ich lege keinen Wert auf Gesamtdeutschland.« Wenn er, im Gegensatz zu vielen westdeutschen Intellektuellen, keine Schwierigkeiten hat, Deutscher zu sein, dann hat das sicher mit seiner Biographie zu tun. Er emigrierte, schloß sich in Frankreich der Résistance an, suchte später Zuflucht in der Schweiz. Schuldgefühle aus der Hitlerzeit belasten ihn nicht, denn er trat damals für ein anderes Deutschland ein. So ist er gern zu Hause in Deutschland, »diesem unglaublich spannenden Land«, ja er vermutet, daß er sich in anderen Ländern, »wo manches viel glatter verläuft«, wahrscheinlich langweilen würde. Das Deutschland, in dem er haust, ist ein großes, umfassendes geistiges Vaterland. Er hütet sich, das der SED peinliche Wort zu nennen, weil nach gängiger Bonner Vorstellung die deutsche Einheit darin schlummert wie dereinst Barbarossa im Kyffhäuser: Kulturnation. Aber wie anders wäre sein Zuhause zu verstehen?

Indes wäre es falsch, aus alledem zu schließen, daß er der DDR die Loyalität verweigere – ganz im Gegenteil: »Ich habe natürlich ein bestimmtes Heimatgefühl in der DDR«, so Stephan Hermlin zu dem Westberliner Verleger Klaus Wagenbach, »einfach deshalb, mag sie nun sein, wie sie will, weil sie die erste staatliche Verkörperung der deutschen Arbeiterbewegung ist, und alles, was diese Bewegung an Elend gekannt hat, ist bei ihr mit drin.« Eine kritische Solidarität also, die er Jahre später im Gespräch mit Günter Gaus unterstrich: Die DDR, sagte er da, brauche eine neue Zeit, »wo öffentliche Kritik sich an öffentlichen Dingen äußern kann«. Die antifaschistische Partei, der er angehöre, sei unvollkommen wie jede andere Partei und habe Fehler begangen. »Ich kann nur darauf drängen, daß diese Bewegung auch mit meiner Hilfe ihre Irrtümer überwindet. Aber ich kann mich nicht von ihr trennen.«

Hermlin mußte sich allerdings fragen lassen, ob er einige dieser Irrtümer nicht selbst mit zu vertreten hat. Nicht nur, daß er zu Zeiten des Kalten Krieges eine scharfe, polemische Feder schrieb. Den 17. Juni 1953 bezeichnete er damals als »schmutzigen faschistischen Putsch«; heute pflichtet er der differenzierten Darstellung der Ereignisse durch Stefan Heym in dessen »Fünf Tage im Juni« bei. Majakovskij, schrieb er, sei von Gegnern der Revolution zu Tode gepeinigt worden; heute räumt er ein, daß es »seine eigenen (und auch meine) Gesinnungsgenossen« waren. Die Bundesrepublik bezeichnete er nach dem Bau der Mauer in einem Brief an Günter Grass als »den gefährlichsten Staat der Welt«. Heute gibt er zu bedenken, er habe vom Staat des Adenauerschen roll-back geredet, nicht aber von der Bundesrepublik, wie sie sich unter Willy Brandt und Helmut Schmidt entwickelte. In einem Gespräch (mit Ulla Hahn) mit der Äußerung über Majakovskijs Tod konfrontiert, bekannte er Scham und Bitterkeit. »Ich könnte mich darauf hinauszureden versuchen, daß ich schlecht informiert war. Aber ich war schlecht informiert, weil ich nicht wirklich informiert sein *wollte*. Viele Jahre hindurch war ich von einer Angst besessen, eine Wahrheit zu erfahren, die mir unvereinbar mit der Sache zu sein schien, für die ich kämpfte. Später erst begriff ich, daß die ›gute Sache‹ nur zu verteidigen war, daß sie erst wirklich zur guten Sache wurde, wenn man ihre Fehler, ihre Irrtümer, ihre Untaten beim Namen nannte.« Was Hermlin damit sagt, brachte Heiner Müller auf den Punkt: »Die Entscheidung gegen Hitler schloß ein das Schweigen über Stalin. Das war ganz klar für die deutsche antifaschistische Emigration.«

Hermlin war auch einer der hohen Priester des Personenkults.

Sicherlich, damals konnte es keiner wissen,
Daß diese Nacht nicht mehr ganz so wie frühere war,
Eine Nacht, wie alle, vom Bellen der Hunde gesplissen,
Und die Wälder wie immer mit Wind in ihrem Haar.

Da werden bewußt Assoziationen an die Geburtsnacht in Bethlehem geweckt, doch der neue Erlöser – »an der Wand über der Wiege hingen beisammen Ahle und Hammer« – kommt unter »grünem grusinischen Mond« zur Welt. Und so endet die 1952 erschienene Ode Hermlins, der seine Lyrik unter anderem an Expressionisten wie Georg Heym geschult hat –, streng die Form, feierlich die Stimmung, überschwänglich der Sinn:

Im Gewölke der Blicke wie eine Schwinge gleitend
Schaun wir durch Explosionen der Knospen die Stadt
Überzogen von Völkern, sich selbst zum Siege geleitend,
Von Propellern entführt und rauschendem Rad.

Aus dem unendlichen Raunen von Inseln und Ländern
Hebt das Entzücken sich mit seiner Botschaft dahin,
Wo die Verheißungen leben und die Epochen verändern,
Namenlos sich die Zeit endlich selbst nennt: STALIN.

Nun hat ein jeder das Recht auf Irrtum. Einer, der auf Hermlin nach dem Krieg großen Einfluß hatte, Johannes R. Becher, brachte Schlimmeres zu Papier. Menschenleiber bilden beim frühen, dem vom Expressionismus geprägten Becher, den »Schotter« für den Fortschritt, »blutübersät ist der Weg«. Die Partei sah er als »Kampfmaschine der Revolution: Sie treibt einen ungeheuren Verschleiß an Menschenzahl und Kraft.« Eine betont freundliche Interpretation vermöchte im Pathos des Becher-Romans »Levisite« vielleicht hellsichtige Vorwegnahme blutiger Despotenherrschaft entdecken, doch leider hält dies gründlicher Prüfung nicht stand. Es gibt in diesem Roman ganze »Heere von Arbeitern«, die immerfort kämpfen und fallen. In einer Studie über »Politiken des Schreibens« mit dem Titel »Der Weg nach oben« hat Michael Rohrwasser verblüffende Parallelen zwischen Becher und Ernst Jünger herausgearbeitet. Beide waren gleichermaßen fasziniert vom Mythischen, von den Massen und der sie zügelnden Disziplin. In der Tat nimmt sich Bechers Klassenkrieg, den er heiligspricht, wie linke Freikorpsdichtung oder wie ein linkes »Stahlgewitter« aus, soldatisch und todessüchtig. »Es gibt in der deutschen Seele, in der Kunst, im Denken und der Literatur eine Art von Verständnislosigkeit für das, was wirklich das Leben ist, für das, was wirklich seinen Zauber, seine Großartigkeit ausmacht, und eine Art von krankhafter und teuflischer Anziehungskraft zum Tode hin.« George Clemenceau schrieb dies in einem Brief an einen Freund und fragte: »Woher das bei ihnen kommt? Ich weiß es nicht . . . Lesen Sie ihre Dichter wieder. Der Tod – der Tod zu Fuß, zu Pferde, überall. In allen Haltungen und Kostümen.« Wer denkt da nicht an Wagner oder an das Nibelungenlied? Doch auch der frühe Becher entspricht ganz dem Klischee, das der rationalistische Franzose von den Deutschen hat. Da marschieren die proletarischen Massen auf, werden dem »großen Klassenkrieg« geweiht und bekunden Todesbereitschaft, als eine »große dunkle Stimme« die Eidesformel spricht: »Frontkämpfer auf! Die Faust gereckt! Wir schwören rot: ›Sieg oder Tod!‹ ›Sieg oder Tod!‹ jauchzt die Menschenmasse.«

Früh wurde Becher Kommunist und damit Teil der großen Kampfmaschine. Und bald dichtet er Hymnen auf die Partei, die Ordnung und Maß in sein expressionistisch-waberndes Denken bringt:

> Was wär ich, ohne daß mich die Partei
> In ihre Zucht genommen, ihre strenge!?
> Ein wilder Spießer, der mit Wutgeschrei
> Sich selbst zerfetzt . . .«

Als im Zuge des Spätstalinismus in der DDR der Personenkult groteske Blüten trieb, ließ DDR-Kulturminister Becher, den Walter Ulbricht einmal den größten lebenden deutschen Dichter nannte, als Barde verklärender Stalin-Hymnen alle Konkurrenten weit hinter sich. Zum Tod des großen Despoten veröffentlichte er folgende »Danksagung«:

Dort wird er sein, wo sich von ihm die Fluten
Des Rheins erzählen und der Kölner Dom.
Dort wird er sein in allem Schönen, Guten,
Auf jedem Berg, an jedem deutschen Strom.

Dort wirst Du, Stalin, stehn, in voller Blüte
Der Apfelbäume an dem Bodensee,
Und durch den Schwarzwald wandert seine Güte,
Und winkt zu sich heran ein scheues Reh.

. . .

Gedenke Deutschland, deines Freunds, des besten.
O danke Stalin, keiner war wie er
So tief verwandt dir. Osten ist und Westen
In ihm vereint. Er überquert das Meer,

Und kein Gebirge setzt ihm eine Schranke,
Kein Feind ist stark genug, zu widerstehn
Dem Mann, der Stalin heißt, denn sein Gedanke
Wird Tat, und Stalins Wille wird geschehn.«

Gemessen an diesem reißerisch-agitatorischen, deutsch-sowjetischen und obendrein pseudosakralen Pathos eines Becher, in dem sich ein (gesamt)deutscher Nationalismus von links, kommunistischer Glaube und die Vergötzung Stalins mischen, wirkt Hermlins Ode auf den Führer der Weltrevolution und seine Partei neuen Typs geradezu feinsinnig. Im Gespräch mit Günter Gaus räumte Stephan Hermlin ein, daß Stalins Name seit dem 20. Parteitag »für rasenden Terror« stehe, »für millionenfachen Mord«. Aber auf die Frage, ob er sich seiner Stalin-Gedichte heute schäme, sagte er: »Nicht im mindesten. Es sind utopische Gedichte, Gedichte, in denen eine Gestalt und ein Name, wenn Sie so wollen, zu Unrecht als Symbol für eine große Sache stehen.« Wenn Millionen und Millionen sowjetischer Soldaten mit dem Ruf »Für die Heimat!«, »Für Stalin!« in den Tod gegangen seien, habe er keinen Grund, seine Gedichte zu verwerfen. Doch Marcel Reich-Ranicki wollte dem Dichter diese Rechtfertigung nicht durchgehen lassen. Auf der Linie der alten Totalitarismus-Theorie argumentierend, schrieb der Kritiker: Mit dem gleichen Recht hätten auch Hitlers Anhänger ihr Idol als Verkörperung einer großen Sache betrachten können.

Das wiederum wies Hermlin voller Empörung in einem Interview mit Wagenbach zurück, in dem er sich gegen eine unerlaubte Gleichsetzung von Kommunismus und Faschismus wehrte. An dieser Auseinandersetzung interessierte weniger, warum Hermlin den Kommunismus für die »große Sache« hielt, die sich unter dem »Zwang von Umständen« zum Schlimmen entwickelte. In der Tat war die Nazi-Ideologie ja rassistisch und allein schon von diesem barbarischen Denkansatz her in sich nicht besserungsfähig. Einen Prager Frühling dagegen hätte es nie geben können, wenn im Marxismus nicht humanistische Ideale steckten, die auf die Freiheit aller zielen, Programmintentionen, die Rebellen gegen die roten Zaren oder die alles erdrückenden Apparate der Parteien für Reformversuche zu Recht bemühen können. Insoweit sich eine regierende kommunistische Partei auf Marx und Engels (und nicht auf Lenin) beruft, bleibt sie, wenn man nur die rechten Klassiker-Passagen bemüht, eben stets am humanistischen Portepe zu packen.

Interessanter ist die Position, die Hermlin in der Sache selbst bezieht. Da erinnert er nicht nur an Majakovskij und Neruda oder Brecht, die alle auf ihre Weise Stalin rühmten oder an Picasso, der zu Stalins 70. Geburtstag ein Porträt des roten Tyrannen schuf. Er erinnert an die Stellung der deutschen Klassiker zur Französischen Revolution – Goethe, Schiller, Herder und Wieland –, die sich von der Generosität ihrer Ideen eingenommen zeigten und sie später unter dem Eindruck des Terrors verwarfen. Von ihrem Urteil differiere einzig das des todkranken, bespitzelten und von der Guillotine bedrohten Georg Forster. »Er beschreibt die Situation, in der sich Frankreich befindet: Massenmord, Korruption, Furcht. Aber er verteidigt auch jetzt noch die Revolution: Sie habe neue Verhältnisse geschaffen, die nicht mehr rückgängig zu machen wären und um derentwillen sich das Ganze gelohnt habe. Im Gegensatz zu ihm, dem organisierten Jakobiner, stehen die anderen Klassiker da als Sympathisanten und Kritiker aus der Ferne. Ihr Standpunkt ist begreiflich, auch ihre Desillusionierung«, sagt Hermlin und kommt dann zum entscheidenden Punkt: »Mein Standpunkt ähnelt eher dem Forsters. Auch ich bin ein direkt Beteiligter.«

Man mag diese Stellungnahme akzeptieren oder ablehnen, eines jedenfalls kann man ihr nicht absprechen: Klarheit und Aufrichtigkeit. Es gibt nicht viele andere Beispiele für den Versuch, die eigene Haltung während Stalins Herrschaft offen und selbstkritisch zu hinterfragen, ohne deshalb mit der Partei zu brechen oder der Sache abzuschwören – jedenfalls nicht in der DDR. Da herrschte bis heute eher die Kunst des Verdrängens oder Verschweigens vor. Einer der wenigen, die über das peinliche Thema ebenfalls Auskunft geben, Jürgen Kuczynski, beschreibt diese Haltung in seinem Buch »Dialog mit meinem Urenkel«. Als er noch an seiner vierzigbändigen »Geschichte der Lage der Arbeiter« schrieb, war Stalin aus den Büchern der Sowjetunion und der Ostblockländer plötzlich verschwunden. Gutachter und Verlag wollten deshalb auch in Kuczynskis neuem Werk alle einschlägigen Stellen, die auf Stalin Bezug nahmen, gestrichen haben. »Ich ging zur Partei«, erzählt er dem Urenkel, »und wir einigten uns auf einen Kompromiß. In der ›Lage der Arbeiter‹ würde ich Stalin positiv oder negativ, je nachdem es mir im einzelnen Fall wissenschaftlich richtig erschien, zitieren, in Artikeln nicht. Du wirst also die groteske Tatsache finden, daß in dieser Zeit meine Bände wohl die einzigen Bücher in der DDR oder Sowjetunion waren, die Zitate von Stalin enthielten.« Sein Kommentar: »Selbstverständlich war diese bei uns allgemeine Behandlung von Stalin nur eine Fortsetzung des ›Stalinismus‹: War jemand in Ungnade gefallen, wurde er nicht mehr erwähnt.«

Wie es komme, hatte Hermlin, auch zur eigenen Entlastung, aber völlig legitim gefragt, daß so viele große Dichter und Künstler damals Stalin rühmten? Er kennt die Antwort, auch wenn er sie so nicht gibt. Nach dem Ersten Weltkrieg mit seinen Massenabschlachtungen vor Verdun und an der Somme gedieh nicht nur das blutige Revolutionspathos eines Becher. Die Zeit war reif für eine neue Offenbarung, die vorgab, sie könne Krieg, Unterdrückung und Ausbeutung für immer und ewig an der Wurzel beseitigen und eine fundamental neue soziale Organisation an die Stelle der verrotteten alten setzen. Es ist das religiöse, das chiliastische Element im frühen Kommunismus, das den beispiellosen Mut von Widerstandskämpfern selbst in aussichtsloser Lage erklärt. Ohne diesen religiösen Charakter sind nicht die Faszination der kommunistischen Weltanschauung auf Künstler und Intellektuelle, und schon gar nicht die Moskauer Hochverratsprozesse der Jahre 1936 bis 1938 mit den erstaunlichen Selbstbeschuldigungen der Angeklagten zu verstehen. In Wahrheit waren sie nicht Revolutions-, sondern Religions-Tribunale, die Angeklagten verhielten sich nicht wie politische Frondeure oder Verräter, sondern wie bußfertige Sünder. Analogien dazu, meint Alexander Rüstow, finden sich nur in mittelalterlichen und barocken Ketzerprozessen, in denen der entsetzliche Druck der Sündenschuld »förmlich Orgien der Selbstbeschuldigung und der Selbstbestrafung« auslöste.

Als einen, der ebenfalls Stalin gerühmt habe, nannte Stephan Hermlin Brecht. Aber eine Ode auf Stalin hat der Stückeschreiber und Lyriker nie verfaßt, auch wenn er in seiner »Erziehung der Hirse« den »großen Ernteleiter Stalin« die Hirse loben läßt. Anders ist das schon mit seinem Stück »Die Maßnahme«, das von drei Agitatoren handelt, welche die Revolution in China vorbereiten sollen. Sie töten einen jungen Genossen, der sich ihnen anschloß, wegen dessen revolutionärer Ungeduld – und mit seinem Einverständnis. Zwar taucht Stalins Name in dem Stück überhaupt nicht auf, aber was da im Dezember 1930 in Berlin, mit der Musik Hanns Eislers, uraufgeführt wurde, nahm die Moskauer Prozesse fast programmatisch vorweg. Der ganz vom Gefühl geleitete junge Genosse, dargestellt von Ernst Busch, will den Erniedrigten und Ausgebeuteten sofort Hilfe bringen. Sein Drängen auf spontane Aktion gefährdet nach Meinung der Agitatoren jedoch die Revolution. Sie berufen sich auf die Lehre der Klassiker und kommen zu dem Schluß, ihn umzubringen. Da der Sturm- und Dranggenosse sich eine andere Zugehörigkeit als zu den Revolutionären, die die Welt verändern, nicht vorstellen kann, unterwirft er sich der Disziplin und willigt in seine eigene Tötung ein.

Hannah Ahrendt, die keinen Zweifel daran läßt, daß sie Brecht für einen der ganz Großen, vor allem auf dem Gebiet der Lyrik hielt, nannte »Die Maßnahme« das einzig wirklich linientreue Stück, das Brecht je schrieb. Kaum habe der Dichter sich mit den Kommunisten eingelassen, da habe er herausgefunden, »daß es keine Gemeinheit geben dürfe, die man nicht zu begehen bereit ist, um die Gemeinheit aus der Welt zu bringen«. Als die KPdSU nach Stalins Ankündigung der Liquidation der rechten und der linken Oppositionen auf dem 16. Parteikongreß 1929 begann, ihre eigenen Miglieder zu ermorden, habe Brecht gemeint, die Partei bedürfe »nun aber auch einer Rechtfertigung zum Liquidieren und zum Töten unschuldiger Menschen«. Brecht hatte nie Freude an dem Stück, mit dem er sich zwischen alle Stühle setzte. Stalins Gegner kreideten ihm die Verteidigung des Tyrannen an, Stalins Anhänger kritisierten ihn und bestritten, daß das Stück mit den Realitäten der Sowjetunion irgend etwas zu tun habe. »Brecht«, meinte Hannah Arendt, »hatte die Regeln des infernalischen Spiels deutlich erkannt und schön (mit »wohllautender Stimme«) besungen und natürlich hoffte er auf Beifall. Nur eine Kleinigkeit hatte er in seinem Eifer übersehen: daß natürlich die Partei verständlicherweise keine Absicht hatte, die Wahrheit bekanntzugeben, und noch dazu von einem ihrer prominentesten Anhänger.«

Gelegentlich geriet der arme B. B. eben in Schwierigkeiten,

weil er für mehr Kommunismus eintrat als die Partei. Und natürlich erging es ihm in politices nicht besser als allen andern Dichtern: Jeder bemühte ihn für die jeweils eigene Sache mit dem, was ihm gerade ins Konzept paßte. Das im Westen meist zitierte Gedicht trägt den Titel »Die Lösung«.

> Nach dem Aufstand des 17. Juni
> Ließ der Sekretär des Schriftstellerverbandes
> In der Stalinallee Flugblätter verteilen
> Auf denen zu lesen war, daß das Volk
> Das Vertrauen der Regierung verscherzt habe
> Und es nur durch verdoppelte Arbeit
> Zurückerobern könne. Wäre es da
> Nicht doch einfacher, die Regierung
> Löste das Volk auf und
> Wählte ein anderes?

Das könnte fast darüber hinwegtäuschen, daß er in der Sache, allen Widersprüchen zum Trotz, Ulbricht in dieser Situation seine Loyalität bekundete. Sein Berliner Ensemble hielt er für Agitationsprogramme im Rundfunk bereit, und an Ulbricht schrieb er: »Die Geschichte wird der revolutionären Ungeduld der Sozialistischen Einheitspartei Deutschlands ihren Respekt zollen. Die große Aussprache mit den Massen über das Tempo des sozialistischen Aufbaus wird zu einer Sichtung und Sicherung der sozialistischen Errungenschaften führen. Es ist mir ein Bedürfnis, Ihnen in diesem Augenblick meine Verbundenheit mit der Sozialistischen Einheitspartei Deutschlands auszusprechen.« Doch in der Solidaritätsadresse steckte noch, typisch für Brecht, Dialektiker und großer Taktiker, der er immer war, der Stachel der Kritik. Daß er die Partei, der er nie formell beigetreten ist, des Fehlers der »revolutionären Ungeduld« bezichtigte und die Führung zum Dialog mit dem Volk aufforderte, den sie bislang nicht gesucht hatte (und den sie auch weiterhin nicht wollte), ärgerte die SED-Spitze. Das »Neue Deutschland« druckte nur den letzten Satz.

Wenn Stephan Hermlin sich in der Stalinfrage auf Georg

Forster beruft, kommt er übrigens Brecht sehr nahe, der nicht moralisch, sondern historisch urteilte und in dem Georgier einen großen revolutionären Tyrannen wie Robespierre sah. Historisch-distanziert mag für den, der genau hinschaut, schon Bertolt Brechts Nachruf auf Stalin vom März 1953 erscheinen. »Den Unterdrückten von allen Erdteilen, denen, die sich schon befreit haben, und allen, die für den Weltfrieden kämpfen, muß der Herzschlag gestockt haben, als sie hörten, Stalin ist tot. Er war die Verkörperung ihrer Hoffnung. Aber die geistigen und materiellen Waffen, die er herstellte, sind da, und da ist die Lehre, neue herzustellen.« Da stand nicht, *seiner* Hoffnung, und es ist nicht *sein* Herzschlag, der da stockt. Brecht beschreibt, was nach seiner Meinung in Millionen Menschen damals vor sich ging. Und wer will, mag sogar herauslesen, daß er der Partei die Abkehr vom Stalinismus wünscht, denn da ist ja die Lehre, um »neue« geistige Waffen herzustellen. Wenn es denn so vieldeutig-schlitzohrig gemeint gewesen ist, dann war es gewiß ein Meisterstück.

Um auf das Wort vom »Staatsdichter« Hermlin zurückzukommen: Er kann auch von schwierigen Zeiten erzählen, die er in der DDR durchgemacht hat; und das nicht nur, weil seine Lyrik immer wieder als formalistisch angegriffen wurde. Als er im Dezember 1962 in der Ostberliner Akademie der Künste einen Lyrik-Abend veranstaltete, ließ er viele junge, meist unbekannte Autoren zu Wort kommen, darunter Günter Kunert, Volker Braun und – Wolfgang Biermann. Er darf deshalb als Entdecker vieler Talente gelten, die sich später gegenüber Partei und Staat als unbotmäßig erweisen sollten. Doch der Ärger setzte für Hermlin früher ein. Verlesen wurden meist kritische Gedichte, deren Auswahl er persönlich besorgt hatte. Schon in der Pause fragten ihn linientreue Freunde, warum er »konterrevolutionäre Gedanken« verbreiten helfe. Die Parteiorganisation der Akademie lud ihn anschließend zweimal, die des Schriftstellerverbands gleich viermal zu mehrstündigen Sitzungen vor, die eher Tribunalen glichen. Da der geistige Terror einschüchternd wirkte, war Hermlin mit Ausnahme von Paul Dessau, der ihn bis zuletzt verteidigte, bald von allen guten Freunden verlassen. Seinen Posten als Sekretär der Sektion Literatur an der Akademie mußte er räumen. Er sah sich »augenblicklich außer Kurs gesetzt«. Erst mit dem Amtsantritt Erich Honeckers sollte sich das wieder ändern.

Unter denen, die Stephan Hermlin auf seiner folgenreichen Veranstaltung »Junge Lyrik – unbekannt und unveröffentlicht« im Dezember im Plenarsaal vorstellte, war ein junger Mann aus Dresden, dem Kritiker später einmal bescheinigen sollten, er habe die »Lust an der List« bei Brecht gelernt. Volker Braun, Jahrgang 1939, ist auf seine Art ein typisches Produkt der marxistischen Erziehung der DDR, die ja nicht immer nur hervorbringt, was sich die Partei von ihr erhofft: ergebene Anhänger des realsozialistischen Systems. Wer seinen Geist schult am dialektischen Scharfsinn der »Klassiker«, wer ihre böse Ironie schätzt und Spaß hat an ihrer erbarmungslosen Kritik, vor der kein noch so schöner Schein besteht, kann auch zum Rebellen werden wie Rudolf Bahro. Oder er entwickelt sich zu einem, der die Widersprüche im Sozialismus aufspürt und an den Pranger stellt, der mit der Elle der Idee Maß nimmt an der Wirklichkeit. Solch ein überzeugter Linker, der gnadenlos genau hinschaut und, was er sieht, in Verse, Prosa oder Dramen packt, ist Volker Braun. Wenn er die Regierenden der SED von links kritisiert, führt er Parteinahme für die gemeinsame Sache zur eigenen Legitimation ins Feld. Den Sozialismus versteht er durchaus dialektisch als etwas Unfertiges, in Entwicklung Begriffenes, als Prozeß, in den er mit seiner Stimme eingreifen will. Und die Elle, mit der er mißt, liefert kein geringerer als der junge Marx mit dem Satz, den nicht zufällig Heiner Müller in der »Hamletmaschine« zitiert: Daß es nämlich gelte, »alle Verhältnisse umzuwerfen, in denen der Mensch ein erniedrigtes, ein geknechtetes, ein verlassenes, ein verächtliches Wesen ist«. Brauns Gedichte und Essays sind mit unbotmäßigen Gedanken gespickt, und so bleiben seine Werke oft Jahre ungedruckt, ehe sie in der DDR erscheinen. In einem Essay über

Rimbaud findet sich das erstaunliche, für Braun beinahe programmatische Bekenntnis: »Der Kommunismus, als Erbteil des Klassenkampfes, mit der Menschheit und der Natur beladen, bleibt im Sozialismus subversiv wie die Poesie: Wir wissen, worauf wir uns eingelassen haben.«

Wir drehten Braun bei den Proben zu seinem Nibelungen-Drama, die er vor der Uraufführung im Deutschen Nationaltheater in Weimar persönlich überwachte. Gleich drei Ebenen hat der unbequeme Autor in diesem komplizierten Stück ineinander geflochten: Die Welt der Sagen, die wahre Geschichte der Burgunden und die Ost-West-Spannung der Gegenwart. Wie nahezu alles von Braun, steckte auch dieses Werk voller Anzüglichkeiten, durch die sich die Kulturfunktionäre herausgefordert fühlten. Unter dem Eindruck der Stationierungsdebatte wollte er die Vernichtung eines Volkes zeigen, »das mit offenen Augen in ein Messer rennt« – eine mythische Vision von Untergang. Aber mit der historischen Situation, die er für das Volk der Burgunden auf der Bühne rekonstruierte, bereitete er Funktionären Verlegenheit, die Rückschlüsse auf das Hier und Heute zogen. Denn die Burgunden werden zwischen zwei mächtigen Reichen, dem der Hunnen im Osten und dem der Römer im Westen, zerrieben und vernichtet. Und für ihren Untergang sind sie mitverantwortlich, denn sie kämpfen auf beiden Seiten, sie führen also Bruderkrieg. Brauns Siegfried aber, ein freier Franke, wird Opfer eines politischen Mordes: Er engagiert sich nur für die Selbstbestimmung, ist anfangs eine Erfindung, ein Wunschheld und eine Sagengestalt, die mit ihrer Kraft und dem Zauber der Jugend dem Volk der Burgunder den Weg aus der Not weisen soll. Aus dieser Projektionsfigur der Volksseele wird zum Schluß der Mann mit dem Schwert, Siegfried der Schlächter, der sich auf den katalaunischen Feldern mißbrauchen läßt. Im Denkansatz zumindest wurde da die Bündnisloyalität der beiden Burgunderparteien hinterfragt – auch der östlichen. Vielleicht ist dies die Erklärung, warum das Drama lange auf seine Uraufführung warten mußte.

Seinen Einstand als Dramatiker hatte Volker Braun mit

dem Schauspiel »Die Kipper« gegeben, das vom Aufstieg und Fall des Hilfsarbeiters Paul Bauch in einem Braunkohle-Tagebau handelt. Der Autor verarbeitete darin vor Ort Erlebtes, denn vor dem Philosophiestudium war er als Maschinist im Bergbau tätig gewesen und hatte die »Widersprüche des Sozialismus« unter härtesten Bedingungen erfahren. »In dem Bereich«, läßt Braun den Betriebsleiter sagen, »ist Sozialismus nicht ganz möglich. Das ist ein Rest von Barbarei, darüber redet man nicht.« Nicht nur solcher Sätze wegen erlebte das 1965 mit Hilfe der Schauspieler und Regisseure Matthias Langhoff und Manfred Karge konzipierte Stück erst 1972 seine Uraufführung. Als zu deutlich auch wurde dem Publikum der unversöhnliche Gegensatz aufgezeigt, der zwischen den Erfordernissen des sozialistischen Aufbaus und der freien Entfaltung der Persönlichkeit besteht. Kaum in Magdeburg vorgestellt, sollten »Die Kipper« alsbald in allerhöchste Ungnade fallen. Erich Honecker persönlich monierte auf dem 9. Plenum des ZK Ende Mai 1973, daß in einigen neueren Werken von Bühne und Film die Aufbauleistung der DDR-Bürger herabgewürdigt werde. Als ein Beispiel zitierte er aus Brauns »Kippern« den Satz, die DDR sei der »langweiligste Staat der Welt«. Für Spannung, so hätte Braun sicherlich kontern können, sorgen allein die Attacken einer mächtigen Parteibürokratie, die gegen vergleichsweise schwächliche Gegner wie ihn, gleich mit tausendfachem overkill zu Felde ziehen. Warum eigentlich? Braun selbst sagte mir: »Die Literatur ist hier keine Angelegenheit am Rande, weil hier die Meinungen der Leute ein wenig mehr gefragt sind, weil es den Staat sozusagen beschäftigt, was wir von uns halten . . . Darum bleibt die Literatur kein Gemurmel. Sie beunruhigt, sie spaltet die Leser. Es sind Erwartungen in sie gesetzt und Befürchtungen. Der hohe Stellenwert hat Vor- und Nachteile.«

Einer der unerträglichen Nachteile ist zweifellos die Zensur. Braun argumentierte auf einer Linie mit Heiner Müller oder auch Hans Mayer, der in seinen Erinnerungen schreibt: »In Leipzig hatte die Literatur mitsamt ihren Literaten als Bestandteil der Politik zu gelten. In Westdeutschland jedoch nahmen die Mächtigen in Bund und Ländern die Literatur nicht ernst: schon gar nicht im eigenen, im politischen Bereich. Da wirkte immer noch, aus historischer Ferne, das Strukturschema des Kaiserreichs ins politische Gründungskonzept der Bundesrepublik Deutschland. Nach wie vor hielt man am Prinzip ›einer machtgeschützten Innerlichkeit‹ fest.«

Erheblichen Ärger handelte sich Braun mit seinem Roman »Hinze und Kunze« ein, der vom Gespräch zwischen einem Fahrer, Hinze, und seinem Chef, Kunze, handelt, genauer: vom Widerspruch zwischen Führern und Geführten, Arbeitern und Funktionären in der DDR, für den der Autor einmal die Formulierung Herr und Knecht gebraucht. »Der Herr und sein Knecht«, heißt es da, »ritten durch die preußische Prärie, die Bäume standen dünn in Reih und Glied, wie herbestellt...« Typisch für den dialektisch-zugespitzten Erzählstil Volker Brauns ist die Beschreibung der sozialen Gegensätze: Die soziale Pyramide ist durch die Revolution zwar auf den Kopf gestellt, und doch hat sich wenig verändert. Es gibt weiter oben und unten: »Die Ortschaften, die sie passierten, schienen gereinigt, der gröbste Mist hinter den Aufstellwänden sekretiert. Der Herr war ein Arbeiter- und Bauernkind, sein Vater ein arbeitsloser Transportarbeiter und Frontsoldat unter dem Regime, hatte sich nach dem Umsturz in der ersten Stunde hervorgetan unter Tage. Der Knecht war so günstiger sozialer Herkunft nicht, er entstammte besseren Kreisen, der guten Stube eines Angestellten, welcher im Siebenjährigen Krieg gefallen war und seiner Witwe mehrere Söhne hinterlassen hatte und diesen nichts, als seine vom Munde abgesparte Bibliothek mit den Werken des Herrn Diderot, des Genossen Lenin und der Freunde der Freikörperkultur.«

Insoweit der Roman eine neue Klassengesellschaft schildert, die in der DDR entstanden ist, läßt er sich Günter de Bruyns »Neuer Herrlichkeit« an die Seite stellen. Der DDR-Autor de Bruyn erzählt darin die Liebesgeschichte Viktors, eines jungen Diplomaten und Doktoranden, der als Sohn eines hohen Parteifunktionärs zu den Privilegierten der neuen Gesellschaft gehört und sich in ein einfaches, sehr irdisches, naives Mädchen vom Lande verliebt. Im Grunde geht es um die uralte Geschichte: Ein junger Mann aus bestem Haus gerät an die falsche Freundin mit unpassenden Eltern. Daß der einflußreiche Vater die Liebe zerstört, indem er die Abberufung Viktors ins Ausland durchsetzt, hat in diesem Roman zwei Gründe: Erstens, und darin steckt der wichtigste Teil der Kritik, hat die Geliebte, das Arbeitermädchen Thilde, nicht die rechten Voraussetzungen für eine Diplomatenfrau – ihr fehlen Bildung und Umgangsformen. Früher hätte man gesagt: Bitte keine Mesalliance! Zweitens hat Thilde eine Mutter im Westen. Familiäre Westkontakte aber sind, wie der mächtige Vater aus dem Apparat aus Intimkenntnis weiß, dem Aufstieg des Sohns in Staat und Partei hinderlich. Der Opportunist und Schwächling Viktor beugt sich dem Vater, der die Geliebte damit in die Kaste der Unberührbaren verweist. De Bruyns Roman erschien in der DDR in kleiner Auflage und war im Handumdrehen vergriffen. Der Autor, schrieb ein Kritiker in der »Sächsischen Zeitung«, habe wohl »ein wenig die Gesellschaftsordnung verwechselt«. Doch von Verwechslung konnte natürlich keine Rede sein, dafür hatte der Autor die Parallelen zwischen alter und neuer Gesellschaft viel zu klar und bewußt herausgearbeitet. Volker Brauns satirischer Roman wurde weitaus schärfer angegriffen. Das »Neue Deutschland« kanzelte ihn als »Farce« ab und kreidete dem Autor anarchistische Tendenzen an. Der Stellvertretende Kulturminister Klaus Höpcke, der »Hinze und Kunze« zum Druck freigegeben hatte, wurde von der Partei gerügt, sein für das Verlagswesen zuständiger Abteilungsleiter hatte gar den Hut zu nehmen. Vier Jahre hatte das Manuskript gelegen, ehe es schließlich zur Veröffentlichung freigegeben werden sollte. Als ob er den Ärger geahnt hätte, der auf ihn zukommen würde, fühlte sich der dafür Verantwortliche verpflichtet, »schöngeistige Lesehilfe« beizusteuern, damit die Leser die »satirischen Elemente« des Buchs auch ja nicht mißverstehen sollten. Und vorsichtig meldete Höpcke gar selbst Bedenken an. So monierte er, daß Braun die DDR als das »aschgraue, mit Grünpflanzen getarnte Schlachtfeld« bezeichne und in den Gesprächen, in denen der Funktionär Kunze über seine Westreisen erzähle, die hohe Arbeitslosigkeit in der Bundesrepublik nicht erwähnt werde. Zwiespältig berührt es Höpcke, Minister, »Lesehelfer« und Kritiker in einem, »was Kunzes Kopf bei einer Reise in kapitalistische Gefilde aufnimmt«. Einen »komischen Essay« nannte er das Buch, das sich am Muster von Diderots »Jacques der Fatalist und sein Herr« orientiert, und lobte Brauns Witz und seine Sprachkraft. Einerseits fand er an den Details der Braunschen Zustandsbeschreibung des Sozialismus manches schief, andererseits meinte er, die »Hinze-Kunze-Vorstellungen über die Leitung gesellschaftlicher Prozesse« seien gerade dank der satirischen Überspitzung »diskutierbar gestaltet«. Fazit: DDR-Leser sollten sich hüten, zu »verhinzen und verkunzen«.

Es gibt kaum ein anderes Beispiel für einen solchen ideologischen Eiertanz, den ein für eine Entscheidung verantwortlicher Kulturpolitiker in der DDR aufgeführt hat, um Kritik, die er antizipierte, abzufangen, sich von manchen Passagen im Werk selbst zu distanzieren und doch gleichzeitig die Veröffentlichung zu rechtfertigen. Höpcke übt sich von Zeit zu Zeit in theoretischen Kunstfertigkeiten, so, wenn er sich in der »Deutschen Zeitschrift für Philosophie« über Formprobleme der Kunst ausläßt. Überschrieben war sein Artikel mit der wahrlich anspruchsvollen Frage: »Was macht die Kunst beim ›Sprung der Menschheit . . . in das Reich der Freiheit‹?« Und natürlich wurde darin die Forderung zitiert, welche der Partei- und Staatschef im September 1984 an die Kunst gestellt hatte. »Unsere Zeit«, so Honecker auf einer Begegnung mit Kunst- und Kulturschaffenden, »braucht Kunstwerke, die den Sozialismus stärken, die Größe und Schönheit des oft unter Schwierigkeiten Erreichten bewußt machen, Kunstwerke, in deren Mittelpunkt der aktive, der geschichtsgestaltende Held, die Arbeiterklasse und ihre Repräsentanten stehen . . .« Das klang wie ein Ruf nach einem neuen Kult des Positiven, aber Höpcke weist ihn zurück, wenn auch in indirekter, veschleierter Form, wie sich das gegenüber dem mächtigen Parteichef ziemt. Indem er für das eingreifende Schreiben plädiert, welches das »literarische Feuer unversöhnlicher Kritik« gegen die Kostgänger des bequemen Schlendrians anzünden soll, nimmt er für die Kritik und gegen die Priester der Schönfärberei Partei. »Wenn ein Autor in schöpferischer, produktiver und kritischer Weise zur weiteren Gestaltung des entwickelten Sozialismus beiträgt, weisen wir energisch diejenigen zurück, die daraus im Ganzen oder in Teilen etwas gegen den Sozialismus Gerichtetes destillieren möchten.« Noch in Höpckes Taktieren, auf das er sich meisterhaft versteht, werden Vorzüge und Nachteile eines Systems offenbar, in dem die Kaste der Mandarine bestimmt, was als Kunst freigegeben wird und was nicht. Daß Literatur ernstgenommen wird, mag als ihr Segen gelten, daß gerade deshalb Wort und Punkt und Komma auf die ideologische Waagschale gelegt werden, ist zweifellos ihr Fluch.

Volker Braun wird in Form linker, subversiver Texte, weiter für Sprengstoff sorgen in der DDR. »Solange eine Gesellschaft, sie mag mittlerweile wie immer heißen, auf Gewalt beruht, nämlich solange es ›die da oben und die da unten gibt‹, bedarf es der Gegengewalt, um sie zu verändern.« Der Satz findet sich in einem Büchner-Essay, der in Paris, aber nicht in der DDR erschienen ist, weil der Ostberliner Verlagsleiter nicht nur »Haare in der Suppe fand, sondern gleich den ganzen Schopf.« Wo sich zwar nicht mehr Klassen gegenüberstehen, sondern Individuen in verschiedenen Stellungen einer Pyramide der Verfügungsgewalt, heißt es da »geht der Kampf nicht mehr um den Platz an der Spitze, sondern um die Zertrümmerung der Pyramide«. Und als das neue revolutionäre Element in realsozialistischen Gesellschaften entdeckt er »das Verhältnis von Ausführenden und Bestimmenden, die wieder die Reichen und die Armen sind«. Ein Karl Marx fände Gefallen an dem Dialektiker Braun, diesem Produkt marxistischer Erziehung. Doch regierenden Kommunisten wird er, der das Training des aufrechten Gangs verlangt, stets ein unbequemer Partner bleiben. »Eigene Kontinuität« nannte er dieses Gedicht:

1

Während wir beinahe gekonnt
Um die Ecke biegen, erklären wir ruhig
Daß wir die Richtung beibehalten.

2

Bei all den schönen Schritten nach vorn
Behaupten wir standhaft unsre Position.

3

Ohne mit der Wimper zu zucken
Nicht mal augenzwinkernd
Wechseln wir die Sachen
Und bleiben bei unsern Begriffen.

4

Wir lernen dazu
Was wir immer gewußt haben.
(. . .)

7. Sozialistischer Ikonenkult und Medienpriester

Klosterfelde bei Bernau, ein verschlafener Ort mit 3000 Einwohnern, liegt an der Fernstraße 109, die von Berlin nach Norden führt. Es ist ein märkisches Städtchen wie viele andere, die Bürger leben von der Holz- und Möbelindustrie, und es wäre kaum erwähnenswert, wenn es sich nicht um den Geburtsort eines neuen Wortes handelte, das die deutsche Sprache seit Januar 1983 bereichert. Bis dahin, die Germanisten in Ost und West sind sich darin einig, gab es im Deutschen den Verkehrsunfall und den Verkehrsverstoß, das Verkehrsvergehen und die Verkehrsgefährdung. Seit dem 12. Januar, an dem ADN über ein Ereignis in Klosterfelde berichtete, gibt es auch den »Verkehrszwischenfall«.

Was darunter genau zu verstehen war, offenbarte sich nur westlichen ADN-Abonnenten durch den Vergleich mit der Meldung einer westdeutschen Illustrierten. Der »Stern« nämlich hatte behauptet, in Klosterfelde sei am Silvestertag 1982 ein Attentat auf Erich Honecker verübt worden, als dieser mit seinem Autokonvoi zu seinem Jagdschloß in der Schorfheide fuhr. Ein 41jähriger Ofensetzer habe versucht, einen Teil der Wagenkolonne zu überholen und sich hinter Honeckers grauen Citroën zu setzen. Während dieses Überholmanövers wurde der Wagen des Ofensetzers von einem Begleitfahrzeug von der Straße gedrängt. Anschließend, so der Bericht des Magazins, kam es zu einem Schußwechsel, bei dem ein Polizist aus der Begleitung Honeckers schwer verletzt wurde. Als der Attentäter sah, daß seine Lage aussichtslos war, habe er sich mit der eigenen Waffe erschossen. Nach Angaben des »Stern«

wurden Angehörige und Bekannte des Attentäters durch den Staatssicherheitsdienst zu strengstem Stillschweigen verpflichtet.

Wie die DDR den Vorfall in Klosterfelde behandelte, steht bis heute exemplarisch für eine zentralgesteuerte Medienpolitik, der Glasnost ein unerwünschtes Fremdwort ist. Zunächst galt die Devise, Melden ist Silber, Unterschlagen ist Gold. Man verlautbarte absolut nichts, nicht einmal in der Lokalzeitung erschien ein Hinweis, der die Anwohner, die Schüsse gehört haben müssen, über den Sachverhalt hätte aufklären können. Erst als die Vorabmeldung des »Stern« durch westliche Fernseh- und Hörfunknachrichten auch die DDR erreichte und klar war, daß in Klosterfelde irgend etwas passiert sein mußte, entschloß man sich zu einem Dementi, das jedoch viele Behauptungen des »Stern« bestätigte. Bei ADN schrumpfte der Attentatsversuch unter der Überschrift »Selbstmord nach Fahrerflucht« nun auf den neuen, ominösen Begriff »Verkehrszwischenfall«. Danach hatte der Fahrer eines PKW vom Typ Lada nach einer »schweren Verkehrgefährdung« die Aufforderung der Polizei mißachtet, seine Fahrt zu stoppen und, als er gestellt wurde, das Feuer eröffnet. Vor seiner Festnahme habe er Selbstmord begangen. Nach der DDR-Version war er mit 2,5 Promille gefahren. Die Person Honeckers und dessen Konvoi wurden mit keinem Wort erwähnt. Hatten die Verfasser ihren Lenin schlecht gelesen, der einst forderte »daß wir in unserer ganzen Propaganda und Agitation reinen Wein einschenken müssen«?

Die Darstellung des West-Magazins ließ viele Fragen offen, beispielsweise, woher ein einfacher Ofensetzer wußte, wann der Staatsratsvorsitzende zum Neujahrsurlaub in die Schorfheide fährt, damit er für das Attentat auch pünktlich zur Stelle ist. In dem Dementi von ADN wiederum, das die DDR-Presse am nächsten Tag kommentarlos übernahm, wurde der staunenden Bevölkerung mit keiner Zeile erklärt, warum ein normaler DDR-Bürger mit einer Pistole bewaffnet spazierenfährt und als erster auf eine stattliche Polizeiübermacht schießt. Ohne die Kenntnis der »Stern«-Meldung blieb das DDR-Dementi vollends unverständlich.

Was macht ein in der DDR akkreditierter Korrespondent, wenn er, wie zu vermuten stand, bei einem Anruf in dem für die Volkspolizei zuständigen Ministerium für Inneres belehrt würde, daß es über die ADN-Meldung hinaus zu diesem Vorfall nichts mitzuteilen gebe?

Die Arbeitsmöglichkeiten westlicher Journalisten in der DDR werden durch eine Journalistenverordnung und eine Durchführungsbestimmung geregelt, die im Gesetzblatt der DDR veröffentlicht sind und vor allem das Fernsehen an die Kette legen. Danach ist so ziemlich alles antrags- und genehmigungspflichtig, was an Recherche für eine gute Reportage unerläßlich ist – »journalistische Vorhaben in staatlichen und wirtschaftlichen Organen, Einrichtungen, volkseigenen Kombinaten und Betrieben, Genossenschaften und gesellschaftlichen Einrichtungen und Institutionen sowie Interviews und Befragungen jeder Art«. Nur Außenaufnahmen innerhalb Berlins bedürfen keiner Genehmigung durch die für uns zuständige »Abteilung für journalistische Beziehungen« beim Ministerium für Auswärtiges. Außenaufnahmen in der Republik sind ebenfalls möglich, nur gilt die Auflage, sich »nicht später als 24 Stunden vor Antritt der Reise unter genauer Angabe des Reiseziels und des Reisegrunds« abzumelden. Anträge und Abmeldungen, so die Regel, sind per Telex an das Außenministerium abzusetzen.

Ein Antrag für eine Drehgenehmigung in Klosterfelde, die Interviews mit den Zuständigen der Volkspolizei, mit Verwandten des Ofensetzers, mit dem Bürgermeister und mit Bürgern des Ortes einschloß, war naheliegend. Immerhin harrten gerade nach der ADN-Meldung einige Fragen der Aufklärung. Wie kam ein Ofensetzer in der DDR, die persönlichen Waffenbesitz strengstens untersagt, überhaupt an eine Pistole? Was hatte den 41jährigen Handwerker bewogen, das Feuer auf die Polizei zu eröffnen? Nicht zuletzt: Konnte ein Mann mit 2,5 Promille Alkohol im Blut a), die Aussichtslosigkeit seiner Lage erkennen und b), war er noch fähig, sich selbst zu erschießen? Im Westen wären ganze Reporterheere ausgeschwärmt, um Motivforschung zu betreiben. Da die DDR den ihr peinlichen Vorfall offenkundig herunterspielen wollte, hätte mir ein Antrag mit Sicherheit eine Ablehnung eingebracht. Zudem erforderte die Bearbeitung von Anträgen erfahrungsgemäß viel Zeit. Mit einer Antwort, so wollte es der sozialistische Gang, war bestenfalls in einigen Tagen zu rechnen, und da wäre selbst eine wider Erwarten erteilte Zustimmung für einen aktuellen Bericht zu spät gekommen. Um wenigtens Bilder vom Tatort zu erhalten, meldete ich mich, nicht ganz der 24-Stunden-Vorschrift entsprechend, telefonisch noch für denselben Tag zu »Außenaufnahmen entlang der Fernstraße 109 nördlich Berlin« ab. Der Ort Klosterfelde wurde dabei bewußt nicht genannt. Der zuständige Funktionär nahm die Mitteilung am Telefon ohne Einwand, aber mit dem Kommentar entgegen: »Na, da können wir ja heute abend vielleicht etwas sehen.« Klang da etwa versteckte Kritik an der eigenen, gezielt vernebelnden Informationspolitik durch?

Wir drehten gerade die erste Einstellung, das Ortsschild mit der Straße, auf der sich alles abgespielt haben mußte, da stiefelte ein Mann vom Acker auf uns zu, überzeugte sich, daß wir tatsächlich vom Westfernsehen waren, sah sich vorsichtig um, ob wir auch nicht beobachtet wurden und sagte: »Da hinten, bei dem Haus an der Ecke müßt ihr drehen – da ist alles passiert.« Interviews vor der Kamera waren nach der Journalistenverordnung nicht möglich, aber mehrere Bürger von Klosterfelde sprachen uns bei unseren Außenaufnahmen an, kamen ins Erzählen und gaben uns Tips. Diese Erfahrung wiederholte sich übrigens in der DDR. Nach dem Motto, zeigt wenigstens ihr, was hier Sache ist, erhielten wir immer wieder Hinweise – meist auf Mißstände. So, als ich für einen Bericht über ein Festival der winzigen sorbischen Minderheit, dem in Nachahmung von Stalins Nationalitätenpolitik in der DDR früh beinahe übertriebene offizielle Förderung zuteil wurde, im mittelalterlichen Bautzen drehte und Passanten empfahlen: »Haltet doch die Kamera nicht nur auf die übertünchte Fassade, schaut auch mal in den Hinterhof!« Da bot sich in der Tat ein Bild schlimmsten Verfalls, es gab kaum noch Putz, der von den Wänden hätte bröckeln können.

Langsam rundete sich das Bild durch die unaufgeforderte Mithilfe der Bürger von Klosterfelde. Nach DDR-Maßstäben war der Handwerksmeister Paul Essling vermögend. Er besaß nicht nur ein stattliches Haus, auf seinem Grundstück hatte er einen Karpfenteich angelegt, und er hielt sich privat ein Pferd. Anwohner, die ihn kannten, bezeichneten ihn als jähzornig und unberechenbar. Offenbar hatte er eine schwierige Scheidung hinter sich und war obendrein mit seiner neuen Freundin zerstritten. Sie, die im nahegelegenen Wandlitz wohnte, hatte er Silvester im Zorn verlassen und befand sich auf der Rückfahrt, als die Autokolonne Honeckers an ihm vorüberbrauste. Um der Nummer 1 den Weg freizumachen, winkt Volkspolizei die anderen Verkehrsteilnehmer rücksichtslos beiseite. Das muß den ohnehin cholerischen Paul Essling besonders aufgebracht haben. Bei einer Kaminreparatur hatte er erfahren, wie die Mitglieder des Politbüros, durch elektronisch überwachte Zäune und militärische Bewachung vom realexistierenden Sozialismus abgeschirmt, in relativem Luxus in ihrem Getto bei Wandlitz lebten. Seither, behaupteten Nachbarn, schimpfte er maßlos auf die Führungsspitze der DDR. Essling versuchte also, es »denen« in halsbrecherischer Fahrt zu zeigen, überholte die letzten Polizeifahrzeuge des Honeckerkonvois, suchte zum Wagen des Generalsekretärs aufzuschließen und wurde dabei am Eingang der Ortschaft auf eine Wiese abgedrängt. Soweit eine einigermaßen schlüssige Rekonstruktion des Geschehens an diesem Silvesterabend. Strittig blieb, ob der Ofensetzer tatsächlich das Feuer eröffnete. Einige Klosterfelder behaupteten, die Volkspolizisten hätten ihn erschossen, kaum daß er aus seinem Wagen geklettert sei. Er habe keine Chance gehabt, auch nur einen Schuß abzugeben. Die These von einem Attentat, das ja Planung und Vorbereitung erfordert, wurde durch diese Recherchen nicht gestützt.

In den Medien der DDR gab es keinen Versuch, die Hintergründe aufzuhellen, es blieb bei der offiziellen, für alle Leser, die sich nicht aus westlichen Quellen informierten, unverständlichen ADN-Meldung. Diese Nachrichtenpolitik, die offensichtlich zu spät einen Mittelweg zwischen Verschweigen und Zugeben suchte, bescherte vielen Zeitungen in der Provinz Zuschriften, welche die Redaktionskollegen in Verlegenheit brachten. Da fragte beispielsweise eine junge Leserin bei einem SED-Bezirksorgan an, warum die unter der Überschrift »Selbstmord nach Fahrerflucht« veröffentlichte Information erst zwei Wochen nach dem Ereignis ins Blatt gerückt wurde. Die kritische junge Frau wollte weiter wissen, was denn eigentlich mit »einer schweren Gefährdung des Straßenverkehrs« gemeint gewesen sei, nach der der Fahrer des Lada Fahrerflucht beging. »Fahrerflucht ist doch wohl ein strafbares Verhalten nach einem Verkehrsunfall. Was ereignete sich aber konkret?« Die DDR kennt das sogenannte Eingaberecht, das Institutionen und Behörden die Beantwortung von Bürgeranfragen innerhalb von 14 Tagen zwingend vorschreibt. Um keine Schriftstücke aus der Hand zu geben, die das Blatt im Westen der Lächerlichkeit preisgeben könnten, pflegte diese Provinzzeitung die Praxis, kritische Leserzuschriften mit Hausbesuchen von Redakteuren zu beantworten. Dabei sollten dann nicht nur Skepsis gegenüber der Berichterstattung ausgeräumt, sondern auch die potentiellen Zweifler am rechten Glauben wieder auf den Pfad der Parteitugend zurückgeführt werden. Der in diesem Fall auserkorene Journalist, selbstverständlich Mitglied der SED, war um seine Aufgabe nicht zu beneiden. Wie die meisten seiner Kollegen in den Etagen unterhalb der Chefredaktion, war er der Auffassung, daß die von seiner Zeitung pflichtgemäß abgedruckte Meldung gegen alle Regeln des Journalismus verstieß. Wie sollte er der Leserbrief-Schreiberin, bei der es sich offensichtlich um eine Abiturientin handelte, plausible Antworten auf Fragen geben, die er selbst vergebens stellte? Für seinen Chefredakteur gab es da keine Probleme. Daß die Information so spät erfolgte, hatte schlicht damit zu tun, daß es sich um die »Antwort auf eine Lüge handelte«. Und auf die Frage nach einem möglichen Attentat, so die Anweisung an den Redakteur, war sofort die einschüchternde Gegenfrage zu stellen, woher die Schreiberin diese Vermutung habe; sie werde sich doch nicht etwa aus westlichen Medien informieren?!

»Die Tätigkeit von Presse, Rundfunk und Fernsehen ist ein wesentliches Element der politischen Massenarbeit«, heißt es in einem Beschluß des Politbüros vom Jahr 1977, und: »Es ist ihre Grundaufgabe, als kollektiver Propagandist, Agitator und Organisator zu wirken.« Wann immer die kollektive Agitation durch seine Zeitung sich als unwirksam erwies, schickte der Chefredakteur dieser Provinzzeitung seinen Lesern den persönlichen Agitator ins Haus, gelegentlich mit Spezialaufträgen versehen, die dem besonderen Engagement und den Launen dieses absolutistisch herrschenden Provinz- und Medien-Fürsten entsprangen. Als einer seiner Redakteure eine Reportage über das Standesamt der Bezirkshauptstadt vorlegte, die auf die besondere Beliebtheit christlicher Namen bei den Eltern im realexistierenden Sozialismus schließen ließ – bei den Mädchen hielt Maria die Spitzenstellung, gefolgt von Christine, Christiane und Ruth, bei den Jungen standen Lukas und Johannes obenan – untersagte er den Abdruck. Der Reporter wendete ein, er habe doch nur über Tatsachen berichtet und die Wahrheit geschrieben, doch er wurde barsch beschieden: »Mag sein, aber wir müssen die Wahrheit ja nicht immer drucken.« Und umgehend erhielt er den Auftrag, alle seine Kollegen und Freunde, die demnächst Familienzuwachs erwarteten, gegen die Wahl christlicher Vornamen zu beeinflussen, besser: zu agitieren, wie man in der DDR so gerne sagt.

Von der DKP zu einer Vortragsreihe in eine westdeutsche Landeshauptstadt eingeladen, durfte ein Redakteur dieses Blattes seine erste Westreise unternehmen. Wieder zu Hause, zeigte er sich geschockt vom Zustand der Partei, deren Gast er gewesen war: Die DKP-Stellungnahmen, die seine Zeitung dem SED-Brauch entsprechend, stets als wichtige Äußerung der »progressiven Kräfte« in der Bundesrepublik an prominenter Stelle veröffentlichte, stammten »von einem winzigen Zirkel«, der »aus Fußkranken und Greisen« bestand, wie er zu seinem Entsetzen entdeckte. Als er dies erzählte, war er noch voller Zorn, weil man ihn gezwungen hatte, mit einem Kollegen zu reisen, mit dem er – Vertrauen ist gut, Kontrolle ist besser – selbst nachts das Zimmer teilen mußte: »In diesen 10 Tagen bin ich länger ununterbrochen mit diesem Menschen zusammengewesen als je mit meiner Frau.« Als wichtigsten Eindruck von dieser Westreise notierte er für sich, daß die westliche Gesellschaft zwar ernste Probleme habe, etwa mit der Arbeitslosigkeit, aber sie prägten nicht den Alltag, in dem herrsche vielmehr eine Atmosphäre des Wohlstands vor. In den Berichten, die er für sein Blatt verfaßte, fand sich davon nichts. Er erhielt die Weisung, nur über das Elend der Arbeitslosigkeit zu schreiben. Das Foto vom Arbeitsamt, in seiner Reportage meist als »Ort der zerstörten Hoffnungen« apostrophiert, wurde so beschnitten, daß die davor parkenden Westautos nicht mehr zu sehen waren.

Wer an die Presse westlicher Demokratien gewohnt ist, dem wird es schwerfallen, diesen sozialistischen Journalismus überhaupt ernst zu nehmen, zumal, wenn er erfährt, daß er sich dem »bürgerlichen Journalismus« haushoch überlegen glaubt. Und wer dann den Gründen dieser wahrlich stolzen Selbsteinschätzung nachspürt, dem halten die überzeugten Marxisten-Leninisten umgehend etliche, auch bei uns kritisierte Auswüchse und Schwächen westlicher Medien wie in einem Zerrspiegel vor. Den im Westen immer wieder gegen sie erhobenen Vorwurf der Parteilichkeit und des Mangels an Objektivität ertragen sie gelassen, weil aus ihrer Sicht die bürgerliche Presse, gerade wenn sie sich oft schon im Untertitel als unabhängig, überparteilich oder unparteiisch anpreist, ihre Parteinahme für die Interessen der Bourgeoisie und des Kapitals nur geschickt verbirgt. Westlicher Journalismus, so steht es im Lehrbuch über »Theoretische Grundfragen des sozialistischen Journalismus« der Karl-Marx-Universität Leipzig, versucht, die »Blockade der richtigen Erkenntnis der Welt«, indem er »eine verwirrende Vielfalt für die weltanschauliche und politische Orientierung irrelevanter Informationen vermittelt, falsche Kriterien und falsche Denkmuster vorgibt und rational schwer faßbare Vorurteile aufbaut«. Aus der Sicht der Marxisten-Leninisten betreiben im Westen marktbeherrschende Multimedia-Konzerne »raffinierte Volksverführung«, indem sie »die Massen« mit einem »Konglomerat nichtiger und wichtiger Informationen, Klatsch und Tratsch, Pornographie und Verbrechen, Halbwahrheiten, Stereotypen und Verleumdungen« erschlagen. Die Konzerne prägen mit dieser Form der indirekten, »unpolitischen« Propaganda »im Klasseninteresse des Monpolkapitals liegende, für die Massen im Sozialismus und im Kapitalismus aber objektiv falsche Leitbilder«. Damit nicht genug, suchen sie durch »Lüge, Suggestion und geistigen Terror« obendrein, die »Loyalität zu einem den objektiven Interessen des Volkes gerade entgegengesetzten System« zu sichern.

Nun liegt gewiß in der westlichen Medienlandschaft vieles im argen, doch fiele es leichter, sich mit dieser Kritik auseinanderzusetzen, wenn die, die sie vorbringen, für den »sozialistischen Journalismus« nicht die Rolle eines blind ergebenen Helfershelfers der SED-Führung postulierten. Nach diesem Verständnis haben Journalisten vor allem Propagandisten und Agitatoren zu sein, wobei die Propagandaarbeit der Verbreitung und Vertiefung der rechtgläubigen Lehre, die Agitation unmittelbar konkreten Fragen der Politik gilt. Agitation hat also mit der praktischen Seite der Politik zu tun, und dies vor allem im Rahmen der Taktik; Propaganda soll die Erkenntnis der objektiven Lage und der Interessen der Arbeiterklasse durch die Massen und die Kenntnis des Marxismus-Leninismus befördern. Sozialistischer Journalismus ist somit der wichtigste Transmissionsriemen zwischen der Führungsspitze und den Massen, und er dient, so wiederum das Lehrbuch der Karl-Marx-Universität, »als Instrument des Zentralismus, der einheitlichen, disziplinierten Durchführung der von den Führungsorganen der Partei beschlossenen Politik. Sein Wirken im Auftrage der Partei wird daran gemessen, daß er entschieden und konsequent die Partei und das Parteiprinzip verteidigt.«

Freilich ist die Parteilichkeit, zu der sich die Marxisten-

Leninisten offen bekennen, von besonderer Art – über ihr schwebt ein Heiligenschein. Nach der Glaubenslehre, der sie sich verschrieben haben, hilft ihre Einseitigkeit ja nicht nur allen arbeitenden Menschen; sie ist im Gegensatz zur bürgerlichen Parteilichkeit nicht verhüllt, sondern offen und deshalb ehrlich; und sie trägt zum Fortschritt bei, weil sie den entwicklungsgeschichtlichen Prozeß fördert und beschleunigt, der nach den Gesetzen des dialektischen Materialismus in die klassenlose Gesellschaft mündet, in der die eigentliche, von jeglicher Unterdrückung und Ausbeutung befreite Geschichte der Menschheit ja erst beginnen soll. Proletarische Parteilichkeit in Form einer bewußten und offenen Parteinahme für die Interessen und Ziele der Arbeiterklasse und des gesellschaftlichen Fortschritts auf der Grundlage des Marxismus-Leninismus wird deshalb von der SED zum Prinzip erhoben. Eine Parteilichkeit, die den gesellschaftlichen Fortschritt unterstützt, bewerten die leninistischen Scholastiker als »wahrhaftig«, wie umgekehrt die historische Wahrheit als parteiisch im Interesse der Arbeiterklasse erscheint – ein Interesse, welches sie, und nicht nur hier liegt der Pferdefuß, anmaßend von Fall zu Fall selbst bestimmen. Der Weg in die klassenlose Gesellschaft aber führt, so will es das Dogma, über die Diktatur des Proletariats, also über den Sieg der Arbeiterklasse, und dieser Sieg wiederum ist ohne die zielgerichtete Führung durch die Avantgarde oder das »Hirn der Klasse«, die marxistisch-leninistische Kaderpartei, nicht zu erringen. So betrachtet sich der sozialistische Journalist als Mitstreiter in einem revolutionären weltgeschichtlichen Prozeß, so versteht sich seine Rolle als Propagandist und Agitator, so erklärt sich seine Unterstellung unter die Autorität der Partei, die die politische Linie vorgibt.

Nun ist es eine Sache, die Macht im Staate zu erringen, und eine andere, nach dem Sieg im Klassenkampf den Sozialismus aufzubauen. Für die Phase des Ringens um die Macht mag die Bindung des sozialistischen Journalisten an die Disziplin der Partei, deren Mitglied er ja ist, als Agitator und Propagandist noch verständlich erscheinen. Aber müßte sich sein Rollenver-

ständnis nicht ändern, wenn die Partei die Diktatur des Proletariats errichtet hat? Müßte dann nicht die sozialistische Presse zur Tribüne werden, die eine offene Diskussion unter Sozialisten über den besten Weg ermöglicht, der beim Aufbau
des Sozialismus einzuschlagen ist, zu einem sozialistischen
Forum, auf dem auch Mißstände und mögliche Führungsfeh-
ler angeprangert werden?

Mit eben diesen Argumenten forderten während des Prager
Frühlings eine Gruppe von Journalisten der tschechoslowaki-
schen Parteiblätter die Unabhängigkeit von Spitze und Apparat der Partei. Ihre Begründung: »Die Zeitung ist das Organ
der ganzen herausgebenden Organisation... über sie kann
nicht ausschließlich das führende Organ irgendeiner politischen oder gesellschaftlichen Organisation verfügen.« Eine
andere Gruppe vertrat eine weitergehende Konzeption und
verlangte die »autonome Stellung der Redaktionen« gegenüber der gesamten Partei. Sie berief sich auf den Zwang der
Redaktion, täglich auf aktuelle Ereignisse reagieren zu müssen. Konkret hieß das: Wir können mit Kommentaren nicht
immer warten, bis das Politbüro die politische Linie festgelegt
hat. Außerdem sind wir überzeugte Sozialisten und erwachsene Menschen, also durchaus in der Lage, von einem gesicherten sozialistischen Standpunkt aus Ereignisse zu kommentie-
ren, ohne die Leitparolen eines Politbürokraten abwarten zu
müssen.

Im Zeichen von Glasnost und Perestroika gibt es in Moskau
Ansätze zu einer öffentlichen Diskussion auf einer sozialistischen Basis, die keiner in Frage stellen will. Doch die DDR,
die sich mit Truppen an der Strafaktion gegen die CSSR betei-
ligte, hält dogmatisch an der Unterordnung der Zeitungen
unter die jeweilige Leitung der Partei fest. Sie beruft sich dabei
auf Lenin, der die straffe und konsequente Kontrolle der Journalisten durch die Partei gefordert hatte. Nun mochte Lenins
berühmte These von der »Notwendigkeit jeder Revolution, bei
Strafe ihres Untergangs die konterrevolutionäre Propaganda
zu unterdrücken«, in Jahren des Kampfes und des Bürgerkrie-
ges berechtigt sein. Die SED aber praktiziert die Diktatur des

Proletariats über viele Jahrzehnte, die Machtfrage stellt sich seit langem nicht mehr für sie. Dennoch fürchtet sie offene Auseinandersetzungen wie der Teufel das Weihwasser. Noch die geringfügigste Abweichung von der vorgegebenen Linie wird disziplinarisch geahndet, selbst wohlgemeinte, konstruktive Kritik mit dem Bannstrahl belegt. Als die »Ostseezeitung«, das Parteiblatt der SED-Bezirksleitung Rostock, einen Artikel veröffentlichte, in dem zu lesen stand, Vollbeschäftigung sei auch in einer sozialistischen Gesellschaft kein Gottesgeschenk, läuteten die Alarmglocken im großen grauen Haus in Ostberlin. Immerhin legte die Formulierung die Schlußfolgerung nahe, Arbeitslosigkeit sei auch im realexistierenden Sozialismus zwischen Elbe und Oder denkbar. Dabei hatte der Verfasser, ein Wirtschaftswissenschaftler, nur warnen wollen. Seine These lief darauf hinaus, daß die Vollbeschäftigung und das ebenso umfangreiche wie kostspielige sozialpolitische Programm von Partei und Staat auf Dauer nur durchzuhalten seien, wenn *alle gute* Arbeiten leisteten. Sein Artikel war als ein Beitrag für die Kampagne der Partei zur Steigerung der Arbeitsproduktivität gedacht. Doch die Formulierung, befanden die Zensoren des ZK, arbeite »dem Feind« in die Hände, der Autor ziehe das von der Verfassung garantierte Recht auf Arbeit in Zweifel. Weil sie »kleinbürgerlichen und opportunistischen Auffassungen« Raum gegeben habe, erhielt die »Ostseezeitung« eine Parteirüge. Wochen später erfolgten Umbesetzungen in den Chefetagen der Redaktion.

Selbstverständlich wissen die Politökonomen der DDR und die Parteiführung über den Zusammenhang zwischen niedriger Arbeitsproduktivität und Sicherheit des Arbeitsplatzes, auf den das Rostocker Blatt hingewiesen hatte, bestens Bescheid. Das belegt kein geringerer als der renommierte Altkommunist Jürgen Kuczynski, Ökonom, Gesellschaftswissenschaftler und Verfasser einer »Alltagsgeschichte des deutschen Volkes«. In seinem Buch »Dialog mit meinem Urenkel« erzählt er eine Begebenheit, die klarmacht, gegen welches Tabu das gerüffelte Blatt verstoßen hatte:

»Ich glaube, es war 1948 oder 1949, als ich zu irgendeinem Punkt, der Wirtschaftsfragen betraf, in eine Sitzung des Politbüros gerufen wurde. Es wurde von der geringen Effektivität der Arbeit gesprochen, die nicht nur auf das vielfach so ungenügende technische Niveau zurückzuführen wäre. Ich meinte, daß die Sicherheit des Arbeitsplatzes zu dieser ungenügenden Arbeitsproduktivität beitrüge, und erinnerte an Lenins Worte, daß die Menschen nach der Revolution erst lernen müßten, wie anders als im Kapitalismus sie sich jetzt zu verhalten hätten – im Kapitalismus, in dem es darauf angekommen wäre, gegen die Arbeitshetze Widerstand zu leisten, ja sich möglichst wenig anzustrengen.« Die Sicherheit des Arbeitsplatzes, legte Kuczynski seinen Genossen vom Politbüro dar, verführe zur Senkung der Arbeitsleistung, denn es könne einem ja nichts passieren. »Die Genossen nickten und stimmten mir zu«, fährt er fort. »Und dann, in der sich unmittelbar anschließenden Pause, seufzte ich leise vor mich hin: ›Nur ein Prozent Arbeitslosigkeit, und die Arbeitsleistung wie der Lebensstandard steigen sofort um zwei Prozent‹. Du hättest sehen sollen, wie die Genossen plötzlich über mich herfielen: ›Das kommt überhaupt nicht in Frage!‹ – ›Das muß man mit Propaganda schaffen!‹ – ›Das ist eine Erziehungsfrage!‹ Natürlich hatten die Genossen recht. Lieber größere Aufbauschwierigkeiten im Augenblick... als dem Kapitalismus und seinen Arbeitsdruckmethoden Einlaß zu gewähren.«

Die Arbeitsproduktivität in der DDR liegt noch immer um 30 Prozent unter der der Bundesrepublik, und der Satz, »das muß man mit Propaganda schaffen«, gilt deshalb noch vierzig Jahre später; sehr effektiv kann diese Propaganda über die Jahrzehnte also kaum gewesen sein. Kuczynski selbst kennzeichnete sie als »nicht selten überflüssig aufdringlich oder langweilig«, und träumt von einer Welt, die derlei banalen Agitprop nicht mehr nötig hat: »Es wird auch einmal Zeiten geben, in denen die Menschen ohne ständige Propaganda und politische Erziehung, nur auf Grund ihrer Lebensverhältnisse, gute Kommunisten sein werden.« Solche Umstände und solche Zeiten liegen offenbar in weiter Ferne. Die SED erblickt in den »Generalthemen Steigerung der Arbeitsproduktivität und Festigung der sozialistischen Staatsmacht« auch heute das »Hauptbewährungsfeld« und die »Qualifizierungsstrecke« für den sozialistischen Journalismus.

In der Praxis heißt dies, alle DDR-Medien bleiben in einer Dauerkampagne für die Beweihräucherung der Führung und für die Hebung der Arbeitsproduktivität eingespannt, was sie nicht nur für westlichen Geschmack ungenießbar macht. Wenn der Paternalismus, wie der Dramatiker Heiner Müller einmal sagte, die Krankheit der Kommunistischen Partei ist, dann gehört die SED auf die Intensivstation. Um die Arbeiter zu höheren Leistungen anzuspornen, produziert das »Neue Deutschland« pathetische agitatorisch gedrechselte Schlagzeilen für Vorgänge und Ereignisse, die anderswo kaum berichtenswert sind. »Mähdrescher rollen bis der Nachttau Einhalt gebietet«, lautete eine Aufmacherüberschrift auf der ersten Seite. Darunter wurde vermerkt, daß die »Erntekapitäne«, wie die Fahrer der Maschinen heißen, das gute Wetter nutzten und Überstunden machten, um die Ernte einzubringen. Wenn in der DDR Schlagzeilen macht, was für jeden Bauern seit alters her selbstverständlich ist, läßt dies nicht Rückschlüsse auf eine laxe Arbeitsmoral der LPG-Bauern zu? Oder klopft die SED sich gelegentlich selbst auf die Schulter und suggeriert sich und den Massen, wie brav und fleißig sie doch sind? Im Januar 1987 brachte eine Periode ungewöhnlich scharfen Frosts Schwierigkeiten in der Energieversorgung, weil der Abbau von Braunkohle im Senftenberger Revier gefährdet schien. Tagelang kündeten die Schlagzeilen von einem heroischen Kampf – da »meisterten die Werktätigen die extremen Wetterbedingungen«, ihr Einsatz war »selbstlos«, mit »vereinter Kraft« boten sie »der Kälte Paroli«, und »vollbrachten« selbstverständlich in diesem »Kräftemessen mit dem Winter« stets große, gelegentlich auch »kräfteverzehrende Leistungen«. Da sich Stromausfälle nicht völlig vermeiden ließen, forderten die Parteizeitungen unter dem Motto »Unser Ziel im Wettbewerb ist ein erfüllter Januarplan« in großer Aufmachung Initiativen für Sonderschichten an, um Planrückstände aufzuholen. Da wurde herausgestellt, daß der Karusselldreher Klaus Döll in Erfurt mit einem »persönlichen Planangebot... zwölf Prozent Teile für Kugeldrehkräne über den Plan« fertigen wollte; an der Stelle, an der sonst der Leitartikel steht, druckte das »Neue Deutschland« einen Brief des Magdeburger Stahlbau-Brigadiers Karl Spiller an den »werten Genossen Honecker«, der ebenfalls eine Selbstverpflichtung enthielt: »Ich, mein Kollektiv und annähernd alle Produktionsarbeiter haben sich bereit erklärt, an den Wochenenden Sonderschichten zu fahren und vom 2- in das 3-Schichtsystem überzugehen«; und voller Stolz wurde gemeldet, daß auch noch einiges normal funktionierte: »Exportgüter gingen pünktlich auf die Reise.« Es handelte sich um Anlagen für die Aufzucht von Saatgut für den wichtigsten Handelspartner Sowjetunion.

»Ihr im Westen denkt immer, bei uns steht Politik ganz oben an«, sagte mir einmal ein DDR-Journalist, der Einfluß und Einblick hat, »dabei dreht sich bei uns alles fast ausschließlich um die Ökonomie.« In der Tat spiegeln die Medien geradezu eine Obsession der politischen Führung auf Wirtschaftsfragen wider. Fast zwei Drittel aller Inlandsmeldungen haben wirtschaftspolitische Relevanz. Wer genau zwischen den Zeilen liest, kann sich ein einigermaßen verläßliches Bild von der Wirtschaftslage machen, auch wenn die Summe, mit der die DDR bei westlichen Banken in der Kreide steht, weiter als Staatsgeheimnis gehütet wird. So manche Information, die man im ersten Bericht schmerzlich vermißt – etwa die Höhe des Schadens, der in einem Betrieb durch den harten Frost entstanden ist –, wird in nachfolgenden Artikeln nachgeliefert – als stolze Erfolgsmeldung, derzufolge die Werktätigen in aufopferungsvollem Einsatz den Planrückstand von drei Tagen aufgeholt haben.

Sprachlich kommen diese Nachrichten schwerfällig und unverständlich, ja gravitätisch gestelzt daher, man liebt blumige Adjektive: »Liebevoll und ideenreich« ehrten die Volkskunstschaffenden anläßlich des 40. Jahrestages der Befreiung »Befreiertat und Bruderbund«. Die Gesellschaft für Sport und Technik unterhielt Funkverbindung mit »Heldenstädten« der

Sowjetunion. Kontakte sind immer herzlich, die Gespräche ergebnisreich, die Kampfgemeinschaft ist stets verschworen, das Gedenken feierlich, der Bruderbund unverbrüchlich, das Bekenntnis eindrucksvoll, die Grundlage bewährt. Die Führung bedient sich fast schon rührend-altfränkischer Anreden: Das Grußtelegramm Erich Honeckers zum III. Parteitag der kubanischen Kommunisten war an die »teuren Genossen« adressiert, denen er zu ihrer »großartigen Bilanz« gratulierte und »brüderliche Kampfesgrüße« übermittelte. DDR-Bürger dachten da etwas bitter an die grünen Orangen, die Castro ihnen im Tausch gegen Industriegüter schickt. Und wenn das ZK einem verdienten Genossen im Parteiblatt zum 80. Geburtstag gratuliert, ist der Glückwunsch an den »werten« Genossen gerichtet.

Was das Lesen dieser Presse so erschwert, was vor allem aber die Fernsehnachrichten so ungenießbar macht, ist das beinahe byzantinische Protokoll, an dem die kommunistischen Parteien festhalten. Der Brauch bestimmt, daß alle Teilnehmer einer politischen Konferenz mit sämtlichen Ämtern in Partei und Staat aufgeführt werden. Wenn das Führungstrio der SED, Erich Honecker, Willi Stoph und Horst Sindermann irgendwo gemeinsam erscheinen, geht allein für die hölzern wirkende Aufzählung der Titel, die da heruntergebetet werden, ein Viertel der Zeit verloren, die die Tagesschau für einen normalen Reporterbericht zur Verfügung hält. Dabei dürfte jedem DDR-Bürger hinlänglich bekannt sein, daß der eine Generalsekretär der SED und Vorsitzender des Staatsrats ist (im militärischen Kontext wird auch seine dritte Funktion, die des Vorsitzenden des nationalen Verteidigungsrates, hinzugefügt), der andere Mitglied des Politbüros und Vorsitzender des Ministerrats und daß es sich bei dem dritten um den Präsidenten der Volkskammer handelt, der ebenfalls dem Politbüro angehört. Vollends zu bemitleiden sind die Nachrichtensprecher der Aktuellen Kamera bei Gipfelkonferenzen des Ostblocks, denn da nehmen die Staats- und Regierungschefs, die Außen-, die Verteidigungsminister und die Oberkommandierenden der Streitkräfte von gleich sieben Staaten teil, was in der Regel bedeutet, daß mindestens 35 Namen mitsamt den Ämtern verlesen werden, ehe die Substanz der Meldung gebracht wird, und die ist obendrein in meist schwer verständlichem bürokratischen Verlautbarungsstil abgefaßt. »Die Rekordleistung«, notierte Stefan Heym in einer Analyse der »Aktuellen Kamera« voll bösem Spott, »kam bei dem Bericht über die Ordensverleihung an die Kosmonauten Bykowskij und Axjonow in Berlin, als der Sprecher die Namen sämtlicher bei dem Festakt anwesenden Würdenträger verlas, sowjetischer wie deutscher, in summa 43 Namen mitsamt allen akademischen, Regierungs- und Parteititeln in genau 108 Sekunden bei fünfmaligem Atemholen.« Heym schrieb dies 1971, aber das einschläfernde, betäubende Ritual am sozialistischen Hofe ist bis heute gleich geblieben.

Kein Zweifel, der Aktualitätsbegriff dieses Journalismus folgt anderen Prinzipien als der unsrige. Ist im Westen ein schleichender Trend zu mehr Unterhaltung und Sensation vorherrschend, gilt im Osten das Prinzip einer fast schon bornierten Seriosität um den Preis der Langeweile – einer Seriosität, die sich oft in der kritiklosen Wiedergabe von nicht enden wollenden amtlichen Mitteilungen erschöpft. In der Theorie beruft man sich gern auf Bertold Brecht, der einmal schrieb, es komme darauf an, mit Hilfe der Wahrheit die »Dinge der Welt handhabbar zu machen«. Aber Brecht, Provokateur, Agitator und Neuerer der Bühne, hatte dabei gewiß nicht Langeweile im Sinn. Handhabbar, heißt es im Lehrbuch, wird die Wahrheit nur, wenn die Menschen »nicht in einem Wust wahrer Informationen ersticken, sondern wenn sie wirklich jene erhalten, die für ihr Denken und Handeln nützlich sind«. Was nützlich ist, bestimmt die Abteilung für Agitation und Propaganda im Zentralkomitee.

Nun muß, da Nachrichtensendungen zeitliche, Zeitungsseiten räumliche Grenzen gezogen sind, auch jeder Redakteur im Westen das Bild der Welt für seine Leser und Zuschauer »handhabbar« machen, also manipulieren. Er wählt aus der Fülle des Materials die Meldungen aus, die ihm wichtig und interessant erscheinen. Der »Bildzeitungs«-Redakteur gaukelt den Lesern vor, daß Luis Trenker seine Tochter enterbt, sei die wichtigste Nachricht des Tages. Doch hat der Konsument zumindest die Wahl. Wer der Nachrichtenselektion von »Bild« mißtraut, greift zu besseren Blättern, die sich, wenn auch mit erkennbaren politischen Vorgaben, in Nachrichtenauswahl und Hintergrundberichten um ein einigermaßen korrektes Bild der Wirklichkeit bemühen. In der DDR aber werden Meldungen verbreitet, »die produktiv und damit wesentlich für das Denken und Handeln der Volksmassen bei der Durchsetzung ihrer objektiven Interessen sind, die dazu beitragen, die politische Linie der Partei der Arbeiterklasse durchzusetzen«. Zwar gibt es Zeitungen der Blockparteien, aber in den wichtigen politischen Aufmachern, Berichten und Kommentierungen unterscheidet sich »Die neue Zeit« der CDU oder »Der Morgen« der NDPD kaum vom »Neuen Deutschland«. Eine zentral gesteuerte Medienpolitik, die im Zweifel selbst vorschreibt, wie wichtige Reden oder ADN-Korrespondenzen zu placieren sind, sorgt für lähmende Monotonie im DDR-Blätterwald. Nuancen finden sich allerdings im Feuilleton oder im Lokalteil, bei Theaterkritiken und Buchrezensionen.

»Produktiv und wesentlich« ist, was höhere Arbeitsleistungen stimuliert oder Erfolge in Aussicht stellt. Wenn das Kosmetikkombinat Berlin verspricht, eine neue Pflegeserie, darunter Vollplast-Deoroller in 3 Varianten und ein neues Schaumcremebad zu produzieren, ist das dem »Neuen Deutschland« einen Dreispalter wert, für die Tatsache, daß der Präsidentschaftskandidat Kurt Waldheim in Österreich wegen seiner Nazivergangenheit heftig umstritten ist, erübrigte das Parteiorgan keine Zeile, die »Aktuelle Kamera« kein Wort. Nach Waldheims Wahl wurde ein Lebenslauf veröffentlicht, der auf westliche Leser wie eine Satire wirken mußte: »Dr. Kurt Waldheim wurde 1918 geboren. Er studierte an der Universität Wien, wo er zum Doktor der Rechte promovierte, und an der Wiener Konsularakademie. Seine diplomatische Laufbahn begann er 1945.« Das las sich, wie von Waldheim bestellt oder geschrieben, die Zeit als deutscher Offizier im Kriege wurde einfach übersprungen. Nur »Horizonte«, ein außen-politisches Monatsblatt, erwähnte die Auseinandersetzung um Waldheims Verhalten nach dem Anschluß Österreichs, wobei betont distanziert von »angeblicher Nazivergangenheit« die Rede war. Die Erklärung dafür lieferte Erich Honecker am Tag nach Waldheims Wahl, als er telegraphisch seine »herzliche Gratulation« übermittelte. »Wir haben ein gutes Verhältnis zu Österreich«, kommentierte ein DDR-Kollege das gesammelte Schweigen im Fall Waldheim, »das wollten wir nicht belasten. Und wie sollen wir unseren Leuten erklären, daß unsere Nummer 1 einem Mann Glückwünsche schickt, den wir vorher durch den Kakao gezogen haben?«

Daß außenpolitische Rücksichten allemal Vorrang haben vor der Information, lehrt auch die Art, in der die Greenpeace-Affäre in den DDR-Medien behandelt wurde. Die »Rainbow-Warrior« von Greenpeace, die zum französischen Atomtestgebiet bei dem Mururoa-Atoll auslaufen sollte, war im Juli 1985 im neuseeländischen Auckland vom französischen Geheimdienst versenkt worden. Es kam zu erheblichen Spannungen zwischen Frankreich und Neuseeland, in der französischen Öffentlichkeit gingen die Wogen hoch, die Pariser Regierung steckte in einer tiefen Krise, doch die DDR-Medien hielten den Fall für nicht erwähnenswert. Erst als Verteidigungsminister Hernu Ende September zurücktrat und Premierminister Fabius die Aktion der französischen Agenten in der Assemblée Nationale öffentlich eingestand, veröffentlichte das »Neue Deutschland« eine 24-Zeilen-Meldung auf Seite 5. »Wir sind eben nett«, meinte ein DDR-Chefredakteur. Natürlich hatte diese Nettigkeit, die die eigenen Bürger entmündigt, guten Grund: Der französische Sozialist Laurent Fabius war der erste Regierungschef der drei Garantiemächte für Westberlin, der mit Erich Honecker in dessen Amtssitz am Marx-Engels-Platz konferierte – in Ostberlin, wo nach Auffassung der westlichen Wächter über den Viermächtestatus die DDR-Regierung ihren Sitz eigentlich gar nicht haben darf.

»Ich frage gelegentlich im großen grauen Haus, was haltet ihr von der Sache?« erzählte mir der Kollege, dem ich die »Nettigkeit« verdanke. »Wenn die Antwort kommt: Darüber

wird diskutiert; oder: Es hat Diskussionen gegeben, heißt das
soviel wie: Laß besser die Finger davon.« Über Aids hatten
»Spiegel« und »Stern« schon mehrere Titelgeschichten gebracht, die neue Krankheit war seit Monaten Thema in der
Tagespresse und in Fernsehdiskussionen, der »Weltspiegel«
brachte erste Reportagen über die Diskriminierung von Aids-
Infizierten an amerikanischen Schulen – für die DDR-Medien
existierte die Immunschwäche nicht. Erst als das Politbüro
darüber diskutiert und sich auf eine Linie geeinigt hatte, die
festlegte, wie die DDR-Bevölkerung zu informieren sei, erschien endlich der erste Artikel. Er war gut vorbereitet, umfassend und betont sachlich gehalten. Die Nachrichtenpolitik
zielte in diesem Fall offensichtlich darauf, unnötige Aufre-
gung, ja Hysterie zu vermeiden, wie sie im Westen auf der
Tagesordnung war. Doch all das verfehlte die Wirkung, denn
es kam zu spät. Längst rissen die bevormundeten DDR-Bürger ihre Witze über die neue Seuche. Frage: »Warum gibt es
bei uns kein Aids?« Antwort: »Das ist wie mit dem Smog:
Unsere Grenze ist so dicht, daß da nichts rüberkommt.«

Die regierenden deutschen Kommunisten nehmen für sich
in Anspruch, daß bei ihnen andere Spielregeln gelten als in
der bürgerlichen Gesellschaft. Das stimmt in der Tat. Bad
news, good news, dieser Satz, nach dem gute Nachrichten in
der Regel keine Nachrichten sind, wurde von der SED auf den
Kopf gestellt. Unverzüglich und in geradezu epischer Breite
berichtet die »Aktuelle Kamera«, sobald für Partei und Staat
Erfreuliches mitzuteilen ist. Wenn an einem Tag drei neue
Botschafter dem DDR-Staatsratsvorsitzenden ihre Beglaubi-
gungsschreiben überreichen, läßt es sich die Hauptnachrich-
tensendung des DDR-Fernsehens nicht nehmen, die wichtigsten Protokollszenen nacheinander auf den Schirm zu bringen. Dreimal fahren dunkelblaue Limousinen vor dem Staats-
ratsgebäude vor, dreimal werden Flaggen aufgezogen, Nationalhymnen intoniert, dreimal schreiten »außerordentliche
und bevollmächtigte Botschafter«, wie der mit öliger Stimme vorgetragene, vollmundig-pathetische Text hervorhebt,
die Front der Ehrenformation des Wachregiments »Feliks

238

Dzierzynski« ab, verneigen sich vor der Fahne mit dem DDR-
Emblem und schütteln danach Erich Honecker die Hand. Im
Westen wäre so etwas für das Fernsehen schlicht ein Anathe-
ma, Zeitungen brächten bestenfalls eine Kurznotiz. Kein
Zweifel: Dieser Staat hat Komplexe wegen seiner schwierigen
Kindheit. Wenn das DDR-Fernsehen geradezu im Zeremo-
niell badet, dann nach dem Motto, »nun sind wir doch wer«.
Die zeitraubende Wiederholung des immer Gleichen macht
nur für den Sinn, der noch immer schmerzlich einen Nach-
holbedarf an Anerkennung verspürt. Treffend sprach Klaus
Bölling, der die Zeremonie als zweiter bundesdeutscher Vertreter über sich ergehen lassen mußte, von einer »Selbstinsze-
nierung der DDR, bei der die Missionschefs eigentlich nur als
Statisten gebraucht wurden«.

Stark autosuggestive Züge trägt eine andere Selbstinszenie-
rung, die zum Gedenken an die Ermordung Karl Liebknechts
und Rosa Luxemburgs am 15. Januar 1919 stattfindet. Da
marschiert das Politbüro an der Spitze einer wie immer
»machtvollen« Kampfdemonstration zur Gedenkstätte der Sozialisten auf dem Zentralfriedhof Berlin-Friedrichsfelde. Auch
hier, Jahr für Jahr am zweiten Sonntag im Januar die Wiederholung des immer Gleichen. Wenige Minuten vor neun Uhr
klettern die Mitglieder der Parteiführung am S-Bahnhof
Frankfurter Allee aus ihren geheizten Staatskarossen und setzen sich vor die »Kolonne der 250 000« Werktätigen. Die sind
zum größeren Teil Mitglieder der Partei und haben schon
Stunden vorher nach einem »Aufmarschplan« Aufstellung
genommen, der von allen Zeitungen veröffentlicht wurde und
– »günstige Möglichkeiten der Anfahrt« eingeschlossen – bis
ins Detail regelt, wann auf welchem Stellplatz sich die Angehörigen der Betriebe und wissenschaftlichen Institute, Mini-
sterien und zentralen Verwaltungen einzufinden haben. Da
ist nicht nur nachzulesen, wer zu »Marschsäule I« oder zu
»Marschsäule III« gehört, da steht auch, welche »Werktätigen
aus den Bereichen der Kreisleitungen« (der SED) das Spalier
zu bilden haben. Das auf dem XI. Parteitag 1986 gewählte
Politbüro weist ein statistisches Durchschnittsalter von 64

Jahren auf, für so manchen betagten Genossen stellt der Drei-einhalb-Kilometer-Marsch bei Wind und Wetter – einmal zeigte das Thermometer 18 Grad minus an – eine beachtliche physische Leistung dar, nicht jedoch für den Generalsekretär. Als ob er es genieße, seine in der Tat erstaunliche Fitness vor aller Augen und zahllosen Kameras demonstrativ zur Schau zu stellen, schreitet Erich Honecker munter voran, die russische Pelzmütze keck und angeschrägt auf dem Kopf wie Trenck der Pandur aus alten Ufa-Zeiten. Mal ballt er die rechte Hand zum »Thälmanngruß«, mal winkt er huldvoll; sichtlich findet er Spaß daran, die alten Lieder der Arbeiterbewegung anzustimmen, singt aus voller Kehle mit und strahlt, als ob er sich einer glücklichen Jugend im Wiebelskirchener Schalmeienzug erinnerte. Selbstverständlich überträgt das DDR-Fernsehen dieses Stunden während Spektakel live. Doch damit nicht genug, hat die »Aktuelle Kamera« am Abend gleich 25 von 30 Minuten Sendezeit für einen Zusammenschnitt des »Aufmarschs der Hunderttausenden« reserviert. Kommentar und Bildauswahl machen deutlich, was die sozialistische Wallfahrt zu den Gräbern im Bewußtsein der Zuschauer bewirken soll. Winkende Mütter und Väter im Spalier halten fähnchenschwenkende Kinder im Arm, ein Sprechchor intoniert Hochrufe auf das Zentralkomitee und seinen Generalsekretär, und plötzlich – Schnitt – ist dieser im Bild, freundlich lächelnd, zurückwinkend, Seit' an Seit' mit den Genossen vom Politbüro; danach – Schnitt – sind wieder die glücklichen Familien vom Straßenrand auf dem Schirm. Der dazu gehörige Text erläutert: »Das Vertrauensverhältnis von Partei und Volk ist enger denn je. Wahre Menschlichkeit, Gleichberechtigung und Freiheit, soziale Sicherheit und Frieden bestimmen das Antlitz unserer Gesellschaft.« In Großaufnahme werden die von den Marschsäulen mitgeführten Transparente vorgestellt: »Mein Arbeitsplatz – Mein Kampfplatz für den Frieden« lautet eine der vorgestanzten Parolen, die sich immer wieder findet. Da die Partei lehrt, der Friede muß bewaffnet sein, marschiert eine Gruppe der FDJ mit der Losung: »Mein Beitrag zum Frieden: Ich werde Berufsoffizier.« Und da auch die traditionellen Selbstverpflichtungen nicht fehlen dürfen, schleppen Studenten den Spruch: »Unser Ziel: Die besten Ergebnisse zur Abschlußprüfung« über die »breite Magistrale« durch das Spalier der »Bürger aller Generationen«, die sich laut Kommentar versammelt haben: »Veteranen des revolutionären Kampfes der Arbeiterklasse, Aktivisten der ersten Stunde und junge Erbauer der entwickelten sozialistischen Gesellschaft.« Zum Abschluß paradieren die Kampfgruppen der Arbeiterklasse vor der Parteiführung, ein Musikzug der NVA spielt auf, doch so mancher Kämpfer rückt ins Bild, dessen pflichtgemäß eingeübte martialische Attitüde und grimmig-entschlossener Blick so recht nicht zu dem Bauch passen will, der sich unter der Uniformjacke wölbt. »Arbeiter, Ingenieure und Wissenschaftler in den Uniformen der Kampfgruppen sorgen dafür, daß sich das Vaterland gedeihlich weiterentwickelt«, sagt der Sprecher weihevoll. »Schutz des Sozialismus und Erhaltung des Friedens sind nicht voneinander zu trennen.«

Geballte 25 Minuten lang führte diese Reportage eine heile DDR-Welt vor, wie die Parteispitze sie sich erträumt und die doch nur eine artifizielle ist. Die Männer vom Politbüro wollen geliebt werden wie alle Politiker. Das kunstvoll in Szene gesetzte Schauspiel trägt den Titel »Einheit von Partei und Volk«, doch über die wahren Beziehungen zwischen Führung und Geführten sagt es so gut wie nichts. Da werden lediglich Wunschgedanken der Führung nach einer fast mystischen Verschmelzung von oben und unten oder von »Herr und Knecht«, um das Wort des DDR-Autors Volker Braun aufzunehmen, in der Form uralter Beschwörungsrituale zelebriert. Es ist ein Kultus, dessen Priester in der Heilsgewißheit leben, daß die Welt sich der marxistisch-leninistischen Theorie zufolge mit fast naturwissenschaftlicher Gesetzmäßigkeit auf ihre Ziele zubewegt, und er schließt die Beweihräucherung der führenden Persönlichkeiten bewußt mit ein. Viereinhalb Minuten lang war Erich Honecker, der als einziger SED-Politiker in der Bevölkerung über einige Popularität verfügt, in dieser Reportage bildfüllend präsent, doch wer regelmäßig das

»Neue Deutschland« verfolgt, dem schien er beinahe unterre-
präsentiert.

In einem Bericht des »Neuen Deutschland« vom Mai 1986
über eine Reise des Staatschefs in die Provinz war Erich Honecker gleich zehnmal im Bild zu sehen: Dreimal auf der
ersten Seite – winkend auf der Tribüne; im weißen Techniker-
kittel im »VEB Mikroelektronik Karl Marx« und, weniger
prosaisch, mit Gärtnerinnen und Melkerinnen in alten Bau-
erntrachten. Dreimal auf Seite drei: Vor dem Modell des neu-
geplanten Stadtteils Erfurt Süd-Südost; als Redner auf der
Tribüne mit kernig-entschlossenem Blick; einen Blumen-
strauß von einer hübschen jungen Werktätigen empfangend.
Viermal auf Seite vier: Eine Hundertschaft der Kampfgruppe
abschreitend; einen Händedruck mit einer Werktätigen in einem Büromaschinenwerk tauschend; schließlich in der »LPG
Fahner-Obst« ein Apfelbäumchen pflanzend.

Wer dies für eine stattliche Strecke hält, sei gewarnt. Zweimal im Jahr, bei der Eröffnung der Frühjahrs- und Herbst-
messe, wird Leipzig in den Augen der DDR zum Nabel der
Welt. Da mögen anderswo Sintfluten hereinbrechen oder Präsidenten stürzen, der Rundgang, mit dem der Generalsekretär
und Staatsratsvorsitzende die Messe eröffnet, ist das alles
überragende Ereignis, das Fernsehnachrichten und Zeitungsseiten füllt. Im »Neuen Deutschland« vom 2. September 1985
zählte ich 27 Fotos, die Honecker auf den verschiedenen Mes-
seständen zeigten, bei der Frühjahrsmesse 1986 waren es
schon 31, doch das Personenkult-Barometer kletterte weiter
auf Hoch. Die Rekordmarke wurde im März 1987 erreicht, als
das Parteiorgan den Generalsekretär auf der ersten Seite
gleich fünfmal porträtierte (davon dreimal mit den westdeutschen Politikern Bangemann, Strauß und Diepgen), insgesamt
sah er sich in dieser Ausgabe 43mal abgebildet.

Als in der DDR akkreditierter Korrespondent konnte ich's
zufrieden sein, denn diese Form der Nachrichtengebung sichert dem eigenen System, vom »Tal der Ahnungslosen« um
Dresden und der Gegend um Greifswald, wo man ARD und
ZDF nicht empfangen kann, einmal abgesehen, die absolute

Priorität bei den Zuschauern in der DDR – sie werden den West-Sendern geradezu in die Arme getrieben. Und doch bedrängten mich Zweifel. Erich Honecker macht den Eindruck eines Realpolitikers, sein oft glanzloser Stil ist trocken, sachlich und nüchtern. Mochte dieser durch und durch uneitle, jeder Show abgeneigte Stil auch auf persönliche Scheu zurückzuführen sein, die Unbeholfenheit, die aus ihm sprach, wirkte nicht unsympathisch. Der sozialistische Ikonenkult, den die SED-Medienpriester mit seiner Person betreiben, konnte ihm schlechterdings nicht verborgen bleiben. Ein Wort des Generalsekretärs hätte genügt, ihn sofort zu beenden. Warum sprach er es nicht? Ich fragte einen, von dem ich wußte, daß er ihm vertraut. Dessen Antwort: »Werden Sie einmal 75, vielleicht ändern auch Sie sich bis dahin und sind voller Stolz auf das, was Sie geleistet haben.« Überzeugend klang das nicht.

8. Die DDR und Perestroika

Die DDR gibt westlichen Beobachtern manche Rätsel auf. Etliche lassen sich lösen, ist man nur lange genug mit den »Mühen der Ebenen« vertraut, die schon Bertolt Brecht bespöttelte. Zu den schier unlösbaren Rätseln aber zählt die geradezu fieberhafte Aktivität, welche Partei- und Staatsführung vor Kommunal- und Volkskammerwahlen entwickeln. Da werden selbst Politbüro-Mitglieder, die fernab der grauen Alltagsrealitäten in ihrem selbsterwählten Sicherheitsghetto in Wandlitz leben, plötzlich zu Politikern, wenn nicht zum Anfassen, dann doch zum Anhören und Ansehen vor Ort. Den ganzen Mai 1986 schwärmte die Elite von Partei und Staat bis in die letzten Winkel der DDR aus, um am 8. Juni ein stattliches Ergebnis der Wahlen zur Volkskammer einzufahren. Dabei stand dies bis auf wenige Prozentpunkte hinter dem Komma von vornherein fest, hatte doch die Einheitsliste seit 1950 regelmäßig über 99 Prozent der Stimmen erhalten. Dennoch schien, glaubte man den Medien, alles einem spannenden, schier unglaublichen Höhepunkt entgegenzustreben. Minister, die die Kollektive der Werktätigen in den großen Betrieben besuchten (und welche Minister taten das nicht?) führten Dialoge, die immerzu »vertrauensvoll«, hatten Begegnungen, die stets »herzlich« waren. Sie trafen fortwährend auf DDR-Bürger, die für Republik und Sozialismus »an jedem Tag das beste« gaben, deren Heimat »immer schöner« wurde und die deshalb den »gemeinsam eingeschlagenen Weg« fortsetzen wollten. Sie sprachen mit Jugendbrigaden, die gelobten, »voller Tatkraft die ökonomische Strategie der Partei« zu verwirklichen und sich »ohne Tempoverlust auf die Meisterung der Schlüsseltechnologien« vorzubereiten. Handwerker der PGH Birkenwerder im Bezirk Potsdam verhießen, die Reparaturleistungen für Haushaltsgeräte über den Plan zu erhöhen, die Mitglieder der PGH Metall Neuruppin stellten in Aussicht, »mehr Stoßdämpfer zu regenerieren«. »Es lassen sich«, versicherte der Korrespondent des »Neuen Deutschland« dieses Mal überaus glaubwürdig, »alle Verpflichtungen« dieser Handwerkerversammlung gar nicht aufzählen. Beteuerungen, mit Blick auf den 8. Juni 1986 mehr und besseres zu schaffen, kamen auch von den Streitkräften. Unteroffizier Mario Wagenschwanz, so meldete die Zeitschrift »Volksarmee«, rief als FDJ-Sekretär seine Einheit dazu auf, »30 Wachen ohne Vorkommnisse« zu leisten. Soldat Rudolf Lenke setzte sich zum Ziel, im Rahmen des sozialistischen Wettbewerbs den Titel »Bester Wachsoldat« zu erringen. Major Hans-Jürgen Horn versprach, die zur Wehrübung eingezogenen Reservisten so zu drillen, daß sie »vom ersten Tage an gefechtsbereit« seien. Und der Unteroffizier und Panzerfahrer Olaf Mundt versicherte, wegen ihrer konsequenten Friedenspolitik könne die Partei sich auf ihn als Kommandant eines T-55 jederzeit verlassen.

Sind all diese Anstrengungen und Mühen nicht wahrhaft erstaunlich, wenn man bedenkt, daß die Entscheidung, welche politischen Kräfte die Macht im Staat ausüben, nach marxistisch-leninistischer Sicht ein für allemal getroffen ist? Danach liegt die Macht unwiderruflich bei der SED, die zusammen mit den ihr verbündeten Parteien und Massenorganisationen der Nationalen Front dem Wähler eine Einheitsliste vorlegt, auf der bestenfalls dieser oder jener Kandidat gestrichen werden kann. Nach Auffassung der SED erfolgt der eigentliche Wahlakt mit der Aufstellung des Kandidaten, so daß der Wahltag selbst nur den formellen Endpunkt einer »großen Wahlbewegung« bedeutet, die an der Basis beginnt. Doch gerade das erhebt ihn in den Rang eines »politischen Festtags«, an dem Führung und Geführte einander Harmonie und Eintracht demonstrieren. Schließlich sollen Wahlen, so die

246

Präambel des Wahlgesetzes, dazu beitragen, »die entwickelte sozialistische Gesellschaft zu gestalten und so die grundlegenden Voraussetzungen für den allmählichen Übergang zum Kommunismus zu schaffen«.

Wie so etwas im einzelnen abläuft, erläuterte ein CDU-Kandidat für die (Ost-)Berliner Stadtverordneten-Versammlung einem befreundeten westdeutschen Pfarrer, der mit der »immer wieder verbreiteten Klischeevorstellung« in die DDR gekommen war, »wir dürften nicht von einer Wahl sprechen, weil wir doch lediglich einen Einheitsstimmschein« in die Urne werfen. »Da hilft nur eins«, schrieb der Kandidat in der Wochenzeitung »Sonntag« – nämlich: »in medias res zu gehen. Als ein christlicher Demokrat unseres Landes, der seit zwei Jahrzehnten Abgeordneter ist ... hatte ich verständlicherweise genügend Belege und Beweise für das Funktionieren unserer sozialistischen Demokratie parat: Nachdenklichkeit trat in sein Gesicht, als ich ihm die verschiedenen Etappen erläuterte, die ich – gleich allen Kandidaten – bis zur Wahl am 8. Juni zu durchlaufen habe. Prüfung durch das Arbeitskollektiv, durch die Kollegen – davon wußte er nichts, das kannte er in seinem Lande nicht. Auch nicht, daß damit eine (Voraus-)Wahl stattfindet. Etliche Kandidaten konnten nicht das Vertrauen ihrer Kollegen erringen und schieden aus dem Kreis der Abgeordneten-Anwärter aus.« Nun werden die Kandidaten in der Tat von den Kollektiven, in denen sie tätig sind, geprüft, aber Ablehnungen sind seltene Ausnahmen und keinesfalls die Regel. Bei den Kommunalwahlen 1984 fielen von insgesamt 263 000 Kandidaten nur rund 800 durchs Netz. Die Aufstellung der Kandidaten obliegt auch nicht den Kollektiven, sondern den Ausschüssen der Nationalen Front, und nominiert wird nur, wer zuvor – und das schließt Wahlbewerber der Blockparteien ein – von den örtlich zuständigen SED-Kreissekretären gründlich auf Zuverlässigkeit durchleuchtet wurde. Ist die anschließende Prüfung durch die Arbeitskollektive geschehen, stellen sie sich auf »öffentlichen Vorstellungen« den in der Regel harmlosen Fragen von Wählern. Danach kommen sie dann auf die Einheitsliste der Nationalen Front und – werden automatisch gewählt.

Übrigens steckt im Wahlgesetz der DDR auch ein Stück von der marxschen Konzeption des Rätesystems, denn der Abgeordnete ist formell an einen Wählerauftrag gebunden und kann theoretisch von den Wählern in der laufenden Wahlperiode abberufen werden. In der Praxis ist ein solcher Rückruf nie erfolgt, und Wähleraufträge, die nicht den übergeordneten »gesamtgesellschaftlichen Interessen« entsprechen, haben natürlich keine Chance. Die ganzen Energien, die in westlichen Demokratien der Kampf miteinander um Mehrheit und Macht konkurrierender Parteien verschlingt, werden im realen Sozialismus darauf verwendet, eine möglichst hohe Wahlbeteiligung zu erzielen, damit die Zustimmung des Volks zur Politik der Führung wieder einmal »überwältigend« erscheint. So wetteifern die einzelnen Wahlkreise miteinander, wer auch den letzten Wähler an die Urne bringt, und das so früh es irgend geht. Viele »Hausgemeinschaften« rücken geschlossen an, kaum daß die Türen der Wahllokale geöffnet sind. Eine Studentin in Leipzig erschien eine Viertelstunde nach fünf, also immer noch gute 45 Minuten vor Ende der Wahl. Am nächsten Tag wurde sie zum Parteisekretär zitiert und geradezu bösartig befragt, warum sie nicht früher gekommen sei. In den Nachrichtensendungen am Wahltag gab es laufend Zwischenberichte, wer im Kampf um die möglichst totale Mobilisierung der Wähler zur Stunde gerade vorne lag. Die »Aktuelle Kamera« zeigte Wahllokale, in denen die »Bürger den Wahlakt vollziehen«, aber der Kamerastandpunkt war so geschickt gewählt, daß die Wahlkabine, die längst nur noch als Formalie existiert, nie ins Bild geriet. Da war eine Gruppe von Diakonissen zu sehen: Sie traten ein, gaben ihre Wahlbenachrichtigung ab und nahmen den Zettel mit den Wahlvorschlägen entgegen; das Stück Papier würdigten sie nicht eines Blickes, falteten es zusammen und steckten es in die Urne. Bei den Kommunalwahlen 1984 drehte ich in einem Wahllokal in Berlin-Pankow. Als wir kurz nach 12 Uhr eintrafen, hatten schon »achtzig Prozent ihrer Bürgerpflicht genügt«, wie der örtliche Wahlleiter mir stolz erzählte. In einer Ecke des geräumigen Klassenzimmers sah ich die Wahlkabine stehen – weit entfernt von der Urne und dem Tisch, an dem der Wähler seinen Stimmzettel erhält. Wer da von dem Recht hätte Gebrauch machen wollen, einige Kandidaten zu streichen oder den Wahlvorschlag ungültig zu machen, wäre mehr als aufgefallen: Der Gang zur Kabine wäre einem Spießrutenlauf gleichgekommen. Ich fragte den Wahlleiter: »Hat einer von den achtzig Prozent, die schon gewählt haben, die Kabine benutzt?« »Nein, heute noch niemand«, antwortete er und meinte: »Das ist ein großer Vertrauensbeweis.« Freunde in Leipzig sagten: »Der Gang zur Urne ist ein Akt der Erniedrigung. Hinterher schämen wir uns jedesmal. Aber es bringt viel überflüssigen Ärger, wenn man nicht hingeht. Und wer geht, befolgt dann auch das offene Ritual. Er benutzt nicht die Kabine, er faltet den Zettel offen; er streicht keinen Kandidaten und steckt ihn einfach in die Urne.« Es gibt nicht den geringsten Zweifel, daß gerade intelligente DDR-Bürger die offene Stimmabgabe nicht nur deshalb vorziehen, weil sie sich damit vor Repressalien schützen. Das ist sicherlich ein wichtiges Motiv. Ebenso wichtig aber ist die Überzeugung, daß sie, wenn sie nicht die Kabine benutzen, dazu beitragen, diese laut DDR-Verfassung allgemeinen, gleichen und geheimen Wahlen als eine Farce zu entlarven. Wenn das auch schlitzohrig gedacht ist, tröstet es doch manchen über den »Akt der Erniedrigung« hinweg.

Ist der Wahlakt eine Farce, gerät dem DDR-Fernsehen die Wahlberichterstattung zur Groteske. Da wurde nach westlichem Muster eigens ein Wahlstudio eingerichtet, das die neuesten Meldungen von der dramatischen Schlacht verbreitete, die um die Dezimalstellen hinter dem Komma der 99 Prozent tobte. Als Gewinner ging aus ihr am 8. Juni 1986 der Wahlkreis Nordhausen-Sondershausen mit einer Wahlbeteiligung von 99,96 Prozent und einem Ja-Stimmenanteil von 99,98 Prozent hervor. Die in diesem Wahlkreis zuständigen Genossen nähern sich bedenklich der Hundertprozentmarke und müssen aufpassen, daß sie bei den nächsten Wahlen, in denen sie gewiß den eigenen Rekord noch einmal überbieten wollen, nicht mehr Ja-Stimmen als Wähler zählen. Immerhin erlaubte selbst dieser Wahlausgang einige Rückschlüsse auf die unterschiedliche Stimmung in der Bevölkerung. Gemessen am DDR-Durchschnitt – Wahlbeteiligung 99,73, Ja-Stimmen 99,94 Prozent – lagen die Ergebnisse einiger Berliner Wahlkreise deutlich darunter. Im traditionellen Arbeiterbezirk Prenzlauer Berg gingen nur 97,7 Prozent zur Wahl, auch waren überdurchschnittlich viele Gegenstimmen (0,18 Prozent; DDR: 0,06 Prozent) zu verzeichnen. Im Rahmen einer Wahlbewegung, die auf totale Mobilmachung aller Wähler zielt, sind das schon beachtliche Signale. Allerdings hatten in den riesigen, verwitterten Mietskasernen und ihren Hinterhöfen am Prenzlauer Berg immer mehr Ausreisewillige gelebt als in anderen Stadtbezirken oder DDR-Regionen. Wer einmal Antragsteller ist, wie das auf DDR-isch heißt, bringt sicher leichter den Mut auf, den Spießrutenlauf zur Wahlkabine zu wagen, den Stimmzettel ungültig zu machen oder gar sein Nein darauf zu vermerken. Für die Behörden ist er ohnehin ein Gezeichneter, so daß er sich kaum noch zusätzliche Unannehmlichkeiten einhandeln dürfte – im Gegenteil: Sein Wählerverhalten könnte als Beweis für die Annahme dienen, daß es sich bei ihm um einen jener völlig Verstockten handelt, die man besser ziehen läßt, weil sie doch nicht in die sozialistische Gesellschaft zu integrieren sind. So liefert die große Zahl derer, die Honecker in den Jahren vor den letzten Volkskammerwahlen ausreisen ließ, vielleicht die Erklärung dafür, daß die Nein-Stimmen gegenüber den 81er Wahlen um mehr als die Hälfte zurückgingen. Nur 7502 Wähler der DDR, das sind ganze 0,6 Prozent, stimmten 1986 mit Nein, 1981 waren es noch 16645, was einem Anteil von 0,14 Prozent der abgegebenen Stimmen entsprach.

Versuche, den Bürgern wenn schon nicht die Wahl zwischen verschiedenen Programmen, dann doch zwischen mehreren Personen für eine Position zu erlauben, steht die DDR-Führung weiterhin ablehnend gegenüber. Die ungarischen Kommunisten haben sich schon vor Jahren zu einer Wahlreform entschlossen, die zwingend vorschreibt, daß für einen Sitz mehrere Bewerber kandidieren müssen. Das führte dazu, daß mancher unbeliebte Parteisekretär sich plötzlich im Parlament oder in seiner regionalen Ratsversammlung nicht wiederfand. An der Vorherrschaft der Partei änderte sich dadurch jedoch nichts. Aber selbst, als Gorbatschow dazu überging, das neue Prinzip der Ungarn in einigen sowjetischen Regionen bei den Parteiwahlen der KPdSU auf seine Tauglichkeit zu testen, war die Resonanz in der DDR negativ, wann immer ich auf das Beispiel des südosteuropäischen Bruderlands zu sprechen kam. Als Begründung wurde da einmal die Tatsache genannt, daß es schon jetzt schwer falle, Kandidaten für die insgesamt 204 000 Abgeordnetenpositionen zu finden, die auf den verschiedensten Ebenen des Staates zu besetzen sind. Ich müsse auch bedenken, daß weitere 400 000 DDR-Bürger in sogenannten ständigen Kommissionen und Aktivs der örtlichen Volksvertretung säßen, um den gewählten 204 000 zuzuarbeiten. Außerdem erforderten Nationale Front, Elternaktivs sowie Arbeiter- und Bauerninspektionen zahllose zusätzliche ehrenamtliche Mitarbeiter. Jeder dritte DDR-Bürger, erklärte Erich Honecker auf dem SED-Parteitag 1986, erfülle eine ehrenamtliche Position. Das klingt beinahe so, als erbringe die DDR bereits ein Übersoll an sozialistischer Demokratie.

Ein bißchen überzeugender wirkte da schon der Hinweis auf die Existenz der Blockparteien. Sie respektieren zwar den Führungsanspruch der SED, die ihnen die Zahl ihrer Sitze in der Volkskammer und den Vertretungen der Bezirke, Kreise und Kommunen fest zuweist. Aber in Detailfragen unterscheiden sie sich doch nach Nuancen. Auch wenn sie öffentlich nicht ins Gewicht fällt, spielt derlei Differenzierung hinter verschlossenen Türen, etwa in der Ausschußarbeit der Volkskammer für den Gesetzgebungsprozeß, speziell für das sogenannte Kleingedruckte, gelegentlich eine Rolle. Vor allem im kommunalen Bereich gibt es für die Abgeordneten der Bündnisparteien Möglichkeiten, ihre zumeist pragmatischen Vorstellungen zur Verbesserung der Lebensumstände beizusteuern. Wenn die Mitgliederzahl dieser Parteien in den letzten Jahren wieder eine leicht steigende Tendenz aufweist, hat das natürlich auch damit zu tun, daß für viele die Mitgliedschaft eine relativ problemlose Möglichkeit darstellt, den »Nachweis gesellschaftlicher Aktivität« zu erbringen. Wer einer Blockpartei angehört, ist integriert, ohne daß er der Ideologie des Marxismus-Leninismus Tribut zollen muß. Selbst wenn er in eine Partei geht, die das im realen Sozialismus wahrlich anachronistische Wort »liberal« im Firmenschild führt, beweist er, daß er dazugehört und den Sozialismus akzeptiert. So bekennt sich die LDPD, die Liberal-Demokratische Partei Deutschlands, wie sie noch immer heißt, in ihrem Programm zu den »humanistischen und revolutionär-demokratischen Traditionen des Bürgertums«, aber zugleich kämpft sie »unter Führung der Arbeiterklasse und ihrer Partei für die glückliche Zukunft des ganzen deutschen Volkes«. Wer sich so oder auch christlich-demokratisch auf die Mitarbeit am Aufbau des Sozialismus einläßt, dem steht der berufliche Aufstieg frei, ausgenommen natürlich in die Schlüsselstellungen von Regierung und Armee, Polizei und Wirtschaft, in den Massenorganisationen FDGB und FDJ sowie auf den Gebieten von Erziehung und Wissenschaft. Diese bleiben selbstverständlich Mitgliedern der SED vorbehalten. Mitgliedschaft in Blockparteien beinhaltet das Mindestmaß an Anpassung, das mittlere und gehobene Karrieren sichern hilft, wie sonst nur die Zugehörigkeit zu den Gewerkschaften, zum Kulturbund oder zum Demokratischen Frauenbund. Sie erlaubt den Nachweis, daß man »organisiert« ist, wie die Landessprache den Tatbestand umschreibt, daß man zu den Mitläufern des Sozialismus zählt — mitsamt mancherlei Annehmlichkeiten, die ein solcher Status mit sich bringt. Anders ließe sich die fortdauernde Existenz der National Demokratischen Partei Deutschlands, die 1948 zur Eingliederung von Berufsoffizieren der Wehrmacht und reuigen NSDAP-Mitgliedern in den realen Sozialismus geschaffen worden war, überhaupt nicht erklären: Inzwischen ist sie längst zum Auffangbecken für Handwerker geworden, ganz gleich, ob sie selbständig sind oder sich zu Genossenschaften zusammenschließen mußten. Eine eindeutig klassen- oder schichtenspezifische Funktion erfüllt unter den Bündnisparteien der Nationalen Front allein die Demokratische Bau-

ernpartei Deutschlands, in der rund 100 000 Genossenschaftsbauern vereinigt sind. Ihr war von Anfang an die Aufgabe
zugewiesen, die Bauern für den Aufbau des Sozialismus zu
gewinnen. Konsequent trat sie deshalb als Schrittmacher der
Kollektivierung der bäuerlichen Einzelbetriebe auf. Heute
spielt sie als Organisator der Bauernkongresse der DDR eine
nicht unwichtige Rolle bei der Formulierung der Agrarpolitik.
Vergleicht man die Bauernpartei mit der CDU der DDR, dann
hat letztere eine sehr viel geringere Bedeutung, denn es fehlt
ihr an der rechten Funktion. Ihre Gründer hatten 1945 zwar
durchaus die Absicht, christliche Vorstellungen in eine – demokratische – sozialistische Gesellschaft einzubringen. Doch nach
ihrer Gleichschaltung durch die sowjetische Militäradministration, nach dem Fortgang Jakob Kaisers und Ernst Lemmers,
verwandelte sich die Christlich Demokratische Union Deutschlands, wie sie noch immer heißt, vom Anwalt der Christen
gegenüber der SED in eine Interessenvertretung der SED gegenüber den Kirchen im Land. Sie wurde zur »einschränkungs-
los sozialistischen Partei«, die in allen Konflikten zwischen
SED-Führung und Kirchen Stellung zugunsten der kommunistischen Obrigkeit bezog. Weil sie sehr früh für die Trennung
der DDR-Kirchen von der EKD eintrat, die obligatorische
Wehrerziehung in den Schulen und gar noch die atheistische
Jugendweihe gegenüber den Kirchen verteidigte, kam es zu
Massenaustritten organisierter Christen und zur totalen Ent-
fremdung zwischen CDU und Kirche, obschon die Partei sich
nach dem eigenen Statut ja als die »führende, anleitende und
helfende Kraft der christlichen Bevölkerung der DDR« verstand. Zum Mittler zwischen Staat und Kirche taugte sie damit
selbst in den Augen der SED nicht mehr. Als Erich Honecker
im März 1978 Bischof Albrecht Schönherr an der Spitze einer
Delegation der DDR-Kirchen empfing, als Staat und protestan-
tische Kirchen also ansatzweise Frieden schlossen, waren Par-
teivertreter der CDU daran nicht beteiligt. Erst seit der tiefe
Graben zwischen SED und Kirchen überbrückt ist, wird die
CDU wieder als Partei interessant, die politische Flankendek-
kung für die kirchliche und politische Tätigkeit geben kann.

Nun ist unstreitig, daß alle diese Blockparteien nur von der Gnade der SED existieren, die sie duldet, als Feigenblatt sozialistischer Demokratie benutzt, aber durch Kontingentierung und Begrenzung ihrer Anhänger stets darauf achtet, daß ein gebührender Abstand zwischen ihr als der Massenpartei der Arbeiterklasse und den kleinen Bündnispartnern bestehen bleibt. Die CDU zählt heute rund 120 000, die LDPD 80 000, die NDPD rund 90 000, die SED aber 2,3 Millionen Mitglieder. Mit Ausnahme der Bauernpartei sind sie im Stadium des »entwickelten Sozialismus«, in dem sich die DDR nach offizieller Lehre befindet, eigentlich überflüssig wie ein Kropf. Entstanden waren sie ja sämtlich in der nationalen und gesamtdeutsch-orientierten Frühphase der SED, in der es den Kommunisten vorrangig nicht um den Aufbau des Sozialismus, sondern um eine demokratisch-antifaschistische Ordnung ging, die auf die Grenzen der damaligen Sowjetischen Zone keinesfalls beschränkt bleiben sollte. Immerhin ist die Nationale Front, zu der sich diese Parteien unter sowjetischem Druck formierten, das Produkt jener Volkskongresse der Jahre 1947 und 1948, die sich als gesamtdeutsches Vorparlament verstanden und Volksabstimmungen über die Einheit Deutschlands forderten. Die Blockparteien waren also Instrumente der offensiven Deutschlandpolitik der SED. Vierzig Jahre später spricht Erich Honecker von der DDR als sozialistischem Vaterland, er spielt gegenüber westeuropäischen Besuchern die Rolle eines Garanten der deutschen Teilung, auf der die Nachkriegsordnung Europas beruht, und immer wieder zitiert er genüßlich François Mauriac, der einmal schrieb, er liebe Deutschland so sehr, daß er es gleich zweimal haben wolle. Welchen Sinn hat da die Fortexistenz bürgerlicher Parteiresiduen aus den deutschnationalen Kampfjahren der SED?

Anzunehmen, man wolle sie eines Tages doch wieder offensiv für eine Wiedervereinigungspolitik nach sozialistischem Muster nutzen, hieße, der SED einen Glauben an ihr innewohnende berserkerhafte Kräfte und Möglichkeiten unterstellen, über die sie nach eigener kritischer Selbsteinschätzung nicht verfügt. Und doch bescheinigte der SED-Chef den

Blockparteien auf dem X. Parteitag der SED 1981 sogar wachsende Bedeutung, als er ihren »eigenständigen Beitrag« zur Entwicklung des Sozialismus unterstrich und ihnen einen »stabilen Platz« und eine »langfristige Perspektive« zusicherte. Sicher hatte das auch damit zu tun, daß SED-Theoretiker die Phase des »entwickelten Sozialismus« seit einigen Jahren als eine lang andauernde und eigenständige bezeichnen, so daß der Übergang in den Kommunismus nun in weiter Ferne liegt. Wirtschaft und Gesellschaft müssen also nicht, utopischen Zwängen folgend, sich sprunghaft und gewaltsam fortentwickeln, und die Pragmatiker der kleinen Schritte halten das Heft fest in der Hand. Als ich einige Mitarbeiter von SED-Thinktanks, etwa dem Institut für Politik und Wirtschaft oder der Akademie für Gesellschaftswissenschaften, auf die Honecker-Äußerung ansprach, wurde mir gesagt, man wolle »polnischen Zuständen« vorbeugen. Deshalb bemühe man sich, den Dialog mit allen Schichten der Bevölkerung zu führen, zu intensivieren und sie damit zugleich einzubinden und zu höheren Leistungen zu motivieren. Die Funktion dieser Blockparteien ist also die von Transmissionsriemen zwischen dem sozialistischen Staat und verschiedenen gesellschaftlichen Gruppen, die nach der Erkenntnis der SED auch im »entwickelten Sozialismus« noch partikulare Interessen haben. Damit fand sich die Deutung des westdeutschen DDR-Historikers Dieter Staritz bestätigt, der das wiedererwachte Interesse der DDR-Führung an eigentlich überholten politischen Strukturen auf die Erkenntnis der »Notwendigkeit neuer Interaktionsformen von Staat und gesellschaftlichen Organisationen« zurückführt. Dabei überwiegen nicht ausschließlich ökonomische Motive, es geht der SED auch darum, ihr politisches System zu festigen und zu ergänzen. Deshalb sucht man bewußt Bürgernähe und neue Formen einer »stabilisierenden Partizipation in Städten und Gemeinden«. Gemessen an sowjetischen Zuständen mit ihrer lähmenden Monostruktur, an der auch Michail Gorbatschow vorerst wenig ändern konnte, enthält das Bündnissystem der Nationalen Front immerhin Raum für Vielfalt, mag er noch so bescheiden sein. Es erlaubt, wenn auch in einem von der SED gesetzten Rahmen und auf der Basis einer von ihr prinzipiell bestimmten Politik, Mitwirkung und die Entfaltung persönlicher Initiative. Kurzum: Es trägt dazu bei, der DDR-Gesellschaft einen Grad von Durchlässigkeit und Flexibilität zu geben, die sie gegenüber der sowjetischen noch immer als die weitaus modernere erscheinen läßt.

Den Mitgliedern der LDPD, die Funktionen im Staat und in ihrer eigenen Partei bekleiden, bescheinigen in der DDR stationierte westliche Diplomaten das höchste Maß an Sachkompetenz, ausgenommen die Spitzenmänner der SED. Da ist es gewiß kein Zufall, wenn die bundesdeutschen Liberalen den Kontakt zu den östlichen »Liberaldemokraten« (Wolfgang Mischnick gehörte ihnen an, ehe er aus Dresden in den Westen ging) nie ganz haben abreißen lassen. Überhaupt: Wer nach dieser Schilderung von Volkskammerwahlen meinen sollte, Kontakte zwischen Volkskammer und Bundestag verböten sich, weil es dem östlichen Parlament an der demokratischen Legitimität fehlt, zöge den falschen Schluß. Sicher sind die Wahlen in der DDR so wenig frei wie die in der ČSSR, UdSSR, Polen, Rumänien oder selbst in Ungarn. Aber wenn der deutsche Bundestag offizielle Kontakte mit dem Obersten Sowjet unterhält, warum dann nicht auch mit der Volkskammer der DDR? Etliche der 500 Abgeordneten halten führende Positionen in ihren Berufen, sind Generaldirektoren von Kombinaten oder Ärzte, Mitglieder der Akademie der Wissenschaften oder Künstler. Ein Gespräch mit ihnen kann durchaus ein Gewinn sein. Viele verfügen über einen hohen Wissensstand nicht nur auf ihrem Fachgebiet, und nahezu alle kennen die wahre Lage im Lande besser als so manches Mitglied des SED-Politbüros, das mit vorrückendem Alter immer häufiger dem Hang zum Beschönigen erliegt. So bemühte Erich Honecker nach der 99,94 prozentigen Volkskammerwahl von 1986 ausgerechnet Goethe, um die Lage der von ihm regierten DDR-Bürger zu preisen: »Ein freies Volk auf freiem Grund.« Zitate sind eben nicht nur Glückssache, manchmal verraten sie den gefährlichen Hang, das Reich der Wünsche für die Wirklichkeit zu halten. Volkskammerpräsident Horst Sindermann nannte Honecker in seiner Glückwunschadresse nach der Wiederwahl zum Staatsratsvorsitzenden einen »sozialistischen Staatsmann, der unter dem Volke lebt«. Wer einmal dabei war, wie ein riesiges Polizeiaufgebot sämtliche Fahrzeuge auf Park- und Rastplätze winkt und den Verkehr auf einzelnen Autobahnabschnitten für 20 Minuten stillegt, nur damit die Nr. 1 mit ihrem Konvoi ungehindert zur Messeeröffnung nach Leipzig brausen kann, dem kommt eher der Satz von der DDR als dem letzten deutschen Feudalstaat in den Sinn. Und auf jeden, der die Bewachung der Politbürosiedlung in Wandlitz kennt – im Volksmund heißt sie wegen der von der Führung bevorzugten Automobilmarke »Volvograd« –, wirkt das wie ein schlechter Witz.

Vor allem aus Sicherheitsgründen hatte sich die SED-Spitze 1960 entschlossen, aus Berlin-Pankow vor die Tore der Stadt zu ziehen. Die Pläne für das Reservat Wandlitz reichen also in eine Zeit zurück, in der Berlin Hauptkampfplatz des Kalten Krieges war, die offene, noch nicht durch die Mauer und Beton geteilte Front-Stadt. Walter Ulbricht, so erzählten Genossen aus seiner engsten Umgebung, habe bis ins hohe Alter die Furcht geplagt, er werde durch ein Attentat ums Leben kommen. Die Unterbringung im sogenannten »Städtchen«, einem Sperrgebiet nahe Schloß Niederschönhausen, schien da auf die Dauer nicht sicher genug; der unübersehbare Bretterzaun, der es umgab, und das stattliche Aufgebot an bewaffneter Polizei lieferten politische Angriffsflächen. Nach einer Begegnung mit seinem Vater schrieb John T. Becher in einem Brief an den DDR-Kulturbund-Präsidenten in Ostberlin aus London: »Es ist mir nie gelungen, Dich in Deinem Haus hinter Stacheldraht zu besuchen. Niemals werde ich Antwort geben können auf die Frage so vieler Freunde: Warum lebt Dein Vater hinter Stacheldraht? – Ist das der Schutz vor der Liebe des Volkes?« Dagegen ist die Siedlung, die ab 1958 nördlich Berlin zwischen märkischen Kiefern entstand, jedem zudringlichen Blick entzogen. Sie umfaßt gut zwanzig solide, zweistöckige, eher schmucklose Einfamilienhäuser, ist weitläufig durch eine Betonmauer gesichert und wird von einer Spezialeinheit bewacht. In einer angrenzenden Vorzone, aber deutlich abgesetzt, liegen die Unterkünfte für Fahrer, Dienstpersonal und Soldaten mit eigenen Einkaufsmöglichkeiten. Für die Bewohner der Villen im geschützten Areal gibt es einen gesonderten Supermarkt, Restaurants, Frisier- und Kosmetiksalon, Swimmingpool sowie eine Arztpraxis. Ob es eine Freude ist, in diesem Getto zu leben, zu dem kein normaler Sterblicher Zutritt hat und auf dem Weg ins Schwimmbad oder zum Friseur am Samstag ausgerechnet dem Spitzengenossen zu begegnen, über den man sich auf der Politbüro-Sitzung am letzten Dienstag besonders geärgert hat? Da ist eher anzunehmen, daß kommunistische Disziplin und der Chef der Staatssicherheit, den die Angst vor den Agenten des Klassenfeinds plagt, die führenden Männer der SED auch privat noch in märkischer Abgeschiedenheit zusammenpferchen. Nur lebt man so gewiß nicht als Staatsmann »unter dem Volke«, sondern befördert die phantastischsten Gerüchte über einen unglaublich luxuriösen privaten Lebensstil, der zum Bild der eher biederen Partei-Oberen so recht nicht passen will. Zwar stimmt, daß auch westliche Politiker mehr und mehr vom Volk abgeschirmt leben, seit der politische Terror grassiert. Doch haben die meisten eine private Adresse, und sei sie noch so gut bewacht. Helmut Schmidt bewirtete Valéry Giscard d'Estaing in seinem Hamburger Reihenhaus. Helmut Kohl hatte François Mitterand bei sich in Oggersheim zu Gast. Erich Honecker und die anderen Mitglieder des Politbüros haben noch nie einen hohen Besucher privat »bei sich zu Hause« in ihrem Getto empfangen, das übrigens weder postalisch noch geographisch existiert. Nicht zufällig ist der erste Präsident der DDR in der Erinnerung bei vielen noch populär. Wilhelm Pieck war der letzte regierende Spitzenfunktionär, der in einer Ostberliner Kneipe gesichtet wurde, als er mit Arbeitern einen Korn und eine Molle nahm.

Es fehlte nicht an brüderlichen Umarmungen, als Michail Gorbatschow der DDR seinen ersten, offiziellen Besuch als

Chef der KPdSU abstattete. Weil nach dem vorausgegangenen Parteitag in Moskau, an dem alle Ostblock-Parteiführer teilnahmen, die »Prawda« nicht das obligate Foto des sowjetischen und des ostdeutschen Chefs veröffentlichte, hatten westliche Beobachter gemunkelt, ihr Einvernehmen sei gestört. Wenn es nach der Zahl der Bruderküsse ging, die Erich Honecker und Michail Gorbatschow auf dem Ostberliner Flughafen Schönefeld gravitätisch, aber herzlich miteinander tauschten, schienen alle Zweifel an der Freundschaft ausgeräumt. Schließlich war der Kreml-Herr gekommen, einem persönlichen Triumph Erich Honeckers beizuwohnen: seiner Wiederwahl zum Generalsekretär der SED.

Nicht die Bestätigung als Staatsratsvorsitzender, sondern die als Parteichef ist das Kennzeichen des erfolgreichen Staatsmannes in den politischen Systemen des östlichen Blocks. So bemessen sich Honeckers Legislaturperioden nach den SED-Parteitagen, die ihm das Vertrauen schenken und auf denen die entscheidenden Weichen für Wirtschaft und Gesellschaft gestellt werden. Volkskammer und Staatsrat fallen im wesentlichen die Aufgabe zu, die politischen Direktiven und Grundsatzentscheidungen, welche der Parteitag für die nächsten fünf Jahre beschließt, in Gesetze zu formen und in konkrete Handlungen umzusetzen. Da versteht sich dann auch die zeitliche Abfolge: Tagt der Parteitag im April, wird die Volkskammer als eine Art vollziehendes Organ im darauffolgenden Juni gewählt. Im April 1986 begann Honeckers vierte Legislaturperiode, und nach 15 Jahren an der Spitze erst der Partei, dann bald auch des Staates, gab es keinen Grund, sein Licht unter den Scheffel zu stellen. Seine Amtszeit übertraf bereits die jedes Bonner Regierungschefs, selbst die Konrad Adenauers, welcher der Bundesrepublik in ihren ersten 14 Jahren seinen persönlichen Stempel aufdrückte. Honecker hatte die DDR, aus Bonner Sicht einst »ein Staat, der nicht sein darf«, zu internationaler Anerkennung geführt und es auch verstanden, sie nach innen zu festigen. Bedenkt man die widrigen Umstände, unter denen er als Politiker operieren mußte – der Teilstaat des gespaltenen Deutschland, dem er vorsteht, hatte und hat ungleich schwerer mit der nationalen Frage zu kämpfen als die wirtschaftlich attraktivere Bundesrepublik –, ist ihm der Respekt vor seiner Leistung schwerlich zu versagen. Anders als auf dem Parteitag der KPdSU wenige Monate zuvor überwogen auf dem der SED im Palast der Republik nicht die selbstkritischen, sondern eher die selbstzufriedenen Töne. Gorbatschows Stil der neuen Nüchternheit erwies die SED nur äußerlich ihre Reverenz. Es gab kein Fahnenmeer, keine Transparente und kein Spalier. Wer tagsüber auf der Straße steht, kann nicht arbeiten und drückt die Produktivität – so wohl mögen die Genossen der SED gedacht haben, als sie, unsicher noch, die neue Art übten, die Nummer 1 des Ostblocks zu begrüßen und den rechten Eindruck zu machen. Der radikale Reformer aus Moskau, der da mit betont kleinem Gefolge am Rande des Parteitags als Tourist durch Ostberlin zog, bewirkte vornehmlich eine Revolution des Protokolls. Drinnen, im »Palast«, sprach er von der Notwendigkeit, Schwachstellen bloßzulegen, und verteidigte den selbstkritischen Ansatz, ohne den sein Reformwerk nicht gelingen könnte. Eine Passage seiner Rede hörte sich an, als wollte er den wichtigsten Einwand der deutschen Genossen gegen Glasnost – einen, der freilich nie offen geäußert wird – widerlegen, ohne ihn direkt anzusprechen: »Haben wir die Selbstkritik nicht übertrieben und antikommunistische Propaganda genährt?«, fragte der sowjetische Parteichef und gab umgehend selbst die Antwort: »Nein, wir sind überzeugt, daß wir nicht übertrieben haben. Marx und Engels lehrten, daß die kritische Einstellung zur eigenen Tätigkeit eine unerläßliche Bedingung für den Erfolg einer revolutionären Partei ist. Wir waren bestrebt, nach diesem Vermächtnis zu handeln und haben die volle Unterstützung der Kommunisten, des ganzen Volkes erhalten.« Der Gegensatz zum Tenor des stolzgeschwellten Gastgebers war schwerlich zu übersehen. »Wir haben nicht den geringsten Grund zu verschweigen«, sagte Erich Honecker, »daß unser seit Anfang der 70er Jahre eingeschlagener Kurs der Volkswirtschaft ... sich als richtig erwiesen und bewährt hat.« Zwar gebe es hier und da Rückstände, und vor allem die Produktion von Konsumgütern und Dienstleistungen müssen verbessert werden. Im großen und ganzen aber gelte die Devise: »Es ist zwar noch nicht vollkommen, wir sind jedoch gut vorangekommen.« Wurde hier ein ideologischer Widerspruch zwischen Ostberlin und Moskau offenbar, wie es ihn in Ostberlin nach dem Kriege bisher nie gegeben hatte? Westliche Kommentatoren spekulierten, wie lange es sich der selbstbewußte Erich Honecker wohl leisten könne, das bis dahin gänzlich Unerhörte zu tun – wider den Stachel des Großen Bruders in Moskau zu löcken. Die bundesdeutsche DKP hatte die beschwörende Rede Gorbatschows vor dem Parteitag der KPdSU unter dem Titel »Wir brauchen die Demokratie wie die Luft zum Atmen« im vollen Wortlaut publiziert, das »Neue Deutschland« dagegen nur Auszüge veröffentlicht. Wo war sie geblieben, die jahrzehntealte SED-Parole: »Von der Sowjetunion lernen, heißt siegen lernen!«? Kein Geringerer als der Chefideologe der SED, Kurt Hager, gab Spekulationen Auftrieb mit einem drastischen Vergleich, den er später intern zwar als mißglückt bezeichnete, der von ihm öffentlich aber nie bedauert wurde: Ob die Zeiten vorbei seien, in denen das Land Lenins für die deutschen Kommunisten Vorbild war, fragte ihn ein Interviewer des »Stern«. In Hagers umfänglicher Antwort fand sich die Gegenfrage: »Würden Sie, nebenbei gesagt, wenn Ihr Nachbar seine Wohnung neu tapeziert, sich verpflichtet fühlen, Ihre Wohnung ebenfalls neu zu tapezieren?« Der Satz wirkte auf alle Künstler und Intellektuellen, für die Gorbatschow noch heute ein Hoffnungsträger ist, wie ein Schock. Viele, die glaubten, die Moskauer Reformen würden auf die DDR übergreifen, sahen sich entmutigt und enttäuscht. In der Tat erweckte Hagers Satz von den Tapeten, der auch vom SED-Parteiorgan verbreitet wurde, den Eindruck, als ob die SED Gorbatschows Perestroika nicht als tiefgreifenden Reformversuch betrachte, den es ernstzunehmen galt, sondern als bloßes Übertünchen alter sowjetischer Fassaden. War das eine zufällige Entgleisung? Wohl kaum in einem geschlossenen System, in dem jedes Wort dreimal auf die Goldwaage gelegt wird, ehe es das

Sekretariat des Zentralkomitees zur Veröffentlichung freigibt. Mag es sich nun um eine gezielte Überspitzung oder eine mißglückte Formulierung handeln, die Botschaft des Satzes ist unmißverständlich; sie wird durch den Kontext, in dem er steht, gestützt und besagt soviel wie: Eine selbstbewußte, starke und erfolgreiche SED hat es nicht nötig, jede Moskauer Mode mitzumachen. Wir deutschen Kommunisten sind zwar gute Leninisten und treue Bundesgenossen der Sowjetunion, aber manchmal gehen wir unseren eigenen Weg.

Dabei kann man getrost in Rechnung stellen, daß die SED-Führung mit der Erfahrung des gebrannten Kindes handelt. Zwar hatten die deutschen Kommunisten manche radikale Sünden der Stalinzeit vermieden – etwa Verratsprozesse gegen Westemigranten, die wie in der ČSSR und Ungarn in den Fällen Rudolf Slánský und Lázló Rajk mit Hinrichtungen endeten. SED-Politbüromitglied Paul Merker, Westemigrant und Jude, wurde aus der Partei ausgeschlossen und verhaftet, aber sein Leben blieb verschont und 1956 sah er sich rehabilitiert. Angeblich nur unter sowjetischem Druck fanden sich Wilhelm Pieck und Walter Ulbricht bereit, den offiziellen Antisemitismus der Stalinzeit mitzumachen. Der jüdische Kommunist und Westemigrant Jürgen Kuczynski wurde als Präsident der Gesellschaft für Deutsch-Sowjetische Freundschaft abberufen, nicht ins Zentralkomitee der Partei gewählt und nicht wieder als Kandidat für die Volkskammer aufgestellt; doch als Wissenschaftler durfte er weiter lehren und publizieren. Auch war der Eifer in der DDR nicht allzu groß, alle irrationalen Eingriffe Stalins in die Naturwissenschaften umgehend nachzuvollziehen. Ulbricht persönlich soll die Saat- und Pflanzenzucht-Anstalten in Quedlinburg gehindert haben, die Lehre eines von Stalin zum Biologie-Genie hochgelobten Scharlatans namens Lyssenko in die Tat umzusetzen, der die Mendel'schen Gesetze als faschistisch und bourgeois bezeichnete und mit dem Segen des Zentralkomitees der KPdSU durch seine eigene dilettantische Theorie ablösen konnte. Zumindest zeitweise war es diesem Trofim Lyssenko gelungen, die sowjetische Biologie um fast ein halbes Jahrhundert zurückzuwerfen.

Von der Seuche des Personenkults war die SED freilich nicht minder stark befallen wie der proletarische Musterstaat. Als nach der sensationellen Rede Chruschtschows auf dem XX. Parteitag der KPdSU 1956, in der er die Verbrechen Stalins anprangerte, die Denkmäler des Despoten auch in der DDR gestürzt wurden, schloß sich die SED-Führung der Fortschrittseuphorie und der Siegesgewißheit des neuen Herrn im Kreml umgehend an. Chruschtschows neues Parteiprogramm, dessen Verkündung das »Neue Deutschland« als »Tag der Freude für alle Völker« feierte, gaukelte vor, noch die – damals – »gegenwärtige Generation« des Sowjetvolkes werde den Kommunismus erleben. Bis 1970 sollten die USA in der Pro-Kopf-Produktion überholt, bis 1980 die kommunistische Gesellschaft in der Sowjetunion im wesentlichen aufgebaut und ein »Überfluß an materiellen und kulturellen Gütern« gesichert sein. Es war dieses Beispiel, das den DDR-Chef dazu inspirierte, sich hoffnungslos zu übernehmen, als er das Überholen Westdeutschlands im Pro-Kopf-Verbrauch bis 1961 ankündigte. Im neuen KPdSU-Programm, für das der Realist Gorbatschow verantwortlich zeichnet, wird der Kommunismus wieder nach Utopia verlegt und der Welt des Kapitalismus, die bei Chruschtschow reif schien für den Untergang, erstaunliche Lebenskraft und Anpassungsfähigkeit bescheinigt.

Auch wenn die SED diese extremen Wechselbäder selten bis auf Punkt und Komma mitvollzogen hat, war sie früher doch mehr um den Gleichschritt mit dem Großen Bruder bemüht, als dies heute der Fall ist. Das hat nicht nur mit der Furcht zu tun, nur ja nicht ein zweites Mal alles auf die Karte eines großen Umwälzers im Kreml zu setzen, der dann eines Tages unverhofft von seinen Genossen in die Wüste geschickt wird. Ihren Chruschtschow hatten die deutschen Kommunisten damals ins Herz geschlossen, weil er ursprünglich eine Westberlin-Lösung versprach, die ganz nach dem Geschmack der Ulbricht-Führung war – Abzug der Westmächte und Umwandlung in eine Freie Stadt. Wie ein Schock mag manchen auch der ältere, nicht minder peinliche und abrupte Kurswechsel von 1956 im Gedächtnis sitzen. Als die ostdeutsche Delegation sich auf den Weg zum XX. Parteitag machte, hatte das Zentralkomitee in einer Grußadresse an die sowjetischen Genossen gekabelt: »Es lebe die unbesiegbare Lehre von Marx, Engels und Stalin!« Wieder daheim, mußte der Delegationschef Ulbricht etwas kleinlaut eingestehen: »Zu den Klassikern des Marxismus kann man Stalin nicht rechnen.«

Sicher spielen solche Erfahrungen heute eine Rolle, wenn die SED Gorbatschow Erfolg wünscht, sich im übrigen aber bedeckt hält, was die Übernahme seiner Reformansätze betrifft. Die Männer im Politbüro kennen die Schwerfälligkeit des sowjetischen Apparats und die gewaltigen Beharrungskräfte der mittleren Bürokratie. Sie wissen um die Schwierigkeiten, einen riesigen Vielvölkerstaat wie die UdSSR in Bewegung zu setzen, der im Südosten und Osten Regionen umfaßt, die sich noch auf dem Stand von Entwicklungsländern befinden. Da gilt oft noch der alte Satz: Rußland ist groß und der Zar ist weit ... Wegen zahlreicher Querverbindungen auf verschiedenen Ebenen der Partei sind sie auch in der Lage, die Widerstände richtig einzuschätzen, die einen allzu stürmisch vorwärtsdrängenden Gorbatschow bremsen und ihn nach innen zu Kompromissen und Kurskorrekturen zwingen. In Zeiten der kollektiven Führung, die sich in der Nach-Stalinära durchgesetzt hat, sind selbst herausragende kommunistische Führergestalten, heißen sie nun Gorbatschow, Kadar oder Honecker, in kritischen Situationen auf die Unterstützung der Mehrheit ihres Politbüros angewiesen. Da wäre es unklug, die eigene politische Zukunft nur an eine Person zu binden, die im Augenblick zwar Erfolg haben mag, in Zukunft aber, wie bittere Erfahrung lehrt, schwere Rückschläge erleiden kann. Überdies ist die SED überzeugt, daß der Zustand der DDR viele sowjetische Reformansätze nicht nötig hat, weil in der östlichen deutschen Republik schon vorhanden ist, was Gorbatschow in der Sowjetunion sich geradezu verzweifelt zu schaffen müht. Das wirkt auf den ersten Blick überheblich und selbstgerecht, aber es lohnt sich, die Argumente der regierenden deutschen Kommunisten einmal unter die Lupe zu nehmen. Zuvor allerdings ist zu prüfen, was ein Mann wie Gorbatschow wirklich will.

Faßt man seine wichtigsten Reformen zusammen, dann handelt es sich im wesentlichen um drei radikale Denkansätze. Der erste, Glasnost, soll eine kritische, aber durchaus systemimmanente Öffentlichkeit herstellen. Sie dient dazu, das wichtigste Reform-Element, Perestroika genannt, zu unterstützen. Perestroika hat die Aufgabe, die sowjetische Gesellschaft aufzurütteln, sie leistungs- und verantwortungsbereit zu machen, um die sowjetische Wirtschaft aus ihrem verhängnisvollen Schlendrian zu reißen. Dafür sind persönliche Initiative, Mitdenken und Partizipation des einzelnen auf allen Stufen der Entscheidungsprozesse notwendig. Der dritte Ansatz, das »Neue Denken«, geht von der Erkenntnis aus, daß atomare Kriege nicht zu führen sind. Er stellt deshalb eine lange Phase friedlicher Koexistenz mit den »Kräften des Imperialismus« und dem kapitalistischen Lager in Rechnung und zielt auf ein Ende des Wettrüstens. Das »Neue Denken« soll dem Versuch Gorbatschows, die sowjetische Wirtschaft zu modernisieren, die außenpolitische Flanke sichern und ermöglichen, bitter benötigte Investitionsmittel für moderne Technologien für den zivilen Wirtschaftsbereich vom Rüstungssektor abzuzweigen. Dabei macht der Kreml-Chef selbst immer wieder unmißverständlich klar, daß er kein »closet liberal« ist, wie die Amerikaner sagen, also kein heimlicher Liberaler im westlichen Sinne, der einen Umbau der Sowjetgesellschaft nach pluralistischem Modell erstrebt. Indem er sich immer wieder als Leninist bekennt, gibt er zu verstehen, daß die sozialistische Demokratie, die er im Auge hat, nie die Errungenschaften der Oktoberrevolution in Frage stellen darf. Freier Meinungsstreit, wie er ihn anvisiert, bleibt hauptsächlich auf die Kader der KPdSU beschränkt, und der Kritik in der Presse, die Mißstände anprangern, Korruptionsfälle aufdekken und Übergriffen von Behörden nachspüren darf, ist klar eine Beistandsfunktion zugedacht: Soweit sie bürokratische Hemmnisse beim Namen nennt und bornierte Apparatschiks aufspießt, steigert sie die Leistungsmotivation der einzelnen

Sowjetbürger. Die wirtschaftlich-technische Rückständigkeit der UdSSR, so Gorbatschow in mehreren Reden, hat nicht nur erhebliche Schatten auf die »weltweite Anziehungskraft des Sozialismus« geworfen, hält sie an, wird auch der politisch-militärischen Großmacht-Stellung der Sowjetunion durch ökonomische Erosion schließlich die Basis entzogen. Michail Gorbatschow übernahm eine Großmacht im Niedergang. Sein wichtigstes Reformziel heißt deshalb, durch Modernisierung der Wirtschaft die Weltstellung der Sowjetunion zu behaupten. Zugleich will er das Erbe Lenins, das revolutionäre Experiment einer alternativen Gesellschaft, ins nächste Jahrtausend hinüberretten, und zwar mit verlockender, ja verheißender Ausstrahlungskraft.

Den kühl analysierenden Männern im großen grauen Haus in Ostberlin ist schwerlich verborgen geblieben, daß die Politik des neuen Herrn im Kreml damit ganz unter dem Primat der Wirtschaft und der Innenpolitik steht. Wirtschaftlich aber fühlen sie, die seit vielen Jahren auf ein stetiges Wachstum von real um 4 Prozent zurückblicken können, sich der Sowjetunion zu Recht überlegen. Auch wenn ihr eigenes System meist unter Ächzen und Stöhnen und am Rande der Belastbarkeit funktioniert, bleiben sie allemal die Leistungsstärksten und Effizientesten im ganzen Block. Gelegentlich müssen Reformansätze Gorbatschows in ihren Augen geradezu rührend wirken – etwa, wenn er, um die Misere auf dem Dienstleistungssektor zu bekämpfen, das private Handwerk zuläßt. Die Sowjetunion experimentiert heute mit Ein-Mann-Betrieben und wenigen Genossenschaften, die Beschäftigung von Angestellten ist untersagt. Die DDR fördert das selbständige Handwerk und kleine private Läden, die sie im Gegensatz zur UdSSR nie gänzlich hat absterben lassen, seit vielen Jahren wieder gezielt, und ihre Kleinbetriebe dürfen bis zu zehn Angestellte haben – zweifellos eine bewährtere, effizientere Form als Versuche, die bisher aus Moskau, Leningrad oder Minsk bekannt geworden sind. Wenn Gorbatschow daran denkt, Betriebsdirektoren durch die Belegschaft wählen zu lassen, kann die SED die Ergebnisse erst einmal in Ruhe abwarten – es handelt sich schließlich um begrenzte Pilot-Versuche in einigen Regionen. Ob sie gelingen, ob sich der Ausstoß und die Qualität der Produktion dadurch verbessern werden, wird sich frühestens in drei oder vier Jahren erweisen. Dann steht der SED immer noch frei zu prüfen, was von diesen Experimenten ins eigene System zu übernehmen ist und was besser nicht. Gewiß nicht zufällig stellten die Medien der DDR vor dem Gorbatschow-Besuch den Bericht eines sowjetischen Ökonomen namens Iwanowitsch Forim heraus, der nach einer DDR-Reise meinte, vieles aus dem Erfahrungsschatz der »deutschen Freunde« sei »in unserer«, sprich der sowjetischen, Wirtschaft anwendbar. In der Tat galt die DDR dem sowjetischen Reformer eine kurze Zeit sogar als ökonomisches Modell, bis er erkannte, daß die straffe zentrale Lenkung, in deren Rahmen die Kombinate begrenzte Eigeninitiative entwickeln können, für die überschaubare DDR vielleicht taugt, für die riesige Sowjetunion aber nicht geeignet ist. Da auch die politische Struktur der DDR sich vielfältiger gefächert zeigt als die sowjetische (s. o. über die Nationale Front) und mithin mehr Möglichkeiten der Partizipation bietet, wenn auch im Rahmen eines streng sozialistischen Demokratieverständnisses, sieht die SED-Führung vorerst keinen Grund, Gorbatschows Perestroika auf die DDR zu übertragen.

Honecker und seine Mitstreiter können dabei das alte Prinzip der Eigenständigkeit der kommunistischen Parteien für sich in Anspruch nehmen, die zwar selbstverständlich im Geiste des proletarischen Internationalismus miteinander verbunden sind und den Marxismus-Leninismus als Weltanschauung sowie den Kommunismus als großes Ziel gemeinsam haben. Doch jede Partei, so SED-Chefideologe Hager, »trägt vor ihrem Volk die Verantwortung« und hat nationale Besonderheiten zu berücksichtigen – »einen bestimmten ökonomischen und sozialen Entwicklungsstand, historische und kulturelle Traditionen, geographische und andere Gegebenheiten«. Wenn die Führung der SED in den letzten Jahren vermehrt auf solche Eigenständigkeit pocht, vermag sie sich nicht nur auf die jahrzehntelange Tradition der internationa-

len Arbeiterbewegung, sondern auch auf Michail Gorbatschow persönlich zu berufen, der dieses Prinzip häufig im
Munde führt. Selbst im neuen Programm der KPdSU werden
die Besonderheiten, die Unterschiede des ökonomischen Ni-
veaus, der Größe und der historischen und nationalen Traditionen »jedes einzelnen sozialistischen Landes« ausdrücklich
erwähnt, und wörtlich ist da die »vollständige Wahrung der
Gleichberechtigung und gegenseitigen Achtung der nationalen Interessen« festgeschrieben. Übrigens wird im Westen
häufig die Tatsache übersehen, daß solche nationalen Sonder-
wege bei der Lösung wirtschaftlicher Fragen auch unter Bre-
schnew geduldet wurden. Anders hätten die Ungarn ihre
Wirtschafts-Reformen, die nach dem Geschmack Gorbatschows zu marktwirtschaftlich gerieten und deshalb auf die
Sowjetunion nicht zu übertragen sind, überhaupt nicht entwickeln können.

Die besonderen nationalen Interessen der DDR hatte die
SED-Führung nicht für ihre Art der Wirtschaftslenkung, sondern zur Verteidigung von Erich Honeckers Politik des Dialogs gegen Moskauer Bedenken ins Feld zu führen, und sie tat
das ebenso geschickt wie entschieden. Im Gegensatz zur Haltung der Sowjets, die nach der Raketenstationierung ihre Beziehungen zur Bundesrepublik demonstrativ einfroren, hielt
Honecker hartnäckig am Gespräch mit Bonn fest – auch über
den »Raketenzaun« hinweg, der das deutsch-deutsche Verhältnis zweifellos belastete. Von Moskau wurde er dafür öffentlich gescholten, doch die SED wies in ihren Stellungnah-
men trotzig darauf hin, daß verschiedene Kampferfahrungen
zeitweilig zu Diskussionen und gelegentlich auch zu Mei-
nungsverschiedenheiten zwischen einzelnen kommunistischen Parteien führen könnten. Dabei fand sie die volle Unterstützung der Ungarn, die den Dialog mit dem Westen
ebenfalls nicht abreißen ließen. Es hatte schon besonderen
Signalwert, als das »Neue Deutschland« im November 1985
einen Artikel des ungarischen Parteiideologen Matyás Szürös
aus dem ungarischen Parteiorgan »Népszabadság« übernahm,
in dem, zweifelsfrei an die Moskauer Adresse gerichtet, zu

lesen stand: »Die stärkere Beachtung der nationalen Besonderheiten und der konkreten Gegebenheiten trägt auch der Erkenntnis Rechnung, daß es keine ewig gültigen und ungeachtet der konkreten Bedingungen immer erfolgreichen Lösungen für den Aufbau des Sozialismus gibt... Nach Lenins Auffassung erfordert die Einheit (der sozialistischen Länder – d. V.) nicht die Aufhebung der Unterschiede, die Beseitigung der nationalen Verschiedenheiten (dies ist in der heutigen Lage ein törichter Traum), sondern die Durchsetzung der Prinzipien des Kommunismus auf solche Weise, daß diese Grundsätze in Details richtig modifiziert und, den nationalen sowie nationalstaatlichen Unterschieden entsprechend, richtig gestaltet und angewandt werden.«

Was die Politik des Dialogs angeht, darf die SED sich im nachhinein nicht nur gerechtfertigt fühlen, weil sie in der Sache nach Gorbatschows Amtsantritt recht behalten hat. Zur Zeit Andropows und Tschernjenkos hatten Honeckers Thesen von der »Koalition der Vernunft« und der »Schadensbegrenzung« in Moskau, aber auch in Warschau den Verdacht von zuviel deutsch-deutscher Gemeinsamkeit geweckt und deshalb Anstoß erregt. Doch nun führte der neue Kreml-Chef selbst eine Außenpolitik, für die Moskau Honecker zuvor demonstrativ gerügt hatte. Die ostdeutschen Kommunisten können mit Fug und Recht zudem von sich behaupten, daß wichtige Ansätze des »Neuen Denkens«, jenes dritte Element in der Reformpolitik Gorbatschows, jedenfalls soweit es Fragen der Sicherheit und der Koexistenz im Atomzeitalter betrifft, schon vor ihm in der DDR entwickelt und formuliert worden sind. Die Erkenntnis, daß sich alle Staaten in einer prinzipiell neuen Situation befinden, weil Kriege unführbar geworden sind und die nationale Sicherheit keines Staates mehr unabhängig von der anderer gewährleistet werden kann, wurde in der DDR sehr früh artikuliert. Auch die Opfer und Konsequenzen, die solch »Neues Denken« der eigenen Ideologie abverlangt, werden von den Theoretikern der SED offen angesprochen. Nur, wenn jeder den anderen für prinzipiell friedensfähig hält, ist gemeinsame Sicherheit möglich, sagen die Vor-Neudenker der SED, Professor Otto Reinhold, der Leiter der Akademie für Gesellschaftswissenschaften beim ZK der SED und Professor Max Schmidt, Chef des Instituts für Politik und Wirtschaft, das dem Generalsekretär der SED mit außenpolitischen Expertisen zuarbeitet. In der Praxis zwingt dies die SED zur kritischen Überprüfung ihrer bisherigen Imperialismus-Theorie, die ja besagte, der Imperialismus sei seinem Charakter nach notwendig aggressiv, Sozialismus und Frieden seien dagegen wesenseins. Auch die marxistische Lehre vom gerechten Krieg dürfte insoweit abzuändern sein, als sie vielleicht für Dritte-Welt-Länder weiter gilt, nicht aber für Europa und die entwickelten Nationen, da es in einem Kernwaffenkrieg keine Sieger mehr geben kann. Dieses Neue Denken, das sich aus der Logik des Atomzeitalters entwickelt, zwingt auch zur Überprüfung des Begriffes Koexistenz, denn sie wurde bisher als vorübergehender Waffenstillstand zwischen den zwei Gesellschaftssystemen und als eine spezifische Form des Klassenkampfes verstanden. Als Grundmaxime galt, daß die Gegensätze zwischen den Lagern »unversöhnlich« und »unüberbrückbar« seien. Auch diese Vorstellung unterliegt im Zeichen des »Neuen Denkens« dem Zwang zur Korrektur. Wenn die ideologische Auseinandersetzung jetzt weiter geführt wird, dann unter der Annahme, daß der Kapitalismus noch auf unabsehbare Zeit existieren wird, die Phase der Koexistenz also als eine sehr lange andauernde in Rechnung zu stellen ist. Im Zentrum der Überlegungen steht nicht mehr so sehr der Klassenkampf als vielmehr die Suche nach gemeinsamen Wegen zur Verhinderung des Krieges; der ideologische Angriff wird nicht gegen den Kapitalismus in Gänze, sondern nur noch gegen die »aggressivsten Kreise des Imperialismus« geführt.

Man sollte sich hüten, dieses kritische Hinterfragen geheiligter Lehrsätze des Marxismus-Leninismus gering zu achten. Was solche ideologischen Kehrtwendungen für manche überzeugte Marxisten bedeuten, hat Heiner Müller so formuliert: »Die Vereinfachung: Krieg oder Frieden schließt die Gefahr des Endes der Geschichte ein«, sagte der Dramatiker 1985 in

einem Interview mit der Zeitschrift »Sinn und Form«. Weil
für die Großmächte Krieg nur noch als nuklearer Krieg
denkbar sei, drohten nun die »Ideologien ausgehöhlt, die
Utopien ›gegessen‹«, und die »Ungleichzeitigkeit der Entwicklung« in der Welt festgeschrieben zu werden. »Bloße Verhinderung des Krieges«, so Müller, »wird Verhinderung von Geschichte, Verhinderung von Fortschritt – das ist die Gefahr,
die ich sehe. Status quo als Festschreibung von Hunger, Un-
terentwicklung, Umweltproblemen . . .« Da wirkte die Rede
von Kurt Hager im Oktober 1986 fast wie eine Antwort auf
solche Einwände gegen das »Neue Denken«. Vor Wissen-
schaftlern und Studenten der Humboldt-Universität verteidigte er nämlich die Priorität des gemeinsamen Überlebens
gegenüber dem Klassenkampf. Die Verhinderung der nuklea-
ren Katastrophe und die Sicherung des Weltfriedens, so Hager, sei in der gegenwärtigen Situation sozialem Fortschritt
gleichzusetzen. Was das »Neue Denken« etwa beim Abbau
von Feindbildern für die DDR nach innen bedeutet, wird später zu erörtern sein. Zunächst kommt es darauf an, festzuhalten, daß in der Neubestimmung der Koexistenz und in der
Außenpolitik zwischen Ostberlin und Moskau hautnahe
Übereinstimmung herrscht.

Ganz anders sieht das natürlich aus, wenn es um Glasnost
geht, um Offenheit oder kritische Öffentlichkeit, wie sie Gorbatschow in Moskau will. Gegenüber diesem Element seiner
Reformpolitik sperrt sich die SED so wie gegenüber der Perestroika; und zu ihrer Verteidigung führt sie ihre geographische Lage an der Grenzlinie beider Systeme und, wiederum, besondere nationale Gegebenheiten ins Feld. Schaut man
sich diese Argumente näher an, stechen in der Tat erhebliche
Unterschiede ins Auge. Was der Sowjetunion im Zeichen des
Satellitenfernsehens vielleicht am Ende dieses, spätestens
Mitte des nächsten Jahrhunderts ins Haus stehen dürfte und
dessen Wirkung auf die sowjetische Gesellschaft schwer abzu-
schätzen ist, gehörte ja zu den Existenzbedingungen der DDR
von Anfang an: Die Einstrahlung westlicher Medien, dazu
noch in der eigenen Sprache. Lange, ehe es Fernsehen gab,

hatten die Regierenden der anderen deutschen Republik sich mit einer kritischen Öffentlichkeit herumzuschlagen, die ihren Bürgern oft über Ätherwellen bis ins Detail genau über Mißgriffe der Planung oder Versorgungsschwierigkeiten in einigen Städten und Bezirken, Übergriffe einzelner Funktionäre oder Verhaftungen von Oppositionellen berichtete. Quellen waren und sind Flüchtlinge, Informanten in Ostberlin und, seit Abschluß des Grundvertrages, in der DDR akkreditierte westliche Korrespondenten. In der Sicht der SED sind diese Radio- und Fernsehstationen, die sich mit einem Teil ihrer Programme direkt an die Hörer in der DDR wenden, Hetz- oder Feindsender, Instrumente der ideologischen Diversion und »Leitzentralen der Konterrevolution«. Versuche von Agitatoren und Propagandisten, die eigenen Bürger vom Empfang abzuhalten, blieben meist ergebnislos. Auch eine Kampagne gegen »ideologisches Grenzgängertum«, welche die SED nach Errichtung der Mauer im Zuge ihrer Stabilisierungspolitik nach innen startete, lief schließlich ins Leere. In einer Rede vor dem Kulturbund hatte Kurt Hager gefordert, endlich die »Antenne im Kopf« richtig zu stellen. Die FDJ half nach, startete die »Aktion Blitz contra Nato-Sender« und räumte schlicht die auf Westempfang gerichteten Antennen vom Dach. Inzwischen ist die westdeutsche Industriegesellschaft mit all ihren Verlockungen – Qualitätswaren oder exotische Früchte im Überfluß, nach denen man nicht Schlange stehen muß und die täglich zu haben sind – allabendlich präsent in den Wohnstuben der DDR. Im Kampf um die Antenne im Kopf und die auf dem Dach hat die DDR-Führung längst kapituliert, denn nahezu selbstverständlich werden inzwischen westliche Kanäle in Gemeinschaftsantennen eingespeist. Welche sozialpsychologischen Folgen es hat, wenn die übergroße Mehrheit der DDR-Bürger als Medien-Zaungäste am Leben in der Bundesrepublik, mit seinen Glanz- und Schattenseiten, Reichtum und Arbeitslosigkeit und auch allen politischen Krisen teilhat, bleibt bis heute allerdings im Bereich der Vermutungen. Der Direktor von »Radio Freies Europa«, George Urban, stellte in der »New York Times« die gewagte These auf, das Westfernsehen wirke im Osten systemstabilisierend, weil es eine Art »Ersatzfreiheit« produziere. Die bunten Bilder aus der westlichen Welt vermittelten die Illusion, an der Freiheit der anderen zu partizipieren. »Das Fernsehen«, so Urban, »läßt politische Unterdrückung leichter ertragen, denn es trägt in sich die verführerische Formel, daß es einen leichten Fluchtweg aus dem Herrschaftsbereich des Kommunismus gibt, solange die Flimmerkiste funktioniert . . . Das flimmernde Bild überdeckt die Realität der Unterdrückung.« Wenn diese Behauptung zutrifft, erklärt sie die Gelassenheit, mit der die SED-Führung sich seit etlichen Jahren nicht nur in das Unausweichliche fügt, sondern auch zuläßt, daß es per Kabel in möglichst guter Qualität frei Haus geliefert wird.

Meine Erfahrung bestätigt die Thesen Urbans nur zum Teil. Um völlig stabilisierend zu wirken, enthalten die westlichen Fernseh-Nachrichten und Magazine zu viele bittere Pillen – Wahrheiten, welche die SED gern unterschlägt, was am Arbeitsplatz dann zu heftigen Diskussionen führt. Allerdings kommt ein Mann wie Heiner Müller, von einer völlig anderen Position her urteilend, zu einem weitgehend ähnlichen Schluß wie der Direktor von »Radio Freies Europa«. Als den politischsten Teil des Westfernsehens betrachtet er die Werbung, die einerseits beim ostdeutschen Zuschauer Bedürfnisse wecke. Auf der anderen Seite wirke diese Bestärkung von Konsum- und Kaufgelüsten wie ein großer »Stabilitätsfaktor« in der DDR-Gesellschaft, weil der »Standard der Träume. . . überwiegend westlich« geprägt werde, soweit es Lebensmittel, Waren und Produkte betreffe. Gerade das aber, so Müller, schwächt »jede Möglichkeit, eine linke Opposition aufzubauen«. Wenn der Dramatiker eine weniger materialistische Gesellschaft erträumt – vor allem darauf zielt ja eine »linke Opposition« –, dürfte er unter den Bürgern der DDR wenige Freunde haben. Natürlich stimmt, daß der Standard der Träume ein westlicher ist, und diese Tatsache mag insoweit systemstabilisierend wirken, als sie, ganz im Sinn der SED-Führung, den Leistungswillen hebt. Der einzelne Bürger ist bereit, härter zu arbeiten, um auch in der DDR diesem Niveau möglichst nahe zu kommen. Doch bleibt hier Vorsicht geboten, denn der Warenvergleich lehrt, daß der Abstand sich allen Anstrengungen zum Trotz nicht verringert hat. Das bewegt dann viele dazu, gleich das ganze System in Frage zu stellen.

Entscheidend für unseren Zusammenhang ist jedoch, daß die SED im Gegensatz zur KPdSU in dem von ihr regierten deutschen Staat wegen der starken Einstrahlung westlicher Medien nie über ein Informationsmonopol verfügt hat. An sowjetischen Verhältnissen gemessen, war die DDR-Gesellschaft also immer eine relativ offene und kannte ein gewisses Ausmaß an Glasnost, auch wenn dafür ausschließlich die Medien des Klassenfeindes verantwortlich waren. Paradoxerweise bestärkt diese Tatsache das Politbüro eher in der Tendenz, die eigene Informationspolitik weiterhin restriktiv zu handhaben. Es befürchtet, daß sich Hörfunk und Fernsehen im Westen an ungeschminkten, kritischen Berichten und Auseinandersetzungen in der DDR ausgiebig weiden würden. Vor allem die Angst vor einem Rückhall- oder Verstärkereffekt durch die westlichen Sender bestärkt die SED also in dem Glauben, sich Glasnost nach Moskauer Modell nicht leisten zu können.

Wer annimmt, Erich Honecker könnte in Moskau in Ungnade fallen, weil er nicht alle Reformansätze Gorbatschows eilfertig übernimmt, erliegt freilich einem Irrtum. Einmal nämlich wünscht er dem KPdSU-Chef sicher all das Glück, das er für das Gelingen seines großen Reformwerks braucht (und er hat eine Menge davon nötig), denn es kann auch für die DDR nur zum Vorteil sein, wenn die Sowjetunion zu einem wirtschaftlich effizienteren Partner wird und die Vormacht des realen Sozialismus weltweit an Attraktivität gewinnt. Und zweitens wäre das schlimmste, was dem Reformer im Kreml widerfahren könnte, das Aufbrechen von Unruhen an den Rändern des eigenen Imperiums. Zu den wichtigsten Voraussetzungen für seinen Erfolg nach innen gehört die Stabilität im eigenen Block. Eine Destabilisierung der vorgeschobenen Bastion DDR riefe sofort die Gegner in den eigenen Reihen auf den Plan und müßte seinen Versuch der Perestroika, der Umgestaltung und Demokratisierung (im Sinne Lenins) der sowjetischen Gesellschaft ernsthaft gefährden. Genau das aber ist die Trumpfkarte in der Hand der SED-Spitze, um sich jene Eigenständigkeit zu sichern, die sie für die Aufrechterhaltung der Stabilität im Innern für notwendig hält. Wenn Honecker darauf pocht, er müsse gelegentlich eigene Wege gehen, damit ihm die Zügel nicht aus der Hand gleiten, wird ein Gorbatschow dafür im ureigensten Interesse Verständnis zeigen.

Falls es dafür eines Beweises bedürfte, dann hat ihn die sowjetamtliche Nachrichtenagentur »Tass« erbracht, als sie die Repressionsmaßnahmen gegen die Demonstranten Krawczyk und Klier, Hirsch und Templin ausdrücklich guthieß und von »vorsätzlichen Provokationen einer Gruppe von Personen« sprach, die »in Verletzung der öffentlichen Ordnung die Demonstration zu stören versuchten«. Rechtswidrige Aktivitäten, hieß es da, wurden »als Kampf für Bürgerrechte« hingestellt. »Die falschen Demokratieapostel im Westen« verlangten von der DDR, »daß sie ihre eigenen Gesetze verletzt.« Seit das NKWD auch in Moskau wieder schärfer gegen sowjetische Bürgerrechtsgruppen vorgeht, dürfte es schwerer fallen, sich auf die Liberalität Gorbatschows zu berufen.

Schwierigkeiten stehen der SED auf andere, gefährlichere Weise ins Haus. Es sind ja nicht die Lauen oder die Opportunisten unter ihren Mitgliedern, die heute voller Hoffnung nach Moskau blicken und sich in Parteiversammlungen nicht länger mit Appellen an die proletarische Disziplin oder mit linientreuen Phrasen abspeisen lassen. Gorbatschow mag Verständnis dafür haben, daß die SED-Führung an den Grenzen des sowjetischen Imperiums unter erschwerten Bedingungen operiert und sich gegen Glasnost und Perestroika sperrt. Doch die besten unter Honeckers über zwei Millionen Genossen sehen in dem Chef der KPdSU ein leuchtendes Vorbild, weil sie sich auch für die DDR eine Partei wünschen, in der man endlich frei diskutiert, eine sozialistische Demokratie, in der man Roß und Reiter beim Namen nennen und offen über den besseren Weg zum gemeinsamen Ziel streiten kann. In einer Erweiterten Oberschule in Ostberlin fand sich an einem Novembertag 1987 Lenin plötzlich durch zwei Portraits von »Gorbi« eingerahmt, und darunter stand: »Von der Sowjetunion lernen, heißt denken lernen.« Nur eine Stunde hing die anstößige Parole, dann war sie verschwunden. Die Anspielung war überdeutlich: Das »Neue Denken«, das Gorbatschow nicht nur auf Außen- und Sicherheitspolitik beschränkt wie die SED, sondern umfassender versteht, soll endlich Einzug halten in der DDR.

Es gärt vor allem in den Verlagen und Universitäten. Im Anschluß an die Verhaftungen derer, die am 17. Januar mit dem Transparent von der Freiheit der Andersdenkenden hatten teilnehmen wollen, sahen sich Funktionäre mit unbequemen Fragen konfrontiert: Warum, wollten die einen wissen, erfahren wir tagelang nichts über diese Vorfälle in den eigenen Medien? Und ist, fragten andere, eine Zusammenrottung (derer die Verhafteten verdächtigt worden waren) etwa schon das Schlangestehen beim Warten auf die Straßenbahn?

Trifft das, was Volker Braun über den Kommunismus schrieb, vielleicht auch auf den neuen Mann im Kreml zu? Wird Gorbatschow im realen Sozialismus der DDR so subversiv wie die Poesie? Die Rockfans, die Pfingsten 1986 Unter den Linden zusammenströmten, um ein paar heiße Musikfetzen der Bands auf der anderen Seite des Brandenburger Tores zu erhaschen, stimmten vor der sowjetischen Botschaft Sprechchöre an und riefen »Gorbatschow, Gorbatschow«. Das hinderte die Volkspolizei nicht, äußerst brutal gegen sie vorzugehen.

Gewiß ist die DDR-Führung seit Jahren um eine Politik der stetigen schrittweisen Öffnung bemüht, wie die sprunghaft gestiegene Zahl der genehmigten Westreisen für jüngere DDR-Bürger überzeugend belegt. Es wäre unredlich, dieses Bemühen nicht anzuerkennen. Nur gibt es für diese Politik der Öffnung nach außen nicht das Pendant eines Dialogs mit den kritischer gewordenen, fordernder auftretenden Bürgern nach innen.

Der Reformer in Moskau hat nicht nur in der DDR, sondern

auch in der SED Erwartungen geweckt, die zu Forderungen an die eigene Führung werden, und das Problem wird nicht leichter, wenn die alte Garde aus Altersgründen abtreten muß. Dann nämlich entfällt der sogenannte Antifaschistenbonus. Was das bedeutet, erklärte mir einer, der diesen Bonus selbst gewährt, einmal so: »Für viele Ältere im Apparat gilt noch heute, daß ich ihnen eine kontroverse, nicht immer verständliche Entscheidung abnehme. Ich denke: Nun gut, er hat gelitten, er saß viele Jahre in Brandenburg oder in Buchenwald und urteilt aus bitterer Erfahrung.« Dieser Bonus ist dahin, wenn die älteren ihren Platz räumen werden. Dann wird sich das Binnenklima in der DDR verändern: »Wer regiert, darf von Parteimitgliedern zwar immer Loyalität erwarten, aber er wird begründen müssen, warum er so und nicht anders handelt.« Da bleibt zu hoffen, daß diese Einschätzung sich bald als wahr erweist.

9. Probleme einer posttotalitären Gesellschaft

Ob die übertriebene Präzision des Parademarschs nötig sei, dieses »lächerlich hohe Aufheben der Beine« und das »frei aus den Hüftgelenken ein Loch in die Natur stoßen«, fragte einst der eine sozialistische Patriarch, Friedrich Engels, den anderen, Karl Marx. Beide waren wahrlich keine Pazifisten, aber den preußischen Paradeschritt betrachteten sie als sinnlosen Drill, seine erzieherische Wirkung hielten sie für Aberglauben. Engels diente 1841 als Einjähriger Freiwilliger in jener Kaserne im Berliner Stadtzentrum, die heute das Wachbataillon der Nationalen Volksarmee (NVA) beherbergt. Es trägt seinen Namen und macht jeden Mittwoch die große Wachablösung vor Schinkels Neuer Wache, heute ein Mahnmal für die Opfer des Faschismus und Militarismus, zum Spektakel und zur Volksbelustigung – mit flotten Märschen und eben jenen Exerzitien, die von der Bundeswehr zum alten Eisen geworfen wurden und die der sozialistische Namenspatron so verspottet hatte. Vielleicht, weil königlich-preußische Ausbilder ihn ins zaristische Rußland exportierten und die siegreiche Sowjetmacht ihn für Leo Trotzkis Rote Armee übernahm, wird der Stechschritt heute auch in der DDR gepflegt. Wann immer Erich Honecker und sein Politbüro sozialistische Heerschau halten – an den Geburtstagen der Republik, den Jahrestagen des Mauerbaus oder der Gründung der Nationalen Volksarmee –, marschiert die schimmernde Wehr der deutschen Kommunisten im preußischen Paradeschritt vor der Ehrentribüne der Karl-Marx-Allee vorbei. Der friderizianische Drill, der da gepflegt wird, soll jedoch keineswegs darüber hinwegtäuschen, daß diese Armee die Streitmacht nicht eines Volkes oder einer Nation, sondern die einer Klasse ist, in deren Auftrag zu handeln die SED vorgibt. Zwar ist die Übernahme tradierter militärischer Formen und Symbole dazu gedacht, die Armee neuen Typs im Volk zu verankern, aber das Militärlexikon der SED läßt keinen Zweifel zu, welche neuen soldatischen Tugenden nebst den alten, Gehorsam und Tapferkeit, besonderen Stellenwert besitzen: Haß auf den Imperialismus und Ergebenheit gegenüber der Partei. Wenn die NVA am Vorabend festlicher Tage, etwa dem 40. »Jahrestag der Befreiung« am 8. Mai 1985 feierlich mit Fackeln zum großen Zapfenstreich vor das Mahnmal Unter den Linden zieht, ist das Zeremoniell unverändert konservativ, aber der Inhalt revolutionär. Früher hieß es: »Helm ab zum Gebet« und neben preußischen Märschen erklang das Lied vom guten Kameraden. Heute spielt man das vom kleinen Trompeter, der ein lustiger Rotgardist war. Der Yorcksche Marsch wird geblasen, aber auch die Internationale und Louis Fürnbergs Hymne »Die Partei, die Partei, die hat immer Recht...« Der Fahneneid verpflichtet die Soldaten, den Sozialismus zu schützen, die Befehle der Arbeiter- und Bauernregierung zu befolgen und den Sieg »an der Seite der Sowjetarmee« zu erringen.

Wer die preußisch-sozialistische Militärsymbiose genau studieren und in Erfahrung bringen will, welche Erbteile der deutschen Geschichte diese Klassen- und Partei-Armee für sich in Anspruch nimmt, sollte sich auf den Weg zum Heiligensee nach Potsdam begeben. Dort findet er, wenige Meter vom Cäcilienhof entfernt, in dem die Sieger 1945 die Entmilitarisierung Deutschlands beschlossen, umringt von Waffen sowjetischer Bauart, das Armee-Museum der DDR in dem von Gontard erbauten Marmorpalais, das einmal Sitz von Hohenzollernprinzen war. Wo Königliche Hoheiten früher ihre Gäste begrüßten, in der klassizistischen Eingangshalle, empfängt den Besucher heute ein riesiges DDR-Emblem – Hammer, Zirkel und Ährenkranz –, und der Rundgang belegt, daß das Leitbild der NVA der sozialistisch-militärische Klassenkämpfer ist. Die Tradition, auf die sie sich beruft, beginnt mit den ungeordneten Haufen aufständischer Bauern, und wo, abseits vom Drill, an Preußisches angeknüpft wird, dann natürlich an Scharnhorst, den Reformer, einen Feldwebel- und Bauernsohn, der die (preußische) Volksarmee schuf und die Wehrpflicht einführte. Auch als Erben der 48er Revolution sollen sich Honeckers Kämpfer fühlen und Vorbilder sind selbstverständlich die Soldaten der November-Revolution und der Münchner Räterepublik, die Mitglieder des Roten Frontkämpferbunds und der Internationalen Brigaden im Spanischen Bürgerkrieg. Über die Teilnahme am Widerstand gegen Hitler – sei es als »Kundschafter« der Roten Kapelle, als Überläufer, als Angehöriger des Nationalkomitees »Freies Deutschland« oder Propagandist in den sowjetischen Gräben – führt ihre Traditionslinie dann weiter in die Gegenwart. Und galten konservative Offiziere wie Graf Stauffenberg oder Henning von Tresckow früher als Junker, Militaristen oder Handlanger der Monopolbourgeoisie, werden sie heute bewußt miteinbezogen. Das neue Ostberliner »Wörterbuch zur deutschen Militärgeschichte« bezeichnet das Attentat vom 20. Juli als einen »heroischen Versuch« und als »patriotische, antifaschistische Aktion«.

»Eine Welle der Sympathie und begeisterte Hochrufe empfingen die Soldaten des Volkes«, kommentierte der Sprecher des DDR-Fernsehens Bilder vom sternförmigen Einmarsch der Volksarmee in den großen Saal des Palasts der Republik. Zu den Klängen des Parademarschs, mit Fahnen, gezogenen Säbeln und einem dreifachen »Hurra« entbot die NVA-Ehrenformation dem XI. Parteitag der SED ihren »kämpferischen Soldatengruß«. In der Botschaft der Armee an die Delegierten hieß es unter anderem: »Die entscheidende Quelle unserer Kraft und Stärke ist die Führung durch die marxistisch-leninistische Partei.« Bundesbürger würden ihren Augen nicht trauen, wollte die Bundeswehr ein vergleichbares Spektakel auf den Parteitagen der jeweils in Bonn regierenden stärksten Koalitionspartei veranstalten. In der DDR zählen solche Einmärsche zum gewohnten Ritual der Parteitage der SED wie der Parlamente der Freien Deutschen Jugend. Und es versteht sich von selbst, daß die Soldaten beteuern, »von Liebe zum sozialistischen Vaterland und vom Haß auf die Feinde des Friedens« durchdrungen zu sein. Wie zufällig ist diese Armee, die sich selbst als Instrument der Klasse und den unwiderruflichen Pakt mit der Sowjetunion als Klassenbündnis versteht, auch immer und überall dabei. Zwischen Bockwurstbuden und Bierständen auf einem Stadtteilfest in Marzahn anläßlich der 750-Jahrfeier Berlins entdeckte ich plötzlich Panzer und Haubitzen der NVA, umlagert und neugierig beäugt von Kindern und Jugendlichen. Freundliche Offiziere nahmen sie an die Hand, erklärten die Waffen und ließen einige in das Innere des zur Schau gestellten T-35 klettern. Auf den nationalen Jugendfestivals der FDJ finden sich Schieß-Stände der NVA, in denen Jugendliche ihre Treffsicherheit erproben können. Die Grenztruppen der DDR, die jeden am Entrinnen hindern, der ihr sozialistisches Vaterland ohne Erlaubnis verlassen will, stellen sich als verdiente, glückliche Menschen dar und werben mit ihrem Maskottchen, einem Teddybären in Grenzeruniform. Nebenan, auf einem Stand der Gesellschaft für Sport und Technik (GST) wird gelehrt, wie man Handgranaten wirft. »Erlebnis und Bewährung« lautet die Parole, mit denen diese Organisation für die Vor- und paramilitärische Ausbildung wirbt. Konkret heißt das: Die GST bietet Abenteuer und lockt die Jugendlichen mit Erlebnissen, die anders nicht zu haben sind. Das beginnt ganz harmlos mit Flugzeugmodellen und führt doch systematisch in die Welt der Waffen ein. »Meine Tat für unser sozialistisches Vaterland« steht auf den Wimpeln, die, wie anderswo Papierblumen, mit Luftgewehren in GST-Schießbuden abzuknallen sind.

Sicher hat die NVA wegen der schwachen Jahrgänge Schwierigkeiten wie die Bundeswehr, ihre Sollstärke zu halten und den Nachwuchs an Berufssoldaten zu sichern. Aber die Art, in der sich die SED müht, Wehrbereitschaft, ja Wehrbegeisterung zu wecken, macht gelegentlich den Eindruck, als stünde die Invasion feindlicher Panzerarmeen stündlich bevor. Die Indoktrination beginnt schon im Kindergarten, wo der Stolz »auf die Menschen vermittelt wird, die den bewaffneten Organen angehören oder bereits gedient haben«, auch »Liebe und Zuneigung zu ihnen« soll gefördert werden. Sie wird im Wehrkundeunterricht in der Schule systematisch vertieft. Als »inhaltliche Probleme« der ideologischen Arbeit bezeichnet eine Richtlinie für Pädagogen »die Vermittlung eines realen Bildes vom gemeinsamen imperialistischen Klassengegner und die Erziehung zum Haß auf die den Sozialismus bedrohenden Feinde«. Thälmann-Pioniere versprechen in ihrem Gelöbnis, sie »schützen den Frieden und hassen die Kriegstreiber«; in Ferienlagern üben sie später in Spielzeugpanzern, wie angreifende Feinde im Gegenstoß zurückzuwerfen sind. Die vormilitärische Ausbildung ist für Schüler Pflicht, für Lehrlinge laut Gesetz ein Bestandteil ihrer Berufsausbildung. NVA-Reservisten, so Oberst Rolf Schleicher, Chefredakteur der Wochenzeitung »Volksarmee«, stellen ein »kräftiges Potential bei der wehrpolitischen Erziehung der Lehrlinge« dar und sollen für »Patenschaftsarbeit« an den polytechnischen Oberschulen gewonnen werden.

Nun behauptet jede Armee, gleich ob in Ost oder West, heute von sich, daß sie lediglich der Aufrechterhaltung des Friedens dient – natürlich auch die der DDR. Doch letztere nimmt obendrein für sich in Anspruch, »zum Wohle der Menschen« zu existieren, wie das »Neue Deutschland« zum 30. Jahrestag ihrer Gründung in fetten Lettern in der Hauptschlagzeile verkündete. Nur ist die Erziehung zum Haß, die für ein klares Feindbild sorgen soll, mit dem »Neuen Denken«, das die Führung proklamiert, schwerlich in Einklang zu bringen. »Wissen und Kämpfen« heißt ein Lehrheft für die politische Schulung von NVA-Soldaten, herausgegeben im Jahr 1985 von der Politischen Hauptverwaltung der NVA. Darin wird die Bundeswehr praktisch als Gegenstück zur Klassenarmee der DDR, nämlich als »militärisches Machtinstrument des Monopolkapitals« bezeichnet. Sie könne niemals eine »Armee des Volkes und des Friedens sein, denn sie ist eine Streitmacht der Monopole, ist gleichsam deren bewaffnete Faust«. Als ihr »Klassenauftrag« wird »Sicherung und möglichst Ausdehnung des Macht- und Einflußbereiches des BRD-Monopolkapitals nach außen sowie Unterdrückung aller demokratischen und fortschrittlichen, gegen das staatsmonopolistische Herrschaftssystem gerichteten Kräfte und Bewegungen nach innen« bezeichnet. In summa: Ihrem ganzen Charakter nach ist sie eine »Aggressionsarmee«, und zum Feind des NVA-Kämpfers wird der »verhetzte und aggressionsbereite Waffenträger der Monopolbourgeoisie« erklärt – der Soldat der Bundeswehr. Das alles heißt nicht gerade, den anderen prinzipiell für friedensfähig zu halten, wie es das »Neue Denken« im Interesse des Überlebens der Menschheit ja verlangt. So bleibt abzuwarten, wann die DDR welche Korrekturen an ihrer Agitation nach innen machen wird. Feindbildstilisierung und die dauernden Appelle zur Erhöhung der Kampfkraft sind aus der Sicht der SED vorerst offenbar unerläßlich für die sozialistische Wehrerziehung. Wenn Bundeswehr- und NVA-Offiziere einander inzwischen als Beobachter an Manövern freundlich begegnen, ist das sicher geeignet, persönliche Feindbilder abzubauen. Gewiß gibt es auch in der Bundeswehr Anlaß, manchen liebgewordenen agitatorischen Pappkameraden in der eigenen Reihe kritisch zu überprüfen, ob er nicht einem törichten eifernden und undifferenzierten Antikommunismus entspricht. Aber ganz so simpel wie die NVA hat sie es sich doch selten gemacht. Vorerst nämlich drückt die »Armeerundschau« der DDR Sätze über die sowjetische Atombombe, die ganz dem Schwarz-Weiß-Schema folgen, nach dem das Gewehr in der DDR-Armee eine gute, in der Bundeswehr eine schlechte Sache ist: »Die Todeswaffe verwandelte sich in den Händen des Sozialismus zu einer Garantie für den Frieden, der einmal mehr aus dem Osten kam«.

Die Front machen gegen ein solches Schwarz-Weiß-Denken, das der eigenen Seite das absolut Gute und Richtige, der anderen das absolut Böse und Falsche zurechnet und Gefahren allein vom Gegner drohen sieht, sind die evangelischen Christen in der DDR. Daß es sie noch gibt, wenn auch als aktive Minderheit, zeigt den großen Irrtum, dem Partei und Staat einst aufgesessen sind. Als die SED das Regiment ergriff, glaubte sie, das Problem der Kirchen würde sich in einer Generation erledigt haben, weil die Religion im Sozialismus wie von selbst verschwinde. Inzwischen haben in der Wolle gefärbte Marxisten erkannt, daß Religion Urbedürfnissen der Menschheit entspricht, zumal der Marxismus auf existentielle Fragen, Leid oder Krankheit keine Antwort weiß. So rechnet der atheistische Staat heute mit langen Zeiträumen einer Koexistenz mit den Kirchen. Die Evangelischen wiederum sehen, so formulierte es der sächsische Landesbischof Hempel einmal, »im Kleinerwerden eine von Gott gesetzte Chance, denn Kleinerwerden heißt, sich konzentrieren können«.

Inmitten einer ideologisch genormten und gelenkten Gesellschaft existiert die Kirche in einer Diaspora, und die sich zu ihr bekennen und aktiv einlassen, sind nicht selten benachteiligt in Studium oder Beruf. Manche verstehen dies als Herausforderung, der sie sich bewußt stellen müssen: »Wenn wir zurückgehen ins Neue Testament, dann konnten auch damals Christen nicht ohne Nachteile leben«, sagte mir eine Pastorin, die eine Gemeinde am Rande von Rostock betreut. »Ich halte es nicht für schlecht, wenn man Christsein damit verbindet, daß man wirklich anders ist und vielleicht auch Dinge tun muß, die Nachteile bringen. Auf der anderen Seite möchte ich auch nicht, daß wir uns zu Märtyrern machen.« Viele Theologen, Pfarrer, Diakonie-Schwestern und kirchliche Mitarbeiter leben wie auf einer Insel im sozialistischen Meer, außerhalb des sozialistischen Alltags. Sie lernen auf kirchlichen Seminaren, studieren an kirchlichen Hochschulen und verkehren meist unter Christen. Einige sehen in dieser Isolation Gefahren und sagen: Die Kirche ist ein Raum, in den man im eigenen Land auswandern kann. Das gilt, auch wenn es auf den ersten Blick unglaublich erscheint, sogar für die Forst- und Landwirtschaft, welche die Kirchen auf eigenen Gütern heute noch betreiben. Wenn man so will, sind sie die letzten in der DDR verbliebenen Großgrundbesitzer.

In Seelendorf, idyllisch im Wald gelegen, wohnt der Domstiftsforstmeister von Brandenburg in einem stattlichen alten

Forsthaus. Und wenn es überhaupt noch so etwas gibt im realen Sozialismus, dann stellt er den Gutsherrn alter Art dar, denn wer da lebt in dem winzigen Ort, steht bei ihm in Lohn und Brot. Im Auftrag der Kirche bewirtschaftet er 1700 Hektar Wald und betreibt ein Sägewerk, das die längsten Bretter und Balken in der DDR produziert – für die Erneuerung der Dachstühle von Kirchen und Domen. Wenige Kilometer entfernt, auf Gut Mötzow, werden in kirchlichen Ställen Kälber schlachtreif gezüchtet – auf Rechnung von Domherren, die Stift Brandenburg verwalten, das sich auf eine Schenkung des Sachsenkaisers Otto I. zurückführt. Zu den Traditionen, die kaum einer im Sozialismus noch am Leben wähnt, gehört denn auch der alljährliche feierliche Einzug der Domherren in St. Peter und Paul in Brandenburg, eine der schönsten deutschen Backstein-Basiliken, die Keimzelle Preußens war: Im Talar, die Häupter mit mittelalterlichen Baretten geschmückt und mit Orden angetan, die der große Preußenkönig dem Domkapitel verlieh, weil es im 7jährigen Krieg das Geld für die Aufstellung eines neuen Infanterieregimentes gespendet hatte. Insgesamt verfügen die Kirchen der DDR über 200 000 Hektar Grundbesitz, und der Erlös der christlichen Acker-, Forst- und Viehwirtschaft kommt dem Erhalt kirchlicher Baudenkmäler oder der Diakonie zugute.

Wenn die Kirchen sich solcher Besitztümer noch erfreuen dürfen, wenn ihr Grund und Boden nicht von der Bodenreform erfaßt wurde und das Diakonische Werk mit seinen Krankenhäusern noch existiert, haben sie dies vor allem den sowjetischen Siegern zu verdanken, die sie als antifaschistische Kraft betrachteten. Auf Befehl der sowjetischen Militäradministration (SMA) wurde ihnen deshalb ihr Vermögen, soweit es von den Nazis beschlagnahmt war, zurückerstattet. Die sowjetische Politik folgte in den ersten Nachkriegsjahren dem Konzept eines einheitlichen, nicht von vornherein sozialistischen, aber demokratisch-antifaschistischen Deutschlands, in dem die Kirchen wie die bürgerlichen Parteien ihren legitimen Platz haben sollten. So gründeten die Evangelischen auf ausdrücklichen Wunsch der Sowjets sogar einen zentralen kirchlichen Verlag, obschon der damals dafür zuständige Berliner Bischof Dibelius sich anfänglich gegen diese Idee sträubte. Die Kirche hatte bis dahin noch nie über eine eigene Publikationszentrale verfügt und sich statt dessen auf eine Vielzahl kleiner privater Verlage verlassen. »Aus heutiger Sicht«, versicherte mir der Chef eben dieses Produkts sowjetischen Insistierens, der »Evangelischen Verlagsgesellschaft« in Ostberlin, »war das natürlich ein Segen. Das hat uns viel geholfen, als 1953 die große Anfeindung kam. In der Zeit des Kampfs wirkte diese sowjetische Geburtsurkunde wie eine Lebensversicherung«.

Kampfzeit – das waren die Jahre, in denen die SED durch massive und militante atheistische Agitation zum Kirchenaustritt ermunterte, eine gezielte Entchristianisierung betrieb und erklärte, daß man sich entweder für den Sozialismus oder die Kirche (bzw. Synagoge) zu entscheiden habe: »Zwischen der religiösen Ideologie und der sozialistischen Ideologie«, so das »Neue Deutschland« damals, »gibt es keine friedliche Koexistenz«. Nicht nur sollte die Jugendweihe an die Stelle der Konfirmation treten, die Namensweihe hatte die Taufe, die Eheweihe die kirchliche Hochzeit abzulösen, und ganz offen bediente die SED sich in dem Bemühen, das tradierte Netzwerk volkskirchlicher Bräuche durch ein atheistisches zu ersetzen, sakramentaler Formen, die sie von der Kirche übernahm. Im Zuge dieser konsequenten Säkularisierungspolitik verhinderte die SED damals die Erteilung der Christenlehre in den Schulen, erschwerte jede kirchliche Arbeit außerhalb kircheneigener Räume und schritt teilweise mit Polizeigewalt dagegen ein. Uwe Johnsons »Ingrid Babendererde«, sein Erstlingsroman, der erst nach seinem Tode erschien, ist ein literarisches Dokument jener Zeit. Er handelt von der Auseinandersetzung zwischen FDJlern und Mitgliedern der Jungen Gemeinde in einer mecklenburgischen Kleinstadt und schildert eindringlich die aggressive Indoktrination und Intoleranz der neuen Funktionäre, die ein junges Liebespaar schließlich in den Westen treiben.

An diese Phase der offenen Konfrontation von Staat und

Kirche erinnert sich der Verlagsleiter als die »Jahre des Wilden Ostens«. Als Pastor mit dem Rucksack radelte er damals mit der Jungen Gemeinde über Land und veranstaltete Bibelrüstzeiten. Weil er damit genau jene offene Kirchenarbeit betrieb, welche die SED mit allen Mitteln unterbinden wollte, zog seine christliche Schar wie die Zigeuner durch Sachsen. »Um Auseinandersetzungen mit den Kreisräten zu verhindern«, erzählte er, »blieben wir immer nur ein oder zwei Tage und konnten damit die Meldeordnung umgehen. Ein Motorradfahrer fuhr voraus und machte irgendwo im nächsten Dorf Quartier.« Immer wieder der Mißachtung der Gesetze beschuldigt, wurde er jedoch nie vor Gericht gestellt. Er ist ein Beispiel für viele, die mit Mut und Gottvertrauen, Glück und gescheitem Taktieren unter schwierigsten Umständen wichtige Positionen für Glauben, Gemeindeleben und die Kirchen behaupteten. Wenn ihm heute auf der Leipziger Buchmesse der stellvertretende Kulturminister Höpcke am Stand der Evangelischen Verlagsanstalt beim Rundgang seine Aufwartung macht, dann, sagte er, »wundere ich mich manchmal doch, daß ich inzwischen für höchste Funktionäre gesprächsfähig bin. Wenn die in meine Kaderakte schauten, würde ihnen sicher schlecht.«

Daß Staat und Kirche vor gut einem Jahrzehnt zu einer teils gelassenen, teils gespannten Koexistenz finden konnten, setzte allerdings auch auf christlicher Seite Umdenken voraus. Lange orientierten sich Pastoren und Bischöfe am westlichen Antikommunismus, und weil sie auf der Einheit der Evangelischen Kirchen Deutschlands (EKD) auch noch beharrten, als die SED längst auf Teilungs- und Abgrenzungskurs gegangen war, erschienen sie in den Augen der Funktionäre oft als Verfechter der westlichen Wiedervereinigungsstrategie. Viele hielten den marxistischen Staat für illegitim und schlossen ihrerseits jeden Gedanken an ein friedliches Miteinander aus. Geschwindigkeitsbegrenzungen im Osten, erklärte der nationalkonservative Bischof Otto Dibelius 1959, und er war damals Vorsitzender der EKD, wolle er nicht beachten, denn die Gebote der DDR hätten für ihn keinerlei verpflichtende Kraft.

Für diese abenteuerliche Argumentation berief er sich auf Römer 13 und den Apostel Paulus und behauptete, der totalitäre Staat Ulbrichts sei keine Gewalt, der man Gehorsam schulde, weil er kein Recht kenne und im Sinne des Heiligen Augustinus eher einer »Räuberbande« gleiche. Wenn der Christ in der DDR Verkehrsgebote übertrete, meinte Dibelius, solle er lediglich sorgfältig Ausschau halten, ob er jemanden gefährde. Eine Verkehrsstrafe zahle er »völlig frei von jeglichem Bewußtsein einer Schuld«. Vermutlich denken die meisten Westberliner Transit-Reisenden immer noch so wie ihr Bischof vor bald 20 Jahren, wenn sie über die mit Radarfallen gespickten Autobahnen der DDR mit über hundert Sachen fahren und, falls erwischt, von »räuberischen« Volkspolizei-Jagdkommandos auf geradezu drakonische Weise zur Kasse gebeten werden.

Gingen die meisten DDR-Pastoren auch nicht soweit wie Dibelius in ihrer Ablehnung des Ulbricht-Staates, hielten viele es doch mit einem andern Spruch ihres EKD-Oberhirten, der da lautete: *Nubecula est transitoria*. Das lateinische Sprichwort heißt soviel wie: Es ist ein Wölkchen, das wieder vergeht oder vorüberzieht, und gemeint war natürlich die Deutsche Demokratische Republik, die damit bewußt als ein Staat auf Abruf und als Provisorium apostrophiert wurde. »Das war tatsächlich die Meinung«, erinnerte sich Bischof Albrecht Schönherr in einem Gespräch, »und sie wurde natürlich auch genährt durch das wiederholte Anerbieten einer Wiedervereinigung gerade von der Sowjetunion aus.« Schönherr steht in der Tradition der Bekennenden Kirche, aber er sieht auch die Fehler, die sie begangen hat. »Für die Kommunisten haben wir kein Wort gefunden. Selbst in der Bekenntnissynode zu Barmen wurde ein Ja zur nationalen Erhebung und Treue zum Führer beteuert. Vor allem aber haben wir geschwiegen ... zur Verfolgung der Juden.«

Albrecht Schönherr wurde bald führend unter jenen Kirchenmännern, die schließlich das Konzept von »Gottes Volk im Sozialismus« entwickelten, welches als diametrales Gegenstück zum Denken des Otto Dibelius zu verstehen ist und von kirchlicher Seite aus den Abbau der Konfrontation erleichterte. Wie dieser Kurswechsel sich in ihm selbst vorbereitete, beschrieb der Alt-Landesbischof der Evangelischen Kirche (Ost)-Berlin-Brandenburg mir einmal so: »Ende der 50er Jahre fragte ich mich plötzlich: Glaubst Du heute eigentlich wirklich daran, daß Gott überall regiert, also auch hier, oder ist die DDR ein weißer Fleck Gottes auf der Landkarte? Und dann bin ich hingegangen zu einer Regierungsstelle und habe gesagt, bitte nehmen Sie mich als Bürger der DDR ernst, ich bin kein Partisan des Westens, ich möchte als Christ in der DDR existieren, aber eben als Christ. Und diese Überzeugung haben dann mehrere gehabt. Nachdem 1961 die Trennung so sichtbar wurde, war es notwendig, daß diejenigen, die leitende Verantwortung in der Kirche ausüben, dann auch da existieren, wo diese Verantwortung sich auswirkt – daß sie also nicht von außen her hineinregieren können, sondern daß sie in der Solidarität der Leute leben müssen, für die sie etwas bestimmen.« Solche Überlegungen führten schließlich, zumal eine neue DDR-Verfassung grenzüberschreitende Institutionen nicht mehr zuließ, zur Abnabelung vom Westen und zur Gründung eines DDR-Kirchenbunds. Als es am 6. März 1978 dann zu jener »historischen« Begegnung zwischen Erich Honecker und Vertretern des Kirchenbundes unter Führung von Schönherr kam, war der vorläufige Höhepunkt eines Verständigungsprozesses zwischen Staat und Kirche erreicht: Die Kirche anerkannte ihren Standort im Sozialismus und in einem kommunistisch geführten Staat, der seinerseits im Gegenzug darauf verzichtete, die Wirkungsmöglichkeiten dieser Kirche um jeden Preis einzuschränken. Welche Früchte diese Annäherung tragen kann, wurde im Jahr der großen Lutherfeiern deutlich. Da traten die Protestanten in ihrem atheistisch regierten Staat plötzlich aus ihren Gotteshäusern heraus, füllten in Wittenberg und Eisleben die Plätze und stimmten immer wieder den mächtigen Choral an: »Ein feste Burg ist unser Gott«. Friedrich Engels nannte ihn einmal die Marseillaise des 16. Jahrhunderts.

Nun wird das sichtbar zum besseren gewendete Verhältnis

von Kirche und Staat in der DDR gelegentlich für die Theorie ins Feld geführt, die andere deutsche Republik sei kein totalitäres System mehr, sondern befinde sich längst im Zustand einer posttotalitären Gesellschaft. Um zu verstehen, was das heißen soll, braucht man nur die politische Elle zu bemühen, die Politik-Wissenschaftler entwickelt haben, um an des Totalitarismus verdächtigen Staaten Maß zu nehmen. Danach ist eine Autokratie vom Typ einer totalitären Diktatur ein Einparteienstaat mit einer radikalen Ideologie, der über das Informations- und das Waffenmonopol verfügt, eine terroristische Geheimpolizei unterhält und eine zentral gelenkte Verwaltungswirtschaft hat. Legt man diese Elle an die DDR, ist fraglich, ob sie alle sechs Kriterien in ihrer bisherigen Geschichte einmal erfüllt hat und je ein totalitärer Staat gewesen ist wie etwa das Dritte Reich oder die Sowjetunion. Im Gegensatz zur KPdSU hat die SED, wie wir gesehen haben, auch trotz allergrößter Anstrengungen, die sie in dieser Richtung unternahm, nie völlig das Informationsmonopol besessen. Und obwohl in der DDR unstreitig eine Partei klar die Führung und damit die Herrschaft ausübt, ist die politische Struktur der Gesellschaft doch wenigstens soweit in sich gebrochen, daß von einem eindeutigen Einparteienstaat schwerlich die Rede sein kann. Richard Löwenthal bezeichnet heute selbst die Sowjetunion und China als posttotalitäre Regime, weil der persönliche Despotismus Stalins und Maos erloschen ist und eine Oligarchie regiert – die kollektive Führung des Politbüros, in dem die Macht der Führer nicht wesentlich größer sei als die eines westlichen Ministerpräsidenten über die Mitglieder seines Kabinetts. Jedoch verfügt das Volk in der posttotalitären Staatsform, und das macht den entscheidenden Unterschied zur westlichen Demokratie aus, nicht über die Mittel, die herrschende Gruppe zu stürzen oder abzulösen. Wenn der Satz vom Überholen ohne einzuholen, den Walter Ulbricht einmal seiner Wirtschaft ins Stammbuch schrieb, je Gültigkeit hatte, dann vielleicht hier: Im Wettlauf mit der Sowjetunion hat die DDR ihr östliches Vorbild ja nie eingeholt und dennoch überholt, denn sie war nie völlig totalitär und schon posttotalitär, ehe die Sowjetunion sich dahin entwickelte. Das Beispiel ist, zugegeben, gewagt, denn der Zustand der DDR läßt sich ebensogut als vortotalitär bezeichnen. Sicher hätte die SED das Moskauer Modell des Einparteienstaates mit seiner radikalen Ideologie eines Tages doch übernommen, wenn sich die sowjetischen Verhältnisse in der Nachfolge Stalins nicht geändert hätten.

Nun verfügen die Kirchen in der DDR über weitaus größeren Freiraum als in der Sowjetunion und der ČSSR und sind in organisatorischen und personellen Entscheidungen in der Tat unabhängig von Staat und Partei, und zwar de jure und de facto. Es war ein Monsignore in Ostberlin, der mir einmal erläuterte, daß der Papst, wenn er einen neuen Kardinal für das Erzbistum München-Freising ernennen wolle, sich vorher mit der Bayerischen Staatsregierung ins Benehmen zu setzen und ihr Einverständnis einzuholen habe. Angesichts des Fehlens jeder vertraglichen Regelung genügte gegenüber dem Staatsratsvorsitzenden der DDR dagegen eine freundliche, aber bestimmte Mitteilung, daß der Heilige Vater beschlossen habe, den Bischof Meissner zum Kardinal zu ernennen und damit zum geistlichen Oberhaupt der Katholiken in der DDR zu bestellen. »Die Kirche ist die einzige Institution im Sozialismus«, so der Ostberliner Bischof Forck, »die nicht ohne weiteres in allen Punkten an staatliche Maßnahmen gebunden ist.« Das stimmt, in soweit die Kirche sich als reine Kultkirche versteht und sich auf den Vollzug von Gottesdiensten und Andachten mit Gläubigen innerhalb ihrer eigenen Räume beschränkt. Es stimmt nur sehr bedingt, wenn sie etwa Kirchentage veranstalten will oder wenn sie in den Gemeindesaal lädt, um Existenzprobleme von Christen in der sozialistischen Gesellschaft zu diskutieren und dabei, missionarischem Auftrag folgend, die Türen weit offen hält für alle, die sich nicht zu ihr bekennen. Da kommt es immer wieder zu Reibungen, und sie haben häufig in der vom Staat betriebenen Erziehung zum Haß ihre Ursache.

In eben dem Jahr, in dem Staat und Kirche sich zu einer begrenzten Partnerschaft zusammenfanden, setzte die DDR-

Regierung jenen Erlaß in Kraft, der den obligatorischen Wehrkundeunterricht in den Schulen einführte und an dem sich schnell die Geister scheiden sollten. Die SED zielte darauf ab, die Erziehung zur sozialistischen Persönlichkeit, die Idealnorm aller Pädagogik in der DDR, durch die Bereitschaft, ja Begeisterung für den Wehrdienst zu vervollkommnen. Doch an den zu diesem Zweck in den Schulen vermittelten Feindbildern nahmen viele christlichen Eltern Anstoß. Gegen das sozialistische Pflichtfach Wehrerziehung setzten die Bischöfe, vor allem aber Pastoren an der Basis, die Kontakt zu wehrpflichtigen Jugendlichen hielten, mit Friedensdekaden und -werkstätten ihr christliches Programm einer Erziehung zum Frieden – ein Unternehmen, aus dem nicht nur die eigenständige Friedensbewegung der DDR, sondern schließlich auch jene Bürgerrechtsgruppen hervorgehen sollten, deren Existenz an den Rändern christlicher Gemeinden das eben entspannte Verhältnis von Kirche und Staat immer neuen Belastungsproben aussetzt. Ein wichtiger Faktor, der für Unruhe sorgt und Spannung schafft, ist die Tatsache, daß die DDR die Verweigerung des Wehrdienstes an der Waffe lediglich aus religiösen Gründen anerkennt. Linke, atheistische Pazifisten vom Schlage eines Carl von Ossietzky haben mithin kein Recht, als Bausoldat zu dienen, sondern müssen zwischen vollem Wehrdienst und Gefängnis wählen.

Wenn es so etwas gibt wie spontane, nicht von der Partei gelenkte gesellschaftliche Aktivität, dann in den wenigen, oft genug winzigen Gruppierungen in den evangelischen Gemeinden oder an ihrem Rande. Und wenn sich die DDR schwer tut, mit diesem unerwünschten, bis vor wenigen Jahren unbekanntem Phänomen umzugehen, hat sie das Problem doch selbst geschaffen – durch Gleichschaltung, und ein Übermaß an Agitation, durch Repression und staatliche Geheimniskrämerei. Die Auswirkungen gleichen einer Kettenreaktion: *Weil* unter dem schützenden Dach der Kirchen freier geredet wird als anderswo in der DDR, fühlen sich junge Menschen angezogen, die der genormten, gestanzten Langeweile des Sozialismus überdrüssig sind und aufbegehren. *Weil* die Bischöfe die Verweigerung des Wehrdienstes als christliches Friedenszeugnis bejahen, wurden die Blues-Messen pazifistischer Pastoren wie Rainer Eppelmann und Michael Passauer in der Ostberliner Erlöserkirche zu attraktiven Happenings nicht nur für junge Christen, sondern auch für die Nichtintegrierten, die Nonkonformisten und Aussteiger aus der ganzen Republik. *Weil* die Kirche für einen sozialen Friedensdienst als Wehrdienstalternative eintritt, *weil* die Pfarrämter in der DDR die einzigen Amtsstuben sind, in denen Auskunft erteilt wird, wie der Dienst mit der Waffe verweigert und wie man »Bausoldat« werden kann, zogen die Kirchen immer mehr jüngere Pazifisten an, die keine Christen sind. *Weil* die Kirchen als erste für ökologisches Bewußtsein sorgten in einem Staat, der geradezu brutal an der Priorität der Ökonomie über die Ökologie festhält und exakte Daten über die Umweltverschmutzung – handele es sich nun um die Schwefeldioxydemissionen von Leuna oder den Ascheausstoß von Bitterfeld – in einem geheimgehaltenen Beschluß zur »Geheimsache« erklärte, siedelten sich bei ihnen die ersten Ökozirkel an. *Weil* die Staatssicherheit Teilnehmer an kirchlichen Friedensdekaden oder Umweltseminaren, die nicht zur engeren Gemeinde zählen, antisozialistischer Aktivitäten verdächtigt, unter Druck setzt und bedroht, entstanden Gruppen, die für ihre Menschenrechte kämpfen. *Weil* die bedrängten Bürgerrechtler zu ihrer Verteidigung die Öffentlichkeit der westlichen Medien suchen, wittert der Staat Ansätze einer organisierten innenpolitischen Opposition und greift zu den brutalsten Mitteln der Repression: Er verhaftet, verurteilt, bürgert aus, oder schiebt ab. *Weil* er Bürgerrechtlern wie Stephan Krawczyk, Freya Klier oder Ralf Hirsch nur die Wahl zwischen Haftstrafen oder der »freiwilligen« Ausreise in den Westen ließ, werden die Kirchen zu Sammelbecken ihrer Gesinnungsgenossen, die demokratische Reformen in der DDR erzwingen wollen und die Andacht und Fürbitt-Gottesdienste in Sympathiekundgebungen für die Eingesperrten und Ausgewiesenen verwandeln. In den Räumen der Kirche formieren sich also die, wenn auch bescheidenen Ansätze einer Gegenmacht, deren Ziel es ist, die Politik des Dialogs, welche die SED-Spitze nach außen führt, durch einen offenen Dialog nach innen zu ergänzen, der einer unruhigen Jugend die Chance gibt, sich frei zu artikulieren, ohne daß sie deshalb gleich Sanktionen befürchten muß. Unter diesen Verhältnissen operieren die Kirchenleitungen auf einem schmalen Grat zwischen politischer Opposition und opportunistischer Anpassung. Um den Freiraum für die »offene Gemeindearbeit« zu behaupten, müssen sie nach unten dämpfen, damit sie nach oben abwiegeln können. Dämpfen sie zuviel, bekommen sie Ärger mit der Basis, die sie des Opportunismus verdächtigt. Lassen sie den Gemeinden zu sehr freien Lauf, öffnen sie in den Augen der Obrigkeit, auf deren Unterstützung die Kirche in vieler Hinsicht immer noch angewiesen ist, das Oppositionsventil.

Daß der Staat die geballte Macht seines Repressionsapparates gegen eine Handvoll Abweichler einsetzt, die mit einer Parole von Rosa Luxemburg an einer offiziellen Kampfdemonstration teilnehmen wollen, um auf sich und ihre Sache aufmerksam zu machen, zeigt wie eng die SED die Toleranzgrenze zieht, wenn sie die offizielle, säkulare, wehrhafte Ersatzreligion namens Marxismus-Leninismus in der Öffentlichkeit in Frage gestellt sieht. »Verwerflich wie eine Gotteslästerung«, nannte Heinz Kamnitzer, der Präsident des DDR-Penclubs, in einem Leitartikel des »Neuen Deutschland« das Transparent von Stephan Krawczyk und Ralf Hirsch mit dem Luxemburg-Wort von der Freiheit, die stets die des Andersdenkenden ist, und trieb den religiösen Vergleich bewußt auf die Spitze: »Keine Kirche könnte hinnehmen, wenn man eine Prozession zur Erinnerung an einen katholischen Kardinal oder protestantischen Bischof entwürdigt. Ebensowenig kann man uns zumuten, sich damit abzufinden, wenn jemand das Gedenken an Rosa Luxemburg und Karl Liebknecht absichtlich stört und schändet.« Sind Erich Honecker, Hermann Axen und Kurt Hager, Willi Stoph und Horst Sindermann also doch Kurienkardinäle, wenn sie an der Spitze der alljährlichen Kampfdemonstration zu Ehren Liebknechts und Luxemburgs zu den Größen der »Märtyrer der kommunistischen Partei« wallfahrten?

Es ist dieser militante ideologische Alleinvertretungs-Anspruch des Sozialismus, der als bestimmendes totalitäres Element im »posttotalitären System« der DDR gelegentlich vergessen macht, daß sich hier und dort der Zugriff der Partei gelockert hat und die Chancen, ein nichtkonformistisches Leben zu führen, über die Jahre besser geworden sind – vorausgesetzt, es geschieht unauffällig im Abseits. Paradoxerweise fördert gerade die egalitäre, gleichmacherische Komponente der SED-Politik Subkulturen wie die am Prenzlauer Berg und manche »abseitige« Existenz in Souterrains oder Hinterhöfen: Weil die Mieten und die Grundnahrungsmittel extrem billig sind, können sich junge Schriftsteller und Künstler, einen relativ hohen Grad an Bedürfnislosigkeit und Bereitschaft zum Konsumverzicht vorausgesetzt, eigenständig entwickeln, ohne im offiziellen Kulturstrom mitzuschwimmen. Inzwischen nimmt der Staat auch hin, daß Manuskripte dieser jungen Autoren, die er bei sich nicht zur Veröffentlichung freigibt, im Westen erscheinen – etwa Lutz Rathenows »Im Lande des Kohls«, eine Satire, bei der schon der Titel in die Irre führt. Gemeint ist ja nicht Helmut Kohl, vielmehr herrscht der große Regierer, der 20 Pflicht-Liegestützen täglich zum Wohle der Landesverteidigung befiehlt, im Reiche des Braunkohls – unverkennbar also jener DDR, deren einzige Energiequelle Braunkohle und deren allein das ganze Jahr über verfügbare »Frischgemüse« Weiß- und Rotkohl sind. Für allzuviel Unbotmäßigkeit üben die Funktionäre jedoch oft kleinliche Rache. Weil er zwar »eingreifend schreibt«, aber anders als der Kulturminister das versteht, wurden Rathenow Westreisen mit der Begründung verweigert, der Staat sei daran interessiert, daß Künstler im Ausland auftreten, welche die Kulturpolitik der DDR anerkennen und »sich mit persönlichem Engagement für das Ansehen der DDR einsetzen«. Da hat ein Satiriker wohl nie eine Chance. Immerhin: Daheim bleibt ein Mann wie Rathenow einigermaßen ungeschoren.

Ein Paradebeispiel für Subkultur, die an den Rändern des offiziellen Kulturbetriebs der posttotalitären DDR gedeiht, war jene Galerie, die ein findiger und gewitzter junger Leipziger in einem alten Druckereigebäude in einem Hinterhof betrieb. Von Hauptberuf Modell an der Kunsthochschule mit einem Monatseinkommen von 300 Mark, hatte er sich mit jungen Künstlern zusammengetan und stellte aus, was in keiner offiziellen Galerie zu sehen war. Mit seinen weißgestrichenen, kaum verputzten Ziegelwänden, von Druckerschwärze vollgesogenen rohen Dielen und der spürbaren Werkstatt-Atmosphäre erinnerte der große Raum an ein Loft in Downtown Manhattan. Um die DDR-Gesetze auch peinlich genau zu beachten, fanden formell überhaupt keine Ausstellungen statt. Vielmehr mietete ein Künstler das Atelier für jeweils vier bis sechs Wochen, reiste mit seinen Arbeiten an und öffnete sein »Studio« zweimal wöchentlich »guten Bekannten«. Brief- und Mundpropaganda sorgten für einen regen Strom von Besuchern aus der ganzen Republik. Ein solches, für DDR-Verhältnisse gewagtes Unternehmen ist natürlich nur in einer Grauzone der Legalität möglich, und sein größter Feind heißt Öffentlichkeit. Es gefährdet sich automatisch selbst, wenn es zuviel Aufmerksamkeit erregt. Dabei ist klar, daß in einem Land, dessen Staatssicherheitsdienst über hunderttausend ehrenamtliche »gesellschaftliche Mitarbeiter« verfügt, wie die Spitzel der Firma »Horch-Guck- und Greif« offiziell heißen, den Behörden schwerlich verborgen bleiben konnte, was sich in diesem Leipziger Hinterhof tat. Doch die Kulturfunktionäre entschlossen sich zu einer Politik des amtlichen Wegschauens: Inoffiziell nahmen sie es zur Kenntnis, aber sie schritten nicht dagegen ein. Die »graue« Galerie hatte ihre stille Duldung und genoß damit eine relative Freiheit – auf Widerruf, versteht sich, der nach Belieben jederzeit erfolgen konnte. Nun steht die Leipziger Kulturbürokratie ohnehin in dem Ruf, die liberalste der DDR zu sein. Was sie in der Messestadt zuließ, wäre in Cottbus, Karl-Marx-Stadt oder Magdeburg undenkbar gewesen. Ein solches Liberalitätsgefälle, das auf der oft unterschätzten Entscheidungsbefugnis der Kreis- und Bezirksräte beruht, wirkt als auflockerndes Element in der zentral gelenkten, ideologisch monochromen anderen Republik und läßt hier und da heute zu, was früher gänzlich unmöglich schien.

Als posttotalitär ist auch hervorzuheben, daß Bürger im Rahmen des Eingabe- und Beschwerderechts die Möglichkeit haben, auf persönlich erlittene Drangsal oder Unrecht hinzuweisen und um Abhilfe zu bitten, und ganz offensichtlich müht sich der Staat in letzter Zeit mehr als früher, die eigene sozialistische Rechtsordnung zu wahren. Nur ist diese so verfaßt, daß der Beschwerdesteller immer auf den Petitionsweg verwiesen bleibt und ein Recht zur Klage gegen Übergriffe von Polizei, Behörden oder des Staatssicherheitsdienstes nicht hat, weil es keine Verwaltungsgerichte gibt. Und selbst da ginge es immer nur um das Kleingedruckte innerhalb eines einmal gesetzten realsozialistischen Rahmens, den die Partei prinzipiell für unantastbar erklärt. Wer immer die Führungsrolle der SED öffentlich in Zweifel zieht – und in dem von ihr regierten und bis in den letzten Winkel systematisch kontrollierten und überwachten Staat können, die solches tun, nur von ihr selbst zur Verzweiflung getriebene, verwegene Einzelkämpfer oder von vornherein zersprengte, verlorene Haufen sein – auf den schlägt sie gnadenlos ein, weil sie nicht will, daß sich je wieder die Machtfrage stellt. Das ist der totalitäre Nachhall, der durch die posttotalitäre Gesellschaft weht. Dabei geht es der SED nicht nur um das Dogma, das die Gewalt im Namen der letzten Ziele rechtfertigt. An der Frontlinie beider Bündnis- und Gesellschaftssysteme und in der »Klassenauseinandersetzung mit der Bundesrepublik«, wie ihre Ideologen formulieren, ist sie vom Trauma des 17. Juni und des großen Exodus vor dem Mauerbau geplagt und ihr sitzt die Angst vor »polnischen Verhältnissen« im Genick. Soviel Furcht vor den Gefahren der Destabilisierung ist einmal mehr ein Eingeständnis der eigenen Schwäche. Aber die SED weiß, warum sie auf der Hut sein muß. Ihren eigenen Beteuerungen zum Trotz ist die nationale Frage für die von ihr Regierten nämlich noch ungelöst.

10. Die SED und die Nation:
Wird die DDR ein zweites Österreich?

Ein Hohenzollerndenkmal, welches die deutschen Kommunisten nach dem Kriege nicht von seinem Sockel stürzten, findet sich auf einem Hügel im Vorland des Harzes. Da setzt ein gußeiserner Wilhelm I., die preußische Pickelhaube auf dem Kopf, über einen Barbarossa hinweg, der tief unter ihm, aus Stein gehauen und mit ihm verwachsen, jahrhundertealte deutsche Sehnsüchte verkörpert: den Kaiser, der aus der Höhle des Kyffhäuser kommt, um deutscher Zerrissenheit ein Ende zu machen und das Reich zu einigen. »Kaiser Wilhelm National Denkmal« hieß das Monument früher, das sich breitquadrig-klotzig und in großmäulig-wilhelminischem Stil, weithin sichtbar über der Goldenen Aue erhebt und jahrzehntelang Wallfahrtsstätte nationalistischer Studentenverbindungen und Kriegervereine war.

Daß der alte Wilhelm noch auf dem Kyffhäuser reitet, hat nichts mit jener verspäteten Gerechtigkeit zu tun, die SED-Historiker dem Monarchen im Zuge der Preußen-Renaissance in der DDR widerfahren lassen. So bescheinigte ihm Karl Heinz Börner in einer 1984 erschienenen Biographie nicht nur die Tugenden eines gestrengen Hausvaters: Sparsamkeit, Fleiß, Gewissenhaftigkeit und Einfachheit im öffentlichen Auftreten. Er zitierte auch das anerkennende Urteil des Altliberalen Karl Schurz, das dieser, inzwischen in seiner neuen Heimat Amerika zu Ansehen und Ehren gekommen, seinem ehemaligen Gegner, der die 48er Revolution als »Kartätschen-Prinz« niederwarf, als einen Nachruf widmete: »Kaiser Wilhelm war ohne Zweifel der populärste Monarch, den dieses

Jahrhundert gesehen, ja mehr noch, er war ein wahrhaft po-
pulärer Mann«, denn er habe die »Sehnsucht nach Einheit«
gestillt. Franz Mehring hatte in ihm wenig mehr als einen
bornierten Drillfeldwebel gesehen, Marx und Engels ihn ob
seines schlichten Gemüts voll böser Ironie »Lehmann« genannt. Sie hätten genausogut Meier, Müller oder Schulze
sagen können, denn gemeint war ja, daß dieser Wilhelm mangels eigener politischer Gedanken nur Wachs in Bismarcks
Händen war. Doch das Ergebnis der Zusammenarbeit von
Junker und »Lehmann« respektierten sie schon, auch wenn sie
deren Revolution von oben reichlich »eklig« fanden: »Revolution bleibt Revolution, ob sie von der Krone Preußens gemacht wird oder von einem Kesselflicker«, schrieb Friedrich
Engels und beklagte im gleichen Atemzug, daß in Deutschland »politisch nichts gründlich erledigt« werde: »Sonst wäre
es nicht in zwei Stücke zerrissen, in Österreich und das sogenannte Deutschland.«

Kein Zweifel, »die Klassiker« waren zwar revolutionär-de-
mokratische, nichtsdestoweniger ganz entschiedene Vertreter
des großdeutschen Gedankens. Doch nicht nur, weil es in
ihrem Werk kein Beispiel gibt für eine Politik der Abgrenzung
und Spaltung der Nation, wie sie heute die SED vertritt, ragt
der Kyffhäuser als ein Symbol der Verlegenheit in die politische Landschaft der DDR. Drinnen im Turm, auf drei riesigen
Bronzereliefs, die an ein pseudosakrales Heiligtum gemahnen,
steht der Text der von Johannes R. Becher verfaßten DDR-
Nationalhymne nachzulesen, den man heute so wenig singt
wie bei uns die ersten Strophen des Deutschlandlieds.
Deutschland wird darin als »einig Vaterland« beschworen;
und es gilt, heißt es weiter, »alte Not zu zwingen«, damit
»vereint« erreicht werde, »daß die Sonne schön wie nie über
Deutschland scheint«. Überdauert im Turm nun die Hymne
wie früher im Berg der Kaiser und schläft, bis jene sagenhafte
Zeit anbricht, in der die Zerrissenheit endet und man in der
DDR das Wort von der deutschen Einheit wieder im Munde
führen kann?

Was heute wirklich museal wirkt, war für die deutschen

Kommunisten viele Jahre nach dem Krieg ebenso brennend wie zwingend aktuell. Sie traten ja einmal an, wie der Nationalhymnen-Autor 1945 in seinem »Deutschen Bekenntnis« schrieb, um das geschichtlich Notwendige zu vollstrecken: »Es gilt, das zu tun, was seit 100 Jahren, seit dem Jahre 1848, wir zu tun verabsäumten. Es gilt, das Deutschland zu schaffen, das einzig und allein Bestand hat, das freiheitliche, demokratische.« Schon im Moskauer Exil hatte Becher, der auf die Sowjetunion voll deutschen Kulturhochmuts herabschaute und sich weigerte, je russisch zu lernen, das spätere SED-Programm einer links-nationalen Deutschlandpolitik in Reime gefaßt:

> Ein heimlich Reich, so lag es wie vergangen,
> So lag es wie im Traum und lag gefangen.
> Doch einmal wußten wir, wird es geschehn,
> Da wird des Volkes Wille es erwecken,
> Und alle werden dann das Reich entdecken,
> Das Deutschland heißt. Deutschland wird auferstehn!

»nachbar, euren speikübel!« empörte sich Brecht in seinem kalifornischen Exil, als ihn solch Zeugnis eines deutschen linken Nationalismus aus der Sowjetunion erreichte. In seinem Arbeitsjournal warf er Becher »entsetzlich opportunistischen quark« vor und notierte: ». . . wieder wird der nationalismus der hitler ganz naiv akzeptiert: hitler hatte nur den falschen, becher hat den richtigen«. Doch auch wenn Becher hymnisch übertrieb, wie es seine Art war, spiegelte er getreulich die politische Linie der deutschen Kommunisten wider, die mit Stalins Segen im Exil artikuliert, in den ersten Nachkriegsjahren in die Praxis umgesetzt werden sollte. Es war ja kein Zufall, wenn Radio »Freies Deutschland« in Moskau als Kenn- und Pausenzeichen Ernst Moritz Arndts »Der Gott der Eisen wachsen ließ, der kannte keine Knechte« wählte. Arndt, zusammen mit Theodor Körner der Dichter der deutschen Befreiungskriege, hatte als Mitstreiter des Freiherrn vom Stein in Petersburg auf russischer Seite den Widerstand gegen

Napoleon vorbereitet, und die kommunistischen Emigranten bedienten sich der Parallele. Als das Nationalkomitee Freies Deutschland nicht unter der schwarz-rot-goldenen Fahne von Weimar, sondern der schwarz-weiß-roten der Deutschnationalen gegründet wurde, stellte es sich als später Nachfahre der preußischen Reformer Stein, Clausewitz und Arndt vor. Als Symbol für den ewigen Bruderbund mit der Sowjetunion wird in der DDR noch heute das Bündnis von Russen und Deutschen bemüht, das mit dem Händedruck zweier konservativer Generäle, des Russen Diebitsch und des Preußen Yorck, in Tauroggen seinen Anfang nahm. Die Propaganda des Nationalkomitees wie auch die Literatur, die im Moskauer Exil entstand, belegen einen geradezu erstaunlichen Mangel an Wirklichkeitssinn bei den deutschen Kommunisten, denn sie setzten die Existenz eines anderen, eines besseren Deutschland in Hitlers Reich voraus, das stark genug sei, sich zu erheben, der Front in den Rücken zu fallen und dem Kampf vor allem gegen die Sowjetunion ein schnelles Ende zu machen. Es war dies eine Lieblingsvorstellung, die sie auch gegenüber den sowjetischen Genossen immer wieder betonten. Und weil diese noch immer hohen Respekt vor der einst so mächtigen deutschen Arbeiterbewegung hatten, waren sie zu Beginn des deutsch-sowjetischen Krieges überzeugt, daß es auf deutscher Seite zu massenweisen Übertritten und Desertationen kommen würde. Desto grausamer sahen sie sich getäuscht. Als anläßlich des 40. Jahrestages der Befreiung das Deutsche Theater in Ostberlin Bechers im Exil entstandene »Winterschlacht« aufführte, wurde dieses Defizit an Wirklichkeitssinn anschaulich in Szene gesetzt: Ein Stabsfeldwebel proletarischer Abkunft desertiert in diesem Stück und läuft zu den sowjetischen Linien über; eine deutsche Bürgersfrau entwickelt sich zum NS-Gegner und tötet ihren Mann, einen Richter und Mitglied der SS; beider Sohn, der an der Front steht, wird auf Befehl seines Vorgesetzten hingerichtet, weil er sich weigert, gefangene russische Partisanen zu erschießen. »Es gibt ein Deutschland größenwahnsinniger Machthaber, und es gibt ein anderes Deutschland – ein Deutschland des Volkes«, heißt es in der »Winterschlacht«. Wunschbilder von einer Wehrmacht, die sich von innen her zersetzt und vom deutschen Volk, dessen andere, bessere Hälfte Hitler mitten im Krieg stürzen werde, vermittelten auch andere im Moskauer Exil – Friedrich Wolf zum Beispiel oder Willy Bredel. Es waren auch nicht nur die Schriftsteller, die lange an diesen ihnen lieb gewordenen Illusionen festhielten. Selbst Wilhelm Pieck sprach 1944 noch von einer Erhebung »gegen diese Verbrecherbande« der Nationalsozialisten. Dabei hätten ihn die Erfahrungen, die das Nationalkomitee Anfang 1944 machte, als es über 70 000 in einem Kessel bei Tscherkassy eingeschlossenen deutschen Soldaten zur Desertation und Kapitulation aufforderte, eigentlich eines Besseren belehren müssen: Die Deutschen kapitulierten nicht, sie machten verzweifelte Ausbruchsversuche und kämpften bis zum Schluß.

Solche Wunschvorstellungen bestimmen auch heute noch das Geschichtsverständnis, etwa wenn Jahr für Jahr am 8. Mai die Mitglieder der Partei- und Staatsführung zu den Klängen eines Trauermarschs hinter Volksarmisten im Stechschritt zum sowjetischen Ehrenmal in Treptow ziehen. Die riesige Figur des Rotarmisten mit dem Schwert gemahnt an 20 000 Sowjetsoldaten, die im Endkampf um Berlin ihr Leben ließen. Sie ist ein Symbol des sowjetischen Sieges, aber die DDR nimmt praktisch für sich in Anspruch, daß dies auch der ihre war. Zwar ist die Gedankenführung keineswegs schlüssig, nichtsdestoweniger aber die Behauptung klar: Weil der neue deutsche Staat, der da als Frucht des sowjetischen Sieges entstand, den Antifaschismus in den Rang einer Staatsdoktrin erhob und mit der mächtigen Sowjetunion verbündet ist, zählt er zu den »Siegern der Geschichte«. Wenn das »Neue Deutschland«, das den Aufruf zum 40. Jahrestag der Befreiung veröffentlichte, in fetten Lettern als Zwischenüberschrift auf Seite 1 hervorhebt: »Deutsche Antifaschisten standen in der Front der Sieger« heißt das soviel wie, sie, diese Antifaschisten und, da sie die DDR gründeten und regieren, »wir«, das Staatsvolk der DDR, haben mitgesiegt. Als Erich Honekker im Januar 1988 Paris besuchte, beschwor er als Antifaschist die »Erinnerung an den gemeinsamen Kampf in der Antihitlerkoalition«, der in den freundschaftlichen Beziehungen »unserer Völker« lebendig sei. Praktisch versuchte er damit, die DDR nachträglich in das Bündnis der Weltmächte gegen Hitlers Reich einzubeziehen. Wochenlang vor dem 8. Mai 1985 hatte das SED-Parteiblatt Tag für Tag in riesigen Artikeln über den siegreichen Vormarsch der sowjetischen Truppen auf Berlin berichtet, als ob es Einheiten der eigenen Armee gewesen seien. »Wie das rote Siegesbanner über Berlin gehißt wurde«, lautete die Zeile über einem Artikel, der den Sturmangriff von Soldaten der 3. Stoßarmee »auf den letzten Metern ihres Kampfesweges« gegen den Reichstag schilderte. Wo sich der Ring der Roten Armee um Berlin schloß, in dem Havelstädtchen Ketzin nordwestlich von Potsdam, erinnert eine kleine Gedenktafel an die »Vereinigung der siegreichen Sowjetarmeen«. Sie ist an der ehemaligen Gaststätte »Deutsches Haus« angebracht, in dem sowjetische Offiziere der »Bjelorussischen Front« und der »1. Ukrainischen Front« am 25. April 1945 ein »Vereinigungsprotokoll« unterzeichneten. Auf den Seelower Höhen am westlichen Oderufer, wo das letzte Aufgebot der Wehrmacht den Sowjets eine erbitterte Abwehrschlacht lieferte, um den Durchbruch nach Berlin zu verhindern, hat man den 30 000 Soldaten und Offizieren der »Bjelorussischen Front«, die beim Sturm auf die deutschen Stellungen fielen, ein stolzes Denkmal gesetzt. Für die Thälmann-Pioniere der Städte und Dörfer der Umgebung ist dieses Monument inzwischen eine nationale Weihestätte der DDR: Begleitet von Politoffizieren kommen Abordnungen und legen Blumen und Kränze an den sowjetischen Gräbern nieder. Wie viele deutsche Soldaten gefallen sind, darunter sicher Großväter dieser Pioniere, daran erinnert keine Inschrift, nur vor dem Kulturhaus in Seelow gibt es ein Mahnmal, das pauschal aller Opfer des Faschismus und des Krieges gedenkt. Nicht einmal werden im Seelower Museum die Einheiten der Wehrmacht auf Texttafeln und Bildunterschriften als deutsche, sondern immer als »faschistische« Truppen bezeichnet. Was diese Verdrängung der eigenen Geschichte und die ideologische Vereinnahmung des sowjetischen Sieges für die DDR in den Köpfen von Schülern und Lehrlingen bewirkt, konnte ich an den Ergebnissen einer Umfrage studieren, die mir zum Jahrestag der Befreiung genehmigt wurde. Auf die Frage, wer denn eigentlich den Krieg gegen die Sowjetunion geführt habe, erhielt ich häufig zur Antwort: »Die Faschisten«. Auf meinen Einwand, ob es denn vielleicht die Deutschen, und nicht nur die vom Faschismus überzeugten gewesen seien, erwiderte eine Gruppe Jugendlicher: »Nein, das waren die Faschisten. Es gab ja ebenso viele Antifaschisten wie Faschisten damals unter den Deutschen.« Wer ein solches Verständnis von Geschichte anerzieht, dem dürfte eines Tages wahrscheinlich schwer fallen zu erklären, warum so viele Sowjetsoldaten nicht nur beim Sturm auf die Seelower Höhen, sondern auch in der Schlacht um Berlin überhaupt ihr Leben lassen mußten. Da blieb es am 8. Mai 1985 wieder einmal einem Mann der Kirche vorbehalten, die nötigen Korrekturen am offiziell vermittelten Geschichtsbild anzubringen: Für eine winzige Minderheit aufrechter Antifaschisten stimme, so Landesbischof Leich vor der Thüringer Synode, daß sie in der Front der Sieger standen, nicht aber für die übergroße Mehrzahl der Deutschen auf dem Boden der nachmaligen DDR – die hätten zu den Besiegten gezählt und den 8. Mai damals subjektiv nicht als Tag der Befreiung verstanden, auch wenn er sich inzwischen als ein solcher erwiesen habe.

Zweifellos trifft es zu, daß sich die Bundesrepublik vergleichsweise schwer tat mit der Bewältigung der Vergangenheit. Daß Ex-Nazis wie Globke unter Adenauer ins Innerste der Macht aufsteigen konnten, daß ein ehemaliger NS-Parteigenosse und Volkstumspolitiker wie Oberländer Sitz und Stimme in seinem Kabinett erhielt, daß die Entnazifizierung nur die Oberfläche traf und die Schichten, die den bürgerlichen deutschen Nationalismus getragen und mit ihm Hitler an die Regierung gebracht hatten, ihre wirtschaftlichen Machtpositionen nahezu unangefochten behaupten konnten – das warf schwere Schatten auf den demokratischen Neuanfang im Westen Deutschlands. Nur macht all das den verord-

neten, aufgesetzten und nicht durch Trauerarbeit gewachse-
nen Antifaschismus in der DDR nicht wahrhaftiger, zumal
auch die SED Vergangenheit hat, die zu bewältigen sie versäumt: Die verhängnisvolle Rolle, welche die KPD in der Weimarer Republik für den Aufstieg Hitlers spielte. Folgt man
der Darstellung von SED-Historikern, dann war die KPD in
der Zwischenkriegszeit die alleinige, allzeit zuverlässige Ge-
genkraft gegen den Nationalsozialismus, ein Selbstverständnis, auf dem unter anderem der Führungsanspruch der deutschen Kommunisten im Rahmen der in der DDR praktizierten
»Bündnispolitik« beruht. Nun sollen hier weder die Leiden
der Kommunisten, die zusammen mit linken Sozialdemokraten die ersten Opfer nationalsozialistischer Verfolgung wurden, herabgesetzt noch gar die prinzipielle Feindschaft gegen
Hitler angezweifelt werden. Zu fragen wäre allerdings, inwieweit die KPD durch ihren erbitterten Kampf gegen die
SPD, die sie als Sozialfaschisten und als »Hauptstütze der
Bourgeoisie« noch vor der NSDAP bekämpfte, zur Zersplitte-
rung der linken Kräfte beigetragen hat. Diese Aufarbeitung
geschieht in der DDR, wenn auch millimeterweise. So wird
im vierten Band der 1966 erschienenen »Geschichte der deutschen Arbeiterbewegung« die Teilnahme der KPD an dem
vom deutschnationalen »Stahlhelm« initiierten Volksent-
scheid gegen die sozialdemokratische Regierung Braun in
Preußen inzwischen eine folgenschwere Fehlentscheidung genannt. Nur: Daß die KPD damals entgegen eigenen Bedenken
einer Weisung der kommunistischen Internationale folgte, die
letztlich von sowjetrussischen Nationalinteressen dominiert
war, wird offen nirgendwo ausgesprochen. Wann immer
nämlich eine deutsch-französische Annäherung greifbar nahe
erschien in der Zeit vor 1933, schrillten die Alarmglocken im
Kreml und die KPD erhielt Order, gegen solche Verständi-
gung Front zu machen. Das richtete sich, völlig unabhängig
von der katastrophalen Sozialfaschismus-These, in erster Linie wiederum gegen die Sozialdemokraten als die wichtigste
politische Kraft, die den Ausgleich mit dem »französischen
Erbfeind« anstrebte. Im sowjetischen Interesse suchte die

KPD auch, die NSDAP rechts zu überholen – mit jener »Programmerklärung zur nationalen und sozialen Befreiung des deutschen Volkes« vom August 1930 etwa, in dem sie die Sozialdemokratie anklagte, »Hab und Gut, Leben und Existenz des werktätigen deutschen Volkes meistbietend an die Imperialisten des Auslandes« verkauft zu haben. Da wurde nicht nur die untrennbare Einheit von nationaler Befreiung und sozialer Revolution proklamiert, da wurde die Zerreißung des »Versailler Raubfriedens« und (sehr großdeutsch!) das Selbstbestimmungsrecht für Elsaß-Lothringen, das Sudetenland und »Pommerellen« bis zur Loslösung von Frankreich, der Tschechoslowakei und Polen gefordert. Die Nationalsozialisten bezichtigte man gar des Verrats an der nationalen Sache, weil sie bereit seien, die Interessen der Südtiroler den guten Beziehungen zu Mussolini und dem italienischen Faschismus zu opfern. Sicher spielten bei der Formulierung dieser Erklärung auch wahltaktische Gründe eine Rolle: Die KPD versuchte in das Wählerpotential der NSDAP einzubrechen. Und gewiß setzte dieses nationale Selbstbestimmungsprogramm die westeuropäische Revolution voraus, das Konzept eines Europa freier souveräner Sowjetrepubliken, in dem keine Nation die andere überlagern würde. Die Verteidigung des »Vaterlandes der Werktätigen«, der Sowjetunion, und nationale Selbstbestimmung schlossen in dieser Sicht einander keineswegs aus. Honecker selbst beschreibt in seiner Autobiographie, wie er mit dem Ruf »Heil Moskau!« mit einer KPD-Jugenddelegation auf dem letzten Parteitag der KPD 1929 im roten Wedding Einzug hielt. Dennoch liest sich dieses Befreiungsprogramm heute wie ein kommunistischer Fahrplan für Hitlers Anschluß-Politik, und mit Sicherheit war es dazu geeignet, die nationalistische Stimmung im Reich weiter anzuheizen.

Die Feindschaft der KPD gegen Versailles war ja auch keine taktische, sondern eine prinzipielle Haltung. Schon Lenin hatte von einem »Vertrag von Mördern und Räubern« gesprochen, und Johannes R. Becher schrieb in seiner Ulbricht-Biographie: »Im Kampf gegen den Versailler Vertrag hatte die

Kommunistische Partei Deutschlands die führende Rolle übernommen und war dadurch... zur Partei der deutschen Nation geworden. Diese historische Tatsache gilt es festzuhalten, um nicht dem Irrtum zu verfallen, als hätte die Reaktion, als hätte die Nazipartei irgendwann einmal so etwas wie nationale Interessen vertreten.« Das Wort vom »Raubfrieden«, das so deutschnational klingt, hatte einen Stammplatz auch im Vokabular der deutschen Kommunisten der Weimarer Zeit, und doch ist all dies in der DDR so wenig aufgearbeitet wie die Fernwirkung des Nationalismus eines Ernst Moritz Arndt, den ja gewiß nicht zufällig ebenfalls die Nationalsozialisten in ihre Dienste nahmen: Der Bauernsohn von der Insel Rügen hatte wider die Leibeigenschaft geschrieben, aber er träumte von einem Kaiser an der Spitze eines einigen Reichs und einem »deutschen Gott«. »Wo Zorn vertilgt den welschen Tand, wo jeder Franzmann heißet Feind, wo jeder Deutsche heißet Freund, das soll es sein – das ganze Deutschland soll es sein.« Wenn es stimmt, daß die Deutschen ihre Identität als Nation nur in Abgrenzung und Feindschaft finden konnten, dann sind die Deutschtümelei und das trunkene Reichs-Pathos der patriotischen Traktate und Gedichte Arndts ein Musterbeispiel. Er definierte Deutsches in der Gegnerschaft gegen Frankreich: »Wir wollen heute Mann für Mann mit Blut das Eisen röten, mit Henkerblut, Franzosenblut – o süßer Tag der Rache!« In seinem »letzten Wort an die Deutschen« versprach er gar, »das Franzosenungeziefer« werde bald »vertilgt« sein.

Es waren die Nationalsozialisten, welche die Universität Greifswald auf den Namen Ernst Moritz Arndt tauften, aber die deutschen Kommunisten änderten daran nichts, was nicht nur ihren unbefangenen Umgang mit der deutschen Geschichte belegt. Bis tief in die 60er Jahre hinein verlieh die Nationale Front als Anerkennung »für patriotische Leistungen« eine »Ernst Moritz Arndt Medaille« an wackere Verfechter der deutschen Einheit, auf der unter dem Konterfei des Dichters sein Wort: »Das ganze Deutschland soll es sein« eingraviert ist. In der Nachkriegszeit hatten der Nationalismus Arndts eine politische Funktion – er diente als Waffe gegen die Staatsgründung der Bundesrepublik. Nach all den Jahren, in denen die DDR den Bonner Alleinvertretungsanspruch bekämpfte und um ihre eigene Anerkennung rang, sollte nicht ganz in Vergessenheit geraten, daß sie selbst für sich anfänglich das Alleinvertretungsrecht für die Gesamtnation beansprucht hat. Aus der Sicht der SED war der Bonner »Separat-Staat« eine Art Anschlag gegen die nationale Einheit, seine Beseitigung eine patriotische Pflicht. Die II. Parteikonferenz der SED verabschiedete 1952 eine Entschließung, derzufolge es die »Aufgabe aller friedliebenden und patriotischen Kräfte« war, im Zuge des »nationalen Befreiungskampfes gegen die amerikanischen, englischen und französischen Okkupanten« in Westdeutschland »für den Sturz ihrer Bonner Vasallenregierung« zu sorgen. Dieses östliche Alleinvertretungsrecht wurde auch durch ein unverhülltes, geradezu klassisches Anschlußdenken ergänzt: Wilhelm Pieck, der erste Präsident der DDR, sprach von der »Wiederangliederung der abgespaltenen Gebiete des Westens in die Deutsche Demokratische Republik«. Damit nicht genug, bezeichnete Otto Grotewohl die DDR als den »einzig rechtmäßigen deutschen Staat«, und die erste, weitgehend bürgerlich-demokratische, an Weimar orientierte Verfassung war zweifellos als Modell für Größeres gedacht: Deutschland wurde in ihr ausdrücklich als »unteilbare demokratische Republik« apostrophiert und sie kannte nur eine deutsche Staatsangehörigkeit. Zwar verzichtete die SED schon im November 1954 auf ihren Anspruch, allein für alle Deutschen zu handeln, als sie in einer Regierungserklärung von der »Existenz zweier deutscher Staaten auf deutschem Boden« sprach, aber an der Vorstellung, daß es eine einheitliche deutsche Nation gebe, hielt sie bis Anfang der 70er Jahre fest. Noch die zweite Verfassung aus der Ulbricht-Zeit nannte die DDR 1968 einen »sozialistischen Staat deutscher Nation«, und Artikel 8 betonte ausdrücklich, daß die DDR und ihre Bürger die »Überwindung der vom Imperialismus der deutschen Nation aufgezwungene Spaltung Deutschlands« anstreben – wenn auch jetzt »durch schrittweise Annäherung der beiden deutschen Staaten«. Dies alles belegt, wie tief die Idee der nationalen Selbstbestimmung, die aus den Konzepten der Linken seit der Französischen Revolution nicht mehr wegzudenken ist, in der SED verankert war.

Als Erich Honecker im Rahmen seiner Abgrenzungspolitik das Fortbestehen einer einheitlichen deutschen Nation aufkündigte und 1971 von der Existenz zweier Nationen sprach, stieß er deshalb auf Erstaunen und Unverständnis in den eigenen Reihen. Die überarbeitete Verfassung von 1974, in der jeder Hinweis auf die deutsche Nation getilgt wurde, bezeichnet die DDR nurmehr als »sozialistischen Staat der Arbeiter und Bauern« – im Gegensatz zu den vorausgegangenen wurde sie nur von der Volkskammer verabschiedet und aus Furcht vor möglichen Nein-Stimmen nicht dem Volk zur Abstimmung vorgelegt, auch wenn dies nur die übliche Formalie bedeutet hätte. Wie heftig der neue Kurs umstritten war, belegt jenes Manifest der SED-Opposition aus dem Jahr 1977, in dem von der Sprengkraft der deutschen Frage in der DDR die Rede ist und, in Anlehnung an die frühere, offensive Deutschlandpolitik, freie und geheime Wahlen für eine gesamtdeutsche Nationalversammlung gefordert wurden. War das die Antwort darauf, daß Honecker über die Bundesrepublik und die DDR erklärt hatte, sie verhielten sich »zueinander wie jeder von ihnen zu einem anderen dritten Staat. Die BRD ist somit Ausland und noch mehr: Sie ist imperialistisches Ausland?« Einige Experten glauben seither, einen geordneten Rückzug des Partei- und Staatschefs zu beobachten. So werten sie die Tatsache, daß er in der Ostberliner Seelenbinderhalle die Möglichkeit einer Wiedervereinigung auf sozialistischer Basis ansprach, als Korrektur an der überspitzten Abgrenzungspolitik: »Wenn ... die Werktätigen an die sozialistische Umgestaltung der Bundesrepublik gehen«, hatte Honecker vor SED-Funktionären 1981 ausgeführt, »dann steht die Frage der Vereinigung beider deutscher Staaten vollkommen neu! Wie wir uns dann entscheiden werden, daran dürfte wohl kein Zweifel bestehen.« Doch so ähnlich hatte sich in seinen letzten Jahren auch Walter Ulbricht ausgelassen. Der neuerliche Hinweis auf die vage Wiedervereinigungsoption, die sich die SED auch in der Abgrenzungsphase gegenüber der Bundesrepublik immer offen gelassen hat, wirkte beschwichtigend, aber in der Sache änderte sich nichts: Sozialismus und Kapitalismus sind so schwer miteinander zu vereinen wie Feuer und Wasser, sagt der regierende Saarländer an der Spree, wann immer er von Journalisten vor einer seiner Westreisen auf dieses Thema angesprochen wird.

An der Grundmaxime der neuen Abgrenzungspolitik, wie sie im SED-Programm von 1976 umrissen wurde, hat es jedenfalls keine Abstriche gegeben. Danach entwickelt sich in der DDR eine neue, »die sozialistische deutsche Nation« und ihre »Wesenszüge prägt die Arbeiterklasse«. Sie wird als eine »freie, stabile Gemeinschaft freundschaftlich verbundener Klassen und Schichten« beschrieben, die »von der Arbeiterklasse und ihrer marxistischen Partei geführt wird«. Sie umfasse, heißt es da weiter, »das Volk der Deutschen Demokratischen Republik und ist gekennzeichnet durch den souveränen sozialistischen Staat auf deren Territorium«. Um die theoretische Begründung für diese neue Maxime zu finden, bedurfte es freilich einiger ideologischer Verrenkungen, um die der Mann, der sie zu bewerkstelligen hatte, wahrlich nicht zu beneiden war. Sein Name ist Alfred Kosing, und in der vom Institut für Marxismus-Leninismus herausgegebenen Reihe »Beiträge zur Geschichte der deutschen Arbeiterbewegung« hatte er noch 1962 in einem Aufsatz über »Arbeiterklasse und Nation« das Programm zur nationalen und sozialen Befreiung des Jahres 1930 als »Meilenstein« in der Entwicklung und Vertiefung der »nationalen Konzeption der KPD« gepriesen. In diesem Artikel hieß es nicht nur, der gesellschaftliche Fortschritt sei »nur im Rahmen der eigenen Nation« zu realisieren, sondern es gelte, »die Nation vor den Anschlägen des Imperialismus zu retten und ihre friedliche Zukunft zu sichern«. Bis weit in den Kommunismus hinein, so Kosing damals, behalte die Nation ihre »Bedeutung als Struktur und Entwicklungsform der menschlichen Gesellschaft«. In der in Ostberlin erscheinenden »Deutschen Zeitschrift für Philosophie« vollzog derselbe Autor 13 Jahre später eine dramatische Kehrtwende und setzte sich von der Vorstellung ab, daß die einheitliche Nation trotz staatlicher Trennung durch gemeinsame Sprache, Familienbande und gemeinsam erlebte und zu verantwortende Geschichte fortbestehe. Jetzt, 1974, hieß es plötzlich, Sprache und ethnische Gemeinsamkeiten stellten »sekundäre Strukturformen« dar, die wichtigere und primäre sei die »ökonomische Gesellschaftsformation«. Weil die sozialistischen Produktionsverhältnisse in der DDR uneingeschränkt seit Anfang der sechziger Jahre herrschten, müsse ab diesem Zeitpunkt auch von der Herausbildung einer »sozialistischen Nation mit all ihren Attributen« gesprochen werden. Die ökonomische Grundlage der sozialistischen Nation in der DDR sei die sozialistische Produktionsweise, eine »Umwälzung von geschichtlicher Tragweite«.

Was Kosing da im Auftrag der Partei formulierte, war nicht nur eine gezielte und polemische Absage an das Konzept der Kulturnation, in der die Einheit der Deutschen in Bonner Sicht trotz staatlicher Trennung ja fortbesteht. Es stellte auch den Versuch dar, die DDR in die »internationale sozialistische Gesellschaft« des Ostblocks zu integrieren und in die Lage zu versetzen, unter diesen »sozialistisch organisierten Nationen«, die keine den deutschen vergleichbaren Identitätsprobleme haben, ein gleichberechtigter, national intakter Partner zu sein. Die Begründung, die er für seine Kehrtwendung liefert, liest sich wie ein einziges, eiferndes, entschuldigendes Stakkato: »Wenn nun – und dies ist die Folge spezifischer geschichtlicher Bedingungen – der revolutionäre Umgestaltungsprozeß vom Kapitalismus zum Sozialismus nicht in der ganzen Nation, nicht auf ihrem ganzen Territorium erfolgt, sondern nur einen Teil erfaßt; wenn über einen längeren historischen Zeitraum die Anstrengungen der progressiven Kräfte der Nation es nicht vermögen, die ganze Nation auf den Weg des Sozialismus zu führen; wenn der unter der Herrschaft reaktionärer Klassenkräfte verbleibende Teil sich in einem Separatstaat organisiert und mittels dieses Staates in einem erbarmungslos geführten Klassenkampf versucht, den in der Entwicklung zum Sozialismus befindlichen Teil der Nation zu erdrosseln, auszubeuten und seine historischen Errungenschaften rückgängig zu machen – dann können im Rahmen einer früher einheitlichen Nation zwei Staaten mit entgegengesetzter Gesellschaftsordnung entstehen, dann kommt es in dem Maße, wie die sozialistische Gesellschaft sich entwickelt, zu tiefgreifenden Veränderungen der nationalen Beziehungen, zur Herausbildung qualitativ neuer Beziehungen auf dem Territorium des sozialistischen Staates, zur Entstehung der sozialistischen Nation, während auf dem Territorium des bürgerlichen Staates die kapitalistische Nation bestehen bleibt. Dies ist – auf eine kurze Formel gebracht – im Hinblick auf die Problematik der Nation das Wesentliche der Nachkriegsentwicklung im ehemaligen Deutschland.«

Ganz offen sprach Kosing auch an, was die SED-Führung als Ziel dieses Prozesses im Auge hat: Die Herauslösung einer eigenständigen DDR-Nation aus dem vom deutschen Volk bewohnten Territorium nach dem Beispiel der Deutschen Österreichs. Bürgerliche Historiker tun sich da sicherlich leichter, wenn sie mit Blick auf die deutsche Geschichte feststellen, der nationale Einheitsstaat stelle für die Deutschen eine kurze Episode in ihrer tausendjährigen Geschichte dar, allein wegen ihrer Zahl, ihrer Macht und ihrer Lage in der Mitte Europas bleibe ihnen eine nationalstaatliche Existenz, wie sie für Italiener, Franzosen, Briten und Spanier selbstverständlich sei, versagt. Der deutsche Normalfall sei, wenn nicht die Spaltung der Nation, so doch das Vorhandensein verschiedener deutscher Staaten, und seien es nur das großpreußisch-kleindeutsche Reich und Österreich. Nun nähert sich die SED langsam solchem bürgerlich-historischem Denken an.

Allerdings fragt sich, wie bereitwillig das Staatsvolk der DDR nach jahrzehntelanger Befreiungspropaganda den Weg in die eigenständige sozialistische Nation mitvollzieht. Sicher bilden sich in dem egalitären sozialen Milieu der DDR, die ja stolz darauf ist, keine Ellenbogengesellschaft zu sein, wie die der »kapitalistischen deutschen Nation«, über die Jahre andere

Verhaltensmuster und Formen der sozialen Kommunikation als in der Bundesrepublik heraus. Selbst Sprache entwickelt sich auseinander, wenn Bürokratendeutsch im Osten Nudeln und Kartoffeln als »Sättigungsbeilage«, Hähnchen als »Broiler« und Fähnchen als »Winkelemente« bezeichnet. Aber die Tatsache, daß die Deutschen im Osten sich mit denen im Westen, allen politischen Grenzen zum Trotz, allabendlich im Wohnzimmer zu einer trauten ARD- und ZDF-Zuschauernation wiedervereinigen, bestärkt eine gegenläufige Tendenz. Zwei DDR-Autoren, Helmut Hanke und Thomas Koch, sind diesen Fragen 1985 in den »Weimarer Beiträgen« in einer Untersuchung über Probleme der kulturellen Identität nachgegangen und kommen zu dem Schluß, daß »Ruhe, Festigkeit, Sicherheit der Lebenslage« – es handelt sich um ein Wort von Marx – eine »große Errungenschaft« der DDR-Ordnung seien, aber sie nannten auch den Preis – der heißt nämlich Langeweile: »Mit Bewährungssituation, Krisen und Konflikten, wie sie in der Welt des Kapitals üblich sind, kann der Sozialismus nicht aufwarten.« Übrigens berufen sich Hanke und Koch ausdrücklich auf Günter Gaus, der dem »Staatsvolk der kleinen Leute« eine »unverstellte Kleinbürgerlichkeit« attestierte, und sie entdecken darin einen »durchaus rationalen Kern«. Es sei eben tatsächlich so, daß »die arbeitenden Menschen« in der DDR den Ton angeben. »Eine im internationalen Vergleich – etwa mit vergleichbaren kapitalistischen Industrieländern – verhältnismäßig geringe soziale und kulturelle Differenzierung korrespondiert auf der einen Seite mit weniger ausgeprägten Vorstellungen von gesellschaftlichem Auf- oder Abstieg, der durch das Mithaltenkönnen mit einer bestimmten sozialen Schicht definiert wäre, auf der andern mit der selbstverständlichen Inanspruchnahme tendenziell aller vorhandenen Lebens- und Genußmöglichkeiten durch alle Gesellschaftsmitglieder.« Nur sprechen die beiden Autoren auch den wunden Punkt an, wenn sie feststellen: »Identität ist erreicht, wenn das Volk mit seiner sozialen und nationalen Lebensform einverstanden ist.« Das genau ist die Frage, welche die DDR daran hindern dürfte, schon bald ein zweites Österreich zu werden, das sich aus der deutschen Nation herauslöst und sich als eine neue, eigenständige bildet. Es werde Jahrzehnte dauern, erklärte mir der SED-Historiker Walter Schmidt, »wir sind ja keine Illusionisten, die verkürzten Perspektiven das Wort reden möchten. Aber wir sagen auch ganz deutlich: Das ist keine Zukunftsmusik mehr, sondern das sind real in Gang gesetzte historische Prozesse. Wir haben einen eigenen souveränen Staat, und der hat sein eigenes Territorum. Es entwickelt sich eine sozialistische Nationalkultur, eine sozialistische Lebensweise, und die sozialistische Gesellschaft verbindet sich auf diesem Territorium mit den überkommenen ethnischen Eigenschaften des Deutschen.«

Die wichtigste Voraussetzung für die Bildung dieser sozialistischen deutschen Nation allerdings steht noch aus: Es ist die Anerkennung der DDR durch ihre eigenen Bürger, dadurch vollzogen und Tag für Tag praktiziert, daß sie frei, ohne Zwang und wie selbstverständlich diesen Staat akzeptieren und ihm die Treue halten – bei offenen Grenzen, die dann nicht mehr Festungscharakter haben müssen. Erst wenn die SED ihre DDR lebenswerter macht, wenn sie nach innen mehr Freiheit gewährt, dürfte aus ihr vielleicht so etwas wie ein zweites Österreich werden – kein neutrales, sondern ein sozialistisches, das im eigenen Lager verwurzelt bleibt. Erst mit einer solchen Demokratisierung der DDR nach innen hätte sich die deutsche Frage wirklich von selbst erledigt. Es ist noch ein weiter Weg dahin.

Epilog

Bis auf wenige Möbel, die zum Inventar gehören, hatten die Packer die Dienstwohnung in der Leipziger Straße geräumt. Wir warteten auf die Männer vom Zoll, die Ausfuhrlisten für privates Hab und Gut abzeichnen mußten. Der Fernseher, den der Nachfolger übernehmen würde, lief und brachte die passende Schlußeinstellung nach fünf Jahren DDR: Erich Honekker und Helmut Kohl gemeinsam vor einer Ehrenkompanie der Bundeswehr. Beide wirkten verklemmt. Der SED-Chef stand steif und hölzern da, aber seine Haltung zeugte von Genugtuung. Neben der großen, massigen Gestalt des Bundeskanzlers nahm er sich klein und zierlich aus. Kohl vermittelte das Gefühl, er verspüre ein inneres Unbehagen, als da beide deutschen Nationalhymnen nacheinander erklangen. So richtig glücklich schauten beide deutschen Regenten nicht drein. Wie sollten sie auch?

Der Saarländer kam als Erbe des großdeutschen Sachsen Ulbricht, der in Adenauer stets einen reaktionären rheinischen Separatisten gesehen hatte. Und der Pfälzer fühlte sich als Enkel eben jenes Kanzlers, der Zeit seines Lebens in Ulbricht nur einen konspirativen kommunistischen Umstürzler und Rädelsführer erblickt, dessen Partei er bei sich zu Hause verboten und dessen Regime er, solange er regierte, offiziell einfach nicht zur Kenntnis genommen hatte. Der eine verstand seinen Staat als Rechtsnachfolger des Deutschen Reiches, von dem der andere sagte, daß es im Feuer des letzten Weltkrieges für immer untergegangen sei. Die deutsche Teilung, die da mit Fahnen und Musik, mit Trommelwirbel und

»Präsentiert das Gewehr!« symbolisch und drastisch in Szene
gesetzt und endgültig besiegelt wurde, hatte ursprünglich keiner gewollt.

Ruft man sich in Erinnerung, wie heftig die christlich-de-
mokratische Opposition gegen die sozialliberale Ostpolitik
von Willy Brandt und Walter Scheel Sturm gelaufen ist, dann
wurde vor allem Kohl an diesem Tage einiges abverlangt. Man
spürte, daß er die Zeremonie nicht mochte und sich einer
Pflicht unterzog. Kohl tat an diesem Tag, was nach der Logik
der Deutschlandpolitik irgendwann einmal vollzogen werden
mußte und längst überfällig war: Er empfing den Repräsentanten der anderen deutschen Republik, er entbot ihm die
Ehren, auf die dieser als Chef eines souveränen Staates Anspruch hatte und auf die er offensichtlich Wert zu legen
schien. Der Schmidt-Nachfolger hat das Versprechen gehalten, das er bei seinem Amtsantritt gab, hat deutschlandpoli-
tisch Kontinuität gewahrt und kann auf diesem heiklen Gebiet
inzwischen auch Erfolge vorweisen. Nun war er vor der Ehrenformation der Bundeswehr um Korrektheit und Höflichkeit bemüht, aber, deutlich sichtbar, nicht um mehr. Dafür
habe ich Verständnis. Der Dialog zwischen beiden deutschen
Staaten ist ein Gebot der Vernunft, lieben muß der eine den
anderen deshalb wirklich nicht. Dies war die Stimmung, mit
der ich nach fünf Jahren genauer Beobachtung der DDR den
»ersten Staat der Arbeiter und Bauern auf deutschem Boden«
verließ. In all den Jahren ist es mir kaum möglich gewesen,
am politischen System der ideologisch genormten Gesellschaft »liebenswerte« Eigenschaften zu entdecken – der Preis,
auch der für die soziale Sicherheit, die er bietet, heißt immer
aufs Neue: Verzicht auf die klassischen Bürgerfreiheiten der
Französischen Revolution. Die Bevölkerung wirkt einge-
schüchtert, kaum einer wagt zu sagen, was er denkt, diese
graue Republik ist keine Gesellschaft des offenen Visiers. Nirgendwo wird so geflüstert wie in den Gaststätten der DDR.

Man kann Kultur-Landschaft entdecken und liebgewinnen
an Orten gemeinsamer Geschichte – die Wartburg, vielleicht
die deutscheste aller Burgen, Weimar oder das mecklenburgi-

sche Güstrow, in dem Barlach wirkte und Uwe Johnson zur Schule ging und wo die Zeit stehen geblieben scheint. Schloß Pillnitz kündet vom Glanz und der Pracht des sächsischen Hofes. Wittenberg von der geistigen Revolution, die der Reformator der Deutschen in Gang setzte, als er verkündete, daß jedermann sein eigener Priester sei. Und was wäre die deutsche Musik ohne den Beitrag Sachsens und Thüringens, der Kernländer der Reformation, aus denen Schütz, Bach und Händel, Schumann und Wagner kamen?

Es gibt viele schöne bleibende Erinnerungen – an Theaterabende oder Sommernachmittage unterm Apfelbaum im Oderbruch, an junge Menschen in Friedens-Seminaren, die unerhörte Zivilcourage zeigten, an Weinbauern an der Unstrut und an den Landpastor in Grüneberg, der, beide Beine im realen Sozialismus, seiner märkischen Feldsteinkirche endlich wieder zu einem Dach verhalf. Man kann Menschen schätzen lernen und enge Freundschaften schließen – der realsozialistische Staat ist für Zuwendung nicht gemacht. Dafür zeigt er zu viele häßliche, autoritäre Züge – Geburtsfehler jener Umwälzung der Gesellschaftsordnung, die, entgegen eigenen Bekundungen, nicht vom Volk, sondern – typisch deutsch – wieder einmal als Revolution von oben ins Werk gesetzt worden ist.

Personenregister